HANDBOOK OF SOCIAL ECONOMICS

VOLUME *1A*

INTRODUCTION TO THE SERIES

The aim of the *Handbooks in Economics* series is to produce Handbooks for various branches of economics, each of which is a definitive source, reference, and teaching supplement for use by professional researchers and advanced graduate students. Each Handbook provides self-contained surveys of the current state of a branch of economics in the form of chapters prepared by leading specialists on various aspects of this branch of economics. These surveys summarize not only received results but also newer developments, from recent journal articles and discussion papers. Some original material is also included, but the main goal is to provide comprehensive and accessible surveys.

The Handbooks are intended to provide not only useful reference volumes for professional collections but also possible supplementary readings for advanced courses for graduate students in economics.

KENNETH J. ARROW and **MICHAEL D. INTRILIGATOR**

HANDBOOK OF SOCIAL ECONOMICS

VOLUME 1A

Edited by

JESS BENHABIB

ALBERTO BISIN

MATTHEW O. JACKSON

ELSEVIER

Amsterdam • Boston • Heidelberg • London
New York • Oxford • Paris • San Diego
San Francisco • Singapore • Sydney • Tokyo
North-Holland is an imprint of Elsevier

N·H

North-Holland is an imprint of Elsevier
525 B Street, Suite 1800, San Diego, CA 92101-4495, USA
Radarweg 29, 1000 AE Amsterdam, The Netherlands

First edition 2011

Library of Congress Cataloging-in-Publication Data
A catalog record for this book is available from the Library of Congress

British Library Cataloguing in Publication Data
A catalogue record for this book is available from the British Library

ISBN Vol 1A: 978-0-444-53187-2
ISBN Vol 1B: 978-0-444-53707-2
SET ISBN: 978-0-444-53713-3

For information on all North-Holland publications
visit our website at elsevierdirect.com

Printed and bound by CPI Group (UK) Ltd, Croydon, CR0 4YY
Transferred to Digital Print 2011

CONTENTS-VOLUME 1A

Contributors xv
Introduction xvii

Part I: Social Preferences

1. Nature and Nurture Effects On Children's Outcomes: What Have We Learned From Studies of Twins And Adoptees? **1**
Bruce Sacerdote

1. Introduction and Overview 2
2. The Behavioral Genetics Model 5
3. Canonical Results from the Behavioral Genetics Literature 8
4. Critiques and Challenges to Interpretation of the Behavioral Genetics Results on IQ and Schooling 14
5. Treatment Effects and Regression Coefficients 17
6. Results from Economics on Adoptees 19
7. Putting It All Together: What Does It Mean? 25

References 26

2. Social Norms and Preferences **31**
Andrew Postlewaite

1. Introduction 32
2. The Social Determinants of Preferences 35
3. Reduced Form Preferences: Social Concerns 40
4. Why Not Take the Indirect Preferences as the Primitive? 53
5. Examples Employing Instrumental Concern for Rank 58
6. Concluding Remarks 63

References 65

3. Preferences for Status: Evidence and Economic Implications **69**
Ori Heffetz and Robert H. Frank

1. Introduction 70
2. Features of Status 72
3. Evidence 75
4. Some Economic Implications 84
5. Conclusion 88

References 89

4. Preferences for Redistribution **93**
Alberto Alesina and Paola Giuliano

1. Introduction 94
2. Preferences for Redistribution: Theory 96
3. Empirical Evidence 103
4. Conclusions 127
References 129

5. Theories of Statistical Discrimination and Affirmative Action: A Survey **133**
Hanming Fang and Andrea Moro

1. Introduction 134
2. The Use of Group Averages as a Proxy for Relevant Variables: the Exogenous Differences Literature 137
3. Discriminatory Outcomes as a Result of Coordination Failure 140
4. Discriminatory Outcomes Due to Inter-Group Interactions 147
5. Dynamic Models of Discrimination 162
6. Affirmative Action 163
7. Efficiency Implications of Statistical Discrimination 191
8. Conclusion 195
References 197

6. Social Construction of Preferences: Advertising **201**
Jess Benhabib and Alberto Bisin

1. Introduction 202
2. The Benchmark Economy 204
3. The Equilibrium Effects of Advertising 206
4. The Effects of Advertising in Empirical Work 211
5. Conclusions 218
References 219

7. The Evolutionary Foundations of Preferences **221**
Arthur J. Robson and Larry Samuelson

1. Introduction 222
2. Evolutionary Foundations 225
3. What Sort of Preferences? 235
4. Preferences over What? 263
5. Concluding Remark 297
6. Proofs 298
References 305

8. Social Norms **311**

Mary A. Burke and H. Peyton Young

1. Background 312
2. Norms, Customs, and Conventions 313
3. Characteristic Features of Norm Dynamics 314
4. Social Interactions and Social Norms 317
5. A Model of Norm Dynamics 318
6. Contractual Norms in Agriculture 321
7. Medical Treatment Norms 327
8. Body Weight Norms 331
9. Concluding Discussion 334

References 336

9. The Economics of Cultural Transmission and Socialization **339**

Alberto Bisin and Thierry Verdier

1. Introduction 340
2. Theoretical Studies 342
3. Empirical Studies 371
4. Conclusions 407

References 407

10. Civic Capital as the Missing Link **417**

Luigi Guiso, Paola Sapienza, and Luigi Zingales

1. Introduction 418
2. Definitions of Social Capital 420
3. Accumulation and Depreciation of Civic Capital 423
4. Measuring Civic Capital 429
5. The Origins of Civic Capital 459
6. The Economic Effects of Civic Capital 467
7. Conclusions 476

References 477

11. Does Culture Matter? **481**

Raquel Fernández

1. Introduction 482
2. Some Preliminaries 483
3. The Epidemiological Approach 489
4. The Epidemiological Literature in Economics 497
5. Concluding Questions and Remarks 506

6. Acknowledgement 508
References 508

Part II: Social Actions

12. An Overview of Social Networks and Economic Applications 511
Matthew O. Jackson
1. Introduction 512
2. Social Networks and Networked Markets 514
3. The Structure of Social Networks 521
4. Network Formation 532
5. Modeling the Impact of Networks 550
6. Concluding Remarks 574
References 574

13. Local Interactions 587
Onur Özgür
1. Introduction 588
2. Static Models 589
3. Dynamic Models 618
4. Concluding Remarks 638
References 639

14. Diffusion, Strategic Interaction, and Social Structure 645
Matthew O. Jackson and Leeat Yariv
1. Introduction 646
2. Empirical Background: Social Networks and Diffusion 647
3. Models of Diffusion and Strategic Interaction Absent Network Structure 653
4. Models of Diffusion and Strategic Interaction in Network Settings 657
5. Closing Notes 674
References 675

15. Learning in Networks 679
Sanjeev Goyal
1. Introduction 680
2. Nonstrategic Interaction 684
3. Strategic Interaction 704
4. Concluding Remarks 721
5. Appendix 723
References 724

16. Formation of Networks and Coalitions **729**

Francis Bloch and Bhaskar Dutta

1. Introduction 730
2. One-Stage Models of Coalition and Network Formation 731
3. Sequential Models of Coalition and Network Formation 746
4. Farsightedness 754
5. Group Formation in Real Time 762
6. The Tension between Efficiency and Stability 771
7. Conclusions and Open Problems 774

References 776

17. Matching, Allocation, and Exchange of Discrete Resources **781**

Tayfun Sönmez and M. Utku Ünver

1. Introduction 783
2. House Allocation and Exchange Models 786
3. Kidney Exchange 801
4. School Admissions 821
5. Axiomatic Mechanisms and Market Design 837
6. Concluding Remarks 844

References 848

Index-Volume 1A I1

Index-Volume 1B I41

CONTENTS-VOLUME 1B

Contributors ix

Part III: Peer and Neighborhood Effects

18. Identification of Social Interactions **853**

Lawrence E. Blume, William A. Brock, Steven N. Durlauf, and Yannis M. Ioannides

1. Introduction 855
2. Decision Making in Group Contexts 857
3. Linear Models of Social Interaction 863
4. Social Networks and Spatial Models of Social Interactions 886
5. Discrete Choice Models of Social Interactions 904
6. Experimental Approaches 922
7. Suggestions for Future Directions 934
8. Conclusions 942

References 958

19. Econometric Methods for the Analysis of Assignment Problems in the Presence of Complementarity and Social Spillovers **965**

Bryan S. Graham

1. Introduction 967
2. An Overview of Empirical Matching Models 969
3. Identification and Estimation of one-to-one Matching Models When Match Output is Observed 974
4. Identification and Estimation of one-to-one Matching Models When Match Output is Unobserved: Equilibrium Approaches 1007
5. Segregation in the Presence of Social Spillovers 1029
6. Treatment Response with Spillovers 1044
7. Areas for Further Research 1046

References 1047

20. Peer Effects in Education: A Survey of the Theory and Evidence **1053**

Dennis Epple and Richard E. Romano

1. Introduction 1054
2. Theory 1055
3. Econometric Issues 1093
4. Empirical Evidence: Peer Effects 1110

5. Concluding Remarks 1156
References 1160

21. The Importance of Segregation, Discrimination, Peer Dynamics, and Identity in Explaining Trends in the Racial Achievement Gap 1165
Roland G. Fryer, Jr.

1. Trends in the Racial Achievement Gap 1166
2. Segregation 1167
3. Information-Based Models of Discrimination 1173
4. Peer Dynamics 1177
5. Identity 1186
6. Conclusion 1189
References 1189

22. Labor Markets and Referrals 1193
Giorgio Topa

1. Introduction 1194
2. The Theoretical Literature 1195
3. Direct Evidence on Usage of Informal Search Methods 1198
4. Labor Market Referrals and Neighborhood Effects 1206
5. Randomized and Natural Experiments 1212
6. Directions for Future Research 1216
References 1217

23. Labor and Credit Networks in Developing Economies 1223
Kaivan Munshi

1. Introduction 1224
2. Identification and Estimation of Network Effects 1226
3. Networks, Growth, and Efficiency 1241
4. Conclusion 1253
References 1253

24. Risk Sharing Between Households 1255
Marcel Fafchamps

1. Introduction 1256
2. Efficient Risk Sharing 1257
3. Forms of Risk Sharing 1259
4. The Motives for Risk Sharing 1261
5. Risk Sharing Groups and Networks 1270

6. Conclusion 1275
References 1275

25. Neighborhood Effects And Housing **1281**
Yannis M. Ioannides

1. Introduction 1283
2. Spatial Models of Location with Social Interactions 1287
3. Endogenous Neighborhood and Contextual Effects in Housing Markets 1304
4. Neighborhood Effects and the Geometry of the Canonical Urban Model 1318
5. Hierarchical Models of Location with Social Interactions 1327
6. Conclusion 1336
References 1337

Index-Volume 1B I1
Index-Volume 1A I23

CONTRIBUTORS

Alberto Alesina
Harvard University, Cambridge, MA

Jess Benhabib
New York University, New York, NY

Alberto Bisin
New York University, New York, NY

Francis Bloch
Ecole Polytechnique, Palaiseau, France

Mary A. Burke
Federal Reserve Bank of Boston

Bhaskar Dutta
University of Warwick, Coventry, UK

Hanming Fang
University of Pennsylvania, Philadelphia, PA

Raquel Fernandez
New York University, New York, NY

Robert Frank
Cornell University, Ithaca, NY

Sanjeev Goyal
University of Cambridge, Cambridge, UK

Paola Giuliano
Anderson School of Management, Los Angeles, CA

Luigi Guiso
European University Institute, EIEF & CEPR, Florence, Italy

Ori Heffetz
Cornell University, Ithaca, NY

Matthew O. Jackson
Stanford University, Stanford, CA

Andrea Moro
Vanderbilt University, Nashville, TN

Onur Özgür
University of Montreal, Montréal QC, Canada

Andrew Postlewaite
University of Pennsylvania, Philadelphia, PA

Arthur J. Robson
Simon Fraser University, Burnaby, BC, Canada

Bruce I. Sacerdote
Dartmouth College, Hanover, NH

Larry Samuelson
Yale University, New Haven, CT

Paola Sapienza
Northwestern University, NBER & CEPR, Evanston, IL

Tayfun Sönmez
Boston College, Chestnut Hill, MA

M. Utku Ünver
Boston College, Chestnut Hill, MA

Thierry Verdier
PSE, Paris, France

Leeat Yariv
California Institute of Technology, Pasadena, CA

H. Peyton Young
University of Oxford, Oxford, UK

Luigi Zingales
The University of Chicago Booth School of Business, NBER & CEPR, Chicago, IL

Social Economics: A Brief Introduction to the Handbook

Jess Benhabib
Department of Economics, New York University

Alberto Bisin
Department of Economics, New York University

Matthew O. Jackson
Department of Economics, Stanford University

Contents

Social Preferences xviii
Social Actions xix
Peer and Neighborhood Effects xx
References xxi

Social economics is the study, with the *methods of economics*, of social phenomena in which aggregates affect individual choices.[1] Such phenomena include, just to mention a few, social norms and conventions, cultural identities and stereotypes, peer and neighborhood effects.

A central underpinning of the methods of economics is methodological individualism. In particular, explanations based solely on group choice are unusual and aggregates are generally studied as the result of individual choices. Furthermore, the methods of economics rely mostly, although not exclusively, on a rational choice paradigm. *Social economics* is to be distinguished therefore from *Economic sociology*, which may be thought of as the study, with the methods of sociology, of economic phenomena, e.g., markets. Although there is increasing overlap in these areas of study as it is quite evident in some of the chapters that follow, they are still quite complementary.

The aim of this handbook is to illustrate the intellectual vitality and richness of the recent literature in *social economics* by organizing its main contributions in a series of surveys. Any organization of this literature is somewhat arbitrary. Social economics, for instance, does not lend itself naturally to a classic distinction along the theory/empirical work line, as concepts and measurements are often developed in tight

[1] The term *social economics*, in this sense, was introduced in a collection of essays by Gary S. Becker and Kevin J. Murphy (2000) by the same title.

connection with each other. We have chosen instead to distinguish three subfields, which we call *Social preferences, Social actions*, and *Peer and neighborhood effects.*

SOCIAL PREFERENCES

Traditionally, economists have considered preferences as exogenous parameters for the study of individual choice. This is a tradition rooted in the work of Milton Friedman (1953). Furthermore, economists are typically shy about allowing for heterogeneous preferences. A very influential Occam Razor's argument in favor of restricting economic analysis to identical preferences is e.g., in Stigler and Becker (1977). Finally, economists eschew explanations based on arbitrary beliefs, but rather impose the constraint of rational expectations.[2]

These self-imposed constraints have traditionally limited the scope of economic theory outside of purely economic phenomena, e.g., markets. Most recently, however, many economists have successfully studied various processes of preference formation; that is, have developed theoretical models of endogenous preferences and beliefs. Perhaps, even more foundationally, economists have contributed to the age-old question of identifying nature from nurture effects in individuals' psychological characteristics and attitudes. These contributions are surveyed in Chapter 1 by Bruce Sacerdote.

With regards more specifically to social preferences (preferences which depend on population aggregates), two complementary approaches can be distinguished. Social preferences can be studied either by incorporating social aspects directly in agents' preferences or by explicitly studying mechanisms which induce indirect (reduced form) preferences that depend on population aggregates. Chapter 2, by Andrew Postlewaite, discusses these modeling choices and surveys the literature which obtains social concerns in preferences endogenously from "standard" preferences. Chapter 3, by Robert Frank and Ori Heffetz, surveys instead the theoretical implications of incorporating social status directly into preferences and reports on empirical work, especially with experimental data, supporting such implications. Chapter 4, by Alberto Alesina and Paola Giuliano, reviews the available evidence for the most studied determinants of preferences for redistribution from the General Social Survey and the World Value Survey. They consider both studies in which (income or wealth) inequality enters directly in individuals' utility function as well as studies in which inequality enters indirectly by means of, for instance, externalities in education. Hanming Fang and Andrea Moro, in Chapter 5, study models of statistical discrimination in which social discrimination, segregation, and group inequality result from individuals rationally using observable characteristics of others as a proxy for unobservable ones, as opposed to

[2] A fundamental argument for rational expectation is in Lucas and Sargent (1981).

models in which they obtain as a result of preferences for in-group interactions. Jess Benhabib and Alberto Bisin, in Chapter 6, provide a formalization of the concept of "social construction of preferences," common in social circles outside of economics. In this literature, while individuals display standard preferences in terms of consumption, they are subject to societal influences mainly through advertising.

A different approach to the study of the endogenous formation of preferences is to characterize those systems of preferences that are stable under some specific dynamic selection mechanism. Chapter 7, by Arthur Robson and Larry Samuelson, surveys studies of indirect preferences that survive explicit evolutionary selection mechanisms. Peyton Young and Mary Burke, in Chapter 8, study the evolutionary stability of norms and conventions in coordination games when subjected to adaptive dynamic processes. Chapter 9, by Alberto Bisin and Thierry Verdier, surveys instead theoretical and empirical contributions regarding the transmission of cultural traits, with particular emphasis on the ability of these models to explain the observed cultural heterogeneity.[3] Lugi Guiso, Paola Sapienza and Luigi Zingales, in Chapter 10, survey the literature on social capital, defined as "the set of values and beliefs that help cooperation," which they prefer to label civic capital. The main object of this literature is to study the long-run persistence of differences in social/civic capital and their effect on economic performance. Relatedly, Raquel Fernandez, in Chapter 11, surveys results obtained by the application of an empirical methodology, referred to as the epidemiological approach, designed to identify and measure the persistence of original cultural traits after migration, and hence in a different environment and under a different set of institutions.

SOCIAL ACTIONS

Economists have traditionally studied externalities as well as strategic interactions, that is, environments in which the actions of some agents affect either the set of feasible actions available to other agents or their preferences. Most recently, economists have also made great progress in the study of interactions between agents in small groups or networks. In all these contexts, agents interact "socially," and their actions at equilibrium are *social* in the sense that they are not mediated exclusively by markets. In other words, the literature on *social actions* takes the agents' preferences as given and studies their actions as the equilibrium result of social interactions.

The structure of social interactions, in this literature, typically takes the formal representation of a network. Social interactions are then studied as the equilibrium effect of specific properties of the network. Strategic network formation is the subject of a

[3] While this chapter also surveys the economic literature on identity formation, the reader might also refer to the recent book by George Akerlof and Rachel Kranton (2010).

complementary literature, and there is also a nascent literature on the coevolution of social structure and behavior. In Chapter 12, Matthew Jackson provides an overview of the analysis of social networks, including how social network structure impacts behavior, and how networks are formed. The chapter includes some discussion of relevant results in the mathematics of networks and of the statistical techniques involved in measurement of social network phenomena. Onur Ozgur, in Chapter 13, surveys a class of models, derived from the study of interacting particle systems in statistical mechanics, in which a simple and stark exogenous network structure of social interactions is coupled with fully dynamic equilibrium models that allow for the characterization of the statistical correlation of individual choices. Matthew Jackson and Leeat Yariv, in Chapter 14, survey models of the diffusion of social phenomena, with particular interest on the role of exogenous social structures on diffusion. They discuss contributions from the epidemiology and random graph literatures that help shed light on the spread of social phenomena as infections throughout a society. Relatedly, Sanjeev Goyal, in Chapter 15, surveys the theoretical literature on learning on networks. In this class of models, the precise structure which governs the interactions between individuals affects the generation and dissemination of information that individuals exploit to guide their choices. Chapter 16, by Francis Bloch and Bhaskar Dutta, provides a detailed survey of the theoretical literature regarding endogenous network formation in the context of group (coalition) formation games. Chapter 17, by Tayfun Sonmez and Utku Unver approaches the issue of group formation from the point of view of matching theory. It contains, in particular, a survey of the literature on allocation and exchange of indivisible goods, which has applications e.g., to house allocation, kidney exchange, and school admissions.

PEER AND NEIGHBORHOOD EFFECTS

The peer and network effects induced by social interactions have been studied empirically for several socio-economic phenomena, e.g., crime, school achievement, addiction, employment search, neighborhood segregation, income stratification and several others. This empirical evidence has also spurred a methodological literature regarding the identification of peer and neighborhood effects. This literature opens with Charles Manski(1993)'s paper showing restrictions and assumptions necessary to recover the structural parameters of economies with relevant social interactions from observable behavior.[4]

However, recently several contributions to the literature have developed econometric models, in specific contexts, which are in fact identified under weaker conditions. Larry Blume, William Brock, Steven Durlauf, and Yannis Ioannides survey

[4] See also Glaeser and Scheinkman (2001) for a survey of this issues.

this literature, in Chapter 18, considering linear and discrete choice models as well as social networks structures, accounting for experimental and quasi-experimental methods. Bryan Graham, in Chapter 19, complements the previous chapter by studying the collection of econometric methods for characterizing the distributional effects of policies, which induce changes in peer group structure, as e.g., partner reassignment in one-on-one matching models and social experiments in geographic integration.

Finally, various chapters in the Handbook provide detailed surveys of empirical results regarding peer, family, and neighborhood effects in specific socio-economic contexts of interest. Dennis Epple and Richard Romano, in Chapter 20, survey peer effects on educational outcomes, stressing the theoretical underpinning of identification and empirical analysis. Roland Fryer, in Chapter 21, reports more specifically on the relative importance of various factors, including segregation, discrimination, and peer effects, in explaining the racial achievement gap in the U.S. Giorgio Topa, in Chapter 22, highlights the most robust results in the large literature in economics and sociology concerning peer effects in the labor markets, with special regard to the issue of job referrals. Kaivan Munshi, in Chapter 23, surveys the empirical literature on the relevance of labor and credit networks in shaping economic development, discussing the inefficiencies associated with community-based networks as well as their effect on growth and mobility in developing countries. Marcel Fafchamps, in Chapter 24, concentrates more specifically on identifying the different roles that family and kinship networks play in sharing risk and in entering binding informal arrangements. Yannis Ioannides, in Chapter 25, surveys the literature on neighborhood effects on housing markets, emphasizing how location decisions of individuals implicitly contain a choice component over neighborhood effects, or more generally over social interactions.

REFERENCES

Akerlof, G.A., Kranton, R.E., 2010. Identity Economics: How Our Identities Shape Our Work, Wages, and Well-Being. Princeton University Press, Princeton.

Becker, G.S., Murphy, K.M., 2000. Social Economics: Market Behavior in a Social Environment. Harvard University Press, Cambridge, MA.

Friedman, M., 1953. The Methodology of Positive Economics. In: Essays In Positive Economics. Univ. of Chicago Press, Chicago.

Glaeser, E.L., Scheinkman, J., 2001. Measuring Social Interactions. In: Durlauf, S.N., Young, H.P. (Eds.), Social Dynamics. MIT Press, Cambridge, pp. 83–132.

Lucas Jr., R.E., Sargent, T.J., 1981. Rational Expectations and Econometric Practice. University of Minnesota Press, Minneapolis.

Manski, C., 1993. Identification of Endogenous Social Effects: The Reflection Problem. Rev. Econ. Stud. 60, 531–542.

Stigler, G., Becker, G., 1977. De Gustibus Non Est Disputandum. Am. Econ. Rev. 67, 76–90.

PART One

Social Preferences

CHAPTER 1

Nature and Nurture Effects On Children's Outcomes: What Have We Learned From Studies of Twins And Adoptees?*

Bruce Sacerdote
Dartmouth College and NBER

Contents

I. Introduction and Overview 2
II. The Behavioral Genetics Model 5
III. Canonical Results from the Behavioral Genetics Literature 8
IV. Critiques and Challenges to Interpretation of the Behavioral Genetics Results on IQ and Schooling 14
V. Treatment Effects and Regression Coefficients 17
VI. Results from Economics on Adoptees 19
VII. Putting It All Together: What Does It Mean? 25
References 26
Further Readings 29

Abstract

There is a rich history of using data from twins and from adoptees to control for genetic influences and thereby examine the impact of environment on children's outcomes. The behavioral genetics model is the workhorse of this literature and for a variety of outcomes including IQ scores and personality measures behavioral geneticists find that the bulk of the variance that can be explained is correlated with genetic influences. However, finding that variation in test scores has a large genetic component is quite different than asking whether test scores can be improved by interventions and changes in policy or whether such interventions pass a cost benefit test. Economists have recently begun asking how the intergenerational transmission of educational attainment, income and health vary when a child is being raised by adoptive rather than biological parents. Results suggest that both the biological and the nurturing parents contribute a great deal to the transmission of income and education to their children

JEL Codes: I0, J0, J24

* I thank Christopher Jencks, Anders Björkland, and seminar participants at NYU for their comments on this literature summary. I thank Holt International Children's Services and particularly Laura Hofer and Karla Miller for their help in gathering data and information on international adoptions. The National Science Foundation provided generous funding. I thank Celia Kujala, Anne Ladenburger, Abigail Ridgeway, and Ariel Stern for tireless research assistance and valuable suggestions.

Handbook of Social Economics, Volume 1A
ISSN 0169-7218, DOI: 10.1016/S0169-7218(11)01001-X

Keywords

twins
adoption
intergenerational transmission
nurture
educational attainment

I. INTRODUCTION AND OVERVIEW

A fundamental question in social science has long been the degree to which children's outcomes are influenced by genes, environment, and the interaction of the two. One sensible way to attempt to separate out the effects of genes and environment is to examine data on twins or adoptees since we may be able to make plausible assumptions about the genetic relationships between identical versus fraternal twins, or between parents and their adoptive and non-adoptive children.

I begin this chapter by reviewing the methods used by psychologists and behavioral geneticists to identify the effects of nature and nurture, and I summarize some of the key results from this large literature. I discuss the assumptions underlying the behavioral genetics model and explain some of the challenges to interpreting the results. I use these issues of interpretation to motivate why economists and sociologists have used a different approach to measuring the impact of environment on children's outcomes. And I discuss the results from the recent literature in economics on environmental versus genetic determinants of children's education, income, and health. Finally, I try to bring the results from both literatures together to address the issues of what we do know, what we don't know and whether this work has implications for social policy or other research on children's outcomes.

Behavioral geneticists have estimated the "heritability" of everything from IQ to "shrewdness" to alcoholism. Their most frequently cited result is that genetic factors explain about 50 to 60% of the variation in adult IQ, while family environment explains little of the variation in adult IQ[1]. This finding is incredibly robust (see Devlin, et al. [1994]). But researchers' interpretation of the finding varies. Harris [1998] uses the finding of almost no effect from family environment as a key piece of evidence for her thesis that parents do not have a direct effect on their children's outcomes. Both Hernnstein and Murray [1994] and Jensen [1972] interpreted the lack of measured effects from family environment to mean that policies aimed at improving the home and school environment of children are likely to have small impacts on outcomes.

[1] Studies of young adoptee's IQ find significant effects of family environment, though still only 1/3 as large as the genetic effects. See Cardon and Cherny [1994]. These effects of adoptive family environment appear to be attenuated in adulthood and get even smaller in old age. Plomin et al. [2001].

Jencks et al. [1972], Jencks [1980], and Goldberger [1979] provide a series of reasons why such strong interpretations may be unwarranted. First, understanding the determinants of IQ is different than understanding the determinants of educational attainment, income, and health. Second, the assumptions of the behavioral genetics model may be tilted towards overstating the importance of genes in explaining variation in outcomes. Positive correlation between family environment and genes raises the heritability estimate. Third, family environment is likely endogenous and may depend heavily on genes (Jencks [1980], Scarr and McCartney [1983], Dickens and Flynn [2001]). This endogeneity makes any simple nature nurture breakdown difficult to interpret.

Fourth, noting that variation in a given outcome for some population has a large genetic component is different from saying that the outcome is predetermined or cannot be changed by interventions. Genetic effects can be muted just as environmental effects can be. To take Goldberger's example, a finding that most of the variation in eyesight is due to genes does not imply that we should stop prescribing eyeglasses for people. The use of eyeglasses may add enormous utility for people (and offer an excellent return on investment), regardless of what fraction of eyesight is measured as being environmental.

In other words, knowing what fraction of the existing variance is environmental does not tell us whether a given environmental intervention is doomed to failure or success. Imagine a state with uniformly mediocre schools. Perhaps in that population, school quality doesn't explain any of the variation in student outcomes. But there may be great benefits from introducing a new school with motivated peers, high financial resources and high teacher quality. It is critical to bear in mind that the variance breakdown only deals with variation in the sample. Mechanically, expanding a sample to encompass a broader range of environment (e.g., considering children in both Africa and the US as opposed to the US alone) increases the variation in inputs and outcomes and likely the proportion of the variation in outcomes that is due to environment.

What then do we learn from behavioral geneticists' estimates of the relative contribution of genes, family environment, and non-shared environment? We are getting a breakdown of the variance of the outcome in the current population, assuming a particular structural model. In the case of adoption studies, heritability is a measure of how much more biological siblings resemble each other relative to adoptive siblings. Similarly, in the case of twin studies, heritability is a measure of how much more outcomes for identical twins are correlated relative to outcomes for fraternal twins or other siblings. See the next section for the algebra. If heritability estimates were labeled as the additional correlation in outcomes that is associated with being identical rather than fraternal twins, there might be less misinterpretation of these numbers.

Such a variance breakdown may be worth something to social scientists as an estimate as to whether genetic variation is particularly important in determining an outcome. Even if the functional form of the behavioral genetics model is simplified, the model may still deliver useful relative rankings of how much variation in genes contributes to variation of different outcomes (e.g., height versus age at first marriage.)

Economists and sociologists have suggested several ways to reframe the question so as to use adoption data to estimate some of the causal impacts from family environment without having to know the true model by which outcomes are determined and without having to deliver a complete nature, nurture breakdown. This line of research consists of regressing child outcomes on parental characteristics, i.e., using the more standard approach within economics. For example, Plug and Vijverberg [2003], and Sacerdote [2007] regress adoptee's years of schooling on the mother's years of schooling, family income, and family size. The advantage of using regression is that it tells us which specific parental inputs are most correlated with child outcomes and the slope of the relationships.

Certainly one cannot necessarily take these regressions coefficients as causal due to measurement error, endogenous relationships among variables, and unobservables. But these regressions provide a starting point for understanding which parental inputs matter and how much they matter even in the absence of a genetic connection between parents and children. We can then compare the observed coefficients on parental inputs that we find for adoptees to those that use other sources of variation in family characteristics. For example, Sacerdote [2007] finds little evidence for a direct effect of parental income on adoptees' income and education. This finding is generally consistent with the work of Mayer [1997] and Blau [1999].[2] And one can compare the effects of family size found in adoption studies to those found by Black Devereux and Salvanes [2005b] and Angrist, Lavy, and Schlosser [2005] who use the birth of identical twins and sex preferences as an exogenous shock to family size.

One can also generate separate transmission coefficients for adoptees and non-adoptees by regressing the child's outcome on that of the parent. See Björklund Lindahl and Plug [2006] and Björklund Jäntti and Solon [2007] for transmission coefficients of income (education) from parents to adoptees and non-adoptees. This enables one to see how transmission varies when there is and is not a genetic link to the parents. This work also has the advantage of providing comparability between existing estimates of transmission coefficients from parents to children such as those in Solon [1999], Zimmerman [1992], and Mazumder [2005].

Several bottom lines emerge from my summary of the nature and nurture literature. First, economists who are not already familiar with the literature are generally surprised by how much genes seem to matter, or more precisely stated, how much less adoptees resemble their adoptive parents and siblings than do non-adoptees.[3] Second, the

[2] Mayer [1997] does find evidence for an effect of parental income on college attendance.

[3] In the twins literature, one might say that economists are often surprised by how much more similar are outcomes for identical twins relative to fraternal twins.

estimated effects of family environment on adoptee outcomes are still large in some studies and leave scope for children's outcomes to be affected by changes in family, neighborhood, or school environment. And the importance of family environment can rise significantly when the model is made more flexible. Third, the precise breakdowns of variance provided by behavioral genetics are subject to a number of important issues of interpretation.

Ultimately, the evidence is consistent with the widely held view that both nature and nurture matter a great deal in determining children's outcomes. Parental characteristics matter even in the absence of any genetic connection to their children. A more deeply informed view will also recognize that certain measured parental effects or transmission coefficients from parents to children drop significantly, when one considers adoptees rather than children raised by their biological parents. However, that fact does not negate any of the findings of researchers who measure directly the causal effects of changing school, neighborhood, and family environment on outcomes.

II. THE BEHAVIORAL GENETICS MODEL[4]

In the simplest version of the model, child outcomes (Y) are produced by a linear and additive combination of genetic inputs (G), shared (common) family environment (F) and unexplained factors, which the BG literature often calls non-shared or separate environment, (S). This implies that child's educational attainment can be expressed as follows:

$$\text{Child's years of education (Y)} = \mathrm{G} + \mathrm{F} + \mathrm{S}. \tag{1}$$

The key assumption's here are that nature (G) and shared family environment (F) enter linearly and additively. Separate environment (S) is by definition the residual term and is uncorrelated with G and F. In the simple version of the model, one further assumes that G and F are not correlated for a given child. On the surface, this seems like a strange assumption and one that could perhaps be defended for some subsets of adoptees but not for children being raised by their biological parents. At a deeper level, behavioral geneticists often take F to represent that portion of family environment that is not correlated with genes, and they assume that G represents both the effects of gene and gene-environment correlation. The correlation between G and F can be modeled explicitly. If F itself is endogenous, modeling becomes very difficult. With these caveats in mind, one can already see that the BG breakdown into genes versus family environment is not necessarily an easily interpreted decomposition.

[4] Large portions of the text here are copied from Sacerdote [2007].

With the assumptions of no correlation between G, F, and S, taking the variance of both sides of equation one yields:

$$\sigma^2{}_Y = \sigma^2{}_G + \sigma^2{}_F + \sigma^2{}_S. \tag{2}$$

Dividing both sides by the variance in the outcome (σ_y^2) and defining $h^2 = \sigma^2{}_g/\sigma^2{}_y$, $c^2 = \sigma^2{}_F/\sigma^2{}_y$, and $e^2 = \sigma^2{}_S/\sigma^2{}_Y$ yields the standard BG relationship:

$$1 = h^2 + c^2 + e^2. \tag{3}$$

The variance of child outcomes is the sum of the variance from the genetic inputs (h^2 or heritability), the variance from family environment (c^2) and the variance from non-shared environment (e^2), i.e., the residual. From this starting point, a variety of variances and covariance's of outcomes can be expressed as functions of h, c, and e. The sample moments can then be used to identify these underlying parameters. Consider first the relationship for two adoptees. If one standardizes Y, F,G, S to be mean zero variance one, the correlation in outcomes between two adoptive siblings equals:

$$\text{Corr}\,(Y1, Y2) = \text{Cov}\,(Y_1, Y_2) = \text{Cov}\,(F_1, F_2) = \text{Var}\,(F_1) = c^2. \tag{4}$$

The correlation in outcomes between two non-adoptive siblings equals:

$$\begin{aligned}\text{Corr}\,(Y1, Y2) &= \text{Cov}\,(G_1 + F_1 + S_1, G_2 + F_2 + S_2)\\ &= \text{Cov}\,(G_1 + F_1, 1/2G_1 + F_1) = ½\ h^2 + c^2.\end{aligned} \tag{5}$$

This assumes that non-adoptive siblings share half of the same genetic endowment and the same common environment (see Plomin, et al. [2001] for a discussion). Thus, one can recover the full variance breakdown (h^2, c^2, e^2) from just the correlation among adoptive and biological siblings. By comparing (4) and (5) we see that h^2 = twice the difference in correlations in the outcome between the adoptive and biological siblings. This is the "double the difference" methodology frequently referred to in textbooks or discussions of the BG model (see Duncan et al. [2001]).

Now consider the correlation in outcomes between two identical twins versus the correlation for two fraternal twins. Identical twins are assumed to share all of the same genes and the same family environment; hence, their correlation in outcomes is:

$$\begin{aligned}\text{Corr}\,(Y1, Y2) &= \text{Cov}\,(G_1 + F_1 + S_1, G_2 + F_2 + S_2)\\ &= \text{Cov}\,(G_1 + F_1, G_1 + F_1) = h^2 + c^2.\end{aligned} \tag{6}$$

The algebra for the fraternal twins is the same as the algebra for any two biological (non-adoptive) siblings; hence, the same ½ $h^2 + c^2$ we had in the preceding paragraph. By subtracting (5) from (6) and multiplying by 2, we see that h^2 is twice the difference in correlations between identical and fraternal twins. Thus, the twins' literature has its own "double the difference" methodology.

Of course, one need not stop at finding the analytical solutions for the correlations for twins, adoptive siblings, and full siblings. One can also write down the equations for correlations in outcomes between children and parents, grandchildren and grandparents, between first cousins, and so on. This general model is known as *Fisher's Polygenetic Model.* Behrman and Taubman [1989] provides a nice illustration in that the authors present formulae for the phenotypic (outcome) correlations among 16 different possible pairings of relatives.

Note that as we add more pairings of different relatives, we can incorporate additional parameters and potentially make the model more realistic. (We can add flexibility and identify additional structural parameters.) Goldberger [1979] provides examples of models that allow for gene-environment correlation and use correlations among twins reared together, twins reared apart, adoptive siblings, and the parent-child correlations for twins and adoptees. Frequently the structural models employed are over identified (because there are more pairings of relatives than parameters) in which case the estimation chooses parameters that minimize the sum of squared errors between the sample moments and the fitted values of the sample moments.

In the case of Behrman and Taubman's [1989] model, they allow both for the possibilities of assortative mating and for the effects of dominance versus additive genes. Assortative mating is the notion that couples may positively select on phenotypes (outcomes), i.e., mating is non-random which means that siblings may have more than 50% of the same genes. Dominant gene effects are identified separately from additive effects by comparing correlations in outcomes across types of relatives that would have the same genetic connection under an additive system but need not if dominant effects are present. For example, suppose we had data for full siblings, half siblings, and identical twins, and we assume that all sibling pairs receive the same common environment. Think of the difference in correlation between full siblings and half siblings as identifying the effects of genetic connection. Under an additive system, genetic effects will cause exactly twice as much resemblance in identical twins as is caused among full siblings. If identical twins resemble each other MORE than twice as much, as implied by the other sibling types, one could attribute this "additional" component to the dominance effects of genes.[5]

Behavioral geneticists may also want to allow for the interactive effects of different genes, which is known as *epistasis*. By modeling the correlation among even more pairings of relatives (beyond the three types of sibling pairs mentioned previously), one can have additive genetics effects, dominance effects, and epistasis in the same model.

There are at least three other ways in which the structural modeling can be extended. First, one might assume that the same underlying process gives rise to several

[5] Goldberger [1979], pg. 331 offers the following intuition: "If the individual genes have non-additive effects, then it is only the additive part of the effect that makes for parent-child resemblance. The non-additive part of the effect does contribute to the resemblance of siblings, who may happen to receive the same gene combination."

different outcomes. For example, one might have two verbal test scores on the same set of individuals. One could treat these as yielding two sets of sample moments that can be used to identify the same underlying parameters. Alternatively, one might have a panel of test score outcomes for the same group of relatives over time, and one could posit that the relationship between siblings' outcomes is changing over time in a specific way. See Cherny and Cardon [1994]. Finally, one can also allow for different levels of gene-environment correlation among different relatives (e.g., fraternal and identical twin pairs need not be modeled as having correlation of 1.0 in their family environments).

An important assumption in this modeling is that the various samples used to estimate the relevant covariance's have the same underlying variance in genes and family environment. If for example, adoptive families have a restricted range of family environments (Stoolmiller [1999]), then it may not make sense to combine covariance's from adoptive siblings, non-adoptive siblings, and twins all in the same estimation. Furthermore, the variance breakdown obtained using adoptees may not apply to the general population.

In practice, the results are sensitive to which relative pairs are modeled in the analysis. As noted above, a great deal of weight is often placed on the difference in correlations of outcomes for adoptive siblings versus full siblings or for fraternal versus identical twins. However, if we instead compare parent-child (i.e., intergenerational) correlations to sibling correlations, we get a different answer for h^2, c^2, e^2 than if we compare across sibling types. Solon [1999] notes that the sibling correlation equals the sum of the intergenerational correlation squared plus other shared factors that are nurture based. Björklund and Jäntti [2008] points out that sibling correlations in many outcomes are typically much higher than intergenerational correlations. And, they show that this fact combined with the BG model implies a large nurture based component to outcomes.

III. CANONICAL RESULTS FROM THE BEHAVIORAL GENETICS LITERATURE

As noted earlier, the most voluminous and heavily cited part of the BG literature measures the contributions of genes and family environment to IQ. There are numerous summaries of this IQ literature including Goldberger [1977], Bouchard and McGue [1981], Devlin et al. [1994], Jencks et al. [1972], and Taylor [1980]. Table I shows the mean of the estimated correlations in each of these meta-studies along with the number of individual studies incorporated.

Devlin, Daniels, and Roeder reviewed 212 different studies of the IQ of twins. The mean correlation in IQ for studies of pairs of identical twins was .85. The correlations for fraternal twins were similar to correlations for other siblings and averaged .44. One can see immediately that in a simple model this will generate a high estimated

Table I Correlations in IQ between siblings, adoptive siblings, and identical twins

Meta study authors	Number of studies considered	Correlation for siblings raised together (non-adoptive, non identical twins)	Correlation for adoptive sibs	Correlation for identical twins	Correlation for fraternal twins
Devlin, Daniels and Roeder (1994)	212	0.44		0.85	
Bouchard and McGue (1981)	69	0.45	0.29	0.85	
Golberger (1977)	7	0.51	0.31	0.91	
Jencks et al. (1972)	18	0.54	0.42	0.86	0.58

The table reports results from four surveys of the IQ literature and incorporate hundreds of individual studies of twin and adoptee samples.
Data for Jencks et al. are as summarized by Taylor [1980] p. 46.

heritability; if one assumes that identical twins are twice as genetically related as other full siblings are and have twice the correlation in outcomes, equations (5) and (6) would lead one to conclude that all of the explained variance is genetic. Goldberger (1977) and Jencks et al. [1972] each reviewed a number of twin studies of IQ. The studies they review yielded similar results. In the case of Jencks [1972], the correlation in IQ for identical twins is .86 versus .54 for other siblings.

Bouchard and McGue [1981] examined a large number of twin studies and adoption studies. The adoption studies find significant correlation in IQ between adoptive siblings. The median correlation in IQ for adoptive siblings is .29 while the correlation for biological siblings raised together is .45. However, many of these studies are for adoptees less than age 18. Studies of older adoptive and biological siblings have found that the correlation in IQ among adoptees tends to fall significantly in adulthood while the correlation for biological siblings grows. Plomin et al. [1997, 2001].

Table II translates these sibling correlations into the behavioral genetics decomposition of variance in IQ into portions attributable to variance in genes, family (common) environment and separate environment. The twin designs find that a high proportion of explained variance in IQ is due to genes, and very little is due to family environment. Averaging over more than 200 studies, Devlin et al. show the average finding is that 49% of the variance is genetic and 5% is attributable to family (common) environment. The Bouchard and McGue summary of correlations for twins finds similar results, namely that 54% of variation is genetic and 4% is due to family environment. Non-shared environment (what economists would call the residual or unexplained variance) accounts for a substantial 40–50% of the variation in IQ.

The adoption studies find a larger proportion of variance in IQ attributable to family environment. Cardon and Cherny's [1994] examination of nine-year-olds in the

Table II IQ Results: Implied variance decomposition from the behavioral genetics model

Meta Studies	Variance attributable to additive genetic effects	Variance attributable to non-additive genetic effects	Total genetic	Variance attributable to common environment	Non-shared environment
Devlin, Daniels and Roeder (1994)	0.34	0.15	0.49	0.05	0.46
Golberger (1977)	0.47	0.11	0.58	0.22	0.20
Bouchard and McGue (1981) MZ vs DZ Twins*			0.54	0.04	0.42
Bouchard and McGue (1981) Adoptees*			0.32	0.29	0.39
Individual Studies					
Cherny and Cardon (1994) (For 9 year old Adoptees and Sibs)			0.60	0.16	0.24

*Bouchard and McGue do not calculate estimates of heritability from the sibling correlations they aggregate. Loehlin (1989) does this calculation using the Bouchard and McGue aggregates does not split environmental effects into common (family) and non-shared. I calculated these using the simple version of the BG model in equations (4) and (5).

Colorado Adoption Project found that 16% of the variation in IQ is attributable to family environment, and 60% is due to genes. The Bouchard and McGue summary of IQ correlations for adoptees implies that 29% of the variation is due family environment and 32% is due to genes. Averaging over the studies in Goldberger's [1977] literature summary, which includes both twin and adoption correlations, I find that 22% of the variation in IQ is due to family environment and 58% is due to genetic effects.

There is a disconnect between the twin and adoption literatures with regard to the importance of family environment. One way to resolve this contradiction is to appeal to the findings that family environment effects on adoptees are greatly attenuated in adulthood and that heritability rises with age (Pedersen et al. [1992] and McClearn et al. [1997]). However, another reasonable explanation is that applying the simple version of the behavioral genetics model to pairs of identical and fraternal twins will overstate heritability if identical twins face environments more similar than that faced for other siblings (Feldman and Otto [1997].)[6] Or, identical twins might affect each other's environment more than do fraternal twins. Recall from Section II that *any* factors which make outcomes for identical twins more similar than outcomes for fraternal

[6] Scarr and Carter-Saltzman [1979] provide some evidence that identical and fraternal twins do have similar correlations in family environment.

twins are assigned to genetic effects. The assumption of the structural model is that sibling pairs raised in the same household have the same correlation in family or common environment. One could imagine that parents and teachers would be even more likely to expect or demand similar performance from siblings who are identical twins. Parents may be more likely to provide similar environmental experiences for identical twins. In decomposing sources of earnings variation, Björkland Jäntii and Solon [2005] find that allowing different types of sibling pairs to have different amounts of correlation in family environment greatly lowers the estimated heritability and raises the estimated impacts from family environment.

In Table III, I summarize the existing behavioral genetics studies of variance in years of education. There are far fewer BG studies of education and earnings than of IQ, and the most widely known studies are those done by economists and sociologists.

Table III Years of education: Implied variance decomposition from the behavioral genetics model

Authors and sample	Variance attributable to additive genetic effects	Variance attributable to non-additive genetic effects	Total genetic	Variance attributable to common environment	Non-shared environment
Behrman and Taubman (1989) 2,000 twins pairs and their relatives NAS-NRC sample	0.88 (.002)	−0.01 (.047)	0.88		
Scarr and Weinberg (1994) 59 adoptive sibling pairs and 105 nonadoptive sibling pairs			0.38	0.13	0.49
Teasdale and Owen (1984) 163 pairs of adoptees from Danish National Register	0.678		0.678	0.052	0.270
Behrman, Taubman, and Wales (1977) 2,478 MZ and DZ Twins in the NAS-NRC sample			0.36	0.41	0.23

Scarr and Weinberg (1994) report adoptive and biological sibling correlations. I used equations (4) and (5) to translate this into the decomposition implied by the simplest form of the BG model. Teasdale and Owen report their results in variance of years of education explained by additive genes, common environment and separate environment. I calculated the fractions explained by each factor. The NAS-NRC sample is a National Academy of Science - National Research Council survey of twins performed in 1974.

Behrman and Taubman [1989] use data on twins and their relatives from the National Academy of Science/National Research Council sample. They compute years of schooling correlations for sixteen different pairs of relatives and fit the parameters of their model to match the predicted correlations with the sample correlations. Consistent with twin studies of IQ that find high heritability, Behrman and Taubman find that genetic effects explain 88% of the variation in schooling.[7] Family environment explains little or none of the variance in schooling. Scarr and Weinberg [1994] examine adoptees and find that family environment explains 13% of the variation. However, this study is based on only 59 adoptive sibling pairs. Teasdale and Owen [1984] have 163 pairs of adoptees and find that variance family environment explains 5% of the variation in schooling.

Overall, to the extent that behavioral geneticists have performed nature-nurture decompositions using years of schooling as the outcome, the findings have mirrored the findings of the much larger IQ literature. Genetic effects play a large role, while there is only a small role for family environment. That statement is tempered a bit by the Behrman, Taubman, and Wales study, and Scarr and Weinberg study, though that study had only 59 pairs of adoptive siblings. A different but equally valid interpretation of the results in Table III would be to say genetic effects clearly matter a great deal in determining schooling, but that the portion attributable to family environment changes significantly depending on how one specifies the structural model.

In Table IV, I switch the outcome of interest to earnings and I report results from two different studies. Björkland, Jäntti, and Solon [2005] used a large sample of siblings, twins and adoptees from the Statistics Sweden and Swedish Twin Registry. They derive formulae for the predicted correlations among nine different sibling types. They use weighted least squares to choose parameters to fit best the sample correlations to the predicted correlations from the models. One of the key results from this study is that it matters a great deal whether or not one constrains all sibling types reared together to have the same degree of correlation in family (common) environment. With such a constraint (Model 1), genes explain 28% of the variance in earnings and family environment explains 4%.[8] By adding three additional parameters to allow for differing correlations in family environment among sibling pairs (Model 4), the importance of family (common) environment rises to 16.4% and the genetic effects fall to 19.9%.

[7] The earlier Behrman Taubman and Wales [1975] study used the same data set of twins, but found lower heritability of schooling. This may be precisely because of the different way the two studies modeled correlation in family environment.

[8] These are the numbers for brothers. For sisters, the comparable numbers are 24.5% genetic and 1% common environment.

Table IV Earnings: Implied variance decomposition from the behavioral genetics model

Authors and sample	Variance attributable genetic effects	Variance attributable to common environment	Variance attributable to non-shared environment
Björklund, Jäntti and Solon (2005) Model 1 Swedish Brothers Including Raised Apart, Together, Twins, Adoptees, Half Sibs	.281 (.080)	0.038 (0.037)	0.681
Björklund, Jäntti and Solon (2005) Model 1 Swedish Sisters Including Raised Apart, Together, Twins, Adoptees, Half Sibs	.245 (.080)	0.009 (0.037)	0.746
Björklund, Jäntti and Solon (2005) Model 4 Swedish Brothers Including Raised Apart, Together, Twins, Adoptees, Half Sibs	0.199 (0.157)	0.164 (0.158)	0.637
Behrman, Taubman, and Wales (1975)	0.45	0.13	−0.42

Björklund, Jäntti and Solon estimates the BG parameters to fit the nine sibling correlations in the data from nine sibling types (MZ raised together, MZ apart, DZ together, DZ apart, Full sibs together, full sibs apart, half sibs together, half sibs apart, adoptive sibs). The difference between models 1 and 4 is that model 4 adds parameters to allow for different degrees of environmental correlation among different types of sibling pairs.

Table V shows the results from Loehlin's [2005] summary of the behavioral genetics literature on the determinants of personality traits. Like the IQ research, this is a rich literature and Loehlin considers hundreds of studies. He reports average correlations *between parents and children* for the most commonly measured aspects of personality, namely extraversion, agreeableness, conscientiousness, neuroticism, and openness. With regard to the determinants of personality traits, the literature has reached even more of a consensus than with regard to IQ. The first column is for the correlations between parents and children when their biological parents raise children. Correlations range from .11 to .17. When we consider adoptees and adoptive parents in column 2, the correlations almost disappear, falling to an average of .036. Column 3 reports correlations in traits for adoptees and their biological parents. Here the correlations rise almost to the levels seen in column (1), that is, for the children raised by their biological parents. This evidence (which again is a summary of hundreds of studies) is striking and certainly points strongly in the direction of genes being an important determinant of personality traits.

More recently, economists and other social scientists have begun to estimate the heritability of parameters that are fundamental to economic models of human behavior. For example, Cesarini et al. [2009] and Cesarini et al. [forthcoming] use twins data to estimate the heritability of preferences for risk taking and for fairness. In both cases the authors find substantial genetic influences and only a small role for shared environment.

Table V Behavioral genetics results on personality traits meta study of correlations between parents and children

	Parent child relationship		
	Biological and social	**Social, not biological**	**Biological, not social**
Dimension			
Extraversion	0.14	0.03	0.16
	(117, .010)	(40, .011)	(15, .019)
Agreeableness	0.11	0.01	0.14
	(65, .013)	(16, .021)	(3, .067)
Conscientiousness	0.09	0.02	0.11
	(64, .013)	(26, .012)	(2, .110)
Neuroticism	0.13	0.05	0.11
	(131, .010)	(40, .011)	(21, .022)
Openness	0.17	0.07	0.14
	(24, .028)	(12, .031)	(1 -)

This is a summary of the literature on personality traits and is reprinted exactly from Loehlin (2005) Table 6.3. Number of correlations that were averaged and the implied standard errors are in parentheses.

As a final outcome of interest, I graph in Figure I some of the data from the Grilo and Pogue-Geile [1991] meta study of correlations in weight, height and body mass index among full siblings raised together, adoptive siblings, and twins. Adoptive siblings have almost no correlation in body mass index. Full siblings raised together have a correlation of about .32. Interestingly fraternal twins show similar levels of correlation to other sibling pairs. The correlation in BMI jumps to .72 for identical twins.[9]

IV. CRITIQUES AND CHALLENGES TO INTERPRETATION OF THE BEHAVIORAL GENETICS RESULTS ON IQ AND SCHOOLING

BG results with respect to IQ appear to be quite robust in finding that the genetic effects account for 50 to 60% of the variance in adult IQ. In the twins studies and the studies of adult adoptees, family environment accounts for almost none of the variance.[10] Behrman and Taubman [1989] and Teasdale and Owen [1984] find no role for family environment in explaining years of schooling. What is one to make of these findings? One approach is to accept this finding as not only an accurate

[9] I report the body mass index correlations, which combine data for both same and mixed gender pairs of siblings. It would look only moderately different if I controlled for gender.

[10] Some of the studies of younger adoptees find that up to 16% of the variation in child IQ is attributed to family environment (Cardon and Cherny [1994]). This clearly leaves the question of family environment effects on test scores open to interpretation. Nonetheless both Harris [1998] and Plomin et al. [2001] pp. 176 sum up the literature by stating that effects of family environment on IQ are modest and get smaller or disappear with age.

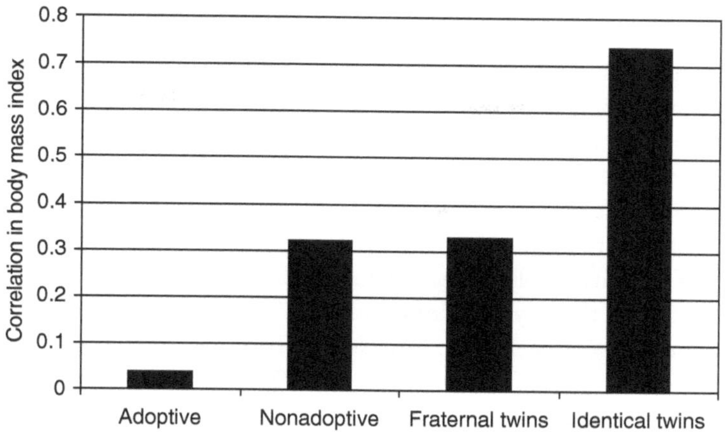

Figure 1 Correlations in Body Mass Index For Four Types of Sibling Pairs *Data are from meta-study done by Grilo and Pogue-Geile [1991]. Numbers for adoptive siblings add results from Sacerdote [2007] since Grilo and Pogue Geile have only one study with BMI figures. All calculations include same and mixed gender pairs.*

estimation of the BG model, but also as having important causal meaning and predictive power for interventions which might affect child test scores, educational attainment or income. This is the approach of Jensen [1972] and Herrnstein and Murrays [1994] who are pessimistic about the ability of social policy to affect inequality of income and schooling.

This view is unsatisfying not only because it makes one unpopular at dinner parties, but more importantly because such conclusions about the real weakness of family influences and other forms of environment like school quality seem to contradict everyday experience. In addition, it is hard to reconcile a view of minimal effects of shared environment with the extensive investments that many parents and school systems make in their children.[11] For example, there is a widespread belief that certain charter schools and certain Catholic schools have large treatment effects on test scores and high school graduation rates. These beliefs have been subsequently confirmed by very careful empirical work on the treatment effects from these schools. See Hoxby and Murarka [2007], Evans and Schwab [1995], and Neal [1997].

One way to handle the apparent contradiction is to note that some BG estimations (particularly those using adoption data for younger adoptees) find a significant role for shared environment in determining income, IQ, and education. Perhaps many of the well measured treatment effects of interventions are working through the 15–20% role

[11] I am assuming here that a large part of school quality is shared between siblings, which strikes me as a reasonable assumption. Parents may of course invest in children for reasons besides producing higher income and levels of education.

assigned to shared environment. In the large Devlin et al., meta study for twins data, the consensus number for the variance explained by family environment is 5%, but the older literature summary by Goldberger [1977] implies an average percent explained by family environment of 22%.

A different approach to reconcile the observed environmental effects on test scores and schooling with the BG decomposition is to note that behavioral geneticists may be working only within a restricted range of environments that are actually observed in the United States or in some other society. Stoolmiller [1999] emphasizes this point and presents corrections for this "restriction of range" problem.

A third reaction to the key BG findings is that one needs to somehow improve the BG structural model so that it not only delivers different estimates of the effects of shared environment, but can also explain other facts such as the Flynn effect. Flynn [1999] notes that IQ scores tend to rise over time. Dickens and Flynn [2001] present an elegant model in which environment responds endogenously to genetic endowments. This can explain a number of facts including the Flynn effect and possibly why the effect of adoptive parents on adoptee's IQ diminishes in adulthood. The Björklund, Jäntti Solon [2005] decomposition for earnings finds that heritability falls significantly once they allow for different shared environment correlations among identical twins relative to fraternal twins.

Generally, there is sizable literature that points out that gene environment interactions or the endogeneity of environment will cause the BG model to understate the importance of shared environment and overstate the importance of genetic factors. See Ridley [2003]. Turkheimer et al. [2003] makes the point that nonlinearities in the relationship between genetic factors and outcomes can cause the BG model to overstate heritability. In particular, they find that measured heritability is lower for children in less advantaged families. Lizzeri and Siniscalchi [2007] point out that if parents are behaving optimally, the learning process for adoptees and non-adoptees will likely differ and that this can lead behavioral genetics' estimates to overstate heritability.

I suggest another approach to understanding the BG results on IQ, schooling and income. This approach follows that of Jencks et al., [1972], Goldberger [1977] and Duncan et al., [2001]. Rather than further trying to upgrade the BG model, one can accept that this is a structural model with strong assumptions and that the model may not be able to deliver causal, out of sample predictions for all environmental interventions of interest to social scientists. The facts from the BG work are that non-adoptive siblings (identical twins) resemble each other much more on certain outcomes than do adoptive siblings (fraternal twins). Clearly, that suggests that genes matter a great deal. We need not proceed from this fact to a full decomposition of outcome variances into the effects of genes that we do not observe or asingle index of shared environment that we do not observe. In addition, if we do implement such a decomposition, one needs to keep in mind that we are decomposing variance within the sample that we have; the causal effects for interventions outside of this range may be bigger or smaller than effects implied by the decomposition. And finally, even if we had the ultimate decomposition, it is unclear that it could be used to make out of sample predictions about the effects of policy changes or the degree to which a shock to an individual will affect her children.

V. TREATMENT EFFECTS AND REGRESSION COEFFICIENTS

Economists tend to be more interested in the associations and causal relationships among variables that we observe directly, such as parental income and children's schooling, and we tend to study children's health, income, education, marital status, and happiness as the outcomes of interest rather than IQ scores and personality traits.

Rubin's causal model [1974] provides an excellent framework for understanding and clarifying what is meant by a "causal effect" or a "treatment effect". According to Rubin (and many empirical economists), in order to measure a causal effect there needs to be an identifiable intervention that could be implemented or not implemented. The causal effect of the treatment on outcome Y for unit i is the difference in potential outcomes that will occur with versus without the treatment being applied. Thus, one wouldn't measure the causal effect from being black or female since that it is not a treatment one could apply or withhold. Similarly, one cannot interpret the BG variance decomposition in a strict causal sense since one cannot literally alter the subjects' genes. Nor can one actually move the family environment of a twin or an adoptee by a standard deviation of the BG index of shared (family) environment since this index is a theoretical concept and not observed.

I take this point very literally in Sacerdote [2007] in which I reduce the problem to estimating the causal effect from an adoptee being assigned to one type of family versus another. For example, I calculate the effects on the adoptee's educational attainment from being assigned to a family in which both parents have college degrees and there are three or fewer children in the family. More formally, I estimate:

$$E_i = \alpha + \beta 1 * T1_i + \beta 2 * T2_i + Male_i + A_i + C_i + \varepsilon_i. \tag{7}$$

Where E_i is educational attainment for child i, $T1_i$ is a dummy being assigned to a family with three or fewer children and high parental education, T2 is a dummy being assigned to a family that either has three of fewer children, OR has one or more college educated parents. A_i is a full set of single year of age dummies, and C_i are a full set of cohort (year of adoption) dummies. The omitted category is children assigned to large families in which neither parent has a college education.

This has the clear disadvantage of only identifying the effect of a discrete jump in family characteristics like parental education that have more variation than simply "college degree or not". However, the advantage is that the result is very easy to explain and interpret. β1 is the causal effect on outcomes from being assigned to a particular family type. The family type includes size, parental education, and all the observables and unobservables correlated with those two characteristics.[12] In such an analysis, there is no attempt to make broader statements about the effects of genes or an overarching index of family environment.

Random assignment of adoptees to families plays a critical role in this analysis. It is the lack of correlation between adoptee pre-treatment characteristics and adoptive family characteristics that allows one to give β1 a causal interpretation.

More broadly, economists and sociologists have used regression to estimate the effects of child and adoptive family characteristics on adoptee outcomes. Examples of this include Plug and Vijverberg [2003], Scarr and Weinberg [1978], and Sacerdote [2002]. A typical equation estimated is of the form:

$$\begin{aligned} E_i = \alpha + \beta 1 * \mathrm{MomsEd}_i + \beta 2 * \mathrm{DadsEd}_i + \beta 4 * \mathrm{Log}\,(\mathrm{Family\ Income})_i \\ + \beta 5 * \mathrm{Birth\ Order}_i + \beta 6 * \mathrm{Male}_i + \varepsilon_i. \end{aligned} \tag{8}$$

Here E_i represents adoptee i's years of education while MomsEd_i and DadsEd_i represent adoptive mother and adoptive father's years of education. If one had similar measures for the biological mother and father, those could clearly be added to the equation as well.

This approach loses the bare simplicity of the treatment effects approach in equation (7) but gains a great deal in allowing the reader to think about *which* adoptive family (or biological family) characteristics are most correlated with adoptee outcomes and how steep the slopes are. Social scientists have long used regression to attempt to separate out the effects of different right hand side variables. Clearly selection, measurement error, collinearity, and unobservables can potentially bias β1−β4 away from the true treatment effects. But these caveats are well understood and presenting the results in the form of regression coefficients is transparent.

Furthermore, the use of regression coefficients in studying the effects of adoptive family characteristics allows a direct comparison of the results to other studies that attempt to examine a particular and exogenous shock to family environment. For instance Blau [1999] and Mayer [1997] present evidence that shocks to income itself have only small effects on child education and income. The results from adoption studies appear to confirm this finding (see the following section).

The final and most common approach used by economists is to calculate transmission coefficients of various outcomes from adoptive and biological parents to adoptees. A transmission coefficient takes the form:

[12] For example, the adoptive families that are large and in which neither parent has a college education may have very different unobserved characteristics than the other families. The quality of the school system might be different or the amount of time spent reading to children might be different, β1 and β2 will incorporate effects from such unobserved characteristics.

$$E_i = \alpha + \delta 1 * E_{Mi} + \gamma * X_i + \varepsilon_i. \quad (9)$$

Where Ei and E_{Mi} are adoptive child's and adoptive (or biological) mother's education respectively and Xi could be a vector of controls for child gender or age. δ1 captures the degree to which additional years of education for the mother are transmitted to the child. Again, the advantage of this approach is that economists already know a great deal about these transmission coefficients, and there is a large amount of literature on transmission coefficients for education and income in general populations. See Solon [1999] and Mazumder [2005].

Calculating transmission coefficients from adoptive parents to adoptees allows us to understand how these transmission coefficients change (are lessened?) when we remove the genetic connection between children and the parents raising them. One can see again why some assumption of random assignment of children to families becomes important. If selection of children into families creates significant positive or negative correlation between the genetic endowments of children and parents, then knowing the transmission coeffient for the adoptees becomes less useful because genetic effects are driving part of δ1.

Similarly calculating δ1 between adoptees and their biological parents is potentially very interesting. This allows us to understand how much of the transmission process remains even when the parents are not involved in raising the child.

VI. RESULTS FROM ECONOMICS ON ADOPTEES

I start by presenting the results on transmissions coefficients since these are the most commonly used tool of economists studying nature and nurture effects. Arguably, the best paper on transmission of education and income to adoptees is Björklund Lindahl, Plug [2006] one which uses a very large sample of Swedish adoptees who were placed with families. This paper literally uses the census of all Swedish adoptees who were born during 1962-1966 (roughly 5,000 adoptees) and a 20% sample of non-adoptees born during the same time period.

Key results from the Björklund Lindahl Plug study are reproduced in Table VI. This table contains transmission coefficients *from* adoptive and biological parents *to* adoptees and non-adoptees. The outcomes considered are years of schooling, a dummy for completing four years of university, annual earnings, and annual income. The first two rows are for non-adoptees, i.e., children raised by their biological parents. For the non-adoptees, we see transmission coefficients of earnings in the range of .24, which are similar to those for single years of income found in the existing income transmission literature. See Solon [1999], Haider and Solon [2006], and Mazumder [2005]. The transmission coefficients for education of .24 also are similar to those found in the OLS specifications in other studies including Black et al. [2005a]. Note that whether

Table VI Transmission coefficients from the Björklund, Lindahl, Plug [2006]

	(1) Years of schooling	(2) Years of schooling	(3) University	(4) University	(5) Earnings	(6) Income
NonAdoptees						
Biological father	.240** (0.002)		.339** (0.004)		.235** (0.005)	.241** (0.004)
Biological mother		.243** (0.002)		.337** (0.004)		
Adoptees						
Biological father	.113** (0.016)		.184** (0.036)		0.047 (0.034)	.059* (0.028)
Biological mother		.132** (0.017)		.261** (0.034)		
Adoptive father	.114** (0.013)		.165** (0.024)		.098** (0.038)	.172** (0.031)
Adoptive mother		.074** (0.014)		.145** (0.024)		
Sum of estimates for bio and adoptive fathers	.227** (0.019)		.349** (0.040)		.145** (0.049)	.231** (0.040)
Sum of estimates for bio and adoptive mothers		.207** (0.021)		.406** (0.039)		

This reproduces most of BLP [2006] Table II. Sample sizes are roughly 2,000 adoptees and 90,000 non-adoptees. Each transmission coefficient is from a separate regression of child's outcome on parents' outcomes for years of schooling, a dummy for having 4 years of university, earnings and income. The latter two variables are averaged over multiple years. All data are from the Swedish National Registry.

one uses the father's education or the mother's education on the right hand side of the regression, the coefficients are nearly identical.

There are several remarkable facts about the results for adoptees. First, there is strong transmission of years of schooling (or university status) from both the adoptive parents and the biological parents. Furthermore, when one considers the effects of the adoptive and biological fathers, the coefficients are roughly equal in magnitude. Transmission of years of schooling from biological fathers to adoptees has a coefficient of .113 and transmission from adoptive fathers to adoptees is .114, and the two transmission coefficients for adoptees add up to .227 which is roughly equal to the .240 transmission coefficient of schooling for the non-adoptees.

This apparent additivity of the transmission from biological parents and nurturing parents is extremely interesting and can be seen in roughly five of the six columns in Table VI. For example, transmission of income from an adoptee' biological father is .06 and .17 from adoptive father's and this adds up to .23. The transmission coefficient for non-adoptees is .24. Björklund, Jäntti, and Solon [2007] explore more deeply this additive property. They find that a simple additive model explains the data quite well. Note that for adoptee earnings, BLP find that adoptive fathers are a more important source of transmission of earnings. For schooling, adoptive and biological fathers seem to matter about equally.

BLP also ask whether there are statistically significant effects from interacting biological and adoptive parent characteristics. They do not find strong evidence of interaction effects. This finding is not surprising given that we already noted above that within their data, the entire transmission coefficient for non-adoptees can be explained by the main effects of adoptive and biological parent characteristics.

Therefore, the bottom line from the BLP study appears to be that transmission of earnings and education works strongly through both biological channels and through environmental channels. To say a bit more about the relative importance of the two channels, I now turn to transmission coefficients found in other adoption studies.

One caveat to the BLP study might be potential selective placement of adoptees into Swedish families and that this might affect their findings on the sources of transmission. For example, positive selection of healthier adoptees into high-income families might cause BLP to overstate how much transmission comes from the nurturing parents. In Sacerdote [2007] I am able to provide transmission coefficients for a set of Korean-American adoptees whose assignment to US families was effectively random. Holt used a queuing system to assign children to families and I provide evidence that this yields quasi-random assignment of children to families.

Table VII provides estimated transmission coefficients from 4 different adoption samples including the BLP study, the Holt study, the National Longitudinal Survey of Youth 1979, and the Wisconsin Longitudinal Study analyzed in Plug [2004]. I report figures for both the transmission of years of education and transmission of a dummy variable for having completed four or more years of college. The upper panel is for the non-adoptees and the lower panel is for the adoptees. These are coefficients for transmission from mothers to children.[13]

For the non-adoptees, the Holt, BLP, NLSY samples deliver transmission coefficients that are roughly in the .25−.40 range. The NLSY numbers tend to be at the higher end of this range. It is possible that this stems from nonlinearities in transmission combined with the greater range of parental education in the NLSY data. The Wisconsin data delivers a large transmission coefficient of .54 for years of education, but the transmission coefficient for "college graduate" status in the WLS sample is .385. This latter number is in line with the results found in the other three samples.

The transmission coefficients from adoptive mothers to adoptees show a different pattern. Both the Holt and the BLP samples of adoptees have coefficients that are

[13] Switching to fathers would not affect the Holt numbers, but it would raise the transmission coefficients for adoptees in the BLP data.

Table VII Transmission of education in five samples of adoptees and non-adoptees

	Transmission of years of education (mother-child)	Transmission of 4 + years college (mother-child)	N
Holt Non-Adoptees	0.315 (0.038)**	0.302 (0.037)**	1,213
Swedish Non-Adoptees	.243 (.002)**	.337 (.004)**	94,079
Swedish NonAdoptees (Holmlund et al.)	.280 (.001)**		570,555
NLSY Non-Adoptees	.401 (.011)**	.440 (.018)**	5,614
WLS Non-Adoptees	.538 (.016)**	.385 (.015)**	15,871
Holt Adoptees	0.089 (0.029)**	0.102 (0.034)**	1,642
Swedish Adoptees	.074 (.014)**	.145 (.024)**	2,125
Swedish Adoptees (Holmlund et al.)	.030 (.010)**		4,603
NLSY Adoptees	.277 (.060)**	.420 (.078)**	170
WLS Adoptees	.276 (.063)**	.178 (.063)**	610

I report transmission coefficients for education and income in the Holt Sample, my calculations from the NLSY79, Björklund et al. [2006] for Sweden, Plug [2004] for the Wisconsin Longitudinal Survey (WLS). The adoptees in BLP's study are ages 35–37 in 1999. The adoptees in Plug's study are ages 23 and older. For the NLSY data I use adoptees ages 28–36 in 1993. Swedish international adoptions are analyzed by Holmlund, Lindahl and Plug [2005].

within one standard error of each other. Transmission of years of education is about .08 and transmission of college status is about .12. The other two samples yield significantly larger transmission from adoptive mothers to children. One natural explanation for this finding is that the two smaller samples (NLSY and WLS) have strong positive selection of adoptees into families in which the healthiest or most naturally able infants were more likely to be adopted by the higher education mothers. On the whole, comparing the transmission coefficients for the adoptees to those for non-adoptees gives the impression that adoptees receive from their adoptive mothers about 1/4 to maybe 1/2 of the transmission effects that non-adoptees receive. The transmission coefficients from adoptive mothers to adoptees are lower than the BLP results using adoptive fathers. Nonetheless, both the biological parents and the nurturing parents matter a great deal. I cannot reject the hypothesis that the two sources of transmission influences are equal in size, though the point estimates of Table VII indicate that transmission to adoptees via nurture is less than half of total transmission to non-adoptees.

Table VIII Transmission of income in the Holt and Swedish samples and the PSID

	Transmission of Log (Income)	N
Holt Non-Adoptees	0.246 (0.080)**	1,196
Swedish Non-Adoptees	0.241** (0.004)	91,932
Panel Study of Income Dynamic Non-Adoptees	0.369** (0.018)	4,160
Holt Adoptees	0.186 (0.111)	1,209
Swedish Adoptees	.172** (0.031)	1,976
Panel Study of Income Dynamic Adoptees	0.096 (0.121)	120

I report transmission coefficients for education and income in the Holt Sample, Björklund et al. [2006] for Sweden and Liu and Zeng [2007] for the Panel Study of Income Dynamics (PSID).

In Table VIII, I report the results on income transmission for the Holt and BLP samples and the Panel Study of Income Dynamics as analyzed by Liu and Zeng [2007]. In the case of BLP, this is transmission of income from fathers to children and averages over multiple years of income for both. In the Holt sample, this is a single survey report in which respondents choose from among ten categories of income. Since I also had administrative data on income at the time of adoption, I instrumented for the survey measure of family income with the administrative measure. In both samples, transmission for non-adoptees is about .24 and transmission for adoptees is about .18. This would indicate that the income transmission process is substantial even without a biological connection between parent and child. Since the measurement of income in the Holt sample is less than ideal, I do not want to lean too heavily on the Holt result in reaching this conclusion. Liu and Zeng [2007] find a larger transmission coefficient for the non-adoptees than do the other two studies and they attribute this fact partially to the fact that they are using earnings for older offspring.[14]

A related and interesting question is how the transmission process from parents to adoptees and non-adoptees differs when one looks across different outcomes. Figure II, graphs transmission coefficients for 9 different outcomes for adoptees and non-adoptees in the Holt sample. The vertical axis is for the transmission coefficient for non-adoptees and the horizontal axis is used for the transmission coefficient for the adoptees. Outcomes close to the 45° degree line such as drinking and smoking are transmitted equally strongly from parents to adoptive and non-adoptive children. Not surprisingly, height is very

[14] Haider and Solon [2006] and Böhlmark and Lindquist [2006] address how the ages at which earnings are measured effects the measured transmission coefficients.

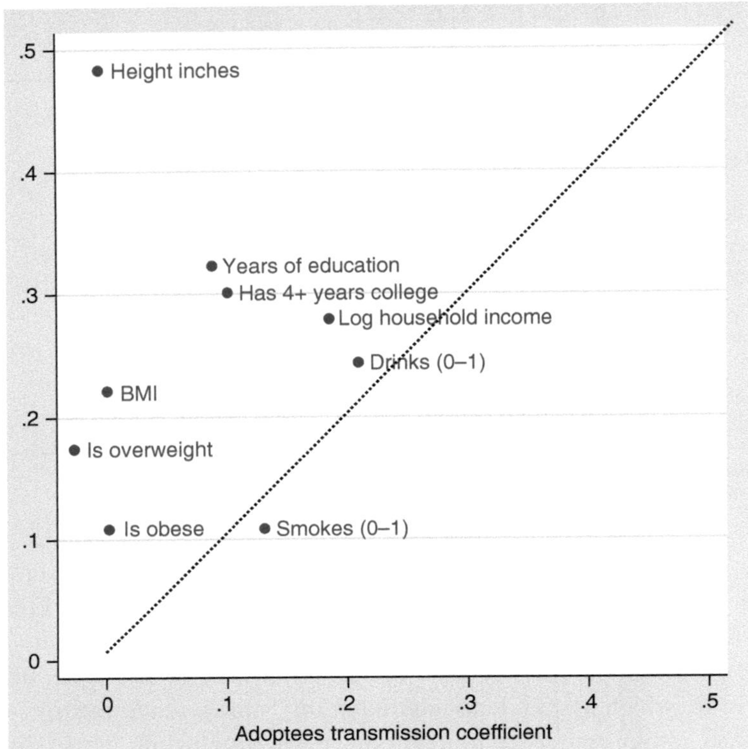

Figure II Comparison of Coefficient of Transmission from Parent to Child *Reproduced from Sacerdote [2007]. Graph shows coefficient from a regression of child's outcome on mother's outcome for adoptees and non-adoptees in the sample.*

heavily transmitted to non-adoptees and not at all to adoptees. The pattern one notices in Figure I is that physical outcomes like obesity and height show very little transmission to adoptees while social outcomes like moderate drinking require no genetic connection for transmission.[15] Education is somewhere in between.

As discussed in the preceding section, one of the advantages of using multiple regressions in this context is that it allows one to regress adoptee outcomes on a host of factors and to potentially make inferences about which factors have the largest and most statistically significant influences on adoptees. I noted this in Sacerdote [2007] for adoptee's years of education and a very clear pattern emerged. The two adoptive family characteristics that are statistically significant predictors of adoptee educational attainment are family size and mother's education. Each additional year of mother's education is associated with an extra .09 years of education for the adoptee. Each

[15] In contrast, a large part of the transmission of alcoholism may be genetic (Cloninger et al. [1981]).

additional child in the family is associated with a statistically significant decrease of .12 years. These facts remain true regardless of what additional controls are added.

The strong finding with regard to family size indicates that either family size is correlated with some important unobservables about the family (as suggested by the findings of Black Devereux and Salvanes [2005b]) or there are indeed direct effects from family size. In fact, in later work, Black Devereux and Salvanes [2007] find that unexpected increases in family size do have significant negative effects on achievement. Family size in the adoption data covaries with other important family characteristics, and thus one cannot be certain that the effects I find are strictly causal effects from family size itself. However, the adoption results are certainly suggestive and push social scientists towards a better understanding of the mechanisms by which family environment affects outcomes.

Consistent with Blau [1999] and Mayer [1997], controlling for other family characteristics there is no direct impact from family income. This remains true regardless of how I employ the four measures of parental income in the data set. For the non-adoptees in the sample, the income measures generate transmission coefficients that resemble those in other data sets so this is unlikely to be purely a story of measurement error.

In order to make some broad causal statements about the effects of family environment on adoptee outcomes, I then asked about the treatment effects on an adoptee from being assigned to a small, high education family. Here, small means three or fewer children and high education means that both parents have college degrees. The measured treatment effects of family environment shifts on adoptee outcomes are quite large. For example, assignment to a small high education family leads to a 16-percentage point increase in the likelihood of graduating from college, relative to assignment to a large family where neither parent has a college degree. That effect is on a mean of about 58% of adoptees graduating from college.

VII. PUTTING IT ALL TOGETHER: WHAT DOES IT MEAN?

A review of the behavioral genetics literature and the recent economics literature on nature and nurture effects yields several conclusions. First, the BG estimates of the heritability of certain outcomes including IQ are quite robust. The canonical result is that adult IQ is about 50% heritable and that for adults, little of the remaining variation is attributable to family environment. The numbers are somewhat similar for decompositions of the variance of educational attainment. Behrman and Taubman [1989] and Teasdale and Owen [1984] find no role for family environment in determining years of education although Behrman, Taubman, and Wales [1977] found substantial effects from family environment on schooling. The finding of no role or only a small role for family environment in determining educational attainment and income also appears to be relatively robust within the BG framework. However as Björklund,

Jäntti, and Solon [2005], Jencks et al. [1972], and Goldberger [1977] and others have noted, that fact need not have major implications for social scientists' investigations of the merits or treatment effects from changes in environment. For example, the variance decomposition may not incorporate the environmental shifts being contemplated.

Furthermore, a tremendous amount of work has recently been done to make the structural BG model more sophisticated. Dickens and Flynn [2001] model the potential endogeneity between genes and environment. Turkheimer et al., [2003] deal with the nonlinear nature in which genes and environment translate into outcomes.

Implementing such decompositions and then applying the results out of sample is so challenging that economists have recently bypassed the problem of fully identifying nature and nurture effects. Instead, we have calculated transmission coefficients from parents to children for adoptees and non-adoptees. This delivers an estimate of how much of the transmission of education, income or some other outcome takes place even in the absence of a genetic connection between parents and children. The resulting picture is one that appears to be quite plausible and to match what we know about the potency of environment from experimental interventions in school characteristics or neighborhood characteristics (see Katz, Kling and Liebman [2001]). For example, Björklund Lindahl and Plug find that about half of transmission of education to adoptees works through biological parents and about half works through adoptive parents.

In some sense, the more we learn about the effects of environment on children's outcomes, the more we see a picture that fits the existing data and parents' intuition. Surely, it would be difficult to deny that genetic effects matter. Just look at how much more biological siblings resemble each other on education and income than do adoptive siblings. At the same time, there are potent environmental effects observed from assigning an adoptee to one type of family versus another. Many social scientists have the intuition that differences in school quality and home environment can explain a lot of inequality of average outcomes that is observed. This intuition may be right. For example, the black-white gap in college completion rates in the US is roughly 15.4 percentage points. Even within the family environment variation observed in the Holt sample, I observe similarly large gaps in Korean-American adoptee outcomes from the assignment to one family environment versus another. Overall, it appears that economists' work with adoptees will help create a consistent picture of what aspects of family environment matter and how much they matter.

REFERENCES

Angrist, J.D., Lavy, V., Schlosser, A., 2005. New Evidence on the Causal Link Between the Quantity and Quality of Children. NBER Working Paper No. 11835, December.

Behrman, J.R., Taubman, P., 1989. Is Schooling 'Mostly in the Genes'? Nature Nurture Decomposition Using Data on Relatives. J. Polit. Econ. XCVII, 1425–1446.

Behrman, J.R., Taubman, P., Wales, T., 1977. Controlling for and Measuring the Effects of Genetics and Family Environment in Equations for Schooling and Labor Market Success. In: Taubman, P. (Ed.), Kinometrics: Determinants of Socioeconomic Success Within and Between Families. North-Holland Pub. Co. Elsevier North-Holland, Amsterdam; New York.

Björklund, A., Jäntti, M., 2008. Intergenerational Income Mobility and the Role of Family Background, forthcoming. In: Salverda, W., Nolan, B., Smeeding, T. (Eds.), Handbook of Economic Inequality. Oxford University Press, Oxford.

Björklund, A., Lindahl, M., Plug, E., 2006. Intergenerational Effects in Sweden: What Can We Learn from Adoption Data? Q. J. Econ. August, forthcoming.

Björklund, A., Jäntti, M., Solon, G., 2005. Influences of Nature and Nurture on Earnings Variation: A Report on a Study of Various Sibling Types in Sweden. In: Bowles, S., Gintis, H., Groves, M.O. (Eds.), Unequal Chances: Family Background and Economic Success. Princeton University Press, Princeton, pp. 145–164.

Björklund, A., Jäntti, M., Solon, G., 2007. Nature and Nurture in the Intergenerational Transmission of Socioeconomic Status: Evidence from Swedish Children and Their Biological and Rearing Parents. NBER Working Paper 12985, March.

Black, S., Devereux, P., Salvanes, K.G., 2005a. Why the Apple Doesn't Fall Far: Understanding Intergenerational Transmission of Human Capital. Am. Econ. Rev. XCV, 437–449.

Black, S., Devereux, P.J., Salvanes, K.G., 2005b. The More the Merrier? The Effect of Family Size and Birth Order on Children's Education. Q. J. Econ. CXX, 669–700.

Black, S., Devereux, P.J., Salvanes, K.G., 2007. Small Family Smart Family? Family Size and the IQ Scores of Young Men. National Bureau of Economics Working Paper Number 13336.

Blau, D.M., 1999. The Effect of Income on Child Development. Rev. Econ. Stat. LXXXI, 261–276.

Böhlmark, A., Lindquist, M.J., 2006. Life-Cycle Variations in the Association between Current and Lifetime Income: Replication and Extension for Sweden. J. Labor Econ. 24 (4), 879–896, Oct.

Bouchard, T.J., McGue, M., 1981. Familial Studies of Intelligence: A Review. Science CCXII, 1055–1059.

Cardon, L.R., 1994. Height, Weight and Obesity. In: DeFries, J.C., Plomin, R., Fulker, D.W. (Eds.), Nature and Nurture During Middle Childhood. Blackwell Press, Oxford, UK.

Cesarini, D., Johannesson, M., Lichtenstein, P., Sandewall, Ö., Wallace, B., Genetic Variation in Financial Decision Making. J. Finance forthcoming.

Cesarini, D., Dawes, C.T., Johannesson, M., Lichtenstein, P., Wallace, B., 2009. Genetic Variation in Preferences for Giving and Risk Taking. Q. J. Econ. CXXIV, 809–842.

Cherny, S., Cardon, L.R., 1994. General Cognitive Ability. In: DeFries, J.C., Plomin, R., Fulker, D.W. (Eds.), Nature and Nurture During Middle Childhood. Blackwell Press, Oxford, UK.

Cloninger, C.R., Bohman, M., Sigvardson, S., 1981. Inheritance of Alcohol-Abuse - Cross-Fostering Analysis of Adopted Men. Arch. Gen. Psychiatry XXXVIII, 861–868.

Devlin, B., Daniels, M., Roeder, K., 1994. The Heritability of IQ. Genetics 137, 597–606.

Dickens, W., Flynn, J.R., 2001. Heritability Estimates versus Large Environmental Effects the IQ Paradox Resolved. Psychol. Rev. CVIII, 346–369.

Duncan, G.J., Boisjoly, J., Harris, K.M., 2001. Sibling, Peer, Neighbor, and Schoolmate Correlations as Indicators of the Importance of Context for Adolescent Development. Demography XXXVIII, 437–447.

Evans, W.N., Schwab, R.M., 1995. Finishing High School and Starting College: Do Catholic Schools Make a Difference? Q. J. Econ. 941–974.

Feldman, M.W., Otto, S.P., 1997. Twin studies, heritability, and intelligence. Science 278 (5342), 1383–1384, Nov. 21.

Flynn, J.R., 1999. Searching for Justice: The discovery of IQ gains over time. Am. Psychol. 54, 5–20.

Goldberger, A.S., 1977. Twin methods: A skeptical view. Kinometrics: Determinants of Socioeconomic Success within and between Families: New York: Elsevier North-Holland, 299–324.

Goldberger, A.S., 1979. Heritability. Economica 46 (184), 327–347, Nov.

Grilo, C.M., Pogue-Geile, M.F., 1991. The Nature of Environmental Influences on Weight and Obesity: A Behavior Genetic Analysis. Psychol. Bull. CX, 520–537.

Haider, S.J., Solon, G., 2006. Life-Cycle Variation in the Association between Current and Lifetime Earnings. Am. Econ. Rev. 96 (4), 1308–1320.

Harris, J.R., 1998. The Nurture Assumption: Why Children Turn out the Way They Do. The Free Press, New York.

Herrnstein, R.J., Murray, C., 1994. The Bell Curve: Intelligence and Class Structure in American Life. The Free Press, New York.

Holmlund, H., Lindahl, M., Plug, E., 2005. Estimating Intergenerational Effects of Education: A Comparison of Methods. University of Stockholm, Mimeo.

Hoxby, C.M., Murarka, S., 2007. New York City's Charter Schools Overall Report. New York City Charter Schools Evaluation Project, Cambridge, MA, June.

Jencks, C., 1980. Heredity, Environment, and Public Policy Reconsidered. Am. Sociol. Rev. 45 (5), 723–736, Oct.

Jencks, C., Smith, M., Ackland, H., Bane, M.J., Cohen, D., Gintis, H., et al., 1972. Inequality: A Reassessment of the Effects of Family and Schooling in America. Basic Books, New York.

Jensen, A.R., 1972. Genetics and Education. Harper and Row, New York.

Katz, L.F., Kling, J.R., Liebman, J.B., 2001. Moving to Opportunity in Boston: Early Results of a Randomized Mobility Experiment. Q. J. Econ. CXVI, 607–654.

Lizzeri, A., Siniscalchi, M., 2007. Parental Guidance and Supervised Learning. Mimeo New York University.

Liu, H., Zeng, J., 2007. Genetic Ability and Intergenerational Earnings Mobility, mimeo, The National University of Singapore and Journal of Population Economics (forthcoming).

Loehlin, JC., 1989. Partitioning Environmental and Genetic Contributions to Behavioral Development. Am. Psychol. XCIV, 1285–1292.

Loehlin, J.C., 2005. Resemblance in Personality and Attitudes Between Parents and Their Children. In: Bowles, S., Gintis, H., Groves, M.O. (Eds.), Unequal Chances: Family Background And Economic Success. Princeton University Press, Princeton and Oxford.

Mazumder, B., 2005. The Apple Falls Even Closer to the Tree than We Thought. In: Bowles, S., Gintis, H., Groves, M.O. (Eds.), Unequal Chances: Family Background and Economic Success. Princeton University Press, Princeton and Oxford.

Mayer, S.E., 1997. What Money Can't Buy: Family Income and Children's Life Chances. Harvard University Press, Cambridge and London.

McClearn, G.E., Johansson, B., Berg, S., Pedersen, N.L., Ahern, F., Petrill, S.A., et al., 1997. Substantial Genetic Influence on Cognitive Abilities in Twins 80 or More Years Old. Science 276 (5318), 1560–1563, Jun. 6.

Neal, D., 1997. The Effects of Catholic Secondary Schooling on Educational Attainment. J. Labor Econ. XV, 98–123.

Pedersen, N.L., Plomin, R., Nesselroade, J.R., McClearn, G.E., 1992. A Quantitative Genetic Analysis of Cognitive Abilities During the Second Half of the Life Span. Psychol. Sci. 3, 346.

Plomin, R., Fulker, D.W., Corley, R., DeFries, J.C., 1997. Nature, Nurture and Cognitive Development from 1–16 Years: A Parent Offspring Adoption Study. Psychol. Sci. 8, 442–447.

Plomin, R., DeFries, J.C., McClearn, G.E., McGuffin, P., 2001. Behavioral Genetics, fourth ed. Worth Publishers, New York.

Plug, E., 2004. Estimating the Effect of Mother's Schooling on Children's Schooling Using a Sample of Adoptees. Am. Econ. Rev. XCIV, 358–368.

Plug, E., Vijverberg, W., 2003. Schooling, Family Background and Adoption: Is It Nature or Is It Nurture? J. Polit. Econ. CXI, 611–641.

Ridley, M., 2003. Nature Via Nurture. Harper Collins, New York.

Rubin, D.B., 1974. Estimating causal effects of treatments in randomized and nonrandomized studies. J. Educ. Psychol. 66 (5), 688–701.

Sacerdote, B., 2002. The Nature and Nurture of Economic Outcomes. Am. Econ. Rev. XCII, 344–348.

Sacerdote, B.I., 2007. How Large Are the Effects From Changes in Family Environment? A Study of Korean American Adoptees. Q. J. Econ. 121 (1), 119–158, Feb.

Scarr, S., Carter-Saltzman, L., 1979. Twin Method: Defense of a Critical Assumption. Behav. Genet. 9 (6), November.

Scarr, S., McCartney, K., 1983. How People Make Their Own Environments: A Theory of Genotype → Environment Effects. Child Dev. 54 (2), 424–435, Apr.

Scarr, S., Weinberg, R., 1978. The Influence of Family Background on Intellectual Attainment. Am. Sociol. Rev. XVIII, 674–692.

Scarr, S., Weinberg, R.A., 1994. Educational and Occupational Achievements of Brothers and Sisters in Adoptive and Biologically Related Families. Behav. Genet. XXIV, 301–325, July.

Solon, G., 1999. Intergenerational Mobility in the Labor Market. In: Ashenfelter, O., Card, D. (Eds.), Handbook of Labor Economics, vol. 3. Elsevier Science B.V.

Stoolmiller, M., 1999. Implications of the Restricted Range of Family Environments for Estimates of Heritability and Nonshared Environment in Behavior-Genetic Adoption Studies. Psychol. Bull, CXV, 392–409.

Taylor, H.F., 1980. The IQ Game. Rutgers University Press, New Brunswick.

Teasdale, T.W., Owen, D.R., 1984. Heredity And Familial Environment In Intelligence And Educational Level—A Sibling Study. Nature CCCIX, 620–622, June.

Turkheimer, E., Haley, A., Waldron, M., D'Onofrio, B., Gottesman, I.I., 2003. Socioeconomic Status Modifies Heritability of IQ in Young Children. Psychol. Sci. XIV, 623–628, November.

Zimmerman, D.J., 1992. Regression toward Mediocrity in Economic Stature. Am. Econ. Rev. 82 (3), 409–429, June.

FURTHER READINGS

Altonji, J.G., Elder, T.E., Taber, C.R., 2000. Selection of Observed and Unobserved Variables: Assessing the Effectiveness of Catholic Schools. National Bureau of Economic Research Working Paper No. 7831.

Angrist, J.D., Lang, K., 2004. Does School Integration Generate Peer Effects? Evidence from Boston's Metco Program. Am. Econ. Rev. XCIV, 1613–1634.

Auld, M.C., 2005. Smoking, Drinking, and Income. J. Hum. Resour. INDENT XC, 505–518.

Behrman, J.R., Mark, R., 1994. Rosenzweig and Paul Taubman, "Endowments and the Allocation of Schooling in the Family and in the Marriage Market. J. Polit. Econ. CII, 1131–1174.

Bowles, S., Gintis, H., Groves, M.O. (Eds.), 2005. Unequal Chances: Family Background And Economic Success. Princeton University Press, Princeton and Oxford.

Cullen, J.B., Jacob, B., Levitt, S., 2005. The Impact of School Choice on Student Outcomes: An Analysis of the Chicago Public Schools. J. Public Econ. LXXXIX, 729–760.

Currie, J., Moretti, E., 2003. Mother's Education and the Intergenerational Transmission of Human Capital: Evidence from College Openings. Q. J. Econ. CXVIII, 1495–1532.

Darwin, C., 1859. On the Origin of Species by Means of Natural Selection. Appleton, New York.

Das, M., Sjogren, T., 2002. The Intergenerational Link in Income Mobility: Evidence from Adoptions. Econ. Lett. LXXV, 55–60.

DeFries, J.C., Plomin, R., Fulker, D.W., 1994. Nature and Nurture During Middle Childhood. Blackwell Press, Oxford, UK.

Dynarksi, S., 2005. Building the Stock of College Educated Labor. National Bureau of Economic Research Working Paper No. 11604.

Flynn, J., 1999. In: KennethArrow, S.B., Durlaf, S. (Eds.), Meritocracy and Economic Inequality. Princeton U. Press, Princeton.

Goldberger, A.S., 1978. The Genetic Determination of Income: Comment. Am. Econ. Rev. CXVIII, 960–969.

Hoxby, C.M., 2000. The Effects of Class Size on Student Achievement: New Evidence from Population Variation. Q. J. Econ. CXV, 1239–1285.

Jacob, B.A., 2004. Public Housing, Housing Vouchers, and Student Achievement: Evidence from Public Housing Demolitions in Chicago. Am. Econ. Rev. XCIV, 233–258.

Jencks, C., Brown, M., 1979. Genes and Social Stratification. In: Taubman, P. (Ed.), Kinometrics: The Determinants of Economic Success Within and Between Families. North Holland Elsevier, New York.

Kling, J.R., Ludwig, J., Katz, L.F., 2005. Neighborhood Effects on Crime for Female and Male Youth: Evidence from a Randomized Housing Voucher Experiment. Q. J. Econ. CXX, 87–130.

Lichtenstein, P., Pedersen, N.L., McClearn, G.E., 1992. The Origins of Individual-Differences In Occupational-Status And Educational-Level - A Study of Twins Reared Apart and Together. Acta Sociol. XXXV, 13–31, Mar.

Loehlin, J.C., Horn, J.M., Willerman, L., 1994. Differential Inheritance of Mental Abilities in the Texas Adoption Project. Intelligence XIX, 325–336.

Loehlin, J.C., Horn, J.M., Willerman, L., 1982. Personality Resemblances Between Unwed Mothers and Their Adopted-Away Offspring. J. Pers. Soc. Psychol. XLII, 1089–1099.

Loehlin, J.C., Willerman, L., Horn, J.M., 1987. Personality Resemblance in Adoptive Families: A 10-Year Followup. J. Pers. Soc. Psychol. LIII, 961–969.

Ludwig, J., Duncan, G.J., Hirschfield, P., 2001. Urban Poverty and Juvenile Crime: Evidence from a Randomized Housing Mobility Experiment. Q. J. Econ. CXVI, 655–680.

Maughan, B., Collishaw, S., Pickles, A., 1998. School Achievement and Adult Qualification Among Adoptees: A Longitudinal Study. J. Child Psychol. Psychiatry XXXIX, 669–685.

Nechyba, T., Vigdor, J., 2003. Peer Effects in North Carolina Public Schools. Mimeo Duke University.

Neisser, U., Boodoo, G., Bouchard Jr., T.J., Boykin, A.W., Brody, N., Ceci, S.J., et al., 1996. Intelligence: Knowns and Unknowns. Am. Psychol. 51, 77–101.

Oreopoulos, P., Page, M., Stevens, A., 2006. The Intergenerational Effects of Compulsory Schooling. J. Labor Econ. 24 (4), 729–760, October.

Plomin, R., DeFries, J.C., Fulker, D.W., 1988. Nature and Nurture During Infancy and Early Childhood. Cambridge University Press, Cambridge, England; New York.

Rouse, C.E., 1998. Private School Vouchers and Student Achievement: An Evaluation of the Milwaukee Parental Choice Program. Q. J. Econ. CXIII, 553–602.

Sacerdote, B.I., 2001. Peer Effects With Random Assignment. Q. J. Econ. CXVI, 681–704.

Taubman, P., 1989. Role of Parental Income in Educational Attainment. Am. Econ. Rev. LXXIX, 57–61.

Teasdale, T.W., Owen, D.R., 1986. The Influence of Paternal Social-Class on Intelligence and Educational-Level in Male Adoptees and Non-Adoptees. Br. J. Educ. Psychol. CVI, 3–12, Feb.

Turkheimer, E., Gottesman, I.I., 1996. Simulating the Dynamics of Genes and Environment in Development. Dev. Psychopathol. 8, 667–677.

Vogler, G.P., Sorensen, T.I.A., Stunkard, A.J., Srinivasan, M.R., Rao, D.C., 1995. Influences of Genes and Shared Family Environment on Adult Body Mass Index Assessed in an Adoption Study by a Comprehensive Path Model. Int. J. Obes. XIX, 40–45.

CHAPTER 2

Social Norms and Preferences,[*,†] Chapter for the *Handbook for Social Economics* edited by J. Benhabib, A. Bisin and M. Jackson

Andrew Postlewaite

Contents

1. Introduction 32
2. The Social Determinants of Preferences 35
   2.1 Internalized preferences 36
   2.2 Reduced form preferences 39
3. Reduced Form Preferences: Social Concerns 40
   3.1 Reduced form social preferences 40
   3.2 Basic model 41
      3.2.1 Two period example 42
      3.2.2 Infinite horizon case 44
   3.3 Concern for relative position 46
      3.3.1 Missing markets 46
      3.3.2 Multiplicity 48
   3.4 Market imperfections and conformity 49
      3.4.1 Endogenizing social groups 51
      3.4.2 Multiplicity of social arrangements 52
4. Why Not Take the Indirect Preferences as the Primitive? 53
   4.1 The case for making relative ranking an argument of the utility function 53
      4.1.1 Experimental support for direct concern for relative position 55
   4.2 Drawbacks in including relative position as an argument of the utility function 55
      4.2.1 What precisely is hardwired? 55
      4.2.2 Parsimony and unity of economic models 56
   4.3 Disadvantages of taking the reduced form preferences as primitive 57
5. Examples Employing Instrumental Concern for Rank 58
   5.1 Conspicuous consumption 58

[*] I want to thank Alberto Bisin, Hal Cole, Olivier Compte, Peter DeMarzo, Hanming Fang, Raquel Fernandez, Ed Hopkins, George Mailath, Peter Norman, Antonio Penta, Arthur Robson, Nikolai Roussanov, Larry Samuelson, David Schmeidler, Yoram Weiss and Ivan Werning for comments on this paper. Support from the National Science Foundation (grant SES-0095768) is gratefully acknowledged.

[†] This paper draws heavily on Postlewaite (1998) and Mailath and Postlewaite (2003), and there is substantial overlap in the discussions there and in this paper.

Handbook of Social Economics, Volume 1A
ISSN 0169-7218, DOI: 10.1016/S0169-7218(11)01002-1

5.2 Labor supply 59
5.3 Investment 61
6. Concluding Remarks 63
References 65

Abstract

Social norms are often posited as an explanation of differences in economic behavior and performance of societies that are difficult to explain by differences in endowments and technology. Economists are often reluctant to incorporate social aspects into their analyses when doing so leads to models that depart from the "standard" model. I discuss ways that agents' social environment can be accommodated in standard models and the advantages and disadvantages of doing so.
JEL Classifications: D01, D03

Keywords

Social norms
social preferences
interdependent preferences
social behavior

1. INTRODUCTION[1]

There is little agreement about what exactly social norms are and how they might be modeled. The term is often used to describe situations in which there is a commonality in behavior in a group of people. However, not every observed commonality is a candidate for the term. No one would describe, as a social norm, the fact that family members regularly eat together. The term is reserved to describe similar behavior within a group that might have been otherwise, that is, behavior that differs from that of a larger population. Nevertheless, even this is not sufficient to delineate what should or should not be included as a social norm. We wouldn't say that it is a social norm that Eskimos wear warmer clothes than do Guatemalans. We understand that it is only rational, given the climate, that Eskimos dress differently than others. Therefore, a minimal criterion for a behavior in a group to be considered a social norm is that it cannot be explained simply as a consequence of optimization to the group's physical environment. I will use the term social norm to describe the behavior of a group if the behavior differs from that of other groups in similar environments. The aim of this

[1] This paper is a discussion of how one can accommodate social aspects of a society in an economic analysis. I will discuss a number of papers to illustrate the points that I want to make, but the paper is not a survey of any particular area.

paper is to clarify how we can model and analyze social norms that generate differences in economic behavior and performance across similar societies.

Most economic analyses begin with an individual agent whose preferences are taken as given. Those preferences determine the agent's choice, and a society's economic behavior is obtained by aggregating the choices of agents in the society. Aggregating the decisions agents in isolation make in this way leaves little room for investigating how the social environment in which agents make decisions affects those decisions: Two communities whose composition and physical environments are the same would necessarily yield the same aggregate behaviors. Yet we often observe groups in similar circumstances behaving quite differently. There are Amish communities in which no house has electricity and there are no automobiles or cell phones that abut "standard" towns in which people live like you and I. What accounts for the wildly different lifestyles? A genetic predisposition to horse and buggy transportation seems unlikely, and many people attribute the difference to differing social norms. The Amish example suggests that it would be foolish to estimate an agent's elasticity of demand for electricity without looking at the social characteristics of the community in which he or she resides.

Social characteristics of a community are important not only for understanding differences across communities, but for understanding decisions within a single community as well. It is commonplace to note that many people are affected by the consumption of others in their buying decisions. Whether it is cars, clothing, housing or jewelry, if everyone around spends more, you are tempted to spend more as well. The term, *keeping up with the Joneses* generates nearly fifteen million hits on Google. An analysis that ignores the social context in which many consumption decisions are made will necessarily be incomplete.

Most economists understand that the social milieu affects peoples' behavior, but are reluctant to incorporate such concerns in their models. Models that include them often allow such a broad range of behavior that there are few, if any, restrictions on equilibrium behavior and, hence, such models have little or no predictive power. Economics is among the most successful social sciences, due in no small part to the modeling methodology employed. Economic models traditionally build on individual maximizing behavior with the (often-implicit) assumption that individuals' utility depends on a quite limited set of arguments.

Thus, there is a tension between the standard methodology of economic modeling and the ability of economic models to capture important effects of the social environment on economic behavior.[2] When we observe very different economic outcomes in societies that are composed of people who are fundamentally the same and who have similar endowments and have access to the same technology, it is profitable to explore how the social environments in those societies differ.

[2] See, e.g., Akerlof (1984), particularly the introduction, for a discussion of the tension.

A successful integration of social concerns into existing economics should maintain individual optimization; one should not simply posit that there is a social norm in the Amish community that individuals should eschew modern conveniences, and that the Amish blindly follow this norm.[3] It is trivial, however, to support observed behavior without abandoning optimization—simply posit that one prefers following a particular social norm.[4] One might posit a norm to cooperate in the prisoners' dilemma if one observed such cooperation, but this is not very productive.[5] As mentioned above, economics has been relatively successful among the social sciences because of the restrictions imposed by the assumptions of the models employed. Models can have predictive power only to the extent that some behavior is inconsistent with the predictions of the model. The central assumption in economics of rational self-interested agents puts no restrictions on behavior unless there are simultaneous restrictions on what might be in the agents self interest. The force of the rational-agent assumption in economics derives from concurrent restrictions on preferences. In interesting economic models, agents' preferences are either unchanging over time, or change in a very structured way depending on history. Similarly, most economic models restrict agents' preferences so that they depend on goods and services consumed by them or their offspring.[6]

The aim of this paper is to describe how economists can incorporate social aspects of societies to understand why we might see very different behavior and economic performance in fundamentally similar societies. There may seem to be a contradiction between saying that the people in two communities are "fundamentally similar," and yet behave differently. There is no contradiction if "fundamentally similar" agents can have different preferences, and I will discuss in the next section how "fundamentally similar" agents may have different preferences and make different choices depending on the social structure of their society. One possibility is that two people may be the same at birth, but that their preferences are shaped by their interactions with others within their different societies as they grow up, so that by the time they are old enough to make economically interesting decisions, what makes them happy or sad is very different. A second possibility is that two people may have the same "deep preferences,"[7] but that the social structures they inhabit provide different future rewards for a given behavior. Preferences over whether to study the Talmud or play

[3] Other disciplines often take adherence to social norms as given. For an economist's survey of the work on social norms by sociologists, see Weiss and Fershtman (1998); for a somewhat different take on this issue by economists, see Burke and Young, this volume.

[4] However, even the simple assumption that an individual's choice can be taken to be his preference might be called into question. For example, there is substantial literature on peoples' desire to commit to future behavior in the belief that they would otherwise make unwise decisions. See the Della Vigna (2009) *JEL* survey for a discussion of this.

[5] I support this view in more detail below.

[6] There are exceptions, of course; see, e.g., Duesenberry (1949), Frank (1985), and Robson (1996), who consider a possible biological basis for such interdependence.

[7] Roughly speaking, what I mean by deep preferences are the things that directly activate pleasurable brain activity.

baseball likely differ systematically across societies. This is, of course, because the future consequences of the decision differ across societies, and preferences should not depend only on the single decision of which of the two activities to engage in, but over the entire paths that the activities lead to. The point is that different people may have the same deep preferences but different reduced form preferences, where what I mean by reduced form preferences is the preferences over the immediate alternatives.

Differing preferences for studying the Talmud and playing baseball in different communities suggests multiple equilibria, and multiplicity of equilibria will indeed play a role in my discussion below. We are familiar with multiple equilibria in the basic models in economics; Arrow-Debreu economies with complete markets can have multiple equilibria, but it is difficult to see how that multiplicity might be thought of in terms of social norms. We will see that *incomplete* markets will be an important ingredient in the relationship between social norms and multiple equilibria.

I discuss in the next section how fundamentally similar people can have different preferences due either to differences in how their social environments shaped their deep preferences or differences in how their social environments generated different reduced form preferences. Following this, I lay out a model illustrating how different social environments can affect growth rates in a more or less standard dynastic growth model. Using the discussion of that model, I discuss the advantages and disadvantages of the modeling methodology.

2. THE SOCIAL DETERMINANTS OF PREFERENCES

Standard economic models typically exclude feelings of affection, envy, and rivalry. Most, perhaps all, economists understand that these restrictions on preferences are unrealistic. There are two primary reasons that economists continue to utilize models that exclude such considerations. First, adding variables that affect individuals' utility weakens the conclusions that can be drawn from the analysis. Second, and in my opinion more important, is that economists have been extremely successful in their attempt to "explain" human behavior using economic models without including such variables. Becker (1976) said this very nicely, "... [the] combined assumptions of maximizing behavior, market equilibrium and stable preferences, used relentlessly and unflinchingly... provides a valuable unified framework for understanding all human behavior" (cf. Becker (1976), p. 5).

This, of course, isn't an argument that other things won't improve our ability to model and understand some aspects of human behavior; rather, it is an argument for pushing the traditionally restricted models in new directions to see how well we can describe human behavior with such simple models. The rational-agent model of optimizing agents with stable preferences has been fruitfully brought to bear on a wide variety of decisions including marriage and criminal behavior (cf. Becker (1976). Research using the model for these problems has proven extremely useful despite substantial initial skepticism of its appropriateness. It is important to understand that applying the rational-agent model to a particular problem does not entail a belief that it is the *only*, or even the most accurate, model of behavior in that setting. What is important is that the model may give us insights that we would miss had we not used the model.

My aim in this paper is to discuss ways that we can incorporate social influences on economic behavior while maintaining the standard modeling restrictions that agents optimize, and what might be included as arguments of agents' utility functions. If similar optimizing agents make different choices, they must have different preferences. Social forces can result in fundamentally similar agents having different preferences in two conceptually different ways. I discuss these next.

2.1 Internalized preferences

"Don't worry that children never listen to you; worry that they are always watching you." — Robert Fulghum

The first, and simplest, way that social forces can affect behavior is through the formation of agents' preferences. Although the bulk of economic analysis takes preferences as exogenously given, for much of the behavior that this paper addresses, preferences are to some degree socially determined in the sense that agents internalize preferences in some domains that reflect those of the society they inhabit. The consequence of this internalization is that agents' deep preferences are influenced by their social environment.[8]

We observe a vast range of behavior that seems to not be in one's narrow self-interest, but easily understood in terms of internalized preferences that are the result of indoctrination.[9] I don't take a pen off my colleague's desk when she is out of the office even when I am positive I won't be caught. If asked why, I would simply say that I would feel bad about myself if I did that. I was brought up to not take other peoples' things (at least not of small value), not to make fun of handicapped people, to tip in restaurants, and to respond positively to requests for small favors. Very likely, the indoctrination took the form of my mother's approval when I behaved in ways she felt appropriate and disapproval when I did not. As with Pavlov's dog, my internal chemistry continues to respond to the external stimuli long after the associated consequences have disappeared.

This is not a novel point of view; as parents, we spend large amounts of time, energy, and money in the belief, or at least the hope, that we can shape our children's preferences, that they will be future-oriented, like classical music, and support their parents in old age. The view has been canonized in the motto attributed to Francis Xavier, "Give me a child until he is seven and I will give you the man."

[8] On this point, see also the discussion in Bowles (1998).

[9] While I focus in this section on indoctrination of children, Yoram Weiss pointed out to me that the formation of internalized preferences does not occur solely in children. A few months of military training seems to dramatically alter the deep preferences of young adults so that they are willing to kill and be killed in ways that would have been inconceivable before training.

It is immediate that endogenous preferences can lead to differences in behavior across groups. If individuals in one group are indoctrinated to "enjoy" work and saving, while those in another group are indoctrinated to dislike work, we would expect to see significant differences in behavior between the groups. Weber (1905) made the argument that religion was one of the many reasons that western cultures differ from eastern cultures. There is recent literature in economics, which is rooted in the notion that peoples' preferences are shaped by the environment in which they are raised.[10]

Bisin and Verdier (2000) analyze a model of cultural transmission in which parents wish to transmit their own traits to offspring and make costly efforts to socialize them, such as spending time with children, attending church, and choosing specific neighborhoods to live in. When parents are of different backgrounds, each parent wishes to transmit his/her own trait to the children. The child's preferences are then determined by the interaction of parents' efforts and the indirect influence of society toward assimilation. Bisin, Topa and Verdier (2004) use this basic idea to carry out an empirical analysis of parental transmission of religious beliefs.[11]

Fernandez, Fogli and Olivetti (2004) suggest that the environment in which men are raised have lasting affects on their preferences. They find that whether a man's mother worked while he was growing up is correlated with whether his wife works, even after controlling for a whole series of socioeconomic variables. They interpret this as preference formation on the men's part – growing up with a working mother affected their preferences for a working wife. Fernandez and Fogli (2005) analyze how fertility and work decisions of second-generation American women were affected by their country of origin. Fernandez and Fogli argue that the cultures of the country of origin with respect to these decisions predict the choices made by the second-generation women.[12]

These papers illustrate how individuals can be acculturated by the society they are in, that is, how their preferences are shaped by the behavior of those they meet. We can distinguish between two different acculturation processes, which we might call active and passive. Acculturation is active when the behaviors that shape the preferences of the young are consciously chosen with the aim to form those preferences in a particular way. Acculturation is passive when the individuals whose behavior shapes the preferences of the young have no particular interest in what preferences might emerge. Men whose mothers worked might be more comfortable with working wives simply because it seems natural, without their mothers having this as a conscious aim, that is, acculturation is passive, while the Jewish parents in Scarsdale who send their children to Hebrew school are engaged in active acculturation.

The distinction is useful because active acculturation typically involves people making costly efforts to affect the preferences of the young, leading to the question

[10] See Benhabib and Bisin (2010) for a discussion of how advertising shapes preferences.

[11] See also Bisin and Verdier (2010) for discussion of this line of work.

[12] See also Fernandez (2007a, 2007b, 2010) for a general discussion of cultural formation and transmission of preferences.

of what the payoffs are to these costly efforts. Parents desire that their children be like them, but this is not the sole motivation for the effort they make to shape their children's values and preferences. There is clearly an interest in socializing children so that they will be successful. Parents define what constitutes success, while what contributes to that success often depends on the community in which the child will live. Tabellini (2008) analyzes a model in which parents rationally choose how to indoctrinate their children. Their choices are guided by external enforcement of behaviors and likely transactions their children will engage in.[13] In such a setting, parents' optimal choices may well depend on the choices of other parents. Your child may do well being cooperative when he will interact primarily with others who are cooperative, but be exploited if others are not. In general, with active acculturation, families' don't face an individual decision problem, but instead are in a game.

This discussion avoids several important issues when examining how social influences affect the formation of preferences. First, suppose that parents actively work to shape their children's preferences. How do parents choose what preferences they desire their children to have? For problems such as investigated by Bisin et al. (2004), we should feel reasonably comfortable assuming that parents want their children to adopt the parents' religion, at least when parents share the same religion.

Considering parents' preferences over the preferences they induce in their children can be more complicated in other problems. We might think that parents want to indoctrinate their children to be honest. This may represent *deep* preferences on the parents' part that their children are honest, or it might be that their deep preferences are that their children be successful and that honest children simply do better in life. While it might be the case that in some social settings it is indeed the case that being congenitally honest is beneficial, there may be others in which it is costly (as Lear's daughter Cordelia learns). Parents' choices about what preferences to instill in their children may depend on other parents' choices.[14] All parents in one group may raise their children to be cooperative, while those in another place raising selfish children, with any set of parents in either place making an optimal choice given the choices of others.

Examining how deep preferences are shaped within a society can provide structure to a deeper understanding of differences in economic performance across societies.[15] It would be interesting to examine *why* different deep preferences arise in different societies: Is it different parental preferences about their childrens' preferences or is it that particular deep preferences have different values depending on others' deep preferences?

[13] See also Lizzeri and Siniscalchi (2008) for a model in which parents rationally shape their children's decision-making process.

[14] Corneo and Jeanne (2009) analyze a model in which parents choose what value systems to instill in their children to maximize their children's expected utility.

[15] See, e.g., Fershtman, Hvide and Weiss (2003) for an argument about how the form of executive compensation is affected by CEOs concerns about their compensation relative to other CEOs.

2.2 Reduced form preferences

The work described above investigates why we might see individuals optimally behaving very differently when in different groups; even if those groups are in very similar physical environments. As I discussed, the interpretation is that the variation in behavior is a consequence of the individuals in different groups having different preferences. At one level, this must be true if we identify the choices people make with their preferred alternatives. However, we need to be cautious about what we mean when we say that an individual "prefers" one thing to another. I came to work today, so by this logic I must prefer working to staying home. Obviously, this doesn't mean that I necessarily like work more than leisure, but rather I prefer working today to staying home primarily because the future consequences of the alternatives are very different. I came to work today because it is part of an equilibrium for which the consequences of "coming to work" and "staying home" differ: they pay me if I come to work, but not otherwise. What we can say is that I have "reduced-form" preferences over my actions today such that working today is preferred to staying home *given the equilibrium in my environment.* My "deep" preferences, that is, my preferences over working versus staying home might be quite different. Holding fixed the actions of all other people, (including paying me whether I show up for work or not) I might well prefer staying home. When I talk about an individual's "preferences," it is important to be clear whether I am talking about his reduced form preferences or his deep preferences where deep preferences are preferences over immediate alternatives, *assuming that the choice doesn't trigger a response from others.* My deep preferences are that I stay home and watch Oprah Winfrey today, while my reduced form preferences that take into account changes in others' actions given my choice are to come to work.[16]

In this taxonomy of deep and reduced form preferences, the internalized preferences discussed in the previous section are deep preferences. I don't take the pen from a colleague's desk, even if I am positive I will not be caught, and I will feel bad making fun of a handicapped individual independent of any future consequences. One should think of the internalized preferences as consequence of indoctrination resulting in a permanent change in the brain activity associated with a particular act.

It may be clear in some problems that preferences are socially influenced, but not obvious whether the socially influenced preferences are internalized preferences or reduced form preferences. Consider for example the Fernandez et al. (2004) paper discussed above, that demonstrated that the wives of men whose mothers worked are more likely to work. One possibility is that this reflects internalized preferences

[16] Distinguishing between "deep preferences" and "reduced form preferences" can be useful, but I don't want to suggest that all choice problems will fall neatly into one or the other category. For example, if I was deciding whether or not to burn down my employer's factory, I would find it hard to think about the choices "holding fixed all other agents' actions."

whereby there is a negative emotion generated in a man whose mother did not work if his wife works, but a positive emotion in a man whose mother worked. Alternatively, it might be that men, whose mothers worked, mate with women from a different pool than men whose mothers' didn't work. It may be that men whose mothers worked come in contact primarily with women who insist on working as a condition of marriage, while men whose mothers' didn't work make no such demand. All men may experience a negative emotion if their wives work, but the reduced form preferences of men whose mothers worked lead to matches with women who work.

It might seem irrelevant whether the change in men's preferences is internalized or reduced form since in either case we have the same outcome – whether a man's mother worked is related to whether his wife works, but the distinction is important. In the case of internalized preferences described above, a woman married to a man whose mother worked is doing him a favor, while in the hypothetical reduced form case; the man is doing a favor for his wife by "letting her work". One would presumably analyze some questions differently in the two cases, for example, bargaining within the family. Additionally, the predicted response in a woman's labor supply decision to a wage change might be different in the two circumstances.[17] I next give a detailed example of how reduced form preferences might exhibit a concern for rank in the wealth distribution when there is no concern in the deep preferences.

3. REDUCED FORM PREFERENCES: SOCIAL CONCERNS

3.1 Reduced form social preferences

In this section, I'll set out a model that illustrates how agents' reduced form preferences can differ in important ways across economies that are identical in all respects except that the equilibrium behavior in the economies differ. In particular, I will demonstrate how people whose deep preferences are completely standard in the sense that they care only about their own consumption and the utility of their children, but whose reduced form preferences exhibit a concern for relative standing.[18]

Cole, Mailath and Postlewaite (1992) (hereafter CMP92) augments a standard growth model with a matching decision between men and women. They assume that individuals care only about their own consumption and their offspring's utility, and that after matching; all consumption within a pair is joint.[19] To the extent that members of

[17] I will return to the advantages of using the framework of reduced form preferences for many problems below.

[18] Some sociologists suggest something like an instrumental argument for why status is important, namely that it provides one with a claim to good treatment from others. This begs the question of why others would give this good treatment? One possible answer is that high status can serve as a coordinating device. That is, high status people may be able to cooperate better when they interact than do others. (See, e.g., Brooks (2001), Okuno-Fujiwara and Postlewaite (1995), and Fershtman and Weiss (1998a, 1998b).)

[19] It isn't important that *all* consumption is joint, only that there is some joint consumption.

either sex have different wealth levels, the joint consumption induces preferences over potential mates: all other things equal, wealthier mates are more desirable.

Since wealthier mates are desirable, a natural process by which men and women might match is that the wealthiest women match with the wealthiest men, that is, the matching process could be positively assortative on wealth. It's clear that this non-market matching decision induces a concern for relative wealth: individuals' consumption depends not only on their own endowment, but also on their position in the wealth distribution of people of the same gender. This concern for relative standing is not in the deep preferences, but is induced in the reduced form preferences because relative standing in the wealth distribution affects individuals' consumption of ordinary goods. Consumption is affected because the obtainable mates depend on one's wealth relative to competitors' in the mating contest. Individuals have a concern for relative standing because relative standing is instrumental in determining ultimate consumption levels.

I will describe the model in more detail next.

3.2 Basic model[20,21]

There are two types of one-period-lived agents, men and women. The agents match into pairs with each pair having two offspring, one male and one female. In addition to the matching decision, agents make standard economic decisions: how to divide their endowment into their own consumption and a bequest to their offspring. Consumption is joint, so agents care about the economic characteristics of potential mates. Men and women are treated asymmetrically in two respects in order to reduce the technical complexity of the model.

First, women are endowed with a non-traded, nonstorable good, while men inherit a second, storable good, which is called *capital*. Women are indexed by $j \in [0, 1]$ and woman j is endowed with j units of the nontraded good. The men are indexed by $i \in [0, 1]$ and are exogenously endowed with capital in the first period.[22]

Second, only the welfare of the male offspring enters the pair's utility function; consequently, parents only make bequests to their sons. A male offspring inherits his father's index, and I will refer to man i, his son, his son's son, and so on, as family line i. Men and women have identical utility functions defined over joint consumption of a matched pair's bundle given by $u(c) + j$, where as c and j are, respectively, the quantities of the male and the female goods. Finally, the utility level of their son enters linearly into each parent's utility function, discounted by $\beta \in (0, 1)$.

The problem facing a couple is, given their wealth (determined by the bequest from the male's parents), how much to consume and how much to bequeath to their son.

[20] The material in this section is taken from Cole, Mailath and Postlewaite (1992) and Postlewaite (1998).

[21] See Corneo and Jeanne (1997, 2001) and Fershtman, Murphy and Weiss (1996) for related models.

[22] Males and females are treated differently only for reasons of tractability.

Their son values the bequest for two distinct reasons. First, it affects the amount he and his descendants can consume and, second, the bequest may affect the quality of his mate. To the extent that their son's match is affected, parents may have an incentive to leave a larger bequest than they otherwise would. Matching is voluntary in the sense that no unmatched man and woman could both improve their situation by moving from their current match. Both men and women prefer wealthier partners, all else equal. It may be, however, that matching with a wealthy partner has adverse implications for the matching prospects of male descendants. For example, they may be punished if their parents deviated from prescribed behavior.

Agents use capital for current consumption and savings. Output is produced according to:

$$c = Ak - k',$$

where k is the initial endowment capital, c is first period consumption, k' is second period capital, and $A > 1$ is a constant. The initial endowment of capital for men in the first period is k_1: $[0, 1] \to R_+$.

3.2.1 Two period example

I can illustrate the instrumental nature of concern for wealth with a two period version of the model described above. Matching will take place in the second period only. Assume that $k_1(\cdot) = k$, i.e., all men have the same initial endowment. Assume that all men have utility function

$$u(c_0) + \beta(u(c_1) + j)$$

where c_0 and c_1 denote respectively the parents' and their son's consumption of the male good and j denotes the endowment of the son's mate.

I assume agents act strategically. Men and women in the second period will maximize their utility, aiming to match with the wealthiest person on the other side of the matching market. Consequently, that matching will be assortative on wealth: the mth percentile male with respect to wealth will match with the mth percentile woman with respect to female endowment. A man's match in the second period thus depends only on his relative position in the wealth distribution in period two. Equilibrium is a description of the consumption-savings decisions of the men in the first period and matching behavior of the men and women in the second period such that no agent has an incentive to deviate from the described behavior.

Since all men in the first period have the same initial wealth and can mimic the decisions of any other man, they must all have the same utility. This is not the case for men in the second period, however. It cannot be the case that bequests to a positive measure of sons are identical. If this were the case, some man would be matched with a woman whose endowment is less than that of a woman matched with a man with the same size bequest by an amount $d > 0$. Then the father of the man whose son matched with the poorer woman could increase his bequest by an arbitrarily small amount, which would ensure that the endowment of the woman in the new match was greater by at least d.

An equilibrium will be a function giving the bequests of each first period man, k_1: $[0, 1] \rightarrow R$ where $k_1(i)$ is the ith father's bequest, where $k_1(i)$ is optimal for father i given other families' choices. Given $k(\cdot)$, let $F(k)$ be the CDF for k, i.e., $F(k)$ is the proportion of families with bequest less than or equal to k.

Then for all i:

$$k(i) \in \text{argmax } u(Ak - k(i)) + \beta[u(k(i)) + F(k(i))]$$

since $F(k(i))$ is the rank in the wealth distribution, so that $F(k(i))$ is the index of the woman i will match with, and hence, the endowment of his mate. The first order conditions for family i are then (assuming $F(\cdot)$ is differentiable):

$$u'(Ak - k(i)) = A\beta u'(Ak(i)) + \beta F'(k(i)).$$

Comparing the first order conditions of a father's bequest decision when that decision affects the son's match with the first order condition when matching considerations are ignored differ only in the additional term $\beta F'(k(i))$ in the former (see Figure 1 below).

$F'(k(i))$ is a measure of the effect of a small change in family i's bequest to their son on the son's position in the wealth distribution in his generation. $F(k(i))$ is the son's position when his parents leave $k(i)$; if they left $k(i) + \Delta$, his position would be approximated for small Δ by $F(k(i)) + F'(k(i)) \cdot \Delta$. When the parents in family i are optimally choosing a bequest to their son, the cost of marginally increasing the bequest is their personal marginal utility of consumption. The benefit of marginally increasing the bequest is the discounted marginal utility of their son's consumption *plus* the marginal increase in his relative wealth position that will increase the wealth of the woman he matches with. F' is strictly positive, and consequently in equilibrium, the marginal utility of the father's consumption is higher when matching is affected by bequests than when it is not; this implies that his consumption is lower in that case, i.e., savings is higher.

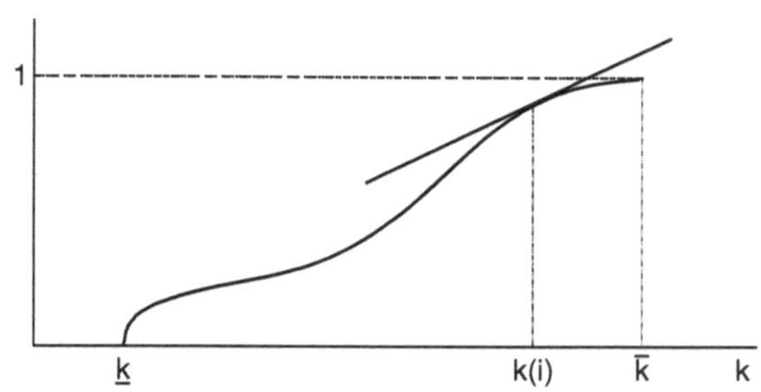

Figure 2.1 Cumulative distribution function F of bequests.

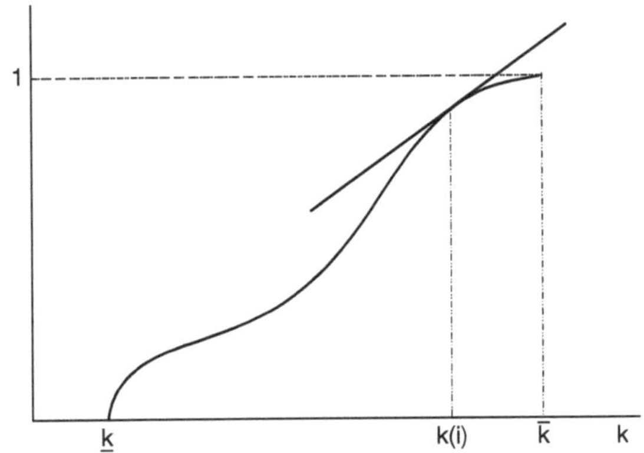

Figure 2.2 A more concentrated wealth distribution.

To summarize, when matching is effected by bequests, people save more. How much more people save when matching considerations are taken into account depends on the dispersion of wealth in the society. When F' is very small, the change in the son's position is small; hence, his parents gain little by increasing their bequest to him. If the distribution of bequests is concentrated, $F'(k(i))$ will, on average, be larger than if the distribution of bequests is dispersed. (See Figure 2.2.)

Consequently, we should expect greater increases in bequests due to concern for rank in societies with more concentrated wealth.[23]

3.2.2 Infinite horizon case

This two period example illustrates how individuals in a society with completely standard deep preferences (that is, with no concern for relative rank) may well have reduced form preferences that exhibit such a concern, and furthermore, how that concern leads to savings that are higher than would be the case absent the matching concern.

The "natural" assortative-on-wealth matching will continue to be consistent with individual agent maximizing behavior when the example is extended to an infinite horizon setting. Other matches, however, may also be consistent with maximizing behavior. CMP92 analyzed an *aristocratic matching,* described as follows. Here, men in the first generation are arbitrarily assigned a rank, with no assumed connection between rank and wealth. The social arrangement prescribes that in each generation, the men with the highest rank match with the wealthiest women; further, people who violate the prescribed behavior will have their male offspring's rank reduced to zero. If all

[23] This depends on the fine details about how concern for relative position is incorporated into the model, however. Hopkins and Kornienko (2004) analyze a somewhat different model and show that greater inequality may provide greater incentives to differentiate oneself and lead to an *increase* in spending because of rank concerns.

others are following the prescribed behavior, the effect of a deviation from the prescriptions of this social arrangement on the male offspring is that he will match with a less wealthy woman. Hence, a wealthy woman for whom the social arrangements prescribe a highly ranked but less wealthy mate who would be tempted to match instead with a richer man could be deterred by the consumption consequences to her son (about whom it is assumed she cares).[24] CMP92 demonstrate that for some economies, there is a Nash equilibrium of the game induced by these social rules that supports the social arrangement.[25]

Thus, with an infinite horizon, in addition to the assortative-on-wealth matching, there can be a matching in which wealth plays no role. There are important economic differences between two societies characterized by the two matching rules that I've described above. Under aristocratic matching, parents have an incentive to leave a bequest to their male offspring because his consumption enters their utility function, but they have no incentive to increase that bequest to improve his matching prospects. This differs from the case in which matching is assortative on wealth, where there is the same incentive for a pair to leave a bequest to the son because his consumption matters to them, but in addition, there is the incentive to increase the bequest because of the effect on matching.

In summary, there can be two societies that are the exact same (as far as the number of individuals, their deep preferences and their endowments) that exhibit very different economic behavior because they are governed by different social arrangements that induce different reduced form preferences. In the economy in which ranking is determined by wealth, couples will save more to benefit their sons. In the other, rank is inherited, and hence independent of wealth, reducing the optimal (from a personal point of view) level of savings; the social arrangements here suppress one of the benefits of forgoing consumption.[26] Any attempt to understand the differences in economic performance in

[24] This point is important: the woman follows the prescriptions of the social arrangements because it is strictly in her interest to do so. To repeat what was said above, we are interested only in social arrangements that are completely consistent with optimizing behavior. This approach to modeling social concerns would be distinctly less interesting if we postulated social arrangements that violated this basic aspect of the standard economic paradigm. I will say more about this below.

[25] See also Cole, Mailath and Postlewaite (1995b, 1997) on aristocratic social norms.

[26] Note that the higher savings when rank is based on wealth is not welfare enhancing. At the point when the agents in any generation are making their consumption-bequest decisions, all parental couples would benefit if everyone ignored the effect of the bequest on their son's rank. When the sons' ranks are taken into account, all couples decrease their consumption from the level they would choose if matching considerations were ignored. The decreases are such that the ranking of the sons after the decreases is the same as if no couple had decreased their consumption. Roughly the couples in any generation are engaged in a prisoners' dilemma situation in which every couple in the generation is worse off than had they ignored ranking considerations (as they do in the aristocratic ranking case). Each of these couples, of course, benefited from their ancestor's increased savings. Welfare evaluations would be altered if we introduced parental concern for daughters' welfare while maintaining our assumption that bequests go only to sons. In this case, an increase in all matched couples' savings would generate a positive externality, as it increases the welfare of all daughters. This would offset, at least partially, the negative externality increased savings imposes on other couples. (I thank Raquel Fernandez for pointing this out.)

these two economies must necessarily fail unless the analysis includes the social arrangements governing matching and an investigation of the incentives they provide.[27]

There are two important features in the equilibria. The first is that even in a simple two-period model non-market activities affect reduced form preferences governing savings. The second is that with an infinite horizon, there can be multiple, qualitatively different equilibria in a society stemming from different social arrangements. In the two-period example agents' deep preferences exhibited no concern about relative position: parents cared only about their consumption and their son's consumption. However, in their reduced form preferences over consumption-bequest choices, relative position *did* matter since their son's consumption was affected by relative position. I will discuss both of these points in some more detail.

3.3 Concern for relative position

3.3.1 Missing markets

A central feature of the model above when matching is assortative on wealth is that agents care about whom they and their offspring match with, but that there is no (direct) market for matching. Consequently, relative position in the wealth distribution determines how well one fares. While matching is an obvious decision that is important but not mediated by a standard market, there are many other decisions that have these properties. Invitations to the White House for dinner, the best seat in the church or synagogue, the table by the window in a restaurant, or seats on the board of trustees at elite universities and museums are a few of the things that people care about, sometimes passionately but they are not priced in the way an intermediate textbook in microeconomics describes markets. To be sure, it is not that money is unimportant in the determination of how these decisions are made; on the contrary, it seems clear that donations affect are called positional goods. Houses in particularly scarce and desirable locations and admission to elite private schools are sometimes called positional goods, that is, goods that will ultimately be consumed by the wealthiest individuals in a society.[28] Positional goods resemble the problem described above but there are important distinctions. First, there may be positional goods even with complete Arrow-Debreu markets. With complete markets, the first welfare theorem holds whether or not there are positional goods: the final allocation, including all savings and effort decisions, is Pareto efficient. There is no real externality in economic decisions other than the standard pecuniary externality, which complete markets mediate

[27] Corneo and Jeanne (1999) analyze a particularly tractable model with similar relative wealth concerns. Hopkins and Kornienko (2006) analyze a growth model in which individuals care about their relative position. There is a substantive difference between Hopkins and Kornienko (2006) (and Hopkins and Kornienko (2004)) and CMP 92. While the focus of all three papers is on the concern for "status," i.e., rank, rank in CMP92 is based on wealth while in the other two papers rank is based on consumption. The competition for position leads to increased consumption when rank is based on consumption rather than increased savings as in CMP92.

[28] See Frank (1985) for a discussion of positional goods.

perfectly. Another way of saying this is that when individuals make decisions, the price vector of marketed goods is the only information an agent needs for decision-making, this is not the case for the problems I have discussed; it is precisely the non-market good – matching – that people care about and can indirectly influence through their market decisions that make them care about other agents' decisions *in addition* to all prices of market goods. There is no reason to expect that when social arrangements rather than markets mediate the allocation of some goods and services the outcome will be Pareto efficient. Indeed, given that for some economic problems, there can be distinct outcomes that can result from different social arrangements; some of these social arrangements will typically be associated with inefficient outcomes.[29]

Another aspect of the approach described here that distinguishes it from the case in which markets are complete is that complete markets greatly limit the scope of societal differences that can be reconciled with equilibrium behavior. The growth model described above in which there are both equilibria, that rank agents by birth and equilibria in which they are ranked by wealth, shows that otherwise identical societies can perform differently as a consequence of different social arrangements. Complete markets, of course, allow multiple equilibria, but it's hard to see how that multiplicity can be linked to differences in underlying social structure.

If the driving force of the argument that social arrangements matter is market imperfections, what are the market imperfections that are so important? I used a specific market imperfection – matching – as the basis of the work described above. As mentioned above, there is a myriad of goods and decisions about which people care about, but that individuals don't purchase through standard markets such as country club memberships and memberships on boards of trustees. These items don't come free, nor are they obtained through a simple market purchase. A large donation is typically a necessary – but not sufficient – condition to be invited to the White House or to the boards of trustees of charities.

CMP92 used matching for both the motivation and the formal modeling of the market imperfection for conceptual reasons. It would be straightforward to assume that there is some good that is allocated through a tournament (for example by relative wealth) instead of being allocated by markets and carry out most of the analysis in those papers. A compelling case for how social arrangements affect economic behavior, however, should provide some explanation for why the allocation of some goods isn't mediated by price. That is, if particular memberships on boards of trustees (or desirable seats in restaurants or invitations to the White House) are particularly desirable, why can't one dial up, ask the price and give a Visa account number?

[29] Becker, Murphy and Werning (2005) analyze a model in which status position can be bought in a market, and show that in their framework, concern for status, leads people to make decisions that result in the same distribution of income, status and consumption for very different initial distributions of income. Their setup differs from that considered here in that it is assumed that people have a direct concern for status.

From a positive point of view, it's clear that for many of the examples above, this isn't the case. From a conceptual point of view, it seems that part of the reason these things are valued is related to the fact that they are *not* bought and sold in a standard way.[30] Nevertheless, if our goal is to understand what seems to be a concern for rank in an entirely standard economic model, any proposed explanation should be based on a clear specification of how any particular behavior affects the goods and services agents consume, uniformly assuming that agents optimize. A proper explanation that relied on the existence of goods or decisions like these should articulate clearly how the system is sustained in the face of optimizing behavior.

The matching decision meets this exacting requirement: there is a clear and plausible link between behavior and consumption and every agent is perfectly optimizing. While I believe that the insights based on this specific market imperfection are widely applicable, it remains an interesting open problem to model carefully how some of the other decisions such as board memberships can be reconciled with fully optimizing behavior in a convincing manner.

3.3.2 Multiplicity

The multiplicity of equilibria in the growth example above stemmed from the fact that in an infinite horizon environment, in any period there can be multiple equilibria in the future continuation problem. In every period, the wealthiest men and the wealthiest women would like to be matched, and if there are no future consequences to consider, matching will be assortative on wealth. The aristocratic equilibrium that resulted in lower savings, introduced such future considerations: when the prescription is that the wealthiest woman to match with the highest ranking man even if he is not the wealthiest, this woman understands that deviating from the prescription entails a cost: her son will not inherit the high rank associated with her prescribed match, and consequently will lose the concomitant desirable match. In the matching in the aristocratic equilibrium, a man's rank enters agents' reduced form utility functions despite the fact that it does not enter directly into their deep utility functions.

The fact that there are multiple equilibria in the infinite horizon dynamic model is not surprising: as in infinitely repeated games, we should expect that the non-uniqueness of continuation play will lead to multiplicity. The insight we get from the multiplicity rests on the plausibility of the behaviors in the different equilibria. That men and women might desire to match with the wealthiest partners possible is eminently reasonable, and any reader of Jane Austen understands the possibility that family background trumps wealth in some social circles. The model above is parsimonious and it is difficult to imagine rankings other than the two I've discussed, but casual observation suggests that

[30] For example, it might be that there is asymmetric information and being invited to serve on a nonprofit board serves a signaling purpose.

education, social skills, athletic ability, and physical attractiveness are given different weights in different social circles. Preferences for mates might be hard-wired, but preferences for other attributes are likely of the reduced form type. Endogenously deriving the preferences for mates or friends with these attributes along the lines of the growth model could be useful in understanding how social structure affects economic behavior.[31]

3.4 Market imperfections and conformity[32]

The concern for rank that I have thus far focused on is perhaps the most compelling example of social concerns that affect economic decisions, but a close competitor would be a concern to conform.[33] The question of whether people are predisposed to behave like those with whom they associate is of central importance to policy questions concerning education, drug control, crime prevention, and welfare (among others). Arguments similar to those above for treating social concerns as reduced form preferences apply here as well. While there are undoubtedly evolutionary arguments for a hardwired concern to be like others, simply putting such a concern into the utility function has disadvantages similar to those discussed above. As I have stressed, adding arguments to the utility function weakens the predictions that can be made. Similar to the arguments concerning rank, we don't know the particular form that a concern to conform will take; is it that we desire to dress like others, talk like others, or engage in the same activities as others? Why is there consensus that some Asian societies exhibit more conformist behavior than Western societies? Again, an explanation that relies on genetic differences is less satisfying than an explanation based on different consequences for conforming or not conforming in different societies.

Analogous to the derivation of a concern for relative position, there are situations in which market imperfections lead naturally to conformist behavior, namely the existence of public goods or public decisions. Many consumption activities are undertaken, at least sometimes, in groups such as dining out, going to concerts and plays, entertaining, sports activities, etc. For group activities, there are common decisions to be taken by the group: how often to eat out and how expensive a restaurant to go to, whether to drive to a nearby ski slope or fly to more exotic distant resort, etc. There is often a price-quality "menu" from which the group can choose, from the cheaper but mundane to expensive and exciting. The group's decision typically reflects the preferences of the individuals in the group.

Suppose the group is homogeneous with one exception: the individuals have different disutilities for working. Because of this heterogeneity, there will be a dispersion of

[31] See, e.g., Mailath and Postlewaite (2006) for an example of such a model.

[32] The discussion in this section stems from discussions with Peter Norman.

[33] See Akerlof (1997) and Bernheim (1994) for examples. As does much of the work on conformism, these papers exogenously assume a desire to conform; in an interesting paper, Morris (2001) derives a reduced form desire to conform.

labor supplied across the group, and *a fortiori,* dispersion in wealth. Suppose the group decision is how expensive a restaurant at which to dine. If the dinner bill is split evenly, a high income group's choices will be more expensive than a low income group'. A consequence is that an individual with a given endowment will likely spend more on dining out as the group he is a member of becomes wealthier.[34]

Consider now an individual's labor-leisure choice problem. When we analyze the agent's reduced form problem, we typically employ his (reduced form) utility function over leisure and money, where the utility of money is the utility derived from the goods on which the money is ultimately spent, including dining out. Consider two agents, Andy and Bob. Suppose Andy dislikes work and prefers to work less and spend less on dining out than Bob who enjoys work and is happy to work more and eat better. If Andy and Bob are in the same dining-out group that splits the bill at the end of the meal, they will necessarily spend the same – more than is optimal for Andy but less than is optimal for Bob. When taking the constraints on their dining expenditures that stem from their dining-out group into account, both Andy and Bob will adjust their labor supply choices from what they might choose in the absence of the public decision. Andy will work more because the marginal utility of money is higher because of his higher, socially determined, dining expense and Bob will work less. In the end, we will see a smaller difference in their labor supply choices than had they not interacted socially.

The point of this example is that his or her social group affects the individual's choice problem, but only because his reduced form preferences will depend on the deep preferences of other individuals with whom he interacts socially. The structure of the problem, including the social arrangements, generates what appears to be a "conformist" tendency in which people's labor supply choices cluster together. For any given group, the wealthier in the group will work less and the poor will work more than they would in the absence of the joint consumption activity. What appears to be conformism is, however, entirely a consequence of the effect of social arrangements on reduced form preferences. The utility functions are standard in that they are devoid of any psychological or sociological desire to be more like others.

As with the growth example above that exhibited qualitatively different economic outcomes depending on the social norm (whether the ranking used in matching was determined by birth or by wealth), different norms in this example can generate different behavior. Social norms will determine how restaurants are chosen in groups: some groups may use something like majority rule, resulting in restaurant expenditures determined by the median wealth individual, some will rotate the restaurant choice among the individuals in the group, making expenditure depend on the variance of the wealth

[34] I take the group or groups of which an individual is a member as exogenous. I discuss below the effect of this assumption.

levels, while other groups may allow individuals to veto restaurants they feel too expensive. Different norms will ultimately result in different equilibrium labor supply choices.

We might expect similar "conformist" behavior in other settings where the social environment is important. Consider a group of young married women without children, each of whom is deciding when to take a leave from work and have a child. Any individual woman might worry that if she were to have a baby, she would be isolated from her friends: it would be difficult to find times that she could join them, and when she did join them she might feel excluded from the conversations about work. The situation is reversed after a number of women in the group have children; now it is the childless woman who will find it difficult to join the others during the day, and will be excluded from the conversation that will naturally center on young children. A casual look at the situation suggests a preference among the women to be conformist, that is, to behave as the others in the group behave. This is correct, but again we need to understand that there is nothing in the deep preferences about wanting to conform; the social environment has induced conformist *reduced form* preferences.[35]

3.4.1 Endogenizing social groups

I will comment on the assumption in the restaurant example that the group to which individuals belonged was exogenous. First, it is obvious that if I modified the example to let individuals choose their social group and if there are sufficiently many people of each ability, people will choose to be in a group with people who are identical to themselves. This is essentially the local public goods result that homogeneous communities are optimal in a simple model like this (cf. Bewley (1981)).

There are several things that mitigate against perfectly homogeneous social groups, however. The whole concept of social groups is somewhat fuzzy. Although the general idea of social groups is compelling, identifying a particular social group and its members precisely is impossible. Abstract social groups, as I am using the term, presumably include some of an individual's relatives, most of whom are exogenously determined. Also included in one's social group are some or all of one's neighbors. The house one purchases is obviously endogenous; the choice is largely determined by the social group to which one wishes to associate. But since the world is not composed of

[35] Neumark and Postlewaite (1998) examine a related question regarding married women's laborforce participation decision. Neumark and Postlewaite carry out an empirical exercise that analyzes a reduced-form model that incorporates into a standard neoclassical framework relative income concerns in women's (or families') utility functions. In this model, the entry of some women into paid employment can spur the entry of other women, independently of wage and income effects. The model is tested by asking whether women's decisions to seek paid employment depend on the employment decisions of other women with whom relative income comparisons might be important. Specifically, that paper looks at the effect of sisters' employment on women's own employment, taking into account the possibility that there may be heterogeneity across families in unobserved variables affecting the employment decision. A variety of tests supports the hypothesis that women's employment decisions are positively affected by a concern about their family income relative income relative to that of their sisters' families.

perfectly homogeneous neighborhoods, some heterogeneity of social groups is unavoidable. Third, even if people initially chose to be in homogeneous social groups, there are substantial transactions costs that prevent easily changing one's social group. Life cycle effects and random shocks will naturally introduce substantial heterogeneity into an initially homogeneous group.

Even with endogenized social groups, we shouldn't necessarily expect the outcome to be perfectly homogeneous groups. The simple model outlined above abstracts from many aspects that are relevant in carefully endogenizing social groups. Folk wisdoms, such as, "It's better to be a big fish in a small pond," suggest advantages of being above average in one's social group while the socially ambitious individual who doggedly attempts to gain entry into groups well above his or her station is a staple of western literature. There is a tension between the desire to be in a homogeneous group to minimize the conflicts on group decisions and the concern from rank discussed above.

There are two points of this example, the first is to provide another illustration that it is not necessary to deviate from traditional economic modeling methodology with standard deep preferences to understand or explain behavior that seems driven by social considerations. Second, by making explicit the relationship between the observed choice (labor supply) and the variables in the deep utility function (dining with friends) we identify a source of heterogeneity of labor supply decisions that we might otherwise overlook.

3.4.2 Multiplicity of social arrangements

There can be a multiplicity of social arrangements with different impacts on economic decisions in this example, as there was in the growth example discussed above. In the restaurant example, I left unspecified the precise manner in which the individuals' preferences over restaurants would be aggregated into a group decision. One possibility is that the system is simply a majority voting system, choosing the median group member's optimum. There is, however, no compelling argument for this particular social arrangement to be canonical. Some groups could be organized by such social arrangements but others could as well be governed by other arrangements. For example, a group could allow any member to "veto" a restaurant as being too expensive. This is equivalent to letting the poorest individual in the group choose the restaurant. These two alternative social arrangements lead to different reduced form utility functions, even if we fixed completely the characteristics of the members of a group. The group governed by a social arrangement in which the restaurant choice is the optimum for the median person will systematically spend more on restaurants than the group for which the restaurant choice is the poorest person's optimal choice. This induces every member of the group to work more; as in the ranking case, any attempt to understand the different economic behavior of two such groups is hopeless unless the social arrangements are part of the analysis.

There is a broader range of social arrangements for this simple example than just how the restaurant is chosen. Once the restaurant choice was made, I assumed that the bill would be split evenly. While plausible, there are clear alternatives. For example, the richer members of the group might pay more than the poorer members.[36] As before, different social arrangements generate different incentives for agents' economic decisions.

I emphasize that there is no canonical way in which we could "correct" the market imperfection. There typically will be an infinite number of social arrangements that can govern group decisions. No one of these Pareto dominates the others, and we should expect that different arrangements emerge in different societies generating different incentives in these societies.

4. WHY NOT TAKE THE INDIRECT PREFERENCES AS THE PRIMITIVE?[37]

There is a natural temptation to use the above arguments about how a concern for rank can arise instrumentally in a standard economic model with market imperfections as a basis for treating the concern as a primitive, which is in the agents' deep preferences. Once we are convinced that agents have such a concern, why not simply write down the utility function with rank as an argument? We would not be violating the bounds of the parsimonious economic paradigm that I argued were important; we would simply put in a footnote saying "We assume that agents have entirely standard preferences but that there are market imperfections that induce a concern for rank; we begin our analysis with those preferences." I will discuss next first some arguments for doing so, and then some disadvantages.

4.1 The case for making relative ranking an argument of the utility function

Every time a friend succeeds, I die a little. —Gore Vidal

The most compelling argument for including relative position as a direct argument in the utility function is that it seems that people often *do* care directly how they rank in an activity. I will argue below that it is often the case that if we look carefully at a particular situation in which people are concerned with rank, we find that there are consequences of ranking above or below other people, and it may be those consequences that matter rather than the rank *per se*. There are, however, many activities where the most inventive analyst would be hard-pressed to identify economically meaningful consequences of one's rank in an activity that nevertheless motivates substantial investment. It isn't difficult to identify with the elation an online video game player might feel when he beats the displayed historic high score even if he is the only person who will ever be aware of the achievement. Winning simply feels good.

[36] This is perhaps more than a plausible alternative since the outcomes that result from social arrangements prescribing equal division of bills can often be Pareto dominated by outcomes made possible by subsidization of the poor by the rich.

[37] The material in this section draws heavily on Postlewaite (1998).

There is a compelling evolutionary argument for an innate concern for relative standing.[38] Human beings are the product of millions of years of evolution and our basic preferences have evolved as a mechanism to induce us to behave in ways that have fitness value, that is, that increase the probability that we survive and have offspring. We have "hard wired" in us certain preferences that promote survival value; for example, our preference for sweet foods has evolved over a long period during which food was scarce and increased consumption of such foods was accompanied by increases in survival. A desire to ascend to the top of a social hierarchy has plausibly had selection value over the course of human evolution and consequently would be similarly hardwired.

Many animals, including those most similar to humans such as apes and chimpanzees, have a hierarchical social structure with top-ranked members faring better than others do. Typically, highly ranked members enjoy better access to food and mating opportunities than those ranked lower. In many species, the ranking of males is determined through physical contests, and there are obvious reasons that females should prefer more highly ranked males to lower ranked. First, almost by definition, highly ranked males are likely to be stronger, and consequently, able to afford better protection for the female and for offspring. Second, if the ability to perform well in the contests that determine rank are heritable, male offspring of a highly ranked male are likely to be highly ranked, and as a result, mate and reproduce well.[39] It follows immediately that if evolution has favored those females who were sensitive to male rank, evolution would necessarily favor males who tried to maximize their rank.

To the extent that humans are the product of this evolutionary process, we should expect them to exhibit at least a residue of this direct concern for rank. The environment that modern humans inhabit may be drastically different from that which conferred an advantage on the largest and fastest of our ancestors, but the genetic structure that evolved when there was an advantage would remain long after the environmental change. Only if the characteristics that were once valuable become disadvantageous might we expect evolutionary forces to eliminate them, and even then, very slowly.

It would thus be natural for humans to be genetically programmed not only to care about food and sex, but also to care about their relative position in groups in which they find themselves. An argument that such hardwiring serves no useful purpose is no more relevant than to point out that it is dysfunctional that an individual's craving for sweets can result in an unhealthy diet; any single individual's preferences are exogenously given, determined by the evolutionary pressures of the past.[40]

[38] See Robson and Samuelson (this volume) for a general treatment of the evolutionary foundations of preferences.

[39] Note that this argument doesn't depend on the characteristics having any inherent benefit; females who mate with males that have (heritable) traits that other females find desirable will find that their male offspring have plentiful mating opportunities. Peacocks' tails are a prototypical biological example of this. This is similar to the discussion of females' concern for male rank in the aristocratic social norm discussed above.

[40] See Maccheroni, Marinacci and Rustichini (2010) for a very nice discussion of why we should consider concern for relative position in the deep preferences and axiomatic foundations of such preferences.

4.1.1 Experimental support for direct concern for relative position

Bault, Coricelli and Rustichini (2007) (BCR) devise a very nice experiment that strongly suggests a direct concern for relative rank. The experimental design aims to distinguish an individual's utility from a random outcome in a two-player condition when there is another person with whom his outcome will be compared and his utility from the same lottery in the absence of a second subject, a one-player condition. The presence or absence of a second player has no effect on the alternatives available to an individual nor on the outcome; the only effect of the second player is that the subject can see whether someone else received more or less money. The experiment is as follows:[41]

In both conditions, the subject has to choose between two lotteries displayed on the screen. The probability of each outcome is described as a sector on a circle. Every point on the circle has equal probability. In the one-player condition, after the subject has made his choice, a square surrounds the lottery he chose. The other lottery is kept on the screen. Then a spinner spins on both circles, and stops randomly at some point on the circle, indicating the outcome. Because this happens on both lotteries, the subject knows the outcome of both lotteries. He is then asked to rate how he feels about the outcome on a fixed scale from −50 to 50. Regret is the event in which the outcome for the chosen lottery is smaller than the outcome on the other lottery, and relief the event in which the opposite happens. The two-player condition is similar except that, after his choice, the subject observes the choice that a subject like him has made out of the same two options available. If the two subjects choose the same lottery and have the same outcome, then they will experience what we can call shared regret or shared relief. If they choose a different lottery, then they might experience envy (if their outcome is lower than the outcome of the other) or gloating (if the opposite occurs). In the experiment, subjects were facing choices made by a computer program.

BCR suggest that for negative emotions, envy seems to be stronger than regret and regret stronger than shared regret: subjects appear to feel worse when they do badly and another does well than when they do badly in isolation. The same is true on good outcomes: people feel better when they've done well and another did badly than when the subjects do well in isolation.

4.2 Drawbacks in including relative position as an argument of the utility function

4.2.1 What precisely is hardwired?

While the evolutionary argument that there is some kind of concern for rank or status hardwired in humans is compelling, it's unlikely that all the determinants of rank are hardwired. As suggested above, sensitivity to characteristics like speed and strength might naturally be the residue of evolutionary forces; it is distinctly less likely that a

[41] From Rustichini (2007).

desire to be the best dressed or to have the most advanced university degrees would be hardwired as a consequence of evolutionary forces. A ranking based on intelligence might be hardwired, but the degree to which one's position in society is enhanced by academic achievement must come from a correlation between academic achievement and intelligence. If the most intelligent individuals in a society choose sports careers, academic achievement won't enhance status as much as in a society in which the most intelligent choose academic careers. In general, while it is probably justifiable to take some kind of a concern for rank as hardwired, we should expect that the degree to which such things as education, wealth or particular occupations to enhance one's status to be culturally determined. Moreover, that relationship is likely to vary across societies, and within a single society, across time.

4.2.2 Parsimony and unity of economic models

I argued above that an advantage of economics modeling is the parsimony of economic models. However, if parsimony were all that mattered one could argue for a parsimonious model that focused on concern for relative position in analyzing a particular problem. There are costs to doing this, even if the resulting model is descriptively more accurate. It is not simply the parsimony of our models that makes economics successful; the fact that we use roughly the same model to analyze all problems in economics plays a huge role. Consider an economist trying to understand why a new lawyer in town would spend a large sum of money to have his name painted in gold paint on the window of his office when he could print his name on a piece of paper and tape it to the window at no cost. A first year economics student who has passed his qualifying exam would be expected to quickly think in terms of signaling: perhaps the lawyer knows he is good, and can signal this belief to others who might be uncertain by paying a large sum for the gold-painted name. The signal is credible since a low ability lawyer would be unwilling to pay this amount since he realizes he will not be able to recoup the cost before his ability becomes known.

The student can come to this possible explanation because he has seen the Spence signaling model (cf. Spence (1973)) in his first-year microeconomics course. His textbook laid out the relatively crude model of an individual who could be of two types choosing how much education to get, and demonstrated the existence of a separating equilibrium characterized by the high ability student acquiring education and the low ability forgoing education.

In many (all?) other social sciences, the Spence signaling model would draw complaints. Some would object that perhaps the low education person might acquire education for the pleasure, and insist that the model be made more realistic by adding this possibility. Others might worry that students often don't know their own ability and that the model should be modified to account for this. Still others might want to incorporate the fact that education is not a one-dimensional object. After the model is modified in response to these concerns, we will have a much more realistic model of education. However, Spence's basic insight about separating equilibria will be obscured to the point that the most sophisticated economists may not recognize the similarity with our lawyer problem. (Indeed, by the time we are done "improving" the Spence model, there may not be any similarity.) The unity of economic analysis that uses a single, simple basic model to analyze a wide variety of problems is hugely valuable. The combination of the same model being used for different problems and the simplicity of the model enables one to transfer insights from the analysis of one problem to other problems.[42] Spence's job market paper has well over four thousand Google Scholar cites, and the basic insight of the model has been applied to nearly every corner of economic analysis. The range of applications would have been greatly reduced had the model been "corrected" to eliminate the glaring discrepancies with the real world.

4.3 Disadvantages of taking the reduced form preferences as primitive

To assess the merits of taking the reduced form preferences as given I first note that it isn't really clear what should really be the primitive arguments of a utility function. In our basic textbooks we are quite comfortable with analyzing the behavior of an agent whose utility function has hamburgers and French fries as arguments. A neurobiologist might argue that that isn't the "true" deep utility function because what really makes an individual happy is neurons firing in the brain; the individual only *seems* to enjoy the hamburger and fries because they cause the neurons to fire in a particular way.[43] In short, he could argue that the preferences over hamburgers and fries are reduced form and that one should look at the utility function over the chemicals in the brain that generate the satisfaction.[44]

Nevertheless, economists are quite content to use these reduced form preferences both for motivation and for empirical work. This is entirely appropriate if we are trying to predict the behavior of an individual when the prices of hamburgers changes or new menu items arise. For these kinds of questions, there is plausibly a stable and exogenous relationship between food bundles and the brain activity they will induce, and we lose nothing by replacing the more complicated pattern of neurons by the more familiar hamburger and fries. We might go wrong, however, if we considered questions in which the relationship between the observable goods – the hamburgers and fries – and the brain

[42] This view of the importance of connecting different parts of a field is not new, as the following quote from G. H. Hardy (1940) makes clear: "The 'seriousness' of a mathematical theorem lies ... in the significance of the mathematical ideas which it connects. We may say, roughly, that a mathematical idea is 'significant' if it can be connected, in a natural and illuminating way, with a large complex of other mathematical ideas."

[43] This discussion is a variant of Lancaster's (1966) argument that a consumer's preferences over goods are derived in the sense that the goods are required only to produce more fundamental characteristics about which the consumer cares.

[44] However, the neurobiologist might find himself being admonished by the physicist who complains that the chemicals are only atoms configured in a particular way, and the deep utility function should be over *them*.

activity wasn't fixed and more or less immutable. For example, if we wanted to investigate the effect of feeding someone a hamburger and fries three times a day for a year, we might expect the pattern to change; what was pleasurable at the beginning might be sickening eventually. There is little lost in beginning an analysis with the reduced form preferences with hamburgers as an argument in predicting demand changes following price increases because the relationship between instrumental and deep preferences varies little over the range of economic circumstances being considered.

In precisely the same way, we could begin with the reduced form preferences including rank concerns for problems in which we believe the relationship between rank and final consumption is fixed and unchanging. However, for many problems the interest in an instrumental concern for rank stems from a belief that the form of the relationship between rank and consumption differs across societies. Different societies may well rank individuals by different characteristics or there may be different sets of goods and services that are not allocated through markets, and hence, serve as motivators to enhance rank. Even if the variable determining rank is fixed, – say wealth – different distributions of that variable will lead to different reduced form preferences.[45] Policy choice may be unlikely to change the relationship between a hamburger and the attendant brain activity, but changes in tax law, say, can easily change the wealth distribution, and consequently, the reduced form preferences. In other words, we have to be aware that these reduced form preferences may not even be fixed within the range of alternatives we are considering in a single analysis.

5. EXAMPLES EMPLOYING INSTRUMENTAL CONCERN FOR RANK

The next section provides several examples that illustrate how an instrumental concern for rank can affect standard economic decision problems.[46]

5.1 Conspicuous consumption

Cole, Mailath and Postlewaite (1995a) (hereafter CMP95) applies the ideas in CMP92 to the question of conspicuous consumption.[47] Economists from Adam Smith to Thorstein Veblen (cf. Veblen (1899)) have noted that much of people's consumption is directed to impressing others. It is typically taken as given that people desire to impress others, consciously or unconsciously treating the question of why people want

[45] See also Hopkins and Kornienko (2010) for a discussion of this point.

[46] This is not by any means an exhaustive list. Furthermore, I restrict attention here only to theory papers. Examples of empirical work that employ reduced form preferences for rank includes Banerjee and Duflo (2008), Botticini (1999) and Corneo and Gruner (2000). There has also been experimental work on the presence of concerns for rank; see, e. g., Ball, Eckel, Grossman and Zame (2001).

[47] See also Bagwell and Bernheim (1996) and Corneo and Jeanne (1997) for a related models of conspicuous consumption. Zenginobuz (1996) analyzes a model in which agents conspicuously contribute to a public good due to a concern for relative position.

to impress others as outside the domain of economics. The model in CMP95 adds asymmetric information to a nonmarket matching decision similar to that described above. Here, wealth is unobservable but still important to potential mates. Individuals with relatively high wealth have an incentive to signal this fact, people will engage in conspicuous consumption to do so even though they are fully rational with standard preferences. Agents conspicuously consume because it's instrumental: in equilibrium, it results in wealthier mates and, consequently, higher consumption. Poorer individuals could, of course, conspicuously consume in the same manner as wealthier individuals but choose not to because of the (relatively) high opportunity cost of doing so. The inferences drawn from consumption patterns are equilibrium inferences.

Again, deriving agents' desire to impress others as instrumental achieves several goals. It again allows an "explanation" of a particular behavior of interest within the standard economic paradigm. Perhaps more importantly, it provides additional structure that has further implications, some of which provide testable hypotheses. For example, if conspicuous consumption serves as a device through which agents can signal their otherwise unobservable wealth, we would expect differing amounts of conspicuous consumption in different environments. In economic situations in which there is very good information about agents' wealth, there is less incentive to conspicuously consume than in situations in which there is poor information about wealth. If one believes that automobiles are a preeminent instrument for signaling wealth and that information about agents' wealth is better in small communities than in large communities, we expect that, *ceteris paribus*, people in large communities would spend more on automobiles than in small communities.[48] Similarly, we would expect that new arrivals to an area would spend more on such items if there were greater uncertainty about their financial status.[49]

These implications focus on the degree of uncertainty as a motivation for signaling. There are also implications that stem from differences in the rewards to signaling. In equilibrium, the incentive to conspicuously consume is to demonstrate one's relative wealth, which determines one's share of the nonmarket benefits of relative rank. If there are few nonmarket benefits, there is little reason to conspicuously consume.[50]

5.2 Labor supply

CMP95 analyzes a two-period model in which individuals are concerned with matching. Again, there is a ranking based on wealth, that is, wealthier individuals will match with wealthier mates. In this model, individuals with differing abilities are faced with a

[48] Similarly, one would expect greater expenditure on other conspicuous consumption items such as expensive watches and clothes.

[49] This is meant to be illustrative; obviously, there is a very serious selection bias in both examples.

[50] Charles, Hurst and Roussanov (2007) documents empirically racial differences in consumption goods, and argue that the differences arise because of different incentives to signal.

labor-leisure choice. Again, the tournament-like competition for mates leads (in equilibrium) to greater effort than would be the case in the absence of the concern for rank. The central point of this model is that an agent responds differently to a lower wage when other agents' wages remain the same than he would if those agents' wages were also lowered.

When all agents' wages are lowered, an individual will face a different wealth distribution than he did previously. If no agent changed his labor supply in the face of a uniform wage decrease, the ranking of agents will be unchanged. If, on the other hand, a single agent's wage was lowered, the wealth distribution of the other agents would be unchanged. A single agent who leaves his labor supply unchanged when his wage alone decreases would see his rank drop, and consequently he would be matched with a less wealthy mate.

In general, when increases in wealth or income lead to secondary benefits due to the social arrangements, agents will respond differently to individual-specific and aggregate shocks. For problems in which the difference is significant, the common practice of using microeconomic data to draw inferences about responses to aggregate shocks presents difficulties that are often overlooked since the micro data may include responses to individual shocks that systematically diverge from responses to the same shock when it is applied uniformly to all agents in a society.

These considerations are particularly relevant for problems such as predicting the effects of income tax. If the secondary benefits that derive from the rank in a society dominate the direct consumption benefit from income, an increase in income tax would have no effect on labor supply since it leaves unchanged the relationship between effort and rank. To the extent that the secondary benefits are important and ignored, there could be a systematic overestimate of the effect of taxes on labor supply.

There is a second potentially interesting effect of tax policy that is typically ignored. The basic interaction between rank and economic decisions stems from the fact that by altering behavior (saving more, working harder, spending more conspicuously) an individual can increase his or her rank in society. This tournament-like effect typically distorts decisions and the magnitude of the distortion depends on the benefits from distorting. Greater secondary benefits will obviously lead to greater distortions. As mentioned above, there is another less obvious determinant of the incentive to distort, namely the dispersion of wealth in the society. In a society with an extremely disparate distribution of wealth, it might take very large changes in my economic decision (saving, labor supply, etc.) to increase my rank by, say, one percent. However, if the wealth distribution is very tight (that is, a relatively equal wealth distribution), the same change in my economic decisions will lead to large increases in rank, and consequently, relatively large secondary benefits. The more equal the wealth distributions, the greater the marginal secondary benefit from distorting economic decisions. The implication for tax policy is that, *ceteris paribus*, tax policies that lead to more equal distributions of income or wealth provide greater incentives to working and saving when agents are concerned about their rank in these dimensions. There is, of course, no reason to think that inducing agents to work and save more leads to an increase in welfare.

5.3 Investment

"I've been saving like crazy. I'm expecting that when I'm 80 and need part-time nursing care, I'm going to be bidding against a lot of people for that." (Wall Street Journal, 3/4/2003, quoting a money manager).[51]

The standard portfolio choice model in finance analyzes an individual's investment choice in isolation, independent of other investors' choices. Concern for relative position introduces a tournament aspect to the investment decision. If all other agents invest in Iraqi Development Bonds, my relative wealth position in the future will be much less variable if I do as well. This adds an important general equilibrium component to the investment problem. In the absence of the concern for relative position, each agent could make his or her investment decision in isolation since others' decisions have no effect on the agent's ultimate consumption. The addition of nonmarket consumption consequences of relative position make the agent's decision depend on the decisions of others.

Cole, Mailath and Postlewaite (2001) (hereafter CMP01) analyze a model in which individuals allocate their initial endowment between two random investments. The returns correlate perfectly across individuals for the first investment, while the second asset is idiosyncratic: for each individual, the returns of the second asset are independent of the first asset, and independent of the returns on all other agents' second assets. All investments have the same distribution of returns. As with the papers discussed above, following the realization of the agents' investments, there is an exogenous incremental utility, which is increasing in the agent's relative position. As discussed above, the increase might stem from matching that is affected by relative position or from other nonmarket decisions affected by relative position.

CMP01 shows how concern for relative position can affect not only the level of investments that people make, but also the composition of their investments. Of particular interest is whether non-market activities provide agents with an incentive to allocate assets in a manner similar to that of other agents or differently from those agents. The issue is whether agents are risk averse or risk loving with respect to their relative position. Suppose each agent invests his entire endowment in the first asset, for which returns are perfectly correlated across individuals. Any agent's initial relative position will then be assured to be unchanged regardless of the performance of the asset since all agents' final wealth holdings will be the same multiple of their initial endowments. Whether any agent has an incentive to deviate from this investment plan

[51] Quote from DeMarzo, Kaniel and Kremer (2004).

depends on how happy he is with his initial relative position. All agents have an incentive to diversify and allocate some of their endowment to their idiosyncratic second asset to reduce risk. However, an agent introduces randomness in his relative position when he unilaterally shifts part of his endowment to his idiosyncratic investment, and the more he invests in the asset the higher will be the variance of his relative position after the random outcomes are realized. How does an agent feel about this increase in variance? This will depend on the rewards that accrue to relative position. Let agents be indexed by $t \in [0, 1]$, $w(t)$ be agent t's wealth, and $g(x)$ be the value that an agent gets if his rank in the wealth distribution is x (that is, $\Pr\{t \mid w(t) \leq x\}$). If g is concave, agents will be risk averse with respect to their rank, and will invest less in their idiosyncratic investment than they would have in the absence of a concern for rank. In essence, the concern for rank leads to herding – a tendency to invest as others do. Notice that this motivation for herding is quite different from that typically investigated in the literature that is driven by informational asymmetries[52]; herding occurs here despite the absence of private information.

CMP01 demonstrates how this phenomenon might explain home-country bias – the fact that individuals inadequately diversify outside their home country.[53] If people's concerns about relative wealth are restricted to comparisons to those in their own country, they will want their investments correlated with those of their compatriots if g is concave. If some agents are constrained to bias their portfolio, (for example, rules that restrict institutions to invest only in home-country companies) this will induce all other agents to bias their portfolios as well.

The concern for relative position will not necessarily lead to conformist investing, however. It was the concavity of g that lead an agent to desire a portfolio that was correlated to others' portfolios. If g is convex, the opposite is the case: agents will be risk loving with respect to relative position.[54] A society in which a few at the top of the ranking receive great benefits while the masses receive little or nothing gives an incentive for risk-taking for an agent not at the top to begin with. He may lose his money, but the decrease in status that accompanies the monetary loss is of little consequence.

Thus, the shape of g within a society – how the non-market benefits are spread among the populace – can have an important effect on risk taking. Societies in which those at the bottom do poorly, while the majority are treated about the same will see less risk taking than those in which the benefits are concentrated at the top.

Subsequent work on the effect of a concern for relative position on financial markets includes DeMarzo, Kaniel and Kremer (2004) who analyze a general equilibrium model with a participation constraint. Suppose individuals in a community want to

[52] See, e.g., Bikhchandani, Hirshleifer and Welch (1992).
[53] See Lewis (1999).
[54] See Gregory (1980), Robson (1992) and Roussanov (2008) for discussions of convexity vs. concavity.

consume a "local good" in the future, but suppliers of this good cannot fully hedge their endowments (e.g., future labor services are not fully collateralizable).[55] Because agents realize that they will compete with others in their community when it comes time to consume the good, they will care about their relative wealth. In equilibrium, agents in their model then have an incentive to herd and choose portfolios similar to those of other agents in the community.

The authors continue this line of work in DeMarzo, Kaniel and Kremer (2008), and show how concern for relative position can also lead to financial bubbles. Here, communities correspond to generational cohorts. Young agents fear that if others in their cohort become rich, their saving activity will drive down future investment returns. In equilibrium this effect leads agents to buy broadly, held assets they know are over-priced in order to preserve their relative position; by not following the crowd, an agent would run the risk of being left behind if the investments perform well.

Robson (1992) shows how an individual might have a direct utility function over wealth itself that is concave, yet have utility that is convex in some wealth regions when the indirect effects of relative wealth are taken into account. Becker, Murphy, and Werning (2005) provide an alternative to relative wealth concern models by assuming a direct concern for status, which can be acquired through purchases of a "status good". They assume that status increases an agent's marginal utility of consumption, and show that in their model this leads to risk taking, but argue that the resulting outcome is optimal.[56] Roussanov (2008) incorporates a concern for relative wealth into a simple model of portfolio choice and shows that this helps explain a range of qualitative and quantitative stylized facts about the heterogeneity in asset holdings among U.S. households. In his model, investors hold concentrated portfolios, suggesting, in particular, a possible explanation for the apparently small premium for undiversified entrepreneurial risk. Consistent with empirical evidence, the wealthier households own a disproportionate share of risky assets, particularly private equity, and experience more volatile consumption growth.

6. CONCLUDING REMARKS

The multiplicity of equilibria for a fully specified economy, where the multiplicity stems from different social norms, is a valuable tool in understanding differences in economic behavior and performance across economies. In a sense, however, this approach simply pushes the indeterminacy one level deeper in that it replaces the explanation "people in different economies have different preferences" with the explanation that they are governed by different social arrangements that induce different reduced form preferences.

[55] Communities may also be generational, as in the quote at the start of the section, with the assumption that tomorrow's nursing care providers are unable to fully hedge their future wage risk today.

[56] See, however, Ray, Robson and Xia (2008) regarding the efficiency of the outcome.

There is, however, additional structure that comes from the instrumental approach. The model above from CMP92 derived an instrumental concern for relative wealth and showed that the reduced form utility function incorporating that concern depends on the distribution of wealth. Policies that lead to changes in the distribution will result in changes in reduced form preferences. The process of explicitly modeling the social arrangements provides structure that leads to new insights and testable hypotheses; simply adding relative wealth as an argument in the utility function would not do this.

Nevertheless, I am sympathetic to a view that the work described above leaves unanswered the basic question of why different economies perform differently. For this, we need an understanding of why different societies are governed by different social arrangements. The modeling approach described here has the potential to do this. I described above how decisions that are not mediated through normal markets could induce a concern for rank, and further, how there could be both equilibria in which people are ranked by birth and by wealth. The additional structure that comes from the specification of the instrumental value of rank has the potential to provide insight into the circumstances when one or another rank would more likely arise.

Consider a variant of the models described above in which some nonmarket decisions induce a concern for rank, but in which people have the opportunity to invest either in physical capital that could be bequeathed to one's children in the standard way or in human capital which could be passed on to one's children through training and teaching. Such a model might well have equilibria in which the ranking that determines the nonmarket decisions is based on either of the two variables.

Suppose there is a small probability that everything an agent owns is confiscated. To the extent that human capital is (at least relatively) freer from the risk of confiscation, it might be more likely to arise as the determinant of ranking than physical capital in the face of confiscation risks. This is not simply because human capital accumulation is necessarily a more efficient way to help one's children in this environment (which it may or may not be depending on the parameters of the problem). Rather, it may be that ranking by human capital is more stable than ranking by physical capital, even if physical capital were more efficient than human capital to offset its greater vulnerability to confiscation. In other words, it may be that social norms based on physical capital simply have lower survivability rates than do social norms based on human capital; if so, we would expect to see human capital rankings in these environments.

The basic point is that some social arrangements are more stable than others are. The fundamentals of one economy may allow a particular social arrangement to survive while the social arrangement might not be sustainable in another.[57] Once again, the additional structure provided by a complete specification of the underlying foundations of the social norms provides implications beyond those that are possible when those arrangements are taken to be outside the scope of analysis.

[57] CMP92 and Brooks (2001) discuss this possibility in detail.

REFERENCES

Akerlof, G., 1984. An Economist's Book of Tales. Cambridge University Press, Cambridge, MA.

Akerlof, G., 1997. Social distance and social decisions. Econometrica 65, 1005–1024.

Bagwell, K., Bernheim, B., 1996. Veblen Effects in a Theory of Conspicuous Consumption. Am. Econ. Rev. 86, 349–373.

Ball, S., Eckel, C., Grossman, P., Zame, W., 2001. Status in Markets. Q. J. Econ. 116, 161–188.

Banerjee, A., Duflo, E., 2008. Marry for what? Caste and Mate Selection in Modern India, mimeo.

Bault, N., Coricelli, G., Rustichini, A., 2007. Interdependent utilities: How social ranking affects choice behavior, mimeo. University of Minnesota.

Becker, G.S., 1976. The Economic Approach to Human Behavior. University of Chicago Press, Chicago.

Becker, G.S., Murphy, K.M., Werning, I., 2005. The equilibrium distribution of income and the market for status. J. Polit. Econ. 113, 282–310.

Benhabib, J., Bisin, A., 2010. The evolutionary foundations of preferences, this volume.

Bernheim, D., 1994. A theory of conformity. J. Polit. Econ. 102, 841–877.

Bewley, T., 1981. A critique of Tiebout's theory of local public expenditures. Econometrica 3, 713–740.

Bikhchandani, S., Hirshleifer, S., Welch, I., 1992. A theory of fads, fashion, custom, and cultural change as informational cascades. J. Polit. Econ. 100, 992–1026.

Bisin, A., Verdier, T., 2000. "Beyond the melting pot": Cultural transmission, marriage, and the evolution of ethnic and religious traits. Q. J. Econ. 115, 955–988.

Bisin, A., Verdier, T., 2010. Cultural transmission and socialization, this volume.

Bisin, A., Topa, G., Verdier, T., 2004. Religious intermarriage and socialization in the united states. J. Polit. Econ. 112, 615–664.

Botticini, M., 1999. Social Norms and Intergenerational Transfers in a Pre-Modern Economy. Florence, mimeo, pp. 1260–1435.

Bowles, S., 1998. Endogenous preferences: The cultural consequences of markets and other economic institutions. J. Econ. Lit. 36, 75–111.

Brooks, N., 2001. The effects of community characteristics on community social behavior. J. Econ. Behav. Organ. 44, 249–267.

Charles, K., Hurst, E., Roussanov, N., 2007. Conspicuous consumption and race, mimeo, University of Chicago.

Cole, H.L., Mailath, G.J., Postlewaite, A., 1992. Social norms, savings behavior, and growth. J. Polit. Econ. 100, 1092–1125.

Cole, H.L., Mailath, G.J., Postlewaite, A., 1995a. Incorporating concern for relative wealth into economic models. Federal Reserve Bank of Minneapolis Quarterly Review 19, 12–21.

Cole, H.L., Mailath, G.J., Postlewaite, A., 1995b. Response to 'Aristocratic equilibria'. J. Polit. Econ. 103, 439–443.

Cole, H.L., Mailath, G.J., Postlewaite, A., 1997. Class systems and the enforcement of social norms. J. Public Econ. 70, 5–35.

Cole, H.L., Mailath, G.J., Postlewaite, A., 2001. Investment and concern for relative position. Rev. Econ. Design 6, 241–261.

Corneo, G., Gruner, H., 2000. Social limits to redistribution. Am. Econ. Rev. 90, 1491–1507.

Corneo, G., Jeanne, O., 1997. Conspicuous consumption, snobbism and conformism. J. Public Econ. 66, 55–71.

Corneo, G., Jeanne, O., 1999. Social organization in an endogenous growth model. Int. Econ. Rev. (Philadelphia) 40, 711–726.

Corneo, G., Jeanne, O., 2001. Status, the distribution of wealth, and growth. Scand. J. Econ. 103, 283–293.

Corneo, G., Jeanne, O., 2009. A theory of tolerance, mimeo.

DellaVigna, S., 2009. Psychology and economics: Evidence from the field. J. Econ. Lit. 47, 315–372.

Demarzo, P., Kaniel, R., Kremer, I., 2004. Diversification as a public good: Community effects in portfolio choice. J. Finance 59, 1677–1715.

Demarzo, P., Kaniel, R., Kremer, I., 2008. Relative wealth concerns and financial bubbles. Rev. Financ. Stud. 21, 19–50.

Duesenberry, J.S., 1949. Income, Saving, and the Theory of Consumer Behavior. Harvard University Press, Cambridge, MA.
Fernández, R., 2007a. Women, work, and culture. J. Eur. Econ. Assoc. 5, 305–332.
Fernández, R., 2007b. Culture as learning: The evolution of female labor force participation over a century, mimeo, New York University.
Fernández, R., 2010. Does culture matter?, this volume.
Fernández, R., Fogli, A., 2005. Culture: An empirical investigation of beliefs, work, and fertility. NBER Working Paper No 11268.
Fernández, R., Fogli, A., Olivetti, C., 2004. Mothers and sons: Preference formation and female labor force dynamics. Q. J. Econ. 119, 1249–1299.
Fershtman, C., Hvide, H., Weiss, Y., 2003. A behavioral explanation of the relative performance evaluation puzzle. Ann. Econ. Stat. 72, 349–361.
Fershtman, H., Murphy, K., Weiss, Y., 1996. Social status, education and growth. J. Polit. Econ. 104, 108–132.
Fershtman, C., Weiss, Y., 1998a. Why do we care about what other people think about us? In: Ben-Ner, A., Putterman, L. (Eds.), Economics, Values and Organization. Cambridge University Press, Cambridge, MA.
Fershtman, C., Weiss, Y., 1998b. Social rewards, externalities and stable preferences. J. Public Econ. 70, 53–73.
Frank, R.H., 1985. Choosing the Right Pond: Human Behavior and the Quest for Status. Oxford University Press, New York.
Gregory, N., 1980. Relative wealth and risk taking: A short note on the Friedman-Savage utility function. J. Polit. Econ. 88, 1226–1230.
Hardy, G.H., 1940. A Mathematician's Apology. Cambridge University Press, Cambridge.
Hopkins, E., Kornienko, T., 2004. Running to keep in the same place: Consumer choice as a game of status. Am. Econ. Rev. 94, 1085–1107.
Hopkins, E., Kornienko, T., 2006. Inequality and growth in the presence of competition for status. Econ. Lett. 93, 291–296.
Hopkins, E., Kornienko, T., 2010. Which inequality? The inequality of endowments versus the inequality of rewards. American Economic Journal: Microeconomics forthcoming.
Lancaster, K., 1966. A new approach to consumer theory. J. Polit. Econ. 74, 132–157.
Lizzeri, A., Siniscalchi, M., 2008. Parental guidance and supervised learning. Q. J. Econ. 153, 1161–1197.
Lewis, K., 1999. Trying to explain the home bias in equities and consumption. J. Econ. Lit. 37, 571–608.
Maccheroni, F., Marinacci, M., Rustichini, A., 2010. Choosing within and between groups, mimeo.
Mailath, G.J., Postlewaite, A., 2003. The social context of economic decisions. J. Eur. Econ. Assoc. 1, 354–362.
Mailath, G.J., Postlewaite, A., 2006. Social assets. Int. Econ. Rev. (Philadelphia) 47, 1057–1091.
Morris, S., 2001. Political correctness. J. Polit. Econ. 109, 231–265.
Neumark, D., Postlewaite, A., 1998. Relative income concerns and the rise of female labor force participation. J. Public Econ. 70, 157–183.
Okuno-Fujiwara, M., Postlewaite, A., 1995. Social norms in random matching games. Games Econ. Behav. 9, 79–109.
Postlewaite, A., 1998. The social basis of interdependent preferences. Eur. Econ. Rev. 1998, 779–800.
Ray, D., Robson, A., Xia, B., 2008. Status and intertemporal choice, mimeo.
Robson, A., 1992. Status, the distribution of wealth, private and social attitudes to risk. Econometrica 60, 837–857.
Robson, A., 1996. A biological basis for expected and non-expected utility. J. Econ. Theory 68, 397–424.
Robson, A., Samuelson, L., 2010. Evolutionary Selection, this volume.
Roussanov, N., 2008. Diversification and its discontents: Idiosyncratic and entrepreneurial risk in the quest for social status, mimeo, Universityof Pennsylvania.
Rustichini, A., 2007. Dominance and competition. J. Eur. Econ. Assoc. 6, 647–656.
Spence, M., 1973. Job market signaling. Q. J. Econ. 87, 355–374.
Tabellini, G., 2008. The scope for cooperation: Values and incentives. Q. J. Econ. 123, 905–950.

Veblen, T., 1899. The Theory of the Leisure Class: An Economic Study of Institutions. Allan and Unwin, London. Reprinted, Modern Library, New York, 1934.
Weber, M., 1905. The Protestant Ethic and the Spirit of Capitalism. Reprinted, Unwin Hyman, London and Boston, 1930.
Weiss, Y., Fershtman, C., 1998. Social status and economic performance: A survey. Eur. Econ. Rev. 42, 801–820.
Zenginobuz, U., 1996. Concern for relative position, rank-order contests, and contributions to a public good. Boğaziçi University Research Papers, ISS EC pp. 97–107.

CHAPTER 3

Preferences for Status: Evidence and Economic Implications*

Ori Heffetz
Cornell University, Johnson Graduate School of Management
oh33@cornell.edu

Robert H. Frank
Cornell University, Johnson Graduate School of Management
rhf3@cornell.edu

Contents

1. Introduction 70
2. Features of Status 72
 2.1 Positionality 72
 2.2 Desirability 73
 2.3 Nontradability 74
3. Evidence 75
 3.1 Positionality 75
  3.1.1 Happiness vs. utility 75
  3.1.2 What does the happiness evidence show? 76
  3.1.3 Social preferences 77
 3.2 Desirability: experimental evidence on status 78
  3.2.1 Status correlates 78
  3.2.2 The effects of status 79
  3.2.3 Do people value status for its own sake? 80
 3.3 Nontradability: evidence on visibility 81
 3.4 Evolutionary considerations: a tie-breaker? 83
4. Some Economic Implications 84
 4.1 Labor market implications 86
5. Conclusion 88
References 89

Abstract

This chapter brings together some of the recent empirical and experimental evidence regarding preferences for social status. While briefly reviewing evidence from different literatures that is consistent with the existence of preferences for status, we pay special attention to

* We thank Catherine Eckel, Ada Ferrer-i-Carbonell, Chaim Fershtman, and Andrew Oswald for useful conversations, comments, and references, and Russell Toth for excellent research assistance. Please direct correspondence to oh33@cornell.edu.

Handbook of Social Economics, Volume 1A
ISSN 0169-7218, DOI: 10.1016/S0169-7218(11)01003-3

experimental work that attempts to study status directly by inducing it in the lab. Finally, we discuss some economic implications.
JEL Codes: C90, D01, D1, D62, Z10, Z13

Keywords

Preferences for status
positional concerns
subjective well-being
conspicuous consumption
positional externalities
relative income
status experiments

1. INTRODUCTION

What are our ultimate objects of desire? Is social status one of them?

In its most abstract form, rational choice theory is general enough to incorporate virtually any assumption about the nature of preferences, including assumptions about the objects over which preferences are defined. Until relatively recently, however, the overwhelming majority of applications of the theory—common examples include models of consumer choice, household behavior, labor markets, the macro-economy, etc.—assumed that the ultimate objects of desire are individually consumed goods (and leisure). Well-being in these applications is a function of the (absolute) amounts consumed of these commodities.

This assumption stands in stark contrast to how psychologists, sociologists, marketers, and researchers in other closely related disciplines view preferences. Recent decades have seen movement by economists on this issue, more of whom are now willing to consider new arguments in the utility function. In this chapter, we focus on one such argument: social status.

The idea that individuals are often motivated in their behavior by a quest for social status is not new. It goes back to the earliest writings known to humanity. It has been a recurring theme, for example, in poetry, literature, religion, and philosophy throughout the millennia, and was a central theme in Western political philosophy well before the birth of economics. This idea—which is manifested in Hobbes's assertion that "men are continually in competition for honor and dignity" (cited in Hirschman 1973)—has been later echoed by economists such as Smith (1776), Marx (1849), Veblen (1899), Duesenberry (1949), and their successors. More recently, social status has increasingly been given attention by economists in both theory and empirical work. Our emphasis in this chapter is on the latter.

Our main goal is to review the growing body of evidence that bears on the hypothesis that people care about status. We stress from the outset that much of the evidence we review is consistent with more general theories, of which a preference for status is but one possible interpretation. For example, as discussed at length below, concerns about status per se and concerns about relative position (relative consumption, relative income) are closely related. Evidence regarding positional concerns is consistent with, but does not require, preferences for status. Positional concerns can be extremely important even in the lack of status concerns. They emerge, for example, when our perception of the quality of a good is determined by comparing it with what we consider a typical good, which in turn depends on what is typically consumed around us (Frank 2007).

One consequence of this 'evidence overlap' is that evidence that is relevant to our topic has been accumulating in several different literatures, from empirical studies of happiness and income to experimental studies of social preferences. We attempt to bring this evidence together and make explicit its relationship with hypotheses regarding preferences for status.

Our second goal is to summarize briefly the economic implications of status seeking. None of these is particularly new: they follow from models and theories that, for the most part, predate the evidence presented in this chapter. Moreover, we again point out that many of these theories were not originally developed with status being their only (or even their main) interpretation, and that their implications do not depend on this interpretation. Examples include early 'modern' models and applications like Pigouvian taxation, Buchanan and Stubblebine's (1962) treatment of externalities, Becker's (1971) analysis of discrimination, Becker's (1974) theory of social interaction, and Frank's (1985a) model of positional goods. Furthermore, as discussed below, some of the main implications of even those theories that were developed specifically to model status are implications of *features* of status (such as its zero-sum nature). Hence, these implications too are mostly interpretation-independent.

Because of this 'model overlap', again, many of the models (and their implications) that can be interpreted as models of status, are surveyed and discussed elsewhere. Although we discuss specific models as they relate to specific evidence or implications, a comprehensive review of the theoretical work that is relevant to status is beyond the scope of this chapter. We also do not review studies from disciplines other than economics (see, e.g., Frank 1999 and Ball and Eckel 1996, 1998, for a partial review of studies in psychology, biology, sociology, social psychology, marketing, and other disciplines). However, we discuss individual studies that are closely related to work in economics.

Finally, an excellent presentation of the main ideas from sociology and their economic applications is given in Weiss and Fershtman's (1998) survey of social status and economic performance. After discussing the definitions, measurement, and determinants of status, the authors review models of status and their economic implications regarding, for example, wages (e.g., Frank 1985b, Chapter 2) and growth. They further discuss equilibrium models and evolutionary models, and conclude by pointing out both the importance of and the lack of empirical evidence: "while it seems intuitively plausible that individuals care about their social standing, the importance given to such considerations relative to monetary returns must be demonstrated empirically" (Weiss and Fershtman 1998). This chapter can thus be viewed as picking up the discussion where Weiss and Fershtman (1998) left it. Indeed, the chapter aims to demonstrate that much has changed in the last decade with respect to evidence. Furthermore, because new experimental evidence on status seems to have gotten less attention (and, for the most part, is not surveyed elsewhere), we review this evidence in special detail, outlining the main findings, their strengths and weaknesses, and what we believe still needs to be done.

The rest of this chapter proceeds as follows. In the next section, we define social status and discuss three of its main features as an argument in the utility function—that it is positional, desirable, and nontradable. In Section 3, we review evidence related to each of these features. In Section 4, we discuss some economic implications, focusing on labor markets as one class of markets where these may be particularly important. Section 5 concludes.

2. FEATURES OF STATUS

We start by discussing features of social status. We focus on three features that we believe are salient, are instrumental to evidence on status, and underlie much of the implications of status. The three are by no means exhaustive. They merely reflect one way in which the evidence presented later can be conveniently arranged.

2.1 Positionality

To set the stage for a discussion of preferences for social status, we first note that status is inherently positional. Of its many definitions, in sociology and other literatures, it is hard to find one that does not use the words "position" or "rank" (the *Merriam Webster Dictionary* indeed uses both, defining status as a "position or rank in relation to others"). Weiss and Fershtman (1998) define social status as "a ranking of individuals (or groups of individuals) in a given society, based on their traits, assets, and actions." They point out that although different members of society may have different rankings, sufficient agreement exists to render status a powerful incentive mechanism. Ball et al. (2001) define it as "a ranking in a hierarchy that is socially recognized and typically carries with it the expectation of entitlement to certain resources." For a definition in sociology, see, e.g., Ridgeway and Walker (1995, p. 281).

The positionality of status is central to the discussion in this chapter, since it underlies both much of the evidence regarding the existence of preferences for status and many of the economic implications of such preferences. Since status is, by definition, positional, it follows that as an object of desire it enters the utility function as a positional good. Following Hirsch (1976), Frank (1985a) defines positional goods as "those things whose value depends relatively strongly on how they compare with things owned by others," and develops a formal model that has become a workhorse in the status and in related literatures. In the model, the utility from consuming positional goods depends both on the amount consumed and on how this amount compares to amounts consumed by others. See Frank (1985b, 1999) for discussions and references, and Clark et al. (2008) for extensions and updates.

One immediate consequence of the positionality of status is that its consumption imposes negative externalities: an increase in someone's relative status automatically translates to a decrease in the relative status of (at least some) others in the relevant reference group. This feature makes the *status game* (Congleton 1989) not unlike a Prisoner's Dilemma, in which an agent's attempt to improve her or his (relative) outcome results in an inefficient equilibrium. A direct implication is that status goods are over-consumed and hence, as is typical in such cases, policy interventions that solve the dilemma could be Pareto improving. We discuss such implications and welfare enhancing policies in Section 4.

2.2 Desirability

One may wonder what makes status desirable (i.e., why it enters the utility function). The second half of the definition in Ball et al. (2001) above provides one potential answer: status typically carries with it the expectation of entitlement to certain resources. In other words, status may be viewed—and desired—merely as an intermediate good. According to this view, status acts as a nonmonetary currency. Like (real) money, it enters agents' (reduced form) utility only as a useful simplification: ultimately, people desire the *resources* that status can buy. Weiss and Fershtman (1998, p. 802) share this approach and give examples:

> *"A person of high status expects to be treated favorably by other individuals with whom he might engage in social and economic interactions. This favorable treatment can take many forms: transfer of market goods, transfer of nonmarket goods (through marriage, for instance), transfer of authority (letting the high status person be the leader), modified behavior (such as deference or cooperation) and symbolic acts (such as showing respect). Because of these social rewards, each individual seeks to increase his social status through group affiliation, investments in assets (including human and social capital) and an appropriate choice of actions".*

Indeed, as Weiss and Fershtman (1998) point out, the question of whether or not to model status as entering the utility function is reminiscent of the question of whether or not to model money as entering the utility function—an old question for monetary economists.

A related approach is found in Ball and Eckel (1996, 1998). Citing research from sociology, the authors point out that status could be valued as a signal (which may or may not be accurate), and that people may react to status in others because it potentially provides economically useful information about individuals—like education in a Spence-type model. Under this interpretation, status seeking could result from a signaling equilibrium, rather than from preferences (or tastes) for status itself.

Proposing yet another (related) approach, Ball et al. (2001) motivate their work with a simple model in which individual utility depends both on consumption and on the status of individuals with whom an individual trades. In their model, status is exogenously distributed, and people desire to *associate* with those with high status. This could be interpreted as an underlying cause and, simultaneously, as an effect, of individuals' (revealed) preference for obtaining status when status is endogenous. Notice, however, that when status is endogenous, association with high status individuals could—while enhancing one's global status (by affiliating with a high status group)—harm one's local status (by worsening one's position relative to one's associates).

Is status then desirable in and of itself, or is it only desired as a means (a currency, a signal, etc.) to achieving other resources? As with education and, ultimately, with money, these two apparently different underlying mechanisms may be harder to distinguish—both conceptually and practically—than they initially seem. Status is probably desired for various reasons at the same time, including that we "simply like it" (its consumption value) and that it can do things for us (its asset value).[1] Can the two be disentangled, e.g. by a clever experimental manipulation in a controlled lab environment? We review work that attempts to do just that. However, social status artificially divorced from some of its essential features may simply cease to be social status as we understand it. We return to this point below when discussing specific studies (see Section 3.2).

2.3 Nontradability

Finally, as discussed above, status is conferred by society, and cannot be directly purchased in an explicit market for status.[2] In other words, it is nontradable. Depending on context, an individual's ability to gain status may be severely limited (for example, when status is hereditary) or less so (for example, when status depends on effort at the workplace). To the extent that one's actions have any effect on one's status, however, these actions have to affect the social perceptions through which status is conferred. In other words, status-seeking activities must be socially visible (either directly or through their socially visible outcomes). As discussed in Section 3.3, this has far-reaching implications.

We emphasize, however, that in calling status nontradable we do not mean to exclude the existence of *implicit* markets for it. For example, an individual can often actively choose

[1] Closely related to these explanations of the desire for status is work on the relationship between status and health, where a key question is whether higher social status improves health (and if so, by how much). See e.g., Rablen and Oswald (2008) for a recent discussion (including a short survey) and new evidence on the longevity of Nobel Prize winners (compared to nominees).

[2] See Becker et al. (2005) for alternative assumptions.

the reference group in which that individual's local status is determined, effectively engaging in transactions in such implicit status markets (Frank, 1984, 1985b). By switching to a firm with a different wage distribution one can influence one's status at the workplace. Similarly, by moving to a different neighborhood one could affect one's local position among one's neighbors. We return to this point when we discuss implications.

3. EVIDENCE

3.1 Positionality

If individuals had preferences for status, and status in turn were conferred on the basis of an individual's economic outcomes such as income, wealth, consumption, etc., then such outcomes (or their combinations) would have to enter the utility function positionally. That is, not only would absolute income and wealth matter, but so too would relative income and relative wealth. Do economic measures like income, wealth, and consumption enter the utility function positionally?

3.1.1 Happiness vs. utility

Although far from providing conclusive answers, a large and growing body of work, referred to in economics as the *happiness* literature, suggests that relative position affects well-being. For example, Frank (1999, Chapter 5) surveys studies that show that different measures of happiness and well-being are often found to correlate positionally with economic variables. These measures range from self-reported happiness questions in surveys to electromagnetic activity levels at different sites in the brain.

Although, as we discuss shortly, the validity of each as a measure of well-being is controversial, they are remarkably consistent with one another. Furthermore, this consistency holds when they compare either across alternative sources or across alternative observable behaviors that are commonly regarded as manifestations of happiness. The former include, for example, an individual's happiness as reported by friends. The latter include increased propensity to initiate social contact with friends and to help others, and decreased propensity for psychosomatic illnesses, absences from work, involvement in disputes at work, and committing suicide.

This cross-measure consistency suggests that these happiness measures may provide evidence regarding the actual shape of the utility function. In a recent comprehensive survey of the happiness literature, Clark et al. (2008, Section 4) return to the discussion regarding the relationship between measures of happiness and the economist's notion of (decision) utility. They point out that since an econometric identification of utility requires data we might never have access to, any discussion is forced to rely on circumstantial evidence. Summarizing different types of such evidence, they cite new studies that show correlation between self-reports and physiological and neurological phenomena (smiles, brain activity), reports by others (who watch pictures or video, or who are friends or family), evaluations by third parties of open-ended interviews, and other measures. They also discuss the correspondence between happiness correlates and observed choice behavior, which reflects on the correspondence between subjective well-being (which is found predictive of future behavior) and utility theory.

Clark et al. (2008) close their discussion by reminding the reader to remain cautious, citing evidence on mispredictions and on the malleability of happiness answers. Similarly, Kahneman and Krueger (2006) argue that while different measures of well-being are useful for different purposes, such subjective measures should not be taken as measuring "utility as economists typically conceive of it." See also Kahneman et al. (2006), and Diamond's (2008) related discussion of the survey questions that are often used in studies that link happiness with income of oneself and with that of others. Diamond (2008) expresses the concern that "such studies may not shed light on the question of how much well-being depends on one's relative standing and how much the respondent looks to relative standing in order to answer the survey question."

3.1.2 What does the happiness evidence show?

With these caveats in mind, the happiness literature provides ample evidence of the positionality of income. For example, Veenhoven (1993) shows the by-now famous example of Japan, where the average reported level of well-being in surveys remained virtually stable over decades during which national income increased dramatically (doubling several times). Known as the Easterlin paradox (Easterlin 1974, 1995), the finding that growth of real national income is not associated with a higher national level of reported happiness has been observed in many Western industrial economies (Easterlin 2005). See Scitovsky (1976) for an early discussion along similar lines.

Other authors have questioned Easterlin's conclusion that, in advanced economies, economic growth does not improve human well-being. Frank (2005), for example, argues that rising per-capita income is associated with lower infant mortality, cleaner environments, better health in old age, and a variety of other clear improvements in well-being, irrespective of whether those improvements are reflected in responses to happiness surveys. Indeed, a widely discussed recent paper by Stevenson and Wolfers (2008) argues that careful analysis of national time-series data reveals a positive relationship between average happiness and per-capita income.

In their survey of the literature, Clark et al. (2008) review studies that document the Easterlin paradox, as well as counterexamples where an aggregate income-happiness correlation does exist (East Germany in the 1990s; see Frijters et al. 2004). Drawing on prior surveys of the empirical literature on happiness and well-being (Kahneman, Diener and Schwartz 1999, Layard 2005, Frank 1999), the authors list the following three stylized facts: (a) cross-section regressions (with or without demographic controls) within a country show a significant income-happiness correlation, with a higher correlation in developing than in developed countries; (b) panel data that control for individual fixed effects show that changes in real incomes are correlated with changes in happiness, with exogenous income variations showing causal effects on happiness (again with larger coefficients in transition than in developed economies); and (c) large samples of cross-time cross-country data show that happiness moves with macroeconomic measures like GDP, growth, and inflation.

Finally, summarizing previous discussions, the authors show how a simple model with social comparisons (where consumption enters the utility function both traditionally and positionally) is consistent with other evidence as well. Such evidence includes, for example, Clark and Oswald (1996), who regress job satisfaction on personal income and on predicted income of a comparison group and find coefficients of equal magnitude but opposite sign. Their finding is consistent with job satisfaction being purely positional in income.

Ferrer-i-Carbonell (2005) conducts a similar exercise with subjective well-being, and she, too, finds a negative coefficient. Furthermore, testing asymmetry, she finds—consistent with Duesenberry's (1949) "demonstration effect"—that individuals tend to compare themselves with others whose incomes are higher than their own. Luttmer (2005) employs richly detailed panel data to confirm the importance of local comparisons. He documents a robust negative association between individual happiness measures and average neighborhood income, a link that does not appear to stem from selection effects. See Clark et al. (2008) for recent evidence from different countries (Latin America, China), with different comparison groups (the wages of coworkers, family, friends), and from experimental studies; Frank (1999, pp. 140–142) for evidence from studies of serotonin in monkeys; Zink et al. (2008) for recent evidence on humans' neural responses (from brain imaging) to hierarchy in a lab-game setup; Solnick and Hemenway (1998, 2005), Alpizar et al. (2005), and Carlsson et al. (2007) for survey evidence on positional concerns; and Alesina et al. (2004) for evidence on the relationship between inequality and happiness.

3.1.3 Social preferences

Finally, positional concerns are closely related to a growing literature on what in the last decade have come to be known as *social preferences*. For surveys and evidence (mostly from lab experiments), see, e.g., Charness and Rabin (2002) and Fehr and Schmidt (2006). Although a discussion of this fascinating literature is beyond the scope of this chapter, we point out that, for example, Frank's (1985a) model of relative concerns is closely linked to (one side of) the Fehr-Schmidt inequity aversion model: an individual whose income is less than her associate's, and who acts to reduce her associate's income, could be viewed as reducing either a positional disadvantage or a disadvantageous inequality.

Interestingly, some lab results suggest that individuals may under some conditions be willing to do the opposite. For example, Charness and Rabin (2002) report that half of their participants chose a payoff of $375 for themselves and $750 for their opponent in a simple choice game in the lab, over the alternative of $400 for themselves and $400 for their opponent. Although one should be cautious regarding any extrapolation from this to real world contexts, such choices (as well as previous findings that the authors review) are predicted by neither positional concerns nor inequity aversion (nor by the standard model with self-interested agents maximizing absolute payoffs for themselves).

3.2 Desirability: experimental evidence on status

A growing body of experimental evidence has shed light on the question of whether status is desirable as a means or as an end. Much of this work has focused on demonstrating that status (or status perceptions) can affect economic outcomes, hence demonstrating that status *could* be desired merely as a means to improved economic outcomes. At the same time, new work attempts to measure directly the extent to which individuals forgo real resources to gain status in a lab context. This work suggests that status may be desired even when it does not result in any economic benefits.

This literature is new and is still quickly evolving. Most of the evidence we review has been published in the last decade (or indeed is yet to be published), and much of it remains only suggestive (but nonetheless interesting). In this section, we review this evidence critically in the hope of helping steer this exciting research in what we believe are promising directions.

3.2.1 Status correlates

Measuring trust through trust game experiments, Glaeser et al. (2000, Table VII) show that individuals with characteristics believed to be correlated with high status systematically realize higher gains. These characteristics include, among others, whether or not a subject's father has a college degree, and "two proxies for 'coolness' or charisma in this [undergraduate] subject population: beers drunk per week and whether the individual has a sexual partner." The authors find, for example, that having a sexual partner positively predicts trusting behavior, and that all status correlates predict a tendency to elicit trustworthiness in others.

The two "coolness" proxies may of course be correlated with trusting and trustworthy behaviors through channels unrelated to charisma or status. As the authors point out, a finding that high-status individuals earn more in the trust game could be driven by many different mechanisms. "For example, high status individuals may elicit trustworthy behavior because they are relatively skilled at socially punishing or rewarding others."

A natural way to confront this issue is to conduct controlled experiments where subjects' social status is directly manipulated. For obvious reasons, such studies present difficult challenges. Next, we describe a few brave attempts to overcome them.

3.2.2 The effects of status

In pioneering work, Ball and Eckel (1996, 1998) and Ball et al. (2001) directly manipulate status in the lab. They artificially award subjects high or low status, and study how it affects economic outcomes in negotiation (ultimatum game) and market ("box design" market game) environments. They show that their manipulation affects behavior and that individuals awarded high statuses in the lab enjoy favorable economic outcomes (improved earnings).

The status manipulation in these experiments involves asking subjects to take an economic trivia quiz, on the basis of which they are assigned either to high-status (Star) or low-status (No Star) groups. Subjects are told that group assignment is "based on their answers" to the quiz. Crucially, however, they are not told that the quiz is graded not according to the correctness of their answers, but rather according to a criterion that makes the assignment into status groups essentially random.[3] High-status group members (Star subjects) are publicly awarded gold stars to wear on their clothing during the experiment, are applauded by No Star subjects, and are visibly given other symbolically-preferential treatment by the experimenters. These manipulations aim to establish their high status.

The authors' finding that Star subjects earn significantly more is intriguing. Interpreting this finding, however, is difficult. The authors distinguish between earned and unearned status and note that in real life, status comes with entitlement (citing Lerner 1970, they refer to just-world theory, according to which "many people believe that in a just world, people get what they deserve and deserve what they get."). Thus, the difficulty is that it is unclear whether subjects perceive Star status as linked to entitlement. While "subjects should think that subjects with stars are more deserving than their no-star counterparts" (Ball and Eckel 1996), subjects "likely considered the test to be unfair" (Ball et al. 2001).

As these observations suggest, the direction of any bias in the authors' findings will depend on whether subjects considered status to have been earned fairly. Furthermore, the very belief by subjects in the existence of *any* (nonrandom) criterion may contaminate the results. If Star subjects are believed to deserve their high status, they are viewed, in effect, as being different from others in their features or behavior. For example, if subjects believe that high-status individuals were more successful in answering the quiz, they might believe high status individuals to be better economists, more intelligent, more intuitive, etc. This may confound the estimated effects of status with the effects of perceptions of these other features.

Recognizing this, Ball et al. (2001) run additional experimental sessions where status is awarded based on a publicly administered lottery, a criterion that subjects

[3] Specifically, grades consist of the total sum of numerical answers to quiz questions (regardless of their correctness), and subjects are divided into groups along the median sum.

should consider "meaningless but fair." They find that when awarded (visibly) randomly, status has a stronger effect on market results.[4] That the effect is found sensitive to implementation confirms the above concerns, and highlights some of the fundamental difficulties underlying the entire status-experiments endeavor. DiNardo (2007) beautifully makes a few related points (especially see his discussion in Section 3.1 "Randomized Controlled Trials," and Section 4 "Just Because We Can Manipulate It Doesn't Mean We Can Learn About It"). One important issue he raises is "the hope that 'how' the treatment is assigned is irrelevant to the effect . . . on the outcome. If the effect of the putative cause is implementation specific, it is often more helpful to abandon the effort to find the effect of the putative cause and 'settle' for the effect of the 'implemented cause.'" As Ball et al. (2001) demonstrate, how status is assigned in the lab is indeed relevant to its effects. Paraphrasing DiNardo (2007), then, the most we may be able to do is describe the causal effect of a Star manipulation administered in one specific way, rather than referring to the measured effect as "the effect of status."

With this in mind, Ball and Eckel (1996, 1998) and Ball et al. (2001) demonstrate the possibility that status and, indeed, other social factors substantially affect economic outcomes. Furthermore, they demonstrate (in the ultimatum game experiments) that these effects may disappear when stakes are increased. In the market experiments, Ball et al. (2001) also find, surprisingly, that when status is awarded privately (that is, other subjects are not aware of a subject's status group), results are reversed: higher status subjects' earnings are *lower* than those of lower status. They nicely summarize this finding: "Although definitive conclusions await further experimentation, this limited evidence implies that status must be publicly revealed to be effective. This suggests that deference by the low-status group is at least as important as confidence on the part of the higher-status group." We further discuss visibility and anonymity in Section 3.3.

Other attempts to study the effects of status in the lab using the Star manipulation include Eckel and Wilson's (2006) attempt to study how status perceptions affect learning, and Kumru and Vesterlund's (2008) study of voluntary contributions. The discussion above underlines the potential high impact of such efforts. Many important questions await further work.

3.2.3 Do people value status for its own sake?

Although it is clear that people might value status because of its instrumental role in securing material benefits, some studies suggest that people also value status for its own sake. Huberman, Loch, and Önçüler (2004), for example, have studied the desire for status in a lab setting where status arguably entails neither access to power nor to

[4] As Ball et al. (2001) note: "This contradicts Hoffman and Spitzer (1985) who show that an earned advantageous role made subjects more willing to exploit their opponents than a randomly assigned advantageous role." Although Hoffman and Spitzer (1985) award power (or power and status) rather than pure status (but see Greenberg and Ornstein 1983), more work is clearly required.

resources. They find that subjects are indeed willing to trade money for temporary status in the lab.

In their cleverly designed experiments, subjects invest game cards (in the experiment's first stage) to win the right to participate in a lottery (in the second stage). The investment is costly because the more one invests in the first stage, the lower are the expected lottery winnings (conditional on participation) in the second stage. Under the "status condition," which is similar to the above Star manipulations, the winner of the right to participate in the lottery is announced publicly, is given a small tag saying "Winner," and is congratulated by all participants with applause. Convincingly arguing that these expressions of status could not be used to gain other resources either in the lab (during the experiment) or outside of it, the authors interpret the higher first-stage investment in the status condition as evidence that participants value status independently of monetary consequences. They run the experiment in five countries (the U.S., Turkey, Hong Kong, Germany, and Finland) and find, for example, significantly stronger reactions to status in Hong Kong than in Finland.[5]

To summarize the discussion in this section regarding the causes behind the desire for status, we quote from the last paragraph of Huberman, Loch, and Önçüler (2004, p. 112):

> *"Under which circumstances may an individual perceive status as a means or as an end? One might reasonably hypothesize that both mechanisms are at work simultaneously all the time. Which one is more important at any given point probably depends strongly on the situation: for example, the size of the rationally recognizable rewards and the salience and nature of the status symbol may influence what is included in a decision to act. This topic would be highly relevant for understanding when one can motivate people with incentives as opposed to emotions, but no theory currently addresses this question; it requires further research".*

3.3 Nontradability: evidence on visibility

The nontradability of status—that it is conferred by society and cannot be directly purchased—implies that the only way to obtain status is through actions that are socially visible (or that have socially visible consequences). Indeed, if we assume that status depends on actions, status-seeking individuals are expected to change their behavior in predictable ways depending on whether their actions are visible to others. The observation that they often do, however, is consistent not only with preferences for status, but also with any preferences where others' opinions are important (e.g., because of considerations of reputation, shame, fear of punishment, etc.). This should be borne in mind when interpreting the evidence below.

Anecdotal evidence that the visibility of actions affects behavior is prevalent and includes many everyday facts, such as the anonymity promised to our experimental

[5] Ball and Eckel (1996, p. 398) claim that "Asian consumers, perhaps because of the structures of their society, tend to be very status oriented." See references there.

subjects and survey participants, and to us as journal referees. More generally, that the private sphere in our lives is so carefully kept separate from the public sphere may suggest that individuals strongly care about society's perceptions of them.

Systematic evidence for this proposition abounds in the economics literature. A recent typical example regarding voluntary giving is Rege and Telle (2004), who show that people contribute substantially more to a public good when both their identity and the amount they gave are made visible to others. Similarly, Ariely, Bracha, and Meier (2007) find that making one's behavior visible to others affects pro-social behavior. They discuss their findings in the context of "image motivation—the desire to be liked and well-regarded by others" but, as discussed above, a desire for status is equally consistent with their findings. For a recent survey see Bekkers and Wiepking (2007, Section 5 "Reputation", pp. 29–31), who review studies that tie charitable giving, generosity, and philanthropic behavior to reputation concerns. For example, they cite studies showing that the likelihood and the size of donations are likely to increase with the social status of the donor and, independently, of the solicitor. Such image-driven giving has come to be referred to as *conspicuous compassion,* a play on Veblen's (1899) term *conspicuous consumption.*

More evidence is provided by economists' studies of awards. As Frey and Neckermann (2008) point out, "all awards share certain essential features," among which are that "awards are always visible, be it via a public ceremony or because the award itself can be publicly displayed." They indeed find, in a vignette experiment on the labor force in an IBM facility, that reported hypothetical contribution to a public good increases not only with the monetary value of the reward but also with the degree of publicity associated with winning the award.

A different approach is taken by Heffetz (2007), who conducts a nationally-representative survey among U.S. households to rank the visibility of thirty-one consumption categories. Using U.S. household expenditure data, he shows that, on average, higher-income households spend larger shares of their budgets on more visible categories. This finding is consistent with Veblen's (1899) conspicuous consumption idea as modeled by Ireland (1994), where consumption is a visible signal sent to society in order to advertise one's income and gain social status. Similarly, Charles, Hurst, and Roussanov (2007) show that black and Hispanic households in the U.S. spend more on visible categories than white ones. They show that most of the difference can be explained by mean income differences in reference groups, as predicted by a similar conspicuous consumption model of status seeking.

Finally, recent evidence from experimental evolutionary psychology establishes causality from anonymity—or, surprisingly, from mere cues of reduced anonymity, when actual anonymity is kept constant—to changed behavior. For example, Haley and Fessler (2005) find that individuals increase generosity in a dictator game when they are presented with a mere visual cue (stylized eyespots on a computer screen, which might remind subjects of the possibility that somebody may be watching them), in spite of no differences in actual anonymity. Kurzban, DeScioli, and O'Brien (2007) show that reducing anonymity causes people to punish more frequently.

Although such findings, like others mentioned above, are often discussed in the context of reputation concerns, they may equally support status interpretations. Haley and Fessler (2005), for example, interpret their findings as showing that we are wired to react to subtle cues of observability, which in turn affect our pro-social behavior.[6] Indeed, in many contexts status is conferred on pro-social individuals (for example, those who are known to be generous, or who punish perceived moral violators).

3.4 Evolutionary considerations: a tie-breaker?

When empirical evidence is consistent with multiple interpretations, we often seek further guidance from *a priori* considerations. Do such considerations have anything useful to say about whether status is valued for its own sake?

The Darwinian model provides a useful framework for thinking about what human and animal nervous systems are molded to do. Robson (2001, Section 2.4 "Preferences for Status") surveys models that can be interpreted as providing a biological basis for preferences for status. Robson and Samuelson (this volume) survey work on the evolutionary foundations of preferences (for example, for positional consumption). Bisin and Verdier (1998) study the intergenerational cultural transmission of such preferences. Departing from the formal approach in these studies, here we briefly discuss some of the main considerations that could favor preferences for status.

According to Darwin, animal drives were selected for their capacity to motivate behaviors that contribute to reproductive success. Reproductive success, in turn, is fundamentally about resource acquisition: other things equal, the more resources an animal has, the more progeny it leaves behind. What matters is not the absolute number of offspring an individual has, but rather how its progeny compares in number with those of other individuals. A specific trait will thus be favored by natural selection less because it facilitates resource acquisition in absolute terms than because it confers an advantage in relative terms.

Frequent famines were an important challenge in early human societies. However, even in the most severe famines, there was always some food. Those with relatively high resource holdings were fed, while others often starved. On the plausible assumption that individuals with the strongest concerns about relative resource holdings were most inclined to expend the effort necessary to achieve high rank, such individuals would have been more likely than others to survive food shortages.

[6] However, as Ellingsen and Johannesson (2007) point out, findings like Haley and Fessler's (2005) could also be viewed as suggesting mechanisms other than respect, esteem, or status seeking, since they demonstrate that people react to a mere eyespots cue rather than to whether they think they are actually being watched.

Relative resource holdings were also important in implicit markets for marriage partners. In most early human societies, high-ranking males took multiple wives, leaving many low-ranking males with none. Even in contemporary societies, sexual attractiveness is strongly linked to relative resource holdings. So here, too, theory predicts that natural selection will favor individuals with the strongest concerns about relative resource holdings.

Do similar considerations say anything about whether people should be concerned about rank per se? In other domains, we see evidence that appetites are favored by natural selection because they promote reproductive success on the average, even though they may fail to do so in specific cases. Extreme thirst, for example, can motivate an irresistible urge to drink, even when the only available liquid is unsuitable for drinking. Thus, if salt water is the only liquid at hand, even an informed scientist might drink it, despite the knowledge that doing so will hasten her or his death. Evolution favored such appetites because they are beneficial on the average. Remaining well hydrated is essential for survival, and individuals suffering from extreme thirst are more likely to expend the effort necessary to find something suitable to drink.

It is plausible to imagine that an appetite for status evolved under similar pressures. Acquiring more status may not always produce rewards sufficient to compensate for the effort necessary to acquire it. Nevertheless, it could have led to sufficiently valuable rewards often enough that the most expedient option was a nervous system that cared about it for its own sake.

That said, much of the evidence discussed in this chapter remains circumstantial and far from conclusive. Overall, it probably raises as many fascinating questions about status as the ones it attempts to answer. The quest for truth continues.

4. SOME ECONOMIC IMPLICATIONS

The most general implications of preferences for status are straightforward: as Ball et al. (2001, p. 162) point out, "If status is desirable, individuals are willing to sacrifice consumption to obtain it" (*consumption* here is interchangeable with *resources*). Combining the desirability of status with the other two features of status highlighted above—its positionality and its nontradability—sharpens this statement. The positionality of status implies that status seeking diverts resources away from welfare-enhancing uses, wasting them—from the point of view of society as a whole—on efforts to win a zero-sum game. The nontradability of status implies that the resulting inefficiencies could be manifest in different (and sometimes unexpected) markets, as they assume a role as implicit status markets.

The main insight is modeled in Frank (1985a): in the existence of positional goods—goods that enter the utility function both as an absolute component and as a relative one—an increase in one's consumption of these goods imposes a negative externality on others. Frank (2007) compares the resulting situation to a military arms race between two nations, where the utility from expenditures on weapons depends heavily on the relative stocks of armaments in the two nations. He notes that a necessary and sufficient condition for equilibrium expenditures on armaments to be inefficiently high from the collective vantage point is that relative position matter more for armaments than for alternative expenditures, e.g., expenditures on consumption goods. In a similar manner, if expenditures on houses are more positional than safety at the workplace, people will accept inefficiently risky jobs (at higher pay than safer ones).

These examples illustrate the familiar result that goods that impose negative externalities tend to be over-consumed. Furthermore, with a utility function that has both a (standard) absolute and a relative consumption components and is—as is usually assumed—concave in absolute consumption, the marginal utility from additional consumption through the absolute term approaches zero as income rises. The relative component hence becomes increasingly important as income rises. Status seeking, on this view, becomes increasingly important with economic growth.

This negative 'positional externality' exists independently of additional externalities that may be imposed by the consumption of specific status-enhancing goods (e.g., the negative externality imposed by a polluting, status-enhancing car). Indeed, Congleton (1989) argues that status games that impose such additional negative externalities "may be replaced by games generating no externalities or, better still, by games generating positive externalities" (e.g., visible contributions to public goods). If he is correct, then the negative positional externality imposed by status seeking may, to some extent, be coupled with a positive externality generated by engaging in specific status-enhancing activities. Fershtman and Weiss (1998) study the conditions under which such coupling—which may or may not be sufficient to achieve efficiency—is evolutionarily stable (in that individuals who care about status survive in the end). As documented above, evidence suggests that individuals engage in both types of status activities: those that impose negative and those that impose positive externalities, in addition to the negative positional externality imposed by any status game.

The insight that positional goods impose a negative externality can be applied in many different contexts.[7] Clark et al. (2008, Section 5) discuss economic and policy implications of relative concerns in the utility function. They discuss implications for economic growth (where the main insight is that with relative concerns, growth above a certain minimum level does not lead to happiness); for income distribution (if the relative term in the utility function is concave, more inequality would mean a less happy society); for labor supply (which would not decline in spite of increasing incomes);[8] for the measurement of

[7] Remember that, as discussed above (e.g., in the Introduction), this insight does not depend on interpreting positional concerns as necessarily stemming from status concerns.

[8] Also see, e.g., Bowles and Park (2005) for evidence on a positive correlation between total hours worked and higher earning inequality, both across countries and over time within countries; and Landers et al. (1996), who find that associates in large law firms state that they would prefer an across-the-board cut of ten percent in both hours and pay.

poverty (poverty may be relative rather than absolute);[9] for saving and investment; and for migration (where, e.g., Stark and Taylor 1991 argue that the reason elites in poor countries do not emigrate is that their relative position would decline if they moved).

Positional concerns have far-reaching implications for taxation. In Frank's (1985a) model, a tax on positional consumption could correct the distortion imposed by the negative externality discussed above. A similar tax could correct the distortion of the under-consumption of leisure in models where leisure is less positional than income. Although the possibility of conspicuous leisure has long been recognized (Veblen 1899), evidence suggests that leisure could in many contexts be less visible (Heffetz 2007) and less positional (Solnick and Hemenway 1998) than consumption. Furthermore, in increasingly mobile societies, conspicuous status symbols that are immediately recognized, portable, and easily transportable increase in importance. Clark et al. (2008) discuss mobility taxes that are meant to correct the imbalance between the increased visibility of conspicuous consumption items and the decreased visibility of conspicuous leisure in mobile societies. See, for example, Boskin and Sheshinski (1978), Ng (1987), Ireland (1998), and Layard (2005) for further discussion of tax remedies for positional externalities; and Frank (2008) for further policy responses to these externalities.[10]

4.1 Labor market implications

Finally, one problem confronting all studies that attempt to apply models of positional concerns to real world contexts is that we never know who is in the reference group. Do people compare themselves with co-workers who occupy adjacent offices? With neighbors? With classmates from high school or college? Although identifying the relevant reference group has always proved a formidable challenge, comparisons with one's co-workers are likely to be important. We therefore close the discussion in this section with applications of positional concerns to labor markets. We hope thus to demonstrate the economic implications of such concerns in the context of one important class of markets.

Much of the evidence above (e.g., regarding the positionality of wages and income in relation to job satisfaction and happiness, and regarding awards among workers) indeed suggests that concerns about local rank may be especially important in the workplace. Other studies suggest that labor markets are affected by positional concerns

[9] See, e.g., Sen's (1999) discussion of what he terms "relative deprivation."

[10] Other related work includes, e.g., work on the economic inefficiencies that result from status seeking as a zero sum game (Congleton 1989); the implications of positional wealth on risk taking behavior (Robson 1992); and the welfare implications of positional income (Ng and Wang 1993). Fershtman et al. (1996) study the implications of status seeking on the distribution of talents in society and hence on growth, and show that the latter may be enhanced by an inequality-reducing redistribution of wealth. Weiss and Fershtman (1998) discuss the economic implications of status seeking behavior on saving, occupational choice, investment in skills and risk taking, and point out that these in turn may affect economic efficiency, growth rates and the distribution of income.

even when the relevant reference group is outside the workplace. In some contexts, such concerns may affect labor outcomes more than traditional factors like local wage and unemployment rates. For example, Neumark and Postlewaite (1998) study labor force participation among a sample of biological full sisters. Although their results are not strongly statistically significant, they estimate that a woman whose sister's husband earns more than her own husband is 16–25% more likely than others to seek paid employment. The authors thus provide some evidence of the wisdom of H. L. Mencken's definition of a wealthy man as one who earns at least one hundred dollars a year more than his wife's sister's husband.

The hypothesis that local rank at the workplace matters has testable implications for the distribution of wages within firms (Frank 1984). If some value high local rank more than others do, then economic surplus is maximized by having workers sort themselves into separate firms in accordance with their respective valuations. Hence, within a firm, the equilibrium distribution of wages will be more compressed than the corresponding distribution of marginal products. In effect, the labor market serves up compensating wage differentials for local rank, much as it does for other nonpecuniary employment conditions. This pattern, which is widely observed, (Frank 1985b, Chapter 4) is inconsistent with models in which local rank has no value.[11]

Loch et al. (2001) explore the managerial implications of status seeking in the workplace, and urge managers to take an active approach. The authors suggest firms can motivate their employees, managing and channeling the status-striving phenomenon "into a powerful motivator serving the goals of the organization." Their advice to managers is closely related to the discussion above regarding the reasons status is desirable: is it desired mostly as a means to an end (e.g., through increased access to resources) or as its own end? Loch et al. (2001) suggest that managers, rather than viewing status as a means and hence trying to eliminate status-seeking behavior by breaking the connection between status and resources, should view status as its own end and manipulate "the environment and the criteria and symbols of status within the organization." Their promise to managers: "We are genetically driven to strive for status, not dollars. . . . If you can create nonmonetary symbols of status within the organization, you will be able to get the benefits of status seeking without the high financial cost."

Ellingsen and Johannesson (2007) further generalize the discussion, and ask why people work. They argue that although economists have been correct to emphasize

[11] Notice the difference between this approach and, e.g., Fershtman and Weiss (1993), who assume that "status is mainly conferred through occupational association." As the authors point out, their alternative approach, which emphasizes global rather than local status (see the related discussion in section 2.2 above), naturally leads to different predictions. In recent work, Fershtman et al. (2003) reemphasize the importance of local status in the workplace. They study the benefits (gains from trade) of cross-individual heterogeneity in status seeking and in what individuals view as their reference group.

the importance of incentives as motivators of work, they have been missing an important part of the picture by almost exclusively focusing on monetary incentives. Discussing evidence dating back to the Hawthorne experiments (conducted during 1924–1932), they note the importance of nonmonetary incentives such as respect and attention given to employees as motivations of work. They point out that respect could be paid by an employer or a manager, as well as by coworkers. This blurs the boundaries between respect and status, as both are something that is desired, is conferred by society, cannot be directly purchased, may be based on personal characteristics, etc. In other words, the "evidence that respect matters in the workplace" they present (including recent interesting experimental work) could be interpreted as evidence for workers' preferences for status.

As discussed previously regarding models that allow for positional consumption, when income rises, the (absolute) consumption benefit approaches zero, and workers are increasingly left with the positional benefit alone. Interpreted as a status component in the utility function, this raises an intriguing question: If workers increasingly work for status, would they not be willing, at least under some conditions, to replace (at least some) monetary income with direct status payments? According to Ellingsen and Johannesson (2007), this indeed seems to be happening. If most extra income is spent on status seeking, an employer could indeed pay directly with status rather than with money. Of course, if competitive pressure led all firms to adopt this strategy, the tendency for the within-firm average wage to equal the within-firm average value of marginal products would be restored.

5. CONCLUSION

In this chapter, we examined the potential of preferences for status to be an important driver of economic outcomes. Over the last decades, abundant evidence has been accumulating that is consistent with the hypothesis that they indeed are. This evidence has been arriving from many—and quite different—research programs. By sampling and discussing some of this evidence, we hope to have established the importance of the social status agenda among economists.

At the same time, we have tried to emphasize that since much of the evidence is also consistent with competing hypotheses, further work is still needed. We also argued that while experimental effort might provide a promising step in answering some of the most intriguing open questions regarding status and status-seeking behavior, attempts at causal demonstrations based on direct manipulation of status in the lab have so far raised more new questions than they have answered. While it may be seen as frustrating by some, this state of affairs guarantees that the status agenda in economics is not likely to disappear in the foreseeable future.

REFERENCES

Alesina, A., McCulloch, R., Tella, R., 2004. Inequality and Happiness: Are Europeans and Americans Different? J. Public Econ. 88, 2009–2042.

Alpizar, F., Carlsson, F., Johansson-Stenman, O., 2005. How Much Do We Care about Absolute Versus Relative Income and Consumption? J. Econ. Behav. Organ. 56, 405–421.

Ariely, D., Bracha, A., Meier, S., 2007. Doing Good or Doing Well? Image Motivation and Monetary Incentives in Behaving Prosocially. Federal Reserve Bank of Boston Working Paper No 07–9.

Ball, S.B., Eckel, C.C., 1996. Buying Status: Experimental Evidence on Status in Negotiation. Psychology and Marketing 13 (4), 381–405.

Ball, S.B., Eckel, C.C., 1998. The Economic Value of Status. J. Soc. Econ. 27 (4), 495–514.

Ball, S.B., Eckel, C.C., Grossman, P.J., Zame, W., 2001. Status in Markets. Q. J. Econ. 116 (1), 161–188.

Becker, G.S., 1971. The Economics of Discrimination, second ed. University of Chicago Press, Chicago, IL.

Becker, G.S., 1974. A Theory of Social Interactions. J. Polit. Econ. 82 (6), 1063–1093.

Becker, G.S., Murphy, K.M., Werning, I., 2005. The Equilibrium Distribution of Income and the Market for Status. J. Polit. Econ. 113 (2), 282–310.

Bekkers, R., Wiepking, P., 2007. Generosity and Philanthropy: A Literature Review. http://ssrn.com/abstract=1015507.

Bisin, A., Verdier, T., 1998. On the Cultural Transmission of Preferences for Social Status. J. Public Econ. 70, 75–97.

Boskin, M., Sheshinski, E., 1978. Optimal Redistributive Taxation when Individual Welfare Depends on Relative Income. Q. J. Econ. 92 (4), 589–601.

Bowles, S., Park, Y., 2005. Emulation, Inequality, and Work Hours: Was Thorstein Veblen Right? Economic Journal 115, F397–F412.

Buchanan, J., Stubblebine, C., 1962. Externality. Economica 29 (116), 371–384.

Carlsson, F., Johansson-Stenman, O., Martinsson, P., 2007. Do You Enjoy Having More than Others? Survey Evidence of Positional Goods. Economica 74, 586–598.

Charles, K., Hurst, E., Roussanov, N., 2007. Conspicuous Consumption and Race. University of Chicago Working Paper.

Charness, G., Rabin, M., 2002. Understanding Social Preferences with Simple Tests. Q. J. Econ. 117 (3), 817–869.

Clark, A.E., Frijters, P., Shields, M.A., 2008. Relative Income, Happiness, and Utility: An Explanation for the Easterlin Paradox and Other Puzzles. J. Econ. Lit. 46 (1), 95–144.

Clark, A., Oswald, A., 1996. Satisfaction and Comparison Income. J. Public Econ. 61, 359–381.

Congleton, R.D., 1989. Efficient Status Seeking: Externalities, and the Evolution of Status Games. J. Econ. Behav. Organ. 11, 175–190.

Diamond, P.A., 2008. Behavioral Economics. MIT Dept. of Economics Working Paper 08-03, (for a special *Journal of Public Economics* forthcoming issue).

DiNardo, J., 2007. Interesting Questions in Freakonomics. J. Econ. Lit. 45 (4), 973–1000.

Duesenberry, J., 1949. Income, Saving, and the Theory of Consumer Behavior. Harvard University Press, Cambridge, MA.

Easterlin, R., 1974. Does Economic Growth Improve the Human Lot? Some Empirical Evidence. In: David, P., Reder, M. (Eds.), Nations and Households in Economic Growth: Essays in Honor of Moses Abramovitz. Academic Press, New York.

Easterlin, R., 1995. Will Raising the Incomes of All Increase the Happiness of All? J. Econ. Behav. Organ. 27 (1), 35–47.

Easterlin, R.A., 2005. Feeding the Illusion of Growth and Happiness: A Reply to Hagerty and Veenhoven. Soc. Indic. Res. 74 (3), 429–443.

Eckel, C.C., Wilson, R.K., 2006. Social Learning in Coordination Games: Does Status Matter? Working Paper.

Ellingsen, T., Johannesson, M., 2007. Paying Respect. J. Econ. Perspect. 21 (4), 135–149.

Fehr, E., Schmidt, K.M., 2006. The Economics of Fairness, Reciprocity and Altruism–Experimental Evidence and New Theories. In: Kolm, S.C., Mercier-Ythier, J. (Eds.), Handbook of the Economics of Giving, Altruism and Reciprocity. Elsevier, Amsterdam, pp. 615–691.

Ferrer-i-Carbonell, A., 2005. Income and Well-being: An Empirical Analysis of the Comparison Income Effect. J. Public Econ. 89, 997–1019.

Fershtman, C., Hvide, H.K., Weiss, Y., 2003. Cultural Diversity, Status Concerns, and the Organization of Work. Working Paper.

Fershtman, C., Murphy, K.M., Weiss, Y., 1996. Social Status, Education, and Growth. J. Polit. Econ. 104 (1), 108–132.

Fershtman, C., Weiss, Y., 1993. Social Status, Culture, and Economic Performance. Economic Journal 103, 946–959.

Fershtman, C., Weiss, Y., 1998. Social Rewards, Externalities, and Stable Preferences. J. Public Econ. 70, 53–73.

Frank, R.H., 1984. Are Workers Paid Their Marginal Products? Am. Econ. Rev. 74, 549–571.

Frank, R.H., 1985a. The Demand for Unobservable and Other Nonpositional Goods. Am. Econ. Rev. 75, 101–116.

Frank, R.H., 1985b. Choosing the Right Pond. Oxford University Press, New York.

Frank, R.H., 1999. Luxury Fever. The Free Press, New York.

Frank, R.H., 2005. Does Absolute Income Matter? In: Porta, P.L., Bruni, L. (Eds.), Economics and Happiness. Oxford University Press.

Frank, R.H., 2007. Falling Behind: How Rising Inequality Harms the Middle Class. University of California Press, Berkeley, CA.

Frank, R.H., 2008. Should Public Policy Respond to Positional Externalities? J. Public Econ. 92 (8–9), 1777–1786.

Frey, B.S., Neckermann, S., 2008. Awards: A View from Psychological Economics.. Institute for Empirical Research in Economics, University of Zurich, Working Paper No. 2008–2.

Frijters, P., Haisken-DeNew, J.P., Shields, M.A., 2004. Investigating the Patterns and Determinants of Life Satisfaction in Germany following Reunification. J. Hum. Resour. 39 (3), 649–674.

Glaeser, E.L., Laibson, D.I., Scheinkman, J.A., Soutter, C.L., 2000. Measuring Trust. Q. J. Econ. 115 (3), 811–846.

Greenberg, J., Ornstein, S., 1983. High Status Job Title as Compensation for Underpayment: A Test of Equity Theory. J. Appl. Psychol. 68, 285–297.

Haley, K.J., Fessler, D.M.T., 2005. Nobody's watching? Subtle Cues Affect Generosity in an Anonymous Economic Game. Evol. Hum. Behav. 26 (3), 245–256.

Heffetz, O., 2007. A Test of Conspicuous Consumption: Visibility and Income Elasticities. Cornell University mimeo.

Hirsch, F., 1976. Social Limits to Growth. Harvard University Press, Cambridge, MA.

Hirschman, A.O., 1973. An Alternative Explanation of Contemporary Harriedness. Q. J. Econ. 87 (4), 634–637.

Hoffman, E., Spitzer, M.L., 1985. Entitlements, Rights and Fairness: Some Experimental Evidence of Subjects' Concepts of Distributive Justice. J. Legal Stud. 14 (2), 259–298.

Huberman, B.A., Loch, C.H., Önçüler, A., 2004. Status As a Valued Resource. Soc. Psychol. Q. 67 (1), 103–114.

Ireland, N., 1994. On Limiting the Market for Status Signals. J. Public Econ. 53, 91–110.

Ireland, N., 1998. Status Seeking, Income Taxation, and Efficiency. J. Public Econ. 70, 99–113.

Kahneman, D., Ed, D., Schwartz, N. (Ed.), 1999. Well-being: Foundations of Hedonic Psychology. Russell Sage, New York.

Kahneman, D., Krueger, A.B., 2006. Developments in the Measurement of Subjective Well-Being. J. Econ. Perspect. 20 (1), 3–24.

Kahneman, D., Krueger, A.B., Schkade, D., Schwartz, N., Stone, A.B., 2006. Would You Be Happier If You Were Richer? A Focusing Illusion. Science 312, 1908–1910.

Kumru, C.S., Vesterlund, L., 2008. The Effects of Status on Voluntary Contribution. Working Paper.

Kurzban, R., DeScioli, P., O'Brien, E., 2007. Audience Effects on Moralistic Punishment. Evol. Hum. Behav. 28 (2), 75–84.

Landers, R., Rebitzer, J., Taylor, L., 1996. Rat Race Redux: Adverse Selection in the Determination of Work Hours in Law Firms. Am. Econ. Rev. 86, 329–348.

Layard, R., 2005. Happiness: Lessons from a New Science. Penguin, London.

Lerner, M.J., 1970. The Desire for Justice and Reactions to Victims. In: Macauley, J., Berkowitz, L. (Eds.), Altruism and Helping Behavior. Academic Press, New York.

Loch, C., Yaziji, M., Langen, C., 2001. The Fight for the Alpha Position: Channeling Status Competition in Organizations. European Management Journal 19 (1), 16–25.

Luttmer, E.F.P., 2005. Neighbors as Negatives: Relative Earnings and Well-being. Q. J. Econ. 120, 963–1002.

Marx, K., 1849. Wage-Labour and Capital.

Neumark, D., Postlewaite, A., 1998. Relative Income Concerns and the Rise in Married Women's Employment. J. Public Econ. 70, 157–183.

Ng, Y., 1987. Diamonds Are a Government's Best Friend: Burden-Free Taxes on Goods Valued for Their Values. Am. Econ. Rev. 77 (1), 186–191.

Ng, Y., Wang, J., 1993. Relative Income, Aspiration, Environmental Quality, Individual and Political Myopia: Why May the Rat-Race for Material Growth be Welfare-Reducing? Math. Soc. Sci. 26, 3–23.

Rablen, M.D., Oswald, A.J., 2008. Mortality and Immortality: The Nobel Prize as an Experiment into the Effect of Status upon Longevity. J. Health Econ., forthcoming.

Rege, M., Telle, K., 2004. The Impact of Social Approval and Framing on Cooperation in Public Good Situations. J. Public Econ. 88, 1625–1644.

Ridgeway, C.L., Walker, H.A., 1995. Status Structures. In: Cook, K., fine, G., House, J. (Eds.), Sociological Perspectives on Social Psychology. Pearson Education, Upper Saddle River, NJ.

Robson, A., 1992. Status, the Distribution of Wealth, Private and Social Attitudes to Risk. Econometrica 60, 837–857.

Robson, A., 2001. The Biological Basis of Economic Behavior. J. Econ. Lit. 39, 11–33.

Robson, A., Samuelson, L., this volume. The Evolutionary Foundations of Preferences.

Scitovsky, T., 1976. The Joyless Economy. Oxford University Press, London.

Sen, A., 1999. Development as Freedom. Alfred A. Knopf, Inc, New York.

Smith, A., 1776. The Wealth of Nations. Reprint 1937, Random House, New York.

Solnick, S.J., Hemenway, D., 1998. Is More Always Better?: A Survey on Positional Concerns. J. Econ. Behav. Organ. 37 (3), 373–383.

Solnick, S.J., Hemenway, D., 2005. Are Positional Concerns Stronger in Some Domains than in Others? American Economic Review, Papers and Proceedings 95, 147–151.

Stark, O., Edward Taylor, J., 1991. Migration Incentives, Migration Types: The Role of Relative Deprivation. Econ. J. 101, 1163–1178.

Stevenson, B., Wolfers, J., 2008. Economic Growth and Subjective Well-Being: Reassessing the Easterlin Paradox. Working Paper.

Veblen, T., 1899. The Theory of the Leisure Class. Reprint 1965, MacMillan, New York.

Veenhoven, R., 1993. Happiness in Nations. Erasmus University, Rotterdam.

Weiss, Y., Fershtman, C., 1998. Social Status and Economic Performance: A Survey. Eur. Econ. Rev. 42, 801–820.

Zink, C.F., Tong, Y., Chen, Q., Bassett, D.S., Stein, J.L., Meyer-Lindenberg, A., 2008. Know Your Place: Neural Processing of Social Hierarchy in Humans. Neuron 58, 273–283.

CHAPTER 4

Preferences for Redistribution*

Alberto Alesina and Paola Giuliano
Harvard University and UCLA

Contents

1. Introduction 94
2. Preferences for Redistribution: Theory 96
   2.1 The basic model 96
   2.2 Expected future income and social mobility 97
   2.3 Inequality indirectly in the utility function 99
   2.4 Inequality directly in the utility function 100
   2.5 Trade offs 101
   2.6 Fairness 102
3. Empirical Evidence 103
   3.1 Data 104
   3.2 Results 105
      3.2.1 The basic model *105*
      3.2.2 Individual characteristics *105*
      3.2.3 Expected future income and social mobility *108*
   3.3 Inequality indirectly in the utility function 111
   3.4 Inequality directly in the utility function 111
      3.4.1 Religion *112*
      3.4.2 Race *114*
      3.4.3 Cultural norms and differences in macroeconomic experiences *114*
      3.4.4 The structure of the family *118*
      3.4.5 Fairness *121*
   3.5 Evidence from the world values survey 121
4. Conclusions 127
References 129

Abstract

This paper discusses what determines the preferences of individuals for redistribution. We review the theoretical literature and provide a framework to incorporate various effects previously studied separately in the literature. We then examine empirical evidence for the US, using the General Social Survey, and for a large set of countries, using the World Values Survey. The paper reviews previously found results and provides several new ones. We

* Prepared for the Handbook of Social Economics. We thank David Laibson, Romain Wacziarg and, especially, Alberto Bisin for very useful comments and suggestions.

Handbook of Social Economics, Volume 1A
ISSN 0169-7218, DOI: 10.1016/S0169-7218(11)01004-5

emphasize, in particular, the role of historical experiences, cultural factors and personal history as determinants of preferences for equality or tolerance for inequality.
JEL codes are: H10, Z1

Keywords

preferences for redistribution
inequality
social mobility
cultural economics

1. INTRODUCTION

Economists traditionally assume that individuals have preferences defined over their lifetime consumption (income) and maximize their utility under a set of constraints. The same principle applies to preferences for redistribution. It follows that maximization of utility from consumption and leisure and some aggregation of individual preferences determines the equilibrium level of taxes and transfers.[1] Note the inter-temporal nature of this maximization problem: preferences for redistribution depend not only on where people are today in the income ladder but also on where they think they will be in the future if redistributive policies are long lasting.

The level of inequality of a society may affect some individuals' income indirectly. For instance, the level of inequality may affect crime and some people may be more or less subject to the risk of criminal activities. But, in addition, individuals have views regarding redistribution that go beyond the current and future states of their pocketbooks. These views reflect different ideas about what an appropriate shape of the income distribution is: in practice, views about acceptable levels of inequality and/or poverty. Explaining the origin of these ideas (which eventually translate into policies via some mechanism of aggregation of preferences) implies bringing into the picture variables that go beyond the current and expected consumption (and leisure) of the individual consumer/worker/voter. Needless to say, standard neoclassical general equilibrium theory can accommodate altruism, i.e., a situation in which one agent cares also about the utility of somebody else. But altruism is not an unpredictable "social noise" to be randomly sprinkled over individuals. Altruism, or, to put it differently, preferences for redistribution that do not maximize private benefits strictly defined, has certain predictable and interesting features. Of course, this does not mean that we ignore individual income, which is indeed very important.

Where do different preferences for redistribution come from? Note that the question of whether or not a government should redistribute from the rich to the poor and how much is probably the most important dividing line between the political left

[1] See Persson and Tabellini (2002) and Drazen (2002) for a broad review of political economic models.

and the political right at least on economic issues. Therefore, answering this question almost amounts to explaining where ideological preferences on economic issues come from, certainly an important, fascinating and difficult task. A few possibilities, nonmutually exclusive of course, have been examined in the literature. First, different preferences may arise from individual history (as emphasized, for instance, by Piketty (1995)). A history of misfortune may make people more risk-averse, less optimistic about their future upward mobility and more inclined to equalize everybody's income, as noted by Giuliano and Spilimbergo (2009) with reference to historical events such as the Great Depression. Second, different cultures may emphasize in different ways the relative merits of equality versus individualism, an issue discussed in detail by Alesina and Glaeser (2004) with reference to a comparison between the US and Europe. Different historical experiences in different countries may lead to various social norms about what is acceptable or not in terms of inequality. Third, indoctrination (for instance, in communist dictatorships) may influence people's views, as emphasized by Alesina and Fuchs-Schündeln (2007) with reference to Germany. Fourth, sometimes parents may purposely transmit "distorted" views about the reality of inequality and social mobility to their children in order to influence their incentives (Benabou and Tirole (2006)). Fifth, the structure and the organization of the family may make people more or less dependent and therefore favorable to government intervention in distributive matters (Todd (1985), Esping Andersen (1999), Alesina and Giuliano (2010)). Sixth, perception of fairness matters. Most people do seem to make a distinction between income acquired by "luck" (broadly defined) and income acquired by "effort" (broadly speaking) and this distinction matters in shaping preferences for redistribution (Alesina and Glaeser (2004), Alesina and Angeletos (2005a). Finally, the desire to act in accordance with public values, or to obtain high social standing could also play a critical role in the determination of preferences for redistributive policies (see Corneo and Gruner (2000, 2002)). We will document these differences and suggest explanations for the persistence of ideologies over time in this area.

In the first part of the paper, we provide a theoretical framework that helps clarify all these various effects in a coherent way. In the second part, we review evidence discussed by others and provide novel results by using the General Social Survey (GSS) for the US and the World Value Survey (WVS) for international cross-country evidence. We begin by showing that individual income indeed matters: richer people are more averse to redistribution. Many other individual characteristics matter as well. In the US, race is an important determinant of preferences for redistribution, a finding consistent with many other previous studies.[2] An interesting observation is that, after controlling for a variety of individual characteristics, women tend to be more favorable to redistribution than men in many different countries and institutional settings. It is hard to reconcile this difference using only economic variables as explanations, while

[2] See Alesina and La Ferrara (2005), Alesina and Glaeser (2004) and the references cited therein.

differences in personalities documented by psychologists may be broadly consistent with this empirical observation[3]. Education is an interesting variable. After controlling for income, it is not clear what one should expect. If individuals that are more educated prefer less redistribution, one may argue that they think about prospects of upward mobility resulting from higher education. On the other hand, education may bias people in favor of more pro-redistributive views as a result of ideology (left-wing views). We find that the first effect prevails in the US, but we investigate interesting interactions between education and political orientation.

We are interested specifically in the determinants of preferences for redistribution, but the modern welfare state has two main objectives: to redistribute from the richer to the poorer and to provide social insurance. Some aspects of the welfare state (think of the progressivity of the income tax) are primarily redistributive, others provide primarily, but not exclusively, social insurance (think of unemployment compensations), others (such as health insurance financed by progressive taxation) have both components, and one could go on. In theory, one can conceptually distinguish the two. Empirically, it is not so simple. Often, but not always, survey questions or any other method to extract individuals' preferences for redistribution cannot distinguish so clearly whether the subjects favor the latter or only social insurance. The problem (we feel) is serious from an empirical standpoint but not fatal, in the sense that preferences for the two are most likely very highly correlated.

The chapter is organized as follows: Section 2 presents some simple formalization that captures the effects sketched above in a reasonably exhaustive way. Section 3 reviews the available evidence on the explanations for preferences for redistribution. We organize the discussion around "variables," e.g., income, education, and race, and we present evidence for the US, cross-national evidence and experimental evidence, whenever available, on each variable. The last section concludes.

2. PREFERENCES FOR REDISTRIBUTION: THEORY

2.1 The basic model

The basic "workhorse" political economic model for preferences for redistribution is provided by Meltzer and Richards (1981), who built upon Romer (1975). In this well-known static model, individuals care only about their consumption (income) and have different productivities. The only tax and transfer scheme allowed is given by lump sum transfers financed with a linear income tax. The median voter theorem aggregates individual preferences and captures a very simple political equilibrium. The simplest possible illustration of this model is as follows. Consider a standard utility function with the usual properties:

$$u_i = u(c_i) \tag{1}$$

[3] See Pinker (2006) for a survey.

where one unit of labor is inelastically supplied and the individual productivity is α_i. Assume that the government uses a linear income tax t on income to finance lump sum transfers and that there is a wastage equal to wt^2 per person which capture the distortionary cost of taxation.[4] Using the government budget constraint, which establishes that every one receives the same lump sum transfer, and defining α^A the average productivity, one can write:

$$c_i = y_i = \alpha_i(1 - t) + \alpha^A t - wt^2 \tag{2}$$

Equation (2) simply states that consumption is the sum of after tax labor income (the first term) plus the lump sum transfer obtained by the government (the second term) reduced by the waste of taxation (the third term).

The equilibrium tax rate is the one that maximizes consumption for the voter with median productivity (α^M):[5]

$$t = \frac{\alpha^A - \alpha^M}{2w} \tag{3}$$

The distance between average and median is, in this model, the critical measure of inequality. The tax rate (and therefore the level of the lump sum redistribution) is higher the larger the difference in productivities (or income, in simplified versions of the model like this one) between the average and the median voter[6].

This is only one particular measure of inequality. There are of course many others measured by different indicators, which would not affect the level of redistribution in this model. In addition, the restriction of the type of redistributive scheme that can be used is also very stringent; a wider available set of policies would lead to different results. However, as we discuss more in the empirical section, the main failure of this model relies on the simplistic assumption about the policy equilibrium, namely the one person one vote rule and the median voter result. Alesina and Rodrik (1994) and Persson and Tabellini (1995) provide two different adaptations of this model to a dynamic environment with growth. However, in these extensions the ranking of individuals does not change in the growth process, that is the profile of the income distribution is invariant over time and the Meltzer-Richards result extends directly.

2.2 Expected future income and social mobility

A departure from the basic model is one in which the ranking of individuals in the income ladder can change; that is, a model where we allow for social mobility, as in

[4] This is of course a simplified version of a model in which the distortionary cost of taxation emerges from an endogenous labor supply.

[5] The result that in this model the median voter result applies is due to Romer (1975).

[6] The level of taxation is also inversely related to the degree of wastage associated with tax distortions. Note that with no tax distorsions the tax level chosen by the median voter would be one.

Benabou and Ok (2001). In their model, individuals care about not only current but also future income. If redistributive policies are long lasting, future income prospects which determine future positions in the income ladder matter in determining current preferences for redistribution. We need at least two periods in the utility function:

$$u_i = u(c_{i1}, c_{i2}) \tag{4}$$

where the second subscript indicates the periods. Individual income is now perturbed by shocks to individual productivity ($y_{i2} = \alpha_i + \varepsilon_{i2}$), where the properties of these shocks are discussed below.[7] The budget constraint for the consumer (ignoring discounting) is:

$$(y_{i1} + E(y_{i2}))(1 - t) + ty_1^A + tE(y_2^A) - 2wt^2 = c_{i1} + c_{i2} \tag{5}$$

which generalizes (2) Note the assumption that the tax rate is decided at the beginning of period 1 and is fixed for period 2. Also period 2 income (productivity) is uncertain so individual i has to vote based upon his expectation about his income relative to average and median income of period 1, which are known, and of period 2, when his position in the income ladder is unknown. In particular, prospects of upward mobility should make somebody below the median of today's income be more averse to redistribution than otherwise. In principle, this effect could be counter-balanced by the prospect of downward mobility, but Benabou and Ok (2001) show that, under certain conditions, prospects of upward mobility (POUM) reduce the demand for redistribution relative to the basic Meltzer-Richards case. They present not only a two period model, but an infinite horizon one. The three key assumptions that deliver this result are: i) tomorrow's expected income is a concave function of today's income; ii) limited risk aversion; and, iii) skewed distribution of the random shocks to income. The concavity of the function of tomorrow's income relative to today's income implies that some of the families that are poorer than the median today will become richer than the median tomorrow, but this effect is declining at an increasing rate with today's income. The assumption on the income shocks prevents the distribution of income to degenerate. The role of low risk aversion is obvious: excessive risk aversion makes too many people too worried about downward mobility.

There are two ways of interpreting the POUM hypothesis. One is as a reminder that people vote on redistribution not only based upon their current income but also based on expected income and that, therefore, social mobility deeply interacts with preferences for redistribution. This is an important point, and we will discuss social mobility extensively below and in the empirical part of this paper. The more stringent interpretation of the POUM hypothesis is an explanation based upon full rationality, and in the median voter spirit, that explains why redistribution is relatively limited

[7] If the shock in period 1 is known before voting for redistribution it is of course irrelevant for the analysis and we assume it away.

despite a relatively poor median voter. This is harder to believe. There are many other reasons why redistribution is limited even in very unequal societies (like the US), and we will examine many of these reasons below. Also, the prediction of the theory seems to be based on a set of fairly restrictive assumptions and functional forms that are very difficult to test empirically. Even remaining in the context of social mobility, other explanations may be more appealing than the POUM hypothesis. One is over-optimism, driven by the fact that many people expect to be richer tomorrow than in a rational equilibrium. Another option is over-optimism as derived from self induced "indoctrination" to convince yourself (or your children) to work hard (Benabou and Tirole (2006)); third, over-optimism about upward mobility may be the result of social indoctrination precisely to prevent the adoption of excessive redistributive policies or the other way around (Alesina and Glaeser (2004)).

2.3 Inequality indirectly in the utility function

A more radical departure from models in which individuals care only about their income/consumption is the one in which the utility function includes some measure of income distribution:

$$U_{it} = \sum_{t=p}^{T} u(c_{it}(\ldots Q_t))$$

where c_{it} is individuals' consumption, Q_t some measure of income inequality and the summation is taken from the present "p" to a final period (possibly infinity). In other words, consumption depends upon a host of standard variables (like labor supply or productivity) and inequality.

This argument in the utility function captures the fact that individual i does not care about inequality per se but only about its effect on her consumption flow. Two observations: First, the dependency of consumption over inequality might be much richer if the model were made dynamic: current consumption may depend on past inequality or even on expected future inequality, but the basic qualitative argument would not change. Second, different individuals may care differently about different measures of inequality, a very important theoretical consideration that will be very hard to take into consideration empirically. More generally, each individual consumption may depend on the entire shape of the income distribution, but for the sake of simplicity of exposition and (especially) of testing, we focus our attention on one specific measure of inequality, say the Gini coefficient.

What would be the sign of the first derivative of that function (i.e., the sign of $\frac{\partial C_t}{\partial Q}$ at different levels of C_t)? In particular, is it possible that even the "rich" may be affected negatively by inequality so that, purely for selfish reasons, they would vote for redistribution? Two arguments have been suggested to justify a negative derivative for the rich:

1) **Externalities in education**. Assume that the average level of education in a country increases the aggregate productivity in the country and that education has positive externalities. Also, assume that more inequality implies that more people are below a level of income that does not allow them to acquire an education (an assumption about imperfection of credit markets is typically needed here). Then, even the rich may favor some redistribution because they would also benefit from an increase in the average level of education[8]. Strictly speaking, the rich should be in favor not of redistribution tout court but especially of publicly supported education, but these models can be also suggestive of conclusions to more general types of redistribution.[9]
2) **Crime and property rights.** A commonly held view is that more inequality leads to more crime, and therefore, by reducing it, the rich would have to spend less on security, since generally their property would be safer. Note that this argument implies that one should observe more redistributions than predicted by both the basic Meltzer-Richards model and its extensions with POUM. However, the implicit assumption to make this work is that it should costs less to the rich to redistribute than to increase spending on security.
3) **Incentive effects.** This channel goes in the opposite direction, which is more inequality has an aggregate social value. In fact, one may argue that more inequality creates incentives to work hard and exercise more effort for most people below the top. To the extent that there are externalities in effort and education acquisition, this may work in favor of society as a whole, since the aggregate level of effort/ investment in education would go up. The strength of this incentive effect is, of course, a very hotly debated empirical question.

Whether channel 3) dominates or not on the other two is of course critical in determining the relationship between inequality and economic efficiency. If channel 3) dominates, there is a trade off between equality and economic efficiency (aggregate level of income/consumption); if channel 1) and 2) dominate there is no such a trade off. Needless to say the trade off does not need to be neither linear nor monothonic, namely it may change shape and its derivative may change sign at different levels of inequality. For a model where this potential nonlinearities are important see Perotti (1993).

2.4 Inequality directly in the utility function

Individuals may have views about "social justice," namely, what constitutes a justifiable level of inequality, or poverty or, generally speaking, views about the distribution of income above and beyond how the latter affects their own income.

[8] See Perotti (1993), Galor and Zeira (1993) and the survey by Benabou (1996) on the issue of redistribution and externalities in education.

[9] Lizzeri and Persico (2004) use a similar argument to justify why the "rich" allowed an extension of the franchise in 19th Century England even though such extensions would have lead to more redistribution.

One way of expressing these preferences that would be useful for our discussion is as follows:

$$U_i = \sum_{p=t}^{T} (\beta^t (u(c_{it}(\ldots Q_t)) - \delta_i (Q - Q_i^*)^2) \tag{6}$$

where Q_i^* represents the ideal level of inequality for individual i and δ_i his/her weight on deviations from it. The quadratic specification is used only for convenience of exposition. The first term in the utility function is the same as in the previous section.

Much of our empirical discussion will be on what determines Q_i^* and δ_i for different individuals. From a theoretical standpoint, we could characterize various possibilities:

a) A "libertarian" view $Q^* = Q^L$ considers a distribution of income (captured by a measure of inequality in short) as determined purely by the market and with no redistribution of any kind from the government.

b) An "efficieny maximizing view" $Q^* = Q^E$, where $Q^E \gtrless \mathbf{Q}^{\mathbf{L}}$ depending on which one of the three channels discussed in the previous section dominates.

c) A "communist view" $Q_i^C = 0$ considers everybody identical; that is this is the distribution obtained by a government who equalizes everybody's income with appropriate tax/transfer schemes.[10]

d) A "Rawlsian view" Q_i^{*R} is the distribution obtained ex post after the government has implemented all the policies that equalize everybody's utility behind a veil of ignorance (Rawls (1971)).

Obviously a fascinating empirical question if what determines preferences, in particular what determines Q^*. We will devote much space to this point in the empirical section.

2.5 Trade offs

Note that someone may face a trade off: on the one hand, excessively market-generated income inequality may reduce his consumption through the effects of $c_i(Q)$ in the first part of the utility function. But, if he has the "libertarian" view he may be willing to give up some consumption to satisfy his ideological goals. In practice, individuals often adjust their beliefs or views in ways that limit these trade offs. Rich people for instance are likely to believe strongly in the beneficial incentive effects of inequality so as to justify in terms of efficiency their preferences for less equality. The opposite applies for those less wealthy and/or left leaning individuals. They tend to disregard the incentive effects of inequality to justify their ideological preferences for equality. This is a more general phenomenon in which when there is uncertainty about the efficiency effects of certain policies, ideological preferences lead people to lean towards the estimates of certain

[10] Actual Communist regimes never achieved that and in fact guaranteed extreme privileges for party members.

economic parameters that justify their ideologies. For instance, right-wingers tend to believe that the elasticity of labor supply to taxes is high and the other way around. A fascinating issue of causality here is obvious, and further research on this point at the border of economics and psychology would be fascinating.[11]

2.6 Fairness

Individuals' views about an acceptable level of inequality are often intertwined with a (possibly vague) sense of what is "fair" and "unfair." As we will show empirically below, people feel that there is a difference between wealth accumulated, for instance, by playing the roulette tables in Las Vegas and wealth accumulated by working one's way up from an entry-level job to a higher-level one with effort, long days at the office and short hours of sleep.

Suppose that individuals' income is due to a combination of effort (e) and luck (l), so that:

$$y_i = e_i + l_i \tag{7}$$

The overall measure of income inequality Q can now be decomposed in Q^e and Q^f, the inequality in the distribution of the effort and the luck parts of income, respectively. Therefore:

$$Q = F(Q^e, Q^f) \tag{8}$$

that is the overall inequality is a function of inequality in income derived from effort and luck. In the previous subsection, we assumed that individuals had an ideal level of Q and no preferences over its two components. But it is also possible (and indeed, it will be the case empirically) that individuals have preferences defined over the two components for a sense of fairness, namely a sense that one is more entitled to retain the sources of his/her effort than income acquired by chance. In this case, we could rewrite the utility function of individual i as follows:

$$U_i = \sum_{t=p}^{T} (\beta^t (u(\ldots c_{it}(Q_t)) - \delta_i^e (Q^e - Q_i^{e*})^2 - \delta_i^l (Q^l - Q^{l*})^2) \tag{9}$$

where $Q_i^M \geq Q_i^{e*} > Q_i^{l*} \geq 0$ for some, and perhaps all, i. These inequalities capture the fact that, at least for some individuals (possibly all of them), a lower level of inequality induced by luck is deemed more desirable than inequality induced by effort. Also, possibly $\delta_i^e \geq \delta_i^l$, if individuals feel more strongly about deviations from optimality for one or the other type of inequality. Note that it makes sense to maintain total inequality in the first part of the utility function, since externalities due to, say, crime, and education depend on total externality rather than its components.

[11] The work by Benabou and Tirole (2006) is related to the issue of adopting certain beliefs because they are useful in order to increase efficiency.

Obviously, what is luck and what is effort, is in practice, an issue on which people may strongly disagree. Is being born smart purely luck? If so, how do we disentangle success in life that results from some combination of effort and intelligence? Being born in a wealthy family is luck, but what if the wealth accumulated by our parents (perhaps at the expenses of care given to us) is the result of great effort?

As we will see below, many people seem to consider this distinction (between effort and luck) relevant to their preferences about social policies and redistribution, even though, if one could investigate people's minds more thoroughly above and beyond simple survey questions, one would discover deep differences in definitions of luck and effort. In addition, the terms effort and luck need to be interpreted broadly. By effort, we mean all activities that require "pain" or a utility cost for the individuals, while luck represents all those factors that deliver income to the individuals without any pain or loss of utility to obtain it. Incidentally, social policies that depend on people's views about luck and effort may in turn create incentives for individuals to put forth more or less effort and therefore generate endogenously different shares of luck-dependent and effort-dependent income. This is the point raised by Alesina and Angeletos (2005a). They derive a multiple equilibria model that is meant to capture a low redistribution (US-style) equilibrium and high redistribution (European-style) equilibrium. In the former, taxes are low, people invest more in effort/hard work, and a higher fraction of income differences amongst people is due to effort. Thus, in equilibrium, people want low redistribution and relatively low taxes. In the European equilibrium, taxes are high, effort and labor supply are low, a larger fraction of income differences is due to differences in luck, and therefore, high taxes and large redistributions are desirable.[12] Note that in equilibrium beliefs about the share of luck and effort in the determination of income differences are correct: In the US, the equilibrium tax is lower, effort is higher, and a larger fraction of income is determined by effort rather than luck, and the other way around.

3. EMPIRICAL EVIDENCE

The goal of this section is to study what determines preferences for redistribution illustrating what we know about the various channels and mechanisms highlighted above. We conduct our analysis using individual level data, as a result we do not provide any evidence on the aggregate relationship between inequality and economic outcomes. Our results focus mostly on the subset of channels with fewer preexisting research; however, we, review available evidence for the most studied determinants of preferences for redistribution. We present two sets of evidence: One for the United States based on results from the General Social Survey, and cross-country evidence based on results from the World Value Survey. We begin by illustrating these two datasets.

[12] Alesina and Angeleots (2005b) present a different version of a similar model in which corruption and connections take the role of luck.

3.1 Data

Starting from 1972, the General Social Survey interviewed a large number of individuals in the US, asking questions about a wide range of opinions, including political behavior, religious preferences, and a wide range of economic beliefs, as well as standard demographics. Each year's sample is an independent cross-section of individuals living in the US, ages 18 and up. We use all data available from 1972 to 2004.

For the cross-country evidence, we use individual data from the World Value Survey (WVS). The WVS covers four waves (1981–84, 1990–93, 1995–97, 1999–2004) and provides questions on beliefs and a large set of demographic and socioeconomic variables. The number of countries varies by wave and goes from a minimum of 20 to a maximum of around 80. We choose questions similar to those in the GSS (exact wording is reported below).

Our variable on preferences for government redistribution is based on the following question from the General Social Survey:[13] "Some people think that the government in Washington should do everything to improve the standard of living of all poor Americans (they are at point 1 on this card). Other people think it is not the government's responsibility, and that each person should take care of himself (they are at point 5). Where are you placing yourself in this scale?" We recode this question so that a higher number means one is more favorable to redistribution.

We measure preferences for redistribution in the World Value Survey by looking at several questions. The closest to the General Social Survey asks the respondent an opinion about the following statement (this question also has the largest coverage, since it has been asked in the last three waves).

a. "Now I'd like you to tell me your views on various issues. How would you place your views on this scale? 1 means you agree completely with the statement on the left; 10 means you agree completely with the statement on the right; and if your views fall somewhere in between, you can choose any number in between. 'People should take more responsibility to provide for themselve (1) versus 'The government should take more responsibility to ensure that everyone is provided for (10)."

We also rely on the following questions for the descriptive evidence (these questions have been asked only in the third wave of the World Values Survey):

b. "Why, in your opinion, are there people in this country who live in need? Here are two opinions: Which comes closest to your view? (1) Poor because of laziness and lack of will power; and (2) Poor because of an unfair society."

c. "In your opinion: (1) Do most poor people in this country have a chance of escaping from poverty, or (2), Is there very little chance of escaping it?"

d. "(1) Do you think that what the government is doing for people in poverty in this country is about too much, (2), The right amount, or (3) Too little?"

[13] This is the same variable used by many others for this purpose; see, for instance, Alesina and La Ferrara (2005).

3.2 Results

3.2.1 The basic model

The basic Meltzer-Richards model has received scant empirical support. Two papers by Alesina and Rodrik (1994) and Persson and Tabellini (1995) noted an inverse correlation between inequality and growth, and they derived this result from a dynamic version of the Meltzer-Richards model. However, work by Benabou (1996) and Perotti (1996) confirmed the negative correlation but found very little evidence that the channel was indeed the tax and transfer scheme suggested by the Meltzer-Richards framework. In fact, the US offers an interesting case in point. This is a country with much (and increasing) inequality and relatively little (and, if anything, decreasing) redistribution, at least until the time of this writing (winter 2009). Alesina and Glaeser (2004) and McCarty, Poole and Rosenthal (2006) discuss in detail the evolution of inequality and redistribution in the US and the political economy of these phenomena. These rejections, however, do not imply immediately that people care about something other than their current income. The political mechanism used by Meltzer and Richards (1981) could be too simplistic if not unrealistic. For instance, with campaign contributions, the rich could count more and tilt the one person/one vote rule in their favor. For recent theoretical and empirical discussions of this point, see Rodriguez (2004), Campante (2007) and Beremboim and Karabarbounis (2008). The latter paper documents how the basic Meltzer-Richards model fails empirically because it does not account for the fact that the very rich may have more weight in the political process, above and beyond the one person/one vote rule and the very poor do not vote so they do not have a weight. However, the authors argue that the Meltzer Richards model could be a good approximation of the evolution of redistributive policies amongst the remaining part of the population.

To put it differently: the rejection of the Meltzer Richards model does not imply that income is not a strong determinant of preferences for redistribution. The relative failure of the model probably relies on the failure of the median voter assumption as an aggregator of social preferences. In fact, in the next section we document that individual income is indeed a strong determinant of preferences for redistribution. As we will see, it is not the only one, and, at least for the US, other determinants, such as race, are also important.

3.2.2 Individual characteristics

We start our analysis by examining the individual determinants of preferences for redistribution in the United States (Table 1). Column one presents our basic specification. All regressions are estimated using OLS for simplicity (similar results are obtained with ordered logic). Results of this type of regression are by now well known, but it is worth briefly reviewing some of the basic facts. First of all, the richer you are, the less you favor redistribution, which is, of course, not surprising. The second striking result from this regression is that, even after controlling for income, marital status, employment status, education, and age, race has a very strong effect: blacks are much more favorable to

Table 4.1 Preferences for Redistribution and Individual Characteristics General Social Survey 1972–2004

	Preferences for redistribution	Preferences for redistribution	Preferences for redistribution
Age	0.061 (0.029)**	0.069 (0.030)**	0.068 (0.030)**
Age squared	−0.014 (0.003)***	−0.013 (0.003)***	−0.013 (0.003)***
Female	0.156 (0.017)***	0.141 (0.017)***	0.134 (0.017)***
Black	0.588 (0.026)***	0.560 (0.027)***	0.565 (0.027)***
Married	−0.049 (0.018)***	−0.012 (0.018)	−0.004 (0.018)
Unemployed	0.111 (0.052)**	0.073 (0.054)	0.072 (0.054)
High school	−0.308 (0.025)***	−0.289 (0.026)***	−0.464 (0.079)***
College and more	−0.378 (0.028)***	−0.375 (0.029)***	−0.984 (0.081)***
Family income	−0.043 (0.004)***	−0.040 (0.004)***	−0.041 (0.004)***
Political ideology		0.152 (0.007)***	0.082 (0.017)***
Political ideology* high school			0.044 (0.019)**
Political ideology* college and more			0.155 (0.019)***
Observations	19512	18135	18135
Rsquared	0.09	0.12	0.13

Notes:

[1] Robust standard errors in parentheses. *significant at 10%; **significant at 5%; *** significant at 1%; all regressions control for year and region fixed effects.

[2] Political ideology is a general measure of ideological selfplacement on a 1-7 scale, where 1 is extremely conservative and 7 is extremely liberal.

redistribution than whites[14]. In order to get some sense of the size of the effect of these individual characteristics, note that a one standard deviation of the black dummy is associated with an increase of preference for redistribution of 17% of a standard deviation of this variable. An increase in a standard deviation of the educational variable (in particular of being in high school) implies an increase of 13% of a standard deviation of preferences for redistribution. Income has a similar impact (10%), while gender could explain only 6% (an increase in standard deviation in the unemployed and married dummy could decrease/increase roughly 2% of the standard deviation of preferences for redistribution.)

Women are more pro-redistribution then men, even though the effect of gender is much smaller than that of race. The fact that, in the US, women are more left wing than men is well known[15], but note that the significant positive coefficient on women remains even when we control in column 3 for political ideology. Thus, there is something about women in addition to ideology that makes them more socially generous than men. The pro-redistributive behavior of women compared to men has also been confirmed in the experimental literature[16]. Differences in redistributive behavior, however, do not seem to be driven by differences in altruism. Andreoni and Vesterlund (2001) found that, when altruism is expensive, women are kinder, but when altruism is cheap, men are more altruistic. They also find evidence that men are more likely to be perfectly selfish or perfectly selfless, whereas women tend to be "equalitarians," who prefer to share evenly.

Even after controlling for income, education enters with a significant and negative coefficient: individuals that are more educated are more averse to redistribution. Perhaps this captures prospects for upward mobility: people invest more in education, holding income constant, to be upwardly mobile. More left-wing individuals are more pro-redistribution even after controlling for income, which already points in the direction of models highlighted above where an ideological dimension matters[17]. Holding income and education constant, people's view about an acceptable level of inequality vary; they care about inequality per se. The interaction between education and ideology is suggestive. Being more left-wing makes people more favorable to redistribution (column 2); moreover, when we do interact education with political ideology, the effect of education reinforces that of political orientation, i.e., having a higher level of education makes more left-wing people even more favorable to redistribution (column 3). Probably we are capturing here the left wing wealthy Democrats made so "famous" in the recent Obama versus Clinton primary contest. Self-identified ideology also plays a role in

[14] The importance of race for redistributive policies in the US is well known, as discussed in detail in Alesina and Glaeser (2004) and many references cited therein.

[15] Alesina and La Ferrara (2005), Inglehart and Norris (2000), Montgomery and Stuart (1999), Shapiro and Mahajan (1986).

[16] For a review on experimental evidence on gender differences in preferences, see Croson and Gneezy (2008).

[17] McCarty Poole and Rosenthal (2006) argue emphatically that income is the only variable that matters in determining political orientation and, therefore, preferences for redistribution, but this result together with all the other significant coefficients in this regression suggests that reality is a bit more complicated.

determining giving behavior in experimental evidence, where right-wing individuals redistribute less and reduce efficiency losses caused by redistribution (Fehr et al. (2006)).

In column 1, unemployed individuals are more favorable to redistribution, but this effect is not robust to alternative specifications. The weakness of this result is interesting: it suggests that the American unemployed may not feel as trapped in poverty as those in other countries (see Alesina and Glaeser (2004) on this point). Age shows an inverted U curve. Individuals are first more favorable, then less favorable, to redistribution. Marital status has an insignificant coefficient.

3.2.3 Expected future income and social mobility

The first extension that we consider of the basic model is the fact that individuals may look at their future prospects of upward mobility. In Table 2, we look at rough proxies for prospects of upward mobility. All the individual controls of column 1 of Table 1 are included; moreover, in column 1, we control for the education of the father, in column 2, for the income of the family when the respondent was 16 and, in columns 3 and 4, for two different measures of social mobility, one based on differences in the years of education between the individual and his/her father and the other defined as a dummy if the occupational prestige of the individual is greater than the one of his/her father[18]. Having a highly educated father reduces the desire for redistribution; the same is true for having a higher income during youth. Social mobility appears to decrease preferences for redistribution, but only when measured by looking at occupational prestige; this result is also found in Alesina and La Ferrara (2005). The impact of father's education is lower than individual education and in the order of 4% of the standard deviation of preferences for redistribution (for a person with a father with a high school degree as compared to a person with a father with less than a high school degree). The impact of family income at 16 is similar (an increase in a standard deviation in the income of the family at 16 is associated with an increase of preferences for redistribution of 4% of a standard deviation of this variable). A one standard deviation increase in social mobility will also decrease preferences for redistribution by 3%.

An experimental test of the POUM hypothesis shows that the preferred taxation declines when the transition matrices are characterized by prospects of upward mobility (Checchi and Filippin (2003)). The authors show that a longer time horizon calls for reduced taxation, because individuals appreciate the freedom of changing the optimal tax when confronted with a different income in the future. Their results are robust when individual factors (such as risk aversion) and framing effects are taken into account.

A history of misfortune in the recent past can change people's views of redistribution. It may make them more risk-averse and less optimistic about upward mobility. This could be interpreted as a learning experience: people realize the importance of government intervention more after experiencing a negative shock. We explore this effect in Table 3. As always, we control for the basic individual determinants of column 1 of Table 1. We look at

[18] For a description of occupational prestige scores in the General Social Survey, see Hodge et al. (1990).

Table 4.2 Preferences for Redistribution, Family Background, and Social Mobility General Social Survey 1972–2004

	Preferences for redistribution	Preferences for redistribution	Preferences for redistribution	Preferences for redistribution
Age	0.042 (0.034)	0.022 (0.043)	0.046 (0.037)	0.034 (0.053)
Age squared	−0.013 (0.003)***	−0.013 (0.004)***	−0.014 (0.004)***	−0.013 (0.005)**
Female	0.157 (0.018)***	0.146 (0.022)***	0.166 (0.019)***	0.117 (0.027)***
Black	0.565 (0.032)***	0.560 (0.038)***	0.559 (0.034)***	0.623 (0.046)***
Married	−0.059 (0.020)***	−0.042 (0.024)*	−0.059 (0.021)***	−0.013 (0.031)
Unemployed	0.091 (0.061)	0.090 (0.069)	0.114 (0.064)*	0.136 (0.088)
High school	−0.314 (0.030)***	−0.328 (0.034)***	−0.328 (0.034)***	−0.284 (0.042)***
College and more	−0.347 (0.034)***	−0.357 (0.039)***	−0.377 (0.043)***	−0.270 (0.049)***
Father with high school	−0.090 (0.022)***	−0.081 (0.026)***	−0.062 (0.030)**	−0.080 (0.033)**
Father with college and more	−0.129 (0.029)***	−0.109 (0.037)***	−0.080 (0.045)*	−0.170 (0.047)***
Family income	−0.047 (0.004)***	−0.046 (0.005)***	−0.047 (0.005)***	−0.054 (0.006)***
Family income at 16		−0.052 (0.015)***		
Mobility (diff. in years of education)			0.006 (0.004)	
Mobility (diff. in occupational prestige)				−0.078 (0.028)***
Observations	15339	10920	14104	7194
R–squared	0.09	0.09	0.09	0.09

Notes:

[1] Robust standard errors in parentheses. *significant at 10%; **significant at 5%; *** significant at 1%; all regressions control for year and region fixed effects.

[2] Mobility measures are defined as a difference in the years of education between the individual and his/her father and as a dummy for whether the occupational prestige of the individual is greater than the one of his/her father.

Table 4.3 Preferences for Redistribution and a History of Misfortune General Social Survey 1972–2004

	Preferences for Redistribution	Preferences for redistribution	Preferences for redistribution
Ever unemployed	0.121		
in the last ten years	(0.020)***		
Trauma last year		0.073 (0.018)***	
Trauma last 5 years			0.039 (0.013)***
Age	0.060 (0.031)**	0.028 (0.042)	0.021 (0.042)
Age squared	−0.012 (0.003)***	−0.011 (0.004)**	−0.010 (0.004)**
Female	0.173 (0.017)***	0.144 (0.023)***	0.144 (0.023)***
Black	0.579 (0.028)***	0.595 (0.035)***	0.599 (0.035)***
Married	−0.047 (0.019)**	−0.003 (0.025)	−0.002 (0.025)
Unemployed	0.053 (0.055)	0.069 (0.075)	0.091 (0.074)
High school	−0.309 (0.026)***	−0.278 (0.033)***	−0.281 (0.033)***
College and more	−0.377 (0.029)***	−0.358 (0.038)***	−0.359 (0.038)***
Family income	−0.041 (0.004)***	−0.049 (0.005)***	−0.050 (0.005)***
Observations	17811	9948	9948
Rsquared	0.09	0.10	0.10

[1] Robust standard errors in parentheses. *significant at 10%; **significant at 5%; *** significant at 1%; all regressions control for year and region fixed effects.

[2] Ever unemployed in the last 10 years is a dummy indicating whether the person has ever been unemployed in the last 10 years; trauma last year/last five years indicate the number of personal traumas (including death of a relative, divorce, unemployment and hospitalization) that the person experienced during the last year/last five years.

different negative experiences: a history of unemployment (defined as a variable equal to 1 if the person has been unemployed in the last 10 years) and two variables indicating the number of personal traumas (including death of a relative, divorce, unemployment and hospitalization) that the person experienced during the last year/last five years. All these variables always have a positive and significant coefficient. An increase in one standard deviation in the "unemployed in the last ten years" dummy is associated with a 5% decline in the standard deviation of preferences for redistribution; the magnitude of the number of traumas last year/last five years is 4% (3%), respectively.

3.3 Inequality indirectly in the utility function

In this subsection of the theoretical discussion we have highlighted several channels through which inequality may affect the level of income of some individuals and as a result the level of aggregate income for a country. The first channel we discussed was that of inequality on education. Perotti (1996) does indeed note a negative correlation in a cross sample of countries between inequality and secondary schooling, a correlation also verified by others especially for poorer countries (see Benabou (1996) for a survey.) The size of aggregate human capital externalities is a hotly debated issue that underlies much of the discussion in the literature on endogenous growth models and it goes beyond the scope of this paper to review this literature. To the extent that there are some positive externalities from aggregate education and if inequality reduces secondary education then this could be a channel of an inverse relationship between inequality and growth.[19]

The second channel emphasizes a direct causation between crime and inequality. Fajnzylber et al. (2002) review the literature and argue that indeed inequality is positively associated with crime. Beremboim and Campante (2008) use Brazilian data and try to disentangle causality. In their data, they do indeed observe a correlation between crime and inequality, but the causality is open to debate. The reverse causality channel goes as follows: those who are more likely to be subject to criminal activities are those who cannot protect their property rights, perhaps the lower middle class, or even the very poor (especially in poor countries most of the crime is amongst the poor.) As a result more crime may actually increases inequality because it does not affect the rich but impoverishes (directly and indirectly) some of the poor. This is a topic that requires further original research.

The third channel emphasizes the incentive effects of inequality. While (almost) nobody would deny some beneficial effects of pay scales at the micro level, the fact that in the aggregate more inequality leads to more efficiency has received relatively little attention. Bell and Freeman (1999, 2001) present evidence on this point and argue that more inequality has lead to stronger incentives to work longer hours; they argue that this may be an explanation of the longer working hours in the US than in Europe.[20]

3.4 Inequality directly in the utility function

Next, we turn to the determinants of preferences for redistribution in which individuals care not only about their income but also about their ideal profile of inequality in society. We have already seen some indirect evidence of this effect in Table 1 when

[19] Rauch (1993) presents evidence consistent with large externalities. Opposite results are discussed in Acemoglu and Angrist (2001) and Rudd (2008) which also includes a survey of the literature. On British data see a recent contribution by Metcalfe and Sloane (2007)

[20] For an overview of the discussion on comparing work hours in the US and Europe, see Alesina, Glaeser and Sacerdote (2005).

we discussed the role of ideological preferences. Left leaning individuals tend to prefer less inequality (in fact it is almost a definition of being left leaning rather than right leaning). But, self proclaimed ideological preferences are only one of the possible determinants of the ideal level of inequality which we have labeled Q_i^* in our theoretical illustration. Other factors are at play and below we examine several of the possible determinants of Q_i^*. In particular, we will focus our analysis on the importance of religion and race and other long lasting determinants of preferences for redistribution, such as differences in historical experiences and cultural differences more generally.

3.4.1 Religion

We begin with religion in Table 4. As above, we include all the individual determinants of column 1 of Table 1. We look not only at the respondent's religion but also at the religious denomination in which he or she was brought up. Overall, compared to atheists,

Table 4.4 Preferences for Redistribution and Religion General Social Survey 1972–2004

	Preferences for redistribution	**Preferences for redistribution**	**Preferences for redistribution**	**Preferences for redistribution**
Age	0.045 (0.034)	0.042 (0.035)	0.043 (0.034)	0.041 (0.035)
Age squared	−0.013 (0.003)***	−0.012 (0.004)***	−0.013 (0.003)***	−0.012 (0.004)***
Female	0.166 (0.018)***	0.142 (0.019)***	0.163 (0.018)***	0.143 (0.019)***
Black	0.593 (0.033)***	0.542 (0.034)***	0.593 (0.033)***	0.544 (0.034)***
Married	−0.049 (0.020)**	−0.011 (0.020)	−0.052 (0.020)***	−0.009 (0.020)
Unemployed	0.080 (0.061)	0.048 (0.064)	0.092 (0.061)	0.055 (0.064)
High school	−0.308 (0.030)***	−0.288 (0.032)***	−0.310 (0.030)***	−0.288 (0.032)***
College and more	−0.351 (0.034)***	−0.337 (0.035)***	−0.354 (0.034)***	−0.340 (0.035)***
Father with high school	−0.091 (0.022)***	−0.084 (0.022)***	−0.090 (0.022)***	−0.084 (0.022)***
Father with college and more	−0.132 (0.029)***	−0.131 (0.029)***	−0.131 (0.029)***	−0.132 (0.029)***
Protestant	−0.136 (0.034)***	−0.035 (0.034)		

Table 4.4 Preferences for Redistribution and Religion General Social Survey 1972–2004—cont'd

	Preferences for redistribution	Preferences for redistribution	Preferences for redistribution	Preferences for redistribution
Catholic	0.012 (0.036)	0.083 (0.036)**		
Jewish	0.059 (0.070)	0.058 (0.070)		
Other religion	0.080 (0.059)	0.098 (0.059)*		
Family income	−0.047 (0.004)***	−0.046 (0.005)***	−0.047 (0.004)***	−0.046 (0.005)***
Ideology		0.155 (0.008)***		0.155 (0.007)***
Protestant at 16			0.005 (0.048)	0.053 (0.048)
Catholic at 16			0.129 (0.050)***	0.154 (0.050)***
Jewish at 16			0.271 (0.080)***	0.210 (0.080)***
Other religion at 16			0.166 (0.079)**	0.158 (0.079)**
Observations	15301	14283	15278	14260
Rsquared	0.09	0.12	0.09	0.12

[1] Robust standard errors in parentheses. *significant at 10%; **significant at 5%; *** significant at 1%; all regressions control for year and region fixed effects.

Protestants appear to be less favorable to redistribution (column1). On the other hand, being raised Catholic or Jewish increases the desire for redistribution (but the effect is not significant). Being brought up in a religious environment has the effect of increasing tastes for redistribution independently of the religious denomination (columns 3 and 4). Note that, when we control for political ideology, all religious denominations appear to be more favorable to redistribution (column 2); being Protestant still has a negative sign but not a significant one. An increase in the standard deviation in the Catholic dummy increases preferences for redistribution of 3% of a standard deviation of this variable. The impact of being raised religiously goes from 3% of a standard deviation of preferences for redistribution for Jewish and other religions to 6% for Catholic. Religious affiliation and participation in religious services (elicited with a multi-item questionnaire) yields no significant influence on social preferences in an experimental setting (Tan (2006)).

3.4.2 Race

A large body of experimental and statistical evidence shows that altruism travels less across racial and ethnic lines. In fact, as it turns out, this is an extremely important determinant of preferences for redistribution. When the poor are disproportionately concentrated in a racial minority, the majority, coeteris paribus, prefer less redistribution. The underpinning of this observation relies in a perhaps unpleasant but nevertheless widely observed fact that individuals are more generous toward others who are similar to them racially, ethnically, linguistically, etc. (see also Luttmer (2001) and Fong and Luttmer (2009)). Evidence for the strength of this channel is quite striking simply looking at our previous regressions on individual characteristics: even after controlling for income, education, gender, age, etc., the race of the respondent is a critical (and large) determinant of preferences for redistribution. In the US, the racial majority (whites) is much less favorable to redistribution than minorities. A large body of literature both in political science and in economics has documented this fact both with reference to the US and as an explanation for cross country comparisons. Alesina and Glaeser (2004) review this literature and make the racial argument a critical determinant of the differences in the more generous redistributive policies of more homogeneous European countries relative to the less racially homogeneous US. But, even within the US the comparison of different redistributive policies in more or less racially homogeneous states is very telling (see Alesina and Glaeser (2004)).

In the language of our approach the acceptable income inequality Q^*_i for individual i in the racial majority is higher if the lower tail of the income ladder is disproportionately filled by racial minorities. Note that this consideration has important consequences for the relationship between immigration and redistribution. To the extent that new immigrants are near the bottom of the income ladder, their arrival should decrease the desired level of redistribution for the locals. This has certainly been a phenomenon at work in the US (Alesina and Glaeser (2004)) but is also beginning to happen in Europe as well with new waves of immigration from Africa and the Middle East. The topic of immigration and redistribution is an excellent one for future research.

3.4.3 Cultural norms and differences in macroeconomic experiences

Preferences for redistribution display large differences across countries, as we discuss below. In this section, we focus on long lasting determinants of preferences for redistribution. In particular, we first focus on the general question of whether individuals bring with themselves the preferences for redistribution of their country of origin. Second, we look at some of the long term differences, including the importance of macroeconomic history or the structure of the family. We examine the importance of culture in the determination of preferences for redistribution by looking at the behavior of immigrants in the US. The approach of using immigrants' behavior has become a common way to isolate the importance of cultural norms.[21] We use as a measure of culture the

[21] See also Giuliano (2007), Alesina and Giuliano (2010), Antecol (2000), Carroll, Rhee and Rhee (1994) and Fernandez and Fogli (2005)

preferences for redistribution in the immigrants' country of origin. We calculate the mean preferences for redistribution in the immigrant country of origin by using a similar question on preferences for redistribution from the World Values Survey. Table 5 presents a variety of specifications, controlling for the usual set of controls (column 1), father education (column 2), income of the family at 16 (column 3) and the two previously described measures of mobility (columns 4 and 5). We specifically control for family background, because a lower level of income or human capital could be the main omitted variable captured by preferences for redistribution in the country of origin. In all our specifications, culture appears to be an important variable in the determination of preferences for redistribution. Our results are in line with those by Luttmer and Singhal (2008), who specifically study the importance of culture in the determination of preferences for redistribution, using evidence drawn from the European Social Survey. A one standard deviation increase in preferences for redistribution in the country of origin is associated with an increase in the standard deviation of preferences for redistribution of about 4%.

Anecdotal evidence suggests that difficult times leave a mark in an individual's beliefs and attitudes. Moreover, research in social psychology points out that differences in historical experiences, especially during youth, can leave a permanent mark in individuals' political and economic beliefs. In particular, social psychologists point out that there is a socialization period in the lives of individuals during which socializing influences have the most profound impact: values, attitudes, and world-views acquired during this time period become fixed within individuals and are resistant to change. Evidence of significant socialization has been found between 18 and 25 years of age (the so-called "impressionable years hypothesis".) In order to investigate the validity of this position (that beliefs that are formed during the initial years of adulthood may change within a generation, but, at the same time, once past a critical age they are more difficult to modify), we follow Giuliano and Spilimbergo (2009) and test whether differences in a history of macroeconomic volatility during youth can have a permanent effect in the determination of preferences for redistribution. In order to do so, we match individual beliefs with the macroeconomic volatility of the region in which the person was living when she was 16. Using the information location of respondents during critical age (the GSS provides the location of the respondent at 16), we construct a measure of macroeconomic volatility during the "impressionable years" range (when the individual was between 18 and 25). For instance, we consider the macroeconomic volatility in New England in the fifties for an individual who was living in Boston at the age of 16 even if she/he is currently living in Los Angeles. A cohort of individuals shares a large amount of experiences, ranging from economic shocks to technological progress to a multitude of unobservable characteristics. This identification strategy, that mainly uses cross-regional variation in individual experiences during critical age, allows distinguishing the impact of a personally experienced macroeconomic history from unrestricted cohort's effects. Macroeconomic volatility, being specific to a given region, vary also within cohorts and not only across cohorts. The specification follows the one

Table 4.5 Preferences for Redistribution and Cultural Origin Immigrants' Regressions General Social Survey 1972–2004

	Preferences for redistribution	Preferences for redistribution	Preferences for redistribution	Preferences for redistribution	Preferences for Redistribution
Preferences for redistrib. in the country of origin	0.063 (0.032)*	0.059 (0.031)*	0.057 (0.032)*	0.067 (0.031)**	0.068 (0.036)*
Age	0.043 (0.033)	0.009 (0.037)	–0.025 (0.050)	–0.010 (0.042)	0.022 (0.062)
Age squared	–0.013 (0.004)***	–0.010 (0.004)**	–0.008 (0.005)	–0.008 (0.005)	–0.013 (0.006)**
Female	0.145 (0.025)***	0.143 (0.030)***	0.147 (0.034)***	0.165 (0.034)***	0.109 (0.039)***
Black	0.360 (0.114)***	0.365 (0.167)**	0.637 (0.182)***	0.428 (0.216)*	0.807 (0.174)***
Married	–0.011 (0.039)	–0.031 (0.035)	0.011 (0.040)	–0.027 (0.040)	0.005 (0.040)
Unemployed	0.201 (0.102)*	0.203 (0.084)**	0.192 (0.087)**	0.222 (0.086)**	0.201 (0.096)**
High school	–0.271 (0.050)***	–0.232 (0.062)***	–0.255 (0.068)***	–0.252 (0.063)***	–0.199 (0.085)**
College and more	–0.313 (0.041)***	–0.230 (0.042)***	–0.222 (0.055)***	–0.261 (0.046)***	–0.115 (0.063)*
Family income	–0.055 (0.006)***	–0.055 (0.006)***	–0.056 (0.007)***	–0.054 (0.007)***	–0.059 (0.011)***
Father with high school		–0.079 (0.041)*	–0.111 (0.045)**	–0.046 (0.041)	–0.122 (0.043)***

Father with college and more		−0.110 (0.033)***	−0.133 (0.040)***	−0.053 (0.039)	−0.259 (0.051)***
Family income at 16			−0.046 (0.025)*		
Mobility (diff. in years of education)				0.006 (0.004)	
Mobility (diff. in occupational mobility)					−0.109 (0.036)***
Observations	7005	5650	4149	5216	2928
Rsquared	0.05	0.05	0.05	0.05	0.05

[1] Standard errors are clustered at the country of origin level. *significant at 10%; **significant at 5%; *** significant at 1%; all regressions control for year and region fixed effects.

[2] Preferences for redistribution in the country of origin are defined as the average at the country level of the following World Value Survey question: "Now I'd like you to tell me your views on various issues. How would you place your views on this scale? People should take more responsibility to provide for themselves (1) vs The government should take more responsibility to ensure that everyone is provided for (10)."

of the previous section but also adds "region at 16" fixed-effects and clusters the standard errors at the "region at 16 level." In all different specifications, a history of macroeconomic volatility during youth appears to be an important component in the determination of preferences for redistribution. We repeat the same exercise for other age ranges[22]. Similarly to Giuliano and Spilimbergo (2009), we do not find evidence of an impact of macroeconomic volatility in the formation of beliefs when the person is older than 26. A one standard deviation increase in macroeconomic volatility during youth is associated with an increase of 3% of a standard deviation of preferences for redistribution (Table 6).

3.4.4 The structure of the family

The organization of the family varies a lot around the world. Family ties are strong in some countries, weak in others. In certain countries nuclear families have been the natural arrangement for decades, in other large families with several generations living together are more common. The relationship between siblings can be more or less even or unequal[23] Different family structures can affect preferences of the desired level of government intervention in redistributive policies, directly or indirectly. Esping Andersen (1999) for instance argues that in societies with close family ties, certain welfare policies are internalized by the family rather than being delegated to the State. Unlucky or even "lazy" youngsters are supported by their parents more in certain societies than in others because of the different family structures. The same applies to impoverished elderly, the sick and disabled, etc. Thus in societies where the family performs these functions, the preferences for government intervention are different (i.e. there is less demand for it) than in countries where the family does not perform such functions. There is obviously an important issue of causality here but family traditions and cultural factors affecting family values are most likely more long lasting and certainly older than the modern welfare state, a post second World War phenomenon by and large. Alesina and Giuliano (2010) present evidence consistent with the role of family ties and preferences of government intervention.

In his fascinating work Todd (1985) argues that the structure of the family, in particular the nature of the hierarchal relations between parents and children, and the nature of the sibling's relations is an important determinant of the tendency for certain societies to be more or less receptive of certain ideologies, say liberalism versus socialism. The latter has of course important implications on the preferences for redistribution. For instance, Todd (1985) argues that it is not an accident that a communist dictatorship took a solid root in Russia rather than in other parts of western Europe. A family structure based on an authoritative head of the family but communal and egalitarian amongst siblings made it easier for a society based upon a dictator and egalitarian policies to be acceptable.

[22] The other age ranges considered are: 10–17, 26–33, 34–41, 42–49, and 50–57. We maintain a period length of 8 years for consistency with the "impressionable years range."

[23] Todd (1985).

Table 4.6 Preferences for Redistribution and a History of Macroeconomic Volatility during Youth General Social Survey 1972–2004

	Preferences for redistribution	**Preferences for redistribution**	**Preferences for Redistribution**	**Preferences for redistribution**	**Preferences for redistribution**
Macrovolatility during 18–25	0.740 (0.286)***	0.653 (0.315)**	0.671 (0.377)*	0.736 (0.322)**	1.222 (0.637)*
Age	0.044 (0.078)	0.059 (0.087)	0.085 (0.109)	0.015 (0.090)	0.046 (0.233)
Age squared	−0.009 (0.010)	−0.012 (0.012)	−0.018 (0.015)	−0.007 (0.012)	−0.005 (0.036)
Female	0.180 (0.020)***	0.200 (0.021)***	0.196 (0.026)***	0.201 (0.022)***	0.177 (0.034)***
Black	0.562 (0.030)***	0.555 (0.038)***	0.526 (0.045)***	0.550 (0.040)***	0.578 (0.057)***
Married	−0.075 (0.021)***	−0.073 (0.023)***	−0.051 (0.029)*	−0.079 (0.024)***	−0.014 (0.037)
Unemployed	0.061 (0.057)	0.038 (0.066)	0.051 (0.075)	0.050 (0.069)	0.076 (0.101)
High school	−0.287 (0.034)***	−0.312 (0.042)***	−0.283 (0.049)***	−0.336 (0.045)***	−0.286 (0.063)***
College and more	−0.392 (0.037)***	−0.410 (0.044)***	−0.375 (0.051)***	−0.449 (0.048)***	−0.358 (0.067)***
Family income	−0.038 (0.005)***	−0.044 (0.005)***	−0.038 (0.006)***	−0.042 (0.006)***	−0.050 (0.008)***
Father with high school		−0.062 (0.022)***	−0.075 (0.027)***	−0.047 (0.022)**	−0.070 (0.034)**

Continued

Table 4.6 Preferences for Redistribution and a History of Macroeconomic Volatility during Youth General Social Survey 1972–2004—cont'd

	Preferences for redistribution	Preferences for redistribution	Preferences for Redistribution	Preferences for redistribution	Preferences for redistribution
Father with college and more		−0.077 (0.068)	−0.114 (0.087)	−0.048 (0.069)	−0.191 (0.138)
Family income at 16			−0.080 (0.017)***		
Mobility (diff. in years of education)				0.012 (0.003)***	
Mobility (diff. in occupational mobility)					−0.023 (0.035)
Observations	12754	10136	6907	9677	4210
Rsquared	0.09	0.09	0.09	0.09	0.08

[1] Standard errors are clustered at the "region of residence at 16" level. *significant at 10%; **significant at 5%; *** significant at 1%; all regressions control for year, actual region of residence and region of residence at 16-fixed effects.

[2] Macroeconomic volatility is measured as the standard deviation of the regional income when the person was between 18 and 25 years old.

3.4.5 Fairness

The final effect, which we emphasized in the theoretical part is the role of fairness and the perception of whether inequality emerges from efforts and ability of different individuals or luck, connections, perhaps corruption, etc. In Table 7, we study the impact of attitudes toward the importance of work versus luck as a driver of success in life and the relevance of fairness in determing prefereces for redistribution. These two beliefs are measured using the following two questions: "Some people say that people get ahead by their own hard work; others say that lucky breaks or help from other people are more important. Which do you think is most important?" Hard work (1) or luck (3); the question takes the value of 2 if hard work and luck are considered equally important" and "Do you think most people would try to take advantage of you if they got a chance (2), or would they try to be fair (1)?" We add these variables to our basic specification of column 1 of table 1. Both beliefs seem to be relevant in determining preferences for redistribution when included separately. When included jointly, only the "work versus luck" variable remains significant. These results are consistent with those of Alesina and La Ferrara (2002) and Fong (2001). Obviously, the questions asked in the GSS do not allow us to disentangle exactly what part of income is attributable to luck or effort according to various individuals. Note also that, controlling for political ideology, does not change the importance of work and luck as a determinant of preferences for redistribution. On the other hand, it seems to undermine the relative importance of fairness, which becomes insignificant.[24] Extensive experimental literature shows that preferences for redistribution may be dictated by a sense of fairness or aversion to inequality (see Durante and Putterman (2007), Frohlich and Oppenheimer (1992), Cowell and Schokkaert (2001), Hoffman and Spitzer (1985)).

3.5 Evidence from the world values survey

In this section, we briefly look at preferences for redistribution using cross-country evidence. Figure 1 presents correlations among several measures of preferences for government redistribution (as defined in the data session) at the country level. All the measures are very strongly correlated; therefore, our results are not simply due to one specific question but are consistent across definitions. It is also apparent from the table that there is a consistent ranking of countries for preferences for redistribution. Eastern European countries are the most pro-government redistribution (a not surprising effect of left-wing ideology), followed by Latin America and Northern European countries. Asian countries, the US, Australia and New Zealand are in the bottom part of the distribution.[25]

As a final step, we perform a within-country analysis to generalize the results outside of the US context. By controlling for country and wave fixed effects, we can limit the possibility that some of the US results depend highly upon the social and historical context of this specific country. Results (reported in Table 8) broadly confirm the

[24] This could be due only to a difference in the sample, since when we restrict the sample to those observations for which we do have data on political ideology, fairness is not significant.

[25] Note that preferences for redistribution were not asked for many countries in Continental and Southern Europe.

Table 4.7 Preferences for Redistribution, Work versus Luck as a Driver of Success, and Fairness General Social Survey 1972–2004

	Preferences for redistribution	Preferences for redistribution	Preferences for redistribution	Preferences for redistribution	Preferences for redistribution	Preferences for redistribution
Fairness	0.038 (0.019)**	0.029 (0.019)			0.027 (0.026)	0.027 (0.026)
Age	0.066 (0.030)**	0.074 (0.031)**	0.006 (0.042)	0.009 (0.042)	0.015 (0.043)	0.019 (0.044)
Age squared	–0.014 (0.003)***	–0.014 (0.003)***	–0.008 (0.004)*	–0.007 (0.004)*	–0.009 (0.004)**	–0.009 (0.004)*
Female	0.158 (0.017)***	0.142 (0.017)***	0.131 (0.024)***	0.115 (0.023)***	0.126 (0.024)***	0.109 (0.024)***
Black	0.587 (0.027)***	0.557 (0.028)***	0.560 (0.036)***	0.544 (0.037)***	0.561 (0.037)***	0.536 (0.038)***
Married	–0.052 (0.019)***	–0.014 (0.019)	–0.022 (0.026)	0.005 (0.026)	–0.031 (0.026)	–0.003 (0.026)
Unemployed	0.113 (0.055)**	0.075 (0.057)	0.109 (0.076)	0.119 (0.076)	0.121 (0.079)	0.129 (0.080)
High school	–0.303 (0.026)***	–0.286 (0.027)***	–0.371 (0.036)***	–0.359 (0.037)***	–0.365 (0.037)***	–0.351 (0.038)***
College and more	–0.375 (0.029)***	–0.373 (0.030)***	–0.430 (0.039)***	–0.427 (0.040)***	–0.427 (0.041)***	–0.420 (0.042)***
Family income	–0.043 (0.004)***	–0.041 (0.004)***	–0.040 (0.006)***	–0.039 (0.006)***	–0.041 (0.006)***	–0.041 (0.006)***

Ideology		0.150 (0.007)***		0.128 (0.009)***		0.130 (0.010)***
Work and luck			0.074 (0.017)***	0.056 (0.017)***	0.070 (0.017)***	0.053 (0.017)***
Observations	18224	16961	9130	8784	8565	8263
Rsquared	0.09	0.12	0.10	0.12	0.10	0.12

[1] Robust standard errors in parentheses. *significant at 10%; **significant at 5%; *** significant at 1%; all regressions control for year and region fixed effects.
[2] *Fairness* is a categorical variable that is the answer to the question: "Do you think most people would try to take advantage of you if they got a chance?" (2) or, "Would they try to be fair?" (1); *Work versus luck* is a categorical variable that is the answer to the question: "Some people say that people get ahead by their own hard work; others say that lucky breaks or help from other people are more important. Which do you think is most important? Hard work? (1), Hard work and luck equally important? (2), Luck most important? (3).

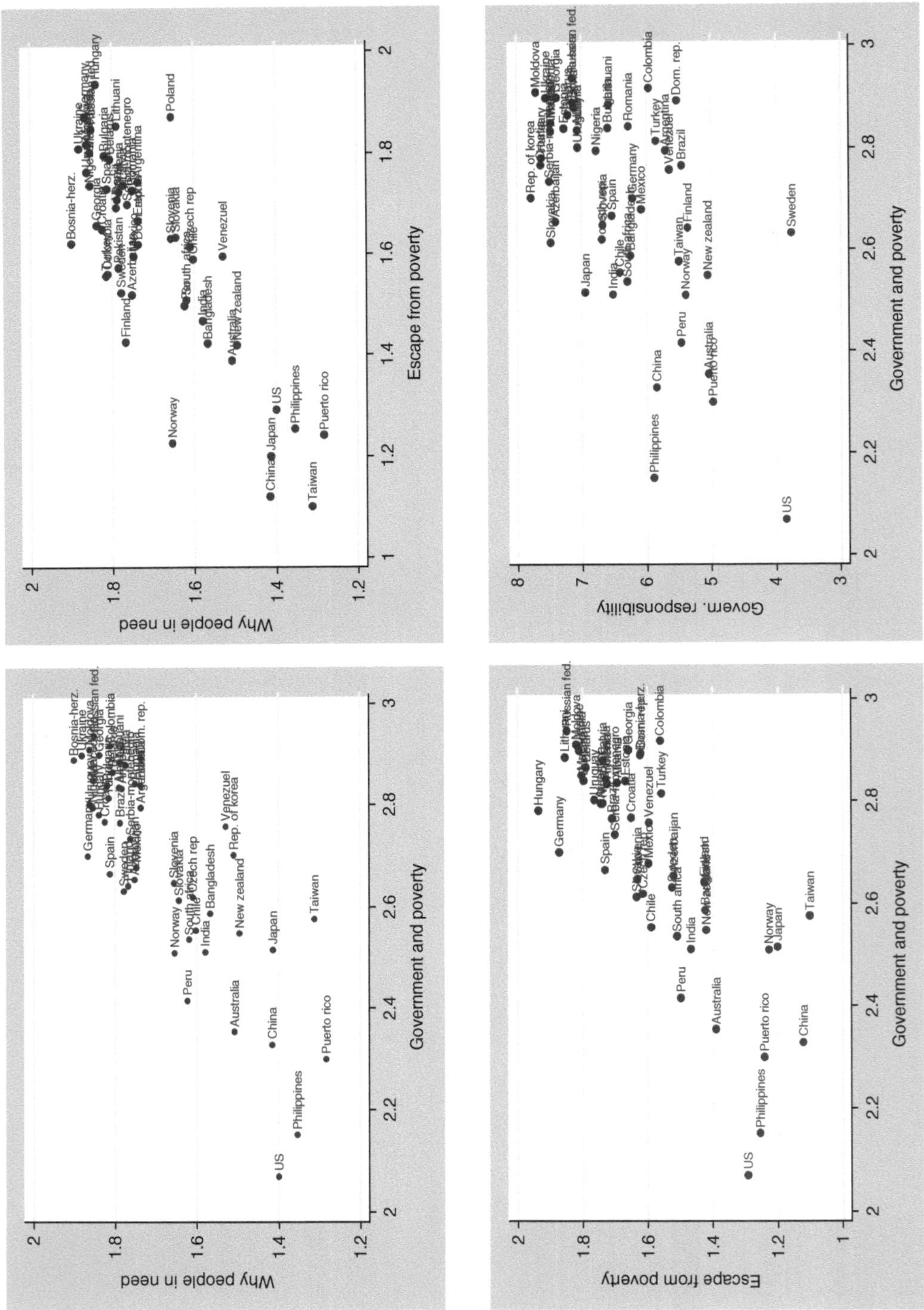

Figure 4.1 Preferences for redistribution and beliefs about the poor.

Table 4.8 Determinants of Preferences for Redistribution World Values Survey

	Pref. for redistribution	Pref. for redistribution	Pref. for redistribution	Pref. for redistribution	Pref. for redistribution	Pref. for redistribution	Pref. for redistribution	Pref. for redistribution
Age	0.067 (0.025)***	0.026 (0.028)	0.025 (0.028)	0.023 (0.028)	–0.003 (0.037)	0.014 (0.068)	0.161 (0.075)**	0.067 (0.025)***
Age squared	–0.007 (0.003)***	–0.003 (0.003)	–0.003 (0.003)	–0.003 (0.003)	0.002 (0.004)	–0.005 (0.007)	–0.014 (0.007)**	–0.007 (0.003)***
Female	0.181 (0.013)***	0.155 (0.015)***	0.154 (0.015)***	0.158 (0.015)***	0.134 (0.019)***	0.144 (0.034)***	0.188 (0.036)***	0.159 (0.029)***
Married	–0.064 (0.015)***	–0.060 (0.018)***	–0.060 (0.018)***	–0.052 (0.018)***	–0.089 (0.023)***	–0.019 (0.042)	–0.071 (0.056)	–0.042 (0.029)
Unemployed	0.305 (0.026)***	0.304 (0.030)***	0.305 (0.030)***	0.300 (0.030)***	0.363 (0.043)***	0.152 (0.057)***	0.404 (0.083)***	0.325 (0.046)***
High school	–0.385 (0.018)***	–0.363 (0.021)***	–0.279 (0.050)***	–0.369 (0.021)***	–0.315 (0.032)***	–0.212 (0.044)***	–0.189 (0.044)***	–0.386 (0.118)***
College and more	–0.542 (0.021)***	–0.509 (0.024)***	–0.715 (0.059)***	–0.513 (0.024)***	–0.490 (0.035)***	–0.330 (0.052)***	–0.389 (0.054)***	–0.520 (0.141)***
Income	–0.258 (0.009)***	–0.238 (0.010)***	–0.237 (0.010)***	–0.237 (0.010)***	–0.242 (0.013)***	–0.215 (0.023)***	–0.329 (0.026)***	–0.246*** (0.039)
Ideology		0.112 (0.004)***	0.110 (0.005)***	0.011 (0.004)***	0.122 (0.005)***	0.063 (0.008)***		
Ideology* high school			–0.016 (0.008)*					
Ideology* college and more			0.038 (0.010)***					
Roman Catholic				–0.068 (0.024)***				
Protestant				–0.210 (0.030)***				

Continued

Table 4.8 Determinants of Preferences for Redistribution World Values Survey—cont'd

	Pref. for redistribution	Pref. for redistribution	Pref. for redistribution	Pref. for redistribution	Pref. for redistribution	Pref. for redistribution	Pref. for redistribution	Pref. for redistribution
Orthodox				0.174 (0.042)***				
Jews				–0.106 (0.120)				
Muslim				–0.040 (0.051)				
Hindu				–0.053 (0.098)				
Buddhist				–0.121 (0.070)*				
Other religion				–0.144 (0.038)***				
Hard work					0.076 (0.004)***			
Fairness						0.026 (0.037)		
Ever been divorced							–0.046 (0.067)	
Macrovolatility during youth (18–25)								0.032 (0.273)
Observations	193956	146166	146166	141285	84028	29556	23320	125128
Rsquared	0.12	0.13	0.13	0.13	0.15	0.11	0.09	0.11

[1] Robust standard errors in parentheses (clustered at the country level in the last column). *significant at 10%; **significant at 5%; *** significant at 1%; all regressions control for wave and country fixed effects.

[1] *Preferences for redistribution* are measured using the following question (on a scale from 1 to 10): "People should take more responsibility to provide for themselves (1) vs The government should take more responsibility to ensure that everyone is provided for (10)". *Ideology* measures the political orientation of the respondent (on a scale from 1 to 10) and it is an answer to the following question: "In political matters, people talk of the left and the right. How would you place your views on this scale, generally speaking? Right (1) versus Left (10). *Work versus luck* is a categorical variable (on a scale from 1 to 10) that is the answer to the question: "Now I would like to tell me your views on the following statement: In the long run, hard work usually brings a better life (1) versus Hard work does not generally bring success – it is more a matter of luck and connections". *Fairness* is a categorical variable that is the answer to the question: "Do you think most people would try totake advantage of you if they got a chance (2), or would they try to be fair (1).

US evidence. Women, youth, the unemployed and left wing people are more pro-redistribution. Income and education reduce the desire for redistribution, but, as in the US, education has a positive effect on redistribution when interacted with political ideology. Believing that luck is more important than work increases the desire for redistribution. Fairness also matters (whereas, in the US, the coefficient has the right sign, but it is not significant). The only measure of personal misfortune found in the World Value Survey asks the respondent if she has ever been divorced (this question was, however, asked only in one wave; therefore, we have a very limited number of observations). We do not find any effect of personal misfortune. Macroeconomic volatility is positively associated with preferences for redistribution but has an insignificant effect. Results for religious denomination are different than in the US. With the exception of the Orthodox, who are strongly pro-redistribution, all the other religious denominations appear to be less favorable to redistribution than atheists.[26]

4. CONCLUSIONS

This paper provides a comprehensive review of the determinants of preferences for redistribution. Our analysis is guided by a theoretical framework and complemented by empirical evidence mostly for the US and (briefly) across countries. Within country analysis is much less likely to be subject to measurement error due to changes in institutional structures of redistributive policies. Preferences for redistribution are determined by personal characteristics such as age, gender, race and socioeconomic status, but they are also a product of history, culture, political ideology and a perception of fairness. In particular, women, youth and African-Americans appear to have stronger preferences for redistribution. Individuals who believe that people try to take advantage of them, rather than being fair, have a strong desire for redistribution; similarly, believing that luck is more important than work as a driver of success is strongly associated with a taste for redistribution.

Preferences for redistribution vary substantially across countries. We show that these differences could be the result of differences in religion, histories of macroeconomic volatility and more generally defined culture.

[26] We also run an alternative specification in which we interact all religious denominations with political ideology. In this case, all religions appear to be less pro-redistribution than atheists. The interaction with ideology is positive, however.

Table A1 Descriptive Statistics General Social Survey 1972–2004

Variable	Obs	Mean	Std. Dev.	Min	Max
Preferences for redistribution	19512	3.12	1.18	1	5
Age	19512	44.54	16.93	18	89
Female	19512	0.55	0.50	0	1
Black	19512	0.13	0.34	0	1
Married	19512	0.54	0.50	0	1
Unemployed	19512	0.03	0.17	0	1
High school	19512	0.53	0.50	0	1
College and more	19512	0.27	0.44	0	1
Income	19512	10.10	2.77	1	12
Polit. ideology	18135	3.88	1.35	1	7
Father with high school	15339	0.36	0.48	0	1
Father with college and more	15339	0.16	0.37	0	1
Income at 16	13620	2.79	0.86	1	5
Mobility (diff. in years of educ.)	14401	2.64	3.87	−16	20
Mobility (diff. in occupat. prestige)	7724	0.47	0.50	0	1
Protestant	19464	0.60	0.49	0	1
Catholic	19464	0.25	0.43	0	1
Jewish	19464	0.02	0.14	0	1
Other religion	19464	0.03	0.18	0	1
Protestant at 16	19432	0.63	0.48	0	1
Catholic at 16	19432	0.28	0.45	0	1
Jewish at 16	19432	0.02	0.14	0	1
Other religion at 16	19432	0.02	0.14	0	1
Fairness	18224	1.39	0.49	1	2
Work and luck	9130	1.45	0.71	1	3
Unemployed in the last ten years	17811	0.32	0.47	0	1
Number of traumas last year	9948	0.47	0.65	0	4
Number of traumas in the last 5 years	9948	1.07	0.88	0	4
Macrovolatility during youth	12754	.0855	.0423	0	.179
Pref. for redistr. in the country of origin	7005	4.99	.667	3.476	7.50

Table A2 Descriptive Statistics World Values Survey

Variable	Obs	Mean	Std. Dev.	Min	Max
Preferences for redistribution	193956	5.80	3.04	1	10
Age	193956	41.27	15.94	15	99
Female	193956	0.51	0.50	0	1
Married	193956	0.65	0.48	0	1
Unemployed	193956	0.08	0.27	0	1
High school	193956	0.33	0.47	0	1
College and more	193956	0.17	0.38	0	1
Income	193956	1.97	0.79	1	3
Ideology	146166	5.43	2.29	1	10
Roman Catholic	141285	0.34	0.47	0	1
Protestant	141285	0.14	0.35	0	1
Orthodox	141285	0.08	0.27	0	1
Jews	141285	0.01	0.09	0	1
Muslim	146166	0.11	0.31	0	1
Hindu	146166	0.03	0.16	0	1
Buddhist	146166	0.01	0.12	0	1
Other religion	146166	0.06	0.24	0	1
Work and luck	84028	4.35	2.84	1	10
Fairness	29556	1.59	0.49	1	2
Ever divorced	23320	0.08	0.27	0	1

REFERENCES

Acemoglu, D., Angrist, J., 2001. How Large are Human Capiutal Externalities. In: Bernanke, B.S., Rogoff, K. (Ed.), NBER Macroeconomics Annual 2000, vol. 15. pp. 9–74.

Alesina, A., Angeletos, G.M., 2005a. Fairness and Redistribution: US vs. Europe. Am. Econ. Rev. 95, 913–935.

Alesina, A., Angeletos, G.M., 2005b. Redistribution, Corruption and Fairness. J. Monet. Econo. 1227–1244.

Alesina, A., Fuchs-Schündeln, N., 2007. Good Bye Lenin (or not?) The Effect of Communism on People's Preferences. Am. Econ. Rev. 97, 1507–1528.

Alesina, A., Glaeser, E., 2004. Fighting Poverty in the US and Europe: A World of Difference. Oxford University Press, Oxford UK.

Alesina, A., Glaeser, E., Sacerdote, B., 2005. Work and Leisure in the United States and Europe: Why so Different? NBER Macroannual 20, 1–64.

Alesina, A., Giuliano, P., 2010. The Power of the Family. Journal of Economic Growth 15 (2), 93–125.

Alesina, A., La Ferrara, E., 2005. Preferences for Redistribution in the Land of Opportunities. J. Public Econ. 89, 897–931.

Alesina, A., Rodrik, D., 1994. Dostributive Polcies and Economic Growth. Q. J. Econ.

Andreoni, J., Vesterlund, L., 2001. Which is the Fair Sex? Gender Differences in Altruism. Q. J. Econ.

Antecol, H., 2000. An Examination of Cross-Country Differences in the Gender Gap in Labor Force Participation Rates. Labour Econ. 7, 409–426.

Baremboim, I., Campante, F., 2008. Does Crime Breed Inequality? Evidence from the Favelas in Rio de Janeiro. unpublished.

Baremboim, I., Karabarbounis, L., 2008. One Dollar One Vote. unpublished.

Bell, L., Freeman, R.B., 2001. The Incentive For Working Hard: Explaining Hours Worked Differences In The US And Germany. Labor Econ. 8 (2), 181–202.

Bell, L., Freeman, R., 1999. Does Inequality Induce Us to Work More. unpublished manuscript.

Benabou, R., 1996. Inequality and Growth. NBER Macroeconomic Annual. MIT Press, Cambridge, MA.

Benabou, R., Ok, E., 2001. Social Mobility and the Demand for Redistribution: the POUM Hypothesis. Q. J. Econ. 116 (2001), 447–487.

Benabou, R., Tirole, J., 2006. Beliefs in a Just World and Redistributive Politics. Q. J. Econ. 121 (2), 699–746.

Campante, F., 2007. Redistribution in a Model of Voting and Campaign Contributions. unpublished.

Carroll, C., Rhee, B., Rhee, C., 1994. Are There Cultural Effects on Saving? Some Cross-Sectional Evidence. Q. J. Econ. 109 (3), 685–699.

Checchi, D., Filippin, A., 2003. An Experimental Study of the POUM Hypothesis. IZA DP 912.

Corneo, G., Gruner, P.H., 2000. Social Limits to Redistribution. Am. Econ. Rev. 90, 1491–1507.

Corneo, G., Gruner, P.H., 2002. Individual Preferences for Political Redistribution. J. Public Econ. 83, 83–107.

Cowell, F., Schokkaert, A., 2001. Risk Perceptions and Distributional Judgements. Eur. Econ. Rev. 45, 941–952.

Croson, R., Gneezy, U., 2008. Gender Differences in Preferences. J. Econ. Lit. 47 (2), 1–27.

Drazen, A., 2002. Political Economy in Macroeconomics. Princeton University Press.

Durante, R., Putterman, L., 2007. Preferences for Redistribution and Perception of Fairness: An Experimental Study. Brown University, mimeo.

Esping- Andersen, 1999. Social Foundations of Poist Industrial Economices. Oxford University Press, Oxford, UK.

Fajnzylber, P., Lederman, D., Loayza, N., 2002. Inequality and Violent Crime. J. Law Econ. 45 (1), 1–40.

Fernandez, R., Fogli, A., 2005. Culture: An Empirical Investigation of Beliefs, Work and Fertility. NBER Working Paper 11268.

Fehr, E., Naf, M., Schmidt, K., 2006. Inequality Aversion, Efficiency, and Maximin Preferences in Simple Distribution Experiments: Comment. Am. Econ. Rev. 96, 1912–1917.

Fong, C., 2001. Social Preferences, Self-Interest, and the Demand for Redistribution. J. Public Econ. 82, 225–246.

Fong, C., Luttmer, E., 2009. What Determines Giving to Hurricane Katrina Victims? Experimental Evidence on Racial Group Loyalty. American Economic Journal: Applied Economics 1 (2), 64–87.

Frohlich, N., Oppenheimer, J., 1992. Choosing Justice: An Experimental Approach to Ethical Theory. University of California Press, Berkeley.

Galor, O., Zeira, J., 1993. Income Distribution and Macroeconomics. Rev. Econ. Stud. 60, 35–52.

Giuliano, P., 2007. Living Arrangements in Western Europe: Does Cultural Origin Matter? J. Eur. Econ. Assoc. 5, 927–952.

Giuliano, P., Spilimbergo, A., 2009. Growing Up in a Recession: Beliefs and the Macroeconomy. NBER WP 15321.

Hodge, R.W., Nakao, K., Treas, J., 1990a. On Revising Prestige Scores for All Occupations. GSS Methodological Report No. 69, NORC, Chicago.
Hoffman, E., Spitzer, L., 1985. Entitlements, Rights and Fairness: An Experimental Examination of Subjects Concepts of Distributive Justice. J. Legal Stud. 14 (2), 259–297.
Inglehart, R., Norris, P., 2000. The Developmental Theory of the Gender Gap: Women and Men's Voting Behavior in a Global Perspective. International Political Science Review XXI, 441–463.
Lizzeri, A., Persico, N., 2004. Why Did the Elite Extend the Suffrage? Democracy and the Scope of Government with an Application to Britain's Age of Reform. Q. J. Econ. May, 451–498.
Luttmer, E., 2001. Group Loyalty and the Taste for Redistribution. J. Polit. Econ. 109 (3), 500–528.
Luttmer, E., Singhal, M., 2008. Culture, Context and the Taste for Redistribution. Harvard University mimeo.
McCarty, N., Poole, K., Rosenthal, H., 2006. Polarized America: The Dance of Ideology and Unequal Riches. MIT Press, Cambridge, MA.
Meltzer, Richard, 1981. A Rational Theory of the Size of Government. J. Polit. Econ. 89, 914–927.
Metcalfe, R., Sloane, P., 2007. Human Capital Spillovers and Economic Performance in the Workplace in 2004: Some British Evidence. IZA DP 2774.
Montgomery, R., Stuart, C., 1999. Sex and Fiscal Desire. University of California, Santa Barbara.
Perotti, R., 1993. Political Equilibrium, Income Distribution and Growth. Rev. Econ. Stud. 60 (4), 755–776.
Perotti, R., 1996. Growth, Income Distribution, and Democracy: What the Data Say. J. Econ. Growth 1 (2), 149–187.
Persson, T., Tabellini, G., 1995. Is ineqwualty Harmful for Growth?
Personn, T., Tabellini, G., 2002. Political Economics: Explaining Economics Policy. MIT Press, Cambridge, Massachusetts.
Pinker, S., 2006. The Blank Slate. Penguin Books.
Piketty, T., 1995. Social Mobility and Redistributive Politics. Q. J. Econ. 110, 551–584.
Rauch, J., 1993. Productivity Gains from Geographic Concentration of Human Capital. J. Urban Econ. 34, 380–400.
Rudd, J., 2008. Empirical Evidence un Human Capuital Spillovers. Unpublished.
Rawls, J., 1971. A Theory of Justice. Belknap Press of Harvard University Press, Cambridge, Massachusetts.
Rodriguez, F., 2004. Inequality, Redistribution and Rent Seeking. Economics and Politics 224–247.
Romer, T., 1975. Individual Welfare, Majority Voting and the Properties of a Linear Income Tax. J. Public Econ. 7, 163–188.
Shapiro, R., Mahajan, H., 1986. Gender Differences in Policy Preferences: A summary of trends from the 1960s to the 1980s. Public Opin. Q. 42–61.
Tan, J., 2006. Religion and Social Preferences: An Experimental Study. Econ. Lett. 90 (1), 60–67.
Todd, E., 1985. The Eplanation of Ideology: Family Structures and Social Systems. Basil Blackwell, Oxford.

CHAPTER 5

Theories of Statistical Discrimination and Affirmative Action: A Survey*

Hanming Fang[§] and Andrea Moro[¶]

Contents

1. Introduction 134
2. The Use of Group Averages as a Proxy for Relevant Variables: the Exogenous Differences Literature 137
   - **2.1** A basic model of signal extraction 137
   - **2.2** Generating average group wage differentials 138
     - *2.2.1 Employers' risk aversion* *138*
     - *2.2.2 Human capital investment* *139*
     - *2.2.3 Tournaments* *139*
3. Discriminatory Outcomes as a Result of Coordination Failure 140
   - **3.1** Origin of equilibrium models of statistical discrimination 140
   - **3.2** Coate and Loury (1993a) 142
     - *3.2.1 The model* *142*
     - *3.2.2 Firms and workers' best responses* *143*
     - *3.2.3 Equilibrium* *145*
4. Discriminatory Outcomes Due to Inter-Group Interactions 147
   - **4.1** Discrimination as group specialization 147
     - *4.1.1 A model with production complementarities and competitive wages* *147*
     - *4.1.2 Cross-group effects* *149*
     - *4.1.3 The effect of group size* *150*
   - **4.2** Discrimination from search frictions 151
   - **4.3** Endogenous group formation 156
   - **4.4** Group interactions from peer effects 161
5. Dynamic Models of Discrimination 162
6. Affirmative Action 163
   - **6.1** A brief historical background 163
   - **6.2** Affirmative action in Coate and Loury (1993a) 165
     - *6.2.1 Modeling affirmative action* *165*
     - *6.2.2 Patronizing equilibrium: an example* *166*

* We thank Alberto Bisin, Jan Eeckhout, Yariv Fadlon, and Kevin Lang for providing comments on an initial draft of this chapter. We also thank our coauthors Glenn Loury and Peter Norman for providing many insights on statistical discrimination and affirmative action.

§ Department of Economics, University of Pennsylvania, 3718 Locust Walk, Philadelphia, PA 19104; Duke University and the NBER. Email: hanming.fang@econ.upenn.edu

¶ Department of Economics, Vanderbilt University, 419 Calhoun Hall, Nashville, TN 37235. Email: andrea.moro@vanderbilt.edu

Handbook of Social Economics, Volume 1A
ISSN 0169-7218, DOI: 10.1016/S0169-7218(11)01005-7

6.3 General equilibrium consequences of affirmative action 170
6.4 Affirmative action in a two-sector general equilibrium model 173
6.5 Role model effects of affirmative action 176
6.6 Color sighted vs. Color blind affirmative action 178
6.6.1 Recent developments in the affirmative action policies related to college admission *178*
6.6.2 Color sighted vs. Color blind affirmative action with exogenous skills *179*
6.6.3 Color sighted vs. Colorblind affirmative action with endogenous skills *183*
6.7 Additional issues related to affirmative action 189
7. Efficiency Implications of Statistical Discrimination 191
7.1 Efficiency in models with exogenous differences 191
7.2 Efficiency in models with endogenous differences 193
7.2.1 The planners' problem *193*
7.2.2 The efficiency of discriminatory equilibria *195*
8. Conclusion 195
References 197

Abstract

This chapter surveys the theoretical literature on statistical discrimination and affirmative action. This literature suggests different explanations for the existence and persistence of group inequality. This survey highlights such differences and describes in these contexts the effects of color-sighted and color-blind affirmative action policies, and the efficiency implications of discriminatory outcomes.

JEL Classification Codes: J150, J160, J700, J780

Keywords

Affirmative Action
Discrimination

1. INTRODUCTION

Statistical discrimination generally refers to the phenomenon of a decision-maker using observable characteristics of individuals as a proxy for unobservable, but outcome-relevant, characteristics. The decision-makers can be employers, college admission officers, health care providers, law enforcement officers, etc., depending on the specific situation. The observable characteristics are easily recognizable physical traits, which are used in the society to broadly categorize demographic groups by race, ethnicity, or gender. But, sometimes the group characteristics can also be endogenously chosen, such as club membership or language.

In contrast to taste-based theories of discrimination (see Becker 1957), statistical discrimination theories derive group inequality without assuming racial or gender animus, or preference bias, against members of a targeted group. In statistical discrimination models, the decision makers are standard utility or profit maximizers; and in most, though not all, models, they are also imperfectly informed about some relevant characteristics of the individuals, such as their productivity, qualifications, propensity to engage in criminal activity, etc., which rationally motivates the use of group statistics as proxies of these unobserved characteristics. While all models of statistical discrimination share these features, there exist important differences, which suggest different explanations for group inequality. This survey is structured to present these explanations and highlight these differences.[1]

The two seminal articles in this literature – Phelps (1972) and Arrow (1973) – which are often cited together, proposed in fact two different sources of group inequality. In Phelps (1972), and the literature that originated from it, the source of inequality is some unexplained exogenous difference between groups of workers, coupled with employers' imperfect information about workers' productivity. In the classic textbook example, if employers believe (correctly) that workers belonging to a minority group perform, on average, worse than dominant group workers do, then the employers' rational response is to treat differently workers from different groups that are otherwise identical. In another example, which is sometimes mentioned in labor economic textbooks, employers believe from past experience that young female workers have less labor market attachment than men, perhaps because of a higher propensity to engage in child-rearing. Therefore, they will be reluctant to invest in specific human capital formation of women, even if women are equally qualified as men. The employers' inability to observe individual's true labor market attachment forces them to rely on the group average. This makes it harder for women to achieve a higher labor market status. We survey this strand of the literature in Section 2.

In the literature that originated from Arrow (1973), average group differences in the aggregate are endogenously derived in equilibrium, without assuming any *ex-ante* exogenous differences between groups. Even in this strand of literature decision makers hold asymmetric beliefs about some relevant characteristic of members from different groups, but the asymmetry of beliefs is derived in equilibrium. This is why these beliefs are sometimes referred to as "self-fulfilling stereotypes". The typical approach in this literature is to design a base model with only one group that is capable of displaying multiple equilibria. When membership to "ex-ante" identical groups is added to the setup, between-group inequality can be sustained as an equilibrium outcome when the discriminated group fails to coordinate on the same equilibrium played by the dominant group. While there are always symmetric, "color-blind" equilibria in which groups behave identically, groups do not interact in these models. This feature, together with equilibrium multiplicity, makes coordination failure possible for one group. We describe these models in Section 3.

[1] For earlier surveys of the related literature with a stronger emphasis on empirical research, see Cain (1986) and Altonji and Blank (1999).

Coordination failure is not the only source of inequality in models with self-fulfilling stereotypes. A recent strand of literature, which we describe in Section 4, emphasizes inter-group interactions in models with complementarities (for example in production technology). Asymmetric equilibria are possible where *ex-ante* identical groups specialize in tasks that have different marginal productivity. These equilibria may exist even when there is a unique symmetric equilibrium. Because of the complementarities, in this class of models there are conflicting interests among groups regarding issues such as affirmative action. Section 4 will also present a model where group inequality emerges as a result of job search frictions instead of informational frictions, and a model where group identities, as well as skill investment decisions, are endogenously chosen.

Most of these models, with some exceptions, are not designed to explain which group ends up being discriminated. Groups are *ex-ante* identical; therefore the focus of these theories lies more in trying to explain the persistence of inequality, rather than its origins, which are implicitly assumed to be based on historical factors. These considerations are more appropriately studied by dynamic models. We survey the small dynamic statistical discrimination literature in Section 5.

In Section 6, we will look at different policy implications from these models, in particular using the models with self-fulfilling stereotypes. Outcome-based policies, such as affirmative action quotas, or the application of disparate impact tests, seem particularly suited to eliminate inequality based on self-fulfilling stereotypes. If the imposition of the quota can eliminate the asymmetric discriminatory equilibria and lead different groups to coordinate on a symmetric outcome, then the temporary affirmative action policy might eliminate inequality. Typically, however, the literature finds that outcomes where inequality persists will remain possible, despite the fulfillment of the policy requirements. While policies may be designed so that only symmetric outcomes remain after their applications, such policies are typically dependent on special modeling assumptions. We also review in this section some interesting theoretical analysis that compares the "color-sighted" and "color-blind" affirmative action policies in college admissions.

Finally, Section 7 presents some considerations regarding the efficiency properties of discriminatory outcomes in statistical discrimination models, and Section 8 concludes.

The concept of statistical discrimination has been applied mostly to labor market examples where employers discriminate against one group of workers. This is why this survey presents mostly labor market related examples, but the reader is advised to consider that the same concepts and theories are applicable to other markets and socio-economic situations. We have chosen for convenience to use racial discrimination of *W(hites)* against *B(lacks)* as the running example because this has been the choice in most of the literature. This choice of notation should not be interpreted as implying that other examples are less relevant, or that racial inequality is the most relevant application of all the theories this survey will describe.

2. THE USE OF GROUP AVERAGES AS A PROXY FOR RELEVANT VARIABLES: THE EXOGENOUS DIFFERENCES LITERATURE

In this section, we describe a simple model where group identity serves as a proxy for unobserved variables that are relevant to economic outcomes. We begin with describing a version of the seminal model of statistical discrimination by Phelps (1972). This model generates inequality from different sources, depending on the details of how the labor market is modeled, and on the nature of the groups' intrinsic differences.

2.1 A basic model of signal extraction

Consider the example of an employer that does not observe with certainty the skill level of her prospective employees, but observes group identity $j \in \{B, W\}$. Workers' skill q is assumed to be equal to the value of their marginal product when employed, and is drawn from a normal skill distribution $N(\mu_j, \sigma_j^2)$. Employers observe group identity and a noisy signal of productivity, $\theta = q + \varepsilon$, where ε is a zero-mean error that is normally distributed according to $N(0, \sigma_{\varepsilon j}^2)$.

In a competitive labor market where all employers share the same type of information, workers are paid the expected productivity conditional on the value of the signal. Each employer infers the expected value of q from θ using the available information, including group identity. The skill and the signal are jointly normally distributed, and the conditional distribution of q given θ is normal with mean equal to a weighted average of the signal and the unconditional group mean (see DeGroot 2004):

$$E(q|\theta) = \frac{\sigma_j^2}{\sigma_j^2 + \sigma_{\varepsilon j}^2}\theta + \frac{\sigma_{\varepsilon j}^2}{\sigma_j^2 + \sigma_{\varepsilon j}^2}\mu_j \tag{1}$$

Intuitively, if the signal is very noisy (that is, if the variance of ε is very high), the expected conditional value of workers' productivity is close to the population average regardless of the signal's value. At the other extreme, if the signal is very precise ($\sigma_{\varepsilon j}$ is close to zero), then the signal provides a precise estimate of the worker's ability.

Phelps (1972) suggested two cases that generate inequality, which is implicitly defined as an outcome where two individuals with the same signal, but from different groups, are treated differently.

Case 1. In the first case, assume that groups' signals are equally informative, but one group has lower average human capital investment, that is, $\sigma_{\varepsilon B} = \sigma_{\varepsilon W} = \sigma_\varepsilon$, and $\sigma_B = \sigma_W = \sigma$, but $\mu_B < \mu_W$. In this case, B workers receive lower wages than W workers with the same signal, because employers rationally attribute them lower expected productivity, after observing they belong to a group with lower productivity.

Case 2. In the second case, the unconditional distributions of skills are the same between the two groups ($\sigma_B = \sigma_W = \sigma$, and $\mu_B = \mu_W = \mu$), but the signals employers receive are differently informative, e.g., $\sigma_{\varepsilon B} > \sigma_{\varepsilon W}$.[2] From this assumption, it follows that B workers with high signals receive lower wages than same-signal workers from the W group, and the opposite happens to workers with low signals.

While this basic model is capable of explaining differential treatment for same-signal workers from different groups, on average workers of the two groups receive the same average wage, unless average productivity is assumed to be exogenously different as in Case 1, which is not an interesting case from a theoretical perspective.

Note also that in this model all workers are paid their expected productivity conditional on available information. Thus, differential treatment of same-signal workers from different groups does not represent "economic discrimination," which is said to occur if two workers with identical (expected) productivity are paid differently.[3,4]

2.2 Generating average group wage differentials

In this section, we present various extensions of Phelps' model that generate different group outcomes. All of these extensions are based on Phelps' "Case 2" assumption of different signal informativeness across groups.[5]

2.2.1 Employers' risk aversion

Aigner and Cain (1977) proposed to incorporate employers' risk aversion into the standard Phelps' setup. Assuming, for example, that employers' preferences are given by:

$$U(q) = a + b\exp(-cq),$$

then employers' expected utility from hiring a worker with signal θ is given by:

$$E(U(q)|\theta) = a - b\exp\left[-cE(q|\theta) + \frac{c}{2}Var(q|\theta)\right].$$

From the properties of the conditional normal distribution we have:

$$Var(q|\theta) = \frac{\sigma_j^2\sigma_{\varepsilon j}^2}{\sigma_j^2 + \sigma_{\varepsilon j}^2},$$

which is increasing in $\sigma_{\varepsilon j}$. This implies that wages are decreasing in $\sigma_{\varepsilon j}$. Therefore the group with the higher noise (e.g., B workers if $\sigma_{\varepsilon B} > \sigma_{\varepsilon W}$) receives, on average, a lower wage. Employers are compensated for the risk factor incorporated in each B worker's higher uncertainty in productivity, measured by the term $cVar(q\,|\,\theta)/2$.

[2] This assumption can be rationalized assuming some communication of language barriers between employers and minorities, see, Lang (1986).

[3] See Stiglitz (1973) and Cain (1986) for early distinctions between statistical and economic discrimination.

[4] In Mailath, Samuelson and Shaked (2000) discussed in Section 4.2, differential treatment of workers with different races features economic discrimination.

[5] An example of an extension to "Case 1" is Sattinger (1998), where it is assumed that groups are homogenous in productivity but their workers differ in the probabilities of quitting their jobs. Firms observe quit rates imperfectly and profit maximization leads them to set unequal employment criteria or unequal interview rates across groups.

2.2.2 Human capital investment

Lundberg and Startz (1983) adopted a different approach, which was later exploited by the literature we will review in Sections 3 and 4. They assumed that worker's productivity q is partly determined by a costly human capital investment choice the worker undertakes before entering the labor market. Specifically, they parameterize $q = a + bX$, where X is human capital investment, b is a parameter common to all workers, and a is drawn from a normal distribution with mean μ and variance σ^2, common to groups B and W. The investment cost is a convex function $C(X) = cX^2/2$. After the human capital investment decision is made, the labor market works as in Case 2 of Phelps' model, that is, groups are assumed to differ in the information of the signal of productivity. Specifically, workers from group j with productivity q receive a signal $\theta = q + \varepsilon_j$ where as before ε_j is drawn from a Normal density $N(0, \sigma_{\varepsilon j}^2)$.

Following (1), group j workers choose human capital investment to solve:

$$\max_{X_j} \int E(q|\theta)d\theta - C(X_j)$$

$$= \max_{X_j} \int \frac{\sigma^2}{\sigma^2 + \sigma_{\varepsilon j}^2}(a + bX_j + \varepsilon_j)d\varepsilon_j + \frac{\sigma_{\varepsilon j}^2}{\sigma^2 + \sigma_{\varepsilon j}^2}\mu - \frac{1}{2}cX_j^2.$$

Thus group j workers' optimal human capital investment is:

$$X_j^* = \frac{b}{c}\frac{\sigma^2}{\sigma^2 + \sigma_{\varepsilon j}^2}, \tag{2}$$

that is, members of the group with the higher signal noise invest less than members from the group with the lower signal noise.[6] Assuming for example that $\sigma_{\varepsilon B}^2 > \sigma_{\varepsilon W}^2$, then in the labor market outcome workers from group B receive lower wages, on average, than workers from group W despite sharing the same distribution of *ex- ante* human capital endowment a. This outcome clearly relies on the existence of some form of heterogeneity across groups, namely, the signal informativeness.

2.2.3 Tournaments

Cornell and Welch (1996) embedded Phelps' "Case 2" assumption in a tournament model. Their observation was that if one group has a more informative signal, then this group's variance of the expected productivity is higher. For example, using Phelps' simple parameterization, workers with signal greater than the average have higher expected productivity if the signal is more precise, whereas the opposite is true for workers with a signal lower than their expected productivity. If labor demand is limited

[6] A version of this model can be written with heterogeneous investment costs. Moro and Norman (2003b) use this parameterization to generate log-normally distributed wages in equilibrium, which are suitable for empirical investigation.

compared to supply (e.g., the pool of candidates for a job is larger than the number of positions available), then jobs will go to the candidates with higher signals. Even if groups receive the same signals on average, the probability that the best signals belong to candidates from the dominant group is higher, which generates group inequality.

This intuition carries to more general paremeterizations. Cornell and Welch (1996) model information by assuming that many signals of productivity are available, all drawn from the same distribution, and assume that members of the dominant group can send employers a larger number of signals than members of the discriminated group. They prove that for any underlying signal distribution, the variance of the expected productivity is higher for the dominant group. As the number of candidates relative to the number of spots increase, the probability that members of the dominant group fill all positions approaches one.

3. DISCRIMINATORY OUTCOMES AS A RESULT OF COORDINATION FAILURE

In the models reviewed in Section 2, race, gender, or any group affiliation, is used in the determination of wages by firms in the competitive market because the distribution of signals about workers' productivity exogenously depends on the group identities. In this section, we review the literature that derives group differences endogenously even when groups share identical fundamentals. Outcomes with inequality can be thought of as the result of a self-fulfilling prophecy, and can be interpreted as group-wide coordination into the different equilibria of a base model in which group identity is ignored.

3.1 Origin of equilibrium models of statistical discrimination

Arrow's (1973) paper laid out the ingredients for a theory of discriminatory outcomes based on "self-fulfilling prophecies" with endogenous skill acquisition. First, the employers should be able to freely observe a worker's race. Second, the employers must incur some cost before they can determine the employee's true productivity (otherwise, there is no need for the use of surrogate information such as race or gender). Third, the employers must have some preconception of the distribution of productivity within each of the two groups of workers.

Arrow proposed the following model. Suppose that each firm has two kinds of jobs, skilled and unskilled, and the firms have a production function $f(L_s, L_u)$ where L_s is skilled labor and L_u is the unskilled labor. Denote with f_1 and f_2 the first derivatives of f with respect to the first and second arguments, respectively. All workers are qualified to perform the unskilled job, but only skilled workers can perform the skilled job.

Skills are acquired through investment. Workers have skill investment cost c, which is distributed in the population according to the cumulative distribution function $G(\cdot)$ which does not depend on group identity. Suppose that a proportion π_W of whites and a proportion of π_B of blacks are skilled, which will be determined in equilibrium. In order to endogenize the skill investment decisions, Arrow proposed the following model of wage differences between the skilled and unskilled jobs. Suppose that workers are assigned either to the skilled job or to the unskilled job. If a worker is assigned to the unskilled job, she receives a wage $w_u = f_2\ (L_s,\ L_u)$, independent of the race group of the worker. If a worker is assigned to the skilled job, then Arrow assumes that the worker will receive a wage contract that pays a group $j \in \{B,\ W\}$ worker wage $w_j > 0$ if that worker is tested to be skilled and 0 otherwise. Finally, the firm must pay a cost r to find out whether or not the worker is skilled. Arrow claims that competition among firms will result in a zero profit condition, therefore,

$$r = \pi_W[f_1(L_s, L_u) - w_W],$$
$$r = \pi_B[f_1(L_s, L_u) - w_B].$$

These imply that:

$$w_W = \frac{\pi_B}{\pi_W} w_B + \left(1 - \frac{\pi_B}{\pi_W}\right) f_1(L_s, L_u).$$

Note that if for some reason $\pi_B < \pi_W$, then $w_B < w_W$. Thus, blacks will be paid a lower wage in the skilled job if they are believed to be qualified with a lower probability. As a result, Arrow (1973) shifted the explanation of discriminatory behavior from preferences to beliefs.

Arrow then provided an explanation for why π_W and π_B might differ in equilibrium even though there are no intrinsic differences between groups in the distribution of skill investment cost $G\ (\cdot)$. Workers invest in skills if the gains of doing so outweigh the costs. Arrow takes the gains to be $w_j - w_u$ for group j workers.[7] Given the distribution of skill investment cost $G\ (\cdot)$, the proportion of skilled workers is $G\ (w_j - w_u)$, namely the fraction of workers whose skill investment cost c is lower than the wage gain from skill investment $w_j - w_u$. Equilibrium requires that:

$$\pi_j = G(w_j(\pi_W, \pi_B) - w_u), \ \text{for}\ j \in \{B, W\}. \tag{3}$$

In a symmetric equilibrium, $\pi_W = \pi_B$, and in an asymmetric equilibrium, $\pi_B \neq \pi_W$. Arrow then notes that the system (3) can have symmetric as well as asymmetric equilibria. The intuition for the asymmetric equilibria is simple: if very few workers invest in a particular group, the firms will rationally perceive this group as unsuitable for the skilled task and equilibrium wages for this group in the skilled job will be low, which will in turn give little incentive for the workers from this group to invest. That is, self-fulfilling prophecies can lead to multiple equilibria. If groups coordinate on different

[7] Note that this is not entirely consistent with the labor market equilibrium conditions. Because $w_u > 0$, and any unqualified worker who is hired on the skilled job will eventually get a wage 0, no unqualified worker should agree to be hired on the skilled job in the first place.

equilibria, then discrimination arises with one group acquiring less human capital and receiving lower wages than the other group.[8]

3.2 Coate and Loury (1993a)

Coate and Loury (1993a) presented an equilibrium model of statistical discrimination where two *ex ante* identical groups may end up in different, Pareto ranked, equilibria. Coate and Loury's model formalizes many of ideas that were originally presented loosely in Arrow (1973), but it assumes that wages are set exogenously from the model.[9] The key element of Coate and Loury's model is that a worker's costly skill investment may not be perfectly observed by firms. Thus, firms may rely on the race of the worker as a useful source of information regarding the worker's skill. This introduces the possibility of self-fulfilling equilibria. If the firms believe that workers from a certain racial group are less likely to be skilled, and thus impose a higher threshold in assigning these workers to higher paying jobs, it will indeed be self-fulfilling to lower these workers' investment incentives, which in turn rationalizes the firms' initial pessimistic belief. Analogously, more optimistic belief about a group can be sustained as equilibrium. This is the source of multiple equilibria in Coate and Loury model. Discriminatory outcomes arise if two groups of identical workers play different equilibria.

As in Arrow's model, *ex ante* discrimination is generated by "coordination failure." It is important to emphasize that in this model there are no inter-group interactions, other than possibly when affirmative action policies such as employment quotas are imposed (see Section 6). In contrast, in the models we discuss in Section 4, inter-group interaction is the key mechanism for discriminatory outcomes for *ex ante* identical groups.

3.2.1 The model

Consider an environment with two or more competitive firms and a continuum of workers with unit mass. The workers belong to one of two identifiable groups, B or W, with $\lambda \in (0, 1)$ being the fraction of W in the population.

Firms assign each worker into one of two task that we respectively label as "complex" and "simple". Coate and Loury assume that wages on the two tasks are exogenous and are as follows: a worker receives a net wage ω if he is assigned to the complex task, and 0 if he is assigned to the simple task. The firm's net return from workers, however, depends on the workers' qualifications and their assigned task, which are summarized in Table 1. Thus the qualification is important for the complex task, but not for the simple task.

Workers are born to be unqualified, but they can become qualified if they undertake some costly *ex-ante* skill investment. Suppose that the cost of skill investment,

[8] Spence (1974) also suggested an explanation for group inequality based on multiple equilibria in his classic signaling model.

[9] This assumption can be relaxed in a model of linear production technology without affecting any of the main insights. New economic insights emerge if wages are endogenized in a model with nonlinear production technology. See Moro and Norman (2003a, 2004) described in Section 4.1.

Table 1 Firms' net return from qualified and unqualified workers in the complex and simple tasks

Worker\Task	Complex	Simple
Qualified	$x_q > 0$	0
Unqualified	$-x_u < 0$	0

denoted by c, is heterogenous across workers and is distributed according to cumulative distribution function (CDF) $G(\cdot)$, which is assumed to be continuous and differentiable. Importantly, $G(\cdot)$ is group independent: workers from different groups share the same cost distribution.

The most crucial assumption of the model is that workers' skill investment decisions are unobservable by the firms. Instead, firms observe a noisy signal $\theta \in [0, 1]$ of the worker's qualification. We assume that the signal θ is drawn from the interval $[0, 1]$ according to PDF $f_q(\theta)$ if the worker is qualified, and according to $f_u(\theta)$ if he is unqualified. The corresponding CDF of f_q and f_u are denoted by F_q and F_u, respectively. To capture the idea that the noisy signal θ is informative about the workers' qualification, we assume that the distributions $f_q(\cdot)$ and $f_u(\cdot)$ satisfy the following Monotone Likelihood Ratio Property (MLRP):

Assumption 1. ***(MLRP)*** *$l(\theta) \equiv f_q(\theta) / f_u(\theta)$ is strictly increasing and continuous in θ for all $\theta \in [0, 1]$.*

It is useful to observe that this assumption is without loss of generality: for any pair of distributions f_q and f_u, we can always rank the signals according to the ratio $f_q(\theta)/f_u(\theta)$ and re-label the signals in accordance to their rankings. As we will see below, the MLRP assumption has two important and related implications. First, it implies that qualified workers, i.e., workers who have invested in skills, are more likely than unqualified workers to receive higher signals; second, it also implies that the posterior probability that a worker is qualified is increasing in θ.

The timing of the game is as follows. In Stage 1, Nature draws workers' types, namely, their skill investment cost c from the distribution $G(\cdot)$; in Stage 2, workers, after observing their type c, make the skill investment decisions, which are not perfectly observed by the firms; instead, the firms observe a common test result $\theta \in [0, 1]$ for each worker drawn respectively from PDF $f_q(\cdot)$ or $f_u(\cdot)$ depending on the worker's skill investment decision; finally, in Stage 3, firms decide how to assign the workers to the complex and simple tasks.

3.2.2 Firms and workers' best responses

The equilibrium of the model can be solved from the last stage. To this end, consider first the firms' task-assignment decision. Suppose that a firm sees a worker with signal θ from a group where a fraction π has invested in skills. The posterior probability that such a worker is qualified, denoted by $p(\theta; \pi)$, follows from Bayes' rule:

$$p(\theta;\pi) = \frac{\pi f_q(\theta)}{\pi f_q(\theta) + (1-\pi)f_u(\theta)}. \tag{4}$$

This updating formula, (4), illustrates a crucial insight: in environments with informational frictions (because workers' skill investment decisions are not perfectly observed by the firms), firms' assessment about the qualification of *a particular worker* with test signal θ depends on their prior about the fraction of *the group* that has invested in skills, i.e., π. Hence, a worker's investment not only increases her own chances of obtaining higher signals and higher expected wages, but also increases the employers' prior of all workers from the same group. This informational externality is the key source of the multiplicity of equilibria in this model.

Now consider the firm's task assignment decision in Stage 3 of a worker with a test signal θ belonging to a group where a fraction π have invested in skills. Using Table 1, the firm's expected profit from assigning such a worker to the complex task is:

$$p(\theta;\pi)x_q - [1 - p(\theta;\pi)]x_u, \tag{5}$$

because with probability $p(\theta;\ \pi)$ the worker is qualified and will generate x_q for the firm, but with probability $1 - p(\theta;\ \pi)$ he is unqualified and will lead to a loss of x_u if he is mistakenly assigned to the complex task. On the other hand, if such a worker is assigned to the simple task, the firm's profit is 0. Thus, the firm will optimally choose to assign such a worker to the complex task in Stage 3 if and only if:

$$p(\theta;\pi)x_q - [1 - p(\theta;\pi)]x_u \geq 0. \tag{6}$$

Using the expression (4) for $p\ (\theta;\ \pi)$, (6) is true if and only if:

$$\frac{f_q(\theta)}{f_u(\theta)} \geq \frac{1-\pi}{\pi}\frac{x_u}{x_q}. \tag{7}$$

Because of the MLRP assumption that f_q/f_u is monotonically increasing in θ, (7) holds if and only if $\theta \geq \widetilde{\theta}(\pi)$ where the threshold $\widetilde{\theta}(\pi)$ is determined as follows. If the equation:

$$\frac{f_q(\theta)}{f_u(\theta)} = \frac{1-\pi}{\pi}\frac{x_u}{x_q} \tag{8}$$

has a solution in (0,1), then $\widetilde{\theta}(\pi)$ is the unique solution (where the uniqueness follows from the MLRP); otherwise, $\widetilde{\theta}(\pi) = 0$ if $f_q(0)/f_u(0) \geq (1-\pi)x_u/(\pi x_q)$, and $\widetilde{\theta}(\pi) = 1$ if $f_q\ (1)/f_u\ (1) \leq (1 - \pi)\ x_u/(\pi\ x_q)$. It is also clear that whenever the threshold $\widetilde{\theta}(\pi) \in (0,1)$, we have

$$\frac{d\widetilde{\theta}}{d\pi} = -l'(\widetilde{\theta}(\pi))\frac{x_u}{x_q}\frac{1}{\pi^2} < 0, \tag{9}$$

where $l(\theta) \equiv f_q(\theta)/f_u(\theta)$. That is, as the prior probability that a worker is qualified gets higher, the firms use a lower threshold of the signal in order to assign a worker to the complex task.

Now we analyze the workers' optimal skill investment decision at Stage 2, given the firms' sequentially rational behavior in Stage 3 as described above.

Suppose that in Stage 3, the firms choose a task assignment that follows a cutoff rule at $\tilde{\theta}$. If a worker with cost c decides to invest in skills, he expects to be assigned to the complex task, which pays $\omega > 0$, with probability $1 - F_q(\tilde{\theta})$ which is the probability that a qualified worker will receive a signal above $\tilde{\theta}$ (recall that F_q is the CDF of f_q). Thus his expected payoff from investing in skills in Stage 2 is:

$$\left[1 - F_q(\tilde{\theta})\right]\omega - c. \tag{10}$$

If he does not invest in skills, the signal he receives will nonetheless exceed $\tilde{\theta}$, and thus will be mistakenly assigned to the complex task with probability $1 - F_u(\tilde{\theta})$ (recall that F_u is the CDF of f_u). Hence his expected payoff from not investing in skills is:

$$\left[1 - F_u(\tilde{\theta})\right]\omega. \tag{11}$$

Hence, a worker with cost c will invest if and only if:

$$c \leq I(\tilde{\theta}) \equiv \left[F_u(\tilde{\theta}) - F_q(\tilde{\theta})\right]\omega. \tag{12}$$

The term $I(\tilde{\theta}) \equiv \left[F_u(\tilde{\theta}) - F_q(\tilde{\theta})\right]\omega$ denotes the benefit, or incentive, of the worker's skill investment as a function of the firms' signal threshold $\tilde{\theta}$ in the task assignment decision. A few observations about the benefit function $I(\cdot)$ can be useful. Note that:

$$I'(\tilde{\theta}) = \omega\left[f_u(\tilde{\theta}) - f_q(\tilde{\theta})\right] > 0 \tag{13}$$

if, and only if $l(\tilde{\theta}) < 1$. Because $l(\cdot)$ is assumed to be monotonic, it immediately follows that $I(\cdot)$ is a single peaked function. Moreover, $I(0) = I(1) = 0$. That is, if the firm assigns all signals (the case $\tilde{\theta} = 0$), or if the firm assigns no signals (the case $\tilde{\theta} = 1$) to the complex task, then workers will have no incentive to invest in skills. Figure 1 depicts one possible function $I(\cdot)$ satisfying these properties.

3.2.3 Equilibrium

Given the workers' optimal investment rule in response to the firms' assignment threshold $\tilde{\theta}$ as specified by (12), the fraction of workers who rationally invests in skills *given a cutoff* $\tilde{\theta}$ is simply the measure of workers whose investment cost c is below $I(\tilde{\theta})$, i.e.,

$$G(I(\tilde{\theta})) = G([F_u(\tilde{\theta}) - F_q(\tilde{\theta})]\omega). \tag{14}$$

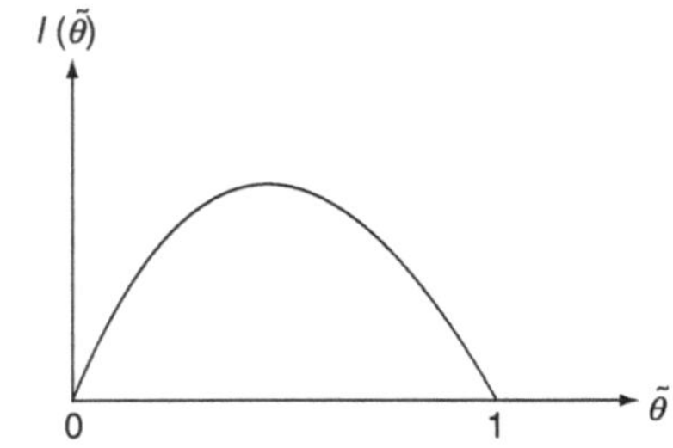

Figure 1 Incentives to invest in skills as a function of the cutoff $\widetilde{\theta}$.

An *equilibrium* of the game is a pair $(\widetilde{\theta}_j^*, \pi_j^*), j \in \{B, W\}$ such that for each j,

$$\widetilde{\theta}_j^* = \widetilde{\theta}(\pi_j^*) \tag{15}$$

$$\pi_j^* = G(I(\widetilde{\theta}_j^*)), \tag{16}$$

where $\widetilde{\theta}(\cdot)$ and $G\,(I(\cdot))$ are defined by (8) and (14) respectively. Equivalently, we could define the equilibrium of the model as $\pi_j^*, j \in \{B, W\}$, which satisfies:

$$\pi_j^* = G(I(\widetilde{\theta}(\pi_j^*))). \tag{17}$$

From the definition of equilibrium, we see that the only way to rationalize discriminatory outcome for the blacks and whites is when the above equation has multiple solutions.

Existence of multiple equilibria is not always guaranteed and depends on the shape of I and G. This possibility can be proven by construction by fixing all parameters of f_q, f_u, and technology parameters x_q, x_u, ω, and finding an appropriate cost distribution G such that the system (15)–(16) has multiple solutions. Note that since G is a CDF, it is an increasing function of its argument. Therefore, the right-hand side of (16) is a monotone transformation of (13). This means that function (16) must be initially increasing, at least in some range of θ near 0, and subsequently decreasing, at least in some range of θ near 1.

We can find a multitude of functions G that ensure multiple equilibria. For example, assume that all workers have a cost of investment zero or positive, so that $G\,(0) = 0$. In this case there is always a trivial equilibrium with $\pi = 0, \widetilde{\theta} = 1$. To ensure existence of at least one interior equilibrium, pick $\theta' \in (0, 1)$, and compute π' by inverting (15). Next, compute $I\,(\theta')$ from (13). If there are a fraction π' of workers with cost less than or equal to $I(\theta')$, then π' is an equilibrium, and there is an infinite number of distributions G that satisfy this condition. Using the same logic, one can construct G functions that are consistent with more than one interior equilibria. This is illustrated in Figure 2, which we drew assuming that there exists some $\widetilde{\theta}$ at which the curve $G\,(I\,(\cdot))$ is higher than the inverse of $\widetilde{\theta}(\cdot)$.

When groups select different solutions to Equation (17), they will display different equilibrium human capital investment, employment, and average wages despite having identical fundamentals regarding investment cost and information technology. Thus, Coate and Loury demonstrate that statistical discrimination is a logically consistent

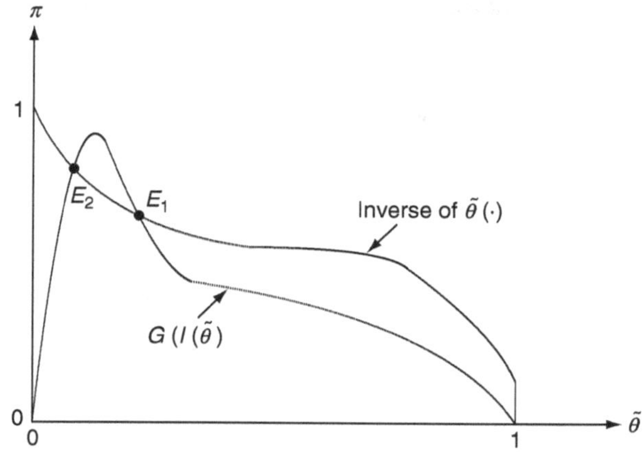

Figure 2 Multiple equilibria in Coate and Loury (1993a).

notion in their model. Discrimination in this model can be viewed as a coordination failure. Equilibria in this model are also Pareto-ranked, as it can be shown that both the workers and the firms would strictly prefer to be in the equilibrium where a higher fraction of workers invests in skills. Group inequality would be eliminated if somehow the blacks and the firms could coordinate on the good equilibrium. Importantly, there is no conflict of interests between whites and blacks concerning the equilibrium selection: if blacks were to coordinate on the better equilibrium, whites would not at all be affected. However, efficiency considerations are somewhat incomplete in this model because wages are set exogenously. We will describe efficiency in equilibrium models of statistical discrimination in more detail in Section 7.

4. DISCRIMINATORY OUTCOMES DUE TO INTER-GROUP INTERACTIONS

In Coate and Loury (1993a), discriminatory outcomes arise in a model where groups could live in separate islands. The privileged group will have no objection whatsoever if the disadvantaged group is able to coordinate themselves into the Pareto dominant equilibrium. In many real-world scenarios, however, we observe conflicts of interest between groups. Models that introduce inter-group interactions in the labor market yield some important insights regarding the potential sources of discrimination. In this section, we describe this literature.

4.1 Discrimination as group specialization

4.1.1 A model with production complementarities and competitive wages

Moro and Norman (2004) relaxed the crucial assumptions guaranteeing group separation in Coate and Loury's model: the linearity of the production technology and the exogeneity of wages. They extended Coate and Loury's framework by assuming a more general technology. In their model output is given by $y(C, S)$, where S is the quantity of workers employed in the simple task, and C is the quantity of *qualified* workers assigned to the complex task; y is strictly quasi-concave, exhibits constant returns to scale and satisfies Inada conditions so that both factors are essential. We use the notation introduced in Section 3.2, and write $x_q(C, S)$ and $x_u(C, S)$ as the marginal products of a *qualified* worker in the complex task, and of any worker employed in the simple task, which now depend on aggregate inputs.

We now characterize the equilibrium in this model. A *Bayesian Nash equilibrium* of the game is a list including the workers' skill investment decision for each cost c, firms task assignment rules, and wage schedules such that every player optimizes against other players' strategy profiles. It can be shown that the optimal task assignment is a threshold rule almost everywhere, where only workers above the threshold $\widetilde{\theta}_j, j = B, W$, are employed in the complex task. Recall that group shares are denoted with λ_j, $j = B, W$. Factor inputs can be computed as follows:

$$S = \sum_{j \in \{B,W\}} \lambda_j \left[\pi_j F_q(\widetilde{\theta}_j) + (1 - \pi_j) F_u(\widetilde{\theta}_j) \right]$$

$$C = \sum_{j \in \{B,W\}} \lambda_j \pi_j \left(1 - F_q(\widetilde{\theta}_j) \right).$$

The thresholds have to be jointly determined for the two groups, because the values of x_q and x_u depend on both groups' assignment rules, given both groups' aggregate investment π_j. The first order conditions are derived from $\max_{\{\widetilde{\theta}_B, \widetilde{\theta}_W\}} y(C, S)$, which are given by:

$$\begin{gathered} \left[\pi_j f_q(\widetilde{\theta}_j) + (1 - \pi_j) f_u(\widetilde{\theta}_j) \right] x_u(C, S) = \pi_j f_q(\widetilde{\theta}_j) x_q(C, S) \\ \Rightarrow \frac{\pi_j f_q(\widetilde{\theta}_j)}{\pi_j f_q(\widetilde{\theta}_j) + (1 - \pi_j) f_u(\widetilde{\theta}_j)} = \frac{x_u(C, S)}{x_q(C, S)}, j = B, W \end{gathered} \tag{18}$$

It shows that the input factor ratio C/S is monotonically increasing with the fraction of investors of any group. To see this, note that, if it decreased when π_j increased, then the right-hand side of (18) would decrease. But then the only way to satisfy the first order condition is to decrease $\widetilde{\theta}_j$, because the left-hand side is decreasing in $\widetilde{\theta}_j$ due to the monotone likelihood ratio property assumed for f_q and f_u. However, if both $\widetilde{\theta}_j$ decrease and π_j increase then the factor ratio increases a contradiction.

To understand how this implication affects group incentives to invest in human capital, note that the incentive to invest in Coate and Loury $[F_u(\widetilde{\theta}) - F_q(\widetilde{\theta})]\omega$ may increase or decrease depending only on the value of $\widetilde{\theta}$, because wages are set exogenously. Moro and Norman instead derive wages in equilibrium as the outcome of firms

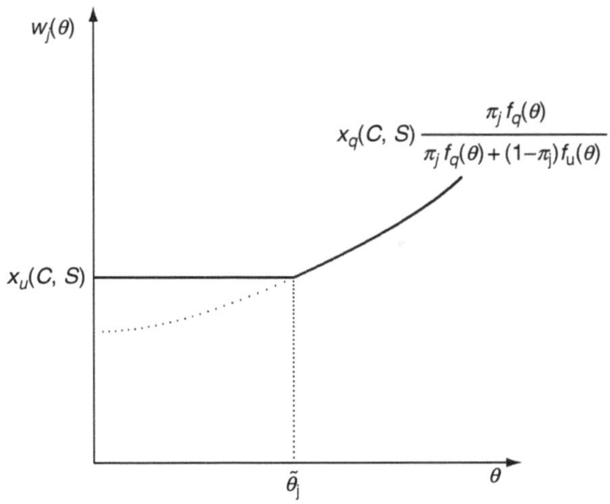

Figure 3 Wage as a function of the signal for group *j*.

competing for workers. It is possible to show that the solution corresponds to wages equal to the expected marginal productivity for almost all $\theta \in [0, 1]$, that is:

$$w_j(\theta) = \begin{cases} x_u(C, S) & \theta < \widetilde{\theta}_j \\ x_q(C, S)\dfrac{\pi_j f_q(\theta)}{\pi_j f_q(\theta) + (1 - \pi_j) f_u(\theta)} & \theta \geq \widetilde{\theta}_j \end{cases}. \quad (19)$$

Figure 3 depicts $w_j(\theta)$. Note that the signal value $\widetilde{\theta}_j$ is the one that equates the marginal products in the two tasks, because the term multiplied by $x_q(C, S)$ is the probability that a worker with signal θ is qualified (see equation (4)).

4.1.2 Cross-group effects

We can now compute incentives to invest and indicate them as a function of the vector of investment of the two groups $\boldsymbol{\pi} \equiv (\pi_B, \pi_W)$:

$$I(\boldsymbol{\pi}) = \int_\theta w_j(\theta) f_q(\theta) d\theta - \int_\theta w_j(\theta) f_u(\theta) d\theta.$$

To understand how groups interact, consider the effect on group-B incentives from an increase in π_W. As π_W increases, as noted above, the factor ratio C/S increases. The effect on the marginal product is to increase x_u and decrease x_q. The threshold $\widetilde{\theta}_B$ increases (at the margin, it becomes relatively more convenient to use W workers for the complex task because their likelihood to be qualified increases). This implies that it is more likely for a B worker to be assigned to the simple task (where wages are independent on the signal). Fewer B workers are assigned to the complex task and their wage is a flatter function of the signal than before. Taken together, these observations imply that incentives to invest in human capital decrease when the investment of members of the other group increase.[10]

This result is crucial because it generates incentives for groups to specialize in employment in different jobs. This creates the possibility for asymmetric equilibria to exist even when there is a unique symmetric equilibrium (symmetric equilibria where groups invest in the same proportion are always a possibility).

One asymmetric equilibrium can be constructed by assuming a distribution of investment cost with $G(0) > 0$, that is, by assuming that a fraction $G(0)$ of workers always invest.[11] Assume $\pi_B^* = G(0)$, and that the employers assign all B workers to the simple task. This is optimal if the marginal product of the group-B worker with signal $\theta = 1$ in the complex task is smaller than her marginal product in the simple task:

$$\frac{\pi_B f_q(1)}{\pi_B f_q(1) + (1 - \pi_B) f_u(1)} x_q(C, S) < x_u(C, S) \tag{20}$$

This inequality holds when $G(0) = \pi_B$ is small enough so that the left hand side is small. Note that this is true for any value of input factors C and S, which are not affected by the value of π_B when this inequality holds, because all B workers are in the simple task. To complete the characterization one has to find the equilibrium investment for group W, π_W. However, once group-B workers' behavior is set, the equilibrium level of π_W^* is just the solution of a fixed-point equation in π_W, which by continuity always exists. The equilibrium level of π_W^* must be interior because both factors are essential. The essentiality of both tasks implies that in equilibrium some group-W workers must be employed in the complex task, which implies that incentives to invest are positive for them, and therefore $\pi_W^* > \pi_B^* = G(0)$.

While other equilibria with both groups at an interior solution are possible, it is important to note that such equilibria cannot be interpreted as group-B's failure to coordinate on a better outcome. It is not possible for group-B workers to re-coordinate and invest as white workers do, because when workers of both groups invest in proportion π_W^*, the optimal factor ratio changes and marginal products are no longer consistent with equilibrium.

4.1.3 The effect of group size

Constant returns to scale imply that only *relative* group size matters. In general, analyzing group size effects would mean comparing different sets of equilibria. Not only the analysis becomes more complicated, but also as one parameter such as relative group size changes,

[10] The effect on incentives of group W of an increase in the same group's investment π_W is instead indeterminate, because we also have to take into account the informational externality that acts within groups. When investment increases in one group, the probability of being qualified of all workers from that group increases. This has a beneficial effect on the slope of the increasing portion of the wage function, which may overcome the negative "price" effect on the marginal products of labor we mentioned when we describe the cross-group effects.

[11] With some additional assumptions, it is possible to ensure that the model displays a unique symmetric equilibrium. See Moro and Norman (1996).

some equilibria may disappear and new ones may appear. Therefore, results depend on the details of the equilibrium selection. Intuitively, as the relative size of one group increases and approaches 1, equilibrium investment for this group will approach the values corresponding to the symmetric equilibria of the model (which are equivalent to the equilibrium of a model with only one group). As for the smaller group, depending on the parameterization either lower or higher investment could be consistent with equilibrium.

Nevertheless, we can rely on the simple corner solution constructed in example at the end of the previous section to understand the importance of group size. Because both factors are essential, as discriminated group becomes larger, it becomes more difficult to sustain the extreme type of task segregation implied by the discriminatory equilibrium constructed in the previous section. To see this, note that as the discriminated group becomes larger, the mass of workers employed in the simple task gets larger, and therefore the ratio or marginal products x_u/x_q gets smaller; eventually, the inequality (20) cannot be satisfied and some group-B workers have to be employed in the complex task. Then the incentives to invest in human capital for B workers become strictly positive.

Hence, in a sense, sustaining extreme segregation in equilibrium against large groups may be difficult, rationalizing the existence of institutionalized segregation, such as apartheid in South Africa, where the larger group was segregated into lower paying tasks before the collapse of apartheid. It can also be shown that the incentives for the small group workers to keep the larger group into the segregation-type of equilibrium gets larger the bigger the large group is. The reason is that the larger the mass of workers employed in the simple task is, the higher is the marginal product in the complex job. This increases the incentives to invest for the small group and their benefits from investment.

4.2 Discrimination from search frictions

All theories of statistical discrimination we have described so far are based on information friction in the labor market: race-dependent hiring policies are followed because race is used as a proxy for information about the workers' skills. However, all workers are paid their marginal product and, given skills, color does not play any additional role in explaining racial wage differences once we control for racial differences in their skill investment decisions. That is, there is no "economic discrimination" in the sense of Cain (1986).

Mailath, Samuelson, and Shaked (2000) proposed a model of an integrated labor market and focused on search frictions instead of information friction.[12] As in Moro and Norman (2004), they can derive discriminatory equilibria from a model that displays a unique symmetric equilibrium, but the distinguishing feature of search frictions is that discrimination arises even when employers have perfect information about workers' productivity.

[12] Early examples of statistical discrimination based on a search framework can be found in Verma (1995) and Rosén (1997). Eeckhout (2006) provides a different rationale for inequality arising in a search-matching environment. See Section (5) for more details.

Consider a continuum of firms and workers. All firms are identical, but each worker belongs to either group B or W. Group identity does not directly affect payoffs. For simplicity, suppose that the fraction of group W workers in the population, λ, is equal to 1/2.

All workers are born unskilled, and they make skill investment decisions before entering the labor market. If one acquires skills, he can enter the skilled labor market; otherwise, he enters the unskilled labor market. The crucial difference from the models we have seen so far is that there is no informational friction, that is, *workers' skill investment decisions are observed to the firms*. An individual's skill investment cost $c \geq 0$ is independently drawn from the distribution $G(\cdot)$. Finally, firms and workers die with Poisson rate δ and new firms and workers replace them so that the total populations of both firms and workers are constant. Time is continuous with interest rate r.

Each firm can hire at most one worker. If a firm employs a skilled worker, regardless of his color, a flow surplus of $x > 0$ is generated; the flow surplus from hiring an unskilled labor is 0.

Search frictions and wage determination. Vacant firms, meaning firms without an employee, and unemployed workers match through searches. Searches are assumed costless for both the firms and the workers. Given the assumption that the surplus for a firm from hiring an unskilled worker is 0, firms will only search for skilled workers. Firms make a key decision of whether to search either groups, or only one group. Suppose that a firm searches for workers of both groups, and suppose that the proportion of the skilled workers in the population is H_I and the unemployment rate of skilled workers is ρ_I, then the process describing meetings between unemployed skilled workers and the searching firm follows a Poisson process with meeting rate $\gamma_F \rho_I H_I$ where the parameter γ_F captures the intensity of firm search. If instead, the firm searches only white workers with intensity γ_F, then the meeting rate between the firm and the white skilled workers is given by $2\gamma_F \rho_I H_I$. Unemployed skilled workers simultaneously search for vacant firms with intensity γ_I and the meetings generated by workers search follow a Poisson process with rate $\gamma_I \rho_F$ where ρ_F is the vacancy rate of the firms. When an unemployed worker and a vacant firm match, they bargain over the wage with one of them randomly drawn to propose a take-it-or-leave-it offer.

Symmetric Steady State Equilibrium. We first characterize the symmetric steady state equilibrium in which firms do not pay any attention to the workers' color so we can treat the workers as a single population. We use subscript I to denote worker related variables in this section. Let V_I denote the value of skills to an individual in equilibrium. Since an individual will invest in skills only if his skill investment cost c is less than V_I, the fraction of skilled workers in the population will be $G(V_I)$. Let H_I be the proportion of skilled workers in the population in the steady state. We must have:

$$H_I = G(V_I) \tag{21}$$

in the steady state. The steady state condition for vacancies ρ_F is given by:

$$2\delta(1-\rho_F) = \rho_F \rho_I H_I(\gamma_I + \gamma_F). \tag{22}$$

In (22), the left hand side represents the rate of vacancy creation because $1 - \rho_F$ is the fraction of firms which are currently occupied, and at the rate 2δ either a worker dies, creating a vacancy at a previously occupied firm, or an occupied firm dies, and is replaced by a new vacant firm. The right hand side is the rate of vacancy destruction because of matches formed due to worker or firm searches. Similarly, the steady state condition for unemployment rate of the skilled worker ρ_I is given by:

$$2\delta(1-\rho_I) = \rho_F \rho_I(\gamma_I + \gamma_F). \tag{23}$$

Finally, we need to derive V_I. Let ω be the expected flow payoff of an employed worker and Z_I be the steady-state value of an employed skilled worker. First, familiar results from dynamic programming give us:

$$(r+2\delta)\ Z_I = \omega + \delta V_I,$$

where the left hand side $(r + 2\delta)\ Z_I$ can be interpreted as the properly normalized flow payoff of an employed worker, which is exactly equal to the wage ω plus, with probability δ, the worker obtains the expected present value of being returned to the unemployment pool by surviving a firm death, V_I. Similarly, when a skilled worker is unemployed, his value V_I is related to Z_I as follows:

$$[\rho_F(\gamma_F + \gamma_I) + r + \delta]\ V_I = \rho_F(\gamma_F + \gamma_I)\ Z_I.$$

On the firm side, let ϕ be the expected flow payoff to an occupied firm, V_F be the steady state value of a vacant firm, and Z_F be the steady state value of a firm who is currently employing a skilled worker. Since $\omega + \phi = x$, the total flow surplus, we know that the total surplus when a vacant firm and an unemployed worker match, denoted by S, must satisfy:

$$(r+2\delta)\ S = x + \delta(V_I + V_F).$$

Since the firm and the worker divide the surplus from the relationship relative to the status quo, given by $S - V_F - V_I$, via Nash bargaining, we have:

$$Z_I = V_I + \frac{1}{2}(S - V_F - V_I),$$

$$Z_F = V_F + \frac{1}{2}(S - V_F - V_I).$$

Thus, we can obtain:

$$V_I = \frac{\rho_F(\gamma_F + \gamma_I)x}{(r+\delta)[(\rho_F + \rho_I H_I)(\gamma_F + \gamma_I) + 2(r+2\delta)]}, \tag{24}$$

$$V_F = \frac{\rho_I H_I(\gamma_F + \gamma_I)x}{(r+\delta)[(\rho_F + \rho_I H_I)(\gamma_F + \gamma_I) + 2(r+2\delta)]} \tag{25}$$

A symmetric steady state is a list (H_I, ρ_I, ρ_F, V_I, V_F) satisfying the steady state conditions (21)–(25). A symmetric steady state is a symmetric equilibrium if the postulated search behavior of the firms, i.e., each firm searches both colors of workers, is optimal. Obviously, since the two groups of workers are behaving identically, any symmetric steady state will indeed be a symmetric equilibrium. With some algebra, Mailath, Shaked, and Samuelson showed that a symmetric equilibrium exists and is unique.

Asymmetric Equilibrium. Now consider the asymmetric equilibrium in which firms search *only white workers*. Under the postulated search behavior of the firms, skilled black workers can be matched to firms only through the worker searches, but the skilled white workers can be matched to firms both through the searches initiated by the workers and the firms. Now first consider the steady state conditions for the postulated asymmetric equilibrium. In this section, we use subscript W and B to denote group-W and group-B related variables respectively.

Let H_W and H_B denote the fraction of skilled workers among white and black population respectively, and let V_W and V_B denote the value of skill for white and black workers respectively. As in the symmetric equilibrium case, the skilled worker steady state conditions are:

$$H_W = \frac{G(V_W)}{2}, \tag{26}$$

$$H_B = \frac{G(V_B)}{2}. \tag{27}$$

Likewise, the vacancies steady state condition will now read:

$$2\delta(1-\rho_F) = 2\rho_F\gamma_F H_W \rho_W + (\rho_W H_W + \rho_B H_B)\gamma_I \rho_F. \tag{28}$$

The white and black unemployment rate steady state conditions are:

$$2\delta(1-\rho_W) = \rho_W \rho_F(\gamma_I + 2\gamma_F). \tag{29}$$

$$2\delta(1-\rho_B) = \rho_B \rho_F \gamma_I. \tag{30}$$

Now we characterize the relevant value functions in an asymmetric steady state. Let ω_j, $j \in \{B, W\}$, be the expected wage of a skilled worker with race j, Z_j be the present value of a race-j employed skilled worker, V_F be the present value of a vacant firm, and $Z_{F,j}$ be the present value of a firm matched with a race-j skilled worker. We have the following relationships:

$$\begin{aligned}(r+2\delta)Z_j &= \omega_j + \delta V_j, j \in \{B, W\},\\ (r+2\delta)Z_{F,j} &= \phi_j + \delta V_F, j \in \{B, W\},\\ (\rho_F\gamma_I + r + \delta)V_B &= \rho_F\gamma_I Z_B,\\ V_B &= \rho_F(\gamma_I + 2\gamma_F)Z_W,\end{aligned}$$

Derivations similar to those for the symmetric steady state yield the following value functions in a white asymmetric steady state:

$$V_F = \frac{x}{(r+\delta)\Delta}\left\{\begin{array}{c}(2\gamma_F+\gamma_I)\rho_F\gamma_I(\rho_W H_W + \rho_B H_B)\\ +2(r+2\delta)[(2\gamma_F+\gamma_I)\rho_W H_W + \gamma_I\rho_B H_B]\end{array}\right\}, \quad (31)$$

$$V_B = \frac{\rho_F\gamma_I[2(r+2\delta) + (2\gamma_F+\gamma_I)\rho_F]x}{(r+\delta)\Delta}, \quad (32)$$

$$V_W = \frac{\rho_F(2\gamma_F+\gamma_I)[2(r+2\delta) + \rho_F\gamma_I]x}{(r+\delta)\Delta}, \quad (33)$$

where $x = \omega_j + \phi_j$, $j \in \{B, W\}$, is the total surplus, and:

$$\begin{aligned}\Delta \equiv\ & 2(r+2\delta)[(2\gamma_F+\gamma_I)(\rho_F + \rho_W H_W) + \gamma_I(\rho_F + \rho_B H_B) + 2(r+2\delta)]\\ & + \rho_F\gamma_I(2\gamma_F+\gamma_I)(\rho_F + \rho_W H_W + \rho_B H_B).\end{aligned}$$

A *white asymmetric steady state* is a list $(H_W, \rho_W, V_W, H_B, \rho_B, V_B, \rho_F, V_F)$ such that the balance equations (26)–(30) and the value functions (31)–(33) hold. It can be verified that in a white asymmetric steady state, black workers face a less attractive value of entering the skilled labor market than do white workers ($V_B < V_W$), and thus fewer black workers than white workers acquire skills ($H_B < H_W$). Black workers thus are at a disadvantage when bargaining with firms and, as a result, firms obtain a larger surplus from black workers ($\omega_B < \omega_W$ and $\phi_B > \phi_W$). Given this pattern of surplus sharing, a vacant firm would prefer to hire a black skilled worker than a white skilled worker ($Z_{F,B} > Z_{F,W}$). Moreover, since it is postulated that firms are only searching for white skilled workers, it must be the case that unemployment rate is higher among blacks than among whites ($\rho_B > \rho_W$).

However, in order for the postulated white asymmetric steady state to be consistent with equilibrium, the firms must find it optimal to only search the white workers. Let V_F $(B|W)$ (V_F $(BW|W)$, respectively) be the value of a firm searching only black workers (searching both black and white workers, respectively) if the other firms are all searching only the white workers. It can be shown that they are respectively given by:

$$V_F(B|W) = \frac{\gamma_I\rho_W H_W Z_{F,W} + (2\gamma_F+\gamma_I)\rho_B H_B Z_{F,B}}{\gamma_I\rho_W H_W + (2\gamma_F+\gamma_I)\rho_B H_B + r + \delta}, \quad (34)$$

$$V_F(BW|W) = \frac{(\gamma_I + \gamma_F)(\rho_W H_W Z_{F,W} + \rho_B H_B Z_{F,B})}{(\gamma_I + \gamma_F)(\rho_W H_W + \rho_B H_B) + r + \delta}. \tag{35}$$

The condition for white asymmetric steady state equilibrium is:

$$V_F \geq \max\{V_F(B|W), V_F(BW|W)\}. \tag{36}$$

Examining the expressions for V_F, $V_F(B|W)$ and $V_F(BW|W)$ as given by (31), (34) and (35), we can see that (36) can be true only if $\rho_B H_B < \rho_W H_W$ in a white asymmetric equilibrium. Since we already know that $\rho_B > \rho_W$ in the asymmetric steady state, it thus must be the case that $H_B < H_W$. That is, to be optimal for the firms to only search for white workers in the white asymmetric equilibrium, there must be a sufficiently low fraction of skilled black workers. That is, the postulated discriminatory search behavior of the firms in favor of whites must generate a sufficiently strong *supply side response* on the part of workers in their skill investment decisions in order for the firms' search behavior to be optimal. The intuition is quite simple: In order for the firms not to search for blacks, and knowing that in equilibrium the wages for black skilled workers are lower, it must be the case that there are a lot fewer black skilled workers in order for the trade-off between a larger surplus from each hired black worker and a smaller probability of finding such worker to be in favor of not searching blacks.

Mailath, Samuelson, and Shaked (2000) show that a sufficient condition for a white asymmetric equilibrium is that when firms' search intensity γ_F is sufficiently large relative to that of the search intensity of the workers γ_I. The intuition for this result is as follows: when firms' searches are responsible for a sufficiently large fraction of the contacts between firms and workers, a decision by the firms not to search the black workers will almost ensure that skilled black workers would not find employment; thus, depressing their incentives to acquire skills, which in turn justifying the firms' decision not to search the black workers. Therefore, this paper shows how search friction might generate group inequality even when employers have perfect information about their workers and would strictly prefer to hire workers from the discriminated group. Holden and Rosén (2009) show in a similar framework that the existence of prejudiced employers may also make it more profitable for nondiscriminatory employers to discriminate.

4.3 Endogenous group formation

The models presented so far assume that individuals' group identities are exogenous. In some situations, group identity is not as immutable as one's skin color or gender, but is defined by characteristics that are more amenable to change, albeit at costs. Fang (2001) presents a model of discrimination with endogenous group formation, where he showed that endogenous group formation and discrimination can in fact coexist, and the resulting market segmentation in the discriminatory equilibrium may lead to welfare improvement. Relative to Coate and Loury (1993a), Fang's model keeps their linear production technology, but endogenizes group identity choices; in addition, wages are set endogenously *à la* Moro and Norman (2003a) (see Section 4.1).

Benchmark Model with No Group Choice. The benchmark is a model without endogenous group choices. There are two (or more) firms, indexed by $i = 1, 2$. They both have a traditional (old) and a new technology at their disposal. Every worker can produce 1 unit of output with the traditional technology. Workers with some requisite skills can produce $x_q > 1$ units of outputs with the new technology, but those without the skills will produce 0. We assume that the firms are risk neutral and maximize expected profits.

There is a continuum of workers of unit mass in the economy. Workers are heterogeneous in their costs of acquiring the requisite skills for the new technology. Suppose for simplicity that a worker is either a *low cost type* whose skill acquisition cost is c_l or a *high cost type* with cost c_h where $0 < c_l < c_h$. The fractions of low cost and high cost workers are λ_l and λ_h respectively with $\lambda_l + \lambda_h = 1$. A worker's cost type is her private information. It is assumed that the workers are risk neutral and that they do not directly care about the technology to which they are assigned.

To dramatize the market failure caused by informational free riding, suppose that it is socially optimal for every worker to invest in skills and use the new technology, i.e., $x_q - c_h > 1$.

The timing of the game and the strategies of the players are as follows. First, workers, observing their cost realization $c \in \{c_l, c_h\}$, decide whether to invest in skills, e: $\{c_h, c_l\} \to \{e_q, e_u\}$. Firms do not perfectly observe a worker's investment decision, instead they observe in the second stage a signal $\theta \in [0, 1]$ about each worker. The signal θ is distributed according to probability density function f_q for qualified workers and f_u for unqualified ones. We assume that $f_q(\cdot)/f_u(\cdot)$ is strictly increasing in θ. In the third stage, the firms compete in the labor market for workers by simultaneously announcing wage schedules as functions of the test signal θ. A pure action of firm i at this stage is a mapping $w_i : [0, 1] \to \Re_+$. Workers then decide for which firm to work after observe wage schedules w_1 and w_2. Finally, each firm allocates its available workers between the old and new technologies using an assignment rule which is a mapping $t_i : [0, 1] \to \{0, 1\}$, where $t_i(\theta) = 1$ (respectively, 0) means that firm i assigns all workers with signal θ to the new (respectively, old) technology.

A *Bayesian Nash equilibrium* of the game is a list including the workers' skill investment decision profile e and offer acceptance rules, and the firms' wage schedules and technology assignment rules $\{w_i(\cdot), t_i(\cdot)\}$ such that every player optimizes against other players' strategy profiles. Wages in equilibrium must be equal to workers' expected marginal product for almost all $\theta \in [0, 1]$, as in equation (19):

$$w_1(\theta) = w_2(\theta) = w(\pi, \theta) \equiv \max\left\{1, \frac{\pi f_q(\theta)}{\pi f_q(\theta) + (1-\pi) f_u(\theta)} x_q\right\}; \tag{37}$$

and the firms' equilibrium assignment rule must be $t_1(\theta) = t_2(\theta) \equiv t(\theta)$, where $t(\theta) = 1$ if for almost all $\theta \in [0, 1]$:

$$\frac{\pi f_q(\theta)}{\pi f_q(\theta) + (1 - \pi) f_u(\theta)} x_q \geq 1.$$

To analyze workers' skill investment decisions in Stage 1, note that the *private benefit* of skill investment when a fraction π of the population is skilled is:

$$I(\pi) = \int_0^1 w(\pi, \theta)[f_q(\theta) - f_u(\theta)]d\theta.$$

Because the private benefit is a function of π, there is *informational free riding*. In fact, the informational free riding problem may lead to $\pi = 0$ being the unique equilibrium outcome. Specifically, define Π_l and Π_h to be the sets of values of π that will respectively induce low and high cost type workers to invest in the skills, that is, $\Pi_l \equiv \{\pi \in [0, 1]: I(\pi) \geq c_l\}$; $\Pi_h \equiv \{\pi \in [0, 1]: I(\pi) \geq c_h\}$. Then it can be shown that any economy where $\Pi_l \neq \emptyset$ and $\min \Pi_l > \lambda_l$; but $\Pi_h = \emptyset$ will have a unique equilibrium with $\pi = 0$. The intuition is analogous to a domino effect: $\Pi_h = \emptyset$ implies that type-c_h workers will never invest in skills, but the presence of the high cost types dilutes the benefit of skill investment for type-c_l types.

Endogenous Group Choices and Discriminatory Equilibrium. Now suppose there is an activity A that workers can undertake. Let $V \in \mathfrak{R}$ be a worker's utility (or disutility if negative) in monetary terms from activity A. Therefore, each worker now has two private characteristics (c, V). Let $H(V|c)$ denote the cumulative distribution of V conditional on the skill acquisition cost c. Importantly, assume that whether a worker undertakes activity A is *observable* to firms. The defining characteristic of a cultural activity is that it is *a priori* completely irrelevant to other economic fundamentals, which is captured by two assumptions: (1). $H(V|c_l) = H(V|c_h) \equiv H(V)$, where H is continuous and strictly increasing in V with support $[\underline{V}, \bar{V}] \subset \mathfrak{R}$; (2) A worker's test signal, and her qualification for the new technology are not affected by whether she undertakes activity A. The game is expanded to include one additional stage where a worker of type (c, V) chooses $j \in \{A, B\}$, where $j = A$ means that she undertakes activity A and $j = B$ that she does not. She derives from activity A (dis)utility V if she chooses $j = A$, and zero utility otherwise. Write the activity choice profile as $g: \{c_l, c_h\} \times [\underline{V}, \bar{V}] \to \{A, B\}$. Workers who choose A will be called *A-workers*, and those who choose B, *B-workers*.

Because of the *a priori* irrelevance of activity A we can suitably augment the equilibrium decision rules of the basic model, and obtain an equilibrium of the augmented model in which activity A plays no role in the firms' wage offer schedules and technology assignments. The activity and skill acquisition choices in this type of equilibrium,

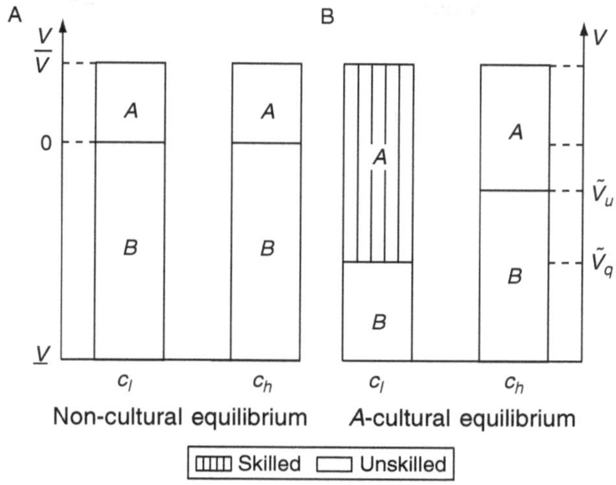

Figure 4 Activity and Skill Acquisition Choices: Fang (2001).

dubbed "non-cultural equilibrium," are pictured in Figure (4a). It is obvious that in the non-cultural equilibrium, no workers are skilled; hence, the new technology is not adopted.

The introduction of the observable activity A allows the firms potential to offer wage schedules and technology assignment rules contingent on whether activity A is undertaken. If firms do use this type of contingent wage schedules then workers may undertake activity A for instrumental reasons. If A-workers are preferentially treated (in a manner to be made precise below), then some workers who intrinsically dislike activity A may choose A to get the preferential treatment. Of course, in equilibrium it must be rational for firms to give preferential treatment to A-workers.

An *A-cultural equilibrium* is defined to be a Bayesian Nash equilibrium of the augmented model in which a positive mass of A-workers are assigned to the new technology, while all B-workers are assigned to the old technology. Now consider an A-cultural equilibrium. Since B-workers are never assigned to the new technology, in this equilibrium the fraction of the skilled among B-workers, denoted by π_B, must be zero. Furthermore, in order for some positive fraction of A-workers to be assigned to the new technology, the proportion of the skilled among A-workers, denoted by π_A, must belong to the set Π_l. An A-cultural equilibrium exists if for some value $\pi_A \in \pi_l$, the population will self-select the activity choices such that the fraction of c_l types among A-workers is exactly π_A.

As before, workers will still be paid their expected productivity. Therefore firm i's sequentially rational wage offer schedule to B-workers, $w_i{}^B$, is:

$$w_1^B(\theta) = w_2^B(\theta) = w(0, \theta) = 1 \text{ for all } \theta \in [0, 1].$$

Suppose that the proportion of the skilled among A-workers is π_A. Then firm i's equilibrium wage schedule to A-workers, w_i^A, is:

$$w_1^A(\theta) = w_2^A(\theta) = w(\pi_A, \theta).$$

For every π_A, the expected wage of a skilled A-worker is $W_q^A(\pi_A) = \int_0^1 w(\pi_A, \theta) f_q(\theta)\, d\theta$, and that of an unskilled A-worker is $W_u^A(\pi_A) = \int_0^1 w(\pi_A, \theta) f_u(\theta)\, d\theta$. We can prove, by simple revealed preference arguments that the activity and skill-acquisition choice profiles under an A-cultural equilibrium, where the proportion of the skilled among A-workers is π_A, must be:

$$e(c, V) = \begin{cases} e_q & \text{if } c = c_l, V \geq 1 + c_l - W_q^A(\pi_A) \\ e_u & \text{otherwise} \end{cases}$$

$$g(c, V) = \begin{cases} A & \text{if } c = c_l, V \geq 1 + c_l - W_q^A(\pi_A) \\ A & \text{if } c = c_h, V \geq 1 - W_u^A(\pi_A) \\ B & \text{otherwise.} \end{cases}$$

Figure (4b) depicts the activity and skill acquisition choices in an A-cultural equilibrium where we have defined $\widetilde{V}_q(\pi_A) = 1 + c_l - W_q^A(\pi_A)$ and $\widetilde{V}_u(\pi_A) = 1 - W_u^A(\pi_A)$ as the threshold disutility values that respectively a skilled and an unskilled worker are willing to incur to be a member of the elites. Note that $W_q^A(\pi_A) - W_u^A(\pi_A) \geq c_l$ because $\pi_A \in \Pi_l$. Since $W_u^A(\pi_A) \gg 1$ whenever there is a positive mass of A-workers assigned to the new technology, we have:

$$\widetilde{V}_q(\pi_A) \ll \widetilde{V}_u(\pi_A) \ll 0. \tag{38}$$

Inequality (38) establishes that in a cultural equilibrium, a single-crossing property of the cultural activity is *endogenously* generated. More specifically, let us denote the *net* benefit to undertake activity A for a skilled and an unskilled worker with the same utility type V respectively by $B(e_q, V; \pi_A) = V - \widetilde{V}_q(\pi_A)$ and $B(e_u, V; \pi_A) = V - \widetilde{V}_u(\pi_A)$. Inequality (38) yields that $B(e_q, V; \pi_A) > B(e_u, V; \pi_A)$ for every type V. In other words, in any A-cultural equilibrium, a skilled worker is more willing than an unskilled one to endure disutility from activity A to be elite, which in turn justifies A-workers as elites. Undertaking activity A becomes a signaling instrument for skilled workers due to the endogenously generated single crossing property.

Fang (2001) provided the necessary and sufficient condition for the existence of A-cultural equilibria. For any $\pi_A \in \Pi_l$, define the proportion of the skilled among A-workers by a mapping $\Psi : [0, 1] \rightarrow [0, 1]$ given by:

$$\Psi(\pi_A) = \begin{cases} \dfrac{\lambda_l(1 - H(\widetilde{V}_q(\pi_A)))}{\lambda_l(1 - H(\widetilde{V}_q(\pi_A))) + \lambda_h(1 - H(\widetilde{V}_u(\pi_A)))} & \text{if } \pi_A \in \Pi_l \\ 0 & \text{otherwise} \end{cases}$$

where the numerator of the fraction is the total mass of skilled A-workers (see the shaded area in Figure 4b) and the denominator is the total mass of A-workers (the area marked "A" in Figure 4b). Every fixed-point of the mapping Ψ will correspond to an A-cultural equilibrium. Notice that by segmenting the labor market into A-workers and B-workers (by whether workers undertake the activity A,) it allows A-workers' skill investment choices depend only on the firms' perception of the proportion of the skilled among A-workers, instead of the firm's perception for the whole population as in the benchmark model. Let $\Delta \equiv \max_{\pi_A \in \Pi_1}[\Psi(\pi_A) - \pi_A]$ be the maximal difference between the function Ψ and the identity map. The necessary and sufficient condition for the existence of at least one A-cultural equilibrium is $\Delta \geq 0$.

Welfare. In a cultural equilibrium, the new technology is adopted by a positive mass of workers. In the mean time, some workers are enduring the disutility of activity A in order to be members of the elites. However, B-workers are exactly as well off as they are in the non-cultural equilibrium. By revealed preferences, A-workers are strictly better off than they are in the non-cultural equilibrium. Thus, any cultural equilibrium Pareto dominates the non-cultural equilibrium.

4.4 Group interactions from peer effects

An alternative source of cross-group interactions is studied by Chaudhuri and Sethi (2008), who extended the standard Coate and Loury's framework assuming that the distribution of the cost of investment in human capital, G, is a function of the mean peer group skill level s, computed as follows:

$$s_j = \eta \pi_j + (1-\eta)\bar{\pi}, j = B, W$$

where $\bar{\pi}$ is the fraction of skilled workers in the whole population and $\eta \in [0, 1]$ measures the level of segregation in the society. Positive spillover in human capital across groups is reflected in the assumption that G is increasing in s_j. Although G is the same across groups, the distribution of the cost of acquiring human capital for a given group is endogenous in this model, and may be different across groups if groups experience different levels of peer quality.

This parameterization allows the investigation of the relationship between integration and discrimination. Chaudhuri and Sethi show that integration may make it impossible to sustain negative stereotypes in equilibrium. To understand the intuition behind the main result, assume that when groups are completely segregated they coordinate on different equilibria. As integration increases, the peer group effect increases the cost of investment for the group with high investment and decreases the cost of investment for the other group; hence, the direct effect is to equalize the fractions of people that invest. Inequality may persist in equilibrium, but under some conditions, if integration is strong enough multiplicity of equilibria disappears and groups acquire the same level of human capital.

5. DYNAMIC MODELS OF DISCRIMINATION

The literature on the dynamic evolutions of discrimination is relatively sparse. Antonovics (2006) considers a dynamic model of statistical discrimination that accounts for intergenerational income mobility. She shows that when income is transmitted across generations through parental investments in the human capital of children, statistical discrimination can lead racial groups with low endowments of human capital to become trapped in inferior stationary equilibria. Fryer (2007) considers a dynamic extension of the Coate and Loury model, more specifically the example that Coate and Loury used to illustrate the potential for patronizing equilibrium with affirmative action as described in Section 6.2.2, by introducing an additional promotion stage after workers are hired. He uses the extension to ask how initial adversity in the hiring stage will affect the subsequent promotions for those minorities who are able to be assigned a job in the firm. The intuition he formalizes in the model can be termed as a possibility of "belief flipping." Specifically, suppose that an employer has negative stereotypes about a particular group, say the minorities, and discriminates against them in the initial hiring practice, relative to another group, say the majorities, for whom the employer has more stereotypes that are positive. Then, conditional on being hired, the minority workers within the firm may be more talented than the majority workers because they were held to a more exacting standard in the initial hiring. As a result, minorities who are hired in the firm may be more likely to be promoted. Fryer's (2007) analysis provides a set of sufficient conditions for the "belief flipping" phenomenon to arise.[13]

Blume (2006) presents an interesting dynamic analysis of statistical discrimination using ideas from evolutionary game theory. This paper adds a learning dynamic to a simplified version of Coate and Loury's static equilibrium model of statistical discrimination. The assignment of workers to firms and the opportunity for firms to experiment generate a random data process from which firms learn about the underlying proportions of skilled workers in the population. Under two plausible, but exogenously specified learning dynamics, long-run stable patterns of discrimination that appear in the data process can be characterized and related to the equilibria of the static model. Blume (2006) shows that long-run patterns of discrimination can be identified with particular equilibria. Although different patterns corresponding to different equilibria are possible, generically only one will be salient for any given specification of parameters.

Blume's (2006) dynamic model is cast in a discrete time setting where in each period, a certain measure of new workers are born and they will have to make unobservable skill investment decisions. A drawback of the discrete time setup is that there

[13] The flipping of the effect of race on the initial hiring probability and subsequent promotion probability may be used as a basis to empirically distinguish statistical discrimination from taste-based discrimination. Altonji and Pierret (2001) proposed and implemented a test of statistical discrimination based on the effect of race on worker wages over time with employer learning.

will be potential multiple equilibria in the skill investment decisions within each cohort due to coordination failure. Levin (2009) avoids this complication by considering a continuous time model where in any instant only one new worker arrives with some probability, thus avoiding the issue of equilibrium multiplicity resulting from coordination problems. As a result, the evolution of the fraction of skilled workers in Levin (2009) is consistent with the optimal behavior of the individuals. He showed that statistical discrimination equilibrium can be persistent even if policies are enacted to improve access to resources for the disadvantaged minorities.

Eeckhout (2006) provides an alternative theory of discrimination based on a search and matching model of a marriage market. This paper generates endogenous segregation in a dynamic environment where partners randomly match to play a repeated prisoner's dilemma game.[14] In this setup, the driving force behind inequality is the use of race as a public randomization device. When cooperation is expected from same-match partners, segregation outcomes might Pareto-dominate color-blind outcomes. Due to random matching, mixed matches always occur in equilibrium, and there may be less cooperation in mixed matches than in same-color matches, but mixed matches may be of shorter duration.

6. AFFIRMATIVE ACTION

6.1 A brief historical background

Affirmative action policies were developed during the 1960s and 1970s in two phases that embodied conflicting traditions of government regulations.[15] The first phase, culminating in the Civil Rights Act of 1964 and the Voting Rights Act of 1965, was shaped by the presidency and the Congress and emphasized nondiscrimination under a "race-blind Constitution." The second phase, shaped primarily by federal agencies and courts, witnessed a shift toward minority preferences during the Nixon administration. The development of two new agencies created to enforce the Civil Rights Act, the Equal Employment Opportunity Commission under Title VII and the Office of Federal Contract Compliance under Title VI of the Civil Rights Act, demonstrates the tensions between the two regulatory traditions and the evolution of federal policy from non-discrimination to minority preferences under the rubric of affirmative action. The results have strengthened the economic and political base of the civil rights coalition while weakening its moral claims in public opinion.

The main goals of the Civil Rights Act of 1964 were "the destruction of legal segregation in the South and a sharp acceleration in the drive for equal rights for women". Title VII, known as the Fair Employment Commission Title or FEPC Title, of the

[14] Fang and Loury (2005a, 2005b) explored a theory of dysfunctional collective identity in a repeated risk sharing game.

[15] See Holzer and Neumark (2000) for a more detailed historical and institutional background of affirmative action's in the U.S.

Civil Rights Act would create the Equal Employment Opportunity Commission (EEOC) to police job discrimination in commerce and industry with the intention to destroy the segregated political economy of the South and enforce nondiscrimination throughout the nation. Title VI of the Act, known as the Contract Compliance Title, "prohibits discrimination in programs receiving funds from federal grants, loans or contracts." The authority to cancel the contracts of failed performers and ban the contractors from future contract work backed contract compliance. The specter of bureaucrats telling businesses whom to hire under Title VII was raised during the congressional debates prior to the passage of the Civil Rights Act. The Senate majority leader of the time, Hubert Humphrey, promised to eat his hat if the civil rights bill ever led to racial preferences. President Lyndon Johnson signed the Civil Rights Act of 1964 into law on 2 July.

But Title VI of the Civil Rights Act of 1964 was the sleeper that led to affirmative action policies. In September 1965, President Johnson issued Executive Order 11246. This order intended to create new enforcement agencies to implement Title VI in the Civil Rights Act, and it repeated nondiscrimination. The Office of Contract Compliance (OFCC) was established by the Labor Department to implement Executive Order 11246. It designed a model of contract compliance based on a metropolitan Philadelphia plan, which required that building contractors submit "pre-award" hiring schedules listing the number of minorities to be hired, with the ultimate goal to make the proportion of blacks in each trade equal to their proportion of metropolitan Philadelphia's workforce (30%). This Philadelphia plan was ruled in November 1968 to violate federal contract law. Nevertheless, in 1971 under the Nixon administration, the Supreme Court affirmed that the minority preferences of the Philadelphia did not violate the Civil Rights Act. The EEOC, in charge of the implementation of Title VII, followed a similar strategy, issuing guidelines to employers to use statistical proportionality in employee testing. In 1972, Congress extended the EEOC's jurisdiction to state and local governments and educational institutions (which were exempt in 1964). Affirmative action became the model of federal hiring practices.

The original rationale for affirmative action was to right the historical wrong of institutional racism and stressed its temporary nature. In 1978, in *Regents of the University of California vs. Bakke*, Supreme Court justice Harry Blackmun was apologetic about supporting a government policy of racial exclusion: "I yield to no one in my earnest hope that the time will come when an affirmative action program is unnecessary and is, in truth, only a relic of the past." He expressed the hope that it is a stage of transitional inequality and "within a decade at most, American society must and will reach a stage of maturity where acting along this line is no longer necessary." Twenty-five years later, however, in her opinion on the case *Grutter vs. Bollinger*, justice Sandra Day O'Connor repeated a similar rhetoric: "The Court expects that 25 years from now, the use of racial preferences will no longer be necessary to further the interest approved today."

6.2 Affirmative action in Coate and Loury (1993a)

Coate and Loury (1993a) analyzed how affirmative action in the form of an employment quota may affect the incentives to invest in skills for both groups and the equilibrium of the model. In particular, it highlights a potential perverse effect of affirmative action: in the so-called "patronizing equilibrium," the incentives to invest in skills by the group A workers – the group that the affirmative action policy is supposed to help, may be reduced in the equilibrium with affirmative action relative to that without affirmative action.

6.2.1 Modeling affirmative action

Coate and Loury (1993a) modeled affirmative action as an employment quota. Specifically, the affirmative action policy requires that the proportion of group B workers on the complex task (which pays a higher wage in their model) be equal to the proportion of group B workers in the population. Recall from Section 3.2, the proportion of white workers in the population is $\lambda \in (0, 1)$. For expositional simplicity, we write $\lambda_W = \lambda$ and $\lambda_B = 1 - \lambda$ below.

Suppose that the proportions of skilled workers are respectively π_B and π_W among groups B and W. Let

$$\rho(\widetilde{\theta}, \pi) \equiv \pi[1 - F_q(\widetilde{\theta})] + (1 - \pi)[1 - F_u(\widetilde{\theta})]$$

be the probability that the firms will assign a randomly selected worker from a group where a fraction π invests in skills to the complex task if the firms use $\widetilde{\theta}$ as the assignment threshold. Now we can write firms' task assignment problem under the employment quota as:

$$\max_{\{\widetilde{\theta}_W, \widetilde{\theta}_B\}} \sum \lambda_j \{\pi_j[1 - F_q(\widetilde{\theta}_j)]x_q - (1 - \pi_j)[1 - F_u(\widetilde{\theta}_j)]x_u\} \quad (39)$$

$$\text{s.t. } \rho(\widetilde{\theta}_W, \pi_W) = \rho(\widetilde{\theta}_B, \pi_B) \quad (40)$$

where in the affirmative action employment quota constraint (40), the left and right hand sides are respectively the probabilities that a random White and Black worker will be assigned to the complex task. Note that when these probabilities are equalized, the fraction of blacks assigned to the complex task will indeed exactly match the fraction of blacks in the population, as stipulated by the employment quota.[16]

An *equilibrium under affirmative action* is a pair of beliefs $(\pi^*{}_B, \pi^*{}_W)$ and cutoffs $(\widetilde{\theta}^*_B, \widetilde{\theta}^*_W)$ such that: (1) $(\widetilde{\theta}^*_B, \widetilde{\theta}^*_W)$ solves problem (39) given $(\pi^*{}_B, \pi^*{}_W)$; (2) $\pi^*_j = G(I(\widetilde{\theta}^*_j))$ for $j = B, W$.

The ideal for an affirmative action policy is to ensure that all equilibria under affirmative action entail homogeneous beliefs by the firms about the investment behavior of the workers from the two groups and lead to a result of race-neutral task assignment

[16] Assuming a law of large numbers holds in this setup.

decisions. The negative stereotypes of the firms regarding the discriminated against group will be eliminated by the affirmative action policy if firms hold homogeneous beliefs.

Coate and Loury (1993a) provide a sufficient condition on the primitives, albeit rather difficult to interpret, for the above ideal of affirmative action to be realized. Let:

$$\hat{\rho}(\tilde{\theta}) \equiv \rho(\tilde{\theta}, G(I(\tilde{\theta}))), \tag{41}$$

where $G(I(\tilde{\theta}))$ is defined in (14), denote the fraction of a group assigned to the complex task if the firms use $\tilde{\theta}$ as the assignment threshold. The affirmative action employment quota constraint (40) requires that $\hat{\rho}(\tilde{\theta}_W) = \hat{\rho}(\tilde{\theta}_B)$. In general $\hat{\rho}(\tilde{\theta}_W) = \hat{\rho}(\tilde{\theta}_B)$ does not necessarily imply $\tilde{\theta}_W = \tilde{\theta}_B$ because $\hat{\rho}(\cdot)$ may not be monotonic (as illustrated in the next section regarding "patronizing equilibrium"). How $\hat{\rho}(\cdot)$ varies with $\tilde{\theta}$ depends on the interaction of two distinct effects. On the one hand, an increase in the threshold $\tilde{\theta}$ makes it harder to be assigned to the complex task for a given fraction of qualified workers, thus leading to a decrease of $\hat{\rho}$; on the other hand, as $\tilde{\theta}$ increases, the workers' skill investment incentives change, leading to changes in the fraction of qualified workers. The net effect is typically ambiguous. However, $\hat{\rho}(\cdot)$ must be decreasing over some part of the domain [0, 1] because $\hat{\rho}(0) = 1$ and $\hat{\rho}(1) = 0$. Thus a sufficient condition under which all equilibria under affirmative action entail homogeneous beliefs about the two groups is that $\hat{\rho}(\cdot)$ as defined in (41) is decreasing on [0, 1].

6.2.2 Patronizing equilibrium: an example

Coate and Loury (1993a) provided an example to demonstrate the possibility of patronizing equilibria under affirmative action. The idea is very simple: to comply with the affirmative action policy (assuming $\pi_B < \pi_W$ is unchanged by the policy for the moment), the standards for blacks must be lowered and the standards for whites must be raised to comply with the employment quota. Thus, it is now easier for blacks to be assigned to the good job (and harder for whites) irrespective of whether or not a particular worker invested in skills. Since the incentives to invest depend on the expected wage difference between skilled and unskilled workers, whether the above change will increase or decrease blacks' incentive to invest in skills depends on the particularities of the distributions f_q and f_u.

Consider the following example. Suppose that the skill investment cost c is uniform on [0, 1]. Assume the following test signal densities for qualified and unqualified workers, respectively:

$$f_q(\theta) = \begin{cases} \frac{1}{1-\theta_q} & \text{if } \theta \in [\theta_q, 1] \\ 0 & \text{otherwise,} \end{cases} \tag{42}$$

$$f_u(\theta) = \begin{cases} \frac{1}{\theta_u} & \text{if } \theta \in [0, \theta_u] \\ 0 & \text{otherwise,} \end{cases} \tag{43}$$

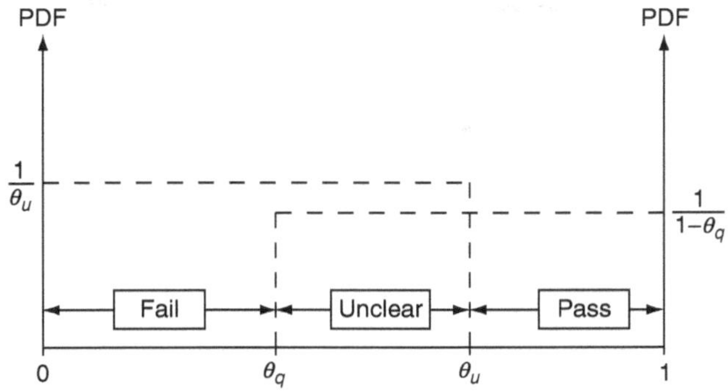

Figure 5 Signal distributions in Coate and Loury's (1993a) example of patronizing equilibrium.

where $\theta_u > \theta_q$. Figure 5 graphically illustrates these two distributions, which are equivalent to the case in which only three test results are possible. If $\theta > \theta_u$, then the signal is only possible if the worker is qualified, thus we call it a "pass" score; if $\theta < \theta_q$, then the signal is only possible if the worker is unqualified, thus we call it a "fail" score; if $\theta \in [\theta_q, \theta_u]$, then the signal is possibly from both a qualified and an unqualified worker, thus we call such a signal "unclear."

Equilibria without Affirmative Action. Let us first analyze the equilibrium of this example with no affirmative action. Clearly, the firm assigns workers with a "pass" score to the complex task and those with "fail" score to the simple task. Now we determine the optimal assignment decision regarding workers with "unclear" scores. It is clear from Figure 5 that the probability that a qualified worker gets an "unclear" score $\theta \in [\theta_q, \theta_u]$ is:

$$p_q = \frac{\theta_u - \theta_q}{1 - \theta_q}; \tag{44}$$

and for an unqualified worker is:

$$p_u = \frac{\theta_u - \theta_q}{\theta_u}. \tag{45}$$

Suppose that the prior that a worker is qualified is π. Then the posterior probability that a worker with an unclear score is qualified is, by Bayes' rule:

$$\xi(\pi) = \frac{\pi p_q}{\pi p_q + (1 - \pi) p_u}. \tag{46}$$

Hence, the employer will assign a worker with unclear scores to the complex task if and only if:

$$\xi(\pi) x_q - [1 - \xi(\pi)] x_u \geq 0,$$

or equivalently,

$$\pi \geq \hat{\pi} = \frac{p_u/p_q}{x_q/x_u + p_u/p_q}. \tag{47}$$

We say that a firm follows a *liberal* policy for group j if it assigns all group j workers with an unclear test score to the complex task, i.e., if $\tilde{\theta} = \theta_q$; we say that a firm follows a *conservative* policy for group j if it assigns all group j workers with an unclear test score to the simple task, i.e., if $\tilde{\theta} = \theta_u$.

In order for a liberal policy to be consistent with equilibrium, it must be the case that the skill investment incentives under the liberal policy will result in the fraction of qualified workers in the group to be larger than $\hat{\pi}$ defined in (47). Note that under a liberal policy, the benefit from skill investment is given by:

$$I(\theta_q) = \omega(1 - p_u)$$

because if the worker is skilled, he will be assigned with probability one to the complex task and if he is unskilled, the probability is p_u. Thus, the proportion of skilled workers in response to a liberal policy is:

$$\pi_l = I(\theta_q) = \omega(1 - p_u). \tag{48}$$

Thus the liberal policy is an equilibrium if $\pi_l > \hat{\pi}$.

Similarly, under a conservative policy, the benefit of skill investment is:

$$I(\theta_u) = \omega(1 - p_q).$$

Hence the proportion of skilled workers in response to a conservative policy is:

$$\pi_c = I(\theta_u) = \omega(1 - p_q). \tag{49}$$

Thus the conservative policy is an equilibrium if $\pi_c < \hat{\pi}$.

To summarize, in the absence of the affirmative action constraint, if $\pi_c < \hat{\pi} < \pi_l$, then the example admits multiple equilibria in that both the liberal policy and the conservative policy could be equilibria. Suppose that the blacks and the whites are coordinated on the conservative and the liberal equilibria, respectively; that is, $(\pi_B, \pi_W) = (\pi_c, \pi_l)$. Clearly, in this equilibrium, firms hold a negative stereotype toward blacks because $\pi_c < \pi_l$.

Equilibria with Affirmative Action. Suppose that the economy is in an equilibrium characterized by $(\pi_B, \pi_W) = (\pi_c, \pi_l)$ described above, and suppose that an affirmative action policy in the form of employment quota as described in Section 6.2.1 is imposed.[17]

[17] It can be verified that the sufficient condition for affirmative action to eliminate discriminatory equilibrium described in the previous section does not hold in this example.

Given that in the pre-affirmative action equilibrium $(\pi_B, \pi_W) = (\pi_c, \pi_l)$, there is a higher fraction of whites on the complex job. In order to comply with the affirmative action employment quota, the firm must either assign more blacks or assign fewer whites to the complex task. Which course of action is preferred will depend on the following calculations. Given $(\pi_B, \pi_W) = (\pi_c, \pi_l)$, if the firm assigns a black worker with a "fail" score to the complex task, it loses x_u unit of profits; however, if the firm assigns a white worker with an "unclear" score to the simple task (instead of the complex task as stipulated under the liberal policy), it loses:

$$\xi(\pi_l)x_q - [1 - \xi(\pi_l)]x_u,$$

where ξ $(\cdot)$ is defined in (46). Notice that if:

$$\lambda[\xi_l x_q - (1 - \xi_l)x_u] > (1 - \lambda)x_u,$$

then the firm would rather put all black workers with "fail" scores to the complex task than to switch white workers with "unclear" scores to the simple task in order to satisfy the employment quota.

Now consider the following assignment policies. For the whites, keep the original liberal policy; namely, assign all workers with "pass" or "unclear" scores to the complex task. Under this policy, the white workers' skill investment decisions in equilibrium will lead to $\pi_W = \pi_l$, same as before. For the black workers, the firms follow the following "*patronizing*" assignment policy: assign all black workers with "pass" or "unclear" scores to the complex task, *and* with probability $\alpha(\pi_B) \in (0, 1)$ assign blacks *with "fail" scores* to the complex task, where $\alpha(\pi_B)$ is chosen to satisfy the employment quota requirement:[18]

$$\alpha(\pi_B) = \frac{\pi_l - \pi_B}{1 - \pi_B}. \tag{50}$$

The firms are "*patronizing*" the blacks in this postulated assignment policy because they are assigning blacks who have "fail" scores to the complex task.

Now consider a black worker's best response if he anticipates being patronized with probability α. If he invests in skills, he will be assigned to the complex task with probability 1; if he does not invest, he will be assigned to the complex task with probability $p_u + (1 - p_u)\,\alpha$. Thus, the return from investing in skills for a black worker is:

$$\omega\{1 - [p_u + (1 - p_u)\alpha]\} = \omega(1 - \alpha)(1 - p_u) = (1 - \alpha)\pi_l$$

where the last equality follows from (48).

[18] That is, to satisfy.

$$\pi_l + (1 - \pi_l)p_u = \pi_B + (1 - \pi_B)[p_u + (1 - p_u)\alpha(\pi_B)].$$

Hence, any (π_B, π_l) where $\pi_l > 1/2$, can be sustained as an equilibrium under the affirmative action policy where firms follow a patronizing assignment policy $\alpha(\pi_B)$ for blacks and a liberal policy for whites if and only if $\pi_B \leq \pi_l$ and π_B satisfies:

$$\pi_B = [1 - \alpha(\pi_B)]\pi_l = \frac{(1 - \pi_l)\pi_l}{1 - \pi_B}. \tag{51}$$

Note that equation (51) admits two solutions for $\pi_B : \pi_B = \pi_l$ or $\pi_B = 1 - \pi_l$. In the first solution, color-blind equilibrium is reached and the employer is liberal toward both groups (at $\pi_B = \pi_l$, it can be seen from (50) that $\alpha(\pi_B) = 0$, thus there is no patronizing). In the second solution, the firms continue to view black workers as less productive in equilibrium and adopt a patronizing assignment policy on the blacks in order to fulfill the affirmative action employment quotas.

Dynamics. Coate and Loury (1993a) further argued that, under a plausible dynamics on the evolution of firms' beliefs about the fraction of blacks who invest in skills specified as system:

$$\begin{aligned} \pi_B^{t+1} &= [1 - \alpha(\pi_B^t)]\pi_l \\ &= \frac{1 - \pi_l}{1 - \pi_B^t}\pi_l, \end{aligned}$$

with initial condition that $\pi_B^0 = \pi_c$, it can be shown using a simple phase diagram that $\pi_B^t \to 1 - \pi_l$ as $t \to \infty$. Thus in some sense, not only is the patronizing equilibrium possible, it could actually be a stable equilibrium outcome. Coate and Loury (1993b) studied the effect of affirmative action in a similar environment, but one where employers also hold prejudicial preferences against minorities. In that case, it is shown that a gradual policy in which representation targets are gradually increased might be more likely to eliminate disparities than radical policies demanding immediate proportional representation.

6.3 General equilibrium consequences of affirmative action

One weakness of Coate and Loury (1993a)'s model is that wages are not determined in a competitive labor market, but are fixed exogenously. Because affirmative action policies change the profitability of hiring workers from different groups, this is not an innocuous assumption. Moreover, workers from the discriminated group face a more favorable task assignment rule, but, conditional on the signal, receive the same wages as before, therefore affirmative action can only be a benefit to them.

Moro and Norman (2003a) study the effect of affirmative action policies in the general equilibrium setting analyzed in Section 4.1, where firms engaged in Bertrand competition for workers determine wages endogenously. Their analysis confirms the perverse incentive effects of government-mandated policies found by Coate and Loury (1993a).

Moreover, it finds perverse effects on equilibrium wages and proves that in some circumstances affirmative action may hurt its intended beneficiaries.

The affirmative action constraint is the same as that assumed in Section 6.2.1, that is, employers are forced to hire the same proportion of workers from both groups in the complex task (and, residually, in the simple task). Employers therefore solve the following problem (assuming for simplicity that groups have identical size):

$$\max_{\widetilde{\theta}_B,\, \widetilde{\theta}_W} y(C,S) = \max_{\widetilde{\theta}_B,\, \widetilde{\theta}_W} y\left(\sum_{j=B,W} \pi_j[1-F_q(\widetilde{\theta}_j)],\ \sum_{j=B,W} [\pi_j F_q(\widetilde{\theta}_j) + (1-\pi_j)F_u(\widetilde{\theta}_j)]\right)$$
$$\text{s.t. } \pi_B F_q(\widetilde{\theta}_B) + (1-\pi_B)F_u(\widetilde{\theta}_B) = \pi_W F_q(\widetilde{\theta}_W) + (1-\pi_W)F_u(\widetilde{\theta}_W).$$

Denote $\hat{\theta}_j(\boldsymbol{\pi}), j = B, W$ as the optimal group-specific cutoff rules that solve this problem for a given vector $\boldsymbol{\pi} = (\pi_B, \pi_W)$. Employers assign all workers with signal above such thresholds to the complex task, and all other workers to the simple task. Observe that from the constraint, it follows directly that if $\pi_B < \pi_W$ then $\hat{\theta}_B(\boldsymbol{\pi}) > \hat{\theta}_W(\boldsymbol{\pi})$. The direct (partial-equilibrium) effect of the policy on the task assignment rule is to force employers to lower the task assignment threshold for the discriminated group, and to raise the threshold for the dominant group. It can be proved that the equilibrium wages are:

$$\hat{w}_j(\theta;\pi) = \begin{cases} p(\hat{\theta}_j(\boldsymbol{\pi}), \pi_j)x_q(\hat{C},\hat{S}) & \text{for } \theta < \hat{\theta}_j(\boldsymbol{\pi}) \\ p(\theta, \pi_j)x_q(\hat{C},\hat{S}) & \text{for } \theta \geq \hat{\theta}_j(\boldsymbol{\pi}) \end{cases} \tag{52}$$

where $\hat{C}, \hat{S}$ are the optimal inputs of the production function computed from the optimization problem satisfying the affirmative action constraint, x_q and x_u are the marginal products of workers in the complex and simple task, and $p(\theta, \pi_j)$ is the probability that a worker with signal θ is qualified, given by (4). This result says that the wage is a continuous function of the signal, that workers in the complex task are paid exactly their marginal products, and that workers in the simple task are paid the wage of the marginal worker. In the simple task, workers are therefore paid above the marginal product if they belong to the dominant group and below their marginal product if they belong to the discriminated group. Figure 6 illustrates the equilibrium wages under the assumption $\pi_B < \pi_W$.

The proof of this result first argues that wages must be continuous, otherwise one employer could exploit the discontinuity and increase profit by offering a slightly higher wage to workers that are cheaper near the discontinuity, and zero to workers that are more expensive. Second, note that there is a difference between quantity of workers in the complex task and their labor input, because not all workers employed in the complex task are productive. If workers in the complex task were not paid their expected marginal product, then employers could generate a profitable deviation that exploits the difference between quantity of workers and quantity of effective

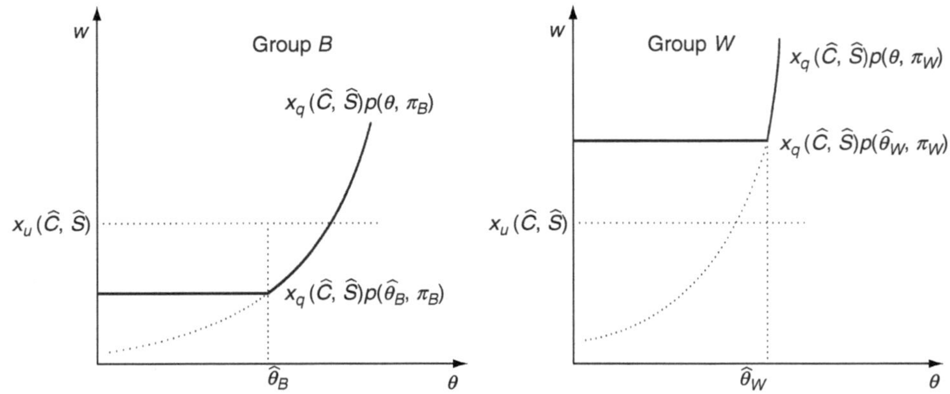

Figure 6 Equilibrium wage schedules under affirmative action in Moro and Norman (2003).

inputs.[19] However, because of continuity, this implies that workers in the simple task are paid above or below the marginal product depending on their group identity. It is not difficult to show from the first order condition of the task assignment problem that the average pay of all workers in the simple task (from both groups) is exactly the marginal product $x_u(\hat{C}, \hat{S})$.

Incentives to invest for group j are:

$$I_j(\boldsymbol{\pi}) = \int_\theta \hat{w}_j(\theta) f_q(\theta) d\theta - \int_\theta \hat{w}_j(\theta) f_u(\theta) d\theta,\ j = B, W \tag{53}$$

and the equilibria are characterized by the solution to the system of fixed-point equations $\pi_j = G(I_j(\boldsymbol{\pi}))$, $j = B, W$, where as usual G is the CDF of the cost of human capital investment. Any symmetric equilibrium of the model without the policy trivially satisfies the affirmative action constraint and therefore is also an equilibrium under affirmative action.

The full equilibrium effects of affirmative action are indeterminate. While it is possible that imposing affirmative action completely eliminates asymmetric equilibria, it is also possible for asymmetric equilibria to exist that satisfy the quota imposed by the policy for reasons similar to those illustrated by the patronizing equilibria derived in Section 6.2.2. A proof may be derived by construction by fixing fundamentals γ, f_q and f_u, and looking for a cost of investment distribution G that satisfies the equilibrium conditions under affirmative action. Note that if $\pi_B = 0$, and $0 < \pi_W < 1$, then from (52) and (53) it must be that $I_B(0, \pi_W) = 0 < I_W(0, \pi_W)$ (all group-B workers are offered zero wage, equivalent to their productivity in the complex task but some are employed in the complex task to satisfy the affirmative action constraint). But then since $I_j(\cdot)$ is

[19] The reader is invited to consult the proof in the original paper for details.

continuous and initially increasing near $\pi_B = 0$, one can find $\pi_B > 0$ such that $0 < \pi_B < \pi_W < 1$ and, at the same time, $0 < I_B(\pi_B, \pi_W) < I_W(\pi_B, \pi_W)$. Hence, one can find a strictly increasing CDF G such that $G(0) > 0$, $G(I_B(\pi_B, \pi_W)) = \pi_B$, and $G(I_W(\pi_B, \pi_W)) = \pi_W$ so that (π_B, π_W) is an equilibrium of the model.

In general, comparing outcomes with and without the policy is difficult because outcomes depend on the equilibrium selection. It is possible to show that the policy may have negative welfare effects for its intended beneficiaries. The negative direct effects on the discriminated group's wages are evident from Figure 6. The picture however hides the full equilibrium effects because factor ratios will change in equilibrium. Unless such factor ratios do not change significantly, expected earnings for group-B decrease. Note also from the figure that the direct effect of the policy is to increase incentives to invest for the discriminated group. This tends to moderate the negative wage effects, but unless this effect is significant, workers in the discriminated groups are made worse-off by the policy.

The wage determination in this model is specific to the modeling assumptions made regarding production and information technologies. In this simplified setting, a slightly more complex policy that combines affirmative action employment quota and racial equality of average wages in each task would be effective in inducing symmetric equilibria. It is not clear, however, whether such a policy would be easily implementable in a more complex environment.[20] Nevertheless, the model is useful to illustrate that affirmative action policies have non-trivial general equilibrium effects.

6.4 Affirmative action in a two-sector general equilibrium model

Fang and Norman (2006) derive similar, but more clear-cut, perverse results in a two-sector general equilibrium model motivated by the following puzzling observation from Malaysia. Since its independence from British colonial rule in 1957, Malaysia protected the Malays by entitling them to certain privileges including political power, while at the same time allowing the Chinese to pursue their economic objectives without interference. This relative racial harmony was rejected in 1970 when the so-called New Economic Policy was adopted, in which wide-ranging preferential policies favoring the Malays were introduced, most important of which is an effective mandate that only the Malays can access the relatively well-paid public sector jobs. However, despite the aggressive preferential policies favoring the Malays, the Malay did not achieve significant economic progress relative to the Chinese; if anything, the opposite seems to be true, that is, the new policy reversed the pre-1970 trend of the narrowing wage gaps between the Chinese and the Malays.

[20] Lundberg (1991), for example, describes how companies may use variables that are correlated with race to evade the imposition of policies that monitor the employment process, such as affirmative action. In that setting, it is shown that policies monitoring outcomes may be more effective in reducing inequality, at the cost of higher production losses from workers' misallocation.

Fang and Norman (2006) considered the following simple model. Consider an economy with two sectors, called respectively the *private* and the *public* sector. The private sector consists of two (or more) competitive firms, indexed by $i = 1, 2$. Firms are risk neutral and maximize expected profits, and are endowed with a technology that is complementary to workers' skills. A skilled worker can produce $x > 0$ units of output, and an unskilled one will, by normalization, produce 0.

The public sector offers a fixed-wage $g > 0$ to any worker who is hired, but there is rationing of public sector jobs: the probability of getting hired in the public sector if a worker applies is given by $\rho_j \in [0,1]$, where $j \in \{A, B\}$ is the worker's ethnic identity. In our analysis below, we treat ρ_j as the government's policy parameter. Government-mandated discriminatory policies are simply modeled by the assumption that $\rho_A \neq \rho_B$. Workers who apply for but are unsuccessful in obtaining public sector employment can return to and obtain a job in the private sector without waiting.

For each ethnic group $j \in \{A, B\}$, there is a continuum of workers with mass λ_j in the economy. Workers are heterogeneous in their costs, denoted by c, of acquiring the requisite skills for the operation of the firms' technology. The cost c is private information of the worker and is distributed according to a uniform [0, 1] distribution in the population of both groups. Workers are risk neutral and do not care directly about whether they work in the public or private sector. If a worker of cost type c receives wage w, her payoff is $w - c$ if she invests in skills, and w if she does not invest.

The events in this economy are timed as follows: In the first stage, each worker in group j with investment cost $c \in [0, 1]$ decides whether to invest in the skills. This binary decision is denoted by $s \in \{0, 1\}$ where $s = 0$ stands for no skill investment and $s = 1$ for skill acquisition. If a worker chooses $s = 1$, we say that she becomes *qualified* and hence she can produce β units of output in the private sector; otherwise she is *unqualified* and will produce 0. As in the other models surveyed in this section, skill acquisitions are *not* perfectly observed by the firms, but in the second stage the worker and the firms observe a noisy signal $\theta \in \{h, l\} \equiv \Theta$ about the worker's skill acquisition decision with the following distributions:

$$\Pr[\theta = h|s = 1] = \Pr[\theta = l|s = 0] = p < 1/2.$$

In the third stage, after observing the noisy signal θ, each worker decides whether to apply for the public sector job. If applying, she is accepted for employment in the public sector with probability ρ_j where j is her ethnic identity. If she was not employed in the public sector, she will, in the fourth stage, return to the private sector, where firms compete for her service by posting wage offers. After observing the wage offers, she decides which firm to work for, clearing the private sector labor market.

The key insight from Fang and Norman (2006) is that 'group j's incentives to invest in skills depend on the probability that they may receive the public sector employment ρ_j. To see this, suppose that at the end of the first stage, a proportion π_j of the group j

population is qualified. Then in the second stage, a total measure $p\pi_j + (1-p)(1-\pi_j)$ of workers receives signal h, among which a measure $p\pi_j$ is qualified and a measure $(1-p)(1-\pi_j)$ is unqualified. Similarly, a total measure $(1-p)\pi_j + p(1-\pi_j)$ of workers receives signal l, among which a measure $(1-p)\pi_j$ is qualified and a measure $p(1-\pi_j)$ is unqualified. Therefore, in the fourth stage, when a firm sees a group j worker with a signal θ, its posterior belief that this worker is qualified, denoted by $\Pr[s=1\mid\theta;\pi_j]$ where $\theta \in \{h, l\}$, is given by:

$$\Pr\left[s=1|\theta=h;\pi_j\right] = \frac{p\pi_j}{p\pi_j + (1-p)(1-\pi_j)}$$
$$\Pr\left[s=1|\theta=l;\pi_j\right] = \frac{(1-p)\pi_j}{(1-p)\pi_j + p(1-\pi_j)},$$

exactly as if there were no public sector. Hence, the equilibrium wage for group j workers with signal $\theta \in \{h, l\}$ when the proportion of qualified workers in group j is π_j, denoted by $w_\theta(\pi_j)$, is:

$$w_h(\pi_j) = \beta\Pr\left[s=1|\theta=h;\pi_j\right] = \frac{\beta p\pi_j}{p\pi_j + (1-p)(1-\pi_j)}$$
$$w_l(\pi_j) = \beta\Pr\left[s=1|\theta=l;\pi_j\right] = \frac{\beta(1-p)\pi_j}{(1-p)\pi_j + p(1-\pi_j)}.$$

Now we analyze the public sector job application decision in the third stage. A group j worker with signal θ applies to the public sector job if $w_\theta(\pi_j) < g$ and does not apply if $w_\theta(\pi_j) > g$ where g is the public sector wage. Defining $\hat{\pi}_\theta$ as the solution to $w_\theta(\hat{\pi}_\theta) = g$ for $\theta \in \{h, l\}$, i.e.,

$$\hat{\pi}_h = \frac{g(1-p)}{g(1-p) + p(\beta-g)}, \hat{\pi}_l = \frac{gp}{gp + (1-p)(\beta-g)}.$$

We can conclude that a group j worker with signal θ applies for a public sector job if and if $\pi_j \leq \hat{\pi}_\theta$.

A worker's incentive to acquire skills in the first stage comes from the subsequent expected wage differential between a qualified and an unqualified worker. With some algebra it can be shown that the incentive to invest in skills for group j workers, denoted by $I(\pi_j, \rho_j)$, is equal to the gain in expected wage from skill investment in the first stage relative to not invest, and is given by:

$$I(\pi_j,\rho_j) = \begin{cases} (2p-1)(1-\rho_j)[w_h(\pi_j) - w_l(\pi_j)] & \text{if } 0 \leq \pi < \hat{\pi}_h \\ (2p-1)\{(1-\rho_j)[w_h(\pi_j) - w_l(\pi_j)] + \rho_j[w_h(\pi_j) - g]\} & \text{if } \hat{\pi}_h \leq \pi < \hat{\pi}_l \\ (2p-1)[w_h(\pi_j) - w_l(\pi_j)] & \text{if } \hat{\pi}_l \leq \pi \leq 1. \end{cases} \quad (54)$$

Notice that the incentive to invest, $I(\pi_j, \rho_j)$, depends also on ρ_j, the probability of public sector employment for group j workers, which is the reason for a government-mandated preferential (or discriminatory) policy in the public sector to matter for the private sector labor market in our model. Indeed, a higher probability of public sector jobs will unambiguously decrease the investment incentives if $\pi < \hat{\pi}_l$ because:

$$\frac{\partial I(\pi_j, \rho_j)}{\partial \rho_j} = \begin{cases} -(2p-1)[w_h(\pi_j) - w_l(\pi_j)] < 0 & \text{if } \pi_j < \hat{\pi}_h \\ (2p-1)[w_l(\pi_j) - g] < 0 & \text{if } \hat{\pi}_h \leq \pi_j < \hat{\pi}_l \\ 0 & \text{otherwise.} \end{cases} \tag{55}$$

The intuition is simple: the public sector does not give any advantage to qualified workers over unqualified workers. As a result, a higher ρ_j always reduces the equilibrium level of π_j.

Now consider an economy where a minority ethnic group, say group A, is subject to government-mandated discrimination in the sense that $\rho_A = 0$; while the majority native group, group B, obtains public sector jobs with probability $\rho_B > 0$. Fang and Norman (2006) show that the discriminated group A, nevertheless, may be economically more successful than the preferred group B. Specifically, when the government marginally increases ρ_B from 0, there is a *direct effect* because now group B will have a higher degree of access to a higher paying public sector and they will less likely enter the private sector. If the public sector wage g is higher than the best private sector wage (i.e., $g > p\beta$), as assumed, this direct effect is a positive for group B. However, there is also a negative *indirect general equilibrium effect* because as ρ_B increases from 0, it also *reduces* the incentives of skill investment, which will in turn lower the expected wages in the private sector for group B. If g is not too high (i.e., $g < 4p\,(1-p)\beta$), then the expected wage of both qualified and unqualified group A workers are higher than those of respective group B workers if $\rho_A = 0$ and $\rho_B > 0$ is sufficiently small. Note that to satisfy the condition $p\beta < g < 4p\,(1-p)\,\beta$, the precision of the test signal p has to be less than 3/4. That the precision in the signal cannot be too high for the negative indirect effect to dominate should be intuitive: A beneficial net effect from being excluded from the public sector can only occur if the informational free riding problem in the private sector is severe enough; and the higher p, the less severe this problem is. It can also be shown that, under the same set of assumptions, not only group B workers have lower expected wages, but also group B workers of all skill investment cost types are economically worse off than their group A counterparts.

6.5 Role model effects of affirmative action

Advocates of affirmative action have often argued that larger representation of minorities in higher paying jobs and occupations can generate role models that can positively influence future generations of minorities in their investment decisions. Chung (2000) formalizes these arguments. Consider a group of individuals who differ in their costs of investment, which take on two possible values c_l or c_h with $c_l < c_h$. In the population, a fraction $\alpha \in (0, 1)$ is of type c_l. An individual's skill investment cost is her private information.

Table 2 Transition matrix of the probability of being hired to the complex job

$p_t \backslash p_{t+1}$	p_1	p_2
p_1	$1-\theta_{12}$	θ_{12}
p_2	θ_{21}	$1-\theta_{21}$

Each individual, upon learning her investment cost type c, makes a binary investment decision. The skill investment decision affects the probability that the individual will obtain a higher paying job. For simplicity, suppose that there are two kinds of jobs, a complex job that pays w and a simple job whose wage is normalized to 0. Suppose that $w > c_h > c_l > 0$.

If an individual invests in skills, then she will obtain the complex job with probability p that is drawn from a two-point distribution $\{p_1, p_2\}$ with $0 < p_1 < p_2 < 1$. Specifically, p follows a discrete-time Markov process as follows. The probability that $p = p_1$ in period 0 is equal to q_0, and q_0 is common knowledge among all individuals; the transition probability $\Pr(p_{t+1} = p_j | p_t = p_i)$ is given in Table 2 where both θ_{12} and θ_{21} lie in (0, 1/2).

Suppose that in each period, one individual makes an investment decision and then receives a job placement. All individuals observe the prior job placements of others, but do not observe their investment decisions.

To characterize the equilibrium investment decisions of the agents, the key is to characterize how the individuals' beliefs about the state of the labor market, whether p is equal to p_1 or p_2, evolve over time. The role model effect in this model refers to the phenomenon that a placement of a minority candidate in the high paying complex job will *increase* subsequent minorities' belief that the labor market condition for skilled workers is in state p_2, and as a result subsequent minorities' incentives to invest in skills increase.

Consider the first individual. Suppose that her belief about the state of the labor market at period 0 being $p = p_1$ is q_0. Assume for simplicity that the skill investment costs c_l and c_h are such that, at the belief that $p = p_1$ with probability q_0, an individual with investment cost c_l will invest in skills, but an individual with cost c_h will not. Moreover, consider a situation following a long history of individuals being placed on the simple job, and as a result the population's belief about the labor market being poor, i.e., $p = p_1$, is at a steady state $q^* \in (0, 1)$. That is, if another individual is observed to be placed on the simple job, the subsequent individual's belief about $p = p_1$ will stay at q^*.[21]

[21] Specifically, q^* solves the unique root in (0, 1) for the following quadratic equation:

$$\alpha(p_2 - p_1)(1-\theta_{12}-\theta_{21})q^2 + [(\theta_{12}+\theta_{21})(1-\alpha p_1) - \alpha(1-\theta_{21})(p_2-p_1)]q - \theta_{21}(1-\alpha p_1) = 0.$$

The exact value of q^* can be easily derived from a steady state condition, and its expression is omitted here.

In the above situation, suppose that the n-th individual is the *very first* one who manages to land a complex job. Upon observing this, the $(n+1)$-st individual will now infer that the n-th individual had invested and thus must have had low skill investment cost. The posterior belief of the $(n+1)$-st individual that the state of the labor market in period n is $p = p_1$ is

$$q_n = \frac{[q^*(1-\theta_{12}) + (1-q^*)\theta_{21}]p_1}{[q^*(1-\theta_{12}) + (1-q^*)\theta_{21}]p_1 + [q^*\theta_{12} + (1-q^*)(1-\theta_{21})]p_2}.$$

It can be shown with some algebra that $q_n < q^*$, that is, upon the observation of a placement on the complex job, the future individuals' belief about the labor market improves. The n-th individual, upon being placed on the complex job, becomes a *role model* for future individuals. If c_h is not too high, this improvement in the belief may lead to those individuals with investment cost c_h to invest in skills as well. Thus a role model may lead to real changes in behavior among future generations. Chung (2000) also analyzed how long the role model effect may last.

However, if the role model effect is indeed an informational phenomenon, then once affirmative action is announced the beliefs of the disadvantaged group regarding the labor market should switch to $p = p_2$, thus there is no additional information about p being conveyed by preferential hiring in favor of the disadvantaged group. Hence, a standard role-model argument in favor of affirmative action is not supported when role-model effects are purely informational. Chung (2000) observes that only when the hiring of minorities have some payoff-relevant effect than anti-discriminatory policies can have a bite, for example when jobs require race-specific know-how, and there are so few minorities employed in positions requiring skills that the returns to such skills are uncertain among minorities.

6.6 Color sighted vs. Color blind affirmative action

6.6.1 Recent developments in the affirmative action policies related to college admission

Race-conscious affirmative action policies in college admission came under a lot of scrutiny ever since the landmark case of *Regents of the University of California vs. Bakke*, 438 U.S. 265 (1978) where the Supreme Court upheld diversity in higher education as a "compelling interest" and held that "race or ethnic background may be deemed a 'plus' in a particular applicant''s file" in university admissions, and at the same time ruled that quotas for underrepresented minorities violates the equal protection clause. In the 1996 case, *Hopwood vs. Texas* the Court banned any use of race in school admissions in Texas. To accommodate the ruling, the State of Texas passed a law guaranteeing entry to any state university of a student's choice if they finished in the top 10% of their graduating class.

Also in 1996, Proposition 209 was passed in California, which mandates that "the state shall not discriminate against, or grant preferential treatment to, any individual or group on the basis of race, sex, color, ethnicity, or national origin in the operation of public employment, public education, or public contracting."[22] Proposition 209 essentially prohibits public colleges and universities in California from using race in any admission or financial aid decision. From 2001, the top 4% of high school seniors are guaranteed admission to any University of California campus under California's Eligibility in Local Context plan. In 1998, Washington state voters overwhelmingly passed Initiative 200, which is almost identical to California's Proposition 209. Florida passed its Talented 20 Plan, which guaranteed Florida high school students who graduate in the top 20% of their class admissions to any of the eleven public universities within the Florida State University System.

Two 2003 Supreme Court cases on affirmative action in admissions are related to the University of Michigan. In *Grutter vs. Bollinger*, the Supreme Court upheld the affirmative action admissions policy of the University of Michigan Law School. The Court's majority ruling, authored by Justice Sandra Day O'Connor, held that the United States Constitution "does not prohibit the law school's narrowly tailored use of race in admissions decisions to further a compelling interest in obtaining the educational benefits that flow from a diverse student body." In *Gratz vs. Bollinger*, on the other hand, the Supreme Court ruled that "the University [of Michigan]'s policy, which automatically distributes 20 points, or one-fifth of the points needed to guarantee admission, to every single 'underrepresented minority' applicant solely because of race, is not narrowly tailored to achieve educational diversity." On the one hand, the court affirmed that the use of race in admission decision is not unconstitutional, but at the same time, in the second case, the court specified that any automatic use of race in the computation of a scoring system used in determining admissions violate the constitution.

6.6.2 Color sighted vs. Color blind affirmative action with exogenous skills

Chan and Eyster (2003) studied the effect of color-blind affirmative action policies on the quality of admitted students when colleges have preferences for diversity.

Applicants. Consider a college who must admit a fraction C of applicants. The applicants belong to two groups, black (B) and white (W), with measure λ_B and λ_W respectively such that $\lambda_B + \lambda_W = 1$. Suppose that the test scores of the applicants (also exchangeably the quality of the applicants), denoted by $t \in [\underline{t}, \bar{t}]$, in group $j \in \{B, W\}$ is drawn from distributions $f_j(\cdot)$, such that $\int_{\underline{t}}^{\bar{t}} f_j(t)dt = 1$. Suppose that black applicants tend to have lower test scores than white applicants.[23] Specifically, assume that the distributions $f_W(\cdot)$ and $f_B(\cdot)$ satisfy the following strict monotone likelihood ratio property:

Assumption 2. f_W (t) / f_B(t) is continuously differentiable and strictly increasing in t for $t \in (\underline{t}, \bar{t})$.

[22] See http://vote96.sos.ca.gov/Vote96/html/BP/209text.htm

[23] See Fryer and Loury (2008), discussed below, for a model that links the distributions of test scores to ex ante investment efforts.

A key implication of this assumption is that higher test scores are more likely coming from white applicants.

Admissions. The admission office observes the applicants' test scores and their group identities, and makes admission decisions subject to the constraint that the fraction of applicants admitted must equal the capacity of the university C. Formally, an admission rule is (r_B, r_W), where $r_j(t) : [\underline{t}, \bar{t}] \to [0, 1], j \in \{B, W\}$ is the probability that a group j member with test score t is accepted, such that $t_j(\cdot)$ is weakly increasing in t. The *admissible* admission rules depend on whether affirmative action is allowed. If it is allowed, then $r_j(t)$ can depend on j; if it is not allowed, then $r_B(t) = r_W(t)$ for all $t \in [\underline{t}, \bar{t}]$. For simplicity, let $N_j(r) = \lambda_j \int_{\underline{t}}^{\bar{t}} r_j(t) f_j(t) dt$ denote the number of group j applicants admitted under rule r.

The admission office's preference is postulated as a weighted average of the total test scores of admitted students and racial diversity. Specifically,

$$U(r) = \sum_{j \in \{B,W\}} \lambda_j \int_{\underline{t}}^{\bar{t}} t r_j(t) f_j(t) dt - \alpha \left| \lambda_B - \frac{N_B(r)}{C} \right| \quad (56)$$

where $\alpha > 0$ captures the admission office's taste for diversity; in particular, the university desires to achieve a racial composition in the student body that is identical to the racial composition of the applicant pool. Note that under (56) the admission office wants to achieve racial diversity whether or not the admission rules have to be -color-blind or are allowed to be color-sighted.

The admission office chooses $\langle r_B(t), r_W(t) \rangle$ among admissible set of admission rules to maximize (56) subject to the constraint that the capacity is reached, i.e.,

$$\sum_{j \in \{B,W\}} \lambda_j \int_{\underline{t}}^{\bar{t}} r_j(t) f_j(t) dt = C. \quad (57)$$

It is clear that restricting the admission office to color-blind admission rules will necessarily lower its attainable payoff; the goal of the analysis is to show how such color-blindness restriction affects the constrained optimal admission rules, and how it affects the test scores of admitted students, i.e., the first term in (56).

Color-Sighted Affirmative Action. When color sighted affirmative action is admissible, the admission office sets a cutoff rule for each group and admits any applicants scoring above her group's cutoff. Let (t_B^*, t_W^*) denote the admission test score threshold for black and white applicants respectively. If we ignore the absolute-value sign in the objective function (56), the admission office solves:

$$\max_{\{t_B, t_W\}} \lambda_B \int_{t_B}^{\bar{t}} \left(t + \frac{\alpha}{C}\right) f_B(t) dt + \lambda_W \int_{t_W}^{\bar{t}} t f_W(t) dt$$

subject to the capacity constraint. If the solution to the above modified problem has the minority group underrepresented, then ignoring the absolute-value sign is not consequential and the solution also solves the original problem. The first order conditions for the above modified problem with respect to t_B and t_W imply that:

$$t_B + \frac{\alpha}{C} = t_W.$$

If under such thresholds (t_B, t_W), minorities are indeed underrepresented, then we have a solution. If minorities are overrepresented, then the solution to the original problem will be thresholds that exactly achieve proportional representation. Thus, given Assumption 2, the optimal color sighted admission rule is a cutoff rule (t_B^*, t_W^*) such that $0 \leq t_W^* - t_B^* \leq \alpha/C$. Blacks are weakly underrepresented.

Color Blind Affirmative Action. A ban on color-sighted affirmative action would require that the same admission rule be used for both groups. Thus, the strict monotone likelihood ratio property would necessarily imply that the minority group will be under-represented among the admitted students as long as the admission rule is increasing in t. Hence the term $\alpha|\lambda_B - \frac{N_B(r)}{C}|$ in the admission office's objective function is simply $\alpha(\lambda_B - \frac{N_B(r)}{C})$. Dropping the constant $\alpha\lambda_B$ and using the fact that $N_B(r) = \lambda_B \int_{\underline{t}}^{\bar{t}} r(t) f_B(t)dt$, we can rewrite the admission office's problem as:

$$\begin{aligned} \max_{r(\cdot)} \; & U(r) = \int_{\underline{t}}^{\bar{t}} r(t)\gamma(t)[\lambda_B f_B(t) + \lambda_W f_W(t)]dt \\ \text{s.t.} \; & \sum_{j\in\{B,W\}} \lambda_j \int_{\underline{t}}^{\bar{t}} r(t) f_j(t)dt = C \end{aligned} \tag{58}$$

where,

$$\gamma(t) \equiv t + \frac{\alpha}{C}\frac{\lambda_B f_B(t)}{\lambda_B f_B(t) + \lambda_W f_W(t)} \tag{59}$$

The function γ defined above represents the increase in the admission office's utility from admitting a candidate with test score t. The first term is its utility from the test score itself, and the second term reflects its taste for diversity. Note that the likelihood that a test score of t is coming from a black applicant is given by the likelihood ratio $\lambda_B f_B(t) / [\lambda_B f_B(t) + \lambda_W f_W(t)]$.

The admission office obviously would like to fill its class with applicants with the highest value of γ. When γ is everywhere increasing in t, it can simply use a threshold rule. The problem is that γ might not be monotonic in t. To see this, note that the monotone likelihood ratio property implies that the second term in the expression $\gamma(\cdot)$ in (59) is strictly decreasing in t, but, in general, nonlinearly, which implies that γ might not be monotonic.

If $\gamma(\cdot)$ is not everywhere increasing in t, the admission office is not able to admit its favorite applicants without violating the constraint that $r(\cdot)$ must be increasing in t.

Chan and Eyster (2003) provides a useful characterization for the optimal color blind admission rule in this case. To describe their characterization, define Γ (t_1, t_2) as the average value of γ over the interval (t_1, t_2):

$$\Gamma(t_1, t_2) \equiv \begin{cases} \frac{\int_{t_1}^{t_2} \gamma(t)[\lambda_B f_B(t) + \lambda_W f_W(t)]dt}{\int_{t_1}^{t_2}[\lambda_B f_B(t) + \lambda_W f_W(t)]dt} & \text{for } t_1 < t_2 \\ \gamma(t_1) & \text{for } t_1 = t_2 \end{cases}.$$

The curves $\gamma(\cdot)$ and $\Gamma(\cdot, \bar{t})$ as a function of t are illustrated in Figure 7. In Figure 7, γ attains its maximum at t_a, but since r must be increasing in t, the admission office cannot admit applicants with test score t_a without also admitting students with higher test scores, even though as shown in the figure, those with higher test scores have lower values of γ. The optimal colorblind admission rule turns out to involve randomization and the optimal random rule depends on $\Gamma(\cdot, \bar{t})$. In Figure 7, $\Gamma(\cdot, \bar{t})$ attains the global maximum at t_m. Thus, the admission office prefers a randomly drawn applicant scoring above t_m to a randomly drawn applicant scoring above other t. If the capacity C is sufficiently small, the admission office will randomly admit applicants with test scores in the interval $[t_m, \bar{t}]$ with a constant probability chosen to fill the capacity. If the capacity is sufficiently large, the admission office will admit all applicants with test scores above t_m with probability 1 and then admit applicants scoring below t_m in descending order of the test score. To summarize, if $\gamma(\cdot)$ as defined in (58) is not everywhere increasing in t, the optimal color blind admission rule must involve randomization for some values of capacity C.

Under random admission rules, applicants with higher test scores are not admitted with probability 1 at the same time that those with lower test scores are admitted with positive probability, the allocation of the seats are thus not efficient in terms of student quality. For any random colorblind admission rule r, one can construct a color sighted threshold admission rule (t_B, t_W) that achieves the same diversity as that under r, but yields higher quality.

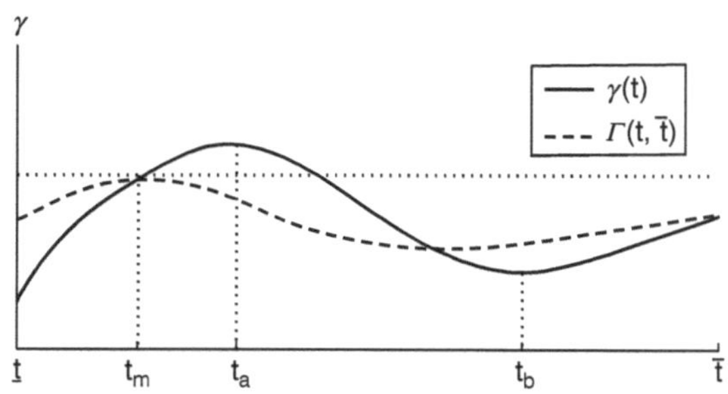

Figure 7 Admission office's preferences over test scores under color-blind admission policy (Figure 1 in Chan and Eyster 2003).

A general equilibrium framework. A similar analysis of the effect of banning Affirmative Action in college admissions, but with colleges competing for students, can be found in Epple, Romano, and Sieg (2008).[24] In their model, colleges care about the academic qualifications of their students and about income as well as racial diversity. Ability and income are correlated with race. Vertically differentiated colleges compete for desirable students using financial aid and admission policies. They show that because of affirmative action minority students pay lower tuition and attend higher-quality schools. The paper characterizes the effects of a ban on affirmative action. A version of the model calibrated to U.S. data shows that a ban of affirmative action leads to a substantial decline of minority students in the top-tier colleges. In an empirical analysis, Arcidiacono (2005) also finds that removing advantages for minorities in admission policies substantially decreases the number of minority students at top tier schools.

6.6.3 Color sighted vs. Colorblind affirmative action with endogenous skills

The analysis of affirmative action in Coate and Loury (1993a) assumed that quotas are to be imposed in the hiring stage. In practice, policymakers who are interested in improving the welfare of the disadvantaged group could potentially intervene in several different stages. For example, in the context of Coate and Loury's model, policymakers could potentially intervene by subsidizing the skill investment of workers from the disadvantaged group. Fryer and Loury (2008) extends the Chan and Eyster (2003) model to add an ex-ante skill investment stage to shed some light on the following question: "Where in the economic life-cycle should preferential treatment be most emphasized; before or after productivities have been determined?"

Recall that in Chan and Eyster (2003)'s model, the test score distribution for group j applicants are assumed to differ by group exogenously. Fryer and Loury (2008) endogenize the differences in $f_j\ (t)$ by assuming that groups differ in the distribution of investment costs, and that the test score distributions $f_j\ (t)$ are related to the investment decisions.

Specifically, let $G_j\ (c)$ be the cumulative distribution of skill investment cost in group j, and let $G(c) \equiv \sum_{j=\{B,W\}} \lambda_j G_j(c)$ be the effort cost distribution in the entire population, with $g_j\ (\cdot)$ and $g\ (\cdot)$ as their respective densities.

Denote an agent's skill investment decision as $e \in \{0, 1\}$. Suppose that the distribution of productivity v, analogous to the test score t in Chan and Eyster (2003), for an agent depends on e, with $H_e\ (v)$ and $h_e\ (v)$ as the CDF and PDF of v if the investment decision is e. If the fraction of individuals in group j who invested in skills is π_j, then the distribution of test scores in group j, again denoted by $F_j\ (v)$, with f being the corresponding density, will be:

$$F_j(v) \equiv F(v; \pi_j) = \pi_j H_1(v) + (1 - \pi_j) H_0(v).$$

[24] See also Epple, Romano and Sieg (2002).

Let $F^{-1}(z;\pi)$ for $z \in [0, 1]$ denote the productivity level at the z-th quantile of the distribution $F(v;\pi)$. Suppose that there is a total measure $C < 1$ of available "slots" that will allow an individual with productivity v to produce v units of output.

Laissez-faire Equilibrium. Fryer and Loury (2008) first analyzed the equilibrium allocation of the productive "slots" and the investment decisions under *laissez-faire*. Let π^m be the fraction of the population choosing $e = 1$ in equilibrium and let p^m be the equilibrium price for a "slot." Clearly,

$$p^m = F^{-1}(1 - C; \pi^m). \tag{60}$$

Given p^m, the ex-ante expected gross return from skill investment is:

$$\int_{p^m}^{\infty} (v - p^m) d\Delta H(v) = \int_{p^m}^{\infty} \Delta H(v) dv \tag{61}$$

where $\Delta H(v) = H_1(v) - H_0(v) \geq 0$. Since agents will invest in skills if and only if the expected gross return from skill investment exceeds the investment cost c, we have the following equilibrium condition:

$$\pi^m = G\left(\int_{p^m}^{\infty} \Delta H(v) dv\right). \tag{62}$$

The *laissez-faire* equilibrium (π^m, p^m) is thus characterized by equations (60) and (62). Note that after substituting the expression of p^m in (60) into (62), and taking G^{-1} on both sides, we have that the *laissez-faire* equilibrium of π^m must satisfy:

$$G^{-1}(\pi^m) = \int_{F^{-1}(1-C;\pi^m)}^{\infty} \Delta H(v) dv, \tag{63}$$

It can be formally shown that the *laissez-faire* equilibrium (π^m, p^m) characterized above is socially efficient. To see this, write an allocation as $\langle e_j(c), \alpha_j(v)\rangle$ where $e_j(c) \in \{0, 1\}$, $\alpha_j(v) \in [0, 1]$ are respectively the effort and slot assignment probability for each type of agent at the two stages. Let $\pi_j \equiv \int_0^{\infty} e_j(c) dG_j(c)$ be the fraction of group j population that invest in skills under effort rule $e_j(c)$. An allocation $\langle e_j(c), \alpha_j(v)\rangle, j \in \{B, W\}$, is feasible if:

$$\sum_{j\in\{B,W\}} \lambda_j \int \alpha_j(v) dF(v;\pi_j) \leq C. \tag{64}$$

An allocation is socially efficient if it maximizes the net social surplus:

$$\sum_{j\in\{B,W\}} \lambda_j \left[\int v\alpha_j(v) dF(v;\pi_j) - \int_0^{\infty} ce_j(c) dG_j(c)\right] \tag{65}$$

subject to the feasibility constraint (64).

We can rewrite the above efficiency problem as follows. Suppose that the fraction of agents investing in skills in some allocation is $\pi \in [0, 1]$, i.e., $\pi = \sum_{\lambda \in \{B,W\}} \int_0^\infty e_j(c) dG_j(c)$. Efficiency would require that the slots are only allocated to those in the top C quantile of the productivity distribution, thus the aggregate production for any given π in an efficient slot allocation rule must be:

$$Q(\pi) = \int_{1-C}^{1} F^{-1}(z; \pi) dz. \tag{66}$$

To achieve a fraction π of population investing, the efficient investment rule $e_j(c)$, $j \in \{B, W\}$, must be that only those in the lowest π-quantile in the effort cost distribution $G(\cdot)$ invest in skills. Thus the least aggregate effort costs to achieve π is:

$$C(\pi) = \int_0^{\pi} G^{-1}(z) dz. \tag{67}$$

Thus the socially efficient π is characterized by the first order condition $Q'(\pi) = C'(\pi)$, which yields:

$$G^{-1}(\pi^*) = \int_{1-C}^{1} \frac{\partial F^{-1}(z;\pi)}{\partial \pi} dz = \int_{F^{-1}(1-C;\pi^*)}^{\infty} \Delta H(v) dv. \tag{68}$$

The characterization for the socially efficient level of π^* is identical to that of the *laissez-faire* equilibrium of π^m provided in (63), thus $\pi^* = \pi^m$. Since it is also obvious that the slot assignment rule under the *laissez-faire* equilibrium allocation is exactly the same as the efficient assignment rule for a given π, we conclude that the *laissez-faire* equilibrium is efficient.

Let ρ_j^* be the faction of group j agents who acquires slots under the *laissez-faire* equilibrium. Under the plausible assumption that $g_B(c)/g_W(c)$ is strictly increasing in c, which, among other things, implies that $G_B(c)$ first order stochastically dominates $G_W(c)$, then the *laissez-faire* equilibrium will have a smaller fraction of the group B agents assigned with slots.

Let us suppose that a regulator aims to raise the fraction of group B agents with slots to a target level $\rho_B \in (\rho^*_B, C]$. Moreover, suppose that the regulator's affirmative action policy tools are limited to $(\sigma_W, \sigma_B, \tau_W, \tau_B)$ where σ_j is the regulator's transfers to group j agents who invest in skills and τ_j is a transfer to group j agents who hold slots. Fryer and Loury (2008) interpret σ_j as intervention at the *ex-ante investment margin*, and τ_j as intervention at the *ex post assignment margin.* It is easy to see that we can without loss of generality set either τ_W or τ_B to zero, because a universal transfer to all slot holders will just be capitalized into the slot price. Let us set $\tau_W = 0$.

Color-Sighted Intervention. First consider the case of color-sighted affirmative action, which simply means that (σ_j, τ_j) can differ by group identity j. Fix a policy

$(\sigma_W, \sigma_B, \tau_B)$, let π_j be the fraction of group j agents who invest in skills, and let p be the equilibrium slot price. We know that only group B agents with v above $p - \tau_B$ will obtain a slot. Thus to achieve the policy goal ρ_B, we must have

$$1 - F(p - \tau_B; \pi_B) = \rho_B,$$

that is,

$$p - \tau_B = F^{-1}(1 - \rho_B; \pi_B). \tag{69}$$

From the slot clearing condition, $\lambda_W \rho_W + \lambda_B \rho_B = C$, we can solve for ρ_W for any policy goal ρ_B, i.e., $\rho_W = (C - \lambda_B \rho_B)/\lambda_W$. The equilibrium slot price p must satisfy:

$$1 - F(p; \pi_W) = \rho_W,$$

or equivalently;

$$p = F^{-1}(1 - \rho_W; \pi_W). \tag{70}$$

A group j agent will invest in skills if his investment cost c, minus the transfer σ_j, is less than the expected benefit from investing. This gives us:

$$\pi_W = G_W\left(\sigma_W + \int_p^\infty \Delta H(v)dv\right) \tag{71}$$

$$\pi_B = G_B\left(\sigma_B + \int_{p-\tau_B}^\infty \Delta H(v)dv\right) \tag{72}$$

For a given pair (π_W, π_B), Equations (69)–(72) uniquely determine the policy parameters $(\sigma_W, \sigma_B, \tau_B)$ and the equilibrium slot price p for whites that will implement the affirmative action target $\rho_B \in (\rho^*{}_B, C]$. What remains to be determined is the constrained efficient levels of (π_W^s, π_B^s) which maximize the social surplus from implementing the policy objective (ρ_W, ρ_B), given by:[25]

$$\sum_{j\in\{B,W\}} \lambda_j \left[\int_{1-\rho_j}^1 F^{-1}(z; \pi_j^s)dz - \int_0^{\pi_j^s} G_j^{-1}(z)dz\right]. \tag{73}$$

Problem (73) is separable by group. Thus, the first order condition for the constrained efficient levels of (π_W^s, π_B^s) is analogous to (68), except that now it is group specific, namely, for $j = B, W$,

[25] (73) is derived analogous to (66) and (67). Note that the transfers and subsidies $(\sigma_W, \sigma_B, \tau_B)$ do not factor into the calculation for social surplus.

$$G_j^{-1}(\pi_j^{s*}) = \int_{F^{-1}(1-\rho_j;\pi_j^{s*})}^{\infty} \Delta H(v)dv. \tag{74}$$

Combining the characterization of (π_W^{s*}, π_B^{s*}) provided in (74) with the (69)–(72), we immediately have the following result: given an affirmative action target $\rho_B \in (\rho^*{}_B, C]$, the efficient color sighted affirmative action policy is:

$$\sigma_W = \sigma_B = 0, \tau_B = F^{-1}(1-\rho_W; \pi_W^{s*}) - F^{-1}(1-\rho_B; \pi_B^{s*}),$$

where $\rho_W = (C - \lambda_B \rho_B)/\lambda_W$, and (π_W^{s*}, π_B^{s*}) satisfy (74).

In other words, when the affirmative action policies can be conditioned on group identity, the regulator will not use *explicit* skill subsidies to promote the access of a disadvantaged group to scarce positions. Of course, by favoring disadvantaged group at the slot assignment stage, skill investment is still *implicitly* subsidized for the disadvantaged. To spell out the intuition for the result, it is useful to note that, due to the noise in the productivity following skill investment, because productivity *vs.* conditional on investment is distributed as H_1 (v), subsidy on the *ex-ante* skill investment will lead to *leakage* in the sense that some black agents may decide to invest in skills as a result of skill subsidy, but may end up with low productivity and be assigned a slot. An *ex post* subsidy on the slot price for the blacks is a more *targeted* policy.

Color Blind Intervention. Now consider the case where policies cannot condition on color, that is, $\sigma_W = \sigma_B = \sigma^c$ and $\tau_W = \tau_B = \tau$. As we discussed earlier, if $\tau > 0$, but the price of slots are allowed to be set in equilibrium, the slot price subsidy τ will be reflected in a higher slot price. Thus in fact, the regulator may as well set $\tau = 0$, but instead *impose a cap p^c for the slot price.* The idea of implementing affirmative action using color blind policy instruments is similar to that detailed in Chan and Eyster (2003): imposing a lower threshold (i.e., a cap on the slot price) and employing randomization. If there are more blacks at the assignment margin p^m identified for the *laissez-faire* equilibrium, the affirmative action goal ρ_B may be achieved because lowering the margin and randomizing the slot assignment for those above the margin favors the blacks.

Let (σ^c, p^c) be the colorblind policy. Suppose that the fraction of individuals who invest in skills under such a policy is π^c in the population and π_j^c within group j. Given the price cap p^c, the total measure of individuals whose productivity v (and thus willingness to pay for a slot) is above p^c is given by $1 - F(p^c; \pi^c)$. Thus the random rationing probability, denoted by α^c, is given by:

$$\alpha^c = \frac{C}{1 - F(p^c; \pi^c)} < 1. \tag{75}$$

The gross returns from investing in skills when slots are rationed is given by $\sigma + \alpha^c \int_{p^c}^{\infty} \Delta H(v)dv$. Thus, the fractions of individuals who invest in skills are:

$$\pi^c = G\left(\sigma + \alpha^c \int_{p^c}^{\infty} \Delta H(v)dv\right), \tag{76}$$

$$\pi_j^c = G_j\left(\sigma + \alpha^c \int_{p^c}^{\infty} \Delta H(v)dv\right) = G_j(G^{-1}(\pi^c)) \text{ for } j = B, W. \tag{77}$$

In equilibrium, the proportion of blacks assigned with a slot is given by $\alpha^c[1 - F(p^c; \pi_B^c)]$. To satisfy the affirmative action target ρ_B, it must be the case that:

$$\rho_B = \alpha^c[1 - F(p^c; \pi_B^c)]. \tag{78}$$

Substituting the expression of α^c from (75) into (78), the affirmative action target constraint can be rewritten as:

$$\rho_B = \frac{C[1 - F(p^c; \pi_B^c)]}{1 - F(p^c; \pi^c)} = \frac{C[1 - F(p^c; G_B(G^{-1}(\pi^c)))]}{1 - F(p^c; \pi^c)}, \tag{79}$$

where the second equality follows from substituting (77) for π_B^c. It can be shown that, for a fixed π^c (and thus fixed π_B^c as well due to (77)), the right hand side is strictly decreasing in p^c. Thus for any target ρ_B, there exists a unique p^c to achieve the target and the price cap p^c is lower, the more aggressive the target ρ_B is.

Because (76) tells us that the skill subsidy σ^c is uniquely determined by (π^c, p^c), we can recast the regulator's problem as choosing (π^c, p^c) to maximize the social surplus given by:

$$\frac{C}{1 - F(p^c; \pi^c)} \int_{p^c}^{\infty} v dF(v; \pi^c) - \int_0^{\pi} G^{-1}(z)dz \tag{80}$$

subject to the affirmative action target constraint (79). Let (π^{c*}, p^{c*}) be the solution to the above problem. From the first order condition to problem (80), Fryer and Loury (2008) showed that σ^{c*} corresponding to (π^{c*}, p^{c*}), which can be derived from (76) as:

$$\sigma^{c*} = G^{-1}(\pi^{c*}) - \frac{C}{1 - F(p^{c*}; \pi^{c*})} \int_{p^{c*}}^{\infty} \Delta H(v)dv$$

is positive if and only if:

$$\frac{f(p^{c*}, G_B(G^{-1}(\pi^{c*})))}{f(p^{c*}, \pi^{c*})} < \frac{g_B(G^{-1}(\pi^{c*}))}{g(G^{-1}(\pi^{c*}))}. \tag{81}$$

Note that the left-hand side term, if multiplied by λ_B, is the relative fraction of blacks among agents on the *ex post* assignment margin p^c; and the right-hand side term, if multiplied by λ_B, is the relative fraction of blacks on the *ex-ante* skill investment margin with $c = G^{-1}(\pi)$. Thus, we have the following result: Given an affirmative action target $\rho_B \in (\rho^*_B, C]$, and let (π^{c*}, p^{c*}) solve problem (80), then the efficient color blind affirmative action policy will involve strictly positive skill investment subsidy $\sigma^{c*} > 0$ if (81) holds at (π^{c*}, p^{c*}).

6.7 Additional issues related to affirmative action

Besides the theoretical examinations of the effects of affirmative action on incentives and welfare, a recent literature asks whether affirmative action policies in college and professional school admissions may have led to mismatch that could inadvertently hurt, rather than, help, the intended beneficiaries. This so-called mismatch literature examines how some measured outcomes, such as GPA, wages, or bar passage rate, etc., for minorities are affected by affirmative action admission policies.[26] A recent paper by Arcidiacono, Aucejo, Fang, and Spenner (2009) takes a new viewpoint by asking why minority students would be willing to enroll themselves at schools where they cannot succeed, as stipulated by the mismatch hypothesis. They show that a *necessary condition* for mismatch to occur once we take into account the minority students' rational enrollment decisions is that the selective university has private information about the treatment effect of the students, and provide tests for the necessary condition. They implement the test using data from the Campus Life and Learning (CLL) project at Duke University. Evidence shows that Duke does possess private information that is a statistically significant predictor of the students' post-enrollment academic performance. Further, this private information is shown to affect subjective measures of students' satisfaction as well as their persistence in more difficult majors. They also propose strategies to evaluate more conclusively, whether the presence of Duke's private information has generated mismatch.

In the class of models where discriminatory outcomes arise because of multiple equilibria and coordination failure, as reviewed in Sections 3 and 4, affirmative action can be interpreted as an attempt to eliminate the Pareto dominated equilibrium where the disadvantaged group coordinates on. One of the problems, as illustrated by the patronizing equilibrium identified by Coate and Loury (1993a) and described in Section 6.2.2, is that affirmative action policies may lead to new equilibrium with inequality. In an interesting paper, Chung (1999) interprets the affirmative action problem as an *implementation* problem and ask whether more elaborate affirmative action policies can be identified that will eliminate the Pareto dominated equilibrium without generating any new undesirable equilibria. Chung (1999) shows that in a Coate and Loury model, a class of policies that combine unemployment insurance and employment

[26] See Loury and Garman (1995), Sanders 2004, Ayres and Brooks 2005, Ho (2005), Chambers et al. (2005), Barnes (2007), and Rothstein and Yoon (2008).

subsidy (insurance-cum-subsidy) can eliminate the bad equilibrium without generating any new undesirable equilibria. The insurance-cum-subsidy policy can be interpreted as follows: each worker from a certain group is offered an option to buy an unemployment insurance package at the time he makes his human capital investment. The insurance is unattractive to any worker unless the probability of being unemployed is sufficiently high; enough workers buying this insurance will trigger a group-wide employment subsidy. A policy like this does not lead to undesirable patronizing equilibrium because the employment subsidies appear only if workers believe the employers are too reluctant to hire them.

Abdulkadiroglu (2005) studies the effect of affirmative action in college admission from the perspective of matching theory. He interprets the college admissions problem as a many-to-one two-sided matching problem with a finite set of students and a finite set of colleges. Each college has a finite capacity to enroll students. The preference relation of each student over colleges is a linear order of colleges, where as the preference relation of each college over sets of students is a linear order of the set of students. He examines the conditions for the existence of stable mechanisms that make truthful revelation of student preferences a dominant strategy with and without affirmative action quotas.

Fu (2006) studies the effect of affirmative action using insights from all-pay auctions. He considers a situation where two students, one majority and one minority, are competing for one college seat. The college wants to maximize test scores, which depends only on the students' efforts. Suppose that the benefit from attending the college is higher for the majority student than for the minority student. The two students compete for the college seat by choosing effort levels. Fu (2006) shows that this problem is analogous to a asymmetric complete information all-pay auction problem where the college can be thought of as the "seller," and the two students the "bidders," the test scores (or the efforts) are the "bids," and the students' benefit from attending the college "values of the object to the bidders." He then uses insights from asymmetric all-pay auctions to show that to maximize the test scores; the college actually should adopt an admission rule that favors the minority students to offset his disadvantage in value from attending the college relative to the majority student.

Hickman (2009) adopts a similar approach by making the college admission problem into an all-pay auction with incomplete information in order to study the effects of types of affirmative action policies on the racial achievement gap, the enrollment gap, and effort incentives. He finds that, in general, quotas perform better than simple admission preference rules. The reason is that preference rules uniformly subsidize grades without rewarding performance, and therefore have a negative effect on effort incentives. In general, however, the details of the admission rule are important, and the optimal policy depends on parameters, which can only be determined empirically.

In a similar vein, Fryer and Loury (2005) use a tournament model to investigate the categorical redistributions in a winner-take-all market and show that optimally designed tournaments naturally involve "handicapping."[27]

7. EFFICIENCY IMPLICATIONS OF STATISTICAL DISCRIMINATION

In models of statistical discrimination, the use of group identity as a proxy for relevant variables is typically the informationally efficient response of an information-seeking, individually rational agent. Efficiency considerations are therefore especially appropriate in these settings, and a small literature has been devoted to analyzing the different sources of inefficiency arising from statistical discrimination. This is in sharp contrast to Becker-style taste discrimination models where efficiency is not an issue. In models where discrimination arises directly from preferences, any limitation in the use of group identity generates some inefficiencies, at least directly.

7.1 Efficiency in models with exogenous differences

In Phelps' (1972) basic model analyzed in Section 2, discrimination has a purely redistributive nature. If employers were not allowed to use race as a source of information, wages would then equal the expected productivity of the entire population conditional on signal θ. Thus, wage equation (1) is replaced by:

$$E(q|\theta) = \frac{\sigma^2}{\sigma^2 + \sigma_\varepsilon^2}\theta + \frac{\sigma_{\varepsilon^2}}{\sigma^2 + \sigma_{\varepsilon^2}}[\lambda\mu_B + (1-\lambda)\mu_W]$$

where λ is the share of group-B workers in the labor market, $\sigma^2 = \lambda^2\sigma_B^2 + (1-\lambda)^2\sigma_W^2$, and $\sigma_\varepsilon^2 = \lambda^2\sigma_{\varepsilon B}^2 + (1-\lambda)^2\sigma_{\varepsilon W}^2$. Assuming a total population size of 1, total product would be equal to average productivity, $\mu = \lambda\mu_B + (1-\lambda)\,\mu_W$. This quantity is the same as when the employers are allowed to discriminate by race. Thus, there is no efficiency gain from discrimination. This equivalence, however, is an artifact of the extreme simplicity of the model and is not robust to many simple extensions.

Suppose, as an illustration, that there are two jobs in the economy, with different technologies. Assume that workers with productivity less than the population average μ are only productive in job 1, and workers with productivity greater than μ are only productive in job 2. In this case, $E(q\,|\,\mu) = \mu$; therefore, it is optimal for firms to allocate workers with signals $\theta < \mu$ to job 1 and workers with signals $\theta \geq \mu$ to job 2. Some mismatches will occur. If populations have different population averages, $\mu_B \neq \mu_W$, then the optimal allocation rule follows thresholds θ_j, $j \in \{B, W\}$ computed to satisfy

[27] Schotter and Weigelt (1992) found evidence that affirmative action may increase the total output in an asymmetric tournament in a laboratory setting. Calsamiglia, Franke, and Rey-Biel (2009) have similar findings in a real-world field experiment involving school children. See Holzer and Neumark (2000) for a detailed survey of available evidence regarding the incentive effects of affirmative action policies.

$E(q \mid \theta_j) = \mu$, which differ by group. Mismatch increases when employers are not allowed to discriminate by race, because race functions effectively as a proxy for productivity.

When human capital investment is endogenous, as in Lundberg and Startz's (1983) version of Phelps' model, efficiency also depends on the human capital investment cost paid by workers. One source of inefficiency of discriminatory outcomes is that the marginal worker from the dominant group pays a higher cost than the marginal worker from the discriminated group. Using the parameterization presented in Section 2.2.2, the marginal worker produces:

$$MP(X) = a + bX^* = a + \frac{b^2}{c}\frac{\sigma^2}{\sigma^2 + \sigma^2_{\varepsilon j}}$$

(see equation 2) after spending $C(X) = cX^2/2$ in investment costs. Hence the net social product of human capital investment in group-j is:

$$\begin{aligned} &MP(X) - MP(0) - C(X) = \\ &a + \frac{b^2}{c}\frac{\sigma^2}{\sigma^2 + \sigma^2_{\varepsilon j}} - a - \frac{b^2}{2c}\left(\frac{\sigma^2}{\sigma^2 + \sigma^2_{\varepsilon j}}\right)^2 = \frac{b^2}{c}\left(1 - \frac{1}{2}\frac{\sigma^2}{\sigma^2 + \sigma^2_{\varepsilon j}}\right) \end{aligned}$$

To generate a discriminatory equilibrium, assume $\sigma^2_{\varepsilon B} > \sigma^2_{\varepsilon W}$. In this case it is efficient to transfer some units of training from high cost W workers to low-cost B workers. In general, a ban on the use of race results in a more efficient solution relative to the statistical discrimination outcome.

However, as Lundberg and Startz (1983) note in their conclusion, this result is not robust, and it is meant to illustrate a more general principle that in a second-best world, as one in which there is incomplete information, "there is no reason to assume that approaching the first best—using more information—is welfare improving. Since the problem of incomplete information is endemic in situations of discrimination, considerations of the second best are a general concomitant to policy questions in this area."

Other papers focus therefore on sources for the opposite outcome, that is showing that statistical discrimination may be efficiency enhancing. This depends on the details of the model specification and sometimes on the parameterization of the model.

Schwab (1986), for example, focused on one specific type of mismatching that statistical discrimination generates. In this paper, workers can pool with other workers in a "standardized" labor market in which individual productivity cannot be detected, and therefore everybody is paid a wage equal to the average productivity in the pool of workers. Workers can, alternatively, self-employ and receive compensation that is an increasing function of their ability. The marginal worker is indifferent between self-employment and the standardized market. However, her productivity in the standardized market must be higher than her wage, because all of the workers in her pool have lower productivity. This is an informational externality, which implies an employment level in the standardized market lower than socially optimal.

Consider adding to this model a second group of workers with higher average ability in the standardized market. In an equilibrium with statistical discrimination, wage in the standardized market will depend on group identity, and will be higher for members of the second group. A ban on statistical discrimination practices will equalize such wage, but will have ambiguous effects on efficiency. It will increase standardized market employment for members of the less productive group, therefore approaching the first-best solution for this group, but the opposite happens for members of the more productive group. The total effect depends on the details of the ability distribution in the two groups.[28]

7.2 Efficiency in models with endogenous differences

The same effects play a role in the equilibrium models of statistical discrimination analyzed in Sections 3 and 4: the efficient allocation of workers to jobs, the role of the informational externalities due to imperfect information. In addition, efficiency may depend on the effects on the cost of human capital investment, and, depending on the technology, the role of complementarities in the production function.

Two broad sets of questions can be asked in this context. First, does the planners' problem solution imply differential treatment across groups? Second, are discriminatory equilibria more efficient than symmetric, nondiscriminatory equilibria?

7.2.1 The planners' problem

A comprehensive analysis of the various effects is performed in Norman (2003), where symmetric outcomes are compared to discrimination in the planners' problem.

Norman adopts a simplified version of the model in Moro and Norman (2004) and shows first that if the planner is allowed to discriminate between groups, then the production possibility frontier expands. This is a direct implication of employers' imperfect information. Assume for simplicity there are only two signals, *H*(igh) and *L*(ow), such that the probability that a qualified worker receives a high signal is $f > 1/2$, whereas the same probability for a low-signal worker is $(1 - f)$. For an intuition, consider the case where groups have equal size, and compare the situations where both groups invest the same amount π with the case where they invest differently, $\pi_B < \pi_W$, but aggregate investment is equal to π.

It is not difficult to see that the production possibility frontier expands with group inequality. Any factor input combination (C, S) with $S > 0$, $C > 0$ achievable in the symmetric case can be improved upon by replacing a high-signal B worker employed in the complex task with a high-signal W worker employed in the simple task.

[28] A similar model is also analyzed in Haagsma (1993), who considers also the effects of varying labor supply.

Substituting these two workers does not change the input in the simple task, but it increases expected input in the complex task because the expected productivity in the complex task is higher for W workers,

$$\frac{\pi_W f}{\pi_W f + (1 - \pi_W)(1 - f)} > \frac{\pi_B f}{\pi_B f + (1 - \pi_B)(1 - f)}. \tag{82}$$

Incomplete information generates misallocation of workers to task. In an asymmetric equilibrium race functions as an additional signal that moderates the informational problem.

However, to generate higher investment in group W the planner has to pay high signal workers from this group a higher premium. Such premium can be "financed" via a transfer or resources from group B, or exploiting the informational efficiency gains. Norman shows with two parametric examples the role of the difference between a linear technology and a technology with complementarities. The crucial result is that when there are complementarities, the discriminatory solution *may* result in Pareto-gains, that is, in an outcome where both groups are better off. On the other hand, when technology is linear, the planner can implement the efficient asymmetric solution only by transferring resources from the discriminated group to the dominant group.

It is possible to illustrate this result with a simple parametric example. Consider a technology given by $y(C, S) = \sqrt{CS}$ with cost of investment equal to 0 for half of the workers of either group, and 0.1 for everybody else. As in the example described above, there are only two feasible signals, H and L, and with $f = 2/3$.

Consider first the situation where the planner is constrained to a symmetric outcome. The advantage of the cost distribution we adopted is that the solution is either $\pi = 1/2$ or $\pi = 1$ so we only need to compare these two cases. When $\pi = 1$ everybody is equally productive in either task, therefore the optimal solution is to assign half the population to each task, and total output is $y = 0.5$. When $\pi = 1/2$, one can easily compute that the optimal solution is to assign all H workers to the complex task and all L workers to the simple task. In this case $C = 2/3 * 1/2$ and $S = 1/2$, which implies $y = 0.5\sqrt{2/3} < 0.5$. Cost of investment is zero when $\pi = 1/2$ and 0.05 when $\pi = 1$. Hence the optimal solution is $\pi = 1$. In this solution, there are 2/3 workers with signal H, hence to implement this outcome, the planner can pay L workers 0 and H workers 3/2. Incentives to invest are 3/2 * (2/3 − 1/3) = 1/2.

To solve for the asymmetric outcome, note that in the symmetric solution 1/2 of the workers are employed in the simple task but do not need to be qualified. Hence, it would be more efficient if we could "tag" half the workers and induce them not to invest in human capital. Using race, the planner can have all W workers replicate what they do in the previous outcome, and all B workers not to invest in human capital. Then, assign all W workers to the complex task and all B workers to the simple task. Output would be the same, but half of the investment costs would be the saved.

This outcome is implementable by paying all B workers 1/2 regardless of their signal, and paying W workers as before. Total wage bill is 1/2 for B workers, and 3/2 * 2/3 * 1/2 = 1/2 for W workers. Because of the savings in investment cost, the B group is more than fully compensated in this outcome.

What this example shows is that complementarities in the production function coupled with specialization allow the planner to reduce investment cost without changing output. This would be impossible in the linear case because less investment implies lower output. Therefore, the gains from specialization cannot be redistributed across groups without breaking incentive compatibility. In a parametric example, Norman shows that even in the linear case there may be efficiency gains from discrimination in the planners' problem (arising from reduced mismatching), but that the added investment for the dominant group must be supported using transfers from the discriminated group.

7.2.2 The efficiency of discriminatory equilibria

Considering the case of the equilibrium model in Moro and Norman (2004) with a linear technology, where discrimination results from coordination failure (see Section 3). Note that equilibria are Pareto-ranked. To see this, the model with a single group of workers displaying two equilibrium levels of human capital investment, $\pi_1 > \pi_2$. Under π_1, wages as a function of θ are weakly greater than under the lower level of human capital investment π_2. Therefore, all workers that either do not invest or that do invest in both equilibria are better off under the high human capital investment equilibrium because they have higher expected wages, which can be computed using (3) by integrating over the relevant distribution of θ, that is f_q for workers that invest, and f_u for workers that do not invest. There is a set of workers that do not invest under π_2, but do invest and pay the investment cost under π_1. To see that even these workers are better-off, note that because they choose to invest, it must be that the benefits outweigh the cost, that is, $\int w(\theta,\pi_1)f_q(\theta) - c \geq \int w(\theta,\pi_1)f_u(\theta)$. The left-hand side however must be greater than the expected wage of non-investors under π_2, $\int w(\theta,\pi_2)f_u(\theta)$. Therefore $\int w(\theta,\pi_1)f_q(\theta) - c > \int w(\theta,\pi_2)f_u(\theta)$; that is, even these workers strictly prefer the higher investment equilibrium.

Hence, because of the linearity in production, separability between groups implies that the discriminatory equilibrium is not efficient. When production displays complementarities, because of effects that are similar to the one displayed in the example illustrated in the planners' problem, we conjecture the possibility that group-wide Pareto gains may exist in discriminatory equilibria relative to symmetric equilibria.

8. CONCLUSION

This chapter surveyed the theoretical literature on statistical discrimination and affirmative action stressing the different explanation for group inequality that have been developed from the seminal articles of Phelps (1972) and Arrow(1973), and their policy implications.

In this conclusion, we highlight some areas for potentially fruitful future research. First, as we mentioned in Section 5, we still have a relatively poor theoretical understanding on the evolution of stereotypes, under what conditions do they arise and lead to permanent inequality, and how the stereotypes are affected by supposedly temporary affirmative action policies. There is not yet any study on how affirmative action policies might change the dynamics of the between-group inequalities. Can temporary affirmative action measures indeed lead to between-group equalities, as proclaimed in Supreme Court justices' opinion in 1978 and 1993? Second, most of the existing literature on affirmative action has studied a quite stylized version of the policy, assuming that employers follow quotas set by the policymaker. In practice, however, the policy maker rarely sets clearly defined quotas. In addition, there exist agency issues between the policymaker (the principal) and the decision-makers (the agent). As an example that should be familiar in the academic world, consider the case of a college dean and a research department that place different weights on their concern for academic excellence and faculty racial or gender diversity. How affirmative action policies should be optimally designed in light of such agency issues is also an important question to study.

Finally, this survey has not made much connection between the theoretical models and the small existing empirical literature related to statistical discrimination theories. Most of the empirical literature on racial and gender inequality focuses on measuring inequality after controlling for a number of measurable factors without attempting to attribute the unexplained residuals to a specific source of discrimination.[29] Some articles attempt to test implications of statistical discrimination directly, with mixed evidence. For example, Altonji and Pierret (2001) test dynamic wage implications of statistical discrimination.[30] Another growing literature attempts to use statistical evidence to distinguish statistical discrimination from racial prejudice, particularly regarding racial profiling in highway stops and searches.[31] In surveying the trends of Black-White wage inequality, Neal (2010) finds that returns to schooling and other test scores are higher for minorities, evidence that he claims to be counterfactual to statistical discrimination theories based on endogenous differential incentives to acquire skills.[32] However, the

[29] Most of these articles assume or suggest that the unexplained differences should be attributed to racial bias. Interested readers should consult the surveys by Altonji and Blank (1999) and Holzer and Neumark (2000).

[30] See also Lange (2007).

[31] See, e.g., Knowles, Persico and Todd (2001), and Anwar and Fang (2006) for evidence on police racial profiling. Fang and Persico (2010) provide a unified framework to distinguish racial prejudice from statistical discrimination that is applicable in many settings.

[32] For additional evidence on returns to aptitude test scores, see Neal and Johnson (1996) and, with more recent data, Fadlon (2010). See also Heckman, Lochner and Todd (2006) for evidence on returns to education controlling for selection bias.

human-capital-based theories that originate from Arrow's (1973) insight depends crucially on *unobserved* human capital investment; therefore, they do not directly imply that returns to *observable* human capital, such as education, should be different or higher for the dominant group. For example, conditional on education, statistical discrimination can predict that members of the discriminated group exert lower learning effort because they have fewer incentives to do so; but returns to schooling might be higher for them. In addition, the theory only predicts that groups have different returns to the skill signals that are *observed by employers*, not to signals observed by the investigator. Even if we interpret education (or any other observable test score) as a signal of skill, a regression of wages on such signals produces estimates that suffer from omitted variable bias whenever firms also use privately observed signals. The size of this bias depends on group fundamentals in ways that might confuse the inference made by the econometrician.[33]

Nevertheless, we believe that studying ways to reconcile empirical facts about wage differences and the typical theoretical predictions of statistical discrimination theories could be a fruitful area of future research. Some attempts at structurally estimating statistical discrimination models find that even stylized versions of these models fit the data quite well. For example, Moro (2003) structurally estimates a model based on Moro and Norman (2004) using Current Population Survey data and finds that adverse equilibrium selection did not play a role in exacerbating wage inequality during the last part of the 20th century. Fang (2006) estimates, using Census data, an equilibrium labor market model with endogenous education choices based on Fang (2001) to assess the relative importance of human capital enhancement versus ability signaling in explaining the college wage premium. Bowlus and Eckstein (2002) estimate a structural equilibrium search model to distinguish the roles of skill differences among groups and employers' racial prejudice to explain racial wage inequality.[34] However, these estimates are not designed to perform model validation. Research addressing the identification issue of how to disentangle different sources of group inequality (being from statistical, taste-based discrimination, or from differences in groups' fundamentals) would be especially welcome.

REFERENCES

Abdulkadiroglu, A., 2005. College Admissions with Affirmative Action. International Journal of Game Theory 33, 535–549.
Aigner, D., Cain, G., 1977. Statistical Theories of Discrimination in the Labor Market. Ind. Labor Relat. Rev. 30 (2), 175–187.
Altonji, J., Blank, R., 1999. Race and Gender in the Labor Market. In: Ashenfelter, O., Card, D. (Eds.), Handbook of Labor Economics, vol. 3C Elsevier, North Holland, pp. 3143–3259 (Chapter 48).

[33] Moro and Norman (2003b) show this point formally.
[34] See also Flabbi (2009) for the case of gender wage differences in a model with both matching and wage bargaining.

Altonji, J., Pierret, C.R., 2001. Employer Learning and Statistical Discrimination. Q. J. Econ. 116 (1), 313–350.
Antonovics, K., 2006. Statistical Discrimination and Intergenerational Income Mobility. mimeo, UC San Diego.
Anwar, S., Fang, H., 2006. An Alternative Test of Racial Profiling in Motor Vehicle Searches: Theory and Evidence. Am. Econ. Rev. 96 (1), 127–151.
Arcidiacono, P., Aucejo, E., Fang, H., Spenner, K.I., 2009. Does Affirmative Action Lead to Mismatch? A New Test and Evidence. NBER Working Paper No. 14885.
Arcidiacono, P., 2005. Affirmative Action in Higher Education: How do Admission and Financial Aid Rules Affect Future Earnings? Econometrica 73 (5), 1477–1524.
Arrow, K.J., 1973. The Theory of Discrimination. In: Ashenfelter, O., Rees, A. (Eds.), Discrimination in Labor Markets. Princeton University Press, pp. 3–33.
Ayres, I., Brooks, R., 2005. Does Affirmative Action Reduce the Number of Black Lawyers? Stanford Law Rev. 57 (6), 1807–1854.
Barnes, K.Y., 2007. Is Affirmative Action Responsible for the Achievement Gap Between Black and White Law Students? Northwest. Univ. Law Rev. 101 (4), Fall, 1759–1808.
Becker, G.S., 1957. The Economics of Discrimination. University of Chicago Press, Chicago.
Blume, L., 2006. The Dynamics of Statistical Discrimination. Econ. J. 116, F480–F498.
Cain, A., 1986. The Economic Analysis of Labor Market Discrimination: A Survey. In: Ashenfelter, O., Layard, R. (Eds.), Handbook of Labor Economics, vol. 1 Amsterdam, North Holland, pp. 693–785 (Chapter 13).
Calsamiglia, C., Franke, J., Rey-Biel, P., 2009. The Incentive Effects of Affirmative Action in a Real-Effort Tournament. Unpublished Working Paper, Universitat Autonoma de Barcelona.
Chambers, D.L., Clydesdale, T.T., Kidder, W.C., Lempert, R.O., 2005. The Real Impact of Eliminating Affirmative Action in American Law Schools: An Empirical Critique of Richard Sander's Study. Stanford Law Rev. 57 (6), 1855–1898.
Chan, J., Eyster, E., 2003. Does Banning Affirmative Action Lower College Student Quality? Am. Econ. Rev. 93 (3), 858–872.
Chaudhuri, S., Sethi, R., 2008. Statistical Discrimination with Peer Effects: Can Integration Eliminate Negative Stereotypes? Rev. Econ. Stud. 75, 579–596.
Chung, K.S., 1999. Affirmative Action as an Implementation Problem. Unpublished Working Paper, University of Minnesota.
Chung, K.S., 2000. Role Models and Arguments for Affirmative Action. Am. Econ. Rev. 90 (3), 640–648.
Coate, S., Loury, G., 1993a. Will Affirmative Action Eliminate Negative Stereotypes? Am. Econ. Rev. 83 (5), 1220–1240.
Coate, S., Loury, G., 1993b. Antidiscrimination Enforcement and the Problem of Patronization. American Economic Review Papers and Proceedings 83 (2), 92–98.
Cornell, B., Welch, I., 1996. Culture, Information, and Screening Discrimination. J. Polit. Econ. 104 (3), 542–571.
DeGroot, M.H., 2004. Optimal Statistical Decisions, first ed. Wiley-Interscience.
Eeckhout, J., 2006. Minorities and Endogenous Segregation. Rev. Econ. Stud. 73 (1), 31–53.
Bowlus, A., Eckstein, Z., 2002. Discrimination and Skill Differences in an Equilibrium Search Model. Int. Econ. Rev. 43 (4), 1309–1345.
Epple, D., Romano, R., Sieg, H., 2002. On the Demographic Composition of Colleges and Universities in Market Equilibrium. American Economic Review Papers and Proceedings 92 (2), 310–314.
Epple, D., Romano, R., Sieg, H., 2008. Diversity and Affirmative Action in Higher Education. J. Public Econ. Theory 10 (4), 475–501.
Fadlon, Y., 2010. Statistical Discrimination and the Implications of Employer-Employee Racial Matches. Unpublished manuscript, Vanderbilt University.
Fang, H., 2001. Social Culture and Economic Performance. Am. Econ. Rev. 91 (4), 924–937.
Fang, H., Loury, G., 2005a. Toward An Economic Theory of Dysfunctional Identity. In: Christopher, B (Ed.), Social Economics of Poverty: On Identities, Groups, Communities and Networks. Routledge, Barrett, London, pp. 12–55.

Fang, H., Loury, G., 2005b. Dysfunctional Identities Can Be Rational. American Economic Review Papers and Proceedings 95 (2), 104–111.
Fang, H., Norman, P., 2006. Government-mandated discriminatory policies. Int. Econ. Rev. 47 (2), 361–389.
Fang, H., 2006. Disentangling the college wage premium: estimating a model with endogenous education choices. Int. Econ. Rev. 47 (4), 1151–1185.
Fang, H., Persico, N., 2010. Distinguishing prejudice from statistical discrimination: a unified framework. mimeo, University of Pennsylvania.
Flabbi, L., 2009. Gender Discrimination Estimation in a Search Model with Matching and Bargaining. Int. Econ. Rev. forthcoming.
Fryer, R., 2007. Belief flipping in a dynamic model of statistical discrimination. J. Public Econ. 91 (5–6), 1151–1166.
Fryer, R., Loury, G., 2005. Affirmative Action in Winner-Take-All Markets. Journal of Economic Inequality 3 (3), 263–280.
Fryer, R., Loury, G., 2008. Valuing Identity: The Simple Economics of Affirmative Action Policies. unpublished manuscript.
Fu, Q., 2006. A Theory of Affirmative Action in College Admissions. Econ. Inq. 44, 420–428.
Haagsma, R., 1993. Is Statistical Discrimination Socially Efficient? Inf. Econ. Policy 5, 31–50.
Heckman, J., Lochner, L., Todd, P., 2006. Earnings Functions, Rates of Returns and Treatment Effects: The Mincer Equation and Beyond. In: Hanusheck, E., Welch, F. (Eds.), Handbook of the Economics of Education, vol. I. North-Holland, pp. 307–458 (Chapter 7).
Hickman, B.R., 2009. Effort, Race Gaps and Affirmative Action: A Game-Theoretic Analysis of College Admissions. Unpublished, University of Iowa.
Ho, D.E., 2005. Why Affirmative Action Does Not Cause Black Students to Fail the Bar. Yale Law J. 114 (8), 1997–2004.
Holden, S., Rosen, A., 2009. Discrimination and Employment Protection. CESifo Working Paper Series No. 2822.
Holzer, H., Neumark, D., 2000. Assessing Affirmative Action. J. Econ. Lit. 38 (3), 483–568.
Knowles, J., Persico, N., Todd, P., 2001. Racial Bias in Motor Vehicle Searches: Theory and Evidence. J. Polit. Econ. 109, 203–228.
Lange, F., 2007. The speed of employer learning. J. Labor Econ. 25 (1), 651–691.
Levin, J., 2009. The Dynamics of Collective Reputation,. BE Journal of Theoretical Economics 9 (1), August 2009.
Lang, K., 1986. A Language Theory of Discrimination. Q. J. Econ. 101 (2), 363–382.
Loury, L.D., Garman, D., 1995. College Selectivity and Earnings. J. Labor Econ. 13 (2), 289–308.
Lundberg, S., 1991. The Enforcement of Equal Opportunity Laws under Imperfect Information: Affirmative Action and Alternatives. Q. J. Econ. 106, 309–326.
Lundberg, S., Startz, R., 1983. Private Discrimination and Social Intervention in Competitive Markets. Am. Econ. Rev. 73 (3), 340–347.
Mailath, G., Samuelson, L., Shaked, A., 2000. Endogenous Inequality in Integrated Labor Markets with Two-Sided Search. Am. Econ. Rev. 90 (1), 46–72.
Moro, A., 2003. The effect of statistical discrimination on black-white wage in-equality: estimating a model with multiple equilibria. Int. Econ. Rev. 44 (2), 457–500.
Moro, A., Norman, P., 1996. Affirmative Action in a Competitive Economy. CARESS Working Paper #96–08, University of Pennsylvania.
Moro, A., Norman, P., 2003a. Affirmative Action in a Competitive Economy. J. Public Econ. 87 (3–4), 567–594.
Moro, A., Norman, P., 2003b. Empirical Implications of Statistical Discrimination on the Returns to Measures of Skills. Ann. Econ. Stat. 71–72, 399–417.
Moro, A., Norman, P., 2004. A General Equilibrium Model of Statistical Discrimination. J. Econ. Theory 114 (1), 1–30.
Neal, D., 2010. Black–white labour market inequality in the United States. In: Durlauf, S.N., Blume, L.E. (Eds.), The New Palgrave Dictionary of Economics. Palgrave Macmillan 2008, The New Palgrave

Dictionary of Economics Online, Palgrave Macmillan. 23 February 2010, DOI: 10.1057/9780230226203.0139.
Neal, D., Johnson, W., 1996. The role of pre-market factors in black-white wage differences. J. Polit. Econ. 104, 869–895.
Norman, P., 2003. Statistical Discrimination and Efficiency. Rev. Econ. Stud. 70 (3), 615–627.
Phelps, E., 1972. The statistical theory of racism and sexism. Am. Econ. Rev. 62, 659–661.
Rosén, Å., 1997. An Equilibrium Search-Matching Model of Discrimination. Eur. Econ. Rev. 41 (8), 1589–1613.
Rothstein, J., Yoon, A., 2008. Mismatch in Law School. Unpublished manuscript, Princeton University.
Sander, R., 2004. A Systemic Analysis of Affirmative Action in American Law Schools. Stanford Law Rev. 57 (2), 367–483.
Sattinger, M., 1998. Statistical Discrimination with Employment Criteria. Int. Econ. Rev. 39 (1), 205–237.
Schotter, A., Weigelt, K., 1992. Asymmetric Tournaments, Equal Opportunity Laws, and Affirmative Action: Some Experimental Results. Q. J. Econ. 107 (2), 511–539.
Schwab, S., 1986. Is Statistical Discrimination Efficient? Am. Econ. Rev. 76 (1), 228–234.
Spence, M., 1974. Job Market Signaling. Q. J. Econ. 87, 355–374.
Stiglitz, J., 1973. Approaches to the Economics of Discrimination. American Economic Review Papers and Proceedings 63 (2), 287–295.
Verma, R., 1995. Asymmetric information, search theory and some commonly observed phenomena. University of Pennsylvania Ph.D. dissertation.

CHAPTER 6

Social Construction of Preferences: Advertising*

Jess Benhabib and Alberto Bisin

Contents

1. Introduction 201
2. The Benchmark Economy 204
   2.1 The economy with monopoly profits 205
   2.2 The economy with free entry and expanding varieties 205
3. The Equilibrium Effects of Advertising 206
   3.1 Advertising and labor 207
   3.2 Advertising and welfare 208
   3.3 Commodification of leisure 209
   3.4 Taking stock 210
4. The Effects of Advertising in Empirical Work 211
5. Conclusions 218

References 219

Abstract

We examine, with the tools of economics, a fundamental tenet of some of the most recent theoretical work in sociology, which we refer to as the *Postmodernist Critique*: preferences are socially constructed, firms exploit their monopoly power through advertising in order to create new (false) needs in consumers, and, as a consequence, consumer spending rises, and so does their supply of labor.

JEL Codes: B41, P1, J20, M37

Keywords

Social construction of preferences
advertising
Postmodernist Critique
work and spend cycle

* Thanks to Benedetto Molinari and Francesco Turino for useful comments. Prepared for the *Handbook of Social Economics*, edited by J. Benhabib, A. Bisin, and M. Jackson, forthcoming in 2010 by Elsevier.

ISSN 0169-7218, DOI: 10.1016/S0169-7218(11)01006-9

1. INTRODUCTION

Individual preferences are in part a social phenomenon. They are the result of the interaction of the individual with parents, teachers, friends, peers. They are influenced by existing social norms and beliefs, by the relative position of the individual, his/her status in different relevant reference groups.

Individual preferences are also possibly influenced by advertising. In fact, a fundamental tenet of some of the most recent theoretical work in sociology is that firms exploit their monopoly power through advertising in order to create new (false) needs, often for "conspicuous consumption." As a consequence, consumer spending rises, and so does their supply of labor.[1]

Concepts like "consumerism," "commodification" of culture, and "manipulation" of preferences have become the central core of what could be called a Postmodernist Critique of the organization of society. Monopoly power and advertising are intended as a form of "manipulation." They interact to "manufacture individual identities," to impose a system of values and preferences to consumers ("consumerism" together with "preferences for status" and "conspicuous consumption") which is not "natural," e.g., it is not supported by psychological and anthropological data.[2] Consequently, the consumption and leisure choices of agents go against their more "fundamental" will ("spontaneous consumer needs" in Galbraith, 1958): consumers are in "psychological denial" regarding their consumption and leisure habits, and desire commodities which are "useless, altered in a senseless way from the point of view of the rational consumer."[3] Consumers' "judgement(s) of taste" are socially determined (through the influence of cultural capital on the set of preference predispositions, called "habitus") so consumers seek "distinction" through "conspicuous consumption," even though they experience such tastes as natural, personal, and individualized.[4] In particular, such "manipulation of preferences," it is argued, induces consumers to reduce the time devoted to leisure activities, and to enter a "work and spend cycle." This is the main contention of J. Schor in *The Overworked American: The Unexpected Decline of Leisure* and *The Overspent American: Why We Want What We Don't Need*, two books which

[1] While this theme has been emphasized e.g., by J. A. Schumpeter in *Business Cycles; A Theoretical, Historical and Statistical Analysis of the Capitalist Process*, chapter III, and by J. K. Galbraith in the *Affluent Society*, it has been adopted and developed recently in Postmodernist circles. See e.g., F. Jameson's *The Cultural Turn*, D. Harvey's *The Condition of Postmodernity*, as well as Leonard (1997) and Anderson (1998). A good survey of the positions of the Postmodernist literature on "consumerism" is Lee (2000), and especially the paper by Campbell, p. 48–72. The importance of monopoly power in the recent development of capitalist society has also been forcefully stressed by Marxist historians, e.g., from P. Baran and P. Sweezy, in *Monopoly Capital,* to E. Mandel, in Late Capitalism, and G. Arrighi, in *The Long Twentieth Century*.

[2] See e.g., M. Douglas and B. Isherwood, *The World of Good*, D. Rushkoff, *Coercion*, M. Sahlins, *Culture and Practical Reason*.

[3] Respectively, Schor, 1998, p. 19, and Mandel, 1972, p. 394 of the English 1978 edition.

[4] See Bourdieu, 1979; p. 101 of the English edition, 1984. The intellectual roots of this argument are in Veblen, 1899, and Duesenberry, 1949.

have received enormous attention in the social sciences (other than economics). Finally, another important aspect of the Critique is the consideration of leisure itself as "commodified": private corporations have dominated the leisure 'market,' encouraging us to think of leisure as a consumption opportunity."[5]

To summarize, the basic argument of the Postmodernist Critique can be reconstructed as follows (obviously considerably simplifying across the wide range of different positions). Exploiting their monopoly power, firms manipulate the preferences of consumers through advertising in order to create new (false) needs. Therefore, profits increase and consumer spending rises, to the point where consumers enter a "work and spend cycle." They reduce the time devoted to leisure activities, or at least they curtail the increase in leisure that would have accompanied productivity and wage increases. Leisure itself is "commodified," and transformed into a form of consumption (e.g., in exotic vacations, eating out, etc.). Not only, it is argued, is the time devoted to leisure reduced because of advertising, but the mere distinction of consumption and leisure is blurred, as our preferences are "manipulated" to choose forms of leisure that are complementary to consumption. Such patterns of behavior, characterized as the "work and spend cycle" and the "commodification of leisure," reduces consumers' overall welfare when welfare is evaluated according to the consumers' ex-ante preferences, that is before advertising takes place.[6]

While it is easy for economists to ignore the Postmodernist literature, especially because of its associated methodological positions,[7] what we have identified as the Postmodernist Critique nonetheless constitutes a coherent statement about economic quantities that can be studied with the tools of economics. Moreover, even if the Postmodernist literature per se is ignored, the Critique we have identified is receiving large attention in the academic profession at large, in the humanities as well as in the social sciences, and in the analyses of many social observers.

In this chapter, we survey theoretical and empirical work regarding advertising as a vehicle for the social construction of preferences. We first posit a model, which can be used to formalize the Postmodernist Critique, from Benhabib-Bisin (2002). We then use this model to organize the existing empirical work relating aggregate advertising and economic activity, bearing therefore directly on the Critique.

[5] See Schor (1992), p. 162: "private corporations have dominated the 'leisure market' . . . How many of us, if asked to describe an ideal week-end, would choose activities that cost nothing?"

[6] Another factor often cited, as a cause of the "work-spend" cycles is a preference for status and/or for conspicuous consumption. We do not discuss this literature here as Frank (2010) takes it up, in these same volumes. In Benhabib-Bisin (2002), we provide a model of the effect of advertising on status which casts some doubts on the ability of this factor to support the Postmodernist Critique.

[7] The improper use of scientific jargon in the Postmodernist literature, for instance, has been exposed by Sokal-Bricmont (1998).

2. THE BENCHMARK ECONOMY

Consider a monopolistic competition economy with differentiated goods. A representative consumer consumes a continuum of goods indexed by i, $i \in [0, I]$. Let $x_i \geq 0$ denote his consumption of good i. The consumer is endowed with one unit of time. Let L, $0 \leq L \leq 1$, denote the share of his/her time he/she devotes to work (hence $1 - L$ denotes the share of time devoted to leisure). The consumer evaluates consumption and leisure plans with a constant elasticity of substitution utility function. He/she maximizes his/her utility in terms of aggregate consumption and leisure goods:

$$\max_{[x_i]_{0\leq i\leq I}, L} \left[(X)^{\frac{\sigma-1}{\sigma}} + (1-L)^{\frac{\sigma-1}{\sigma}} \right]^{\frac{\sigma}{\sigma-1}} \tag{1}$$

where

$$X := \left[\int_0^I \alpha_i (x_i)^{\frac{\theta_i - 1}{\theta_i}} di \right]^{\frac{\int_0^I \theta_i di}{\int_0^I \theta_i di - 1}}, \quad \theta_i > 1 \tag{2}$$

The parameter σ represents the elasticity of substitution between aggregate consumption and aggregate leisure. When $\sigma = 1$ preferences reduce to a Cobb-Douglas aggregator between consumption and leisure, the case often used in macroeconomics; see Browning-Hansen-Heckman (1999) for a survey. The parameter θ_i represents the elasticity of substitution associated with good i; finally α_i represents the intensity level of utility associated with good i.

The consumer's utility maximization is subject to his/her budget constraint, as his/her total expenditures must be financed by earned wages, wL, and by the firms' aggregate profits, π, as firms are owned by the representative consumer:

$$\int_0^I p_i x_i \, di = w\,L + \pi \tag{3}$$

We will restrict the representative consumer to symmetric preferences, $\alpha_i = \alpha$, and $\theta_i = \theta$, independent of i. We can therefore consider only symmetric equilibria. Let E denote the representative consumer's nominal expenditures. Let $x_i = x_i(p_i, p, E; \alpha, \theta)$ denote the demand of good i, evaluated at $p_j = p_{j'} := p$, for all $j, j' \neq i$, and $\alpha_i = \alpha$, $\theta_i = \theta$.[8] Each good $i \in [0, I]$ is produced using labour by a firm which is monopolistically competitive in the good's market and perfectly competitive in the labour market. The wage rate is denoted by w. We adopt the normalization that the production of one unit of good requires $\frac{1}{w}$ units of labor. The parameter w is then an index of the marginal product of labor, as well as the wage rate.

[8] I.e, formally, $x(p_i, p, E, \alpha, \theta) := \text{argmax}\left[\int_0^i \alpha(x_i)^{\frac{\theta-1}{\theta}} di\right]^{\frac{\theta}{\theta-1}}$ subject to $\int_0^i p_i x_i \, di \leq E$, and, as we focus on symmetric equilibria, $p_j = p_{j'} := p$, for all $j, j' \neq i$.

Any firm producing good i chooses price p_i to maximize profits:

$$p_i = p(p, E; \alpha, \theta, w) = \text{argmax}(p_i - 1)x_i$$

subject to:

$$x_i = x(p_i, p, E; \alpha, \theta)$$

We shall study two distinct economies, characterized by appropriate equilibrium concepts. In the first economy the monopoly power of firms translates into monopoly profits. In the second economy, free entry and expanding varieties guarantee that firms make zero profits in equilibrium.

2.1 The economy with monopoly profits

The set of goods produced and consumed in the economy, $[0, I]$, is exogenous. Without loss of generality we normalize $I = 1$. In the general equilibrium context of our model, the firms' profits are redistributed to (and spent by) their owners. The representative agent framework then implies that expenditures are equal to total wages plus total profits: $E = px = wL + \pi$. As a consequence, in equilibrium, $x = wL$.

A *symmetric monopolistically competitive equilibrium with monopoly profits* is composed of allocations $x_i = x$, $X = (\alpha)^{\frac{\theta}{\theta-1}}x$, L, prices $p_i = p$ such that:

$$x_i(p, p, wL + \pi; \alpha, \theta) = x, \pi = (p - 1)x, p = p(p, wL + \pi; \alpha, \theta), x = wL.$$

In turn, at equilibrium each firm producing an arbitrary good i sets price:

$$p = \frac{\theta}{\theta - 1} \tag{4}$$

and the representative consumer's labor L solves,

$$\frac{L}{1 - L} = \frac{1}{w}\left(\frac{p}{w}\right)^{-\sigma} \alpha^{\frac{\theta(\sigma-1)}{\theta-1}}.$$

2.2 The economy with free entry and expanding varieties

Firms face no barriers to entry and the production of each good entails a fixed-cost c, which can consist of fixed production costs as well as advertising costs. In equilibrium there are no profits, as new firms enter the market and expand the varieties produced until it is no longer profitable to do so. Therefore the number of varieties produced, I, is endogenous for this specification of the economy as firms will expand varieties until profits are driven down to zero: $pIx = wL$.

A symmetric monopolistically competitive equilibrium with free entry and expanding varieties is composed of allocations $x_i = x$, $X = (\alpha)^{\frac{\theta}{\theta-1}}x$, L, prices $p_i = p$ and varieties I such that:

$$x_i(p, p, wL; \alpha, \theta) = x, p = p(p, wL; \alpha, \theta), Ix = wL - Ic$$

and profits $\pi = pIx - wL = 0$.

In turn, at equilibrium each firm producing an arbitrary good i sets price:

$$p = \frac{\theta}{\theta - 1}, \tag{5}$$

and the representative consumer's labor L solves,

$$\frac{L}{1-L} = \left(\frac{p}{w}\right)^{1-\sigma} \alpha^{\frac{\theta(\sigma-1)}{\theta-1}}$$

3. THE EQUILIBRIUM EFFECTS OF ADVERTISING

Consider advertising as affecting the preference parameters α and θ. These parameters represent, respectively, a measure of the intensity of preferences for consumption and the elasticity of substitution across consumption goods. Note that changes in θ translate into effects on the elasticity of substitution between consumption and labor.[9] We do not consider the case where advertising affects σ, the elasticity of substitution between consumption and leisure.

We also consider a different channel for advertising to affect preferences, adopted by Molinari-Turino (2009a,b), which operates by inducing a *consumption habit* that modifies the consumption aggregator X. Let X be defined as:

$$X := \left[\int_0^I \alpha_i (x_i - b_i)^{\frac{\theta_i - 1}{\theta_i}} di\right]^{\frac{\int_0^I \theta_i di}{\int_0^I \theta_i di - 1}}$$

where b_i denotes a measure of the habit for good i induced by advertising ($b_i = b$ under symmetry), and $b_i = 0$ with no advertising. A higher b_i requires a higher x_i to guarantee the same "utils" to the consumer; hence the *consumption habit* interpretation of advertising.

Advertising is costly and is the result of the strategic interactions between each firm (producing good) i. For simplicity, we will not explicitly study the advertising game, but we instead posit directly the effects of the Nash equilibrium of the game on the agents' preference parameters:[10]

[9] In addition, we do not attempt here a survey of the economic models of advertising. In particular we do not discuss the view that advertising represents simply "a good or a bad" as in Becker-Murphy (1993), and as a consequence that the amount of exposure to advertising can be freely chosen by the consumer. This view of advertising, while quite compelling, is at odds with the Postmodernist view of the world that we aim at rationalizing in this survey. Also, and again for the sake of our analysis of the Postmodernist critique, we do not either consider informational advertising, i.e., advertising conveying useful information about consumer products; see Becker (1996; ch. 1) and Tirole (1990; p. 290) for an overview.

[10] Conditions on costs guaranteeing that the Nash equilibrium of the game has the posited effects on the parameters can be easily derived; see Benhabib-Bisin (2002).

$$\text{Before advertising} : \alpha = 1 \qquad \theta > 1 \qquad b = 0$$

$$\text{After advertising} : \alpha = \alpha_+ \begin{cases} > & > \\ = 1 & \text{if } \sigma = 1 \\ < & < \end{cases} \quad \theta = \theta_+, 1 < \theta_+ < \theta \quad b = b_+ > 0$$

Notice that, depending on the elasticity of substitution between consumption and leisure, σ, advertising will either increase of decrease α_i, so as to increase the demand for good i, x_i.

3.1 Advertising and labor

We study first the effect on labor, for both economies. Consider first the economy with monopoly profits. In equilibrium,[11]

$$\frac{wL - b_+}{1 - L} = \left(\frac{p_+}{w}\right)^{-\sigma} \alpha_+^{\frac{\theta_+(\sigma-1)}{\theta_+ - 1}}.$$

Consider now the economy with free entry and expanding varieties.

In equilibrium,

$$\frac{\frac{wL}{p_+} - b_+}{1 - L} = \left(\frac{p_+}{w}\right)^{-\sigma} \alpha_+^{\frac{\theta_+(\sigma-1)}{\theta_+ - 1}}.$$

How does advertising affect equilibrium labor L? Let's consider separately the effects of the different advertising channels, intensity on α, elasticity of substitution on θ, and habits on b.

1. *Advertising on α, given equations 4 and 5, and other things equal, has no effect on prices p_+. However, advertising on α increases L, by affecting the relative marginal utility of consumption over leisure, unless $\sigma = 1$ (log preferences), in which case advertising on α has no effects.*
2. *Advertising on θ, other things equal, reinforces any effect of advertising on intensity α. Nevertheless, advertising on θ has also the effect of increasing the price p_+. The price effect has substitution and income effects. In turn, then the price effect decreases L when the substitution effect dominates. This is the case i) in the economy with monopoly profits, where the income effect is compensated by the redistribution of profits to consumers (who own the firm); ii) if $\sigma > 1$ in the economy with free entry. The price effect instead increases L when the income effect dominates, that is, if $\sigma < 1$ in the economy with free entry. The price effect has no effects on L when the income and substitution effect cancel out, that is, in the log case, when $\sigma = 1$.*
3. *Advertising on b, other things equal, increases L. It also increases the price p_+, but the price effect is second order.*

The special case of log by both ex-antes as well as preferences ($\sigma = 1$) is important; see e.g., Prescott (2004), and McGrattan-Prescott (2007). In this case, income and substitution effects cancel out and hence:

[11] Note that $b_+ > 0$ affects equilibrium prices, by affecting the elasticity of substitution for varieties in the representative consumer's demand. In fact, it can be shown that p_+ increases in b_+; see Molinari-Turino (2009b).

1. In *Advertising on* α*, other things equal, has no effect on L.*
2. In *Advertising on* θ*, other things equal, has the effect of increasing the price* p_+*. The price effect decreases L with monopoly profits, but has no effect on L* with free entry.
3. In *Advertising on b increases L. It also increases the price* p_+*, but the price effect is second order.*

3.2 Advertising and welfare

Studying the effects of advertising on consumers' welfare is not straightforward because, as advertising changes consumers' preferences, it is not at all obvious what the reference welfare criterion should be, ex-ante or ex-post with respect to advertising.[12]

Given the preference parameters α, θ, b (we use for simplicity a notation which abuses by postulating symmetry), the representative consumer's equilibrium allocations are denoted by $x(\alpha, \theta, b)$, $L(\alpha, \theta, b)$; and his/her equilibrium utility is denoted $\mathcal{U}(x(\alpha,\theta,b),\ L(\alpha,\ \theta,\ b);\ \alpha,\ \theta,\ b)$. Recall that advertising has the effect of changing his/her preference parameters (α, θ, b) into $(\alpha_+, \theta_+, b_+)$.

We say that the consumer's welfare (weakly) increases due to advertising with respect to ex-post preferences if

$$\mathcal{U}(x(\alpha_+,\theta_+,b_+),L(\alpha_+,\theta_+,b_+);\alpha_+,\theta_+,b_+) \geq \mathcal{U}(x(\alpha,\theta,b),L(\alpha,\theta,b);\alpha_+,\theta_+,b_+). \quad (6)$$

Consumer's welfare (weakly) increases instead due to advertising with respect to ex-ante preferences if

$$\mathcal{U}(x(\alpha_+,\theta_+,b_+),L(\alpha_+,\theta_+,b_+);\alpha,\theta,b) \geq \mathcal{U}(x(\alpha,\theta,b),L(\alpha,\theta,b);\alpha,\theta,b). \quad (7)$$

Several[13] of our welfare comparisons are in fact unambiguous, in the sense that they hold for the partial ordering induced by both ex-ante as well as for ex-post preferences. In an economy in which prices are distorted by monopoly power of firms, in fact, advertising might, depending of the parameters of the economy, either exacerbate such effects, and hence possibly reduce welfare with respect to both ex-ante and ex-post preferences, or it might introduce a form of nonprice competition across firms which mitigates the effects of monopolistic distortions and hence on the contrary unequivocally improves welfare.

How does advertising affect the welfare of the representative agent? We again consider separately the effects of the different advertising channels, intensity on α, elasticity of substitution on θ, and habits on b.

[12] See Dixit-Norman (1978) for an early analysis of advertising in a monopolistic competition economy.

[13] Dixit and Norman (1978) suggest that such partial ordering can be surprisingly effective for the analysis of the effects of advertising. Stigler-Becker (1977) compellingly argues in favor of the formulation of metapreference orderings, which depend on advertising (see also Becker (1996)). The partial ordering just introduced is robust to such formulation in the sense that, in our set up, it generates welfare comparisons, which hold for all metapreference orderings increasing in ex-ante and ex-post preferences (Harsanyi (1954) notes that this is not necessarily the case in general.)
It is important to note that our welfare analysis disregards the direct costs of advertising. Even though such costs are potentially empirically relevant, we abstract from them because they are not an essential element of the Postmodernist Critique.

1. *Advertising on* α, *other things equal, decreases (resp. increases, has no effect on) ex-post welfare if* $\sigma < 1$ (resp. *if* $\sigma > 1$, $\sigma = 1$) *since it uniformly decreases (resp. increases, has no effects on) utility levels. Furthermore, if* $|\alpha_+ - \alpha|$ *is high enough, the representative consumer's welfare decreases with respect to ex-ante preferences (a moderate increase in* α *increases only moderately the labour supply, L, thereby possibly reducing the distortion towards leisure that is induced by monopolistic competition).*
2. *Advertising on* θ, *other things equal, reinforces any effect of advertising on intensity* α. *However, advertising on* θ *has also the effect of increasing the price* p_+. *The price effect always accentuates the negative welfare consequences of monopolistic competition; more so in the economy with free entry, where profits are not redistributed to consumers but rather wasted in expanding varieties.*
3. *Advertising on b, other things equal, reduces ex-ante welfare but has ambiguous welfare results with respect to ex-post preferences.*

Let's study once again the special case of log preferences ($\sigma = 1$), when income and substitution effects cancel out:

1. log *Advertising on* α, *other things equal, has no effects on ex-post or ex-ante welfare.*
2. log *Advertising on* θ, *other things equal, has the effect of increasing the price* p_+. *The price effect has negative welfare consequences.*
3. log *An increase in b, other things equal, reduces ex-ante welfare but has ambiguous welfare results with respect to ex-post preferences.*

3.3 Commodification of leisure

We briefly sketch the extensions of the benchmark model of the previous section required to discuss "commodification of leisure" (see Benhabib-Bisin (2002)). Monopolistically competitive firms can, by advertising, extract rents from the consumers' leisure activities, as leisure is now composed of different market activities. Consider a continuum of leisure activities, indexed by $j \in [0, 1]$. The aggregator of leisure, which enters in the utility function of agents, is

$$L := \left(\int_0^1 L_{jt}^{\frac{\omega_j - r}{\omega_j}} dj \right)^{\frac{\int_0^1 \omega_j dj}{\int_0^1 \omega_j dj - 1}} \quad , \omega_j \geq 1, \forall j \tag{8}$$

where $1 - L_j$ is interpreted as the amount of labour given up to leisure activity j.

A monopolistic firm controls leisure activity j. The fee charged by the firm per unit of leisure time on activity j is denoted q_j; such a fee represents a pure rent, as it is assumed that controlling leisure activity j requires no resources as inputs.

The case in which leisure is merely a non-market activity corresponds to the special case in which all leisure activities are perfect substitutes, $\omega_j = \infty$, for all j. Perfect substitutability in fact implies that no rents can be extracted by controlling the different leisure activities in the market. They might then just as well be interpreted as non-market activities, since the fees imposed by the firms controlling such activities are necessarily zero in equilibrium. If instead, for instance, $\omega_j = \omega < \infty$, for all j, then the demand for market leisure activities is rigid. Consumers will devote some time to each one of such activities in equilibrium, and firms with monopoly power controlling the different leisure activities in the market will charge a positive fee for a profit.

Suppose that advertising by firm j affects ω_j. Before advertising, leisure is composed by non-market activities, $\omega_j = \infty$, for all j. After advertising, "commodification of leisure" is induced and different leisure activities become imperfect substitutes, $\omega_j < \infty$. Consequently, positive rents in the form of positive fees q_j emerge in equilibrium.

The structure of the economy is then as in Section 1. It can be shown that, at equilibrium in the economy with free entry and expanding varieties, after advertising:

$$q_j = q = \frac{1}{\omega - 1}$$

and $L_j = L$ solves:

$$\frac{L}{1-L} = \left(\frac{p_+}{w}\right)^{1-\sigma} + q$$

In this case, if $\sigma < 1$, consistently with the Postmodernist Critique, the "commodification of leisure" and the "work and spend cycle" are associated to an unambiguous reduction in welfare.[14]

3.4 Taking stock

Our analysis of general equilibrium with advertising identifies a set of conditions (or parametrizations of the model) which may lend some support to what we called the Postmodernist Critique. We now summarize our results.

For clarity, we distinguished advertising, which affects the intensity of the preferences from advertising as product differentiation and habit creation. In the first case, advertising may generate a "work-spend cycle" with negative welfare effects for the consumer if the shift in intensity is strong enough and $\sigma < 1$. This effect is though small (resp. null) for σ close (resp. equal) to 1.

Advertising as product differentiation has unambiguous negative welfare effects. If the economy is one of free entry and if the elasticity of substitution between aggregate consumption and leisure is low ($\sigma < 1$), then a "work and spend cycle" associated with negative welfare effects is indeed generated. Finally, when advertising creates habits, the "work-spend cycle" is always generated, but the welfare effects are ambiguous.

Finally, when advertising is aimed at product differentiation and there is free entry that expands product variety and drives profits to zero, the "commodification ofleisure" induces a "work-spend cycle" and also has unambiguous negative welfare effects.

[14] In the economy with monopoly profits "commodification of leisure" increases labor L but it might have positive welfare effects as it provides competition for the monopoly power of good producers.

4. THE EFFECTS OF ADVERTISING IN EMPIRICAL WORK

The pattern of consumption, leisure, and consumers' welfare associated with the Postmodernist Critique depends on *i)* the form taken by advertising, *ii)* the elasticity of substitution between consumption and leisure, *iii)* the existence of monopoly profits in equilibrium. The evidence on *i-iii)* is in general controversial. We attempt a discussion below.

i) The form of advertising. Most of the evidence of the effect of advertising documents that its main role consists in affecting the consumer's perceived difference across physically homogenous goods, rather than the intensity of preferences for consumption goods (see e.g., Arens (1996), and Sutherland, (1993)). This is consistent with the fact that advertising expenditures to sales ratios vary by industry, ranging from 10–20% for drugs, perfumes, and cereals, to practically no advertising in homogenous commodities like beet sugar (see Tirole (1990), p. 289).

ii) Elasticity of substitution between consumption and leisure. Much of the microeconomic empirical evidence consistently documents a σ smaller than 1 (see e.g., Pencavel, 1987). At least restricting to the male population, it is safe to conclude from the evidence that σ is slightly less than 1, according to Browning-Hansen-Heckman (1999). Such a low elasticity may be considered at odds with the implied elasticity of aggregate labour supply. In particular, macroeconomic models are often calibrated with values of σ equal to one, as the average weekly hours per capita remained roughly constant in the U.S. since the '60's while real wage rates increased dramatically in the same period; see e.g., the contributions of Kydland, and of Cooley-Prescott, in Cooley (1995);[15] this argument dates back to Lucas-Rapping (1969), and Ghez-Becker (1975).[16] Prescott (2002, 2004) and Ljungqvist-Sargent (2006) discuss how to reconcile the micro and macro evidence by exploiting the indivisibility of labor.

iii) Monopoly profits in equilibrium. The average return on capital in the U.S. seems to be low, around 4% per annum, suggesting that profits are probably low as well; see Basu (1996). In the U.S., there are few pure monopolies, and in the absence of regulatory restrictions, multimarket firms are the norm (Tirole (1990), p.351). Bresnahan and Reiss (1991)'s empirical results suggest that in general competitive conduct in a market is established after the entry of a second or third firm, with further entry having little effect. It is nonetheless possible that there are variations across industries, and that barriers to entry prevent the dissipation of profits, e.g., in pharmaceuticals. Overall however, the free entry and expanding varieties version of the advertising model where profits are dissipated on fixed costs seems more in line with U.S. market structure.[17]

[15] Leete Guy-Schor (1992) argue though that average yearly hours of those workers who were employed full time in the whole year have actually increased in the period 1969–1989.

[16] Historical data shows however, a negative trend in weekly hours worked in the U.S. until the '60s; see Coleman-Pencavel (1993).

[17] Carroll (2000) extensively documents that the distribution of stock ownership across the population is very unequal. In particular, the "rich" (defined as the top 1% of households by net worth) hold a disproportionate share of their

The Postmodernist Critique seems therefore consistent with a broad calibration of the crucial parameters of the model: advertising as product diversification and habit creation, low substitutability between consumption and labor, $\sigma \leq 1$, and free entry in most sectors. Maintaining the assumption that advertising operates as product differentiation, its main effect is an increase in the price level. The secular rise of real wages $\frac{w}{p+}$ is due to productivity increases, that are increases in w relative to p. Productivity increases that generate higher incomes have the effect of decreasing the labor supply. Advertising may then indeed have offset a tendency towards further increases in the time devoted to leisure activities since the 60s, with a negative effect on welfare. Such an effect of advertising is consistent with the rising trend in advertising expenditures that tracks the observed secular rise of real wages.[18]

Hours and Advertising. To evaluate the Critique more directly we now turn to an overview about what is it known about the relationship between advertising expenditures and hours worked. We concentrate on hours because so does the literature, though the effects of advertising on hours are naturally reflected on consumption and income.

As already noted, historical data show a negative trend in weekly hours worked: in the U.K., for instance, manual workers worked 65 hours per week on average in 1865 and 46 hours in 1960 (see Matthews-Feinstein-Odling Smee (1982). Since then, however, the trend appears broken: on average weekly hours in 1997 were 43.5 (Fraser-Paton (2003), Table 1). A similar picture is painted by hours worked for the U.S.[19]

Can the growth in advertising explain this break of the time trend in hours in the '60s, in the presence of continuous productivity improvements? Per-capita advertising has in fact grown rapidly since the 50s; in the U.S., at an average rate of about 25% per decade (see Cowling-Poolsombat (2007), Table 1; see also Brack-Cowling (1983) for U.S. data since 1919). Advertising expenditures as a share of GNP, however, do not display any significant time trend in the U.S. or in other OECD countries.[20]

Interesting stylized facts characterize also the cross-section of advertising expenditures. While constant in the long run, advertising shares vary significantly across the OECD countries: on average over the period 1984–2005, advertising accounts for 2.27% of GDP in the U.S., while it accounts for 1.54% of GDP in the U.K., 1.49% in Germany and 1.16% in Japan (see Molinari-Turino (2009a), Table 1).[21]

[18] Furthermore, quality adjustments in the advertising services category of the Census could have been quite significant because of technological advances in the communication media, and in fact may have given rise to a secular trend in quality-adjusted advertising expenditures as a fraction of GDP.

[19] See Coleman-Pencavel (1993) for U.S. data from 1940.

[20] See the Statistical Abstract of the United States, published by the US Bureau of Census, Washington D. C., for the years 1980 to 2000, as well as the Historical Statistics of the United States: Colonial Times to 1970, Bicentennial Edition also published by US Bureau of Census. See also The European Business Readership Survey (1998) of the Financial Times, available online at: http://www.asianmediaaccess.com.au/ftimes/adspend/gdp.htm.

[21] The period 1984–2005 is chosen to facilitate comparability across countries, but in fact the advertising share in the U.S. displays no trend since the 50s.

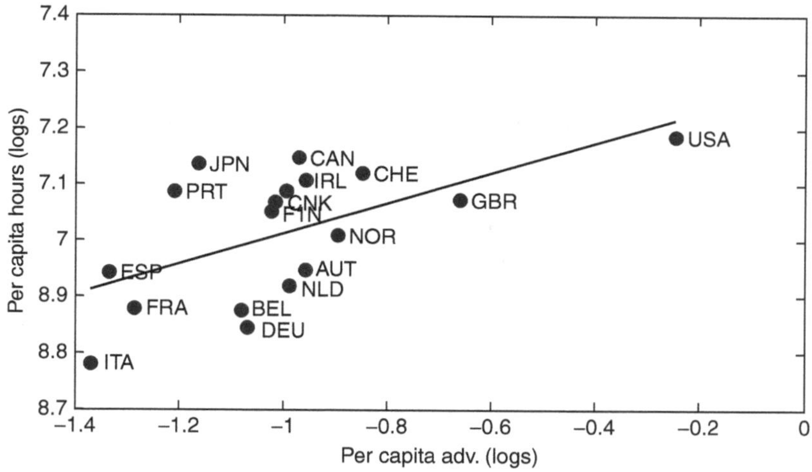

Figure 1 Scatter plot: Log of per capita hours against per capita advertising. Period 1996-2005. Taken from Molinari-Turino (2009a), Figure 2, Panel C.

Most importantly for our objectives, per-capita advertising is positively correlated with per-capita hours in a cross-section of 18 OECD countries over the period 1996–2005: the estimated elasticity is .269% (see Fig. 1).[22]

Let's discuss the time series and cross-section evidence in turn. Several studies have looked at the time series of advertising and either GDP or consumption or hours with the aim of uncovering casual effects. Brack-Cowling (1983) have time series regressions of U.S. hours worked on wage and advertising, for the period 1919–1976, which they interpret as an estimate of the long-run labour supply.[23] Interpreting correlations causally, they conclude that over their time-series advertising had the effect of increasing labor supply in the order of 27%. More recently, Fraser-Paton (2003) studied the relationship between hours, wage, and advertising in the U.K. over the period 1952–97 as a vector cointegration analysis (a Vector Error Correction Mechanism, VECM, to be precise). They obtain a strong positive correlation of advertising and hours (.19 for male weekly hours, .186 for female weekly hours, .24 for male yearly hours).[24] These elasticities imply large effects: the increase in hours worked for males over their time series, associated with the changes in per-capita advertising, is estimated to be between

[22] Per-capita advertising is positively correlated as well with per-capita GDP and per-capita consumption; Molinari-Turino (2009a, Table 2).

[23] It is of course hard to identify labor supply from labor demand effects. Schor (1992) for instance interprets related evidence of increasing hours worked in the U.S. as a demand effect, due to firms' monopsonistic power over labor. Some evidence for labour demand effects is found in survey data for the U.K., when workers report preferences for working shorter hours at the prevailing wage; see Stewart-Swaffield (1997). For arguments in favor of supply effect explanations, see also George (1997).

[24] A negative correlation for female yearly hours is considered evidence of mis-specification.

21% to 46%. Interestingly, the correlation of hours and wage is estimated to be negative. A similar Vector Cointegration analysis is applied by Cowling-Poolsombat (2007) to the U.S. over the period 1952–2002. However, to the vector of hours worked, wage, and advertising, Cowling-Poolsombat (2007) add taxes (the effective marginal tax rate as computed by Prescott (2004)). Their analysis also produces a strong positive correlation of advertising and hours (.124 for male weekly hours, .171 for female weekly hours, and .263 for yearly manufacturing production hours), stronger than the negative correlation between hours and taxes. In contrast to Fraser-Paton (2003), the correlation of hours and wage is estimated to be positive.[25]

While the evidence just surveyed is suggestive of a strong correlation between hours and advertising, a causal relationship is much harder to identify. To this end, Fraser-Paton (2003) also produce some Granger causation tests which provide evidence of unidirectional causation from per capita advertising to (male weekly, female weekly, and male yearly) hours.[26]

A more structural attempt at studying the time-series relationship between advertising and several macroeconomic variables of interest (hours, consumption, GDP) is due to Molinari-Turino (2009a) who calibrate a dynamic extension of the model we introduced in Section 1.[27] More specifically, they embed the monopolistic competition model of advertising of Section 1 into a neoclassical growth model with capital accumulation and a labor-intensive advertising sector. They restrict the analysis to advertising in the form of consumption habits. The calibration they adopt is standard in the Real Business Cycle literature for the U.S. economy,[28] augmented with a productivity parameter and a preference parameter for the advertising sector to fit the ratio of advertising to GDP (see Molinari-Turino (2009a), Table 3).[29] At the parameters of the calibration, comparative statics exercises on the steady state of the economy show that an increase in advertising (through an increase in the productivity of advertising, other things equal) induces an increase in the price mark-up and an increase in hours. With no advertising, the representative agent would decrease equilibrium hours in the steady state by about 10%. Furthermore, the structural analysis of Molinari-Turino (2009a) has the advantage that, using the model, the welfare effects of advertising can be investigated. In fact, it is shown that at the parameters of the calibration advertising has negative welfare effects (both ex-ante and ex-post): the representative agent is worse-off with advertising than without. The calibration in Molinari-Turino (2009a) is therefore

[25] The measure of hours in Fraser-Paton (2003) includes overtime, while that of Cowles-Poolsombat (2007) does not.

[26] Bidirectional Granger causality between advertising and consumption has been also documented; see e.g., Jung-Seldon (1995) for the U.S. and Philip (2007) for India.

[27] In Molinari-Turino (2009b) essentially the same calibration is used to study the effect of advertising at business cycle frequencies.

[28] As in Prescott (1986) and e.g., Ravn-Schmitt Grohe-Uribe (2006).

[29] A degree of freedom is exploited in the calibration; this is apparent by comparison with the more parsimonious specification of the model in Molinari-Turino (2009b).

consistent with the Postmodernist Critique and the *work-and-spend cycle:* advertising increases hours worked and decreases welfare.

We can also ask if advertising can help to explain some additional puzzling data. McGrattan-Prescott (2007) have documented that the rise in hours in the U.S. in the period 1990–2005 cannot be reconciled with a neoclassical growth model under the calibration which is standard in Real Business Cycle and the observed labor productivity. Essentially labor productivity is too flat to produce the observed growth in hours. While they show that an extension of the model, which accounts for non-tangible investment, jointly with independent (though indirect) measures of such investment, does well to fit the data, advertising could, in principle, provide a complementary explanation.

Molinari-Turino (2009a) apply the calibrated model to *the U.S. boom of the '90's* by means of a Business Cycle Accounting exercise along the lines of Chari-Kehoe-McGrattan (2007). Using data on investment, GDP, advertising expenditures, and taxes (as in McGrattan-Prescott (2007) for comparison), their methodology produces predictions about hours worked which can be compared with actual data. As documented by McGrattan-Prescott (2007), the benchmark neoclassical growth model under the calibration standard in Real Business Cycle predicts a counterfactual decline of hours in the '90s. The addition of advertising manages to predict a very moderate positive trend, without however coming close to match the actual increase: advertising contributes just about 60% to the explanation the peak of actual hours with respect to the benchmark (see Fig. 2).

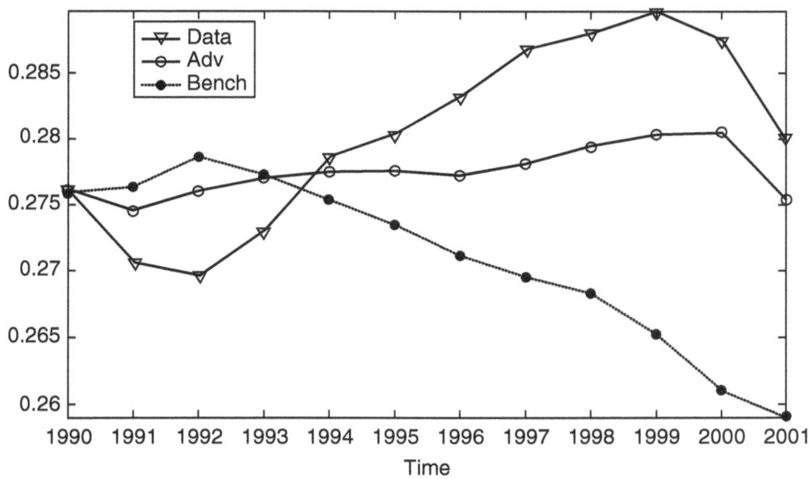

Figure 2 Hours worked during the U.S. boom in the 1990s. Model's prediction vs. actual data. All the data taken from McGrattan-Prescott (2007). Bench refers to the model without advertising. Taken from Molinari-Turino (2009a), Figure 5.

Much less has been done in the literature to explain the cross-country correlation between per-capita advertising and hours in the OECD. Once again, Molinari-Turino (2009a) attack this issue. They show that, not surprisingly, changes in the productivity parameter of advertising can produce enough variation in advertising shares to fit the OECD data. More importantly, they attempt to show that advertising can contribute to explain puzzling data, in this case the *differences in U.S. vs. European hours*. Prescott (2004)[30] has documented large differences in average hours between the U.S. and Europe in the nineties. He has also documented that a model with a large elasticity of substitution of labor could explain the data due to the variation of effective tax rates between the U.S. and Europe. Others, e.g., Alesina-Glaeser-Sacerdote (2005), Bisin-Verdier (2004), Blanchard (2004), Ljungqvist-Sargent (2006), Rogerson (2006), have produced distinct explanations of the data, which involve differences in preferences, work ethic norms, social security systems and labor market regulations, which would require less controversial elasticities of substitution of labor. Finally, George (1997), and Cowling-Poolsombat (2007) have suggested that advertising could contribute to the explanation of the puzzle, since the U.S. displays larger advertising shares than European countries. Molinari-Turino (2009a) evaluate the contribution of advertising to Prescott (2004)'s explanation of the U.S.-Europe difference in hours at the calibrated parameters (but at a lower elasticity of labor supply than Prescott's), by varying advertising productivity to fit each country's advertising share. Advertising is shown, in fact, to improve the fit of the model, contributing about 50% to the explanation of the difference in hours worked between the U.S. and Germany, France, Italy, U.K. (see Molinari-Turino (2009a), Table 5).

The theoretical models and the empirical work we surveyed adopt the standard definition of a household as a single agent. In other words, they do not distinguish between male and female labor supply (or between other demographic characteristics). Furthermore, these models and the empirical work do not account for home-production. The empirical work, in particular, adopts measures of hours worked which only include hours worked in the market. Nevertheless, are these assumptions adequate? Are labor and leisure accurately measured? Is the aggregation across demographics and across different forms of labor innocuous? We discuss these issues in turn.

First of all, large shifts have indeed occurred in the composition of average weekly hours across the population since World War II; McGrattan-Rogerson (2008) extensively document trends in average weekly hours, disaggregated along demographic lines. Leete Guy-Schor (1992) decompose the trends in hours with respect to

[30] See also Prescott (2002).

employment status. For instance, while average weekly hours substantially increased for families of two or more in the U.S. since the 60s, they have decreased for males and increased for females; see McGrattan-Rogerson (2008). Not much is known about the factors driving such compositional shifts in hours worked. Similarly, a recent extensive review of the evidence by Browning-Hansen-Heckman (1999) concludes that the preference parameter that controls the response of labor supply to real wages is poorly estimated, that it varies significantly with demographics, labor force status, and the level of consumption, and that the evidence is inconsistent with a uniform parameter value that is constant across the population.

Furthermore, adopting measures of hours worked which only include hours worked in the market, disregarding home-production, is of course problematic if the composition of hours in the market and in home-production changes over time and across countries. There is evidence that it is so. By using data from time-use surveys, Aguiar-Hurst (2007) are able to document accurately changes in the allocation of time in the market and in home-production for males and females in the U.S. in the period 1965–2003. They document a decrease total (market plus home production) hours worked for both males (driven by decreasing hours in the market) and females (driven by decreasing hours in home production) over this period (see Fig. 3).

While the reduction in the slope of the decreasing time trend of total hours is observed after 1975, more disaggregated data suggest a need to reassess the evidence on the relationship between advertising and hours based only on market hours. Also relevant for such a re-evaluation is the evidence from time-diaries indicating that it is the highly educated that have increased their average weekly hours at work; see Aguiar-Hurst (2006), Figure 6a and 6b; see also Robinson-Godbey (1997).

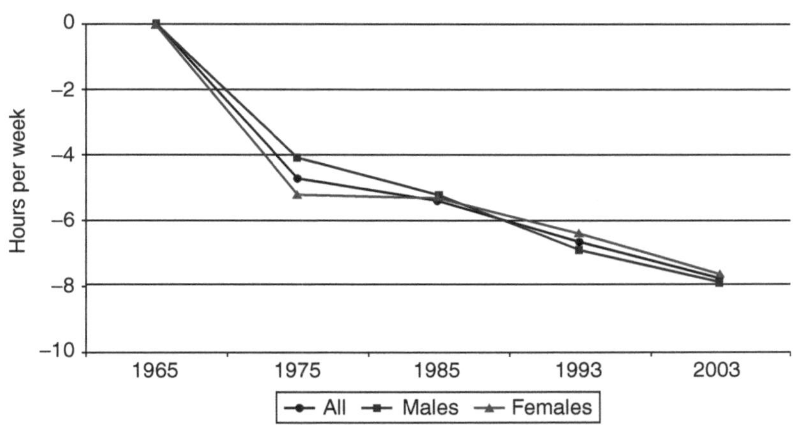

Figure 3 Time spent in total work by sex, conditional on demographics; Change in hours per week relative to 1965. Taken from Aguiar-Hurst (2007), Figure 3.

Finally, time diaries provide us with both time series and cross-country data on the composition of leisure activities. While to the best of our knowledge, no analysis of time-series data at this level of decomposition is available, Alesina-Glaeser-Sacerdote (2005) use data from the Multinational Time Use Survey to decompose "sleep" from other leisure activities in a cross-section of OECD countries; see Table 17. Averaging over the period 1992–1999, it is shown that in the U.S. the time devoted to sleep is, e.g., 5 hours per week less than in France and 3 hours less than in the U.K. Since the U.S. has the highest advertising share in the OECD (and U.K. the second highest) and since "sleep" is the prototypical leisure activity which is not "commodified," the rankings are suggestive of advertising producing "commodification of leisure" at the expense of sleep.

5. CONCLUSIONS

We identified a Postmodernist Critique of the organization of society. This Critique suggests that the interaction of monopoly power and advertising creates negative welfare effects for consumers. In particular, advertising takes the form of the "manipulation of preferences," leads consumers to "work and spend cycles" and subjects them to the "commodification of leisure."

We studied the interaction of monopoly power and advertising in a simple general equilibrium model, constructed to satisfy the basic postulates of this Critique (especially in terms of the effects of advertising on consumers' preferences) and we identified specifications and parameter configurations of our model that give rise to equilibria which could support the Postmodernist Critique.

While we discussed some of the available empirical evidence pertaining to key aspects of our specification that supports, and is consistent with the Postmodernist Critique, more extensive formal empirical studies are necessary before a stand can be taken on the its relevance. In particular, it may be important to assess more precisely the effects of the component of advertising that is emphasized in the Critique, that of the "manipulation of preferences," relative to the informational content of advertising. The empirical relevance of the distortion induced by advertising and identified by the Postmodernist Critique, relative to the many distortions and frictions present in the U.S. economy (from incompleteness of financial markets and borrowing constraints, to asymmetric information and distortionary taxes) also remains to be established.

Finally, our whole analysis has been conducted under the Postmodernist postulate that advertising directly affects the consumer's preferences. The cognitive and psychological effects of advertising are not yet well understood, and the contrary view (associated with Gary Becker), that the level of advertising is determined by the supply and demand of rational consumers and firms needs to be better evaluated in view of the Postmodernist Critique.

REFERENCES

Aguiar, M., Hurst, E., 2007. Measuring Trends in Leisure: The Allocation of Time Over Five Decades. Q. J. Econ. 122, 969–1006.

Alesina, A., Glaeser, E., Sacerdote, B., 2005. Work and Leisure in the U.S. and Europe: Why So Different?. CEPR 5140.

Anderson, P., 1998. The Origins of Postmodernity. Verso, London.

Arens, W., 1996. Contemporary Advertising. Irwin, Chicago.

Arrighi, G., 1994. The Long Twentieth Century. Verso, London.

Basu, S., 1996. Procyclical Productivity: Increasing Returns or Capacity Utilization? Q. J. Econ. 111, 719–751.

Becker, G.S., 1996. Accounting for Tastes. Harvard Univ. Press, Cambridge.

Becker, G.S., Murphy, K., 1993. A Simple Theory of Advertising as a Good or Bad. Q. J. Econ. 108, 941–964.

Benhabib, J., Bisin, A., 2002. Advertising, Mass Consumption, and Capitalism. mimeo, NYU.

Bisin, A., Verdier, T., 2004. Work Ethic and Redistributive Taxation in the Welfare State,. mimeo, NYU.

Blanchard, O., 2004. The Economic Future of Europe,. NBER 10310; forthcoming in Journal of Economic Perspectives.

Bourdieu, P., 1984. Distinction: A Social Critique of the Judgement of Taste. Harvard University Press, Cambridge (original edition, in French, 1979).

Brack, J., Cowling, K., 1983. Asvertising and Labour Supply: Workweek and Workyear in U.S. Manufacturing Industries, 1919–76. Kyklos 36, 285–303.

Bresnahan, T.F., Reiss, P.C., 1991. Entry and Competition in Concentrated Markets. J. Polit. Econ. 99, 977–1009.

Browning, M., Hansen, L.P., Heckman, J.J., 1999. Micro Data and General Equilibrium Models. In: Taylor, J.B., Woodford, M. Handbook of Macroeconomics, vol. I. Elsevier Science, New York.

Campbell, C., 2000. The Puzzle of Modern Consumerism. In: Lee, M.J. (Ed.), op. cit.

Carroll, C.D., 2000. Portfolios of the Rich. mimeo.

Chari, V.V., Kehoe, P.J., McGrattan, E.R., 2007. Business Cycle Accounting. Econometrica 75 (3), 781–836.

Coleman, M.T., Pencavel, J., 1993. Changes in Work Hours of Male Emplyees, 1940–1988. Ind. Labor Relat. Rev. 46 (2), 262–283.

Cooley, T., 1995. Frontiers of Business Cycle Research. Princeton University Press, Princeton.

Cowling, K., Poolsombat, R., 2007. Advertsing and Labour Supply: Why Do Americans Work Such Long Hours? Warwick Economics Research Paper 789.

Dixit, A., Norman, V., 1978. Advertising and Welfare. Rand J. Econ. 1–17.

Douglas, M., Isherwood, B., 1978. The World of Goods. Routledge, London.

Duesenberry, J.S., 1949. Income, Saving, and the Theory of Consumer Behavior. Harvard University Press, Cambridge.

Fraser, S., Paton, D., 2003. Does Advertising Increase Labour Supply? Time Series Evidence for the U.K. Appl. Econ. 35, 1357–1368.

Frank, R., 2010. Status and Conspicuous Consumption, forthcoming. In: Benhabib, J., Bisin, A., Jackson, M. (Eds.), Handbook of Social Economics. Elsevier, New York.

Galbraith, J.K., 1958. The Affluent Society. Houghton Mifflin, Boston.

George, D., 1997. Working Longer Hours: Pressure from the Boss or Pressure from the Marketers? Rev. Soc. Econ. 55 (1), 33–65.

Ghez, G., Becker, G.S., 1975. The Allocation of Time and Goods over the Life Cycle. Columbia University Press, New York.

Jameson, F., 1998. The Cultural Turn. Verso, London.

Harsanyi, J., 1954. Welfare Economics of Variable Tastes. Rev. Econ. Stud. 21, 204–213.

Harvey, D., 1989. The Condition of Postmodernity. Blackwell, Oxford.

Jung, C., Seldon, B.J., 1995. The Macroeconomic Relationship Between Advertising and Consumption. South. Econ. J. 61, 577–587.

Lee, M.J. (Ed.), 2000. The Consumer Society Reader. Blackwell, Oxford.
Leete Guy, L., Schor, J., 1992. The Great American Time Squeeze: Trends in Work and Leisure, 1969–1989. Economic Policy Institute Briefing Paper.
Leonard, P., 1997. Postmodern Welfare: Reconstructing and Emancipatory Project. SAGE Publications, London.
Ljungqvist, L., Sargent, T., 2006. Do Taxes Explain European Employment? Indivisible Labor, Human Capital, Lotteries, and Savings. In: NBER Macroeconomics Annual 2006, vol. 21. National Bureau of Economic Research, Inc., Boston, pp. 181–246.
Lucas Jr., R.E., Rapping, L.A., 1969. Real Wages, Employment and Inflation. J. Polit. Econ. 77, 721–754.
Mandel, E., 1978. Late Capitalism. Suhrkamp Verlag, Berlin, London, 1972 (in German); English edition by Verso.
Matthews, R.C.O., Feinstein, C.H., Odley Smee, J.C., 1982. British Economic Growth 1856 to 1973. Clarendon Press, Oxford.
McGrattan, E.R., Prescott, E.C., 2007. Unmeasured investment and the puzzling U.S. boom in the 1990s. NBER Working Paper 13499.
McGrattan, E.R., Rogerson, R., 2008. Changes in the distribution of family hours worked since 1950. Federal Reserve Bank of Minneapolis, Research Department Staff Report 397.
Molinari, B., Turino, F., 2009a. Advertising, labor supply and the aggregate economy: A long run analysis. Universidad Pablo de Olavide wp.econ, n. 09.16.
Molinari, B., Turino, F., 2009b. Advertising and business cycle fluctuations. Istituto Valenciano de Investigaciones Economicas, AD Working Paper 2009–09.
Pencavel, J., 1987. Labor Supply of Men: A Survey. In: Ashenfelter, O., Layard, R. (Eds.), Handbook of Labor Economics, vol. I. Elvevier Science, Amsterdam.
Philip, A.P., 2007. The Relationship between Advertising and Consumption in India: An Analysis of Causality. In: International Marketing Conference on Marketing & Society, 8–10 April 2007. IIMK.
Prescott, E.C., 1986. Theory Ahead of Business Cycle Measurement. Federal Reserve Bank of Minneapolis Quarterly Review Fall, 9–22.
Prescott, E.C., 2002. Prosperity and Depression. Am. Econ. Rev. 92, 1–15.
Prescott, E.C., 2004. Why Do Americans Work So Much More than Europeans? Federal Reserve Bank of Minneapolis Quarterly Review 28, 2–13.
Ravn, M., Schmitt Grohe, S., Uribe, M., 2006. Deep Habits. Rev. Econ. Stud. 73, 196–218.
Robinson, J.P., Godbey, G. (Eds.), 1997. Time for Life: The Surprising Ways Americans Use Their Time. Pennsylvania State University Press, University Part, PA.
Rogerson, R., 2006. Understanding Differences in Hours Worked. unpublished text of plenary session at SED 2005.
Rushkoff, D., 1999. Coercion. Riverside Books, New York.
Sahlins, M., 1976. Culture and Practical Reason. University of Chicago Press, Chicago.
Schor, J., 1992. The Overworked American: The Unexpected Decline of Leisure. Basic Books, New York.
Schor, J., 1998. The Overspent American: Why We Want What We Don't Need. HarperCollins, New York.
Schumpeter, J.A., 1964. Business Cycles; A Theoretical, Historical and Statistical Analysis of the Capitalist Process. McGraw-Hill, New York, first edition 1939.
Sokal, A.D., Bricmont, J., 1998. Fashionable Nonsense: Postmodern Intellectuals' Abuse of Science. St. Martins Press, New York.
Stewart, M.B., Swaffield, J.K., 1997. Constraints on the Desired Hours of Work of British Men. Econ. J. 107, 520–535.
Sutherland, M., 1993. Advertising and the Mind of the Consumer. Allen & Unwin, St Leonards, NSW.
Tirole, J., 1990. The Theory of Industrial Organization. MIT Press, Cambridge.
Veblen, T., 1899. The Theory of the Leisure Class. Penguin, Macmillan, New York and London.

CHAPTER 7

The Evolutionary Foundations of Preferences*

Arthur J. Robson
Department of Economics Simon Fraser University 8888 University Drive, Burnaby, BC, Canada V5A 1S6
Robson@sfu.ca

Larry Samuelson
Department of Economics Yale University 30 Hillhouse Avenue, New Haven, CT 06520-8281, USA
Larry.Samuelson@yale.edu

Contents

1. Introduction 222
2. Evolutionary Foundations 225
   2.1 Evolution and economic behavior 225
   2.2 The rules of evolution 226
   2.3 Evolution and utility functions 227
   2.4 Evolutionary mismatches 230
   2.5 The indirect evolutionary approach 231
3. What Sort of Preferences? 235
   3.1 Risk 236
      3.1.1 Attitudes toward risk 236
      3.1.2 Risk and status 243
      3.1.3 Implications 246
   3.2 Time 247
      3.2.1 A simple beginning: semelparous life histories 248
      3.2.2 Extensions 251
      3.2.3 Environmental capacity 251
      3.2.4 Iteroparous life histories 252
      3.2.5 Consumption 255
      3.2.6 Heterogeneous choices 256
      3.2.7 Nonexponential discounting 257
      3.2.8 Implications 262
4. Preferences over What? 263
   4.1 Context 264
      4.1.1 A model 266
      4.1.2 Utility 267

* We thank Andrew Postlewaite for helpful discussions and comments. Arthur Robson thanks the Canada Research Chair Program and the Social Sciences and Humanities Research Council of Canada and Larry Samuelson thanks the National Science Foundation (SES-0549946 and SES-0850263) for financial support.

Handbook of Social Economics, Volume 1A
ISSN 0169-7218, DOI: 10.1016/S0169-7218(11)01007-0

4.1.3 Choice-set dependence 269
4.1.4 Implications 271
4.2 Status 272
4.2.1 Information and relative consumption 273
4.2.2 Adaptive utility and relative consumption 278
4.2.3 Implications 287
4.3 Group selection 290
4.3.1 The haystack model 292
4.3.2 Selection among equilibria 294
4.3.3 Group selection and economics 295
4.3.4 Implications 297
5. Concluding Remark 297
6. Proofs 298
6.1 Proof of Proposition 1 298
6.2 Proof of Proposition 2 302
References 305

Abstract

This paper surveys recent work on the evolutionary origins of preferences. We are especially interested in the circumstances under which evolution would push preferences away from the self-interested perfectly-rational expected utility maximization of classical economic theory in order to incorporate environmental or social considerations.
JEL Codes: D0, D8

Keywords

Preferences
Evolution
Evolution of Preferences
Risk
Status
Discounting
Hyperbolic Discounting
Relative Consumption
Group Selection

1. INTRODUCTION

This essay on the evolutionary foundations of preferences is best introduced with an example. The example in turn requires some notation, but this seemingly technical beginning will set the stage for an ensuing discussion that is more intuitive.

We are interested in a setting in which consumption must be distributed across periods in the face of uncertainty. Suppose that time is discrete, indexed by $\{0, 1, 2, \ldots\}$. A state $\omega \in \Omega$ is first drawn from the finite set Ω, with $\rho(\omega)$ giving the probability of state ω.

The consumption bundle in period t is drawn from a set C and given by $c_t(\omega)$, being a function of the period and the realized state. The consumption profile, identifying a consumption bundle for each period, is then $\{c_t(\omega)\}_{\omega\in\Omega,\, t\in\{0,1,\ldots\}}$. Let $\boldsymbol{c}$ denote a typical such consumption profile and $\mathcal{C}$ the set of such profiles. How do we model preferences over the set $\mathcal{C}$?

The most common approach in economics is to assume there exists an increasing utility function $u : C \rightarrow \Re$, allowing preferences over $\mathcal{C}$ to be represented by the discounted-sum-of-expected-utility function $U : \mathcal{C} \rightarrow \Re$, given by

$$U(\boldsymbol{c}) = \sum_{t=0}^{\infty}\sum_{\omega\in\Omega} D^t u(c_t(\omega))\rho(\omega), \tag{1}$$

where $D \in (0, 1)$ is the discount factor. Dating at least to Samuelson (1937), this model is so familiar as to require no explanation and no second thoughts when pressed into service.

Why is this a useful representation? From an analytic point of view, (1) is compelling for its tractability. The additive separability across time and states, the stationarity of the discounting, and the stationarity of the function u over time and states all make analysis and computation easier. For example, this maximization problem exhibits the consistency property that lies at the heart of dynamic programming. Computationally, a single function u is much easier to simulate or estimate than one such function for each period or state. At the very least, one might view (1) as an ideal point of departure for a study of behavior, however unrealistic it turns out to be, perhaps with the goal of subsequently examining the robustness of its more interesting implications to more flexible specifications.

From a normative point of view, (1) can be viewed as an expression of rationality. Within periods, the expected utility formulation is implied by Savage's (1972) axioms, often defended as foundations of rationality (with Allais (1953) and Ellsberg (1961) giving rise to a vast literature questioning their positive applicability). For example, a person whose behavior is characterized by (1) can never fall prey to a money pump, a criterion typically regarded as essential for rationality (cf. Nau and McCardle (1990)). Looking across periods, it is once again reassuring that the resulting behavior is consistent, in the sense that an optimal consumption plan at time t is the continuation of the optimal plan at time $t' < t$. This ensures that recommendations based on (1) cannot lead to conflicting advice.

From a positive point of view, however, (1) is less convincing, doing both too little and too much. This representation does too little in the sense that it leaves important questions open. What is the shape of the function u? Are people risk-neutral, risk-averse, risk-seeking, or something more complicated? How are risk attitudes related to observable characteristics of either the decision maker or her environment? The representation does too much in the sense that it places a great deal of structure on preferences. Do people really discount in such a stationary fashion? Are their preferences linear in probabilities? Do they think in terms of probabilities at all? Are their preferences really so separable? Once we go beyond these points to open the deeper question of what enters the utility function, all sorts of questions arise. Are people really concerned only with their own consumption and nothing else? How might various aspects of their environment, including perhaps the consumption of others, affect their preferences?

One possible response to these questions is empirical. Bolstered by evermore-plentiful data as well as powerful experimental techniques, we can simply observe behavior and infer the corresponding preferences. In doing so, one could usefully draw on the rich revealed-preference literature in psychology as well as economics.[1]

Our thinking on this point is that empirical work on preferences and behavior is essential. However, the specification of preferences is sufficiently complicated, and poses sufficient identification issues, that we have little hope of making progress by pursuing a *purely* empirical approach. However much data we have, we can hope to make sense of it only in the context of theoretical models.[2] But, where do we find these models? Building models is something at which economists excel, and economists are seldom idle when there are new models to be produced. As one might expect, the analysis of of preferences is no exception.[3] The difficulty is that if we do not restrict ourselves to some simple form such as (1), it seems that anything goes, and we can provide theoretical foundations for anything. How do we impose discipline on the resulting theoretical exercise?

This quest for discipline is perhaps the ultimate motivation for (1). Whatever its disadvantages, it clearly imposes a great deal of structure on the analysis. As a result, when faced with behavior seemingly inconsistent with (1), a common reaction is to preserve (1) while searching for features of the environment to account for the proposed behavior. Postlewaite (1998) states the case for doing so quite clearly. By allowing departures from (1) as explanations, not only may we acquire sufficient explanatory power as to rob the resulting exercise of any substance, but the ease with which we can thereby accommodate observed behavior may distract attention from aspects of the environment that actually lie behind the behavior. If allowed to work freely with models in which people simply prefer not to purchase used durable goods such as automobiles, we may never have discovered the lemons phenomenon (Akerlof (1970)). It may thus be better to stick with (1), trading the constraints imposed, and its potential lack of realism for the concreteness it brings to our inquiry.

The point of departure for this essay is the belief that we must both sometimes impose more structure on (1), as well as sometimes move beyond this formulation, and that we require solid theoretical foundations for both. We suggest seeking the required theoretical discipline in evolutionary models. In particular, we view human preferences as having been shaped by years of evolutionary selection. When thinking about whether (1) is a reasonable representation of preferences, or which more specific

[1] See Rabin (1998) for an introduction to work at the intersection of psychology and economics.

[2] See Gilboa and Samuelson (2009) for an abstract discussion of this point.

[3] Camerer, Loewenstein and Rabin (2004) provide a good point of entry into this literature.

or more general models might be useful alternatives, our first step is to ask what sorts of preferences are likely to emerge from this evolutionary process. The more readily can we provide evolutionary foundations for a model of preferences, the more promise we see in using this model in theoretical and applied economic analyses.

This approach to preferences raises a collection of methodological issues that are discussed in Section 2. Sections 3 and 4 provide illustrations from the literature. Section 3 concentrates on the functional form assumptions built into (1), including the expected-utility criterion that is applied within periods and the exponentially discounted summation that aggregates utility across periods. Section 4 examines arguments that are likely to appear in the utility function beyond an agent's own consumption. Section 5 very briefly concludes.

2. EVOLUTIONARY FOUNDATIONS

2.1 Evolution and economic behavior

Is it reasonable to talk about evolution and human behavior at all? A large literature, referred to as evolutionary game theory, has grown around evolutionary models of behavior.[4] The presumption behind evolutionary game theory is that human behavior, whether in games (and hence the name) or decision problems, typically does not spring into perfect form as the result of a process of rational reasoning. Instead, it emerges from a process of trial and error, as people experiment with alternatives, assess the consequences, and try new alternatives. The resulting adaptive processes have been modeled in a variety of ways, from Bayesian to reinforcement learning, from cognitive to mechanical processes, from backward to forward looking processes, all collected under the metaphor of "evolutionary game theory."

This literature has provided valuable insights into how we interpret equilibria in games, but we have a fundamentally different enterprise in mind when talking about the evolution of preferences in this essay. We take the word "evolution" literally to mean the biological process of evolution, operating over millions of years, which brought us to our present form.[5] The driving force behind this evolution is differential survival and reproduction. Some behavior makes its practitioners more likely to survive and reproduce than others, and those behaviors most conducive to survival are the ones we expect to prevail. Our task is to identify these behaviors.

This view would be uncontroversial if we were talking about the evolution of physical characteristics. A giraffe who can reach more leaves on a tree is more likely

[4] See, for example, Fudenberg and Levine (1998), Hofbauer and Sigmund (1998), Mailath (1998), Samuelson (1997), van Damme (1991, Chapter 9), Vega-Redondo (1996), Weibull (1995) and Young (1998).

[5] We have no doubt that cultural evolution is also vitally important. We expect the techniques we examine to transfer readily to models of cultural evolution, often with simply a reinterpretation. We find interpretations in terms of biological evolution more straightforward, and hence tend to adopt them. Henrich, Boyd, Bowles, Camerer, Fehr, Gintis and McElreath (2001) and Henrich, Boyd, Bowles, Camerer, Fehr and Gintis (2004) provide interesting points of departure into the study of cultural evolution and economic behavior.

to survive, and hence evolution gives us giraffes with long necks. A bat that can detect prey is more likely to survive, and so evolution gives us bats capable of echolocation. Porcupines are more likely to survive if they are not eaten, and so have evolved to be covered with sharp quills. The list of such examples is virtually endless.

Behavior can also confer an evolutionary advantage, with a similarly long list of examples. African wild dogs enlarge their set of eligible prey, and hence their chances of survival, by hunting in packs. Vampire bats reduce their likelihood of starvation by sharing food. Humans enhance the survival prospects of their offspring by providing food for their young. If different members of a population behave differently, then those whose behavior enhances their survival can be expected to dominate the population. The relentless process of differential survival will thus shape behavior as well as characteristics.

Doesn't this commit us to a strong form of biological determinism? Is our behavior really locked into our genes? We think the answer is no on both counts.[6] Nature alone does not dictate behavior. However, there is a huge gap between the assertion that genetic factors determine every decision we will ever make and the assertion that biological considerations have no effect on our behavior. We need only believe that there is some biological basis for behavior, however imprecise and whatever the mechanics, for the issues raised in this essay to be relevant.[7]

2.2 The rules of evolution

We will often refer to "evolution" as if referring to a conscious being. We will use phrases such as "evolution selects" or "evolution prefers" or "evolution maximizes" or even "evolution believes." It is important to be clear at the beginning that we attribute no consciousness and no purpose to evolution. We have in mind throughout the standard, mindless process of mutation and selection studied by biologists. We suppose that individuals in a population may have different types, whether these are manifested as different physical characteristics or different behavior. These different types reflect genetic endowments that arose initially from undirected, random mutations. Some of these types will make their possessors more likely to survive, while others will be detrimental. Over time, this process of differential survival will cause a larger proportion of the population to be characterized by the former types, and it is this process that lies behind our analysis.[8] If allowed to run unchecked, the pressures of differential survival will eliminate those types that are less likely to survive and produce a population

[6] Ridley (2003) introduces the voluminous literature that has grown around these sometimes controversial questions.

[7] The evidence that there is some such connection is both wide-ranging and fascinating. For two examples, see Dreber and Hoffman (2007) and Knafo, Israel, Darvasi, Bachner-Melman, Uzefovsky, Cohen, Feldman, Lerer, Laiba, Raz, Nemanov, Gritsenko, Dina, Agam, Dean, Bronstein and Ebstein (2007).

[8] We suggest Dawkins (1989), Ridley (1993) and Williams (1966) as accessible introductions to evolutionary theory, and Hofbauer and Sigmund (1998) for a more precise examination of the conditions under which the outcome of an evolutionary process can be modeled as the solution to an optimization problem.

consisting only of those whose behavior is most conducive to survival. As a result, it is often convenient to model the *outcome* of an evolutionary process as the solution to a maximization problem. This convention is familiar to economists, who routinely model consumers, firms, governments, and other entities as maximizers, bolstered by the view that this maximization may be the outcome of an adaptive process rather than conscious calculation. We proceed similarly here when talking about evolution, without any illusions that there is purposeful behavior behind this maximization.

The idea that an evolutionary perspective might be helpful in studying behavior is by no means unique to economists. The field of evolutionary psychology has grown around this view of behavior.[9] We can learn not only from the successes of evolutionary psychology, but also from its difficulties. Gould and Lewontin (1979) criticize evolutionary psychology as being an exercise without content. In their view, a clever modeler can produce an evolutionary model capable of producing any behavior. To reinforce their point, they refer to the resulting models as "just-so" stories. As we have already noted, of course, an analytical approach capable of explaining everything in fact explains nothing. If an evolutionary approach is to be useful, we must address the just-so critique.

Economists are also adept at constructing models, and the criticism that we can concoct models rationalizing any imaginable sort of behavior is not a new one. How do we reconcile Gould and Lewontin's argument with our assertion that evolutionary models are designed to impose discipline on our study of preferences? In our view, the ability to fix a characteristic of behavior and then construct an evolutionary rationale for that behavior is only the first step. If we can go no further, we have typically learned very little. An obvious next step is to fit the model into its place in the existing body of evolutionary theory. Simple and direct models constructed from familiar and inherently plausible evolutionary principles tend to be convincing, while convoluted models taking us well beyond the usual evolutionary considerations are reasonably greeted with skepticism. Moving beyond this informative but subjective evaluation, our goal should be to construct models that generate predictions beyond those of the target behavior, especially predictions that we could take to data. The more fruitful is a model in doing so, the more useful will it be.

2.3 Evolution and utility functions

The preceding subsections have referred frequently to the evolution of behavior, while our title refers to the evolution of preferences. How should we think about evolution shaping our behavior? In one view, evolution would simply program or "hard-wire" us with behavior, equipping us with a rule indicating what to do in each possible circumstance. Alternatively, we might think of evolution as equipping us with utility functions and instructions to maximize utility whenever called upon to make a choice.

[9] Barkow, Cosmides and Tooby (1992) provide a wide-ranging introduction.

Most of what we discuss in this essay requires no choice between these alternatives, and requires us to take no stand on the countless intermediate constructions that combine aspects of both types of model. Our focus will primarily be to identify *behavior* that confers evolutionary advantage. We will then frequently describe this behavior in terms of the preferences with which it is consistent. However, this description is a matter of convenience rather than an assertion about causality.

Taking this approach keeps us squarely within the revealed-preference approach to behavior. Among the fundamental building blocks of economic theory is an assumption that behavior satisfies the consistency conditions captured by the revealed-preference axioms. However, it is often insightful to describe this behavior in terms of preferences, and then convenient to use these preferences as the point of departure for subsequent models of behavior. Similarly, it is behavior that matters to evolution, but there often will be much to be gained by describing this behavior in terms of preferences.[10]

No amount of introspection will tell us the extent to which our behavior is hard-wired, and the extent to which we have discretion. Reading a restaurant menu and choosing a meal makes us feel as if we have conscious control over our actions. However, there is no particular reason why that same feeling could not accompany an inevitable action, or why we might not make choices without being aware of what we are doing. Pursuing these distinctions runs the risk of recreating a long-running discussion of whether we have free will, and how we would know whether we have. This is a fascinating topic, but one that has bedevilled philosophers for centuries and that would only be a hopeless diversion here.

At the same time, we think there are good a priori grounds for thinking of evolution as designing us to be utility maximizers rather than simply hard-wiring us with behavior, and Section 4.2.2 relies on a view of utility maximization as a process that shapes our choices. Robson (2001) offers an argument for the evolutionary utility of utility functions, beginning with the assumption that environments fluctuate more quickly than evolution can respond. Simply telling people to hunt rabbits is risky because they may encounter situations in which deer are more readily available. With hard-wired behavior, an evolutionary response to such situations would require a deer-hunting mutation, or perhaps several if the first few such mutations are unlucky. This must then be followed by a process of selection that may be fast compared to length of time humans have been developing, but may be quite slow compared to the length of time it takes for a shock to the weather or to the population of predators to once again make rabbits relatively plentiful. By the time the new hard-wired behavior has spread into the population, it may well be out of step with the environment. A more flexible

[10] This emphasis on behavior as the primitive object of analysis distinguishes the evolutionary approach from much of behavioral economics, where the process by which choices are made often takes center stage. See Camerer (2003) and Gul and Pesendorfer (2008) for a discussion of these issues.

design would give the agent the ability to observe and collect information about her environment, coupled perhaps with an instruction of the form "hunt the relatively more plentiful prey." This type of contingent behavior will be effective as long as evolution can reasonably anticipate the various circumstances the agent may face. However, this may require taking account of a list of contingencies prohibitively long for evolution to hit upon the optimum via trial-and-error mutations. A more effective approach may then be to endow the agent with a goal, such as maximizing caloric intake or simply feeling full, along with the ability to learn which behavior is most likely to achieve this goal in a given environment. Under this approach, evolution would equip us with a utility function that would provide the goal for our behavior, along with a learning process, perhaps ranging from trial-and-error to information collection and Bayesian updating, that would help us pursue that goal.[11]

If this were the case, however, why would we attach utility to activities such as eating? Evolution necessarily selects for that behavior which leads to the most effective propagation, so why don't we have preferences solely over offspring, or some appropriate trade-off between the quantity and quality of offspring, or some other measure of descendants? One difficulty is that simply giving us preferences over offspring gives rise to a small-sample learning process. Human offspring come relatively rarely and provide relatively sparse feedback. Opportunities to eat are much more frequent and provide a much richer flow of information. An agent designed with the goal of producing healthy adult offspring, and then left to learn the details of doing so by trial-and-error, may not learn soon enough to do any good. An agent whose goal is to be well nourished may acquire enough experience soon enough to make good use of this information. Defining utilities in terms of offspring thus gives us an objective that quite faithfully captures the relevant evolutionary criterion, but gives us little means of learning how to accomplish this objective. Defining utilities in terms of intermediate goods such as consumption gives us an objective that only approximates evolution's—in some environments we will mechanically pursue additional consumption even though circumstances are such that doing so retards reproduction—in return for giving us the means to effectively learn how to accomplish this objective. The choice of which arguments to place in a utility function thus reflects a

[11] There are, of course, other aspects of our preferences that evolution may prefer to place outside our learning. Many people have a deep-seated fear of snakes (cf. Mineka and Cook (1993) and Pinker (1997, pp. 388–389)), but few of us are afraid of mushrooms. Since both can be potentially fatal and both can be eaten, this combination is by no means obvious. To see why we may have come to such a state, imagine that being bitten by a poisonous snake is very unlikely to happen but likely to be fatal if it does, while ingesting a poisonous mushroom is more likely to occur but less likely to be fatal. Then evolution may optimally leave it to her agents to sort out which mushrooms are dangerous, while being unwilling to take chances on encounters with snakes. In general, evolution should make us fear not simply things that are bad for us, but rather things whose danger we may underestimate *without* discovering our error before they kill us. Samuelson and Swinkels (2006) pursue these possibilities.

delicate evolutionary balancing act, one that we believe merits further study. As a first step, there is much to be learned about this evolutionary trade off simply from observing how evolution has solved this problem, i.e., observing what enters our utility functions.

Utility functions carry risk for evolution as well as benefits. Evolution has equipped us with preferences over many things—basic needs, such as food, sleep, safety, sex, and shelter, as well as more complicated items such as our relationship with others and our position in our community—that evolution has chosen because of the resulting salutary effects on our fitness. The fact that we have cognitive abilities that allow us to predict the effects of our actions, and to choose actions whose effects fare well in terms of our preferences, suggests that the resulting behavioral flexibility is also evolutionarily advantageous. At this point, however, a conflict can arise between evolution's preferences and our preferences. We have been designed to maximize our utility or "happiness," while evolution does not care whether we are happy, instead viewing happiness simply as a means for producing evolutionarily valuable ends. Maximizing happiness must on average lead to good evolutionary outcomes, or our utility functions would be designed differently, but this still leaves room for conflict. Evolution has given us a taste for sex, but over the course of having children we may notice some of the sometimes less desirable effects, leading to birth control practices that can thwart evolution's goals. It is important to bear the potential for such conflict in mind when confronted with behavior that seems otherwise inexplicable.

2.4 Evolutionary mismatches

There are two complementary approaches to thinking about the evolutionary foundations of behavior. One is based on the observation that we currently live in an environment much different from that in which we evolved. As a result, behavior that was well suited for our evolutionary environment may fit quite awkwardly into our current one. For example, food was likely to have been in perpetually tenuous supply over the course of our evolutionary history, and the only technology for storing it was to eat it. An instruction of the form "eat all you can whenever you can" accordingly may have made good evolutionary sense. This presumably explains why so many of us struggle to keep our weight down in our modern world of abundance. Similarly, predators were probably not only a threat during much of our evolutionary history, but also one that often left little leeway for learning. Ascertaining which animals are dangerous by trial-and-error is a process fraught with danger, even if most animals pose no threat. A deep-seated fear of predators was accordingly quite useful for survival. This presumably explains why children in our modern urban society are much more likely to fear wild animals than electrical outlets, even though the latter pose a much greater threat.

We refer to these types of observations as "evolutionary mismatch" models. This is clearly a useful perspective.[12] However, our interest will typically lie not in such mismatch stories, but in examining behavior that is well adapted to its environment. We will accordingly be especially interested in tracing various features of behavior to features of the environment in which the behavior could have evolved. For example, we will examine how the nature of the uncertainty in the environment affects intertemporal preferences. Mismatches are clearly important, but we believe that a good understanding of how preferences are tailored to the environment in which they evolved is an essential first step in understanding their effects in mismatched environments. If nothing else, allowing ourselves to indulge in mismatch explanations gives us yet one more degree of freedom in constructing our models, while the goal throughout is to use evolutionary arguments to restrict such freedom.

It is important throughout to distinguish evolutionary mismatches from the potential conflict, noted in Section 2.3, between evolutionary goals and the results of our utility maximization. The latter conflict readily arises in the environment in which we evolved. Evolution finds it expedient to give us utility functions because it is prohibitively difficult to dictate every aspect of our behavior. However, once this step is taken, the prospect arises that the resulting utility maximization will sometimes lead to counterproductive outcomes, even before we consider the effects of thrusting the agent into a new environment.

2.5 The indirect evolutionary approach

We distinguish the work described in this essay from a body of literature that has come to be called the "indirect evolutionary approach." It is worth making this distinction carefully. The indirect evolutionary approach grew out of evolutionary game theory. In the simplest evolutionary-game-theory model, players are characterized by the actions they take in the decision problem or game of interest. We might think of the players as being programmed to take such actions. As play progresses, a revision protocol induces a process by which the players switch their actions. For example, players may randomly choose a new action whenever their realized payoff falls below an aspiration level, or players may switch after each period to the action that would have been a best response to the previous-period average population action, or may switch only in randomly-drawn periods to actions that are best responses to an average of the play of their previous opponents, and so on. One can imagine an endless list of such revision protocols. A central question in evolutionary game theory concerns the extent to which we can characterize the outcome of such revision protocols over the course of repeated play. Will the people be directed to behavior that appears to be "rational?" For example, will their behavior satisfy the revealed preference axioms? Will it

[12] See Burnham and Phelan (2000) for a wealth of examples.

maximize a simple objective? Will people eschew dominated strategies? Will the process induce population behavior that can be rationalized by a concept such as Nash equilibrium? Will the resulting behavior satisfy more refined equilibrium concepts?

The point of departure for the indirect evolutionary approach is to note that throughout the rest of economics, we typically model people as being characterized by preferences rather than simply actions, with these preferences inducing actions through a choice procedure such as utility maximization. Taking this idea literally in an evolutionary context, we can think of people as maximizing utility given their preferences, with their preferences adjusting over time according to a revision protocol. The evolutionary process now shapes behavior through its effect on preferences, and it is this indirect link that gives rise to the name indirect evolutionary approach, pioneered by Güth (1995) and Güth and Yaari (1992).

The indirect evolutionary approach has been embraced by many because of its ability to explain seemingly anomalous preferences. To see what is involved, it is useful to start with an example. Consider the following game:[13]

	L	R
T	6, 2	4, 4
B	5, 1	2, 0

(2)

This game has a unique Nash equilibrium, given by (T, R), with payoffs (4,4).[14]

Now suppose that, before the game begins, player 1 could commit to playing B, and player 2 can observe whether such a commitment has been made. The game proceeds as before if no commitment is made, and otherwise player 1 is locked into B and 2 is left to choose an action. Essentially, a commitment gives us a new game with a sequential structure in which player 1 moves first. This new structure is valuable for player 1. By committing to B, 1 can ensure player 2 will choose a best response of L, giving player 1 a payoff of 5. It is clear that player 1 would jump at the chance to commit.

The observation that commitments can be valuable has a long history, beginning with von Stackelberg (1934, translated into English in Peacock (1952)) and playing a prominent role in Schelling (1980). Early theories of bargaining, including Binmore (1980) and Crawford and Varian (1979), explore the power of commitment more formally, as does Frank (1987). While it is straightforward to see that it can be valuable to make commitments, it is less clear just how one does so.

Now let us think of a population of player 1s and another population of player 2s. Players from these populations are repeatedly matched to play the game given by (2). The indirect evolutionary approach assumes that the payoffs in (2) are "material payoffs" or "fitnesses." These payoffs are relevant in evolutionary terms. Evolution induces

[13] The subsequent discussion follows Samuelson (2001),

[14] This is the unique rationalizable outcome, since strategy T strictly dominates B and R is a strict best response to T.

behavior by endowing agents with preferences over the actions T and B (for player 1s) and L and R (for player 2s). These preferences need not match the fitnesses given in (2), but it is fitnesses and not preferences that govern the evolutionary process. Agents whose behavior leads to high fitnesses will reproduce relatively rapidly and the population will ultimately be dominated by such preferences. In particular, an agent may choose an action that performs wonderfully from the point of view of the agent's preferences, all the while wasting away in the population because the action yields a low fitness. Evolution can thus mislead her agents, in the sense that preferences need not match fitnesses, but cannot fool herself, in that high fitnesses remain the ticket to evolutionary success.

Is there any reason for preferences to be anything other than fitnesses in such a setting? The key here is the assumption that preferences are observable, in the sense that when two players meet, each player can observe the other's preferences. The two matched players then play a complete-information version of the game given by (2), with their behavior governed by their preferences, and with the evolutionary implications of their behavior governed by the fitnesses given in (2). Suppose that player 2s have preferences that match fitnesses, as do some player 1s. However, the population also includes some player 1s whose preferences make B a strictly dominant strategy, effectively committing themselves to B. In response to the former types of player 1, player 2 will choose R, giving 1 a payoff of 4. In response to the latter, player 2 will choose L, giving 1 a payoff of 5. As a result, the population will eventually be dominated by player 1s committed to playing B. There is thus evolutionary value in equipping agents with preferences that do not reflect their fitnesses.

Bolstered by results such as this, the indirect evolutionary approach has been interpreted as providing foundations for a collection of empirical, experimental, or introspective findings that appear inconsistent with material self-interest, including the endowment effect, altruism, vengeance, punishment, and so on.[15] These results are intriguing, but raise two questions. First, initial applications of the indirect evolutionary approach typically considered only a few possible preference specifications, often including preferences that match material fitnesses and one or more "commitment preference" alternatives that are tailored to the game in question. In considering (2), for example, we considered the possibility that 1 might be committed to B, but there are many other possible preference specifications. What happens if they are present as well? Player 2, for example, would like to commit to R, for much the same reason that 1 finds it valuable to commit to B. What if there are also player 2s who are so committed? What if the entire collection of preference specifications were allowed? Would we be confident that the commitment types emerging from simple models would also be selected from such a crowd?

More importantly, it was critical in the preceding argument that players could observe each other's preferences. Being committed to B is an advantage to player 1 only

[15] See Ostrom (2000) for an introduction.

because it affects player 2's behavior, inducing 2 to switch to *L*. Ely and Yilankaya (2000) and Ok and Vega-Redondo (2000) confirm that if preferences are not observable, any limit of behavior in their indirect evolutionary models must constitute a Nash equilibrium in material fitnesses. The indirect evolutionary approach with unobservable preferences then gives us an alternative description of the evolutionary process, one that is perhaps less reminiscent of biological determinism, but leads to no new results.

Preferences are not typically high on the list of things taken to be observable in economic analysis. Is it reasonable to assume that people can identify one another's preferences? Frank (1988) argues that we do often have good information about the preferences of others, and that there is a technological basis for such information. Our preferences are determined partly by emotions such as anger or embarrassment that are beyond our conscious control, expressed by involuntary changes in our facial expressions and body language. If one is prone to blushing when the center of attention, how much good does it do to remind oneself not to blush? Who can keep flashes of anger out of their eyes? Our preferences may then often be an open book free for others to read. At the same time, Güth (1995) shows that preferences need not be *perfectly* observable in order for the indirect evolutionary approach to have nontrivial implications. It suffices that player 2 *sometimes* be able to discern player 1's preferences and react to them. As Güth notes, it is a seemingly quite strong assertion that this is never the case, arguably as unrealistic as the assumption that people can always observe one another's preferences.

To evaluate these considerations, we must return to the evolutionary context. The standard argument is that we can observe preferences because people give signals—a tightening of the lips or flash of the eyes—that provide clues as to their feelings. However, the emission of such signals and their correlation with the attendant emotions are themselves the product of evolution. A complete version of the indirect evolutionary approach would then incorporate within the model the evolution of preferences *and* the evolution of the attendant signals. In (2) for example, player 1 prefers (*T, L*) to (*B, L*). Evolution thus has an incentive not only to produce player 1s who are visibly committed to playing *B*, but also a version of player 1 whose signals match those emitted by those player 1s committed to *B*, inducing *L* from player 2, but who then plays *T*. What prevents the appearance of such a mimic? We cannot simply assume that mimicry is impossible, as we have ample evidence of mimicry from the animal world, as well as experience with humans who make their way by misleading others as to their feelings, intentions and preferences.[16] If such mimics did appear, of course, then presumably player 2s would at least eventually learn that player 1s appearing to be committed to *B* are not always so, and would then no longer respond to such apparent commitment by playing *L*. This opens the door for a new type of player 1 to appear, emitting a new signal that is reliably

[16] For introductions see Harper (1991) and Maynard Smith (1998, pp. 85–87).

associated with a commitment to B and hence inducing L from player 2. Then the incentive to produce a new mimic appears, and on we go. It appears as if the result could well be a never-ending cycle, as in Robson (1990).

In our view, the indirect evolutionary approach will remain incomplete until the evolution of preferences, the evolution of signals about preferences, and the evolution of reactions to these signals, are all analyzed within the model. Perhaps there are outcomes in which players can effectively make commitments by exhibiting the appropriate observable preferences, and there is some force barring the evolutionary pressure to produce mimics, giving us a stationary outcome featuring effective commitment. Perhaps instead the outcome is the sort of cyclical arms race envisioned by Robson (1990), with our current situation being a point along this cycle in which some aspects of preferences are at least partially observable. The implications of these scenarios could well be quite different. Further work is required before we have a good idea of what these implications might be. Given the presence of mimics in the natural world, the topic is clearly important. However, without more work along these lines, we regard the indirect evolutionary approach as incomplete.

3. WHAT SORT OF PREFERENCES?

A representation of preferences such as (1) combines a number of different features, including the choice of what to include as the arguments of the utility function, attitudes toward risk, and trade-offs between consumption at different times. We find it most convenient to address these features separately. We begin in this section by taking it for granted that we can reasonably think of preferences as being defined over a single homogeneous consumption good. We then break our investigation into two parts.

First, we strip away intertemporal considerations to focus on preferences over consumption within a single period. What form do we expect the function $u(c)$ to take? What attitudes toward risk might have evolved? How might risk attitudes vary with one's circumstances or characteristics?

Second, we examine preferences over intertemporal tradeoffs. How do we expect preferences to be aggregated over time? Should we expect preferences to be reasonably approximated by an additively separable utility function, as in (1)? If so, should we expect people to discount the future exponentially? At what rate? If not, how might we expect their discounting to depart from exponential? These questions are all the more pertinent in light of the recent explosion of interest in behavioral economics, much of which is built on the presumption that agents do *not* discount exponentially (cf. Frederick, Loewenstein and O'Donoghue, (2002)).[17]

[17] See Ainslie (1992), Loewenstein and Prelec (1992), and Loewenstein and Thaler (1989) for treatments of present-biased preferences. See Rubinstein (2003) for an alternative perspective. Early studies of present bias and self-control by Pollak (1968), Schelling (1984), and Strotz (1956) have engendered a large literature. For a few examples, see Elster (1985), O'Donoghue and Rabin (1999a, 1999b), and Thaler and Shefrin (1981).

3.1 Risk

3.1.1 Attitudes toward risk

The expected utility theorem has pride of place in the economic theory of behavior under risk. Whether one believes that expected utility-maximization faithfully describes behavior or not, its salience in economic analysis is inescapable.

At first blush, it seems that evolution would surely induce preferences that can be characterized by expected utility maximization.[18] To focus on choice under risk, let us consider a setting in which agents have to choose a lottery from a set of possible lotteries, with the outcome of their selected lottery determining the number of their offspring. The lottery choice is the behavior that is shaped by evolution, being a heritable feature that is passed on from one generation to the next. We then think of a population made up of a number of different types of people, with each type characterized by their choice of economic lottery. All risk is independent across types and individuals, a case that we refer to as "idiosyncratic" (as opposed to "aggregate") risk. For simplicity, we adopt the common assumption that all reproduction is asexual, or "parthenogenetic."[19]

Lotteries are defined over a set of allocations C. The bundle $c \in C$ produces the same expected offspring $\Psi(c)$, regardless of the type of agent, i.e., regardless of the lottery from which this bundle was drawn. Hence, ex ante menus have no ex post consequences. Let q_k^i be the probability that the lottery chosen by type i produces the outcome c_k^i. It follows that the expected number of offspring of type i is then

$$\sum_k q_k^i \Psi(c_k^i).$$

Since the population is large and all risk is idiosyncratic, this is also the growth rate of type i. Thus, the most successful type will be the type that maximizes this criterion. But this is simply the maximization of expected utility, where the role of the von Neumann-Morgenstern utility function u is played by the biological production function Ψ.

This evolutionary foundation for expected utility maximization is critically dependent on all the risk being idiosyncratic or independent across individuals. There seems no compelling reason why all risk should be idiosyncratic. One often begins with hunter-gatherers when thinking about evolution, in an effort to imagine the circumstances under which much of the evolution affecting our current behavior has occurred. Some of the risk in a hunter-gatherer society undoubtedly concerned the weather, which clearly is a

[18] This section draws on Robson (1996).

[19] We emphasize that are not under the illusion that human reproduction is asexual, nor do we believe that one can consistently ignore the sexual nature of reproduction when studying evolution. However, models of sexual reproduction are significantly more complicated, and doing justice to sexual reproduction often leaves little analytic headroom to consider other issues. It is thus common practice to effectively focus on an issue of interest by working with asexual reproduction.

shared form of risk. This remained a source of correlated risk as people made the shift to agriculture, perhaps becoming all the more important in the process. In a modern setting, there continue to be important shared risks. Aggregate shocks in the weather have escalated to the possibility of global climate change sufficiently serious as to threaten our survival, while recent events have made it all too clear that social institutions such as financial markets give rise to new sources of correlated risks.

Intuitively, idiosyncratic risk corresponds to having a separate, personal coin flipped for each individual in each period. To keep things simple, let us assume that aggregate risk gives us the opposite extreme in which a single public coin is flipped in each period—heads everyone wins, tails everyone loses. What difference would this make?

To answer this question, let us warm up by considering a related puzzle. An investor must choose between three alternatives:

(1) Investment 1 pays $(3/2)^{52} \simeq \$1{,}400{,}000{,}000$;

(2) Investment 2 pays the expected value of the following lottery. One begins with a balance of one dollar. One then goes through a well-shuffled deck of cards, with 26 black and 26 red cards, successively turning over each card. Each time a red card turns up, the current balance is doubled, while each time a black card comes up, there is no change in the running total;

(3) Investment 3 matches Investment 2, except that the 52 draws are taken from an infinite deck of cards, half red and half black, much like the decks used by casinos to thwart card counters at the blackjack table.

The expected value of Investment 1 is trivially $(3/2)^{52}$, since there is no randomness here. What is the expected return from turning over the first card in Investment 2? 3/2. After that, things get more complex, because it depends now on whether the first draw was red or black. Surely it can't be too bad to take the Investment 2? Surely, the expected value of the Investment 2 is something close to \$1,400,000,000, even if this is not the exact value.

Compared to the first alternative, Investment 2 is terrible. Indeed, the "lottery" defining Investment 2 involves no uncertainty at all. The payoff is exactly $2^{26} = (\sqrt{2})^{52} \simeq \$67,000,000$, because there are 26 red cards and the doubling effect of each red card is independent of where it arises in the deck. A priori, each card in the deck is equally likely to be red or black, so that the first draw generates an expected value of 3/2. However, the subsequent draws are not independent across cards, and this dependence matters.

Now consider Investment 3. This investment really is a lottery, with realizations that are independent across cards. It no longer matters to subsequent draws whether the first draw is red or black, since there is an infinite number of each color. It is not hard to show that the expected value of the lottery after 52 draws is $(3/2)^{52}$, matching that of the first alternative. To a risk-neutral investor, the two options are then precisely equivalent. A risk-averse investor would choose the first alternative in order to avoid the risk inherent in the third.

Nothing that is fundamental in these comparisons depends upon there being only 52 cards, with a similar comparison holding for any finite number T of draws. The lesson to be learned from this example is that when computing the effect of a series of random variables that accumulate multiplicatively, correlation matters. Notice that if instead the investments were additive—the first adding 3/2 to the running total in each period, and the second being equally likely to add 0 or add 2—then correlation would be irrelevant. The expected payoff of both alternatives would be (3/2) T. Indeed, the correlation induced by the 52-card deck, by eliminating any randomness from the problem, would make the two alternatives identical. The infinite deck would preserve the expected value, but make the third alternative riskier.

Now let us turn to an evolutionary setting where analogous forces will appear. We consider a population consisting of two types of infinitely-lived individuals, who differ in the lotteries that govern their number of offspring. In each period, type 1 has either 2 offspring, an event that occurs with probability 1/2, or has only a single offspring, also with probability 1/2. Importantly, all of the risk here is idiosyncratic, meaning that it is independent across all individuals and dates. Type 2 similarly has either 1 or 2 offspring, with each alternative occurring with probability 1/2. However, the risk is now aggregate—either all the type 2 individuals alive at a particular date have two offspring, or they all have only a single offspring—though it remains independent across dates.

One's first reaction here might well be that there should be no difference in the evolutionary success of the two types. From an individual's point of view, the various lotteries involved in each type are identical, making one or two offspring equally likely in each period, independently of how many offspring have appeared in the previous period or are expected to appear in subsequent periods. Nonetheless, the two types of individuals face decidedly different evolutionary prospects.

If the population is sufficiently large, then with very high probability, the population ends each period with half again as many type 1s as it began. Because the offspring lotteries are independent across periods, this is an immediate implication of the law of large numbers. Hence, the number of type 1s grows essentially deterministically by a factor of 3/2 in every period, with the number of type 1s at date T being arbitrarily close to $N(T) = (3/2)^T$ (normalizing $N(0)$ to equal 1). The corresponding continuously-compounded growth rate is $\frac{1}{T}\ln N(T) = \ln(3/2)$. The type-1 individuals are thus essentially facing the first alternative in our investment problem.

The number of type 2s is inescapably random, even when the population is extraordinarily large, since in each period a single flip of the offspring coin governs the outcome for every individual. These draws are independent over time, so type 2s are facing the third investment option, played with an infinite deck. It is then not hard to calculate the expected type-2 population size $\widetilde{N}(T)$ at time T, finding that $E(\widetilde{N}(T)) = (3/2)^T$. This matches the expression for type 1, confirming that the expected number of descendants under each scheme are the same. However, type 2s face risk, with the realized number of type 2s being $\widetilde{N}(T) = 2^{\tilde{n}(T)}$, where $\widetilde{N}(0) = 1$ and $\tilde{n}(T)$ is the random variable describing the number of heads in a sequence of T flips of a fair coin.

What is the effect of this risk? We can calculate a continuous, deterministic growth rate that reliably describes the behavior of the population as T gets large. In particular, $\frac{1}{T} \ln \widetilde{N}(T) = \frac{1}{T} \tilde{n}(T) \ln 2 \to \frac{1}{2} \ln 2 = \ln \sqrt{2}$, with probability one, as $T \to \infty$ (again, by the strong law of large numbers). Hence, while the expected number of type 2s matches the expected number of type 1s, with arbitrarily high probability the realized number of type 2s performs as in Investment 2. Of course, $\sqrt{2} < 3/2$ which implies that with probability one, the ratio of type-1 to type-2 agents goes to infinity. In a strong sense, then, the first type outperforms the second.

What lies behind this comparison? The correlation in the outcomes of Investment 2, whereby every red card calls forth a compensating black card, forces its payoff below that of Investment 1. The independent draws of Investment 3 break this correlation, but over long periods of time the numbers of red and black cards are nonetheless very nearly equal. On outcomes where this is the case, the payoff of Investment 3 falls below that of Investment 1, and similarly the numbers of type 2s fall behind those of type 1s. Investment 3 achieves an expected payoff matching that of Investment 1 by riskily attaching extraordinarily large returns to extraordinarily unlikely events (involving preponderances of red cards). From an evolutionary point of view, this strategy is deadly. With probability arbitrarily close to 1 (for large T), type 2s become a vanishingly small proportion of the population, despite the fact that the expected values of the two are precisely the same. Indeed, with probability one the mean number of type-2 agents grows faster than does the number of type-2 agents itself!

An early use of the word "martingale" was to describe the following betting strategy, mentioned by Casanova in his memoirs: Bet \$1 on a fair coin (or 1 sequin in Casanova's memoirs).[20] If you win, quit, in the process having gained \$1. If you lose, bet \$2 on the next throw. If you win, quit, having gained \$2 − \$1 = \$1. If you lose, bet \$4 on the next throw, and so on. This strategy is claimed to ensure you win \$1.[21]

The martingale betting strategy shares some features with our erstwhile type 2s. Consider the possible outcomes of the martingale strategy after a maximum of $T + 1$ flips of the fair coin. One possibility is that you have lost every flip. That is, you might have

[20] A sequin was a small gold coin used in Italy. Its value became debased over time, and the word entered English with its current meaning of a dress ornament.

[21] Casanova initially did well with this system, writing that "Before leaving, M– M– asked me to go to her casino, to take some money and to play, taking her for my partner. I did so. I took all the gold I found, and playing the martingale, and doubling my stakes continuously, I won every day during the remainder of the carnival. I was fortunate enough never to lose the sixth card, and, if I had lost it, I should have been without money to play, for I had two thousand sequins on that card. I congratulated myself upon having increased the treasure of my dear mistress, who wrote to me that, for the sake of civility, we ought to have a supper 'en partie carrée' on Shrove Monday. I consented." (This quotation is from Chapter 21 of *The Complete Memoirs of Jacques Casanova de Seingalt, Volume Two: To Paris and Prison*, translated by Arthur Machen, published by G. P. Putnam's Sons of New York, and available at http://www.gutenberg.org/files/2981/2981-h/v2.htm.)

lost $1 + 2 + \ldots + 2^T = 2^{T+1} - 1$.[22] The probability of this loss is the probability of $T + 1$ heads, or $\left(\frac{1}{2}\right)^{T+1}$. The only other possibility is that you have won, possibly stopping at some earlier time S. If you win, the amount won is always $1 = 2^S - (1 + \ldots + 2^{S-1})$. The probability of winning must be $1 - \left(\frac{1}{2}\right)^{T+1}$. The expected change in wealth is $-\left(\frac{1}{2}\right)^{T+1}(2^{T+1} - 1) + 1 - \left(\frac{1}{2}\right)^{T+1} = 0$, as one would expect—you can't string together a finite series of finite fair bets, no matter how you do it, and expect to do any better than breaking even.[23]

In the limit as $T \to \infty$, however, this is no longer true. The probability of losing tends to zero and that of winning tends to one. In the limiting distribution to which this process converges, you win \$1 for sure. Thus, the limit of the means, \$0, is not equal to the mean of the limiting distribution, \$1. How can this happen? The distribution after a finite number of flips puts a very small probability weight on a very large loss. This yields a non-vanishing contribution to the mean. In the limit, however, the probability of this loss converges to zero, giving us an upward jump in the mean "at the limit."

In our simple biological example, the mean of the type 2 population is similarly (if inversely) held *up* by very small probabilities of very large populations. In the limit, these probabilities vanish, so the growth of the population is overestimated by the mean. Despite having the same mean, the population almost surely fares worse under aggregate uncertainty (the type 2s) than under individual uncertainty (type 1).

The implication of this difference is that evolutionarily optimal strategies should be more averse to aggregate risk than to equivalent idiosyncratic risk, in the sense that people should be less willing to accept lotteries incorporating aggregate risks. From an individual point of view, this may seem bizarre. Why should I be on the verge of undertaking an investment, only to balk upon learning that many other people will share my realizations? However, we can expect evolution to have learned via experience that such investments are to be shunned, and can expect this to be reflected in our preferences.

The example can be recast as an economic choice as follows. Suppose that bundles c_1 and c_2 induce the offspring levels 1 and 2, so $\Psi(c_1) = 1$ and $\Psi(c_2) = 2$, where Ψ is the common production function for expected offspring. Now individuals must choose between lottery 1 and lottery 2. Lottery 1 yields c_1 and c_2 each with probability 1/2, where all this risk is independent. Lottery 2 also yields c_1 and c_2 each with probability 1/2, but now all this risk is aggregate. From an expected utility point of view, these two

[22] To confirm this expression, suppose it holds after losing T times. It follows that it holds after losing $T + 1$ times because $1 + 2 + \ldots + 2^{T+1} = 2(2^{T+1}) - 1 = 2^{T+2} - 1$.

[23] It seems that Casanova came to a similar conclusion, writing in Chapter 24 that, "I still played on the martingale, but with such bad luck that I was soon left without a sequin. As I shared my property with M– M– I was obliged to tell her of my losses, and it was at her request that I sold all her diamonds, losing what I got for them; she had now only five hundred sequins by her. There was no more talk of her escaping from the convent, for we had nothing to live on! I still gamed, but for small stakes, waiting for the slow return of good luck."

lotteries should be equivalent. Indeed, even from the perspective of any decision theory that applies the apparently weak notion of "probabilistic sophistication," these two lotteries should be equivalent. But, it is not enough here to consider only one's own payoffs and the associated probabilities, as such sophistication requires. One must also consider how the uncertainty affects others. That is, preferences are interdependent. In an evolutionary environment, individuals should prefer lottery 1 to lottery 2.

The most general case that can easily be analyzed is as follows. Given an aggregate environment z, each type i faces an idiosyncratic economic lottery where $q_k^{i,z}$ is the probability of receiving a commodity bundle $c_k^{i,z}$. We let $\Psi(c)$ be the expected offspring from bundle c for any state and any type, where any underlying risk here is also idiosyncratic. Hence $\sum_k q_k^{i,z}\Psi(c_k^{i,z})$ is the expected offspring of type i in state z. If each state z has probability ρ_z, then the long run limiting exponential growth rate of type i is

$$\sum_z \rho_z \ln\left(\sum_k q_k^{i,z}\Psi(c_k^{i,z})\right). \tag{3}$$

Hence the type that maximizes this expression should be favored by natural selection. In particular, we see the preference for idiosyncratic rather than aggregate risk in our example, since

$$\ln\left((1/2)\Psi(c_1) + (1/2)\Psi(c_2)\right) > (1/2)\ln\Psi(c_1) + (1/2)\ln\Psi(c_2),$$

by the strict concavity of the function ln.

What are the behavioral implications of the distinction between aggregate and idiosyncratic risk? People may strictly prefer to take idiosyncratic lotteries for reasons that are quite distinct from a conventional explanation in terms of the convexity of the von Neumann-Morgenstern utility. Perhaps the simplest example of this is due to Cooper and Kaplan (2004). Consider the evolutionary success of a parthenogenetic animal. Suppose the probability of a snowy winter is $\rho \in (0, 1/2)$ and hence the probability of a clear winter is $1 - \rho \in (1/2, 1)$. The animal is hunted by predators that it hopes to escape by blending indistinguishably into its surroundings. As a result, animals with dark coats survive clear winters but die in snowy winters, while those that develop white coats survive snowy winters but die in clear ones. Clearly, a type that always has a dark coat is doomed to extinction with the first white winter, and one that always has a white coat is doomed by the first clear winter. Suppose the chameleon-like strategy of changing colors with the nature of the winter is infeasible. Then consider a type whose members randomize—choosing a white coat with probability π and a dark coat with probability $1 - \pi$. That is, all individuals of this type are genetically identical, where this means merely that they choose their winter color from the same idiosyncratic lottery, but experience different ex post outcomes. The overall growth rate of this type is then

$$r = \rho \ln \pi + (1 - \rho) \ln (1 - \pi),$$

which is readily shown to be maximized by choosing $\pi = \rho$. In particular, such "probability matching" allows this type to avoid extinction.

This argument is developed further by Bergstrom (1997), who casts the story in terms of squirrels who might similarly adopt a mixed strategy in saving food for a winter of variable length. Even if the long and harsh winters were extraordinarily rare, a pure type that stored enough food only for shorter and milder winters would be doomed to extinction, while a pure strategy of saving for the longest and harshest of winters is very wasteful, consuming resources and incurring risks to accumulate food that virtually always goes unused. The optimal response is a mixture in which only a small fraction of the population stockpiles sufficient food to ensure the worst of winters, allowing the population to avoid extinction while most members also avoid overwhelmingly wasteful accumulation.

Cooper and Kaplan (2004) interestingly interpreted individuals who choose a white coat in their model after the flip of their coin as being "altruistic." Why? The probability of such an individual dying in their model is higher than the probability of death for an individual with a dark coat, simply because $1 - \rho > 1/2 > \rho$. The apparent altruism thus arises out of a choice that seems to decrease an agent's probability of survival, while protecting the population from extinction. Why would such an agent ever make such a choice? Why not maximize the probability of survival? Before we can interpret this choice as altruism, we must make sure of the correct notion of fitness (as a biologist would put it) or, equivalently, the correct utility function.

Grafen (1999) offers a resolution of the apparent altruism puzzle raised by Cooper and Kaplan. Consider a continuum of agents of size 1. Suppose π of these agents choose white and $1 - \pi$ choose dark. Now consider the choice of a small mass of individuals of size ε. If they choose white, the *expected fraction* of the population they will constitute at the end of the winter is $\frac{\rho\varepsilon}{\pi}$, which equals ε if $\rho = \pi$. If they choose dark, the *expected fraction* of the population they will constitute is $\frac{1-\rho}{1-\pi}\varepsilon$, which again equals ε if $\rho = \pi$. Each individual of the type that randomizes $(\rho, 1 - \rho)$ thus maximizes the expected fraction of the population it will comprise, and this expected fraction of the population is the appropriate notion of biological fitness. Death brings zero fitness no matter what the state of the population, but when you survive, it matters how large you loom in the population.

To reinterpret this from an economic point of view, the result is that the usual selfish preferences are inadequate in explaining behavior in the face of aggregate uncertainty. It is instead important to consider not only the likelihood of death, but also how well you are doing when you do survive *relative to others*. The the appropriate notion of utility must then be interdependent. See Curry (2001) for an analysis of this interdependence.

3.1.2 Risk and status

It is a common observation that people exhibit risk-aversion when making some choices while also exhibiting risk-preference in other cases. People buy both insurance and lottery tickets. The standard explanation for this behavior begins with Friedman and Savage (1948), who suggested that the typical von Neumann-Morgenstern utility function is concave over low values of wealth but then becomes convex over higher values. People with such utility functions would seek insurance protection against downside risk, while at the same time buying lottery tickets that promise a small probability of a large increase in wealth. One can account for the observation that actual lotteries have a nontrivial array of prizes, rather than a single grand prize, by assuming that there is a final range of wealth over which von Neumann-Morgenstern utility is again concave.

The Friedman-Savage explanation views utility as being defined over absolute wealth levels. The difficulty here is that absolute wealth levels have changed dramatically over a relatively short period of our recent history. If a Friedman-Savage utility function supported the simultaneous purchase of insurance and gambling in a particular society at a particular date, then growing wealth levels would make it difficult to use the same utility function in explaining similar phenomena at a later date. Indeed, if utility functions are stable, then the market for insurance should wither away, as the number of individuals in the requisite low range of wealth decrease. Lotteries may also have diminishing prizes over time, since a lower prize would attain the same target level of final wealth. Nothing in our current experience suggests that the demand for insurance has dissipated as our society has gotten wealthier, or that lottery prizes are deteriorating.

The preceding argument relies on a particularly simple utility function, and one could come closer to a consistent model of behavior with a more elaborate function. In the process, of course, one must worry about constructing ever-more-sophisticated models that ultimately collapse under the weight of their complexity, just as epicycles ultimately gave way to a more parsimonious planetary model. A seemingly more likely explanation is that utility functions have changed over time. Increasing wealth has not vitiated the need for insurance because utility functions have ratcheted up along with wealth levels. While intuitive, this explanation alone is discomforting in its reliance on the exogenously generated shifting of utility functions. Why do our utility functions change as our society gets wealthier? When is this shift likely to be especially pronounced, and when is it likely to be attenuated? What implications does it have for behavior, and for economic policy?

Robson (1992) (see also Robson (1996)) offers a model that allows us to address these types of questions. The key ingredient is that people care not only about their absolute wealth, but also about their position in the wealth distribution.[24] There are

[24] A similar convention is helpful in accounting for patterns of consumption as a function of wealth or income, as was pointed out long ago by Duesenberry (1949). See Rabin (2000) and Cox and Sadiraj (2006) for another discussion of whether utility is usefully defined over absolute wealth levels.

many reasons why people might care about how their wealth compares to that of others. For the purposes of this discussion, we simply assume that people care about "status," which in turn is determined by their place in the wealth distribution. We close this section with some examples of the considerations that might give rise to such a concern for status, deferring a more careful discussion to Section 4.2.

We suppose that an individual with wealth w attains status $S = F(w)$, where F is the continuous cumulative distribution function describing the wealth distribution in the relevant population. The population is represented by a continuum, normalized to have size 1. Hence, status is the proportion of individuals that the individual outranks in terms of wealth. The individual has a von Neumann-Morgenstern utility function that is concave in w but convex in S. The convexity of S, indicating that increases in status are especially valuable near the upper end of the wealth distribution, will lead to risk-seeking behavior over some wealth levels.

For convenience, let us work with a particular functional form, given by:

$$u(w, S) = \ln w + kS^{\beta},$$

where $k > 0$ and $\beta \geq 2$. Suppose, for simplicity, that the wealth distribution is uniform on the interval of wealth levels $[0, \gamma]$, and hence is given by:

$$\begin{aligned} & F(w) = w/\gamma \text{ for all } w \in [0, \gamma] \\ \text{and} \quad & F(w) = 1 \text{ for all } w > \gamma. \end{aligned}$$

In a more complete model, of course, one would want the distribution of wealth levels to be endogenous, but a partial-equilibrium approach will serve us well here.

Suppose now that we condense the utility function so that it takes only wealth as an argument by defining $v(w) = u(w, F(w))$. Then it follows that:

$$\begin{aligned} & v''(w) < 0 \text{ for all } w \in (0, \widetilde{w}), \quad \text{where } \widetilde{w} = \frac{\gamma}{(\beta(\beta-1)k)^{1/\beta}} \\ & v''(\widetilde{w}) = 0 \\ & v''(w) > 0 \text{ for all } w \in (\widetilde{w}, \gamma) \text{ and} \\ & v''(w) < 0 \text{ for all } w > \gamma, \end{aligned}$$

where we assume that $\beta(\beta - 1)k > 1$ so that $\widetilde{w} < \gamma$.

This example yields the concave-convex-concave utility described by Friedman and Savage. The convexity of $u(w, S)$ in S is needed to obtain the intermediate range of wealth, $(\widetilde{w}, \gamma)$, over which $v(w)$ is convex. The concavity of $u(w, S)$ in w yields the concavity of $v(w)$ over the initial and final ranges $(0, \widetilde{w})$ and (γ, ∞). The latter range appears despite the status effect because $f(w) = 0$ on (γ, ∞). Note that the first inflection point, $\widetilde{w}$, can fall anywhere in $(0, \gamma]$, depending on the values of the parameters.

This model allows us to capture behavior that is risk-averse over some income ranges and risk seeking over others, without such counterfactual implications as the prediction that the insurance industry will wither away as a society becomes wealthier. Consider, for example, a uniform multiplicative shift in the wealth distribution, represented by an increase in γ. The inflection point $\widetilde{w}$ is subject to the same multiplicative shift, so the same individual lies on the watershed between risk-aversion and risk-preference. Similarly, this model is consistent with prizes in lotteries that grow over time in step with the growth of the wealth distribution. That is, the wealth level γ marking the transition from risk-preference to risk-aversion is subject to this same shift.[25] To an analyst using models based on utility functions of the form $v(w)$ to study the economy, it would look as if the parameters of the utility functions are adjusting at about the same rate as wealth is growing, in the process coincidentally preserving the qualitative features of behavior. In fact, however, there would be nothing exogenous in the seemingly shifting utilities.

If the von Neumann-Morgenstern utility of wealth alone has a concave-convex-concave shape, as in Friedman and Savage, and individuals have access to a variety of fair bets, then individuals in an intermediate range will find it attractive to take gambles whose outcomes will put them either into a low initial range of wealth or a high terminal range (e.g., Friedman (1953)). As a result, the middle class should disappear. However, Robson (1992) shows that if the von Neumann-Morgenstern utility also depends on status, this redistribution of wealth will end before the middle class is completely depopulated. Robson (1992) also discusses how a concern with status in this sense involves an externality. If we contemplate the effects of an increase in our wealth, we take into account the effect this has in increasing our status, but we neglect the effect it has in lowering other individuals' status. There may well then be too much gambling. Less obviously, there may instead be too little—there are distributions of wealth that are stable, in the sense that no one wishes to take any fair bet, despite the existence of fair bets that induce a Pareto improvement.

How might the concern with status that lies at the heart of this model have evolved? We only sample the many possibilities here. For example, Robson (1996) considers how a concern for status and an attendant risk-preference might arise in a polygynous setting, where females choose males based on their wealth. Cole, Mailath and Postlewaite (1992) suggest that concerns for status may arise because some goods in our economy are allocated not by prices, but by nonmarket mechanisms in which status plays a role. Cole, Mailath and Postlewaite suggest the "marriage market" as a prime such example, where access to desirable mates often hinges on placing well in a status ordering that depends importantly on wealth. Additional points of entry into the literature include Becker, Murphy and Werning (2005), Frank (1999), and Ray and Robson (2010).

[25] This argument can be immediately generalized to utility functions of the form $u(w, S) = \ln w + v(S)$, where v is any increasing differentiable function and to an arbitrary continuous cumulative distribution function of wealth F.

What form might a concern with status have? There are two intriguing possibilities. If access to desirable mates lies behind a concern for status, then evolution may have designed us with utility functions that depend directly on absolute wealth and mates. The contest for mates may give rise to behavior that makes it look as if people have a concern for relative wealth, but this concern would be instrumental rather than intrinsic (cf. Postlewaite (1998)). Hence, status may be important, while the standard economists' inclination to work with "selfish" preferences, or preferences only over one's own outcomes may still have a solid biological foundation. Alternatively, constraints on the evolutionary design process, perhaps rising out of information or complexity considerations, may cause evolution to find it easier or more expeditious to simply design us with preferences over relative wealth, trusting that this will lead (perhaps more reliably) to the appropriate outcomes. In this case, the concern with relative wealth is intrinsic and we are pushed away from the familiar selfish preferences.

Determining which aspects of our preferences are instrumental and which are intrinsic is an important and challenging question. We return to the possibility that status may play a role in preferences in Section 4.2.

3.1.3 Implications

Where do we look for the implications of these evolutionary models, implications that Section 2.2 suggested should be the signature of the evolutionary approach? One obvious point stands out here. People should evaluate idiosyncratic and aggregate risks differently.

A standard finding in psychological studies of risk attitudes is that a feeling of control is important in inducing people to be comfortable with risk.[26] Risks arising out of situations in which people feel themselves unable to affect the outcome cause considerably more apprehension than risks arising out of circumstances people perceive themselves to control. People who fear flying think nothing about undertaking a much more dangerous drive home from the airport.[27] The risk of a meteor strike that eliminates human life on Earth is considered more serious than many other risks with comparable individual death probabilities. Why might this be the case? The first task facing evolution in an attempt to induce different behavior in the face of idiosyncratic and aggregate risks is to give us a way of recognizing these risks. "Control" may be a convenient stand-in for an idiosyncratic risk. If so, then our seemingly irrational fear of uncontrolled risk may be a mechanism inducing an evolutionarily rational fear of aggregate risk.

[26] See Slovic, Fishhoff and Lichtenstein (1982) for an early contribution to this literature and Slovic (2000) for a more recent introduction.

[27] Indeed, Gigerenzer (2002, p. 31) suggests that direct death toll in the September 11, 2001 attack on New York's World Trade Center may have been surpassed by the increased traffic deaths caused by the subsequent substitution of driving for air travel.

3.2 Time

We now turn our attention from the within-period considerations, captured by the function $u(c)$, to the question of intertemporal trade-offs. In doing so, we strip away all considerations of the nature of $u(c)$ by focussing on preferences over offspring. Hence, the agents in our model will do nothing other than be born, have offspring, and then die. In addition, no notion of the quality of offspring will enter our discussion. Agents will differ only in the number and timing of their offspring.

Our motivation in constructing such a model is to work with as close a link as possible between the model and the criteria for evolutionary success. The ultimate goal of evolution is successful reproduction. As simple as this sounds, "reproduction" is a multifaceted process and "success" involves managing a variety of tradeoffs. We eliminate many of these tradeoffs by working with a world of homogeneous offspring, focussing attention on the twin objectives of having many offspring and having them quickly. How does evolution balance "many" versus "quickly?" We view this as the obvious place to look for clues to how our preferences treat intertemporal tradeoffs, and so this becomes the focus of our analysis.

Evolution must not only identify the preferred mix of number and timing of offspring, but also solve the problem of how to induce this behavior. As faulty as it is, introspection suggests that evolution has not accomplished her goal by having us make constant calculations as to whether our next restaurant choice will increase or decrease the number of children we expect, or whether our choice of what car to drive will advance or postpone our next child. Instead, evolution works through utility functions that attach rewards to a host of intermediate goals, such as being well nourished. How and why evolution has done this is again an important and fascinating question, but is swept out of sight here.

Our basic notion is that of a "life history." A life history specifies the number of offspring born to an agent at each of the agent's ages. We assume that such life histories are heritable. The evolutionary approach proceeds by asking which life history will come to dominate a population in which a variety of life histories is initially present. In particular, we imagine mutations regularly inserting different life histories into a population. Some cause the group of agents characterized by such a life history to grow rapidly, some lead to slow rates of growth. The life history leading to the largest growth rate will eventually dominate the population. Having found such a life history, we will be especially interested in characterizing the implicit intertemporal trade-offs.

The question of why people discount is an old one. It seems intuitively obvious that future consumption is less valuable than current consumption, but why is this the case? A good place to start in one's search for an answer is the work of Fisher (1930, pp. 84–85), who pointed to one reason future rewards might be discounted—an intervening death might prevent an agent from enjoying the reward. This gives us a link between mortality and discounting that has often reappeared (e.g., Yaari (1965)), and that will again arise in our model. Hansson and Stuart (1990) and Rogers (1994) (see also Robson and Szentes (2008)) point to a second factor affecting discounting. They construct models in which evolution selects in favor of people whose discounting reflects the growth rate of the population with whom they are competing. Our first order of business, in Section 3.2.1, is to put these ideas together in the simplest model possible, leading to the conclusion that evolution will induce people to discount exponentially at the sum of the population growth rate and mortality rate. We then consider a sequence of variations on this model.

3.2.1 A simple beginning: semelparous life histories

We begin by considering only *semelparous* life histories, in which an organism reproduces at a fixed, single age (if it survives that long) and then dies.[28] We do not view this model as a realistic foundation for understanding discounting, but it does introduce the relevant evolutionary forces.

A life history in this context is simply a pair (x, τ), where x is the agent's expected number of offspring and τ is the age at which these offspring are produced. The agents in this environment live a particularly simple life. They wait until age τ, possibly dying beforehand, and then have x offspring. At that point, the parents may die or may live longer, but in the latter case do so without further reproduction. We need not choose between these alternatives because the possibility of such a continued but barren life is irrelevant from an evolutionary point of view. Agents who survive past their reproductive age may increase the size of the population at any given time, but will have no effect on the population growth rate. As a result, any mutation that sacrifices post-reproduction survival in order to increase the number of offspring x or decrease the age τ at which they are produced will be evolutionarily favored, no matter what the terms of the trade-off.

In the parlance of evolutionary biology, the particularly simple life histories of these agents earn them the title of "Darwinian dolts" (cf. Stearns and Hoekstra (2005), p. 219). In particular, if reproduction is affected by aggregate risks, such as predators or plagues that threaten survival to reproductive age, famines that threaten the ability to produce offspring, or climatic fluctuations that threaten offspring survival, then a semelparous life history can expose its practitioners to costly risk. Nonetheless, there is much to be learned from Darwinian dolts.

We examine a group of agents whose members are all characterized by a particular life history (x, τ). We will speak throughout as if a life history is a deterministic relationship, with each age-τ parent having precisely x offspring. The interpretation is that x is the *expected* number of offspring born to age-τ parents. As long as the group size

[28] This section is based on Robson and Samuelson (2007).

is sufficiently large and the random variables determining the number of offspring born to each parent are independent, then the average number of offspring will be very close to x and x will provide a very good approximation of the behavior of the evolution of the population.[29] The life history (x, τ) is presumably the result of various choices on the part of the agent, such as where to seek food, what food to eat, when to mate, what sort of precautions to take against enemies, and so on, all of which have an important effect on reproduction, but which do not appear explicitly in our model.

An agent who delays reproduction increases the risk of dying before reaching reproductive age. In particular, an agent choosing (x, τ) survives for the length of time τ required to reach reproductive age with probability $e^{-\delta\tau}$, where δ is the instantaneous death rate. If and only if the agent survives, the x offspring appear.

Consider a population characterized by strategy (x, τ), of initial size N_0. How large will this population be at time $t > 0$? Let us follow a dynasty, meaning a cohort of agents initially of some age τ', who have offspring when they reach age τ, with these offspring then having their offspring upon reaching age τ, and so on. From time 0 until time t, there will have been approximately (depending on the cohort's initial age and integer problems) t/τ intervals during which this dynasty will have first shrunk by factor $e^{-\delta\tau}$, as the population is whittled away by death while awaiting its next opportunity to reproduce, and then multiplied itself by x as it reproduces. The population at time t is thus

$$N_0 (e^{-\delta\tau} x)^{\frac{t}{\tau}}.$$

The growth factor for this population is then $e^{-\delta}(x)^{\frac{1}{\tau}}$.

If the population is characterized by a variety of life histories, then evolution will select for the value (x, τ) that maximizes $e^{-\delta}(x)^{\frac{1}{\tau}}$ or, equivalently, that maximizes

$$\frac{\ln x}{\tau}. \tag{4}$$

Hence, evolution evaluates births according to the function $\ln(\cdot)$ and discounts them hyperbolically. The equilibrium population will grow exponentially at the growth rate $-\delta + \frac{\ln x}{\tau}$.

Have we just discovered an evolutionary foundation for the hyperbolic discounting that lies at the core of much of behavioral economics? Caution is in order on several counts. First, the phrase "hyperbolic discounting" is used to denote a variety of discounting patterns, many of which do not match (4). Perhaps the most common of these is the "$\beta - \delta$" formulation, in which payoffs in period t are discounted to the present (period 0) at rate $\beta\delta^{t-1}$, with $\beta > \delta$. As a result, the delay between

[29] For typical limit theorems underlying this type of deterministic approximation, see Benaïm and Weibull (2003). The case of a continuum of agents raises technical problems. See Al-Najjar (1995) for a discussion.

the current and next periods is weighted especially heavily, with subsequent delays being equivalent. In contrast, the preferences given by (4) represent hyperbolic discounting in the literal sense, in that period-t payoffs are discounted to the present by the factor $1/t$. This discounting pattern is common in biological models of foraging (e.g., Houston and McNamara (1999, Chapter 4), Kacelnik (1997), Bulmer (1997, Chapter 6), but less common in economics. Second, hyperbolic discounting is especially intriguing to behavioral economists for its ability to generate preference reversals. In contrast, no incentive for preference reversals arises in the present evolutionary context. Indeed, we have not yet built a rich enough set of choices into the model to talk about preference reversals. We have simply identified the criterion for finding the optimal tradeoff between the delay to reproduction and the number of attendant offspring.

More importantly, we need to think carefully about making the leap from (4) to individual preferences. The preferences captured by (4) are relevant for asking a number of questions about the comparative statics of evolution. For example, these preferences are the appropriate guide if we want to know which of two populations, characterized by different life histories, will grow faster, or which of two mutants will be most successful in invading a population. Suppose, however, that we are interested in using preferences to describe the choices we see in a particular population. Let (x, τ) be the equilibrium life history, giving rise to a population that grows exponentially at rate $r = \ln(e^{-\delta}x^{\frac{1}{\tau}}) = -\delta + \frac{1}{\tau}\ln x$. Then consider the alternative strategy $(\tilde{x}, \tilde{\tau})$. Suppose this alternative strategy is feasible but not chosen (and hence gives a lower growth rate $\tilde{r}$). What preferences would we infer from this observation? We could assume that preferences are given by (4). However, we could also assume that the agents evaluate births linearly and discount exponentially at rate $-(\delta + r)$, so that (x, τ) is evaluated as $e^{-(\delta + r)\tau} x$. In particular, to confirm that such preferences rationalize the choice of (x, τ), we need only note that[30]

$$e^{-(\delta+r)\tau}x > e^{-(\delta+r)\tilde{\tau}}\tilde{x} \Leftrightarrow e^{-(\delta+r)\tau}x > e^{-r\tilde{\tau}}e^{\tilde{r}\tilde{\tau}}e^{-(\delta+\tilde{r})\tilde{\tau}}\tilde{x}$$
$$\Leftrightarrow r > \tilde{r}.$$

Exponential discounting, at the sum of the death and optimal growth rates, thus characterizes the preferences with which evolution will endow her agents. This representation of preferences is intuitive. There are two costs of delaying reproduction. One of these is simply that death occurs at rate δ. The other is that a given number of offspring will comprise a smaller fraction of a population growing at rate r. The sum of these two rates is the rate at which delaying births causes an agent to fall behind the population.

[30] The second inference follows from the observation that $e^{-(\delta+r)\tau}x = 1 = e^{-(\delta+\tilde{r})\tilde{\tau}}\tilde{x}$.

3.2.2 Extensions

With this basic result in hand, we consider six respects in which this analysis is limited, and hence warrants generalization:

1. Once the optimal strategy has spread throughout the population, the population will grow exponentially at the resulting growth rate. In practice, we do not expect populations to grow without bound, and so a model with some constraints on population size would be more reasonable.
2. We have allowed agents to reproduce only once, while we expect situations to be important in which agents can reproduce more than once.
3. Even if reproduction is the ultimate issue of concern to evolution, all of our experience as well as our economic literature suggests that we have preferences over many other things, commonly lumped together in economic models under the label of consumption.
4. The agents in our model are homogeneous, with every agent facing the same set of choices and making the same optimal choice. How do we incorporate heterogeneity into the model?
5. All of the uncertainty in the model is idiosyncratic, and hence washes out in the analysis of the population. What if there is aggregate uncertainty?
6. One motivation for studying evolutionary foundations for discounting is to glean insights into models of hyperbolic discounting, present bias, and preference reversal. We have found a hint of hyperbolic discounting in preferences that are relevant for evolutionary comparative statics, but none in the induced individual behavior. Does an evolutionary perspective lock us into exponential discounting?

The following sections examine each of these points in turn.

3.2.3 Environmental capacity

The discount rate in our analysis is tied closely to the population growth rate. A more rapid population growth induces a higher discount rate, while a population that shrinks sufficiently rapidly will induce negative discounting (in which case reproduction is better deferred). If the population growth rate is zero, agents will discount at the death rate δ.

The difficulty here is that we do not expect populations to grow without bound. If nothing else, an exponentially growing population will eventually produce a physical mass of agents too large to fit on the Earth, even neglecting any considerations of whether the planet can sustain them.[31] In some instances, resource constraints may not bind for a long time. One might then argue that an unconstrained model is a reasonable approximation of our evolutionary past, even if not a good guide to our future.

[31] Pursuing this point into the more fanciful, the space occupied by an exponentially growing population will eventually contain a sphere whose radius expands at a rate exceeding the speed of light, ensuring that we cannot alleviate the problem by travel to other planets (at least under our current understanding of physics). Finding oneself too heavily involved in such arguments is a reliable sign that something is missing from one's model.

However, we must be wary of appealing to the latter type of short-run argument when interpreting a theory whose predictions consist of limiting results. Perhaps more to the point, it seems likely that environmental constraints restricted human growth rates to be near zero throughout much of our evolutionary past.

Nothing in our analysis changes if we modify the death rate δ to reflect environmental constraints on the population size. We can do so while retaining all of the analysis in Section 3.2.1, as long as we interpret the death rate appearing in our model as the steady-state rate that balances population growth and environmental constraints.

In particular, notice that the discount rate in our exponential-discounting representation of preferences, given by

$$\delta + r = \frac{1}{\tau} \ln x,$$

is *independent* of the death rate. If an increasing population size uniformly increases the death rate, the growth rate will exhibit a corresponding decrease, leaving the discount rate unaffected. The discount rate is affected only by the life-history specification (x, τ). In a sense, we have thus turned the views of Fisher (1930) and Yaari (1965) on their heads. Instead of being a primary reason for discounting, death has nothing to do with the appropriate discount rate.[32]

3.2.4 Iteroparous life histories

We can easily generalize the analysis to *iteroparous* life histories, in which an individual may have offspring at more than one age. Among other advantages, such a life history may allow individuals to diversify some of the (unmodeled, in our analysis) aggregate risks that might make semelparity particularly precarious.

It is convenient here to let time be measured discretely. Let each agent live for T periods, producing x_τ offspring in each period $\tau = 1, \ldots, T$. A life history is then a collection $(x_1, x_2, \ldots, x_T)$, where some of these entries may be zero.

Our basic tool for keeping track of the population is a *Leslie* matrix (Leslie (1945, 1948)), given in this case by

$$\begin{bmatrix} e^{-\delta}x_1 & e^{-\delta} & 0 & \ldots & 0 & 0 \\ e^{-\delta}x_2 & 0 & e^{-\delta} & \ldots & 0 & 0 \\ \vdots & \vdots & \vdots & & \vdots & \vdots \\ e^{-\delta}x_{T-1} & 0 & 0 & \ldots & 0 & e^{-\delta} \\ e^{-\delta}x_T & 0 & 0 & \ldots & 0 & 0 \end{bmatrix}.$$

[32] We must be careful here to distinguish proximate and ultimate causes. The latter are the evolutionary considerations that shape the optimal life history, while the former are the mechanisms by which evolution induces the attendant optimal behavior. The death rate does not appear among the ultimate causes of discounting.

Each row $\tau = 1, \ldots, T$ in this matrix corresponds to the fate of agents of age τ in the population in each period. The first entry in this row indicates that these agents have x_τ offspring, which survive to become the next period's 1-period-olds at rate $e^{-\delta}$. The second term in the row indicates that at rate $e^{-\delta}$, the agents of age τ themselves survive to become one period older.

Letting X be the Leslie matrix, the population at time t is given by

$$N'(t) = N'(0)X^t, \tag{5}$$

where $N'(t)$ is a (transposed) vector $(N_1(t), \ldots, N_T(t))$ giving the number of agents in the population of each age $1, \ldots, T$ at time t. The fate of the population thus hinges on the properties of X^t. The Perron-Frobenius theorem (Seneta (1981), Theorem 1.1]) implies that the Leslie matrix has a "dominant" eigenvalue ϕ that is real, positive, of multiplicity one, and that strictly exceeds the modulus of all other eigenvalues.[33] This eigenvalue is the population growth factor, and its log is the corresponding growth rate, in the sense that (Seneta (1981, Theorem 1.2))

$$\lim_{t\to\infty} \frac{X^t}{\phi^t} = vu',$$

where the vectors u and v are the strictly positive left ($u'X = \phi u'$) and right ($Xv = \phi v$) eigenvectors associated with ϕ, normalized so that $u'v = 1$ and $\sum_{\tau=1}^{T} u_\tau = 1$.[34]

Evolution must select for behavior that maximizes the eigenvalue ϕ, or equivalently, that maximizes the long-run growth rate $\ln \phi$. This eigenvalue solves the characteristic equation

$$\begin{vmatrix} e^{-\delta}x_1 - \phi & e^{-\delta} & 0 & \ldots & 0 \\ e^{-\delta}x_2 & -\phi & S & \ldots & 0 \\ \vdots & \vdots & \vdots & & \vdots \\ e^{-\delta}x_{T-1} & 0 & 0 & \ldots & e^{-\delta} \\ e^{-\delta}x_T & 0 & 0 & \ldots & -\phi \end{vmatrix} = 0,$$

or, equivalently,

$$\Phi = x_1 + \frac{x_2}{\Phi} + \frac{x_3}{\Phi^2} + \ldots + \frac{x_T}{\Phi^{T-1}}, \tag{6}$$

[33] We assume that the Leslie matrix X is primitive, in that there exists some $k > 0$ for which X^k is strictly positive. A sufficient condition for this is that there exist two relatively prime ages τ and τ' for which x_τ and $x_{\tau'}$ are both nonzero.

[34] Regardless of the initial condition $N'(0)$, the proportion of the population of each age τ approaches u_τ. The vector v gives the "reproductive value" of an individual of each age, or the relative contribution that each such individual makes to the long run population.

where

$$\Phi = \frac{\phi}{e^{-\delta}}.$$

Equation (6) gives us our basic description of preferences. Evolution will endow an agent with preferences (or more precisely, would endow an agent with behavior consistent with such preferences) whose indifference curves are described by the right side of (6), with ϕ corresponding to the optimal growth rate. In particular, choices $(x_1, \ldots, x_T)$ that lead to a smaller value on the right side of (6) would lead to a lower growth rate and would be optimally rejected by the agent.

As with the case of semelparous life histories, we can draw two kinds of conclusions from these results. First, we can ask questions about "evolution's preferences" or "evolutionary comparative statics," addressing the relative performance of alternative populations or alternative mutants within a population. Here, we once again recover hints of hyperbolic discounting, seen in the fact that the evolutionary criterion for evaluating alternative life histories, given by (6), contains our previous results for semelparous life histories as a special case. In particular, it is immediate from (6) that evolution is indifferent over two semelparous strategies (x_1, τ_1) and (x_2, τ_2) if and only if $x_1^{\frac{1}{\tau_1}} = x_2^{\frac{1}{\tau_2}}$. This confirms that the semelparous analysis is a special case of this more general model. Preferences over the remaining iteroparous strategies are captured by connecting indifferent semelparous strategies with linear indifference surfaces. More generally, this population growth rate is a complex function of the fertility profile. If we let $\Phi = \Phi(x_1, x_2, \ldots)$ be the function implicitly defined by (6), then the marginal rate of substitution between x_t and x_{t+1} is Φ itself, which is a strictly increasing function of *each* x_τ for $\tau = 1, \ldots, T$. It is then immediate that there can be no additively separable representation of evolution's preferences.

Alternatively, we can ask about the behavior we would observe from agents. Agents can once again be induced to make optimal choices via exponentially discounting offspring at the sum of the death and optimal growth rates. Letting $(x_1, \ldots, x_T)$ be the optimal fertility profile and Φ be implicity defined by (6), we have

$$1 = \frac{x_1}{\Phi} + \frac{x_2}{\Phi^2} + \ldots + \frac{x_T}{\Phi^T}.$$

Now suppose an alternative fertility/utility profile $(x'_1, \ldots, x'_T)$ is feasible but is not chosen because it gives a smaller growth rate. Then

$$\frac{x_1}{\Phi} + \frac{x_2}{\Phi^2} + \ldots + \frac{x_T}{\Phi^T} = 1 > \frac{x'_1}{\Phi} + \frac{x'_2}{\Phi^2} + \ldots + \frac{x'_T}{\Phi^T}.$$

The agent's behavior is thus again consistent with exponentially discounted preferences, with a discount rate given by the sum of the death rate and population growth rate.

3.2.5 Consumption

Economists are typically interested in preferences over consumption rather than births and mortality. Perhaps the simplest way to transform a model of preferences over fertility and mortality rates into a model of preferences over consumption is to assume that births are a function of consumption, so that preferences over consumption are those induced by the underlying preferences over births. Notice that in doing so, we are not assuming that every visit to a restaurant requires a quick calculation as to whether steak or fish is more likely to lead to more offspring. Instead, our presumption is that evolution simply gives the agent preferences over steak and fish, with evolution shaping these preferences to reflect the required calculation.

Consider for simplicity the case in which age-τ births depend only on age-τ consumption.[35] Formally, let $f_\tau(c_\tau)$ give age-τ births as a function of age-τ consumption c_τ. Suppose that all the f_τ are strictly increasing and concave.

For any consumption vector $c = (c_1, \ldots, c_\tau)$, an indifference curve is defined by (from (6)),

$$1 = \frac{f_1(c_1)}{\Phi} + \ldots + \frac{f_\tau(c_\tau)}{\Phi^\tau} + \ldots + \frac{f(c_{T-1})}{\Phi^{T-1}} + \frac{f_T(c_T)}{\Phi^T}, \tag{7}$$

where ϕ is constant on a particular indifference surface. A higher value of ϕ corresponds to a higher indifference curve, so that consumption plan $(c'_1, \ldots, c'_T)$ is preferred to $(c_1, \ldots, c_T)$ if and only if

$$1 = \frac{f_1(c_1)}{\Phi} + \ldots + \frac{f_T(c_T)}{\Phi^T} < \frac{f_1(c'_1)}{\Phi} + \ldots + \frac{f_T(c'_T)}{\Phi^T}.$$

It follows readily that evolution's indifference surfaces over consumption bundles $(c_1, \ldots, c_T)$ have the usual shape, in the sense that evolution's preferences can be described by a utility function $U(c_1, \ldots, c_T)$ that is strictly increasing and quasi-concave.

This gives us the beginnings of an extension from models of reproduction to models of consumption. As long as period-τ reproduction is a function only of period-τ consumption, preferences over consumption will once again be described by an exponentially-discounted sum of utilities. In practice, of course, period-τ births will depend on the entire history of consumption. At the very least, one must have consumed enough to survive until period τ in order to reproduce at that age. Period-τ births are thus implicitly a function of consumption at all preceding ages. This in turn opens the possibility that the induced preferences over consumption may exhibit complicated discounting patterns. There is much that remains to be done in terms of exploring this connection between reproduction and consumption, including especially the implications for discounting.

[35] See Robson, Szentes and Iantchev (2010) for more involved specifications.

3.2.6 Heterogeneous choices

We have hitherto implicitly assumed that all of our agents face the same feasible set and choose the same alternative from that feasible set. How do we incorporate some heterogeneity into the model? In addressing this question, we keep things simple by retaining our basic framework of choice of reproductive life histories.

Suppose that each agent entering our model is randomly and independently (over time and agents) assigned one of N feasible sets, with p_n the probability of being assigned to the nth feasible set, and with $(x_1(n), \ldots, x_T(n))$ the life history chosen when faced with the nth feasible set. Some agents may find themselves in the midst of plenty and face relatively rich feasible sets, while others may face harder circumstances and more meager feasible sets. The Leslie matrix associated with this population is given by

$$\begin{bmatrix} e^{-\delta}\sum_{n=1}^{N} p(n)x_1(n) & e^{-\delta} & 0 & \ldots & 0 & 0 \\ e^{-\delta}\sum_{n=1}^{N} p(n)x_2(n) & 0 & e^{-\delta} & \ldots & 0 & 0 \\ \vdots & \vdots & \vdots & & \vdots & \vdots \\ e^{-\delta}\sum_{n=1}^{N} p(n)x_{T-1}(n) & 0 & 0 & \ldots & 0 & e^{-\delta} \\ e^{-\delta}\sum_{n=1}^{N} p(n)x_T(n) & 0 & 0 & \ldots & 0 & 0 \end{bmatrix}.$$

The agent's preferences can be derived from the corresponding characteristic equation, or

$$1 = \frac{\sum_{n=1}^{N} p(n)x_1(n)}{\Phi} + \frac{\sum_{n=1}^{N} p(n)x_2(n)}{\Phi^2} + \frac{\sum_{n=1}^{N} p(n)x_3(n)}{\Phi^3} + \ldots + \frac{\sum_{n=1}^{N} p(n)x_T(n)}{\Phi^T}$$

$$= p(1)\left(\frac{x_1(1)}{\Phi} + \frac{x_2(1)}{\Phi^2} + \ldots + \frac{x_T(1)}{\Phi^T}\right) + \ldots + p(N)\left(\frac{x_1(N)}{\Phi} + \frac{x_2(N)}{\Phi^2} + \ldots + \frac{x_T(N)}{\Phi^T}\right).$$

In each of these choice situations, it follows that the optimal decision is consistent with exponential discounting, where the discount rate now depends on the overall *population* growth rate. Hence, those agents facing relatively meager feasible sets will apply a discount factor seemingly higher than would be warranted from consideration of that feasible set alone, while those facing a quite rich feasible set would apply a discount factor seemingly too low. Given the discount factor, however, we would observe a collection of choices that could together be rationalized as maximizing the same exponentially discounted utility function.[36]

[36] One can well imagine more complicated ways in which heterogeneity might be incorporated into the model, requiring a more sophisticated model. The tools for addressing such questions are provided by the theory of structured populations, as in Charlesworth (1994).

3.2.7 Nonexponential discounting

The message to emerge from our analysis thus far is that we can expect to see agents evaluating intertemporal trades according to an exponentially discounted utility function. Depending on one's point of view, this represents good news or bad news. On the one hand, it directs attention to the most common model of intertemporal choice in economics. At the same time, it provides little insight into departures from exponential discounting.

There are three obvious possibilities for exploring foundations of nonexponential discounting. Section 3.2.5 raises the first. Even if reproduction is discounted exponentially, the relationship between reproduction and consumption may be complicated and may induce nonexponential discounting of consumption. This possibility remains relatively unexplored.

Second, Sozou (1998) and Dasgupta and Maskin (2005) show that if the realization of a future consumption opportunity is subject to uncertainty, then the result can be a present bias in discounting. As illustrated by such proverbs as "a bird in the hand is worth two in the bush," the idea that one should discount uncertain prospects is quite familiar.

Sozou supposes that there is a constant hazard rate that an opportunity to consume in the future may disappear before the proposed consumption date arrives. Someone else may consume the resource beforehand, or a predator may in the meantime block access to the resource. In the absence of any additional complications, this uncertainty has a straightforward effect on the agent's behavior. Future payoffs are again exponentially discounted, with the relevant discount rate now being the sum of the death rate, population growth rate, and disappearance rate.

Sozou further assumes that the agent is uncertain about the hazard rate of consumption disappearance, updating her prior belief about this value as time passes. Suppose, for example, the agent initially compares one unit of consumption at time 0 with c units at time $t > 0$, and discounts (taking into account the likelihood that the latter will disappear before time t arrives) the latter at rate 10%. Now suppose that time $t/2$ has arrived, and the agent must again compare a unit of current (i.e., time $t/2$)) consumption with the same c units of consumption at time t. If this choice is to be meaningful, it must be the case that over the interval $\left[0, \frac{t}{2}\right]$, the future consumption opportunity did not vanish. This is good news, leading the agent to conclude that the probability of disappearance is not as high as the agent's prior distribution indicated. As a result, the agent's discount rate will now be lower than the 10% relevant at time 0.

More generally, let c_τ denote consumption at time τ. The agents in Sozou's model apply a higher discount factor when comparing c_0 and c_1 than when comparing c_τ and $c_{\tau+1}$: if the latter choice is still relevant at time τ, then the agent will infer that the hazard rate at which consumption opportunities disappear is lower than originally suspected. As a result, the discount rate decreases as one considers choices further and further into the future, introducing a present bias into discounting.

Sozou's model will not generate preference reversals, the strikingly anomalous choices that have fueled much of the interest in present-biased preferences. In a typical preference reversal, an agent prefers $c_{\tau+1}$ from the choice $\{c_\tau, c_{\tau+1}\}$ when choosing at time 0, but then prefers c_τ when making the choice at time τ. Invoking some stationarity, the standard route to constructing a preference reversal is to assume that the agent prefers c_0 from $\{c_0, c_1\}$ at time 0 as well as prefers $c_{\tau+1}$ from the choice $\{c_\tau, c_{\tau+1}\}$; coupled with an assumption that the agent makes the choice from $\{c_\tau, c_{\tau+1}\}$ at time τ precisely as she does the choice $\{c_0, c_1\}$ at time 0. It is this latter assumption that does not hold in Sozou's model. If the choice from $\{c_\tau, c_{\tau+1}\}$ is relevant at time τ, then the agent infers that the hazard rate at which consumption opportunities disappear is not as large as originally suspected. This only reinforces the patience that prompted the agent to originally prefer $c_{\tau+1}$ from the choice $\{c_\tau, c_{\tau+1}\}$. Discount rates are thus not constant, but we would not observe the type of inconsistency in behavior that would induce the agent to take steps to restrict future choices.

In Dasgupta and Maskin (2005), there is again the possibility that a consumption opportunity might disappear before it arrives, but the hazard rate at which this happens is constant and known. In the absence of any other considerations, we would then simply have constant discounting at this hazard rate (plus the relevant death and growth rates). On top of this, however, Dasgupta and Maskin add some additional uncertainty about *when* as well as whether the consumption will be realized. An opportunity to consume c_τ at time τ in fact gives the consumption at time c_τ with high probability, but with the remaining probability gives a consumption opportunity whose timing is distributed over the interval $[0, \tau]$ (all conditional on not having disappeared in the meantime). Fortuitous circumstances may bring the opportunity early.

Now consider two consumption opportunities, one promising consumption c_τ at time time τ and one promising $c_{\tau'}$ at time $\tau' > \tau$. Suppose that at time 0, the agent prefers opportunity $(c_{\tau'}, \tau')$. If this is to be the case, then we must have $c_{\tau'} > c_\tau$, since it would not be worth waiting longer for a lower reward. Now consider what happens as time passes. The dates τ and τ' at which the consumption opportunities will be realized draw nearer. This increases the value of each option, but this effect alone does not change the relative ranking of the two consumption prospects. The probability that either one is realized is scaled upward by a common factor reflecting that an interval has passed without the consumption disappearing. The other effect is that this same interval has passed without either consumption opportunity arriving early. This decreases the value of each option, but especially decreases the value of option $(c_{\tau'}, \tau')$, since it involves the larger quantity of consumption and hence its early arrival is a relatively lucrative outcome. Thus, as time passes, the relative ranking shifts toward (c_τ, τ). If the two bundles are sufficiently closely ranked to begin with, and if the prospect of early arrival is sufficiently important, preferences will reverse to bring (c_τ, τ) into favor as time passes.

Dasgupta and Maskin's analysis thus provides us with an evolutionary account of preference reversals. At the same time, it does not give rise to the sorts of inconsistency and commitment issues that appear in behavioral models. The preference reversal as time τ draws near reflects an optimal response to the changing time-profile of the consumption opportunities. As a result, an agent would never have an incentive to preclude such reversals. Preference reversals have excited interest from behavioral economists largely because people often take costly measures to avoid them. We build rigidities into our lives to ensure that currently-optimal choices are not undone by future preference shifts. Dasgupta and Maskin's agents would welcome any preference reversals they encounter.

Dasgupta and Maskin sketch an extension of their model that gives rise to commitment issues. Very roughly speaking, they suppose that evolution has endowed people with preferences that are appropriate for the distributions of early consumption arrivals that were common over the course of our evolutionary history. Then they consider an agent facing a choice that the agent knows to involve distributions atypical of this history. An agent who simply expresses her preferences may then find herself confronted with a preference reversal, which she would regard as inappropriate, given her knowledge of how the distribution of early arrivals has shifted. Given the opportunity, the agent would rationally strive to prevent such a reversal, giving rise to incentives for commitment reminiscent of behavioral models. This gives us a mismatch model of preference reversals. Must evolutionary models of preference reversals necessarily involve mismatches, or are there circumstances under which evolutionary design calls for preference reversals in the environment giving rise to that design? If the latter type of models can be constructed, is there any reason to prefer them to mismatch models? Do their implications differ? These are open and interesting questions.

The preferences emerging from the models of Sozou (1998) and Dasgupta and Maskin (2005) give rise to a delicate issue of interpretation. First, an essential feature of both models is that consumption opportunities are subject to uncertainty. Each model begins with the assumption that the evolutionary objective is to maximize total consumption, with discounting reflecting the uncertainty inherent in pursuing a consumption opportunity. In short, it is better to consume now rather than later because the later opportunity may disappear before it can be realized. However, the analysis of Sections 3.2.1–3.2.4 suggests that even in the absence of uncertainty (and in the absence of death), we can expect discounting, so that maximizing total consumption is not an obvious point of departure. Fortunately, building the type of considerations uncovered in Sections 3.2.1–3.2.4 into the models of Sozou or Dasgupta and Maskin appears to be straightforward.

Second, our underlying view is that evolution shapes our behavior, with preferences being an analytical tool we choose to represent this behavior. The standard approach in constructing this representation is to use preferences and feasible sets to capture different aspects of an agent's choice problem, with the feasible set describing the alternatives and constraints on the choice. In particular, the standard approach would view consumption opportunities subject to uncertainty and consumption opportunities without uncertainty as different objects, with preferences first defined in the absence of uncertainty and then extended to uncertain outcomes, perhaps via an expected utility calculation. In using discounting to capture the effects of uncertainty about consumption, the models of Sozou and Dasgupta and Maskin blur the distinction between the feasible set and preferences.

In some cases, this blurring may be precisely what is required. In particular, suppose our evolutionary model of behavior incorporates the mismatch possibility that preferences evolved in one environment but may be applied in another. If this is the case, then we must know not only the choices induced by evolution, but also the process by which these choices are induced. Thus, we have no alternative but to model the mechanics of the agents' decision-making. It may well be that evolution has responded to some of the uncertainty in our environment by altering our discounting rather than our representation of the feasible set. Notice, however, that establishing the process by which choices are implemented is a taller order than describing the choices themselves.

An alternative possibility under which preferences may no longer exhibit exponential discounting is explored by Robson and Samuelson (2009), and returns us to the distinction between idiosyncratic and aggregate risk examined in Section 3.1. We have assumed in Sections 3.2.1–3.2.6 that the uncertainty faced by the agents is idiosyncratic. It seems reasonable to imagine that aggregate uncertainty may well have been an important feature of our evolutionary environment. Periods in which the weather was harsh, food was scarce, disease was rampant, or predators were prevalent, may have had an impact on a population. What effect does this have on our analysis of time preference?

To capture the possibility of aggregate uncertainty, we assume that in each period t, a Leslie matrix $X(t)$ is drawn from a distribution over such matrices, with $X(t)$ then describing the fate of the population, in terms of both reproduction and death, during that period. A period of particularly harsh weather may be characterized by a Leslie matrix with high death rates, while a period in which food is quite plentiful may be characterized by favorable survival rates. The matrix $X(t)$ may itself contain values that are the averages of idiosyncratic uncertainty, but as before this will have no effect on the analysis.

Given an initial population $N'(0) = (N_1(0), \ldots, N_T(0))$ with $N_\tau(0)$ of agents of age τ, the population at time t is then given by (cf. (5))

$$N'(t) = N'(0)\widetilde{X}(1)\widetilde{X}(2)\cdots\widetilde{X}(t),$$

where $\widetilde{X}(t)$ is the random Leslie matrix in time t. We thus have a product of random matrices, a much less tractable object than the product of the fixed Leslie matrices arising in (5). It is not even immediately obvious that such a product has an appropriate limit. Fortunately, there are quite general theorems establishing the limiting growth rates of such products (e.g., Furstenberg and Kesten (1960, Theorem 2) and Tanny (1981, Theorem 7.1)), but the model is still considerably less tractable than the case of idiosyncratic uncertainty.

Aggregate uncertainty opens up all sorts of new possibilities for discounting patterns. We present here a simple example to illustrate some of these possibilities, leaving a more systematic analysis to Robson and Samuelson (2009). Suppose that there are T possible Leslie matrices, $X_1,\ldots,X_T$. Under Leslie matrix X_τ, only offspring born to parents of age τ survive, with expected offspring per parent denoted by x_τ. The Leslie matrices are drawn independently across periods and are equally likely in any given period. In each period and under every Leslie matrix, all existing agents face an idiosyncratic death risk, with death rate δ.

We thus have a rather extreme form of aggregate uncertainty, but one that significantly simplifies the resulting calculations, while driving home the point that aggregate uncertainty can lead to new results. Section 6.1 proves the following:

Proposition 1 *Almost surely,*

$$\lim_{t\to\infty}\frac{1}{t}\ln u'\widetilde{X}(1)\ldots\widetilde{X}(t)v = \ln S + \frac{\sum_{\tau=1}^{T}\ln x_\tau}{\sum_{\tau=1}^{T}\tau}. \tag{8}$$

Preferences are thus represented by the *undiscounted* sum of the logs of the offspring in each state. In contrast to our previous findings, there is no impatience here, no matter what the population growth rate (given by (8)) and death rate. A reduction in fertility at age τ reduces the growth rate via its effect on the term $\sum_{\tau=1}^{t}\ln x_\tau$, while the extent of this reduction does not depend upon the age in question.

We can push this example somewhat further. Suppose $T = 2$, to keep the calculations simple, and that instead of being independent across periods, the environment is drawn from a symmetric Markov process with persistence α, i.e., with probability α the environment in period t is the same as in period $t-1$, and with probability $1-\alpha$ the environment changes from period $t-1$ to period t. Section 6.1 proves:

Proposition 2 *Almost surely,*

$$\lim_{t\to\infty}\frac{1}{t}\ln u'\widetilde{X}(1)\ldots\widetilde{X}(t)v = \frac{2\alpha\ln x_1 + \ln x_2}{2+2\alpha}.$$

For the case of $\alpha = 1/2$, or no persistence, we have Proposition 1's result that there is no discounting. Assuming $\alpha > 1/2$ generates impatience, while assuming $\alpha < 1/2$, so that environments are negatively correlated, generates negative discounting—the future is weighted more heavily that the present.

What lies behind the result in Proposition 1? Consider the generation of agents born at some time t, and for the purposes of this illustration only assume there is no death before age T.[37] Given the convention that only one age class reproduces in any period, these newborns all have parents of the same age, with any such age τ being equally likely, and with each parent giving rise to x_τ offspring.[38] These parents in turn all had parents of the same age, with any such age τ' being equally likely, and with each parent giving rise to $x_{\tau'}$ offspring. Continuing in this fashion, the number of agents born at time t is given by a product $x_\tau x_{\tau'} x_{\tau''} \ldots$, where the sequence $\tau, \tau', \tau'', \ldots$ identifies the age of the parents reproducing in the relevant period. Because the age to reproduce in each period is uniformly drawn from the set $\{1, 2, \ldots, T\}$, over long periods of time each age will appear with very close to the same frequency in the string $\tau, \tau', \tau'', \ldots$, with that frequency being $1/T$. Hence, the number of births at time t is proportional to a power of $x_1 x_2 \ldots x_T$. In light of this, evolution will seek to maximize $\ln[x_1 x_2 \ldots x_T]$, leading to the no-discounting result. If expected offspring are equal across ages, then evolution is indifferent as to where an increment to expected offspring appears.

It is clearly an extreme assumption that only one age of parent has offspring in any given state of the environment. We present this result not for its realism, or because we would like to suggest that evolutionary models should lead us to expect that people do not discount, but to illustrate how aggregate uncertainty can lead to new and counterintuitive results. In Robson and Samuelson (2009) we first show that if aggregate uncertainty bears equally on all survival rates, then we have a wedge between the rate of discounting and the sum of the growth and mortality rates. We then consider cases in which the extent of aggregate uncertainty in the environment is relatively small, unlike the model we have just presented. This reflects a belief that results emerging from models with relatively modest doses of aggregate uncertainty are a better point of departure for our analysis than models with drastic specifications of uncertainty. We present plausible, but by no means universal, conditions for aggregate uncertainty to lead to a present bias in discounting. Once again, however, this present bias leads to neither preference reversals nor a desire for commitment. The search for evolutionary foundations of preference reversals and commitment remains an important area of research.

3.2.8 Implications

Our search again turns to implications. We can start with the observation that discounting in general has nothing to do with death rates. An increase in the death rate simply induces a corresponding decrease in the growth rate (for fixed fertilities $(x_1, \ldots, x_T)$), leaving discounting unchanged. Higher fertility should thus correspond to higher discounting; holding the death rate constant, but higher death rates (holding fertility constant) should

[37] Since death rates are equal across ages, introducing death before age T involves only a normalization of the following calculations.

[38] It is this property that fails, vitiating the argument leading to Proposition 1, when births are not so perfectly synchronized.

not. An attempt to verify these comparative static predictions would give rise to valuable and exciting research.

Looking a bit beyond our model, the remarks of the previous paragraph correspond to cross-population comparisons of discounting, in the sense that we would need to compare different populations whose discount factors have been adapted by evolution to their various circumstances. Suppose in contrast that we examine different types within a population. Here, the relevant terms in the discount factor are the average growth rate of the population and the death rate of the particular type in question. As a result, agents with higher death rates within a population should exhibit higher discount rates. Wilson and Daly (1997) find just such a relationship.

Finally, the models suggest that evolution may more readily lead to non-exponential discounting, often in the form of a present bias, than to generate preference reversals. This suggests that experimental or empirical evidence may accordingly more readily exhibit declining discount factors than preference reversals. It is then perhaps unsurprising that some investigations do not find a great willingness to pay for the ability not to reverse preferences (e.g., Fernandez-Villaverde and Mukherji (2001)).

4. PREFERENCES OVER WHAT?

Our next selection of topics takes us somewhat deeper into preferences, asking what we should expect to find as the arguments of the function u. The standard assumption throughout much of economics is that u depends only on an agent's own consumption, as in (1). At the same time, there is considerable suspicion that other factors also enter our preferences. As we have explained above, the goal is to incorporate such possibilities while retaining some discipline in our work. This section examines three dimensions along which an evolutionary analysis is helpful.

Our guiding principle is that to understand our utility function, we must think through the constraints on what evolution can do in designing us to make good decisions. In each of the cases we describe in this section, in the absence of such constraints, we would come back to a standard utility function defined only over an individual's own consumption. However, if something prevents the construction of such a perfect utility function, then evolution may optimally compensate by building other seemingly anomalous features into our utility function. Intuitively, we have an evolutionary version of the theory of the second best.[39]

[39] Beginning with Lipsey and Lancaster (1956), the theory of second best has become a pillar of welfare economics, noting that if some of the conditions for an optimal outcome fail, and then moving closer to satisfying the remaining conditions may not improve welfare. In our context, we can first imagine a first-best or unconstrained design that would lead to evolutionary success for an agent. The idea is then that if feasibility constraints preclude implementing some features of this design, it may not be optimal to insist on all of the remaining features.

Under this approach, the analysis will be no more convincing than the case that can be made for the constraints. In this sense, Gould and Lewontin's (1979) critique of evolutionary psychology recurs with some force, since one suspects that a judiciously chosen constraint will allow anything to be rationalized.

In response, before even embarking on this line of research, we should be willing to argue that it is prohibitively costly for evolution to enhance significantly our cognitive powers. Otherwise, we would expect evolution to simply have done away with whatever constraints might appear in our decision-making. Evolutionary psychologists routinely appeal to limits on our cognitive capabilities, finding evidence for these limits in the relatively large amount of energy required to maintain the human brain (Milton (1988)), the high risk of maternal death in childbirth posed by infants' large heads (Leutenegger (1982)), and the lengthy period of human postnatal development (Harvey, Martin and Clutton-Brock (1986)).

Notice that there is no question of evolution's designing us to solve some problems of inordinate complexity. The human eye and the attendant information processing is an often-cited triumph of biological engineering. Our argument requires only that evolution cannot ensure that we can solve *every* complex problem we encounter, and that she will accordingly adopt information-processing shortcuts whenever she can. "In general, evolved creatures will neither store nor process information in costly ways when they can use the structure of the environment and their operations upon it as a convenient stand-in for the information-processing operations concerned." (Clark (1993, p. 64)).[40]

We should also expect to see evidence that humans often make mistakes in processing complicated information. For example, psychologists have conducted a wealth of experimental studies suggesting that people are poor Bayesians (e.g., Kahneman and Tversky (1982)).

4.1 Context

This section, borrowing from Samuelson and Swinkels (2006), examines one respect in which our utility seemingly depends upon more than simply what we consume, but with a perhaps somewhat unusual perspective. It is common to think of our utilities as depending not only on what we consume, but also on what we have consumed in the past, or on what others consume. Instead, we consider here the possibility that our utility also depends upon what we could have consumed, but did *not* choose. A salad may be more attractive when the alternative is oatmeal than when it is steak,

[40] LeDoux (1996) discusses the incentives for evolution to arm us with a mix of "hard-wired" and cognitive responses to our environment, arguing that many of our seemingly hard-wired reactions are engineered to economize on information processing.

and toiling away at the office may be more bearable on a cold, cloudy day than a warm, sunny day.[41]

It is no surprise, of course, that choices typically depend on the set of alternatives. Who would doubt that it is more tempting to skip work on a warm, sunny day than on a cold bitter one? There is little point in continuing if this is the extent of our insight. However, the key points of our analysis are that the presence of unchosen alternatives affects not just our choices but also our preferences over those choices, and their ability to do so depends upon their salience. We may happily work in a windowless office on a brilliant spring day, but find that such work is much less satisfying when the office has a panoramic view. Knowing that one can order dessert is different from having the dessert cart at one's table. Knowing that it's nice outside is different than being able to see the sun and feel the warm breeze.[42]

As we have suggested, our evolutionary model will revolve around a constraint on evolution's ability to design agents. We assume in this case that evolution cannot equip her agents with a perfect prior understanding of the causal and statistical structure of the world. Our belief here is that the complexity of a perfect prior is simply out of reach of a trial-and-error mutation process.[43] Nor can the agents themselves be trusted to infer this information from our environment. An agent cannot learn the relationship between specific nutrients and healthy births by trial and error quickly enough to be useful, and we certainly cannot learn quickly enough that even many generations of ample food might still be followed by famine in the next year.[44]

[41] Gardner and Lowinson (1993), Loewenstein (1996), Mischel, Shoda and Rodriguez (1992), and Siegel (1979) examine the importance of salient alternatives. The possibility that preferences over objects may depend on the set from which they are chosen has attracted theoretical and experimental attention from psychologists (e.g., Tversky and Simonson (1993) and Shafir, Simonson and Tversky (1993)). Gul and Pesendorfer (2001) present a model of such preferences centered on the assumption that resisting tempting alternatives is costly. Laibson (2001) examines a model in which instantaneous utilities adjust in response to external cues. Our interest here is not so much the mechanism by which this interaction between the set of alternatives and the utility of particular alternatives is generated, but rather the question of why evolution might have endowed us with such preferences in the first place.

[42] In a similar vein, psychologists have suggested that our behavior is driven partly by a collection of utility-altering visceral urges (Loewenstein (1996)). It is again straightforward to appreciate why we have urges reflecting direct evolutionary consequences such as hunger, thirst, or fatigue (Pluchik (1984)). We consider here the less obvious question of why the strength of these urges can depend on the set of unchosen consequences.

[43] For example, it is difficult to randomly create an agent who knows not only that the probability of a successful birth from a random sexual encounter is about 2% (Einon (1998)), but also how this probability varies systematically with health, age, and other observable features of the mate.

[44] This constraint is well-accepted in other areas of study. Focusing on reactions to danger, LeDoux (1980, pp. 174–178) notes that evolution deliberately removes some responses from our cognitive control precisely because her prior belief is strong. "Automatic responses like freezing have the advantage of having been test-piloted through the ages; reasoned responses do not come with this kind of fine-tuning."

4.1.1 A model

An agent in this model enters the environment and must either accept or reject an option. Accepting the option leads to a lottery whose outcome is a success with probability p and a failure with probability $1-p$. Rejecting the option leads to a success with probability q and a failure with probability $1-q$. This is the only decision the agent makes. As usual, this leaves us with a ludicrously simple evolutionary model, but one that allows us to focus clearly on the important features of the problem.

We might think of the option as an opportunity to consume and success as reproducing. The parameters p and q are random variables, reflecting the benefits of eating and the risks required to do so in any given setting. The probability of success may be either increased ($p > q$) or decreased ($p < q$) by accepting the option.

The agent is likely to have some information about the likely values of p and q. For example, the agent may know whether the game is plentiful, whether food is nearby but guarded by a jealous rival, or whether a drought makes it particularly dangerous to pass up this opportunity. However, the agent is unlikely to know these probabilities precisely. We model this by assuming that the agent observes a pair of scalar signals s_p about p and s_q about q. The probabilities p and q are independent, as are the signals s_p and s_q. In addition, p and s_q are independent, as are q and s_p. Hence, each signal gives information about one (and only one) of the probabilities. We assume that s_p and s_q are informative about p and q and satisfy the monotone likelihood ratio property with respect to p and q respectively, so that (for example) $E\{p|s_p\}$ is increasing in s_p.

Evolution designs the agent to have a rule ϕ for transforming signals into estimates of the probability of success. We assume that ϕ is continuous and strictly increasing. The crucial restriction in our model—the imperfection that makes this an interesting setting for examining utility functions—is that the agent must use the *same* rule ϕ for evaluating all signals. In this simple setting, the result is that the agent must have one process for evaluating both the signal s_p and the signal s_q, rather than a separate evaluation rule for each signal. If, for example, p and q come from different processes and with information of varying reliability, proper Bayesian updating requires that different updating rules be applied to s_p and s_q. Our assumption is that evolution cannot build this information about the prior or signal-generation process into the agent's beliefs, and hence that the agent has a single belief-formation rule ϕ.[45]

Evolution's goal is to maximize the probability of a success. In pursuit of this goal, evolution can design a utility function for the agent, with utility potentially derived both from the outcome of the agent's action and from the action itself. A success leads

[45] Without this restriction, the solution to the problem is again trivial. Evolution need only attach a larger utility to a success than to a failure, while designing the agent to use Bayes' rule when transforming the signals he faces into posterior probabilities, to ensure that the agent's choices maximize the probability of success.

to an *outcome* (e.g., successful reproduction) that yields a utility of x. A failure gives the agent a utility that we can normalize to zero. In the absence of any constraints, evolution would need only these two tools. Given the agent's imperfect information process, it is potentially relevant that the *act* of accepting the option (e.g., eating the food) yields a utility of y.[46]

4.1.2 Utility

We view evolution as choosing values x and y that maximize an agent's probability of success. No generality is lost by taking $x = 1$. The question is the choice of y. If $y = 0$, then utilities are attached only to outcomes and not to actions. In this case, we would be motivated to eat not because we enjoy food, but because we understand that eating is helpful in surviving and reproducing. If y is nonzero, then actions as well as outcomes induce utility.

The optimal decision rule from an evolutionary perspective is to accept the option whenever doing so increases the probability of success, or

$$\text{accept } \textit{iff } p - q > 0. \tag{9}$$

The agent will accept the option whenever it maximizes utility, or

$$\text{accept } \textit{iff } y + \phi(s_p) - \phi(s_q) > 0. \tag{10}$$

Consider

$$E\{p - q \mid \phi(s_p) - \phi(s_q) = t\}.$$

This is the expected success-probability difference $p - q$ conditional on the agent having received signals that lead him to assess this difference at t. To make our results easier to interpret, we assume throughout that the signal generating process ensures

$$\frac{dE\{p - q \mid \phi(s_p) - \phi(s_q) = t\}}{dt} \geq 0, \tag{11}$$

so the expected difference in success probabilities $p - q$ is weakly increasing in the agent's assessment of this difference.[47]

We then have the following characterization of the optimal utility function:

Proposition 3 *The fitness-maximizing y satisfies*

$$E\{p - q \mid \phi(s_p) - \phi(s_q) = -y\} = 0. \tag{12}$$

[46] Attaching another utility to the act of rejecting the option opens no new degrees of freedom at this stage.

[47] This is an intuitive assumption and it is easy to find either examples in which it is satisfied or sufficient conditions for it to hold, but it is *not* simply an implication of our monotone-likelihood-ratio-property assumption.

In particular, the agent's fitness is maximized by setting $y = 0$ if and only if

$$E\{p - q \mid \phi(s_p) - \phi(s_q) = 0\} = 0. \tag{13}$$

To see why this should be the case, we need only note that when conditions (11) and (13) hold, setting $y = 0$ ensures that the agent's choice rule (10) coincides with the (constrained) optimal choice rule (9). There is then no way to improve on the agent's choices and hence setting $y = 0$ is optimal. More generally, let us fix a value of y and then consider the expectation $E\{p - q|\phi(s_p) - \phi(s_q) = -y\}$, which is the expected difference in success probabilities at which the agent is just indifferent between accepting and rejecting the option. If this expectation is positive, then the expected probability of success can be increased by increasing y, and if this expectation is negative, then the expected probability of success can be increased by decreasing y, giving the result.

From (13), if the agent interprets his signals correctly, then there is no evolutionary value in attaching utilities to actions. The agent will make appropriate choices motivated by the utility of the consequences of his actions. The agent will still sometimes make mistakes, but without better information, there is no way to eliminate these mistakes or improve on the expected outcome.

From (12), if the agent does not interpret his signals correctly, then evolution will attach utilities to his actions in order to correct his inferences at the *marginal* signal, i.e., at the signal at which the expected success probabilities are equal. The agent must be indifferent ($y + \phi(s_p) - \phi(s_q) = 0$) when his signal would lead a perfect Bayesian to be indifferent ($E\{p - q|\phi(s_p) - \phi(s_q) = -y\} = 0$).

An initial expectation might be that evolution should attach utilities only to the things evolution "cares" about, or outcomes, rather than actions. As Proposition 3 confirms, we have rendered this suboptimal by giving the agent an unreliable understanding of how actions translate into outcomes. Evolution then compensates by attaching utilities to actions. One might then expect utilities to reflect the *average* evolutionary value of the various actions. Those that often lead to success should get large utilities; those that are less productive should have smaller utilities. However, Proposition 3 indicates that this intuition need not hold, for two reasons. First, we can expect utilities to be attached to actions only to the extent that agents sometimes misunderstand the likelihoods of the attendant outcomes. If the outcomes are correctly assessed, then actions, no matter how valuable, need receive no utility. Optimal utilities thus reflect not the evolutionary value of an action, but the error the agent makes in assessing that evolutionary value. Second, one might think that fitness would be maximized by a utility function that corrected this error *on average*. As (12) makes clear, what counts is the error the agent makes in the marginal cases where he is indifferent between two actions.

We illustrate by constructing an example in which the agent on average overestimates the value of accepting the option, but evolutionary fitness is nonetheless improved by setting $\gamma > 0$, pushing him to accept the option more than he otherwise would. Let

$$E\{p - q|\phi(s_p) - \phi(s_q) = t\} = a + bt,$$

with $a > 0$ and $b > 0$. Solving (12), the optimal utility is

$$\gamma = \frac{a}{b}. \tag{14}$$

Assume that $\phi(s_p) - \phi(s_q)$ is large on average and that $b < 1$. Because $\phi(s_p) - \phi(s_q)$ is on average large and $b < 1$, the agent on average overestimates the value of the option. However, since $\gamma = a/b > 0$, the agent's fitness is maximized by pushing the agent even more toward acceptance. We see here the importance of the agent's marginal beliefs: When $\phi(s_p) - \phi(s_q) = -a/b$ (so that $E\{p - q|\phi(s_p) - \phi(s_q)\} = 0$), the agent *underestimates* the relative value of the option (thinking it to be negative), even though he overestimates it on average.

It follows from (14) that, as one might expect, a choice with a large expected value (large a) will tend to have a large utility. It is thus no surprise that we have a powerful urge to flee dangerous animals or eat certain foods. However, there is also a second effect. The smaller is b, the larger is γ. The point is that the less informative is the agent's information, holding fixed his average assessment, the more negative is the relevant marginal signal. When b is near zero, evolution effectively insists on the preferred action. While blinking is partly under conscious control, our utility functions do not allow us to go without blinking for more than a few seconds. It would seem that we are unlikely to have reliable information suggesting that this is a good idea.

4.1.3 Choice-set dependence

We have reached a point where evolution might optimally attach utilities to actions, but have said nothing about how utilities might depend upon the set of salient alternatives. In this section, we show how a setting where the agent makes different mistakes in different contexts creates evolutionary value for a utility function that depends on things that have *no* direct impact on evolutionary success. Rather, their role is to tailor utility more closely to the specific informational context at hand. How any given feature optimally affects utility depends on both its direct evolutionary impact and how it correlates with errors in information processing.

Suppose that the environment may place the agent in one of two situations. The success probability when rejecting the option is q in either case, with success probability p_1 and p_2 when accepting the option in situations 1 and 2. The corresponding signals are s_q, s_{p_1} and s_{p_2}. We initially assume that, as before, the agent derives a utility of 1 from a success, 0 from a failure, and utility γ, *the same value in both situations*, from the act of accepting the option.

For example, suppose that in situation 2, accepting the option entails an opportunity to eat a steak. As we have shown, evolution optimally attaches a utility y to steak satisfying

$$E(p_2 - q \mid \phi(s_{p_2}) - \phi(s_q) = -y) = 0.$$

Now suppose that in situation 1, accepting the option entails eating a steak at the end of a hunting trip. The agent is likely to have quite different sources of information about these two situations and thus to make quite different errors in processing this information. In particular, the hunter may have an idea of what hazards he will face on the hunting trip before achieving consumption and how these will affect the probability p_1. Only coincidentally will it then be the case that $E(p - q|\phi(s_p) - \phi(s_q) = -y$, steak on hand) equals $E(p - q|\phi(s_p) - \phi(s_q) = -y$, steak to be hunted). However, if these two are not equal, the agent's expected fitness can be increased by attaching different utilities to accepting the option in the two situations.

How can evolution accomplish this? One possibility is to attach utilities to more actions. The agent can be given a taste for meat, a disutility for the physical exertion of hunting, and a fear of the predators he might encounter. However, there are limits to evolution's ability to differentiate actions and attach different utilities to them—what it means to procure food may change too quickly for evolution to keep pace—and the set of things from which we derive utility is small compared to the richness of the settings we face. As a result, evolution inevitably faces cases in which the same utility is relevant to effectively different actions. This is captured in our simple model with the extreme assumption that y must be the same in the two situations. The critical insight is then that the agent's overall probability of success can be boosted if utility can be conditioned on some other reliable information that is correlated with differences in the actions.

Assume that in situation 2, a utility of z can be attached to the act of *foregoing* the option. We say that an option with this property is *salient*. In practice, an option is salient if its presence stimulates our senses sufficiently reliably that evolution can tie a utility to this stimulus, independently of our signal processing.[48] In our example, the presence of the steak makes it salient in situation 2. The question now concerns the value of z. If fitness is maximized by setting $z \neq 0$, then there is evolutionary advantage to tailoring the utility gradient between accepting and rejecting the option to the two situations, and we have "choice-set dependence." Only if $z = 0$ do we have a classical utility function.

Proposition 4 *The optimal utility function (x, y, z) does **not** exhibit choice-set dependence (sets $z = 0$) if and only if there exists t^* such that*

$$E\{p_1 - q \mid \phi(s_{p_1}) - \phi(s_q) = t^*\} = E\{p_2 - q \mid \phi(s_{p_2}) - \phi(s_q) = t^*\} = 0. \qquad (15)$$

[48] The importance of salient alternatives is well studied by psychologists (Gardner and Lowinson (1993)), Mischel, Shoda and Rodriguez (1992), Siegel (1979) and is familiar more generally—why else does the cookie store take pains to waft the aroma of freshly-baked cookies throughout the mall?

To see why this is the case, we note that if (15) holds, then the agent's estimates of the success probabilities in the two situations he faces are equally informative at the relevant margin. Setting $z = 0$ and $y = -t^*$ then ensures that (12) holds in both situations, and there is thus no gain from choice-set dependence. Conversely, suppose that the agent's beliefs are differentially informative in the two situations (i.e., (15) fails). Then fitness can be enhanced by attaching different utility subsidies in the two situations. This can be accomplished by choosing y to induce optimal decisions in situation 1 and $y - z$ (and hence $z \neq 0$) to induce optimal decisions in situation 2. The result is choice-set dependence.

For example, using choice-set dependence to boost the relative attractiveness of steak when it is available ($z < 0$), in contrast to simply increasing the utility of steak across the board (increasing y), might reflect a situation in which evolution finds it beneficial to grant substantial influence to the agent's beliefs about the consequences of production, while allowing less influence to his beliefs about consumption.

4.1.4 Implications

Our model of the evolution of choice in the face of coarse priors tells us that evolution will generally find it useful to exploit choice set dependence. Anyone who has ever said, "Let's put these munchies away before we spoil our dinner," or more generally "I don't keep junk food in the house because I know I'd eat too much if I did," has practical experience with choice-set dependence. Best of all is to be without the temptation of a pantry full of sinfully delicious snacks. Once they are there, eating is the preferred choice. Worst of all is looking at the food, constantly knowing it is there, without indulging.[49] In essence, such an individual is engaged in the sort of evolutionary conflict described in Section 2.3. If the agent's utility function perfectly captured the evolutionary goals it was designed to pursue, there would be no conflict, but the same complexity that forces evolution to resort to the device of a utility function also makes it difficult to design a perfect utility function. As a result, the utility function sometimes pulls the individual in a direction unintended by evolution. This gives rise to a potentially intricate game, in which evolution resorts to devices such as context dependence to reinforce her desired ends, while the agent seeks refuge in devices such as hiding (or not buying) the junk food.

Which alternatives are salient in any given context is again the result of evolution. As it turns out, a sizzling steak is salient while a steak in the grocer's freezer is not. Potato chips on the table are salient; those in the pantry are less so. What is salient reflects both the technological constraints faced by evolution and the incremental value of tailoring utility to specific contexts.

[49] Thaler (1994, p. xv) tells of a request to put tempting munchies aside, coming from a group of people seemingly well acquainted with decision theory, and explains it with much the same preferences.

Choice-set dependence can give rise to internal conflict and problems of self-control. For example, suppose the agent begins by choosing between an unhealthy but gratifying meal and a diet meal. Situation 1 corresponds to a lonely meal at home, with a refrigerator full of health food and nary an ounce of fat in sight. Situation 2 corresponds to a steakhouse with a supplementary dieter's menu. Suppose that evolution has designed our preferences so that the act of choosing steak is subsidized when it is salient. Then the agent may prefer situation 1 even if there is some cost in choosing situation 1, in order to ensure that he rejects the steak.

Economists have recently devoted considerable attention to issues of self-control, with present-biased preferences being a common route to self-control problems. Our best intentions to reap the benefits of a healthy diet may come to nothing if our preferences continually put excessive weight on the immediate gratification of the dessert tray. It is accordingly interesting to note that choice-set dependence has implications for self-control beyond those of present bias. First, difficulties with self-control can arise without intertemporal choice. One can strictly prefer junk food that is hidden to that which is exposed, knowing that one will find it painful to resist the latter, all within a span of time too short for nonstandard discounting to lie behind the results. More importantly, because our utility for one choice can be reduced by the salient presence of another, it may be valuable to preclude temptations that one *knows* one will resist. Someone who is certain she will stick to a diet may still go to some lengths not to be tempted by rich food.

When gut instincts and dispassionate deliberations disagree, the "rational" prescription is to follow one's head rather than one's heart. In our model, a strong utility push in favor of an action indicates either that the action has been a very good idea in our evolutionary past or that this is a setting in which our information has typically been unreliable. There is thus information in these preferences. The truly rational response is to ask how much weight to place on the advice they give.

4.2 Status

We now return to the consideration of status, on which we touched briefly in Section 3.1.2. The concept of status runs throughout our ordinary lives. We readily categorize people as being of high status or low status, and talk about actions as enhancing or eroding status.

We will examine a particular, narrow view of status as arising out of relatively high consumption. People's preferences often appear to depend not only on their own consumption, but also on the consumption of others, so much so that "keeping up with the Joneses" is a familiar phrase. Frank (1999), Frey and Stutzer (2002a, 2002b), and Neumark and Postlewaite (1998) highlight the importance of such effects, while the suggestion of a link between desired consumption and one's past consumption or the consumption of others is an old one, going back to Veblen (1899) and Duesenberry (1949).

There are two basic approaches to explaining such relative consumption effects. One retains the classical specification of preferences, building a model on the presumption that people care directly only about their own consumption. However, it is posited that some resources in the economy are allocated not via prices and markets but according to status. In addition, it is supposed that one attains status by consuming more than do others, perhaps because the ability to do so is correlated with other characteristics that are important for status. A flashy sports car may then be valued not only for its acceleration, but also for its vivid demonstration that the driver has spent a great deal of money. Tuna may taste better than caviar, but fails to send the same signal. The resulting behavior will be readily rationalized by preferences in which people care about their consumption and about how their consumption relates to that of others. For example, Cole, Mailath and Postlewaite (1992) construct a model in which competition for mates induces a concern for status, around which a subsequent literature has grown.

The second alternative explanation is that evolution has directly embedded a concern for status into our preferences. We focus on this second possibility here, both because it is relatively unexplored and because it naturally suggests links to evolutionary foundations. As usual, our models of this possibility evolve around some constraint on evolution's ability to shape behavior. We consider two possible sources of relative consumption effects, arising out of two such constraints.

4.2.1 Information and relative consumption

Our first examination of relative consumption effects emphasizes information considerations, and ultimately hinges on an imperfection in information processing. The basic idea here is that relative consumption effects may have been built into our preferences as a means of extracting information from the behavior of others. We present a simple model of this possibility here, expanded and examined more thoroughly in Samuelson (2004) and Nöldeke and Samuelson (2005).

The idea that one can extract information from the actions of others is familiar, as in the herding models of Banerjee (1992) and Bikhchandani, Hirshleifer and Welch (1992). In our case, agents observe their predecessors through the filter of natural selection, biasing the mix of observations in favor of those who have chosen strategies well-suited to their environment. An agent's observed behavior thus mixes clues about the agent's information with clues about his evolutionary experience, both of which enter the observer's inference problem. The problem then resembles that of Banerjee and Fudenberg (2004) and Ellison and Fudenberg (1993, 1995) more than pure herding models.

At the beginning of each period $t = 0, 1, \ldots$, the environment is characterized by a variable $\theta_t \in \{\underline{\theta}, \bar{\theta}\}$. The events within a period proceed as follows:

1. Each member of a continuum of surviving agents gives birth, to the same, exogenously fixed, number of offspring. Each offspring is characterized by a parameter ε, with the realized values of ε being uniformly distributed on $[0,1]$.

2. Each newborn observes n randomly selected surviving agents from the previous generation, discerning whether each chose action $\underline{z}$ or $\bar{z}$.
3. All parents then die. Each member of the new generation chooses an action $z \in \{\underline{z}, \bar{z}\}$.
4. Nature then conducts survival lotteries, where $h : \{\underline{z}, \bar{z}\} \times [0, 1] \times \{\underline{\theta}, \bar{\theta}\} \to [0, 1]$ gives the probability that an agent with strategy z and characteristic ε survives when the state of the environment is θ. Again, we assume no aggregate uncertainty.
5. Nature draws a value $\theta_{t+1} \in \{\underline{\theta}, \bar{\theta}\}$.

We interpret the actions $\underline{z}$ and $\bar{z}$ as denoting low-consumption and high-consumption lifestyles. The survival implications of these actions depend upon individual characteristics and the state of the environment. Some agents may be better-endowed with the skills that reduce the risk of procuring consumption than others. Some environments may feature more plentiful and less risky consumption opportunities than others may. These effects appear in the specification of the survival probabilities $h(z, \varepsilon, \theta)$, given by

$$h(\underline{z}, \varepsilon, \theta) = \frac{1}{2}$$

$$h(\bar{z}, \varepsilon, \bar{\theta}) = \frac{1}{2} + b(\varepsilon - q) \tag{16}$$

$$h(\bar{z}, \varepsilon, \underline{\theta}) = \frac{1}{2} + b(\varepsilon - (1 - q)), \tag{17}$$

where $0 < q < 1/2$ and, to ensure well-defined probabilities, $0 < b < 1/(2(1 - q))$. The low-consumption action $\underline{z}$ yields a survival probability of $\frac{1}{2}$, regardless of the agent's characteristic or state of the environment. The high-consumption action $\bar{z}$ yields a higher survival probability for agents with higher values of ε and yields a higher survival probability when the state is $\bar{\theta}$.

The environmental parameter θ follows a Markov process, retaining its current identity with probability $1 - \tau$ and switching to its opposite with probability $\tau < \frac{1}{2}$.

An agent's strategy identifies an action as a function of the agent's characteristic ε and information. Strategies (but not characteristics or actions) are heritable and are thus shaped by natural selection.

Our interest concerns cases in which fluctuations in the state θ are not perfectly observed by the agents and are sufficiently transitory that Nature cannot observe them.[50] It follows from the monotonicity of (16)–(17) that an optimal strategy must take the form of a cutoff $\varepsilon^*(\cdot)$, conditioned on the agent's information, such that action $\bar{z}$ is chosen if and only if $\varepsilon > \varepsilon^*(\cdot)$.

[50] If the state θ can be observed, then evolution faces no constraints in designing strategies to maximize the survival probabilities given by (16)–(17), and observations of the previous generation are irrelevant for behavior.

Let ψ_t be the proportion of strategy $\bar{z}$ among those agents who survived period $t-1$. Then a period-t newborn observes $\bar{z}$ on each survivor draw with probability ψ_t and observes $\underline{z}$ with probability $1-\psi_t$. Let $\Psi_{\mathcal{E}}(\psi_t, \theta_t)$ be the proportion of surviving period-t agents who chose $\bar{z}$, given that (*i*) these agents, as new-borns, drew observations from the distribution described by ψ_t (*ii*) the period-t state of the environment relevant for Nature's survival lotteries is θ_t, and (*iii*) every agent's decision rule is given by the decision $\mathcal{E} = \{\varepsilon^*(n), \ldots, \varepsilon^*(0)\}$. We can describe our system as a Markov process (ψ_t, θ_t) defined on the state space $[0,1] \times \{\underline{\theta}, \bar{\theta}\}$. Letting Θ denote the transition rule governing the state θ, $(\Psi_{\mathcal{E}}, \Theta)$ denotes the transition rule for the process (ψ_t, θ_t), where:

$$\begin{aligned}\psi_{t+1} &= \Psi_{\mathcal{E}}(\psi_t, \theta_t)\\ \theta_{t+1} &= \Theta(\theta_t).\end{aligned}$$

The optimal strategy $\varepsilon^*(\cdot)$ maximizes

$$\int_{\Theta\times\Psi} \rho(\theta,\psi)\ln\left(\int_K f(k|\theta,\psi)p(\varepsilon^*(k),\theta)dk\right)d\theta d\psi, \tag{18}$$

where ρ is the stationary distribution over states $(\theta, \psi) \in [0,1] \times \{\underline{\theta}, \bar{\theta}\}$, f is the distribution over the number (k) of $\bar{z}$ agents observed when sampling the previous generation (given the state (θ, ψ)), and p is the probability that an agent characterized by decision rule ε^* (i.e., chooses $\bar{z}$ if and only if $\varepsilon > \varepsilon^*$) survives in state θ. Notice in particular the ln that appears in this expression. The fluctuating state of the environment subjects the agents to aggregate uncertainty. This objective is then the adaption of (3) to this somewhat more complicated setting.

The key question in characterizing an optimal strategy is now the following: if the agent observes a relatively large value of k, is the environment more likely to be characterized by $\underline{\theta}$ or $\bar{\theta}$? Let $\rho(\bar{\theta}|k)$ be the posterior probability of state $\bar{\theta}$ given that an agent has observed k agents from the previous generation choosing $\bar{z}$. These updating rules are an equilibrium phenomenon. The expectation is that an agent observing more instances of high consumption will think it more likely that the state is $\bar{\theta}$ and hence be more willing to choose high consumption, i. e., that $\varepsilon^*(k)$ should be decreasing in k. We say that a strategy $\{\varepsilon^*(n),\ldots,\varepsilon^*(0)\}$ is *admissible* if it exhibits this property.

Let the function $\rho_{\mathcal{E}}(\bar{\theta}_t|k,t)$ give the probability that the state in time t is $\bar{\theta}$, given a time-t observation of k values of $\bar{\theta}$. The role of k in this probability balances two considerations—the extent to which an observation of a large k indicates that the previous-period state was relatively favorable for strategy $\bar{z}$ (i.e., was $\bar{\theta}$), and the probability that the state may have changed since the previous period. Samuelson (2004) proves:

Lemma 5 *There exists a value* $q* \in (0,\frac{1}{2})$ *such that for any* $q \in (q*,\frac{1}{2})$ *and any admissible* $\mathcal{E}$, *there exist probabilities* $\rho_{\mathcal{E}}(\bar{\theta}|k)(k = 0,\ldots,n)$ *satisfying, for all initial conditions,*

$$\lim_{t\to\infty} \rho_{\mathcal{E}}(\bar{\theta}_t|k,t) = \rho_{\mathcal{E}}(\bar{\theta}|k).$$

The $\rho_{\mathcal{E}}(\bar{\theta}|k)$ *satisfy* $\rho_{\mathcal{E}}(\bar{\theta}|k+1) > \rho_{\mathcal{E}}(\bar{\theta}|k)$.

The restriction that $q > q^*$ ensures that the population can never get too heavily concentrated on a single action, either $\bar{z}$ or $\underline{z}$. This in turn ensures that changes in the environmental state are reflected relatively quickly in the observed distribution of actions, and hence that the latter is informative.[51]

The inequality $\rho_{\mathcal{E}}(\bar{\theta}|k+1) > \rho_{\mathcal{E}}(\bar{\theta}|k)$ indicates that observations of high consumption enhance the posterior probability that the state of the environment is $\bar{\theta}$. This is the foundation of relative consumption effects.

Equilibrium is a specification of ε that is optimal in the induced stationary state. Hence, in defining equilibrium, we use the limiting probabilities $\rho_{\mathcal{E}}(\bar{\theta}|k)$ to evaluate the payoff of a strategy. This reflects an assumption that the process governing the state of the environment persists for a sufficiently long time that (*i*) evolution can adapt her agents to this process, and (*ii*) the limiting probabilities $\rho_{\mathcal{E}}(\bar{\theta}|k)$ are useful approximations for evolution of the information-updating problem facing the agents. Nöldeke and Samuelson (2005) show that:

Proposition 6 *There exists* $q* \in (0, \frac{1}{2})$ *and* $\tau^* > 0$ *such that for any* $q \in (q*, \frac{1}{2})$ *and* $\tau \in (0, \tau^*)$, *an equilibrium with an admissible strategy* $\{\varepsilon^*(n), \ldots, \varepsilon^*(0)\}$ *exists. In any such equilibrium,* $\varepsilon^*(k+1) < \varepsilon^*(k)$.

Agents are more likely to choose high consumption, i.e., choose $\bar{z}$ for a wider range of ε, when k is large. Observations of high consumption, by increasing the expectation that the environment is in a state favorable to high consumption, increase an agent's propensity to choose high consumption. A revealed preference analysis of behavior would thus uncover relative consumption effects, in which agents optimally exploit information by conditioning their consumption on observations of others' consumption.

It is important to note that an agent's survival in this model depends only on the agent's own consumption. The route to genetic success is to choose optimal consumption levels, regardless of the choices of others. The consumption levels of others are relevant only because they serve as valuable indicators of environmental information that neither the agents nor Nature can observe.

There are many ways Nature could induce the optimal behavior characterized by Proposition 6, from hard-wired stimulus-response machines to calculating agents who understand Bayes' rule and their environment and who make their decisions so as to maximize the expected value of a utility function defined in terms of only their own

[51] To see how this could fail, consider the extreme case of $q = 0$. In this case, it is possible that virtually the entire population chooses $\underline{z}$. A change from state $\underline{\theta}$ to $\bar{\theta}$ will then not produce a noticeable change in the distribution of actions for an extraordinarily long time, causing this distribution to be relatively uninformative.

consumption. Our argument thus far accordingly provides no reason to believe that relative consumption effects are built directly into preferences, and no reason why we should care about which of the many observationally-equivalent methods Nature might have chosen to implement such behavior.

The next step in the argument returns us to the observation that Nature faces a variety of obstacles in inducing behavior that will maximize expected utility. Suppose that in addition to the number k of preceding agents observing high consumption, the agent also observes a signal ξ that is more likely to take on high values when the environment is $\bar{\theta}$. Suppose also that the agent does not process this signal perfectly. In Samuelson (2004), this imperfect-information processing assumption is made operational by assuming that the agent observes an informative signal ξ, as well as an uninformative signal ζ, but does not recognize this distinction, instead simply processing all signals as if they were informative. Recognizing that both ξ and ζ play a role in the agent's information, evolution finds the agent's information less informative than does the agent. She thus reduces the sensitivity of the agent's actions to his information. This reduced sensitivity can be accomplished by a utility function that discourages the agent from straying too far from a target action $\hat{\varepsilon}(k)$ that depends upon the agent's observation of others' consumption. In particular, evolution can make the agent's utility depend upon his value of ε, his action ($\underline{z}$ or $\bar{z}$), and the number k of high-consumption agents observed in the previous period (the relative consumption effect). Consider a value ε^* and the posterior belief $\hat{p}_{\mathcal{E}}(\theta|k,\xi,\zeta)$ that would make the cutoff ε^* optimal given perfect information processing. Given that the agent is sometimes responding to an uninformative signal, evolution now has an incentive to boost the agent's marginal utility at ε^* above zero (i.e., $\varepsilon^* < \varepsilon(k)$) if the agent has received a large signal convincing him that $\bar{\theta}$ is quite likely; or depressed below zero (i.e., $\varepsilon^* > \hat{\varepsilon}(k)$), if the agent has received a small signal. Evolution thus requires that the agent observe more persuasive information than would be the case with errorless information processing before straying too far from a consumption strategy that makes high consumption more likely when more instances of high consumption have been observed. Evolution accomplishes this by not only inducing the agent's behavior to respond to the behavior of others, but by using the ability to make the agent's utility respond to the behavior of others.

We now have relative consumption effects built directly into preferences, in order to induce relative consumption effects in behavior. Notice that the case for the preference effect is somewhat more tenuous than for the behavioral effect. We can expect relative consumption effects in behavior whenever agents face environmental uncertainty. Relative consumption effects in preferences are one solution to a particular constraint in Nature's design problem. However, the general principle remains that if Nature cannot ensure the agent processes information perfectly, then she will find it advantageous to compensate by manipulating other features of the agent's decision-making apparatus, with relative consumption effects in preferences being one possible result.

4.2.2 Adaptive utility and relative consumption

Our next approach views relative consumption effects as arising out of constraints on the technology for translating choices into utilities that evolution can build into her agents. This line of work, beginning with Robson (2001, pp. 17–19), brings us back to an old question in economics—is utility reasonably viewed as a cardinal or ordinal concept?

The concept of cardinal utility traces back to the English philosopher and lawyer Jeremy Bentham (1791). Bentham believed that utility derived from pleasure or pain, and proposed to make judgments about policy by summing these utilities across the individuals involved. The result was his maxim "the greatest good for the greatest number," which, as Paul Samuelson is said to have remarked, has too many "greatests" in it to be implementable. Whatever the value of the maxim, the point of view was clear, namely, that utility was a physical process whose properties we could discover and whose nature would provide clues as to how and why people make choices.

The view that utility is a cardinal notion, perhaps based on some measurable concept of pleasure, raises a number of awkward questions. Perhaps as a result, subsequent economists pared back the notion of utility to take refuge in an ordinal interpretation. In the context of consumer theory, it was realized that utility simply did not need to be cardinal—one needed only indifference curves and an appropriate set of labels. That such stripping down was philosophically a good idea was justified by an appeal to "Occam's Razor." Although matters are less cut-and-dried in the original context of welfare theory, most economists also became skeptical of interpersonal comparisons based on cardinal utility, often settling finally for a weak welfare criterion that is independent of any such comparisons—Pareto efficiency. This is associated with a clear minimal view of utility, as simply a description of choice, devoid of any physical or extraneous causal features.

This reliance on ordinal utility, while convenient from both a conceptual and technical point of view, has begun to falter in response to recent work in psychology and behavioral economics. As this work has illustrated an evermore complicated and subtle array of choice behavior, it has been natural to seek explanations in the process by which these choices are made, in the course of which utility once again often plays the role of a mechanism rather than description.[52] For example, psychologists discuss how a burst of intense pleasure stems from a positive outcome, such as winning the lottery, but this pleasure subsides quickly, with the winner ending up feeling only slightly better than before winning. Analogously, the intense sadness that arises from a negative outcome, such as becoming the victim of a crippling accident, tends to fade away, so

[52] Recent experiments have provided fascinating evidence of the link between utility and chemical processes in the brain. See, for example, Zaghloul, Blanco, Weidemann, McGill, Jaggi, Baltuch and Kahana (2009).

that one ends up feeling only somewhat worse than before the accident.[53] In both cases, the dominant effect is that if you were happy before, you will be happy now; if you were miserable before, you will be miserable now. Taken at face value, these findings seem to suggest that people should not particularly mind running the risk of a catastrophic accident and should not buy lottery tickets. Why take precautions to avoid only a slight loss, or incur costs in search of a slight gain? However, people do try to avoid being maimed and do buy lottery tickets.

Putting these considerations together, we consider here a model of utility with three features. Utility is a physical process that translates actions and choices into rewards, typically described as pleasure. In addition, these rewards are adaptive. Whether an experience makes you happy or sad depends on what you were expecting, on what you had before, and on what those around you are receiving. Moreover, this adaption is not always perfectly anticipated. We buy lottery tickets because we anticipate the resulting utility boost, without recognizing that it will be adapted way, and avoid accidents for similar reasons.

It will be helpful to begin with an analogy. Consider an old-fashioned, analog voltmeter, with a needle that is moved along a scale by an electrical current. To get an accurate reading from a voltmeter, one must first estimate the range into which the unknown voltage falls. If the range is set too high and the resulting voltage is in fact quite low, the needle hardly budges and the voltmeter produces no useful information. If the range is set too low, the meter self-destructs as the needle pegs against its upper end and the unexpected surge of current burns out the meter. Only if the range is set right can you obtain useful information. The problem is that the voltmeter, like all real measuring devices, has limited sensitivity.

The suggestion here is that one might think similarly about utility. The ultimate rewards that motivate our choices are provided by chemical flows in our brain. There are limits to the strength of these flows. In addition, we are likely to have limited perceptual discrimination, being unable to tell the difference between roughly similar perceptual stimuli.

Consider the following example. An individual must choose between two lotteries over real numbers, with larger outcomes being better than smaller ones. Each lottery is an independent draw from the same known continuous cumulative distribution function F. The individual must choose a lottery *after* the draws are made. The choice then seems stunningly simple—there is no need to worry about expected values, or risk, or anything else. Just pick the larger number. However, suppose that the individual can only perceive whether each realization is above or below some threshold c. Evolution creates incentives to make the right choice by attaching hedonic utilities to the perceived outcomes, being high when an outcome above c is selected and otherwise low. If the outcomes of both lotteries lie above or both lie below c, the choice is made

[53] Attention was drawn to this phenomenon by Brickman, Coates and Janoff-Bulman's (1978) study of lottery winners and paraplegics, and has become the subject of a large literature. See Loewenstein and Schkade (1999) and Frederick and Loewenstein (1999) for introductions and Gilbert (2007) for a popular account.

randomly, so that with probability 1/2 the individual makes a mistaken choice, failing to choose the larger value.

What value of c minimizes the probability of error, given the distribution F from which choices are made? This probability of error is

$$\begin{aligned} PE(1) &= (1/2)\Pr\{x_1, x_2 < c\} + (1/2)\Pr\{x_1, x_2 > c\} \\ &= (1/2)(F(c))^2 + (1/2)(1 - F(c))^2 \\ &= (1/2)y^2 + (1/2)(1 - y)^2, \end{aligned}$$

where x_1 and x_2 are the outcomes of the two lotteries and $y = F(c)$. This is a convex function. The first-order condition for this minimization problem is

$$\frac{dPE(1)}{dy} = y - (1 - y) = 0,$$

so that one should choose c so that $y = F(c) = \frac{1}{2}$. Hence, it is optimal to choose c to be the median of the distribution described by F. In particular, it is optimal to set a threshold that adapts to the circumstances in which it is to be used, as captured by F.

We view this simple example as a metaphor for the problem evolution faces when designing utility functions. In the absence of any constraints, evolution would simply give the agent the utility function x, and would be confident of optimal decisions. An ordinal view of utility would be perfectly adequate. The view of utility as arising out of a process for transforming choices into rewards introduces constraints, in that values of x that are quite similar might induce sufficiently similar rewards that the agent sometimes ranks them incorrectly.[54] We have taken this to the extreme here of assuming that the agent can only distinguish high from low. This in turn gives rise to a design problem. If the utility function is going to give rise to imperfections, then evolution will want to influence and allow for those imperfections. This gives us our first look at the first of the three features we would like to build into our model of adaptive utility.

Before looking for the next feature, namely the adaptive part, we pause to elaborate on our first example. There is clearly a long way to go from this example to models of utility functions. To begin, the probability of error is not the convincing objective here. After all, some errors involve a very large gap between the x that is chosen and the optimal x, and some involve a very small gap. A more plausible objective would be to identify fitness with x and then maximize the expected value of the x that is received.[55] Now the value of the threshold c should be set at the mean of the distribution rather than the median. Having done this, an obvious next question is to ask what

[54] The psychology literature is filled with studies documenting the inability of our senses to reliably distinguish between small differences. For a basic textbook treatment, see Foley and Matlin (2009).

[55] The identification of fitness with x is relatively innocuous, in the sense that, if fitness were a monotonically increasing function of x, we could easily find the cumulative distribution function over fitness that is implied by the given distribution over x. This does not make a significant qualitative difference.

happens if the agent is somewhat more sophisticated than being able to identify only a single threshold for the value of x.

Netzer (2009) examines this problem further, considering the case in which the individual maximizes the expected payoff and has an arbitrary number of perception thresholds available. We will continue here with the illustrative and more tractable problem of minimizing the probability of error, now considering the more general case in which the individual has N threshold values

$$c_1 < c_2 < \ldots < c_N.$$

The probability of error is now

$$\begin{aligned} PE(N) &= (1/2)(F(c_1))^2 + \ldots + (1/2)(F(c_{n+1}) - F(c_n))^2 + \ldots + (1/2)(1 - F(c_N))^2 \\ &= (1/2)(y_1)^2 + \ldots + (1/2)(y_{n+1} - y_n)^2 + \ldots + (1/2)(1 - y_N)^2, \end{aligned}$$

where $y_n = F(c_n)$ for $n = 1, \ldots, N$. This is again a convex function of $(y_1, \ldots, y_N)$ so that satisfying the first-order conditions is still necessary and sufficient for a global minimum. These first-order conditions are

$$\begin{aligned} &\frac{\partial PE(N)}{\partial y_1} = 0 \text{ so } y_2 - y_1 = y_1 - 0 \\ &\frac{\partial PE(N)}{\partial y_n} = 0 \text{ so } y_{n+1} - y_n = y_n - y_{n-1}, \quad \text{for } n = 2, \ldots, N-1 \\ &\frac{\partial PE(N)}{\partial y_N} = 0 \text{ so } 1 - y_N = y_N - y_{N-1}. \end{aligned}$$

Hence, the solution is

$$y_1 - 0 = k, y_{n+1} - y_n = k, \text{ for } n = 2, \ldots, N-1 \text{ and } 1 - y_N = k.$$

It must then be that $k = 1/(N+1)$, so that

$$y_n = F(y_n) = n/(N+1), \text{ for } n = 1, \ldots, N.$$

For example, if $N = 9$, the thresholds should be at the deciles of the distribution.

What is the probability of error $PE(N)$ when the thresholds are chosen optimally like this? We have

$$PE(N) = \overbrace{\frac{1}{2(N+1)^2} + \ldots + \frac{1}{2(N+1)^2}}^{N+1\text{terms}} = \frac{1}{2(N+1)} \to 0, \text{ as } N \to \infty.$$

It is thus clearly advantageous to have as many thresholds as possible, i.e., to be able to perceive the world as finely as possible. Unfortunately, the ability to measure the world more precisely is biologically costly. Suppose the individual incurs a cost that is proportional to the probability of error as well as a cost $c(N)$ that depends directly on N, so that more thresholds are more costly. The total cost is then

$$PE(N) + c(N),$$

which should be minimized over the choice of N. If $c(N) \to 0$, in an appropriate uniform sense, it follows readily that $N \to \infty$ and $PE(N) \to 0$. As costs decline, the resulting choice behavior is exactly as conventionally predicted.

This exercise gives us some quite useful insights into how evolution would design a utility function to cope with a particular decision problem. One of the seemingly obvious but important lessons is that the optimal utility function depends upon the characteristics of the problem, in this case captured by the distribution F. Suppose evolution has to cope with different decision problems—sometimes one specification of F, sometimes another. Evolution would then like to tailor the utility function to each such problem, just as a different specification of F in our first example would give rise to a different utility function. To do so, however, evolution needs to "know" what problem the agent is facing.

This leads naturally to the second feature we seek in our analysis of adaptive utility and relative consumption effects, namely the relative consumption effects. The agent's past consumption or the consumption of others provides clues about the agent's decision environment and the choices the agent is likely to face. Evolution uses these clues to adjust the agent's utility, giving rise to a utility function that conditions current utilities on past consumption.

In examining this process, we follow Rayo and Becker (2007). Their model gives rise to two effects, namely,

(1) Habituation—utility adjusts so that people get used to a permanent shift, positive or negative, in their circumstances, and

(2) Peer comparisons—people are concerned with relative income or wealth.

What these have in common is a specification of utility in terms of a reference point that is determined either by one's own past consumption, or by the past and present consumption of peers. These are the relative consumption effects.

Rayo and Becker (2007) again view utility as hedonic, as a biological device that induces appropriate actions by an individual. In particular, evolution chooses the mapping from material outcomes into pleasure in the most effective way possible. In the present context, this most effective way involves the construction of a reference point that reflects the individual's expectations of the world. As in Robson (2001), there is a metaphorical principal-agent problem here, with evolution as the principal and the individual as the agent. Evolution "wishes" the individual to be maximally fit, and she has the ability to choose the utility function of the agent to her best advantage. The key ingredients of the model are a limited range of utility levels that are possible, and a limited ability to make fine distinctions.[56]

Consider an agent who must choose a strategy $x \in X$. This might be interpreted as a method of hunting, for example, or more generally the pursuit of consumption. Once x is chosen, an output y is determined, with

$$y = f(x) + s$$

where the strictly concave function f represents the technology that converts the agent's consumption into output, and s is the realization of a random variable $\tilde{s}$ that has a zero mean and a continuous, unimodal density g, with $g' = 0$ only at its maximum. The agent must choose x before knowing the realization of $\tilde{s}$.

Evolution designs a utility function $V(y)$, attaching utilities to outputs, with the goal of maximizing the expected value of y. Notice that several familiar elements appear in this problem. First, evolution chooses a utility function to motivate the agent, rather than simply specifying or hard-wiring the optimal choice of x. The latter option is prohibitively difficult, compared to the trial-and-error capabilities of evolution, or rendered impossible by a tendency for the technology f to change at a pace too rapid for evolution to supply corresponding adjustments in her prescription of x.[57] Second, while evolution's goal is the maximization of offspring, the variable y may represent directly observable intermediate goods such as money or food. Evolution then attaches utilities to values of y to induce choices that in turn have the desired effects in terms of offspring.

The agent's objective is to maximize

$$E\{V|x\} = \int V(f(x) + s)g(s)ds$$

over the choice of $x \in X$.

The first important constraint in the model is that there are bounds on V so that

$$V \in [\underline{V}, \bar{V}],$$

[56] Robson (2001) argues that utility bounds and limited discrimination between utilities will induce evolution to induce adaptive utility functions that strategically position the steep part of the utility function. Trémblay and Schultz (1999) provide evidence that the neural system encodes relative rather than absolute preferences, as might be expected under limited discrimination. See Friedman (1989) for an early contribution and Netzer (2009) and Wolpert and Leslie (2009) for work that is more recent.

[57] We could capture this assumption more explicitly by writing the technology as $f(x, z)$, as do Rayo and Becker, where z represents features of the environment that affect the technology available to the agent and hence the agent's optimal actions, while assuming that the agent observes z, but the possible values of z are too many and too complex for evolution to incorporate in the agent's utility function. Although the maximizer x then varies with the state z, the simplest Rayo and Becker formulation assumes that the maximized value of f does not. As we discuss briefly below, relaxing this assumption generates "S-shaped" utility functions rather than the step function derived for the simplest case. We omit z here in order to simplify the notation.

which we can then normalize so that $V \in [0, 1]$. The constraints might ultimately reflect the fact that there are a finite number of neurons in the brain, and hence limits on the positive and negative sensations evolution can engineer the agent to produce. These upper and lower constraints on V will typically be binding, in that evolution would benefit from a wider range of emotional responses. It is expensive, however, to enlarge the range, and so this range must be finite and evolution must use the range optimally.

The second constraint is that the agent has only limited discrimination in distinguishing utilities. This takes the precise form that, if

$$|E\{V|x_1\} - E\{V|x_2\}| \leq \varepsilon,$$

then the individual cannot rank x_1 and x_2. Hence all choices within ε of $\max_{x \in X} E\{V|x\}$ are "optimal." It is assumed that the agent randomizes uniformly, or at least uses a continuous distribution with full support, over this satisficing set. Of course, evolution would also prefer a smaller value of ε, but this is again expensive, and she will have to optimize given the optimal $\varepsilon > 0$.

Let x^* maximize $f(x)$. Then the agent thus chooses a value x from a satisficing set $[\underline{x}, \bar{x}]$, where

$$E\{V|x^*\} - E\{V|\underline{x}\} = E\{V|x^*\} - E\{V|\bar{x}\} = \varepsilon.$$

Evolution's goal is then to minimize the size of this satisficing set. The first step toward solving this problem is to note that evolution will maximize the difference in utilities between the optimal choice and the choice that lies just on the boundary of the satisficing set:

Lemma 7 *If V^* minimizes the satisficing set $[\underline{x}, \bar{x}]$, then V^* solves*

$$\max_{V(\cdot)\in[0,1]} E\{V|x^*\} - E\{V|\underline{x}\} \tag{19}$$

or, equivalently,

$$\max_{V(\cdot)\in[0,1]} E\{V|x^*\} - E\{V|\bar{x}\}.$$

To verify this claim, suppose that it is not the case. Then, given the candidate optimum V^* and the attendant satisficing set $[\underline{x}, \bar{x}]$, there exists some other utility function $V \neq V^*$ such that

$$E\{V|x^*\} - E\{V|\underline{x}\} > E\{V^*|x^*\} - E\{V^*|\underline{x}\} = \varepsilon,$$

with, of course, an analogous inequality for $\bar{x}$. Then the alternative utility function V would give a smaller satisficing set, yielding a contradiction. This gives the result, and in the process a simple characterization of evolution's utility design problem.

It is now relatively straightforward to characterize the optimal utility function:

Proposition 8 *There exists a value* $\hat{y}$ *such that the optimal utility function* V^* *is given by*

$$V^*(y) = \begin{cases} 1 & y \geq \hat{y} \\ 0 & y < \hat{y} \end{cases}$$

where $\hat{y}$ *solves*

$$g(\hat{y} - f(x^*)) = g(\hat{y} - f(\underline{x})) = g(\hat{y} - f(\bar{x})).$$

To establish this, we recall that evolution's optimal utility function must minimize the satisficing set, which in turn implies that it must maximize the difference $E\{V|x^*\} - E\{V|\underline{x}\}$ (cf. (19)). Writing the expectations in (19) and then changing variables to obtain the right side of the following equality, the utility function must be chosen to maximize

$$\int [V(f(x^*) + s) - V(f(\underline{x}) + s)]g(s)ds = \int V(y)[g(y - f(x^*)) - g(y - f(\underline{x}))]dy.$$

Now the solution is clear. The smallest possible values of utility, or 0, should be assigned to values of y for which $g(y - f(x^*)) - g(y - f(\underline{x})) < 0$ and the largest possible utility, or 1, assigned to values of y for which $g(y - f(x^*)) - g(y - f(\underline{x})) > 0$. Our assumptions on g ensure that it has a "single-crossing" property, meaning that (since $f(x^*) > f(\underline{x})$) there is a value $\hat{y}$ that $g(y - f(x^*)) - g(y - f(\underline{x})) < 0$ for all smaller values of y and $g(y - f(x^*)) - g(y - f(\underline{x})) > 0$ for all larger values. This gives the result. Notice that we could just as well have used $\bar{x}$ throughout this argument.

Evolution thus designs the agent with a "bang-bang" utility function, choosing a cutoff $\hat{y}$ such that outcomes above this cutoff induce the maximum possible utility, while those below minimize utility. As $\varepsilon \to 0$, the satisficing set collapses around x^* and the value of $\hat{y}$ approaches $f(x^*)$. Evolution thus becomes arbitrarily precise in penalizing the agent for choosing suboptimal values of x^*, as we would expect, as the agent's perceptual imprecision disappears.

What lies behind this result? Because of the agent's perceptual errors, evolution would like the utility function to be as steep as possible, so that the agent is routinely choosing between alternatives with large utility differences and hence making few mistakes. However, the constraints $\underline{V}$ and $\bar{V}$ on utility make it impossible to make the utility function arbitrarily steep everywhere. Evolution responds by making the utility function steep "where it counts," meaning over the range of decisions the agent is likely to encounter, while making it relatively flat elsewhere to squeeze the function into the utility bounds.

In the simple model presented here, making the utility function steep where it counts takes the extreme form of a single jump in utility. More generally, one might expect a smoother, S-shaped utility function to be more realistic than the cliff shape or bang-bang utility function we have derived. Notice first that the expected utility $E\{V|x\}$ that guides the agent's decisions has such an S shape. In addition, Rayo and Becker (2007) show that an S shape would arise if deviations from a given reference level V_0 were costly. Alternatively, it might be that the agent knows more about the output technology than does evolution. Now evolution might not be able to target $E\{y|x^*\}$, instead having to smooth out V to provide strong incentives over a range of possible $E\{y|x^*\}$'s.[58]

Where do we see relative considerations in this model? We have the obvious beginnings of relative consumption effects in the need for evolution to tailor the utility function to the problem the agent faces, in order to position the "steep spot" at the appropriate place. Now suppose that output is given by

$$y = f(x) + s + w,$$

where w is a random variable whose value is observed by the agent before he makes his choice but is not observed by evolution, and s is again drawn subsequently to the agent's choice. The random variable w may capture aspects of the agent's environment that make high output more or less likely, while s captures idiosyncratic elements of chance and luck that affect the agent's output. Then evolution will condition the utility function on any variables that carry information about w. If the agent is involved in a sequence of choices and there is persistence in the value of w, then evolution will condition the agent's current utility function on past realizations of the agent's output. A higher previous output will mean that it takes a higher current output to hit a given utility level. If the agent can observe others who are also affected by w, then evolution will condition the agent's utility function on the output of others. Observing higher output from one's neighbors will mean that a higher output must be produced to hit a given utility level. Relative consumption effects thus become the rule. Without such effects, trends in the value of w could eventually render the utility function irrelevant for the environment, with most choice occurring in a range where the utility function is virtually flat. All decisions would look equally good or bad and the individual's incentives would disappear.

For example, Rayo and Becker present a case in which $\hat{y}_t = y_{t-1}$. Hence, the individual is happy if and only if current output exceeds last period's output. Notice that in this case, the agent is punished as severely for bad luck as she would be for a bad decision. In equilibrium, the agent's decisions would be inevitably optimal and happiness would be purely a matter of luck.

[58] Footnote 57 raised the possibility of incorporating an environmental variable z into the agent's technology, which would then be $f(x, z)$. As long as z affects only the shape of f, and hence the identity of the maximizer x^*, but not the value of the maximum $f(x^*, z)$, our previous analysis goes through without change. If z also affects the maximum $f(x^*, z)$, then the result is a smoother specification of the optimal utility function.

This gives us the second of our desired features, namely a utility function that adjusts to reflect relative consumption effects. Finally, we can ask whether agents will anticipate these future adjustments when making their current choices, or will they remain unaware of such changes. Equivalently, will the agents be sophisticated or naive (cf. O'Donoghue and Rabin (1999)). Robson and Samuelson (2010) argue that evolution will optimally design agents to be at least partially naive. The intuition is straightforward. Suppose agents make intertemporal choices. Evolution then has conflicting goals in designing future utilities. On the one hand, they must be set to create the appropriate tradeoffs between current and future consumption, so that agents have appropriate investment incentives. On the other hand, once the future is reached, evolution would like to adjust the utility function to create the most effective current incentives.

These forces potentially conflict. Suppose that current investment can create lucrative future payoffs. Evolution would like to promise high future utilities, in order to induce such investment. Once the investment has been made and the future reached, however, evolution would like to ratchet the entire utility function down, to continue to create incentives. However, an agent who anticipates this will not undertake the current investment. The solution? Make the agent naive, so that she has current investment incentives in anticipation of lucrative future payoffs, which are subsequently and unexpectedly adjusted to heighten subsequent incentives.

4.2.3 Implications

In each of the two preceding subsections, we find utility functions that are defined over the consumption of others as well as one's own consumption, providing foundations for preferences that are not purely "selfish." In each case, these relative consumption effects implicity incorporate useful environmental information into the agent's utility maximization.

Why do we care about such relative consumption effects? What behavior might we expect to observe that is consistent with relative consumption effects? Why do we care whether they might enter preferences directly? We take these questions in reverse order.

Our current world is much different from the ancestral environment in which our preferences evolved. If we were concerned only with the ancestral environment, then our interest would not extend beyond the behavior that maximizes fitness. We would be interested in whether behavior exhibited relative consumption effects, but we could ignore imperfections such as the agent's noisy information processing that have only a minor impact (or, in the case of our simple model, no impact) on the constrained-optimal behavior implemented by evolution. If we are concerned with our current world, however, then we must recognize that these imperfections can have an important impact on the mechanism by which evolution induces her optimal behavior, and that the implementing mechanism can in turn have an important impact on the behavior that appears once the agents are transplanted from the ancestral environment to our much different modern environment. For example, perfect Bayesians will never erroneously imitate uninformative consumption decisions. Relative consumption effects that are embedded in preferences may cause agents in a modern environment to condition their behavior on a variety of uninformative or misleading signals, regardless of the uncertainty they face. It makes a difference what sort of behavior evolution has programmed us to have, and how the programming has been done.

What would we expect to see in a world of relative consumption effects? First, we should either see evidence that evolution designs agents to consciously or unconsciously make use of environmental cues in shaping consumption decisions. Experiments have shown that some animals condition their fat accumulation on day length, a source of information that is reasonably reliable in natural environments but that can be used to manipulate feeding behavior in laboratory settings (Mercer, Adam and Morgan (2000)). A variety of young animals, including humans, have been shown to be more likely to consume foods that they have observed others consuming (Smith (2004, Section 2.1)). More striking is recent evidence that a low birth weight puts one relatively at risk for subsequent obesity (Petry and Hales (2000), Ravelli, van der Meulen, Osmond, Barker and Bleker (1999)). The conventional interpretation is that poor maternal nutrition is a prime contributor to a low birth weight as well as a prime indicator of a meager environment, so that a low birth weight provides information to which the optimal reaction is a tendency to store more bodily food reserves.

In addition, we should observe an inclination to conform to the behavior of others that will sometimes appear to be unjustified on informational grounds. Psychologists again commonly report a taste for conformity (Aronson (1995, Chapter 2), Cialdini (1988, Chapter 4)), even in situations in which one would be extremely hard-pressed to identify an objective information-based reason for doing so.[59]

Our model of relative consumption effects directs attention to conformity effects that initially appear somewhat counterintuitive. The model suggests that relatively low-productivity agents will strive to increase consumption, while high productivity agents will attenuate their consumption, both avoiding being too conspicuously different. The latter finding contrasts with the popular view of relative consumption effects as creating incessant incentives to consume more in order to "keep up with the Joneses." Do we expect internet billionaires to lie awake at night, desperately searching for ways to dispose of their wealth to look more like ordinary people? Notice first that information-based relative consumption effects are consistent with outcomes in which some people happily, even gloatingly, consume more than others, perhaps much more.

[59] The work of Asch (1956) is classic, in which an apparent desire to conform prompted experimental subjects to make obviously incorrect choices when matching the lengths of lines, while denying that they were influenced by the choices of others.

Higher-productivity agents optimally consume more than lower-productivity agents, both in the model and in the world. The billionaire need not lie awake at night.

More importantly, the behavior predicted by the model is that agents who observe others consuming more should themselves consume more. But this is typically what one means by "keeping up with the Joneses." Information-based relative consumption effects imply not that we must observe people endeavoring to reduce their consumption, but rather observe people whose characteristics lead to high consumption levels should strive less vigorously to keep ahead of the Joneses than they would to catch up if the Joneses were ahead.

Preferences incorporating relative consumption effects give rise to the risk that agents will react to others' consumption in ways that do not reflect the informational content of their surroundings, leading to outcomes that are inefficient (conditional on the environment). Evolution may have optimally incorporated these risks in the ancestral environment in which our preferences evolved, but new problems appear as agents apply their behavioral rules to a modern industrial society for which they are likely to be a poor match.[60] In addition, to the extent that evolution has responded to this risk, she has done so to maximize the fitness of her agents. From our point of view, it is utility and not fitness that counts. Studying evolutionary foundations allows us to gain insight into the difference between evolution's preferences in the ancestral environment and our preferences in our current world, in turn helping us assess modern social developments or policy interventions.

For example, it is likely that the observations which motivate information-based relative consumption effects are stratified, with evolution finding it optimal for her agents to react more strongly to the generally more relevant consumption of others who appear to be "like them" than to people whose circumstances are quite different. Hence, we may be unfazed by comparisons with internet billionaires, but may be much more conscious of how our consumption compares with that of our colleagues. However, the concept of likeness on which such stratification is based is likely to be both endogenous and liable to manipulation. The development of modern advertising and mass communications may accentuate the visibility of high consumption levels and hence the inefficiencies caused by relative consumption effects. Information and communication technologies may thus bear a hidden cost.

Suppose next that we consider an inequality policy designed to decrease the variation in individual productivities, perhaps by enhancing the productivity of those at the bottom of the income and consumption scale. This will tend to compress the distribution of consumption levels. Consumers will thus observe others who look more like themselves, attenuating the distortions caused by information-based relative income effects.

[60] For example, Frank (1999) argues that relative consumption effects lead Americans to undersave, overconsume luxury goods, and underconsume leisure and public goods.

In contrast, if agents seek status that is tied to conspicuous consumption, then compressing the distribution of consumption increases the returns to investing in status, since a given increase in consumption now allows one to "jump over" more of one's contemporaries. The result can be a ruinous race to invest in status, possibly making everyone worse off (Hopkins and Kornienko (2004)). Policy prescriptions can thus depend critically on whether relative consumption effects arise out of information or status concerns.

4.3 Group selection

Much of the recent interest in more sophisticated models of preferences has been motivated by the belief that people are not as relentlessly selfish as economic models might have us believe. People donate to charity, they vote, they provide public goods, they come to the aid of others, and they frequently avoid taking advantage of others. Such "other-regarding" behavior is often invoked as one of the distinguishing and puzzling features of human society (e.g., Seabright (2005)). At first glance, however, evolutionary arguments appear particularly unlikely to generate other-regarding behavior. Where else would the survival of the fittest lead, but to relentless self-interested behavior? Upon closer reflection, there is ample room for evolution to generate more complex and other-regarding preferences. Perhaps the leading candidate for doing so is the familiar concept of group selection, by which evolution can seemingly design individuals whose behavior is beneficial to the group to which they belong. It is accordingly only natural that we touch here on the idea of group selection.

It is uncanny how close Darwin came to the modern view of biological evolution, given that a detailed understanding of the mechanics of genetic inheritance lay far in the future. In particular, he emphasized that a certain variation would spread if this variation led to greater reproductive success for *individuals* and was inherited by their descendants. We now have a better understanding of the genetics behind the inheritance, as well as a more nuanced view of whether it is the individual, the gene, or something else that is the appropriate unit of selection, but the basic understanding remains the same.

At the same time, Darwin occasionally wandered away from models of evolution based in the fates of individuals, into what would now be called "group selection." Thus, he thought an individual human might engage in behavior that is beneficial to the survival of a group, even if this behavior had a fitness cost to the individual. To what extent can group selection help us explain our preferences?[61]

There is a "folk wisdom" appeal to group selection, and this mechanism was once routinely invoked in popular accounts of natural selection. For example, the idea that a predator species was doing a prey species a favor by eliminating its weakest members represented one of the more fanciful extremes in applying "group selection" arguments. More scientifically, the English experimental biologist Wynne-Edwards (1962, 1986)

[61] This section is based on Robson (2008).

opened the modern discussion of group selection by providing a clear and explicit manifesto on group selection, in the process becoming a favorite target for those wishing to preserve a focus on the individual (or gene). For example, he argued that birds limit the size of their clutches of eggs to ensure that the size of the population does not exceed the comfortable carrying capacity of the environment. That is, individuals act in the best interest of the species, with those that do so most effectively being evolutionarily rewarded by the resulting success of their species.

Williams (1966) effectively devastated these early group selection arguments. If a new type of individual does not so obligingly limit her clutch, for example, why would this more fertile type not take over the population, even though the result is disastrous for the population's standard of living? After all, the profligate egg-layer inevitably has more offspring than her more restrained counterparts do, even if the result is counterproductive overcrowding. This challenge to the logic of group selection was complemented by doubts as to the need for group selection. For example, one can find compelling arguments as to why it is in the interests of an individual to limit her clutch size. It might be that, beyond a certain point, an increase in the number of eggs reduces the expected number of offspring surviving to maturity, because each egg then commands a reduced share in parental resources. A finite optimum for clutch size is then to be expected. Thus, observations suggesting that clutch sizes are limited do not compel a group selection interpretation. As a collection of similar observations accumulated, some biologists were tempted to argue that evolutionary theory could dispense with group selection entirely. Dawkins (1989) has been especially insistent in rejecting group selection, in the process going further in the other direction by arguing for the primacy of the gene rather than individual as a still more basic unit of selection.

Subsequent work suggests that there certainly are phenomena best understood at the level of the gene, but at the same time has uncovered cases in which evolution appears to proceed at different levels. Consider, for example, meiotic drive, also known as segregation distortion. This refers to any process which causes one gametic type to be over-represented or under-represented in the gametes formed during meiosis, and hence in the next generation. A classic example of meiotic drive concerns the *T* locus in mice. This locus controls tail length, but also the viability of the mouse. The following facts apply—*TT* homozygotes have normal long tails, *Tt* heterozygotes have short tails, which is presumably somewhat disadvantageous, and *tt* homozygotes are sterile. If this were the whole story, there would be unambiguous selection against the *t* allele. However, the wrinkle is that the *Tt* heterozygotes transmit the *t* allele with about probability 90% to their sperm, rather than the usual Mendelian 50%. Hence, when the *t* alelle is rare, this strong meiotic drive will overcome the slight fitness disadvantage of short tails and the frequency of the *t* allele will increase. Eventually, the *tt* homozygotes will occur with appreciable frequency, and there will be an equilibrium mixture of the two alleles. The evolutionary processes governing tail length in mice thus mixes considerations that arise at two levels of selection: positive selection for t haplotypes at the level of the gene, but negative selection for tt individuals at the level of the organism. However, if selection can operate at both the genetic and individual level, might it not sometime also operate at the group level?

We want to be clear in recognizing the primacy of the gene as the unit of evolutionary selection. It is genes that carry characteristics from one generation to the next, and only through genes can characteristics be inherited. At the same time, genes are carried by individuals, and which genes are relatively plentiful can depend upon the fate of their host individuals. But could not the fate of these individuals depend upon the groups to which they belong?

We address these issues by examining the interplay between individual and group selection. Again, we emphasize the importance of beginning with the perspective of the gene. However, there are many cases where the interests of the gene and the individual do not conflict. In addition, it is often difficult to give concrete form to the notion of the gene as the unit of selection, given our ignorance of the details of the transformation of genes into individual traits, particularly for complex behavioral characteristics.[62] Hence, despite the theoretical primacy of the gene, we believe we can usefully simplify the analysis by restricting attention here to the comparison between individual level and the group level of selection.

4.3.1 The haystack model

In order to fix ideas, we consider the classic haystack model, offered by Maynard Smith (1964) to study the issue of individual selection versus group selection. Our account simplifies the standard model in several ways. Perhaps most importantly, reproduction here is assumed here to be asexual.

There are a number of haystacks in a farmer's field, where each haystack is home to two mice. Each pair of mice plays the prisoners' dilemma, choosing between the usual two alternatives—cooperate or defect—and then dies. However, each individual leaves behind a number of offspring equal to her payoff in the prisoners' dilemma. The heritable characteristic of an individual is her choice to either cooperate or defect, so we can think of the population as being divided between cooperators and defectors. In particular, offspring inherit their mother's choice of strategy.

After this initial play of the prisoners' dilemma by the haystack's founding pair, there are a number $T-1$ of subsequent stages of play, where the mice in each haystack are paired at random, play the prisoners' dilemma, and then die, while giving rise to further offspring in numbers determined by their prisoners'-dilemma payoffs.

[62] Grafen (1991) advocates finessing such detailed questions on the genetic basis of individual variation, an argument refereed to as his "phenotypic gambit."

The number of individuals within the haystack choosing each strategy then grows in an endogenous fashion, as does the overall size of the group. Every so often, once a year, say, the haystacks are removed, and the mice are pooled into a single large population. Now pairs of mice are selected at random from the overall population to recolonize the next set of haystacks, and excess mice die.

To give an example, consider the following version of the prisoners' dilemma:

	C	D
C	2, 2	0, 4
D	4, 0	1, 1

As a further simplification, suppose that there are a large number of haystacks and therefore individuals, although this assumption facilitates group selection and hence is not innocent. Suppose that the initial fraction of C's in the population is $f \in [0,1]$. Hence the fraction of haystacks that are colonized by 2 C's is f^2; the fraction that are colonized by 2 D's is $(1-f)^2$; and the fraction that have one of each is $2f(1-f)$. There are T rounds of play within each haystack. It follows that each pair of C's gives rise to 2^{T+1} descendants, who are also C's. Each pair of D's gives rise to just 2 D's. Each pair of one C and one D gives rise to 4 D's.

At the end of the T periods of play, and hence just as the haystacks are disrupted, the new fraction of C's in the population is,

$$f' = \frac{2^{T+1}f^2}{2^{T+1}f^2 + 8f(1-f) + 2(1-f)^2}. \tag{20}$$

Let us check first what happens if $T = 1$. In this case, $f' < f$ if and only if

$$4f < 4f^2 + 2(1-f)(3f+1) = 2 + 4f - 2f^2 \Leftrightarrow f < 1.$$

That is, in this case, the D's will increase, and $f \rightarrow 0$. This is not surprising, since with $T = 1$, we simply have an elaborate description of the usual prisoners' dilemma—the extra generality available in the structure of the haystack model is not used. Pairs are broken up immediately so that there is no opportunity to exploit the relatively high total payoffs for the haystack/group that arise from two initial C's.

When there is more than one generation per haystack cycle, these relatively high total payoffs may quickly outstrip those from any other possible starting combination of mice. In particular, if $T \geq 3$, then we have $f' > f$ as long as f is close enough to 1. To see this, we use (20) to conclude that more cooperators than defectors will emerge from the haystacks if

$$2^{T+1}f > 2^{T+1}f^2 + 8f(1-f) + 2(1-f)^2 = 2^{T+1}f^2 + 2(1-f)(3f+1)$$

which in turn holds if

$$T(f) = 2^{T+1}f^2 + 2(1-f)(3f+1) - 2^{T+1}f < 0.$$

Moreover, there is some $f < 1$ sufficiently large as to satisfy this inequality for all $T \geq 3$, an observation that follows immediately from noting that

$$T(1) = 0, \text{ and } T'(1) = 2^{T+2} - 8 - 2^{T+1} = 2^{T+1} - 8 > 0.$$

Hence, in this case, the relatively high growth rate of groups founded by cooperators is sufficiently strong as to allow cooperation to dominate a population whose initial proportion of cooperators is sufficiently large. Cooperation is rescued in the prisoners' dilemma by group selection.

Maynard Smith's intention in examining this model was to give the devil his due by identifying circumstances under which group selection might well have an effect. At the same time, he regarded the analysis as making it clear that the assumptions needed to make group selection comparable in strength to individual selection would be unpalatable. First, in order for group selection to be effective in the haystack model, there must obviously be a number of groups, preferably a large number.

Second, there must be a mechanism that insulates the groups from one another. Only then can a cooperative group be immune to infection by a defecting individual, and hence be assured of maintaining its greater growth rate. Groups must thus be isolated from the appearance of migrating D's as well as D mutants. Third, even with the temporary insulation of each haystack in this model, cooperation will only evolve if there are sufficient rounds of play within each haystack, so that cooperation amasses a sufficient advantage as to survive the next sampling.

While there is some room to relax these assumptions, and one might hope that alternative models are more amenable to group selection, a reasonably widespread view within biology is that group selection is logically coherent but of limited importance.[63] The requirements of a large number of groups, sufficient isolation of groups, barriers to migration and mutation, and differential group success rates, all combine to limit the applicability of group selection. Intuitively, a loose description of the problem with group selection is that it relies too heavily upon the assumption that a bad choice will lead to *group* extinction. There is clearly scope in reality for individual selection, since individuals die frequently, but the idea that groups face extinction sufficiently often as to potentially overwhelm the strength of individual selection strikes many as less plausible.

4.3.2 Selection among equilibria

Much of the initial attention was devoted to the possibility of group selection leading to different results than would individual selection, as in the prisoners' dilemma. This

[63] See Sober and Wilson (1998) for a forcefully argued alternative view.

debate left many skeptics as to the effectiveness and importance of group selection. However, there is a compelling alternative scenario in which group selection may well operate robustly, in any species. This is as a mechanism to select among equilibria (Boyd and Richerson (1985, 1990)).

Consider a population that is divided into various subpopulations, largely segregated from one another, so that migration between subpopulations is limited. The members of each subpopulation are randomly matched to play the same symmetric game, which has several symmetric equilibria. For example, suppose the game is the simplest 2 × 2 coordination game:

	A	B
A	2, 2	0, 0
B	0, 0	1, 1

Individual selection ensures that some equilibrium is attained within each subpopulation. In general, some subpopulations would play the A equilibrium, and some would play the B equilibrium. Each of these configurations is internally robust. That is, if there were the occasional B arising by mutation in an A subpopulation, it would find itself at a disadvantage and would die out. Similarly an A mutant in a B population would die out, despite the ultimate advantage of getting to the all-A configuration. Alternatively, a small group of individuals may occasionally migrate from one subpopulation to another. If the newcomers did not match the prevailing action in their new subpopulation, the newcomers will once again disappear.

Now consider the competition between subpopulations. The A subpopulations grow faster than do those that play B. It is then reasonable to suppose the B populations will eventually die out completely. That is, group selection is free to operate in a leisurely fashion to select the Pareto superior equilibrium. There is no tension here between the two levels of selection, and hence no calculations that need to be made about the number of groups or rates of mutation and migration. Indeed, given enough time, virtually any group structure will lead to a population dominated by the Pareto superior equilibrium. The implication, in Boyd and Richerson's (1985, 1990) view, is that group selection theories have missed the boat by concentrating on the prisoners' dilemma. The true strength of group selection may be not to motivate behavior at odds with individual selection, but as a force mitigating between various contenders for the outcome of individual selection.

4.3.3 Group selection and economics

Why does group selection matter in economics? Group selection is one of the most obvious mechanisms for generating preferences in humans to behave in the social interest rather than that of the individual. At stake then is nothing less than the basic nature of human beings.

As an economist, one should be skeptical of the need to suppose that individuals are motivated by the common good. Economic theory has done well in explaining a wide range of phenomena based on selfish preferences, and so the twin views of the individual as the unit of selection and as the extent of the considerations that enter one's utility function are highly congenial to economists. Furthermore, to the extent that armchair empiricism suggests that non-selfish motivations are sometimes present, these seem as likely to involve malice as to involve altruism. For example, humans seem sometimes motivated by relative economic outcomes, which apparently involve a negative concern for others. Finally, group selection is a potentially blunt instrument that might easily "explain" more than is true.

There are, nevertheless, some aspects of human economic behavior that one is tempted to explain by group selection. For example, human beings are often willing to trade with strangers they will likely never see again, behavior that might be analogous to cooperating in the one-shot prisoners' dilemma. Indeed, there is no shortage of reliable data showing that human beings are capable of such apparently irrationally cooperative behavior, in appropriate circumstances. Whatever the underlying reasons for this, it is a significant factor in supporting our modern economic and social structure.

One possibility is that we are simply mistaken in likening this behavior to cooperation in the prisoners' dilemma. It might be that we trade with others rather than simply trying to seize their goods because there are effective sanctions for behaving otherwise. Alternatively, it is sometimes argued that the structure of the hunter-gatherer society's characteristic of our evolutionary past helps account for cooperative behavior in modern settings. Hunter-gatherer societies were composed of a large number of relatively small groups, and individuals within each group were often genetically related. Perhaps, so the argument goes, we acquired an inherited psychological inclination towards conditional cooperation in such a setting, partly perhaps because of group selection. The group selection argument here gets a boost not only from a setting in which small, relatively isolated groups are likely to have been the norm, but from the fact that the members of these groups were likely to be related, allowing group selection to free ride on the forces of kin selection.[64] The resulting cooperative inclinations may then have carried over into modern societies, despite genetic relatedness now being essentially zero on average.

It is hard to believe, however, that hunter-gatherers never encountered strangers, and that it wasn't important to both keep track of who was a stranger and to adjust one's behavior accordingly. If there were good reasons to condition on this distinction, why would corresponding different strategies not have evolved? Why wouldn't we now use the "defect against strangers" response nearly always? Even if we did somehow acquire a genetic inclination to cooperate in archaic societies, shouldn't we now be in the process of losing this inclination in modern large and anonymous societies?

[64] See Eshel (1972) for a discussion of the relationship between kin selection and group selection.

Sober and Wilson (1998) push energetically for a rehabilitation of group selection within biology. They argue that kin selection—the widely accepted notion that individuals are selected to favor their relatives—should be regarded as a special case of group selection. Proceeding further, they note that what matters most fundamentally is the likelihood that altruistic individuals will be preferentially matched with other altruistic individuals. They offer kin selection as one obvious circumstance under which this will be the case, while arguing that there are many others. While kin selection is widely accepted, one must remember that the mechanisms for achieving the preferential matching of altruistic individuals are quite different for kin selection and group selection. In the end, a skeptical view of the importance of group selection appears to be common among biologists.

4.3.4 Implications

Of all the topics considered in this essay, group selection has perhaps the widest range of potential applications. With the appropriate model, group selection allows us to rationalize almost any behavior. This may explain why biologists, though readily conceding the logical coherence of group selection arguments, typically exhaust all other avenues before turning to group selection as an explanation.[65] We view finding ways to assess group selection arguments, and to separate those circumstances in which group selection is an essential element of an explanation from those in which it provides a convenient alternative story, as one of the foremost challenges facing those working on evolutionary foundations of economic behavior.

5. CONCLUDING REMARK

This essay has addressed a broad subject area, and has all too predictably touched only a fraction of it, despite consuming many pages. We believe there is much to be learned, and much yet to be done, in studying the evolutionary foundations of economic behavior. Pursuing these topics should bring economists increasingly into contact with work in biology and psychology, both of which have much to offer. We have no doubt that we can continue to produce elegant evolutionary models. Will they remain simply nice models, or will they serve as the basis for the type of applied work that motivates our interest in them? This key question remains unanswered. An affirmative answer will require moving beyond the theoretical foundations with which this essay has been concerned to demonstrate that these models are useful in addressing particular applied questions. Can they help us get better estimates of patterns of risk aversion or discounting? Can they help us design more effective economic institutions? There is clearly much work still to be done.

[65] One is reminded in this respect of Wilson's (1985) caution to economists that reputation models may well make things too easy to explain.

6. PROOFS

6.1 Proof of Proposition 1

We provide the proof for the case in which $N(0) = (\frac{1}{T}, \ldots, \frac{1}{T})$. Relaxing this assumption requires only more tedious notation.

Fix a time t. Let τ_t identify the event that the period-t Leslie matrix features $x_\tau \neq 0$ (and all other $x_{\tau'} = 0$). We say in this case that environment τ_t has been drawn in period t. Then only parents of age τ_t reproduce in period t, having x_{τ_t} offspring. There are $S^{\tau_t} N_0(t - \tau_t)$ such parents, so that we have

$$N_0(t) = S^{\tau_t} x_{\tau_t} N_0(t - \tau_t).$$

We can perform this operation again. Let $\tau_{t-\tau_t}$ be the environment drawn at time $t - \tau_t$. Then we have

$$N_0(t) = S^{\tau_t} x_{\tau_t} S^{\tau_{t-\tau_t}} x_{\tau_{t-\tau_t}} N_0(t - \tau_t - \tau_{t-\tau_t}).$$

Continuing in this fashion, we have

$$N_0(t) = S^t x_{\tau_t} x_{\tau_{t-\tau_t}} x_{\tau_{t-\tau_t-\tau_{t-\tau_t}}} x_{\tau_{t-\tau_t-\tau_{t-\tau_t}-\tau_{t_{t-\tau_t-\tau_{t-\tau_t}}}}} \cdots \frac{1}{T},$$

for a sequence $\tau_t, \tau_{t-\tau_t}, \tau_{t-\tau_t-\tau_{t-\tau_t}}, \tau_{t-\tau_t-\tau_{t-\tau_t}-\tau_{t_{t-\tau_t-\tau_{t-\tau_t}}}}, \ldots$ with the property that τ_t is the environment drawn in period t, $\tau_{t-\tau_t}$ is the environment drawn in period $t - \tau_t$, $\tau_{t-\tau_t-\tau_{t-\tau_t}}$ is the environment drawn in period $t - \tau_t - \tau_{t-\tau_t}$, and $\tau_{t-\tau_t-\tau_{t-\tau_t}-\tau_{t_{t-\tau_t-\tau_{t-\tau_t}}}}$ is the environment drawn in period $t - \tau_t - \tau_{t-\tau_t} - \tau_{t_{t-\tau_t-\tau_{t-\tau_t}}}$, and so on. The $1/T$ represents the initial mass of parents of the appropriate age, and the sequence $\tau_t, \tau_{t-\tau_t}, \ldots, \tau_{t'}, \tau_{t''}$ has the properties

$$\tau_t + \tau_{t-\tau_t} + \ldots + \tau_{t'} < t \tag{21}$$

$$\tau_t + \tau_{t-\tau_t} + \ldots + \tau_{t'} + \tau_{t''} \geq t. \tag{22}$$

Hence, the final environment in this sequence, $\tau_{t''}$, causes offspring to survive who are born to a generation of parents that were alive at time 0. The age of these parents at time 0 depends upon the period in which $\tau_{t''}$ is drawn, and the realization of $\tau_{t''}$, and may be any of the generations alive at time 0. Since there are $1/T$ of each age at time 0, the final $1/T$ is applicable regardless of which time-0 age is relevant.

We can then write

$$N_0(t) = \frac{1}{T} S^t \prod_{\tau=1}^{T} x_\tau^{r_\tau(t)}$$

and hence, taking logs and then dividing by t,

$$\frac{1}{t}\ln N_0(t) = \ln S + \sum_{\tau=1}^{T}\frac{r_\tau(t)}{t}\ln x_\tau - \frac{\ln T}{t}, \tag{23}$$

where $r_\tau(t)$ is the number of times environment τ is drawn in the sequence $\tau_t, \tau_{t-\tau_t}, \tau_{t-\tau_t-\tau_{t-\tau_t}}, \tau_{t-\tau_t-\tau_{t-\tau_t}} - \tau_{t_{t-\tau_t-\tau_{t-\tau_t}}}, \ldots, \tau_{t''}$. Our analysis then rests on examining the numbers $r_1(t), \ldots, r_T(t)$. Notice that so far, we have made no use of independence assumptions, having only rearranged definitions. Independence plays a role in examining the $r_\tau(t)$.

Intuitively, the argument now proceeds along the following lines:

- As t gets large, each of the $r_\tau(t)/t$ converges to the same limit as does R_t/Tt, where R_t is the total number of draws in the sequence, i.e., the proportion of periods featuring a draw of environment τ is very nearly the same for all $\tau = 1, \ldots, T$. This follows from the observations that each environment is equally likely and environments are drawn independently each time one is drawn, and gives

$$\lim_{t\to\infty}\sum_{\tau=1}^{T}\frac{r_\tau(t)}{t}\ln x_\tau = \lim_{t\to\infty}\sum_{\tau=1}^{T}\frac{R_t}{Tt}\ln x_\tau.$$

- From (21)–(22), the total number of draws R_t is determined approximately (with the approximation arising out of the fact that the parents of those offspring who survive as a result of draw $\tau_{t''}$ may be older than 1 at the beginning of the process, and with the approximation thus becoming arbitrarily precise as the number of draws increases) by

$$\sum_{\tau=1}^{Tt}\frac{R_t}{T}\tau = \frac{R_t}{Tt}\sum_{\tau=1}^{T}\tau = 1.$$

- This is the statement that the total of the reproductive lengths drawn in the course of the sequence $\tau_t, \tau_{t-\tau_t}, \tau_{t-\tau_t-\tau_{t-\tau_t}}, \tau_{t-\tau_t-\tau_{t-\tau_t}} - \tau_{t_{t-\tau_t-\tau_{t-\tau_t}}}, \ldots, \tau_{t''}$ must equal t. This gives

$$\lim_{t\to\infty}\sum_{\tau=1}^{T}\frac{r_\tau(t)}{t}\ln x_\tau = \frac{\sum_{\tau=1}^{T}\ln x_\tau}{\sum_{\tau=0}^{T}\tau}.$$

Inserting this in (23) gives (8), the desired result.

Our first step in making this argument precise is to confirm that the random draws determining the environments in the sequence $\tau_t, \tau_{t-\tau_t}, \tau_{t-\tau_t-\tau_{t-\tau_t}}, \tau_{t-\tau_t-\tau_{t-\tau_t}} - \tau_{t_{t-\tau_t-\tau_{t-\tau_t}}}, \ldots, \tau_{t''}$ are independent. This is not completely obvious. While the environment is determined independently in each period, the identities of the periods at which the draws are taken in this sequence are endogenously (and hence randomly) determined, potentially vitiating independence.

To examine this question, we construct a model of the stochastic process determining the environment. Consider the measure space $([0,1], \mathcal{B}, \lambda)$, where λ is Lebesgue measure and $\mathcal{B}$ is the Borel σ-algebra. We now model the process determining the environment by letting $\xi(1)$ be a random variable defined by

$$\omega \in \left(\frac{\tau-1}{T}, \frac{\tau}{T}\right) \Rightarrow \xi(1)(\omega) = \tau, \quad \tau = 1, \ldots, T.$$

We then define $\xi(2)$ by

$$\omega \in \left\{\left(h + \frac{\tau-1}{T^2}, h + \frac{\tau}{T^2}\right) \text{ for some } h \in \{0, 1, \ldots, T\}\right\} \Rightarrow \xi(2)(\omega) = \tau, \tau = 1, \ldots, T.$$

Continuing in this fashion gives a countable sequence of random variables that are independent and that each are equally likely to take each of the values 1,2,. . .,T. We interpret $\xi(t)$ as determining the environment at time t. But it is now a straightforward calculation that

$$Pr\{\xi(t) = \tau, \xi(t-i) = \tau'\} = \frac{1}{T^2}$$

for any τ and τ', and hence that $\xi(t)$ and $\xi(t-\tau_t)$ are independent. This in turn ensures that the sequence $\tau_t, \tau_{t-\tau_t}, \tau_{t-\tau_t-\tau_{t-\tau_t}}, \tau_{t-\tau_t-\tau_{t-\tau_t}-\tau_{t_{t-\tau_t-\tau_{t-\tau_t}}}}, \ldots, \tau_{t''}$ is independent.

Let

$$K \equiv \sum_{\tau=1}^{T} \tau.$$

Our goal is to show that with probability one,

$$\lim_{t\to\infty} \frac{r_\tau(t)}{t} = \frac{1}{K}, \tag{A5}$$

which combines with (26) to imply (15), giving the desired result.

We now construct a model of the process determining the frequencies $r_\tau(t)$. To do this, consider again the measure space $([0,1], \mathcal{B}, \lambda)$, where λ is Lebesgue measure and $\mathcal{B}$ is the Borel σ-algebra. Let $\zeta(1)$ be a random variable defined by

$$\omega \in \left(\frac{\tau-1}{T}, \frac{\tau}{T}\right) \Rightarrow \zeta(1)(\omega) = \tau, \quad \tau = 1, \ldots, T.$$

We then define $\zeta(2)$ by

$$\omega \in \left\{\left(h + \frac{\tau-1}{T^2}, h + \frac{\tau}{T^2}\right) \text{ for some } h \in \{0, 1, \ldots, T\}\right\} \Rightarrow \zeta(2)(\omega) = \tau, \tau = 1, \ldots, T.$$

Continuing in this fashion again gives a countable sequence of random variables that are independent and that each are equally likely to take each of the values 1,2, . . . ,T.

In particular, having fixed t, we think of $\zeta(1)$ as describing the draw of the environment at time t. Then, noting that $\zeta(2)$ is independent of $\zeta(1)$ and has the same distribution as $\xi(t-\tau_t)$ regardless of the value of τ_t, we think of ζ_2 as describing the draw of the environment at time $t-\tau_t$. Similarly, $\zeta(3)$ describes the draw at time $t-\tau_t-\tau_{t-\tau_t}$, and so on. The frequencies $r_\tau(t)$ thus are determined by the draws from the collection $\zeta(1),\ldots,\zeta(\hat{t}(t))$ for some number $\hat{t}(t)$. The time $\hat{t}(t)$ is randomly determined and is given by

$$\hat{t}(t) = \max\{t : \sum_{s=0}^{t-1}\tau_s < t\}. \tag{A6}$$

Then $r_\tau(t)$ is the number of times environment τ is drawn by the random variables $\zeta(1),\ldots,\zeta(\hat{t}(t))$.

Fix $\varepsilon > 0$ and define $t'(t)$ (hereafter typically written simply as t') to satisfy

$$t'(t)\left(\left(\frac{1}{T}-\varepsilon\right)K + T^2\varepsilon\right) = t. \tag{A7}$$

Notice that $t > t'(t)$ (this is equivalent to $T^2 > K$) and that t' is linear and increasing in t. Intuitively, $t'(t)$ will be useful because (as we will see) with high probability $t'(t) < \hat{t}(t)$, i.e., with high probability, the random stopping time has not yet been encountered by time $t'(t)$.

Let $\rho_i(t')$ be the number of times environment i is drawn by the random variables $\zeta(1),\ldots,\zeta(t')$. Then choose t and hence $t'(t)$ sufficiently large that, with probability at least $1-\varepsilon$, we have

$$\frac{1}{T}-\varepsilon < \frac{\rho_\tau(t')}{t'} < \frac{1}{T}+\varepsilon \tag{A8}$$

for $\tau = 1,\ldots,T$. The weak law of large numbers ensures the existence of such t. Let $\Sigma \subset [0,1]$ be the event that these inequalities hold (and note that $\lambda(\Sigma) \geq 1-\varepsilon$). For our purposes, the key characteristic of Σ is that on Σ,

$$t'\left(\left(\frac{1}{T}-\varepsilon\right)K + T\varepsilon\right) \leq \sum_{s=1}^{t'}\zeta(s) \leq t'\left(\left(\frac{1}{T}-\varepsilon\right)K + T^2\varepsilon\right) = t. \tag{A9}$$

The term $\sum_{s=1}^{t'}\zeta(s)$ is the sum of the realizations of the t' random variables $\zeta(1),\ldots,\zeta(t')$. The left term is the smallest value this sum can take on Σ, which is obtained by first assuming that every value $i \in \{1,\ldots,T\}$ appears just often enough to attain the minimum frequency $\frac{1}{T}-\varepsilon$ (giving the term $\left(\frac{1}{T}-\varepsilon\right)K$), and then that all additional draws $(t'(1-(\frac{1}{T}-\varepsilon)T) = t'T\varepsilon$ of them) all give environment 1. The third term is the largest value this sum can take on Σ, which is obtained by first assuming that every value $i \in \{1,\ldots,T\}$ appears just often enough to attain the minimum frequency $\frac{1}{T}-\varepsilon$ (giving the term $(\frac{1}{T}-\varepsilon)K$), and then that all additional draws $\left(t'\left(1-\left(\frac{1}{T}-\varepsilon\right)T\right) = t'T\varepsilon\right.$ of them) all give environment T. Comparing with (A6), (A9) is the statement that on Σ, $t'(t) < \hat{t}(t)$, and hence on Σ, all of the random variables $\zeta(1),\ldots,\zeta(t')$ are relevant.

We now put bounds on $r_\tau(t)/t$. First, note that (using (A7) for the first equality)

$$t - t'\left(\left(\frac{1}{T} - \varepsilon\right)K + T\varepsilon\right) = t'\left(\left(\frac{1}{T} - \varepsilon\right)K + T^2\varepsilon\right) - t'\left(\left(\frac{1}{T} - \varepsilon\right)K + T\varepsilon\right)$$
$$= t'(T^2 - T)\varepsilon.$$

Then, on Σ, we have

$$\frac{\rho_\tau(t')}{t} \le \frac{r_\tau(t)}{t} \le \frac{\rho_\tau(t') + t'(T^2 - T)\varepsilon}{t}.$$

In particular, a lower bound on $r_\tau(t)$ is given by assuming that no further draws of environment τ occur past time t', giving $r_\tau(t) = r_\tau(t')$. An upper bound is given by assuming that every subsequent draw is environment τ, and that there are $t - t'\left(\left(\frac{1}{T} - \varepsilon\right)K + T\varepsilon\right) = t'(T^2 - T)\varepsilon$ such draws.

Inserting lower and upper bounds for $\rho_\tau(t')$ (given that we are in Σ) in the appropriate places, this is (cf. (A8))

$$\frac{t'\left(\frac{1}{T} - \varepsilon\right)}{t} \le \frac{r_\tau(t)}{t} \le \frac{t'\left(\frac{1}{T} + \varepsilon\right) + (T^2 - T)\varepsilon}{t}$$

and, using (A7),

$$\frac{\frac{1}{T} - \varepsilon}{\left(\frac{1}{T} - \varepsilon\right)K + T^2\varepsilon} \le \frac{r_\tau(t)}{t} \le \frac{\frac{1}{T} + \varepsilon + (T^2 - T)\varepsilon}{\left(\frac{1}{T} - \varepsilon\right)K + T^2\varepsilon}.$$

There thus exist constants $0 < \underline{c} < \bar{c}$ such that, for any sufficiently small ε and for all sufficiently large T,

$$\Pr\left\{\frac{1}{K} - \underline{c}\varepsilon < \frac{r_\tau(t)}{t} < \frac{1}{K} + \bar{c}\varepsilon\right\} \ge 1 - \varepsilon$$

which implies (A5).

6.2 Proof of Proposition 2

The Leslie matrices identifying the two environments are:

$$A: \begin{bmatrix} Dx_1 & D \\ 0 & 0 \end{bmatrix}$$

$$B: \begin{bmatrix} 0 & D \\ Dx_2 & 0 \end{bmatrix}.$$

The transition matrix between environments, M, is given by

$$\begin{bmatrix} \alpha & 1-\alpha \\ 1-\alpha & \alpha \end{bmatrix}.$$

We then note that the stationary distribution of the matrix M attaches probability 1/2 to each environment. We consider the case in which the initial environment is drawn from this stationary distribution, so that the prior expectation for any period is also this distribution. (If the initial environment is drawn from some other distribution, we need only let the process run sufficiently long that it is usually near the stationary distribution.) Note that

$$M^2 = \begin{bmatrix} \alpha^2 + (1-\alpha)^2 & 2(1-\alpha)\alpha \\ 2(1-\alpha)\alpha & \alpha^2 + (1-\alpha)^2 \end{bmatrix} = \begin{bmatrix} 1-2(1-\alpha)\alpha & 2(1-\alpha)\alpha \\ 2(1-\alpha)\alpha & 1-2(1-\alpha)\alpha \end{bmatrix}.$$

We now construct a backward chain. Note first

$$\begin{aligned}\Pr(s_{t-1}=A|s_t=A) &= \frac{\Pr(s_t=A|s_{t-1}=A)\Pr(s_{t-1}=A)}{\Pr(s_t=A|s_{t-1}=A)\Pr(s_{t-1}=A)+\Pr(s_t=A|s_{t-1}=B)\Pr(s_{t-1}=B)} \\ &= \frac{\alpha\frac{1}{2}}{\alpha\frac{1}{2}+(1-\alpha)\frac{1}{2}} \\ &= \alpha.\end{aligned}$$

Similarly,

$$\begin{aligned}\Pr(s_{t-2}=A|s_t=B) &= \frac{\Pr(s_t=B|s_{t-2}=A)\Pr(s_{t-2}=A)}{\Pr(s_t=B|s_{t-2}=A)\Pr(s_{t-2}=A)+\Pr(s_t=B|s_{t-2}=B)\Pr(s_{t-2}=B)} \\ &= \frac{2(1-\alpha)\alpha\frac{1}{2}}{2(1-\alpha)\alpha\frac{1}{2}+(1-2(1-\alpha)\alpha)\frac{1}{2}} \\ &= 2(1-\alpha)\alpha.\end{aligned}$$

The backward chain, giving the state in either period $t-1$ or $t-2$ as a function of the current state (the former if the current state is A, the latter if B), is then given by

$$\begin{bmatrix} \alpha & 1-\alpha \\ 2(1-\alpha)\alpha & 1-2(1-\alpha)\alpha \end{bmatrix}.$$

We now reverse our view of the process, starting our numbering at the end, and think of this as a forward chain, giving the state in period $t+1$ as a function of the state in period t. The stationary distribution of this chain solves

$$[p, 1-p]\begin{bmatrix} \alpha & 1-\alpha \\ 2(1-\alpha)\alpha & 1-2(1-\alpha)\alpha \end{bmatrix} = \begin{bmatrix} p \\ 1-p \end{bmatrix},$$

giving

$$\begin{aligned} p\alpha + 2(1-\alpha)\alpha(1-p) &= p \\ 2(1-\alpha)\alpha(1-p) &= p(1-\alpha) \\ 2\alpha(1-p) &= p \\ 2\alpha - 2\alpha p &= p \\ p &= \frac{2\alpha}{1+2\alpha} \\ 1-p &= \frac{1}{1+2\alpha}. \end{aligned}$$

Now we fix a time T and calculate how many draws t will be taken from the forward chain by time T, which is given by

$$\left[\frac{2\alpha}{1+2\alpha} + \frac{1}{1+2\alpha}2\right]t = T.$$

Our expression for the population at time T is then given by

$$\begin{aligned} N_T &= (x_1^p x_2^{1-p})^t \\ &= \left(x_1^{\frac{2\alpha}{1+2\alpha}} x_2^{\frac{1}{1+2\alpha}}\right)^{\frac{T}{\frac{2\alpha}{1+2\alpha}+\frac{2}{1+2\alpha}}} \end{aligned}$$

and hence

$$\begin{aligned} \frac{1}{T}\ln N_T &= \ln\left(x_1^{\frac{2\alpha}{1+2\alpha}} x_2^{\frac{1}{1+2\alpha}}\right)^{\frac{1+2\alpha}{2+2\alpha}} \\ &= \ln\left(x_1^{\frac{2\alpha}{2+2\alpha}} x_2^{\frac{1}{2+2\alpha}}\right) \\ &= \frac{2\alpha \ln x_1 + \ln x_2}{2+2\alpha}. \end{aligned}$$

REFERENCES

Ainslie, G.W., 1992. Picoeconomics. Cambridge University Press, Cambridge.

Akerlof, G.A., 1970. The market for lemons: Quality uncertainty and the market mechanism. Q. J. Econ. 89, 488–500.

Al-Najjar, N.I., 1995. Decomposition and characterization of risk with a continuum of random variables. Econometrica 63 (5), 1195–1264.

Allais, M., 1953. Le comportement de l'homme rationnnel devant le risque, critique des postulats et axiomes de l'école Américaine. Econometrica 21, 503–546.

Aronson, E., 1995. The Social Animal. W. H. Freeman and Company, New York.

Asch, S.E., 1956. Studies of independence and conformity: A minority of one against a unanimous majority. Psychol. Monogr. 70 (416).

Banerjee, A., 1992. A simple model of herd behavior. Q. J. Econ. 107, 797–817.

Banerjee, A., Fudenberg, D., 2004. Word-of-mouth learning. Games Econ. Behav. 46, 1–22.

Barkow, J.H., Cosmides, L., Tooby, J., 1992. The Adapted Mind. Oxford University Press, Oxford.

Becker, G.S., Murphy, K.M., Werning, I., 2005. The equilibrium distribution of income and the market for status. J. Polit. Econ. 113 (2), 282–310.

Benaïm, M., Weibull, J., 2003. Deterministic approximation of stochastic evolution in games. Econometrica 71 (3), 873–903.

Bentham, J., 1791. Principles of Morals and Legislation. Doubleday, London.

Bergstrom, T.C., 1997. Storage for good times and bad: Of rats and men. Mimeo, University of California, Santa Barbara.

Bikhchandani, S., Hirshleifer, D., Welch, I., 1992. A theory of fads, fashion, custom, and cultural exchange as information cascades. J. Polit. Econ. 100, 992–1026.

Binmore, K., 1980. Nash bargaining theory III. STICERD Discussion Paper 80/15, London School of Economics.

Boyd, R., Richerson, P.J., 1985. Culture and the Evolutionary Process. University of Chicago Press, Chicago.

Boyd, R., Richerson, P.J., 1990. Group selection among alternative evolutionarily stable strategies. J. Theor. Biol. 145, 331–342.

Brickman, P., Coates, D., Janoff-Bulman, R., 1978. Lottery winners and accident victims: Is happiness relative? J. Pers. Soc. Psychol. 32 (8), 917–927.

Bulmer, M., 1997. Theoretical Evolutionary Ecology. Sinauer Associates, Inc., Sunderland, MA.

Burnham, T., Phelan, J., 2000. Mean Genes. Perseus Publishing, Cambridge.

Camerer, C., 2003. Behavioral Game Theory: Experiments in Strategic Interaction. Russell Sage Foundation and Princeton University Press, Princeton.

Camerer, C., Loewenstein, G., Rabin, M. (Eds.), Advances in Behavioral Economics. Russell Sage Foundation, New York, 2004.

Charlesworth, B., 1994. Evolution in Age-Structured Populations. Cambridge University Press, Cambridge.

Cialdini, R.B., 1988. Influence: Science and Practice. Scott, Foresman and Company, Boston.

Clark, A., 1993. Microcognition. MIT Press, Cambridge, Massachusetts.

Cole, H.L., Mailath, G.J., Postlewaite, A., 1992. Social norms, savings behavior, and growth. J. Polit. Econ. 100, 1092–1125.

Cooper, W.S., Kaplan, R.H., 2004. Adaptive "coin-flipping": A decision theoretic examination of natural selection for random individual variation. J. Theor. Biol. 94 (1), 135–151.

Cox, J.C., Sadiraj, V., 2006. Small- and large-stakes risk aversion: Implications of concavity calibration for decision theory. Games Econ. Behav. 56 (1), 45–60.

Crawford, V.P., Varian, H., 1979. Distortion of preferences and the Nash theory of bargaining. Econ. Lett. 3, 203–206.

Curry, P.A., 2001. Decision making under uncertainty and the evolution of interdependent preferences. J. Econ. Theory 98 (2), 357–369.

Dasgupta, P., Maskin, E., 2005. Uncertainty and hyperbolic discounting. Am. Econ. Rev. 95 (4), 1290–1299.

Dawkins, R., 1989. The Selfish Gene. Oxford University Press, Oxford.
Dreber, A., Hoffman, M., 2007. Portfolio selection in utero. Mimeo, Stockholm School of Economics and University of Chicago.
Duesenberry, J.S., 1949. Income, Saving, and the Theory of Consumer Behavior. Harvard University Press, Cambridge, Massachussetts.
Einon, D., 1998. How many children can one man have? Evol. Hum. Behav. 19, 413–426.
Ellison, G., Fudenberg, D., 1993. Rules of thumb for social learning. J. Polit. Econ. 101, 612–643.
Ellison, G., Fudenberg, D., 1995. Word-of-mouth communication and social learning. Q. J. Econ. 110, 95–126.
Ellsberg, D., 1961. Risk, ambiguity, and the Savage axioms. Q. J. Econ. 75, 643–669.
Elster, J., 1985. Weakness of will and the free-rider problem. Econ. Philos. 1, 231–265.
Ely, J.C., Yilankaya, O., 2000. Nash equilibrium and the evolution of preferences. J. Econ. Theory (2), 255–272.
Eshel, I., 1972. On the neighbor effect and the evolution of altruistic traits. Theor. Popul. Biol. 3, 258–277.
Fernandez-Villaverde, J., Mukherji, A., 2001. Can we really observe hyperbolic discounting?. Mimeo, University of Pennsylvania.
Fisher, I., 1930. The Theory of Interest, as Determined by Impatience to Spend Income and Opportunity to Invest It. MacMillan, New York.
Foley, H.J., Matlin, M.W., 2009. Sensation and Perception. Allyn and Bacon, Boston.
Frank, R.H., 1987. If homo economicus could choose his own utility function, would he want one with a conscience? Am. Econ. Rev. 77, 593–604.
Frank, R.H., 1988. Passions within Reason. Norton, New York.
Frank, R.H., 1999. Luxury Fever. Free Press, New York.
Frederick, S., Loewenstein, G., 1999. Hedonic adaptation. In: Kahneman, E.D.D., Schwartz, N. (Eds.), Well-Being: The Foundations of Hedonic Psychology. Russell Sage Foundation Press, New York, pp. 302–329.
Frederick, S., Loewenstein, G., O'Donoghue, T., 2002. Time discounting and time preference: A critical view. J. Econ. Lit. 40 (2), 351–401.
Frey, B.S., Stutzer, A., 2002a. Happiness and Economics: How the Economy and Institutions Affect Human Well-Being. Princeton University Press, Princeton.
Frey, B.S., Stutzer, A., 2002b. What can economists learn from happiness research? J. Econ. Lit. 40, 402–435.
Friedman, D., 1989. The S-shaped value function as a contrained optimum. Am. Econ. Rev. 79 (5), 1243–1248.
Friedman, M., 1953. Choice, chance, and the personal distribution of income. J. Polit. Econ. 61 (4), 277–290.
Friedman, M., Savage, L.J., 1948. The utility analysis of choices involving risk. J. Polit. Econ. 56 (4), 279–304.
Fudenberg, D., Levine, D.K., 1998. Theory of Learning in Games. MIT Press, Cambridge.
Furstenberg, H., Kesten, H., 1960. Products of random matrices. Annals of Mathematical Statistics 31 (2), 457–469.
Gardner, E.L., Lowinson, J.H., 1993. Drug craving and positive/negative hedonic brain substrates activated by addicting drugs. Seminars in the Neurosciences 5, 359–368.
Gigerenzer, G., 2002. Calculated Risks. Simon and Schuster, New York.
Gilbert, D., 2007. Stumbling on Happiness. Vintage Books, New York.
Gilboa, I., Samuelson, L., 2009. Subjectivity in inductive inference. Cowles Foundation Discussion Paper 1725, Tel Aviv University and Yale University.
Gould, S.J., Lewontin, R.C., 1979. The spandrels of San Marco and the Panglossian paradigm: A critique of the adaptionist programme. Proc. R. Soc. Lond.Ser. B 205, 581–598.
Grafen, A., 1991. Modelling in behavioural ecology. In: Krebs, J.R., Davies, N.B. (Eds.), Behavioral Ecology: An Evolutionary Approach. Blackwell Scientific Publications, Oxford, pp. 5–31.
Grafen, A., 1999. Formal Darwinism, the individual-as-maximizing-agent analogy, bet-hedging. Proc. R. Soc. Lond. Ser. B 266, 799–803.

Gul, F., Pesendorfer, W., 2001. Temptation and self-control. Econometrica 69 (6), 1403–1436.
Gul, F., Pesendorfer, W., 2008. Mindless economics. In: Caplin, A., Shotter, A. (Eds.), The Foundations of Positive and Normative Economics. Oxford University Press, New York.
Güth, W., 1995. An evolutionary approach to explaining cooperative behavior by reciprocal incentives. International Journal of Game Theory 24, 323–344.
Güth, W., Yaari, M.E., 1992. Explaining reciprocal behavior in simple strategic games: An evolutionary approach. In: Witt, U. (Ed.), Explaining Process and Change. University of Michigan Press, Ann Arbor, pp. 23–34.
Hansson, I., Stuart, C., 1990. Malthusian selection of preferences. Am. Econ. Rev. 80 (3), 529–544.
Harper, D.G.C., 1991. Communication. In: Krebs, J.R., Davies, N.B. (Eds.), Behavioural Ecology. Blackwell Scientific Publications, London, pp. 374–397.
Harvey, P.H., Martin, R.D., Clutton-Brock, T.H., 1986. Life histories in comparative perspective. In: Smuts, B.B., Cheney, D.L., Seyfarth, R.M., Wrangham, R.W., Struhsaker, T.T. (Eds.), Primate Societies. University of Chicago Press, Chicago, pp. 181–196.
Henrich, J., Boyd, R., Bowles, S., Camerer, C., Fehr, E., Gintis, H., 2004. Foundations of Human Sociality. Oxford University Press, Oxford.
Henrich, J., Boyd, R., Bowles, S., Camerer, C., Fehr, E., Gintis, H., McElreath, R., 2001. In search of Homo Economicus: Behavioral experiments in 15 small-scale societies. Am. Econ. Rev. 91 (2), 73–78.
Hofbauer, J., Sigmund, K., 1998. Evolutionary Games and Population Dynamics. Cambridge University Press, Cambridge.
Hopkins, E., Kornienko, T., 2004. Running to keep in the same place: Consumer choice as a game of status. Am. Econ. Rev. 94 (4), 1085–1107.
Houston, A.I., McNamara, J.M., 1999. Models of Adaptive Behavior. Cambridge University Press, Cambridge.
Kacelnik, A., 1997. Normative and descriptive models of decision making: Time discounting and risk sensitivity. In: Bock, G.R., Cardew, G. (Eds.), Characterizing Human Psychological Adaptations. John Wiley and Sons, New York, pp. 51–70.
Kahneman, D., Tversky, A., 1982. Judgement under uncertainty: Heuristics and biases. In: Kahneman, D., Slovic, P., Tversky, A. (Eds.), On the Psychology of Prediction. Cambridge University Press, Cambridge, pp. 48–68.
Knafo, A., Israel, S., Darvasi, A., Bachner-Melman, R., Uzefovsky, F., Cohen, L., et al., 2007. Individual differences in allocation of funds in the dictator game associated with length of the arginine vasopressin 1a receptor RS3 promoter region and correlation between RS3 length and hippocampal mRNA. Genes Brain Behav. OnlineEarly Article, doi: 10.1111/j.1601-183X.2007.00341.x.
Laibson, D., 2001. A cue-theory of consumption. Q. J. Econ. 116 (1), 81–120.
LeDoux, J., 1996. The Emotional Brain. Simon and Schuster, New York.
Leslie, P.H., 1945. On the use of matrices in certain population mathematics. Biometrica 33 (3), 183–212.
Leslie, P.H., 1948. Some further notes on the use of matrices in population mathematics. Biometrica 35 (1–2), 213–245.
Leutenegger, W., 1982. Encephalization and obstetrics in primates with particular reference to human evolution. In: Armstrong, E., Falk, D. (Eds.), Primate Brain Evolution: Methods and Concepts. Plenum Press, New York, pp. 85–95.
Lipsey, R.G., Lancaster, K., 1956. The general theory of second best. Rev. Econ. Stud. 24 (1), 11–32.
Loewenstein, G., 1996. Out of control: Visceral influences on behavior. Organ. Behav. Hum. Decis. Process. 65, 272–292.
Loewenstein, G., Prelec, D., 1992. Anomalies in intertemporal choice: Evidence and an interpretation. Q. J. Econ. 107, 573–598.
Loewenstein, G., Schkade, D., 1999. Wouldn't it be nice? Predicting future feelings. In: Kahneman, D., Diener, E., Schwarz, N. (Eds.), Well-Being: The Foundations of Hedonic Psychology. Russell Sage Foundation, New York, pp. 85–105.
Loewenstein, G., Thaler, R., 1989. Anomalies: Intertemporal choice. J. Econ. Perspect. 3, 181–193.
Mailath, G.J., 1998. Do people play Nash equilibrium? Lessons from evolutionary game theory. J. Econ. Lit. 36, 1347–1374.

Maynard Smith, J., 1964. Group selection and kin selection. Nature 201, 1145–1147.
Maynard Smith, J., 1998. Evolutionary Genetics, second ed. Oxford University Press, Oxford.
Mercer, J.G., Adam, C.L., Morgan, P.J., 2000. Towards an understanding of physiological body mass regulation: Seasonal animal models. Nutr. Neurosci. 3, 307–320.
Milton, K., 1988. Foraging behavior and the evolution of primate cognition. In: Byrne, R.W., Whiten, A., (Eds.), Machiavellian Intellegence: Social Expertise and the Evolution of Intellect in Monkeys, Apes and Humans. Clarendon Press, Oxford, pp. 285–305.
Mineka, S., Cook, M., 1993. Mechanisms involved in the operational conditioning of fear. J. Exp. Psychol. Gen. 122, 23–38.
Mischel, W., Shoda, Y., Rodriguez, M.L., 1992. Delay of gratification in children. In: Loewenstein, G., Elster, J. (Eds.), Choice over Time. Russell Sage, New York.
Nau, R.F., McCardle, K.F., 1990. Coherent behavior in noncooperative games. J. Econ. Theory 50 (2), 424–444.
Netzer, N., 2009. Evolution of time preferences and attitudes towards risk. Am. Econ. Rev. 99 (3), 937–955.
Neumark, D., Postlewaite, A., 1998. Relative income concerns and the rise in married women's employment. J. Public Econ. 70, 157–183.
Nöldeke, G., Samuelson, L., 2005. Information-based relative consumption effects: Correction. Econometrica 73, 1383–1387.
O'Donoghue, T., Rabin, M., 1999a. Doing it now or later. Am. Econ. Rev. 89 (1), 103–124.
O'Donoghue, T., Rabin, M., 1999b. Incentives for procrastinators. Q. J. Econ. 114 (3), 769–816.
Ok, E., Vega-Redondo, F., 2000. On the evolution of individualistic preferences: An incomplete information scenario. J. Econ. Theory 97 (2), 231–254.
Ostrom, E., 2000. Collective action and the evolution of social norms. J. Econ. Perspect. 14 (3), 137–158.
Peacock, A.T., 1952. The Theory of the Market Economy. William Hodge, London.
Petry, C.J., Nicholas Hales, C., 2000. Long-term effects on offspring of intrauterine exposure to deficits in nutrition. Hum. Reprod. Update 6, 578–586.
Pinker, S., 1997. How the Mind Works. W. W. Norton, New York.
Pluchik, R., 1984. Emotions: A general psychoevolutionary theory. In: Scherer, K.R., Ekman, P. (Eds.), Approaches to Emotion. Erlbaum, Hillsdale, NJ, pp. 197–219.
Pollak, R.A., 1968. Consistent planning. Rev. Econ. Stud. 35 (2), 201–208.
Postlewaite, A., 1998. The social basis of interdependent preferences. Eur. Econ. Rev. 42 (3–5), 779–800.
Rabin, M., 1998. Psychology and economics. J. Econ. Lit. 36, 11–46.
Rabin, M., 2000. Risk aversion and expected-utility theory: A calibration theorem. Econometrica 68, 1281–1292.
Ravelli, A.C.J., van der Meulen, J.H.P., Osmond, C., Barker, D.J.P., Bleker, O.P., 1999. Obesity at the age of 50 y in men and women exposed to famine prenatally. Am. J. Clin. Nutr. 70, 811–816.
Ray, D., Robson, A.J., 2010. Status, intertemporal choice, and risk-taking. Technical report. New York University and Simon Fraser University.
Rayo, L., Becker, G., 2007. Evolutionary efficiency and happiness. J. Polit. Econ. 115 (2), 302–337.
Ridley, M., 1993. The Red Queen. Penguin Books, New York.
Ridley, M., 2003. Nature via Nurture: Genes, Experience, and What Makes Us Human. Harper Collins Publishers, New York.
Robson, A.J., 1990. Efficiency in evolutionary games: Darwin, Nash, and the secret handshake. J. Theor. Biol. 144, 379–396.
Robson, A.J., 1992. Status, the distribution of wealth, private and social attitudes to risk. Econometrica 60 (4), 837–857.
Robson, A.J., 1996. A biological basis for expected and non-expected utility. J. Econ. Theory 68 (2), 397–424.
Robson, A.J., 1996. The evolution of attitudes to risk: Lottery tickets and relative wealth. Games Econ. Behav. 14, 190–207.
Robson, A.J., 2001. The biological basis of economic behavior. J. Econ. Lit. 39 (1), 11–33.
Robson, A.J., 2001. Why would nature give individuals utility functions? J. Polit. Econ. 109 (4), 900–914.

Robson, A.J., 2008. Group selection. In: Durlauf, S.N., Blume, L.E. (Eds.), New Palgrave Dictionary of Economics. Palgrave Macmillan, New York.

Robson, A.J., Samuelson, L., 2007. The evolution of intertemporal preferences. Am. Econ. Rev. 97 (2 (May)), 496–500.

Robson, A.J., Samuelson, L., 2009. The evolution of time preference with aggregate uncertainty. Am. Econ. Rev. 99, 1925–1953.

Robson, A.J., Samuelson, L., 2010. The evolutionary optimality of decision and experienced utility. Working paper, Simon Fraser University and Yale University.

Robson, A.J., Szentes, B., 2008. Evolution of time preference by natural selection: Comment. Am. Econ. Rev. 98 (3), 1178–1188.

Robson, A.J., Szentes, B., Iantchev, E., 2010. The evolutionary basis of time preference: Intergenerational transfers and sex. Mimeo, Simon Fraser University and the London School of Economics.

Rogers, A.R., 1994. Evolution of time preference by natural selection. Am. Econ. Rev. 84 (2), 460–481.

Rubinstein, A., 2003. "Economics and Psychology"?: The case of hyperbolic discounting. Int. Econ. Rev. 44, 1207–1216.

Samuelson, L., 1997. Evolutionary Games and Equilibrium Selection. MIT Press, Cambridge.

Samuelson, L., 2001. Introduction to the evolution of preferences. J. Econ. Theory 97, 225–230.

Samuelson, L., 2004. Information-based relative consumption effects. Econometrica 72 (1), 93–118.

Samuelson, L., Swinkels, J., 2006. Information and the evolution of the utility function. Theoretical Economics 1, 119–142.

Samuelson, P., 1937. A note on the measurement of utility. Rev. Econ. Stud. 4, 155–161.

Savage, L.J., 1972. The Foundations of Statistics. Dover Publications, New York (originally 1954).

Schelling, T., 1980. The Strategy of Conflict. Harvard University Press, Cambridge, MA (first edition 1960).

Schelling, T., 1984. Self-command in practice, in policy, and in a theory of rational choice. Am. Econ. Rev. 74 (1), 1–11.

Seabright, P., 2005. The Company of Strangers: A Natural History of Economic Life. Princeton University Press, Princeton.

Seneta, E., 1981. Non-Negative Matrices and Markov Chains. Springer Verlag, New York.

Shafir, E., Simonson, I., Tversky, A., 1993. Reason-based choice. Cognition 49, 11–36.

Siegel, S., 1979. The role of conditioning in drug tolerance and addiction. In: Keehn, J.D. (Ed.), Psychopathalogy in Animals: Research and Treatment Implications. Academic Press, New York.

Slovic, P., 2000. The Perception of Risk. Earthscan Publications, London.

Slovic, P., Fishhoff, B., Lichtenstein, S., 1982. Why study risk perception? Risk Anal. 2 (2), 83–93.

Smith, T.G., 2004. The McDonald's equilibrium: Advertising, empty calories, and the endogenous determination of dietary preferences. Soc. Choice Welfare 23 (3), 383–413.

Sober, E., Wilson, D.S., 1998. Unto Others. Harvard University Press, Cambridge, Massachusetts.

Sozou, P.D., 1998. On hyperbolic discounting and uncertain hazard rates. Proc. R. Soc. Lond.Ser. B 265 (1409), 2015–2020.

Stearns, S.C., Hoekstra, R.F., 2005. Evolution: An Introduction, second ed. Oxford University Press, Oxford.

Strotz, R.H., 1956. Myopia and inconsistency in dynamic utility maximization. Rev. Econ. Stud. 23 (3), 165–180.

Tanny, D., 1981. On multitype branching processes in a random environment. Adv. Appl. Probab. 13 (3), 464–497.

Thaler, R.H., 1994. Quasi-Rational Economics. Russell Sage Foundation, New York.

Thaler, R.H., Shefrin, H.M., 1981. An economic theory of self-control. J. Polit. Econ. 89 (2), 392–406.

Trémblay, L., Schultz, W., 1999. Relative reward preference in primate orbitofrontal cortex. Nature 398, 704–708.

Tversky, A., Simonson, I., 1993. Context-dependent preferences. Manag. Sci. 39, 1179–1189.

van Damme, E., 1991. Stability and Perfection of Nash Equilibria. Springer-Verlag, Berlin.

Veblen, T., 1899. The Theory of the Leisure Class. MacMillan, New York.

Vega-Redondo, F., 1996. Evolution, Games, and Economic Behavior. Oxford University Press, Oxford.

von Stackelberg, H., 1934. Marktform und Gleichgewicht. Julius Springer, Vienna.
Weibull, J.W., 1995. Evolutionary Game Theory. MIT Press, Cambridge.
Williams, G.C., 1966. Adaptation and Natural Selection. Princeton University Press, Princeton.
Wilson, M., Daly, M., 1997. Life expectancy, economic inequality, homicide, and reproductive timing in Chicago neighborhoods. Br. Med. J. 314 (7089), 1271.
Wilson, R.B., 1985. Reputations in games and markets. In: Roth, A.E. (Ed.), Game-Theoretic Models of Bargaining. Cambridge University Press, Cambridge, pp. 27–62.
Wolpert, D.H., Leslie, D.S., 2009. The effects of observational limitations on optimal decision making. NASA Ames Research Center and Department of Mathematics, University of Bristol.
Wynne-Edwards, V.C., 1962. Animal Dispersion in Relation to Social Behavior. Oliver and Boyd, Edinburgh.
Wynne-Edwards, V.C., 1986. Evolution Through Group Selection. Blackwell Scientific Publications, Oxford.
Yaari, M.E., 1965. Uncertain lifetime, life insurance, and the theory of the consumer. Rev. Econ. Stud. 32 (1), 137–158.
Young, P., 1998. Individual Strategy and Social Structure. Princeton University Press, Princeton.
Zaghloul, K.A., Blanco, J.A., Weidemann, C.T., McGill, K., Jaggi, J.L., Baltuch, G.H., Kahana, M.J., 2009. Human substantia nigra neurons encode unexpected financial rewards. Science 323, 1496–1499.

CHAPTER 8

Social Norms

Mary A. Burke and H. Peyton Young
Forthcoming in *The Handbook of Social Economics*, edited by Alberto Bisin, Jess Benhabib, and Matthew Jackson. Amsterdam: North-Holland.

Contents

1. Background 312
2. Norms, Customs, and Conventions 313
3. Characteristic Features of Norm Dynamics 314
   Local conformity/global diversity 314
   Conformity warp 315
   Punctuated equilibrium 316
   Long-run stability 316
4. Social Interactions and Social Norms 317
5. A Model of Norm Dynamics 318
6. Contractual Norms in Agriculture 321
7. Medical Treatment Norms 327
8. Body Weight Norms 331
   The model 331
   Predictions and evidence 333
9. Concluding Discussion 334
References 336
Further Reading 338

Abstract

Social norms are customary or ideal forms of behavior to which individuals in a group try to conform. From an analytical standpoint, the key feature of social norms is that they induce a positive feedback loop between individual and group behavior: the more widely that a norm is practiced by members of a group, the more strongly others are motivated to practice it too. In this chapter we show how to model this type of process using evolutionary game theory. The theory suggests that norm dynamics have several distinctive features. First, behavior within a group will be more uniform than if people optimized solely according to their personal preferences, that is, individual choices will be shifted in the direction of the average choice (*conformity warp*); second, there will be greater variability between groups than within groups (*local conformity/global diversity*); third, norm dynamics tend to be characterized by long periods of inertia punctuated by occasional large changes (*punctuated equilibrium*). We study these and other effects in the context of three examples: contractual norms in agriculture, norms of medical practice, and body weight norms.
JEL Classification: C73, D02

Handbook of Social Economics, Volume 1A
ISSN 0169-7218, DOI: 10.1016/S0169-7218(11)01008-2

Keywords

Norm
convention
increasing returns
dynamical systems
stochastic stability
evolutionary game theory

1. BACKGROUND

Social norms and customs shape many economic decisions, but they have not always been at the forefront of economic analysis. Indeed, social influences were more prominently acknowledged by the founders of the discipline than by neoclassical theorists of the last century. J.S. Mill, for example, argued that custom was a potent force in setting the terms of contracts and also the wages paid to labor: "[T]he division of produce is the result of two determining agencies: competition and custom. It is important to ascertain the amount of influence which belongs to each of these causes, and in what manner the operation of one is modified by the other. . . Political economists in general, and English political economists above others, have been accustomed to lay almost exclusive stress upon the first of these agencies; to exaggerate the effect of competition, and to take into little account the other and conflicting principle." [Mill, 1848, Book II, Chapter IV].

Later, Marshall pointed to the effects of custom on the dynamics of economic adjustment, suggesting that they would make adjustment *sticky* and *punctuated by sudden jumps*: "The constraining force of custom and public opinion. . . resembled the force which holds rain-drops on the lower edges of a window frame: the repose is complete till the window is violently shaken, and then they fall together. . ." [Marshall, 1920, p. 641].

Unfortunately, the difficulty of making such dynamic arguments precise led to their being put on the back burner for many years. Meanwhile an opposing view took hold in which individuals' choices were treated as if they were mediated only by prices and self-regarding preferences; norms, customs, and social influences were treated as secondary effects that could be safely ignored. This position was stated in a particularly stark form by Frank Knight as one of the pre-conditions for perfect competition: "Every person is to act as an individual only, in entire independence of all other persons. To complete his independence he must be free from social wants, prejudices, preferences, or repulsions, or any values which are not completely manifested in market dealing." [Knight, 1921, p.78]

In recent decades there has been a return to the earlier point of view, which acknowledges that individual choices are mediated by norms, customs, and other forms of social influence. The aim of this chapter is to provide an overview of recent work that shows how to incorporate norms into economic models, and how they affect the dynamics of economic adjustment. Given space limitations it is impossible to do justice to the many varied ways in which norms have been modeled in the recent literature; [1] instead, we shall focus on a trio of models that illustrate the approach in three different settings: contractual norms in agriculture, norms of medical practice, and body weight norms. While the specific mechanisms of norm enforcement differ across these cases, it turns out that certain qualitative features of the dynamics cut across many different applications, just as Marshall suggested.

2. NORMS, CUSTOMS, AND CONVENTIONS

We define a *social norm* as a standard, customary, or ideal form of behavior to which individuals in a social group try to conform. We do not believe it is fruitful to draw a distinction between norms and conventions, as some authors have tried to do. In our view there is no simple dichotomy between the two concepts, based for example on whether or not the behavior is enforced by third parties. We would argue that there is a constellation of internal and external mechanisms that hold norms in place, and that the salience of these factors varies from one situation to another. In some societies, for example, it is a norm to avenge an insult. A person who is insulted and does not avenge his honor will lose social status and may be severely ostracized. In this case the norm is held in place by third-party sanctions.[2] However, consider the norm against littering in public areas. People are often in a situation where they can litter without being observed, nevertheless they may refrain from doing so because they would not think well of themselves. In this case, the norm is held in place by an internalized sense of proper or moral conduct.

As a third example, consider the norm of extending the right hand in greeting. This solves a simple coordination problem: there is no need for third party enforcement or internalized codes of conduct. Thus one might say it is "merely" a convention, but this distinction is not particularly useful, because the desire to conform may be just as strong for conventions as for norms. Furthermore, adhering to convention does more than solve a coordination problem, it signals one's attentiveness to the nuances of social interaction. Extending one's left hand would not only cause a momentary coordination failure, it would raise questions about what the act might mean.

[1] Contributions that we will not have space to consider in detail include Akerlof [1980, 1997], Becker and Murphy [2000], Bicchieri [2006], Coleman [1987], Elster [1989], Hechter and Opp [2001], Lewis [1969], Schotter [1981], and Ullman-Margalit [1977]. For a survey of modeling and identification issues in the presence of social interactions see Durlauf and Young [2001]. Postlewaite (this volume) discusses the interaction between preferences and social norms.

[2] Experimental evidence suggests that subjects are willing to punish norm violators even at some cost tothemselves [Fehr, Fischbacher, and Gächter, 2002; Fehr and Fischbacher, 2004a,b].

We prefer, therefore, to view social norms as encompassing both conventions and customs, and not to draw fine distinctions between them according to the mechanisms that hold them in place. The key property of a social norm from a modeling standpoint is that it induces a positive feedback loop between expectations and behaviors: the more widely that members of a social group practice a behavior, the more it becomes expected, thus reinforcing adherence.

In its simplest form, this type of feedback loop can be modeled by a coordination game. Suppose that members of a group interact randomly and in pairs, and that each interaction involves playing a coordination game with two actions: Left and Right. A norm is a situation in which the population in general plays one or the other, and everyone has come to expect this. In other words, a social norm corresponds to a pure equilibrium of a coordination game that is played repeatedly by members of a population, with the proviso that the equilibrium is not conditional on who is playing. Note that this framework can be extended to include more complex games in which the equilibrium involves punishments for deviation. The relevant point is that the equilibrium holds at the *population* level, inducing common expectations and behaviors for an interaction that is repeated over time by members of a social group. The framework can be extended still further by incorporating both individual and interactive terms into the analysis. In other words, an agent's utility may derive in part from his idiosyncratic preference for a particular action, and in part from the extent to which the action dovetails with the actions of others. This set-up allows one to explore the interaction between positive feedback loops due to social norms, and (possibly negative) feedback loops induced by competing demands for ordinary consumption goods.

3. CHARACTERISTIC FEATURES OF NORM DYNAMICS

Before turning to specific applications, however, we wish to draw attention to certain characteristic features of models in which social norms play a role. We shall single out four such features: local conformity/global diversity, conformity warp, punctuated equilibrium, and long-run stability. We briefly discuss these features below without specifying the models in detail; these will be considered in subsequent sections.

Local conformity/global diversity

When agents interact in a social group and there are positive feedback effects between expectations and behaviors, there will be a tendency for the population to converge to a common behavior, which can be interpreted as a social norm. Frequently, however, there are alternative behaviors that can form an equilibrium at the population level (e.g., different coordination equilibria in a pure coordination game), so there is indeterminacy in the particular social norm that will eventually materialize. Suppose that society is composed of distinct subgroups or "villages" such that social interactions occur within each village but not between them. Starting from arbitrary initial conditions, different villages may well end up with different norms. That is, there will be near-uniformity of behavior within each village and substantially different behaviors across villages. This is the *local conformity/global diversity effect.* It turns out that this effect is present even when society is not partitioned into distinct villages: it suffices that ties across subgroups are relatively weak, or that the strength of interactions falls off with geographic (or social) distance. This effect is discussed in two of our case studies: the choice of agricultural contracts and the choice of medical practices, where in both cases the effect has strong empirical support.

Conformity warp

When social interactions are not present, agents usually optimize based on their personal preferences, that is, their actions are determined by their "types." For example, people vary considerably in their natural body weights, depending on genetic inheritance and other factors such as age, education level, and idiosyncratic preferences for food and exercise. Absent social norms, weight would be determined solely by such individual factors, together with economic constraints such as food prices. If, however, a social norm about appropriate or desirable body weight is in force within a group, its members will try to conform to the norm, which implies that *some people make choices that are warped away from the choices they would make if there were no norm.*

Testing for this effect empirically is complicated by the fact that the "warp" could arise from some unobserved common factor rather than from a social norm. For example, in a region in which food prices are low, people will tend to be heavier than they would in an environment with more expensive food. While it may be possible to control for food prices, other common factors may be unknown or unobservable. However, if there is an observable *exogenous* factor that affects individual weight, such as a genetic marker, one can use the group prevalence of that factor as an instrument for the group's average weight and test whether average weight affects individual weight, controlling for the genetic marker at the individual level. If social body weight norms are operative, the weights of those in the genetic minority will be warped away from what would be predicted based on their genetic type, towards the size predicted by the group's average genetic makeup.[3]

We first identified this warping effect in connection with the choice of agricultural contracts [Young and Burke, 2001]. In that setting, a natural predictor of contract choice (absent social effects) is the soil quality on a given farm. (Higher soil qualities produce naturally higher yields, which should be reflected in improved terms for the landowner.) What we find, however, is that contract choice is remarkably uniform

[3] For this to be a valid instrument, the group average trait must have no direct effect on the individual, controlling for her own trait, and must not predict other, unobserved individual traits that affect weight.

across farms with different soil qualities that are located in the same region (a regional norm). Moreover, the terms of a regional norm correspond more or less to the average soil quality within that region. Consequently, regional outliers (farms with exceptionally low or high soil quality for that region) tend to have contracts whose terms differ substantially from the terms that would hold if they were the only farms (or if social interactions were not present). A similar phenomenon arises in regional variations in medical treatment, as we discuss in the second case study below.

Punctuated equilibrium

One consequence of increasing returns is that a social norm, once established, may be quite difficult to dislodge even when circumstances change. In particular, incremental changes in external conditions (e.g., prices) may have no effect, because they are not large enough to overcome the positive feedback effects that hold the norm in place. In short, it may take a very large change in conditions before a norm shift is observed, which is precisely the effect to which Marshall was referring in his raindrops example.

A second way in which norms can shift is through the accumulation of many small changes in behaviors. The process is analogous to mutation: suppose that, by chance, some doctors in a particular region happen to experiment with a new procedure. Their experience will rub off on their colleagues, who may then be more inclined to try it than they otherwise would be. If enough of these (positive) experiences accumulate, a tipping point is reached in which an existing treatment norm is displaced in favor of a new one. Note that, unlike an exogenously induced norm shift, this type of shift will appear to be spontaneous.

Long-run stability

The incorporation of stochastic shocks into the dynamic adjustment process leads to the striking prediction that some norms are much more likely than others to be observed over the long run. The reason is that the likelihood of norm displacement, due to an accumulation of small stochastic shocks, depends on the "depth" of the basin of attraction in which the norm lies. This fact can be exploited to estimate the probability that different norms will be observed in the long run, using techniques from the theory of large deviations in stochastic dynamical systems theory [Freidlin and Wentzell, 1984; Foster and Young, 1990; Young, 1993a; Kandori, Mailath, and Rob, 1993]. Moreover when the shocks have very small probability and are independent across actors, the theory shows that only a few norms (frequently a unique norm) will have nonnegligible long-run probability. These norms are said to be *stochastically stable* [Foster and Young, 1990].

This effect is discussed in some detail in our case study on contractual norms in agriculture. Here the theory makes two specific predictions: i) contractual terms will tend to be locally uniform even though there is substantial heterogeneity in the quality of the inputs (labor and land), which in neoclassical theory would call for similar heterogeneity in the contracts, and ii) contractual terms may differ markedly between regions, with sharp jumps observed between neighboring regions, rather than more or less continuous variation.

4. SOCIAL INTERACTIONS AND SOCIAL NORMS

Models involving social interactions have proved particularly useful in capturing a variety of phenomena that exhibit local uniformity, together with diversity in average behavior across regions or groups that exceeds the variation in fundamentals across such units. Relevant examples include the use of addictive substances, dropping out of school, and criminal behavior [Case and Katz,1991; Glaeser, Sacerdote and Scheinkman, 1996]. The framework constitutes a tractable and powerful way to describe variation in social norms across societies and over time—allowing for considerable within-group heterogeneity—where the distribution of behaviors and the social norm exhibit mutual causality. A *social interaction* occurs when the payoff to an individual from taking an action is increasing in the prevalence of that action among the relevant set of social contacts. As we illustrate in three examples below, the choice model is not a pure coordination game. Rather, agents trade off private incentives against social rewards or penalties, and conformity may be incomplete. Interactions may be either local or global—in the latter case, agents optimize against the mean action of the entire population, whereas in the former the social interaction occurs only with a local subset of the population. The assumption that agents benefit from behaving similarly to others—an example of strategic complementarity—gives rise to a *social multiplier*, such that the effect of variation in fundamentals is amplified in the aggregate relative to a situation involving socially isolated choices.[4]

Social interactions may accelerate shifts in social norms over time initiated by technological change and other shocks—that is, interactions may lead to punctuated equilibria. For example, Goldin and Katz [2002] link the birth control pill, via direct effects as well as indirect, social multiplier effects, to the dramatic increases in women's career investment and age of first marriage in the 1970s. Contraception has also been linked to the large increase in out-of-wedlock births since the 1960s [Akerlof, Yellen and Katz, 1996]. The technology's direct impact served, via social interactions, to erode the social stigma against such births. As shown below, there is evidence that social multiplier effects have magnified the impact of falling food prices on obesity rates in the United States in recent decades and led to a larger value of the social norm for body size [Burke and Heiland, 2007].

[4] Canonical models of social interactions are provided by Brock and Durlauf [2001], Becker and Murphy [2000], and Glaeser and Scheinkman, [2003]. See Burke [2008] and Glaeser, Sacerdote, and Scheinkman [2003] for further discussion of social multipliers.

5. A MODEL OF NORM DYNAMICS

We turn now to the question of how social norms arise in the first place. If they represent equilibrium behaviors in situations with multiple equilibria, how does society settle on any particular one starting from out-of-equilibrium conditions? To model this situation, imagine a population of players who interact over time, where each interaction entails playing a certain game G. For expositional simplicity we shall assume that G is a two-person game; the general framework extends to the n-person case. We shall make the following assumptions:

i) Players do not necessarily know what is going on in the society at large; their information may be local, based on hearsay, and on personal experience.

ii) Players behave adaptively—for the most part, they choose best replies given their current information.

iii) Players occasionally deviate from best responses for a variety of unmodeled reasons; we represent these as stochastic shocks to their choices.

iv) Players interact at random, though possibly with some bias toward their geographical or social "neighbors."

We wish to examine how behaviors evolve in such a population over time starting from arbitrary initial conditions. In particular, we would like to know whether behaviors converge to some form of population equilibrium (a social norm), and, if so, whether some norms are more likely to emerge than others are.

To be concrete, let us assume that G is a symmetric two-person coordination game, where each player chooses an action from a finite set X. Given a pair of actions, (x,x'), denote the payoff to the first player by $u(x, x')$, and the payoff to the second player by $u(x', x)$. We assume that each of the pairs (x, x) is a strict Nash equilibrium of the one-time game.

Now consider a population of n players who interact pairwise. The "proximity" of two players i and j is given by a weight $w_{ij} \geq 0$, where we assume that $w_{ij} = w_{ji}$. We can think of w_{ij} as the relative probability that two players will interact, or the importance of their interaction, or some combination thereof.

Consider a discrete-time process with periods $t = 1, 2, 3, \ldots$. At the end of period t, the *state* of the system is given by an n-vector $\boldsymbol{x}(t)$, where $x_i(t) \in X$ is the current strategy choice by player i, $1 \leq i \leq n$. The state space is denoted by $\mathbf{X} = X^n$. Assume that players update their strategies asynchronously: at the start of period $t+1$, one agent is chosen at random to update. Call this agent i. Given the choices of everyone else, which we denote by $\boldsymbol{x}_{-i}(t)$, the expected utility of agent i from choosing action x is defined to be

$$U_i(x, \boldsymbol{x}_{-i}(t)) = \sum_j w_{ij} u(x, x_j(t)).$$

Assume that i chooses a new action $x_i(t+1) = x$ with a probability that is non-decreasing in its expected utility, where all actions have a positive probability of being chosen. A particularly convenient functional form is the logistic response function

$$P[x_i = x] = e^{\beta U_i(x, \boldsymbol{x}_{-i}(t))} / \sum_{x' \in \boldsymbol{X}} e^{\beta U_i(x', \boldsymbol{x}_{-i}(t))}.$$

This is also known as a *log-linear response function*, because the difference in the log-probabilities of any two actions is a linear increasing function of the difference in their expected payoffs [Blume, 2003; Young, 1998a].[5]

This adjustment rule is convenient to work with because the Markov learning process has a stationary distribution that takes an especially simple form. Define the potential function $\rho : \boldsymbol{X} \rightarrow R$ such that for every state $\boldsymbol{x} \in \boldsymbol{X}$,

$$\rho(\boldsymbol{x}) = \sum_{i,j} w_{ij} u(x_i, x_j).$$

Theorem. The unique stationary distribution of the Markov learning process is

$$\mu(\boldsymbol{x}) = e^{\beta\rho(\boldsymbol{x})} / \sum_{x' \in \boldsymbol{X}} e^{\beta\rho(\boldsymbol{x}')}, \qquad (1)$$

that is, from any initial state, the long-run frequency of state $\boldsymbol{x}$ is $\mu(\boldsymbol{x})$.

Corollary. When β is high (agents best respond with high probability), the state(s) that maximize potential are the most probable, and when β is very large the state(s) that maximize potential have probability close to one. These are known as the *stochastically stable states* of the evolutionary process [Foster and Young, 1990].[6]

Many variants of this approach have been discussed in the literature. One variation is to suppose that each agent reacts to a random sample of current (or past) choices by other agents [Young, 1993a]. This captures the idea that agents typically have limited information based on personal experience and local contacts. Other variations are obtained by assuming that deviations from best response follow a distribution that differs from the logistic. For example, one could assume that all non-best response strategies are chosen with equal probability (mutations are purely random). Under this assumption the long-run dynamics cannot be expressed in a simple closed form such as (1); nevertheless it is reasonably straightforward to characterize the states that have high probability in the long run [Young, 1993a].

The evolutionary approach can also be adapted to non-symmetric games involving two or more players. Given an n-person game G, assume that the population can be divided into n disjoint subpopulations, one for each "role" in the game. In each period a set of n individuals is selected at random, one from each subpopulation, and they play

[5] This is a standard representation of discrete choice behavior, and can be justified as a best-response function when an agent's utility is subjected to a random utility shock that is extreme-value distributed [Mcfadden, 1974; Durlauf, 1997; Brock and Durlauf, 2001].

[6] This term can be stated quite generally as follows: a state of a perturbed Markov chain is stochastically stable if its long-run probability is bounded away from zero for arbitrarily small perturbations.

G. As in the previous models, each agent best responds with high probability to an estimate of the frequency distribution of choices by other agents [Young, 1993a].

Different stochastic adjustment rules can yield different predictions about the specific equilibria that are most likely to emerge over the long run. For certain important classes of games, however, the predictions are reasonably consistent across a wide range of modeling details. We mention two such results here.

A two-person game G is a *pure coordination game* if each player has the same number of strategies, and the strategies can be indexed so that it is a strict Nash equilibrium to match strategies, i.e., when one player uses his k^{th} strategy, the other's unique best response is her k^{th} strategy. Note that this definition does not presume that the players' strategies are the same, or that they have the same payoff functions.

A natural example of such a game arises when players must first agree on the rules of the game. Consider, for example, a two-person interaction in which the rules can take m different forms. Before they can interact, the players must agree on the rules that will govern their interaction. If they agree on the kth set of rules, they play the game and get the expected payoffs (a_k, b_k). If they fail to agree their payoffs are zero. Assume that all versions of the game are worth playing, that is, $a_k, b_k > 0$ for all k. This is a pure coordination game. A population-level equilibrium in which everyone plays by the same set of rules can be viewed as a social norm. It can be shown that, under a fairly wide range of stochastic best response rules, such a process will select an *efficient norm*: an equilibrium whose payoffs are not strictly dominated by the payoffs in some alternative equilibrium [Kandori and Rob, 1995; Young, 1998b].[7]

A second general result applies to 2×2 games, that is, two-person games in which each player has exactly two strategies. We can write the payoff matrix of such a game as follows:

$$\begin{bmatrix} a_{11}, b_{11} & a_{12}, b_{12} \\ a_{21}, b_{21} & a_{22}, b_{22} \end{bmatrix}$$

Assume that this is a coordination game, that is,

$$a_{11} > a_{21},\ b_{11} > b_{12},\ a_{22} > a_{12},\ b_{22} > b_{21}$$

Equilibrium (1, 1) is *risk dominant* if $(a_{11} - a_{21})(b_{11} > b_{12}) > (a_{22} - a_{12})(b_{22} - b_{21})$, whereas equilibrium (2, 2) is *risk dominant* if the reverse inequality holds strictly. Notice that this definition coincides with efficiency if the off-diagonal payoffs are zero (as in a pure coordination game), but otherwise risk dominance and efficiency may differ. It can be shown that, under fairly general assumptions, the risk dominant equilibrium is stochastically stable in an evolutionary process based on perturbed best responses [Blume, 2003].

[7] Moreover, when the set of feasible payoffs approximates a convex bargaining set, and the perturbations are uniformly distributed, the stochastically stable equilibrium corresponds very closely to the Kalai-Smorodinsky solution [Young, 1998a,b].

Although evolutionary models of norm formation differ in certain details, they have several *qualitative implications* that hold under a wide range of assumptions. Assume that a given type of interaction can be represented as a coordination game in which the alternative equilibria correspond to different potential norms. Assume also that the evolutionary process is based on random interactions with some form of perturbed best responses by the agents. Under quite general conditions, a given population or "society" will eventually find its way toward *some* equilibrium; in other words, a social norm will become established with high probability. Within such a society there will be a high degree of uniformity in the way that people behave (and expect others to behave) in this type of interaction, though there may not be *perfect* uniformity due to the presence of idiosyncratic behaviors (mutations). Second, different societies (or subgroups that have limited interactions with one another) may arrive at different norms for solving the same type of coordination problem, due to chance events and the vagaries of history. Putting these two phenomena together, we can say that social norms lead to a high degree of conformity locally (within a given society), and possibly much greater diversity globally (among societies). This is known as the *local conformity/global diversity effect* [Young, 1998a].

Another general phenomenon predicted by evolutionary models is that social norms can spontaneously shift due to stochastic shocks. Such shifts may be precipitated by an accumulation of small changes in behaviors and expectations (mutations), by an external shock that suddenly changes agents' payoff functions, or by some form of coordinated action (e.g., a social movement). The theoretical models discussed above focus on the effect of small chance events, but the other two mechanisms are certainly important in practice. A common implication of all of these mechanisms, however, is that shifts will tend to be very rapid once a certain threshold is crossed. The reason is that the linkage between expectations and behaviors induces a highly nonlinear feedback effect: if enough people change the way that they do things (or the way they expect others to do things) everyone wants to follow suit, and the population careens toward a new equilibrium. In other words, once a norm is in place it tends to remains so for a long time, and shifts between norms tend to be sudden rather than gradual. This is known as the *punctuated equilibrium effect* [Young, 1998a].[8]

6. CONTRACTUAL NORMS IN AGRICULTURE

The framework outlined above has potential application to any situation in which social norms influence agents' decisions. In this section we apply the theory of social norms to the domain of economic contracts. In particular, we use it to illuminate

[8] The use of this term in biology is more specialized and somewhat controversial. Here we employ it merely to describe the qualitative behavior of the stochastic process over time.

the pattern of crop sharing contracts found in contemporary U.S. agriculture [Young and Burke, 2001].[9]

A *share contract* is an arrangement in which a landowner and a tenant farmer split the gross proceeds of the harvest in fixed proportions or shares. The logic of such a contract is that it shares the risk of an uncertain outcome while offering the tenant a rough-and-ready incentive to increase the expected value of that outcome.[10] When contracts are competitively negotiated, one would expect the size of the share to vary in accordance with the mean (and variance) of the expected returns, the risk aversion of the parties, the agent's quality, and other relevant factors. In practice, however, shares seem to cluster around "usual and customary" levels even when there is substantial heterogeneity among principal-agent pairs, and substantial and observable differences in the *quality* of different parcels of land. These contractual customs are pinned to psychologically prominent focal points, such as 1/2-1/2, though other shares—such as 1/3-2/3 and 2/5-3/5—are also common, with the larger share going to the tenant.

A striking feature of the Illinois data is that the above three divisions account for over 98% of all share contracts in the survey, which involved several thousand farms in all parts of the state. An equally striking feature is that the predominant or customary shares differ by region: in the northern part of the state the overwhelming majority of share contracts specify 1/2-1/2, whereas in the southern part of the state the most common shares are 1/3-2/3 and 2/5-3/5 [Illinois Cooperative Extension Service, 1995].[11] Thus, on the one hand, uniformity *within* each region exists in spite of the fact that there are substantial and easily observed differences in the soil characteristics and productivities of farms within the region. On the other hand, large differences exist *between* the regions in spite of the fact that there are many farms in both regions that have essentially the same soil productivity, so in principle they should be using the same (or similar) shares. The local interaction model discussed in the previous section can help us to understand these apparent anomalies.

Let us identify each farm i with the vertex of a graph. Each vertex is joined by edges to its immediate geographical neighbors. For ease of exposition we shall assume that the social influence weights on the edges are all the same. The *soil productivity index* on farm i, s_i, is a number that gives the expected output per acre, measured in dollars, of the soils on that particular farm. (For example, $s_i = 80$ means that total net income on farm i is, on average, \$80 per acre.) The contract on farm i specifies a share x_i for the tenant, and $1-x_i$ for the property owner, where x_i is a number between zero and one. The tenant's

[9] Applications of the theory to the evolution of bargaining norms may be found in Young [1993b] and Young [1998a, Chapter 9].

[10] Stiglitz [1974] identified this basic rationale for sharecropping contracts.

[11] This north-south division corresponds roughly to the southern boundary of the last major glaciations. In both regions, farming techniques are similar and the same crops are grown – mainly corn, soybeans, and wheat. In the north, the land tends to be flatter and more productive than in the south, though there is substantial variability within each of the regions.

expected income on farm i is therefore $x_i s_i$ times the number of acres on the farm. For expositional convenience let us assume that all farms have the same size, which we may suppose is unity. (This does not affect the analysis in any important way.)

Assume that in each period one farm (say i) is chosen at random and the contract is renegotiated. The property owner on i offers a share x_i to the tenant. The tenant accepts if and only if his expected return $x_i s_i$ is at least w_i, where w_i is the reservation wage at location i. The expected monetary return to the landlord from such a deal is $v_i(x_i) = (1 - x_i)s_i$.

To model the impact of local custom, suppose that each of i's neighbors exerts the same degree of social influence on i. Specifically, for each state $\boldsymbol{x}$, let $\delta_{ij}(\boldsymbol{x}) = 1$ if i and j are neighbors and $x_i = x_j$; otherwise let $\delta_{ij}(\boldsymbol{x}) = 0$. We assume that i's utility in state x is $(1 - \boldsymbol{x}_i)s_i + \gamma\sum_j \delta_{ij}(\boldsymbol{x})$, where γ is a *conformity parameter*. The idea is that, if a landlord offers his tenant a contract that differs from the practices of the neighbors, the tenant will be offended and may retaliate with poorer performance (given the non-contractibility of some aspects of the relationship). Hence the landlord's utility for different contracts is affected by the choices of his neighbors. The resulting potential function is

$$\sum_i (1 - x_i)s_i + (\gamma/2)\sum_{i,j} \delta_{ij}(\boldsymbol{x}).$$

The first term, $\sum_i (1 - x_i)s_i$, represents the total *rent to land*, which we shall abbreviate by $r(\boldsymbol{x})$. The expression $c(\boldsymbol{x}) = (1/2)\sum_{i,j} \delta_{ij}(\boldsymbol{x})$ represents the total number of edges (neighbor-pairs) that are coordinated on the same contract in state x, and thus measures the conformity in state x. Thus, the potential function can be written

$$\rho(\boldsymbol{x}) = r(\boldsymbol{x}) + \gamma c(\boldsymbol{x}).$$

As in (1) it follows that the stationary distribution, $\mu(\boldsymbol{x})$, has the classic Gibbs form

$$\mu(\boldsymbol{x}) \propto e^{\beta[r(\boldsymbol{x}) + \gamma c(\boldsymbol{x})]}.$$

It follows that *the log probability of each state* $\boldsymbol{x}$ *is a linear function of the total rent to land plus the degree of local conformity*. Given specific values of the conformity parameter γ and the response parameter β, we can compute the relative probability of various states of the process, and from this deduce the likelihood of different geographic distributions of contracts. In fact, one can say a fair amount about the qualitative behavior of the process even when one does not know specific values of the parameters.

We illustrate with a concrete example. Consider the hypothetical state of Torusota shown in figure 1. In the northern part of the state—above the dashed line—soils are evenly divided between High and Medium quality soils. In the southern part they are

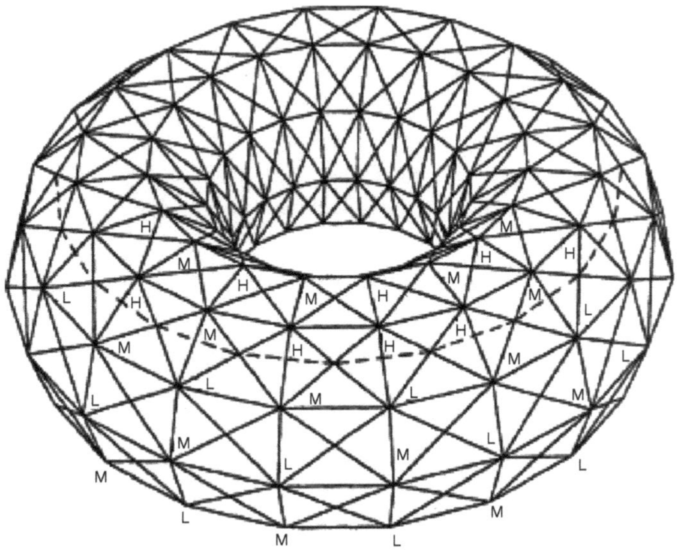

Figure 1 The hypothetical state of Torusota. Each vertex represents a farm, and soil qualities are High (H), Medium (M), or Low (L).

evenly divided between Medium and Low quality soils. The soil types are interspersed, but average soil quality is higher in the north than it is in the south.[12] Let n be the number of farms. Each farm is assumed to have exactly eight neighbors, so there are 4n edges altogether. Let us restrict the set of contracts to be in multiples of 10%: $x = 10\%$, $20\%, \ldots, 90\%$. (Contracts in which the tenant receives 0% or 100% are not considered.) For the sake of concreteness, assume that High soils have index 85, Medium soils have index 70, and Low soils have index 60. Let the reservation wage be 32 at all locations.

We wish to determine the states of the process that maximize the potential function $\rho(\boldsymbol{x})$. The answer depends, of course, on the size of γ, that is, on the tradeoff rate between the desire to conform with community norms and the amount of economic payoff one gives up in order to conform.

Consider first the case where $\gamma = 0$, that is, there are no conformity effects. Maximizing potential is then equivalent to maximizing the total rent to land, subject always to the constraint that labor earns at least its reservation wage on each class of soil. The contracts with this property are 40% on High soil, 50% on Medium soil, and 60% on Low soil. The returns to labor under this arrangement are: 34 on H, 35 on M, and 36 on L. Notice that labor actually earns a small premium over the reservation wage ($w = 32$) on each class of soil. This *quantum premium* is attributable to the discrete nature of the contracts:

[12] This is qualitatively similar to the dispersion of soil types in Illinois, which is analyzed in some detail in Young and Burke [2001].

no landlord can impose a less generous contract (rounded to the nearest 10%) without losing his tenant. Except for the quantum premium, this outcome is the same as would be predicted by a standard market-clearing model, in which labor is paid its reservation wage and all the rent goes to land. We shall call this the *competitive* or *Walrasian* state $\boldsymbol{w}$.

Notice that, in contrast to conventional equilibrium models, our framework actually gives an account of how the state $\mathbf{w}$ comes about. Suppose that the process begins in some state x^0 at time zero. As property owners and tenants renegotiate their contracts, the process gravitates towards the equilibrium state $\boldsymbol{w}$ and eventually reaches it with probability one. Moreover, if β is not too small, the process stays close to $\boldsymbol{w}$ much of the time, though it will rarely be *exactly* in equilibrium.

These points may be illustrated by simulating the process using an agent-based model. Let there be 100 farms in the North and 100 in the South, and assume a moderate level of noise ($\beta = 0.20$). Starting from a random initial seed, the process was simulated for three levels of conformity: $\gamma = 0$, 3, and 8. Figure 2 shows a typical distribution of contract shares after 1000 periods have elapsed. When $\gamma = 0$ (bottom

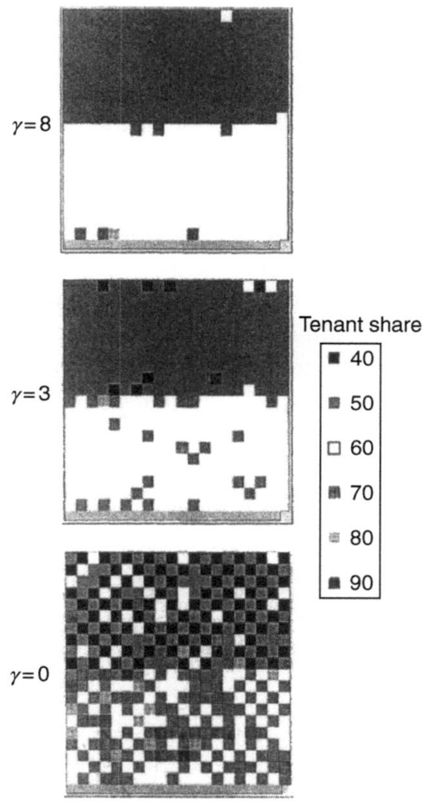

Figure 2 Simulated outcomes of the process for n = 200, β = 0.20.

panel), the contracts are matched quite closely with land quality, and the state is close to the competitive equilibrium. When the level of conformity is somewhat higher (middle panel), the dominant contract in the North is 50%, in the South it is 60%, and there are pockets here and there of other contracts. Somewhat surprisingly, however, a further increase in the conformity level (top panel) does not cause the two regional customs to merge into a single global custom; it merely leads to greater uniformity in each of the two regions.

To understand why this is so, let us suppose for the moment that everyone is using the *same* contract x. Since everyone must be earning their reservation wage, x must be at least 60%. (Otherwise Southern tenants on low quality soil would earn less than $w = 32$.) Moreover, among all such global customs, 60% maximizes the total rent to land. Hence, the 60% custom, which we shall denote by $\boldsymbol{y}$, maximizes potential among all global customs. But it does not maximize potential among all states. To see why this is so, let $\boldsymbol{z}$ be the state in which everyone in the North uses the 50% contract, while in the South everyone uses the 60% contract. State $\boldsymbol{z}$'s potential is almost as high as $\boldsymbol{y}$'s potential, because in state $\boldsymbol{z}$ the only negative social externalities are suffered by those who live near the North-South boundary. Let us assume that the number of such agents is about $\sqrt{n}$, where n is the total number of farms. Thus the *proportion* of farms near the boundary can be made as small as we like by choosing n large enough. However, $\boldsymbol{z}$ offers a higher land rent than $\boldsymbol{y}$ to all the Northern farms. To be specific, assume that there are $n/2$ farms in the north, which are divided evenly between High and Medium soils, and that there are $n/2$ farms in the south, which are evenly divided between Medium and Low soils. Then the total income difference between $\boldsymbol{z}$ and $\boldsymbol{y}$ is $7n/4$ on the Medium soil farms in the north, and $8.5n/4$ on the High soil farms in the north, for a total gain of $31n/8$. It follows that, if γ is large enough, then for all sufficiently large n, the regional custom $\boldsymbol{z}$ has higher potential than the global custom $\boldsymbol{y}$.[13]

While the details are particular to this example, the logic is quite general. Consider any distribution of soil qualities that is heterogeneous locally, but exhibits substantial shifts in average quality between geographic regions. For intermediate values of conformity γ, it is reasonable to expect that potential will be maximized by a distribution of contracts that is uniform locally, but diverse globally—in other words the distribution is characterized by *regional customs*. Such a state will typically have higher potential than the competitive equilibrium, because the latter involves substantial losses in social utility when land quality is heterogeneous. Such a state will typically also have higher potential than a global custom, because it allows landlords to capture more rent at relatively little loss in social utility, provided that the boundaries between the regions are not too long (i.e., there are relatively few farms on the boundaries).

[13] A more detailed calculation shows that $\mathbf{z}$ uniquely maximizes potential among *all* states whenever γ is sufficiently large and n is sufficiently large relative to γ.

In effect, these regional customs form a compromise between completely uniform contracts on the one hand, and fully differentiated, competitive contracts on the other. Given the nature of the model, we should not expect perfect uniformity within any given region, nor should we expect *sharp* changes in custom at the boundary. The model suggests instead that there will be occasional departures from custom within regions (due to idiosyncratic influences), and considerable variation near the boundaries. These features are observed in the empirical distribution of actual share contracts [Young and Burke, 2001].

7. MEDICAL TREATMENT NORMS

A prominent stylized fact about medical treatment is the phenomenon of "small area variations" [Wennberg and Gittelsohn, 1973, 1982]. The usage rates of caesarian section [Danielsen et al., 2000], beta blockers [Skinner and Staiger, 2005], tonsillectomy [Glover, 1938], and invasive coronary treatments [Burke et al., 2010; Chandra and Staiger, 2007}, among many other procedures, have been found to vary widely across small regions (such as hospital areas, counties, or cities) well in excess of the underlying variation in patient characteristics and other factors that predict treatment intensity [Phelps and Mooney, 1993]. Such variations suggest the presence of local medical treatment norms, norms that can be explained using a model adapted from Burke et al. [2010] in which medical decisions are subject to social influences, as described below.

In general, the best treatment for any given patient cannot be determined with certainty, either because scientific knowledge is lacking or because outcomes depend on unobservable patient characteristics. Even in cases in which clear medical practice guidelines exist, such guidelines are not followed uniformly. For example, medical guidelines recommend the administration of beta (β) blockers, an inexpensive, off-patent drug treatment invented in the 1950s, following acute myocardial infarction (AMI, or heart attack), a recommendation that is contraindicated in only about 18% of cases. Beta blockers have been shown in clinical trials to reduce post-AMI mortality by 25% or more [Gottlieb et al., 1998], and yet their usage rate was found to vary across states from a low of 44% in Mississippi to a high of 80% in Maine [Jencks et al., 2000]. Consistent with the presence of treatment variations, there is evidence that physicians respond more strongly to practice recommendations made by local peer "opinion leaders" than to impersonal recommendations such as professional practice guidelines and results of clinical trials [Soumerai et al., 1998; Bhandari et al., 2003].

To capture these facts, we model medical decisions in which the recent actions of local peers influence the subjective assessments of treatment efficacy. In this decision framework, regional treatment norms can emerge, such that a given local norm will be the treatment that is (objectively) "best" for the dominant patient type in the region. Minority-type patients may suffer welfare losses under such norms—a case of "conformity warp." The following exposition shows how regional norms emerge within a very simple, one-dimensional topology, but the results can be extended to higher-dimensional spaces.

Assume that physicians are located along a line. We index physicians by the set of integers, Z. Each physician $x \in Z$, has two neighbors, $\{x - 1, x + 1\}$. There are two types of patients, denoted α and β, and two treatments, A and B. At any given location, patients arrive one at a time at random intervals in continuous time, are treated instantaneously by the physician at that location, and then leave. The patient type is also random (between α and β), and the probability that a patient is of a given type may vary with the treatment location, as described below. The time lapse between patient arrivals at any location (the inter-arrival time) is distributed exponentially with parameter λ, which we take to be 1 without loss of generality. These assumptions ensure that at most a single treatment decision occurs at any given time at a random location in Z.

Each treatment can result in either "success" or "failure." The payoff to the patient in the event of success (or failure) is the same regardless of which procedure was used, and we normalize these payoffs to 1 (success) and 0 (failure). We assume that the true probability of success of a given procedure on a given patient type is not known with certainty by either the physician or the patient. Given this uncertainty, the physician at a given location makes a subjective assessment of the success probability of a given treatment for a given patient based on the patient's type, which we assume is observed with certainty, and based on the most recent treatment choice at each of the two adjacent treatment locations. The physician chooses a treatment, z, to maximize this subjective probability, $\pi(z; h, LR)$, where h is patient type, and LR is the local history pair. For example, $\pi(A; \alpha, AB)$ denotes the physician's assessment of the probability of success of procedure A on an α -type patient, given that one of that doctor's neighbors used treatment A at her last treatment opportunity and the doctor's other neighbor last used treatment B.[14] Under the assumed payoffs to the patient in the events of success and failure, the success probability represents the expected welfare of the patient, *as the physician assesses it*, in the case of risk neutrality. In this model, the recent choices of nearby peers send a signal concerning which treatment is best. We assume all doctors make treatment decisions according to the same payoff function, $\pi(.)$, and patients have no explicit input into the treatment choice.

The *state* of the system is an infinite sequence, *. . .AABBBABAAABA. . .*, where the letter at each location indicates the most recent treatment choice made by the physician at that site. The set of states is denoted by Ω. At random dates the state changes as the value at one location changes from A to B or vice versa. The process is a continuous time Markov chain, $X(t)$, and we are interested in the stationary (or equilibrium, or

[14] The subjective assessments depend on the doctor's own patient's type, but not on the neighboring doctors' patient types, types which we presume cannot be observed by the given doctor.

invariant) distributions of this process—meaning a distribution over the set of states to which the system converges in the long-run—rather than in the transient states.

We assume that the physician payoffs, π *(.)*, depend on the patient's type and on the local treatment history in the following way:

(i) For patients of type α, treatment A has a higher expected payoff if one or both neighbors used A at their respective last treatment opportunities, while B has a higher expected payoff if both neighbors last used B.

(ii) For patients of type β, procedure B has a higher expected payoff if one or both neighbors last used procedure B, while A has a higher expected payoff if both neighbors last used A.

An example of payoffs that satisfy these two conditions is given below. For a patient of type α, the payoffs are as follows:

$$\pi(A; \alpha, BB) = 0.3; \pi(B; \alpha, BB) = 0.4$$
$$\pi(A; \alpha, AB) = 0.4; \pi(B; \alpha, AB) = 0.3$$
$$\pi(A; \alpha, AA) = 0.5; \pi(B; \alpha, AA) = 0.2$$

Similarly, for a patient of type β, the assumed payoffs are:

$$\pi(A; \beta, BB) = 0.2; \pi(B; \beta, BB) = 0.5$$
$$\pi(A; \beta, AB) = 0.3; \pi(B; \beta, AB) = 0.4$$
$$\pi(A; \beta, AA) = 0.4; \pi(B; \beta, AA) = 0.3$$

Observe that a patient of type α will receive treatment A if the local history is either AB or AA, but will receive treatment B if the local history is BB. A type-β patient will receive treatment B if the local history is either BB or AB, and treatment A only if the local history is AA. The physicians in this model are not motivated to conform for conformity's sake, but the choices that emerge may appear as if such motives were in play.

An equilibrium distribution involving regional treatment norms exists provided payoffs satisfy conditions (i) and (ii) and provided the distribution of patient types exhibits sufficient variation across different regions of the treatment space [Burke et al., 2010]. For example, partition the set of treatment locations (Z) into two regions: the negative integers constitute the West, while the non-negative integers constitute the East. If patients arriving at locations in the West are of type α with probability *greater* than one-half, and if patients arriving in the East are of type α with probability *less* than one-half, the existence of an equilibrium involving regional norms is guaranteed. To be precise, there exists a long-run distribution over the set of states for which the support is S, the set of all states of the form .....AAAAAABBBBBBB..... (an infinite string of A's followed by an infinite string of B's). The states in S differ only in the position of the boundary between A's and B's, which can drift randomly to the left or to the right one unit at a time because treatment choice at each of the two boundary locations (i.e., the highest-numbered "A" location and the lowest-numbered "B" location) depends on which type of patient arrives. In addition, it can be shown that the system converges to the set of states involving regional norms from a very broad set of initial states.

The results suggest that the procedure performed on a patient depends on the demographic mix in that region, a prediction found to hold for cardiac treatment in the state of Florida. Because this dependence on the patient mix derives from subjective treatment choices, such choices may entail welfare losses for patients as a result of "conformity warp." Consistent with the model's predictions, we observe that a 75-year-old heart patient is more likely to receive an invasive treatment—either coronary angioplasty or bypass surgery—in Tallahassee, a city with a relatively high proportion of younger cardiac patients (62 and under), than in Fort Lauderdale, a city with a comparatively older patient population [Burke, et al., 2010]. Since surgery becomes riskier with age, 75-year-olds in Tallahassee are likely to have worse outcomes than 75-year-olds in Fort Lauderdale, even with no difference in the average competence of physicians across the locations.

In the context of the model, physicians may persist in holding incorrect beliefs about the efficacy of different treatments. In the confirmatory bias model of Rabin and Schrag [1999], individuals seek out evidence that confirms an initial hypothesis and discount evidence that contradicts initial beliefs. In addition, learning about relative payoffs to different treatments may require experimentation, which is likely to be costly in the case of discrete treatment choices such as whether or not to perform surgery [Bikhchandani, et al., 2001].

There is an alternative interpretation of this model in which the social influence reflects productivity spillovers among physicians. In this interpretation, described in Burke et al. [2010] and Chandra and Staiger [2007], a given doctor's objective probability of success increases with its usage rate among her local peer group. Regional treatment norms also emerge in this case but the welfare implications are different. For example, β patients in a predominantly α region will receive treatment A rather than treatment B, but may in fact be better off—assuming they can't switch location—because the local physicians have less experience, and so less expertise, in treatment B than treatment A. While the counterfactual is difficult to observe, Chandra and Staiger [2007] find, for example, that the quality of non-invasive care (or "medical management") for heart attack patients was worse in locations that had a high propensity to apply invasive heart treatments. Consistent with this finding, the model implies that β patients would be better off if they could be transferred (at minimal cost) to a location with relative expertise in treatment B. The aggregate welfare implications of local productivity spillovers depend on the distribution of patient types across and within locations, the strength of the spillover, the cost of transferring patients across locations, and on the extent to which physicians choose their locations on the basis of prior specialization.

8. BODY WEIGHT NORMS

The norms discussed so far have pertained to choices—such as contractual arrangements and medical treatments—over which people exert a high degree of control. There are also norms governing aspects of appearance, such as body weight or size, over which individuals have relatively less control. Like other social norms, body size norms tend to exhibit both local uniformity and global diversity. Different body size norms are possible, depending on the underlying economic, social, and physiological factors of the relevant population. Like other types of social norms, size norms may be enforced by social sanctions or by self-imposed sanctions. However, social norms governing body size differ from some other norms in that they compel conformity in aspirations to a greater extent than they do conformity in physical outcomes. That is, a body size norm should be thought of as a shared reference point or standard against which actual sizes are judged.

We illustrate the distinctive features of body weight norms, first within a theoretical model of norm formation and then by examining the relevant empirical evidence, focusing on the case of women in the United States during the past 20 years. The model is constructed with contemporary Western society in mind and embeds two key assumptions: (1) the ideal size portrayed in the dominant popular media is thinner than the average woman and close to being underweight in relation to public health standards and (2) despite the idealization of absolute thinness, individuals assess themselves on a relative weight scale, such that the de facto reference point or norm is a value that is thinner than average by some fixed fraction.

Why should relative weight comparisons matter? One possibility is that people compete for scarce goods, such as marriage partners and high-status jobs, on the basis of appearance. For example, Averett and Korenman [1996] find that a woman's probability of getting married and her spouse's income (if married) are both lower if she is overweight or obese than if she is not. Other penalties accruing to overweight women include elevated depression risk [Ross, 1994; Graham and Felton, 2006] and reduced wages and job status [Cawley, 2004; Conley and Glauber, 2005]. Furthermore, there is evidence that both obese women and extremely underweight women experience social stigmatization based on their weight [Puhl and Brownell 2001, Mond et al. 2006].

The model

The model, adapted from Burke and Heiland [2007], consists of a population of heterogeneous individuals that constitutes an interacting social group. Each individual cares about how her own weight, W_i, compares to the group's weight norm, M. In particular, the individual experiences a disutility cost of $-J\ (W_i - M)^2$ for a deviation from the norm, where the parameter J indexes the strength of the desire to conform to the norm.[15] The group norm, M, is defined as a given fraction, ξ, of group average

[15] This general specification of social interactions is due to Brock and Durlauf [2001].

weight, $\overline{W}$, where $0<\xi<1$, such that $M \equiv \xi\overline{W}$. The norm is therefore subject to variation across groups and over time with factors that shift average weight in the group. The norm has the intuitive effect of lowering the variance of weight in the population, even though not everyone will conform to the norm exactly.[16]

In addition to the disutility of deviating from the weight norm, each individual receives positive utility from consumption of food and nonfood goods. The per-period utility-maximization problem can be expressed as follows:

$$\max_{F_{it},C_{it}} U_t[F_{it}, C_{it} | W_{i,t-1}] = G[F_{it}, C_{it}] - J(W_{it}[F_{it}, W_{i,t-1}, \varepsilon_i] - M_{t-1})^2,$$

subject to the per-period budget constraint: $pF_{it} + C_{it} \leq Y_{it}$.

The function $U[\cdot]$ is assumed to be jointly concave in F_{it} and C_{it}, which represent individual i's food and nonfood consumption, respectively, for period t. $W_{i,t-1}$ represents body weight as of period $t-1$, which is given by past actions. Biological heterogeneity is captured by ε_i, a stationary idiosyncratic shock to the individual's resting (or basal) metabolism.[17] The function $G[\cdot]$ is the private component of utility, which is strictly increasing and strictly concave in C_{it}. $G[\cdot]$ is strictly concave but not necessarily monotonic in F_{it}, such that the marginal utility of one-period food consumption may become negative beyond a certain level. Body weight enters utility only through the social interaction or norm-reference term, $J(W_{it}[F_{it}, W_{i,t-1}, \varepsilon_i] - M_{t-1})^2$. The coefficient J represents the intensity of conformity preference, which may reflect both third-party enforcement and self-monitoring or internalization. The time subscript on M implies that agents observe the value of the weight norm as of period t-1 and take this as fixed in the period-t optimization problem—that is, they do not forecast the equilibrium norm that will emerge in period t. However, the individual does anticipate her period-t weight as a function of period-t food intake and period-t-1 weight, and assesses the norm-deviation cost for period-t weight. Through this latter channel, the weight norm influences the consumption decision.

Aside from taking into account the effect of current food consumption on end-of-period weight, individuals are myopic: at the beginning of each period, F_{it} and C_{it} are chosen to maximize the one-period utility function subject to the one-period budget constraint, taking $W_{i,t-1}$, M_{t-1}, and the relative price of food, p, as given. Under a set of relatively weak assumptions on the functional form of $G[\cdot]$ and on the magnitude of J, it can be shown that successive optimization of the one-period problem results in convergence to a *stable weight*, W_{is}, for any vector $(M, Y_i, p, \varepsilon_i)$. That is, holding the

[16] In Bernheim's [1994] model of conformity, a non-zero fraction of the population conforms exactly to the (endogenous) norm in equilibrium, despite idiosyncratic variation in preferences within the conforming group. Our model does not share this feature, as body weight varies continuously with the individual endowment.

[17] Resting metabolism is the caloric expenditure (per day, for example) required to sustain involuntary bodily functions in a resting state. Aside from calories burned in the digestion of food, assumed to be a fixed fraction of calories consumed, resting metabolism is the only source of energy expenditure in the model.

norm, prices, and income fixed and beginning from any initial weight, each individual will converge to a stable, myopically optimal vector, (C_{is}, F_{is}, W_{is}), that is unique (given ε_i) and not path-dependent.[18]

The equilibrium norm satisfies the fixed-point condition, $M = \xi \overline{W}_s(M, p)$, where $\overline{W}_s(M, p)$ is the mean stable weight that arises when individuals take the norm to be M and the food price to be p. ($\overline{W}_s$ depends also on the respective population distributions of income and the idiosyncratic shock.) Under the functional form specified in Burke and Heiland [2007], an equilibrium exists and is unique for each combination of the food price and the vector of metabolic shocks. Despite myopia at the individual level, the system will converge to equilibrium from any initial weight distribution following repeated one-period optimization and norm updating, as described above.

Predictions and evidence

The model implies that the equilibrium weight distribution and weight norm will vary with the distribution of metabolic shocks, the income distribution, the relative food price, the strength of social interactions, and with the strength of absolute preference for thinness (which is stronger the lower is ξ). In addition, social interactions magnify the effect of variation in fundamentals on outcomes: a shock to fundamentals has a direct effect on weight values, as well as an indirect effect that occurs because the norm adjusts to the change in average weight, and norm adjustments in turn lead to additional adjustments to individual weight. To take a specific example, the model predicts that an exogenous decline in the relative price of food, as occurred in the United States between 1976 and 2002 [Cutler et al., 2003; Chou et al., 2004; Burke and Heiland, 2007], will result in an increase in average weight in the population and, correspondingly, an increase in the weight norm or reference standard.

We find strong evidence in support of the model in data on weight perceptions collected by the Centers for Disease Control (CDC) as part of its National Health and Nutrition Examination Survey (NHANES). In both the NHANES III, which aggregates data collected between 1988 and 1994, and the NHANES 1999–2004, subjects were asked whether they considered themselves to be either "underweight," "about right," or "overweight." Consistent with our assumption that contemporary American culture prizes thinness in women, the data reveal a bias toward self-classification as overweight relative to an individual's objective weight status under the CDC classification system. In NHANES III, 40% of normal-weight women classified themselves as "overweight," and only 43% of underweight women actually considered they were

[18] This stable weight does not coincide with the weight that optimizes a dynamic programming problem with the same per-period utility function. However, the qualitative results are robust to a specification involving forward-looking behavior. See Burke and Heiland [2007].

"underweight." While the same qualitative bias is observed in the later survey, the data reveal a rightward-shift in weight norms between the earlier and later surveys. In the 1999–2004 survey, the share of normal-weight women that classified themselves as overweight fell to 33% and the share of underweight women that self-classified as underweight rose to 50%. In addition, the share of overweight women who classified themselves as "overweight" fell from 85% to 79% between the surveys. These cross-survey differences are significant at the .05 level and cannot be explained based on changes in demographic and socioeconomic characteristics between survey waves [Burke, Heiland, and Nadler 2010].

The model also predicts that different weight norms will arise in different social groups, given differences in fundamentals between the groups that lead to differences in average weight levels. Since social interactions and cultural identification tend to cut strongly along racial and ethnic lines in the United States, and because the mean BMI of African-American women is significantly greater than that of white American women, we expect to observe a higher weight norm among black (non-Hispanic) women relative to whites. In the weight perception data described above, we find that African-American women are significantly less likely, by approximately half, than white women to consider themselves overweight, controlling for actual BMI, age, educational attainment, income, and marital status; black women are also more than twice as likely as white women to consider themselves underweight, controlling for the same factors [Burke and Heiland 2008]. Consistent with these differences in perception, Graham and Felton [2006] find that obesity is associated with elevated depression risk for white American women but not for African-American women, and Averett and Korenman [1999] find that obesity predicts low self-esteem among white women but not among black women in the United States.

In light of the apparent temporal and ethnic variation in body weight norms, it is difficult to argue that women's weight aspirations are based primarily on a desire for optimal health, or, as some evolutionary biologists have argued [Pinker 1997], that appearance norms reflect hard-wired preferences. In fact, to minimize overall mortality risk, recent evidence suggests that individuals should target the overweight (but not obese) BMI range of 25–29.9 [Flegal et al. 2005].

9. CONCLUDING DISCUSSION

We began this chapter with a quotation from Alfred Marshall about the dynamics of social norms. Marshall pinpointed two features of norm dynamics that occur in many different settings: stickiness and punctuated change. Both arise from the positive feedback loop that a norm sets up between expectations and behaviors. When people expect that most other members of the population will adhere to a norm, it is in their interest to adhere to it also. Therefore, small deviations from equilibrium tend to die out, whereas occasional large deviations can push the dynamics onto a radically different trajectory.[19]

Such large deviations come from a variety of sources. One is technological change. Norms of medical practice eventually respond to the introduction of new techniques and procedures, but often do so only after a long period of initial resistance. The theory also shows why adoption may occur at different times in different subpopulations, so that at any given time norms of practice may differ quite radically in different communities. Another source of norm shifts comes from changes in relative prices. As food becomes less expensive, people tend to eat more and average body weight increases. The increased prevalence of heavy people induces a shift in expectations about what is an appropriate or "normal" body weight, so that now people eat more because food is cheaper and because there is less stigma attached to being heavy. Note that in this case the change in weight norms will tend to be continuous, whereas technological change occurs in discrete jumps. In both cases, however, an initial change that is relatively small can lead to relatively large (and rapid) changes in outcome due to the norm's amplification effect.

A third source of norm shifts arises from spillover effects between different spheres of social interaction. Economic changes may lead to greater female labor force participation, which leads to a decline in marriage and childbearing rates; the result may be a change in norms and expectations that affect both women and men, including women who choose not to enter the labor force. Thus, one norm shift begets another.

The incorporation of social norms into economic models provides a rich set of predictions and hypotheses that can be tested empirically. This presents a number of methodological challenges, because it is often difficult to obtain data that are rich enough to separate social feedback effects from common unobservables and also from endogenous selection into groups (homophily); for a discussion of these issues see Manski [1993], Moffitt [2001], Brock and Durlauf [2001a, 2001b], Glaeser and Scheinkman [2001]. The most promising types of data are event studies that detail the timing of individual decisions as a function of individual characteristics, background economic variables, and (most importantly) the decisions of other members of the relevant social group at each point in time. In other words, one must look at the dynamics of behavior at the level of individual agents rather than aggregate cross-sectional data to tease out social feedback effects. The models we have described in preceding sections provide clues about what to look for; it remains for empirical researchers to take up the challenge.

[19] Lindbeck, Nyberg, and Weibull [1999] study changes in attitudes toward public transfers using a model of this type.

REFERENCES

Akerlof, G.A., 1980. A theory of social custom, of which unemployment may be one consequence. Q. J. Econ. 94, 749–775.

Akerlof, G.A., 1997. Social distance and social decisions. Econometrica 65, 1005–1027.

Akerlof, G.A., Yellen, J.L., Katz, L.M., 1996. An analysis of out-of-wedlock childbearing in the United States. Q. J. Econ. 111, 277–317.

Averett, S., Korenman, S., 1996. The Economic Reality of the Beauty Myth. J. Hum. Resour. 31, 304–330.

Averett, S., Korenman, S., 1999. Black-White differences in social and economic consequences of obesity. Int. J. Obes. 223 (2), 166–173.

Becker, G., Murphy, K., 2000. Social Economics: Market Behavior in a Social Environment. Belknap-Harvard University Press, Cambridge, MA.

Bernheim, D., 1994. A theory of conformity. J.Polit. Econ. 102, 841–877.

Bhandari, M., et al., 2003. A randomized trial of opinion leader endorsement in a survey of orthopedic surgeons: effect on primary response rates. Int. J. Epidemiol. 32, 634–636.

Bicchieri, C., 2006. The Grammar of Society: The Nature and Dynamics of Social Norms. Cambridge University Press, New York.

Bikhchandani, S., Chandra, A., Goldman, D., Welch, I., 2001. The Economics of Iatroepidemics and Quackeries: Physician Learning, Informational Cascades and Geographic Variation in Medical Practice. (Draft). Los Angeles, CA: University of California, Los Angeles, Anderson School of Business.

Blume, L.E., 2003. How noise matters. Games Econ. Behav. 44, 251–271.

Brock, W., Durlauf, S., 2001. Discrete Choice with Social Interactions. Rev. Econ. Stud. 68 (2), 235–260.

Brock, W.A., Durlauf, S., 2001a. Interactions based models. In: Heckman, J., Leamer, E. (Eds.), Handbook of Econometrics, vol. 5. North-Holland, Amsterdam.

Brock, W., Durlauf, S.N., 2001b. Discrete choice with social interactions. Rev. Econ. Stud. 68, 235–260.

Burke, M.A., 2008. Social Multipliers. In: Durlauf, S., Blume, L. (Eds.), The New Palgrave Dictionary of Economics. second ed. Palgrave-Macmillan Ltd, London.

Burke, M.A., Fournier, G.M., Prasad, K., 2010. Geographic Variations in a Model of Physician Treatment Choice with Social Interactions. J. Econ. Behav. Organ. 73, 418–432.

Burke, M.A., Heiland, F., 2008. Race, Obesity, and the Puzzle of Gender-Specificity. Federal Reserve Bank of Boston working paper.

Burke, MA., Heiland, F., 2007. Social Dynamics of Obesity. Econ. Inq. 45 (3), 571–591.

Burke, M.A., Heiland, F.k., Nadler, C., 2010. From "Overweight" to "About Right": Evidence of a Generational Shift in Body Weight Norms. Obesity 18, 1226–1234.

Case, A.C., Katz, L.F., 1991. The Company You Keep: The Effects of Family and Neighborhood on Disadvantaged Youths. NBER Working Paper 3705.

Cawley, J., 2004. The impact of obesity on wages. J. Hum. Resour. 39, 451–474.

Chandra, A., Staiger, D., 2007. Productivity Spillovers in Health Care: Evidence from the Treatment of Heart Attacks. J. Polit. Econ. 115 (1), 103–140.

Chou, S.Y., Grossman, M., Saffer, H., 2004. An economic analysis of adult obesity: results from the Behavioral Risk Factor Surveillance System. J. Health Econ. 23, 565–587.

Coleman, J.S., 1987. Norms as social capital. In: Radnitzky, G., Bernholz, P. (Eds.), Economic Imperialism: The Economic Approach Applied Outside the Field of Economics. Paragon House, New York.

Conley, D., Glauber, R., 2005. Gender, body mass and economic status. NBER working paper 11343.

Cutler, D.M., Glaeser, E.L., Shapiro, J.M., 2003. Why have Americans become more obese? J. Econ. Perspect. 17, 93–118.

Danielsen, B., Castles, A.G., Damberg, C.L., 2000. Variation in Risk-Adjusted Cesarian Section Rates by California Region and Hospital Characteristics, Abstracts of the Academy of Health Services Research Health Policy Meeting.

Durlauf, S.N., 1997. Statistical mechanical approaches to socioeconomic behavior. In: Brian Arthur, W., Durlauf, S.N., Lane, D. (Eds.), The Economy as a Complex Evolving System, vol. II. Addison-Wesley, Redwood City CA.

Durlauf, S.N., Peyton Young, H. (Eds.), 2001. Social Dynamics. The Brookings Institution, Washington DC.
Elster, J., 1989. Social norms and economic theory. J. Econ. Perspect. 3 (4), 99–117.
Fehr, E., Fischbacher, U., 2004a. Third party punishment and social norms. Evol. Hum. Behav. 25, 63–87.
Fehr, E., Fischbacher, U., 2004b. Social norms and human cooperation. Trends Cogn. Sci. 8 (4), 185–190.
Fehr, E., Fischbacher, U., Gächter, S., 2002. Strong reciprocity, human cooperation, and the enforcement of social norms. Hum. Nat. 13, 1–25.
Flegal, K.M., Graubard, B.I., Williamson, D.F., Gail, M.H., 2005. Excess deaths associated with underweight, overweight, and obesity. J. Am. Med. Assoc. 293, 1861–1867.
Foster, D.P., Peyton Young, H., 1990. Stochastic evolutionary game dynamics. Theor. Popul. Biol. 38, 219–232.
Freidlin, M.I., Wentzell, A.D., 1984. Random Perturbations of Dynamical Systems. Springer-Verlag, Berlin.
Glaeser, E.L., Sacerdote, B., Scheinkman, J.A., 1996. Crime and Social Interactions. Q. J. Econ. 111 (2), 507–548.
Glaeser, E., Sacerdote, B., Scheinkman, J., 2003. The social multiplier. J. Eur. Econ. Assoc. 1, 345–353.
Glaeser, E., Scheinkman, J., 2001. Measuring social interactions. In: Durlauf, S.N., Peyton Young, H. (Eds.), Social Dynamics. The Brookings Institution, Washington DC (Chapter 4).
Glaeser, E., Scheinkman, J., 2003. Non-market interactions. In: Dewatripont, M., Hansen, L.P., Turnovsky, S. (Eds.), Advances in Economics and Econometrics: Theory and Applications, Eighth World Congress. Cambridge University Press, Cambridge.
Glover, A.F., 1938. The Incidence of Tonsillectomy in School Children. Proc. R. Soc. Med. 31, 1219–1236.
Goldin, C., Katz, L., 2002. The power of the pill: oral contraceptives and women's career and marriage decisions. J. Polit. Econ. 110, 730–770.
Gottlieb, S., McCarter, R., Vogel, R., 1998. Effect of Beta-Blockade on Mortality among high-risk and low-risk patients after myocardial infarction. N. Engl. J. Med. 339 (August 20), 489–497.
Graham, C., Felton, A., 2006. Variance in Obesity across Cohorts and Countries: A Norms-Based Explanation Using Happiness Surveys. Brookings CSED working paper number 42.
Hechter, M., Opp, K.D. (Eds.), 2001. Social Norms. Russell Sage Foundation, New York.
Illinois Cooperative Extension Service, 1995. Cooperative Extension Service Farm Leasing Survey 1995. Department of Agricultural and Consumer Economics, Cooperative Extension Service, University of Illinois at Urbana-Champaign.
Jencks, S.F., et al., 2000. Quality of Medical Care Delivered to Medicare Beneficiaries: A Profile at State and National Levels. J. Am. Med. Assoc. 284 (13), 1670–1676.
Kandori, M., Mailath, G., Rob, R., 1993. Learning, mutation, and long-run equilibria in games. Econometrica 61, 29–56.
Kandori, M., Rob, R., 1995. Evolution of equilibria in the long run: a general theory and applications. J. Econ. Theory 65, 29–56.
Knight, F.H., 1921. Risk, Uncertainty, and Profit. Houghton-Mifflin, Boston and New York.
Lewis, D., 1969. Convention: A Philosophical Study. Harvard University Press, Cambridge MA.
Lindbeck, A., Nyberg, S., Weibull, J., 1999. Social norms and economic incentives in the welfare state. Q. J. Econ. 114, 1–35.
Manski, C., 1993. Identification of endogenous social effects: the reflection problem. Rev. Econ. Stud. 60, 531–542.
Marshall, A., 1920. Principles of Economics, ninth ed. Macmillan, London and New York.
McFadden, D., 1974. Conditional logit analysis of qualitative choice behavior. In: Zarembka, P. (Ed.), Frontiers in Econometrics. Academic Press, New York.
Mill, J.S., 1848. [1929]. Principles of Political Economy. Longmans Green, London.
Moffitt, R.A., 2001. Policy interventions, low-level equilibria, and social interactions. In: Durlauf, S.N., Peyton Young, H. (Eds.), Social Dynamics. The Brookings Institution, Washington DC (Chapter 3).

Mond, J., Robertson-Smith, G., Vetere, A., 2006. Stigma and eating disorders: is there evidence of negative attitudes towards anorexia nervosa among women in the community? J. Ment. Health 15 (5), 519–532.
Phelps, C.E., Mooney, C., 1993. Variations in medical practice use: causes and consequences. In: Arnould, R.J., Rich, R.F., White, W. (Eds.), Competitive Approaches to Health Care Reform. The Urban Institute Press, Washington, DC.
Pinker, S., 1997. How the Mind Works. W.W. Norton and Company, New York.
Puhl, R., Brownell, K.D., 2001. Bias, Discrimination, and Obesity. Obes. Res. 9 (12), 788–805.
Rabin, M., Schrag, J.L., 1999. First Impressions Matter: A Model of Confirmatory Bias. Q. J. Econ. 114 (1), 37–82.
Ross, C.E., 1994. Overweight and Depression. J. Health Soc. Behav. 35, 63–79.
Schotter, A., 1981. The Economic Theory of Social Institutions. Cambridge University Press, New York.
Skinner, J., Staiger, D., 2005. Technology Adoption from Hybrid Corn to Beta Blockers. NBER Working Paper 11251.
Soumerai, S.B., et al., 1998. Effect of Local Medical Opinion Leaders on Quality of Care for Acute Myocardial Infarction: A Randomized Controlled Trial. J. Am. Med. Assoc. 279 (17), 1358–1363.
Stiglitz, J.E., 1974. Incentives and Risk Sharing in Sharecropping. Rev. Econ. Stud. 41 (2), 219–255.
Ullmann-Margalit, E., 1977. The Emergence of Norms. Oxford University Press, Oxford.
Wennberg, J., Gittelsohn, A., 1973. Small area variations in health care delivery. Science 182, 1102–1108.
Wennberg, J., Gittelsohn, A., 1982. Variations in Medical Care Among Small Areas. Sci. Am. 182, 1102–1108.
Young, H.P., 1993a. The evolution of conventions. Econometrica 61, 57–84.
Young, H.P., 1993b. An evolutionary model of bargaining. J. Econ. Theory 59, 145–168.
Young, H.P., 1998a. Individual Strategy and Social Structure: An Evolutionary Theory of Institutions. Princeton University Press, Princeton NJ.
Young, H.P., 1998b. Conventional contracts. Rev. Econ. Stud. 65, 773–792.
Young, H.P., Burke, M.A., 2001. Competition and custom in economic contracts: a case study of Illinois agriculture. Am. Econ. Rev. 91, 559–573.

FURTHER READING

Cheung, S.N.S.,1969. The Theory of Share Tenancy. University of Chicago Press, Chicago.

CHAPTER 9

The Economics of Cultural Transmission and Socialization

Alberto Bisin* and Thierry Verdier**
*New York University and NBER
**PSE and CEPR*

Contents

1. Introduction 340
2. Theoretical Studies 342
   2.1 Population dynamics 343
      2.1.1 Cultural heterogeneity 345
   2.2 Socialization mechanisms 346
      2.2.1 Geographic spread 348
      2.2.2 Homogamous marriages 349
      2.2.3 Fertility 351
      2.2.4 Self-segregation 352
      2.2.5 Identity formation 352
   2.3 Multidimensional cultural traits 355
   2.4 Cultural transmission and social interactions 359
      2.4.1 Cultural transmission and trade 362
      2.4.2 Cultural transmission and institutions 363
      2.4.3 Cultural transmission and collective action 365
   2.5 Cultural transmission of beliefs 369
3. Empirical Studies 371
   3.1 Cultural heterogeneity 371
   3.2 Resilience of cultural traits 374
   3.3 Population dynamics 377
      3.3.1 Long term persistence 384
      3.3.2 Immigration and assimilation 389
   3.4 Socialization 392
      3.4.1 Imperfect empathy 394
      3.4.2 Vertical vs. oblique/horizontal transmission 394
      3.4.3 Marriage 395
      3.4.4 Neighborhood and school choice 399

* We have collaborated on the study of cultural transmission for more than a decade, while socializing our own children. Many have helped and encouraged us over the years, many more than we can thank here. We owe special thanks however to D. Acemoglu, A. Alesina, G.S. Becker, J. Benhabib, L.L. Cavalli Sforza, P.A. Chiappori, E. Glaeser, E. Ok, A. Postlewaite, J.A. Scheinkman and to our co-authors on this topic, J. Olivier, E. Patacchini, M. Thoenig, G. Topa, Y. Zenou.

Handbook of Social Economics, Volume 1A
ISSN 0169-7218, DOI: 10.1016/S0169-7218(11)01009-4

3.4.5 Collective socialization mechanisms 400
3.4.6 Cultural substitution 400
3.4.7 Cultural distinction 404
4. Conclusions 407
References 407

Abstract

This paper presents a survey of the theoretical and empirical literature on cultural transmission and socialization. It has been prepared for the *Handbook of Social Economics*, edited by Jess Benhabib, Alberto Bisin, and Matt Jackson, to be published by Elsevier Science in 2010.
JEL Codes: Z1, D01, D03

Keywords

cultural transmission
socialization
identity formation
assimilation
integration

1. INTRODUCTION

Preferences, beliefs, and norms that govern human behavior are partly formed as the result of heritable genetic traits, and are partly transmitted through generations and acquired by learning and other forms of social interaction. Therefore, cultural transmission is an object of study of several social sciences, such as evolutionary anthropology, sociology, social psychology, and economics. In this paper, we define culture to represent those components of preferences, social norms, and ideological attitudes which

> *depend upon the capacity for learning and transmitting knowledge to succeeding generations.*
> Merriam Webster's Online Dictionary.

Cultural transmission arguably plays an important role in the determination of many fundamental preference traits, like discounting, risk aversion and altruism.[1] It certainly plays a central role in the formation of cultural traits, social norms, and ideological tenets, like e.g., attitudes towards family and fertility practices, and attitudes in the job market. Relatedly, distinct cultural traits determine how individuals interpret and react to common (e.g., strategic) choice environment.[2] It is, however, the

[1] The decomposition of the cultural (or environmental) and genetic effects on cognitive and psychological traits is the object of a large literature, typically referred to as *nature/nurture*, which spans from behavioral genetics to the social sciences. Sacerdote (2010), in this *Handbook*, surveys this literature. The role of evolutionary selection in the formation of preferences is surveyed by Robson and Samuelson (2010) for this *Handbook*.

[2] See e.g., Henrich, Boyd, Bowles, Camerer, Fehr, and Gintis (2004) for cooperative behavior in 15 small scale societies; Cameron, Chauduri, Erkal, and Gangadharan (2009) for a corruption game in Melbourne, Delhi, Jakarta, Singapore. In this *Handbook*, Fernandez (2010) surveys the *Does-culture-matter?* literature in detail.

pervasive evidence of the resilience of ethnic and religious traits across generations that motivates a large fraction of the theoretical and empirical literature on cultural transmission. In the U.S., for instance, persistent ethnic and religious diversity in what social scientists until the 1960s expected to turn into a 'melting pot,' are very well documented. In fact, immigrants all over the world generally strive to maintain various traits of the culture of the country of origin. Several ethnic and religious communities in the U.S., e.g., Orthodox Jews, even observed a *cultural renaissance* after being declared *endangered*. Outside the United States, Basques, Catalans, Corsicans, and Irish Catholics in Europe, Quebecois in Canada, and Jews of the Diaspora have all remained strongly attached to their languages and cultural traits even through the formation of political states which did not recognize ethnic and religious diversity. Similarly, e.g., in Africa, various forms of tribal distinction persisted and even thrived after the creation of overarching national institutions. Finally, various measures of social capital display very long-run hysteresis, of the order of hundreds of years: historical events like the constitution of free-city-state in the Middle Ages, the quality of political institutions in the nineteenth century Europe, the slave trade in West Africa, Ottoman domination, all have effects which seem to persist up until the present.

In this article, we concentrate on intergenerational transmission of culture. We conceptualize cultural transmission as the result of interactions between purposeful socialization decisions inside the family ("direct vertical socialization') and other socialization processes like social imitation and learning which govern identity formation ('oblique and horizontal socialization"). Cultural traits are then endogenous in this context. But how to think about agents who choose their children's and/or their own preferences? Is it even logically consistent to think of agents choosing their own preferences? Which preference order applies to this choice? George Stigler and Gary Becker's famed *De gustibus non est disputandum* paper addresses some of these methodological questions. They favor postulating an identical meta-preference ordering each agent actual preferences. This methodological standpoint has generated a rich and interesting literature and several important applications; see Becker (1996) and Becker and Murphy (2000) for book-length surveys. On the other hand, by restricting the determinants of heterogeous preferences across agents to differences in the technologies which constrain preference choices, this class of models is at a loss e.g., to deal with cultural transmission. For instance, how to explain the widespread observation of purposeful actions by parents limiting their children integration into extraneous dominant cultures? In turn, these models can hardly produce the resilience of ethnic and religious traits we tend to observe.

Bisin and Verdier, in a series of papers, deviating from identical meta-preferences, introduce a fundamental friction in parental altruism, *imperfect empathy*, which is sufficient to sustain a theory of cultural transmission by biasing parents towards their own cultural traits. More specifically, *imperfect empathy* requires that while parents are altruistic with respect to their children, they evaluate their choice using their own (the parents' - not the children's) preferences. For instance, religious parents care about the social and economic success of their children, but would regret their having to accept secular norms and attitudes to achieve it. These models of cultural transmission have implications regarding the determinants of the persistence of cultural traits and more generally regarding the population dynamics of cultural traits. The persistence of cultural traits or, conversely, the cultural assimilation of minorities, is determined by the costs and benefits of various family decisions pertaining to the socialization of children in specific socio-economic environments, which in turn determine the children's opportunities for social imitation and learning.

This article reviews the main contributions of models of cultural transmission, from theoretical and empirical perspectives. It presents their implications regarding the long-run population dynamics of cultural traits, and discusses the links between the economic and other approaches to cultural evolution in the social sciences as well as in evolutionary biology. Furthermore, it discusses how to extend the economic theory of cultural transmission to the analysis of several important aspects of the dynamics and propagation of beliefs and values.

2. THEORETICAL STUDIES

The first formal theoretical contributions to the modeling of cultural transmission are due to Cavalli-Sforza and Feldman (1981) and to Boyd and Richerson (1985), who apply models of evolutionary biology to the transmission of cultural traits. Their analysis contains a simple elegant stylized model of the cultural transmission mechanism, together with a clear terminology, which are extensively adopted by most of the subsequent literature.

Consider a *dichotomous cultural trait* in the population, $\{a, b\}$. Let the fraction of individuals with trait $i \in \{a, b\}$ be q^i. *Reproduction* is *a-sexual* and each parent has one child. Cultural transmission is the result of *direct vertical* (parental) socialization and *horizontal/oblique socialization* in society at large.[3] More specifically,

i) Direct vertical socialization to the parent's trait, say i, occurs with probability d^i;

ii) If a child from a family with trait i is not directly socialized, which occurs with probability $1 - d^i$, he/she is horizontally/obliquely socialized by picking the trait of a role model chosen randomly in the population (i.e., he/she picks trait i with probability q^i and trait $j \neq i$ with probability $q^j = 1 - q^i$).

The cultural transmission mechanism introduced by Cavalli Sforza and Feldman (1981) is then summarily represented by the following system of equations for P^{ij}, the probability that a child from a family with trait i is socialized to trait j:

[3] *Horizontal* socialization refers to socialization resulting from interactions between members of the children population, while *oblique* socialization is due to interactions between children and members of their parents' population. This distinction turns out to be relatively unimportant in the literature.

$$P^{ii} = d^i + (1-d^i)q^i$$
$$P^{ij} = (1-d^i)(1-q^i) \tag{1}$$

Bisin and Verdier (2000, 2001) introduce parental socialization choice in Cavalli Sforza and Feldman (1981)'s model. Consequently, direct socialization probabilities, d^i, d^j, are endogenously determined. Parental socialization choice is motivated by *imperfect empathy*, which is a form of altruism biased towards the parents' own cultural traits: parents care about their children's choices, but they evaluate them using their own (the parents' – not the children's) preferences.

More specifically, let X denote an abstract choice set, comprising all choices relevant to an individual's economic and social life. Cultural traits are represented by preferences: each individual (parent or child) chooses $x \in X$ to maximize $u^i : X \rightarrow \mathfrak{R}$, for cultural trait $i \in \{a, b\}$. Let V^{ij} denote the utility to a cultural trait i parent of a type j child, $i, j \in \{a, b\}$. Then

Imperfect empathy: *For all i, j,* $V^{ij} = u^i(x^j)$, *where* $x^j = argmax_{x \in X}\, u^j(x)$.[4]

As long as V^{ii}, V^{ij} are independent of q^i, imperfect empathy implies $V^{ii} \geq V^{ij}$, with $>$ for generic preferences $u^i(x)$, $u^j(x)$. More generally, when individuals interact socially, V^{ii}, V^{ij} will be a function of q^i. This case is studied in Section 2.4.

When $V^{ii} > V^{ij}$ parents have an incentive to socialize their children to their own cultural trait. But socialization requires parental resources, e.g., time spent with children, private school tuition, church contributions, and so on. Let $C(d^i)$ denote socialization costs, where d^i is the probability of direct socialization of parents with trait i to the i trait. The value of parental socialization choice is then represented by:

$$W^i(q^i) = \max_{d^i \in [0,1]} -C(d^i) + P^{ii}V^{ii}(q^i) + P^{ij}V^{ij}(q^i), \text{ s. t. 1), and 2).}^5$$

Assuming for simplicity quadratic socialization costs, $C(d^i) = \frac{1}{2}(d^i)^2$, we obtain

$$d^j = d(q^i, \Delta V^i) = (1-q^i)\Delta V^i, \tag{2}$$

where $\Delta V^i = V^{ii} - V^{ij}$ measures the relative value of child with the same cultural trait as the parents; we refer to ΔV^i as the *cultural intolerance* of trait i.

2.1 Population dynamics

Consider first Cavalli Sforza and Feldman (1981). The system of equations (1) for P^{ij}, the probability that a child from a family with trait i is socialized to trait j, imply the following dynamics of the fraction of the population with trait i, in the continuous time limit:

[4] To avoid trivial cases, we assume $x^a \neq x^b$.

[5] The socialization choice of parents is independent of their choice of $x \in X$. This is due to preference separability.

$$\dot{q}^i = q^i(1-q^i)(d^i - d^j). \tag{3}$$

Equation (3) is a simple version of the replicator dynamics in evolutionary biology for a two-trait population dynamic model. Formally, it is a *logistic differential equation.* If $(d^i - d^j) > 0$ cultural transmission represents a selection mechanism in favor of trait i, due to its differential vertical socialization. This selective mechanism is all the more powerful (i.e., the speed of selection is higher) when there is enough variation in the population, which is captured by the term $q^i(1-q^i)$, reflecting the variance of types in the population. We say that the stationary state of the population dynamics q^{i*} is culturally homogeneous if either $q^{i*} = 0$ or $q^{i*} = 1$. We say instead that q^{i*} is culturally heterogeneous if $0 < q^{i*} < 1$. Let $q^i(t, q^i_0)$ denote the solution path of the differential equation which describes the population dynamics, so that $q^i(t, q^i_0)$ is the value of q^i at time t when, at time $t = 0$, q^i takes the value q^i_0.

A first obvious result coming from (3), as in Cavalli Sforza and Feldman (1981), is the following:

Suppose (d^i, d^j) are exogenous and $d^i > d^j$.[6] *In this case, the stationary states of the population dynamics are culturally homogeneous. Moreover, $q^i(t, q^i_0) \to 1$, for any $q^i_0 \in (0, 1]$. If instead $d^i = d^j$, $q^i(t, q^i_0) = q^i_0$, for any $t \geq 0$.*

In other words, the selective mechanism of cultural transmission, as modeled by Cavalli Sforza and Feldman (1981), can hardly explain the observed resilience of cultural traits (except in the knife hedge non-generic case in which $d^i = d^j$). Boyd and Richerson (1985) extend Cavalli Sforza and Feldman (1981)'s analysis to allow for frequency dependent direct socialization probabilities:

$$d^i = d(q^i), d^j = d(1-q^i),$$

generating more interesting and complex population dynamics. But in Boyd and Richerson (1985), while direct socialization probabilities are frequency dependent, they are nonetheless exogenous.[7]

Economic models of cultural transmission also predict frequency dependent socialization probabilities, but purposeful parental socialization decisions restrict the class of consistent frequency dependent socialization. The dynamics of the fraction of the population with cultural trait i is then determined by equation (3), evaluated at $d^i = d(q^i, \Delta V^i)$, $d^j = d(1-q^i, \Delta V^j)$ as in (2):

Suppose (d^i, d^j) are endogenously determined as in equation (2). The stationary states of the population dynamics are $(0, 1, q^{i*})$, where q^{i*} is culturally hetrogeneous. Moreover, the culturally hetrerogenous stationay state is globally state, that is, $q^i(t,q^i_0) \to q^{i*}$, for any $q^i_0 \in (0,1)$.

[6] Obviously, the case $d^j > d^i$ is symmetric, as i and j are arbitrary.

[7] There is a lively interesting literature in anthropology and biology which studies cultural transmission as the outcome of exogenous evolutionary rules. While we do not discuss this literature in detail as it exudes from our purposes, we refer the reader to e.g., Henrich (2001), Gallo, Barra, and Contucci (2009), and Enquist, Ghirlanda, Eriksson (2010).

The economic model of cultural transmission in Bisin and Verdier (2001) predicts then cultural heterogeneity and is therefore consistent with the observed resilience of cultural traits. But, how general is this result? What does explain cultural heterogeneity?

2.1.1 Cultural heterogeneity

Intuitively, cultural heterogeneity might obtain when parents belonging to a cultural minority face relatively higher incentives to socialize their children to their own trait. Formally, this is the case socialization mechanisms which satisfy the following property.

Cultural substitution: for any $\Delta V^i > 0$, $d^i(q^i, \Delta V^i)$ *is a continuous, strictly decreasing function in* q^i, *and, moreover,* $d^i\,(1, \Delta V^i) = 0$.

We say that direct vertical transmission acts as a cultural substitute to oblique transmission, when parents have fewer incentives to socialize their children the more widely dominant are their traits in the population. In the limit of a perfectly homogenous populations of type i, parents of type i do not directly socialize their children. As a consequence the socialization pattern moves the system away from full homogeneity: $q^i = 0$ and $q^i = 1$ are locally unstable stationary states of (3), and the basin of attraction of the unique steady state associated to heterogeneous population, q^{i*}, is the full interval (0, 1). Bisin and Verdier (2001) show the following:

Cultural heterogeneity obtains generally whenever direct vertical socialization is a substitute to oblique/horizontal socialization.

When $d^i(q^i, \Delta V^i)$ is instead increasing in q^i, socialization efforts of parents of type i are typically larger the more frequent their trait in the population. Direct vertical and oblique transmissions are linked in some degree by cultural complementarity in this case. Strong enough forms of cultural complementarity can drive the dynamics of the distribution of the traits in the population towards homogeneity.

We illustrate the role of cultural substitution versus complementarity in the population dynamics of cultural traits with two examples of different socialization mechanisms from Bisin and Verdier (2001).

Cultural substitution example: It's the family. Suppose children are exposed simultaneously to their parent's trait, say i, and to the trait of an individual picked at random from a restricted population, composed of a fraction τ_2^i of agents with trait i (the population of neighbors, friends, school peers, and teachers). The parent's direct socialization effort is denoted $\tau_1^i \in [0, 1]$, and controls the children's internalization of the parent's trait. If the two traits match (i.e., if the child internalizes his parent trait, i, and the trait of the individual in the restricted population is also i), then the child is socialized to trait i. Otherwise, with probability$(1-\tau_1^i\tau_2^i)$, the child picks a trait from the population as a whole. The probability that a child of a type i father is directly socialized (by exposure to the parent and to the restricted pool) is then:

$$d^i = \tau_1^i \tau_2^i$$

Suppose both the direct socialization effort,$\tau_1^i \in [0,1]$, and the segregation effort, $\tau_2^i \in [0,1]$, are chosen by parents. If preferences and socialization costs satisfy some regularity assumptions (see Bisin and Verdier, 2001), direct vertical and oblique transmission are substitutes for such transmission mechanisms and the long run state of the population dynamics is culturally heterogeneous.

Cultural complementarity example: It takes a village. Suppose children are first exposed simultaneously to the parent's trait and to the trait of a role model from the population with which he/she is matched randomly. If the parent and the role model are culturally homogeneous, the child is directly socialized to their common trait, otherwise the child is matched a second time randomly with a role model from the population, and adopts his/her trait. Vertical and oblique transmissions are not cultural substitutes in this example. With quadratic socialization costs, in this case,

$$d(q^i, \Delta V^i) = (q^i)^2(1 - q^i)\Delta V^i.$$

This socialization effort is clearly non monotonic in q^i and exhibits a range of q^i for which there is cultural complementary.[8]

A simple analysis of the population dynamics implies that

$$q^i(t, q_0^i) \rightarrow 0, \textit{ for any } q_0^i \in \ [0, q^{i^*});$$
$$q^i(t, q_0^i) \rightarrow 1, \textit{ for any } q_0^i \in \ (q^{i^*}, 1], \textit{for } 0 < q^{i^*} < 1.$$

Summarizing, the economic cultural transmission model in Bisin and Verdier (2000, 2001) allows for population dynamics of the distribution of cultural traits which converge to a heterogeneous distribution, and can be therefore providing an explanation of the observed resilience of e.g., ethnic and religious traits. This is the case, in particular, when direct and oblique socialization mechanisms are cultural substitutes. Figures 1 and 2 illustrate the starkly different population dynamics in the leading models in Cavalli Sforza and Feldman (1981) and in Bisin and Verdier (2000, 2001):

2.2 Socialization mechanisms

The cultural transmission model we described abstracts from many important details regarding socialization mechanisms. Direct socialization probabilities are the results of several different effort choices of parents, e.g., in terms of time and resources dedicated to their children. Socialization effort is more effective e.g., when the parents in the family share the cultural trait to socialize the children to, when teachers in school, other adults and the children peers all reinforce the socialization effort of parents. Socialization is a fundamental family activity and as such, it might motivate individuals to prefer homogamous marriages (along relevant cultural traits) and particular fertility patterns. It also might motivate families to the consideration of various cultural aspects when choosing schools for their children, when choosing the neighborhood where they reside in, when choosing

[8] Indeed $\frac{\partial d(q^i, \Delta V^i)}{\partial q^i} \gtreqless 0$ as $q^i \lesseqgtr \frac{2}{3}$.

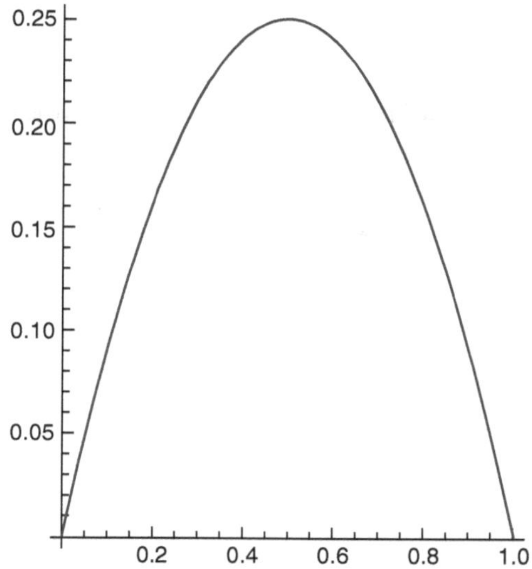

Figure 1 Dynamics with cultural substitution in Cavalli Sforza and Feldman (1981): $\dot{q}^i$ as a function of q^i.

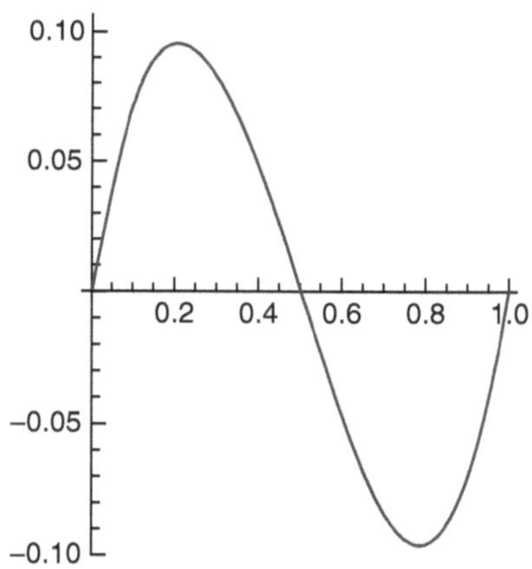

Figure 2 Dynamics with cultural substitution in Bisin and Verdier (2001): $\dot{q}^i$ as a function of q^i.

with civil and social organizations they are member of, and so on. More generally, parental socialization requires the active participation of the children themselves, who ultimately form their identities and preferences in the social environment they interact with. This in turn motivates parents to pro-actively intervene in shaping their children social environment, once again through the choice of schools, neighborhood, peers, and so on.

In this section, we survey the theoretical contributions to the cultural transmission literature whose focus is to expand the analysis to consider several different socialization mechanisms.

2.2.1 Geographic spread

Cultural traits diffuse geographically, e.g., because the population carrying the trait moves, typically while expanding economically or militarily. Let l denote the distance (e.g., the radial distance in two dimensions) from an initial location. Let $q(l, t)$ denote the fraction of agents of type i at location l. Rendine, Piazza, and Cavalli Sforza (1986), extending the cultural transmission model to geographic diffusion (in the continuous time approximation), obtain the following partial differential equation

$$\frac{\partial q^i}{\partial t} = q^i(1-q^i)(d^i-d^j) + m\frac{\partial^2 q^i}{\partial l^2} \tag{4}$$

where m is the diffusion coefficient. This equation, known in evolutionary genetics as Fisher-Kolmogorov equation, has a constant traveling wave solution

$$q^i(l,t) = w^i(l-\alpha t)$$

which is monotonic and satisfies $\lim_{z\to-\infty} w^i(z) = 1$ and $\lim_{z\to\infty} w^i(z) = 0$. Figure 3 illustrates the dynamics associated to a stationary constant traveling wave, for $m = .001$ and $d^i - d^j$ equal to .5.

Furthermore, for any initial condition $q^i(l, 0)$ satisfying regularity conditions which appear natural in this context,[9] $q^i(l, t)$ evolves to a travelling wave with speed $\alpha = 2\sqrt{(d^i - d^j)m}$. This asymptotic solution can be accurately approximated as

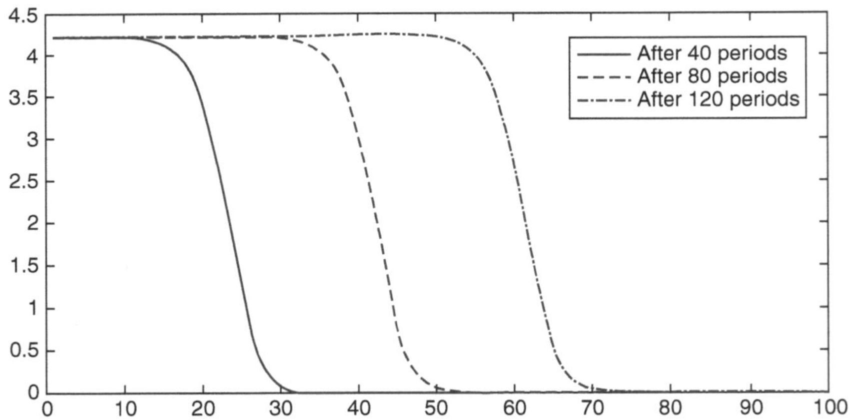

Figure 3 Constant traveling wave: Each curve represents the wave at a time *t*, with the variable *l* on the *x*-axis

[9] The condition are the following:

$q^i(l,0) \geq 0$ and continuous in l, $q^i(l,0) = \begin{cases} 1 & \text{if } l \leq l_1 \\ 0 & \text{if } l \geq l_2 \end{cases}$ for some $l_1 < l_2$.

$$w^i(z) \approx \frac{1}{1+e^{\frac{z}{\alpha}}};$$

see Murray (1989), p. 283.

The geographical spread model assumes diffusion on the part of only population i and, most importantly, it assumes away any interaction between the two populations. These extensions are possible, though an analytic characterization of the resulting dynamics has yet to be derived.[10] Suppose at any location l at time t live two interacting populations, characterized by their distinct cultural traits, a, b. Let their density be denoted, respectively, $Q^a(l, t)$ and $Q^b(l, t)$ respectively.[11] Suppose population Q^a diffuses geographically, while population Q^b does not. Furthermore, assume the populations interact socially, at any location l. The result of such interactions is the adoption of trait Q_a, on the part of individuals of type b, at an instantaneous rate proportional to $Q^a(l, t) \cdot Q^b(l, t)$. Finally, suppose that the highest sustainable population densities at any location l and time t are, respectively, P^a and P^b. Under these assumptions, the dynamic population equations (in the continuous time approximation) are a version of the Lotka-Volterra equation for interaction geographically structured populations,[12]

$$\begin{aligned} \frac{\partial Q^a}{\partial t} &= \alpha_a Q^a\left(1-\frac{Q^a}{P_a}\right)+\gamma Q^a Q^b + m\frac{\partial^2 Q^a}{\partial l^2} \\ \frac{\partial Q^b}{\partial t} &= \alpha_b Q^b\left(1-\frac{Q^b}{P_b}\right)-\gamma Q^a Q^b. \end{aligned} \tag{LV}$$

To the best of our knowledge, nobody has studied the cultural transmission model with geographic diffusion when $d^i - d^j$ is a function of q^i, as in the economic model of cultural transmission. Based on the analysis of Murray (1989), ch. 11.5 (especially p. 304), we conjecture existence and stability (for appropriate initial conditions) to a monotonic travelling wave $w^i(z)$ such that $\lim_{t\to\infty} w^i(z) = q^{i*}$, $0 < q^{i*} < 1$. Similarly, nobody has studied the Lotka-Volterra model with endogenous α_a, α_b, m, γ.

2.2.2 Homogamous marriages

Marriages are formed in the marriage market anticipating their role in the direct socialization of children. Bisin and Verdier (2000) study a marriage market in which homogamous marriages (that is, marriages in which spouses share the same cultural trait) are valued because they are more effective socialization mechanism. The simplest model

[10] See Aoki et al. (1996) for numerical solutions.

[11] Clearly,

$$q^i(l,t) = \frac{Q^i(l,t)}{Q^a(l,t)+Q^b(l,t)}, \quad i = a, b.$$

[12] For an introduction to these reaction-diffusion systems, see Murray (1989), ch. 12, 14, 15.

is developed under the extreme assumption that only homogamous marriages are endowed with a direct socialization technology. In this case, the expected utility of child of for a type i parent in a heterogamous marriage, not endowed with a direct socialization technology, is simply

$$W^{i,Het}(q^i) = q^i V^{ii} + (1-q^i) V^{ij}.$$

The corresponding expected utility for a type i parent in an homogamous marriage,

$$W^{i,Hom}(q^i) = \max_{d^i}[d^i + (1-d^i)q^i] V^{ii} + (1-d^i)(1-q^i) V^{ij}] - C(d^i),$$

depends on the parent's socialization choice. Consequently, the option to socialize children provided by homogamous marriages is valued by individuals in the marriage market:

$$W^{i,Hom}(q^i) - W^{i,Het}(q^i) \geq 0.$$

The marriage market is then modeled to allow each individual to affect the probability to be married homogamously. Suppose the marriage market contains a restricted pool in which marriages, if they occur, are homogamous (churches, ethnic clubs, and various other cultural institutions may serve this purpose). An individual of trait i can enter the restricted pool and marry homogamously with probability α^i, which is chosen at a cost $H(\alpha^i)$. With probability $1-\alpha^i$ the individual enters instead a common pool, composed of all individuals who have not been matched in marriage in their own restricted pools, and is married there with a random match. Let A^i be the fraction of individuals of type i who are matched in their restricted pool. The probability of homogamous marriage of an individual of type i is given by

$$\pi^i(\alpha^i, A^i, A^j, q^i) = \alpha^i + (1-\alpha^i)\frac{(1-A^i)q^i}{(1-A^i)q^i + (1-A^j)(1-q^i)}. \tag{5}$$

An individual with trait i chooses $\alpha^i \in [0, 1]$, for given A^i, A^j, q^i, to maximize

$$\pi^i(\alpha^i, A^i, A^j, q^i)[W^{i,Hom}(q^i) - W^{i,Het}(q^i)] - H(\alpha^i). \tag{6}$$

The maximization of (6) for each agent of type i provides an optimal α^i as a function of A^i, A^j and q^i. Under convexity and regularity assumptions, Bisin and Verdier (2000) show the existence of a unique symmetric Nash equilibrium of the marriage game, where all individuals of type i choose the same marital segregation effort $\alpha^i = \alpha^i(q^i)$ and $A^i = \alpha^i(q^i)$. At equilibrium, the probability of homogamous marriage for agents of type i is then $\pi^i(q^i) = \pi^i(\alpha^i(q^i), \alpha^i(q^i), \alpha^j(q^j), q^i)$. The population dynamics, in turn, are:

$$\dot{q}^i = q^i(1-q^i)(d^i\pi^i - d^j\pi^j), \tag{7}$$

evaluated at $d^i = d^i(q^i)$ and $\pi^i = \pi^i(q^i)$. The selective forces for cultural transmission, therefore, account for the differential "effective" efforts of vertical transmission, $d^i\pi^i$, which reflect the fact that only homogamous marriage can successfully bias the transmission of their cultural trait.

Bisin and Verdier (2000) show that at equilibrium, when homogamous marriages act as a socialization mechanism, cultural substitution applies to this "effective" vertical cultural transmission $d^i\pi^i$:

For any $0 < q^i < 1$ and for $i \in \{a, b\}$, in equilibrium, i) the probability of matching in the restricted pool for agents of type i, $\alpha^i(q^i)$, and the direct socialization probability of homogamous families of type i, $d^i(q^i)$, are strictly positive; ii) the homogamy rate of the population of type i is greater than the homogamy rate associated with random matching, $\pi^i(q^i) > q^i$; and iii) the probability of successful socialization for a family of type i is greater than the oblique socialization rate, $P^{ii}(q^i) > q^i$. Furthermore, iv) $\alpha^i(q^i)$ and $d^i(q^i)$ are decreasing in the fraction of the population with trait i, q^i.

Consequently, the population dynamics of the trait distribution, when homogamous marriages act as a socialization mechanism, induce a stationary distribution, which is culturally heterogeneous:

The culturally homogeneous stationary states of the population dynamics, (0, 1), are locally unstable. There always exists a culturally heterogeneous stationary state, q^{i*}, which is locally stable, that is, such that $q^i(t, q_0^i) \rightarrow q^{i^*}$, for any q_0^i in an appropriate neighborhood of q^{i*}.[13]

In summary, in an environment in which individuals search for homogamous marriages for their benefits in terms of socialization, the cultural substitution properties of socialization mechanisms are preserved.

2.2.3 Fertility

Fertility, as an endogenous choice of parents, also interacts with socialization, if for no other reason that socialization costs naturally increase with the number of children to socialize. Consider for instance the cultural transmission model, extended to allow for parental choice of reproductive pattern. Let $N^i \geq 0$ denote the number of children chosen by parents with trait i, at cost $c(N^i)$. To better illustrate the effects of endogenous fertility, consider the extreme case in which direct socialization is exogenous. In this case, parents of type i then choose $N^i \geq 0$ to maximize:

$$-c(N^i) + N^i(P^{ii}V^{ii} + P^{ij}V^{ij}),$$

where $P^{ii}\ V^{ii} + P^{ij}V^{ij}$ can be interpreted as the expected *quality* of one child,[14] and is independent of N^i. It follows then that the parents of a cultural majority will choose relatively high fertility rates, since in this case their children are of high-expected quality, that is, they will inherit their trait with high probability. The choice of reproduction patterns, as a consequence, will tend to introduce cultural complementarity in the socialization mechanism: $N^i(q^i)$ will tend to be increasing.

[13] If the culturally heterogeneous stationary state q^{i*} is unique, $q^i(t, q_0^i) \rightarrow q^{i^*}$, globally, for $q_0^i \in (0, 1)$.

[14] See Becker and Lewis (1973) for this terminology.

However, more generally, fertility will interact with direct socialization and hence parents, when choosing direct children socialization, incur a classic quantity/quality (of children) trade off. Assuming for simplicity socialization costs linear in N^i, parents of type i choose $d^i \in [0, 1]$, and $N^i \geq 0$ to maximize:

$$-c(N^i) - N^i C(d^i) + N^i(P^{ii}V^{ii} + P^{ij}V^{ij}), \tag{8}$$

where P^{ii} and P^{ij} are as in (1). The dynamics of the distribution of traits in the population is then determined by

$$\dot{q}^i = q^i(1-q^i)(d^i n^i - d^j n^j),$$

where $n^i = \frac{N^i}{N^i+N^j}$ and d^i are determined at equilibrium. Bisin-Verdier (2001) show that, under some regularity conditions, with endogenous fertility:

The stationary states of the population dynamics are (0, 1, q^{i*}), where q^{i*} is culturally heterogeneous. Moreover, the culturally heterogeneous stationary state is globally stable, that is, $q^i(t, q_0^i) \rightarrow q^{i^*}$, for any $q_0^i \in (0, 1)$.

In other words, the quantity/quality trade-off is sufficient to re-establish the dynamics associated to cultural substitution, over-riding the cultural complementarity due to endogenous fertility.

2.2.4 Self-segregation

The socialization model we introduced interacts direct vertical transmission in the family with oblique transmission, in society: if a child is not directly socialized, he/she picks the trait by random matching in society (i.e., trait i with probability q^i and trait j with probability $q^j = 1-q^i$). More generally, however, the cultural composition of society is at least partly under the control of parents: they in fact choose schools, neighborhood, peers, and so on. Abstracting from details, the transmission probabilities could be more generally written as,

$$\begin{aligned} P^{ii} &= d^i + (1-d^i)Q^i \\ P^{ij} &= (1-d^i)(1-Q^i), \end{aligned} \tag{9}$$

where the composition of the social environment of the child, Q^i, could be specified as a function of the population share q^i and a costly parental intervention, say s^i. Examples of a model along these lines are Bisin-Verdier (2001; Section 2.2.2, *Do not talk to strangers*) and Saez Marti and Sjogren (2008).

2.2.5 Identity formation

While parents directly make various socialization choices to influence the preference formation of their children, vertical socialization is nonetheless in general limited by the children's role in forming their own cultural *identity*. An interesting literature on identity in economics is rapidly emerging, stirred by the contribution of Akerlof and

Kranton (2000).[15] This literature evolved with particular emphasis on the formation of oppositional identities, namely situations where minority individuals adopt cultural categorizations and prescriptions defined in opposition to the categorizations and prescriptions of the mainstream group. Akerlof and Kranton (2000) discuss how a student's primary motivation is his or her identity and how the quality of a school depends on how well students fit in the school's social setting. Austen-Smith and Fryer (2005) focus on the tension faced by individuals between signaling their type to the outside labor market and signaling their type to their peers: signals that induce high wages can be signals that induce peer rejection. Relatedly, Battu, Mwale and Zenou (2007) show that some ethnic minorities may reject the majority's norms of behavior even if this implies a penalty in the labor market.[16]

More generally, the study of ethnic identity formation has a long theoretical and empirical tradition in social sciences, with Cross (1991), Phinney (1990), Ferdman (1995) in developmental psychology, Stryker (1968) in symbolic interactions sociology, Tajfel (1981), Tajfel and Turner (1979), Turner et al. (1987) in social psychology, and Brewer (1999) in political psychology. Abstracting from many specific details, two opposing views characterize the theoretical analysis of identity formation in the social sciences. A first group of social scientists argues that ethnic identity is reduced by assimilation and contact across cultures.[17] Underlying this reasoning is the basic principle that group identity is driven by a motive for inclusiveness and *cultural conformity*. The alternative view considers that ethnic minorities are motivated in keeping their own distinctive cultural heritage to generate a sense of positive *distinctiveness* from individuals who are part of that group.[18] According to this view, the group identity formation is motivated by a *cultural distinction* mechanism that allows individuals to reduce the psychological costs associated with cultural differences.[19]

When identity formation is characterized by cultural distinction, social interactions across groups might induce the formation of stronger oppositional identities on the part of minorities. An interesting example is Darity, Mason and Stewart (2006). They study a formal model of the relationship between wealth accumulation and racial identity to evaluate the persistence of racial identity as a social norm. More precisely, they consider a large population of agents divided into two groups distinct by a racial characteristic

[15] See also Akerlof and Kranton (2010).

[16] See also, for instance, Cook and Ludwig (1997), Ferguson (2001), Fryer (2004), Fryer and Torelli (2005), Patacchini and Zenou (2007).

[17] *Assimilation theories*, in political science and sociology (Gordon, 1964; Moghaddam and Solliday 1991), *contact theory* in social psychology (Allport, 1954) are the prominent theories of this line of thought.

[18] These ideas have been expressed by the theories of *multiculturalism* (Glazer and Moynihan, 1970; Taylor and Lambert, 1996), and *conflict* (Bobo, 1999). At a broader level, this view is also related to the *social identity theory* in social psychology (Tajfel, 1981; Turner, 1982; and Abrams and Hogg, 1988).

[19] *Cultural distinction*, as defined here, is a property of individual preferences. It is related but distinct from *cultural substitution* (see Section 2), which is a property of socialization mechanisms.

(e.g., color of skin, shape of eyes, etc.) that cannot be changed by deliberate choice. Individuals however differentiate themselves also along an endogenous dimension, their racial identity. *Individualists* attempt to live a race-free life, even though their exogenous social group characteristic is in fact observable. *Racialists*, on the other hand, choose to identify strongly with their social group. In each time period, individuals are randomly matched in pairs and interact in socio-economic activities. Agents' productivity in these interaction depends on the mutual compatibility of their identities. Racialists are altruistic toward members of their own social group, but antagonistic toward members of the other group. Individualists, on the other hand, are neither altruistic nor antagonistic toward any agent they interact with, socially. Within each social group, the division between individualists and racialists evolves endogenously. The population frequencies evolve in response to average payoffs by category, according to a standard replicator dynamics. The paper provides conditions on intra-group and inter-group interactions, matching parameters, and initial conditions, such that a racialist or individualist identity norm dominates in each group.

The replicator dynamics mechanism of identity formation is exogenously assumed in Darity, Mason and Stewart (2006). Bisin, Patacchini, Verdier, and Zenou (2010) model instead the economics of identity formation, along the lines of the cultural transmission literature. In addition, they offer an explicit formal definition of cultural distinction and complementarity to develop their different implications regarding identity formation. Consider for simplicity the case of a child socialized to a minority cultural trait, i. Minority individuals have psychological costs $C(I^i, q^i)$ of interacting with the majority that depend both on identity I^i and the fraction q^i of individuals of group i in the neighborhood. These psychological costs can be reduced by identity formation I^i.

More precisely, consider that identity I^i can take two possible discrete values (i.e., $I^i \in \{0, 1\}$). The intensity v^i with which a cultural trait i is adopted by children is then simply the probability of acquiring the minority identity (after successful parental socialization), $v^i = prob\{I^i = 1\}$, and it is modeled as a choice of the agent. The utility cost of developing identity v^i, $J(v^i)$ is increasing and convex, in the same units of the psychological costs $C(I^i, q^i)$.

The psychological costs of interactions can only be felt by individuals that do not acquire a strong ethnic identity (i.e., in the case $I = 0$). Formally $C(I^i, q^i)$ takes the simple form:

$$C(I^i, q^i) = (1 - I^i)c(1 - q^i).$$

The two polar cases, cultural distinction and cultural conformity, are then simply captured as follows:

Cultural distinction: *$c(1-q^i)$ is increasing in the proportion of the majority $1-q^i$.*
Cultural conformity: *$c(1-q^i)$ is decreasing in $1-q^i$.*

The identity formation choice of an individual has then different properties in the two cases. In particular, Bisin, Patacchini, Verdier, and Zenou (2010) show that:

The distinctive characteristics of cultural distinction is that identity v^i is decreasing in q^i, for q^i large enough.

Bisin, Patacchini, Verdier and Zenou (2010) extend the theoretical analysis of this paper by explicitly interacting cultural transmission and identity formation. They also draw the population dynamics implications of the model and show that both cultural substitution and cultural distinction induce resilience and persistence of minoritarian traits. More specifically, in Bisin, Patacchini, Verdier and Zenou (2010), after being socialized to a particular trait (directly or indirectly), the intensity with which an individual identifies to that trait (i.e., his cultural *identity*) is his personal choice, that is, it is not transmitted by the family. Choosing the intensity of an identity is conceptualized as a form of cultural distinction. Specifically, parents decide how much to invest in socializing their children to their own ethnic trait anticipating the possible peer effects favoring assimilation and their children's future identity choice. Formally, the optimal parental transmission effort d^i and child identity intensity effort v^i are the solution of the following problem:

$$\max_{v,d} -P^{ii}(d,q^i)(1-v^i)c(1-q^i) - [1-P^{ii}(d,q^i)]c(1-q^i) - H(d) - J(v^i)$$

with P^{ii} (d, q^i) given by (1).

As a result, the identity of an individual turns out to notably depend on the ethnic composition of the neighborhood in which he/she is raised and his/her personal negative experiences related to ethnicity. The prevalence of an oppositional culture in the minority group can be sustained if and only if there is enough cultural segmentation in terms of role models, the size of the minority group is large enough, the degree of oppositional identity it implies is high enough, and the socio-economic opportunity cost of the actions it prescribes is small enough. The model also identifies sufficient conditions on economic fundamentals such that ethnic identity and socialization effort are more intense in mixed rather than in segregated neighborhoods.[20]

2.3 Multidimensional cultural traits

The cultural transmission model we described only refers to single dichotomous cultural traits, abstracting from several interesting issues related to the cultural space. In fact cultural traits are often multidimensional. For instance, a religious trait is composed of common ethical values and common preferences along many dimensions, from food to art. Religious traits also come in different forms, one for each reference religious

[20] Finally the model also allows for attitudes of the majority group, e.g., racism, which might induce its reaction into forms of oppositional identity of the minority. As it turns out, racism by the majority and minority integration present natural complementarities that may give rise to social multiplier effects and/or multiple social steady state equilibria.

denomination. Furthermore, cultural traits can in general be adopted with different intensity along different dimension, e.g., an individual can share most values of the Catholic church while feeling unease with the mandate for priests' celibacy.

While the model of cultural transmission has not been extended to account for several of these richer cultural spaces, Montgomery (2009) has exhaustively studied the case of cultural traits taking many different forms.[21] When the leading model of economic cultural transmission is extended to a N traits, the population dynamics is governed by

$$q^j = q^i\left(d^i - \sum_{j=1}^{N} d^j q^j\right)$$
$$d^i = \sum_{j=1}^{N} q^j \Delta V^{ij},$$

where $\sum_{j=1}^{N} q_j = 1$ and $\Delta V^{ij} = V^{ii} - V^{ij}$.[22] While Montgomery (2009) studies more general environments, it is pedagogically convenient to restrict the analysis to the symmetric case, where $\Delta V^{ij} = \Delta V^{ik}$, $\forall\, j,\, k \neq i$, and hence traits can be ranked in terms of their cultural intolerance. Abusing notation, we let then $\Delta V^{ij} \equiv \Delta V^i$ and, without loss of generality, we order traits so that

$$\Delta V^1 \geq \Delta V^2 \geq \ldots \geq \Delta V^N.$$

Let F_k denote a k-dimensional subsets of $\{1,\ldots,N\}$. We say that a stationary distribution supports F_k, and we denote it $q(F_k)$, if it is contained in the appropriate simplex:

$$q(F_k) \in \left\{q \in S^N | q^i = 0, \text{ for } i \notin F_k\right\}.$$

A cultural group i is not supported by a stationary state if it is not intolerant enough relatively to the other groups:

A stationary distribution which supports F_k exists if

$$\Delta V^i > [k-1] G^{F_k}, \forall i \in F_k \tag{10}$$

where $\frac{1}{G^{F_k}} \equiv \sum_{i \in F_k} \frac{1}{\Delta V^i}$.

G^{F_k} can be in fact considered a measure of the cultural intolerance of the traits belonging to F_k; e.g., if $\Delta V^i = \Delta V$ for all $i \in F_k$, $G^{F_k} = \frac{\Delta V}{k}$.

Montgomery (2009), exploiting techniques developed for the *replicator dynamics* in evolutionary game theory, proves that culturally heterogeneous stationary distributions tend to be supported in the N-trait case as well:

[21] See also Bisin, Topa and Verdier (2009); but Montgomery (2009)'s results are stronger.

[22] In a more recognizable matrix form:
$\dot{\mathbf{q}} = diag(\mathbf{q})(\Delta_{\mathbf{q}} - \mathbf{q}'\Delta_{\mathbf{q}})$, where $\mathbf{q} = [q^i]$ and $\Delta = [\Delta V^{ij}]$.

Any culturally homogeneous distribution, $q(F_1)$ is locally unstable. Furthermore, the stationary distribution $q(F_{k^*})$, where F_{k^*} is the largest subset of cultural groups $\{1,\ldots,N\}$ which is supported by a stationary distribution, is globally stable.[23]

A simple corollary of this result is that,

If

$$\sum_{i=1}^{N} \frac{1}{\Delta V^i} > \frac{N-1}{Min_i\{\Delta V^i\}}, \quad (Symmetry)$$

there is a unique globally stable stationary state $q(F_N)$.

Note that this condition is stricter for larger N: in the limit, for $N \to \infty$, it requires symmetric preferences across cultural groups: ΔV^i independent of i. This corollary then identifies symmetry of the parents' preferences for children as a factor which facilitates the stability of heterogeneous stationary distributions of traits in the population.

So far, only cultural transmission models with a discrete number of traits were presented. There is however, a well-established tradition in evolutionary biology and anthropology to consider continuous traits models of cultural transmission. These models postulate a dynamics of cultural traits which is driven by exogenous linear mixing; see e.g., Cavalli-Sforza (1973), Otto, Christiansen and Feldman (1994). More specifically, let $B^i(t)$ denote the value of trait i associated to a representative individual at time t. Formally, $B^i(t)$ is a stochastic process whose dynamics is governed by:

$$\dot{B}^i = (1 - d^i)(\bar{B} - B^i) + \varepsilon^i$$

where ε^i is an independently and identically distributed random shock with zero mean and constant variance σ; and d^i is an exogenous parameter which represents the speed of adjustment of the process to its mean. More complex and interesting models along these lines are discussed in Boyd and Richerson (1985).

Extending the analysis to the case of endogenous cultural transmission is a non-trivial exercise. Keeping track of the time evolution of the mean and the variance of the distribution of continuous traits, a central insight of these approaches is to derive conditions for the long-term persistence of cultural variation in the population. Bisin and Topa (2003) suggest a model of endogenous transmission in a continuous trait setting which assumes that the value of the trait of a child of type i, B^i is constructed as a weighted average between a target value B^{*i} and the mean value of the trait in the population $\bar{B}$,

$$\dot{B}^i = (1 - d^i)(\bar{B} - B^{i*}) + \varepsilon^i$$

As in the discrete trait model, parents could spend effort to isolate the influence of friends, peers, and society at large on their children's value of the trait, that is, by

[23] Since $\Delta V^1 \geq \Delta V^2 \geq \ldots \geq \Delta V^N$, $F_k = \{1,\ldots,k\}$.

choosing d^i, which is then interpreted as the direct vertical socialization choice of parents and is assumed costly (with cost $C(d^i) = \frac{1}{2}(d^i)^2$, for simplicity). Socialization preferences would depend on the context. For instance, suppose agents of type i consider the trait favorably (i.e., parents like their children to possess the trait in the highest expected value). Parents of type i would then maximize utility by solving

$$\max_{d^i} E(B^i) - C(d^i)$$
$$s.t.\dot{B}^i = (1-d^i)(\bar{B} - B^{*i}) + \varepsilon^i$$

The solution of the problem is $d^i = (B^{*i} - \bar{B})$, and parental socialization effort satisfies a form of *cultural substitution*: it declines with the influence of the social environment as captured by the mean value of trait in the population, $\bar{B}$. For instance, the target B^{*i} might correspond to the maximum possible value of the trait given the family characteristics of type i. Suppose, by means of illustration, that the target value B^{*i} is directly related to the cultural trait value of the parent:

$$B^{*i} = aB^i, a > 0.$$

This could be the case, e.g., if parents had a limited or costly technology to set the socialization target based on their own cultural trait value, B^i.

Interesting socialization preferences in this context are studied by Pichler (2010), who lets parents explicitly choose also the socialization target B^{*i}.[24] As an illustration, consider the following special case of Pichler (2010)'s model. Assume parents of type i face a disutility which increases in the distance between the value of the trait of their children, B^i, and the socialization target they set. Assume also that socialization costs are higher the larger the distance between the target and the parents' own trait value, and quadratic for simplicity, $C(d^i, B^{*i} - B^i) = \frac{1}{2}(B^{*i} - B^i)^2 + \frac{1}{2}(d^i)^2$. Fixing exogenously d^i, the parental socialization problem is

$$\max_{B^{*i}} -\frac{1}{2}E(B^i - B^{*i})^2 - C(d^i, (B^{*i} - B^i))$$
$$s.t.\ \dot{B}^i = (1-d^i)(\bar{B} - B^{*i}) + \varepsilon^i$$

and, B^{*i} is a weighted average of B^i and $\bar{B}$. Consequently, once again, cultural substitution obtains. This is the case also when parents choose direct socialization d^i optimally.

In either Bisin and Topa (2003) and Pichler (2010), the dynamics of B^i is characterized by a non-linear stochastic different equation with a (global) interaction term, $\bar{B}$, of the form

$$\dot{B}^i = f(B^i, \bar{B}) + \varepsilon^i,$$

[24] Along these lines is also the work in progress of Panebianco (2010) and Vaughan (2010).

for some map f. Conditions for existence and uniqueness of a non-degenerate ergodic distribution in cultural traits can be obtained. Results on ergodicity for stochastic processes in this class, with (local and global) interactions have been obtained, e.g., by Follmer and Horst (2001) and Horst and Scheinkman (2006).[25]

In the simple case of Bisin and Topa (2003), for example, the inter-generational dynamics of the trait is characterized by the following stochastic non-linear dynamic difference equation:

$$B^i_{t+1} = (aB^i_t - \bar{B}_t)(aB^i_t - \bar{B}_t) + \bar{B}_t + \varepsilon^i_t.$$

and the study of ergodicity requires tracking the evolution of $\bar{B}_t$ as well as of the variance, of B^i_t.[26]

The previous models are specific in many dimensions. It would be important to extend this approach to more general structures of cultural traits and processes of cultural transmission.

2.4 Cultural transmission and social interactions

In the cultural transmission models we described so far, parental socialization depends on the parents' relative value of child with the same cultural trait as theirs, ΔV^i, which we referred to as the *cultural intolerance* of trait i. In fact, the ΔV^i's have been treated as exogenous preference parameters in the theoretical work we have surveyed up to this point. In many contexts of interest, however, this is too restrictive an assumption. The endogeneity of ΔV^i can originate in many different environments. For instance, when individuals interact on markets, their indirect utility may depend on economic variables such as prices and incomes or policy outcomes that depend on the type of society and therefore on the distribution of cultural traits that prevails in such society. Similarly, in strategic and matching interactions contexts, the payoffs that an individual may obtain are likely to be influenced by the distribution of cultural traits in the population. In all of these situations, it is reasonable to expect cultural intolerance, ΔV^i, to be endogenous.

While the implications of the endogeneity of ΔV^i for socialization and population dynamics need be derived case-by-case, a reduced form analysis is however useful, to clarify what to look for in the examples. Suppose for instance that each individual (parent or child) chooses $x \in X$ to maximize $u^i(x, q^i)$, for $i \in \{a, b\}$ so that, under *imperfect empathy*, direct parental socialization for types i depends on $\Delta V^i\ (q^i) = u^i(x^i, q^i) - u^i(x^j, q^i)$. The first fundamental implication of the endogeneity of ΔV^i is the following:

25 More generally, for stochastic stability and ergodicity of non-linear stochastic difference equations, see the classic treatment in Meyn and Tweedie (2009).

26 Tahbaz-Salehi and Karahan (2008) study a dynamic process determined by preferences for assortative marriages along cultural lines and cultural transmission as averaging across parents. Not surprising melting pot represents a possible stationary state in this model.

When cultural intolerance ΔV^i depends on q^i, imperfect empathy does not necessarily imply that $\Delta V^i(q^i) \geq 0$.

In fact, socialization to the parents' trait might put the children at a disadvantage in the child social environment, represented by q^i. While *imperfect empathy* is manifested as a preference on the part of parents for sharing their cultural traits with their children, such a preference depends on the economic and social conditions, which parents expect for their children. Different economic and social conditions could in principle lead parents to socialize their children to a trait different from their own.

Furthermore, when cultural intolerance is endogenous, the dynamic system for the evolution of cultural traits can be written as:

$$\dot{q}^i = q^i(1-q^i)[d(q^i, \Delta V^i(q^i)) - d(q^j, \Delta V^j(q^j))]$$

While *cultural substitution* is still sufficient to guarantee population dynamics which converge to cultural heterogeneity, an additional assumption on $\Delta V^i(q^i)$ is necessary to produce direct socialization maps $d^i(q^i)$ satisfying cultural substitution:

Strategic substitution: *The social environment is characterized by strategic substitution if,*

$$\frac{\partial}{\partial q^i}\Delta V^i(q^i) < 0.$$

It is easy to see then that, if direct and oblique socialization mechanisms are culturally substitutes:

In a social environment characterized by strategic substitution, the stationary states of the population dynamics are $(0, 1, q^{i*})$, where $0 < q^{i*} < 1$. Moreover, $q^i(t, q^i_0) \to q^{i*}$, globally, for any $q^i_0 \in (0,1)$.

Strategic substitution guarantees that cultural minorities will face relatively larger gains from socialization, independently of the socialization mechanism. In the case of strategic complementarity, on the contrary, cultural minorities face smaller (even possibly negative) socialization gains. Depending on the strength of cultural substitution, therefore, in this case minorities might or might not assimilate culturally to the majority. *Strategic substitution example: Preferences for status.* An example of strategic substitution is the case of preferences for social status studied by Bisin and Verdier (1998). Suppose the expenditures on conspicuous consumption necessary to achieve a given level of social status increase with the fraction of individuals in the population who care about status. In this case, the socialization gains to preferences for status are higher the smaller is the fraction of the population sharing these preferences. In this context therefore, strategic substitution obtains and hence socialization mechanisms will tend to satisfy cultural substitution.

Strategic complementarity example: Corruption. An interesting example of strategic complementarity, albeit only for a subset of parameter values, is represented by Hauk and Sáez-Martí (2002)'s study of the cultural transmission of ethical values regarding corruption. Honest and potentially dishonest agents interact. Each agent is randomly matched to a principal, who in turn assigns him/her to either a project with a high payoff to the principal if the agent is honest, but more conducive to corrupt behavior, or to a safe project whose payoff is low but independent of corruption. Furthermore, for a price, the principal can acquire a signal on the values of the agent he/she is matched to. In this environment, a parent's intolerance towards different values regarding corruption will depend on the strategy of principals in the population, e.g., acquiring the signal and separating project assignments or pooling all agents into the same project. The strategy of principals, in turn depends on the distribution of values in the population of agents. Let σ^p denote the pooling strategy to associate the safe project to all agents and σ^s the separating strategy of offering the high payoff project to all agents who have been signaled as honest. Let also i denote honest agents. Hauk and Sáez-Martí (2002) show that, under particular assumptions about the role of honesty and corruption in the agents' payoffs from strategic interactions, each principal's optimal strategy involves acquiring the signal and separating project assignments when honest agents are a large enough fraction of the population:

$$\sigma(q^i) = \begin{cases} \sigma^s & \text{if } q^i > q^* \\ \{\sigma^s, \sigma^p\} & \text{if } q^i = q^* \\ \sigma^p & \text{if } q^i < q^* \end{cases}$$

Since honest agents have higher payoff on average when principals choose the separating strategy, the socio-economic interaction in this environment is essentially one of *cultural complementarity*, and the population dynamics is biased away from cultural heterogeneity: under specific assumptions, Hauk and Sáez-Martí (2002) find two locally stable distributions of the population, one corresponding to low corruption and the other to high corruption.

Several papers explore the transmission of various distinct cultural traits along the lines of this section: developing a model of the specific socio-economic interaction of interest, obtaining a reduced form for $\Delta V^i(q^i)$, applying the cultural transmission model to study the population dynamics.[27] A non-exhaustive list include: Olcina and Penarrubia (2004) for other-regarding preferences in hold-up contexts; Escriche, Olcina, and Sánchez (2004) for family-related preferences and gender labor market discrimination; Francois (2002), Francois and Zabojnik (2005) and Estrella López (2003)

[27] Some other papers also investigate cultural transmission without the imperfect empathy assumption. See for instance Lindbeck and Nyberg (2006) for the transmission of work norms and social insurance, Epstein (2006) for transmission of extremism; Kuran and Sandholm (2008) for cultural hybridization, Corneo and Jeanne (2009) for a theory of tolerance formation, Dessi (2008) and Adriani and Sonderegger (2009) for an information-based theory of intergenerational transmission of values.

for social capital; Saez-Marti and Zenou (2005) and Senik and Verdier (2007) for work values and ethnic labor market discrimination; Francois (2006) and Bidner and Francois (2009), for the evolution of informal institutions; Frot (2008) for cultural transmission through friendship formation; Hiller (2008a) for preferences for autonomy and work organization; Hiller (2008b) for pro-social preferences and corporate culture; Baudin (2008) for fertility; Ponthiere (2008) for lifestyles transmission and longevity; Melindi Ghidi (2009) for political ideology; Correani, Di Dio, and Garofalo (2009) for tolerance; Frot (2009) and Michaud (2008) for work values and social/unemployment insurance. We cannot discuss them in any detail, for obvious space limitations. We chose to select instead a few papers, which focus on general important themes regarding the interactions of cultural transmission with trade, institutions, and collective action mechanisms.

2.4.1 Cultural transmission and trade

An interesting class of models studies strategic substitution in the context of trade models where standard *Walrasian price effects* obtain on demand. The analysis of these models is mostly relevant, for instance, in the case of international trade of e.g., ethnic goods. The following simple 2 × 2 exchange economy illustrates the argument. Suppose agents have all the same endowment vector $\omega = (\omega_l)_{l=1,2}$, differing instead in their preferences over the two goods: preferences of agents of type i are biased in favor of good i. For instance, assume agents i have well behaved preferences u^i (x_1, x_2) such that, $\forall x_1, x_2$,

$$\frac{\partial u^1(x_1,x_2)}{\partial x_1} > \frac{\partial u^2(x_1,x_2)}{dx_1}, \frac{\partial u^2(x_1,x_2)}{\partial x_2} > \frac{\partial u^1(x_1,x_2)}{dx_2}.$$

Under these assumptions, it is straightforward to show that strategic substitution obtains: the larger the fraction q^i of individuals with preference trait i, the larger the total demand and the market clearing price for good i, the smaller the cultural intolerance of parents of type i.

The market clearing relative price of good 1, p, will be determined by the market clearing condition:

$$z(p) = q^1 x_1^1(p) + (1 - q^1)x_1^2(p) - \omega_1 = 0, \tag{11}$$

where $z(p)$ is the total excess demand for good 1 in the economy and $x_1^i(p)$ is the individual i's demand function for good 1. From equation (11) it is clear that the price p is a function $p(q^1)$. Indeed, given that individuals of type 1 do prefer good 1, $p(q^1)$ will, under general robust conditions, be an increasing function of q^1. When preferences of individuals of type 1 (respectively type 2) are sufficiently biased towards good 1 (respectively good 2), then one can show that $\Delta V^i(q^i)$ is decreasing in q^i and strategic substitution obtains. Cultural heterogeneity will tend to apply to preferences for ethnic goods in exchange economies. The same results obtain, *a fortiori*, in production economies with increasing marginal costs

Olivier, Thoenig, and Verdier (2008), on the other hand, model cultural goods, in general, as goods that generate a group-identity externality: keeping goods' prices constant, the larger the size of the group sharing the same culture, the larger the utility benefit to identify to that cultural group, and the larger also the cultural intolerance ΔV^i. In this context, the strategic substitution effect on ΔV^i arising from Walrasian price effects is compensated by strategic complementarities due to the group-identity externality. As such, this effect promotes cultural homogeneity.

More generally, strategic complementarities and cultural homogeneity in trade economies will typically hold, e.g., with increasing returns in production and market power. Maystre, Thoenig, Olivier and Verdier (2009), who study the transmission of a preference for a specific differentiated good whose varieties are produced under monopolistic competition provide an example. In this context, the larger the size of the group with a preference for a good, the larger the market size and the entry of firms producing differentiated varieties of that good. Increased varieties in turn make it relatively more attractive to acquire and transmit preferences for this good, leading once again to strategic complementarity.

2.4.2 Cultural transmission and institutions

Another interesting class of models studies strategic substitution in socio-economic environments in which individual randomly match to interact strategically. Consider for instance the case of an ethical norm, which imposes a psychological cost when an individual does not play cooperatively in situations like e.g., the *Prisoner's Dilemma* (these are also called *norms of pro-sociality*).[28] If individuals are matched randomly to interact, the gains to transmit the norm for pro-sociality tend to be higher when many individuals in the population share the norm, $\Delta V^i(q^i)$ is increasing; see Bisin, Topa, and Verdier (2004).

Relatedly, Tabellini (2008b) studies the cultural transmission of a norm which imposes a psychological cost when an individual does not play cooperatively in situations like e.g., the Prisoner's Dilemma, but such that the cost declines in some measure of cultural distance of the opponent (e.g., costs are high only when the opponent is part of the family or of the tribe; accordingly, these norms have been called *norms of limited morality*, and in extreme case, *immoral familism*).[29] More precisely, Tabellini (2009), following Dixit (2004), considers a continuum of one period lived individuals uniformly distributed on the circumference of a circle. The density of individuals per unit

[28] Bowles (2001) and Bowles and Gintis (1998, 2002, 2003) develop cultural evolutionary models of norms of cooperation but in contexts with exogenous cultural transmission and standard replicator dynamics.

[29] The distinction between norms of limited or general morality is due to Banfield (1958)'s study of Lucania, in the South of Italy. See also Platteau (2000).

of arc length is 1. Each individual is randomly matched with another located at distance y with probability $g(y) > 0$. Two matched individuals observe their distance and play a prisoner's dilemma game. Besides material payoffs, each individual enjoys a psychological benefit d that decays with distance at exponential rate $\theta > 0$: the psychological gain of playing cooperation against an opponent located at distance y is $de^{-\theta y}$. Two types of player are characterized by different decay parameters θ_i ($i = 1, 2$) with $\theta_2 > \theta_1$. Hence a *general morality* player, with $i = 1$, values cooperation more than a *limited morality* player, with $i = 2$, at any positive distance y.

For a given fraction q^1 of general morality players, the equilibrium is such that individuals play cooperatively only with opponents which are close enough in cultural space (namely individuals of type i play cooperatively when matching with individuals at a distance $y \leq Y_i$). Obviously, the distance cut-off is higher for individuals who have adopted a general morality, as opposed to a limited morality, norm: $Y_2 < Y_1$. Moreover, the upper threshold $Y_1 = Y_1(q^1)$ depends positively on the fraction of general morality players q^1 in the population. This is the case because when playing, individuals do not observe their opponent type. Hence general morality players bear the risk of cooperating against cheating opponents, specifically when $y > Y_2$. A larger fraction of general morality players reduces this risk, inducing conversely a larger range of matches over which cooperation can be sustained. This element generates therefore a strategic complementarity in the Prisoner's Dilemma game: individuals are more willing to cooperate the higher the fraction of general morality individuals in the population.

Extending Bisin, Topa, and Verdier (2004), Tabellini (2009) embeds this prisoner's dilemma structure into a version of the cultural transmission model with imperfect empathy. A parent's of type i at time $t-1$ evaluates his child of type j in the equilibrium of the matching game as

$$V^{ij} = u^j(\theta_j, q^1) + d\int_0^{Y_j} e^{-\theta_i z} g(z)dz$$

where $u^j(\theta_j, q^j)$ represents the expected equilibrium material payoff of a child of type j in the prisoner's dilemma game with random matching when the fraction of general morality agents is q^1. The second term is the parent's evaluation of his child's expected psychological benefits of cooperating in matches of distance smaller than Y_j. Note that because of imperfect empathy, this term is evaluated with the preference parameter θ_i of the parent. Specifically, the cultural intolerance of a general morality parent, ΔV^1, can be written as

$$\Delta V^1 = \underbrace{u^1(\theta_1, q^1) - u^2(\theta_2, q^1)}_{A} + \underbrace{d\int_{Y_2}^{Y_1} e^{-\theta_1 z} g(z)dz}_{B}. \tag{12}$$

The first term, A, captures the difference in the expected material payoff between a limited and a general morality child. This term is negative, as general morality induces behavior that is more cooperative and is dominated by non-cooperation from a pure material payoff point of view. The second term, B, reflects instead the expected benefit of extending the scope of the child's cooperative behavior to a larger range of matches, evaluated with the parent's values, θ_1. This term is positive, as enlarging the scope of cooperative behavior increases the direct psychological benefit as perceived by the parent. Hence (12) reflects the tradeoff that a general morality parent faces in terms of cultural transmission of his values.

Importantly, ΔV^1 depends positively on the actual fraction q^1 of general morality individuals in the generation of the offspring. Indeed, a higher anticipated fraction of general morality agents in the children's generation makes cooperation less costly in terms of material payoffs and more worthwhile in terms of psychological benefits. In this context then, the gains from socialization to a general morality norm are higher in societies where such norms are prevalent and strategic complementarity obtains.[30]

2.4.3 Cultural transmission and collective action

An important feature of cultural transmission processes, especially in the case of socioeconomic interactions, is that group size effects and parents' expectations about the dynamics of these group sizes have strong implications for socialization choices. Issues of collective action and coordination of expectations within and across cultural groups arise then naturally and are important determinants of the type of long run social outcomes that may prevail in society. Collective action mechanisms for cultural transmission and socialization include, e.g., parties, churches, communities, lobbies, and clubs.

A few papers consider such collective mechanisms in detail. In a series of papers, Gradstein and Justman (2002, 2005) consider the role of education in promoting a common culture within society. In particular, Gradstein and Justman (2002) consider the implications of the cultural content of education for economic growth. Specifically they show that when different cultural groups separately determine the social content of their school curricula, excessive polarization may result which leads to less than optimal growth. On the other hand, the optimal trajectory involves school curricula converging towards a middle ground. The authors then investigate how different modes of political implementation of centralized schooling through representative democracy

[30] However, Tabellini (2009) shows that in his model $\Delta V^1 > 0$, namely that the non-economic benefits of cooperation as perceived by general morality parents always outweigh the material costs. The model therefore displays positive incentives to transmit the general morality norm across generations and under specific assumptions on the transmission mechanism, which bias the process somewhat towards the general morality trait, the population dynamics converges to a distribution which contains a positive fraction of individuals sharing the general morality norm, notwithstanding strategic complementarity.

can lead to excessive polarization in some cases and overly rapid homogenization in others.

Dixit (2009) also considers the role of education in the transmission of values and norms, though the focus of the paper is on norms of pro-sociality. In this context, school financing is a collective action problem addressed by majority voting. More precisely, the model considers an economy where final output is produced using two complementary inputs, a public good and private individual effort. The public good is financed by contributions of individuals. If individuals have a *pro-social component in their preferences* that internalizes the welfare of others to some extent, a larger quantity of the public good will be provided. More specifically, consider a society populated by n individuals, labeled $i \in \{1, \dots n\}$. Each individual can exert two types of efforts: private x_i, and public z_i. The income of individual i is given by

$$y^i = (1 + \bar{z})x^i, \text{ with}$$
$$\bar{z} = \frac{1}{n}\sum_{i=1}^{n} z^i$$

A selfish individuals with utility

$$u^i(y^i, x^i, z^i) = y^i - h(x^i + z^i),$$

for regular convex cost of effort $h(x^i + z^i)$, will choose $z^i = 0$ at equilibrium (provided n is large enough). An individual with *pro-social* preferences of the form

$$v_i = u_i + \gamma \sum_{j \neq i} u_j, \quad \gamma > 0$$

might instead more efficiently choose $z^i > 0$; e.g., when γ is large enough.

Consider a society in which parents are (perfectly) altruistic towards their own children, discounting their utility at rate δ. In this case, parents might collectively choose to socialize them to pro-social preferences, that is, to a $\gamma > 0$, even if socialization is costly, e.g., because of school contributions. Dixit (2009) discusses different socialization outcomes, depending on whether parents have themselves pro-social preferences. When parents are selfish, the preferred level of education γ of any dynastic parent is positive if parental altruism is strong enough, that is, δ large enough. In this case, if parents have homogeneous preferences so that any collective choice mechanism induces the same socialization outcome, children will be socialized by schools to norms of pro-sociality.[31]

[31] Assuming that parental altruism is increasing in income, the intergenerational transmission of pro-sociality might remain stuck in a poverty trap where collective action is determined by relatively poor agents who would rather not invest in schools favoring the transmission of norms of pro-sociality and hence, in turn, inducing a higher growth of income.

Several interesting contributions to the literature focus on a specific collective action mechanism, *majority voting*, in different political economy environments. Bisin and Verdier (2000) considers the cultural transmission of preferences for a good whose provision is determined by voting, e.g., a public good. For any generation, socialization preferences depend on the parents' expectations regarding the political aggregation of the distribution of preferences in their children's population, which will vote on public good provision. On the other hand, the outcome of voting in any period depends on the present distribution of traits in the population, which in turn is determined by past parents' socialization. Under perfect foresight assumptions, the dynamics of the distribution of preferences, and of political outcomes, depends very much on initial conditions. For unbalanced initial preference distributions, the dynamics display a tendency to homogeneity in the end distribution of preferences, while for relatively balanced initial distributions; the dynamics display multiple equilibrium paths generated by self-fulfilling expectations. These paths have very different long run consequences in terms of both cultural values and policy outcomes.[32]

Tabellini (2009)'s model of cultural transmission of morality norms, discussed before, also allows for voting on the constitution of external legal enforcement institutions. In this setting Tabellini (2009) shows how formal enforcement mechanisms may interact differentially with local and general morality norms. Under majority rule voting, inefficient legal institutions may lead to an equilibrium path where such inefficiency reduces the gains to transmit norms of general morality across generations, which in turn reinforces the political support for an inefficient legal system.

Another example regarding the interaction of cultural transmission and voting is Bisin and Verdier (2005), which investigates the relationship between transmission of a work ethic and redistributive policies. The paper shows how heavily redistributive policies, like e.g., welfare states policies, limit the gains for transmitting work ethic norms, which in turn induce political support for the welfare state (and eventually its own demise, as redistribution is moot as long as work ethic norms disappear in the population).

More precisely, the paper considers preferences for work ethic in a context in which income redistribution is obtained through simple majority voting. Agents have quasilinear preferences over consumption, c, and hours worked, l:

$$u^i(c, l) = c + \theta_i v(1 - l), \quad \text{with } \theta_i > 0.$$

for some well behaved preference for leisure map v. Agents differ in terms of their preferences for leisure, parameterized by θ^i, for $i \in \{1, 2\}$. Agents of type 1 are characterized by lower preferences for leisure at the margin, $\theta_1 < \theta_2$, that is, by a better *work ethic.*

[32] The fact that equilibrium paths are highly dependent on self-fulfilling expectations provides a role for ideologies as programmatic coordination expectation devices that help to select a particular path of cultural values and political power structure in society.

Before-tax income is redistributed in each period, and redistribution decisions are taken by majority voting of the mature generation under the constraint that the work ethic parameter θ_i is private information of individual agents, that is, it is not observable in the labor market (see Mirrlees, 1971, for the pioneering analysis of redistribution in economies with adverse selection). Let $R^i(q^1_{t+1})$ and $l^i(q^1_{t+1})$ denote respectively the after tax income and induced work effort of an individual of type i following the optimal redistributive scheme voted in period $t + 1$, which depends on the fraction of agents with a work ethic, q^1_{t+1}.

When agents of type i represent the majority of the population, they vote for an income redistribution scheme which is incentive compatible with the work behavior of private agents and maximizes their representative utility. Bisin and Verdier (2005) show that in this context, minorities have no socialization incentives:

$$\Delta V^i(q^i_{t+1}) = 0, \quad \text{for } q^i_{t+1} < 1/2.$$

On the contrary, the socialization incentives of the majority are strictly positive and increasing in the fraction of the other (minority) group

$$\Delta V^i(q^i_{t+1}) \text{ is decreasing in } q^i_{t+1}, \quad \text{for } q^i_{t+1} > 1/2$$

With quadratic socialization costs, direct socialization d^i has the therefore the following form:

$$d^i = \begin{cases} (1 - q^i_t)\Delta V^i(q^i_{t+1}) & \text{if } q^i_{t+1} \geq 1/2 \\ 0 & \text{if } q^i_{t+1} < 1/2 \end{cases},$$

as minority agents have no incentives to spend resources to socialize their children to their own work ethic norm.

Bisin and Verdier (2005) characterize the path q^i_t of the population dynamics as well as the equilibrium level of redistribution and taxation starting from an initial fraction q^i_0 of individuals of type i. They show in particular that, when one preference type is strongly majoritarian in society, then the politics of redistribution lead to a homogenization towards that preference. On the contrary, when the initial distribution of preferences for leisure is sufficiently balanced and diversified, then the dynamics of the evolution of preferences may follow various paths depending on the type of self-fulfilling expectations individuals coordinate on at equilibrium.

Very limited is the theoretical research studying cultural transmission and other collective choice mechanisms, like religious organizations, firms, political parties, armies, gangs, etc. Interestingly, such institutions might have different objective functions and operate by means of different socialization strategies, including prices, weapons, ideas, and belief-manipulations. An example is provided by Dessi' (2008) who studies collective memory as the outcome of belief-manipulation on the part of nation-states when individual have imperfect memory.

In addition, different modes of socialization, individual versus collective, may compete with each other. For instance, state propaganda may compete with direct family socialization. These interactions in turn may affect the policies and social actions undertaken by future generations, leading in the end to different socio-cultural trajectories. Looking at how such socialization organizations and their different modes of functioning can be integrated in cultural transmission models remains an avenue for future research.

2.5 Cultural transmission of beliefs

Cultural transmission relates more generally to the transmission of cultural traits, values, preferences. In practice, in the models we surveyed, cultural transmission pertains to the transmission of preferences: cultural traits and values are projected in the space of preference traits.

In fact, in many instances of interest, we can think of cultural transmission as the transmission of beliefs or ideologies. That is, preferences are identical across agents, but different cultural types have a different model of the socio-economic environment.[33] Guiso, Sapienza, and Zingales (2008) build a simple model of the transmission of beliefs about trustworthiness, motivated by the literature we survey in this chapter. It is pedagogically convenient however here attempt at a generalization which better highlights how cultural transmission models can be adapted to study the transmission of beliefs. We only sketch a model, avoiding details.

Let X denote an abstract choice set, comprising all choices relevant to an individual's economic and social life. Let $\theta \in \Theta$ denote a parameter unknown to agents. Each individual has preferences represented by $u : X \times \Theta \to \mathrm{R}$. Individuals have distinct probability distribution over θ. Let p_t^i denote the probability distribution shared by all individuals (parents and children) of type $i \in \{a, b\}$ at time t. At time t, children of type i choose $x \in X$ to maximize

$$E_{i,t}[u(x;\theta)] = \int_{\Theta} u(x;\theta)dp_t^i.$$

They then observe the realization of a signal of θ, ζ^i and update to the posterior p_{t+1}^i, which they enter time $t+1$ with.

Let V^{ij} denote the utility to a type i parent of a type j child, $i, j \in \{a, b\}$. Analogously to imperfect empathy, we require

Imperfect learning: For all $i, j \in \{a, b\}$, $V^{ij} = E_{i,t}\,[u(x^j;\,\theta)]$, *where* $x^j = \arg\max_{x\in X} E_{j,t}\,[u(x;\,\theta)]$. Learning is imperfect in the sense that agents of type i disregard the

[33] For example, an interesting literature has attributed the support for the welfare state in Europe, and the lack of support in the U.S., to heterogeneous beliefs about the fairness of social competition and about what determines income inequality, individual effort or luck; see Alesina and Angeletos (2005).

information which has lead individuals of type j to p_t^j, and vice versa. As long as V^{ii}, V^{ij} are independent of q^i, imperfect updating implies $V^{ii} \geq V^{ij}$, with $>$ for generic utility function $u(x;\, \theta)$.

Applying the economic socialization model to this general environment is now straight forward, and, with quadratic socialization costs,

$$d^i = d(q^i, \Delta V^i) = (1 - q^i)\Delta V^i.$$

As an illustration, suppose $\Theta = \{\theta_0,\, \theta_1\}$ and, abusing notation, p_t^i is the probability, according to the posterior of agents of type i, that $\theta = \theta_0$. The signal ζ takes value in Θ, and is distributed to assign probability $p > \frac{1}{2}$ to the true value of θ, which we take to be θ_0 without loss of generality.

In this simple learning environment, trivially, each type's posterior converges to the truth,

$$p_t^i \rightarrow 1,^{34} \quad \text{for any } i\ \{a, b\},$$

and as a consequence,

$$\Delta V^i \rightarrow 0.$$

In this environment it is of interest to study the dynamics of the *average beliefs* in the population,

$$b(t, q_0^i, p_0^i, p_0^j) = q_t^i p_t^i + (1 - q_t^i) p_t^j.$$

It follows that

While average beliefs converge to the truth, $b(t; q_0^i, p_0^i, p_0^j) \rightarrow 1$; *direct vertical socialization slows down convergence.*

It should be clear that, as in the case of cultural transmission, endogenous cultural intolerance, $\Delta\ V^i(q^i)$, could drastically affect the dynamics. In the particular case of the transmission of beliefs of trustworthiness, as in Guiso, Sapienza, and Zingales (2008), the untrustworthy type, say type j, does not engage in social interaction and hence does not receive any signal. As a consequence, type j individual do not learn, $p_t^j = p^j$. Furthermore, the trust game is characterized by strategic complementarity (the more trustworthy individuals in the population, the higher their incentives to socially interact):

$$\Delta V^i(q^i), \text{ with } \frac{d\Delta V^i(q^i)}{dq^i} > 0.$$

[34] Formally, the notion of convergence is convergence in probability, as from the Martingale Convergence Theorem. We choose here an imprecise notation in the advantage of simplicity.

It is straightforward in this case to construct examples where, by selecting appropriate initial conditions (q_0^i, p_0^i, p^j), we obtain average beliefs which do not converge to the truth and a population of trustworthy types which tends to vanish,

$$b(t; q_0^i, p_0^i, p^j) \to p^j, \; q^i(t; q_0^i, p_0^i, p^j) \to 0.$$

3. EMPIRICAL STUDIES

As we noted in the Introduction, cultural transmission as a field of study in the social sciences is largely motivated by the observation that cultural traits in general, and religious and ethnic traits in particular, tend to be quite resilient in the population. The fundamental manifestation of this phenomenon is cultural heterogeneity, the world's geographical fractionalization by ethic and religious traits, at any given time. It is then appropriate to start a survey of empirical studies of cultural transmission by substantiating this observation. We should also stress at the outset, however that cultural heterogeneity is not a curiosum of culture studies. It is heavily correlated to many relevant socio-economic phenomena (from the provision of public goods to civil wars), so much so that the fractionalization index is now a constant feature e.g., of growth regressions; see Alesina and La Ferrara (2005) for a survey.

Similarly, the recent debate over the *clash of civilization*, as spurred by Huntington (1992), has been informed by the study of ethnic and religious diversity and by different measures of ethnic and religious fractionalization. For instance, using genetic distance as a proxy for ethnic diversity, Spolaore and Wacziarg (2010) obtain the surprising result that a one standard deviation increase in genetic distance between two populations is associated to a 23% reduction in the probability of conflict between them from 1816 and 2000.

3.1 Cultural heterogeneity

The categorization and analysis of different cultural traits is the object of study of cultural anthropology, as a separate discipline. Ethnology, in particular, concerns the comparison and contrast of different cultural traits catalogued by ethnographic studies. Referring to any manual of cultural anthropology like, e.g., Rapport and Overing (2007), for a more in-depth analysis and for references, it will suffice in this survey to report on aggregate measures of cultural heterogeneity along the ethnic and religious dimensions.

Ethnolinguistic diversity is documented by the ethnolinguistic fractionalization index, as computed from the classifications based on the *Atlas Narodov Mira*, the *Encyclopedia Britannica*, or *the Ethnologue database*.[35] Consider a country j with $i = 1, \ldots N$,

[35] The *Ethnologue database* e.g., contains 6,909 language descriptions organized by continent and country; see Lewis (2009). Of course we are side-stepping here the difficult *what-is-a-language* issue.

ethnolinguistic groups, each representing share s_{ij} in the country's population. The fractionalization index of country j takes values from 0 to 1 (with 1 corresponding to maximal fractionalization) and is defined as:

$$ELF_j = 1 - \sum_{i=1}^{N} s_{ij}.$$

Figure 4 reports the distribution of the fractionalization index by country according to the Ethnologue database. As an illustration, Chad, with an index close to 1, has 135 languages spoken inside its borders.

But, even an impressionistic look at the heterogeneity of languages spoken around the world is striking. See e.g., the case of Asia in Figure 5, where each red dot represents the geographic center of a distinct language.

Other fractionalization indexes, e.g., indexes of ethnic, language, and religion fractionalization, display a similar picture, as shown in Table 1. In particular it is notable that religious fractionalization is higher than ethnolinguistic fractionalization as well as than both ethnic and language fractionalization measured distinctly.

Even limiting the analysis to the main religions, fractionalization is substantial. The Encyclopedia Britannica World Book 1999's list of ten major religions, in Figure 6, contains seven religious denominations (which themselves can be subdivided in several

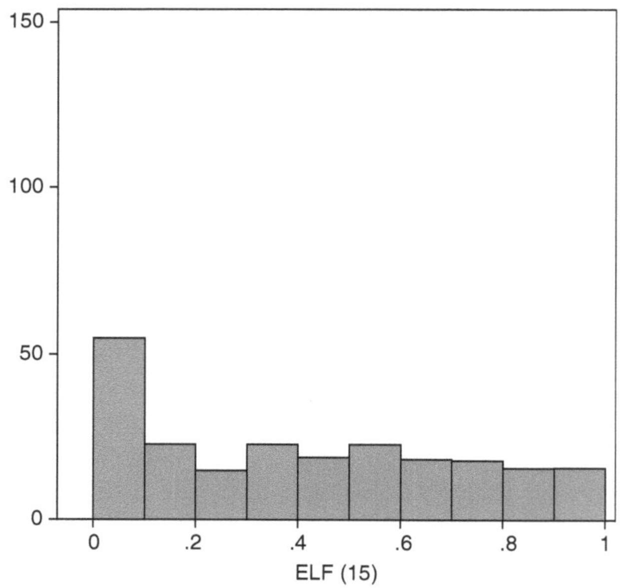

Figure 4 Cross-Country Distribution of the Ethnolinguistic Fractionalization Index. Source: Desmet, Ortuno-Ortin, and Wacziarg (2009).

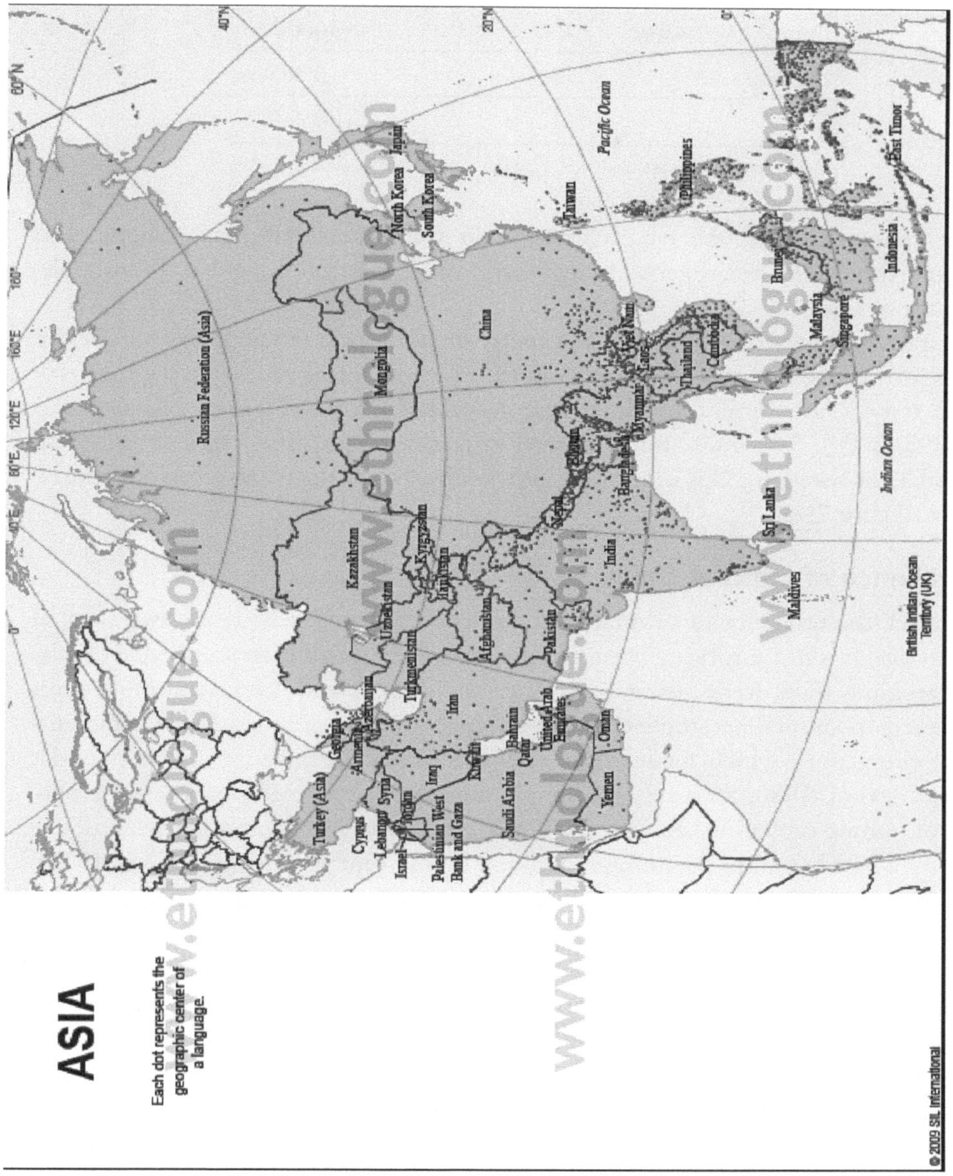

Figure 5 Languages spoken in Asia. Source: www.Ethnologue.com

Table 1 Sample Means of Fractionalization Indexes.

Variable	# of Observations	Sample Mean
Religion	198	0.439
Ethnic	180	0.435
Language	185	0.385
ELF	112	0.418

Source: Alesina, Devleeschauwer, Easterly, Kurlat, and Wacziarg (2003).

different denominations: like e.g., Christians in Catholics, Orthodox, Coptic, and others) and three very heterogeneous aggregations: Chines folk religions, Ethnic religions, New-religions.[36]

Cultural heterogeneity is not only a property of ethnic and religious traits. Tabellini (2008), for instance, constructs a cross-country index of social values, an aggregate of trust and respect, specifically, obtained from World Value Surveys data (waves 1981, 1990, 1995, 2000). The index is normalized to take values in [0,1], e.g., almost 0 for Brazil and 1 for Sweden. This index also shows substantial dispersion across the world, as seen in Figure 7.

3.2 Resilience of cultural traits

As we noted, the resilience of cultural traits and cultural heterogeneity are two sides of the same coin. It is not surprising then that the evidence regarding the resilience of ethnic and religious traits across generations is quite pervasive and it nicely complements the evidence on cultural heterogeneity. For instance, the fast assimilation of immigrants into a 'melting pot', which many social scientists predicted until the 1960s (see, for example, Gleason, 1980, for a survey), simply did not materialize. Moreover, the persistence of 'ethnic capital' in second- and third-generation immigrants has been documented by a vast literature on immigration and ethnic capital (see e.g., Borjas, 1992), and recently also by "epidemiological" studies on culture (see e.g., Fernandez and Fogli, 2009, and Giuliano, 2006). Orthodox Jewish communities in the United States constitute another example of the strong resilience of culture (see Mayer, 1979, and the discussion of a 'cultural renaissance' overcoming the predicted complete assimilation of Jewish communities in New York in the 1970s). Outside the United States, Basques, Catalans, Corsicans, and Irish Catholics in Europe, Quebecois in Canada, and Jews of the Diaspora have all remained strongly attached to their languages and cultural traits even through the formation of political states which did not recognize their ethnic and religious diversity. Most recently, several empirical studies have documented that immigrants in Europe, and especially so those of Muslim faith, appear to integrate

[36] The tenth group is Atheism and nonreligion.

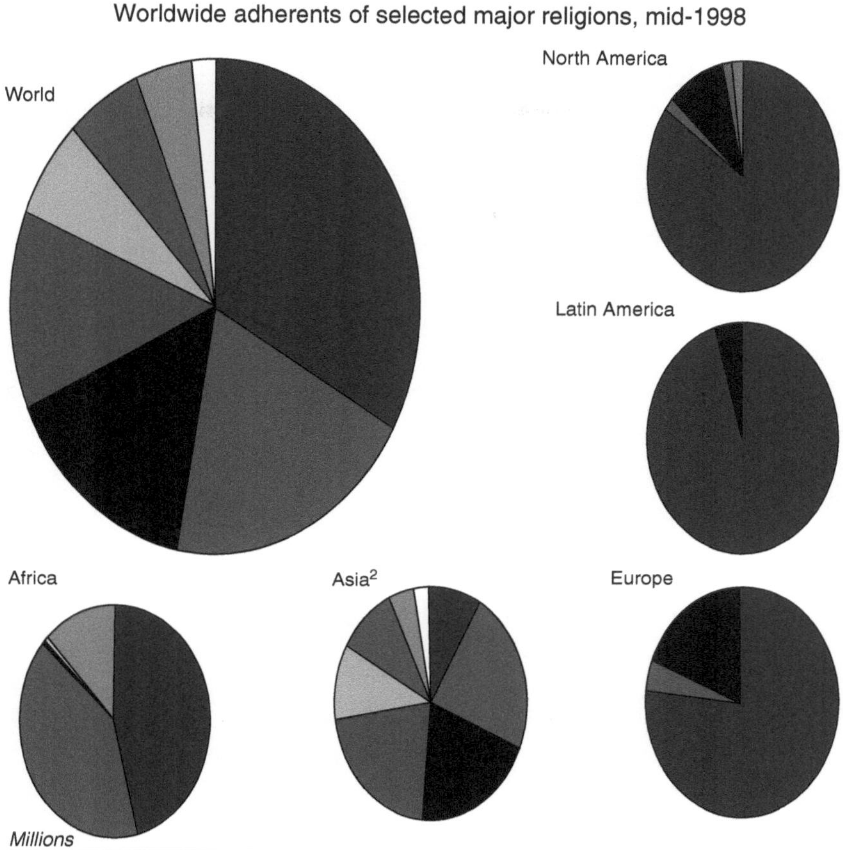

Millions

	Africa	Asia[2]	Europe	Latin America	North America	World
Christians	356.27	308.19	558.73	462.97	256.88	1,943.04
Muslims	315.00	812.25	31.40	1.62	4.35	1,164.62
Atheists and nonreligious	4.90	726.13	131.44	17.97	29.07	909.51
Hindus	2.41	755.85	1.38	0.79	1.27	761.70
Chinese folk religionists	0.03	377.86	0.25	0.18	0.84	379.16
Buddhists	0.14	349.07	1.52	0.62	2.45	353.80
Ethinic religionists[b]	97.20	148.45	1.26	1.23	0.42	248.56
New-religionists[2]	0.03	98.60	0.16	0.60	0.76	100.15
Jews	0.23	4.24	2.53	1.12	6.00	14.12
Confucianists	0	6.23	0.01	0	0	6.24
Total	776.21	3.58,6.87	728.68	487.10	302.04	5,880.90

Source: Encyclopedia Britannica World Book, 1999.
[a] Asia includes Middle East and Central Asia.
[b] Followers of local tribal, animalistic, or shamanistic religions.
[c] Followers of primarily crisis or syncrotistic religions and movements, all founded since 1800 and most since 1995.

Figure 6 Major religions. Source: Encyclopedia Britannica.

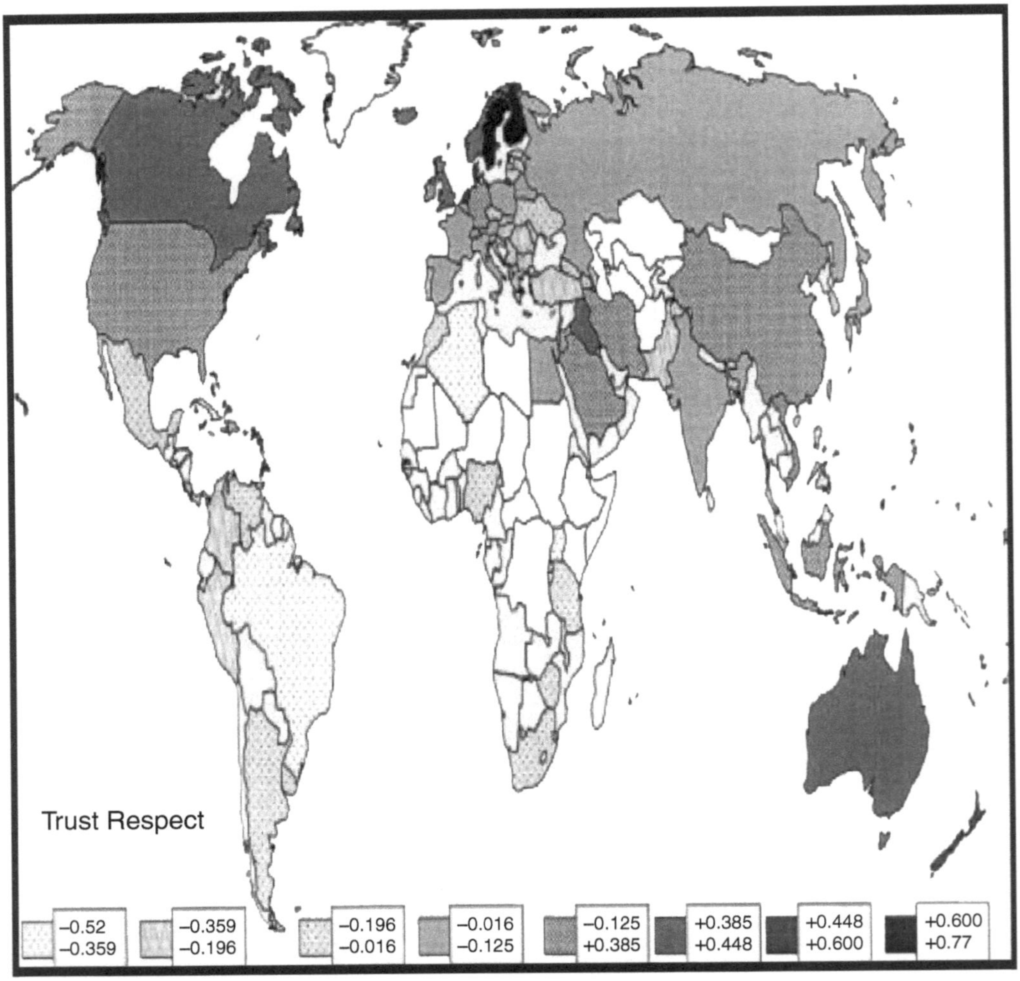

Figure 7 Trust and Respect index by country. Source: Tabellini (2008).

culturally at very slow pace; see Algan, Bisin, Manning and Verdier (2010) for a comprehensive analysis of the data. Finally, various measures of social capital display very long-run hysteresis, of the order of hundreds of years: for instance, Guiso, Sapienza and Zingales (2007, 2008) reconduct the contemporary variation of social capital in Italy to the experience of free-city-state in the Middle Ages, Tabellini (2005, 2008a, 2008b) links cross-country variation in measures of trust to the quality of political institutions in the nineteenth century, Nunn and Wantchekon (2009) link variation in measures of trust in West Africa to the slave trade, Grosjean (2009) finds a cross-regional relationship between institutional corruption in the present and an history of Ottoman domination.

It is convenient to organize empirical studies of cultural transmission along two main dimensions. The first distinguishes *population dynamics studies* from *socialization studies*; while the second one distinguishes *structural* and *non-structural methodologies.*

Population dynamics studies aim at measuring directly the resilience of cultural traits, the speed of cultural transmission. *Socialization studies* aim instead at identifying the most relevant properties of socialization mechanisms, e.g., cultural substitution vs. complementarity, which the theory suggests are related to the resilience of cultural traits.

A large part of the empirical work on cultural transmission adopts a *structural methodology*, linking estimates to the theoretical models we surveyed. *Structural population dynamics studies*, for instance, exploit the observation of the population dynamics of a trait in history, a time series of q_t^i, to estimate the speed of transmission, $\frac{q_{t+1}^i - q_t^i}{q_t^i}$, as well as direct socialization rates $(d^i - d^j)$ from a discrete time version of the population dynamics as in equation (3). The time series of the population dynamics q_t^i is obtained from archeological anthropology and/or historical and ethnographic data. Methods from evolutionary genetics and historical linguistics have also been exploited to produce time series of the population dynamics.

Structural socialization studies typically exploit instead the observation, at a time *t*, of a cross-section of population distributions by trait as well as socialization rates P^{ii}, P^{ij}, P^{ji} to estimate the vertical socialization rates d^i, d^j as well as the deep preference parameters of the model, ΔV^i, ΔV^j, from a version of the cultural transmission equations, e.g., (1)

Finally, interesting empirical properties of cultural transmission are also uncovered by means of *non-structural methods*, as in the case of *historical case-studies* of population dynamics, *migration* and *epidemiological studies.*

3.3 Population dynamics

Let $t = 0, 1, \ldots, \infty$ index discrete time. The population dynamics equation for the leading cultural transmission model we have discussed, in the discrete time formulation adopted in empirical studies, is

$$q_{t+1}^i - q_t^i = q_t^i(1 - q_t^i)(d^i - d^j),$$

with parental socialization conditions

$$d^i = d(q_t^i, \Delta V^i) = (1 - q_t^i)\Delta V^i.$$

Identification of $d^i - d^j$ at time *t* only requires observing two data points from a sequence of population shares $\{q_t^i\}$ over time *t*. A longer sequence will in general allow the identification of the deep preference parameters of the model, ΔV^i, $i = a, b$.

Examples of this approach abound, though in this literature, parental socialization conditions are typically disregarded and $d^i - d^j$ is assumed constant over time. In this case, the population dynamics displays logistic growth:

$$q_t^i = \frac{q_0^i}{(1 - q_0^i)e^{-(d^i - d^j)t} + q_0^i}.$$

Stark (1984, 1997), for instance, adopts this method to estimate the spread of the Mormon Church and of early Christianity in the Roman Empire.[37] In the case of early Christianity, population shares from 40 to 350 *C.E.* (Common Era) are obtained from secondary sources and are imprecisely estimated. The resulting estimates of $d^i - d^j$ are .43 per decade for Mormons and .4 for Christians.

Botticini and Eckstein (2005, 2007) study the cultural transmission of preferences for education to explain the historical occupational choices of Jews in favor of urban skilled trades rather than farming. They argue that preferences for education constitute a component of Judaism since the reform after destruction of the Temple in 70 CE and, as such, have been directly transmitted across generations. Botticini and Eckstein (2004) provide a wealth of historical evidence for the transmission of preferences for education by Jews from the first century to the eight century, when the occupational transition and urbanization of Jews occurs. Such evidence includes rabbinical discussions and rulings in the Talmud regarding education and teachers, demographic data (e.g., education levels among Jewish farmers before the 8th century), archeological findings on the building of synagogues in farming villages in Eretz Israel between the 3rd and 5th century. Furthermore, consistently with cultural substitution, high socialization rates have been historically supported as Judaism represented a minority in the Diaspora, even more so after the transition to urban occupations, in which education is an advantage.[38] Using Botticini and Eckstein (2007)'s data on population shares and voluntary conversions of Jews a small negative $d^i - d^j$, of the order of $-.007$, $-.003$ per decade, depending on the region, can be estimated from the 2nd to 7th century. Such negative net socialization rates are due, according to Botticini and Eckstein (2007), to the cost of socializing children to Judaism (which required educating them) in subsistence farming economies. While socialization rates for the period between the 9th and the 12th century cannot be estimated for the difficulty of taking into account of massacres and forced conversions of Jews, Botticini and Eckstein (2007)

[37] In fact, Stark's estimates are based on exponential rather than logistic growth. The exponential equation is a reasonable approximation to the logistic for q^i close to 0, as is the case in both his applications.

[38] Kuznet (1960, 1972) provides an explanation of the occupational history of the Jews which also relies on the economics of minorities (cultural substitution, in our terminology), but where the cultural trait transmitted is the occupation itself.

provide evidence suggesting institutional reforms in favor of education, e.g., mandatory primary schooling for boys, and positive net socialization rates (with no voluntary conversions).

A related approach, to account for geographic diffusion, has been adopted in series of pathbreaking papers by L.L. Cavalli Sforza and his coauthors[39] to study the Neolithic transition in Europe.[40] Let $l = \infty, \ldots, 0, \ldots, \infty$ index discrete location x_l. In this context, population dynamics in the model is governed by the discrete time analogue of (4):

$$q^i_{t+1,l} - q^i_{t,l} = q^i_{t,l}(1 - q^i_{t,l})(d^i - d^j) - mq^i_{t,l} + \frac{m}{2}(q^i_{t,l-1} + q^i_{t,l+1}) \tag{13}$$

where m is the diffusion coefficient. Identification of $d^i - d^j$ at time t at location l only requires observing $q^i_{t,l}$ at two points in time t for three locations l. More generally, a whole sequence $\{q^i_{t,l}\}$ over both l and t indentifies separately ΔV^i, $i = a, b$, and m. As we noted in the previous section, however, the dynamics of (13) converges to a traveling wave with constant speed $\alpha = 2\sqrt{(d^i - d^j)m}$, which is then identified by data on a sequence of dates t at which locations l first displays $q^i_{t,l} > 0$.

This is the method adopted by Ammerman and Cavalli Sforza (1971, 1984), exploiting radio carbon dating estimates of early farming in 53 archeological sites (from Clark, 1965). First, they document that the statistical relationship between the advent of farming at a site and the distance of the site from the ancient city of Jericho, considered the center of diffusion of farming, is consistent with a constant radial speed of diffusion, as assumed by the diffusion model (13). The radial speed of advance is then approximately estimated at 25 km per generation (see Figure 8, taken from Ammerman and Cavalli Sforza (1984) and based on more extensive later data confirming this finding).[41]

Independent estimates of the parameters (d^i-d^j) and m can be obtained from archeological, historical, and anthropological data. Ammerman and Cavalli Sforza (1984) exploit a range of estimates of the rate of growth of early human establishments in a geographical location for d^i-d^j and of the mean square distance between the birth locations of spouses in early farmer's populations for m. Their preferred calibration has

[39] The first paper is Ammerman and Cavalli Sforza (1971). An early book length treatment is contained in Ammerman and Cavalli Sforza (1984).

[40] These studies exploit method and concepts from biology, linguistics, and archeological anthropology. A complete survey would require space and competence we do not possess. We feel content with examples that illustrate these methodologies and some of their results.

[41] Gkiasta, Russell, Shennan, and Steele (2003) re-examine Ammerman and Cavalli Sforza (1971)'s regression with data on 508 Neolithic sites and 207 Mesolithic sites, producing a slightly higher radial speed estimate of 32.5 km per generation.

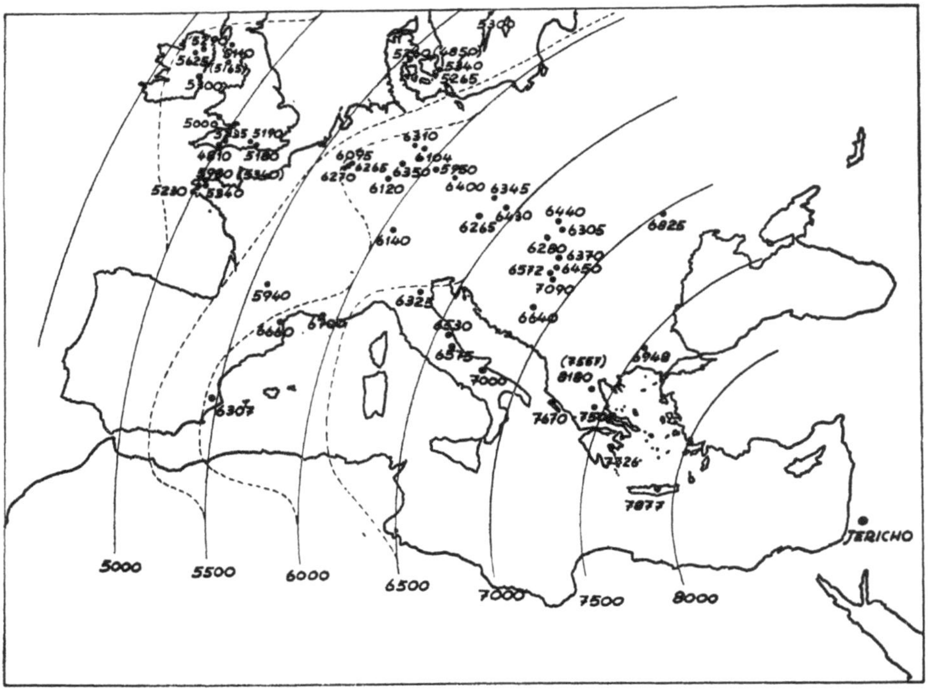

Figure 8 The spread of early farming in Europe. Source: Ammerman and Cavalli Sforza (1984).

$d^i - d^j = .5$ (equivalent to 2.7% population growth per year) and $m = .04$ (equivalent, using the diffusion interpretation, to a mean square distance between the birth location of spouses of 31 km). A wave of advance moving radially at a speed of 25 km per generation is quite in accordance with the model at this calibration.

Subtle identification problems when fitting the geographical diffusion model with data on the advent of farming need be addressed, however, to provide an answer to some of the more fundamental questions regarding cultural transmission: Which transmission mechanisms are responsible for the spread of Neolithic culture (including e.g., sedentary dwellings) and farming technologies? Did the adoption of a dominant technology, farming, require cultural transmission in the form of parental socialization? In other words, a wave of advance of farming could be obtained simply by technological adoption, without any intermarriage across farmers and hunters and without any movement of people. It becomes then of interest to distinguish adoption through cultural transmission and intermarriage (what the literature refers to as *demic diffusion*) from a simple technological adoption process.

To address this identification issue, Rendine, Piazza, and Cavalli Sforza (1986) calibrate a discretized version of the geographic spread reaction-diffusion dynamics in (LV).

Let i denote farmers and j denote hunter-gatherers. Let $Q^i_{l,t}$ be the number of people of type i in location l at time t and $Q^j_{l,t}$ be the number of people of type j in location l at time t. The discrete population dynamics satisfy the following Lotka-Volterra equations,

$$Q^i_{l,t+1} - Q^i_{l,t} = \delta_i Q^i_{l,t}\left(1 - \frac{Q^i_{l,t}}{P_i}\right) + \gamma Q^i_{l,t} Q^j_{i,t} - m Q^i_{l,t} + \frac{m}{2}\left(Q^i_{l-1,t} + Q^i_{l+1,t}\right)$$

$$Q^j_{l,t+1} - Q^j_{l,t} = \delta_j Q^j_{l,t}\left(1 - \frac{Q^j_{l,t}}{P_j}\right) - \gamma Q^i_{l,t} Q^j_{l,t}.$$

The parameter m captures then demic diffusion, through intermarriage, while γ represents technological adoption. The identification issue involves then distinguishing the effects of γ and m on the simulated population dynamics and on the geographical spread. In their simulation Rendine, Piazza, and Cavalli Sforza (1986) pick time units t to represent a generation (25 years). They also set locations l to span a (two dimensional) map of Europe (hence velocity in the simulation need be interpreted as radial velocity) so that the distance between two adjacent locations is 156 km. Initial conditions are set so that $t = 0$ is 400 generations (10,000 years) ago, by the advent of farming in the fertile crescent; $l = 0$ is the location of the city of Jericho, so that geographical distance is measured as kilometers from Jericho. At $t = 0$, Jericho and the adjacent locations are filled to capacity with farmers, $Q^i_{l,0} = P_i$, $Q^j_{l,0} = 0$, $l = -1, 0, 1$, and the rest of Europe with hunter-gatherers $Q^i_{l,0} = 0$, $Q^j_{l,0} = P_j$, $1 > 1$ and $1 < -1$. Furthermore, the calibrated parameters are chosen, as in Ammermann and Cavalli Sforza (1984), from archeological, historical, and anthropological data. Farmer societies are assumed much denser than hunter-gatherers, $P_i = 8$ and $P_j = .3$ (in thousands), and much faster growing, $\delta_i = .5$ (equivalent to 2.7% population growth per year) and $\delta_j = .25$. Furthermore the migration rate is $m = .04$, as in Ammermann and Cavalli Sforza (1984). We have reproduced here, in Figures 9 and 10, Rendine, Piazza, and Cavalli Sforza (1986)'s simulations.[42]

Rendine, Piazza, and Cavalli Sforza (1986) argue convincingly that γ and m cannot be identified with data on the speed the wave of advance. But an interesting property of diffusion models is that the faster is the wave the less steep is the wave front (that is, the shorter is the minimal distance between loci with $q^i > 0$ and loci with $q^i = 0$). The following simulation, in Figure 11, makes it clear that in fact γ and m could be identified with more detailed data on the wave, in particular with data on its steepness at the boundary: keeping the migration rate m constant, a higher γ induces a steeper wave at the boundary, that is, a faster assimilation of hunter-gatherers from their first interaction with farmers at any location.

[42] Thanks to Giorgio Topa for help with the simulation of the Lotka-Volterra system.

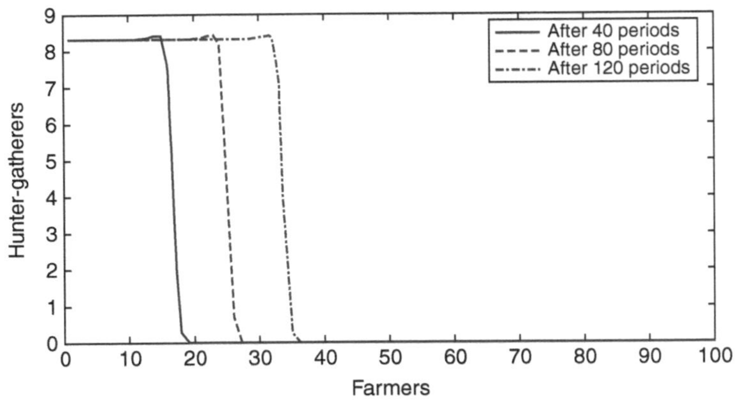

Figure 9 Evolution of farmers

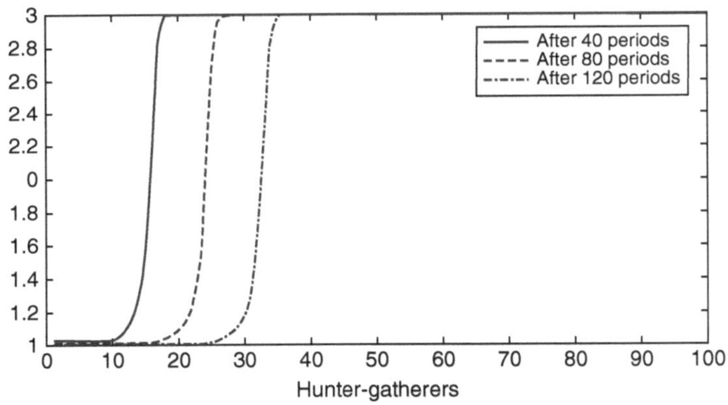

Figure 10 Evolution of hunter-gatherers

Rendine, Piazza, and Cavalli Sforza (1986) pioneer instead a different methodology to identify γ and m, which exploits theory and data on genetic evolution. Since only marriage involves genetic admixture, superimposing a genetic evolution model to the population dynamics of equation (13), allows in principle to identify the relative components of diffusion due to marriage and to technological adoption with data on genetic heterogeneity by location at any point in time.[43] Consider a diploid gene, that

[43] An important related literature exists on gene-culture coevolution. Its main focus, however, is the evolution of traits which share genetic and cultural aspects, as in the case of adult lactose absorption and drinking the milk of domesticated animals; see Aoki, Shida, and Shigesada (1996) for an application to the spread of agriculture, and Aoki (2001) and Feldman and Laland (1996) for recent surveys. For some important applications of this literature to the nature-nurture question, see Cavalli Sorza and Feldman (1973) and Otto, Christialsen, and Feldman (1995).

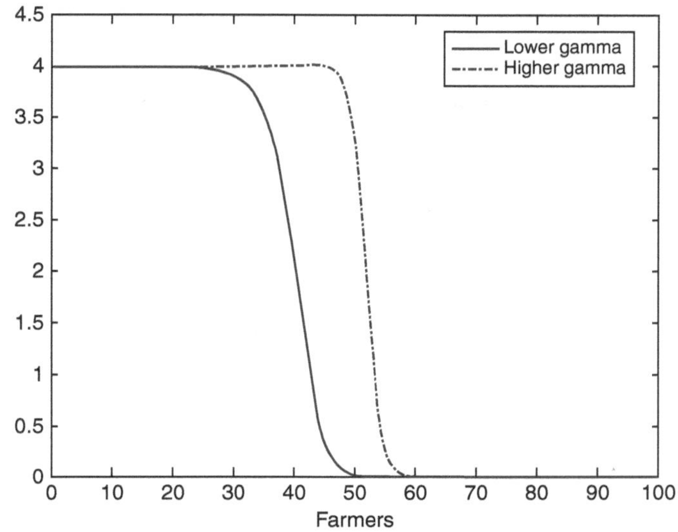

Figure 11 Comparative statics exercise on the steepness of the wave of advance with respect to γ.

is a gene with two alleles, g, g'. Let $q_{l,t}^{i,g}$ (resp. $q_{l,t}^{j,g}$) denote the fraction of individuals in the i population with allele g at location l at time t (resp. the fraction of individuals in the j population with allele g at location l at time t). Naturally, $q_{l,t}^{i,g} = 1 - q_{l,t}^{i,g'}$ and $q_{l,t}^{j,g} = 1 - q_{l,t}^{j,g'}$. Assume that marriages are necessarily homogamous with respect to each population i, j. In this context, gene frequencies change over time because of geographical spread, as long as adjacent locations have different gene frequencies. More precisely, we can express the dynamic gene frequency as follows:

$$q_{l,t+1}^{i,g} = \frac{1}{Q_{l,t+1}^{i}} \left[\begin{array}{c} \delta_l Q_{l,t}^{i} \left(1 - \dfrac{Q_{l,t}^{i}}{P_i}\right) q_{l,t}^{i,g} + \gamma Q_{l,t}^{i} Q_{l,t}^{j} q_{l,t}^{j,g} + \\ + \dfrac{m}{2}\left(Q_{l-1,t}^{i} q_{l-1,t}^{i,g} + Q_{l+1,t}^{i} q_{l+1,t}^{i,g}\right) - m Q_{l,t}^{i} q_{l,t}^{i,g} \end{array} \right]. \tag{14}$$

Gene frequencies are $\frac{1}{2}$ for any gene at $t = -N$ (N not reported) and they are left subject to drift only, in a population of hunter-gatherers, up to the advent of farming at $t = 0$, when it then follows (14). Simulating the population dynamics jointly to their genetic evolution produces a geographical gradient in gene frequencies (*genetic cline*, in the literature) consistent with the observed geographical gradient, from the Middle east to Europe, associated to 20 diallelic genetic forms for which data was available (these include e.g., the Rh as well as the HLA genes). Different simulations with smaller diffusion parameter m, even when compensated by a larger technological adoption parameter γ, apparently generate too flat genetic clines. This is interpreted as evidence that demic diffusion (and intermarriage), as opposed to technological adoption, has played a fundamental role in the Neolithic transition.

More recently, phylogenetic methods from evolutionary biology have been adapted, along the lines of Rendine, Piazza, Cavalli Sforza (1986), in sophisticated studies of cultural and physical migration as well as of historical linguistics; see Cavalli Sforza, Menozzi, and Piazza (1994), Forster and Renfrew (2006), Peregrine, Peiros, and Feldman (2009). Also, for a more critical overview of this literature, sharing similar methods, see Rogers and Cashdan (1997) and Borgerhoff Mulder, Nunn, and Towner (2006).

3.3.1 Long term persistence

An important recent literature has documented the long-term persistence and long lasting effects of institutions on socio-economic outcomes.[44] For instance, Acemoglu, Johnson, and Robinson (2001), following North and Thomas (1973) and North (1990a,b), study protection of property rights and limitations on the power of the executive, while La Porta, Lopez de Silanez, Shleifer and Vishny (1997) study legal origin. Others, like e.g., Tabellini (2008a), following Bainfield (1958), attribute the persistence of institutions to indicators of individual values and beliefs, such as trust and respect for others. Guiso, Sapienza, and Zingales (2008), following Putnam (1993), stress instead the long lasting effects of institutions, the constitution of free city-states in medieval Italy in their study, on values and beliefs like trust. Relatedly, Durante (2009) documents the effects of historical institutions favoring cooperation and social insurance on trust in Europe. Other striking and interesting examples of long term persistence of values and institutions include the effect of the slave trade on trust (Nunn and Wantchekon, 2009), of Ottoman domination on corruption (Grosjean, 2009), of a history of civil conflict and violently play in soccer (Miguel, Saiegh, and Satyanath, 2008), of the Chinese writing system on the adoption of collective values (Mo, 2007), of medieval family systems on various indicator of demographic and economic development (Duranton, Rodríguez-Pose, and Sandall, 2007), of prevalence of herding on a "culture of honor" (Grosjean, 2010), of pogroms in 1349 in Germany (following the Black Death) on various measures of anti-Semitism in the 20's and 30's (Voigtländer and Voth, 2010), of early historical use of animal plough agriculture on female labor force participation (Alesina, Giuliano, and Nunn, 2010).

The motivation of these papers typically consists in identifying a *cause* of present day values and institutions, which are conducive to economic growth: Is it *institutions*? Is it *values*? Or, *culture*? To this end it is not sufficient, while nonetheless very interesting, to document the statistical correlation between past institutions, values, and cultural traits and present-day socio-economic outcomes. To identify causal effects the various

[44] Several fascinating papers explore the role of genetic evolution and especially of genetic diversity in explaining the variation in populations' economic and demographic success; see Galor and Moav (2002), Galor (2005), Ashraf and Galor (2010).

measures of possible original institutions, values, and cultural traits are instrumented in a regression of present-day socioeconomic outcomes. For instance, settlers' mortality instruments for protection of property rights and limitations on the power of the executive in Acemoglu, Johnson, and Robinson (2001), since in countries with high settler's mortality colonial institutions where designed to extract value rather than to induce growth. Tabellini (2008a) instead instruments culture and values in the distant past in Europe with within country variation in literacy rates at the end of the 18th century and other indicators of political institutions between the 17th and the 19th century, so as to implicitly control for political institutions, which do not vary within countries. Guiso, Sapienza, and Zingales (2008) instrument the constitution of a free city-state in medieval Italy with dummies indicating cities which were the seat of a bishop before the turn of the millennium (typically, cities which were more independent from the Holy Roman Empire) and cities with an Etruscan origin (typically, cities enjoying a strategic military defense position). Finally, Durante (2009) instruments historical institutions favoring cooperation and social insurance with historical year-to-year variability in precipitations and temperature.

A different approach to the long-term persistence of institutions, one that, by recognizing the endogeneity and interdependence of institutions, values, and culture, would exploit more directly the structural implications of cultural transmission models. We are not aware of any papers which systematically investigate culture and institutions adopting this approach. For instance Tabellini (2008), while explicitly modeling the interaction of values and political institutions, as we have seen, does not exploit the structural restrictions of the model but rather documents the statistical correlation between a measure of self-reported trust for U.S. citizens (from GSS survey data) and indicators of political institutions in their ancestor's country between the 17th and the 19th centuries. Similarly, Guiso, Sapienza, and Zingales (2008) model explicitly the transmission of beliefs, but document the persistence of trust (from both World Value Survey data as well as from German Socio-Economic Panel data) without linking it structurally to the medieval political institutions in Italy the effects of which motivate their analysis.

An exemplary advantage of the adoption of structural methods to the empirical analysis of long term persistence of values, e.g., in Guiso, Sapienza, and Zingales (2008)'s data on Italian cities, would consist in exploiting the important aspect that values seem to persist *at the level of geographical units* even after centuries of intense migration patterns, e.g., across cities in Italy. This has, in principle, important un-exploited implications on the nature of the mechanism, which governs the transmission of values.

Bisin and Verdier (2005) also do not attempt at a structural empirical analysis of their model of the interaction between the cultural transmission of norms of work ethic and the institutions of the welfare state. However, Ljunge (2010) represents an important step in this direction, tackling directly the implication of Bisin and Verdier (2005)'s model that, under initial conditions not unlike the socio-economic environment of northern Europe in the 70's, the political support for the welfare state will tend to intensify over time while work ethic norms will weaken. Using registry data on individual panels over the period 1974 to 1990 in Sweden, Ljunge (2010) estimates that exposure to the institutions of the welfare state can account for a large fraction of the younger generations' higher demand for social insurance benefits, the discretionary take up of sick leave benefits, in particular; see Figure 12.[45]

Another step in the direction of evaluating empirically the structural implications of cultural transmission in a socio-economic environment where institutions and culture, values, and beliefs are jointly determined is contained in Doepke and Zilibotti (2008) and in Fernandez-Villaverde, Greenwood, and Guner (2010).

Doepke and Zilibotti (2008) propose and provide empirical evidence for a theory of the success of the middle class during the British Industrial Revolution which relies on the reinforcement between its cultural traits favoring patience and a work ethic and the technology and market institution of early capitalism. In their model, altruistic parents shape their children's preferences, in particular concerning their patience and the work ethic. Parents' incentives to invest in their children patience increases in the steepness of the children's future income profile. At the same time, a relatively patient child will tend to favor professions characterized by a steep income profile. Relatedly, parents whose children will rely mostly on labor income will tend to socialize them to a strong work ethic and children with a strong work ethic will work harder and obtain high labor income. In this context, society will tend to become endogenously stratified into *social classes* defined by occupations and their associated preferences: artisans,

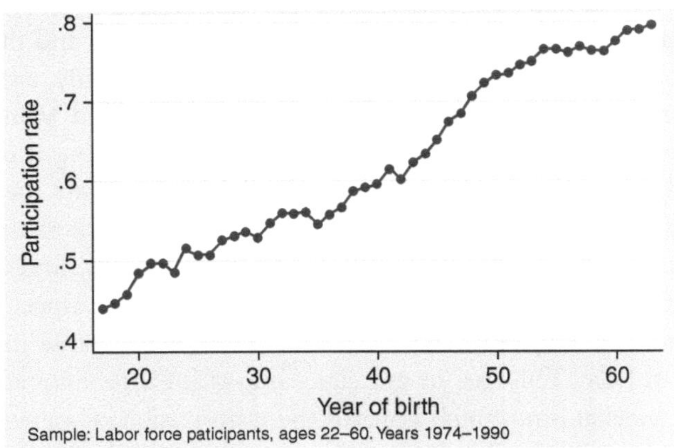

Figure 12 Sick leave participation rate by cohort in Sweden. Source: Ljunge (2010).

[45] For other recent important work along these same lines, see Alesina, Algan, Cahuc, and Giuliano (2010) on the interactions between family values and regulation of labor market; and Nannicini, Stella, Tabellini, and Troiano (2010) on the interaction between norms of generalized trust and political accountability in election.

craftsmen, and merchants will tend to be patient and will display a strong work ethic, while the landed upper class will tend to cultivate tastes for present consumption and leisure. The advent of the *spirit of capitalism*, and the new technologies associated with the Industrial Revolution, is the shock that selects the preferences of artisans, craftsmen, and merchants in Doepke and Zilibotti (2008). The model is shown to be consistent with several important historical facts regarding i) the predominantly middle class origin of the first industrialists; ii) the lack of involvement of landowners in the financing of new enterprises; iii) the catching-up of the wealth of non-landed entrepreneurs in manufacturing, commerce, and finance, with respect to the landed upper class.

While Doepke and Zilibotti (2008) informally argue for the consistency of their model with some statistical regularities pertaining to the Industrial Revolution, Fernandez-Villaverde, Greenwood, and Guner (2010) take more formally and directly their model of the Sexual Revolution to data. The Sexual Revolution in the U.S. is manifested by the fraction of women who have engaged in premarital sex by age 19: such fraction went from 6% in 1900 to about 75% nowadays. Importantly, the change in sexual behavior has been accompanied by a corresponding, while lagged, change in values regarding pre-marital sex: for instance, 15% of women in 1968 had a permissive attitude toward premarital sex, when 40% of 19 year-old females had experienced it; this attitude spread to 45% by 1983, when 73% of 19 year olds had had pre-marital sex. Fernandez-Villaverde, Greenwood, and Guner (2010)'s model interacts parental socialization with the children's choices regarding pre-marital sex and a marriage market equilibrium. Pre-marital sex, in the model, is costly because it possibly induces out-of-wedlock births, which negatively affects marriage prospects. The model is calibrated and, when its reaction to a technological shock which drastically improves the contraceptive technology (thereby reducing the probability of out-of-wedlock births as a consequence of pre-marital sex) is simulated, it is shown to account for both the sexual revolution as well as for the lagged increase in permissive attitudes toward pre-marital sex.

Finally, a series of contributions study the effect of human genetic diversity between populations on different current economic variables of interest. Because genetic mixing across populations is an effect of heterogamous marriages and diffusion, as in the analyses of the Neolithic transition discussed in Section 3.3, genetic distance is appropriately interpreted as a proxy for cultural distance. This literature exploits data collected by Cavalli Sforza, Menozzi, and Piazza (1994; see pp. 75–76 and Figure 13 below) on allele frequencies in different populations. Genetic distance between two populations is measured as the probability that two alleles at a given genetic locus selected at random from the two populations will be different.[46]

[46] The genetic loci sampled are chosen to be relatively neutral with respect to evolutionary selection. This measure of genetic distance can then also be interpreted as a measure of distance from the most recent common ancestors of the two populations.

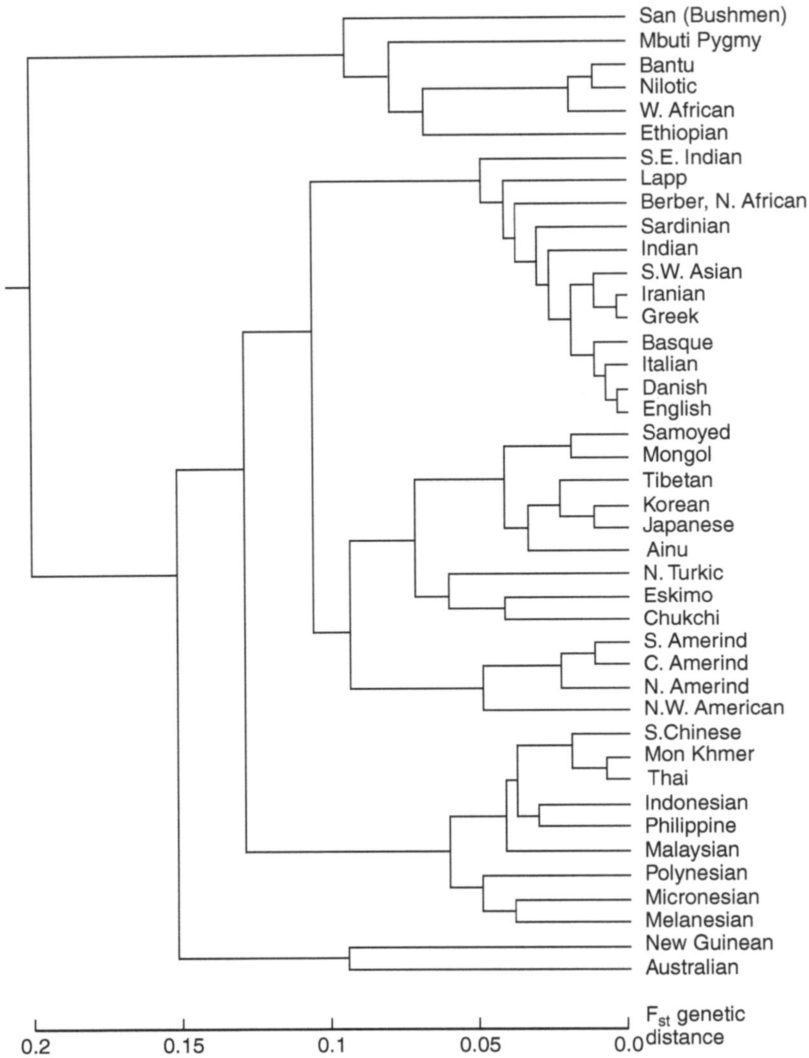

Figure 13 Genetic Distance Between 42 Populations. Source: Cavalli Sforza, Menozzi, and Piazza (1994).

In this literature, notably, Guiso, Sapienza and Zingales (2009) use genetic distance between European populations as an instrument for trust in trade gravity regressions.[47] Desmet, Ortuno-Ortiz, and Wacziarg (2009) document the close relationship between genetic distance and cultural differences as measured by several answers to the World

[47] Giuliano, Spilimbergo, and Tonon (2006) however dispute the effect of genetic distance on trade volume after controlling for geography.

Values Survey regarding norms, values and cultural characteristics. Spolaore and Wacziarg (2009) construct worldwide measures of genetic distance between 137 countries and the U.S., considered to embed the technological frontier in 1995, and correlate them with income levels. In cross-country regressions they document then a positive correlation between genetic distance from the frontier and income levels.

3.3.2 Immigration and assimilation

The cultural transmission of ethnic and religious traits if often studied, somewhat indirectly, focusing on the behavior of immigrants. The dynamic pattern of cultural and socio-economic integration of immigrants to the receiving country contains evidence of the parental socialization (or lack thereof) to the traits which characterize their origin. Countless ethnographic studies have been produced about the immigrant experience in sociology and anthropology, at least since the photographic documentation about, *How the other half lives*, in New York, by Jacob Riis in 1890.[48] Starting in the late 1950s and 1960s, many of them discredit the view that immigrants naturally assimilate in a melting pot and focus instead on their struggles to socialize children to their ethnic and religious traits.

We concentrate in this survey on econometric studies of the integration pattern of immigrants. A fundamental tool of this analysis are assimilation indexes.[49] One such index has been recently proposed by Vigdor (2008). It measures the residual of the probability that an individual is an immigrant, appropriately rescaled from 0 to a 100 (maximal assimilation), when the probability is obtained under a linear probit prediction model. A measure of the speed of assimilation can then be ascertained from the graph in Figure 14, which reports the index as a function of *years in the U.S.* at different period in time (1900, 1910, 1920, 2006), that is, for different cohort of immigrants.

An extensive analysis of Census data from the point of view of Vigdor's assimilation index indicates that, for instance, immigrants in the U.S. in the past quarter-century have assimilated more rapidly than immigrants a century ago, even though Mexicans appear to assimilate at a slower rate than other immigrant groups before them.

Other measures of integration are obtained by comparing first and second-generation immigrants to natives of similar demographic and economic characteristics. Borjas (1995), for instance, studies residential segregation in Census 1970 and NLSY data. He documents a large variation in segregation rates across ethnic groups (first generation):

[48] See e.g., the following *classic studies*, with no claims to exhaustivity whatsoever, W. C. Smith's *Americans in the Making* (1939), M. Hansen's *The Immigrant in American History* (1941), Whyte's *Street Corner Society* (1943), Handlin's *The Uprooted* (1951) and *Boston's Immigrants* (1959), J. Higham's *Strangers in the Land* (1955), O. Herberg *Protestant-Catholic-Jew* (1955), Glazer and Moynihan's *Beyond the Melting Pot* (1963), Gordon's *Assimilation in American Life* (1964), Mayer (1979).

[49] We generally prefer the word *integration* to the more charged *assimilation*. They are effectively synonyms, however, and we use the latter when so is done in the literature.

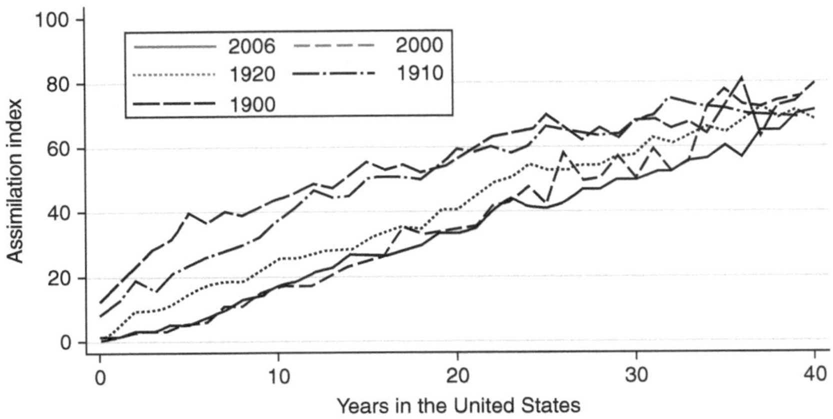

Figure 14 Assimilation by years in the U.S. Source: Vigdor (2008).

e.g., 2.6% for Greeks, 2.2% for Jamaicans, 15.3% for Italians and 22.6% for Mexicans in the 1970 Census. Similarly, he documents a large variation in first-second generation differences in segregation rates: Italians go from 15.3% to 12.1%, Mexicans from 22.6% to 18.1%, while Cubans from 21.3% to 4.7%.

More formally, the integration literature typically relies on waves of cross sectional data (like e.g., Census data) to construct synthetic cohorts and distinguish integration from the effects of age at migration and cohort.[50] Consider a general trait y_i of an individual i in a fixed country j (the destination country). Let X_i represent individual specific controls and let I_k be a dummy taking value 1 if the individual is an immigrant from country of origin k (and 0 for natives). The regression

$$y_i = \beta_0 + \beta_1 X_i + \sum_k I_k \begin{pmatrix} \delta_k + \gamma_{1,k}\, \textit{age at migration} + \gamma_{2,k}\, \textit{year of migration} + \\ + \gamma_{3,k}\, \textit{length of stay} \end{pmatrix} + \varepsilon_i$$

identifies the speed of integration of immigrants from country k with $\gamma_{3,k}$, the coefficient of *length of stay*.[51] Furthermore, when data to distinguish second and third generation immigrants are available, let I_k be a first generation dummy, that is, 1 if the individual is a first generation immigrant from country of origin k (and 0 for second generation and natives); and let II_k be a second generation dummy, 1 if the individual

[50] See Borjas (1999) for a discussion of the identification problems arising when cohort effects are not accurately controlled for.

[51] We abstract here from several measurement issues that are dealt with in different ways in this literature, e.g., the definition of second generation and of country of origin.

is a second generation immigrant from country of origin k (and 0 otherwise).[52] In this case, the regression is:

$$y_i = \beta_0 + \beta_1 X_i + \sum_k \begin{pmatrix} \delta_k + \gamma_{1,k}\, age\ at\ migration + \gamma_{2,k}\, year\ of\ migration + \\ + \gamma_{3,k}\, length\ of\ stay \end{pmatrix} I_k + \varepsilon_i + \sum_k \theta_k II_k$$

and θ_k identifies the second generation effect.

Following some variant of this methodology, measures of economic integration for the U.S. and Canada have been constructed using earnings, (log) wage rates, skills (see e.g., LaLonde and Topel, 1997 and Borjas, 1999, for surveys). Other measures of assimilation, which focus more on cultural dimensions, have been constructed using intermarriage rates (Pagnini and Morgan, 1990; Meng and Gregory (2005); Bisin, Patacchini, Verdier, Zenou, 2008), or English proficiency (see Chiswick and Miller, 1992), ethnically-revealing names (Arai, Besancenot, Huynh, and Skalli, 2009), civic participation (Aleksynska, 2007), ethnic job specialization (Mandorff, 2005), self-reported measures in survey data (Dustmann, 1996; Bisin, Patacchini, Verdier, Zenou, 2008; Manning and Roy, 2009).

A recent empirical literature has studied the behavior of immigrants with a different perspective. This literature, which goes by the name of *epidemiological approach*,[53] is motivated as an attempt to isolate cultural traits of the origin countries, which affect the behavior of immigrants (including second-generation immigrants) in the destination countries. In this sense, the literature provides evidence that *culture matters*. In the process of documenting that culture matters, however, these studies indirectly measure the persistence of ethnic and religious traits, which immigrants maintain from their original backgrounds.

Consider a sample of individuals born in country j, including natives and second-generation immigrants from country of origin k. Consider a general trait y_i of an individual i in country j, and let Y_k be measure of the mean value of the trait in the country of origin. Ideally, the mean Y_k should be measured at the beginning of the immigration wave to country j which resulted in the second generation immigrant population in the sample. In this case Y_k is interpreted to instrument from culture. The regression

52 Panel data are necessary to correct for the survivorship bias due to return migration and cohort heterogeneity; see e.g., Hu (2000).

53 See Fernandez (2007b) for a methodological discussion of the approach, as well as Fernandez (2010), in this Handbook, for a more detailed survey.

$$y_i = \beta_0 + \beta_1 X_i + \sum_k \gamma_k Y_k + \varepsilon_{ij}$$

identifies the effects of country k's culture with γ_k, the coefficient of Y_k.[54]

Data regarding several behavioral traits of interest are have been collected and analyzed using the *epidemiological approach*; see Fernandez and Fogli (2006a,b) for female labor supply and fertility, Giuliano (2007) for living arrangements of 18–30-year-olds, Tabellini (2005) and Guiso, Sapienza, and Zingales (2008) for social capital, Algan and Cahuc (2007, 2009) and Tabellini (2008) for trust.

Statistics like the average speed of integration and the correlation between the speed of integration and the prevalence of the ethnic group in the country as a whole or in specific geographical areas, e.g., states could be produced with the data employed in the epidemiological literature. They would give a better picture of cultural transmission of ethnic and religious traits.

While the immigration literature provides much needed empirical evidence on integration, results cannot be interpreted to indicate the (causal) determinants of the speed of integration. In particular, properly identifying the determinants of integration would require identifying cross-cultural variations in attitudes towards integration on the part of immigrants from the incentives to integration, which depend on the socio-economic conditions of the destination country.[55] Furthermore, this literature cannot address the important issue of changes in the speed of integration across generations, as little is known about third generations. Finally, the speed of integration depends on the cultural trait of interest, as for instance language assimilation is much faster than religious assimilation (Jasso, 2009).

3.4 Socialization

A large empirical literature in sociology and economics concerns socialization mechanisms directly. It addresses a few general questions, like, Are relevant cultural traits and preferences correlated across generations? Which socialization mechanisms are more responsible for cultural transmission?

The answer to the first question tends to be positive for many traits; from specific traits, like use of salt in food, to general preferences and attitudes, like generosity. Cavalli Sforza, Feldman, Chen, and Dornbusch (1982) document high intergenerational correlations in a pool of Stanford students (and their parents) for many traits, including religious and political affiliation and attitudes, superstitions, and habits

[54] In several instances the effects of culture are restricted to be equal across country of origin, $\gamma_k = \gamma$, for any k.

[55] Meng and Gregory (2005) address this issue for Australia by measuring the earning gap in favor of intermarried immigrants. Arai and Thoursie (2006) measure for Sweden, the earning gap obtained by those immigrants who change their name to a more Swedish-sounding name. Avitabile, Clots-Figueras, and Masella (2009) relate immigrants' propensity to integrate to a more favorable citizenship legislation in Germany. See also Hatton and Leigh (2007) for a discussion of these issues.

(including use of salt in food). Among the most interesting and recent studies, high correlations are found in risk and discounting preferences (Arrondel, 2009), risk and trust attitudes (Dohmen, Falk, Huffman, and Sunde, 2006, on the 2003 and 2004 waves of the German Socio-Economic Panel), attitudes towards supporting own parents in old age (Jellal and Wolff, 2002a), attitudes towards supporting own children (Jellal and Wolff, 2002b), attitudes toward work, welfare, and individual responsibility (Baron, Cobb-Clark, and Erkal, 2008, from Youth in Focus Project data on Australian administrative social security records between 1993–2005), and generosity (Wilhelm, Brown, Rooney, and Steinberg, 2008). The relation between parents' and children's fertility behaviors is also very well documented; see e.g., Murphy and Knudsen (2002), Murphy and Wang (2001), Tymicki (2005) and the references therein. Similarly, a strong intergenerational correlation between gender role attitudes is also well documented (see Farre' and Vella, 2007, on a sample of mother-child pairs from the NLSY79; Fernandez, Fogli, and Olivetti, 2004, on a sample of mother-son pairs from the GSS). On the other hand, Cipriani, Giuliano, Jeanne (2007) find no correlation in attitudes towards cooperation in an experiments with young children (and their parents).

With regards to the socialization mechanisms most responsible for cultural transmission, some of the stylized facts include the following: religious and ethnic traits are usually adopted in the early formative years of children's psychology, and family, peers and role models play a crucial role in determining their adoption (Clark and Worthington 1987, Cornwall 1988, Erickson 1992, Hayes and Pittelkow 1993); children of mixed religious marriages have weaker religious commitments and are less likely to conform to any parental religious ideology or practices (Hoge and Petrillo, 1978, Hoge, Petrillo and Smith, 1982, Heaton 1986, and Ozorak 1989); the effect of homogamy on socialization is strong, though it vanishes if socialization effort is controlled for (Hayes and Pittelkow, 1993); schools and other collective socialization mechanisms are perceived as effective socialization instruments (O'Brien and Fugita, 1991, for Japanese; Mayer, 1979, for Jews; Tyack, 1974, for Germans; and, more recently, Glazer, 1997, for African-Americans).

Of course, intergenerational correlations and revealed preferences for the ethnic composition of schools cannot be interpreted directly as measures of successful socialization, because of several daunting identification problems. In particular, these include the issues associated to the nature/nurture problem (see Sacerdote, 2010, in this *Handbook* for a survey of the literature in economics and in behavioral genetics). Detailed empirical analyses of the properties of socialization mechanisms can nonetheless shed light on several fundamental questions arising in the study of cultural transmission, How is cultural heterogeneity explained? What are its determinants?

The theoretical work on cultural transmission we surveyed identifies *cultural substitution* between *vertical and oblique/horizontal transmission* as a general component of socialization mechanisms, which induce heterogeneity, especially in socio-economic environments characterized by *strategic substitution*. In addition, *cultural distinction* in identity formation mechanism of minorities acts in a related manner. Importantly, however, all these implications rely on the assumption of *imperfect empathy* and on the distinction between *vertical and oblique/horizontal transmission.*

Do we observe imperfect empathy, vertical and oblique/horizontal transmission, cultural substitution, strategic substitution, and cultural distinction? We next survey the empirical literature dedicated to address these specific questions.

3.4.1 Imperfect empathy

Evidence for *impure altruism* (a general form of *imperfect empathy*) is found in the empirical analysis of *inter vivos* transfers (see e.g., Altonji, Hayashi, and Kotlikoff, 1997, and Laferrere and Wolff, 2006). Survey data can also be taken to bear indirect light on the issue: in the response to NORC's General Social Survey's question, 'Which three of the qualities listed would you say are the most desirable for a child to have?' 'obedience' is cited on average across the sample more than, (in order) 'self-control', 'success', 'studiousness', 'cleanliness', and less often only than 'honesty.'

3.4.2 Vertical vs. oblique/horizontal transmission

Booth and Kee (2009) estimate count data quantile regression models using the British Household Panel Survey to distinguish vertical and oblique transmission of fertility rates, finding strong evidence for substantial vertical transmission. Branas-Garza and Neuman (2007) exploit data from the International Social Survey Programme: Religion II (ISSP) on church attendance and prayer habits of parents in Spain and Italy to study the effect of a specific vertical transmission mechanism – exposure to religiosity – on fertility preferences and practice of children. The major finding is that such effects are pronounced, though maternal and paternal effects are different. Collado, Ortuno-Ortin, and Romeu (2005) introduce a novel methodology to identify vertical transmission in consumption choices, lacking consumption data for both parents and children. Analyzing the correlation between the geographical distributions of surnames and consumption choices, they conclude that the data suggest a very significant vertical transmission of preferences regarding food items and no vertical transmission for non-food goods. Aleksynska (2007) adopts the synthetic cohort methodology to study the cultural transmission of immigrants to the European Union with European Social Survey and World Values Survey data). In particular she is interested in determining whether the observed levels of immigrants' civic participation depends relatively more on the levels of natives' civic participation in the same countries or in the country of origin. Notwithstanding selection issues, the evidence in favor of country of destination effect suggests horizontal transmission leading to the solicit internalization of the norms of the host country. Uslaner (2008) similarly tests whether an individual generalized trust is relatively more transmitted from parents to children, obtained by ethnic heritage (where their grand-parents came from), or by horizontal and oblique transmission (the proportion of people of different ethnic backgrounds in a state), finding strong evidence in favor of direct vertical socialization and ethnic heritage.

Many empirical studies concern the determinants of female labor force participation, to identify cultural components. Fernandez and Fogli (2009) show that the variation in the work behavior of second-generation American women can be explained, in part, by the level of female labor force participation in their parents' country of origin. Moreover, Fernandez (2007b) shows that the attitudes towards women's work in the parental country of origin has important explanatory value for second-generation American women's work behavior in the U.S. Fernandez, Fogli, and Olivetti (2004) identify a vertical transmission mechanism: sons of working mothers seem to display a preference for working wives, relatively to sons of non-working mothers. Fernandez (2007a), and Fogli and Veldkamp (2008) find evidence for a horizontal transmission and learning in a variety of data, from calibration to survey and labor market data.

3.4.3 Marriage

Chiswick (2008) studies the determinants of ethnic intermarriage by means of a binomial logistic regression using 1980 U.S. Census data. Interestingly, the paper constructs measures for the *availability ratios for potential spouses* and for *group size*. It then documents lower intermarriage rates the greater the availability ratio and the larger the size of the group, a property generally consistent with choice theoretic marriage markets. Evidence for homogamous marriage as a socialization mechanism can be indirectly gauged from the fact that most religious denominations include rules favoring homogamy (Smith 1996) and that most conversions are attributable to the desire of establishing homogamy (Greeley, 1979; Branas-Garza, Garcia-Munoz, and Neuman, 2007). Furthermore, Becker (2009) provides evidence, from the Preschool Education and Educational Careers among Migrant Children project on naming patterns of Turkish parents in Germany, that intermarriage strongly decrease the probability of Turkish names.

A more detailed non-linear analysis of this dependence is necessary, however, to identify the properties of marriage as a socialization mechanism. Bisin, Topa, and Verdier (2004) attempt this endeavor, producing an empirical analysis of the endogenous marriage model in Section 2.2.2. Exploiting the geographic variation in the distribution of religious traits in the U.S., Bisin, Topa, and Verdier (2004), estimate the model by matching simulated inter-marriage rates π^{ij} and socialization rates P^{ij}, at a given moment in time, with the corresponding empirical moments. The data are from the General Social Survey (GSS), 1972–1996, with respect to 4 religious groups: Protestants, Catholics, Jews, and the residual group, Others ($i,j = P, C, J, O$). The geographical unit of variation is a U.S. state (for 23 of them). Information on socialization rates P^{ij} is obtained from a special module on religion of the GSS. The structural parameters of the model are the intolerance parameters ΔV^{ij}, for any i and j, and the parameters of the cost functions for socialization and entrance in the restricted marriage pool. Furthermore, they test the model against different alternatives that restrict the role of marriage as a socialization mechanism, finding support for socialization as a major incentive for religious homogamy in marriage.

The observed intermarriage rates by religious trait in the U.S. data are a stark indication of the prevalence of religious homogamy. Figure 15 displays the probability of homogamous marriage, in the data, as a function of the religious shares, by U.S. state, for the four religious groups analyzed in the study (Protestants, Catholics, Jews, and others).

Note that points on the 45°-line in the graph represent the marriage rates which would be obtained by random matching, by religious share. Data points above the 45°-line are then to be interpreted as raw evidence for the prevalence of homogamy.

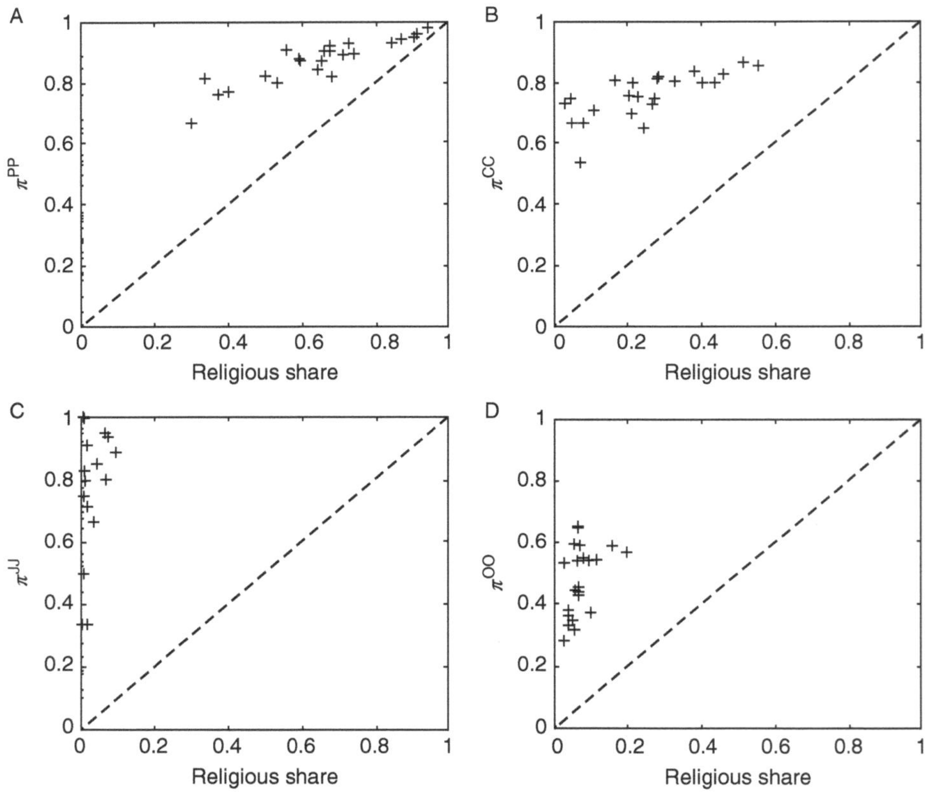

Figure 15 Probability of homogamous marriage as a function of the religious shares, by U.S. state. a: Protestants; b: Catholics; c: Jews; d: Others. Source: Bisin, Topa, and Verdier (2004).

Table 2 Socialization rates for selected marriage types. Source: Bisin, Topa, and Verdier (2004).

	Protestants	Catholics	Jews	Others
PP marriage	.9179	.0284	0	.0537
CC marriage	.0850	.8571	.0034	.0544
JJ marriage	.0370	0	.9259	.0370
OO marriage	.3231	.0462	0	.6308
PC marriage	.5116	.3140	0	.1744
PO marriage	.7100	.1000	0	.1900
CO marriage	.1667	.5000	0	.3333

NOTE.–Each cell reports the sample probability that a child in the row marriage is a member of the column religious group. P = Protestants, C = Catholics, J = Jews, and O = Others.

Similarly, socialization rates are also very high, along the religious dimension; especially in homogamous marriages; see Table 2.

The endogenous marriage model fits these data quite well, as illustrated by Figure 16 and Table 3 (see the paper for formal statistics).

The significant positive intolerance parameters (with the exception of the parameter describing attitudes toward Jews of the residual group, Others)[56] estimated by Bisin, Topa, and Verdier (2004) are consistent with homogamous marriage to be perceived (and chosen) by agents as a socialization mechanism.

The estimated model of marriage and socialization is based on the behavioral assumption that marriage and socialization are endogenously determined as economic decisions of agents who have preferences for children with their own religious attitudes. But Bisin, Topa, and Verdier (2004) also formally assess the relevance of economic behavior to explain the observed socialization and marriage rates by conducting some statistical test to compare the performance of the model to several alternative specifications that make different behavioral assumptions; namely, a first specification in which marriage segregation choices are endogenous but socialization is exogenous, a second specification in which both marriage and socialization are exogenous, and a third specification in which the value of a homogamous marriage is exogenous and independent of the religious share. The rankings of the Sargan test of the over-identifying restrictions reported in the paper suggest that none of the three alternative models fits the data nearly as well as the baseline model (p-values vary between .02 and .0017, compared with .11 in the baseline model estimate).[57]

[56] The most striking estimates are those describing the intolerance parameters of Jews, which are about four times as high as those of any other religious group.

[57] A formal statistical test comparing the baseline to the alternative specifications requires a procedure to compare non-nested models. The results of one such test produced in the paper confirm the Sargan test rankings.

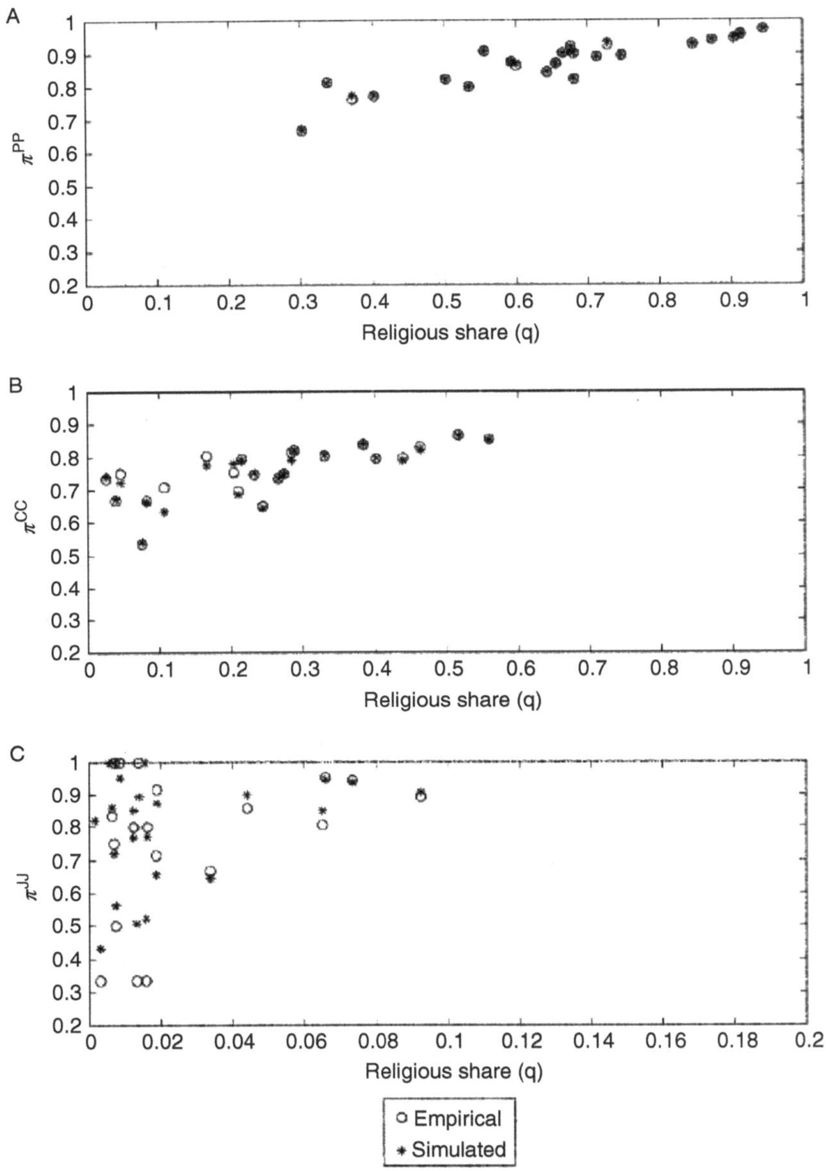

Figure 16 Fit of the endogenous marriage model: Homogamous marriage probabilities. a: Protestants; b: Catholics; c: Jews. Source: Bisin, Topa, and Verdier (2004).

Table 3 Fit of the endogenous marriage model: Socialization rates. Source: Bisin, Topa, and Verdier (2004).

	Protestants	Catholics	Jews	Others
	A. Empirical Frequencies			
PP marriage	.9179	.0284	0	.0537
CC marriage	.0850	.8571	.0034	.0544
JJ marriage	.0370	0	.9259	.0370
OO marriage	.3231	.0462	0	.6380
PC marriage	.5116	.3140	0	.1744
PO marriage	.7100	.1000	0	.1900
CO marriage	.1667	.5000	0	.3333
	B. Simulated Frequencies from the Model			
PP marriage	.9227	.0349	.0031	.0394
CC marriage	.1078	.8293	.0065	.0564
JJ marriage	.0308	.0220	.9291	.0180
OO marriage	.1472	.0712	.0078	.7738
PC marriage	.4855	.3409	.0165	.1571
PO marriage	.5168	.1378	.0131	.3323
CO marriage	.3051	.3425	.0192	.3333

NOTE.–Each cell reports the sample probability that a child in the row marriage is a member of the column religious group. P = Protestants, C = Catholics, J = Jews, and O = Others.

In summary, parameter estimates in Bisin, Topa, and Verdier (2004) are consistent with Protestants, Catholics, and Jews having a strong preference for children who identify with their own religious beliefs and making costly decisions to influence their children's religious beliefs.

3.4.4 Neighborhood and school choice

Ioannides and Zanella (2007) study the determinants of household decisions to change residence, using geocodes to merge micro data from the PSID with data at the level of census tracts from the 2000 U.S. Census. They identify parental concerns about children socialization, within neighborhoods and schools, off of households' revealed preferences over attributes of neighborhoods. They find strong evidence that households with children (but not those without) are more likely to move neighborhoods with commonly perceived characteristics which are more conducive to the transmission of parental cultural traits.

Relatedly, Kremer and Sarychev (2000) produce evidence that school choice (as opposed to a public school system) is correlated with cultural segregation, as parents choose their children schools as part of their vertical socialization effort.

3.4.5 Collective socialization mechanisms

Evidence about the empirical relevance of collective socialization mechanisms, especially school, is sparse but not surprisingly clear-cut, at least for some specific traits like language; see e.g., Aspachs-Bracons, A., I. Clots-Figueras, and P. Masella, 2007, and Aspachs-Bracons, A., I. Clots-Figueras, J. Costa-Font, and P. Masella, 2008, for the Catalan and the Basque case. Hryshko, Luengo-Prado, and Sorensen (2006) find that, in the Panel Study of Income Dynamics, state-level compulsory schooling laws that boosted parents' education made children less risk averse through adulthood, suggesting an horizontal transmission mechanism operating through public schooling (for the parents) and associated to vertical socialization of children.

3.4.6 Cultural substitution

The literature addressing the issue of cultural substitution has typically a structural flavor. Even without time series data the cultural transmission model can in fact be identified and estimated through cross sectional data on socialization frequencies across different populations.

Identification of cultural intolerances ΔV^i, requires the observation of socialization probabilities P^{ii}, P^{ij} at a point in time for different populations characterized by different population shares q^i. Several papers undertook this approach, whose main difficulty however consists in requiring the exogeneity of q^i. In fact, in empirically work, the residents of different geographic units, like counties, census tracts, or states, constitute the populations. As long as individuals choose where to reside and base their choice on the cultural composition of the geographic unit, the exogeneity of q^i is called into questions. Various data dependent methods to deal with this issue have been developed in the literature.

The first paper to structurally estimate an economic model of cultural transmission is Bisin, Topa, and Verdier (2004), which we discussed in Section 2.2.2. While the aim of the paper is to test the behavioral assumption that marriage and socialization are endogenously determined as economic decisions of agents, the structural estimates of the parameters of the model provide evidence which can distinguish between cultural substitution and complementarity. In particular, the parameter estimates for the cost of socialization and marriage segregation reveal a strong dependence on religious shares, which could be interpreted as partial evidence for some form of cultural complementarity. In fact, the estimated direct socialization as a function of the religious share is not negatively sloped in the entire domain, as would be required for cultural substitution; see Figure 17.

Nonetheless it is clear from the figure that socialization rates of small religious minorities (with religious shares close to 0) are much higher than what random socialization in the population would imply (the same is true for marriage homogamy with respect to random matching, not reported here). To better understand the implications of the model estimates with respect to religious heterogeneity, Bisin, Topa, and Verdier (2004) simulate the population dynamics of the distribution by religious group,

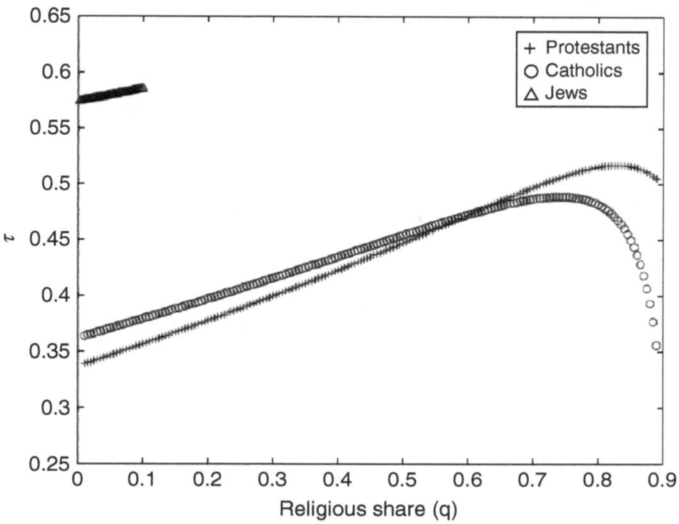

Figure 17 Socialization as a function of the religious share. Source: Bisin, Topa, and Verdier (2004).

over time, using the estimated structural parameters and the empirical religious composition of several U.S. states as initial conditions.[58] Results are reported in Figure 18. Note that two different stationary distributions of the population by religious trait are attractive for different sets of initial conditions: one has a large majority of Protestants (about 90%) and a minority of the residual group, Others (about 10%); the other is uniquely composed of Jews.

The simulations therefore support some cultural heterogeneity at the stationary state of the population dynamics. In particular, they are in stark contrast to those emerging from linear extrapolations of current trends: in particular, the *triple melting pot* (along the religious dimension) and the *vanishing of American Jews* hypotheses, suggested, respectively by Herberg (1955) and Dershowitz (1997) and often aired in the sociological literature, are not supported.

Namoro and Roushdy (2008) also test cultural substitution directly, on data on the preference for fertility of married Egyptian women. In particular, Namoro and Roushdy (2008) estimate structurally (1),

$$P^{ii} = d(q^i) + (1-d(q^i))q^i,$$

for $i = l, h$, where l (resp. h) denotes the low (resp. high) fertility preference trait. Given data on q^i and P^{ii} (as well as on a series of covariates) across 26 administrative

[58] The authors caution the reader that these simulations are only aimed at illustrating the implications of the estimation results and should not be interpreted as direct forecasts of the future prevalence of the different religious denominations; p. 645

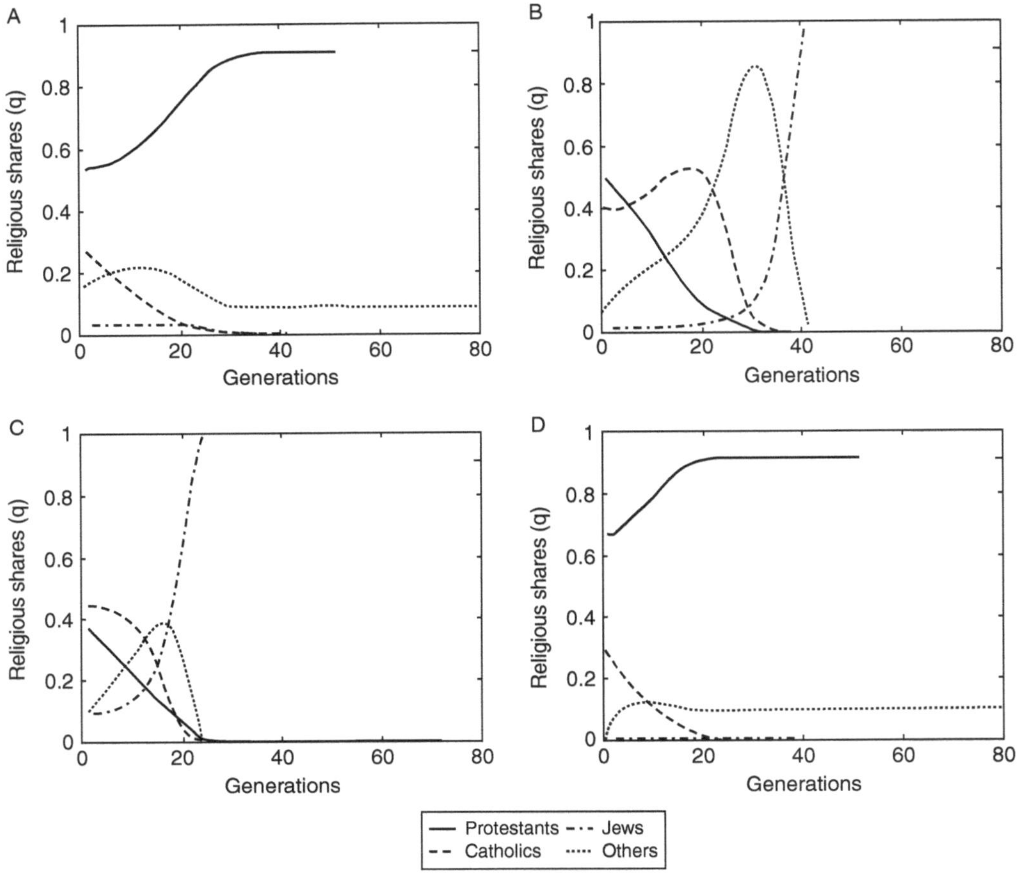

Figure 18 Simulated population dynamics. Initial conditions: a, California; b, Illinois; c, New York; d, Texas. Source: Bisin, Topas, Verdier (2004).

localities (Governatorates), $d(q^i)$ is estimated non-parametrically and the resulting negative slope is evidence for cultural substitution.

Cohen-Zada (2006) pursue an empirical analysis of U.S. county data (from the Religious Congregations and Membership in the U.S., 2000, and various years of the School and Agency Survey and of the Private School Survey) on Catholic and private school enrollment to explicitly test for cultural substitution, that is, to test whether the demand for separate religious schooling declines with the share of the religious minority. Cultural substitution is already evident from raw correlations; see Table 4, which displays an inverted U-shaped relationship between enrollment in Catholic schools and the share of Catholics in the population, by county.

Table 4 Enrollment in Catholic schools out of total enrollment. Source: Cohen-Zada (2006).

Catholic share in the population	Number of observations	Average Catholic enrollment rate
0%–10%	3352	0.527%
10%–20%	1307	2.504%
20%–30%	708	4.722%
30%–40%	376	6.702%
40%–50%	174	6.719%
50%–60%	129	8.210%
60%–70%	49	7.887%
70%–80%	27	6.901%
80%–90%	14	3.639%
90%–100%	7	0.000%

Patacchini and Zenou (2004) also speak to the identification of cultural substitution vs. complementarity. They study the vertical transmission of preferences for education, under the assumption that both educated and uneducated parents wish to transmit preferences for education to their children, to positively affect their educational attainment, but educated parents are most effective at doping so, other things equal. An important property of the data Patacchini and Zenou (2004) exploit, the UK National Child Development Study (NCDS), is that it allows them to construct a direct measure of parental socialization effort, based on qualitative information on the parent's interest in his/her child's education. Imputing a measure of neighborhood quality from Census data on the distribution of education levels by ward, Patacchini and Zenou (2004) can study the relationship between parental socialization effort and neighborhood quality. Assuming that residential location is exogenous, Patacchini and Zenou (2004) interpret their evidence that parents invest more in socializing their children when living in a high quality neighborhood as evidence for cultural complementarity. If residential location were endogenous, and parents moved to neighborhoods with desirable characteristics in terms of socialization, as e.g., documented by Ioannides and Zanella (2008) and Kremer and Sarychev (2000), then Patacchini and Zenou (2004)'s result would instead be consistent with cultural substitution, as parental effort and neighborhood choice could both represent distinct direct vertical socialization instruments. An additional interesting result of Patacchini and Zenou (2004) regards the differential socialization effort, on average, between high and low educated parents. Consistently with imperfect empathy joined with the assumption that educated parents are more efficient in socializing their children to preferences for education, low-educated parents spend significantly less time than their educated counterparts, other things equal, in socializing their offspring; in fact, in this case, only the quality of the neighborhood has a significant impact on their children's educational attainment.

This structural evidence for *cultural substitution* is also consistent with several empirical studies studying the link between identity and segregation. Using a nationally representative sample of more than 90,000 students from 175 schools who entered grades 7 through 12 in 1994 in the U.S. (the National Longitudinal Study of Adolescent Health), Fryer and Torelli (2005) find that "acting white" behaviors among blacks (i.e., the higher the test score, the less popular a student is) are more developed in racially mixed schools.[59] Munshi and Wilson (2008) combine data from the U.S. census and the National Longitudinal Survey of Youth 1979 (NLSY79) to identify a negative relationship across counties in the Midwest of the United States between ethnic fractionalization in 1860 and the probability that individuals have professional jobs or migrated out of the county by 2000; see Figure 19.

Furthermore, Munshi and Wilson (2008) also document a positive correlation between ethnic (and religious) fractionalization and better functioning religious and parochial institutions, suggesting an important role of churches in the transmission of ethnic traits.[60]

3.4.7 Cultural distinction

Bisin, Patacchini, Verdier, and Zenou (2010) study instead identity formation, aiming at distinguishing *cultural conformity* from *cultural distinction*.[61] They exploit the Fourth National Survey of Ethnic Minorities (FNSEM) of the U.K. The dataset oversamples Caribbean, Indian, Pakistani, African-Asian, Bangladeshi, and Chinese and contains a direct survey question about respondents' identification with their own ethnic group and additional (indirect) information about different dimensions of identity (e.g., attitudes towards inter marriage, importance of religion and other aspects of individuals' ethnic preferences).

To better address the possible endogeneity of residential decisions Bisin, Patacchini, Verdier, and Zenou (2010) proceeds in steps, from a non-structural probit analysis of

[59] Anthropologists have also observed that social groups seek to preserve their identity, an activity that accelerates when threats to internal cohesion intensify. Thus, groups may try to reinforce their identity by penalizing members for differentiating themselves from the group. The penalties are likely to increase whenever the threats to group cohesion intensify; for an early analysis of these issues, see Whyte (1943).

[60] Anthropologists have also observed that social groups seek to preserve their identity, an activity that accelerates when threats to internal cohesion intensify. Thus, groups may try to reinforce their identity by penalizing members for differentiating themselves from the group. The penalties are likely to increase whenever the threats to group cohesion intensify; for an early analysis of these issues, see Whyte (1943).

[61] Other empirical studies on identity formation include Battu and Zenou (2010), Constant, Gataullina and Zimmermann (2009), Nekby and Rödin (2009), and Manning and Roy (2009). We do not discuss them in detail because they take a more descriptive approach.

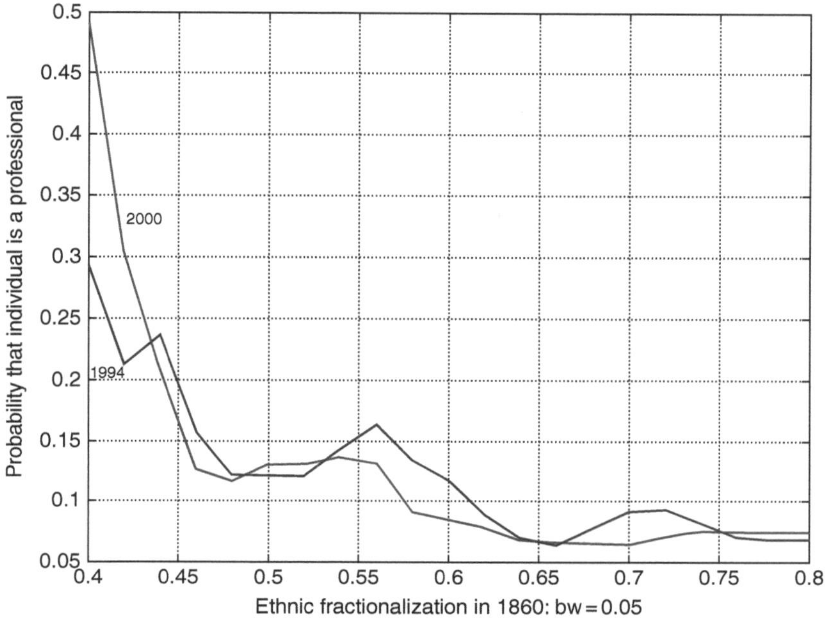

Figure 19 Relationship between ethnic fractionalization in 1860 and the probability that individuals have professional jobs. Source: Munshi and Wilson (2008).

identity and homogamy in terms of ethnic composition to fully structural models of ethnic integration. The probit displays a negative relationship between ethnic identity and the share of the ethnic group in the neighborhood, for those neighborhoods in which the share is above 20%, a result consistent with cultural distinction, see Figure 20.[62]

The structural analysis of identity formation exploits the identity formation choice model (extended to jointly determine identity and homogamy in marriage) outlined in Section 2.2.5. The model produces a map between identity ν^i and the psychological costs of interacting with the majority $c(q^i)$. A non-parametric estimate of $c(q^i)$ under the restrictions of the model is also consistent with ethnic identity being formed as a *cultural distinction* mechanism, and so is a structural estimate of the model parameterized to formally nest *distinction* and *conformity* and to allow individuals to choose the neighborhood where to reside depending on its ethnic composition.[63]

[62] The analysis uses a self-reported measure of "importance of religion" as a proxy for ethnic identity. The use of the other proxies leads to similar results.

[63] Also, recent studies of the *Islamic Revival*, the surge in Islamic participation in the world since the 1970s, suggest interpretations which are consistent with cultural distinction, inasmuch as the decline of social mobility and the impoverishment of the middle-class in Islamic countries, relatively to the economic success of West, have intensified the religious revival of Islam; see Carvalho (2009) and references therein.

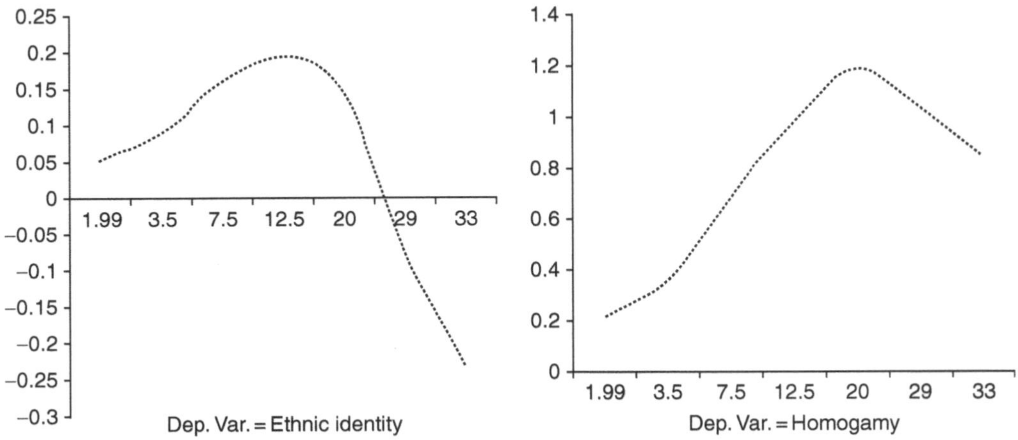

Figure 20 Non linear effect of neighborhood ethnic composition on identity and homogamy. Source: Bisin, Patacchini, Verdier, and Zenou (2010).

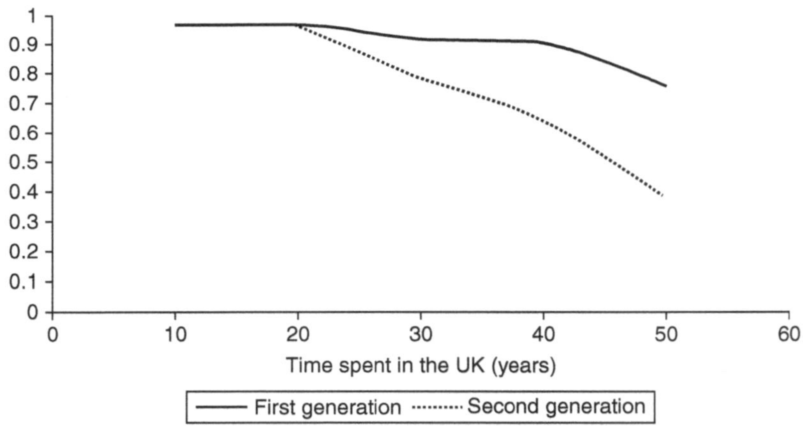

Figure 21 Predicted identity as a function of time in the U.K. Source: Bisin, Patacchini, Verdier, and Zenou (2010).

The speed of integration predicted by the structural model at the estimated parameter values can be gauged upon from Figures 21 and 22, reporting predicted identity and homogamy, respectively, as a function of time spent in the U.K. The ethnic homogamy rate, for instance, is predicted to decline less than 10% between first and second immigration immigrants.

Finally, *cultural distinction* is also consistent with the literature on participation in social activities as a function of segregation and fractionalization, as in Alesina and La Ferrara (2000), Putnam (2007), Letki (2008), and Fumagalli and Fumagalli (2010).

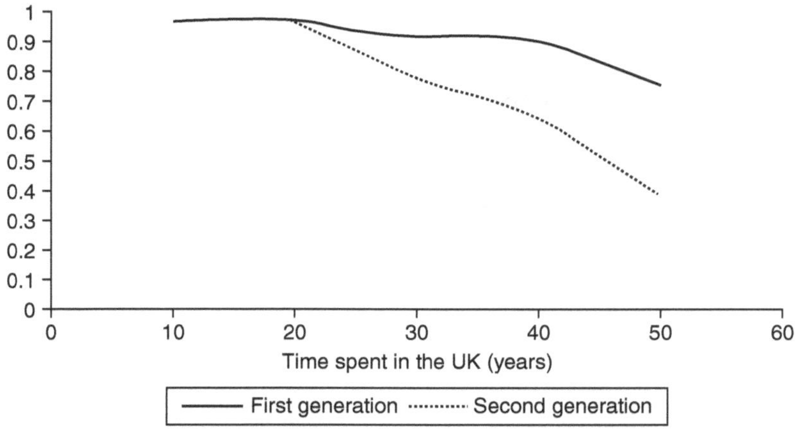

Figure 22 Predicted homogamy as a function of time in the U.K. Source: Bisin, Patachini, Verdier, and Zenou (2009).

4. CONCLUSIONS

This article has reviewed the main contributions of models of cultural transmission, from theoretical and empirical perspectives. The literature reviewed has developed a set of workhorse models to study the dynamics of cultural traits, values, and beliefs. These models have been extended in several dimensions of interest and have been put to data in several different contexts.

This literature has been successful in providing a better understanding of the cultural heterogeneity, which characterizes the human condition, as well as of the cultural resilience of ethnic and religious traits, which has been repeatedly observed in human history. Furthermore, this literature has advanced our understanding of the patterns of cultural integration of immigrants and of the properties of various socialization mechanisms.

Finally, the interaction of cultural traits and institutions along human history and its effect on present socio-economic condition of populations is a fascinating topic, which is now being explored, both theoretically and empirically along the lines and with the models surveyed in this paper.

REFERENCES

Abrams, D., Hogg, M., 1988. Social Identifications: A Social Psychology of Inter-group Relations and Group Processes. Routledge, London.

Acemoglu, D., Johnson, S., Robinson, J.A., 2001. The Colonial Origins of Comparative Development: An Empirical Investigation. Am. Econ. Rev. 91, 1369–1401.

Adriani, F., Sonderegger, S., 2009. Why Do Parents Socialize Their Children to Behave Pro-socially? An Information-based Theory. mimeo, University of Bristol.

Akerlof, G.A., Kranton, R.E., 2000. Economics and Identity. Q. J. Econ. 115, 715–753.
Akerlof, G.A., Kranton, R.E., 2010. Identity Economics: How Identities Shape Our Work, Wages, and Well-Being. Princeton University Press, Princeton.
Aleksynska, M., 2007. Civic Participation of Immigrants: Cultural Transmission and Assimilation. mimeo, Universita' Bocconi.
Alesina, A., Angeletos, G.M., 2005. Fairness and Redistribution: US versus Europe. Am. Econ. Rev. 95 (4), 960–980.
Alesina, A., La Ferrara, E., 2000. Participation in heterogeneous communities. Q. J. Econ. 115 (3), 847–904.
Alesina, A., La Ferrara, E., 2005. Ethnic Diversity and Economic Performance. J. Econ. Lit. 43, 762–800.
Alesina, A., Devleeschauwer, A., Easterly, W., Kurlat, S., Wacziarg, R., 2003. Fractionalization. J. Econ. Growth 8 (2), 155–194.
Alesina, A., Algan, Y., Cahuc, P., Giuliano, P., 2010. Family Values and Regulation of Labor. CEPR Discussion Paper 7688.
Alesina, A., Giuliano, P., Nunn, N., 2010. On the Origins of Gender Roles: Women and the Plough. Work in progress.
Algan, Y., Bisin, A., Manning, A., Verdier, T. (Eds.), 2010. Immigration and cultural integration in Europe, forthcoming. CEPR, Oxford University Press, Oxford.
Algan, Y., Cahuc, P., 2007. Social Attitudes and Economic Development: AN Epidemiological Approach. CEPR Discussion Papers 6403.
Algan, Y., Cahuc, P., 2009. Civic Virtue and Labor Market Institutions. Am. Econ. J.: Macroeconomics 1 (1), 111–145.
Allport, G.W., 1954. The nature of Prejudice, Cambridge. Perseus Books, MA.
Altonji, J., Hayashi, F., Kotlikoff, L., 1997. Parental Altruism and Inter Vivos Transfers: Theory and Evidence. Journal of Political Economy 105 (6), 1121–1166.
Ammerman, A.J., Cavalli Sforza, L.L., 1971. Measuring the Rate of Spread of Early Farming in Europe. Man 6 (4), 674–688.
Ammerman, A.J., Cavalli Sforza, L.L., 1984. The Neolithic Transition and the Genetics of Populations in Europe. Princeton University Press, Princeton.
Aoki, K., 2001. Theoretical and Empirical Aspects of Gene-culture Coevolution. Theor. Popul. Biol. 59, 253–261.
Aoki, K., Shida, M., Shigesada, N., 1996. Travelling Wave Solutions for the Spread of Farmers into a Region Occupied by Hunter-gatherers. Theor. Popul. Biol. 50, 1–17.
Arai, M., Thoursie, P., 2006. Giving up Foreign Names: An Empirical Investigation of Surname Change and Earnings. mimeo, Stockholm University.
Arai, M., Besancenot, D., Huynh, K., Skalli, A., 2009. Children's First Names and Immigration Background in France. mimeo, Stockholm University.
Arrondel, L., 2009. My Father Was Right: The Transmission of Values Between Generations. Paris School of Economics Working Paper 2009–12.
Ashraf, Q., Galor, O., 2010. The "Out of Africa" Hypothesis, Human Genetic Diversity, and Comparatibe Economic Development. mimeo, Brown University.
Aspachs-Bracons, A., Clots-Figueras, I., Masella, P., 2007. Identity and Language Policies. mimeo, Universidad Carlos III.
Aspachs-Bracons, A., Clots-Figueras, I., Costa-Font, J., Masella, P., 2008. Compulsory Language Educational Policies and Identity Formation. J. Eur. Econ. Assoc. 6 (2–3), 434–444.
Austen-Smith, D., Fryer, R.D., 2005. An Economic Analysis of 'Acting White' Q. J. Econ. 120, 551–583.
Avitabile, C., Clots-Figueras, I., Masella, P., 2009. The Effect of Birthright Citizenship on Parental Integration Outcomes. mimeo, University of Mannheim.
Banfield, E., 1958. The Moral Basis of a Backward Society. Free Press, Glencoe, IL.
Baron, J.D., Cobb-Clark, D.A., Erkal, N., 2008. Cultural Transmission of Work-Welfare Attitudes and the Intergenerational Correlation in Welfare Receipt. mimeo, IZA, Bonn.

Battu, H., Zenou, Y., 2010. Oppositional Identities and Employment for Ethnic Minorities: Evidence from England. Economic Journal 120 (542), pp. F52–F71, 021.

Battu, H., Mwale, M.D., Zenou, Y., 2007. Oppositional Identities and the Labor Market. J. Popul. Econ. 20, 643–667.

Baudin, T., 2008. A Role for Cultural Transmission in Fertility Transitions. mimeo, Paris School of Economics University of Paris I Panthéon-Sorbonne.

Becker, B., 2009. Immigrants' Emotional Identification with the Host Society. Ethnicities 9 (2), 200–225.

Becker, G.S., 1996. Accounting for Taste. Harvard University Press, Cambridge, MA.

Becker, G.S., Lewis, H.G., 1973. On the Interaction Between the Quantity and Quality of Children. J. Polit. Econ. 81 (2), 279–288.

Becker, G.S., Murphy, K.M., 2000. Social Economics. Harvard University Press, Cambridge, MA.

Bidner, C., Francois, P., 2009. Cultivating Trust: Norms, Institutions and the Implications of Scale. mimeo, University of British Columbia.

Bisin, A., Topa, G., 2003. Empirical Models of Cultural Transmission. J. Eur. Econ. Assoc. 1 (2), 363–375.

Bisin, A., Verdier, T., 1998. On the Cultural Transmission of Preferences for Social Status. J. Public Econ. 70, 75–97.

Bisin, A., Verdier, T., 2000. Beyond the Melting Pot: Cultural Transmission, Marriage and the Evolution of Ethnic and Religious Traits. Q. J. Econ. 115, 955–988.

Bisin, A., Verdier, T., 2001. The Economics of Cultural Transmission and the Dynamics of Preferences. J. Econ. Theory 97, 298–319.

Bisin, A., Verdier, T., 2005. Work Ethic and Redistribution: A Cultural Transmission Model of the Welfare State. mimeo, New York University.

Bisin, A., Topa, G., Verdier, T., 2004. Cooperation as a Transmitted Cultural Trait. Ration. Soc. 16, 477–507.

Bisin, A., Patacchini, E., Verdier, T., Zenou, Y., 2008. Are Muslims Immigrants Different in terms of Cultural Integration? J. Eur. Econ. Assoc. 6, 445–456.

Bisin, A., Patacchini, E., Verdier, T., Zenou, Y., 2010. Bend It Like Beckham: Ethnic Identity and Integration. mimeo, NYU.

Bisin, A., Topa, G., Verdier, T., 2009. Cultural Transmission, Socialization and the Population Dynamics of Multiple State Traits Distributions. International Journal of Economic Theory 5 (1), 139–154, issue in honor of Jess Benhabib.

Bobo, L.D., 1999. Prejudice as a Group Position: Microfoundations of a Sociological Approach to Racism and Racial Relations. J. Soc. Issues 55, 445–472.

Booth, A.L., Kee, H.J., 2009. Intergenerational Transmission of Fertility Patterns. Oxf. Bull. Econ. Stat. 71 (2), 183–208.

Borgerhoff Mulder, M., Nunn, C.L., Towner, M., 2006. Cultural Macroevolution and the Transmission of Traits. Evol. Anthropol. 15, 52–64.

Borjas, G.J., 1992. Ethnic Capital and Intergenerational Income Mobility' Q. J. Econ. 57, 123–150.

Borjas, G.J., 1995. Ethnicity, Neighborhoods, and Human Capital Externality. Am. Econ. Rev. LXXXV, 365–390.

Borjas, G.J., 1999. The economic analysis of immigration. In: Ashenfelter, O.C., Card, D. (Eds.), Handbook of Labor Economics vol. 3, Part 1. pp. 1697–1760.

Botticini, M., Eckstein, Z., 2005. Jewish Occupational Selection: Education, Restrictions, or Minorities? J. Econ. Hist. 65 (4), 922–948.

Botticini, M., Eckstein, Z., 2007. From Farmers to Merchants, Conversions and Diaspora: Human Capital and Jewish History. J. Eur. Econ. Assoc. 5 (5), 885–926.

Bowles, S., 2001. Individual Interactions, Group Conflicts and the Evolution of Preferences. In: Durlauf, S., Young, H.P. (Eds.), Social Dynamics. MIT Press, Cambridge MA, pp. 155–190.

Bowles, S., Gintis, H., 1998. The Moral Economy as Community: Structured Populations and the Evolution of Prosocial Norms. Evol. Hum. Behav. 19 (1), 3–25.

Bowles, S., Gintis, H., 2002. Social Capital and Community Governance. Economic Journal 112, 419–436.

Bowles, S., Gintis, H., 2003. Origins of Human Cooperation. In: Hammerstein, P. (Ed.), Genetic and Cultural Evolution of Cooperation. MIT Press, Cambridge, MA.
Boyd, R., Richerson, P., 1985. Culture and the Evolutionary Process. University of Chicago Press, Chicago, IL.
Branas-Garza, P., Neuman, S., 2007. Parental Religiosity and Daughters' Fertility: The Case of Catholics in Southern Europe. Rev. Econ. Household 5 (3), 305–327.
Branas-Garza, T., Garcia-Munoz, P., Neuman, S., 2007. Unraveling Secularization: An International Study. IZA Discussion Paper 3251.
Brewer, M., 1999. The Psychology of Prejudice: Ingroup Love or Outgroup Hate? J. Soc. Issues 55 (3), 429–444.
Cameron, L., Chauduri, A., Erkal, N., Gangadharan, L., 2009. Propensities to Engage in and Punish Corrupt Behavior: Experimental Evidence from Australia, India, Indonesia, and Singapore. J. Public Econ. 93, 843–851.
Carvalho, J.P., 2009. A Theory of the Islamic Revival. mimeo, University of Oxford.
Cavalli-Sforza, L., Feldman, M., 1973. Models for cultural inheritance, I: Group mean and within group variation. Theor. Popul. Biol. 4, 42–55.
Cavalli Sforza, L.L., Feldman, M., 1973. Cultural Versus Biological Inheritance: Phenotypic Transmission from Parent to Children. Am. J. Hum. Genet. 25, 618–637.
Cavalli Sforza, L.L., Feldman, M., 1981. Cultural Transmission and Evolution: A Quantitative Approach. Princeton University Press, Princeton, NJ.
Cavalli Sforza, L.L., Feldman, M., Chen, K.H., Dornbusch, S.M., 1982. Theory and Observation in Cultural Transmission. Science 1, 218 (4567), 19–27.
Cavalli Sforza, L.L., Menozzi, P., Piazza, A., 1994. The History and Geography of Human Genes. Princeton University Press, Princeton, NJ.
Chiswick, B.R., 2008. Ethnic Intermarriage among Immigrants: Human Capital and Assortative Mating. IZA Discussion Paper 3740.
Chiswick, B.R., Miller, P.W., 1992. Language in the Labor Market: The Immigrant Experience in Canada and the United States. In: Chiswick, C.U. (Ed.), Immigration, Language and Ethnic Issues: Canada and the United States. American Enterprise Institute, Washington D.C., pp. 229–296.
Cipriani, M., Giuliano, P., Jeanne, O., 2007. Like Mother Like Son? Experimental Evidence on the Transmission of Values from Parents to Children. IZA Discussion Paper 2768.
Clark, M., 1965. Hopewell Type Figurines. Central States Archaeological Journal 12, 120–122.
Clark, C.A., Worthington, A., 1987. Family Variables Affecting the Transmission of Religious Values from Parents to Adolescents: A Review. Family Perspective XXI, 1–21.
Cohen-Zada, D., 2006. Preserving Religious Identity through Education: Economic Analysis and Evidence from the US. J. Urban Econ. 60.
Collado, M.D., Ortuno-Ortin, I., Romeu, A., 2005. Vertical Transmission of Consumption Behavior and the Distribution of Surnames. mimeo, Universidad de Alicante.
Constant, A.F., Gataullina, L., Zimmermann, K.F., 2009. Ethnosizing Immigrants. J. Econ. Behav. Organ. 69, 274–287.
Cook, P.J., Ludwig, J., 1997. The Burden of Acting White: Do Black Adolescents Disparage Academic Achievement. J. Policy Anal. Manage.
Corneo, G., Jeanne, O., 2009. A theory of tolerance. J. Public Econ. 93, 691–702.
Cornwall, M., 1988. The Influence of Three Agents of Religious Socialization. In: Thomas, D.L. (Ed.), Religion and Family Connection: Social Science Perspectives. Brigham Young University Press, Provo, UT.
Correani, L., Di Dio, F., Garofalo, G., 2009. The Evolutionary Dynamics of Tolerance MPRA Paper 18989. University Library of Munich, Germany.
Darity Jr., W., Mason, P.L., Stewart, J.B., 2006. The Economics of Identity: The Origin and Persistence of Racial Identity Norms. J. Econ. Behav. Organ. 60, 283–305.
Dershowitz, A., 1997. The Vanishing American Jew: In Search of Jewish Identity for the Next Century. Little, Brown.

Desmet, K., Ortuno-Ortiz, I., Wacziarg, R., 2009. The Political Economy of Ethnolinguistic Cleavages. NBER Working Paper 15360.
Dessi, R., 2008. Collective Memory, Cultural Transmission and Investments. Am. Econ. Rev. 98 (1), 534–560.
Dixit, A., 2004. Trade expansion and contract enforcement. J. Polit. Econ. 111 (6), 1293–1317.
Dixit, A., 2009. Socializing Education and Pro-Social Preferences. mimeo, Princeton University.
Doepke, M., Zilibotti, F., 2008. Occupational Choice and the Spirit of Capitalism. Q. J. Econ. 123 (2), 747–793.
Dohmen, T., Falk, A., Huffman, D., Sunde, U., 2006. The Intergenerational Transmission of Risk and Trust Attitudes. IZA Discussion Paper 2380.
Durante, R., 2009. Risk, Cooperation and the Economic Origins of Social Trust: An Empirical Investigation. mimeo, Brown University.
Duranton, G., Rodriguez-Pose, A., Sandall, R., 2007. Family Types and the Persistence of Regional Disparities in Europe. Bruges European Economic Research Papers 10.
Dustmann, C., 1996. The Social Assimilation of Immigrants. J. Popul. Econ. 9, 37–54.
Enquist, M., Ghirlanda, S., Eriksson, K., 2010. Modeling the Evolution and Diversity of Cumulative Culture, forthcoming. Philosophical Transactions of the Royal Society B.
Epstein, G., 2006. Extremism within the Family. IZA Discussion Paper No. 2199.
Erickson, J.A., 1992. Adolescent Religious Development and Commitment: A Structural Equation Model of the Role of Family, Peer Group, and Educational Influences' J. Sci. Stud. Relig. XXXI, 131–152.
Escriche, L., Olcina, G., Sánchez, R., 2004. Gender Discrimination and Intergenerational Transmission of Preferences. Oxf. Econ. Pap. 56 (3), 485–511.
Estrella López, O., 2003. Social Capital and Government in the Production of Public Goods. mimeo, Universidad Autónoma de Barcelona.
Farre', L., Vella, F., 2007. The Intergenerational Transmission of Gender Role Attitudes and Its Implications for Female Labor Force Participation. IZA Discussion Paper 2802.
Feldman, M.W., Laland, K.N., 1996. Gene-culture Coevolution Theory. Trends Ecol. Evol. 11 (11), 453–457.
Ferdman, B.M., 1995. Cultural Identity and Diversity in Organizations: Bridging the Gap between Group Differences and Individual Uniqueness. In: Chemers, M.M., Oskamp, S., Costanzo, M.A. (Eds.), Diversity in Organizations: New Perspectives for a Changing Workplace. Sage, Thousand Oaks, CA, pp. 37–61.
Ferguson, 2001.
Fernandez, R., 2007a. Culture as Learning: The Evolution of Female Labor Force Participation over a Century. mimeo, NYU.
Fernandez, R., 2007b. Women, Work, and Culture. J. Eur. Econ. Assoc. 5 (2–3), 305–332.
Fernandez, R., 2010. Does Culture Matter? In: this Handbook, chapter 11.
Fernandez, R., Fogli, A., 2009. Culture: An Empirical Investigation of Beliefs, Work, and Fertility. Am. Econ. J.: Macroeconomics 1 (1), 146–177.
Fernandez, R., Fogli, A., 2006a. Fertility: The Role of Culture and Family Experience. J. Eur. Econ. Assoc. 4 (2–3), 552–561.
Fernandez, R., Fogli, A., 2006b. Culture: An Empirical Investigation of Beliefs, Work, and Fertility. American Economic Journal: Macroeconomics 1 (1), 146–177.
Fernandez, R., Fogli, A., Olivetti, C., 2004. Mothers and Sons: Preference Formation and Female Labor Force Dynamics. Q. J. Econ. 119, 1249–1299.
Fernández-Villaverde, J., Greenwood, J., Guner, N., 2010. From Shame to Game in One Hundred Years: Economic Model of the Rise in Premarital Sex and its De-Stigmatization. IZA DP No. 4708.
Fogli, A., Veldkamp, L., 2008. Nature or Nurture? Learning and the Geography of Female Labor Force Participation. NBER Working Papers 14097.
Follmer, H., Horst, U., 2001. Convergence of locally and globally interacting Markov chains. Stochastic Processes and Applications 96 (1), 99–121.

Forster, P., Renfrew, C., 2006. Phylogenetic Methods and the Prehistory of Languages. McDonald Institute for Archeological Research, Cambridge University Press, Cambridge.
Francois, 2006. Norms and the Dynamics of Institution Formation. mimeo, University of British Columbia.
François, P., 2002. Social Capital and Economic Development. Routledge, London.
Francois, P., Zabojnik, J., 2005. Trust Social Capital and the Process of Economic Development. J. Eur. Econ. Assoc. 3 (1), 51–94.
Frot, E., 2008. Cultural Transmission through Friendship Formation. mimeo, Stockholm Institute of Transition Economics.
Frot, 2009. The Rise and Fall of Social Insurance. mimeo. Available at SSRN, http://ssrn.com/abstract=1517343.
Fryer, 2004. An Economic Approach to Cultural Capital. mimeo, Harvard.
Fryer, R.G., Torelli, P., 2005. An Empirical Analysis of 'Acting White'. NBER Working Paper No. 11334.
Fumagalli, E., Fumagalli, L., 2010. Like oil and water or chocolate and peanut butter? Ethnic diversity and social participation of young people in England. mimeo, University of Essex.
Gallo, I., Barra, A., Contucci, P., 2009. Parameter Evaluation of a Simple Mean-Field Model of Social Interaction. Mathematical Models and Methods in Applied Sciences 19, 1427–1439.
Galor, O., 2005. The Demographic Transition and the Emergence of Sustained Economic Growth. J. Eur. Econ. Assoc. 3 (2–3), 494–504.
Galor, O., Moav, O., 2002. Natural Selection And The Origin Of Economic Growth. Q. J. Econ. 117 (4), 1133–1191.
Giuliano, P., 2006. Living Arrangements in Western Europe: Does Cultural Origin Matter? J. Eur. Econ. Assoc. 4.
Gkiasta, M., Russell, T., Shennan, S., Steele, J., 2003. Neolithic transition in Europe: The radiocarbon record revisited. mimeo.
Glazer, N., 1997. We Are All Multiculturalists Now. Harvard University Press, Cambridge, MA.
Glazer, N., Moynihan, D.P., 1970. Beyond the Melting Pot: The Negros, Puerto Ricans, Jews, Italians and Irish of New York City. MIT Press, Cambridge, MA.
Gleason, P., 1980. American identity and Americanization. In: Stephan, T., Ann, O., Oscar, H. (Eds.), Harvard Encyclopedia of American Ethnic Groups. Harvard University Press, Cambridge, MA.
Gordon Milton, M., 1964. Human Nature, Class, and Ethnicity. Oxford University Press, New York.
Gradstein, M., Justman, M., 2005. The Melting Pot and School Choice. J. Public Econ. 89 (5–6), 871–896.
Gradstein, M., Justman, M., Education, 2002. Social Cohesion and Growth. Am. Econ. Rev. 92, 1192–1204.
Greeley, A., 1979. Crisis in the Church: A Study of Religion in America. Thomas More Press.
Grosjean, P., 2009. The Role of History and Spatial Proximity in Cultural Integration: A Gravity Approach. mimeo, University of California, Berkeley.
Grosjean, P., 2010. A History of Violence: Testing the 'Culture of Honor' Hypothesis in the US South. mimeo, University of San Francisco.
Guiso, L., Sapienza, P., Zingales, L., 2007. Long-Term Persistence. NBER Working Paper.
Guiso, L., Sapienza, P., Zingales, L., 2008. Social Capital and Good Culture. Marshall Lecture, J. Eur. Econ. Assoc. 6 (2–3), 295–320.
Guiso, L., Sapienza, P., Zingales, L., 2009. Cultural Biases in Economic Exchange? The Quarterly Journal of Economics 124 (3), 1095–1131.
Hatton, T.J., Leigh, A., 2007. Immigrants Assimilate as Communities, Not just as Individuals. mimeo, University of Essex.
Hauk, E., Sáez-Martí, M., 2002. On the Cultural Transmission of Corruption. J. Econ. Theory 107, 311–335.
Hayes, B., Pittelkow, Y., 1993. Religious Belief, Transmission, and the Family: An Australian Study. J. Marriage Fam. 55, 755–766.
Heaton, T., 1986. How Does Religion Influence Fertility? The Case of Mormons. J. Sci. Study Relig. 28, 283–299.

Henrich, J., 2001. Cultural Transmission and the Diffusion of Innovations: Adoption Dynamics Indicate That Biased Cultural Transmission Is the Predominate Force in Behavioral Change. American Anthropologist 103 (4), 992–1013.
Henrich, J., Boyd, R., Bowles, S., Camerer, C., Fehr, E., Gintis, H. (Eds.), 2004. Foundations of Human Sociality: Economic Experiments and Ethnographic Evidence from Fifteen Small-Scale Societies. Oxford University Press, Oxford.
Herberg, W., 1955. Protestant-Catholic-Jew. Doubleday, New York, NY.
Hiller, V., 2008a. Work organization and preferences dynamics. mimeo, Paris School of Economics-Université Paris I - Panthéon Sorbonne.
Hiller, V., 2008b. Corporate Culture, Labor Contracts and the Evolution of Cooperation. mimeo, Paris School of Economics-Université Paris I - Panthéon Sorbonne.
Hoge, D.R., Petrillo, G.H., 1978. Determinants of Church Participation and Attitudes among High School Youth. J. Sci. Study Relig. XVII, 359–379.
Hoge, D.R., Petrillo, G.H., Smith, E.I., 1982. Transmission of Religious and Social Values from Parents to Teenage Children. J. Marriage Fam. XLIV, 569–580.
Horst, U., Scheinkman, J.A., 2006. A limit theorem for systems of social interactions. forthcoming Journal of Mathematical Economics.
Hryshko, D., Luengo-Prado, M.J., Sorensen, B.E., 2006. Childhood Determinants of Risk Aversion: The Long Shadow of Compulsory Education. mimeo, University of Alberta.
Hu W.Y., (2000), Immigrant Earnings Assimilation: Estimates from Longitudinal Data. The American Economic Review, 90 (2), Papers and Proceedings 368-372.
Huntington, S.P., 1992. The Clash of Civilizations. Foreign Aff. 72, 22–49.
Ioannides, Y., Zanella, G., 2007. Searching for the Best Neighborhood: Mobility and Social Interactions. mimeo, Tufts University.
Ioannides, Y., Zanella, G., 2008. Searching for the Best Neighborhood: Mobility and Social Interactions. Discussion papers Tufts University. no 0720, Department of Economics, Tufts University.
Jasso, G., 2009. Ethnicity and Immigration of Highly Skilled Workers in the United States. IZA Discussion Paper 3950.
Jellal, M., Wolff, F., 2002a. Cultural Evolutionary Altruism: Theory and Evidence. European Journal of Political Economy 18, 241–262.
Jellal, M., Wolff, F., 2002b. Altruistic Bequests with Inherited Tastes. International Journal of Business and Economics 1 (2), 95–113.
Kremer, M., Sarychev, A., 2000. Why Do Governments Operate Schools? mimeo, Harvard University.
Kuran, T., Sandholm, W., 2008. Cultural Integration and Its Discontents. Rev. Econ. Stud. 75, 201–228.
Laferrère, A., Wolff, F.C., 2006. Microeconomic models of family transfers'. In: Kolm, S.C., Mercier Ythier, J. (Eds.), Handbook on the Economics of Giving, Reciprocity and Altruism, vol. 2. Elsevier, North-Holland, pp. 889–969.
LaLonde, R.J., Topel, R.H., 1997. Economic Impact of International Migration and the Economic Performance of Migrants. In: Borjas, G.J., Freeman, R.B. (Eds.), Immigration and the Workforce: Economic Consequences for the United States and Source Areas. University of Chicago Press, Chicago, pp. 67–92.
La Porta, R., Lopez-De-Silanes, F., Shleifer, A., Vishny, R., 1997. Legal Determinants of External Finance. J. Financ. 52–3, Papers and Proceedings, 1131–1150.
Letki, N., 2008. Does Diversity Erode Social Cohesion? Social Capital and Race in British Neighbourhoods. Polit. Stud. 56, 99–126.
Lewis, M.P. (Ed.), 2009. Ethnologue: Languages of the World. sixteenth ed. SIL International, New York.
Lindbeck, A., Nyberg, S., 2006. Raising Children to Work Hard: Altruism, Work Norms, and Social Insurance. Q. J. Econ. 121 (4), 1473–1503.
Ljunge, M., 2010. Sick of the Welfare State? Lagged Stigma and Demand for Social Insurance. mimeo, University of Copenhagen and SITE.
Mandorff, M., 2005. Ethnic Specialization. Ph. D. Dissertation, University of Chicago.

Manning, A., Roy, S., 2009. Culture Clash or Culture Club? The Identity and Attitudes of Immigrants in Britain. Economic Journal forthcoming.
Maystre, N., Olivier, J., Thoenig, M., Verdier, T., 2009. Product-Based Cultural Change: Is the Village Global? CEPR Discussion Paper 7438, C.E.P.R.
Mayer, E., 1979. From Suburb to Shetl: The Jews of Boro Park. Temple University Press, Philadelphia, PA.
Melindi Ghidi, P., 2009. A Model of Ideological Transmission with Endogenous Paternalism. Universite' Catholique de Louvain Discussion Paper 2009–43.
Meng, X., Gregory, R.G., 2005. Intermarriage and the Economic Assimilation of Immigrants. J. Labor Econ. 23, 135–176.
Meyn, S., Tweedie, R.L., 2009. Markov Chains and Stochastic Stability, second ed. Cambridge University Press, Cambridge.
Michaud, J.B., 2008. Unemployment Insurance and Cultural Transmission: Theory & Application to European Unemployment. mimeo, Centre for Economic Performance, London School of Economics.
Miguel, E., Saiegh, S.M., Satyanath, S., 2008. National Cultural Norms and Soccer Violence. NBER Working Paper 13968.
Mirrlees James, A., 1971. An Exploration in the Theory of Optimum Income Taxation. Rev. Econ. Stud. 38 (114), 175–208.
Moghaddam, F.M., Solliday, E.A., 1991. Balanced Multiculturalism and the Challenge of Peaceful Coexistence in Pluralistic Societies. Psychol. Dev. Soc. J. 3, 51–71.
Montgomery, J.D., 2009. Intergenerational Cultural Transmission as an Evolutionary Game. mimeo, University of Wisconsin.
Mo, P.H., 2007. The Nature of Chinese Collective Values: Formation and Evolution. International Journal of Chinese Culture and Management 1 (1), 108–125.
Munshi, K., Wilson, N., 2008. Identity, Parochial Institutions, and Occupational Choice: Linking the Past to the Present in the American Midwest. NBER Working Paper 13717.
Murphy, M., Knudsen, L.B., 2002. The Intergenerational Transmission of Fertility in Contemporary Denmark: The Effects of Number of Siblings (Full and Half), Birth Order, and Whether Male or Female. Popul. Stud. (Camb.) 56, 235–248.
Murphy, M., Wang, D., 2001. Family-level Continuities in Childbearing in Low-Fertility Societies. Eur J Popul 17, 7596.
Murray, J.D., 1989. Mathematical biology. Springer Verlag, Berlin.
Namoro, S.D., Roushdy, R., 2008. Intergenerational Transmission of Fertility Preferences: A Test of the Cultural Substitution Assumption. mimeo, University of Pittsburgh.
Nannicini, T., Stella, A., Tabellini, G., Troiano, U., 2010. Social Capital and Political Accountability. mimeo, Universita' Bocconi.
Nekby, L., Rödin, M., 2009. Acculturation Identity and Employment among Second and Middle Generation Immigrants. J. Econ. Psychol. forthcoming.
North, D.C., 1990a. Institutions, Institutional Change, and Economic Performance. Cambridge University Press, New York, NY.
North, D.C., 1990b. A Transactions Cost Theory of Politics. J. Theor. Polit. 2 (4), 355–367.
North, D.C., Thomas, R.P., 1973. The Rise of the Western World: A New Economic History. Cambridge University Press, Cambridge.
Nunn, N., Wantchekon, L., 2009. The Slave Trade and the Origins of Mistrust in Africa. NBER Working Paper 14783.
O'Brien, J., Fugita, S., 1991. The Japanese American Experience, Bloomington: Indiana University Press.
Olcina, G., Penarrubia, C., 2004. Hold-up and Intergenerational Transmission of Preferences. J. Econ. Behav. Organ. 54, 111–132.
Olivier, J., Thoenig, M., Verdier, T., 2008. Globalization and the Dynamics of Cultural Identity. J. Int. Econ. 76, 356–370.
Otto, S.P., Christiansen, F.B., Feldman, M.W., 1994. Genetic and Cultural Inheritance of Continuous Traits. Morrison Institute for Population and Resource Studies, Working Paper 0064, Stanford University.

Ozorak, E., 1989. Social and Cognitive Influences on the Development of Religious Beliefs and Commitment in Adolescence. J. Sci. Study Relig. 28, 448–463.
Pagnini, D.L., Morgan, S.P., 1990. Intermarriage and Social Distance among U.S. Immigrants at the Turn of the Century. Am. J. Sociol. 96 (2), 405–432.
Panebianco, F., 2010. Driving While Black: A Theory of Interethnic Integration and Evolution of Prejudice. Eurodiv Paper 70.2010.
Patacchini, E., Zenou, Y., 2004. Intergenerational Education Transmission: Neighborhood Quality and/or Parents' Involvement? Stockholm Research Institute of Industrial Economics, Working Paper 631.
Patacchini, E., Zenou, Y., 2007. Intergenerational Education Transmission: Neighborhood Quality and/or Parents' Involvement? IZA Working Paper 2608, Institute for the Study of Labor (IZA).
Peregrine, P.N., Peiros, I., Feldman, M., 2009. Ancient Human Migrations: A Multidisciplinary Approach. University of Utah Press, Salt Lake City, UT.
Phinney, J.S., 1990. Ethnic Identity in Adolescents and Adults: Review of Research. Psychol. Bull. 108, 499–514.
Pichler, M., 2010. The Economics of Cultural Formation of Preferences. Institute of Mathematical Economics, Bielefeld University Working Paper 431.
Platteau, J.P., 2000. Institutions, Social Norms, and Economic Development. Routledge, London.
Ponthiere, G., 2008. Unequal Longevities and Lifestyles Transmission. mimeo, Paris School of Economics.
Putnam, R.D., 1993. Making Democracy Work. Princeton University Press, Civic traditions in modern Italy, Princeton, NJ.
Putnam, R., 2007. E Pluribus Unum: Diversity and Community in the Twenty First Century; The 2006 Johan Skytte Prize Lecture. Scan. Polit. Stud. 30, 137–174.
Rapport, N., Overing, J., 2007. Social and Cultural Anthropology: The Key Concepts, second ed. Routledge, London.
Rendine, S., Piazza, A., Cavalli Sforza, L.L., 1986. Simulation and Separation by Principal Components of Multiple Demic Expansions in Europe. Am. Nat. 128 (5), 681–706.
Riis, J., 1890. How the Other half Lives: Studies among the Tenements of New York. Charles Scribner's Sons, New York, NY.
Robson, A., Samuelson, L., 2010. Evolutionary Selection of Preferences. this Handbook, chapter 7.
Rogers, A.R., Cashdan, E., 1997. The Phylogenetic Approach to Comparing Human Populations. Evol. Hum. Behav. 18, 353–358.
Sacerdote, B., 2010. Nature/nurture. In: this Handbook, chapter 11.
Saez-Marti, M., Sjögren, A., 2008. Peers and Culture. Scand. Journal. of Economics 110 (1), 73–92.
Sáez-Martí, M., Zenou, Y., 2005. Cultural Transmission and Discrimination. mimeo, Research Institute of Industrial Economics, Stockholm.
Senik, C., Verdier, T., 2007. Segregation, Entrepreneurship and Work Values: The case of France. PSE Working Paper, pp. 2007–2037.
Smith, R.C., 1996. Two Cultures One Marriage. Andrews University Press, Berrien Springs, MI.
Spolaore, E., Wacziarg, R., 2009. The Diffusion of Development. Q. J. Econ. 124 (2), 469–529.
Spolaore, E., Wacziarg, R., 2010. War and Relatedness. mimeo, UCLA.
Stark, R., 1984. The rise of a new world faith. Rev. Relig. Res. 26, 18–27.
Stark, R., 1997. The rise of Christianity. HarperCollins, San Francisco.
Stryker, S., 1968. Identity Salience and Role Performance: The Relevance of Symbolic Interaction Theory for Family Research. Journal of Marriage and Family 30 (4), 558–564.
Tabellini, G., 2005. Culture and Institutions: Economic Development in the Regions of Europe. IGIER Working Paper.
Tabellini, G., 2008a. Institutions and Culture. Presidential address, J. Eur. Econ. Assoc. 6 (2–3), 255–294.
Tabellini, G., 2008b. The Scope of Cooperation: Normes and Incentives. Q. J. Econ. 123 (3), 905–950.
Tahbaz-Salehi, A., Karahan, F., 2008. Marriage, Intergenerational Cultural Transmission, and the Evolution of Ethnic and Religious Traits. mimeo, University of Pennsylvania.

Tajfel, H., 1981. Human Groups and Social Categories: Studies in Social Psychology. Cambridge University Press, Cambridge.

Tajfel, H., Turner, J.C., 1979. An Integrative Theory of Intergroup Conflict. In: Austin, W.G., Worchel, S. (Eds.), The Social Psychology of Intergroup Relations. CA Brooks/Cole, Monterey, pp. 33–47.

Taylor, D.M., Lambert, W.E., 1996. The Meaning of Multiculturalism in a Culturally Diverse Urban American Area. J. Soc. Psychol. 136, 727–740.

Turner, J.C., 1982. Towards a Cognitive Redefinition of the Social Group. In: Tajfel, H. (Ed.), Social Identity and Intergroup Relations. Cambridge University Press, Cambridge, pp. 15–44.

Turner, J.C., Hogg, M.A., Oakes, P.J., Reicher, S.D., Wethrell, M.S., 1987. Rediscovering the Social Group: A Self-categorization Theory. Blackwell, Oxford.

Tyak, D., 1974. The One Best System: A History of American Urban Education. Harvard University Press, Cambridge MA.

Tymicki, K., 2005. Intergenerational Transmission of Fertility: Review of Up to Date Research and Some New Evidence from Bejsce Parish Register Reconstitution Study, 18th 20th centuries, Poland. mimeo, accessible online at http://paa2006.princeton.edu/do.

Uslaner, E.M., 2008. Where You Stand Depends Upon Where Your Grandparents Sat: THe Inheritability of Generalized Trust. Public Opin. Q. 72 (4), 725–740.

Vaughan, D., 2010. Conformity and Cultural Transmission: The Assimilation of Hispanic Americans in the United States. NYU, in progress.

Vigdor, J., 2008. Measuring Immigrant Assimilation in the United States. Duke University, Civic Report 53.

Voigtländer, N., Voth, J., 2010. Persecution Perpetuated: The Medieval Origins of German Anti-Semitism in the 1920s and 1930s. Work in progress.

Whyte, W.F., 1943. Street Corner Society. University of Chicago Press, Chicago, IL.

Wilhelm, M.O., Brown, E., Rooney, P.M., Steinberg, R., 2008. The Intergenerational Transmission of Generosity. J. Public Econ. 92, 2146–2156.

CHAPTER 10

Civic Capital as the Missing Link

Luigi Guiso
European University Institute, EIEF & CEPR

Paola Sapienza
Northwestern University, NBER & CEPR

Luigi Zingales
University of Chicago, NBER & CEPR

Contents

Introduction 418
1. Definitions of Social Capital 420
   1.1 The sociologists' definitions 421
   1.2 The political scientists' definition 422
   1.3 Social capital as civic capital 422
2. Accumulation and Depreciation of Civic Capital 423
   2.1 Civic capital as norms of cooperation: the Tabellini model 424
   2.2 Civic capital as trusting beliefs: the GSZ model 424
   2.3 Civic capital as civic education: the Aghion et al. (2010) model 425
   2.4 The accumulation of civic capital through socialization 426
   2.5 The effects of religion 426
   2.6 Depreciation of civic capital 427
   2.7 "La Mala Educacion" 428
   2.8 Values and beliefs as long lasting civic capital 428
3. Measuring Civic Capital 429
   3.1 Direct measures: values 429
      3.1.1 Survey measures of values 429
      3.1.2 Experimental measures of values 437
   3.2 Direct measures: beliefs 440
      3.2.1 Measuring trust in surveys 440
      3.2.2 Measuring trust in trust experiments 451
      3.2.3 Other beliefs 452
   3.3 Indirect measures 452
   3.4 Are these measures useful? 453
4. The Origins of Civic Capital 459
   4.1 Correlates of civic capital 459
   4.2 Natural experiments 463
      4.2.1 History 463
      4.2.2 Geography 466
   4.3 Field experiments 466

Handbook of Social Economics, Volume 1A
ISSN 0169-7218, DOI: 10.1016/S0169-7218(11)01010-0

5. The Economic Effects of Civic Capital 467
5.1 Civic capital and identification 468
5.1.1 Past history as a source of instruments 469
5.1.2 Movers and cultural portability as an identification strategy 471
5.1.3 Using field experiments to identify the effect of civic capital 475
6. Conclusions 476
References 477

Abstract

This chapter reviews the recent debate about the role of social capital in economics. We argue that all the difficulties this concept has encountered in economics are due to a vague and excessively broad definition. For this reason, we restrict social capital to the set of values and beliefs that help cooperation, which for clarity we label *civic capital*. We argue that this definition differentiates social capital from human capital and satisfies the properties of the standard notion of capital. We then argue that civic capital can explain why differences in economic performance persist over centuries and discuss how the effect of civic capital can be distinguished empirically from other variables that affect economic performance and its persistence, including institutions and geography.
JEL Codes: A1, A12, D1, O15, Z1

Keywords

Civic capital
trust
trustworthiness
cultural norms
economic performance

INTRODUCTION

Since its introduction by Bourdieu in 1972, the term 'social capital' has gained wide acceptance in social sciences and economics in particular. Economists have used social capital to explain an impressive range of phenomena: economic growth (Knack and Keefer 1997; Knack & Zak, 1999), size of firms (La Porta et al., 1997; Bloom et al., 2009) institution's design and performance (Djankov, Glaeser, La Porta, Lopez-de-Silanes, and Shleifer (2003)), financial development (Guiso, Sapienza, and Zingales (GSZ henceforth), 2004; 2008a), crime (Glaeser, Sacerdote, and Scheinkman, 1995), the power of the family (Alesina and Giuliano, 2007), innovation (Fountain, 1997), and the spread of secondary education (Goldin and Katz 2001). This list touches only a very minor subset of the topics that have been linked to social capital. New Economic Papers, a weekly announcement service of new economic papers, shows that every couple of weeks between 20 and 30 new papers come out that directly or indirectly rely on social capital to explain some economic phenomenon, for a total of 600 papers in 2008![1]

[1] See http://www.socialcapitalgateway.org/eng-archive2008.html a web site that also provides numerous references to the social capital literature and information on initiative and conferences on social capital. Those interested in subscribing to NEP can do so at http://lists.repec.org/mailman/listinfo/nep-soc.

However, this success has been achieved at the cost of a lot of ambiguity in the use of the term. From time to time, social capital has been identified as "the aggregate of the actual or potential resources which are linked to possession of a durable network of more or less institutionalized relationships of mutual acquaintance and recognition," (Bourdieu, 1986) and "features of social life—networks, norms, and trust—that enable participants to act together more effectively to pursue shared objectives" (Putnam, 1993). This ambiguity has also fostered very different views of the ultimate role played by social capital in society. While some, including Putnam (1993), identify social capital as necessarily a positive value, others, such as Bourdieu, emphasize the negative aspects of social capital, such as its fostering of privileged cliques or even gangs.

In his critique to Fukuyama (1995), Solow (1995) effectively summarizes the weaknesses of the current definitions of social capital. "If 'social capital' is to be more than a buzzword"–he writes–"the stock of social capital should somehow be measurable, even inexactly." Furthermore, if it has to retain the term 'capital', social capital has to have a non-negative economic payoff. In other words, for social capital to continue to be useful in the economic discourse we need to abandon this ambiguity and elaborate a definition that distinguishes social capital from standard human capital and explains the mechanisms through which social capital can be accumulated and depreciated.

After reviewing why the prevailing definitions of social capital do not fit these criteria, in this chapter we introduce a definition of social capital as *civic* capital, i.e., *those persistent and shared beliefs and values that help a group overcome the free rider problem in the pursuit of socially valuable activities*. This definition has several advantages. First, it clearly identifies the cultural norms and beliefs that matter: only those that help members of a community to solve collective action problems. As such, social capital has a positive economic payoff. It also clarifies why the definition deserves the word "capital"—because it is durable. Third, as we will show not only does this definition satisfy Solow's critique, but it can be easily incorporated into standard economic models, such as Tabellini (2008b).[2]

Besides dispensing with the ambiguities of the concept that exist in other definitions, we argue and document that our definition can overcome one of the main shortcomings of social capital: measurement. Values and beliefs can be measured either through laboratory experiments and/or in standard surveys, though not without problems. These social capital measures have been widely collected, often by social scientists other than economists, and are now readily available for several years and many countries in such popular surveys as the World Values Survey, the European Social Survey, the General Social Survey, and Eurobarometer. Furthermore, in recent years field experiments helped highlight the usefulness of a cultural based definition of social capital and lab experiments have contributed in identifying its components.

[2] The term civic capital has also been used by Djankov et al. (2003) in a related meaning. They define civic capital as the "location of the institution possibility frontier" in the trade-off between disorder and dictatorship. As a result, they do not deal directly with the measurement problem.

Finally, we argue that civic capital is the missing ingredient in explaining the persistence of economic development. Civic capital is empirically and theoretically correlated, with the notion of social infrastructure introduced by Hall and Jones (1999) to explain the high labor productivity of developed economies. In addition, civic capital is highly persistent, since all the methods for its transmission (interfamily transmission, formal education, and socialization) take long time. For this reason, communities/countries that, for an historic accident, are rich in civic capital enjoy a comparative advantage for extended periods.

The purpose of this chapter is not to review the immense literature on social capital but rather to give a new perspective on the concept in a way that is particularly useful to economists. Hence, we cannot do justice to even a small number of the many papers written of the topic. Durlauf and Fafchamps (2005) provide an excellent critical assessment of the conceptual issues that emerge in the social capital literature with a focus on the statistical and empirical problems, suggesting some solutions.

The rest of the chapter proceeds as follows. Section 1 discusses various concepts of social capital and highlights their limitations, showing why many do not conform to Solow's requirements. In this section, we also introduce our new definition of social capital as civic capital and explain how it overcomes the common critiques. Section 2 deals with the measurement of civic capital and how it can be addressed. Section 3 discusses the origins of civic capital and reviews what we know about its formation. Section 4 reviews the debate about the effects of civic capital discussing issues of identification that this raises. Finally, Section 5 concludes with a tentative discussion on how civic capital can be changed and what policies can affect its accumulation.

1. DEFINITIONS OF SOCIAL CAPITAL

In his critique of Fukuyama (1995), Solow (1995) writes "if 'social capital' is to be more than a buzzword, something more than mere relevance or even importance is required. Those cultural and social formations should be closely analogous to a stock or inventory, capable of being characterized as larger or smaller than another such stock. There needs to be an *identifiable process of 'investment'* that adds to the stock, and possibly a *process of 'depreciation'* that subtracts from it. The stock of *social capital should somehow be measurable,* even inexactly. Observable changes in it should correspond to investment and depreciation (emphasis added)." As an analogy with "human capital" Solow would also like the concept of social capital to be definable in a way that investment in social capital corresponds to "spending resources now to produce an object that will contribute to production (and profit) in the future." Finally, a new term is warranted only if social capital is distinct from other well-established forms of capital, in particular human capital.

In this section we will review the most prominent definitions of social capital used by sociologists, political scientists, and economists. As we will argue these definitions do not satisfy "the Solow criteria" described above.

1.1 The sociologists' definitions

In sociology, social capital refers to the advantages and opportunities accruing to people through membership in certain communities. Bourdieu (1986), credited for having introduced this concept, defines social capital as "the aggregate of the actual or potential resources which are linked to possession of a durable network of more or less institutionalized relationships of mutual acquaintance and recognition" (Bourdieu, 1986).[3] Similarly, Coleman (1990) describes social capital as a resource of individuals that emerges from social ties and their belonging to a certain community.

This definition satisfies most of the Solow criteria. An individual can invest in cultivating relationships and the value of these relationships can deteriorate over time, if they are not maintained (Glaeser, Laibson, and Sacerdote, 2002). The stock of these relationships can be (and has been) measured (for a review, see Wasserman and Faust, 1997) and so can their economic payoff (see for example Hochberg et al., 2007).

This definition fails in the "social" dimension. Bourdieu's social capital is accumulated by individuals, possessed by the individuals, dissipated by individuals. In other words, it is not substantially different from the definition of human capital. If we do not consider human capital as just the set of notions learned at school, but also as the set of acquaintances and relationships you accumulate at school and outside of school—that is if we slightly expand it to include not only *what* you know but also *who* you know—then the notion of human capital can fully account for the notion of social capital championed by Bourdieu.

Some (e.g., Coleman, 1990) identify the specificity of social capital in the externality involved in the investment process. When A invests in a relationship with B, B also acquires a relationship with A, however, this externality is not unique to social capital either. As the modern literature on economic growth points out, even investments in physical capital generate important externalities and so do investments in human capital.

A related definition, endorsed by Coleman (1990) and (at least in part) by Putnam (1993) is that social capital is the set of relationships that support effective norms. "Effective norms that inhibit crimes in a city make it possible for women to walk freely outside at night and for old people to leave their homes without fear," (Coleman, 1990). In the language of economists, social capital is the mechanism of social enforcement (see Spagnolo, 1999).

In this acceptation, social capital can be both a "good" and a "bad." As Portes (1998) points out, a high level of social capital can lead to exclusion of outsiders and punishment of people who deviate from a downward leveling social norm. In many ghettos, for instance, individuals seeking to join the middle-class mainstream are subject to continuous verbal attacks by the rest of the community (e.g., Bourgois, 1995). This alternative definition of social capital fails the Solow's criteria in many dimensions. First, it is very hard to distinguish inputs from outputs. While we can measure the

[3] Coleman instead attributes the introduction to the term to Loury (1977).

degree of effectiveness of social norms, we cannot easily measure the inputs that deliver this outcome. The network of relationships is not sufficient because this network is useless if they do not share the same social norm. Hence, the stock of social capital so defined should be measured as a combination of the power of the existing networks and the strength of shared norms in these networks. We are not aware of any attempt in this direction. Second, as Portes (1998) stresses, in this interpretation social capital may become a social liability.[4] Finally, it is not clear what investment and depreciation means in this context. Is the establishing of new relationship an investment or a disinvestment? It depends, if these relationships "close" the network in the sense of Coleman (1990), these investments strengthen the norms and so represent an investment. However, if they open the network, making its members less subject to social pressure, then they represent disinvestment. Furthermore, depending on the shared norms and the goal in mind, this "investment" can increase or decrease social welfare. Hence, this is not a viable definition from an economic point of view.

1.2 The political scientists' definition

In more recent years, the concept of social capital has been adopted and adapted by political scientists like Putnam (1993) and Fukuyama (1995). Since this is the definition that triggered Solow's criticisms, it is not surprising that it fails Solow's criteria in many respects. Even in this case, it is very difficult to distinguish inputs from outputs. Measuring social capital in terms of the level of cooperation or obedience to the law is ambiguous because both these behaviors are also driven by other considerations (economic payoff, legal enforcement, etc.) that are difficult to measure with any degree of precision. If obedience to the law is stronger in the United States than Brazil even after controlling for differences in law enforcement, is it because the United States has more social capital than Brazil or because the amount of law enforcement is poorly measured (as is likely to be the case)? This definition in terms of outcomes also makes it difficult to determine what is an investment or depreciation in the stock of social capital. If we cannot measure the stock separately from the outcome, how can we measure accumulation in the stock?

This problem has been recognized by Putnam, who in "Bowling Alone" (2000) defines "social capital" as "social networks and the norms of reciprocity and trustworthiness that arise from them," to distinguish conceptually between social capital and its consequences.

1.3 Social capital as civic capital

Building on GSZ's (2006) definition of culture, we define social capital as those persistent and shared beliefs and values that help a group overcome the free rider problem in

[4] Alternatively. social capital can be an asset for some and a liability for others. as it may be the case with certain social clubs with limited membership. Guiso and Zingales (2007) find that social interactions between firms and bankers in an exclusive club facilitates access to credit to members but this may come at the expense of restricted credit availability for non-members. See also Dessì and Ogilvie (2004) for a similar argument in relation to the diffusion of merchant guilds.

the pursuit of socially valuable activities. This definition is similar to the one advanced by Putnam and Fukuyama, but makes it clear that social capital is not about networks or just about values, but about values and beliefs, which are shared by a community and persist over time, often passed on to its members through intergenerational transmissions, formal education, or socialization. Our definition of social capital is similar to the Almond and Verba (1963) concept of civic culture, which they define as "a set of beliefs, attitudes, norms, perceptions and the like, that support participation." Unlike Almond and Verba (1963), however, our definition of civic is not restricted to political participation, but applies more generally to any type of economic interaction.

The greatest advantage of narrowing down the definition is that it makes civic capital easily measurable. As we will review below, both beliefs and values can be (and have been) measured through surveys and experimental work. Thus, when a community has more (or stronger) values that foster cooperation, we can say that the community has capital that is more civic. As we will see in the Tabellini (2008b) model investment in civic capital is the amount of resources that parents spend to teach more cooperative values to their children. A deterioration of this set of values can be seen as depreciation of civic capital.

Since we consider as civic capital only values and beliefs that *help a group overcome the free rider problem in the pursuit of socially valuable activities,* by definition civic capital has a non-negative economic payoff. In other words, civic capital purposefully excludes from the definitions those values that favor cooperation in socially deviant activities, such as gangs.

Finally, civic capital so defined is very different from traditional human capital. First, the process of investment is social. It is parents and other members of a community that instill values and beliefs in an individual, not the individual himself. Second, these values and beliefs do not represent civic capital if other members of the community do not share them. The set of values and beliefs shared by Swedes (which represent the civic capital of the Swedish nation) might be a liability if carried by a Swede to Italy. In fact, Butler, Giuliano and Guiso (2009) find that because cultural beliefs persist, immigrants from high trust countries are more likely to be cheated (and lose) than immigrants from low trust countries.

Our definition of civic capital not only nicely fits Solow's requirements, but it can also be easily incorporated into standard economic models (as did the definition of human capital introduced by Becker (1964) and Ben-Porath (1967)). In the next sections we are going to see some examples.

2. ACCUMULATION AND DEPRECIATION OF CIVIC CAPITAL

One of the key requirements for a meaningful economic definition of social capital imposed by Solow is the existence of an *identifiable process of 'investment'* that adds to the stock, and a *process of 'depreciation'* that subtracts from it.

In this section we discuss how civic capital fulfills this requirement and how the process for the accumulation of social capital is consistent with methodological individualism (the paradigm of economics) and thus can be easily incorporated in standard economic models. At the same time, this discussion will show that the process of accumulating (and depreciating) civic capital is different from that of accumulation and depreciation of human capital because it has a social dimension to it.

2.1 Civic capital as norms of cooperation: the Tabellini model

Tabellini (2008b) builds a very interesting model of the cultural transmission of cooperative values. He relies on and extends the value transmission framework first developed by Bisin and Verdier (2000, 2001) and Bisin et al. (2004), in which parents optimally choose what values to pass onto their children but, in so doing, assess their children's welfare in terms of their own values. In Tabellini's model, this creates a strategic complementarity between norms and behavior. If more people cooperate, then the payoff from cooperation increases and this expands the scope of cooperation. In turn, an expansion in the scope of cooperation makes it easier for parents to transmit good values to their children.

In Tabellini's model, the effect of any institutional change (such as the quality of law enforcement) is amplified and protracted over time because of cultural transmission. Most importantly, when individuals are allowed to choose their institutions through voting, the equilibrium shows path dependence: if initial conditions are favorable, then individuals will transmit values of generalized cooperation and choose strong legal enforcement; if initial conditions are unfavorable, then individuals will opt for values of limited cooperation and limited enforcement.

2.2 Civic capital as trusting beliefs: the GSZ model

To explain persistence over time, GSZ (2008c) focus on the transmission of beliefs over time. Specifically, since trust is a key ingredient in virtually all economic transactions, they build an overlapping-generations model in which parents decide how much trust to transmit to their children

Economic models are generally silent on how people acquire priors (i.e., probability distributions over events with which they have no experience), GSZ (2008c) posit that intergenerational cultural transmission plays a major role in the formation of such priors. To analyze the possible distortions in this process, they build an overlapping-generations model where children absorb the prior from their parents and then, after experiencing the real world, transmit it (updated) to their own children. The reason why this overlapping-generations model is not identical to an infinitely living agent is that parents do not weigh future and current benefits exactly the same way as children do.

This intergenerationally transmitted prior affects each individual decision regarding whether to trust other members of the society and participate in an anonymous exchange. If the trust is well founded then an individual reaps substantial gains from trade. However, if it is not, she will face a major loss. As a result, a pessimistic prior will induce individuals to withdraw from the market and not invest. This strategy does minimize losses, but it will prevent any update on the trustworthiness of the rest of society.

To protect children from costly mistakes, parents transmit conservative priors to them, from a social point of view, these priors are excessively conservative because parents do not fully incorporate the value of their children learning from experience. In this context, GSZ (2008c) show that, if the net benefits of cooperation are not sufficiently high, then a society starting with diffuse priors will be trapped in equilibrium of mistrust. Interestingly, starting from this situation, a positive large shock to the benefit of cooperation can permanently shift the equilibrium to a cooperative one even when the shock is temporary.

This result could rationalize Putnam's (1993) conjecture that the differences in civic capital between the North and the South of Italy could be due to the free city-state experience that ended more than five centuries ago. Furthermore, it can rationalize the long-lasting effect of a history of good institutions even after these institutions have vanished. In the context of GSZ (2008c) model, better legal enforcement can be captured as a reduction in the cost of being cheated. Even a temporary reduction in this cost can permanently increase the level of cooperation as the good experience is transmitted across generations. This effect can also explain the long-lasting effect of bad colonial institutions (Acemoglu, Johnson, and Robinson 2001) or of legal origin (La Porta, Lopez de Silanes, Shleifer, and Vishny 1998).

One limitation of GSZ model is that it assumes that trustworthiness is exogenously given and is not affected by the prevailing level of trust. In reality, there could be two channels through which beliefs can affect trustworthiness. First, a receiver who knows that the sender expects him to cheat, is more likely to cheat, as shown by Reuben et al. (2009). Thus, mistrust breeds mistrust. Second, social pressure will make it easier to teach children to be trustworthy (a value), when the expectation (a belief), is that most people will be trustworthy. Both these effects would strengthen the results of the model and the persistence of the equilibrium. These effects also show the complementarity between the GSZ model and Tabellini's (2008b) model. Tabellini addresses the transmission of values, while GSZ address the transmission of beliefs. Both form social capital.

Note that the beliefs accumulated in this way are perfectly rational, in the common use of the word rational, which requires beliefs to be Bayesian. In fact, the Bayesian paradigm does not deal with the process of belief formation and does not address the question of the rationality of beliefs (Gilboa, Postlewaite, and Schmeidler, 2004). Hence, this approach allows us to integrate our definition of civic capital, which includes beliefs, into standard economic models.

2.3 Civic capital as civic education: the Aghion et al. (2010) model

Aghion et al. (2010), document a very strong correlation between mistrust and the level of regulation. Their explanation for this phenomenon is that there is a substitution between civic capital and regulation. In countries with high level of civic capital, the externalities associated with production are reduced because people raised with civic values are less likely to pollute and create externalities. People that are more civic are also those who trust others more. When people are not civic, then the only way to restrict the externalities is through regulation, hence the correlation between mistrust and regulation. In Aghion et al.'s model, civic capital is a set of virtues that you learn in school.

While authors do not develop the process for the accumulation of civic capital, this aspect can be easily inserted in their model. The economic payoff of a higher level of civic capital in their model is very high, since a higher level of civic capital leads to a reduction of production externalities with lower costs of regulation. However, this payoff occurs for everybody, regardless of the amount of effort they spent in transmitting certain values and beliefs to their children. Hence, the need for some form of public financing for education, an aspect present in all countries.

2.4 The accumulation of civic capital through socialization

Another important form of accumulation of civic capital is socialization. Immigrants in the United States, for example, slowly converge toward the U.S. mean of values and beliefs. In part, this can be the result of exposure to the U.S. type (and/or quantity) of education. In part, it can be the result of socialization with U.S. values and beliefs. Ichino and Maggi (2000), for example, show that Southern Italian workers who move to the North exhibit a work ethic more similar to the Northern ones, while Northern workers who move to the South quickly converge to the lower work ethic standards present in the South. Similarly, GSZ (2004) show that the use and availability of financial instruments is partly responsive to the level of social capital prevailing in the province where a person was born, but partly to the level of social capital prevailing in the province where a person lived. This finding suggests that people do adapt their norms and beliefs in response to the social pressure of the community they live in.

The pressure of socialization in the formation (and deterioration) of civic capital is very different, which can explain the asymmetry in the speed of adaptation of Southern workers moving to the North and Northern workers moving to the South found by Ichino and Maggi (2000). In the case of beliefs, a trusting person will quickly find out at his own expense that the environment does not deserve the level of trust he has. By contrast, it will take longer for a mistrusting individual to realize he is missing trading opportunities by not trusting (see GSZ, 2008c).

In the case of values, the process is more complicated. If civic values are completely embedded in preferences, they should not be modified by socialization. If, however, civic values are supported, at least in part, by the desire to conform to others, then socialization can lead to changes. Exactly how and how fast these values can improve and deteriorate because of social pressure is a topic for future research.

2.5 The effects of religion

Another potential source for the accumulation of social capital is religion. Religion is both a source of moral values and an engine of socialization. As GSZ (2003) show, people who have been raised religiously tend to trust other more and to have stronger moral values, independent of the religion they have been raised into. Similarly, actively religious people trust more and have stronger moral values than non-active ones.

Religions might differ in the extent they are able to build trust and help accumulate civic capital. As Putnam (1993) claims, less hierarchical religions might foster horizontal ties among its followers and promote civic capital more. For example, most protestant religions delegate decision rights to the local parish level, teaching people to take responsibility and internalize the common good of their small community. By contrast, the Catholic religion does not share these features.

One aspect of religion that can undermine the development of civic capital is the intolerance it spreads among its followers. As GSZ (2003) show, religious people are more intolerant of diversity than non-religious ones, regardless of the type of religion, albeit some religions are worse than others. This intolerance may represent an obstacle to the development of trust and common shared values in countries with different ethnicities.

2.6 Depreciation of civic capital

Physical capital mostly depreciates with use. Human capital does not depreciate with use (in fact it can appreciate with use), but it can depreciate with age, both for the obsolescence of the knowledge accumulated and for the obsolescence of the brain that acquired it. While there is not much literature on the depreciation of civic capital, we can certainly say that civic capital does not depreciate with use, in fact, like human capital, it tends to increase with use. Reduction in the stock of civic capital is likely to take place in three ways.

One way is the change in the economic or social factors that foster the formation and transmission of civic capital. For example, a great influx of immigrants of a different ethnicity can lead to an increase in racial differences that tend to undermine civic capital (Alesina and La Ferrara, 2002). Similarly, an increase in income inequality can have the same effect. In the same way, a dramatic reduction in the benefits from cooperation can have a similar effect.

The stock of civic capital can also be reduced by some major historical event that generates an enduring level of mistrust. Nunn and Wantchekon (2009), for instance, show that the slave trade left a legacy of mistrust in the populations whose leaders sold some of their people to slave traders. Similarly, the high level of distrust present in some countries (like Argentina and Brazil) could be the result of dictatorships that favor citizens spying on their fellow citizens.

Finally, civic capital can be depreciated by some salient episodes that change people's beliefs and/or change the perception of the moral acceptability of certain behaviors. While we are not aware of any systematic evidence in this sense, the generalized mistrust that ensued following the Madoff scandal is suggestive in this direction (Tatro, 2009).

2.7 "La Mala Educacion"

An important aspect, which has not been analyzed very much but should be, is whether different styles of education have different returns in terms of civic capital. For instance, Frank et al. (1993) show experimental evidence indicating not only that economics students tend to exhibit a more selfish behavior, but also that economic training tends to make students behave more selfishly both in the lab and in the field. This is hardly surprising. While economics is only a positive theory of human behavior, it is often presented with a normative flavor to it. Not contributing in a public good game is the "rational" strategy, while cooperating is deemed the wrong (often labeled "irrational" or "stupid') strategy. It is hard not to see a normative aspect in this teaching.

More generally, the style of education, emphasizing joint projects, civic value, and cooperation, can foster the creation of civic capital in the formative years. By contrast, a more competitive, individualistic, and not socially oriented teaching style can reduce the effect of education on civic capital.

2.8 Values and beliefs as long lasting civic capital

All these examples show that our definition of civic capital as the set of values and beliefs that foster cooperative behavior fulfills Solow's requirements. This capital can be accumulated in an investment process that is similar to, but distinct from, the investment of physical or human capital. When parents put (costly) effort in transmitting certain values and priors to their offspring, they invest in civic capital. When the formal education process tries to instill certain values and beliefs in the younger generations, it spends (mostly public) resources to accumulate civic capital. When individuals ostracize and reprimand behaviors they deem to be antisocial, they spend time and effort to teach certain values and beliefs to their fellow citizens, because they are well aware that only a few free riders can destroy a cooperative equilibrium and thus they intervene to preserve the benefit of cooperation. This accumulation process is consistent with methodological individualism (the paradigm of economics) and thus easily incorporated in standard economic models, but is different from human capital because it has a social dimension to it: civic values and beliefs have a return only if shared by other members of the community.

Even more than physical and human capital, civic capital takes time to accumulate and has increasing returns to scale. It takes time to accumulate because two of the three ways in which it is accumulated (intergenerational transmission and formal education) require the passage of a generation to have an effect. It has increasing returns to scale because the payoff from an individual investment in civic capital positively depends upon the prevailing level of civic capital in a community. The combination of these two factors makes civic capital a leading potential explanation for persistence in the level of development observed around the world. We are going to return to this in Section 5, after having discussed how civic capital can be measured and how it has accumulated over time.

3. MEASURING CIVIC CAPITAL

Traditionally, the measurement of social capital has been a very contentious issue. Precisely because the concept is so complex and multidimensional, we can find many different measures in the literature, which capture the many dimensions of these various definitions. One good example of this complexity is a recent attempt by the World Bank to design questionnaires to obtain measures of civic capital that will be implemented primarily in developing countries. They identify six families of variables, each meant to capture one dimension of social capital: "Groups and Networks," "Trust and Solidarity," "Collective Action and Cooperation," "Information and Communication," "Social Cohesion and Inclusion," and "Empowerment and Political Action" (see Grootaert et al. 2005). Of course, the ambiguity that is reflected in the various definitions is also evident in these measures.

The multidimensionality of the social capital concept has induced many authors to try to measure it by looking at outcomes, e.g., the level of economic cooperation or the diffusion of newspaper readership (Putnam 1993). One problem with these measures is that they are contaminated by other factors. For example, is the level of trust a New Yorker exhibits in her daily economic behavior the result of good law enforcement or the product of a high level of social capital? Similarly, the diffusion of cooperative firms across different communities may reflect different tax incentives to set up cooperative firms or patterns of industrial specializations (it is difficult to run an oil company as a cooperative) rather than the strength of cultural values and beliefs that can sustain a high level of cooperation and exchange.

In this section, we show that our narrower definition lends itself to easier measurements. We can directly measure both values and beliefs and, even if we want to resort to outcome-based measures, we can more easily isolate more accurate proxies.

3.1 Direct measures: values

3.1.1 Survey measures of values

Several surveys such as the World Values Survey, the European Social Survey, the General Social Survey, Eurobarometer, and the German Socio Economic Panel (among others) collect direct measures of values and beliefs. One important advantage is that some (though not all) of these surveys collect data for many countries. The most recently available wave of the World Values Survey conducted in 2005 includes 56 countries worldwide. Pooling the 1995–97 and 1999–2000 waves, it covers 80 countries. Because of its broad geographical coverage, and its longer tradition, the WVS has been widely used in the social capital literature, and has often acted as a reference for other surveys that aim to collect information on values and beliefs.

Not all values measured in the WVS are relevant for our definition of civic capital, rather only those that induce individuals to cooperate are useful. One way to identify the relevant questions is to focus on those values that induce people to dislike actions that obtain private benefits at high social costs. For instance, people's opinions about cheating on taxes, free riding on public goods, cutting in line, littering and similar behaviors can all be good indicators for the prevalence of morality norms and thus of people's willingness to internalize the public good. The common features across all these measures is that they are value judgments on activities that result in the appropriation of (possibly limited) private benefits at the expenses of (possibly much larger) costs imposed on other members of society.

To illustrate how some of these norms can provide a measure of civic capital, we use the responses individuals gave on the WVS when asked: "Please tell me for each of the following statements whether you think it can always be justified, never be justified, or something in between, using this card." Answers range from 1–10, where 1 = never justifiable and 10 = always justifiable. We chose to focus on seven questions that capture how much people value the public good. These questions were: "Claiming government benefits to which you are not entitled" (var 1); "Avoiding a fare on public transport" (var 2); "Cheating on taxes if you have a chance" (var 3); "Accepting a bribe in the course of their duties" (var 4); "Lying in your own interest" (var 5); "Throwing away litter in a public space" (var 6); "Speeding over the limit in built-up areas" (var 7).

To make these variables reflect increases in civic capital, we recoded them so that 10 means "never justifiable" and 1 means "always justifiable." The sample means for these variables are summarized in Table 1, Panel A, which also shows the number of countries for which these variables are available.[5] As the mean values show, there is a general dislike for opportunistic behaviors, but there is ample variation in the intensity of the values. Interestingly, as Panel B shows, all these values are positively correlated consistent with answers reflecting a general norm of "good behavior," but the correlation is far from perfect, suggesting that each one has some independent information.

To summarize these values in a single index of civic capital, we have extracted the first principal component using the three variables (1, 2 and 4) that are available for most countries. All individual measures are also highly correlated with the principal component (Table 1, panel B). Table 2 reports the country means of variables 1, 2 and 4 as well as the principal component for all countries for which they are simultaneously available and Figure 1, Panel A plots the values across countries of the principal component. There is wide variation with a tendency for more economically developed countries to have higher civic values.

One issue with these specific measures is that people may have poor incentives to reveal their true values: after all, why one should not please the interviewer by saying

[5] While variables 1, 2, and 4 are available for at least 79 of the 81 countries covered by the two rounds, the other variables have a lower geographical coverage.

Table 1 Measuring Civic Values. Values reported are based on the following question: *"Please tell me for each of the following statements whether you think it can always be justified, never be justified, or something in between, using this card."* Answers are in the range 1-10, with 1 = never justifiable and 10 = always be justifiable. We have recoded the answers so that 10 means never justifiable and 1 always justifiable. *"Claiming government benefits to which you are not entitled"* (var 1). *"Avoiding a fare on public transport"* (var 2). *"Cheating on taxes if you have a chance"* (var 3). *"Accepting a bribe in the course of their duties"* (var. 4). *"Lying in your own interest"* (var 5). *"Throwing away litter in a public space"* (var 6). *"Speeding over the limit in built-up areas"* (var 7).

Panel A

Civic capital measures	Mean	Median	Sd	N. of observations	N. of countries covered
1. Claiming government benefits you are not entitled to	8.70		2.20	108,829	79
2. Avoiding a fare on public transport	8.53		2.40	90,977	64
3. Cheating on taxes	8.72		2.25	111,490	80
4. Accept a bribe	9.30		1.68	113,190	81
5. Lying in your own interest	8.20		2.23	40,386	33
6. Throwing away litter in a public place	9.16		1.63	40,674	33
7. Speeding over the limit in built-up areas	8.71		1.74	40,510	33
8. Principal component of civic values 1.3 & 4					
Tabellini (2009) cultural capital indicators					
1. Respect	0.69		0.46	118,319	81
2. Obedience	0.38		0.49	118,315	81
3. Control	6.67		2.51	110,484	80
4. Prinicipal component of norms	-5.86e-09		1.05	110,308	80
Main beliefs					
Generalized trust	0.27		0.44	114,203	81
Fairness	0.42		0.49	49,872	37

Panel B cross correlations among civic capital measures

Civic Variable	1 Gov. benefits	2 Avoid a fare	3 Cheat on taxes	4 Accept bribe	5 Lying	6 Littering	7 Speeding	8 PC 1.3 & 4
1. Claiming gov. benefits	1							
2. Avoiding a fare	0.28	1						
3. Cheating on taxes	0.43	0.37	1					
4. Accepting a bribe	0.32	0.34	0.39	1				
5. Lying in own interest	0.30	0.37	0.44	0.40	1			
6. Littering	0.23	0.34	0.21	0.30	0.27	1		
7. Speeding	0.24	0.38	0.30	0.31	0.29	0.34	1	
8. PC 1.3 & 4	0.73	0.45	0.82	0.74	0.50	0.32	0.37	1

that he considers littering in public spaces "never justifiable" even if he is one that actually litters? This could explain the average high values of the indexes in Table 2. Furthermore, it is plausible that those who lie to the interviewer are precisely the ones with lower civic values, as telling the truth at own cost is a dimension of civicness—a tendency that would bias the index towards low geographical variability.

One way to verify that these measures are not biased is to compare them with other measures of values that are presumably less subject to this problem. For instance, Tabellini (2009) constructs measures of cultural capital using the answers to three WVS

Table 2 Measures of civic capital

Country name	Claim government benefits	Cheat on taxes	Accept a bribe	Principle component of civic values
Greece	6.96	7.84	9.07	−0.75
Indonesia	7.12	9.46	9.55	−0.11
Mexico	7.28	8.69	8.87	−0.49
Philippines	7.40	7.84	7.66	−1.10
Peru	7.51	8.89	9.28	−0.25

Continued

Table 2 Measures of civic capital—cont'd

Country name	Claim government benefits	Cheat on taxes	Accept a bribe	Principle component of civic values
Belarus	7.52	6.78	7.91	−1.31
France	7.62	7.96	8.92	−0.59
Chile	7.67	8.83	8.95	−0.34
Armenia	7.76	7.32	8.87	−0.77
Brazil	7.80	7.41	6.98	−1.36
Estonia	7.80	7.82	9.07	−0.53
Algeria	7.98	8.99	9.54	−0.01
Macedonia	8.01	8.70	9.51	−0.04
Venezuela	8.02	9.18	9.38	−0.02
Slovakia	8.09	8.85	8.08	−0.53
Georgia	8.09	8.26	9.25	−0.29
Luxembourg	8.13	7.65	9.18	−0.47
Slovenia	8.18	8.66	9.22	−0.17
Ukraine	8.20	7.59	8.98	−0.53
Singapore	8.23	8.96	9.25	−0.08
Iran	8.30	9.53	9.74	0.28
El Salvador	8.31	9.09	9.53	0.08
Montenegro	8.37	8.45	9.67	−0.01
Argentina	8.40	9.12	9.73	0.19
Belgium	8.45	7.39	9.02	−0.52
Lithuania	8.51	7.16	8.92	−0.62
Azerbaijan	8.58	7.38	8.14	−0.78
Spain	8.62	8.75	9.35	0.01
Taiwan	8.63	9.04	9.43	0.12
Poland	8.64	8.86	9.47	0.09
South Africa	8.65	8.77	9.09	−0.07

Continued

Table 2 Measures of civic capital—cont'd

Country name	Claim government benefits	Cheat on taxes	Accept a bribe	Principle component of civic values
Finland	8.65	8.45	9.56	0.00
India	8.66	8.86	9.12	0.00
Switzerland	8.67	8.35	9.41	−0.07
Russia	8.75	8.02	9.22	−0.21
Puerto Rico	8.81	8.99	9.67	0.23
Dominican Republic	8.81	9.05	9.11	0.10
United States	8.83	8.78	9.44	0.09
China	8.87	9.43	9.66	0.34
Vietnam	8.87	9.69	9.85	0.49
Serbia	8.88	8.91	9.71	0.25
Latvia	8.88	8.64	9.32	0.03
Austria	8.91	8.90	9.43	0.14
Japan	8.91	9.54	9.47	0.33
Sweden	8.92	8.58	9.15	−0.04
Northern Ireland	8.92	8.64	9.44	0.09
Portugal	8.95	8.56	9.22	−0.01
Germany	9.00	8.63	9.06	−0.04
Uganda	9.01	7.42	8.76	−0.47
United Kingdom	9.03	8.57	9.22	0.01
Nigeria	9.03	8.97	9.09	0.07
Colombia	9.05	9.08	9.51	0.25
Albania	9.08	9.12	8.62	−0.03
Italy	9.12	8.61	9.50	0.15
Canada	9.12	8.98	9.45	0.22
New Zealand	9.13	8.69	9.54	0.19
Bulgaria	9.17	9.01	9.37	0.22

Continued

Table 2 Measures of civic capital—cont'd

Country name	Claim government benefits	Cheat on taxes	Accept a bribe	Principle component of civic values
Ireland	9.17	8.71	9.60	0.21
Romania	9.18	8.21	9.48	0.03
Egypt	9.18	9.42	9.86	0.49
Uruguay	9.19	9.24	9.71	0.40
Czech Republic	9.19	8.98	8.82	0.03
Morocco	9.20	9.75	9.86	0.59
Iceland	9.25	8.77	9.73	0.29
Australia	9.29	8.84	9.73	0.32
Zimbabwe	9.29	9.44	9.77	0.50
Bosnia	9.33	9.24	9.63	0.40
Jordan	9.36	9.49	9.88	0.57
Hungary	9.36	8.91	8.41	−0.09
Norway	9.36	8.29	9.68	0.17
Croatia	9.38	8.26	9.29	0.03
Pakistan	9.47	9.81	9.85	0.68
Netherlands	9.51	8.26	9.44	0.11
Denmark	9.62	9.00	9.85	0.49
Malta	9.64	9.47	9.90	0.63
Bangladesh	9.65	9.94	9.97	0.79
Turkey	9.76	9.82	9.88	0.75
Israel			9.58	0.00
Mean	8.68	8.70	9.29	−0.02
Standard deviation	0.65	0.68	0.53	0.43
Correlation with principal component	0.75	0.86	0.87	

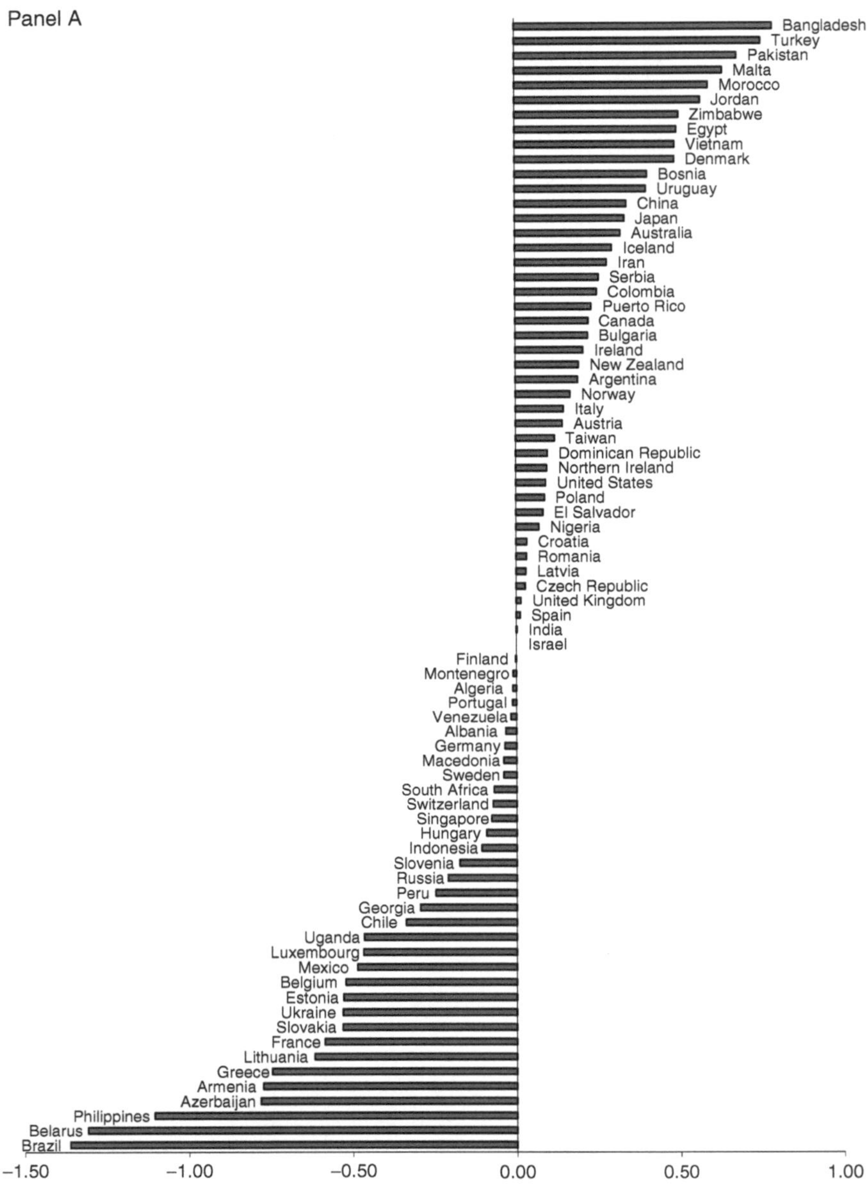

Figure 1 ***Civic capital across countries.*** Panel A figure shows the principal component across countries of the indexes 1, 2 and 4 of civicness described in Table 1. Panel B shows the principle component of the three indicators of cultural capital (respect, obedience, and control) used by Tabellini (2009) and described in Table 1.

questions aimed at capturing cultural traits that ought to encourage welfare enhancing social interactions: *respect, obedience*, and *control*. The variable *respect* is defined as being equal to 1 if the respondent indicates the quality "tolerance and respect for other people" as being one of the top five qualities children are encouraged to learn at home. A high share of people that value respect is taken as a sign of a stronger culture of extended morality. *Obedience* is the fraction of people that regards obedience as an important quality that children should be encouraged to learn. According to Tabellini (2009), higher values of this index indicate lower cultural capital, since a coercive cultural environment stifles individual initiative and cooperation within a group. Finally, *control* is the answer to the question "Some people feel they have completely free choice and control over their lives, while other people feel that what we do has no real effect on what happens to them." The idea is that in hierarchical societies, where people can only count on their family members and the rest of society is perceived as inimical, success is perceived more as the result of luck instead of personal effort.

Table 1, Panel A reports summary statistics for these three indicators and Figure 1, Panel B shows the variation across countries of their first principle component, which again shows a lot of diversity and a clear correlation with the level of a country's economic development.[6] These measures are less subject to reporting bias. Interestingly, both the principal component based on the civicness values and on Tabellini's values are highly positively correlated.

3.1.2 Experimental measures of values

The values that are at the base of civic capital can also be measured through controlled experiments, either in the lab or in the field. Camerer and Fehr (2003) provide a very useful overview of the methodologies for measuring social norms in a variety of games that involve cooperation.

A typical game that can be informative about peoples' adherence to norms of civic behavior is the public good game. People in a group of N (the number of participants in the experiment) are each given a sum S; each participant can contribute this endowment to a common fund managed by an administrator. If the administrator receives more than a given (and known) threshold $0 < \lambda < 1$ of the overall endowments $N \times S$, for instance 80%, than everyone receives back more than S—e.g., twice as much, a measure of the return for cooperation—otherwise they receive nothing. Individually, each participant has an incentive to ride free, keep S and hope the others will all contribute to the fund, reaping the benefits of the public good. If more than λN participants ride free, however, no public good can be produced and all lose. Hence, *shared* norms of extended morality and civicness can temper individual incentives and lead the majority to cooperate by contributing their endowment. The stronger these

[6] Tabellini (2009) also uses trust as a measure of civic cultural traits and in constructing his principle component.

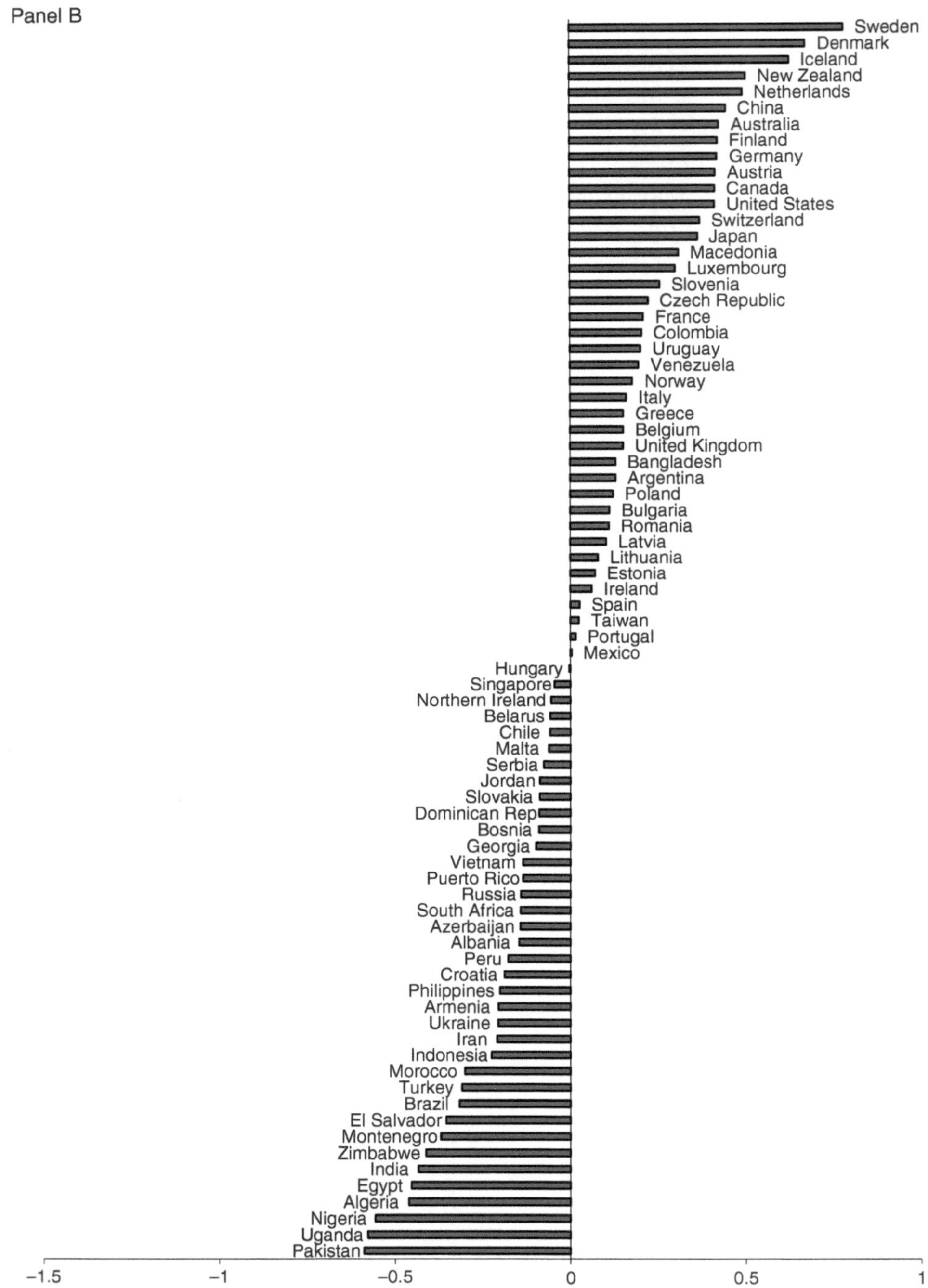

Panel B ***Cultural capital.***

Panel B shows the principal component of the three indicators of cultural capital—respect, obedience and control—used by Tabellini (2009) and described in Table 1.

norms are, the larger λ is, and the higher the civic capital in the group is, making it easier to produce the public good. Thus λ can be seen as a continuous measure of the civic norms of a community. If the game is played in different communities, differences in λ can be used to study the effect of civic capital on outcomes, as done by Carpenter and Seki (2005), Karlan (2005), and Fehr and Leibbrandt (2008).

Compared to survey-based measures of norms, such as those illustrated above, measures of civic capital obtained from experimental games have several advantages. First, the game imposes some structure, which facilitates interpretation of the behaviors observed or the answers obtained. This is not often the case when individuals are asked qualitative questions of the sort illustrated above, as is common in many surveys. Obviously, better-designed survey questions can reduce the relevance of this problem. For instance, a question such as: "*If 90% of the members of your community contribute $10 to a city hall project, including you, you could all reap a benefit that is worth $50 (for instance you and your family have access to a new park). But if less than 90% contribute, then the project fails. Would you contribute your 10 dollars?*" comes close to replicating the public good game and can thus be more easily interpreted than qualitative questions on free riding.

A second advantage of experimental games measures is that answers can be made incentive compatible by having participants play with real money and providing them with appropriate monetary incentives, although paying subjects who participate in a survey is both unpractical and expensive. It is unpractical because it is difficult to manage a large number of small payments, and it is expensive because even small payments can turn into large sums when the number of respondents runs into the tens of thousands.

On the other side, experiments have limitations that surveys do not. Perhaps the most important one is the difficulty of running experiments on representative samples or even on samples other than undergraduates at major universities. If one is concerned in obtaining a measure of the predominant cultural values of a large society, issues of representiveness may be of first order importance.

Levitt and List (2007) have questioned the validity of using laboratory experiments to measure social preferences. In their view, several factors distort the behavior of subjects in the lab. In particular, Levitt and List (2007) claim that lab experiments are biased by the so-called "experimenter effect." Subjects in the lab may sometimes try to please the experimenter, responding to subtle social cues that the investigator provides in the instructions and administration of the game (Rosenthal, 1976; Hoffman et al., 1994). This critique is particularly strong when applied to measures of social preferences as the subjects may be induced to "look good" in the eyes of the experimenter by exhibiting pro-social behavior, even if they would behave as self-interested individuals outside the laboratory.

However, Baran et al. (2010) find a strong correlation between the reciprocity measure in a trust experiment and reciprocity manifested through a "give back" donation campaign in an MBA program. Most importantly, they show that the behavior in the field is correlated with the social desirability scale, a questionnaire-based index that measures how much a person tries to please others, while behavior in the lab is not. This evidence suggests that the experimenter effect if it exists is not so pronounced in standard economic games.

3.2 Direct measures: beliefs

Willingness to cooperate and act together with others depends critically on one's beliefs about the opponent's behavior. In particular, beliefs about the "fairness" and the "trustworthiness" of other people one may find herself interacting with are key ingredients in many economic (and non-economic) transactions. If members of a community have reasons to believe others are unfair, they may be reluctant to grant coordination and decision power for fear of abuse. Similarly diffuse mistrust beliefs can discourage people's willingness to invest and hamper economic success. Thus, fairness and, even more so, trust have attracted the attentions of economists and social scientists interested in studying the effects of cultural capital. Besides relevance, from the measurement point of view there is one important reason to pay attention to fairness and trust beliefs: they are much less ambiguous concepts and because of this easier to measure and, as we see, to compare.

In particular, trust can be given a very specific probabilistic content. As stated by Gambetta (2000), "When we say we trust someone or that someone is trustworthy, we implicitly mean that the probability that he will perform an action that is beneficial. . .is high enough for us to consider engaging in some form of cooperation with him." Gambetta's (2000) definition of trust makes two important points: first, trust, being a belief, can be measured as a probability; since probabilities are cardinal, they have a very specific quantitative content. Thus, as a measure of civic capital one can say whether there is more or less of it in a given community by comparing the average probability that people trust other members of the community with the average in another community. Second, higher values of this probability enhance cooperation, as implied by civic capital. Because of these features, trust has been widely used in the literature as a measure of social capital.

3.2.1 Measuring trust in surveys

When measuring trusting beliefs, it is important to distinguish between personalized trust and generalized trust. Personalized trust is the trust that one has towards a well identified individual—e.g., her boss, her fund manager, or a specific classmate. Generalized trust is instead the trust that a given person has toward a generic and unknown (randomly drawn) member of a broader community, such the other Americans or people of another country (e.g., the trust the French have towards the British).

Most research has focused on generalized trust, since the earlier rounds of the WVS only asked one question pertaining to that: "Generally speaking, would you say that most people can be trusted or that you need to be very careful in dealing with people?" with *'Most people can be trusted'* and *'Need to be very careful'* as possible answers. In this question, "people" means other people of the same country. These dichotomous qualitative answers are particularly useful to characterize the fraction of people that express trust in a community.

Figure 2 shows how this measure varies across countries. There are three interesting features to notice. First, there is enormous variability in the fraction of people that trust others; this ranges from as low as 3% in Brazil to as high as 67% in Denmark.

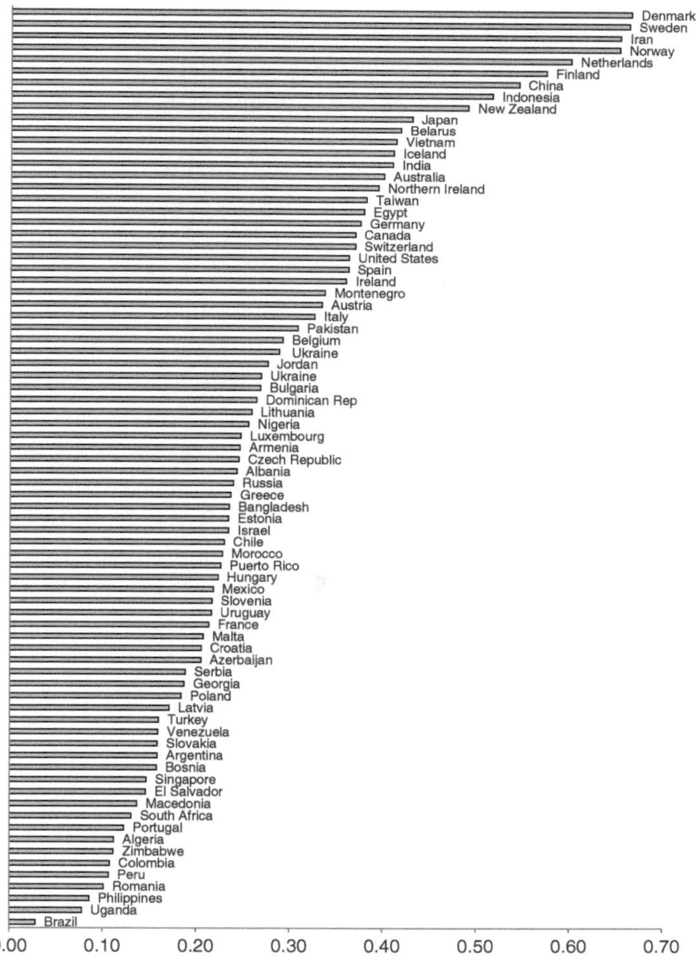

Figure 2 ***Trust beliefs across countries.*** The figure shows the proportion of people that when asked the WVS trust question answer that most people can be trusted.

Second, there is a very strong correlation, visible at glance, between average trust and a country's level of economic development, which has obviously attracted the attention of economists and that, prima facie, is consistent with civic capital having an economic payoff. Third, average generalized trust correlates well with the principle components of the indicators for civic capital (Figure 3, Panel A), and that of generalized morality (Figure 3, Panel B), which is evidence that all these measures capture the underlying civic capital.

The last wave of the WVS also includes some questions about personalized trust: "I'd like to ask you how much you trust people from various groups," which include a) the family; b) the neighbors; c) people one knows personally; d) people one meets for the first time. Answers are provided on a 1–4 scale ranging from no trust to complete trust and trust somewhat in between.

Table 3 shows mean country values for these measures of trust. Not surprising, trust in family members is higher than in people one knows personally, which in turns is higher than trust in neighbors, and trust in strangers. Equally unsurprising, at the country level, generalized trust (fraction of people who respond that most people can be trusted) is most highly correlated with trust towards strangers, then with trust towards neighbors, trust towards somebody one knows, and finally with the trust toward a family member. More interestingly, there is relatively little cross-country variation in the trust in family (st. dev of 0.1 with a mean of 3.8), while trust in strangers has more variability (st. dev of 0.26. with a mean of 2.0).

If we want to measure a country's or a community's civic capital, which is the right measure of trust? From a theoretical point of view, the right measure is generalized trust. For institutions and markets to work properly, people need to trust strangers. High levels of personal trust not joined by high levels of generalized trust are generally the result of strong in-group ties (e.g., Greif, 1993). Hence, high trust towards people one is close to—such as the family members or people that one knows personally—relative to trust towards people one meets for the first time can be taken as a weak norms index of generalized morality (Banfield, 1958; Alesina and Giuliano (2010).

One possible limitation of the WVS question is that people can only say whether they trust or not, but cannot express the intensity of the belief. Some surveys allow for a richer spectrum of answers: for instance, the recently constructed US trust index (Sapienza and Zingales, 2009) is based on the WVS questions, but allows people to answer on a scale between 1 ("I do not trust them at all") and 5 ("I trust them completely"). The European Social Survey allows for an even finer partition with answers to the WVS questions on a scale between 0 (no trust at all) and 10 (complete trust). Intensity of beliefs can be useful to get a better characterization of their distribution within a population and thus provide an indication of how homogeneous, and thus *shared*, these beliefs are within a certain community. Figure 4 shows the distributions of trust for the 26 countries surveyed in round II of the European Social Survey

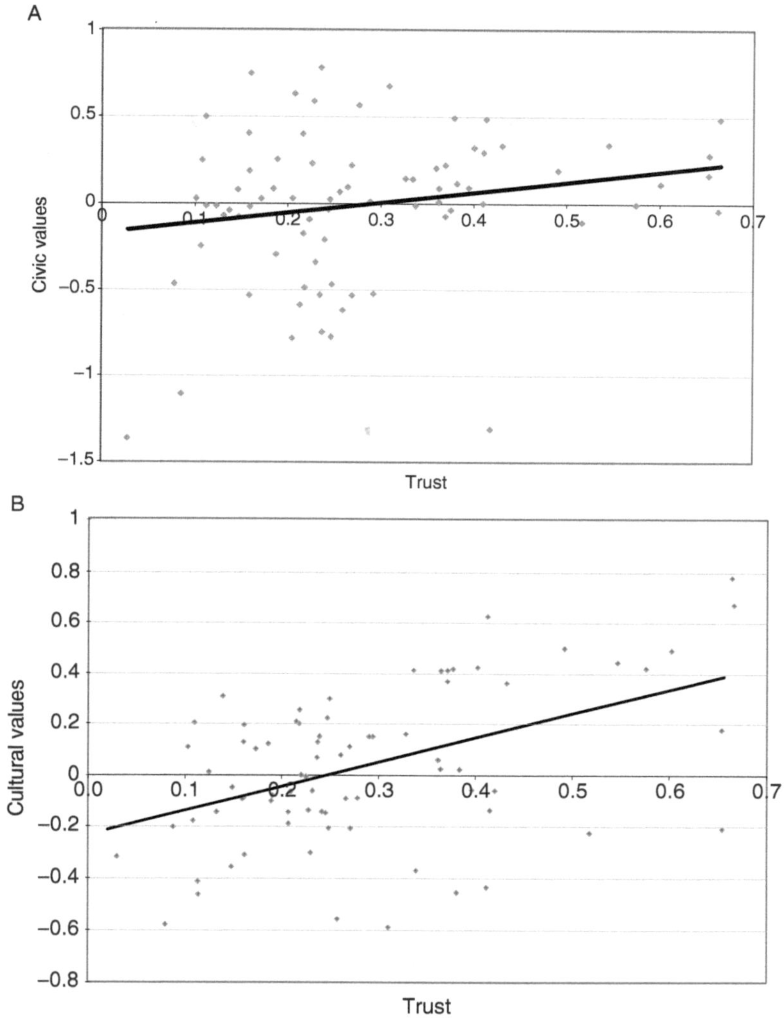

Figure 3 ***Trust and cultural values.*** Panel A shows the scatter plot and the regression line between generalized trust in the WVS and principal component of civic values; Panel B shows the plot and regression lines between trust and the principal component of the three measures of Tabellini's (2009) cultural values.

used by Butler et al. (2009). Several points are worth noting: a) in all countries people hold heterogeneous beliefs with some people trusting a lot and some not trusting at all; b) the shape of the distributions differ markedly across countries not only their means; c) the degree of heterogeneity also differs across countries with distributions more concentrated in the Scandinavian countries which have also a high level of average trust.

Table 3 Personalized versus generalized trust

Country	Trust Family	Trust people Know personally	Trust Neighbourhood	Trust stranger	Generalized trust	Family - stranger	Personally know - stranger	Neighbourhood - stranger
France	3.74	3.62	3.12	2.32	0.19	1.42	1.30	0.80
Britain	3.84	3.48	2.96	2.35	0.30	1.49	1.13	0.61
West Germany	3.77	3.19	2.84	2.10	0.41	1.67	1.09	0.74
Italy	3.86	2.72	2.73	1.93	0.29	1.92	0.79	0.80
Netherlands	3.54	3.16	2.82	2.03	0.44	1.51	1.12	0.79
Spain	3.91	3.25	2.92	2.11	0.20	1.79	1.14	0.81
USA	3.71	3.26	2.90	2.30	0.40	1.40	0.96	0.60
Mexico	3.68	2.84	2.50	1.68	0.16	1.99	1.16	0.82
South Africa	3.82	3.01	2.86	2.04	0.17	1.78	0.97	0.82
Australia	3.82	3.40	2.89	2.39	0.48	1.43	1.01	0.49
Sweden	3.93	3.47	3.29	2.69	0.68	1.24	0.79	0.60
Argentina	3.87	3.18	2.84	2.07	0.17	1.80	1.12	0.77
Finland	3.90	3.39	3.21	2.47	0.59	1.44	0.92	0.75
South Korea	3.87	2.97	2.76	1.87	0.30	2.00	1.10	0.89
Poland	3.70	2.96	2.80	2.06	0.19	1.64	0.90	0.75
Switzerland	3.79	3.28	3.01	2.41	0.51	1.38	0.87	0.61

Brazil	3.59	2.68	2.48	1.64	0.09	1.94	1.04	0.84
Chile	3.82	2.73	2.56	1.67	0.12	2.14	1.06	0.89
India	3.83	3.04	3.21	2.03	0.23	1.82	1.01	1.18
East Germany	3.77	3.16	2.88	1.97	0.28	1.81	1.19	0.91
Slovenia	3.79	2.99	2.70	1.71	0.18	2.09	1.28	0.99
Bulgaria	3.89	3.13	2.90	1.98	0.22	1.91	1.15	0.92
Romania	3.73	2.54	2.47	1.76	0.20	1.98	0.79	0.71
China	3.87	3.02	3.12	1.91	0.52	1.96	1.11	1.21
Taiwan	3.86	3.11	2.92	2.06	0.24	1.80	1.04	0.86
Turkey	3.95	2.93	2.86	1.77	0.05	2.18	1.16	1.09
Ukraine	3.76	2.97	2.84	1.91	0.28	1.87	1.07	0.93
Russia	3.90	3.03	2.73	1.75	0.27	2.15	1.27	0.98
Peru	3.69	2.43	2.20	1.49	0.06	2.19	0.94	0.71
Ghana	3.64	2.76	2.73	1.88	0.09	1.75	0.87	0.85
Moldova	3.78	2.84	2.53	1.71	0.18	2.08	1.13	0.82
Thailand	3.78	2.82	3.04	1.90	0.42	1.88	0.92	1.14
Indonesia	3.79	3.05	2.89	2.00	0.43	1.80	1.05	0.89
Vietnam	3.88	2.85	3.20	2.10	0.52	1.79	0.74	1.09
Colombia	3.79	2.74	2.56	1.71	0.14	2.08	1.03	0.85
Serbia	3.91	3.11	2.79	2.01	0.15	1.90	1.09	0.77

Continued

Table 3 Personalized versus generalized trust—cont'd

Country	Trust Family	Trust people Know personally	Trust Neighbourhood	Trust stranger	Generalized trust	Family - stranger	Personally know - stranger	Neighbourhood - stranger
New Zealand	3.90	3.57	3.11		0.51		3.57	3.11
Egypt	3.96	3.33	3.42	2.09	0.18	1.87	1.24	1.33
Morocco	3.89	3.11	3.28	1.89	0.13	2.00	1.22	1.39
Jordan	3.96	3.00	3.24	1.95	0.31	2.02	1.05	1.29
Cyprus	3.86	3.04	2.75	1.66	0.13	2.19	1.38	1.09
Trinidad	3.66	2.95	2.59	1.84	0.04	1.82	1.11	0.74
Andorra	3.80	3.13	2.42	1.90	0.21	1.90	1.23	0.52
Malaysia	3.84	2.85	2.94	1.78	0.09	2.06	1.07	1.16
Burkina Faso	3.79	2.73	2.92	2.01	0.15	1.78	0.72	0.91
Ethiopia	3.86	2.80	3.12	2.08	0.24	1.77	0.72	1.04
Mali	3.90	3.12	3.18	2.23	0.17	1.68	0.89	0.95
Rwanda	3.69	2.99	3.13	2.19	0.05	1.50	0.80	0.94
Zambia	3.59	2.67	2.66	1.75	0.12	1.84	0.92	0.91

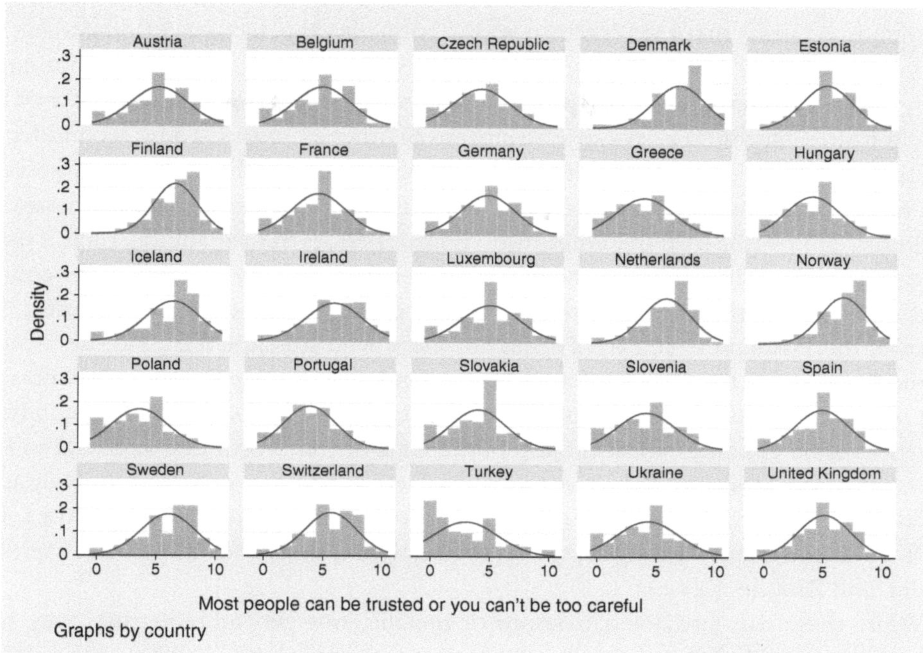

Figure 4 Trust beliefs: density functions by country. Source: *Butler et al. (2009) based on the European Social Survey Wave II.*

One large scale survey—Eurobarometer—has collected information on trust since the rise of the European Union and it does so with a very interesting twist. In order to monitor the sentiments of the Europeans as the process of integration and enlargement of the E.U. evolved, Eurobarometer has asked respondents of different nationalities to report not only how much they trust their fellow citizens, but also how much they trust the citizens of each of the countries in the European Union. More specifically, they were asked the following: "I would like to ask you a question about how much trust you have in people from various countries. For each, please tell me whether you have a lot of trust, some trust, not very much trust or no trust at all." The set of countries sampled varies over time with the enlargement of the European Union: there were 5 in 1970 (France, Belgium, The Netherlands, Germany, and Italy), when the first survey was conducted, and it had grown to 17 in 1995, the last survey to which we have access.[7]

[7] In some of the surveys, this same question was also asked with reference to citizens of a number of non-European Union countries, including the United States, Russia, Switzerland, China, Japan, Turkey, and some Eastern and Central European countries, which at the time were perspective entrants into the Union (Bulgaria, Slovakia, Romania.,Hungary, Poland, Slovenia, and Czech Republic). See Guiso, Sapienza and Zingales (2009) and the online appendix to the paper for details.

Following GSZ (2009) who first used these data, we have re-coded the answers to the trust question setting them as 1 (no trust at all), 2 (not very much trust), 3 (some trust), and 4 (a lot of trust), and have then aggregated responses by country and year computing the mean value of the responses to each survey. Table 4 shows the average level of trust that citizens from each country have toward citizens of other countries. There is considerable variation in the level of trust exhibited from one country to another. The average level of trust ranges from a minimum trust of 2.13 (the trust of Portuguese toward Austrians) to a maximum of 3.69 (the trust of Finns toward Finns). Besides this variability, Table 4 shows three regularities. First, there are systematic differences in how much a given country trusts and how much others (see the last row and last column of Table 4) trust it. For instance, the Portuguese and the Greeks are those who trust the least and the Swedish are those who trust the most. Second, there is tendency of people from one country to trust more their fellow citizens. Third, there is a correlation between trusting and being trusted. Nordic countries are at the top of the level of trustworthiness and tend to trust others the most. While not definitive proof, this fact suggests that people excessively apply the level of trustworthiness of their own compatriots to people from other countries. This result is also consistent with experimental evidence in Glaeser et al. (2002) and Sapienza, Toldra, and Zingales (2008).

While these data provide a measure of specific, not generalized, trust, they have been used to shed light on the cultural determinants of trust (GSZ, 2009). With regard to civic capital formation, one interesting issue that can be studied with these data is whether political inclusion can affect the beliefs people have about the trustworthiness of other populations that before were not part of the same political entity.

As in every survey, there may be some doubts about the way people interpret the trust question. In a trust game (see below), the level of trust maps into the amount of money one is willing to risk. In the Eurobarometer survey, this mapping is missing. One can address this doubt by asking the trust question to eliminate the ambiguity that may be present in the wording of the WVS-trust question. For instance in one of the modules of the 2003 Dutch National Bank Household survey (DNB survey), a sample of 1,990 individuals were asked both the WVS question and the following one: "Suppose that a random person you do not know personally receives by mistake a sum of 1000 euros that belong to you. He or she is aware that the money belongs to you and knows your name and address. He or she can keep the money without incurring in any punishment. According to you what is the probability (a number between zero and 100) that he or she returns the money?" This question maps trust into a probability that a generic person behaves honestly, allowing for a clear interpretation and a natural metric for measuring trust beliefs. Answers to this question are positively correlated with the WVS question, suggesting that the latter indeed captures beliefs about the trustworthiness of fellow citizens.

In recent surveys, it is becoming more standard to ask trust questions in such a way that they better reflect people's assessment about the probability of being cheated

Table 4 The trust matrix

		Trust From															
		Aus	**Bel**	**UK**	**Den**	**NL**	**Fin**	**Fra**	**Ger**	**Gre**	**Ire**	**Ita**	**Nor**	**Por**	**Spa**	**Swe**	**Average**
TRUST TO	Aus	3.56	2.83	2.89	3.22	2.90	3.29	2.70	2.98	2.32	2.93	2.66	.	2.13	2.65	3.53	2.90
	Bel	2.95	3.28	2.91	3.18	3.18	3.07	3.07	2.84	2.60	2.93	2.64	3.18	2.66	2.73	3.23	2.96
	UK	2.61	2.84	3.29	3.22	3.00	3.18	2.55	2.69	2.34	2.81	2.51	3.27	2.66	2.31	3.43	2.85
	Den	2.95	3.01	3.13	3.39	3.29	3.30	2.96	2.97	2.56	2.99	2.70	3.53	2.66	2.73	3.57	3.05
	NL	2.95	2.90	3.16	3.33	3.28	3.14	2.94	2.90	2.55	3.00	2.77	3.26	2.70	2.85	3.33	3.00
	Fin	2.94	2.92	2.98	3.20	3.25	3.69	2.91	2.85	2.42	2.92	2.78	.	2.18	2.71	3.49	2.95
	Fra	2.62	2.92	2.32	2.86	2.72	2.92	3.18	2.85	2.78	2.81	2.66	2.93	2.91	2.37	3.04	2.79
	Ger	3.09	2.75	2.62	3.12	2.84	2.89	2.74	3.50	2.31	2.78	2.63	2.99	2.54	2.66	3.13	2.84
	Gre	2.52	2.45	2.54	2.61	2.59	2.68	2.53	2.51	3.21	2.50	2.40	2.52	2.41	2.47	2.88	2.59
	Ire	2.55	2.75	2.61	3.02	2.80	2.92	2.72	2.59	2.55	3.33	2.37	3.01	2.51	2.57	3.26	2.77
	Ita	2.43	2.40	2.51	2.53	2.35	2.51	2.43	2.36	2.33	2.65	2.80	2.65	2.55	2.61	2.81	2.53
	Nor	3.00	2.91	3.06	3.50	3.30	3.48	2.97	2.92	2.40	2.93	2.78	.	2.22	2.79	3.65	2.99
	Por	2.50	2.53	2.74	2.67	2.74	2.67	2.59	2.48	2.60	2.65	2.32	2.60	3.29	2.51	2.97	2.66
	Spa	2.58	2.59	2.47	2.66	2.64	2.61	2.68	2.66	2.71	2.64	2.64	2.56	2.59	3.32	2.86	2.68
	Swe	3.05	2.99	3.03	3.41	3.34	3.35	2.99	2.99	2.51	2.92	2.89	.	2.24	2.84	3.59	3.01
	Average	2.82	2.80	2.82	3.06	2.95	3.05	2.80	2.81	2.55	2.85	2.64	2.95	2.55	2.67	3.25	

by an anonymous opponent. For instance the 2005 Mexican Family Life Survey—a newly designed multi-thematic survey that interviews over 40,000 Mexican citizens—asks the following probabilistic question: "If you lost your wallet with $200 pesos in it, how probable is it that you will get it back with all of your money and everything else inside it if someone who lives close to you found it?" with answers between 0 (will not get it back for sure) and 100 (get it back for sure). Probabilistic trust questions have the advantage of increasing comparability of the answers both across people and social groups and, since their elicitation requires reference to an explicit event (such as returning a lost wallet), avoids the "vagueness" that may characterize questions like the ones asked in the WVS.

A second doubt about the WVS question is that it may reflect people's ability to detect others' trustworthiness. The 2003 DNB also asks respondents "How good are you (very good, good, not very good, and not good at all) in detecting people who are trustworthy?" Answers to this question are not correlated with those to the trust question, suggesting the latter does not reflect differences in ability to detect trustworthiness, but rather the subjective probability that a random person is trustworthy.[8]

Perhaps, a more serious objection raised against questions of the sort asked in the WVS is that they may be poor measures of trust beliefs and rather reflect some combination of beliefs about others trustworthiness (what we would like to be picking up) and individual preferences—a point forcefully made by Fehr (2009). Actual trust behavior, as measured for instance by the amount of money that a person would be willing to lend to an unknown individual, obviously depends both on the belief the lender has about the borrower's trustworthiness as well as on the lender's willingness to bear the risk that the borrower does not repay. When faced with "social risk"—that is the risk that a loss is caused by another person rather than nature—what matters is betrayal aversion (Bohnet and Zeckhauser, 2004), that is the dislike for the risk of being cheated, not risk aversion. By using the German Socio-Economic Panel (which collects measures of trust, risk preferences, and betrayal aversion). Fehr (2009) finds that the people who are more risk averse and more betrayal averse also trust less, where trust is measured as in the WVS. This finding is consistent with answers to these questions reflecting also individual preferences, perhaps because when asked people mentally simulate the act of trusting rather that isolating their belief about others' trustworthiness. If risk aversion and betrayal aversion were heterogeneous across individuals, but not across cultures, then one could still use variation in average, generalized trust

[8] Another criticism to the WVS trust question is that the respondents have the choice between trusting and being cautious rather than between trust and distrust. Hence, it may be mixing two different phenomena,trust and cautiousness (see Yamagishi, Kikucki and Kosugi. 1999), which may be not be mutually exclusive. One implication is that the interpretation of the WVS trust question may differ among societies if cautiousness does even if they trust equally (Miller and Mitamura, 2003). The simplest way to deal with this issue is to change the wording of the question and askfor an example. "How much do you trust other people in your country?" providing an appropriate scale, as done fro instance by Naef and Shupp (2009) using the German Socio-Economic Panel.

measures of the WVS-type for cross-countries comparisons. However, evidence from six countries (Brazil, China, Oman, Switzerland, Turkey, and the United States) collected by Bohnet et al. (2008) seems to suggest that risk and betrayal preferences do differ, though the sample sizes are not large enough to draw strong conclusions (see also Naef and Schupp, 2009). These findings suggest that when designing survey questions to measure trust beliefs, wording should be such that it is clear to the respondent what one is concerned about: his beliefs about others' trustworthiness. In this regard, probability questions of the type asked in the Mexican survey could be a step ahead.

3.2.2 Measuring trust in trust experiments

As with preferences, one can use lab or field experiments to measure trust. Since Berg, Dickhaut, and McCabe (1995) first proposed it, the trust game has become a routine tool to obtain measures of trust. In a trust game an individual, the sender, is endowed with a sum of money E. He is paired with another player (typically anonymous), the receiver. The sender has to choose how much of his endowment he wants to send to the receiver. If he sends $0 \leq S \leq E$ the sum is multiplied by a factor $\lambda > 1$ (typically 2 or 3) before reaching the receiver; this is meant to capture the creation of surplus from trusting and investing. The receiver then decides, without the sender observing his action, how much of the sum he gets, λS, he wants to return to the sender. The fraction of the endowment sent—S/E—is bounded between 0 and 1 and provides a *behavioral* measure of trust that has a clear interpretation. The trust game also allows researchers to obtain a measure of trustworthiness, by taking the fraction of λS that is returned to the sender.

The main advantage of the trust game is that one can obtain a more easily interpretable measure of trust. Furthermore, since one can ask the sender to also report his expectations about the amount she thinks the receiver will return, the trust game allows researchers to neatly separate beliefs and preferences (the latter being embedded in the behavioral trust). This has helped clarify the meaning of the WVS questions and provide some external validity to it. Glaeser et al. (2002), for instance, argue that the World Values Survey trust question is not correlated with the sender behavior in the standard trust game but reflects instead correlated behavioral trustworthiness in the game. However, Sapienza, Toldra, and Zingales (2008) argue that the sender behavior in the trust game is not a good measure of trust beliefs, because, being a behavioral measure, it is also affected by other regarding preferences. Using the sender's expectation about the receiver's behavior, Sapienza, Toldra, and Zingales (2008) show that this expectation strongly correlates with the World Values Survey trust question and other similar trust questions.[9] To better understand what survey and trust game measures actually mean, Naef and Shupp (2009) have a randomly selected group of the German

[9] There is very large literature that uses the trust game to measure trust behavior and less often, trust beliefs. A good account of this literature is provided by Fehr (2009) and Naef and Shupp (2009).

Socio-Economic Panel play a standard trust game. They find that trust in the experiment is best correlated with the survey measure of trust when people are asked how much they trust strangers. This is useful as it is precisely trust in anonymous members of a community that civic capital is about.

3.2.3 Other beliefs

Though a large literature has focused on trust, other beliefs, such as fairness or expectations about others' corruption, are likely to be as important in encouraging extended social interactions and willingness to cooperate with others. Several surveys now ask questions about expected fairness and other potentially important beliefs. For instance, the last round of the WVS obtains a qualitative measure of expected fairness by asking: "Do you think most people would try to take advantage of you if they got a chance, or would they try to be fair? Please show your response on this card, where 1 means that "people would try to take advantage of you" and 10 means that "people would try to be fair."[10] Fairness beliefs are positively correlated with trust, but correlation is far from perfect (on the 2005 WVS the correlation with country averages of generalized trust is 0.6 and with trust towards people met for the first time it is 0.43).

Summing up, this discussion has shown that once social capital is redefined as civic capital, that is as the set of beliefs and preferences that are shared by a community and that facilitate community members' achievement of common interest goals, it can be measured. We can obtain measures for the diffusion of civicness norms and generalized moralities as well as measures of trust beliefs and fairness that help characterize the stock of civic capital in a community, which is required by Solow in his criticism of social capital. These measures are far from being free of problems; there are issues of interpretation, comparison across countries, selection of which indicators to use, etc. But these issues are probably no more severe that the ones that one we face when building a measure of aggregate physical capital, as shown by the capital controversy debate of the 1960s to which Solow himself contributed with the same constructive criticism that he has provided to the social capital debate.

3.3 Indirect measures

As we discussed earlier, outcome-based measures of civic capital are difficult to interpret because the effects of other institutions contaminate them. When we observe that Swedes evade taxes less than Brazilians do, we do not know to what extent this is the effect of Sweden's higher social capital or superior tax enforcement. For an outcome-based measure to qualify as a good indicator of civic capital, the relationship between the input (civic capital) and the measured output should be stable and unaffected by other factors, such as legal enforcement. These conditions are not generally present. There are, however, particular situations where they are likely to be met.

[10] The fairness questions started to be asked in the WVS 2000 wave but answers were dichotomous; other surveys, notably the ESS and the GSS,ask also beliefs about fairness.

One such instance is donation of blood or organs. Since there is no economic payoff to either donation and there is no legal obligation to donate, the decision to donate can be seen as a direct measure of how much people internalize the common good. Donating organs and/or blood provides insurance to others, with no direct compensation for the person providing it. Therefore, it is the ultimate example of valuing the common good. For these reasons, GSZ (2004) and GSZ (2008b) use them as measures of civic capital.

Another example is voter turnout. Since there is no direct economic payoff to voting, this measure captures the extent to which people in a community are willing to pay a personal cost to enhance the common good. For this reason, Putnam (1993) uses electoral participation in referenda as a measure of the underlying civicness.

Consistent with the idea that these measures are capturing the same underlying norms, they tend to be highly correlated. Figures 5 and 6 plot the distribution of participation in referenda and blood donation across the 95 Italian provinces. As Figure 5 shows, voter turnout is higher in the north of Italy (north of the Apennines), weaker in the center (from the Apennines to Rome), and very weak in the south (south of Rome). It is indeed this difference within Italy that attracted the attention of Banfield (1958) first and Putnam (1993) subsequently. Figure 6 shows the geographical distribution of the indirect measure based on blood donation. The geographical pattern that we see in Figure 6 is very similar to the one shown in Figure 5 using a very different indicator. Despite the different nature of these variables, their cross-correlation is as high (0.64), as one would expect if indeed they were the reflection of the same set of cultural norms for civic behavior. Notice however that the correlation is far from perfect, suggesting that indirect indicators are affected by measurement error. Hence if one were to rely on measures of this sort in applied work, one could gain some insights by obtaining several indirect indicators and looking at common components (see Tabellini (2009)).

Another example of a legitimate outcome-based measure of civic capital is Fisman and Miguel's (2007) paper on parking violations by United Nations officials in Manhattan. Until 2002, diplomatic immunity protected U.N. diplomats from parking enforcement actions. Only cultural norms prevent U.N. diplomats from parking illegally. Hence, the number of parking violations per diplomat is a good measure of the strength of the social norms in each country. As Fisman and Miguel (2007) show, this measure is correlated with other, less clean, outcome-based measures such as corruption.

3.4 Are these measures useful?

Economists are interested in civic capital because they think might help explain differences in economic development. Thus, a necessary, albeit not sufficient condition, for these measures to be of interest is that they are correlated with indicators of economic and institutional performance. To check whether this is the case, Table 5 looks at the correlation between these measures and several economic (Panel A) and institutional indicators (Panel B).

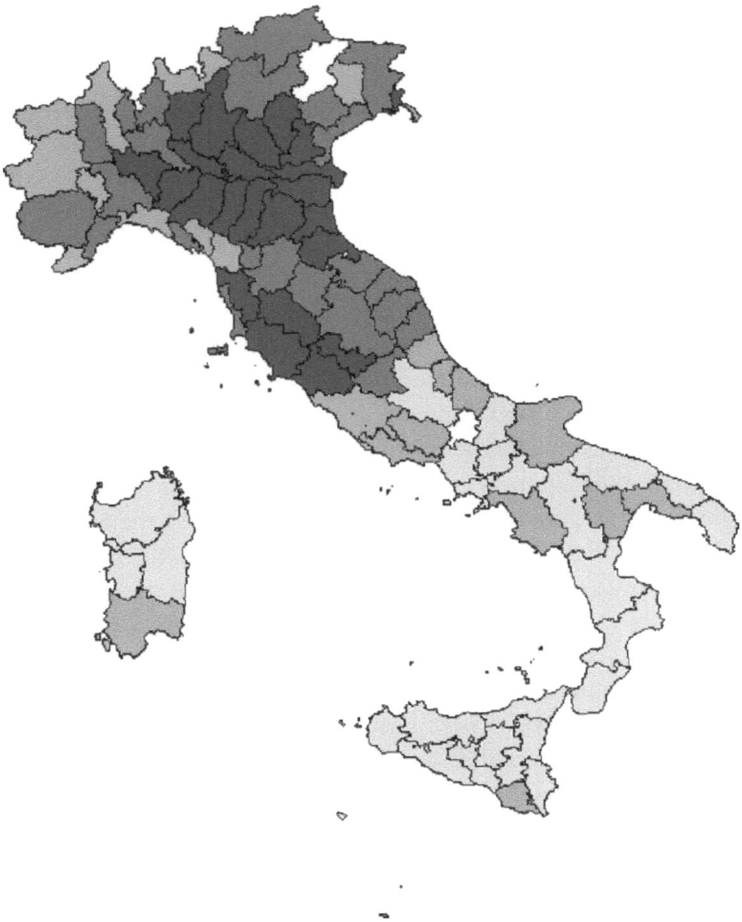

Figure 5 ***Referenda turnout across Italian provinces.*** Voter turnout as a province is the average percentage of people that participated in all the referenda that occurred in Italy between 1946 and 1989. Referenda cover a very broad set of issues, ranging from the choice between republic and monarchy (1946) to divorce (1974) and abortion (1981), from hunting regulation (1987) to the use of nuclear power (1987) and to public order measures (1978, 1981). Darker areas correspond to higher social capital.

To begin with we look at the correlation between income per capita in 2007 and three sets of civic capital measures: a measure of expectations (trust in stranger), a survey-based measure of norms (the principle component of the answers to three World Value Survey questions on values), and an outcome-based measure (the number of parking violations per U.N. diplomat). As Table 5A shows, both trust and parking violations have a statistical significant correlation with productivity, no matter whether we measure productivity per capita or per worker. By contrast, the principal

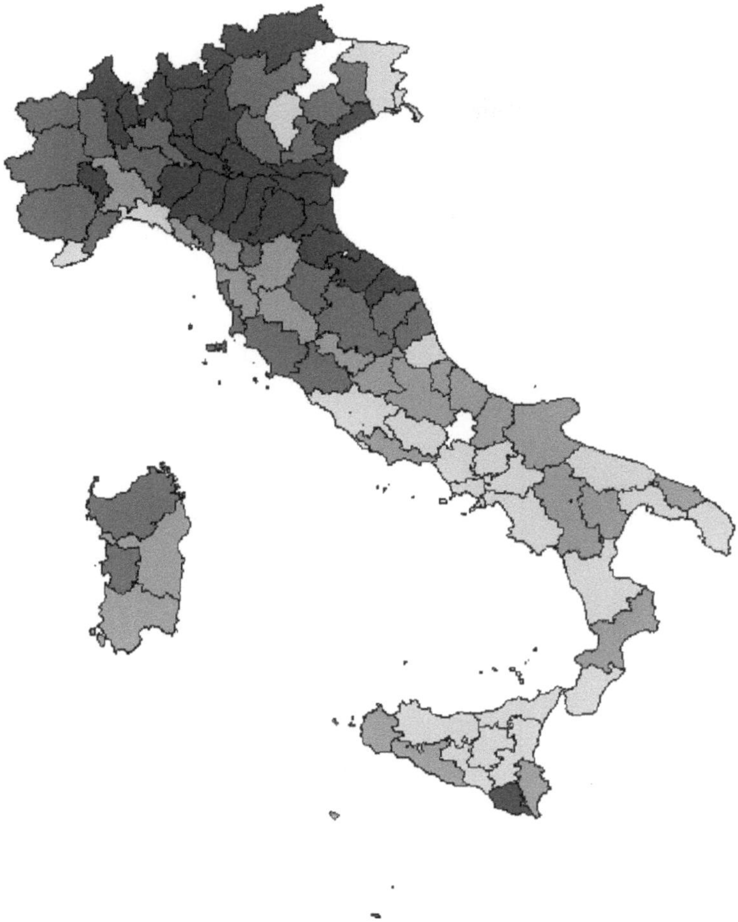

Figure 6 ***Blood donation across Italian provinces.*** Number of blood bags per million inhabitants; the indicator ranges from 0 to .11; darker areas correspond to provinces with more social capital. Source: GSZ (2004).

component of norms does not appear to be correlated. If we substitute trust in strangers with the general trust question, the effect is similar, but weaker.

As Figure 7 shows, this effect of trust appears to be limited to the more developed countries. While there is a very strong correlation between trust and economic development for countries with a per capital GDP above $20,000, there is no correlation below that level. One possible explanation is that trust is particularly useful in more sophisticated transactions. For example, one can effectively run a sugar plantation without much trust, while it is difficult to engage in financial transactions without it.

Table 5 Civic capital and economic development

Panel A. Productivity

Variables	Real GDP per capita (1)	Real GDP per worker (2)	Real GDP per capita (3)	Real GDP per worker (4)
Trust toward strangers	22.184***	37.183***		
	[6.331]	[11.329]		
Violation	−144.8***	−239.6***	−133.1***	−227.4**
	[44.90]	[82.90]	[47.93]	[90.51]
Principal component civic values	−701.7	−1.138	−189.6	−139.9
	[986.4]	[1.814]	[967.4]	[1.814]
Generalized trust			26.044**	36.470*
			[11.135]	[19.970]
Constant	−25.587**	−38.744*	11.775***	25.946***
	[12.535]	[22.553]	[3.392]	[6.199]
Observations	42	42	45	45
R-squared	0.31	0.264	0.257	0.193

Notes: GDP figures refer to 2007 (Source: Penn World Table 6.3). Trust and civic values data are from the World Values Survey. Violation is the number of parking violations per U.N. diplomat (Source: Fisman and Miguel, 2007).
Robust standard errors in brackets, *** $p<0.01$, ** $p<0.05$, * $p<0.1$.

Panel B. Government efficiency

	Bureaucratic delays		Corruption		Tax compliance		GADP	
Variables	**(1)**	**(2)**	**(3)**	**(4)**	**(5)**	**(6)**	**(7)**	**(8)**
Trust toward strangers	2.321***	1.497**	4.765***	3.720***	1.550**	0.869	0.327***	0.237***
	[0.505]	[0.537]	[0.946]	[0.717]	[0.626]	[0.560]	[0.0984]	[0.0449]
Violation	−0.0134***	−0.00504	−0.0218**	−0.00873	0.00119	0.00691*	−0.00171**	−0.00018
	[0.00387]	[0.00430]	[0.00882]	[0.00655]	[0.00428]	[0.00387]	[0.000763]	[0.000336]
Principle component civic values	0.073	0.0186	−0.17	−0.122*	−0.214	−0.254	0.0301	−0.00029
	[0.223]	[0.149]	[0.110]	[0.0699]	[0.206]	[0.166]	[0.0342]	[0.0130]
Log of GDP		0.820***		1.117***		0.624***		0.132***
		[0.260]		[0.259]		[0.188]		[0.0144]
Constant	0.136	−6.105***	−2.89	−11.46***	−0.129	−4.777***	0.0403	−1.027***
	[0.974]	[2.040]	[1.854]	[1.875]	[1.252]	[1.657]	[0.187]	[0.127]
Observations	28	28	38	38	27	27	37	37
R-squared	0.359	0.604	0.428	0.676	0.175	0.425	0.349	0.85

Notes: Bureaucratic delays (red tape) data is the average of the years between 1972 and 1995. The scale is from 0 to 10 and low ratings indicate lower levels of red tape in the bureaucracy of the country (Source: La Porta et al., 1999). Corruption refers to corruption in government. Low ratings indicate "high government officials are likely to demand special payments" and "illegal payments are generally expected toward lower levels of government" in the form of "bribes connected with import and export licenses, exchange controls, tax assessment, policy protection or loans." The scale is from 0 to 10 and data refer to the average of the years between 1982 and 1995 (Source: La Porta et al., 1999). Data for tax compliance refer to 1995. The scale is from 0 to 6, where higher scores indicate higher compliance (Source: La Porta et al.,1999), GADP is the index of government anti-diversion policies (Source: Hall and Jones, 1999). It is an equal-weighted average of 5 categories for the years 1986–1995: i) law and order, ii) bureaucratic quality, iii) corruption, iv) risk of expropriation, v) government repudiation of contracts. Each of the 5 categories has higher values for governments with more effective policies for supporting production. The index is measured on a scale from 0 to 1. Trust and civic values data are from the World Values Survey. Violation is the number of parking violations per UN diplomat (Source: Fisman and Miguel, 2007).
Robust standard errors in brackets, *** p<0.01, ** p<0.05, * p<0.1.

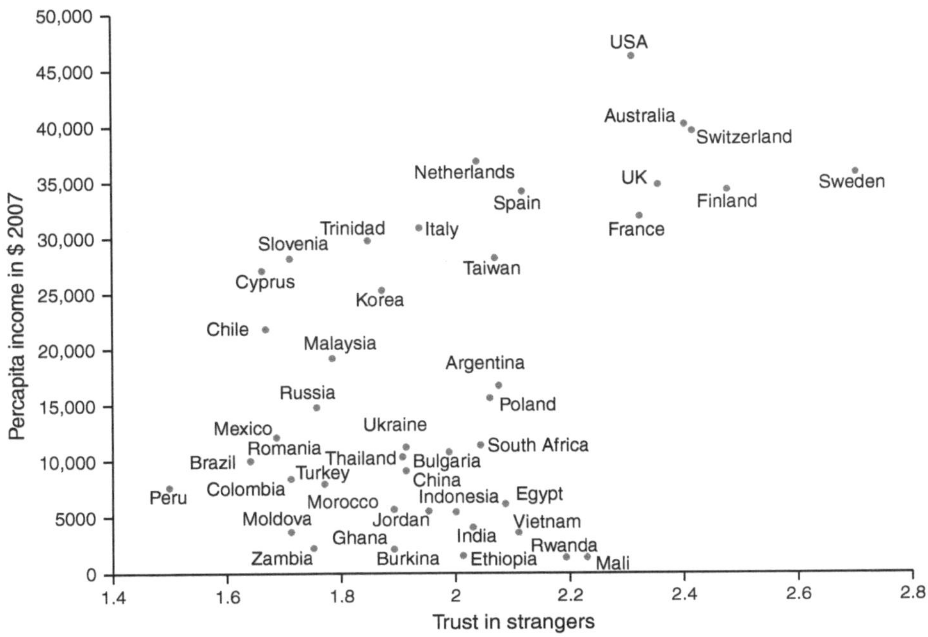

Figure 7 ***Trust and economic development.*** The figure shows the scatter plot of trust toward people one meets for the first time (WVS 2005–2008) and Gross Domestic Product per capita in 2007 (Penn World data). Trust in people one meets for the first time can take four possible values: 1 (do not trust at all), 2 (trust very little), 3 (trust), 4 (trust completely).

Consistent with this hypothesis, GSZ (2009) find that mutual trust between countries is more important in the international trading of more differentiated goods.

In Table 5B we correlated various institutional measures with the same right-hand side variables. To distinguish between the direct effect of civic capital and its indirect effect via a generalized increase in income per capita, for each left-hand side variable we report two regressions, one controlling for income per capita, the other not.

The main result is that trust seems to be positively correlated with all the measures of institutional development, from bureaucratic delays to corruption, from tax evasion to an index of government anti-diversion policies. This correlation is statistically different from zero, regardless of whether we control for per capita income. By contrast, the measure of parking violations is negatively correlated with the measure of institutional development, but this correlation becomes statistically insignificant when we control for per capita income. Finally, the survey-based measure of norms is not correlated with any measure of institutional development.

In sum, if we are interested in studying the effect of civic capital on economic outcomes, the survey-based measure of trust seems to be the most promising indicator. By contrast, a survey-based measure of norms does not seem to add any value. One plausible explanation is that people are more inclined to distort their answers to questions regarding moral values because they are sensitive to the judgment of the interviewer. The advantage of the trust question instead is that it does not have any obvious answer that is more socially acceptable.

4. THE ORIGINS OF CIVIC CAPITAL

In Figures 1 and 2, we show the enormous variability in values and beliefs across countries. This raises the question of where these differences in civic capital come from. This is a very difficult question since it is the same as asking what factors may trigger the adoption and diffusion of cultural norms for generalized morality and cooperation among members of a community. In this section, we start by showing some cross-country evidence on the main correlates of civic capital. As in all cross-country regressions, it is impossible to make any causal statement. To try to address the causality, we will resort to reviewing some within country studies that shed more light on this dimension.

4.1 Correlates of civic capital

We will start by analyzing the one dimension of civic capital that appears more correlated with economic performance: trust in strangers. For this variable we rely on the World Value Survey measure, hence our sample is constrained by the WVS country coverage. To account for possible feedback effects between economic performance and civic capital, in studying the correlates of civic capital we will control for log of GDP per capita (measured in 1997).

As described in Section 2, one of the potential sources of accumulation of civic capital is education. To capture the level of education accumulated over time, we measure the primary enrollment in the 1920a as computed by Benavot and Riddle (1988). As Table 6A shows, this is positively and significantly correlated with of measure of civic capital: today's level of trust in strangers. One standard deviation increase in 1920 enrollment is associated with a 70% standard deviation increase toward trust toward strangers.

In column 2 we add the level of ethnic fractionalization. As Alesina and La Ferrara (2002) show, ethnic diversity is negatively correlated with trust. We find the same coefficient, but it is not significant in this regression. In column 3 we also control for the number of years a country has been a democracy since independence. As we argued, historical experience of political participation has a positive effect on civic capital. As predicted, the effect is positive, but it is not statistically significant. Ethnic fractionalization, however, becomes significant. Finally, in column 4 we control for the prevalence of two hierarchical religions: Catholicism and Islam. The percentage of Catholics in a country is negatively correlated with trust, while the percentage of Muslims not. When we include these controls, the effect of years of democracy since independence turns significant. Together these variables account for 45% of the cross-country variation of civic capital, supporting all the various channels of accumulation of civic capital reported in Section 2.

In Table 6B we show the same set of regressions with the parking violation measure of civic capital taken from Fisman and Miguel (2007). The educational level appears to be

Table 6 Where does civic capital come from?
Panel A. The sources of trust

	Trust toward strangers			
Variables	**(1)**	**(2)**	**(3)**	**(4)**
Enrollment rate in 1920	0.00660*** [0.00140]	0.00646*** [0.00137]	0.00417* [0.00226]	0.00474** [0.00229]
Ethnic fractionalization		−0.249 [0.163]	−0.340** [0.152]	−0.303** [0.139]
Years of democracy since independence			0.00147 [0.00120]	0.00186* [0.000991]
Percentage Catholic				−0.00269** [0.00101]
Percentage Muslim				0.000141 [0.00112]
Log of GDP	−0.0786* [0.0429]	−0.0983** [0.0453]	−0.110** [0.0432]	−0.103** [0.0490]
Constant	2.523*** [0.368]	2.801*** [0.411]	2.933*** [0.387]	2.896*** [0.456]
Observations	44	43	42	42
R-squared	0.245	0.285	0.313	0.449

Notes: Trust figures are from the World Values Survey. Enrollment rate is the fraction of people aged 5 to 14 enrolled in primary education in 1920 (Source: Benavot and Riddle, 1988). Years of democracy since independence is the number of years since independence in which the country has been democratic. A country is defined as democratic in a specific year if in that year the variable polity2 in the Polity IV dataset is strictly positive. Ethnic fractionalization reflects the probability that two randomly selected people from a given country will not belong to the same ethno-linguistic group (Source: Alesina et al., 2003). The higher the number, the more fractionalized the society. The definition of ethnicity involves a combination of racial and linguistic characteristics. Percentage Muslim and percentage Catholic identify the percentage of the population in each country that belonged to Roman Catholic or Muslim religions in 1980 (Source: La Porta et al., 1999).
Robust standard errors in brackets, *** $p<0.01$, ** $p<0.05$, * $p<0.1$.

Panel B. The sources of respect for rules

	Parking violations			
Variables	**(1)**	**(2)**	**(3)**	**(4)**
Enrollment rate in 1920	−0.216** [0.0917]	−0.197** [0.0920]	−0.145 [0.113]	−0.0841 [0.106]
Ethnic fractionalization		16.24 [10.17]	15.93 [10.34]	16.44 [10.03]

Continued

Table 6 Where does civic capital come from?—cont'd

Panel B. The sources of respect for rules—cont'd

	Parking violations			
Variables	**(1)**	**(2)**	**(3)**	**(4)**
Years of democracy since independence			−0.0641 [0.0492]	−0.0357 [0.0496]
Percentage Catholic				−0.0253 [0.0439]
Percentage Muslim				0.165* [0.0919]
Log of GDP	−4.355** [1.782]	−2.334 [1.836]	−1.726 [1.906]	−1.356 [2.010]
Constant	60.95*** [15.71]	35.13** [17.70]	30.96* [18.17]	22.07 [19.09]
Observations	131	130	128	128
R-squared	0.114	0.124	0.128	0.168

Notes: Violation is the number of parking violations per U.N. diplomat (Source: Fisman and Miguel, 2007). Enrollment rate is the fraction of people aged 5 to 14 enrolled in primary education in 1920 (Source: Benavot and Riddle, 1988). Years of democracy since independence is the number of years since independence in which the country has been democratic. A country is defined as democratic in a specific year if in that year the variable polity2 in the Polity IV dataset is strictly positive. Ethnic fractionalization reflects the probability that two randomly selected people from a given country will not belong to the same ethno-linguistic group (Source: Alesina et al., 2003). The higher the number, the more fractionalized the society. The definition of ethnicity involves a combination of racial and linguistic characteristics. Percentage Muslim and percentage Catholic identify the percentage of the population in each country that belonged to Roman Catholic or Muslim religions in 1980 (Source: La Porta et al., 1999).
Robust standard errors in brackets, *** $p<0.01$, ** $p<0.05$, * $p<0.1$.

Panel C. The sources of moral norms

	Principal component of civic values			
Variables	**(1)**	**(2)**	**(3)**	**(4)**
Enrollment rate in 1920	0.0207 [0.0124]	0.0197 [0.0128]	0.00908 [0.00893]	0.0149 [0.0100]
Ethnic fractionalization		−0.687 [0.657]	−0.948 [0.661]	−1.075 [0.663]
Years of democracy since independence			0.00844 [0.00919]	0.00914 [0.00978]
Percentage Catholic				−0.0092 [0.00996]

Continued

Table 6 Where does civic capital come from?—cont'd
Panel C. The sources of moral norms—cont'd

	Principal component of civic values			
Variables	**(1)**	**(2)**	**(3)**	**(4)**
Percentage Muslim				0.00878* [0.00486]
Log of GDP	−0.44 [0.437]	−0.458 [0.439]	−0.55 [0.534]	−0.506 [0.517]
Constant	3.548 [3.555]	3.982 [3.521]	4.821 [4.355]	4.332 [4.303]
Observations	46	45	44	44
R-squared	0.055	0.058	0.084	0.155

Civic values data are from the World Values Survey. Enrollment rate is the fraction of people aged 5 to 14 enrolled in primary education in 1920 (Source: Benavot and Riddle, 1988). Years of democracy since independence is the number of years since independence in which the country has been democratic. A country is defined as democratic in a specific year if in that year the variable polity2 in the Polity IV dataset is strictly positive. Ethnic fractionalization reflects the probability that two randomly selected people from a given country will not belong to the same ethno-linguistic group (Source: Alesina et al., 2003). The higher the number, the more fractionalized the society. The definition of ethnicity involves a combination of racial and linguistic characteristics. Percentage Muslim and percentage Catholic identify the percentage of the population in each country that belonged to Roman Catholic or Muslim religions in 1980 (Source: La Porta et al.. 1999). Robust standard errors in brackets, *** $p<0.01$, ** $p<0.05$, * $p<0.1$.

negatively associated with the number of parking violations per diplomat, albeit this effect is significant only when we do not insert too many controls. Besides that, only the percentage of Muslims is positively correlated with the number of parking violations.

Finally, in Table 6C we show that the principal components of the civic values measured via survey are not correlated with any of the variables above, except for the percentage of Muslims in the country, which has a positive effect.

A more elaborated analysis of the relationship between political history and civic capital is provided by Tabellini (2009). He focuses on variation in norms and beliefs across regions of Europe. He measures civic capital with the level of the WVS trust and with the principal component of the measures of obedience, respect, and control discussed in Section 3. Since he uses within country variation, he can rule out (by inserting country level fixed effects) that current cultural values reflect heterogeneous formal institution, as would be case, for instance, if legal codes offer different degrees of legal protections which in turn affect the willingness of individuals to trust their counterparts in a trade.

The key idea, reminiscent of Putnam (1993) and Banfield (1958), is that autocratic and hierarchical regimes that perpetuate due to to imposition and brutal force rather than consensus are natural vehicles for the creation of a culture of mistrust. Because they subdue individuals, they are inimical of self-determination and individual autonomy, which discourages individual initiative and willingness to collaborate and join forces with others that do not belong to the narrow family circle. In such environment widespread illiteracy is seen as reinforcement of these negative attitudes "...because it isolates individuals and it reduces their ability to control and understand the external environment."

Consistent with distant political history playing a role, Tabellini (2009) finds that historically more backward regions—that is regions with higher illiteracy rates more than 200 years ago and with a long history of relatively poor political institutions—tend to have worse cultural traits today: they have lower generalized trust, less respect for others, less confidence in the individual and a lower value of these indicators together as measured by their first principal component. Thus, a long history of bad political climates can result in cultural norms that are adverse to extended exchanges, that is in a lower value of civic capital.

One big advantage of the Tabellini (2009) study is that it shows that general political histories can be behind the differences in cultural norms and beliefs that dominate current societies. The shortcoming of this general approach is that its measure of political institutions—an index of constraints on the executive—can reflect far too many historical episodes, which affected the limits rulers had in exercising their power in the distant past and thus be unable to provide a clear description of how these norms are set up and adopted.

4.2 Natural experiments

While interesting, these correlations do not provide a reliable test of the determinants of civic capital. To do so, the literature has relied on a combination of natural and field experiments. In what follows we will provide a brief description of the methodology and the findings.

4.2.1 History

As discussed in Section 2, large shocks to the benefits of cooperation can induce a change in the norms and beliefs that support cooperative behavior. History can provide some natural experiments in this sense.

One such a shock is represented by the collapse of the Holy Roman Empire at the beginning of the second millennium. As the opportunities for trade expanded, the North and South of Italy were subjected to two very different treatments. While the South was governed by an efficient and autocratic monarchy (the Norman Kings), the North was left in power vacuum. In some northern cities, the response to the lack of government was the formation of small groups of individuals who agreed with an informal pact to provide mutual help and collaborate to solve problems of common interest. Slowly, more stable institutions started to emerge from these agreements. In the mid-twelfth century, a new word came into use to describe them: "commune." The word *commune* is a synonym for republic (*res publica*, i.e.,common property) and is used with this meaning. This sense of responsibility for the common good that citizens of independent towns developed and consolidated over two centuries of self-government is the "civicness" Putnam refers to and the limits to the power of the executive that Acemoglu and Johnson (2005) deem necessary for development.

Putnam (1993) uses this historical episode to justify today's large differences in civic capital between the North and the South of Italy, which we reported in Figures 5 and 6. Appealing as it may seem, Putman's explanation is just an inference based on only two data points. In a recent contribution GSZ (2008b) try to overcome this problem.

Rather than just comparing civic capital between the North and South of Italy, GSZ exploit variation *within* the North. As Figure 8 shows, not all major cities located in the North at the turn of the first millennium actually became free cities: some did not and either remained under the control of the emperor (at least for a while) or fell under the control of one of feudal lords that survived the communal experience and that even gained power relative to the emperor. Furthermore, not all cities that became free cities enjoyed independence and self-government for the same length of time. GSZ exploit this variation to test whether civic capital today is affected by a distant episode in history. They find that Center-Northern cities that became free cities have significantly higher levels of civic capital today. For example, the number of voluntary associations is 25% higher in cities that were free city-states which is consistent with Putnam's conjecture.

This correlation by itself, however, is insufficient to attribute this variation to historical experience. History may be a proxy for some unobservable characteristics that affect both the chances a city became independent in the middle ages and the level of civic capital today. To address this problem, GSZ find two instruments that affect the cost of becoming independent at that time, but that are unlikely to affect the level of civic capital today: whether a city was the seat of a Bishop and whether the Etruscans had founded the city. The first variable captures the variation in the cost of coordination, since it is documented (Tabacco, 1987) that the presence of a bishop facilitated the necessary coordination of the prominent local families to provide the public goods and made it easier to transform a city into an independent commune. The second variable is a proxy for how easy a city was to defend. Since the Etruscans, a pre-Roman civilization, was organized as free city states, they chose to locate their cities in positions that were easy to defend.

Using two instruments GSZ are able to confirm that cities that became a commune have capital that is more civic today. Furthermore, since the affirmation of the Norman Kingdom in the South prevented the formation of free city-states in the area they can then test the validity of their instruments by looking at their effect there. That these instruments have no effect in the South suggests as GSZ find is evidence of the validity of the exclusion restriction, lending strong support to Putnam conjecture.

Nunn and Wantchekon (2009) provide a very interesting historical natural experiment of how civic capital can be destroyed. They focus on the slave trade to explain mistrust within Africa. They argue that today's level of trust among different African

Figure 8 ***Historical map of Italy around year 1167.*** The bold line marks the border of the Holy Roman Empire of Germany. All the towns marked with a full dot were commune. The Southern part of Italy, not belonging to the Empire was under the Norman Kingdom of Sicily.

ethnicities is the reflection of the past exposure to the risk of being captured and sold as slave between the 15th and early 19th centuries. Because of the high payoff of selling people to slave traders, indigenous groups sold even people of their same ethnic group, close friends, and relatives—those who are less likely to expect to be betrayed and are thus easier to be surprised. Nunn and Wantchekon (2009) argue that this engendered a climate of suspicion that may have resulted in an evolution of mistrust towards others and towards local leaders.

To assess the effects of this historical experience Nunn and Wantchekon (2009) use data from the 2005 wave of the Afrobarometer, a survey similar to the Eurobarometer and the World Values Survey that covers 17 African countries. They find that Africans whose ancestors faced a higher chance of being captured and sold as slaves today trust their relatives, neighbors, and local council less. This conclusion is further strengthened by instrumenting the intensity of the slave trade with the distance from the coast.

4.2.2 Geography

A second source of "natural" shocks to the benefit of cooperation is provided by geographical environments. The efficient exploitation of certain natural resources can only be achieved if several people, possibly a whole community, are willing to cooperate.

For example, in mountainous areas where the main crop is slow-growing trees it is impossible to support a fragmented land ownership without a very high degree of cooperation, since farmers need to take turns in cutting their trees and then pool and divide the proceeds. As Ostrom (1990) shows, this solution requires a considerable amount of cooperation and mutual trust. This experience of cooperation and trust, repeated over centuries, can increase the level of civic capital. By contrast, sheep breeding does not require any cooperation to be efficiently carried out. Shepherds can do most of the work alone or with the help of just a few relatives. In these areas, generalized trust is typically low and cooperatives are few.

Durante (2009) provides an example of this approach. He shows that areas of Europe with higher climate variability have higher level of trust. In his view, this correlation arises because climate variability generates a higher need for insurance, which can only be delivered if there is enough cooperation.

4.3 Field experiments

An alternative approach to identify the causal determinants of civic capital is field experiments. These experiments have the advantage of a truly exogenous and properly randomized treatment. However, they do not have the luxury of sustaining this treatment for a long period. To the extent that civic capital needs time to form, these experiments are bound to fail to find any effect.

One such an experiment took place within the Conditional Cash Transfer program (CCT) in Colombia called Familias en Acciòn. As part of its objectives, beneficiary mothers participate in the so-called '*Encuentros de Cuidado*' where they discuss topics of mutual interest and collaboration is encouraged. This experience can foster civic capital if treated people earn the benefits of mutual trust through experimentation and extrapolate this knowledge to other collective action decisions not directly subsidized by the program.

To test whether this is actually the case, Attanasio et al. (2009) compare people's behavior in a public good game between two similar villages, one treated with the CCT program for two years and the other not.[11] They find that the fraction of people who contribute to the public good is 30 percentage points larger in the treated village. This result is consistent with the hypothesis that people in the treated village accumulate civic capital, which becomes productive when an opportunity to use it arises.

Of course, there are caveats here as well. First, the treatment and control, while similar, were not randomly selected, though the results Attanasio et al. (2009) obtain are robust to controlling for observables. Second, it is unclear whether the observed difference in behavior is long lasting. What would happen if the program stopped? How long should the program last in order for the observed behavior to be ingrained into the culture of the beneficiaries? Thus, while field experiments may prove useful in addressing some of the questions about the formation of civic capital, they are unlikely to be able to replace field data that rely on large surveys and historical episodes.

5. THE ECONOMIC EFFECTS OF CIVIC CAPITAL

Civic capital as defined in this paper exhibits strong correlation with level-measures of economic development, such as GDP per capita. This is remarkable since economic models have proved able to explain at best only half of the massive differences in GDP per capita across countries with differences in (traditional) factor endowments. The other half is the Solow residual when applied to levels (instead of growth rates) of GDP and identifies the "measure of our ignorance" in the cross-sectional dimension (see Caselli (2005) for an excellent survey).

In an early attempt at finding the missing factor that could bridge the "measure of ignorance," Hall and Jones (1999) argue that one should focus on differences across countries in what they call *social infrastructure*, that is the set of institutions and government policies that result in "...an environment that supports productive activities and encourages capital accumulation, skill acquisition, invention, and technology transfer." Obviously, not only formal institutions of the sort first emphasized by North (1990) can contribute to provide such an environment but also informal mechanisms,

[11] The game was played in two stages. In each stage participants were given a token. They could keep the token or contribute it to the public good. Keeping it results in a $5 return; contributing it returns 40 cents for each person that contributes his token. Each experiment session gathers 25 people. Thus, if less than 12 contribute, not contributing is a dominant strategy. whatsoever. Free riding is always return maximizing. Social and private surplus is maximized if all contribute.

Table 7 Civic Capital and Social Infrastructure

Variables	Social infrastructure (1)	Log of labor productivity (2)
Trust toward strangers	0.393***	0.982*
	(0.128)	(0.506)
Violation	−0.003***	−0.009**
	(0.001)	(0.004)
Principal component civic values	0.037	0.204
	(0.037)	(0.158)
Constant	−0.214	7.252***
	(0.266)	(1.015)
Observations	40	38
R-squared	0.297	0.193

including the trust market participants have on each other and the cultural norms of respect for others they were educated to follow.

As Table 7 shows, there is a strong correlation between the measures of social infrastructure (as defined empirically by Hall and Jones (1999)) and our measures of civic capital. The same is true if we directly run the labor productivity (the dependent variable in Hall and Jones (1999)) and our measures of civic capital.

The empirical challenge is to find convincing sources of exogenous variation in our measures of civic capital that can overcome the potential failure of the exogeneity assumption either because civic capital may reflect the working of institutions (e.g., trust more where legal structure is better), or be correlated with unobserved factors that also affect performance (e.g., education quality), or because it is at least partially reverse-caused by current economic forces (Glaeser, Laibson, and Sacerdote (2002)).

As noticed by Durlauf (2002), one impediment to the search of valid instruments is that while these papers "...often employ instrumental variables to account for the endogeneity of social capital [they] typically do not incorporate a separate theory of the determinants of social capital formation..." and thus "one cannot have much confidence that unobserved heterogeneity is absent in the samples under study."

5.1 Civic capital and identification

One of the advantages of narrowing down the definition of social capital to the set of cultural norms and beliefs that make cooperation among individuals easier is that it can help pin down the causal economic effects of civic capital by suggesting potential identification strategies. As we showed in Section 3, this definition of civic capital allows itself to be incorporated into standard economic models that provide explanations of its accumulation, which can be used to provide identification restrictions when testing the effects of social capital on economic outcomes.

In much of the literature that studies the effect of social capital on economic performance, a key problem is how to separate the effect of social capital from that of formal institutions. As the model by Tabellini (2008b) implies, the cultural values that promote cooperation and exchange and pro-market institutions are complementary, implying that countries with strong values and high trust also choose institutions that support these values making them attractive to the population. Hence, in cross-countries estimates it is hard to distinguish between the effect of social capital on income per capita (or growth) from that of institutions.

The work by Knack and Keefer (1997)—which has the great merit of having brought to economists' attention the potential relevance of trust beliefs and civic capital for understanding cross-country differences in economic success—is a good example of this problem. They use cross country variation in GDP levels and growth, and in levels of generalized trust and civic capital from the WVS (similar to the ones discussed in Section 4) and find that indeed countries with higher GDP per capita and higher growth rates do indeed have higher civic capital and higher levels of trust. Higher trust does not necessarily reflect an effect of cultural norms as it may capture better institutional design: in countries with stronger legal protection, it is natural that people trust each other more, and so trust may be picking up the effect of better institutions rather than higher civic capital. Controlling for institutional quality (as they indeed do) may not suffice to capture the effect if institutions are not properly measured or some relevant dimension of institutions is not controlled for. Instrumenting trust with ethno-linguistic diversity, as Knack and Keefer (1997) do, could in principle provide a way out but raises the issue of what is the basis for excluding ethno-linguistic diversity from the growth regression and for arguing that it is a good causal predictor of cultural capital. Absent a theory of social capital formation, it is hard to tell.

Inspired by the notion of civic capital and the theoretical models of Section 3, the recent literature has followed two approaches to deal with this issue. The first relies on the theoretically grounded link between past political institutions and current cultural traits to find appropriate instruments. The second is based on movers and the idea of "cultural portability." A third, less developed approach that has been followed relies on field experiments. We discuss them in turn.

5.1.1 Past history as a source of instruments

As discussed in Section 4 long-term historical episodes are a casual source of civic capital accumulation and, if properly isolated, they can be good candidates for acting as instruments for today norms and beliefs shared by a community. In fact, since culture is transmitted slowly from one generation to the next, distant but relevant historical episodes can have predictive power on today's norms and beliefs.

This is the strategy followed by Tabellini (2009) to identify the effect of civic capital on economic growth and development. As we have discussed in Section 4. Tabellini (2009) shows that differences across regions of Europe in the current endowment of civic capital can be explained by differences in long-term history, such as the literacy rates that prevailed at the end of the 19th century and indicators of political institutions in the period from 1600 to 1850. Using these measures as instruments, he finds that regions with higher endowments of civic capital have higher GDP per capita today and have experienced faster GDP growth. The contribution of civic capital is also large, as it can explain much of the difference in GDP per capita between Lombardy—one of the most economically developed regions of Italy—and the backward regions in the Italian South, and contribute half of a percentage point to the growth differential of the two areas between 1977 and 2001.

Since Tabellini (2009) uses regional variation and these regions are part of countries with common institutional design, he can exclude that civic capital captures the effect of *formal* institutions as country fixed effects absorb them. Furthermore, controls for current levels of education and for the historical level of economic development suggest that civic capital is unlikely to reflect persistent differences in human capital and in productivity. The key for identification is that the historical instruments do not have a direct effect on today's output but affect the latter only because they affected the cultural traits of these populations centuries ago which are then reflected—through intergenerational transmission—in today's culture. We will return to this assumption below.

GSZ (2008b) rely on a similar strategy to identify the effect of civic capital on average per capita income. After having shown that a history of communal independence explains differences across cities in the North of Italy, they use this variation to identify the effect of civic capital on GDP per capita in year 2001, instrumenting today's civic capital with the history of independence. Indeed, they find that differences in civic capital can explain a good fraction of the differences in income per capita across towns in the North of Italy, as shown in Figure 9. Since they look at variation across cities of an area that has long shared the same formal institutions, they can exclude that differences in civic capital reflect differences in institutions rather than in shared values and beliefs. However, while both in Tabellini (2009) and GSZ (2008b), one can rule out that civic capital reflects differences in formal institutions, one cannot exclude that differences in culture across regions capture differences in the *actual performance* of institutions that are formally the same (this possibility is less likely in GSZ (2008b) since the area they look at is also quite homogeneous along these dimensions).

There is however a more serious problem with this approach that invests the validity of the exclusion restriction for the instrument(s) for civic capital. For the instruments to be valid, it must be that the historical episodes that built up civic capital did not at the same time foster the accumulation of other forms of capital that have

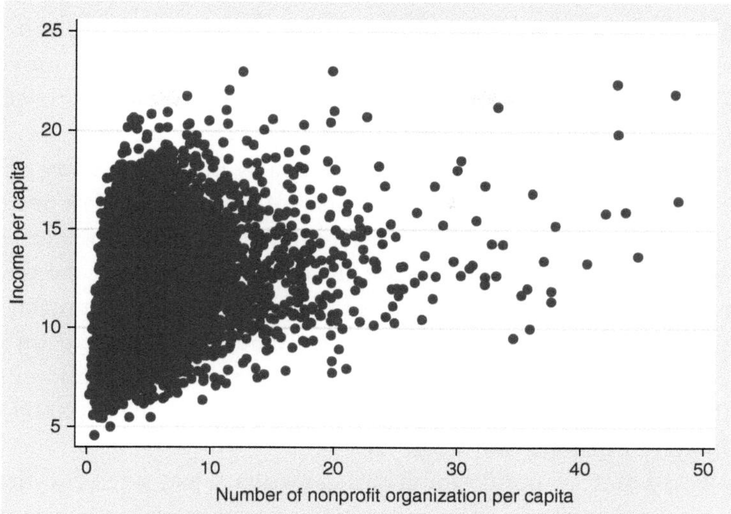

Figure 9 The effect of social capital on income per capita across cities in Northern Italy.

lasted up to today and still exert a direct effect on income. For instance, in the GSZ (2008b) context, having been a free city in the 13th century may have resulted in accumulated assets of some sort that still *directly* affect income today, besides affecting it indirectly because of its boost on civic capital. Using the Bishop city and the Etruscan city indicators, which proved to be good instruments for the historical determinants of civic capital, is not a solution either. In fact, even if they affect civic capital only because they facilitated the emergence of the free city (and thus qualify as instruments in a civic capital regression), they also boosted all the unobservable assets that may continue to affect a city's income today (which may invalidate them as instruments in an income regression). The only way to account for this is to obtain direct measures of these assets and try to control for them.[12] The general point is that historical shocks to civic capital could have also shocked other types of capital that are as persistent as civic capital and which may have an independent, direct effect on income.

5.1.2 Movers and cultural portability as an identification strategy

An alternative strategy to identify the effect of civic capital on economic outcomes and separate it from the effect that institutions—both their design and their actual functioning—have on the economy is to rely on one unique feature of cultural norms and beliefs that is embedded in the models of Section 3: once ingrained in the brain of

[12] For instance, GSZ (2008) address this issue by controlling for the most likely type of asset (besides social capital) that free cities created and that still generates income: historical attractions and arts that result in a richer tourist industry in the city, captured by the number of annual visitors to the city (scaled by population).

individuals norms and beliefs tend to move with them and continue to affect their actions when people locate in a new environment, where different norms and beliefs prevail. On the other hand, institutions are not portable: they do not move with *single* individuals as they leave their country or region, though they can be transplanted when *many* people move to colonize a new country. Therefore focusing on movers' and using information on the prevailing norms and beliefs in their country of origin, one can separate the effect of civic capital from that of institutions. The institutions that matter are those of the country or region where the person lives; the norms and beliefs that matter—given cultural persistence—are *also* those of the place were the person originates. This approach, known sometimes as the epidemiological approach (Fernandez, 2007), has been successfully used in the recent emerging literature on culture and economics to identify the effect of other cultural norms on economic outcomes e.g., by Carroll, Rhee C, and Rhee B, (1999), GSZ (2004), Giuliano (2007), Ichino and Maggi (2000), and Fernandez and Fogli (2009).[13]

There are two points to notice about this approach. First, since also the norms and beliefs of the place where the person interacts may matter for his/her economic decisions, this approach is likely to provide a lower bound estimate of the effect of civic capital. Second, the set of norms and beliefs that foster cooperation may even be caused by the institutions in the country of origin (which would be consistent with Tabellini (2008a), finding that trust attitudes of third generation U.S. immigrants is explained by the political institutions prevailing around or before 1900 in the ancestor's country of origin), but if they affect mover's behavior in the country of destination it is because beliefs and norms matter independently of the institutions that forged them.

GSZ (2004) rely on this idea to identify the effect of civic capital on financial development, measured by the intensity people rely on financial markets. The authors use data on individual Italian investors and their reliance on financial instruments, knowing where they live and make their decisions as well as their place of birth. This allows them to identify the movers. The great variation in civic capital within Italy, illustrated in Figures 5 and 6, offers a good opportunity for testing while the fact that they rely on within country variation implies that formal institutions are held constant. Thanks to the presence of movers, differences in the actual working of institutions—such as the efficiency of the local courts, which may affect people's beliefs and their choices as well, and that were a problematic issue with the previous strategy—can be perfectly controlled for by inserting dummies for the place where they live and make decisions.

[13] Several studies do indeed document that cultural norms and beliefs are carried over when people move and persists in the new environment. Rice and Feldman (1997) and Putnam (2000) document that the civic values of US-immigrants are correlated with those in the country of origin of their ancestors and Guiso, Sapienza, and Zingales (2006) show that trust of second generation immigrants to the US varies with the country of origin of the ancestors and is strongly correlated with trust currently prevailing their. Uslaner (2008) provides similar evidence but adds that the generalized trust of today's Americans depends more strongly on the trust inherited from their ancestors than on the trust of the people they currently live close to.

They find that civic capital in the province where movers come from has very strong effects on the use and availability of financial contracts in the province where they live: people that moved from provinces with higher civic capital make larger investments in stocks, rely more on checks to settle transactions and have an easier access to the loans market, consistent with this people being willing to take more social risk as they trust more and to deserve more credit for being more trustworthy.

These results also help us better understand the channels through which higher civic capital can result in higher GDP per capita: because it fosters financial development and, through it, economic growth. This result is also consistent with Osili and Paulson (2004) which finds that participation in stock markets of second generation Americans depends on the institutions in the ancestors' country of origin which have promoted cultural beliefs conducive to higher trust and by GSZ (2008a) who find that in a sample of Dutch investors people who trust more invest more in stocks.

In a recent contribution, Algan and Cahuc (2010) make an ingenious use of the movers approach to obtain time variation in trust, which they then use to eliminate the unobserved formal and informal institutions that pose identification problems in cross-country regressions. To describe this strategy, consider the nature of the problem in a cross-country regression of income per capita at time t in country c:

$$Y_{ct} = \alpha_0 + \alpha_1 S_{ct} + \alpha_2 X_{ct} + \alpha_3 F_c + \alpha_4 F_t + \nu_{ct}$$

where S_{ct} is a measure of civic capital such as trust as measured in the WVS, that (by assumption) varies across countries and over time, X_{ct} is a vector of controls that vary across countries and over time and F_c and F_t are country and time fixed effects which absorb the effects on per capita GDP of time-invariant institutions and factor endowments and aggregate time varying productivity. Obviously, what matters for output at time t is the civic capital prevailing at time t (i.e., the set of norms and beliefs of the generation that is currently active in the labor market).

The problem with this regression is that those norms and beliefs are most likely correlated with the contemporaneous error term ν_{ct} – for instance because positive current shocks to productivity, particularly if permanent, also affect the level of trust of the current generation. However, due to cultural persistence and the fact that values and priors of the current generation (the one responsible for today's GDP) are acquired from the previous generation, if one could observe the trust of the previous generation—call it S^I_{ct}—one could use it to replace S_{ct} in the GDP per capita regression. Since these are the beliefs of the previous generation and they where transmitted when today GDP was not yet produced, it is reasonable to assume they are orthogonal to ν_{ct}.

The clever idea of Algan and Cahuc (2010) is to use the attitudes of different cohorts of second-generation Americans whose ancestors migrated from various countries to obtain an estimate of the inherited component of the beliefs of the active generation in each of the countries of origin. In fact, the beliefs of, say, today's Italians living in Italy are correlated with the beliefs of second-generation Americans of Italian origin. However, while the beliefs of the Italian population have evolved according to what has happened in Italy meanwhile, those of Italian-Americans only respond to shocks to the U.S. economy. Hence, it should be the case that they are orthogonal to the error term in the GDP regression. Inherited trust is estimated for two (benchmark) periods, 1935–38 and 2000–2003, using data from U.S. General Social Survey and information on the age and ancestry of the respondents, under the assumption of a generation gap of 25 years.[14] They then attach these estimates to each of the countries in their sample and run a regression for GDP per capita as:

$$Y_{ct} = \alpha_0 + \alpha_1 S^I_{ct} + \alpha_2 X_{ct} + \alpha_3 F_c + \alpha_4 F_t + \nu_{ct}$$

where t includes data on GDP per capita in 1935 and 2000 (using a 10-year centered average).

Since the regressions include country fixed effects, any persistent difference across countries that affects both its productivity and its cultural norms and beliefs such as the nature and quality of its institutions is captured by these fixed effects, and only the time variation in inherited trust is used to identify the causal effect of civic capital on income. Controlling also for changes in the quality of institutions and changes in education (to make sure that changes in inherited attitudes do not reflect remote changes in these variables), they find that civic capital has a positive and statistically significant effect on GDP per capita. Furthermore, these effects are also sizeable, as illustrated in Figure 10, which reproduces Algan and Cahuc's (2010) Figure 6, which shows the percent change in per capita GDP relatively to the level observed in 2000–2003 that a country would have experienced if the level of inherited trust in that country were the same as the ones inherited by the current Swedes. For instance, GDP per capita in Russia and Mexico would have been around 60% higher had these countries inherited as much trust as the Swedes, lending support to the famous statement by Kenneth Arrow (1972) who wrote "... it can be plausibly argued that much of the economic backwardness in the world can be explained by the lack of mutual confidence" (p. 357).[15]

[14] With the information available in the GSS Algan and Cahuc (2010) can identify second, third and fourth generation American-born with foreign ancestors. They use the beliefs of all to obtain their estimates of inherited trust. Inherited trust in 1935–1938 reflects the beliefs of second generation Americans born before 1910 (i.e., whose parents arrived for sure one generation before 1935) of third generation Americans born before 1935 and of fourth generation Americans born before 1960. In the same way, inherited attitudes in 2000–2003 are those inherited by: second generation Americans born between 1910 and 1975, by third generation born after 1935 and by fourth generation Americans born after 1960.

[15] Of course, as in GSZ also in this case this strategy is likely to yield a lower bound estimate of civic capital since the estimated effects only uses the inherited component of trust.

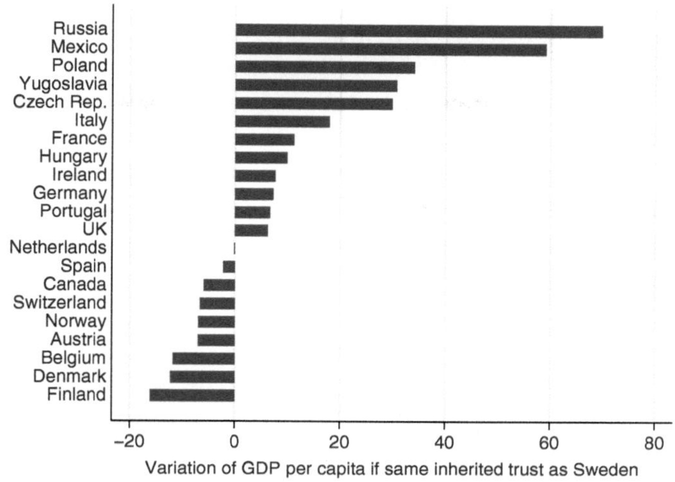

Figure 10 ***The causal effect of civic capital on per capita GDP.*** The figure shows the predicted variations in GDP per capita over the period 2000–2003 in a given country if it had the same level of inherited social attitudes as Sweden, as estimated by Algan and Cahuc (2010).

5.1.3 Using field experiments to identify the effect of civic capital

A third and so far less investigated strategy to identify the economic effects of civic capital are to rely on field experiments where one obtains both measures of civic values which can be contrasted with observed behavior. A good example of how this strategy can be used is offered by Karlan (2005) who uses a field experiment conducted on a sample of borrowers that participated in the Peruvian microcredit program Foundation for International Community Assistance.

Karlan (2005) first obtains experimental measures of trustworthiness from a trust game as discussed in Section 3, and finds that players identified as trust-worthier in the game are more likely to repay their loans one year later. This result is consistent with the idea that because civic capital disciplines borrowers and investors behaviors, it promotes financial development and, through this channel, economic development. Furthermore, since the measures of trustworthiness that Karlan (2005) uses are obtained from a field experiment were institutions play no role by construction, differences in trustworthiness across individuals can only reflect differences in the preferences and values that people have and that result in different incentives to default. This evidence further provides support that higher civic capital has economic real effects.

What is missing in Karlan (2005) is the link between the behaviour of the receiver in the trust game and its underlying values. Butler et al. (2009) provides such a link. They run a trust game experiment and in a separate questionnaire they ask participants in the experiment to report how much effort on a scale between 0 and 10 their parents put in teaching them a set of civic values such as always behave as a model citizen (e.g., by not throwing trash on the ground) or be fair with others. They find that players whose parents put more efforts in teaching civic values are more trustworthy when playing as receivers in the trust game.

In sum, we believe that much progress has been made to pin down the causal effects of civic capital on economic outcomes and identification strategies have benefited from the narrower definition of social capital and the simultaneous theoretical advances that have followed. None of the strategies is free of problems but they do not seem more serious than the ones one meets when addressing issues of causality in other domains—such as, for instance, the estimation of production functions. Each of these strategies has its merits and shortcomings; so for instance, field experiments are likely to provide more controlled evidence but while they can speak about the channels through which civic capital may affect the economy, they are likely to be less useful at providing estimates of its overall effect on a country output. The other two approaches, though exposed to stronger exogeneity requirements, are better designed to provide such an estimate.

6. CONCLUSIONS

The growing literature on social capital has been plagued by ambiguity on what social capital is. This ambiguity has made it difficult for this concept to be fully accepted in the mainstream economic debate. In this chapter, we propose a narrower definition of social capital that satisfies the criteria for an economic definition of capital (Solow, 1995) and clearly differentiates social capital from physical and human capital. We argue that this so-defined civic capital is an important omitted factor of production. In fact, it can help explain the Solow residuals when applied to levels (instead of growth rates) of GDP.

While we consider this avenue very promising, we are very aware that much remains to be done. First, our definition is still far from delivering measures that can be readily used in national accounts. The most promising component of such a measure is trust. Trust is well-founded economically, it is easy to measure, and seems to be correlated with the variables of interests. Other survey-based measures of values seem less satisfactory. While some outcome-based measures look promising, more work needs to be done to obtain reliable and consistent measures.

The second important area for future research is the mechanisms through which civic capital accumulates and depreciates. The evidence gathered so far seems to suggest that a positive shock to the benefits of cooperation can have effects that last several centuries. What ensures such a high degree of persistence, however, remains unclear. A better understanding of these mechanisms is crucial if we want to think about designing policies that might foster the formation and preservation of civic capital. However, a better understanding is also crucial in avoiding policies that, while producing short-term benefits, undermine civic capital, with negative long-term effects. For example, a tax pardon, which grants immunity for past tax evasions in exchange for a small fee, can be a very smart fiscal policy in the short term, since it will increase tax revenues without increasing the marginal tax rates, but it might deteriorate the stock of civic capital of a nation, with very negative long-term consequences.

The political economy of civic capital formation is per se a very important and unexplored area for future research. In a democracy with periodic elections and frequent turnover, the politicians' horizon will be short, much shorter than the time of formation of civic capital. This might explain why it is so difficult for a country to accumulate civic capital and why it remains low even among some economically developed countries.

REFERENCES

Acemoglu, D., Johnson, S.H., 2005. Unbundling Institutions. J. Polit. Econ. 113, 949–995.

Acemoglu, D., Johnson, S., Robinson, J., 2001. The Colonial Origins of Comparative Development: An Empirical Investigation. Am. Econ. Rev. 91 (5), 1369–1401.

Aghion, P., Algan, Y., Cahuc, P., Shleifer, A., 2010. Regulation and Distrust. Q. J. Econ. 125 (3), 1015–1049.

Alesina, A., La Ferrara, E., 2002. Who Trusts Others? J. Public Econ. 85 (2), 207–234.

Alesina, A., Devleeschauwer, A., Easterly, W., Kurlat, S., Wacziarg, R., 2003. Fractionalization. J. Econ. Growth 8, 155–194.

Alesina, A., Giuliano, P., 2007. The power of the family. J. Econ. Growth 15, 93–125. DOI:10.1007/s10887-010-9052-z.

Alesina, A., Giuliano, P., 2010. The Power of the Family. J. Econ. Growth forthcoming.

Algan, Y., Cahuc, P., 2010. Inhereted Trust and Growth. Am. Econ. Rev. forthcoming.

Almond, G., Verba, S., 1963. The Civic Culture: Political Attitudes and Democracy in Five Nations. Princeton University Press, Princeton, NJ.

Attanasio, O., Pellerano, L., Polanía Reyes, S., 2009. Building Trust? Conditional Cash Transfer Programmes and Social Capital. Fisc. Stud., Institute for Fiscal Studies 30 (2), 139–177.

Banfield, E.C., 1958. The Moral Basis of a Backward Society. Free Press, New York.

Baran, N., Sapienza, P., Zingales, L., 2010. Can we infer social preferences from the lab? Evidence from the trust game. NBER Working Paper 15654, January.

Becker, G., 1964. Human Capital: A Theoretical and Empirical Analysis, with Special Reference to Education. University of Chicago Press, Chicago.

Berg, J., Dickhaut, J., McCabe, K., 1995. Trust, Reciprocity and Social History. Games Econ. Behav. 10, 122–142.

Benavot, A., Riddle, P., 1988. The Expansion of Primary Education, 1870–1940: Trends and Issues. Sociol. Educ. 61 (3), 191–210.

Ben-Porath, Y., 1967. The Production of Human Capital and the Life Cycle of Earnings. J. Polit. Econ. 75 (4), 352–365.

Bisin, A., Verdier, T., 2000. Beyond the Melting Pot: Cultural Transmission, Marriage and the Evolution of Ethnic and Religious Traits. Q. J. Econ. 115 (3), 955–988.

Bisin, A., Verdier, T., 2001. The Economics of Cultural Transmission and the Evolution of Preferences. J. Econ. Theory 97 (1), 298–319.

Bisin, A., Topa, G., Verdier, T., 2004. Cooperation as a Transmitted Cultural Trait. Working paper. New York University.

Bloom, N., Sadun, R., Van Reenen, J., The organization of firms across countries. NBER Working Paper No. 15129.

Bohnet, I., Zeckhauser, R., 2004. Trust Risk and Betrayal. J. Econ. Behav. Organ. 55, 467–484.

Bohnet, I., Greig, F., Herrmann, B., Zeckhauser, R., 2008. Betrayal Aversion: Evidence from Brazil, China, Oman, Switzerland, Turkey and the United States. Am. Econ. Rev. 98, 294–310.

Bourdieu, P., 1972. Outline of a Theory of Practice. Cambridge University Press, Cambridge.
Bourdieu, P., 1986. The forms of capital. In: Richardson, J.G. (Ed.), Handbook of Theory and Research for the Sociology of Education. Greenwood Press, New York, 241–258.
Bourgois, P., 1995. In Search of Respect: Selling Crack in El Barrio. Cambridge University Press, New York.
Butler, J., Giuliano, P., Guiso, L., 2009. The Right Amount of Trust. NBER working paper 15344.
Camerer, C., Fehr, E., 2003. Measuring Social Norms and Preferences using Experimental Games: A Guide for Social Scientists. In: Boyd, H., Camerer, B., Gintis, F., McElreath, (Eds.), Foundations of Human Sociality – Experimental and Ethnographic Evidence from 15 Small-Scale Societies. Working Paper version at: http://www.iew.unizh.ch/wp/iewwp097.pdf.
Carpenter, J., Seki, E., Do social preferences increase productivity? Field experimental evidence from fishermen in Toyama Bay. Econ. Inq. no. doi: 10.1111/j.1465-7295.2009.00268.x.
Caselli, F., 2005. Accounting for Cross-Country Income Differences. In: Aghion, P., Durlauf, S. (Eds.) Handbook of Economic Growth. North Holland, Amsterdam.
Carroll, C.D., Rhee, C., Rhee, B., 1999. Does Cultural Origin Affect Saving Behavior? Evidence from Immigrants. Econ. Dev. Cult. Change 48 (1), 33–50.
Coleman, J., 1990. Foundations of Social Theory. Harvard University Press, Cambridge MA.
Dessì, R., Ogilvie, S., 2004. The Political Economy of Merchant Guilds: Commitment or Collusion?
Djankov, S., Glaeser, E., La Porta, R., Lopez-de-Silanes, F., Shleifer, A., 2003. The New Compartive Economics. J. Comp. Econ. 31, 595–619.
Durante, R., 2009. Risk, Cooperation and the Economic Origins of Social Trust: An Empirical Investigation. Working Paper.
Durlauf, S.N., Fafchamps, 2005. Social Capital. In: Handbook of Economic Growth. North Holland, Amsterdam.
Durlauf, S., 2002. On the Empirics of Social Capital. Econ. J. 112, 459–479.
Fernandez, R., 2007. Women, Work and Culture. J. Eur. Econ. Assoc. 5 (2–3), 305–332.
Fernandez, R., Fogli, A., 2009. Culture: An Empirical Investigation of Beliefs, Work and Fertility. American Economic Journal: Macroeconomics 1 (1), 146–177.
Fehr, E., Leibbrandt, A., 2008. Cooperativeness and Impatience in the Tragedy of the Commons. IZA DP 3625.
Fehr, E., 2009. On the Economics and Biology of Trust. Presidential address at the 2008 meeting of the European Economic Association J. Eur. Econ. Assoc.
Fisman, R., Miguel, E., 2007. Corruption, Norms and Legal Enforcement: Evidence from Diplomatic Parking Tickets. J. Polit. Econ. 115 (6), 1020–1048.
Fountain, J.E., 1997. Social capital: A Key Enabler of Innovation in Science and Technology. In: Branscomb, L.M., Keller, J. (Eds.), Investing in Innovation: Toward a Consensus Strategy for Federal Technology Policy. MIT Press, Cambridge MA.
Frank, R., Gilovich, T., Regan, D., 1993. Does Studying Economics Inhibit Cooperation? J. Econ. Perspect. 7, 159–171.
Fukuyama, F., 1995. Trust: The Social Virtues and the Creation of Prosperity. Free Press, New York.
Gambetta, D., 2000. Can We Trust Trust? In: Gambetta, D. (Ed.), Trust: Making and Breaking Cooperative Relations. University of Oxford, Oxford, 213–237.
Gilboa, I., Postlewaite, A., Schmeidler, D., 2004. Rationality of Belief. Or Why Bayesianism is Neither Necessary Nor Sufficient for Rationality. PIER Working Paper No. 04–011; Cowles Foundation Discussion Paper No. 1484.
Giuliano, P., 2007. Living Arrangements in Western Europe: Does Cultural Origin Matter? J. Eur. Econ. Assoc. 5 (5), 927–952.
Glaeser, E.L., Sacerdote, B., Scheinkman, J.A., 1995. Crime and Social Interactions. Q. J. Econ. 111, 507–548.
Glaeser, E.L., Laibson, D., Sacerdote, B., 2002. An Economic Approach to Social Capital. Economic Journal 112, 437–458.
Goldin, C., Katz, L., 2001. Human Capital and Social Capital: the Rise of Secondary Schooling in America, 1910–1940. In: Rotberg, R. (Ed.), Patterns of Social Capital. Cambridge University Press, Cambridge.

Greif, A., 1993. Contract Enforceability and Economic Institutions in Early Trade: the Maghribi Traders' Coalition. Amer. Econ. Rev. 83 (3), 525–548.
Grootaert, C., Narayan, D., Nyhan Jones, V., Woolcock, M., 2005. Measuring Social Capital: An Integrated Questionnaire. World Bank working paper 18.
Guiso, L., Sapienza, P., Zingales, L., 2003. People's Opium? Religion and Economic Attitudes. J. Monet. Econ. 50 (1), 225–282.
Guiso, L., Sapienza, P., Zingales, L., 2004. The Role of Social Capital in Financial Development. Am. Econ. Rev. 94 (3), 526–556.
Guiso, L., Sapienza, P., Zingales, L., 2006. Does Culture Affect Economic Outcomes? J. Econ. Perspect. 20, 23–48.
Guiso, L., Sapienza, P., Zingales, L., 2008a. Trusting the Stock Market. J. Finance 63 (6), 2557–2600.
Guiso, L., Sapienza, P., Zingales, L., 2008b. Long-Term Persistence. NBER Working Paper W14278.
Guiso, L., Sapienza, P., Zingales, L., 2008c. Social Capital as Good Culture. J. Eur. Econ. Assoc. 6 (2–3), 295–320.
Guiso, L., Sapienza, P., Zingales, L., 2009. Cultural Biases in Economic Exchange? Q. J. Econ. 3 (124), 1095–1131.
Guiso, L., Zingales, L., 2007. The Value of Social Networks in Bank Lending. University of Chicago. mimeo.
Hall, R.E., Jones, C.I., 1999. Why do some countries produce so much more output per worker than others? Q. J. Econ. 114 (1), 83–116.
Hochberg, Y.V., Ljungqvist, A., Lu, Y., 2007. Whom you know matters: Venture capital networks and investment performance. J. Finance 62, 251–301.
Hoffman, E., McCabe, K., Shachat, K., Smith, V., 1994. Preferences, Property Rights, and Anonymity in Bargaining Games. Games Econ. Behav. 7, 346–380.
Ichino, A., Maggi, G., 2000. Work Environment and Individual Background: Explaining Regional Shirking Differentials in a Large Italian Firm. Q. J. Econ. 115 (3), 1057–1090.
Karlan, D., 2005. Using Experimental Economics to Measure Social Capital and Predict Financial Decisions. Am. Econ. Rev. 95, 1688–1699.
Knack, S., Keefer, P., 1997. Does social capital have an economic impact? A cross-country investigation. Q. J. Econ. 112 (4), 1252–1288.
Knack, S., Zak, P., 1999. Trust and Growth. Claremont University Working Paper.
La Porta, R., Lopez de Silanes, F., Shleifer, A., Vishny, R., 1997. Trust in Large Organizations. Am. Econ. Rev. 87 (2), 333–338.
La Porta, R., Lopez de Silanes, F., Shleifer, A., Vishny, R., 1998. Law and Finance. J. Polit. Econ. 1131–1150.
La Porta, R., López de Silanes, F., Shleifer, A., Vishny, R., 1999. The Quality of Government. Journal of Law Economics and Organizations 15, 222–279.
Loury, G.C., 1977. A dynamic theory of racial income differences. In: Wallace, P.A., La Mond, A.M. (Eds.), Women, Minorities, and Employment Discrimination. Lexington Books, Lexington MA, 153–186.
Levitt, S.D., List, J.A., 2007. What Do Laboratory Experiments Measuring Social Preferences Reveal About the Real World? J. Econ. Perspect. 21 (2), 153–174.
Miller, A.S., Mitamura, T., 2003. Are Surveys on Trust Trustworthy? Soc. Psychol. Q. 66, 62–70.
Naef, M., Schupp, J., 2009. Can we Trust the Trust Game? A Comprehensive Examination. Working Paper 5. Royal Holloway College, London.
North, D.C., 1990. Institutions, Institutional Change and Economic Performance. Cambridge University Press, Cambridge.
Nunn, N., Wantchekon, L., 2009. The Slave Trade and the Origins of Mistrust in Africa. Am. Econ. Rev. forthcoming.
Ostrom, E., 1990. Governing the Commons: The Evolution of Institutions for Collective Action. Cambridge University Press, Cambridge.
Osili, U.O., Paulson, A., 2004. Institutional Quality and Financial Market Development: Evidence from International Migrants in the U.S., Federal Reserve Bank of Chicago WP, 2004–2019.

Portes, A., 1998. Social Capital: Its Origins and Applications in Modern Sociology. Annu. Rev. Sociol. 24, 1–24.

Putnam, R.D., 1993. Making Democracy Work. Princeton University Press, Princeton NJ.

Putnam, R., 2000. Bowling alone: The collapse and revival of American community. Simon and Schuster, New York.

Rice, T.W., Feldman, J., 1997. Civic Culture and Democracy from Europe to America. J. Polit. 59, 1143–1172.

Rosenthal, R., 1976. Experimenter effects in behavioral research (enlarged ed.). Irvington Publishers, New York.

Reuben, E., Sapienza, P., Zingales, L., 2009. Is Mistrust Self-Fulfilling? Econ. Lett. 100, 89–91.

Sapienza, P., Toldrà, A., Zingales, L., 2008. Understanding Trust. Working Paper.

Sapienza, P., Zingales, L., 2009. The Chicago Booth/Kellogg School Financial Trust Index dataset. http://www.financialtrustindex.org/.

Solow, R., 1995. Trust: The Social Virtues and the Creation of Prosperity (Book Review). New Repub. 213, 36–40.

Spagnolo, G., 1999. Social Relations and Cooperation in Organizations. J. Econ. Behav. Organ. 38, 1–25.

Tabellini, G., 2008a. Institutions and Culture. J. Eur. Econ. Assoc. Presidential Lecture to the European Economic Association.

Tabellini, G., 2008b. The Scope of Cooperation: Values and Incentives. Q. J. Econ. 905–950.

Tabellini, G., 2009. Culture and institutions: economic development in the regions of Europe. J. Eur. Econ. Assoc. forthcoming.

Tabacco, G., 1987. La città vescovile nell'alto Medioevo. In: Rossi, P., Comunita', E. (Eds.), Modelli di città. Strutture e funzioni politiche, Torino, pp. 327–345.

Tatro, Q., 2009. Madoff's Far-reaching Fallout, Minyanville Markets http://www.minyanville.com/businessmarkets/articles/C-SKF-all-APPL-qid/1/12/2009/id/20613.

Uslaner, E.M., 2008. Where You Stand Depends Upon Where Your Grandparents Sat: The Inheritability of Generalized Trust. Public Opin. Q. 72.

Wasserman, S., Faust, K., 1997. Social network analysis: methods and applications. Published/Created: Cambridge University Press, Cambridge; New York.

Yamagishi, T., Kikuchi, M., Kosugi, M., 1999. Trust gullibility and social intelligence. Asian Journal of Social Psychology 2 (1), 145–161.

CHAPTER 11

Does Culture Matter?

Raquel Fernández
New York University, CEPR, NBER, IZA

Contents

1. Introduction 482
2. Some Preliminaries 483
   2.1 Some experimental evidence 488
3. The Epidemiological Approach 489
   3.1 An example 492
      3.1.1 A simple model *492*
      3.1.2 Empirical issues *494*
4. The Epidemiological Literature in Economics 497
   4.1 Women's work, fertility, and gender preferences 497
   4.2 Family ties, political engagement, and labor market regulation 499
   4.3 Corruption, redistribution, and violence 501
   4.4 Within-country migration: shirking and financial participation 503
   4.5 Cultural change and changes in economic outcomes 504
5. Concluding Questions and Remarks 506
Acknowledgement 508
References 508

Abstract

This paper reviews the literature on culture and economics, focusing primarily on the epidemiological approach. The epidemiological approach studies the variation in outcomes across different immigrant groups residing in the same country. Immigrants presumably differ in their cultures but share a common institutional and economic environment. This allows one to separate the effect of culture from the original economic and institutional environment. This approach has been used to study a variety of issues, including female labor force participaiton, fertility, labor market regulation, redistribution, growth, and financial development among others.
JEL Nos: O10, Z1, D01, D1

Keywords

Culture
Beliefs
Preferences
Norms

Handbook of Social Economics, Volume 1A
ISSN 0169-7218, DOI: 10.1016/S0169-7218(11)01011-2

1. INTRODUCTION

Societies differ markedly in their economic outcomes. This is evidenced in a variety of ways: from different choices of redistributive policies and social security provisions to differences in aggregate outcomes such as average savings rates, fertility rates, or women's participation rate in the formal labor market. As shown in cross-country opinion polls, social attitudes also vary. On average, across countries people hold different views of, for example, the role that luck versus merit plays in generating income, the degree of social obligation one has towards others, or the importance of thrift as a moral virtue. These differences in social attitudes tend to be correlated with the differences in cross-country economic outcomes. For example, countries in which people value thrift also tend to have higher savings rates. Guiso, Sapienza, and Zingales (2006) find that a one-standard-deviation increase in the share of people who value thriftiness is associated with an increase in the national saving rate of 1.8 percentage points.[1] Similarly, countries that hold a more traditional view of women's role tend to have lower female labor force participation and higher fertility. For example, using attitude data from the World Value Survey (WVS), one finds that the percentage of individuals in a country that think that housework is as fulfilling as having a job is negatively and significantly correlated with female labor force participation (LFP) across countries.[2] Lastly, countries in which people tend to think that luck plays a fundamental role in the income process also have higher redistribution. Alesina and Angeletos (2005) show that the share of respondents in each country who believe that luck determines income is highly correlated with that country's spending in social welfare as a proportion of GDP.

Is the correlation between social attitudes and economic outcomes due entirely to economic and institutional differences across societies or are potentially systematic differences in social beliefs playing a causal role? More generally, what role do differences in the distribution of social preferences and beliefs (what I will henceforth call *culture*) play in explaining the variation in economic outcomes be it at the level of countries, social groups (e.g., ethnic or socioeconomic groups), or over time?

For a long period of time, questions regarding the role of culture in economic outcomes were largely absent in economic research. This was primarily the result of the absence of an empirical methodology that would allow one to investigate this issue. In particular, it reflected the difficulty in finding an approach that was capable of distinguishing the effects of culture from those of the economic and institutional environment in which economic decisions are taken. Did differences in aggregate outcomes across countries, for example, arise because they had different economic and institutional environments or because social attitudes were different? Standard approaches to this question, such as the use of cross-country regressions on a large variety of variables that are meant

[1] This is calculated from answers to survey questions from the World Value Survey.

[2] These calculation use data from the WVS and from the OECD as reported in Fernández (2007b).

to capture economic and institutional differences across countries, identify culture with the regression residual. However, this approach is fraught with problems of omitted variables and endogeneity, compounded by mismeasurement.

In the last decade there have been a variety of new approaches that provide more persuasive evidence that culture matters. Some of the evidence comes from historical case studies that have attempted to use "natural experiments" to identify the effect of culture (e.g., Botticini and Eckstein (2005) or Greif (1994)). Some evidence has been provided by experiments showing that, on average, individuals from different social groups play different strategies in games such as the dictator game or public goods game (e.g. Henrich, Boyd, Bowles, Camerer, Fehr, Gintis, and McElreath (2001)). Better instruments for culture have also strengthened the case in favor of culture's impact on economic outcomes (see, e.g. Tabellini (2010) and Guiso, Sapienza, and Zingales (2004)). Finally, a large portion of evidence has come from following what I have called "the epidemiological approach" (see Fernández (2008)) to which this chapter is mostly devoted. The epidemiological approach attempts to separate culture from the environment by studying the outcomes of individuals whose cultures potentially differ, but in a common economic and institutional setting.

This chapter will primarily focus on the epidemiological approach to culture although some of the experimental and historical evidence will also be reviewed. A chapter by Guiso, Sapienza and Zingales in this handbook provides a more thorough review of the literature that uses instrumental variables, particularly for understanding social capital, and Fernández (2008) reviews several of the historical case studies. This chapter is organized as follows: the next section provides a definition as well as some historical evidence for how cultures differ, and reviews some of the experimental literature. Section 3 develops a theoretical framework for the epidemiological approach and discusses the empirical challenges in the context of an example. Section 4 reviews the epidemiological literature and the last section concludes.

2. SOME PRELIMINARIES

Before proceeding with a review of the literature on culture and economics, a definition of culture is useful, even if it is left somewhat vague.[3] In general terms, we may think of culture as a body of shared knowledge, understanding, and practice. According to the Merriam Webster Dictionary, culture is: "the integrated pattern of human knowledge, belief, and behavior that depends upon the capacity for learning and transmitting knowledge to succeeding generations;" and "the customary beliefs, social forms, and material traits of a racial, religious, or social group; (and) the set of shared attitudes, values, goals, and practices that characterizes an institution or organization."

[3] There is no agreed upon definition. By 1950, Kroeber and Kluckhohn (1952) provided over 150 definitions.

Economists model individuals as economic agents who make choices in an economic and institutional environment, given their preferences and beliefs. Consider two hypothetical societies faced with identical institutional and economic settings. Suppose that, despite these identical environments, these societies end up with different outcomes, reflecting the fact that their inhabitants made different choices. We would like to say that these choices differed because these societies possessed different cultures, i.e., because they differ in their distributions of preferences and beliefs across individuals. Thus, for the purposes of what I will be discussing, a more useful working definition is to consider *differences in culture* as systematic variation in beliefs and preferences across time, space, or social groups.

Why should societies differ in their distributions of preferences and beliefs? This can happen for a variety of reasons. One possibility is that differences arise because actions are taken in an environment that resembles a game with multiple equilibria. In this case, non-identical outcomes are simply the result of the different strategies chosen by individuals reflecting their different expectations about the equilibrium outcome. Alternatively, the agents across the two societies could possess different priorities about, for example, the payoffs to various actions, which could have resulted from different histories (obtained, for example, from different realization sequences of aggregate shocks).[4]

It may be useful to explicitly note here that nothing in this conception of culture considers it as either irrational, static, or slow changing. In particular, a definition of culture that considers the latter to be slow-moving (see, e.g. Guiso, Sapienza, and Zingales (2006)[5]) is rejected. The speed of cultural change depends on how quickly social beliefs and preferences change over time, which in turn depends on the environment broadly speaking, including the opportunities which determine individuals' learning pace, their interactions with others, and particular historical experiences. A salient example of a cultural change that began slow and accelerated considerably is seen in the social attitudes towards married women working. As shown in Figure (1) below (from Fernández (2007a)), beliefs in the US of the propriety of a married woman working if she had a husband "capable of supporting her" evolved dramatically over the 20th century, going from under 20% of the population being in favor of this in 1936 to less than 20% being against it in the 1990s.

Different historical experiences have important repercussions on individuals' beliefs and preferences. As shown by Alesina and Fuchs-Schundeln (2007), for example, Communism had a significant effect on the beliefs of people who lived under it. The authors study German attitudes towards the role of the state in two main areas of social

[4] See Fernández (2007a) for a model of cultural change as a process of endogenous intergenerational learning. If societies obtained different shocks, that would lead them to learn at different rates and would give rise to different actions on average.

[5] Guiso, Sapienza, and Zingales (2006) define culture as "those customary beliefs and values that ethnic, religious, and social groups transmit fairly unchanged from generation to generation."

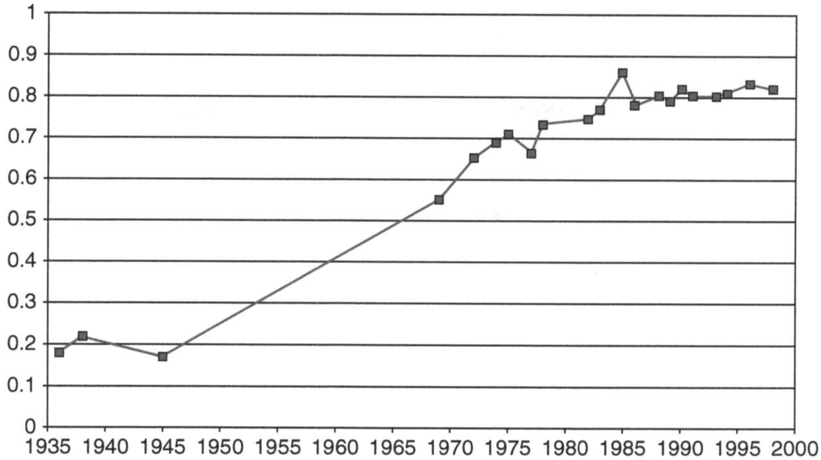

Figure 1 Fraction that approves of wife working if husband can support her. *(Data Source: WVS.)* Picture from Fernández (2007a).

security: the extent of state provision desired in case of unemployment or illness and the extent to which the state should provide financial security for families, old-age or for people needing care.[6] They find that if an individual lived in East Germany prior to reunification, she/he is much more likely to favor government provision for financial security for all of the areas mentioned above, after controlling for traits such as age, education level and type, gender, number of children, marital status, occupation, income, among others. This is independent of whether the responder lived in the former East or West Germany at the time of the survey.

The allocation of land titles to squatters in Argentina in 1989, as shown in DiTella, Galiani, and Schargrodsky (2006), likewise provides vivid testimony to the power of past experience. Hundreds of squatter families occupied an area of wasteland in the outskirts of Buenos Aires which belonged to many different private owners. The government attempted to redistribute the land to the squatters by buying it, but not all private owners were willing to sell. The squatters who had settled on tracts bought by the government obtained full property rights. The authors argue that this can be viewed as a case of random assignment and they provide evidence that the family heads in the group that received land titles are similar in age, gender, education levels, and ethnic origin to the ones in the group that did not. Despite the economic similarities across the two groups (those with land titles and those without), answers to survey questions regarding individualism, materialism, and trust differed markedly across them, with the group that received property rights demonstrating beliefs which are more

[6] The answers for each question ranged from 1 to 5 which correspond to "only the state," "mostly the state," "state and private forces," "mostly private forces," and "only private forces."

aligned with those of the general Buenos Aires population. Namely, the squatters who were granted property rights were more likely than their counterparts without these rights to believe that success can be achieved alone, that money is important to happiness and that one can, in general, trust other people. Interestingly, however, the beliefs of the two groups regarding the role of merit do not differ significantly (perhaps reflecting the role of luck in determining who obtained property rights).

A last example is provided by Giuliano and Spilimbergo (2009) who use survey questions to show that an individual's (regional) location at age 16 affects her/his adult attitudes. In particular, individuals who grew up in an area affected more severely by recession were more likely to believe in luck and redistribution and to have less confidence in institutions such as Congress and the executive branch of the federal government.[7]

In addition to history, there is abundant evidence that attitudes are transmitted from parents to children. For example, Dohmen, Falk, Huffman, and Sunde (2008) use German data to show that a child's propensity to trust and her/his attitudes towards risk (as measured in answers to survey questions at age 23) is strongly positively correlated with parental attitudes.[8] Farré and Vella (2007) use a sample of mother-child pairs to show that mothers transmit their attitudes regarding women's role in the labor market to their children. On the other hand, Cipriani, Giuliano, and Jeanne (2007) do not find a significant correlation in the way in which parents and their children play public goods games, but their sample is quite small.[9]

As noted in the introduction, there is plenty of evidence that economic outcomes and social beliefs are correlated. At the national level, for example, the extent to which executives believe that labor relations are good is correlated with union density across countries as shown in Figure (2) from Aghion, Algan, and Cahuc (2008).[10] A different example is provided by Figure (3) from Alesina and Giuliano (2007) that shows a negative correlation across between the strength of family ties and the ratio of girls to boys in tertiary education.[11]

[7] Specifically, the authors use the answers to questions in the GSS which asked the individual whether she believed in government intervention to reduce income inequality and improve standards of living, as well as questions that asked inviduals to express the degree of confidence in various government branches and whether luck is a driver of success.

[8] The results for risk remain significant and strong even after controlling for region where individual lived for the last 15 years, religion, ethnicity, subjective health status, income, and years of schooling, as well as a dummy for whether the family lived in East Germany before 1989. Interestingly, the mother's attitudes towards trust have a much stronger correlation with those of the child and the effects of both parents' attitudes decrease with birth order.

[9] The authors conduct the experiment with 38 parent-children pairs recruited from the same public elementary school in Washington, DC.

[10] The authors use executives' responses across more than 50 countries to the statement "Labor/employer relations are generally cooperative" from the *Global Competitiveness Reports*.

[11] To measure the strength of family ties, the authors use answers to a series of question in the World Value Survey that attempt to assess how important the family is in a person's life, the degree to which one should love and respect one's parents regardless of their characteristics, and whether parents have a duty to do their best for their children even at the expense of their own well-being.

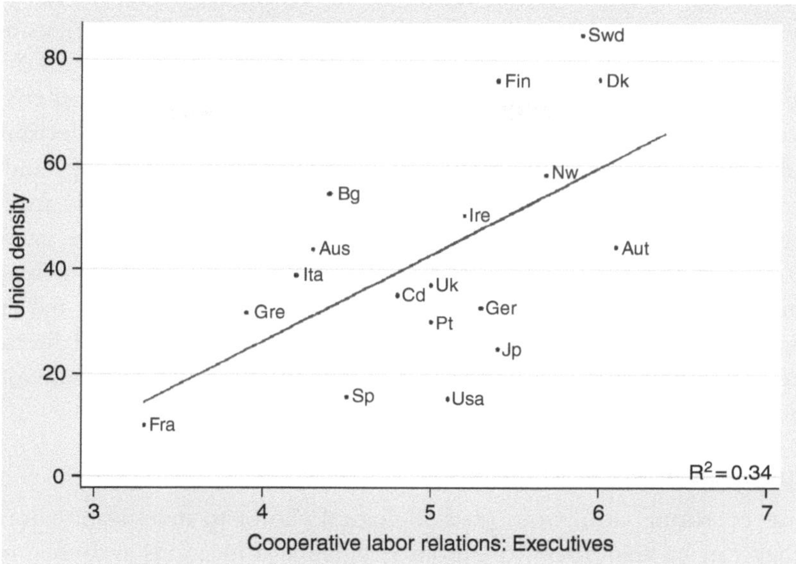

Figure 2 Correlation between union density and executives' beliefs that the labor relations are cooperative. *(Data Sources: OECD and GRC 1999 database.) Picture from Aghion, Algan and Cahuc (2008).*

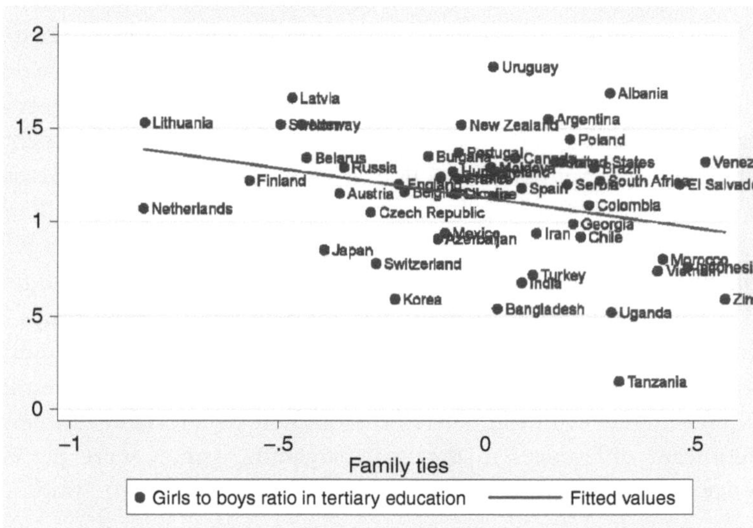

Figure 3 Relationship between strength of family ties and the ratio of girls to boys in tertiary education. *(Data Source: WVS.) Picture from Alesina and Giuliano (2007).*

A significant correlation between attitudes and outcomes is also found at the individual level within the same national environment. For example, Vella (1994), using Australian data, shows that attitude variables are correlated with the extent of a woman's involvement in market work and Farré and Vella (2007) find that a mother's attitudes towards working women is correlated with her daughter's labor market decisions as well as those of her son's spouse. Dohmen, Falk, Huffman, Sunde, Schupp, and Wagner (2005) show that risk attitude measures from survey questions in Germany are correlated with a variety of risky behavior including traffic offenses, portfolio choice, smoking, risk in occupational choice, participation in sports, migration and overall life satisfaction.

Of course, correlation does not imply causation. Before turning to the epidemiological approach, the next section reviews some of the experimental literature that attempts to show the effect of culture by comparing the decisions of individuals from different societies who face identical controlled environments.

2.1 Some experimental evidence

Experiments constitute an obvious methodological choice to investigate cultural differences as they can be transposed to various geographical locations and conducted with locally recruited samples.[12] Overall, however, the prevalence of small sample sizes and the fact that many experiments are conducted with college students makes it difficult to control for individual characteristics that may potentially differ in important ways across various groups. Below I give a brief review of some of the work in this area.

Evidence suggestive of cultural differences in players' choices of strategies in a given game is found by many authors. For example, Chuah, Hoffmann, Jones, and Williams (2007) and Chuah, Hoffmann, Jones, and Williams (2009) use the ultimatum game to investigate whether UK and Malaysian subjects exhibit differential behavior when bargaining within and across their national groups. They find stronger evidence of "home country bias" on the part of Malaysians. Namely, Malaysian students offered higher shares to their countrymen than UK proposers gave to theirs, whereas Malaysians gave lower offers to UK nationals than to their own countrymen. UK proposers, on the other hand, did not change their offers when bargaining with Malaysians. Neither nationality was punished or rewarded for using different strategies, as the authors found that the rejection rates were not different for the two groups.

Roth, Prasnikar, Okuno-Fujiwara, and Zamir (1991) compared how individuals in four international cities play market games versus bargaining games. Interestingly, they found no cultural differences in the behavior of individuals in market games, whereas there were significant differences in the way bargaining games were played, giving greater credence to a cultural explanation.[13] Henrich (2000) finds that the

[12] Roth, Prasnikar, Okuno-Fujiwara, and Zamir (1991) point out, however, various problems with experimental design in multinational experiments, namely, how to control differences in languages, currencies and experimenters.

[13] They study market behavior using first price auctions, where all buyers have the same valuation. As predicted by standard theory, they found that the seller obtained the entire surplus.

Machiguenga tribe of the Peruvian Amazon, when playing the ultimatum game, makes significantly smaller offers than a control group in Los Angeles and that the former also has a lower rejection rate. In post game interviews, tribal members explained that they accepted low offers because they did not want to reject any money. The proposers also expected their low offers to be accepted.

Henrich, Boyd, Bowles, Camerer, Fehr, Gintis, and McElreath (2001) summarizes the results of experiments conducted in 15 small-scale societies in various countries. They had individuals play various games, including the ultimatum, dictator and public goods game and found important differences across societies in the average outcomes. They argue that this may reflect differences in culture that arise from different structures of production requiring a smaller or greater degree of cooperation among individuals.

Does the fact that different societies play these games differently reflect different cultural attitudes? Even leaving aside the (critically) important issue of whether these results are driven by systematic differences in individual characteristics, a meta-analysis of 37 papers conducted by Oosterbeek, Sloof, and van de Kuilen (2004), which includes 75 results from ultimatum game experiments, finds that differences in game outcomes are not reflected in variations in attitudes. The authors use answers to several questions in WVS to construct a measure of average attitudes across countries that reflect the respect for authority, trust, and competition. They regress the outcomes (e.g. the share offered and the rejection rate) on variables such as the amount offered, regional dummies, the Gini coefficient in the country, GDP per capita and the average attitude as constructed from the WVS. They tend to find that attitudes are insignificant in explaining the variation. Of course, it is quite possible that the attitudes chosen by the authors are not capturing the cultural features that are relevant for these outcomes or that the demographic groups from which the experimental subjects are drawn do not have the average attitudes of their countries. Nonetheless, this finding suggests that one must be cautious about the cultural interpretation of experimental results based on small samples and on subjects whose individual characteristics are not controlled for.

3. THE EPIDEMIOLOGICAL APPROACH

The essence of what I call the epidemiological approach is the attempt to identify the effect of culture through the variation in economic outcomes of individuals who share the same economic and institutional environment, but whose social beliefs are potentially different. Very often, the focus is on the economic behavior of immigrants or their descendants, but this need not always be the case (see, e.g., Fisman and Miguel (2007) and Miguel, Saiegh, and Satyanath (2008)).[14] This approach is reminiscent of that used by epidemiologists

[14] Studying outcomes for the second generation rather than the first-generation immigrants offers some advantages. It avoids some of the confounding difficulties that first-generation immigrants are more likely to suffer to varying degrees such as the ability to speak the host country language and the prevalence of ties with non-immigrating family members. These factors are likely to be less important for the second generation.

(hence the name) who, in order to attempt to distinguish the genetic contribution to disease from the physical (including cultural, e.g. diet) environmental contribution, study various health outcomes for immigrants and compare them to outcomes for natives.[15]

To understand the strengths and weaknesses of an epidemiological approach to medical issues, suppose that the incidence of, say, heart disease differs markedly between two countries (the source and host countries). If the incidence of heart disease in immigrants converges to that of the natives in the host country, the difference between the two countries is unlikely to be driven by genetics and instead results from the environment. Failure to find convergence, on the other hand, does not imply the opposite. Even when the environment is the sole responsible, there are still many ways to sustain differential levels of heart disease. For example, cultural assimilation may occur slowly (for instance, if immigrants maintain the same dietary patterns as in the source country), or living in the source country at a young age may confer some degree of immunity, or selection into immigration may be correlated with a particular health outcome.

In economics, unlike in medicine, the epidemiological approach attempts to distinguish between cultural versus environmental factors contributing to individual variation (and thus the environment now includes the economic and (formal) institutional settings that may affect outcomes, but excludes culture). The reasoning underlying this strategy is that (i) parents transmit their cultural beliefs to their children; (ii) cultural beliefs vary across (immigrant) groups in a systematic fashion reflecting culture in the country of origin; (iii) individuals who live in the same country or in the same appropriately defined geographical area, face similar economic and formal institutional environments. The idea is thus that individuals from different cultures will take different actions despite facing identical environments.

The basic empirical exercise uses data on individuals that live in one given country but whose parents were born in some other country – the country of ancestry. With this data one can estimate the probability that an individual i from country-of-ancestry c takes some action, y_{ic},

$$y_{ic} = \beta_0 + \beta_1 X_i + \beta_2 Y_c + \varepsilon_i \tag{1}$$

in which X_i is a vector of individual characteristics, Y_c is a proxy for culture in country c, and ε_i is an error term. Thus, X_i can consist of demographic information such as gender and age as well as measures of household income, education, etc. The primary variable of interest is the one that attempts to capture culture in the country of ancestry. Although it is possible to simply use a country-of-ancestry dummy for this variable, a superior strategy is to use a variable that more directly reflects the cultural attitudes of interest. For example, if y_{ic} is a labor force participation decision for a woman whose parents were first generation immigrants, then Y_c could be the female LFP in her parents' home country.

[15] See, for example, the classic study by Marmot, Syme, Kagan, Kato, Cohen, and Belsky (1975). The methodological basis for this approach to culture in economics is developed in Fernández (2008) and the explanation offered here follows closely the one laid out there.

One may question the epidemiological approach described above for a variety of grounds. First, parents are not the only (nor necessarily even the most important) transmitters of culture; the relationships and institutions of the local environment (schools, local institutions, neighborhood, etc.) will also impact an individual's beliefs. Culture, furthermore, is socially constructed: to be replicated, the behavior may require the incentives – rewards and punishments – provided by a larger social body.[16] Second, although studying the descendants of immigrants rather than immigrants directly allows one to avoid some potential problems (see footnote 14), it also means that the impact of culture from the source country is likely to have been attenuated over time. Both of these factors will lead to an underestimation of the effect of culture on economic outcomes in the above specification. Nonetheless, for a wide variety of issues, there appears to be a significant correlation between attitudes in the home country and attitudes expressed by immigrants and their descendants. This can be seen, for example, in the attitudes towards trust as shown in Figure (4) from Guiso, Sapienza, and Zingales (2006), or in

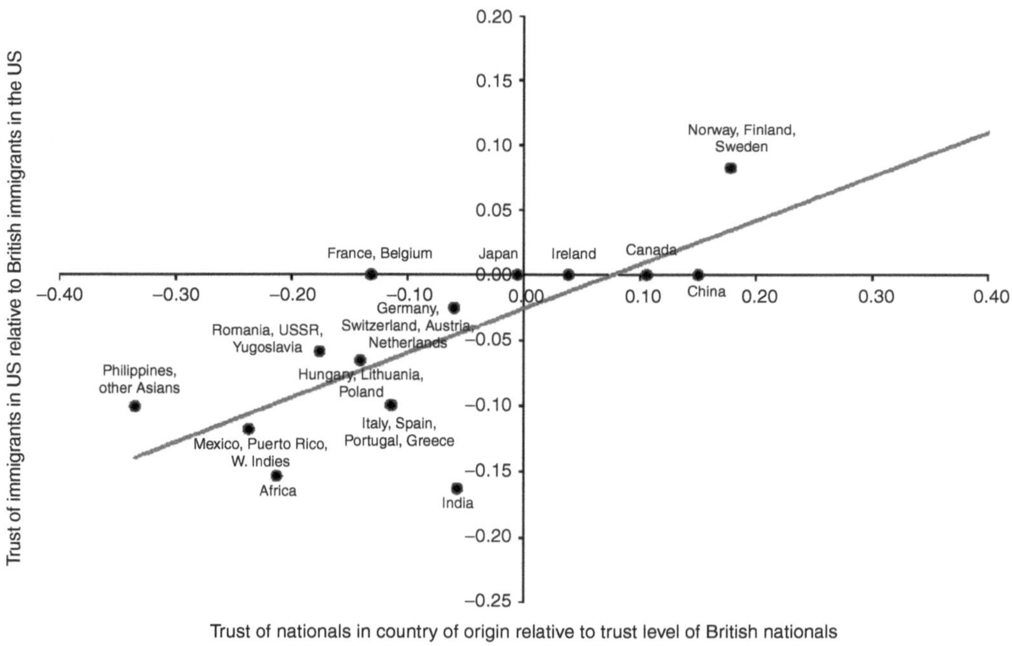

Figure 4 Correlation between trust level of country of origin and trust level of immigrants relative to Great Britain. *(Data Sources: World Values Survey, General Social Survey.) Picture from Guiso, Sapienza and Zingales (2006).*

16 Fernández and Fogli (2009) show that, in fact, the impact of culture appears to be greater for the descendants of those immigrant groups that have a greater tendency to cluster in the same neighborhood.

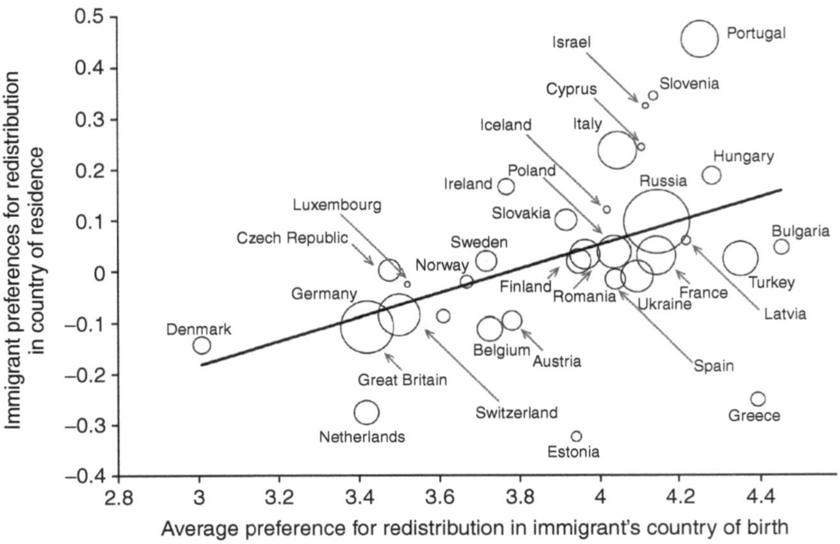

Figure 5 Preferences for redistribution by immigrant group and country of birth. *(Data Source: ESS.) Picture from Luttmer and Singhal (2010).*

the attitudes towards redistribution in Figure (5) from Luttmer and Singhal (2010).[17] Third, immigrants (and their descendants) from different countries may face different economic and institutional environments within the host country. Fourth, immigrants are not a random sample of a source-country's population. I will discuss the potential problems that the last two concerns pose for the estimation strategy in greater detail below, in the context of an example.

3.1 An example

In order to understand the strengths and weaknesses of the epidemiological approach to culture, I will develop it in greater detail in the context of a simple model of a married woman's decision to work in the formal labor market.

3.1.1 A simple model

Let's start with the work decision of a (married) woman i in country k. For simplicity, I model solely the extensive margin and treat the utility from consumption and disutility

[17] As a measure of trust, Guiso, Sapienza, and Zingales (2006) use the answer to the binary question in WVS "Generally speaking, would you say that most people can be trusted or that you have to be very careful in dealing with people?" to construct a dummy which takes a value 1 if the person answered that people could be trusted. Luttmer and Singhal (2010) measure preferences for redistribution using the European Social Survey (ESS). Individuals are given the statement "the government should take measures to reduce differences in income levels" and the responses are measured in a scale of 1 to 5, ranging from strong disagreement to strong agreement.

from working as separable. Thus, a woman's work decision can be thought of as the solution to the maximization of the following utility function:

$$U(c, v_i) = u(c) - \mathbf{1}v_i$$

where u is a strictly increasing, concave utility function, $\mathbf{1}$ is an indicator function that takes the value one if she works and zero otherwise, c is household consumption, and v_i is woman i's disutility from working.

A woman's consumption is the sum of her labor income (if she works), w_f, and her husband's wages, w_h (i.e., consumption is a public good at the household level). Husbands are assumed to always work. For simplicity, the level of wages is taken as exogenous and identical for individuals within the same country but is potentially different across countries. Thus,

$$c = w_{hk} + \mathbf{1}w_{fk}$$

The disutility of work, v_i, varies across women and is assumed to be a random draw from a country-specific distribution with mean m_k and variance σ^2, with a cdf denoted by G_k (m_k, σ). Thus, for simplicity, differences in culture across countries with respect to women's work are modeled as (exogenous) differences in the mean of the distribution that characterizes the disutility of working. Note that there are two sources of heterogeneity in the model: a within-country heterogeneity across women in the same country reflected in the fact that they obtain different preference draws from a given distribution, and cross-country heterogeneity reflected in the mean of the preference distribution from which women obtain individual-level preference draws.

Given wages in country k, w_{hk} and w_{fk}, and the distribution of preferences in the country, G_k, we can solve for the level of female labor force participation in that country, L_k. It is given by the cdf evaluated at v_k^*, i.e.,

$$L_k = G_k(v_k^*)$$

where

$$v_k^* \equiv v^*(w_{hk}, w_{fk}) = u(w_{hk} + w_{fk}) - u(w_{hk})$$

is the level of disutility from work in country k which makes a woman indifferent between participating in the labor market or not.

If, for concreteness, we assume that G is a normal distribution and $\Phi(x)$ is the standard normal cumulative distribution evaluated at x, then $L_k + \Phi\left(\frac{v_k^* - m_k}{\sigma}\right)$. To summarize, the women that choose to work are those whose disutility of working lies below the critical level v_k^*, which depends only on the wages in that country, w_{hk}, w_{fk}.

Note that both culture and the economic/institutional environment play a role in determining the level of women's labor force participation. Culture matters since it shifts the distribution from which preferences are drawn, by changing m_k (without affecting v_k^*).[18] Cultures that have more negative views about women working, i.e., those with higher values of m_k, will have, ceteris paribus, lower female LFP, i.e.,

$$\frac{\partial L_k}{\partial m_k} = -\phi\left(\frac{v_k^* - m_k}{\sigma}\right)\frac{1}{\sigma} < 0 \tag{2}$$

where $\phi(x)$ is the pdf associated with standard normal distribution $\Phi(x)$.

Economic/institutional differences across countries also matter. In this simple framework these differences are reflected in wages and thus affect v_k^*. In particular, $\frac{\partial L_k}{\partial w_{fk}} = \frac{1}{\sigma}\phi\left(\frac{v_k^*-m_k}{\sigma}\right)u'(w_{hk} + w_{fk}) > 0$ and $\frac{\partial L_k}{\partial w_{hk}} = \frac{1}{\sigma}\phi\left(\frac{v_k^*-m_k}{\sigma}\right)[u'(w_{hk} + w_{fk}) - u'(w_{hk})] < 0$. Thus an increase in female wages will lead to an increase in a country's level of female LFP whereas an increase in the male wage leads to a decrease.

Next, consider a random sample of women from different countries of ancestry k, ($k = 1, 2, \ldots, n$), all living in the same country j. Suppose that these women are identical in all but their cultural beliefs. In particular, suppose that they are endowed with identical husbands (i.e., they do not differ in their earnings) and that they face the same formal institutional environment so that their market wages, w_{f_j}, w_{h_j}, are the same. Hence v^* will be the same across all women, even though they have different countries of ancestry. We will also assume that culture is transmitted perfectly by parents, i.e., these women inherit the same v_i draws as their (foreign-born) mothers. The proportion of women who will work, however, will differ across countries of ancestry k since each of their v_i are drawn from different distributions. In particular, assuming a normal distribution for G, the proportion of women from ancestry k who work in country j is given by $L_{kj} = \Phi\left(\frac{v_j^*-m_k}{\sigma}\right)$. Note that, as shown in equation (2), women whose mothers were born in countries that have less favorable views of working women will be less inclined to work, as their disutilities v_i will be drawn from distributions with higher values of m. Thus, from a theoretical perspective, culture not mattering requires the distribution of distribution of preferences/beliefs to be identical across countries ($m_k = m, \forall k = 1, \ldots..n$).

3.1.2 Empirical issues

Because cultural differences (m_k) are not observable, in order to conduct an empirical analysis akin to equation (1) one needs to find variables which can function as proxies for cultural attitudes. In the context of the model above, a good proxy for a woman's culture could be the level of married women's LFP in her country of ancestry or a measure of attitudes in that country towards married women who work.[19]

[18] In more general models, culture will also affect v_k^* by affecting, for example, the supply of labor and through it, wages.

[19] See Fernández and Fogli (2009) for the former and Fernández (2007a) for the latter.

There are several important issues that must be addressed before one can conclude that a statistically significant coefficient on the cultural proxy in equation (1) constitutes even moderately persuasive evidence that culture matters. First, there are many sources of heterogeneity across women other than their cultural beliefs. To the extent that these sources of heterogeneity are orthogonal to culture, it is simple to include them in the vector of individual characteristics. The comparative statics of equation (2) will then still be valid. Many of these characteristics, however, are endogenous outcomes that may well be influenced by culture. In the context of a woman's work decisions, her desire to acquire higher levels of education, the state/neighborhood where she lives, and the characteristics of her husband are a few of the more salient variables that may be influenced by culture. Thus, by including them in a regression one is effectively testing whether culture has an influence on work outcomes beyond the ways in which it is already reflected in these choices. It is important to note that in this case the failure to find a significant coefficient on the cultural proxy is not an indication that culture does not matter.

Second, these women may not be randomly selected in the sense that their immigrant parents may be a selected sample from the distribution of beliefs in the country of ancestry. Thus, the cultural attitudes which were transmitted to their descendants may not be representative of the country's culture. Once again, a finding of an insignificant coefficient on the cultural proxy cannot lead one to rule out the possibility that culture matters. The interpretation of a significant coefficient on the cultural proxy, on other hand, depends on the issue being studied. In the case of women's work outcomes, selection would invalidate this finding only if parents from different countries came from systematically different parts of an otherwise identical distributions of beliefs and preferences across countries. For a positive coefficient on the cultural proxy of female LFP to be driven by selection would require countries to have identical distributions of preferences but that those parents (immigrants) from high female LFP countries be drawn from a different part of the distribution than the ones from low female LFP countries. In particular, it would require the former to be drawn disproportionately from the low disutility-of-labor portion of the distribution and the opposite for latter. How reasonable this possibility is depends upon the issue being studied. It is worth noting, in any case, that selection is a problem for all empirical methodologies, as even random experiments can suffer from the possibility of attrition with selection on unobservable variables.

Third, and perhaps the most critical issue, is whether there exists an omitted variable that varies in a systematic fashion across country of origin for purely economic reasons. In the context of our example of married women's LFP, variables such as her education, her husband's income, and her geographic location are all likely candidates that might reflect underlying economic differences across individuals rather than culture. Thus, controlling for these characteristics is important in this regard as well, despite their potential endogeneity.

While controlling for observed individual characteristics is straightforward (assuming that the data is available), the issue of unobserved heterogeneity remains; there may well be an omitted variable that is correlated with the country of ancestry. How to deal with this possibility depends on the question that is being studied. Tackling this issue is fundamental, however, as the ability of the new epidemiological literature to be persuasive depends on how well this issue is addressed.

In the case of culture and female LFP, the most likely candidate for an omitted variable is unobserved human capital. For example, it is possible that women with higher levels of (unobserved) human capital would choose to supply more labor to the market since their wages are higher. The most direct way to test for the presence of different human capital levels is via a Mincer regression on wages. After controlling for the usual variables in a Mincer regression (schooling, experience, experience squared and location), the cultural proxy should not have additional explanatory power for women's wages. If it does, then it is more likely that unobserved human capital is responsible for the correlation between culture and women's labor supply. Other possible variables that one can use to control for an individual's unobserved human capital (assuming that individual IQ or individual test scores are unavailable) include proxies for the quality of education of the parents or parental human capital. In order to do this, one can employ either direct measures of the latter's education or average test scores on standardized international tests (a la Hanushek and Kimko (2000)) in the country of ancestry as a measure of the parents' quality of education.[20]

Fourth, it should be noted that although using variables related to the economic outcome of interest is in many ways a superior approach to the "black box" of a country dummy, there may be issues with this alternative. On the one hand, making use of an economic variable is preferable since it facilitates formulating alternative hypotheses regarding the critical issue of a potentially omitted variable. On the other hand, the variable used as a cultural proxy may itself not reflect cultural differences across countries since this source of variation may be swamped by their economic and institutional differences. For example, one could imagine a country which despite having more conservative attitudes towards women working, could also have higher female wages or a better child-support mechanism, resulting in an overall higher female-LFP-rate than that in a less conservative country. Using alternative proxies (or more directly a country dummy) will eliminate this concern.

It should be noted explicitly that the epidemiological approach is biased towards finding that culture does not matter. As mentioned previously, the fact that parents are only one source of cultural transmission among many and that they may have cultural attitudes that differ from the average ones in the country of ancestry, implies

[20] Fernández and Fogli (2009) conduct a large battery of tests, including the ones mentioned above, to persuade the reader that an omitted variable is not responsible for their results.

that one is more likely to rule the cultural proxy insignificant. Thus, just like the absence of convergence in disease does not provide definitive evidence in favor of genetics, the absence of a significant coefficient on the cultural proxy does not imply that only the economic and institutional setting matters.

4. THE EPIDEMIOLOGICAL LITERATURE IN ECONOMICS

The first paper to use the epidemiological approach was Carroll, Rhee, and Rhee (1994). They used individual-level data on immigrants to Canada to investigate whether cross-country differences in savings rates were culturally driven. They estimated individual consumption levels as a function of permanent income, demographics, and region of origin. The authors found that although recent immigrants tended, on the whole, to save less than native-born Canadians, their saving patterns did not vary significantly by region of origin. Given this negative finding, it is perhaps not surprising that for some time no further attempts were made using this methodology. In more recent years, however, the epidemiological approach has been used to study the impact of culture on various economic outcomes such as women's work, fertility, labor market regulation, corruption, redistribution, and financial participation to name a few topics. Below I review some of this literature.

4.1 Women's work, fertility, and gender preferences

Not surprisingly, issues which concern women (e.g. female labor force participation and fertility) have been a popular focus for work in culture and economics since attitudes towards women have evolved significantly over the last century across most of the developed countries.

Reimers (1985) is an early attempt to examine the role of ethnicity in married women's labor force participation in the United States. Using a standard regression approach with ethnicity dummies, she finds mixed results regarding the importance of ethnicity for female LFP. The women in the sample she studies have been in the US for varying time periods, however, which is perhaps partially responsible for these results.

Antecol (2000) uses male and female LFP in the country of ancestry to examine whether culture plays a role in determining the inter-ethnic gender gap in labor force participation rates in the United States. She studies both first-generation immigrants and second and higher-generation individuals, which she groups into the same category. The results are suggestive that ethnicity matters although the absence of key individual-level variables leaves open the possibility that the results could be driven by omitted factors such as education or differences in parental background that lead to systematic variations in unobserved human capital.

The concern above is mitigated in Fernández and Fogli (2009) who use various measures of parental education and unobserved human capital (including average test scores in the country of ancestry and wages as described in the prior section) to rule out this alternative transmission channel. They show that culture plays a quantitatively significant role in explaining variation in women's work and fertility outcomes. The authors also examine whether it is her or her husband's country-of-ancestry that drives their results. Interestingly, they find that both matter but, if anything, the husband's culture has a larger impact on his wife's labor supply than her own cultural background.

An alternative to proxying culture with aggregate economic variables from the country-of-ancestry (such as female LFP above) is to make use of indicators of social attitudes prevalent in those countries. The important issue of reverse causality discussed previously is avoided by using the epidemiological approach. The first paper to do this is Fernández (2007a). She uses the attitudes towards women's work expressed by individuals in the woman's country of ancestry as a cultural proxy to study the work outcomes of second-generation American women. She finds that cross-European variation in answers to questions about women's role in the 1990 WVS has explanatory power for the 1970 work outcomes of second-generation American women from these countries of ancestry, even after controlling for individual differences such as those in education, location, and husband's characteristics.[21] Figure (6) from Fernández (2007b) shows the raw correlation between the cultural proxy (in this case, female labor force participation in 1990 in the country of ancestry) and the 1970 work outcome for second-generation American women from that country of ancestry, measured in hours worked per week.[22]

Another strand of literature focuses on the effect of culture over another important outcome for women, fertility. This literature includes, for example, Guinnane, Moehling, and Ó'Gráda (2006) who study Irish fertility in the United States in 1910, and Blau (1992) who examines the fertility behavior of first-generation immigrant women in the United States. These investigations are based on immigrants directly and therefore face the usual issues associated with immigration such as selection and the possible disrupted and delayed fertility behavior. The analysis of Fernández and Fogli (2006) and Fernández and Fogli (2009) mitigates these concerns by studying second-generation American women. Using past values of the total fertility rates from the woman's country of ancestry as a cultural proxy, they find that the latter has explanatory power for fertility outcomes, leading them to conclude that culture plays an important role.

On a related issue, Almond, Edlund, and Milligan (2009) investigate the role of culture in son preference. The authors note that sex ratios at birth are above the biologically normal level in a number of Asian countries. They investigate whether this is a result due to traditional economic reasons associated with poverty and/or to the existence of a rural or

[21] The WVS statements with which individuals are asked to agree or disagree (with various degrees of intensity) are: 1. Being a housewife is just as fulfilling as working for pay; 2. Having a job is the best way for a woman to be an independent person.

[22] Note that if the way in which culture evolves is relatively stable across countries, it is possible to use future levels of the outcome as a cultural proxy, e.g., female LFP in 1990 is used to explain work behavior in 1970.

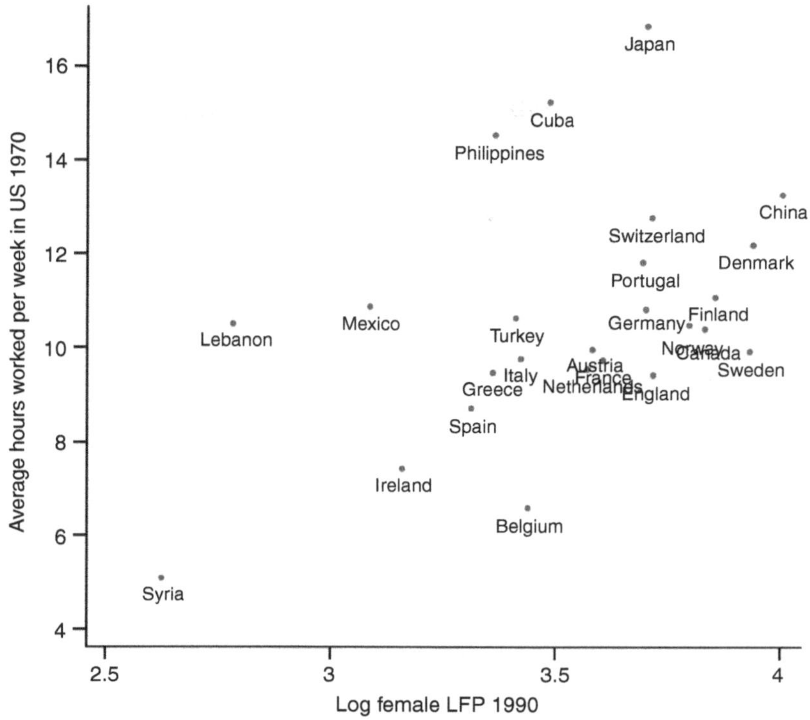

Figure 6 Hours worked and culture (Female LFP in 1990). *(Data Source: ILO and US Census.) Picture from Fernández (2007).*

discriminatory environment that renders sons more valuable, or whether it is instead due to culture. To do this, they use an epidemiological approach and study Asian immigrants to Canada. They find that sex ratios for these immigrants rise with parity (i.e., with the number of children) if there was no previous son. In particular, those families whose first two children were girls are significantly more likely both to have a third child and for that child to be a boy, if they originally emigrated from India, China, Korea, or Vietnam. Since these immigrants no longer live in rural environments and poverty is presumably no longer an issue, culture is likely to be responsible for these results.[23]

4.2 Family ties, political engagement, and labor market regulation

The type of relationships people possess may have a cultural component, which can affect economic outcomes. For example, the degree of attachment to one's family may influence one's political attitudes or lead to economic concessions as individuals may have greater stakes in remaining in the same location. Relatedly, the perceived

[23] Unfortunately, they do not control for household income explicitly.

quality of the relationship between workers and management may also have important economic consequences.

In a series of papers, Giuliano and various coauthors establish that there is cross country variation in how families are viewed and that these views are correlated with a series of political and economic outcomes. First, as shown in Giuliano (2007), the living arrangements of second-generation immigrants in the US tend to follow the cross-European cultural patterns from their country of ancestry. In particular, individuals of Southern European descent in the US are more likely to live with their parents during the ages of 18 to 33 than the descendants of immigrants from other European countries.

Second, Alesina and Giuliano (2009) use questions in the WVS to construct a measure of the average "strength" of family ties across European countries.[24] They first show that, within a country, individual answers to these questions have predictive value for an individual's political participation and general interest in politics.[25] Next, they follow the epidemiological approach by using the country-level measure of the strength of family ties as a cultural proxy for second-generation nationals. That is, within a given host country, say Germany, second-generation Germans are associated with the Turkish value of the strength of family ties if their parents came from Turkey and with the Italian value if their parents came from Italy. Using host country dummies and data from European Social Survey, the authors show that the cultural proxy has explanatory power for within-country variation in political attitudes of individuals from different countries of ancestry.[26] In particular, they find that second-generation immigrants are themselves less likely to be interested in politics if their father's country of origin had a high average level of family ties. Their analysis includes a series of individual-level characteristics such as education categories, employment status, and a measure of family income. The fact that they consider second-generation immigrants across 32 destination countries strengthens the analysis as it is less likely that the results are driven by some special feature of a destination country. They interpret their finding as evidence of the importance of "amoral familism" in which strong family ties have a negative influence on social capital.

The strength of family ties also matters for labor market outcomes. Using the CPS from various years, Alesina, Algan, Cahuc, and Giuliano (2010) show that second-generation Americans whose parents come from countries with stronger family ties

[24] The authors use answers to a series of questions in the World Value Survey that attempt to assess how important the family is in a person's life, the degree to which one should "love and respect" one's parents regardless of their characteristics, and whether parents have a duty to do their best for their children even at the expense of their own well-being.

[25] To assess the latter, the authors use questions which ask respondents about their general interest in politics and their interest in engaging in political conversations with friends. Political action is measured using a list of political activities that the respondent has engaged in.

[26] The authors use questions concerning political attitudes in the ESS, which are very similar to the ones mentioned in footnote (25). For further details, see Alesina and Giuliano (2009).

tend to have lower geographic mobility, a higher probability of unemployment, and lower hourly wages even after controlling for individual characteristics such as age, education, marital status, gender, and number of children as well as state fixed effects. They interpret this result as evidence that individuals who have a more family-focused culture are less able to take advantage of labor market opportunities due to their lower willingness to move away from their family in response to adverse local conditions.

Culture can also impact the labor market at the institutional level. Aghion, Algan, and Cahuc (2008) argue that bad labor relations and low unionization rates lead governments to set more stringent minimum wage policies in order to better protect workers. In a series of cross-country comparisons, they first show that the stringency of the state's regulation of the minimum wage in OECD countries is negatively correlated with both executives' and workers' beliefs in the quality of labor relations, whereas the unionization rate is positively correlated with these beliefs. They next use an epidemiological approach to show that there exists a cultural component to an individual's attitudes towards unions and her/his likelihood of belonging to a union. In particular, they examine the relationship between two cultural proxies for the country of ancestry - union density and a composite measure of state regulation of minimum wage - and two outcomes for second generation immigrants in the US: the degree of confidence an individual expresses about labor unions as well as the probability that the respondent belongs to a union.[27] They control for various individual-level characteristics but their use of the General Social Survey significantly restricts the number of countries of ancestry (twelve only) and provides only rough categories for critical variables such as income. Thus, although their finding that union density and minimum wage legislation in the country of ancestry has a significant impact on both an individual's confidence in unions and her/his probability of participating in one (in the US) is suggestive, it is also open to other interpretations. For example, it may be that an individual's occupation may be more or less prone to being unionized in a way that is correlated with her/his country of ancestry.

4.3 Corruption, redistribution, and violence

Is there a link between culture and the extent to which countries engage in redistribution?[28] Luttmer and Singhal (2010) take a step towards establishing this link by using an epidemiological approach to show that individual preferences for redistribution exhibit a cultural component. They study (mostly European) immigrants to 32 European host countries and show that preferences for redistribution in the country of origin can

[27] The authors construct a composite index to measure the degree of state regulation of the minimum wage. It is a combination of stringency measures, such as the existence of minimum wage legislation, and the "level" of the minimum wage, which the authors measure as the ratio of the minimum wage over the median wage in the economy. For further details, see Aghion, Algan, and Cahuc (2008).

[28] For of a review of this literature, see Alesina and Giuliano (this volume).

help explain the variation in the immigrants' preferences for redistribution in the host country.[29] This result holds even after controlling for several individual characteristics such as income, education, employment status, and host country fixed effects.[30] The fact that the authors consider immigrants across 32 destination countries strengthens the analysis as it makes it less likely that the results are driven by some special feature of a destination country. The cultural effects are large in the sense that a one-standard deviation increase in the average preference for redistribution across birth countries is associated with a greater than one-standard-deviation decrease in the log of household income.

A rather different take on the epidemiological approach is Fisman and Miguel (2007). The authors investigate the parking behavior of United Nations officials in Manhattan. As in studies based on immigrants or their descendants, this work follows an epidemiological approach by studying a select group of individuals (UN officials) in the same geographical environment (Manhattan). Until 2002, diplomatic immunity protected U.N. diplomats from parking enforcement prosecution, so their actions were presumably constrained by cultural norms alone. The authors find that diplomats from countries with high levels of corruption (based on existing survey-based indices) accumulated significantly more unpaid parking violations.

Fisman and Miguel's finding is intriguing as it seems to indicate that countries with high levels of corruption also have cultures which facilitate corrupt behavior. Does the failure to pay parking tickets when one is not legally required to do so, however, indicate corruption? An alternative explanation may be that highly corrupt countries face a different set of social problems that are far more serious than parking violations, leading to a culture in which these comparatively trivial issues are ignored. Moreover, even if one accepts the authors' interpretation of their results, an important remaining issue is whether the UN officials from countries with different levels of corruption face different likelihoods of punishment at home. If they do, then it would be unclear whether culture or economic rewards/punishments underlie their findings since this would imply that the institutional setting in which these officials operate may not truly be one and the same (the UN and Manhattan) but may also involve the institutions from their country of origin.[31]

Violence may also have a cultural component. By studying individuals from different nationalities who are all involved in the same activity – soccer – Miguel, Saiegh, and Satyanath (2008) find an ingenious way to keep the environment constant. The authors examine the relationship between a country's history of civil war and a soccer player's

[29] Preferences for redistribution are measured by the average answer to the ESS question which asks respondents how strongly they agreed/disagreed with the statement that "the government should take measures to reduce differences in income levels".

[30] A similar analysis, but for second-generation immigrants to the US rather than Europe, is performed by Alesina and Giuliano (this volume).

[31] The authors only deal with this issue partially by ascertaining that the length of a diplomat's tenure is uncorrelated with the number of parking violations early in her/his career.

propensity to engage in violence on the soccer field as evidenced in his incidence of yellow and red cards (indicating a violent foul) when playing in one of six major European leagues. These leagues include players from 70 countries and all continents.

Controlling for a variety of important characteristics such as the position and league played in, the number of games, the quality of play (goals scored), etc., Miguel et al. find that players from countries with higher civil war incidence accumulate a greater number of yellow and red cards. The inclusion of continent dummies to some extent helps rule out alternative explanations such as racial discrimination by the referees. While it may be that, as in the study of parking violations and corruption, different home institutions are responsible for this behavior (e.g., perhaps future coaching opportunities on a home team depend on the degree to which violence is punished domestically), this concern seems less pressing in this arena than in the former study.

4.4 Within-country migration: shirking and financial participation

Different cultures can coexist within the same country, particularly across different geographical regions. Ichino and Maggi (2000) use movers from and to different regions of Italy in an attempt to investigate the role of culture in the higher incidence of shirking found in Southern versus Northern Italian employees. As shown by the authors, the rate of absenteeism in the South is almost double that in the North of the country. The authors' results are suggestive of a role for culture in this phenomenon since, when faced with a common environment, and after controlling for several individual and local characteristics, individuals born in the South but working in the North continue to have greater shirking rates than comparable Northern workers.

Guiso, Sapienza, and Zingales (2004) also study movers within Italy to attempt to identify the effect of civic capital on financial development. They use indicators of how much people rely on financial markets, such as the use of checks, reliance on cash, stock holdings and access to credit markets, as these are presumably correlated with financial development. They measure civic capital in an ingenious fashion, using not only the degree of electoral participation but also the quantity of voluntary blood donations in each province.[32] As in the prior study, the use of movers allows the authors to control for cross-regional variations in the efficiency of institutions.[33]

Guiso et al. use a dummy variable for the individual's place of residence and another one for the individual's origin to identify the effect of her/his culture. They find that people who were originally from provinces with higher civic capital make larger investments in stocks, rely more on checks to settle transactions, and have easier access to loans. It should be noted that while the authors interpret the latter finding as resulting from trustworthiness, it is also consistent with discrimination.

[32] This is the number of 16 oz blood bags per individual in each province in 1995.

[33] As an example of institutional cross-variation, the completion of similar courtroom trials can range from 1.4 to 8.3 years across different regions of Italy.

4.5 Cultural change and changes in economic outcomes

As discussed previously, there is no reason to believe, a priori, that culture changes only slowly. Algan and Cahuc (2010) exploit time variation in measures of individual trust to show that trust can impact economic growth. Suppose that income per capita Y in country c at time t can be written, in a cross-country regression form, as:

$$Y_{ct} = \alpha_0 + \alpha_1 S_{ct} + \alpha_2 X_{ct} + F_c + F_t + \varepsilon_{ct}$$

where S_{ct} measures the country average of social attitudes of individuals who live in country c in period t; X_{ct} denotes a vector of average characteristics of the population and past economic development of the economy; F_c stands for country fixed effects and captures all other time invariant specific features in the country such as legal origins, endowments, or past institutions with long-lasting effects; F_t stands for period fixed-effects common to all countries and ε_{ct} denotes an error term.

The problem with the specification above is that contemporaneous social attitudes, S_{ct}, are likely to be correlated with the unobserved error term (if, for example, higher per-capita income increases trust). Here is where the authors employ the epidemiological approach.[34] Assuming that contemporaneous social attitudes are formed both by attitudes inherited from previous generations as well as by the contemporaneous environment allows the authors to write:

$$S_{ct} = \gamma_0 + \gamma_1 S_{c,t-1} + \gamma_2 X_{ct} + \Phi_c + \Phi_t + v_{ct}$$

where Φ_c and Φ_t stand for country and time dummies respectively; $S_{c,t-1}$ denotes the social attitudes of the prior generation; and v_{ct} is an error term. The assumption that social attitudes from period $t-1$ do not directly affect Y_{ct}, along with the assumption that $v_{ct} \perp S_{c,t-1}$, allows the authors to identify the parameters of the system of equations.

Given that standardized cross-country databases on social attitudes of earlier generations are not available, the authors proxy the inherited attitudes of people living in country c at time t by the social attitudes that Americans born in the US inherited from forebears coming from country c. As shown by Guiso, Sapienza, and Zingales (2006) (see Figure (4)), there is a positive correlation between the trust levels of immigrants and their descendants in the US and trust levels in the country of ancestry.[35] Using the fact that the GSS identifies whether one's parents or grandparents were born outside the US, the authors use variation in the arrival times of the individual's ancestors to the US to proxy for attitudes in two different time periods: 1935–1938 and 2000–2003. Note that this strategy deals not only with the lack of historical data on trust attitudes but also ensures that contemporaneous events that might affect attitudes

[34] In fact, a prior version of this paper was titled "Social Attitudes and Economic Development: An Epidemiological Approach".

[35] The authors use the answers to simple binary question on trust. See footnote (17).

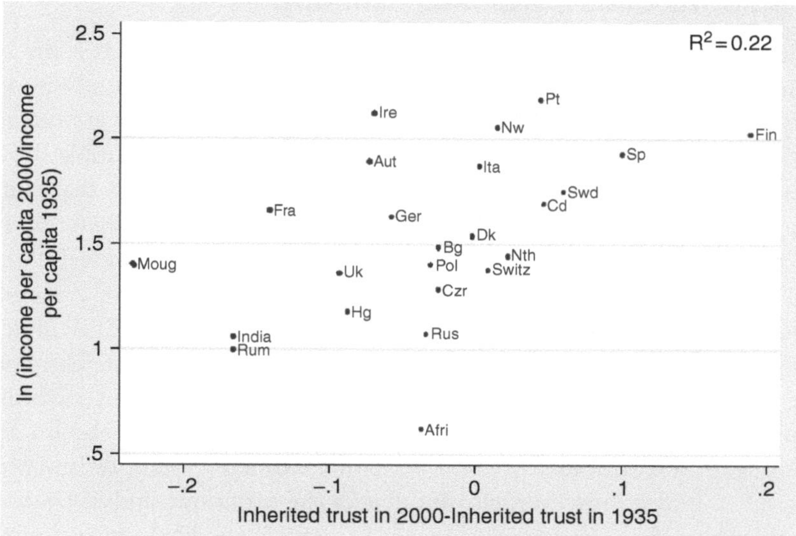

Figure 7 Correlation between change in income per capita and change in inherited trust between 2000 and 1935. *(Data Sources: Maddison database and GSS 1977–2004.) Picture from Algan and Cahuc (2010).*

in the country of ancestry do not affect the cultural proxy, which is the inherited portion of culture for second, third, and forth generation Americans.[36]

The authors first show that the level of trust transmitted from the source countries has changed over the two time periods. They then demonstrate that the change in trust explains a significant portion of the variation in change in per capita income for the 24 countries in their sample (Figure 7 above shows how these vary across the sample countries). This is an intriguing finding. The causal interpretation relies on inherited attitudes and contemporaneous economic outcomes not being codetermined by some common factors, however. The authors attempt to mitigate this concern by using longer time lags between the outcomes and the inherited attitudes. A theory that would allow us to understand why trust changed over time and to identify the sources of change in the data would further strengthen their finding.

[36] Assuming generations of 25 years, inherited trust in 1935–1938 would be relected in the beliefs of second-generation Americans born before 1910 (i.e., whose parents arrived for sure one generation before 1935), of third-generation Americans born before 1935 and of fourth-generation Americans born before 1960. In the same way, inherited attitudes in 2000–2003 are those inherited by: second-generation Americans born between 1910 and 1975, by third-generation born after 1935 and by fourth-generation Americans born after 1960. For the authors, second-generation Americans are those whose both parents were born in the US; third-generation Americans at least two grand-parents but not all immigrated to the US; and fourth-generation Americans had all grand-parents born in the US.

5. CONCLUDING QUESTIONS AND REMARKS

The empirical work on culture has evolved considerably over time. It is my belief that the evidence that culture matters for a large variety of economic outcomes is by now sufficiently strong that most readers would find it convincing. There are many exciting questions left open, however. We would like to understand, for example, how culture propagates and evolves. The evidence presented in this paper shows that cultural preferences and beliefs have a life of their own in the sense that, even when removed from the environment in which they originated, they continue to exercise influence over individual outcomes. The evidence also shows, however, that there is some convergence over time both in economic outcomes and in attitudes. This indicates, not surprisingly, that culture changes in response to a new environment. Culture and the economic environment are. moreover, unlikely to be independent variables. Take, for example, attitudes towards premarital sex; these are likely to depend on contraceptive technology, the availability of abortion, and a woman's ability to support a family on her own.[37] Culture, however, also influences the economic and institutional environment. A culture that considers sex to be shameful is less likely to make contraception or abortion easily available.[38] Thus culture and the economic and institutional environment interact and influence one another. Studies of this interaction would be an important addition to the literature.

Related to the topic discussed above is the question of why culture sometimes changes quickly and at other times glacially. This may be, at least in part, a response to the pace of change in the technological environment. This is not the only possibility, however. As shown in Fernández (2007a), cultural change can also arise from people endogenously learning about their environment. The author develops a dynamic model of culture in which individuals hold heterogeneous beliefs regarding the relative long-run payoffs for women who work in the market versus the home. These women do not know the long-term consequences of market work for their marriages and their children's welfare. Their beliefs, however, and those of their descendants, evolve rationally via an intergenerational learning process in which they learn about the long-term payoffs from working by observing (noisy) private and public signals.

The process described above generically generates an S-shaped figure for female labor force participation, which is what is found in the data. The S shape results from the dynamics of learning. When either small or large proportions of women work, learning is very slow and the changes in female labor force participation are also small. When the proportion of women working is close to 50%, rapid learning and rapid changes in female LFP take place. Thus, a learning model is also able to explain why

[37] See Fernández-Villaverde, Greenwood, and Guner (2010) for an interesting study of this issue.

[38] For example, although the FDA approved the first oral contraceptive in 1960, it was not until the Supreme Court's decision in 1972 that it became available to unmarried women in all states.

culture changes at times slowly and at other times quickly, giving rise to an evolution in social attitudes similar to that shown in Figure (1).

It is also important to gain a deeper understanding of when cultural differences are simply manifestations of multiple equilibria versus when they reflect a deeper disagreement. As discussed in Postlewaite (this volume), for example, the concern with rank, which varies across societies, may not indicate fundamental differences in preferences but arise instead from selecting different equilibria in a model of multiple equilibria.

In the model developed by Cole, Mailath, and Postlewaite (1992), individuals have standard preferences over consumption and their children's utility. Individuals are assigned some initial distribution of wealth, and men in the first generation are arbitrarily assigned a social rank which has no assumed correlation with wealth. The social arrangement (i.e., the equilibrium behavior) prescribes assortative matching between men's rank and women's wealth, with the highest ranked man matching with the wealthiest woman, etc.. The punishment for violating this prescription (which only women would be tempted to do) is that the rank of the male offspring from such a union would be reduced to zero. This implies that these sons will be matched with relatively poor women. Thus, a woman will rationally choose to match with a less wealthy but higher-ranked man if the decrease in her son's future consumption due to her deviation is sufficiently large.

The authors show that the behavior described above in which rank matters (called "aristocratic matching") is an equilibrium for some parameters of the infinite-horizon model. There is also always an equilibrium, however, in which aristocratic rank plays no role and individuals sort simply on the basis of wealth, with the wealthiest man marrying the wealthiest woman etc. It is important to note that these two societies will look very different not only because they give rise to different marital patterns, but also because they will give rise to different savings and bequest levels. In particular, in the aristocratic matching equilibrium, parents have less of an incentive to leave a large bequest to their male offspring since the bequest itself does not change their son's match in the marriage market. This is not so in the equilibrium in which both sexes match on wealth alone. Thus, one would expect families to save more in the latter equilibrium, changing fundamental economic outcomes.

As noted in Fernández (2008) in a slightly different context, behavioral differences arising from true differences in preferences versus those which are simply manifestations of multiple equilibria may be more difficult to distinguish in reality. It is likely that over time, the concerns for aristocratic rank (like the preferences for blue eyes in Mailath and Postlewaite (2003)) evolve in such a way that they become incorporated in deep preferences or beliefs. This would make them more robust in the sense that small changes in the environment would not necessarily eliminate this equilibrium even if it were no longer tenable as equilibrium behavior with standard preferences.

This raises the important question of where preferences and beliefs come from and the extent to which cultural transmission is purposeful, that is, optimizing on the part of an individual or her parents.[39,40] Lastly, it should be noted that if cultural variations are manifestations of endogenous differences in preferences rather than reflections of either different priors (as in Fernández (2007a)) or multiple equilibria arising from standard preferences (as in the Cole, Mailath, and Postlewaite (1992) paper discussed above), this raises difficulties for welfare analysis. Once preferences are endogenous, the standard welfare theorems no longer apply leaving open the question of how policies should be evaluated. This is an important question that requires further investigation.

ACKNOWLEDGEMENT

The author wishes to thank Joyce Cheng Wong for excellent research assistance and the NSF and the Russell Sage Foundation for financial support.

[39] Cultural transmission may well be involuntary. Fernández, Fogli, and Olivetti (2004) show that whether a man's mother worked while he was growing up is positively correlated with whether his wife works, even after controlling for a whole series of socioeconomic variables. They interpret this as preference transmission, but whether it is voluntary – optimizing – or simply by example is an open question.

[40] See Bisin and Verdier (2000) for a model in which parental effort affects the probability with which children inherit their parents' preferences. See Bisin and Verdier (this volume) and Postlewaite (this volume) for excellent reviews of this literature.

REFERENCES

Aghion, P., Algan, Y., Cahuc, P., 2008. Can Policy Interact with Culture? Minimum Wage and the Quality of Labor Relations. mimeo.

Alesina, A., Algan, Y., Cahuc, P., Giuliano, P., 2010. Family Values and the Regulation of Labor. mimeo.

Alesina, A., Angeletos, G.M., 2005. Fairness and Redistribution. Am. Econ. Rev. 95 (4), 960–980.

Alesina, A., Fuchs-Schundeln, N., 2007. Goodbye Lenin (or Not?): The Effect of Communism on People's Preferences. Am. Econ. Rev. 97, 1507–1528.

Alesina, A., Giuliano, P., 2007. The Power of the Family. Working Paper 13051, NBER.

Alesina, A., Giuliano, P., 2009. Family Ties and Political Participation. mimeo.

Alesina, A., Giuliano, P., (this volume): Preferences for Redistribution. in this volume..

Algan, Y., Cahuc, P., 2010. Inherited Trust and Growth. Am. Econ. Rev. forthcoming.

Almond, D., Edlund, L., Milligan, K., 2009. Son Preference and the Persistence of Culture: Evidence from Asian Immigrants to Canada. Working Paper 15391, NBER.

Antecol, H., 2000. An Examination of Cross-Country Differences in the Gender Gap in Labor Force Participation Rates. Labour Econ. 7 (4), 409–426.

Bisin, A., Verdier, T.A., 2000. Beyond The Melting Pot: Cultural Transmission, Marriage, And The Evolution Of Ethnic And Religious Traits. Q. J. Econ. 115 (3), 955–988.

Bisin, A., Verdier, T.A., (this volume): Cultural Transmission and Socialization. in this volume..

Blau, F.D., 1992. The Fertility of Immigrant Women: Evidence from High Fertility Source Countries. In: Borjas, G., Freeman, R. (Eds.), Immigration and the Workforce: Economic Consequences for the United States and Source Areas. University of Chicago Press, Chicago.

Botticini, M., Eckstein, Z., 2005. Jewish occupational selection: education, restrictions, or minorities? J. Econ. His. 65 (922–948).

Carroll, C.D., Rhee, B.K., Rhee, C., 1994. Are there cultural effects on saving? Some cross-sectional evidence. Q. J. Econ. 109 (685–699).

Chuah, S.H., Hoffmann, R., Jones, M., Williams, G., 2007. Do Cultures Clash? Evidence from Cross-National Ultimatum Game Experiments. J. Econ. Behav. Organ. 64, 35–48.

Chuah, S.H., Hoffmann, R., Jones, M., Williams, G., 2009. An economic anatomy of culture: Attitudes and behaviour in inter- and intra-national ultimatum game experiments. J. Econ. Psychol. 30, 732–744.

Cipriani, M., Giuliano, P., Jeanne, O., 2007. Like Mother Like Son? Experimental Evidence on the Transmission of Values from Parents to Children. IZA Discussion Papers 2768.

Cole, H.L., Mailath, G.J., Postlewaite, A., 1992. Social norms, savings behavior, and growth. J. Polit. Econ. 100 (1092–1125).

DiTella, R., Galiani, S., Schargrodsky, E., 2006. The Formation of Beliefs: Evidence from the Allocation of Land Titles to Squatters. mimeo.

Dohmen, T.J., Falk, A., Huffman, D., Sunde, U., 2008. The Inter-generational Transmission of Risk and Trust Attitudes. Working Paper 2307, CESifo.

Dohmen, T.J., Falk, A., Huffman, D., Sunde, U., Schupp, J., Wagner, G.G., 2005. Individual Risk Attitudes: New Evidence from a Large, Representative, Experimentally-Validated Survey. IZA Discussion Papers 1730.

Farré, L., Vella, F., 2007. The Intergenerational Transmission of Gender Role Attitudes and its Implications for Female Labor Force Participation. IZA Discussion Papers 2802, IZA.

Fernández, R., 2007a. Culture as Learning: The Evolution of Female Labor Force Participation over a Century. mimeo.

Fernández, R., 2007b. Women, Work and Culture. J. Eur. Econ. Assoc. 5 (2–3), 305–332.

Fernández, R., 2008. Culture and Economics. In: Durlauf, S., Blume, L. (Eds.), New Palgrave Dictionary of Economics. second ed. Palgrave Macmillan, Basingstoke and New York.

Fernández, R., Fogli, A., 2006. Fertility: The Role of Culture and Family Experience. J. Eur. Econ. Assoc. 4 (2–3), 552–561.

Fernández, R., Fogli, A., 2009. Culture: An Empirical Investigation of Beliefs, Work and Fertility. American Economic Journal: Macroeconomics 1 (1), 146–177.

Fernández, R., Fogli, A., Olivetti, C., 2004. Mothers and sons: preference formation and female labor force dynamics. Q. J. Econ. 119 (1249–1299).

Fernández-Villaverde, J., Greenwood, J., Guner, N., 2010. From Shame to Game in One Hundred Years: An Economic Model of the Rise in Premarital Sex and its De-Stigmatization. mimeo.

Fisman, R., Miguel, E., 2007. Corruption, Norms, and Legal Enforcement: Evidence from Diplomatic Parking Tickets. J. Polit. Econ. 115 (6), 1020–1048.

Giuliano, P., 2007. Living Arrangements in Western Europe: Does Cultural Origin Matter? J. Eur. Econ. Assoc. 5 (5), 927–952.

Giuliano, P., Spilimbergo, A., 2009. Growing Up in a Recession: Beliefs and the Macroeconomy. NBER Working Paper 15321.

Greif, A., 1994. Cultural beliefs and the organization of society: a historical and theoretical reflection on collectivist and individualist societies. J. Polit. Econ. 102, 912–950.

Guinnane, T.W., Moehling, C.M., Gráda, C.Ó., 2006. The Fertility of the Irish in the United States in 1910. Explor. Econ. Hist. 43 (3).

Guiso, L., Sapienza, P., Zingales, L., 2004. The Role of Social Capital in Financial Development. Am. Econ. Rev. 94, 526–556.

Guiso, L., Sapienza, P., Zingales, L., 2006. Does Culture Affect Economic Outcomes? J. Econ. Perspect. 20, 23–48.

Hanushek, E.A., Kimko, D.D., 2000. Schooling, Labor-Force Quality, and the Growth of Nations. Am. Econ. Rev. 90 (5), 1184–1208.
Henrich, J., 2000. Does Culture Matter in Economic Behavior? Ultimatum Game Bargaining Among the Machiguenga of the Peruvian Amazon. Am. Econ. Rev. 90 (4), 973–979.
Henrich, J., Boyd, R., Bowles, S., Camerer, C.F., Fehr, E., Gintis, H., et al., 2001. In search of Homo economicus: Behavioral experiments in 15 small-scale societies. Am. Econ. Rev. 91 (2), 73–78.
Ichino, A., Maggi, G., 2000. Work Environment and Individual Background: Explaining Regional Shirking Differentials in a Large Italian Firm. Q. J. Econ. 115, 1057–1090.
Kroeber, A., Kluckhohn, C., 1952. Culture. Meridian Books, New York.
Luttmer, E.F., Singhal, M., 2010. Culture, Context, and the Taste for Redistribution. mimeo.
Mailath, G., Postlewaite, A., 2003. The social context of economic decisions. J. Eur. Econ. Assoc. 1 (354–362).
Marmot, M.G., Syme, S.L., Kagan, A., Kato, H., Cohen, J.B., Belsky, J., 1975. Epidemiologic studies of coronary heart disease and stroke in Japanese men living in Japan, Hawaii and California: prevalence of coronary and hypertensive heart disease and associated risk factors. Am. J. Epidemiol. 102, 514–525.
Miguel, E., Saiegh, S.M., Satyanath, S., 2008. National Cultures and Soccer Violence. mimeo.
Oosterbeek, H., Sloof, R., van de Kuilen, G., 2004. Cultural Differences in Ultimatum Game Experiments: Evidence from a Meta-Analysis. Experimental Economics 7, 171–188.
Postlewaite, A., (this volume): Social Norms and Preferences. in this volume.
Reimers, C.W., 1985. Cultural Differences in Labor Force Participation Among Married Women. American Economic Association Papers and Proceedings 75 (2), 251–255.
Roth, A.E., Prasnikar, V., Okuno-Fujiwara, M., Zamir, S., 1991. Bargaining and Market Behavior in Jerusalem, Ljubljana, Pittsburgh, and Tokyo: An Experimental Study. Am. Econ. Rev. 81 (5), 1068–1095.
Tabellini, G., 2010. Culture and Institutions: Economic Development in the Regions of Europe. J. Eur. Econ. Assoc. forthcoming.
Vella, F., 1994. Gender Roles and Human Capital Investment; The Relationship between Traditional Attitudes and Female Labor Market Performance. Economica 61, 191–211.

PART *Two*

Social Actions

CHAPTER 12

An Overview of Social Networks and Economic Applications*

Matthew O. Jackson[†]
Written for the *Handbook of Social Economics*[‡]

Contents

1. Introduction 512
2. Social Networks and Networked Markets 514
    2.1 Some background on networked markets 514
        2.1.1 Social networks in labor markets 514
        2.1.2 Other networked markets 517
    2.2 Social networks in learning and diffusion 518
3. The Structure of Social Networks 521
    3.1 Definitions and graph terminology 522
    3.2 Degree distributions 523
    3.3 Average distances and small worlds 526
        3.3.1 Clustering 527
        3.3.2 Homophily 529
4. Network Formation 532
    4.1 Random networks 533
        4.1.1 Poisson random networks 533
        4.1.2 The small world model 533
        4.1.3 Preferential attachment 534
        4.1.4 Richer sequential link formation models 535
    4.2 Models for statistical analysis 535
        4.2.1 Exponential random graph models and p models* 536
        4.2.2 Fitting random and strategic models 540
        4.2.3 Community detection 540
    4.3 Strategic network formation 543
    4.4 Mixing random and strategic models 549
5. Modeling the Impact of Networks 550
    5.1 Diffusion 551
    5.2 Learning 551
    5.3 Bargaining and trade through networks 560

* Financial support from the NSF under grant SES–0647867 is gratefully acknowledged. Thank you to Matthew Elliott, Carlos Lever, and Yves Zenou for comments on earlier drafts.
† Department of Economics, Stanford University, Stanford CA 94305, USA and the Santa Fe Institute, Santa Fe NM 87501, USA.
‡ Edited by Jess Benhabib, Alberto Bisin, and Matthew O. Jackson, forthcoming, Elsevier Press.

Handbook of Social Economics, Volume 1A
ISSN 0169-7218, DOI: 10.1016/S0169-7218(11)01012-4

5.4 Peer interactions and games on networks 565
5.5 Labor markets 573
6. Concluding Remarks 574
References 574
Further Readings 582

Abstract

In this chapter, I provide an overview of research on social networks and their role in shaping behavior and economic outcomes. I include discussion of empirical and theoretical analyses of the role of social networks in markets and exchange, learning and diffusion, and network games. I also include some background on social network characteristics and measurements, models of network formation, models for the statistical analysis of social networks, as well as community detection.
JEL Classification Codes: D85, C72, L14, Z13

Keywords

Social Networks
Network Games
Graphical Games
Games on Networks
Diffusion
Learning
Network Formation
Community Detection

1. INTRODUCTION

The people with whom we interact on a regular basis, and even some with whom we interact only sporadically, influence our beliefs, decisions and behaviors. Examples of the effects of social networks on economic activity are abundant and pervasive, including roles in transmitting information about jobs, new products, technologies, and political opinions. They also serve as channels for informal insurance and risk sharing, and network structure influences patterns of decisions regarding education, career, hobbies, criminal activity, and even participation in micro-finance. Beyond the role of "social" networks in determining various economic behaviors, there are also many business and political interactions that are networked. Networks of relationships among various firms and political organizations affect research and development, patent activity, trade patterns, and political alliances.[1] Given the many roles of networks in economic activity, they have become increasingly studied by economists.

[1] References to studies on some of these subjects are provided below. Related chapters on labor markets (Topa (this volume)), networks in developing countries (Munshi (this volume)), risk sharing (Fafchamps (this volume)), diffusion and social structure (Jackson and Yariv (this volume)), learning (Goyal (this volume)) provide additional references, and Jackson (2008) provides a more detailed look at some applications and an extensive bibliography.

There are two important aspects of the study of networks from an economist's perspective. The first iunderstanding is how network structure influences economic activity. Some examples of questions examined in the literature provide an idea of why this is an important issue:

How does the role of social networks in disseminating job information affect wages and employment?

How do terms of trade in networked markets depend on the network structure and compare to centralized markets?

How are education and other human capital decisions influenced by social network structure?

Will the networks that are formed be the efficient ones in terms of their implications for economic activity?

The second important aspect of the study of networks from an economist's perspective is that economic tools are very useful in analyzing both network formation and network influence, and these tools are quite complementary to those from the many other disciplines that also study social networks. That is, even beyond the eventual implications for economic activity and welfare, what can we say about how people will self-organize and why certain patterns will emerge? For example, why do people tend to associate with other people who are similar to them along a number of dimensions and what will this imply for behavior? Why is the social distance between people (in terms of the shortest path in the social network in which they are embedded) so small even in very large societies?

In this chapter, I provide background on networks, both in terms of how they influence social and economic activity as well as how they can be modeled and analyzed. In doing so, I cover areas branching out from what an economist might usually be exposed to because the study of networks is so naturally interdisciplinary and multidisciplinary. Part of this is due to the fact that networked interactions have wide-ranging applications, from purely social, to economic, to political, and even to biological. This is also partly due to the diverse set of tools that are useful in analyzing networks, including: anthropological case studies, sociological survey methods, mathematical analyses of random graphs, techniques from statistical physics as well as computer science for analyzing complex interactive systems, and models of strategic interaction from economics. Given the broad scope of network analysis, the chapter can only provide an introduction to and glimpse of the research in this area, discussing a few examples of the empirical and theoretical literature and giving a feel for the importance of the subject.[2]

[2] See Jackson (2008) for a much more detailed look at some of the topics covered here, as well as many that are not discussed here.

2. SOCIAL NETWORKS AND NETWORKED MARKETS

I begin with a discussion of some of the various settings in which networked interactions are prominent and important.

2.1 Some background on networked markets

Although we often idealize markets as centralized, many goods and services are contracted upon through networks of bilateral relationships. A manufacturer might have specific relationships with a few suppliers of raw materials, that also supply other firms and possibly even the manufacturer's competitors. Firms subcontract and out-source some of their business. The terms of trade, prices and products that emerge in such a world can depend on who is connected to whom. To understand this, it is useful to note the ingredients that comprise an idealized market: large numbers of well-informed agents in semi-anonymous settings, goods that are observable and of verifiable qualities, and contracts that are fully specified and costlessly enforced. In reality, even very large markets involve frictions that lead them to be at least partly decentralized. For example, in many labor markets jobs come with various idiosyncrasies (including location, skills required, work environment, compensation, etc.), as do workers in terms of their backgrounds. Such heterogeneity in the market means that information can be critical in properly matching workers to positions.[3] Social networks fill such a role, both in communicating information to workers about the specifics of various job opportunities, as well as communicating information to firms about the potential fit of various workers; mitigating substantial search frictions. This role of enhancing a matching is not specific to labor markets, as the same can be said of a broad range of markets, as most goods and services involve some heterogeneity both in terms of what is supplied and what is demanded. Also, this is not the only role that networks play in labor and other markets. Repeated interactions with specific partners help mitigate a number of problems related to moral hazard and adverse selection, and thus long-term economic relationships with known partners can dominate shorter-term anonymous transactions.

In this section I begin with a discussion of a few of the many studies that illustrate these roles of networks in market settings, and then I go on to discuss the more general roles of social networks in diffusing information and in shaping behavior.

2.1.1 Social networks in labor markets

The role of social networks in labor markets deserves our attention for at least two reasons: first, because of the central role networks play in disseminating information about job openings they place a critical role in determining whether labor markets function

[3] For example, see Pissarides (2000).

efficiently; and second, because network structure ends up having implications for things like human capital investment, as well as inequality. As such, this application is a great example of why economists should care about networks and why networks deserve careful study and should be incorporated into our modeling of markets. As this topic is also discussed in Topa (This volume) and Munshi (This volume), I will keep this discussion rather brief.[4]

The fact that social networks are an important conduit of information about and access to jobs is evident to anyone who has ever looked for employment in almost any profession. The role of networks in labor markets has been extensively documented, with early studies including that of Myers and Shultz (1951) who interviewed textile workers in a New England mill town. Myers and Shultz observed that 62% of the interviewees had found out about and applied to their first job through a social contact, while only 23% had applied directly on their own and 15% had found their job through an agency, ads, or other means. This sort of pattern is not specific to the textile industry, but is typical. There are some variations in the role of networks as a source of job information as we make comparisons across professions, locations, ethnicities of workers, and other attributes; but networks play a substantial role in essentially all of the labor markets that have been studied, regardless of the skill level, location, or population of workers (e.g., see Rees and Shultz (1970), Montgomery (1991), Pellizzari (2009), Corcoran, Datcher, and Duncan (1980), and Bentolila et al. (2009)).[5]

The fact that information about jobs is passed through a social network becomes interesting because of its implications for wage and employment dynamics and patterns. As a starting point, models of social networks in labor markets imply that peoples' wages and employment will be related to that of their friends and acquaintances. The basic driver for this is that unemployed workers will generally obtain more job information if their social contacts are employed than if their social contacts are unemployed. This gives rise to robust and strong forms of correlation in the wages and employment of linked individuals in a network, as studied in some detail by Calvó-Armengol and Jackson (2004, 2007). Although the theoretical implications can be cleanly established, testing for such correlations is not so easy since there is an absence of longitudinal data sets that include detailed social network observations together with employment and wage data. As such, much of the empirical work testing for social influence on wages and employment has tried to proxy for the social network by using some other observable such as the proximity of individuals, their ethnicity, or other

[4] For a more extensive background, the reader is also referred to the survey article by Ioannides and Datcher-Loury (2004), and Chapter 10 in Jackson (2008).

[5] The resilience of networks as job contact information conduits is the subject of an analysis by Casella and Hanaki (2008), and there is even evidence that the use of social networks as information sources is positively related to unemployment, as found by Galeotti and Merlino (2008) looking at U.K. data.

attributes. For example, Bayer, Ross and Topa (2005) make use of census data to demonstrate higher correlation in employment among people living in the same city block compared to correlations among those living on different city blocks (but still close enough to avoid a geographical employment effect), and controlling for workers' characteristics. Thus, an individual's employment outcome is not simply based on (observed) characteristics or the employment of the general geographic area, but also the state of employment of his or her peers at very close proximity. This is not conclusive evidence for social network effects, as one cannot completely rule out some other unobserved characteristic that accounts for employment outcomes and also is related to peoples' tendency to live on the same city block, but it provides evidence that goes beyond previous studies. This challenge of alternative explanations of unobserved characteristics that are correlated with social interaction is endemic to peer effect studies, and in particular has pushed studies of social effects in labor markets to be increasingly detailed and careful in their design with the intent of ruling out other potential explanations for observed patterns.[6]

In addition to the correlation of wage and employment outcomes across agents, the fact that jobs are accessed through social networks has implications for the time series of employment. In particular, as Calvó-Armengol and Jackson (2004) point out, duration dependence in unemployment arises in a networked model of employment. Duration dependence (e.g., see Schweitzer and Smith (1974) and Heckman and Borjas (1980)) refers to the stylized fact that the longer a given individual is unemployed, the higher the chance that the individual will still be unemployed in the next period, even after controlling for various characteristics of the individual. There are various reasons for duration dependence given in the labor economics literature, including characteristics about the worker that potential employers can observe but the researcher cannot (a form of "unobserved heterogeneity"), so that conditioning on a longer spell of unemployment it is more likely that the worker is unattractive to employers. It can also be that workers lose skills from being out of work, or that longer spells of unemployment are correlated with unobserved local labor market conditions (see Lynch (1989) for more discussion and references). The role of social networks as a conduit of information about jobs adds a new facet to understanding duration dependence. Duration dependence arises in a job-contact network context, because longer spells of unemployment are more likely to occur to an agent who has fewer (employed) friends, all else held equal. Thus, the longer we see an agent being unemployed, the lower the conditional probability that the agent has many employed friends, and so the lower the probability that the agent will have access to job information in the near future.

[6] For some other clever recent approaches to isolating social effects, see Laschever (2007), Munshi (2003), and Beaman (2007), as well as the discussion in Topa (This volume).

Beyond the implications for employment and wages, studies of job contact networks also have led to other observations and implications. Perhaps the best-known example of this is Granovetter's (1973) observation of the "strength of weak ties." Granovetter interviewed people in Amherst Massachusetts and asked not only how they found out about their jobs, but also how frequently they interacted with the people through whom they heard about their jobs. He called relationships "strong" if the two people interacted at least twice per week on average, "medium" if the pair interacted less than twice per week but more than once per year, and "weak" if they interacted less than once per year. Based on 54 interviewees who found their most recent job through a social contact, Granovetter found that 16.7% had found their job through a strong tie, 55.7% through a medium tie, and 27.6% through a weak tie. While people might tend to have many more medium and weak ties than strong ones, it is still significant that people with whom an individual interacted so infrequently could play such an important and instrumental role. Granovetter (1973) goes on to discuss that the importance of weak ties can be in part traced to the fact that they often connect an individual to parts of a social network to which that individual would otherwise be quite far from. Thus, weak ties play a sort of bridging role, and can provide access to information that an individual might not find through other means. Much of the impact of Granovetter's work has come from the wide application and evaluation of the "strength of weak ties" idea in other contexts, and the important observation that the strength of ties have consequences, and so it can be useful to keep track of tie strength.

Additional implications of networked labor markets beyond their direct impact on employment and wages concern things like workers' decisions to drop out of the labor force, and decisions invest in education and other forms of human capital. As Calvó-Armengol and Jackson (2004, 2007, 2009), point out, the fact that social networks are important in conveying job information results in complementarities in investment decisions between friends and acquaintances. As more of an agent's friends are in the labor market, an agent has a better chance of hearing about jobs, which increases that agent's payoff from remaining in the labor force and may also increase that agent's returns from education. Modeling these implications of networked labor markets is discussed in more detail below in Section 5.5.

2.1.2 Other networked markets

Beyond labor markets, there are many other market settings where networks of relationships play an important role. An interesting and illustrative example is that of the garment industry. Uzzi's (1996) study of the New York garment industry uncovered several aspects of the role of networks. In that industry there are a set of firms that manufacture garments and others that are contracting to buy particular garments. A typical relationship involves a contractor coming to a manufacturer with a given design and contracting to buy a given number of garments produced to the design specification.

Some such arrangements are straightforward, whereas others are more complex and involve some idiosyncracies in production potentially requiring special investments, uncertainties, or other things that might lead to less than perfect contracting. Uzzi's interviews suggest that some relationships function well as one-time "arm's length" or "market" interactions, while others are "special" or "close" and involve repeated interaction, trust, fine-grained information transfer, and joint problem solving. Uzzi (1996) also explores the extent to which having close relationships versus market relationships is related with a firm's survival. In particular he examines data from 1991 from the International Ladies Garment Workers' Union which cover most of the active firms in New York in that year. Uzzi then documents that 125 of the 479 contractors with complete records in the data set failed to survive during this year. He regresses whether or not a firm survives on a variable that keeps track of the extent to which a firm is involved in close and repeated relationships, as well as a series of other background variables (geographic location, age of the firm, size of the firm, network centrality measures, and other neighborhood variables). He finds a positive and significant relationship between the survival variable and the variable measuring how concentrated a firm's contracts are. A firm that has completely dispersed contracts (so no repeat business) is almost twice as likely to exit the market in the year as a firm that is completely monogamous and contracts with only one other firm.

Clearly, there are many potential explanations for the correlation between a firm's survival and how many other firms it contracts with, and so we cannot deduce the causal relationship from these data.[7] Nevertheless, whatever the causal chain, there is still a statistically significant negative relationship between the degree of a firm in terms of how many other firms it contracts with and the firm's chance of survival. Thus, network structure is playing some role, either affecting the survival rate, or being an outcome of the survival prospects of a firm, or relating to some other unobserved characteristic that affects the survival rate. Some of the models discussed below provide specific hypotheses about how firm characteristics relate to the network structure, as well as the terms of trades. These models, together with further empirical and experimental studies, should help us to better understand the role of networks of relationships in various markets.

2.2 Social networks in learning and diffusion

Another important role of social networks is in influencing learning, as well as the diffusion of technology, opinions, and behaviors. This is discussed in more detail in Goyal (This volume) and Jackson and Yariv (This volume), and I will mention a few of the primary points here.

[7] The role of networks of relationships between firms and their survival is still not extensively modeled. Some work on this appears in Allen and Babus (2007), but it is still an under-developed area of study, especially given the potential role of network structure in financial contagions.

Given the obvious importance of the diffusion of a technology, product, disease, or opinion, diffusion has been extensively studied from a variety of perspectives. There are early studies such as Ryan and Gross's (1943) research on the diffusion of hybrid corn seed among farmers, and Hagerstrand's (1970) study of the diffusion of the telephone, as well as a range of other case studies (see Rogers and Rogers (2003)). In terms of some of the interesting issues, on a most basic level there is a simple question of establishing that a given individual's behavior is influenced by that of his or her social contacts. There are many different challenges in such an analysis. If we observe that an individual's behavior is correlated with that of his or her friends and acquaintances can we conclude that they influenced it? There is an ever-looming question that we may not have observed all of the characteristics that influence behavior. That is, if we see that two friends both buy a new product, one after the other, can we conclude that one's purchase had an influence on the other? The difficulty is that there can be many things that influence these individuals' decisions, such as their age, income, education, ethnicity, exposure to advertising, and so forth. To the extent that we can observe *all* of the relevant factors affecting behavior, we can test for peer influence then by seeing whether a peer's purchase of a product leads to an increase (or decrease) in an individual's propensity to purchase after accounting for all of those other factors. Of course, the difficulty is that we generally will not have observed all such factors. This is exacerbated by the fact that people's friendships tend to correlate with how similar they are, something termed "homophily" and discussed in more detail below. So, it could be that the individuals happen to be friends because they share some trait, and it is that trait which causes them both to buy the product. If we do not observe that trait we could mistakenly conclude that one's purchase influenced the other's.[8]

Overcoming this problem requires some clever collection of data or experimental analysis. A nice example of this using field data is a study of social learning by Conley and Udry (2001, 2004a, b, c). They examine the use of fertilizer by pineapple farmers. In particular, they show that changes in the amount of fertilizer used by a given farmer are related to the success or failure of similar past changes in fertilizer use by other farmers. Having controlled experiments can substantially narrow down the range of explanations for observed peer correlations. For example, Hesselius, Johansson, and Nilsson (2009) examine absences in the workplace based on a randomized rule affecting about 3000 workplaces in Göteborg Sweden. Randomly assigned agents were allowed to have longer spells of absence from work (14 days) without having to produce a doctor's certificate than was the rule for the general population (8 days). This resulted not only in an

[8] For an interesting recent study showing how strongly homophily can bias studies of such peer influence, see Aral, Muchnik, and Sundararajan (2009).

increase in absences for the treated individuals (those allowed the extra time before producing a doctor's certificate), but also for nontreated individuals conditional on being in a workplace with many treated individuals. Interestingly, the affect of how many other treated individuals there were in the workplace did not significantly influence treated individuals' behavior. This allows them to distinguish between various ways in which the peer effects might work, ruling out things like enjoying time together and being more consistent with a fairness effect or related peer effect on preferences. This sort of study shows the power of (field) experiments in identifying peer effects.[9]

Of course, an alternative technique to working with controlled data is a structural approach where one works with a model that makes pointed predictions about patterns in the data depending on the mechanism at work. This can offer an improved understanding of the mechanisms at work in peer effects and diffusion, but depends on the plausibility of the model. For example, Banerjee, Chandrasekhar, Duflo and Jackson (2010) fit models of diffusion to patterns of microfinance participation in a set of villages in rural India. They take advantage of differences in predicted patterns of behavior as a function of the diffusion of basic information (awareness of microfinance) compared to peer effects (where agents are reluctant to participate unless they have a personal acquaintance who endorses microfinance). Based on such models, they investigate how patterns of microfinance are affected by both peer effects and information diffusion.

Another challenge faced in studying peer effects comes from dealing with problems where one does not directly observe the network of who interacts with whom, but instead proxies for this with aggregated behavior by a given individual's peers. This can lead to identification problems, such as the reflection problem pointed out by Manski (1993) and discussed in more detail in the chapters by Blume et al. (This volume) and Durlauf (This volume).[10]

Beyond establishing the fact that individuals are influenced by their peers, we also wish to better understand how this depends on an individual's "position" in the network. An early study in this direction is by Coleman, Katz, and Menzel (1966) who examined the time at which different doctors first prescribed a new drug to one of their patients. Coleman, Katz, and Menzel first interviewed doctors to map out a social network in terms of whom they would turn to for advice and whom they had contact with socially. Coleman, Katz, and Menzel also kept track of the first date at which a doctor prescribed the new drug to a patient. They divided their sample of doctors into

[9] Taking advantage of randomized programs in the field has proven to be a useful strategy in identifying various peer effects, not only operating through preference interactions but also through the diffusion of information. For example, see Duflo and Saez (2003) and Bayer, Hjalmarsson, and Pozen (2009).

[10] See Bramoullé, Djebbari and Fortin (2009) for a discussion of how network information can overcome the reflection problem.

three groups: those named by at least three other doctors as an advisor or friend, those named by one or two other doctors as an advisor or friend, and those not named by any other doctors as an advisor or friend. They then tracked what fraction of the doctors in each of these three groups had prescribed the drug at least once. Essentially their finding was that the most highly connected group (named by three or more other doctors) had the greatest fraction who had prescribed the drug by each date, and the second most highly connected group was second, and the unconnected group lagged behind in the fraction that had prescribed the drug. Thus, according to one measure of how "connected" a doctor is, more connected doctors were significantly more likely to be prescribing this new drug at an earlier date. So, we see that position seems to matter; although it is not clear why it matters. Subsequent studies have worked to sort out why this might have occurred, and there one faces the same challenges as discussed above in interpreting these data (see Jackson (2008) for some discussion and references to follow ups). It is possible that there are other factors that lead doctors to begin prescribing a new drug, such as their exposure to drug companies' marketing, or doctors' attitudes towards change, and so forth; and these other factors could be spuriously correlated with the connectedness of the doctors. Again, by specifying the mechanism that one believes might be at work, one can then begin to distinguish between some of the potential explanations via more detailed observations, or controlled experiments in lab or field settings. Regardless of whether network position is directly causal, or only indirectly related via some other attributes, it is of interest to understand why network position ends up being related to activity.

The list of settings where peer effects, or network effects more generally, have been found to be important is a long and varied one. It includes a range of things from criminal behavior (Reiss (1980), Glaeser, Sacerdote and Scheinkman (1996), Kling, Ludwig and Katz (2005), Patacchini and Zenou (2008)), to education (e.g., Calvo-Armengol, Patacchini and Zenou (2009)), to risk-sharing and loan behavior (Fafchamps and Lund (2003), De Weerdt (2004), Karlan, Mobius, Rosenblat, Szeidl (2009)), to obesity (Christakis and Fowler (2008), Fowler and Christakis (2008), and Halliday and Kwak (2009)). (See Fafchamps (This volume), Ioannides (This volume), Jackson and Yariv (This volume), Munshi (This volume), Sacerdote (This volume), and Topa (This volume), for more examples and background on empirical evidence.)

3. THE STRUCTURE OF SOCIAL NETWORKS

I now turn to discussing what is known about social networks in terms of their basic structure and how they can be usefully quantified. These issues are of interest from a pure social science perspective to those studying how humans self-organize, as well as a basic toolbox for those wishing to further study the role of network structure in economic interactions.

3.1 Definitions and graph terminology

I begin with some definitions and terminology that will allow us to talk about network structure. Much of this terminology emerges from standard graph theory, with some variation in terms across disciplines.[11]

A network is represented as a graph on a set N of *nodes*, with a finite number of members n. Nodes are also sometimes referred to as vertices, agents, or players.

A *graph* or *network* is a pair $(N, \mathbf{g})$, where $\mathbf{g}$ is an $n \times n$ adjacency matrix on the set of nodes, where g_{ij} indicates the relationship between nodes i and j. For most of the discussion here I focus on cases where $g_{ij} \in \{0, 1\}$ so that a relationship is either present ($g_{ij} = 1$) or absent ($g_{ij} = 0$), although weighted and/or directed (as well as dynamic!) cases are clearly of interest as well.

A graph is *undirected* if $\mathbf{g}$ is required to be symmetric so that $g_{ij} = g_{ji}$, and is *directed* otherwise. Whether or not a network is directed or undirected depends on the application. In applications where mutual consent is required to maintain a relationship (friendships, alliances, partnerships, contracts, and so forth) it will often be most appropriate to represent these as an undirected graph, while there are other applications where unilateral relationships are possible (such as one author citing another or a web page linking to another).

It is generally useful to use the notation $ij \in \mathbf{g}$ to indicate that $g_{ij} = 1$ and $ij \notin \mathbf{g}$ to indicate that $g_{ij} = 0$, and one can represent a graph by the set of links that are present (so one could alternatively represent $\mathbf{g}$ by its set of links). I alternatively view $\mathbf{g}$ as a matrix or a set of links depending on which is more convenient, and thus abuse notation in what follows.

A relationship between two nodes i and j, represented by $ij \in \mathbf{g}$, is referred to as a link. Links are also referred to as edges or ties in various parts of the literature; and sometimes also directed links, directed edges, or arcs in the specific case of a directed network.

A *walk* in a network $(N, \mathbf{g})$ refers to a sequence of nodes, $i_1, i_2, i_3, \ldots, i_{K-1}, i_K$ such that $i_k i_{k+1} \in \mathbf{g}$ for each k from 1 to K. The *length* of the walk is the number of links in it, or $K-1$. For example, see Figure 1.

A *path* in a network $(N, \mathbf{g})$ is a walk in $(N, \mathbf{g})$, $i_1, i_2, i_3, \ldots, i_{K-1}, i_K$, such that all the nodes are distinct.[12]

A *cycle* in a network $(N, \mathbf{g})$ is a walk in $(N, \mathbf{g})$, $i_1, i_2, i_3, \ldots, i_{K-1}, i_K$, such that $i_1 = i_K$.

A network $(N, \mathbf{g})$ is *connected* if there is a path in $(N, \mathbf{g})$ between every pair of nodes i and j.[13]

[11] See Chapter 2 in Jackson (2008) for additional background and references.

[12] Standard definitions of paths, formally define them as subnetworks of the original network, in which case they are not simply sequences of nodes, but need to be specified as sets of nodes together with sets of links. The definitions here simplify notation, and for the purposes of this chapter, the difference is inconsequential.

[13] Each of these definitions has an analog for directed networks, simply viewing the pairs as directed links and then having the name directed walk, directed path, and directed cycle. In defining connectedness for a directed network one often uses a strong definition requiring a directed path from each node to every other node.

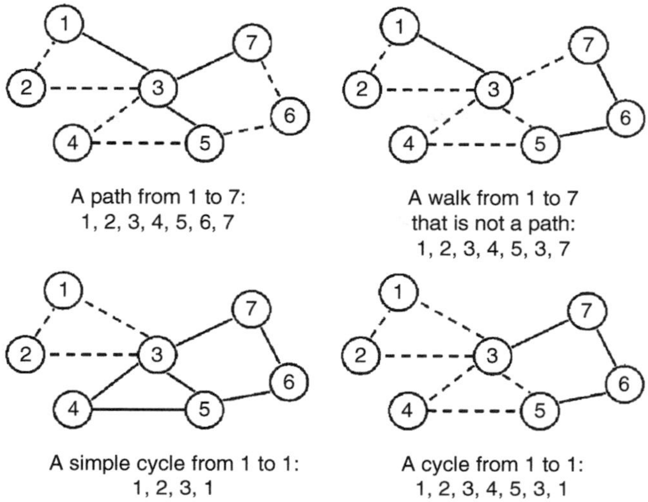

Figure 1 Paths, Walks, and Cycles.

A *component* of a network $(N, \mathbf{g})$ is subnetwork $(N', \mathbf{g}')$ (so $N' \subset N$ and $\mathbf{g}' \subset \mathbf{g}$) such that there is a path in $\mathbf{g}'$ from every node $i \in N'$ to every other node $j \in N'$ ($j \neq i$), and such that every node $l \in N$ such that $l \notin N'$ has no link in $\mathbf{g}$ to any node in N'. Thus, a component of a network is a maximal connected subgraph, so that the subgraph is connected and there is no way of expanding the set of nodes or links in the sub-graph and still having it be connected (e.g., see Figure 2).

The *distance* between two nodes in the same component of a network is the length of a shortest path (also known as a *geodesic*) between them.

The *neighbors* of a node i in a network $(N, \mathbf{g})$ are denoted[14]

$$N_i(\mathbf{g}) = \{j | ij \in \mathbf{g}\}$$

The *degree* of a node i in a network $(N, \mathbf{g})$ is the number of neighbors that i has in the network, so that $d_i(\mathbf{g}) = |N_i(\mathbf{g})|$.[15]

3.2 Degree distributions

While the information contained in a full specification of all relationships, $(N, \mathbf{g})$, is sometimes very useful, it is generally too cumbersome when there are many nodes, and so descriptive statistics that capture facets of the network are used. For instance, knowing the average degree in the network $\sum_i d_i(\mathbf{g})/n$ gives some idea of the density

[14] For the remaining definitions, I omit dependence on the set of nodes N, so for instance I write $N_i(\mathbf{g})$ rather than $N_i(N, \mathbf{g})$, as generally the set of nodes will be fixed and so only the set of connections will be varying.

[15] Unless otherwise stated, let us suppose that $g_{ii} = 0$, so that nodes are not linked to themselves.

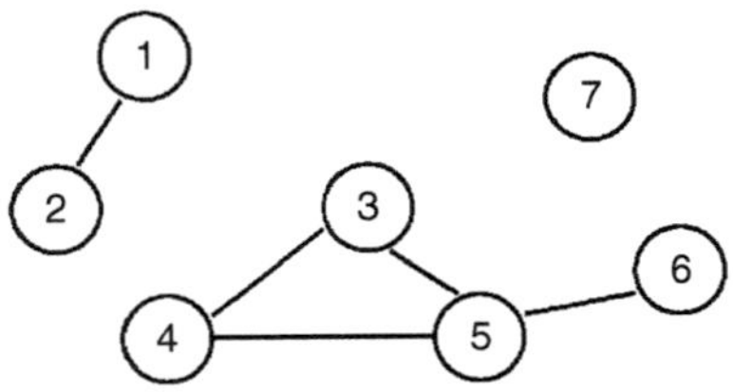

Figure 2 A Network with 3 Components.

of the connections in a network. However, often we need richer information and the distribution of the degrees of the nodes provides more substantial information about network structure.

The *degree distribution* of a network (N, $\mathbf{g}$) is the frequency distribution P of the degrees in the network. $P(d)$ indicates the fraction of nodes that have degree d.

Degree distributions vary across applications. One extreme distribution corresponds to a *regular network* such that all nodes have the same degree. A useful benchmark is a network where each link is formed at random with the same probability p and independently of all other links in the network. In that case, the probability that a given node has degree d has a binomial distribution described by

$$\binom{n-1}{d} p^d (1-p)^{n-1-d}. \tag{1}$$

For large n and relatively small p, a standard approximation of a binomial distribution by a Poisson distribution applies and the probability that a node has d links is approximately

$$\frac{e^{-(n-1)p}((n-1)p)^d}{d!}. \tag{2}$$

Such networks where all nodes are formed uniformly at random with the same probability have been studied extensively in random graph theory, including seminal papers by Erdös and Rényi (1959, 1960, 1961) and many others.[16] They are often referred to as "Poisson random graphs," due to the (approximate) degree distribution. They serve a useful benchmark and exhibit many properties that are common to many random graph models:[17]

- when p is very low (well below $1/n$) most nodes are completely isolated and only a few nodes are linked as pairs,

[16] See the book by Bollobás (2001) for a overview of this literature.

[17] See Jackson (2008) for more detailed discussion and background. This class of networks is also referred to as Bernoulli random graphs, and even simply "G(n,p)."

- as p increases (above $1/n$) a network begins to emerge in the sense that some nodes have more than one link and a large component (referred to as the *giant component* begins to emerge and dominate the network,[18] and cycles begin to occur,
- as p increases further (beyond $\log(n)$) the isolated nodes disappear and network begins to coalesce into a single connected component.

Another useful benchmark distribution is a power distribution such that

$$P(d) = cd^{-\gamma}$$

for some parameter γ and normalizing constant c, where the distribution is generally truncated at some upper bound. In settings where such degree distributions are prevalent it is often said that a *power law* is satisfied, and the distributions are referred to as being *scale-free*. The scale-free property refers to the fact that $P(d)/P(d') = P(kd)/P(kd')$ for a rescaling by a factor k. Such distributions have been found in a variety of settings, with prominent examples being the distributions of wealth noted by Pareto (1896) (for whom the related Pareto distribution is named), word usage, and city sizes (often referred to as Zipf's law - Zipf (1949)). An example of such a distribution in a network context was noted by Price (1965), who examined the network of citations among articles. Albert, Jeong and Barabasi (1999) and Huberman and Adamic (1999) found that portions of the world wide web (examining links between web pages) fit a power distribution.

Power distributions have the nice feature that the frequency distribution can be rewritten as

$$\log(P(d)) = \log(c) - \gamma \log(d)$$

and so are linear when viewed on a log-log plot. An important feature of such a distribution is that it has "fat tails" relative to a Poisson distribution. Thus, the frequency of very high and very low degree nodes is greater than if links were formed uniformly at random, and correspondingly the frequency of nodes with degrees near the center of the distribution is lower than if links were formed uniformly at random. This distinction can lead the network to have very different properties, as very high degree nodes can serve as "hubs" and play prominent roles in different contexts as I discuss below.

There are many examples of networks whose degree distribution have fat tails, and so it sometimes said that a power law is satisfied by many networks (e.g., see Barabasi (2002)). Nevertheless, social networks exhibit a full spectrum of degree distributions across different applications, ranging from one extreme where the distribution of links is nearly as if they were formed uniformly at random (e.g., matched well by distributions of romances among

[18] There will generally only be one large component as it is very unlikely to have two components that each has many nodes in them but with absolutely no links between the two components.

high school students in the Add-Health data set), and another extreme where there the distribution is nearly scale-free (e.g., the www from Albert, Jeong, and Barabasi (1999) and Huberman and Adamic (1999)). Thus, although many networks have fatter tails than one would see uniformly at random, when statistically fitting degree distributions they can come out somewhere between the extremes of a scale-free and being formed uniformly at random, as discussed by Jackson and Rogers (2007a).[19,20]

3.3 Average distances and small worlds

How far apart are nodes on average in a network? Consider an individual who has 100 people with whom he or she is in regular contact. If each of them has 100 (different) people with whom they are in contact with, and so forth, than as a rough approximation the individual is at a distance of at most 2 from 10000 people, and at a distance of at most 3 from a million people, and 4 from 100 million people. With this sort of reasoning, there are on the order of $\bar{d}(\bar{d}-1)^{k-1}$ nodes at a distance of k from a given node if each node has $\bar{d}$ neighbors on average. With such expansion one reaches approximately n nodes by moving out k steps where

$$\bar{d}^k = n$$

or

$$k = \log(n)/\log(\bar{d}).$$

This calculation is a rough one in at least two ways: first, it presumes that all people have the same number of friends and most applications exhibit substantial heterogeneity; and second, it does not account for cycles in the network in that there may be some overlap in the friends of friends. Still this calculation shows us why distances between nodes in social networks can be quite small relative to the number of nodes, since neighborhoods tend to expand exponentially as we radiate outwards from a given node. Perhaps surprisingly, $\log(n)/\log(\bar{d})$ is a very accurate estimate of the average distance between nodes and the diameter for a wide set of random networks, including the Poisson random graphs as originally shown by Erdös-Renyi (1959, 1960), networks with other sorts of degree distributions (e.g., see Chung and Lu (2002)), and even quite general ones where there are heterogeneous types of nodes and link formation is type dependent (see Jackson (2008b)).

19 See also Pennock et al. (2002) for other examples.

20 There are also some interesting measurement biases to keep in mind here. If an interview process estimates links, degree can be underestimated either by some cap imposed by the interview or the memory of the interviewee; while if degree is estimated by some computer program that "crawls" from one web page to another then it can be biased towards finding larger degree nodes. There are techniques for limiting such biases, but measurement error is an endemic challenge in network estimation.

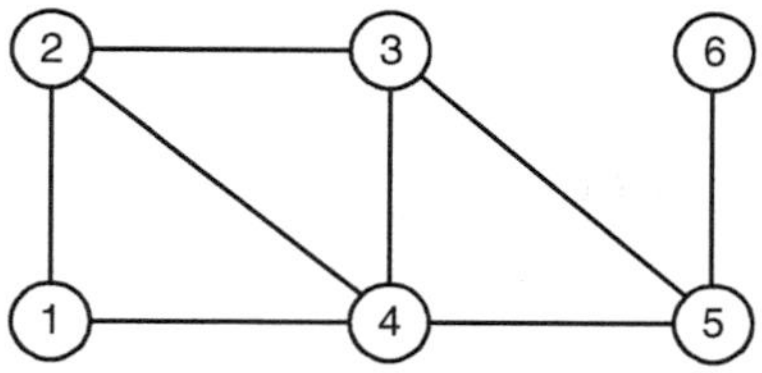

Figure 3 Clustering is 1 for node 1, is 2/3 for nodes 2 and 3, is 1/2 for node 4, 1/3 for node 5, and 0 for node 6.

Small average distances and diameter relative to the number of nodes has also been extensively explored empirically. One of the earliest and most famous experiments in the social network literature was conducted by Milgram (1967) and shed light on this phenomenon. Milgram had people in one part of the United States try to get a letter to a person in another part of the United States. The subjects were told limited information about the target, such as the target's name and some information about where the target lived (but not an address), and then were instructed to send the letter to someone who might be able to forward it to someone, who could forward it to someone, etc., with the intent of eventually finding someone who knew the target and could get it directly to the target. Roughly a quarter of the letters made it to their targets, with a median number of five links. This sort of result has also been many follow up studies on larger data sets, across countries, and with more detailed analyses of what strategies people used in selecting to whom they forwarded messages (e.g., see Watts (2004)). The small-world phenomenon applies not just to acquaintance networks, but also to things like links on web pages (e.g., see Adamic (1999)) and a variety of other networks (e.g., see Watts (1999, 2004)). The small average distances in networks has important implications for things like diffusion and contagion.

3.3.1 Clustering

An aspect of networks that can be important in social and economic settings is the extent to which relationships are transitive: that is, the extent to which if node i is linked to node j, and j is linked to k, then i is linked to k. The frequency with which such transitivity is present is referred to as *clustering* and is measured in various ways. For any given node, such as the node j above, we can measure the clustering relative to that node by measuring the fraction of all pairs of nodes that are both linked to j that are linked to j that are linked to each other (e.g., see Figure 3). Averaging this measure of clustering across nodes then gives an idea of the extent to which such transitivity exists in a network.[21]

[21] That is, the clustering for node j is $\sum_{k \in N_j(g), i \in N_j(g), k \neq i} g_{ik} / \sum_{k \in N_j(g), i \in N_j(g), k \neq i} g_{jk} g_{ji}$. One can then average this across nodes. Alternatively, one can simply examine the overall fraction of pairs of adjacent links that are completed: $\sum_{i \neq j \neq k \neq i} g_{jk} g_{ji} g_{ik} / \sum_{i \neq j \neq k \neq i} g_{jk} g_{ji}$.

There are various reasons as to why clustering can be important in a network. For instance, it impacts how the extent to which connections reach out to new nodes and so can affect information transmission. It can also impact how able a group is to monitor and enforce behaviors. For example, suppose that without any threat of punishment or loss of future access, an individual might have an incentive to cheat another individual in a transaction. If there is no clustering, and information only travels by word of mouth, then it might be that if an individual cheats another then he or she only faces retribution and punishment from that individual. If instead, there is substantial clustering, then the cheated individual might inform other people who are also involved in relationships with the cheating agent who can aid in retribution and punishment. The importance of clustering traces back to the pioneering social network research of Simmel (1908), and Coleman (1988) provides specific discussion of the role of clustering (or more general forms of "closure") in enforcing social norms.[22]

As Newman (2003) points out, there are a number of observed social networks that have much higher clustering than would be present in, for instance, a Poisson random network. For example, Newman discusses how networks of who has co-authored with whom in various research areas exhibit clustering rates ranging from around 15–50%, while a Poisson random networks of similar size and density would have clustering close to zero.

Clustering can be traced to a variety of sources: it occurs quite naturally if friends meet new friends via their current friends (see Jackson and Rogers 2007a). Institutional structures and geography can also affect who meets whom or who might benefit from interacting with whom.[23]

Recently, Jackson, Rodriguez-Barraquer and Tan (2009) proposed an alternative measure of closure within a network that they call *support*. A link ij in a network g is *supported* if there exists a node k who is a neighbor of both i and j, so that $ik \in g$ and $jk \in g$. One can then measure the fraction of links within a network that are supported.

Superficially, support and clustering seem to be similar measures, as they both involve triads. Nonetheless, they are quite different, and support can be quite higher than clustering. For example, consider a network with links $\{12, 13, 23, 14, 15, 45\}$. In this network all links are supported and so the support measure is 1. However, only 1/3 of the pairs of friends of agent 1 are friends with each other (e.g., 2 is a friend of 3, but not of 4 or 5). Thus, the clustering in this network is much lower than the support measure.

Jackson, Rodriguez-Barraquer and Tan (2009) find that a theoretical model of favor exchange leads to specific predictions about support levels within a network, but does not make predictions about clustering. Their model is based on examining the incentives for agents to perform costly favors for each other. In cases where the threat of losing one

[22] See Ali and Miller (2009) for a game-theoretic model of the role of clustering in enforcing cooperative behavior.

[23] For more discussion of potential sources of clustering, see Watts (1999), Jackson and Rogers (2005), and Carayol and Roux (2003).

friend is not enough to induce an agent to perform a favor, having common friends can provide incentives for agents to cooperate and perform costly favors via the threat of ostracism. Based on the insights from such a theory, Jackson, Rodriguez-Barraquer and Tan analyze data concerning exchange of favors, as well as other relationships from 75 rural Indian villages. They find significantly higher levels of support than clustering, and that the fraction of links that are supported is higher when one examines relationships based on favor exchange than other sorts of more "hedonic" relationships.

3.3.2 Homophily

Beyond, the patterns of degrees, average distance, clustering, and other such measures that only concern network architecture, there are also patterns that relate to how links depend on other characteristics of nodes. For instance, if nodes are people, then they have identities that include things like their age, gender, ethnicity, profession, education level, as well as other behavioral attributes such as what their hobbies are, whether they smoke, their political attitudes, and so forth. When we keep track of these various characteristics of nodes, then we see further patterns in terms of which nodes are linked to which other ones. In particular, one of the most extensively studied and documented aspects of social networks structures is that nodes tend to be more frequently linked to other nodes that are similar to themselves in terms of their characteristics than to nodes that are less similar to themselves in characteristics. This is referred to as homophily, as originally named by Lazarsfeld and Merton (1954). McPherson, Smith-Lovin and Cook (2001) provide an overview of the many dimensions on which homophily has been observed and also discuss some of the potential reasons for it.

Homophily can impact behavior and welfare in a variety of ways.[24] For example, it can affect workers' decisions of whether to drop out of the labor force. In particular, such decisions depend on the decisions of a worker's friends and colleagues and are often complementary: the greater the drop-out rate of a worker's social neighbors, the more attractive it becomes for the worker to drop out. When there is substantial homophily in a network, different groups can be quite isolated from each other and it might be that many individuals of one group drop out, while very few of another group drop out, even when the groups are otherwise similar (e.g., see Calvó-Armengol and Jackson (2004), Jackson (2007), as well as the following discussion). Homophily can similarly affect decisions of whether to invest in education (e.g., see Calvó-Armengol and Jackson (2009)). Homophily can also affect the speed of learning (e.g., see Golub and Jackson (2008)), as well as a variety of other network attributes (e.g., Currarini, Jackson, Pin (2007), Bramoullé and Rogers (2009)), and in field experiments has been found to affect things like how generous agents are towards each other (e.g., see Goeree et al. (2008), Exelle and Riedl (2008), and Leider et al. (2007)).

[24] See Jackson (2007) for more discussion of some of the effects mentioned here.

A simple measure of homophily is as follows. Let us partition the set of nodes N into groups according to their characteristics, $N_1,\ldots, N_i,\ldots N_m$, where all nodes in some group N_i have the same characteristics and nodes from different groups have different characteristics. Let n, and $n_1,\ldots,n_i,\ldots n_m$ be the respective cardinalities. First let us examine how many links form in the network **g** compared to how many could have formed, and denote this proportion by $p(\mathbf{g})$; so,

$$p(\mathbf{g}) = \frac{\sum_{j\in N} d_j(\mathbf{g})}{n(n-1)},$$

where $d_j(\mathbf{g})$ is node j's degree. Next, let us do the same calculation but now seeing what proportion of links between nodes of the same types occur in the network **g** compared to how many could have occurred and denote this by $p_s(\mathbf{g})$, where

$$p_s(\mathbf{g}) = \frac{\sum_{i=1,\ldots,m} \sum_{j,k\in N_i} g_{jk}}{\sum_{i=1,\ldots,m} n_i(n_i-1)}.$$

Then let us define the homophily in the network to be

$$h(\mathbf{g}) = \frac{p_s(\mathbf{g})}{p(\mathbf{g})}$$

so that $h(\mathbf{g})$ is how relatively prevalent links among same-type nodes are compared to links in the network overall. If this measure turns out to be 1, then there is no bias in the link formation relative to these characteristics, at least on average. If the measure is above 1, then we observe what is generally referred to as *inbreeding homophily*, so that links are more likely to be formed within groups than across groups. It is also possible to have "out-breeding," so that links across groups are relatively more likely than within groups, as would be the case in some sorts of trading networks or other bipartite networks. We can also examine similar measures group by group. That is, for a group $N_i \subset N$ we can define

$$p^i(\mathbf{g}) = \frac{\sum_{j\in N_i} d_j(\mathbf{g})}{n_i(n-1)} \quad \text{and} \quad p^i_s(\mathbf{g}) = \frac{\sum_{j,k\in N_i} g_{jk}}{n_i(n_i-1)}.$$

Then we define the homophily of group $N_i \subset N$ to be $h^i(\mathbf{g}) = \frac{p^i_s(\mathbf{g})}{p^i(\mathbf{g})}$.

As an illustration of homophily, Table 1 reports friendship patterns among high school students in the Adolescent Health data set that is based on interviews with over 90,000 students at a representative sampling of U.S. high schools including urban and rural, private and public, large and small, religious and secular schools, from a variety of geographical regions, and including different ethnic and socio-economic mixes of students. Looking at 84 of the schools that had substantial network data, the following

Table 1 : Homophily in High School Friendships.

	Groups Defined by:		
	Race	Sex	Grade
average homophily ($h(g)$) across schools	1.4	1.2	4.0
minimum homophily across schools	.99	1.0	1.5
maximum homophily across schools	2.7	1.5	5.6
standard deviation of homophily across schools	.43	.08	.90

data summarizes the average of the homophily measure defined above, $h(g)$, across the 84 different high schools (so 84 networks or different g's):[25]

From Table 1 we see that, on average across the schools, students are 4 times more likely to form friendships with a student in their own grade than with students overall, and are 1.4 more likely to form friendships with students of their own race than with students overall, and so forth. In these data and comparing across these characteristics, the strongest bias in relationships is by grade (that is, by year in school and so roughly by the students' age), with weaker biases by race and gender.[26,27,28]

Homophily can occur for various reasons. For example, one would expect substantial age-based homophily in friendships of children due to the grouping of students into classes in schools so that most of their contact is with other students of nearly the same age. Homophily can also be driven by preferences: students may prefer to associate with other students of the same age since their interests and maturity will be similar. The role of biases in contact as a source of homophily is discussed by Allport (1954), Blau (1977), Feld (1981), Rytina and Morgan (1982), and the role preferences for associating with individuals with similar traits, behaviors, or backgrounds is discussed by Cohen (1977), Kandel (1978), Knoke (1990), and Currarini, Jackson and Pin (2006, 2009, 2010) and Bramoullé and Rogers (2009). There are also other reasons that homophily might arise, including competition among groups (Giles and Evans (1986)), social norms and culture (Carley 1991)), institutional and organizational pressures (Meeker an Weiler (1970), Khmelkov and Hallinan (1999), Kubitschek and Hallinan (1998), Stearns (2004)). Empirical work based on models that allow for more

[25] These data come from a joint project with Ben Golub, although we did not report them in the paper Golub and Jackson (2008). For more background on these data see Golub and Jackson (2008).

[26] There are some measurement issues here. For example, subjects were asked to name up to five male friends and five female friends. So, a subject with fifteen male friends and five female friends would end up only naming five of each. Most subjects ended up below the caps, but there is some censoring of the data.

[27] These data also contain information about intensity of relationships, including the number of various activities that pairs of individuals reported participating in together. If one looks only at relationships such that there are more than three interactions in a week, then the homophily along all dimensions becomes much more pronounced.

[28] There are also various ways of normalizing homophily measures. For some discussion see Coleman (1958).

than one source of homophily as in Currarini, Jackson and Pin (2009, 2010) and van der Leij and Buhai (2008) helps identify sources of homophily and can help explain various patterns of homophily.

Beyond some of the patterns discussed above, there are a variety of other patterns that can be important in various settings. For instance, we consider the diffusion of a disease through a network can be affected by whether or not high degree nodes are linked to other high degree nodes or to low degree nodes. Similarly, there are relationships between clustering and degree, degree and homophily, and a variety of other patterns in networks.[29]

Understanding network structure is not simply interesting in its own right, but also because of its implications for decision-making and economic behavior. For example, as a society becomes more homophilous and groups become more segregated, the reaching of a consensus in word-of-mouth learning can slow significantly (e.g., see Golub and Jackson (2008)). I discuss some such implications below, but first begin with a discussion of how networks form and why they exhibit some of the features mentioned above.

4. NETWORK FORMATION

Given the impact of network structure on various behaviors, it is important to understand how networks are formed and why they might have certain characteristics.

The literature on network formation has adopted three main approaches:

- One approach originates in random graph theory and is process-based. Such models begin with the classic work of Erdös and Rényi (1959, 1960, 1961), and provide an understanding of how certain observed features of networks (such as fat-tailed degree distributions, high clustering, low diameter, and other properties) can be traced to processes governing how links form.
- The second approach is based on building statistical models for working with social network data. This approach develops models that are versatile in terms of estimation. That is, these are models that enable one to estimate which patterns and correlations among various features appear in social network data.
- The third approach is based economic fundamentals presuming that agents choose their relationships based on the payoffs that emerge as a function of the network. Such modeling incorporates game theoretic techniques and can help indicate why certain structures emerge.

Clearly, these approaches stem from very different perspectives and goals, and they offer different insights into social networks. Let me discuss each approach in turn.[30]

[29] See Jackson (2008) for more background.

[30] Parts of Section 4.1 on random networks were co-written with Leeat Yariv and originally appeared in Jackson and Yariv (This volume), but the section was a better fit here. Thank you to Leeat for her work on it and grace in moving it here.

4.1 Random networks

Random network models originate in the random graph literature where the main focus is on how specific assumptions about the random emergence of links leads to various properties of network structure. These models analyze the outcomes of particular (stochastic) algorithms by which links are created.[31] The following are some of the canonical models (see Newman 2003 and Jackson 2008 for more background).

4.1.1 Poisson random networks

This is the most basic random graph model that was mentioned above, and was independently proposed by Solomonoff and Rapoport (1951), Gilbert (1959), and Erdös and Rényi (1959, 1960, 1961) who discovered some of the seminal results on the properties of the random graphs. Given a finite set of nodes N, a link between nodes i and j is formed independently of all other pairs of nodes with a given probability p. The degree of any given node thus follows a binomial distribution, and as the number of nodes becomes large (provided p does not grow too quickly), this is well-approximated by a Poisson distribution.

The main insights from this literature are that there are specific thresholds in terms of the link probability, such that the networks have distinct properties above and below the thresholds. As mentioned before, there is a threshold at $p = 1/n$ (where each node expects to have a single neighbor) at which some cycles and a giant component emerge. That is, if p over $1/n$ goes to 0, then with a probability going to 1 there are no cycles and no component containing more than a vanishing set of nodes, while if p over $1/n$ goes to infinity, then with a probability going to 1 there are cycles and a (single) giant component containing a nonvanishing fraction of the networks. Such "large network" thresholds and properties are the primary basis for analysis of random networks.

4.1.2 The small world model

Watts and Strogatz (1998) noted that basic random network models failed to capture an important feature of many observed networks: the combination of relatively small diameters and high levels of clustering. Unless each node is connected to a nontrivial fraction of all other nodes (which is clearly not true of most large social networks), a Poisson random network will have vanishing clustering. So, in order to maintain the small diameters of a (connected) Poisson random network, but also to obtain high clustering, Watts and Strogatz (1998) constructed a model in which nodes are initially connected according to a highly clustered lattice. For example, think of having nodes located on a circle, and each connected to neighbors that are of distance k steps or lower on the circle. This initial configuration has high clustering, but will not have a

[31] The focus is largely on identifying simple procedures generating certain classes of degree distributions. The literature has also tackled the converse question having to do with the feasibility of general degree distributions in a network. The configuration model and various relatives (see Bender and Canfield (1978) and Chung and Lu (2002)) are such that nodes are connected in a manner to realize a pre-specified degree distribution.

small diameter. Next, some fraction of links are severed and reconnected uniformly at random. That is, a given link is removed with probability π and then rewired to a node chosen uniformly at random from those to which it is not already connected. The probability π is a measure of the randomness of the network. For $\pi = 0$, the network is a type of lattice, while for $\pi = 1$ the network is effectively a Poisson random network. The small world model is so named since even for small re-wiring probabilities π, the distance between any two nodes on the network is significantly smaller than in the original lattice and similar to the average distance of a Poisson random network, but while keeping the high clustering of the lattice. As Watts and Strogatz (1998) show, there is a fairly wide range of parameters for which the network maintains the dual properties of high clustering of the lattice and relatively low average distance between nodes of a Poisson random network.

4.1.3 Preferential attachment

While the Watts and Strogatz (1998) model exhibits high clustering and small average distances, it does not match some other characteristics of observed social networks. In particular, the degree distribution can be quite unlike that of most observed networks as it looks like a mix between a regular network (where all nodes have the same degree) and a Poisson random network, and certainly does not exhibit the fatter tailed distributions seen in some applications. In order to generate degree distributions with such fat tails, like a power distribution, one needs other sorts of formation processes.

An early version of such a process is suggested by Price (1976) in the context of citation networks, and Barabási and Albert (1999) show how a simple model can be applied quite generally to result in networks where the degree distribution is scale-free; that is, satisfies a power law so that the frequency of degree d is proportional to $d^{-\gamma}$ for a parameter γ. The two essential features of the model[32] are that (i) nodes enter over time, and so we can index them by their date of birth $i = 1, 2, .., n$, and (ii) each newborn node forms a given number of links, say m, to the existing nodes in a manner that Barabási and Albert (1999) refer to as "preferential attachment." The idea is that the newborn node i chooses which m of the existing nodes $1, \ldots, i - 1$ to link to with probabilities proportional to the number of links that those nodes already have. For example, if node $j < i$ has 10 links and node $k < i$ has 5 links, then node i is twice as likely to attach a given link to node j as to node k. This sort of process exhibits a "rich-get-richer" pattern so that nodes that have high degree grow in degree over time more rapidly than nodes with low degree, leading to the fat-tails in the distribution. Such networks end up with a sort of "hub-and-spoke" pattern to them, with some nodes with very high degrees that act like "hubs" and help

[32] The study of power distributions has a rich history, and these features of the model reflect those found to generate power laws in other settings. See Mitzenmacher (2004) for an overview.

connect the large number of small degree nodes to the rest of the network. These networks can have even smaller average distances than in Poisson random networks with similar average degree.

4.1.4 Richer sequential link formation models

While the preferential attachment model provides insight into what might generate fat-tailed degree distributions, it exhibits negligible clustering in large networks and hence also fails to match many observed networks when considering the broader set of characteristics that they exhibit. Moreover, as pointed out by Pennock et al. (2002), many observed networks have degree distributions that lie somewhere between that of a Poisson random network and one formed by preferential attachment.

Models developed by Vazquez (2003) and Jackson and Rogers (2007a) span between uniformly random link formation and something like preferential attachment. The key to these models is that they have some combination of links formed uniformly at random and others that are based on existing network structure. For instance, by first finding some nodes uniformly at random, and then finding others by meeting some of those nodes friends, the friends of friends that are met will tend to be those who have many friends. That is, if we locate nodes by meeting friends of friends, then a node with twice as many friends as another node is twice as likely to be found via such a process. Thus, one ends up with a sort of preferential attachment because nodes are found via the existing network structure. As the ratio of how many links are formed through uniformly random meetings, and how many are formed by searching through the existing network, these models span a set of degree distributions, with extremes of a scale-free distribution and a growing version of the Erdös-Renyi uniformly random world. Moreover, as Jackson and Rogers (2007a) point out, some versions of these models also have naturally high clustering, as well as correlations in degrees among neighbors, decreasing clustering with degree, and other features matching observed networks. For example, high clustering emerges naturally since some links are formed via meeting friends of friends, and such links naturally result in a triad and so result in clustering. Such models can be fit to observed networks to estimate the extent to which links are formed uniformly at random versus through meetings determined by the existing network, as shown by Jackson and Rogers (2007a). In fitting such models to data, it becomes clear that degree distributions are quite varied, with some friendship networks looking almost uniformly random and some other networks exhibiting formation based on existing network structure like a friends of friends meeting process.

4.2 Models for statistical analysis

Although some of the random-graph-style models listed above can be used in empirical analyses of social networks, they are stark in terms of the characteristics they incorporate. They are useful for understanding how social networks come to exhibit some features that they do, but the models need to be enriched in order to examine things like homophily or how various node characteristics, and specific local network patterns, influence network formation. Such an emphasis has led to the development of another class of models for network analysis are that I will refer to as "statistical models," since they were developed specifically for the empirical analysis of social networks. As social networks are naturally complicated, models that look for regularities, patterns, and uncover various formation properties, can be vital to understanding social networks. This is a large topic on its own, and so here I offer overviews of a couple of the most prevalent classes of statistical models: exponential random graph models and community detection models.

4.2.1 Exponential random graph models and p^* models

The starting point of exponential random graph models, called "ERGMs" for short, is to express the probability, $\Pr(\mathbf{g})$, that a given network $\mathbf{g}$ arises as a function of a set of K different statistics of the network $\{s_k(\mathbf{g})\}_1^K$. For instance, the statistics could include the number of links in the network, the number of triads (completely connected triples of nodes) in the network, and so forth. The purpose of doing this is to test for various correlation patterns. For example, are networks with certain patterns, e.g., clustering or other forms of closure, more likely to appear than networks without such patterns? While such models are not necessarily well-suited for identifying causal relationships, they can be quite useful for identifying certain patterns in networks.

A standard formulation of this class of models one where

$$\Pr(\mathbf{g}) = \frac{\exp(\sum_k \beta_k s_k(\mathbf{g}))}{c(\boldsymbol{\beta})}, \tag{3}$$

So, the probability that a given network is formed depends on certain patterns that it exhibits, which are specified as the statistics s_k's on the right hand side.

For example, the special case of Erdös-Rényi random graphs with a probability of a link of p is expressed by setting $K = 1$ and letting $s_1(\mathbf{g})$ be the number of links in the network. In that case,

$$\Pr(\mathbf{g}) = p^{s_1(\mathbf{g})}(1-p)^{n(n-1)/2-s_1(\mathbf{g})}.$$

If we let $\beta_1 = \log(p/(1-p))$ and $c(\boldsymbol{\beta}) = (1-p)^{-n(n-1)/2}$, then this is expressed as in the form of (3).

More generally, the point of allowing for a range of statistics in (3) is to investigate other patterns that might be present in the network. In the Erdös-Rényi random graph setting the links are independent and so any clustering that occurs is simply uniformly at random and simply occurs based on the link probability. As already discussed, clustering in many observed social networks is significantly higher than would occur uniformly at random. Allowing for richer statistics to govern network formation probability, allows one to incorporate a range of dependencies into a network. For example, if we want to see whether clustering is statistically significant, possibly in the presence of other attributes of a network, then we can include a statistic s_k which counts the number of triads in the network. Other statistics that are often included are the number of various types of "stars", where there is some node connected to some given number of other nodes. For instance if we are examining a network of marriages, then we should not see any stars, whereas in networks that are nearly scale-free we would expect to see some very large stars. Some of the seminal work on this subject, by Frank and Strauss (1986), built a model that included triangles and various stars.

There are several practical difficulties in estimating an ERGM. The first of these depends on the model's specification. In looking at the model specification in (3) we see that the network appears on both the left and implicitly on the right hand sides of the expression. Since this is a nonlinear specification, it is generally not possible to reduce this to a simple expression. Moreover, when estimating an ERGM we are nominally working with a single observation as we generally see only one realized network, **g**. Thus in order for this to make statistical sense, implicitly there must be much more information that we take advantage of than just one observation, and in particular the formulation in terms of statistics generally includes information about local parts of the network (links, triads, local star formations, etc.) that can lead to many implicit observations in a single network. For example, in the case of an Erdös-Rényi random graph, we can think of the observation taking place at the link level, and so we have $n(n-1)/2$ independent observations if there are n nodes. This allows for a very accurate estimation of the link probability. The extent to which we are at one extreme with the observed network as a single datum, or the other extreme with each link being an independent observation, or somewhere in between, depends on the specification of the ERGM and how rich and interdependent the statistics $s_k(\mathbf{g})$ are. If the statistics involve large parts of the network, or correlations between various portions of the network, then we cut down on the number of independent observations that are in the single network. The richer the model becomes in terms of interdependencies, the fewer implicit observations there are from a given network on which to estimate the model.

Beyond limitations of observations, a central difficulty in estimating the coefficients in (3), and one that is often most limiting in practice, comes from the fact that the normalizing coefficient $c(\boldsymbol{\beta})$ is effectively impossible to compute for large networks. In particular, for the right hand side of (3) to be a probability it must be that when we sum the expression in (3) across networks $\mathbf{g}$ that it sums to 1. Thus, the normalizing coefficient must satisfy

$$c(\boldsymbol{\beta}) = \sum_{\mathbf{g}} \exp\left(\sum_k \beta_k s_k(\mathbf{g})\right).$$

The summation on the right hand side is over all possible networks, of which there are $2^{n(n-1)/2}$ in the undirected case and $2^{n(n-1)}$ in the directed case. With only 30 nodes, this is already more than 2^{435} networks in the undirected case, which is more than the estimated number of atoms in the universe (on the order of 2^{270})! Thus, unless there is some intuitive way to deduce the normalizing coefficient, one is forced to avoid the use of the normalizing coefficient in estimating the coefficients in (3). Thus in order to estimate a model of the form (3), we have to get around calculating the normalizing coefficient.

To get work around the normalizing coefficient, it is useful to work at the link level and to think about the probability that a given link ij takes on a certain value conditional on the rest of the network:

$$\Pr(g_{ij} = 1|\mathbf{g}_{-ij}) = \frac{\exp\left(\sum_k \beta_k s_k(g_{ij} = 1, \mathbf{g}_{-ij})\right)}{\exp\left(\sum_k \beta_k s_k(g_{ij} = 1, \mathbf{g}_{-ij})\right) + \exp\left(\sum_k \beta_k s_k(g_{ij} = 0, \mathbf{g}_{-ij})\right)}.$$

We no longer have the normalizing parameter in this equation. We can similarly deduce the odds ratio

$$\frac{\Pr(g_{ij} = 1|\mathbf{g}_{-ij})}{\Pr(g_{ij} = 0|\mathbf{g}_{-ij})} = \frac{\exp\left(\sum_k \beta_k s_k(g_{ij} = 1, \mathbf{g}_{-ij})\right)}{\exp\left(\sum_k \beta_k s_k(g_{ij} = 0, \mathbf{g}_{-ij})\right)}.$$

Thus, the log odds ratio is

$$\log\left(\frac{\Pr(g_{ij} = 1|\mathbf{g}_{-ij})}{\Pr(g_{ij} = 0|\mathbf{g}_{-ij})}\right) = \sum_k \beta_k [s_k(g_{ij} = 1, \mathbf{g}_{-ij}) - s_k(g_{ij} = 0, \mathbf{g}_{-ij})].$$

or

$$\log\left(\frac{\Pr(g_{ij} = 1|\mathbf{g}_{-ij})}{\Pr(g_{ij} = 0|\mathbf{g}_{-ij})}\right) = \sum_k \beta_k \Delta s_k(g_{ij}, \mathbf{g}_{-ij}), \tag{4.2.1}$$

where $s_k(g_{ij}, \mathbf{g}_{-ij}) = s_k(g_{ij} = 1, \mathbf{g}_{-ij}) - s_k(g_{ij} = 0, \mathbf{g}_{-ij})$. (4.2.1) looks almost like a standard logit calculation used in a logistic regression. If the links were independent of each other, then this would be a standard logistic regression. Indeed, one technique for estimating the coefficients in (3) is a "pseudolikelihood" technique, where one effectively ignores the interdependencies in (4.2.1) and works with a formulation of the form:

$$\log\left(\frac{\Pr(g_{ij} = 1)}{\Pr(g_{ij} = 0)}\right) = \sum_k \beta_k \Delta s_k(g_{ij}, \mathbf{g}_{-ij}),$$

where we have eliminated the conditional distributions on the left hand side. This can then be maximized by mimicking standard techniques of maximum likelihood.

Unfortunately, this can lead to (very) inaccurate estimates since it is ignoring the interdependencies that were the real purpose for exploring such a model in the first place, and conditions for it to be a reasonable technique are not well understood (e.g., see van Duijn, Gile, and Handcock (2009)).

What has led to the recent surge in the use of ERGMs are advances in Monte Carlo simulation have provided techniques for estimating such models, and in particular MCMC (Markov chain Monte Carlo) techniques, which are becoming increasingly manageable and in some cases much more accurate than the pseudolikelihood techniques that ignore dependencies. A key technique along this line was introduced by Snijders (2002) and in a different variation by Handcock (2003). Let me describe the basic ideas.

The method relies on generating a distribution of different *g*'s that emerges for any given specification of **$\boldsymbol{\beta}$s**. Then one can search over the set of **$\boldsymbol{\beta}$s** (more on this below) to find one that leads to the highest likelihood of getting a network that looks similar to the observed *g*. So, how do we generate a distribution of different *g*'s for a given specification of $\boldsymbol{\beta}$? We can do this by fixing a starting network $\boldsymbol{g}^{\mathbf{0}}$. Then we randomly pick a link to change, *ij*. Then, based on (4.2.1), one can randomly put the link *ij* in or out with with the appropriate probability given the profile of parameters $\boldsymbol{\beta}$ and given the $\mathbf{g}^{\mathbf{0}}_{-ij}$. This leads to a new network $\boldsymbol{g}^{\mathbf{1}}$. Now, let us iteratively do this, cycling through the different links *ij* (possibly randomly). This results in a Markov chain over the resulting networks, and over time, the probability that we visit any given network approaches that of its steady-state distribution. Provided the model is such that only a small number of networks get visited very frequently (the critical condition for this technique to work well), then this will converge reasonably well in a limited time and so for each given $\boldsymbol{\beta}$ we get an estimation of the relative likelihood of different networks. Then we search across $\boldsymbol{\beta}$'s by various techniques (e.g., Metropolis-Hastings algorithm or Gibbs Sampling, etc., see Snjiders et al. (2006)) to find a specification that leads to the highest likelihood of the observed network or something similar to it.

These techniques may or may not end up overcoming the difficulties in estimating the ERGM model. Even with an MCMC method, we are still only sampling relatively few networks relative to the huge number possible (recall that there are 2^{435} networks on just 30 nodes...). As such, the Markov chain might not converge to the steady state distribution, or even close to it, in a reasonable time. This problem is particularly acute if networks that are quite different from each other can have similar likelihoods and/or there are local basins of attraction among networks (e.g., the distribution over networks is multi-modal) which can happen quite easily when there are complementarities or interdependencies among links. With very large data sets or challenging specifications of an ERGM this can be almost hopeless. There are many researchers working on improving techniques, but there are still many cases without convergence in reasonable time. This can make the output from such analyses difficult to interpret, and some of the significance tests that have been developed should be interpreted with the appropriate caution since some of them are based on asymptotic properties that may not be be well-satisfied in practice.

In spite of the challenges that accompany their estimation, the use of ERGM and related models is rapidly increasing since they help researchers detect a multitude of network patterns and can be tailored to look for very specific sorts of effects. Moreover, in addition to statistics about network structure, we can also include various observed attributes of agents such as socio-economic and demographic data as independent variables affecting the likelihood of links.

4.2.2 Fitting random and strategic models

Quite complementary to statistical models such as the ERGMs, there are important reasons for also using "structural estimation" methods of network analysis based on more foundational models. The point is a familiar one: structural models can help disentangle causal relationships into which other models might offer little insight. As an example, consider homophily. Working with the adolescent Health data set discussed above various researchers, including Moody (2001) and Goodreau, Kitts, Morris (2009), have fit statistical network models and found that races have different propensities to form friendships with each other. While such analyses show that propensities to form friendships depend on whether the students are of the same race, such models cannot identify whether such homophily is due to preferences for same-race friendships, or instead due to differences in how frequently students of different races meet each other, or some combination of both. Is the lower rate of inter-racial friendships due to the segregation of students through the classes and activities that they participate in, so that students rarely interact with students of other races, or do students prefer to form friendships with others of their own race? Currarini, Jackson and Pin (2009, 2010) develop models of network formation that allow for biases in both preferences and meeting probabilities. Through a characterization of equilibrium conditions, Currarini, Jackson and Pin show that preference biases can be identified from patterns in the number of friendships formed based on the mix of races in a school, and biases in meeting probabilities can be identified via patterns in the homophily as a function of racial composition of a school. They find that both preference and meeting biases are significant and that the extent and structure of these biases differ significantly across races.

Of course, any model, statistical or structural, necessarily omits some relationships and thus can lead to incorrect conclusions. This makes it important to combine the use of statistical models, which help uncover patterns and critical correlations among variables, with structural models that can help identify the factors underlying the patterns.

4.2.3 Community detection

Another type of statistical modeling of network analysis relates to "community structure" and detection. The basic idea is that a society has natural underlying "communities" that the researcher wants to discover from examining social network data. This can be seen as a special case of detecting some latent structure that generates or influences observed behaviors or data; an idea that has a long history in anthropology and sociology (e.g., see Lévi-Strauss (1958) and Lazarsfeld and Henry (1968)). As an illustration, given a network of scientific collaborations one might wish to identify the natural communities or disciplines that influence the relationships, as those might not coincide with standard disciplinary boundaries and organizations. Or, one might have data on a labor market and wish to investigate whether there are biases in hiring. Such techniques can also be useful in reducing very large networks to smaller networks between communities. The literature evolved to include a variety of approaches to detecting or identifying the communities that underly a network. I will not survey that literature here (see Newman (2004) and Chapter 13 in Jackson (2008) for more background), but let me provide a quick summary of the landscape.

Let us think of a community structure as a partition of the set of nodes, with each element of the partition referred to as a community. The idea of community detection is to uncover the community structure from an observed network. This has its roots in what is known as "block modeling" where one identifies blocks of nodes that are comparable or equivalent, as introduced by Lorrain and White (1971) and White, Boorman and Breiger (1976). It is rare to find nodes that are completely interchangeable in a network (so that their relationships with all other nodes is identical), and so strict definitions of equivalence are often too restrictive to be useful in identifying communities of nodes. Thus, one needs to loosen the approach to categorizing nodes as belonging to the same community or class of nodes. An early and popular method for doing this is based on an algorithm called CONCOR (for "convergence of iterated correlations"), as developed by Breiger, Boorman, and Arabie (1975). CONCOR is based on correlation patterns among the connections that nodes have. The idea is that if two nodes are have similar connections, then they should belong to the same community. Thus, CONCOR loosens the idea of two nodes having identical relationships with other nodes to instead having a high level of correlation in their relationships. CONCOR iterates on this idea, studying the correlation patterns in the correlation patterns among nodes, with the idea that nodes in the same community should not only have similar connections, but also similar correlation patterns with other nodes, and correlation in correlation patterns, and so forth. There is a whole class of loosely related approaches that build up communities by grouping similar nodes together where similar is based on some measurement of the similarity of their connection patterns. Communities coalesce as nodes are groups of nodes are declared similar, and so one ends up with a hierarchy of communities depending on when one stops the process. A variety of such methods is known as *hierarchical clustering.*

Another branch of community detection methods originates from the computer science literature and amounts to repeatedly bissecting a network. This works by, for instance, minimizing the number of links between two comparably sized groups (see Newman (2004) for background on some of those algorithms). Here the idea is not so much based on similarity of nodes, but instead based on a notion that separate communities should have few links between them. A related approach in terms of a starting point that communities should be sets of nodes with few links between them is based on edge removal. For example, Girvan and Newman (2002) developed a popular algorithm that repeatedly deletes links from a network based on finding links that have very high measures of betweenness. The premise is that a high betweenness score means that a link must be joining two disjoint groups, which could naturally be different collections of communities. As one iteratively removes edges, the network naturally fragments and the resulting component structure leads to a partition of the set of nodes, which can be thought of as a community structure.

Each of the previously described methods faces a question of when to stop. One can either continue bissecting until each node is its own community, or one can keep putting nodes together in groups building up until all the nodes are in one community. Part of the difficulty with using these methods stems from the fact that there is no natural underlying notion of exactly what communities are or how the network was formed, and so the decision of when two nodes should be in the same or different communities is somewhat subjective.

A very different approach is based on a model of the role of community structures in generating a network. The idea is based on a random network formation model. As a simple example, consider a simple variation on a Poisson random network, where instead of all links forming with the same probability nodes within the same community are linked to each other with a higher probability than nodes in different communities. With such models, community detection becomes a natural statistical exercise (e.g., see Holland, Laskey, and Leinhardt (1983), Snijders and Nowicki (1997)). This has been referred to as *a posteriori block modeling*, in the sociology literature.[33] Essentially, there is homophily, but the researcher does not directly observe the communities that underly the homophily and so seeks to recover it. A class of such community detection techniques based on maximum likelihood estimation have been axiomatized by Copic, Jackson, and Kirman (2009).

The basic challenge facing community detection techniques is similar to that facing the estimation of ERGMs: the potential number of community structures is a factorial function of the number of nodes and so exhaustive search for one that was most likely to generate the data is impossible when the network involves more than a handful of

[33] A more general form of this is referred to as "latent space estimation," (e.g., see Hoff, Raftery, and Handcock (2002) and Hoff (2006)) where there may be a more specific spatial structure (where this may be a "social space") that underlies the interconnection of nodes that one wishes to recover or detect based on social network data. An obvious case is where individuals belong to multiple groups at once, or have various attributes that affect their interconnectivity, rather than each residing in a single community.

nodes. Thus, methods that are based on underlying models of community structure (e. g., the likelihood methods) have solid foundations but face difficulties in implementation, while in contrast methods that are defined by their algorithms can be quite tractable but can also be very ad hoc and difficult to interpret.

4.3 Strategic network formation

A completely different approach to modeling network formation originates in the economics literature and examines the consequences of agents' choices of relationships. The basic premise is that agents choose relationships in order to maximize their well-being. These may be individuals choosing friendships that make them happy or otherwise benefit them, or firms choosing other firms with which to transact, or firms choosing which workers to hire, and so forth.

Externalities abound in network settings, as agents are generally impacted not only by their choice of friends, but also their friends' choices of friends, and so forth. For example, in a co-authorship relationship an author is affected by how many other researchers with whom his or her co-author communicates. Those other relationships impact both the co-author's experience and knowledge and also affect how busy the co-author might be, and thus such co-author of co-author relationships can have both positive and negative external effects. As another example, in terms of obtaining information and favors, an individual might prefer, all else held equal, to be friends with someone who has a larger number of contacts rather than a smaller number of contacts. A country that forms a military alliance with another country will care about which other military alliances are in place. It is easy to see that in many, if not most, networked settings an individual's decision of whom to maintain relationships with has both direct effects on those involved in the relationship and indirect effects on others in the network. Thus, understanding which relationships will tend to emerge when individuals react to such incentives is paramount to understanding which networks we expect to see and what the consequences will ultimately be for the society's welfare.

An early model that incorporated individual decision making in a network setting is due to Boorman (1975) who examined a labor market setting and the trade-offs between maintaining "strong" and "weak" ties. Boorman was interested in understanding the tradeoff that individuals faced in terms of maintaining a few strong ties versus many weak ties. Examples of individual choice of relationships also emerged in the cooperative game theory literature, including the formation of a graph in a context where the network of connections would affect the structure of the cooperative game and thus ultimately the payoffs of different agents, as studied by Aumann and Myerson (1988).

The modeling of strategic formation in a general network setting originates in a paper by Jackson and Wolinsky (1996), who modeled payoffs to individuals as a function of the network, and then examined individual incentives to form networks. The literature on this subject is covered in more detail in Bloch and Dutta (This volume) (see also Jackson (2003, 2008)), and so here I just present an example that introduces some of the ideas and themes.

The main thrust of the early literature on this subject was to understand if and when individual incentives to form and maintain links would lead to socially efficient networks. The following example, from Jackson and Wolinsky (1996), illustrates some of the basic ideas and themes. It is one of the simplest possible cases where we begin to see network externalities emerge as it has just three agents, but it makes the issues very clear.

Each agent is a node and gets a payoff that depends on the network structure that emerges in the society. The payoff that an agent gets can depend on the full configuration of the network; for instance, agent 1′s payoff might be affected by whether agents 2 and 3 are friends. A simple example of possible payoffs to nodes is pictured in Figure 4.

The arrows in Figure 4 indicate the incentives that agents have to add or delete links. An arrow points from one network to another network where some link is added whenever both of the agents involved in that link would weakly benefit from adding the link to the network with at least one of them benefiting strictly. An arrow points from one network to another network where some link is deleted if one of the

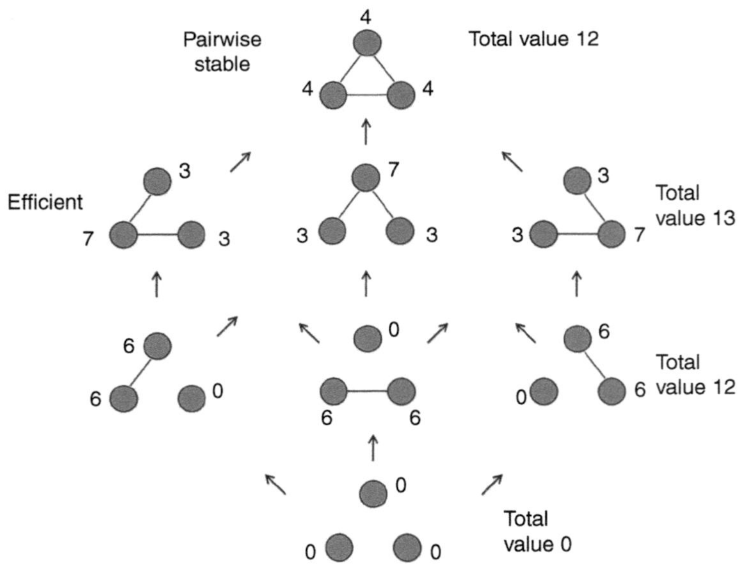

Figure 4 Payoffs to each node as a function of the network. Two-link networks result in the maximal overall payoffs. The arrows indicate changes networks that benefit both nodes associated with adding a link or at least one node who can delete a link. The unique pairwise stable network in this simple example is the complete network.

two agents involved in the link would strictly benefit from deleting it. Sequences of such arrows leading from one network to another is what has been called an "improving path" by Jackson and Watts (2002), and any network with no arrows leaving it is a called a pairwise stable network, as defined by Jackson and Wolinsky (1996).[34]

If just two agents are connected, so that there is just one link in the network, then those two agents benefit equally from the relationship and each of their payoffs is 6. Adding a second link leads to an increase in payoff for the center node, but with a lower marginal payoff than the first link. The center node ends up with a payoff of 7 and the peripheral nodes get a payoff of 3 each. Here we see the incentives to form links: Starting a one-link network, if a second link is added, then the agent who now has two links has seen an increase in his or her payoff (7 compared to 6), and the newly linked peripheral player gets a payoff of 3, which is better than being isolated with a payoff of 0. There is a negative externality, however, from the addition of this second link. One of the agent's payoff goes down from 6 to 3 from the addition of the second link. The peripheral agents lose value from each other's presence. Such an effect could be present in a variety of settings, whenever agents compete with each other for the attention of the resources of an agent to whom they are both connected. Overall, however, the total payoff for the society is highest with two links: the benefit to the center node and second peripheral node outweigh the loss in payoff to the first peripheral node from the addition of the second link. This is not the end of the story however. The two peripheral agents now have an incentive to add the third possible link, as their payoffs each go up, from 3 to 4. Again, this has a negative externality, as even though each of their payoffs goes up, the center agent's payoff goes down from 7 to 4. In fact, adding the third link in the society reduces total payoff from 13 to 12. Effectively, the third link's cost outweighs its marginal contribution to the society. Nonetheless, the two peripheral agents end up gaining by adding the third link. This sort of effect can be present in many bargaining situations, where without the third link the center agent is in a strong bargaining position, and with the third link that agent's position is weakened and so the other agents have an incentive to add the third link to strengthen their bargaining position even though it is destructive in an overall sense for the society. This example exhibits negative externalities, in the sense that adding a link generally reduces the payoff of the third agent who is not involved in the link. In this example, the incentive is for agents to keep adding links and the the unique pairwise stable network is the complete network.

[34] There are a variety of different solutions that can be used to model network formation, and many of them coincide in this example. For more background, see the chapter by Bloch and Dutta (This volume), and Chapters 6 and 11 in Jackson (2008). Bloch and Jackson (2006) provide comparisons of many of the solution concepts.

We can also consider a different variation on this simple example that has the same total payoff to society as a function of the network, but a different allocation of the payoffs to the agents in the two-link networks, as pictured in Figure 5. Here, in a two-link network the peripheral agents get a higher payoff than the center agent, who bears a higher total cost from maintaining two relationships rather than just one. In this case, we no longer see the incentive for the peripheral agents to add the third link, and so with this modified allocation of payoffs we no longer see an incentive to over-connect relative to what is efficient. However, in passing from a one-link to a two-link network, the center node bears most of the marginal cost of forming the second link and ends up with a lower payoff in the two-link network than in a one-link network. Thus, the center node would prefer to sever one of the links in a two-link network. In this variation of the example, the only pairwise stable networks are now the one-link networks, as we see via the arrows in Figure 5.

By changing the allocation of the payoffs in the two-link networks we saw a change from the pairwise stable networks being over-connected to being under-connected relative to that which maximizes society's total payoff. Is there any way in which we could allocate the payoff between the center agent and the two peripheral agents in the two-link networks so that they would be pairwise stable? It turns out that there

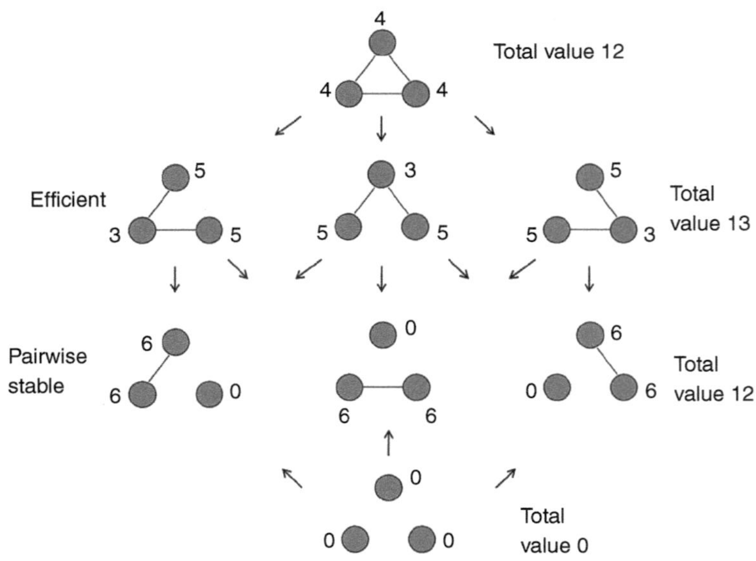

Figure 5 Payoffs to each node as a function of the network. Two-link networks result in the maximal overall payoffs. The arrows indicate changes in the network that benefit both nodes associated with adding a link, or one of the nodes involved in deleting a link. The pairwise stable networks are the one-link networks.

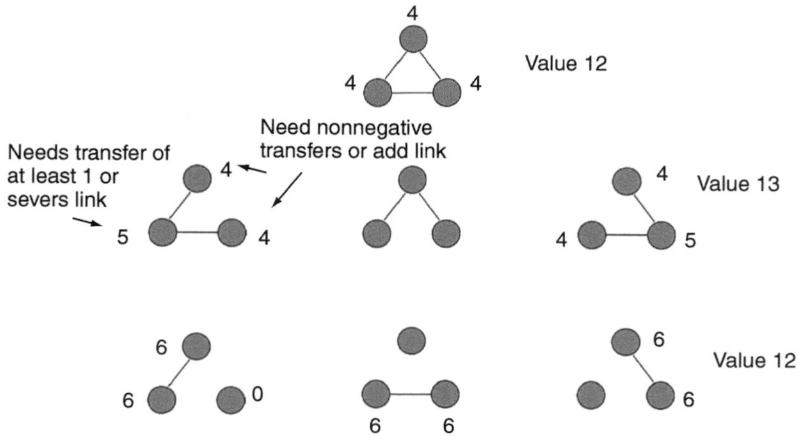

Figure 6 The impossibility of maintaining the total utility maximizing network as being pairwise stable, regardless of transfers between the peripheral nodes and center node.

is no way that this can be done without treating the peripheral players unequally![35] This was shown in Jackson and Wolinsky (1996) and is seen in Figure 6. We need to give each of the peripheral agents at least a payoff of 4 in order to avoid over-connection, and we need to give the center agent a payoff of at least 6 to avoid under-connection. This sums to 14, which is greater than the total payoff of 13, which is available.

This example provides a glimpse of some of the issues that arise in strategic network formation. The tension between individual incentives and societal value is not new to economists, but there are new facets to it here. Generally, such inefficiencies arise in settings with some asymmetries of information or an inability to bargain. Here, even with full information and ability to reallocate payoffs up to some symmetry constraints,[36] we cannot reconcile individual incentives with economic efficiency.[37]

This goes counter to what economists think of as a form of the "Coase theorem": namely that with the ability to bargain or make transfers conditional on the setting,

[35] One can solve the problem with unequal allocations, as discussed by Dutta and Mutuswami (1997). In this example, for instance, on a two-link network give the center 6, and then give one peripheral agent 6 and the other 1. Such a network would be pairwise stable.

[36] There is also a hidden constraint here in that I have not mentioned reallocating value on one-link networks. If we can give disconnected agents some of the payoffs from the network, then we can avoid the difficulty here. While that might be feasible in some cases, it is not in others. This corresponds to a component balance condition in Jackson and Wolinsky (1996).

[37] There is also a question of which notion of efficiency is appropriate. Here we are considering maximizing the total payoff rather than using a notion of Pareto efficiency. However, the tension here generalizes to a version of Pareto efficiency that allows for reallocation of payoffs up to the symmetry and balance constraints, as argued in Jackson (2003).

fully efficient outcomes should be obtained. The complexity of network settings, and in particular of the multilateral bargaining and multiple incentive constraints that need to be satisfied simultaneously, means that the simple logic of the Coase theorem in bilateral settings does not generalize to all multilateral settings. Whether or not transfers lead to efficient networks being stable depend on the nature of the externalities and the transfers available (e.g., see Jackson and Wolinsky (1996), Dutta and Mutuswami (1997), Currarini and Morelli (2000), Bloch and Jackson (2007)). It also depends on how agents behave when forming links, as it might be a dynamic process and they might be farsighted and anticipate each other's reactions to their actions (e.g., see Mauleon and Vannetelbosch (2004) and Page, Wooders and Kamat (2005)), or they might be able to form links unilaterally (e.g., see Bala and Goyal (2000) and Dutta and Jackson (2000)). Broader surveys of this central and broad question of the tension between individual incentives and societal efficiency appear in Bloch and Dutta (this volume) and Jackson (2003, 2008).

Before moving on, let me make an important comment on strategic models of network formation. Such an approach to modeling is not only useful for examining trade-offs between incentives and efficiency, but it also provides insight into some observed phenomena, like the small worlds referred to in Sections 3.3 and 4.1.2. For example, suppose that agents are located in some space, which might correspond to physical geography, but might also relate to their characteristics, such as age, profession, education, religion, etc., with closer agents being more similar than ones farther away. If the costs of links are low in terms of forming connections to nearby agents, then one would tend to see very dense connections on a local level, and thus high clustering. Links between agents that are farther apart would tend to be more costly to maintain and thus would be rarer given the higher cost. However, if there were no links that covered large distances, then there would be very substantial payoffs to such links, as they would provide closer access for an agent to many other agents that are far away. Thus, we would expect some long distance links to emerge, and at least a few such links should emerge precisely because they shorten the diameter of the network. In fact, as long as costs of long-distance links are not overwhelming, the diameter of the network is limited, since if we end up with too big a distance between some sets of nodes, then there would be substantial gains from at least one pair forming a link. Thus, a strategic formation model, with quite natural assumptions about costs and benefits can explain *why* we might expect small world network phenomena. This point appears in various forms in Johnson and Gilles (2000), Carayol and Roux (2003) and Jackson and Rogers (2005).

Thus strategic models of network formation are complementary to random-graph and statistical models of network formation, not only in their methods and approach, and the settings to which they might apply, but also in the types of insights that they provide into which network structures should emerge and why.

4.4 Mixing random and strategic models

Jackson (2005b) discusses the contrast and complementarities between random network and strategic models of network formation, and the need for some hybrid models. Serendipity plays a role in the relationships that people form, but so does choice. The relative roles of choice and chance can depend on the setting, and it can also be that the randomness that determines who meets whom is not uniform but depends on the context and the evolution of some process. It can also be that the choices that individuals make given their meeting opportunities end up being critical to determining the patterns of links that emerge. There are a few models of network formation that incorporate both randomness and choice, but still relatively few such models, especially given the insights that they can generate. Let me discuss a few of them.

One of the best-known such models is due to Schelling (1978), who considered a preference-based model of neighborhood formation taking into account agents' preferences to be close to other agents who are similar to themselves. Schelling devised a simple model illustrating how a city consisting of agents with different attributes (e.g., religion, race, age, etc.) who are initially integrated can "tip" into a highly segregated state just due to slight biases in preferences. This phenomenon turns out to be quite robust and provides important insights into homophily.

Schelling's basic model can be described as follows. Think of a city constructed as a checkerboard with 64 squares representing possible locations where an agent can reside. There are two agent types: green and red. Assume the number of agents is smaller than 64 and that they are initially randomly distributed on the board. Suppose now that each agent is content if a fraction greater than $\alpha \in (0,1)$ of his or her immediate neighbors is of his or her type. For instance, if $\alpha = \frac{1}{4}$, and all of the eight adjacent squares are occupied, than the player is content if at least two of the adjacent squares are occupied with agents of the same type. Schelling considered a simple dynamic in which at each stage one agent is randomly selected and can move if he or she is not content, and then moves to one of the nearest squares where she would be content.[38] Schelling inspected the effects of the initial constellation of parameters (distribution of players and taste parameters α's). Even very integrated initial constellations can shift to very segregated ones with even slight preference biases towards being with own type: one individual moving can tip his or her former neighbors' neighborhoods past a threshold, which leads them to move, and leading to chain reactions.

As mentioned above, a model designed to directly investigate roles of choice and chance, Currarini, Jackson, and Pin (2009, 2010) consider a model in which individuals have types and preferences over the types of their friends. Friendships are formed through a random meeting process, but that process and the resulting friendships that form are influenced by individual decisions, and so there are two sources of bias that

[38] One can consider a variety of algorithms, with similar results. For instance, see Fagiolo, Valente and Vriend (2007).

could potentially lead to homophily: bias in whom people wish to befriend, and biases in whom they meet.[39] They find that both of these biases are needed within the model in order to generate patterns that are consistent with two empirical facts that Currarini, Jackson and Pin identify in the data on high school friendships: As an ethnic group forms a larger percentage of a school it exhibits higher per-person average numbers of friends, and while almost all groups are homophilistic relative to the base-rate demographics, the most inbred groups are those which form middle-sized proportions of their school. They also find that these biases can differ significantly across races. Thus, at least in one setting there is some evidence suggesting that both choice and chance play important roles in determining the network that emerges, and they are responsible for different properties of the emerging network and understanding the roles of choice and chance can help explain differences in network structure across races.

Given that models that incorporate nontrivial randomness and heterogeneity along with individual choice can be very hard to solve analytically, one can work with simulations. For example, Carayol, Roux and Yildizoglu (2006, 2008) solve large versions of a connections model originating in Jackson and Wolinsky (1996) and are able to match some moments of various data. Such simulations provide a promising technique in fitting such models to data. The class of such models is also growing, both in terms of the development of more general statistical models (e.g., see Christakis, Fowler, Imbens and Kalyanaraman (2010)) and the fitting of existing models to data (e.g., the papers of Carayol, Roux and Yildizoglu (2006, 2008) mentioned above and that of Comola (2009)).

5. MODELING THE IMPACT OF NETWORKS

As discussed in the introduction, network structure is important because it impacts behavior and ultimately the welfare of a society. In understanding, modeling and measuring these sorts of effect, it is useful to distinguish between two sorts of situations. In one sort of situation, the impact on behavior is somewhat mechanical and not strategic. For example, in understanding the diffusion of a disease or an idea, or information about jobs, and so forth, network structure matters mainly as a conduit, and the transmission can be modeled probabilistically. In other situations, such as the trade of goods and services, the adoption of a technology, the provision of local public goods, and other decision making that is influenced by friends and acquaintances, network structure also matters but with the added features of strategic interactions between networked agents. In the first case where a network serves mainly as a conduit, much of the resulting behavior can be traced directly to network structure and attributes and some information about the process of diffusion or interaction. In the second case, the interaction between

[39] Currarini, Jackson, and Pin (2009, 2010) do not model what underlies the preference to link with others with similar characteristics. For recent models leading to such a bias, see Peski (2007) and Baccara and Yariv (2009).

network structure and outcomes can be more complicated requiring some dynamic and/ or equilibrium analysis. Let me discuss some of the issues in analyzing these sorts of effects and process, partly in the contexts of some more specific applications.

5.1 Diffusion

There are many situations where an idea, disease or behavior is transmitted from one person to another. Network structure is the primary determinant of whether diffusion occurs to a significant fraction of the society, how quickly diffusion occurs, what fraction ends up affected, and other related questions. This subject is discussed in Jackson and Yariv (This volume), and so I refer the interested reader there for more detail, and just outline some basic points here. It is useful to start with the simplest case. Consider a situation where some nodes are initially "infected" with a disease, idea, or behavior. Suppose that then they spread this to each of their neighbors, and then those neighbors spread it to their neighbors, and so forth. In that case, it is clear that the extent of diffusion will depend on which nodes are initially affected and which components of the network they lie in. If the network is connected, then all nodes will eventually be "infected". If not, then the extent of the diffusion will be determined by the component structure of the network. Thus, a direct description of the components is enough to understand the extent of diffusion in this simple case. Component structure of random graphs (and strategically formed graphs) is something that is well studied and so predictions are easy to make for this simple case. This is discussed in more detail in Jackson and Yariv (This volume).

Of course, in many cases of interest, it might be that some nodes are immune to the infection, or would never choose to adopt the behavior, etc. It could also be that interaction among nodes is probabilistic or that transmission has some inherent randomness. Simple variations of diffusion incorporating variation in nodes immunity can be analyzed simply by deleting those nodes that would be immune to infection or face prohibitively high costs of adoption and considering the subnetwork that remains. Some situations where there is stochastic transmission can be incorporated via variations that allow for links to only be present with certain probabilities. It might also be that nodes can recover and become immune to becoming infected, or that nodes need repeated exposure in order to become infected. There are a variety of such models that have come out of studies of epidemiology, as well as diffusion (again, see Jackson and Yariv (This volume) for background). These sorts of analyses show how network structure can directly translate into predictions about emergent behaviors in a society.

5.2 Learning

Word-of-mouth is an important means of communication and formation of opinions about subjects ranging from political elections to consumer products (see Katz and

Lazarsfeld (1955) for seminal research on these subjects). Modeling the effects of network structure on how we learn and what opinions we hold involves complications relative to the pure diffusion setting above. The most obvious difference is that individuals no longer fall into simple categories such as "infected" or not, but instead might have beliefs or opinions that vary more continuously and are influenced in more complicated ways by interaction with their neighbors. As Goyal (This volume) discusses this subject,[40] I simply focus on the major themes here.

How social learning works depends on a number of facets of the setting, including:

- Is the learning observational, so that agents see others' decisions, or do agents directly communicate?
- Does new information come in over time or just once?
- Do agents repeatedly act or communicate?
- Is the interaction simultaneous or in sequence?
- How do agents process information, via Bayesian updating or via some other process?
- Do some agents have more precise information than others?

There are also a number of questions that we can answer about social learning:

- Does the society reach a consensus and eventually hold similar beliefs and/or make similar decisions?
- How much influence does each agent have over societal outcomes and how does that depend on network position?
- Do individuals end up accurately aggregating initially decentralized information?
- How quickly is information aggregated and how does that depend on network structure?

It is useful to begin by describing a benchmark model that comes from the seminal work on social learning of Banerjee (1992) and Bikhchandani, Hirshleifer and Welch (1992). That model is observational and sequential: each agent sees one piece of information, makes a decision just once, and agents arrive in sequence with each agent getting to observe the choices (but not the information) of all of the previous agents. Agents choose between two actions, say A and B. Each agent $i \in \{1,2,\ldots\}$ sees a signal $s_i \in \{A, B\}$ that provides the agent with information about which action offers a higher payoff. Banerjee describes an example where agents are deciding between two restaurants, A and B. One restaurant has a better chef and all agents would like to go to the restaurant with the better chef, and they each get an independent, equally accurate, but noisy signal about which restaurant has the better chef. Let us suppose that an agent's signal is correct in telling him or her which restaurant has the better chef with a probability $p > 1/2$, and suppose that without any signals the prior is that each restaurant is

[40] For additional background, see Sobel (2000) and Jackson (2008).

equally likely to have the better chef. Agents arrive in sequence and can see the other agents in each restaurant before making their choice. Suppose also, that in the case of indifference, an agent follows his or her own signal.[41] Agents can deduce the first agent's information from observing her choice. Suppose, without loss of generality, that the choice is *A*. Now the second agent makes a choice. Since that agent follows his or her signal when indifferent, we can also deduce the second agent's choice from his choice. So, if the third agent observes that the first two choices were *A, A*, then she knows that there were two signals that indicated that *A* has the better chef. Regardless of the third agent's signal, she will choose *A*, since there are at least two signals in favor of *A* and at most one in favor of *B*. Thus, the third agent's choice will be *A* and will not provide any information about that agent's signal. That will be true from then on, so the society will then "herd" to the *A* restaurant. Agents will all observe that it has all of the agents, and correctly infer that it is more likely to be the better restaurant, based on what they can deduce from others' actions. If, instead the second agent saw a *B* signal, then that agent would have chosen *B* and so the first two choices would be *A, B* and would effectively cancel each other out. Those choices could effectively be ignored, and so it would be as if we started the process all over again. Almost surely, the society will eventually herd so that agents ignore their information and all end up going to the restaurant that ends up having at least two more agents than the other restaurant.

This benchmark case illustrates some of the potential outcomes of social learning. First, a consensus is eventually reached and agents end up all making the same decision. Second, and quite importantly, it is not necessarily the correct decision. It could be that restaurant *B* happens to have the better chef, but that the first two agents get signals saying that *A* has the better chef, and society herds on restaurant *A* even though it has the worse chef. Third, there can be some randomness in the process, so it might take some time before the herd forms, depending on the particular realization of the sequence of signals.

The conclusions in this canonical social learning example are sensitive to specifics of the setting. To begin with, suppose that agents got to observe previous agents' signals rather than their actions. In that case, by a law of large numbers, the probability that agents would be going to the restaurant with the better chef would converge to one over time. Even without seeing signals, if periodically some agents do not observe anything and make choices just based on their own information, then simply observing such agents would eventually lead to accurate information about which restaurant had the better chef.[42] Allowing some agents to have arbitrarily accurate

[41] This does not affect the qualitative conclusions, but helps simplify the analysis.

[42] It is not even necessary that later agents know who these agents are, but just what fraction of the agents will make such choices, as then they can deduce from long enough histories whether an "incorrect" herd has occurred by noting whether there is a large enough set of agents who have gone against the herd.

signals can overcome herding, as they will have accurate enough information to lead them to go against a mistaken herd, and then this can be seen by subsequent agents providing they see the order in which actions are taken before them and are confident in the rationality of those agents. Allowing for heterogeneous preferences, and other idiosyncratic preferences that favor particular types of restaurants, can also change the results. These are the subjects of a set of papers such as Bikhchandani, Hirshleifer and Welch (1998), Smith and Sorensen (2000), Çelen and Kariv (2004, 2005), and Acemoglu et al. (2008). For example, Acemoglu et al. (2008) provide results on how social learning depends on how neighborhoods of which agents observe which other agents develop over time, and also on how accurate various agents' signals are. Although the results show that conclusions about social learning are somewhat case-specific, the results do have nice intuitions about things like the precision of information and who observes whom.

This canonical herding model has a sequentiality to it that means that social network structures do not play a prominent role. Social network structure can begin to play more of a role once agents either repeatedly take actions or repeatedly communicate with each other. A variation on the above model was investigated by Bala and Goyal (1998) and can be described as follows. Instead of taking actions just once, each agent takes an action at every date. Agents do not get signals about which is the better restaurant, but instead have experiences each time they eat, and those experiences are somewhat random but are correlated with the skill of the chef. If agents were simply acting alone, this would be a classic "two-armed-bandit" problem. For some number of periods agents would experiment and sample each of the restaurants, and eventually they would settle in to one of the restaurants.[43] However, agents are also connected to each other in a social network so that they observe their friends' choices and experiences at each date. Agents are boundedly rational so they do not infer anything from which choices their friends make,[44] but instead they just keep track of the quality of all of the meals that they and their friends have experienced over time. A fairly intuitive and direct conclusion in such a setting is that the long run average outcome of all the agents will be the same. The idea is that if some agent is enjoying consistently better meals than one of his or her friends, then it must be that the agent is going to the better restaurant more frequently than his or her friend, but then that friend would come to observe this over time and so should change restaurants. Again, this does not imply that the agents all end up going to the better restaurant, but instead that there will be a consensus and in the long run all agents who lie in the same component of the network

[43] This, of course, abstracts away from things like preferences for variety or non-stationary restaurant quality.

[44] This poses a challenging Bayesian updating problem. If I see that a friend changes restaurants, that could tell me something about what she has learned from her friends, who could be people that I do not know. How should I weight that in my decisions? Bayes' rule provides an answer, but one that quickly becomes intractable even in very simple networks.

will eventually end up going to the same restaurant.[45] Another similarity to the canonical herding setting is that the conclusions depend on the specific assumptions (e.g., see Ellison and Fudenberg (1995), Gale and Kariv (2003), Rosenberg, Solan and Vieille (2007), Mueller–Frank (2009), Acemoglu, Dahleh, Lobel, Ozdaglar (2008), among others), but the basic idea that agents converge to some consensus action will carry through provided there is not too much heterogeneity in the payoffs across agents (so, for instance, agents are similar enough in what they view as a good or bad meal and restaurants treat agents similarly), and there is enough repeated viewing of neighbors' actions over time.

A challenge of Bayesian learning in social settings, both for the agents and the modeler, is that the updating becomes quite complex very quickly.[46] Even after a few periods, one is faced with a rather complicated inference problem of deducing what an agent's action indicates about that agent's friends' information. Even with a handful of agents in the simplest settings, this quickly becomes intractable. Choi, Gale, and Kariv (2005, 2007) have done some laboratory experiments on simple variations on three agent networks and found that although the strategies that agents employ show qualitative features of those employed in an equilibrium setting with fully Bayesian rational agents, the strategies of individual agents can deviate substantially, especially when the computations involved become more complicated.

A leading alternative to Bayesian updating in network settings is a model that was partly described in work by French (1956) and Harary (1959), and was more completely specified and developed by DeGroot (1974). It has been used and extended by Besag (1974), Krause (2000), Friedkin and Johnsen (1997), DeMarzo, Vayanos, and Zwiebel (2003), Lorenz (2005), and Golub and Jackson (2008, 2010), among many others. I will refer to it as the *DeGroot model.*

The DeGroot model is simple and tractable, and has a number of nice properties that make it a useful benchmark both in terms of positive and normative features. The setting is one where agents observe signals just once and then repeatedly communicate with each other and update their beliefs after every round of communication. The social network is described by a weighted and possibly directed "trust" matrix $\mathbf{T} \in [0, 1]^{n \times n}$.

The idea is that T_{ij} is the weight that person i places on person j's opinion. The matrix is (row) stochastic, so that $\sum_j T_{ij} = 1$ for each i, so these are really relative weights.

[45] If the restaurants happen to have exactly the same average quality, then it is possible that the agents frequent different restaurants but they will still enjoy the same quality of meals on average. But provided there is a difference the restaurants, then agents will converge to picking the same restaurant, almost surely.

[46] This presumes some bounds on communication. If every agent can tell neighbors exactly what they have seen in every period, and what they have heard from their neighbors about all of their information, and so forth, then there is no inference problem. Such communication is obviously burdensome, and it becomes especially complicated when information is not in the form of simple signals, but in terms of subjective perceptions of the world.

A simple version of this model is where society is described by an undirected social network $\mathbf{g}$, with $g_{ij} = 1$ indicating that i and j are linked, and then setting[47]

$$T_{ij} = \frac{g_{ij}}{d_i(\mathbf{g})}, \tag{4}$$

where recall that $d_i(g)$ is i's degree. Thus, i places equal weight on each of his or her friends. Of course, this is just an example, and more generally agents might place different weights on different friends based on frequencies of interaction, envisioned reliability, affinity, or other reasons.

In the DeGroot model, agents begin with some initial opinions described by a belief $b_i(0) \in [0, 1]$ and then update these over time. The updating rule is just

$$b_i(t) = \sum_i T_{ij} b_j(t-1)$$

which can be written as

$$\mathbf{b}(t) = \mathbf{T}\mathbf{b}(t-1)$$

or

$$\mathbf{b}(t) = \mathbf{T}^t\mathbf{b}(0).$$

We easily see why this model is so tractable, and provides a useful benchmark, since working with a matrix raised to a power allows us to draw on substantial mathematical structure and knowledge and so there is much that can be said about the process that is not so easily deduced about nonlinear processes, such as Bayesian updating.

There are many interpretations of this process. For example, one interpretation is that each agent is trying to estimate some unknown parameter μ. The initial signals (the $b_i(0)$s) are independently distributed with mean μ. If these were normally distributed signals, then at least at a first step Bayesian updating would be such that each agent would take a weighted average of his or her neighbors' signals, where the weights would be related to the precision of various friends' signals. With equal precision, the weights would be exactly those in (4). The divergence from Bayesian behavior comes from the fact that agents do not adjust their updating rule over time to account for the network structure: some friends may be talking to more people over time than others, and so forth. Despite this boundedly rational behavior, there are still many situations where the society eventually reaches a consensus that correctly approximates the unknown μ, as shown by Golub and Jackson (2010). Whether or not the DeGroot process converges to accurate estimate (and hence the Bayesian estimate) depends on how well balanced the relative weights are that different groups of agents place on each

[47] This presumes that the degree of i is not 0, and to fix ideas let us consider a case where we allow $g_{ii} = 1$ so that each agent pays attention to his or her own opinion.

other. If there is sufficient balance in the weights then an accurate consensus is reached over time, while if things are too imbalanced then some small subset of agents' information can dominate the eventual consensus. Another very different interpretation of this process is one of myopic best responses: Instead of beliefs, the b_is represent some behavior and each agent wants to match the average behavior of his or her friends (e.g., as in some of the peer effects models like Manski (1993)).

There are several nice aspects of this process. Beyond the models tractability, it allows the network to enter in a nontrivial way. In the analysis of observational learning, the conclusions that a consensus was reached in the society did not really depend on network structure, and the nature of the consensus might depend on the network structure, but in ways that researchers have not been able to deduce. In contrast, the limiting behavior of (4) is very easily analyzed and depends on the network structure in interesting and intuitive ways.

To get a feeling for this, let us examine a simple example, as shown in Figure 7. This corresponds to a network where each agent is connected to him or herself, and there are also links between agents 1 and 2, and between agents 1 and 3. Each agent places equal weight on each friend when updating.

We see how the DeGroot updating works for this case, when starting with an initial belief vector of $\mathbf{b}(0) = (0, 1, 0)$, so that agent 2 has an initial belief of 1 and the others have an initial belief of 0. In this case, agent 1′s first period belief is the average of these beliefs, and so it becomes 1/3. Agent 2 averages beliefs of 1 and 0 and ends up at a new belief of 1/2, while agent 3 averages two beliefs of 0 and so stays at 0. So the new beliefs are $\mathbf{b}(1) = (1/3, 1/2, 0)$. We now repeat this process and then beliefs become $\mathbf{b}(2) = (5/18, 5/12, 1/6)$, and iterating in this way the beliefs eventually converge to $\mathbf{b}(\text{limit}) = (2/7, 2/7, 2/7)$, as pictured in Figure 8. This limit has a natural interpretation. Note that in this network agents 2 and 3 each have two links, while agent 1 has

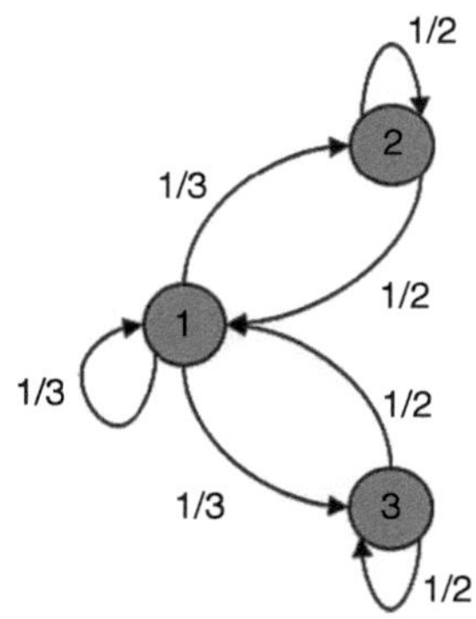

$$T = \begin{bmatrix} 1/3 & 1/3 & 1/3 \\ 1/2 & 1/2 & 0 \\ 1/2 & 0 & 1/2 \end{bmatrix}$$

Figure 7 The DeGroot updating process for a case where agent 1 has links to all agents and agents 2 and 3 just link to agent 1 and themselves, and where agents equally weight all of their friends, as in (4).

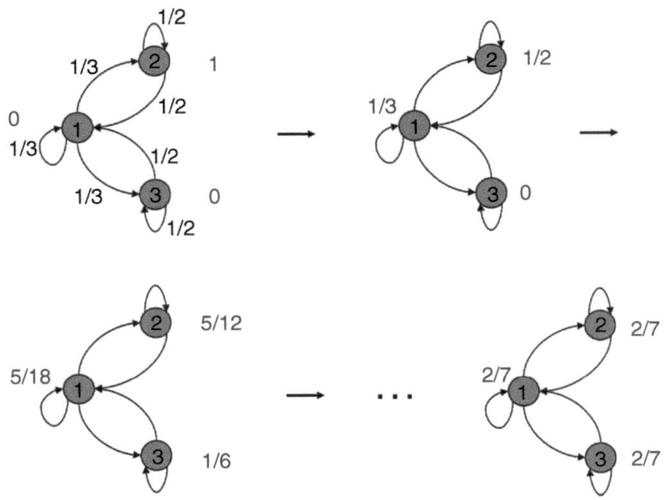

Figure 8 The DeGroot updating process over time for the system in Figure 7 when agent 2 starts with belief 1 and the other agents start with belief 0.

three links. There is a total of seven links, and each agent's "influence" turns out to be proportional to the number of links that the agent has. Here agent 2 has 2/7 of the links and that is agent 2′s influence. Agent 2 is the only agent with a positive initial belief, and the limit point is 2/7 times agent 2′s initial belief, plus 2/7 times agent 3′s initial belief and 3/7 of agent 1′s initial belief.

This example illustrates a couple of features of the DeGroot process.

First, the agents' beliefs converge to a consensus. This will be true of any strongly connected component such that there is a directed path from each agent to every other agent, and such that the component is aperiodic[48] (for which it is sufficient that at least one agent place some weight on his or her own opinion). Thus, under very weak conditions, the society will reach a consensus in the DeGroot model. The intuition behind this result is straightforward: if we have not already reached a consensus then some agent who holds the highest belief at some point in time must be communicating with someone with a lower belief, and so that high-belief agent's belief will decrease, and similarly the agents with the lowest beliefs will have their beliefs move up over time. Since these are weighted averages of previous beliefs, they do not overshoot, and so the set of beliefs contracts over time (presuming the connectedness and aperiodicity conditions discussed above are satisfied).

Second, the influence that each agent has on the final consensus depends in very intuitive ways on the network structure. In the setting of (4) where agents place equal

[48] This requires that the least common divisor of the length of all the cycles in the component be one.

weights on each of their friends, the influence of an agent is proportional to his or her degree. An agent with twice as many friends as another agent has twice the influence on the eventual consensus. More generally, the influence will be related to the unit (left-hand) eigenvector of the trust matrix **T**, that is, the unique vector **s** such that $\mathbf{sT} = \mathbf{s}$. This has the nice intuition that an agent's influence is related to the influence of those agents who trust him or her. Beyond this application, it also provides some foundation for eigenvector-based definitions of centrality that date to Katz (1953), and also is the reasoning behind things like Google's page rank system (e.g., see Langville and Meyer (2006)).

Thus, we see that network structure plays an intuitive and tractable role in the DeGroot model of updating. This tractability enables a number of questions to be answered. To get a feeling for this, let us change the network in Figure 8 to include links between all of the agents, then we see that both the relative influences of the agents, the consensus, and the speed of convergence changes, as pictured in Figure 9.

Although very simple, this example shows that network structure affects both the consensus reached and how quickly it is reached. Understanding speed of convergence is important as a society may have limited iterations on communication, and so understanding the factors that affect rate of convergence can give an idea of the extent to which a consensus might emerge in the DeGroot model. As one might expect intuitively, the main thing that slows convergence is a split of the network into two or more

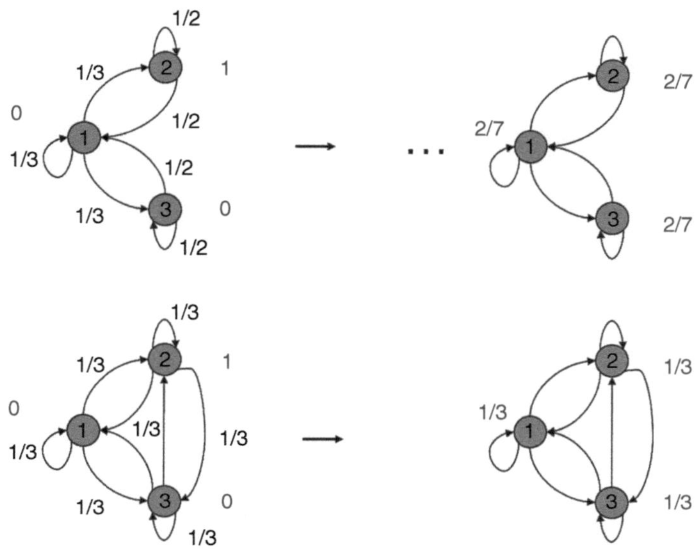

Figure 9 The DeGroot updating process for two different configurations: In the top setting agents 2 and 3 are not friends and the process is slower to converge to a consensus, in the bottom setting there is a complete network and consensus occurs in the first period.

groups that communicate more intensely within group than across groups. This is studied by Golub and Jackson (2008) who provide details as to when and to what extent homophily slows the convergence process. They show how the DeGroot updating process can be slowed by homophily due to the fact that convergence is dependent on the relative distribution of communication across groups, while there are other processes, such as those that simply depend on shortest paths in a network, which are unaffected by homophily.

There are many other questions that can be studied in the context of the DeGroot model and its variations. For example, Demarzo, Vayanos, and Zwiebel (2003) show how communication along many dimensions at once can reduce to convergence along a single dimension, providing insight into why complicated political landscapes often reduce to unidimensional discourses, where agents have the approximately the same relative positions in terms of their updated beliefs compared to the average belief across different dimensions after sufficient discourse time. The technical details of the proof involve working with the spectral decomposition of the trust matrix, but the intuition can be seen fairly easily from examples. As an illustration, suppose that society is divided into three groups, agents in group 1 talk evenly to all agents in groups 1 and 2, agents in group 3 talk evenly to all agents in groups 2 and 3, and agents in group 2 talk evenly with all agents. Agents in the middle group 2 will be at the average opinion, while agents in group 1 will be biased in a direction that under-weights group 3′s average opinion, and group 3 agents will be biased in a direction that under-weights group 1′s average opinion. Whatever the issue, groups 1 and 3 will be on opposite extremes and group 2 in the middle, and they will reach a consensus as groups 1 and 3 slowly move in towards the central group 2 average opinion.

The Bayesian and DeGroot analyses discussed above represent just some of the many in this growing area of analysis. Recent work has led to fuller understandings of what leads to a society to a consensus opinion or behavior and what the consensus will be, as well as how influential each agent in the society is. There are still many issues that remain open, including understanding issues of strategic transmission of information when agents have incentives to misrepresent or distort their information to try influence the eventual outcome (e.g., see Hagenbach and Koessler (2009), Lever (2010) and Acemoglu Ozdaglar, and ParandehGheibi (2009)), costly information acquisition in such contexts, endogenous formation of networks in the context of learning, and developing alternative models between the rational and DeGroot-style models (e.g., Jadbabaie, Sandroni, and Tahbaz-Salehi (2009)).

5.3 Bargaining and trade through networks

Another important application of network analysis is to understand how terms of trade and transactions are affected by the network of relationships through which they take place. Moreover, once we understand how network structure affects trade we can then explore the incentives for agents to form trading networks and to see whether they lead to competitive or efficient outcomes.

In order to fix ideas, let us examine settings where there is some cost to establishing communication between a potential buyer and seller. This cost might reflect many things. It could represent the opportunity cost of time spent learning about a product, adjustments for compatibility, or simply establishing and/or maintaining lines of communication. In a first stage, agents form a network of relationships and then in a second stage the agents can bargain and transact, but only with agents to whom they are linked.

The key to understanding the efficiency of trading networks comes through understanding the "externalities" in such settings and the splits of the gains from trade. Usually, we do not think of there being any externalities in the exchange of private goods. The consumption of a good by one agent does not affect another agent. However, when trading opportunities depend on which relationships are present in a society, choices of network ties have external effects. Thus, the (Pareto) efficiency that is the hallmark of the competitive exchange of private goods no longer applies when goods can only be traded through established relationships. The fact that inefficiencies arise when there is some limitation on the potential transactions that can occur is not new, as we see in the extensive literature on search. Moreover, such frictions serve as the basis for understanding various labor market imperfections, as well as macroeconomic phenomena (see Rogerson, Shimer, and Wright (2005) for a recent survey). However, the way that inefficiencies arise and manifest themselves in network settings provide new insights into trading frictions, price dispersion, and bargaining power.

To get a feeling for some of the analysis in the literature, let us start with the simplest setting. Consider a benchmark case where each agent is either a "buyer" or a "seller". When buyer i and seller j transact there is a total value to the transaction of v_{ij}. The value of that transaction can be split between them in any way. We can capture this via a price p so that the value of the transaction to the seller is p and to the buyer is $v_{ij} - p$. Buyers can only transact with sellers and vice versa, and each agent can participate in at most one transaction.

Let us start with a case where the transactions are homogeneous, so that the value of any transaction between a buyer and seller is 1 (so, all the v_{ij}s are 1) and where the cost is $1/2 > c_s > 0$ to the seller for each link, and $1/2 > c_B > 0$ to each buyer involved in a link. Clearly, the efficient network is to have pairs of linked buyers and sellers, so that no agent has more than one link and the number of links is equal to the minimum of the number of buyers and the number of sellers.[49] Extra links waste cost, and given that

[49] This takes an ex post perspective. From an ex ante point of view, if, for instance there are more buyers than sellers the buyers are not sure of which transaction might take place ex post, then one could imagine extra links being good from a buyer's perspective. However, networks with extra links are Pareto dominated by randomly choosing which links get formed and then transacting at the expected value on the links that forms.

the total cost of a link is less than its value it makes sense to maximize the number of transactions taking place.

To see the basic issues that arise regarding efficiency, consider an example with just one seller and two buyers. The fact that the two-link network is inefficient does not prevent it from forming. Whether it forms when the buyers and sellers choose the links will depend on the the expected values that each of the agents gets as a function of the network structure. The key point is that we should expect the price that the seller gets (presuming the bargaining occurs after the network is formed and held fixed) to be higher when there are two links than when there is just one. If the bargaining takes place after the links have formed and the agents ignore the sunk costs of link formation, then with symmetry in the bargaining game, we would expect $1/2 - c_i$ to be the payoff to each of the agents in a single-link network. This is indeed the outcome of an alternating bargaining game like a variation on the Rubinstein-Stahl bargaining game considered in the network bargaining study of Corominas-Bosch (2004), if we examine the limit as the (common) discount factor goes to 1, or we randomize in terms of who gets to make the first offer and examine the expected value of the bargaining. In the two-link network, we should expect that the seller will obtain a greater expected share of the transaction than in the one-link network, although exactly how much better the seller is will depend on the bargaining protocol. Let this share be $v \geq 1/2$, so that the payoffs are as pictured in Figure 10. The value of v determines which network we should expect to form.

If $1 - 2c_B > v > 1/2 + c_S$, then the unique pairwise stable network is the two-link network, as both the unlinked-buyer and seller gain from adding a second link to the network. If instead, $v > 1 - 2c_B$ or $1/2 + c_S > v$, then the one-link networks are the pairwise stable ones, as in the first case the buyers have a negative value from the two-link network and in the second case the seller is better off in a one-link network than a two-link network.

Which of these cases ensues depends on the specifics of the bargaining protocol. In an extreme case where the seller can get the buyers to bid against each other as in a sort of reverse Bertrand competition, the seller would extract all of the surplus when there are two links formed, and so $v = 1$, then only the efficient networks are pairwise stable, as the buyers would benefit from severing a link from the two-link network. This is the outcome under a core definition of trade (see Rochford

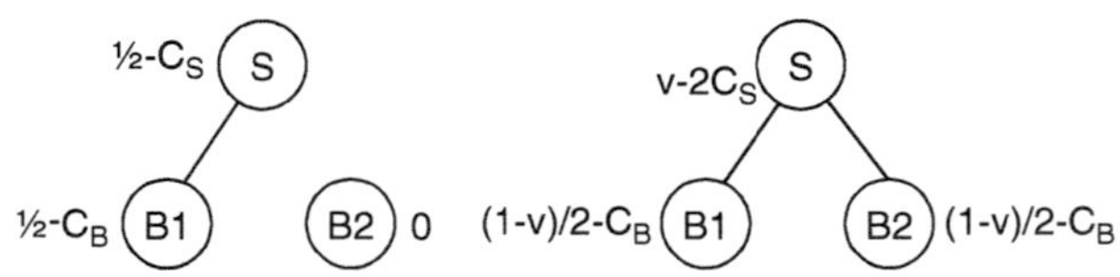

Figure 10 Payoffs to buyers and sellers as a function of the network.

(1984), Sotomayor (2006), and Elliott (2009)) or else under the Corominas-Bosch (2004) alternating offer bargaining (with a limiting discount factor).

If in contrast, if the bargaining power in the two-link network is less extreme, but still favors the seller to some extent so that $1 - 2c_B > v > 1/2 + c_S$, then the two-link network will be the unique pairwise stable network. It is interesting to note that the seller would actually benefit from committing to lower his or her bargaining power if v exceeds $1 - 2c_B$. By committing to a bargaining procedure that leads to a v such that $1 - 2c_B > v > 1/2 + c_S$, the seller will obtain a greater surplus than if the bargaining procedure is more extreme.

Even in this very simple example, we see the role of the externalities and the potential for resulting inefficiencies. The buyers do not internalize the impact on each other of their decisions to form links. When we get to more complicated networks, how the allocation of utilities depends on the network structure depends on having a well-specified prediction for the bargaining outcome, and different bargaining protocols can lead to different conclusions regarding the efficiency of the stable networks.

Let me discuss a few of the ways in which such settings have been modeled. Corominas-Bosch (2004) examines settings such as those above where there is an identical value of 1 to each potential buyer-seller transaction. The prediction of the outcome of the bargaining depends on the network in a way that keeps track of relative balance of buyers and sellers in various subnetworks and is based on an alternating move bargaining game. A clever algorithm identifies which buyers and sellers are evenly matched and which ones end up extracting full surplus. In that setting, if both buyers and sellers bear link costs (and without too much asymmetry in their costs) and the discount factor in the bargaining is high enough, then the only pairwise stable networks are the efficient ones, as buyers or sellers on the long side of the market do not get enough surplus to cover link costs.

Kranton and Minehart (2001) allow for heterogeneity in the realization of various buyers' valuations after links are formed and study settings where sellers' items are all identical and simultaneously auctioned off. They show that then the marginal expected value to a buyer from adding a link is exactly that link's social expected value. In that case, if only buyers pay costs (so that $c_S = 0$) then the network will be efficient, but if sellers pay costs it may not. Depending on the cost to sellers, the resulting network can be over- or under-connected relative to what would be total surplus maximizing (see Jackson (2003)). There are two effects: one is that sellers see changes in the relative competition in bidding as links are added and so have an incentive to add links, and the other is that the change in a seller's surplus can differ from the change in social value from adding a link, and so their incentives to add links can be distorted in either direction from the social incentive; compounded by the fact that buyers and seller are also internalizing only part of the cost of a link.

The model of Elliott (2008) allows for a full heterogeneity in each buyer-seller transaction value. This presents a challenge in predicting the relative splits of surplus as a function of the network or in working with any specific bargaining protocol. Elliott uses a core definition to sort this out, which provides a multiplicity of predictions as to the values realized to buyers and sellers as a function of the network, but the core has well-defined endpoints in terms of maximum and minimum outcomes for buyers and sellers. Through an illuminating algorithm, Elliott traces out how the determination of relative shares can be traced to chains of outside options that buyers and sellers have. Elliott also presents interesting results on the "price of anarchy," a term due to Papadimitriou (2001) and Roughgarden and Tardos (2002), which examines the extent to which the total surplus of the society can be dissipated when agents form the network. He shows that the full level of surplus can be dissipated by the inefficient network formation of the agents involved. He also traces the inefficiencies to over-investment (to improve bargaining position)[50] and under-investment where beneficial networks fail to form in cases where the agents do not see enough value from a transaction to cover their personal cost. Which form of inefficiency emerges depends on whether link costs are exogenous or can be negotiated.

Kakade et al. (2004b) (as well as Kakade, Kearns and Ortiz 2004a) examine a model of exchange on random graph-generated network structures. Their interest is in the extent to which there can exist price dispersion and how this depends on network structure. They examine a simple general equilibrium model, reminiscent of the Corominas-Bosch model described above, but where goods are fully divisible, so that a seller quotes a price so that she sells exactly her unit supply of the good, and buyers exchange their unit supply of money until they have exhausted it. Kakade et al. (2004) find, roughly, that if the network is sufficiently symmetric in that buyers all have similar numbers of connections, and similarly for sellers, then there will be low levels of price dispersion, but as asymmetry increases so that some sellers have high degrees while others do not (or similarly for buyers), then substantial variation in prices can be observed across different parts of a network.

Beyond these models there are many other important questions to be investigated. For example, in the above analyses buyer-seller transactions occur just once and are exclusive, but one can also studysettings where there are repeated transactions, or where there are multiple goods for sale. For example, Manea (2008) (see also Abreu and Manea (2008)) examines a model similar to the setting described above, except that any two agents can transact and once two agents transact, they are replaced by new agents. The bargaining game is such that each period a different link is recognized and then one of the agents is randomly selected to make an offer for trade to the other agent. This gives agents bargaining power in proportion to the number of links that they have, and although it does not directly correspond to any particular application, it

[50] See Jackson (2003, 2004) for more discussion of how externalities in determining allocations and how bargaining can lead to systematic over-connection of networks.

provides a tractable model in which to examine the above issues of allocations as a function of network structure and the efficiency of network formation. One can also examine models of oligopoly on networks as in Nava (2008) to see when it is that competitive outcomes are reached and how that depends on network structure, or to see what incentives firms have to enter each other's markets as in Lever (2010), as well as to understand the role of middlemen in determining profits and achieving economic efficiency (e.g., Blume et al. (2007)), or the role of collaboration among firms (Goyal and Joshi (2003)).

Beyond the models above, and the empirical studies referred to in Section 2.1, there are also a number of experimental studies regarding how surplus is split among agents in network situations who negotiate over potential transactions. Charness, Corominas-Bosch and Frechette (2005) provide some direct tests of the Corominas-Bosch model. Although the model does not fit exactly, they do find that the predictions of the model are accurate in terms of the directions of changes in surplus as a function of network changes. This comes on the heels of a fairly large literature on "exchange theory," which evolved from general forms of dyadic exchanges in Homans (1958, 1961), to more direct economic applications as in Blau's (1964), and eventually included explicit consideration of social network structure as in Emerson (1962, 1967) and Cook and Emerson (1978) (see Cook and Whitmeyer (1992) for an overview). The exchange theory literature includes many experiments examining various network configurations and the exercise of bargaining power by agents as a function of their position in a network.

The growing catalog of studies on exchange through networks have shown that, beyond the basic point that network structure affects outcomes, full efficiency only arises in some specific circumstances. Looking across the studies one sees a theme that parallels one from the industrial organization literature: conclusions can be sensitive to details of the interaction. Nonetheless, there are some underlying regularities. Externalities are generally negative: agents have incentives to add relationships that might not be needed for efficient transactions but improve their bargaining power, and to the extent that agents do not fully see the value of potential transactions they may hurt others by not adding relationships that are needed to reach efficiency. Better connected agents (in precise network-defined senses) are relatively favored, and more asymmetric degree distributions can lead to greater inequality in outcomes. Looking forward, it seems that there is substantial promise in bringing network-based models of transactions to empirical studies of bargaining and trade, and measuring levels of inefficiencies. Given recent market failures, it also seems clear that a deeper understanding of interconnected liabilities and correlations in investments and financial contagion is needed.

5.4 Peer interactions and games on networks

Beyond direct transactions through a network, there are many other contexts where agents make decisions that are influenced by the decisions of their friends and acquaintances. This includes whether we drop out of the labor force, what political opinions we hold, which music we listen to, whether or not we engage in criminal activity, and which products we buy, among a myriad of other behaviors. Once the payoff to the decision of one agent from a given choice depends on the actions of his or her neighbors, the decisions can be modeled as a game.

Simple variations of games on networks were studied in the computer science with respect to showing how hard it can be to compute Nash equilibria in n person games.[51] In particular, Kearns, Littman and Singh (2001) introduced a class of games, that they called graphical games, such that each agent chooses between two actions 0 and 1 and an agent's payoff depends not only on his or her choice, but also on the decisions of his or her neighbors in a social network. The concern of that early literature was how hard it was to compute equilibria in cases where players' payoffs as a function of their neighbors' actions could be quite arbitrary. Despite the original paper's results on the difficulties of computing equilibria in some graphical games with large numbers of players, the basic model is quite useful as a device for understanding peer effects and strategic peer interactions. In particular, in many situations with peer effects there is substantial structure in the way that payoffs behave, so that actions are strategic complements or substitutes. This makes equilibria much more manageable and interesting.

Some aspects of such games are discussed in other chapters by Goyal (This volume) and Jackson and Yariv (This volume),[52] and so I just provide some illustrations of the central themes here.

It is useful to start with an example studied by Morris (2000) that provides some interesting insights. Consider a situation where agents are choosing two actions 0 and 1, which might be technologies, languages, fashions, etc. An agent can only choose one of the two and suppose that an agent prefers action 1 if and only if a fraction of at least q of his or her neighbors chooses action 1 and otherwise prefers action 0, where $1 > q > 0$.[53] For instance, it might only be worthwhile to adopt a new technology if a sufficient fraction of the agent's neighbors adopt it. There are clearly multiple (strict) Nash equilibria to this game: if all agents choose action 1, then each agent will strictly prefer to take action 1; while if all agents choose action 0 then all agents strictly prefer to take action 0. When is it that equilibria exist where some agents take action 0 and others take action 1?[54]

In Figure 11 we see an illustration of the multiplicity of equilibria in a setting where agents wish to match the majority of their neighbors' actions (with a preference for action 0 if an agent's neighbors are evenly split). In particular, it is possible to have

[51] Some specific examples of games on networks had been studied earlier, such as Ellison's (1993) and Young's (1998) studies of coordination games played between players in various lattice configurations (and see Jackson and Watts (2002b) and Goyal and Vega-Redondo (2005) for coordination games on more general and endogenous network structures).

[52] See Chapter 9 in Jackson (2008) for more background and detail.

[53] Letting q be an irrational number ensures that agents are never indifferent.

[54] I restrict attention to pure strategy equilibria in this discussion.

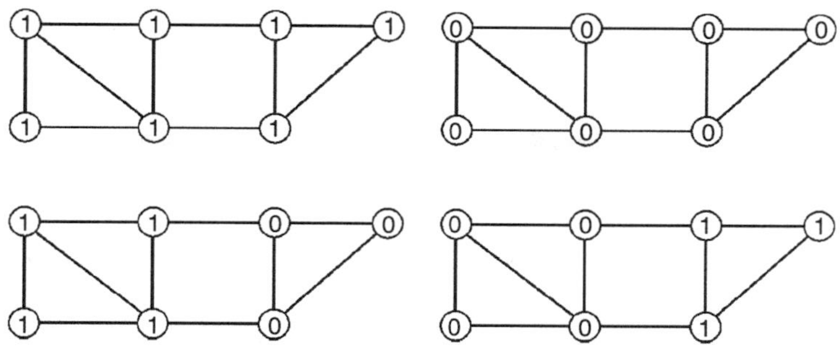

Figure 11 Equilibria when agents are willing to take action 1 if and only if more than half of their neighbors do.

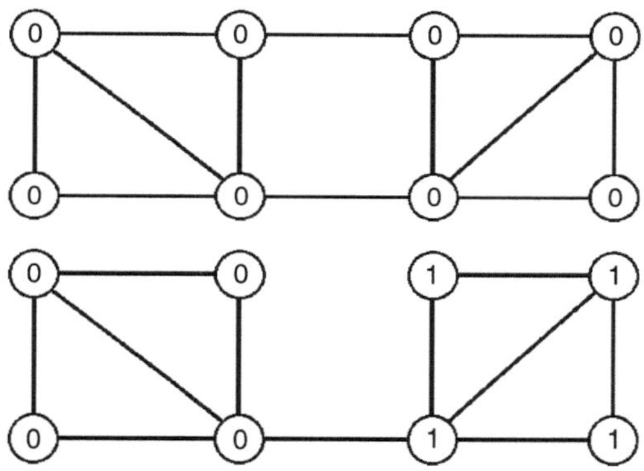

Figure 12 A game such that agents are willing to take action 1 if and only if more than 70% of their neighbors do. In the top network there does not exist an equilibrium where some agents play action 1 at the same time that other agents play action 0, while in the bottom network there exists such an equilibrium.

equilibria where both actions are played simultaneously by different agents in the same component of a network, as we see in the two networks in the bottom part of Figure 11.

The survival of both actions at the same time in an equilibrium is not always possible. We see that in the top network in Figure 12 for a situation where agents are only willing to take action 1 provided more than 70% of their neighbors do. However, by severing one of the links we obtain a network, as pictured in the bottom of Figure 12, where there are two sufficiently isolated groups so that both actions can be sustained in equilibrium.

In general, the ability of a society to sustain equilibria where both actions are played by different segments of the society depends on the network structure and the preferences of the agents. As one can intuit from the above examples, one needs to find a splitting of the society such that each of the two groups of the society are sufficiently inward-looking. This is captured through an intuitive definition of "cohesiveness" introduced by Morris (2000). A group of agents is r-cohesive if each agent in the group has a fraction of at least r of his or her neighbors in the group. In order to have an equilibrium played with both actions played in a game where action 1 is preferred if and only if more than a fraction q of an agent's neighbors take action 1, there must exist a partitioning of the agents into two groups: one group is more than q cohesive and ends up playing action 1, and the other group is at least $1 - q$ cohesive and plays action 0. Morris also provides conditions under which if some small segment of a society is fixed to select action 1, that action will eventually spread to the entire society if agents (iteratively) best respond to their neighbors' actions.

There are variations on this sort of coordination game that have been studied in the statistical physics literature with the best known version being what is called the "voter model." That model dates to Clifford and Sudbury (1973) and was named by Holley and Liggett (1975). Early versions of the voter model were on lattices, but more recent studies have examined general network structures. The simplest version of the model is one where a node is randomly selected and then a neighbor is randomly selected and the node's state of 0 or 1 is changed to match the neighbor. Over time, if the number of nodes is finite and all nodes are path connected, the society will eventually reach a consensus and stay there, although the random time to reaching a consensus can depend on the network.[55] Many variations on the voter model have been considered, including ones where nodes match the majority of their neighbors. See Castellano, Fortunato, and Loreto (2009) for a survey.

These examples provide a flavor of the types of results that emerge from games on networks. In many situations there is an inherent multiplicity of equilibria and thus many ways in which behavior might evolve, and so the challenge is to get a handle on the set of possible outcomes. Despite the multiplicity, some settings still have some nice intuitions and results that can be derived. For example, in games with strategic complementarities, such as the examples above, where an agent's incentive to take a higher action increases as more of an agent's neighbors take higher actions, then the existence of pure strategy equilibria is guaranteed and some of the equilibria are quite easy to compute.[56] Moreover, in such settings a variety of dynamics naturally tend towards equilibrium behavior.

[55] The idea behind the proof that a consensus will eventually be reached, for any network, is quite simple. With a finite number of nodes and a connected network, we can pick some node and then there is a positive probability that each one of its neighbors will be picked and matched to it before being matched to any other nodes, and then a positive probability that subsequently their neighbors will be picked and matched to those nodes before being matched to any other nodes, and so forth. Although the aggregate probability that some specific node's state will eventually overtake the whole network can be quite small, over time the needed sequence of matchings will eventually take place. So, with probability one the system will eventually reach a consensus.

[56] The equilibria form a lattice, and the maximal and minimal equilibria are easily found. For example, start with all agents at the highest action. If some agents then strictly prefer to take a lower action, change their action. Iterating on this process, will eventually lead to a point where no agent wishes to lower his or her action. This is the maximal equilibrium in that it has higher actions for each agent than in any other equilibrium. Analogously, one can find a minimal equilibrium. For more details, see Jackson (2008).

There are also many applications where there is a nice relationship between network structure and equilibrium structure, such as the cohesiveness of different subgroups in the network and the sustainability of multiple actions in one equilibrium.

The analysis above pertains to a special case, and more generally agents might care about more than just the proportion of agents taking a given action. For example, it might be an absolute number of an agent's neighbors that matter, so that an agent might be willing to take action 1 provided at least some fixed number of the agent's neighbors take the action. For example, an agent might be willing to learn a new language if the agent has at least some number of friends who speak the language, or might be willing to take up a certain hobby if at least some number of friends partake in the hobby. In such cases, agents' decisions can depend on their degrees and the degrees of their neighbors, and so forth.

Beyond games of strategic complements, another important class of games on networks is that of strategic substitutes. In games of strategic substitutes, if the actions of an agent's neighbors increase, then the agent has a stronger preference for lower actions. This applies in many settings of local public good provision. For example, consider an example of buying a particular book. If an agent has a friend who buys the book, then the agent can free-ride and borrow the book and so does not need to buy it. This reversal in the direction of peer effects does not result in a simple variation on games of strategic complements: the analysis of games of strategic substitutes is quite different. In games of strategic complements, agents' preferences move together, while in games of strategic substitutes interactions and dynamics can be more complicated and existence and computation of equilibria can be significantly more challenging. Bramoullé and Kranton (2007b) provide an analysis of a class of such games, and show, among other things, that slight variations in network structure can lead to dramatic changes in equilibrium structure.

The multiplicity of equilibria, and the sensitivity to network structure, depends on the information structure. In the above discussions each agent is choosing an action that must be a best response given knowledge of his or her friends' actions. There are many applications where agents have less specific information when making a choice. In buying a new software program, an agent might not even know exactly with whom he or she might interact in the future, but might only have some idea of the number of interactions he or she is likely to have. The agent's decision may need to be based on some idea of the overall prevalence of the compatibility of the program with choices of other agents in the population. Galeotti et al. (2010) and Jackson and Yariv (2007) examine such settings and show that an incomplete information setting can actually simplify the analysis of games on networks. In particular, results can be derived showing how agents' actions vary with their degree. For instance, suppose that it is only worthwhile for an agent to adopt a new technology if he or she expects to have at least k future neighbors adopt it. Then agents who expect to have more future interactions are more likely to exceed that threshold and thus have a stronger incentive to adopt the technology. This implies a monotonicity in decisions such that agents who expect to have more future interactions are those who will adopt and those who expect to have fewer interactions will not. Thus there is a threshold, such that the adopting agents are those who expect to have more than that number of interactions. This translates into a series of results of how equilibrium structure varies with the society's degree distribution, as changes in the distribution that increase the number of agents above the threshold lead to increased adoption, and changes that reduce the number of agents above the threshold lead to decreased adoption. Details are discussed in Jackson and Yariv (This volume).

As one adds more structure to the payoff structure to a game on a network, one can begin to obtain an explicit calculation of equilibrium. A nice example is a model by Ballester, Calvó-Armengol, and Zenou (2006) and is such that agents choose an intensity of an action from a continuum, and where there are local strategic complementarities and global substitution effects. In particular, Ballester, Calvó-Armengol, and Zenou work with a simple quadratic payoff structure that makes explicit equilibrium calculation quite easy, and yet insightful. The payoff structure captures an application of criminal behavior, where agents find increased benefits from engaging in crime as their friends' criminal activity increases, but there is also an overall competitive effect so that increased criminal activity on average in a society reduces the benefits to any individual's criminal behavior. Ballester, Calvó–Armengol, and Zenou show how equilibrium actions intuitively relate to a network centrality measure. Although the assumed functional form for payoffs is special, it encapsulates basic factors influencing choices and allows for a tractable analysis of how changes in network structure lead to changes in behavior.[57]

While our knowledge of peer effects is growing, the complexities involved mean that there is still much to be learned. Useful tools in this area of research are laboratory and field experiments, where one can directly measure how agents' behaviors change as network structure is changed, or as a function of their position in a network. The use of experiments to study social networks has a long history including the seminal work of Milgram (1967) on small worlds and studies of exchange theory such as that of Cook and Emerson (1978). There is a growing literature using experiments to study strategic network formation (e.g., see Callander and Plott (2005), Pantz and Zeigelmeyer (2003), Falk and Kosfeld (2003), Goeree, Riedl, and Ule (2003) and Charness and Jackson (2007)), learning (e.g., Choi, Gale, and Kariv (2005, 2009) and Celen, Kariv and Schotter (2004), and as well as interaction on networks (see Kosfeld (2003) and Jackson and Yariv (this volume) for additional background).[58] In terms of studying how network structure influences behavior,

[57] For other examples of some of the advantages of working continuum models, see Rogers (2006) and Bloch and Dutta (2009).

[58] There is also a growing use of field experiments in combination with social network data, such as those by Duflo and Saez (2003), Karlan, Mobius, Rosenblat, and Szeidl (2009), Dupas (2010), Beaman and Magruder (2010), and Feigenberg, Field, and Pande (2010), Baccara, Imrohoroglu, Wilson, and Yariv (2010).

Goeree et al. (2008) and Leider et al. (2007) show that giving behavior in dictator games is related to social distance, with agents being more generous to those who are nearby. Other examples include Kearns et al. (2009) who examine how a society's ability to reach a consensus in choosing an action depends on the network configuration and various agents' payoffs from their actions.

Another important aspect of strategic behavior in network settings that has been looked at but is far from being understood is the coevolution of networks and behavior. Much of the literature that I have discussed to this point focuses either primarily on the formation of a network or on the influence of a network on behavior. It is clear that there is feedback: People adjust their behaviors based on that of their friends and they choose their friends based on behaviors. Kandel (1978) provides interesting evidence suggesting that both effects are present in friendship networks, so that over time agents adjust actions to match that of their friends and are more likely to maintain and form new friendships with other individuals who act similarly to themselves. There has been some modeling of this in the context of the coevolution of behavior and networks in coordination games by Jackson and Watts (2002b), Goyal and Vega-Redondo (2005), and Ehrhardt, Marsili, and Vega-Redondo (2006), Fosco and Mengel (2009).[59] A message that emerges from those studies is that when networks co-evolve with actions, the actions that emerge can differ from what one sees with a fixed network. There is also a nascent literature on repeated games on networks, that provides insight into both how individuals behave and what sort of network structures are necessary to promote cooperation and pro-social behavior (e.g., see Jackson, Rodgrigez-Barraquer, and Tan (2010) and the references therein).

To get a feeling for this, consider the simple coordination game in Table 2.

Now let us consider this in the context of a social network. Each agent plays this game with each of his or her neighbors, and the agent just chooses one action, so that if the player chooses A then that is played against every one of the agent's neighbors. This game has two strict Nash equilibria: one where all players choose A, and another where all players choose B.

Table 2 A Coordination Game. The first entry in each cell is the payoff to Player 1 based on the combination of actions played.

		Player 2: A	Player 2: B
Player 1	A	1, 1	−2, 0
	B	0, −2	0, 0

[59] See also Jackson and Watts (2010) for an equilibrium analysis of a choice of partners together with a choice of behavior in a matching setting.

Let us take a closer look a the incentives for various play in the context of a complete network, so that all agents play the game with every other agent. In this example playing B leads to a sure payoff of 0, whereas playing A can lead to 1, but could also lead to a payoff of −2. Playing B is the better response if an agent expects more than one third of the other players to play B, while A is the better response if an agent expects less than one third of the other players to play B. Thus, if one starts with uniform uncertainty about what the other players are doing, B is the better response. In this sense every agent playing B is known as the "risk dominant" equilibrium. Refinements of equilibrium, such as stochastic stability, have found that if we add a bit of noise to the play of agents, and we examine a dynamic process where agents adjust their actions over time but with occasional errors so that the process never settles down completely, then play visits the "risk-dominant" equilibrium more often (e.g., see Kandori, Mailath and Rob (1993) and Young (1993)). The reasoning behind this is that if a society begins by all playing A, if one third of the population happened to tremble and switch to action B, then it would become a (myopic) best response for all players to play B. So errors made by one third of the population can lead away from the equilibrium where all play A. In contrast, if the society is playing equilibrium B, then it takes trembles by two thirds of the population to switch to A before it becomes a best response to play A. So, there is a precise sense in which it takes more perturbations to the system to transition from B to A than to move in the reverse direction, and so the equilibrium where all agents play B is more "robust," in at least one particular sense. This is not great news for the society, since the equilibrium where all play A leads to a higher payoff for everybody involved.

However, as Jackson and Watts (2002b) point out, this conclusion is dependent upon the network structure. Consider the same game but played by a society arranged in a "star" network such that there is one central agent who plays with every other agent, and the peripheral agents only play with the central agent. Then, it is much easier to transition between the two equilibria. Whatever action is chosen by the center of the star becomes the best response for all the other agents in the society. Here the society can transition back and forth between the two equilibria quite easily, simply by changing the action of the central agent, as the other agents' (myopic) best responses are to match whatever the central agent does.[60] This leads both of the equilibria to be stochastically stable.

This example illustrates that network structure can influence the play of a society, even in terms of selecting among (strict) Nash equilibria. This is true a fortiori when one endogenizes the network along with the play of the game. This echoes a point

[60] Intuitively, if the center of the star is forwardlooking, then he or she can actually consciously choose to steer the society towards one of the equilibria by choosing that action. Formalizing such behavior requires a careful definition of forward-looking behavior, and modeling it for all agents. For example, see and Mauleon and Vannetelbosch (2004) and Page, Wooders, and Kamat (2005) for such definitions.

of Ely (2002), who studied the outcome of such games when agents could choose to change where they lived. All it takes is some agent to locate at an empty location and play A to have other agents want to move there, as they will then be playing equilibrium A rather than equilibrium B at their own location. When one endogenizes a network structure, agents have similar incentives: to form links with others who are playing action A and to sever links with those playing B. Exactly what emerges depends on a number of details including the cost structure to links, whether agents get a payoff that depends on the number of people they play with and not just the average play, how many links can be changed at once, and whether mutual consent is required to form a link (see Jackson and Watts (2002b) and Goyal and Vega-Redondo (2005) for more). There are also questions as to the relative rates at which actions change compared to network structure, and that can affect the overall convergence to equilibrium, as one sees in Ehrhardt, Marsili, and Vega-Redondo (2006), as well as Holme and Newman (2006) and Gross and Blasius (2008).

5.5 Labor markets

To see an illustration of the insights generated by analyzing games on networks, let us return to the role of social networks in labor markets. There are a variety of decisions that agents take, whether or not to drop out of the network, whether to become educated, whether to look for employment, and so forth, for which the payoff can be heavily influenced by the decisions and situations of an agent's friends. If an agent's friends have all dropped out of the labor force, then that makes it difficult for the agent to get information about job openings and so worsens that agent's future employment prospects and makes dropping out relatively more attractive. As Calvó-Armengol and Jackson (2004) point out, this is a (graphical) game where agents' decisions to be in the labor force or to drop out are strategic complements. The insights from games on networks are then very useful. If we begin with two groups of agents who have many inward connections and few cross group connections, and we start one group with many drop-outs and the other group with few drop outs, then we can see very different outcomes for the two groups, similar to what we see in the bottom of Figure 5.4. Agents react to their neighbors' decisions and some subgroups end up with high participation in the labor force while others end up with high drop-out rates. When coupled with historical patterns and initial conditions, this can help explain the significant differences in drop-out rates that are exhibited across races. In particular, as Jackson (2007) points out, given racial homophily patterns, so that individuals of a given race tend to be connected to others of the same race, very different drop out rates can emerge for different races, even after controlling for all individual characteristics. This can lead to persistent inequality across different social groups, and not just in drop out rates: the individuals of a race with a low participation rate who happen to be in the labor force, will then have less access to job information leading to more unemployment spells, worse matches with employers, and lower wages (see Arrow and Borzekowski (2004) for more on wage effects). Thus, such network-based complementarities lead to an explanation for some of the differences in labor force participation rates and employment outcomes that have been widely documented by Card and Krueger (1992), Chandra (2000), and others.

In addition to helping us to understand different behaviors across groups, these complementarities in decisions can also have implications for intergenerational correlations in behavior. For example, Calvó-Armengol and Jackson (2009) show that if a child's social network has overlap with that of his or her parents, that can lead the child's decisions regarding how much education to pursue to be correlated with that of the parent, even without any direct parental influence. This extends beyond education to any behavior that sees a network influence, and can have implications for general forms of social mobility. These examples show the usefulness of the theory of strategic interaction in networked settings.

6. CONCLUDING REMARKS

The study of social and economic networks has expanded rapidly in the past decades and naturally cuts across many disciplines. It is an exciting area not only because of the explosion of "social networking" that has emerged with the internet and other advances in communication, but because of the fundamental role that social networks play in shaping human activity. Social network analysis has already taught us a great deal and it holds tremendous potential for future application, especially in economics. Moreover, beyond the applications, and as I hope that this survey illustrates, the increasingly sophisticated tools emerging in a variety of fields promise to continue to improve our modeling and understanding of the patterns of human interaction.

REFERENCES

Abreu, D., Manea, M., 2008. Bargaining and efficiency in networks. mimeo, Princeton University.

Acemoglu, D., Dahleh, M., Lobel, I., Ozdaglar, A., 2008. Bayesian learning in social networks. NBER Work. Pap. No. W14040.

Acemoglu, D., Ozdaglar, A., ParandehGheibi, 2009. Spread of (Mis)Information in Social Networks. forthcoming. Games Econ. Behav.

Adamic, L.A., 1999. The SmallWorldWeb. In: Proceedings of the ECDL. Lecture Notes in Computer Science 1696. Springer-Verlag, Berlin.

Albert, R., Jeong, H., Barabási, A.L., 1999. Diameter of the World Wide Web. Nature 401, 130–131.

Ali, S.N., Miller, D.A., 2009. Cooperation and Collective Enforcement in Networked Societies. mimeo.

Allen, F., Babus, A., 2007. Networks in Finance. In: Kleindorfer, P., Wind, J. (Eds.), Network-Based Strategies and Competencies. Wharton School Publishing, Philadelphia. forthcoming.

Allport, W.G., 1954. The Nature of Prejudice. Addison-Wesley, Cambridge, MA.

Aral, S., Muchnik, L., Sundararajan, A., 2009. Distinguishing Influence Based Contagions from Homophily Driven Diffusion in Dynamic Networks. Proc. Natl. Acad. Sci.

Arrow, K.J., Borzekowski, R., 2004. Limited Network Connections and the Distribution of Wages. Federal Reserve Board Publication 41, Washington, D.C.

Aumann, R., Myerson, R., 1988. Endogenous formation of links between players and coalitions: an application of the Shapley value. In: Roth, A.E. (Ed.), The Shapley Value. Cambridge Univ. Press, New York, pp. 175–191.

Baccara, M., Yariv, L., 2009. Similarity and Polarization in Groups. mimeo.

Baccara, M., Imrohoroglu, A., Wilson, A., Yariv, L., 2010. A Field Study on Matching with Network Externalities. mimeo.

Bala, V., Goyal, S., 1998. Learning from neighbors. Rev. Econ. Stud. 65, 595–621.

Bala, V., Goyal, S., 2000. A model of non-cooperative network formation. Econometrica 68, 1181–1230.

Ballester, C., Calvó-Armengol, A., Zenou, Y., 2006. Whos who in networks: wanted the key player. Econometrica 74 (5), 140–317.

Banerjee, A.V., 1992. A Simple Model of Herd Behavior. Q. J. Econ. 107, 797–817.

Banerjee, A.V., Chandrasekhar, A., Duflo, E., Jackson, M.O., 2010. Social Networks and Microfinance. mimeo, MIT and Stanford University.

Barabási, A., Albert, R., 1999. Emergence of scaling in random networks. Science 286, 509–512.

Barabási, A., 2002. Linked. Perseus Publishing, Cambridge, Mass.

Bayer, P.J., Hjalmarsson, R., Pozen, D., 2009. Building criminal capital behind bars: Peer effects in juvenile corrections. Q. J. Econ. 124, 105–147.

Bayer, P.J., Ross, S.L., Topa, G., 2005. Place of work and place of residence: informal hiring networks and labor market outcomes. Econ. Growth Cent. Discuss. Pap. 927, Yale Univ, New Haven, CT.

Beaman, L., 2007. Refugee Resettlement: The Role of Social Networks and Job Information Flows in the Labor Market. Northeast Univ. Dev. Consort. Conf., 2006. Sess. 20: Migration. mimeo. Yale Univ, New Haven, CT, manuscript.

Beaman, L., Magruder, J., 2010. Who gets the job referral? Evidence from a social networks experiment. mimeo.

Bender, E.A., Canfield, E.R., 1978. The Asymptotic Number of Labelled Graphs with Given Degree Sequences. Journal of Combinatorial Theory A 24, 296–307.

Bentolila, S., Michelacci, C., Suarez, J., 2009. Social Contacts and Occupational Choice, Economica. forthcoming.

Besag, J.E., 1974. Spatial Interaction and the Statistical Analysis of Lattice Systems (with Discussion). J. R. Stat. Soc. Series B 36, 196–236.

Bikhchandani, B., Hirshleifer, D., Welch, I., 1992. A Theory of Fads, Fashion, Custom, and Cultural Change as Informational Cascades. J. Polit. Econ. 100 (5), 992–1026.

Bikhchandani, B., Hirshleifer, D., Welch, I., 1998. Learning from the Behavior of Others: Conformity, Fads, and Informational Cascades. The Journal of Economic Perspectives 12, 151–170.

Blau, P.M., 1964. Exchange and Power in Social Life. Wiley, New York.

Blau, P.M., 1977. Inequality and Heterogeneity: A Primitive Theory of Social Structure. Free Press, New York.

Bloch, F., Dutta, B., 2009. Communication networks with endogenous link strength. Games Econ. Behav. 6 (1), 39–56.

Bloch, F., Jackson, M.O., 2006. Definitions of Equilibrium in Network Formation Games. Int. J. Game Theory 34 (3), 305–318.

Bloch, F., Jackson, M.O., 2007. The formation of networks with transfers among players. J. Econ. Theory 133, 83–110.

Blume, L., Easley, D., Kleinberg, J., Tardos, E., 2007. Trading Networks with Price-Setting Agents. Games Econ. Behav. forthcoming.

Bollobás, B., 2001. Random Graphs, second ed. Cambridge University Press, Cambridge.

Boorman, S., 1975. A combinatorial optimization model for transmission of job information through contact networks. Bell J. Econ. 6, 216–249.

Bramoullé, Y., Djebbari, H., Fortin, B., 2009. Identification of Peer Effects through Social Networks. J. Econom. 150, 41–55.

Bramoullé, Y., Kranton, R., 2007b. Public Goods in Networks. J. Econ. Theory 135 (1), 478–494.

Bramoullé, Y., Rogers, B.W., 2009. Diversity and Popularity in Social Networks. Mimeo.
Breiger, R.L., Boorman, S.A., Arabie, P., 1975. An Algorithm for Clustering Relational Data with Applications to Social Network Analysis and Comparison with Multidimensional Scaling. J. Math. Psychol. 12, 328–383.
Calvó-Armengol, A., Jackson, M.O., 2007. Networks in labor markets: wage and employment dynamics and inequality. J. Econ. Theory 132 (1), 2746.
Calvó-Armengol, A., Jackson, M.O., 2009. Like father, like son: labor market networks and social mobility. Am. Econ. J. Microecon. 1, 124–150.
Calvó-Armengol, A., Patacchini, E., Zenou, Y., 2009. Peer effects and social networks in education. Rev. Econ. Stud. 76, 1239–1267.
Callander, S., Plott, C., 2005. Principles of Network Development and Evolution: An Experimental Study. Study of Public Economics 89, 1469–1495.
Carayol, N., Roux, P., 2003. Collective Innovation in a Model of Network Formation with Preferential Meet. mimeo, Univ. Louis Pasteur/Univ, Toulouse I. (Mimeo).
Carayol, N., Roux, P., Yildizoglu, M., 2006. In search of efficient network structures: the needle in the haystack. Rev. Econ. Des. 11 (4), 434–470.
Carayol, N., Roux, P., Yildizoglu, M., 2008. Inefficiencies in a model of spatial networks formation with positive externalities. J. Econ. Behav. Organ. 67 (2), 495–511.
Card, D., Krueger, A.B., 1992. School Quality and Black-White Relative Earnings: A Direct Assessment. Q. J. Econ. 7 (1), 151–200.
Carley, K.M., 1991. A theory of group stability. Am. Sociol. Rev. 56, 331–354.
Castellano, C., Fortunato, S., Loreto, V., 2009. Statistical physics of social dynamics. Reviews of Modern Physics (eprint arXiv: 0710.3256).
Casella, A., Hanaki, N., 2008. Information channels in labor markets: On the resilience of referral hiring. Journal of Economic Behavior & Organization 66, 492–513.
Celen, B., Kariv, S., Schotter, A., 2004. Learning in Networks: An Experimental Study. Columbia University, University of California at Berkeley, and New York University, mimeo, New York and Berkeley.
Çelen, B., Kariv, S., 2004. Distinguishing Informational Cascades from Herd Behavior in the Laboratory. American Economic Review 94 (3), 484–497.
Çelen, B., Kariv, S., 2005. An Experimental Test of Observational Learning under Imperfect Information. Economic Theory 26 (3), 677–699.
Chandra, A., 2000. Labor-Market Dropouts and the Racial Wage Gap: 19401990. American Economic Review (Papers and Proceedings) 90 (2), 333–338.
Charness, G., Jackson, M.O., 2007. Group Play in Games and the Role of Consent in Network Formation. J. Econ. Theory 136 (1), 417–445.
Charness, G., Corominas-Bosch, M., Frechette, G.R., 2005. Bargaining on networks: an experiment. J. Econ. Theory 136, 28–65.
Choi, S., Gale, D., Kariv, S., 2005. Behavioral aspects of learning in social networks: an experimental study. In: Morgan, J. (Ed.), Advances in Applied Microeconomics, Vol. 13: Behavioral and Experimental Economics. Bepress, Berkeley, CA.
Choi, S., Gale, D., Kariv, S., 2007. Social Learning in Networks: A Quantal Response Equilibrium Analysis of Experimental Data. Univ. Calif. Berkeley, Berkeley.
Christakis, N.A., Fowler, J.H., 2008. The collective dynamics of smoking in a large social network. N. Engl. J. Med. 358 (21), 2249–2258.
Christakis, N.A., Fowler, J.H., Imbens, G.W., Kalyanaraman, K., 2010. An Empirical Model for Strategic Network Formation. mimeo, Harvard University.
Chung, F., Lu, L., 2002. The Average Distances in Random Graphs with Given Expected Degrees. Proc. Natl. Acad. Sci. 99, 15879–15882.
Clifford, P., Sudbury, A., 1973. A Model for Spatial Conflict. Biometrika 60 (3), 581.
Cohen, J., 1977. Sources of peer group homo- geneity. Sociol. Educ. 50, 227–412.
Coleman, J., 1958. Relational analysis: the study of social organizations with survey methods. Hum. Organ. 17, 28–36.

Coleman, J.S., 1988. Social Capital in the Creation of Human Capital. Am. J. Sociol. 94 (Supplement: Organizations and Institutions: Sociological and Economic Approaches to the Analysis of Social Structure), S95–S120.

Coleman, J.S., Katz, E., Menzel, H., 1966. Medical Innovation: A Diffusion Study. Bobbs-Merrill, Indianapolis, Ind.

Comola, 2009. The Network Structure of Informal Arrangements: Evidence from Rural Tanzania. mimeo, Paris School of Economics.

Conley, T.G., Udry, C.R., 2001. Social Learning through Networks: The Adoption of New Agricultural Technologies in Ghana. Am. J. Agric. Econ. 83 (3), 668–673.

Conley, T.G., Udry, C.R., 2004a. Social Networks in Ghana. Economic Growth Center, Yale University, New Haven, Conn. Discussion Paper 888.

Conley, T.G., Udry, C.R., 2004b. Learning About a New Technology: Pineapple in Ghana. Economic Growth Center Working Paper 817, Yale University, New Haven, Conn..

Conley, T.G., Udry, C.R., 2004c. The Adoption of New Agricultural Technologies in Ghana. Am. J. Agric. Econ. 83 (3), 668–673.

Cook, K.S., Whitmeyer, J.M., 1992. Two Approaches to Social Structure: Exchange Theory and Network Analysis. Ann. Rev. Sociol. 18, 109–127.

Copic, J., Jackson, M.O., Kirman, A., 2009. Identifying Community Structures from Network Data. B.E. Press Journal of Theoretical Economics 9 (1) (Contributions), Article 30.

Corcoran, M., Datcher, L., Duncan, G., 1980. Information and influence networks in labor markets. In: Duncan, G., Morgan, J. (Eds.), Five Thousand American Families. 8, Univ. Mich, Ann Arbor, pp. 1–38.

Corominas-Bosch, M., 2004. On two-sided network markets. J. Econ. Theory 115, 35–77.

Currarini, S., Jackson, M.O., Pin, P., 2006. Long Run Integration in Social Networks. mimeo.

Currarini, S., Jackson, M.O., Pin, P., 2009. An economic model of friendship: homophily, minorities and segregation. Econometrica 77 (4), 1003–1045.

Currarini, S., Jackson, M.O., Pin, P., 2010. Identifying the roles of race-based choice and chance in high school friendship network formation. Proc. Natl. Acad. Sci. 107 (11), 4857–4861.

Currarini, S., Morelli, M., 2000. Network formation with sequential demands. Rev. Econ. Des. 5, 229–250.

DeGroot, M.H., 1974. Reaching a consensus. J. Am. Stat. Assoc. 69, 118–121.

DeMarzo, P., Vayanos, D., Zwiebel, J., 2003. Persuasion bias, social influence, and uni-dimensional opinions. Q. J. Econ. 1183, 909–968.

De Weerdt, J., 2004. Risk-sharing and endogenous network formation. In: Dercon, S. (Ed.), Insurance Against Poverty. Oxford Univ. Press, Oxford.

Duflo, E., Saez, E., 2003. The Role of Information and Social Interactions in Retirement Plan Decisions: Evidence From a Randomized Experiment. Q. J. Econ. August 2003, 118 (3), 815–842.

Dupas, P., 2010. Social Learning about New Health Technologies: Experimental Evidence from Kenya. mimeo.

Dutta, B., Jackson, M.O., 2000. The Stability and Efficiency of Directed Communication Networks. Rev. Econ. Design 5, 251–272.

Dutta, B., Mutuswami, S., 1997. Stable networks. J. Econ. Theory 76, 322–344.

Ehrhardt, G., Marsili, M., Vega-Redondo, F., 2006. Diffusion and Growth in an Evolving Network. International Journal of Game Theory 34, 383–397.

Elliott, M., 2009. Inefficiencies in Trade Networks. mimeo, Stanford University.

Ellison, G., 1993. Learning, Local Interaction, and Coordination. Econometrica 61, 1047–1071.

Ellison, G., Fudenberg, D., 1995. Word-of-Mouth Communication and Social Learning. Q. J. Econ. 110, 93–126.

Ely, J.C., 2002. Local Conventions. Advances in Theoretical Economics 2 (1), Article 1.

Emerson, R.M., 1962. Power-Dependence Relations. Am. Sociol. Rev. 27 (3), 140.

Emerson, R.M., 1967. Exchange Theory, Part I: A Psychological Basis for Social Exchange, and Exchange Theory, Part II: Exchange Relations and Networks. In: Berger, J., Zelditch, M., Anderson, B. (Eds.), Sociological Theories in Progress. Houghton–Mifflin, Boston.

Erdös, P., Rényi, A., 1959. On random graphs. Publ. Math. Debrecen. 6, 290–297.

Erdös, P., Rényi, A., 1960. On the evolution of random graphs. Publ. Math. Inst. Hung. Acad. Sci. 5, 17–61.
Erdös, P., Rényi, A., 1961. On the strength of connectedness of a random graph. Acta Math. Acad. Sci. Hung. 12, 261–267.
Exelle, B., Riedl, A., 2008. Directed Generosity in Social and Economic Networks. mimeo Maastricht University.
Fafchamps, M., Lund, S., 2003. Risk-sharing networks in rural Philippines. J. Dev. Econ 71, 261–287.
Fagiolo, G., Valente, M., Vriend, N., 2007. Segregation in Networks. J.Econ. Behav. Organ. 64, 316–336.
Falk, A., Kosfeld, M., 2003. Its All About Connections: Evidence on Network Formation. Institute for the Study of Labor (IZA), Discussion Paper 777, Zurich IEER Working Paper 146, Zurich, Switzerland.
Feigenberg, B., Field, E., Pande, R., 2010. Does Group Lending Increase Social Capital? Evidence from a Field Experiment in India. mimeo.
Feld, S.L., 1981. The Focused Organization of Social Ties. Am. J. Sociol. 86 (5), 1015–1035.
Fosco, C., Mengel, F., 2009. Cooperation through Imitation and Exclusion in Networks. mimeo, Maastricht University.
Fowler, J.H., Christakis, N.A., 2008. Estimating Peer Effects on Health in Social Networks. J. Health Econ. 27 (5), 1400–1405.
Frank, O., Strauss, D., 1986. Markov Graphs. J. Am. Stat. Assoc. 81, 832–842.
French, J., 1956. A Formal Theory of Social Power. Psychol. Rev. 63, 181–194.
Friedkin, N.E., Johnsen, E.C., 1997. Social Positions in In uence Networks. Soc. Networks 19, 209–222.
Gale, D., Kariv, S., 2003. Bayesian learning in social networks. Games Econ. Behav. 45 (2), 329–346.
Galeotti, A., Merlino, L.P., 2008. Endogenous job contact networks. mimeo.
Galeotti, A., Goyal, S., Jackson, M.O., Vega-Redondo, F., Yariv, L., 2010. Network Games. Rev. Econ. Stud. 77, 218–244. http://www.jacksonm.edu/~jacksonm/networkgames.pdf.
Gilbert, E.N., 1959. Random Graphs. The Annals of Mathematical Statistics 30, 1141–1144.
Giles, M.W., Evans, A., 1986. The power approach to intergroup hostility. J. Conflict Resolut. 30 (3), 469–486.
Girvan, M., Newman, M.E.J., 2002. Community Structure in Social and Biological Networks. Proc. Natl. Acad. Sci. 99, 7821–7826.
Glaeser, E., Sacerdote, B., Scheinkman, J., 1996. Crime and social interactions. Q. J. Econ. 111, 507–548.
Goeree, J.K., Riedl, A., Ule, A., 2003. In Search of Stars: Network Formation among Heterogeneous Agents. Institute for the Study of Labor (IZA), Discussion Paper 1754, Bonn.
Goeree, J.K., McConnell, M.A., Mitchell, T., Tromp, T., Yariv, L., 2008. Linking and Giving Among Teenage Girls. mimeo, California Institute of Technology, Pasadena.
Golub, B., Jackson, M.O., 2008. How Homophily Affects the Speed of Contagion, Best Response and Learning Dynamics. Stanford Univ, Stanford, CA, arXiv:0811.4013v2 [physics.soc-ph].
Golub, B., Jackson, M.O., 2010. Naive learning and influence in social networks: convergence and wise crowds. Am. Econ. J.Microecon. 2 (1), 112–149, Feb. 2010.
Goodreau, S.M., Kitts, J.A., Morris, M., 2009. Birds of a Feather, or Friend of a Friend? Using Exponential Random Graph Models to Investigate Adolescent Social Networks. Demography 46 (1), 103–125.
Goyal, S., Joshi, S., 2003. Networks of Collaboration in Oligopoly. Games Econ. Behav. 43, 57–85.
Goyal, S., Vega-Redondo, F., 2005. Learning, Network Formation and Coordination. Games Econ. Behav. 50, 178–207.
Granovetter, M., 1973. The strength of weak ties. Am. J. Sociol. 78, 1360–1380.
Gross, T., Blasius, B., 2008. Adaptive coevolutionary networks: a review. Journal of the Royal Society Interface 5, 259–271.
Hagenbach, J., Koessler, F., 2009. Strategic communication networks. Preprint, Université de Paris I - Sorbonne.
Hagerstrand, T., 1970. What about people in Regional Science? Journal Papers in Regional Science 24 (1), 6–21.

Handcock, M.S., 2003. Assessing Degeneracy in Statistical Models of Social Networks. University of Washington, Seattle Working Paper no. 39 Center for Statistics and the Social Sciences University of Washington.

Halliday, T.J., Kwak, S., 2009. Weight Gain in Adolescents and Their Peers. Econ. Hum. Biol..

Harary, F., 1959. Status and Contrastatus. Sociometry 22, 23–43.

Heckman, J.J., Borjas, G., 1980. Does Unemployment Cause Future Unemployment? Definitions, Questions and Answers from a Continuous Time Model of Heterogeneity and State Dependence. Economica 47 (187), 247–283.

Hesselius, P., Johansson, P., Nilsson, P., 2009. Sick of Your Colleagues Absence? IZA DP No. 3960.

Hoff, P.D., 2006. Multiplicative Latent Factor Models for Description and Prediction of Social Networks. mimeo, University of Washington, Seattle.

Hoff, P.D., Raftery, A.E., Handcock, M.S., 2002. Latent Space Approaches to Social Network Analysis. J. Am. Stat. Assoc. 97, 1090–1098.

Holland, P.W., Laskey, K.B., Leinhardt, S., 1983. Stochastic Blockmodels: First Steps. Soc. Networks 5, 109–137.

Holley, R., Liggett, T., 1975. Ergodic theorems for weakly interacting infinite systems and the voter model. Ann. Probab. 3, 643.

Homans, C.G., 1958. Social Behavior as Exchange. Am. J. Sociol. 62, 597–606.

Homans, C.G., 1961. Social Behavior: Its Elementary Forms. Harcourt, Brace and World, New York.

Huberman, B.A., Adamic, L., 1999. Growth dynamics of the World-Wide Web. Nature 401 (9 SEPTEMBER), 131.

Ioannides, Y.M., Datcher-Loury, L., 2004. Job information networks, neighborhood effects and inequality. J. Econ. Lit 424, 1056–1093.

Jackson, M.O., 2003. The stability and efficiency of economic and social networks. In: Dutta, B., Jackson, M.O. (Eds.), Advances in Economic Design, ed. S Koray, M Sertel. Heidelberg: Springer-Verlag. Reprinted in Networks and Groups: Models of Strategic Formation. Springer-Verlag, Heidelberg, pp. 99–140.

Jackson, M.O., 2004. A survey of models of network formation: stability and efficiency. In: Demange, G., Wooders, M. (Eds.), Group Formation in Economics; Networks, Clubs and Coalitions. Cambridge Univ. Press, Cambridge, UK, pp. 11–57.

Jackson, M.O., 2007. Social Structure, Segregation, and Economic Behavior. Nancy Schwartz Memorial Lecture, given in April 2007 at Northwestern University, printed version:. http://www.stanford.edu/~jacksonm/schwartzlecture.pdf.

Jackson, M.O., 2008. Social and Economic Networks. Princeton Univ. Press, Princeton, NJ.

Jackson, M.O., 2008b. Average Distance, Diameter, and Clustering in Social Networks with Homophily, arXiv:0810.2603v1 [physics.soc-ph]. In: Papadimitriou, C., Zhang, S. (Eds.), the Proceedings of the Workshop in Internet and Network Economics (WINE 2008), Lecture Notes in Computer Science. Springer Verlag, Berlin Heidelberg.

Jackson, M.O., Rodriguez-Barraquer, T., Tan, X., 2010. Social Capital and Social Quilts: Network Patterns of Favor Exchange. mimeo, Stanford University.

Jackson, M.O., Rogers, B.W., 2005. The economics of small worlds. J. Eur. Econ. Assoc. Pap. Proc. 32 (3), 617–627.

Jackson, M.O., Rogers, B.W., 2007a. Meeting strangers and friends of friends: how random are social networks. Am. Econ. Rev. 97 (3), 890–915.

Jackson, M.O., Watts, A., 2002a. The evolution of social and economic networks. J. Econ. Theory 106 (2), 265–295.

Jackson, M.O., Watts, A., 2002b. On the Formation of Interaction Networks in Social Coordination Games. Games Econ. Behav. 41 (2), 265–291.

Jackson, M.O., Wolinsky, A., 1996. A strategic model of social and economic networks. J. Econ. Theory 71 (1), 44–74.

Jackson, M.O., Yariv, L., 2007. The diffusion of behavior and equilibrium structure properties on social networks. American Economic Review (Papers and Proceedings), 97, 92–98.

Jackson, M.O., Watts, A., 2010. Social Games: Matching and the Play of Finitely Repeated Games. Games Econ. Behav. 70 (1), 170–191.
Jadbabaie, A., Sandroni, A., Tahbaz-Salehi, A., 2009. Non-Bayesian Social Learning. mimeo, Northwestern University.
Johnson, C., Gilles, R.P., 2000. Spatial Social Networks. Rev. Econ. Design 5, 273–300.
Kakade, S.M., Kearns, M., Ortiz, L.E., 2004a. Graphical economics. Proc. Annu. Conf. Learn. Theory 23 (3120), 17–32.
Kakade, S.M., Kearns, M., Ortiz, L.E., Pemantle, R., Suri, S., 2004b. Economic Properties of Social Networks, Proc. Neural Information Processing Syst., NIPS. MIT Press, Cambridge, MA.
Kandel, D.B., 1978. Homophily, Selection, and Socialization in Adolescent Friendships. Am. J. Sociol. 14, 427–436.
Kandori, M., Mailath, G., Rob, R., 1993. Learning, Mutation, and Long-Run Equilibria in Games. Econometrica 61, 29–56.
Karlan, D., Mobius, M., Rosenblat, T., Szeidl, A., 2009. Measuring trust in Peruvian shantytowns. mimeo.
Katz, E., Lazarsfeld, P.F., 1955. Personal Influence: The Part Played by People in the Flow of Mass Communication. Free Press, New York.
Katz, L., 1953. A New Status Index Derived from Sociometric Analysis. Psychometrica 18, 39–43.
Kearns, M.J., Littman, M., Singh, S., 2001. Graphical Models for Game Theory. In: Breese, J.S., Koller, D. (Eds.), Proceedings of the 17th Conference on Uncertainty in Artificial Intelligence. Morgan Kaufmann, San Francisco.
Kearns, M.J., Judd, S., Tan, J., Wortman, J., 2009. Behavioral Experiments on Biased Voting in Networks. PNAS 106 (5), 1347–1352.
Khmelkov, V.T., Hallinan, M.T., 1999. Organizational Effects on Race Relations in Schools. J. Soc. Issues 55 (4), 627–645.
Kling, J.R., Ludwig, J., Katz, L.F., 2005. Neighborhood effects on crime for female and male youth: evidence from a randomized housing voucher experiment. Q. J. Econ. 120, 87–130.
Knoke, D., 1990. Networks of Political Action: Towards Theory construction. Soc. Forces 68, 1041–1063.
Kosfeld, M., 2003. Network Experiments. Zuirch IEER Working Paper 152, University of Zurich.
Kranton, R., Minehart, D., 2001. A theory of buyer-seller networks. Am. Econ. Rev. 91 (3), 485–508.
Krause, U., 2000. A Discrete Nonlinear and Nonautonomous Model of Consensus Formation. In: Elaydi, S., Ladas, G., Popenda, J., Rakowski, J. (Eds.), Communications in Difference Equations. Gordon and Breach, Amsterdam.
Kubitschek, W.N., Hallinan, M.T., 1998. Tracking and Students' Friendships. Soc. Psychol. Q. 61 (1), 1–15.
Langville, A.N., Meyer, C.D., 2006. Google's PageRank and Beyond: The Science of Search Engine Rankings. Princeton University Press, Princeton, N.J.
Laschever, R., 2007. The doughboys network: social interactions and labor market outcomes of World War I veterans. Work. Pap., Univ. Ill., Champaign-Urbana.
Lazarsfeld, P.F., Merton, R.K., 1954. Friendship as a Social Process: A Substantive and Methodological Analysis. In: Berger, M. (Ed.), Freedom and Control in Modern Society. Van Nostrand, New York.
Leider, S., Mobius, M.M., Rosenblatt, T., Do, Q.A., 2007. How Much Is a Friend Worth? Directed Altruism and Enforced Reciprocity in Social Networks. revision of NBER Working Paper 13135, National Bureau of Economics Research, Cambridge, Mass..
Lévi-Strauss, C., 1958. Anthropologie structurale. Librairie Plon, Paris.
Lever, C., 2010. Strategic spending in voting competitions with social networks. mimeo.
Lorenz, J., 2005. A Stabilization Theorem for Dynamics of Continuous Opinions. Physica A 355, 217–223.
Lorrain, F., White, H.C., 1971. Structural Equivalence of Individuals in Social Networks. J. Math. Sociol. 1, 49–80.
Lynch, L.M., 1989. The Youth Labor Market in the Eighties: Determinants of Reemployment Probabilities for Young Men and Women. Rev. Econ. Stat. 71, 37–54.
Manea, M., 2008. Bargaining on networks. mimeo, Princeton University.

Manski, C.F., 1993. Identification of Endogenous Social Effects: The Reflection Problem. Rev. Econ. Stud. 60 (419), 431.
Mauleon, A., Vannetelbosch, V.J., 2004. Farsightedness and Cautiousness in Coalition Formation. Theor. Decis. 56, 291–324.
McPherson, M., Smith-Lovin, L., Cook, J.M., 2001. Birds of a feather: homophily in social networks. Annu. Rev. Sociol. 27, 415–444.
Meeker, R.J., Weiler, D.M., 1970. A New School for the Cities.
Milgram, S., 1967. The small-world problem. Psychol. Today 2, 60–67.
Mitzenmacher, M., 2004. A Brief History of Generative Models for Power Lawand Log-normal Distributions. Manuscript available at http://www.eecs.harvard.edu/michaelm/ListByYear.html.
Montgomery, J., 1991. Social networks and labor market outcomes. Am. Econ. Rev. 81, 1408–1418.
Moody, J., 2001. Race, School Integration, and Friendship Segregation in America. Am. J. Sociol. 107 (3), 679–716.
Morris, S., 2000. Contagion. Rev. Econ. Stud. 67, 57–78.
Mueller-Frank, M., 2009. A General Framework for Rational Learning in Social Networks. mimeo, Northwestern University.
Munshi, K., 2003. Networks in the modern economy: Mexican migrants in the U.S. labor market. Q. J. Econ. 118 (2), 549–597.
Myers, C.A., Shultz, G.P., 1951. The Dynamics of a Labor Market. Prentice-Hall, New York.
Newman, M.E.J., 2003. The Structure and Function of Complex Networks. SIAM Review 45, 167–256.
Newman, M.E.J., 2004. Detecting Community Structure in Networks. Phys. Rev. E 69, 066–133.
Page, F., Wooders, M., Kamat, S., 2005. Networks and farsighted stability. J. Econ. Theory 1202, 257–269.
Pantz, K., Ziegelmeyer, A., 2003. An Experimental Study of Network Formation, Garching. mimeo, Max Planck Institute, Germany.
Papadimitriou, C.H., 2001. Algorithms, Games, and the Internet. In: Proceedings of the 33rd Annual ACM Symposium on the Theory of Computing. ACM, New York.
Pareto, V., 1896. Cours dEconomie Politique. Droz, Geneva.
Patacchini, E., Zenou, Y., 2008. The strength of weak ties in crime. Eur. Econ. Rev. 52, 209–236.
Pellizzari, M., 2009. Do friends and relatives really help in getting a good job? Ind. Labor Relat. Rev. forthcoming.
Pennock, D.M., Flake, G.W., Lawrence, S., Glover, E.J., Giles, C.L., 2002. Winners dont take all: characterizing the competition for links on the Web. Proc. Natl. Acad. Sci. U.S.A. 99 (8), 5207–5211.
Peski, M., 2007. Complementarities, Group Formation, and Preferences for Similarity. mimeo.
Pissarides, C.A., 2000. Equilibrium Unemployment Theory, second ed. MIT Press, Cambridge, MA.
Price, D.J.S., 1965. Networks of scientific papers. Science 149, 510–515.
Price, D.J.S., 1976. A general theory of bibliometric and other cumulative advantage processes. J. Am. Soc. Inf. Sci 27, 292–306.
Rees, A.J., Shultz, G.P., 1970. Workers in an Urban Labor Market. Univ. Chicago Press, Chicago.
Reiss, A.J., 1980. Understanding changes in crime rates. In: Indicators of Crime and Criminal Justice: Quantitative Studies. Bur. Justice Stat, Washington, DC.
Rochford, S.C., 1984. Symmetrically Pairwise Bargained Allocations in an Assignment Market. J Econ Theory 34, 262–281.
Rogers, B.W., 2006. A strategic theory of interdependent status. PhD diss., Calif. Inst. Technol.
Rogers, E.M., Rogers, E., 2003. Diffusion of Innovations, fifth ed. Free Press, New York.
Rogerson, R., Shimer, R., Wright, R., 2005. Search-Theoretic Models of the Labor Market: A Survey. Journal of Economic Literature 43, 959–988.
Rosenberg, D., Solan, E., Vieille, N., 2007. Informational Externalities and Emergence of Consensus. HEC School of Management, mimeo, Paris.
Roughgarden, T., Tardos, E., 2002. How Bad Is Selfish Routing? J. ACM 49 (2), 236–259.
Ryan, B., Gross, N.C., 1943. The Diffusion of Hybrid Seed Corn in Two Iowa Communities. Rural Sociol. 8, 1524.
Rytina, S., Morgan, D.L., 1982. The Arithmetic of Social Relations: The Interplay of Category and Network. Am. J. Sociol. 88 (1), 88–113.

Schelling, T.C., 1978. Micromotives and macrobehavior. W. W. Norton, New York.
Schweitzer, S.O., Smith, R.E., 1974. The Persistence of the Discouraged Worker Effect. Ind. Labor Relat. Rev. 27 (2), 249–260.
Simmel, G., 1908. Sociology: Investigations on the Forms of Sociation. Berlin, Duncker and Humblot.
Smith, L., Sorensen, P., 2000. Pathological outcomes of observational learning. Econometrica 68 (2), 371–398.
Snijders, T.A.B., Pattison, P.E., Robins, G.L., Handcock, M.S., 2006. New Specifications for Exponential Random Graph Models. Sociol. Methodol. 36, 99–153.
Snijders, T.A.B., 2002. Markov Chain Monte Carlo Estimation of Exponential Random Graph Models. Journal of Social Structure 3 (2), 240.
Snijders, T.A.B., Nowicki, K., 1997. Estimation and Prediction for Stochastic Block Models for Graphs with Latent Block Structure. Journal of Classification 14, 75–100.
Sobel, J., 2000. Economists' Models of Learning. J Econ Theory 94 (2), 241–261.
Solomonoff, R., Rapoport, A., 1951. Connectivity of Random Nets. Bull. Math. Biophy. 13, 107–117.
Sotomayor, M., 2006. Adjusting prices in the many-to-many assignment game to yield the smaller competitive equilibrium price vector. mimeo, Sao Paolo.
Stearns, E., 2004. Interracial Friendliness and the Social Organization of Schools. Youth Soc. 35 (4), 395–419.
Uzzi, B., 1996. The sources and consequences of embeddedness for the economic performance of organizations: the network effect. Am. Sociol. Rev. 61, 674–698.
van der Leij, M.J., Buhai, I.S., 2008. A Social Network Analysis of Occupational Segregation. Fondazione Eni Enrico Mattei Working Paper 192.
van Duijn, M.A.J., Gile, K., Handcock, M.S., 2009. Comparison of Maximum Pseudo Likelihood and Maximum Likelihood Estimation of Exponential Family Random Graph Models. mimeo.
Vázquez, A., 2003. Growing Network with Local Rules: Preferential Attachment, Clustering Hierarchy, and Degree Correlations. Phys. Rev. E 67 (5), 056–104.
Watts, D.J., 1999. Small Worlds: The Dynamics of Networks Between Order and Randomness. Princeton Univ. Press, Princeton, NJ.
Watts, D.J., 2004. The New Science of Networks. Annual Sociological Review 30, 243–270.
Watts, D.J., Strogatz, S., 1998. Collective dynamics of. small-world.networks. Nature 393, 440–442.
White, H.C., Boorman, S.A., Breiger, R.L., 1976. Social Structure from Multiple Networks. I. Blockmodels of Roles and Positions. Am. J. Sociol. 81 (4), 730–780.
Young, H.P., 1993. The Evolution of Conventions. Econometrica 61, 57–84.
Young, H.P., 1998. Individual Strategy and Social Structure. Princeton University Press, Princeton, N.J.
Zipf, G., 1949. Human Behavior and the Principle of Least Effort. Addison-Wesley, Cambridge, Mass.

FURTHER READINGS

Bala, V., Goyal, S., 2001. Conformism and diversity under social learning. Econ. Theory 17, 101–120.
Banerjee, A.V., Fudenberg, D., 2004. Word-of-Mouth Learning. Games Econ. Behav. 46, 122.
Bearman, P., Moody, J., Stovel, K., 2004. Chains of Affection: The Structure of Adolescent Romantic and Sexual Networks. University of Chicago, Chicago, manuscript.
Bloch, F., 2004. Group and network formation in industrial organization. In: Demange, G., Wooders, M. (Eds.), Group Formation in Economics; Networks, Clubs and Coalitions. Cambridge Univ. Press, Cambridge, UK (Chapter 11).
Bloch, F., Genicot, G., Ray, D., 2008. Informal Insurance in Social Networks. J. Econ. Theory 143 (1), 36–58.
Blume, L., 1993. The Statistical Mechanics of Strategic Interaction. Games Econ. Behav. 5, 387–424.
Bonacich, P., 1972. Factoring and weighting approaches to status scores and clique identification. J. Math. Sociol. 2, 113–120.
Bonacich, P., 1987. Power and centrality: a family of measures. Am. J. Sociol 92, 1170–1182.

Borm, P., Owen, G., Tijs, S., 1992. On the Position Value for Communication Situations. SIAM Journal on Discrete Mathematics 5, 305–320.
Bourdieu, P., 1986. Forms of Capital. In: Richardson, J.G. (Ed.), Handbook of Theory and Research for the Sociology of Education. Greenwood Press, Westport, Conn.
Bramoullé, Y., Kranton, R., 2007a. Risk-sharing networks. J. Econ. Behav. Organ. 64 (34), 275–294.
Brock, W., Durlauf, S.N., 2001. Interactions-Based Models. In: Heckman, J., Leamer, E. (Eds.), Handbook of Econometrics. 5, North-Holland, Amsterdam.
Burt, R., 1992. Structural Holes: The Social Structure of Competition. Harvard Univ. Press, Cambridge, MA.
Calvó-Armengol, A., 2004. Job contact networks. J. Econ. Theory 115, 191–206.
Calvó-Armengol, A., Jackson, M.O., 2004. The effects of social networks on employment and inequality. Am. Econ. Rev. 94 (3), 426–454.
Calvó-Armengol, A., Zenou, Y., 2004. Social Networks and Crime Decisions: The Role of Social Structure in Facilitating Delinquent Behavior. Int. Econ. Rev. 45, 935–954.
Casella, A., Rauch, J., 2002. Anonymous Market and Group Ties in International Trade. J. Int. Econ. 58 (1), 1947.
Christakis, N.A., Fowler, J.H., 2007. The spread of obesity in a large social network over 32 years. N. Engl. J. Med. 357, 370–379.
Coase, R.H., 1960. The problem of social cost. J. Law Econ. 3, 144.
Coleman, J.S., 1990. Foundations of Social Theory. Harvard University Press, Cambridge Mass.
Conley, T.G., Topa, G., 2001. Socio-Economic Distance and Spatial Patterns in Unemployment. Journal of Applied Economics 17 (4), 303–327.
Cook, K.S., Emerson, R.M., 1978. Power, Equity and Commitment in Exchange Networks. Am. Sociol. Rev. 43, 721–739.
Cook, K.S., Emerson, R.M., 1978. Power, Equity and Commitment in Exchange Networks. Am. Sociol. Rev. 43, 721–739.
Corbae, D., Duffy, J., 2009. Experiments with Network Economies. Games Econ. Behav.
Demange, G., Wooders, M., 2005. Group Formation in Economics; Networks, Clubs and Coalitions, G. Cambridge University Press, Cambridge.
Deröian, F., 2003. Farsighted Strategies in the Formation of a Communication Network. Econo. Lett. 80, 343–349.
De Weerdt, J., Dercon, S., 2006. Risk-sharing networks and insurance against illness. J. Dev. Econ. 81, 337–356.
Diestel, R., 2000. Graph Theory. Springer-Verlag, Heidelberg.
Droste, E., Gilles, R.P., Johnson, C., 2000. Evolution of Conventions in Endogenous Social Networks. In: Econometric Society World Congress 2000 Contributed Papers 0594. Econometric Society, Seattle.
Dutta, B., Jackson, M.O., 2003. Networks and Groups: Models of Strategic Formation. Springer-Verlag, Heidelberg.
Dutta, B., Ghosal, S., Ray, D., 2005. Farsighted network formation. J. Econ. Theory 122, 143–164.
Economides, N., 1996. The Economics of Networks. International Journal of Industrial Organization 16 (4), 673–699.
Fong, E., Isajiw, W.W., 2000. Determinants of friendship choices in multiethnic society. Sociol. Forum 15 (2), 249–271.
Freeman, L.C., 2004. The Development of Social Network Analysis: A Study in the Sociology of Science. Empirical Press, Vancouver.
Furusawa, T., Konishi, H., 2005. Free trade networks. Jpn. Econ. Rev. 56, 144–164.
Garg, M., 2009. Axiomatic Foundations of Centrality in Networks. mimeo, Stanford University.
Gilles, R.P., Sarangi, S., 2005. Stable networks and convex payoffs. In: Review of Economic Design.
Goyal, S., 2008. Connections: An Introduction to the Economics of Networks. Princeton University Press.
Granovetter, M., 1978. Threshold models of collective behavior. Am. J. Sociol. 83 (6), 1420–1443.
Granovetter, M., 1985. Economic action and social structure: the problem of embeddedness. Am. J. Sociol. 91 (3), 481–510.
Granovetter, M., 1995. Getting a Job: A Study of Contacts and Careers, second ed. Univ. Chicago Press, Chicago.

Herings, P.J.J., Mauleon, A., Vannetelbosch, V., 2004. Rationalizability for social environments. Games Econ. Behav. 49, 135–156.
Hojman, D., Szeidl, A., 2006. Endogenous networks, social games and evolution. Games Econ. Behav. 551, 112–130.
Holland, P.W., Leinhardt, S., 1977. A Dynamic Model for Social Networks. J. Math. Sociol. 5, 520.
Holme, P., Newman, M.E.J., 2006. Nonequilibrium phase transition in the coevolution of networks and opinions. arXiv:Physics 060303 v3.
Holme, P., Newman, M.E.J., 2006. Nonequilibrium phase transition in the coevolution of networks and opinions. Phys. Rev. E 74, 056–108.
Jackson, M.O., 2005a. Allocation rules for network games. Games Econ. Behav. 51, 128–154.
Jackson, M.O., 2005b. The economics of social networks. In: Blundell, R., Newey, W., Persson, T. (Eds.), Proc. 9th World Congr. Econ. Soc. Cambridge Univ. Press, Cambridge, UK (Chapter 1).
Jackson, M.O., Rogers, B.W., 2007b. Relating network structure to diffusion properties through stochastic dominance. B.E. Press J. Theor. Econ. 7 (1), 1–13.
Jackson, M.O., van den Nouweland, A., 2005. Strongly stable networks. Games Econ. Behav. 51, 420–444.
Jackson, M.O., Yariv, L., 2010. Diffusion, Strategic Interaction, and Social Structure. This volume.
Johari, R., Mannor, S., Tsitsiklis, J.N., 2006. A Contract-Based Model for Directed Network Formation. Games Econ. Behav. 56 (2), 201–224.
Katz, M., Shapiro, C., 1994. Systems Competition and Networks Effects. J. Econ. Perspect. 8, 93–115.
Kearns, M.J., Suri, S., Montfort, N., 2006. An Experimental Study of the Coloring Problem on Human Subject Networks. Science 313, 824–827.
Kets, W., 2008. Networks and Learning in Game Theory. Dissertation, Tilburg University, Tilburg, The Netherlands.
Kirman, A.P., 1983. Communication in markets: a suggested approach. Econ. Lett. 12, 1–5.
Kirman, A.P., Oddou, C., Weber, S., 1986. Stochastic communication and coalition formation. Econometrica 54, 129–138.
Kochen, M., 1989. The Small World. Albex, Norwood, N.J.
Kogut, B., 2000. The Network as Knowledge: Generative Rules and the Emergence of Structure. Strategic Management Journal 21 (3), 405–425.
Lamberson, P.J., 2010. Social Learning in Social Networks. The B.E. Journal of Theoretical Economics: Topics. 10:1, article 36.
Lazarsfeld, P.F., Henry, N.W., 1968. Latent structure analysis. Houghton, Mifflin Co.
Littman, M.L., Kearns, M.J., Singh, S.P., 2001. An Efficient, Exact Algorithm for Solving Tree-Structured Graphical Games, in Advances in Neural Information Processing Systems. MIT Press, Cambridge, Mass.
Lopez-Pintado, D., 2008. Diffusion in complex social networks. Games Econ. Behav. 62 (2), 573–590.
Loury, G., 1977. A Dynamic Theory of Racial Income Differences. In: Wallace, P.A., Le Mund, A. (Eds.), Women, Minorities, and Employment Discrimination. Lexington Books, Lexington, Mass (Chapter 8).
Marsden, P.V., 1987. Core discussion networks of Americans. Am. Sociol. Rev. 52, 122–131.
Marsden, P.V., 1988. Homogeneity in confiding relations. Soc. Netw. 10, 57–76.
Marsili, M., Vega-Redondo, F., Slanina, F., 2007. The Rise and Fall of a Networked Society: A Formal Model. Proc. Natl. Acad. Sci. of the U.S.A. 101, 1439–1442.
Mobius, M.M., Rosenblatt, T.S., 2003. Experimental Evidence on Trading Favors in Networks. mimeo, Harvard University and Wesleyan University, Cambridge, Mass., and Middletown, Conn.
Mobius, M.M., Szeidl, A., 2006. Trust and Social Collateral. Harvard University and the University of California at Berkeley, Cambridge, Mass., and Berkeley.
Mutuswami, S., Winter, E., 2002. Subscription mechanisms for network formation. J. Econ. Theory 106, 242–264.
Myerson, R., 1977. Graphs and cooperation in games. Math. Oper. Res. 2, 225–229.
Nava, F., 2009. Quantity Competition in Networked Markets. mimeo, University of Chicago.
Newman, M.E.J., 2002. The Spread of Epidemic Disease on Networks. Phys. Rev. E 66, 016128.

Newman, M.E.J., Barabasi, A.L., Watts, D.J., 2006. The Structure and Dynamics of Networks: (Princeton Studies in Complexity. Princeton University Press.
Pastor-Satorras, R., Vespignani, A., 2000. Epidemic spreading in scale-free networks. Phys. Rev. Lett. 86, 3200–3203.
Pastor-Satorras, R., Vespignani, A., 2001. Epidemic dynamics and endemic states in complex networks. Phys. Rev. E Stat. Nonlin. Soft. Matter Phys. 63, 066–117.
Patacchini, E., Zenou, Y., 2006. Racial Identity and Education. SSRN Working Papers.
Pattison, P.E., 1993. Algebraic Models for Social Networks. Cambridge University Press, Cambridge.
Pattison, P.E., Wasserman, S., 1999. Logit Models and Logistic Regressions for Social Networks: II. Multivariate Relations. Br. J. Math. Stat. Psychol. 52, 169–193.
Pellizzari, M., 2004. Do friends and relatives really help in getting a job? Cent. Econ. Res. Discuss. Pap. 623. London Sch. Econ.
Putnam, R., 2000. Bowling Alone: The Collapse and Revival of American Community (Simon and Schuster).
Rauch, J.E., 2007. Missing Links: Formation and Decay of Economic Networks. Russell Sage Foundation Publications, NY.
Reiss, A.J., 1988. Co-offending and criminal careers. In: Tonry, M. (Ed.), Crime and Justice: A Review of Research. 10, Univ. Chicago Press, Chicago.
Skyrms, B., Pemantle, R., 2000. A Dynamic Model of Social Network Formation. Proc. Natl. Acad. Sci. U. S. A. 97, 9340–9346.
Slate, J.R., Jones, C.H., 2005. Effects of school size: A review of the literature with recommendations. Essays in Education.
Slikker, M., van den Nouweland, A., 2001. Social and Economic Networks in Cooperative Game Theory. Kluwer Acad. Publ, Norwell, MA.
Snijders, T.A.B., Steglich, C.E.G., Schweinberger, M., 2007. Modeling the Coevolution of Networks and Behavior. In: van Montfort, K., Oud, H., Satorra, A. (Eds.), Longitudinal Models in the Behavioral and Related Sciences. Routledge, New York.
Sobel, J., 2002. Can We Trust Social Capital? J. Econ. Lit. 40, 139–154.
Sundararajan, A., 2005. Local network effects and network structure. New York Univ. Stern.
Tesfatsion, L., 1997. A trade network game with endogenous partner selection. In: Amman, H., Rustem, B., Whinston, A.B. (Eds.), Computational Approaches to Economic Problems. Kluwer Acad. Publ, Norwell, MA, pp. 249–269.
Topa, G., 2001. Social Interactions, Local Spillovers and Unemployment. Rev. Econ. Stud. 68, 261–296.
Vega-Redondo, F., 2007. Complex Social Networks, Econometric Society Monographs. Cambridge University Press, Cambridge.
Wang, P., Watts, A., 2006. Formation of buyer-seller trade networks in a quality differentiated product market. Canadian Journal of Economics 39 (7), 971–1004.
Wasserman, S., Faust, K., 1994. Social Network Analysis: Methods and Applications. Cambridge University Press, Cambridge.
Wasserman, S., Pattison, P., 1996. Logit Models and Logistic Regressions for Social Networks: I. An Introduction to Markov Graphs and P*. Psychometrika 61, 401–425.
Watts, A., 2001. A Dynamic Model of Network Formation. Games Econ. Behav. 34, 331–341.
Watts, A., 2007. Formation of segregated and integrated groups. International Journal of Game Theory 35, 505–519.

CHAPTER 13

Local Interactions*

Onur Özgür
Université de Montréal[†]

Contents

1. Introduction 588
2. Static Models 589
   2.1 Baseline static model 590
   2.2 Continuous choice models 592
   2.3 Multiple equilibria and social multiplier 608
   2.4 Discrete choice models 611
3. Dynamic Models 618
   3.1 Baseline dynamic model 618
   3.2 Rational forward-looking interactions 619
   3.3 Local vs. global dynamics 627
   3.4 Ergodicity 631
   3.5 Myopia vs. rationality 633
      3.5.1 Myopic Interactions *633*
      3.5.2 Does it matter? *635*
   3.6 Rational dynamics and identification 637
4. Concluding Remarks 638
References 639
Further Readings 644

Abstract

Local interactions refer to social and economic phenomena where individuals' choices are influenced by the choices of others who are 'close' to them socially or geographically. This represents a fairly accurate picture of human experience. Furthermore, since local interactions imply particular forms of externalities, their presence typically suggests government action. I survey and discuss existing theoretical work on economies with local interactions and point to areas for further research.

JEL Classification: C3, C33, C62, C72, C73, D9, D62, D50, Z13.

* Prepared for the *Handbook of Social Economics*, edited by Jess Benhabib, Alberto Bisin, and Matt Jackson, to be published by elsevier Science in 2010. I thank Alberto Bisin for his continuous support as a mentor and a friend throughout the years and for long hours that he has spent with me discussing social economics. I am grateful to the Fonds Québécois de la Recherche sur la Société et la Culture (FQRSC) for financial support, Centre Interuniversitaire de Recherche en Economie Quantitative (CIREQ) and Centre Interuniversitaire de Recherche en Analyse des Organisations (CIRANO) for research facilities.

† Department of Economics; e-mail: onur.ozgur@umontreal.ca, http://www.sceco.umontreal.ca/onurozgur

Handbook of Social Economics, Volume 1A
ISSN 0169-7218, DOI: 10.1016/S0169-7218(11)01013-6

Keywords

Conformity
externalities
local interactions
Markov perfect equilibrium
multiple equilibria
rational expectations
social interactions
social multiplier
strategic complementarities

1. INTRODUCTION

Social scientists discovered not so long ago that seemingly unrelated phenomena such as criminal activity, school attendance, out-of-wedlock pregnancy, substance use, adoption of new technologies, fashion and fads, panics and mania display similar empirical features.[1] Some of these features are

- Too much variation across space and time in the observable variables of interest relative to the variation in the observed fundamentals.
- S-shaped adoption (frequencies) of new technologies, behavior, fashion and norms.
- Presence of direct social (non-market) influences on individual behavior.

The response in the economics science has been to build model economies that can generate these empirical features as equilibrium properties. Economists call these phenomena *social interactions*, i.e., particular socio-economic events in which markets do not fully mediate individuals' choices, and each individual's choice might be in part determined by choices of other individuals in his *reference group*. The underlying idea is that individuals do not exist as isolated atoms but rather are embedded within networks of relationships, e.g., peer groups, families, colleagues, neighbors, or more generally any socio-economic group.

In most of the socioeconomic phenomena cited above and in many others, behavior and characteristics of agents who are 'close' to each other in some social or geographical sense, seem to be correlated: Adolescent pregnancy and school drop-out rates are correlated with neighborhood composition in inner city ghettoes (Case and

[1] Glaeser, Sacerdote, and Scheinkman (1996) argue that they can explain the high variance of crime rates across space using local interaction. Crane (1991) finds that both high school drop-out and teenage childbearing rates are related to the local neighborhood characteristics; Haveman and Wolfe (1996) find similar results for drop-out rates. See Nakajima (2007) and Kremer and Levy (2008) for the existence of peer effects in smoking and drinking in teenagers and college students respectively. For technology adoption and local complementarities see Brock and Durlauf (2010), Durlauf (1993), Ellison and Fudenberg (1993). For threshold and herd behavior, multiple equilibria and cycles in fads and fashion see Bikhchandani, Hirshleifer, and Welch (1992) and Pesendorfer (1995). For similar behaviors in market crashes, panics and manias see Shiller (2000).

Katz (1991)); teenagers whose closest friends smoke are more likely to smoke (Nakajima (2007)); Coleman, Katz, and Menzel (1996) show how doctors' willingness to prescribe a new drug diffuses through local contacts; Topa (2001) finds, using Census Tract data for Chicago, that agents are more likely to find a job if their social contacts are employed and that these local spillovers are defined by neighborhood boundaries and ethnic dividing lines. Essentially, most of human interaction that we experience in our daily lives seems to be of similar nature.

The term **local interactions** is coined to refer to such environments where individuals interact with a group of agents close to them in an otherwise large economy. Therefore, in a general economy with local interactions, each agent's ability to interact with others depends on the position of the agent in a predetermined network of relationships, e.g., a family, a peer group, or more generally any socio-economic group. The origin of the term might be traced back to the Physics and Probability of Interacting Particles, where the fundamental question of interest is whether specification of a system at the particle level (local) can determine its global characteristics. In economics, the analogous question is whether social and economic interaction observed at the individual level can determine the properties of economic aggregates of interest.

My main objective in this chapter is to present and discuss existing theoretical work on economies with local interactions. Consequently, this is a review of the methodological contributions and I do not venture to survey the rapidly growing body of applications of local interaction methods. Interested reader should consult Brock and Durlauf (2001b), Durlauf (2004), Glaeser and Scheinkman (2001), Durlauf and Young (2001) and Manski (2000) for excellent surveys of the literature and more.

There does not yet exist what one may call a 'canonical' model of local interactions. Accordingly, there are rough dividing lines that partition the literature. The most important of these is the static vs. dynamic divide. Majority of the existing models are static, consequently static environments are the ones we best understood so far. Having said that, there is a plethora of questions that beg for and a number of theoretical questions that needs to be answered with dynamic models. Another division is along the binary vs. continuous choice line. Mathematical and econometric techniques currently used in each category are quite different. One final division is along the rational vs. myopic modeling choice. Early models of local interactions in economics have been built with myopic agents and under particular behavioral assumptions. This is changing recently. Thus, although I touch upon models with myopic best-responders, my focus is on models with rational agents. For all these reasons, I chose to follow similar division lines in this article.

2. STATIC MODELS

I start with a review of the existing static literature for two main reasons. Firstly, most of the important features of economies with local interactions we know of have been discovered originally in static environments, e.g., cross-sectional correlation of behavior, multiple equilibria, social multiplier. Secondly, this is clearly the most natural order to proceed in and once the reader has the necessary understanding of the aforementioned features, it is simpler to appreciate the delicate aspects of dynamic models and their equilibrium properties.

2.1 Baseline static model

In this section, I present a baseline model that will prevail throughout the chapter. I will use the same notation throughout although the original notation used in the articles that I present might be different. The framework is flexible enough to accommodate a variety of different economies of interest. The theoretical object of study is a class of local interaction economies, represented by the tuple $\mathcal{E} = (\mathbb{A}, X, \Theta, N, P, u)$. I describe below what each of these elements is.

Agents are represented by a countable set $\mathbb{A}$ and the letters a, b, c ... are used for generic agents. In most of the literature, $\mathbb{A}$ is assumed to be a finite set.[2] Each agent $a \in \mathbb{A}$ makes his choices from a common **action set** X. Depending on the question at hand, structure will be given to X; for example it might be an interval of the real line as in Glaeser and Scheinkman (2003) and Bisin and Özgür (2009a,b) (*continuous choice*) or a binary choice set as in Brock and Durlauf (2001a), and Glaeser, Sacerdote, and Scheinkman (1996) (*discrete choice*).

Any exogenous heterogeneity at the individual level (such as family background, observed or unobserved role model or peer group characteristics, individual ability and traits) will be captured by the common **type space** Θ. We will let θ^a be agent a's type, a random variable with support on the set Θ and $\theta := (\theta^a)_{a\in\mathbb{A}}$ be the vector of types for all individuals. At this point, no restriction is made on the admissible probabilistic structure on this set. Yet, the baseline model is general enough to incorporate economies where individual characteristics are correlated (observably or in a hidden way) across agents and time.

When all agents observe the realization of θ, we call the economy one with **complete information**. Otherwise, we say that the economy is with **incomplete information**. Typically, all results for complete information economies I will report will also apply to economies with incomplete information, unless it is mentioned otherwise.

There might be exogenous determinants of individual behavior affecting all agents. These latter will be presented by the **parameter** $p \in P$. When one is interested in modeling aggregate influences (e.g., global interactions, general equilibrium effects) one can extend the notion of equilibrium to allow for an endogenous p. Typically in those cases, p will be an aggregator of some sort.

[2] Notable exceptions are Föllmer (1974), Durlauf (1993), Bisin, Horst and Özgür (2006), and Horst and Scheinkman (2006).

Now that the underlying physical setup and choice sets are in place, I can introduce preferences. One novelty of the local interaction models is the local structure that allows agents' preferences to be affected by the choices of 'close' (geographically or socially) agents they care about. Consequently, in order to introduce individual preferences on the choice sets, one needs to be precise about who cares about whom. For an agent $a \in \mathbb{A}$, his **reference group** is given by $N(a) \subset \mathbb{A}$. Thus,

$$N : \mathbb{A} \to 2^{\mathbb{A}}$$

is a "neighborhood" operator that maps each agent $a \in \mathbb{A}$ to his reference group, $N(a) \subset \mathbb{A}$, the set of agents whose choices affect a's utility directly. Since the baseline model of this section is static, no time index appears. With dynamic models of Section 3, one can allow for intertemporal changes in the reference group of an agent a, i.e., $N : \mathbb{A} \times \{,2,\ldots\} \to 2^{\mathbb{A}}$.

Given the neighborhood structure, the preferences of an agent $a \in \mathbb{A}$ are represented by a **utility function** u^a of the form

$$\left(x^a, \{x^b\}_{b\in N(a)}, \theta^a, p\right) \to u^a\left(x^a, \{x^b\}_{b\in N(a)}, \theta^a, p\right)$$

Typical assumptions made in the literature on the utility function are: it is sufficiently smooth with respect to arguments and cross-arguments; that it is concave with respect to agent a's (own) choice. I will be more precise about these when I discuss particular models. Finally, one needs an equilibrium concept to close the model. The one that will be used throughout Section 2 is the following.

Definition 1 *An equilibrium for a static economy with local interactions and complete information,* $\mathcal{E} = (\mathbb{A}, X, \Theta, N, P, u)$, *is a family of choice maps* $\{g^a\}_{a\in\mathbb{A}}$ *such that, for each agent* $a \in \mathbb{A}$, *given* θ *and* p,

$$g^a(\theta, p) \in \arg\max_{x^a\in X} u^a\left(x^a, \{g^b(\theta, p)\}_{b\in N(a)}, \theta^a, p\right)$$

Notice that this definition assumes that agents, before making their choices, observe the characteristics of other agents and the value of the parameter p. More importantly, each agent a anticipates that any other agent b's choice will be dictated by the behavioral rule (strategy) $g^b : \Theta^{\mathbb{A}} \times P \to X$. For static environments, observing characteristics only of a smaller number of agents (say of one's peers only) is not a fundamental problem as long as the probabilistic structure is common knowledge. The equilibrium concept can be extended in a straightforward manner to incomplete information scenarios. However, in dynamic contexts, the nature of the restrictions that one imposes on the probabilistic structure becomes an important issue, as we will see in Section 3.

Remark 1 (Global interactions) *One might want to model phenomena where agents' preferences depend on some aggregate of individual choices, e.g., increase in average achievement in the* *classroom might have a positive effect on individual achievements; or the fact that a majority of the population behaves according to a particular social norm might affect behavior at the individual level. In other words, one might want to model the direct dependence of p on x, the action profile, such that $p(x)$ enters into the utility function of an agent. With a finite number of agents, this is a straightforward extension of the local interaction models. It is in that sense that global interaction is a special case of local interaction. However, with an infinite number of agents, one needs to be careful about continuity issues as we will see in Section 2.2 when we look at Horst and Scheinkman (2006).*

Remark 2 (Social Space) *To introduce the notion of reference groups means to endow the set of agents with the structure of a graph. Some in the literature stop at that point and use a binary relation and the properties of this latter to model interactions (Morris (2000)); some others look at mean-field interactions only (Brock and Durlauf (2001)). However, one may go further and model the interaction on a lattice and interpret it as a social space and the associated norm as representing social proximity, e.g., Akerlof (1997), Föllmer (1974), Bisin and Özgür (2010). The advantage of the lattice structure is that the mathematical theory of Markovian interaction on lattices is well developed.*

The methods used to study economies with discrete and continuous choices being quite different, there is a rough division in the literature along that line. On each side of the line, there exists a sufficient number of social and economic phenomena that justifies the respective modeling choice. I start in the next section with the continuous choice models.

2.2 Continuous choice models

Some socio-economic phenomena have been naturally modeled using continuous choice in economics. Education is one such phenomenon (Bénabou (1993, 1996), Durlauf (1996a, 1996b)); since its quantity and frequency matters, addiction to substance use is another (Becker and Murphy (1988), Gul and Pesendorfer (2007)). Moreover, models with continuous actions are mathematically simpler to analyze since they yield themselves to differentiable methods. I survey in this section some of the mostly cited methodological contributions to the literature.

Föllmer (1974)

In the early 70s, general equilibrium economists (see Hildenbrand (1971), Malinvaud (1972), and Bhattacharya and Majumdar (1973)) took an interest in the following questions: How should the demand theory and the general equilibrium analysis, as we know them, be modified if individuals' preferences are allowed to be random? Can one always find prices that clear the markets? In particular, does the randomness die out at the aggregate when we look at large economies or limits of finite economies, so that one can use standard results from classical general equilibrium theory?

Hildenbrand (1971) formulated answers to the above questions under the hypothesis that the probability laws governing individual preferences and endowments are random but *independent* across agents. Consider the following class of economies. The set of agents $\mathbb{A}$ is countable. For an agent $a \in \mathbb{A}$, $\preceq (a)$ denotes his *preferences*, an element in the set $\mathcal{P}$ of continuous complete preorderings on the *commodity space* $\mathbb{R}^l_+$, and $e(a) \in \mathbb{R}^l_+$ his *initial endowment*. Let $w(a) := (\preceq (a), e(a)) \in \mathcal{S} := \mathcal{P} \times \mathbb{R}^l_+$ be agent a's *state* and $\mathcal{S}$ the *set of possible states*. To avoid measure theoretical technicalities, let $\mathcal{S}$ be a finite set[3] and the individual preferences be monotonic and strongly convex (regularity conditions). In this environment, the map

$$w : \mathbb{A} \to \mathcal{S}$$

is called the *state of the economy*. Let Ω be the set $\mathcal{S}^{\mathbb{A}}$ of all possible states and $\mathcal{F}$ the σ-field generated by the individual states $w \to w(a), a \in \mathbb{A}$. Hildenbrand shows that given some regularity conditions, one can choose a price system p such that

$$\lim_{|\mathbb{A}|\uparrow\infty} \frac{1}{|\mathbb{A}|} \sum_{a\in\mathbb{A}} \zeta(w(a), p) = 0, \text{ in probability,} \tag{1}$$

where $|\mathbb{A}|$ is the number of agents and ζ $(w(a),p)$ is the excess demand of agent $a \in \mathbb{A}$ at prices p and individual state $w(a)$. It is not very surprising that randomness alone does not seriously affect the existence of price equilibria. Malinvaud (1972), and Bhattacharya and Majumdar (1973)) take the analysis one step further by dropping independence but imposing conditions on the underlying probability space $(\Omega, \mathcal{F})$ (e.g., strong mixing) that guarantee a suitable law of large numbers. Any conditions on the underlying stochastic structure of the economy are then encoded in to the probability law μ on the probability spaceΩ $(\Omega, \mathcal{F})$.

Föllmer (1974) argues that conditions imposed directly on μ cease to be purely *microeconomic*, since local knowledge on individual laws is not enough to determine the aggregate μ; one needs to know the probabilities governing the joint behavior of all sub-populations in the economy. He rather asks '*Can one always find prices that clear the markets along with an aggregate probability law for a large economy just on the basis of microeconomic data (local specifications)*?

To that end, let $\eta : \mathbb{A} \backslash \{a\} \to \mathcal{S}$ be the *environment* of an agent $a \in \mathbb{A}$. The **local characteristics** of agent a are given by a probability kernel $\pi_a(\cdot|\eta)$, i.e., $\pi_a(s|\eta)$ is the probability that agent a's state is s given his environment η. Let Π be the collection of local (*microeconomic*) characteristics of the economy. Call any probability measure μ on $(\Omega, \mathcal{F})$ which is compatible with Π, i.e.,

$$\mu[w(a) = s|\eta] = \pi_a(s|\eta), \mu - a.s. \qquad (a \in \mathbb{A}, s \in \mathcal{S})$$

[3] This is generalizable and the general version would require some compactness assumption.

a global (macroeconomic) **phase** of the economy. We say that the local characteristics are **consistent** if they admit at least one global phase.[4]

Definition 2 *A price p is said to* **stabilize** *the phase* μ *of an economy* $\mathcal{E}$ *if*

$$\lim_{n\to\infty}\frac{1}{|\mathbb{A}_n|}\sum_{a\in\mathbb{A}_n}\zeta(w(a),p)=0,\ \mu-\textit{almost surely}$$

whenever $(\mathbb{A}_n)$ *is an increasing sequence of subsets of agents which exhausts* $\mathbb{A}$[5]. *We say that* p stabilizes the economy $\mathcal{E}$ *if* p *stabilizes each phase* μ *of* $\mathcal{E}$.

Markovian Interaction. Föllmer uses the following class of economies to show that (i) even short range interaction may propagate through the economy and may indeed 'become an important source of uncertainty' and (ii) if the local interaction is 'strong' enough, the microeconomic characteristics may no longer determine the global probability law which governs the joint behavior of all economic agents; and in that case a given global phase typically will not satisfy a law of large numbers like in equation (1). Let

$$\mathbb{A}:=\mathbb{Z}^d:=\{a=(a_1,\ldots,a_d)|\ a_i \text{ is integer}\}$$

for some $d\geq 1$ and the reference group of an agent a is given by

$$N(a):=\{b\in\mathbb{A}|\ \|\ b-a\ \|=1\}$$

where $||\cdot||$ is the usual Euclidean norm. Thus each agent has $2d$ *immediate neighbors*. Call this economy *Markovian* if local characteristics are consistent and they satisfy

$$\pi_a(\cdot|\eta)=\pi_a(\cdot|\eta'),\ \text{if}\,\eta \text{ and } \eta' \text{coincide on } N(a)$$

that is, each agent a's state is influenced by the states only of those agents in his *reference group*. The economy is *homogeneous* if Π is translation invariant. A phase μ is called *homogeneous* if μ is a translation invariant measure[6] Let $\Phi(\mathcal{E})$ be the set of all phases of the Markovian economy $\mathcal{E}$; similarly, let $\Phi_0(\mathcal{E})$ be the set of all homogeneous phases of $\mathcal{E}$. Consistency of the local characteristics imply (Spitzer (1971)) that

$$|\Phi(\mathcal{E})|\geq|\Phi_0(\mathcal{E})|\geq 1$$

[4] If $\mathbb{A}$ is finite then the macroeconomic phase is uniquely determined by the local characteristics; see Spitzer (1971). Similarly, under the independence assumption, as in Hildenbrand (1971), there exists a unique global phase μ given by the product measure on $(\Omega,\mathcal{F})$with marginals $\mu_a(\cdot)=\pi_a(\cdot|\eta), a\in\mathbb{A}$.

[5] This does not only mean that $\cup\mathbb{A}_n=\mathbb{A}$ but also that the subsets $\mathbb{A}_n$, are 'good representatives' of $\mathbb{A}$. That is, that they expand to $\mathbb{A}$ in approximately the same manner as the subsets $\mathbb{B}_n=\{a\in\mathbb{A}:\ \ \|\ a\ \|\ \ \leq n\}$. To be precise, it requires $\mathbb{A}_n\subset\mathbb{B}_n$ and the existence of some integer N and some $\delta>0$ such that $\mathbb{A}_n$ is the disjoint union of at most N boxes parallel to the axes of the lattice $\mathbb{A}$ and satisfies $\mathbb{A}_n||\mathbb{B}_n|^{-1}\geq\delta$.

[6] For $a\in\mathbb{A}$, consider the shift operator T^a: $\Omega\to\Omega$ defined by $T^a w(b)=w(a+b)$. Translation invariance of Π means $\pi_{a+b}(\cdot|\eta)=\pi_a(\cdot|\eta\circ T^b)$ where $\eta\circ T^b(c)=\eta(b+c), (a,b,c\in\mathbb{A})$. Translation invariance of μ means that $\mu\circ T^a=\mu, a\in\mathbb{A}$.

and both inequalities might be strict. This means that although the underlying structure is homogeneous, the global probability measure might not be ($|\Phi(\mathcal{E})| > |\Phi_0(\mathcal{E})|$) and in particular the individual measures μ_a might be different (*symmetry breakdown*). Moreover, multiple consistent global phases are possible ($|\Phi(\mathcal{E})| > 1$) for the same local characteristics (*phase transition*). Let us call each extreme point[7] of $\Phi_0(\mathcal{E})$ a *pure phase.*[8] The following theorem states that given a pure phase for the economy, there always exists a price vector p such that aggregate excess demand vanishes when the economy gets large.

Theorem 1 *Any pure phase can be stabilized. In particular one can equilibrate the economy as soon as it admits only one phase.*

This is an affirmative answer to only one part of the question that Föllmer asked. The most important second part is not answered yet: do local characteristics determine the global phase? To this end, assume that local conditional probabilities $\pi_a(\cdot|\eta)$ are all strictly positive. Then thanks to a theorem by Averintzev (1970), the local characteristics are consistent if and only if they can be written in the following form

$$\pi_a(s|\eta) = Z(a,\eta)^{-1}\exp\left(\gamma(a,s) + \sum_{b\in N(a)} U\,(a,b,s,\eta(b))\right) \tag{2}$$

where $Z(a,\eta)$ is a normalization factor to guarantee that $\sum_s \pi_a(s|\eta) = 1$. The function U satisfies

$$U(a,b,\cdot,\cdot) = 0 \quad \text{if} \quad b \notin N(a)$$

which corresponds to the Markov property[9] and homogeneity of Π is equivalent to

$$U(a+c,b+c,\cdot,\cdot) = U(a,b,\cdot,\cdot), \gamma(a+c,\cdot) = \gamma(a,\cdot)$$

One may interpret this as γ representing the own-effect and the coupling factors $U(a,b,s,s')$ representing the *intensity of interaction* between the agents a and b when their respective states are s and s'. The representation in (2) is unique if one lets

$$\gamma(\cdot,s_0) = U(\cdot,\cdot,s_0,\cdot) = U(\cdot,\cdot,\cdot,s_0) = 0$$

for some reference state s_0. With this normalization one has $U = 0$ if and only if there is no interaction at all, in which case there is no phase transition. A much weaker condition is given by the following

7 An extreme point of a convex set $\Phi(\mathcal{E})$ in a real vector space is a point in $\Phi(\mathcal{E})$ which does not lie in any open line segment joining two points of $\Phi(\mathcal{E})$.

8 Föllmer argues that both $\Phi(\mathcal{E})$ and $\Phi_0(\mathcal{E})$ are metrizable simplices with respect to the weak topology on the space of measures over the compact space Ω (Choquet (1969), Georgii (1972)). Thus, by Choquet's integral representation theorem, each phase (resp. each homogeneous phase) can be written as a mixture of extreme points in $\Phi(\mathcal{E})$ (respectively $\Phi_0(\mathcal{E})$).

9 Follmer argues that if we replace this condition by $\sum_b \max_{s,s'} U(a,b,s,s') < \infty$, we get an economy with infinite range interactions where interactions 'decay at infinity' and thanks to Georgii (1972), the results of this section remain valid.

Theorem 2 (Spitzer (1971), Dobrushin (1968)) *There exists a* unique *(no phase transition) global probability measure (phase) consistent with local conditional probabilities if either*
(i) $\max|U(\cdot,\cdot,\cdot,\cdot)|$ *is small enough, i.e., if the local interaction among economic agents are sufficiently* weak, *or*
(ii) $d = 1$, *i.e., the local interaction structure is one-dimensional.*

So, one should expect multiple phases when the local interaction is strong and complex enough. Moreover, when multiple phases exist, there is an infinity of non-pure phases due to the convexity of $\Phi(\mathcal{E})$; hence Theorem 1 is of no great use either. Finally, Föllmer demonstrates through an economic reinterpretation of well known example in Statistical Mechanics what sort of complications might arise when the conditions in Theorem 2 are violated.

Example 1 (Ising Economies) *Let $\mathcal{E}$ be a homogeneous Markov economy with two goods and $\mathbb{A} = \mathbb{Z}^2$. Let $e(a) = e := (e_1, e_2) \in \mathbb{R}^2_{++}$ (endowments are not random) and assume that π_a is rotation invariant, i.e., each agent $a \in \mathbb{A}$ reacts in the same way to neighbors in any direction. Moreover, assume that an agent either wants to consume as much as good 1 and does not care about good 2 (type $w(a) = +1$) or the other way around (type $w(a) = -1$).*

Due to rotation invariance, representation in (2) takes the form

$$\pi_a(\pm 1|\eta) = Z(\eta)^{-1}\exp\left(\pm\left(\gamma + J\sum_{b\in N(a)}\eta(b)\right)\right)$$

Follmer calls the case $J > 0$ *cyclic* (*conformity*) and $J < 0$ *acyclic* (*nonconformist, against the trend*). Consider a $\mu \in \Phi_0(\mathcal{E})$. At price p, agent a's excess demand is

$$\zeta(+1,p) = \left(\frac{p_2}{p_1}e_2, -e_2\right) \text{ respectively } \zeta(-1,p) = \left(-e_1, \frac{p_1}{p_2}e_1\right)$$

so his expected excess demand (given $\mu_1 = \mu[w(a) = +1]$ and $\mu_2 = \mu[w(a) = -1]$) vanishes if

$$\mu_1\left(\frac{p_2}{p_1}e_2, -e_2\right) + \mu_2\left(-e_1, \frac{p_1}{p_2}e_1\right) = (0,0)$$

which implies the necessary condition

$$\frac{p_2}{p_1} = \frac{e_1}{e_2}\frac{\mu_2}{\mu_1} \tag{3}$$

Due to a result in Spitzer (1971), when $J > 0$ and $\gamma \neq 0$, there is a unique phase which can be stabilized by Theorem 1. Now, assume that $\gamma = 0$. By a result in Georgii (1972), there is a critical value J_0 (that depends on the dimension of interaction d) such that for $J > J_0$, there are exactly two phases, say μ^1 and μ^2 that satisfy

$$\frac{\mu_1^1}{\mu_2^1} = \frac{\mu_1^2}{\mu_2^2} > 1, \tag{4}$$

Denoting expectation with respect to μ^i by E^i ($i = 1{,}2$), we have by Theorem 1

$$\frac{1}{|\mathbb{A}_n|}\sum_{a\in\mathbb{A}_n}\zeta(w(a),p) \rightarrow E^i[\zeta(w(0),p)] \quad \mu^i - \text{almost surely}, \quad i = 1, 2.$$

Unfortunately, equations (3) and (4) combined imply that there does not exist a price $p \in \mathbb{R}_+^2$ which makes the right side of the above equation vanish simultaneously for μ^1 and μ^2. Hence, we cannot stabilize the economy. Follmer shows that actually the situation is even worse than that as summarized in

Theorem 3 *A cyclic Ising economy where $\gamma = 0$ and with strong and complex interaction can almost never be stabilized.*

Overall, apart from being a contribution to the general equilibrium theory of random economies, the most important impact of Föllmer (1974) on the economics science has been the introduction and reinterpretation of mathematical methods used in Statistical Mechanics (Probability and Physics of Interacting Particles) in economies with local interactions. Interested reader should consult the standard reference in Mathematics for Interacting Particle Systems Liggett (1985). Durlauf (2008) is a nice reading with many more references.

Glaeser and Scheinkman (2003)

The main contribution of Glaeser and Scheinkman (GS henceforth) is the exploration of the common mathematical structure in existing models of static social interactions. They provide conditions under which equilibria exist and are unique. They give sufficient conditions for the existence of multiple equilibria and social multiplier effects, and ergodicity of the large economy limits. Finally, they discuss possible approaches to measurement and estimation of interaction effects. With the exception of a small section on 'mean field' interaction (average population action as an argument in the utility) with binary choice, all results are obtained for **continuous choice**.

Formally, they study economies with a finite number of agents $\mathbb{A} = \{1, \ldots, n\}$, each of whom is subject to a taste shock θ^a with support on a set Θ. The common action set, X, is an interval of the real line. Although they allow for multiple reference groups for each agent a, i.e., $N_k^a \subset \mathbb{A}\setminus\{a\}, k = 1, \ldots, K > 1$ s.t. $N(a) = \cup_k N_k^a$, to accomodate some examples in the literature, their results are presented for a single reference group ($K = 1$). The utility function of agent a is defined as

$$u^a\left(x^a, \{x^b\}_{b\in N(a)}, \theta^a, p\right) := u^a(x^a, \bar{x}_1^a, \ldots, \bar{x}_K^a, \theta^a, p)$$

where

$$\bar{x}_k^a := \sum_{b \in \mathbb{A}} \gamma_k^{ab} x^b$$

with $\gamma_k^{ab} \geq 0, \gamma_k^{ab} = 0$, if $b \in N_k^a, \sum_b \gamma_k^{ab} = 1$, and $p \in P$ is a vector of parameters.

Agents, when making choices, observe $\bar{x}^a$, the summary statistics of other agents' actions ($K = 1$). Given u^a that is twice continuously differentiable with $u_{11}^a < 0$, agent a's optimal interior choice is given by

$$u_1^a(x^a, \bar{x}^a, \theta^a, p) = 0 \tag{5}$$

Since $u_{11}^a < 0, x^a = g^a(\bar{x}^a, \theta^a, p)$ is well defined and

$$g_1^a(\bar{x}^a, \theta^a, p) = -\frac{u_{12}^a(x^a, \bar{x}^a, \theta^a, p)}{u_{11}^a(x^a, \bar{x}^a, \theta^a, p)} \tag{6}$$

Given this structure, an equilibrium always exists if the following holds.

Proposition 1 *Given a pair $(\theta, p) \in \Theta \times P$, suppose that for each $a, g^a(\bar{x}^a, \theta^a, p) \in I \subset X$, whenever $\bar{x}^a \in I$, where I is a closed and bounded interval. Then, there exists at least one equilibrium.*

One commonly used practice in the literature to generate multiple equilibria, e.g., Cooper and John (1988), is to introduce strategic complementarity into the utility functions. GS show, through an example, that strategic complementarity is *not* necessary for multiplicity. They also prove that, under standard regularity conditions, existence of a continuum of equilibria, such as in Diamond (1982), is non-generic in their economies[10]. A sufficient condition for a unique equilibrium, in these economies, is what they call the **Moderate Social Influence** (MSI) condition: The effect of a change in own action on own marginal utility is greater (in absolute value terms) than the effect on the latter of a change in average reference group action, i.e.,

$$\left|\frac{u_{12}^a(x^a, \bar{x}^a, \theta^a, p)}{u_{11}^a(x^a, \bar{x}^a, \theta^a, p)}\right| < 1 \tag{7}$$

This latter implies (although it is stronger than) from equation (6) that at the equilibrium profile, $|g_1^a(\bar{x}^a, \theta^a, p)| < 1$ for each agent a, which in turn implies uniqueness.

Proposition 2 *If for a given (θ, p), MSI holds for all $a \in \mathbb{A}$, then there exists at most one equilibrium.*

If, in addition to MSI, one assumes strategic complementarity $(u_{12}^a > 0)$, one can show that there is a **social multiplier:** a change in the value of a parameter, say p^1 will

[10] The issue of multiplicity is studied in more detail in Section 2.3 along with the construction of the particular example in GS.

have a *direct* effect going through the optimal choice g^a and an *indirect* effect going through the average reference group choice, $\bar{x}^a$. If each g^a has a positive partial derivative with respect to p^1, this will be amplified through the increased averages that increase the marginal utility of each agent for any (θ, p), due to strategic complementarity[11]

The next interesting question they ask is: Can individual shocks determine aggregate outcomes for large groups? Generically, **ergodicity** depends on the details of the interaction structure unlike the other results that they obtain. Nevertheless, economies with i.i.d shocks and local interactions tend to behave ergodically. GS provide sufficient (but not necessary) conditions for the average action of a large population to be independent of the particular realization of the individual shocks.

Proposition 3 *Suppose that the following conditions hold*

1. *θ^a is i.i.d across agents.*
2. *u^a (hence g^a) is independent of a (ex ante homogeneous preferences).*
3. *$N(a) := \mathbb{A}\backslash\{a\}$.*
4. *The interaction weights $\gamma^{a,b} := \frac{1}{n-1}$.*
5. *Action set X is bounded.*
6. *MSI holds uniformly, that is*

$$\sup_{\bar{x}^a, \theta^a} |g_1(\bar{x}^a, \theta^a, p)| < 1.$$

Let $x_n(\theta, p)$ denote the equilibrium when the population size is n and agent a's shock realization is θ^a. Then there exists an $\bar{x}(p)$ such that, with probability one,

$$\lim_{n \to \infty} \sum_{a=1}^{n} \frac{x_n^a(\theta, p)}{n} = \bar{x}(p)$$

One problem that is at the heart of empirical work in the literature is the empirical description of reference groups. GS touch upon the existing approaches to that question in the literature, namely: (i) models that take as an agent's reference group other individuals who are close to him geographically, e.g., Bénabou (1993), Glaeser, Sacerdote, and Scheinkman (1996); (ii) models that use random graph theory to treat particular reference groups as realizations of a random process, e.g., Kirman (1983), Ioannides (1990); (iii) models that treat individual incentives for the formation of reference groups, e.g., Jackson and Wolinsky (1996), and Bala and Goyal (2000).

Finally, GS give a tour of the empirical approaches that have been and that might be used to detect, measure, and estimate social interactions empirically. The three methods they consider are: (i) using the variance of group averages; (ii) regressing individual outcomes on group averages; and (iii) using the social multiplier.

[11] I will formulate this argument in Section 2.3 and compare it with similar results in other cited work.

Bisin, Horst, and Özgür (2006)

Bisin, Horst, and Özgür (BHÖ henceforth) consider general economies with static as well as dynamic local and global interactions. Here, I will present their study of static economies. Their most important contribution, that is, the study of the rational expectations equilibria of dynamic local and global interaction economies with rational forward looking agents is studied in section 3.2. Here is their contribution in a nutshell:

(i) For the static complete and incomplete information economies with local interactions, they provide conditions for existence, uniqueness, and Lipschitz continuity of equilibrium. Moreover, in their setup of the complete information economies with local interactions, BHÖ show that the law of the configuration of the endogenous choices of agents is a **Gibbs measure**[12] specified by a family of conditional probability distributions (agents' behavioral rules) given neighbors' equilibrium choices.

(ii) For the dynamic economies with forward looking rational agents with both local and global interactions, they show existence and Lipschitz continuity of stationary Markov equilibria. To do that, they use a novel separation argument to treat local and global equilibrium dynamics as independent processes and give conditions for these economies to converge to a unique probability law independent of initial conditions.

(iii) Finally, for a class of local conformity and habit formation economies, they characterize equilibria in closed form and study the effects of rationality, information, and dynamics on the existence (or suppression) of social multiplier effects.

Formally, they consider economies with a large number of agents; $\mathbb{A}$ is countably infinite to be precise[13]. Hence each agent is 'insignificant' compared to the rest of the economy in the spirit of common general equilibrium abstraction. Types, θ^a, are i.i.d. across agents, with law ν, and support Θ. For each agent a, $N(a) = \{a+1\}$, i.e., the local interaction structure is one-sided. BHÖ use this particular form to study in an abstract way economies where interactions are directed (e.g., hierarchical interactions in organizations, local conformity and role model interactions)[14] The preferences of each agent a are represented by the utility function

$$(x^a, x^{a+1}, \theta^a) \rightarrow u(x^a, x^{a+1}, \theta^a)$$

which is assumed to be continuous and strictly concave in its first argument. Prior to his choice, each agent $a \in \mathbb{A}$ observes the realization of his own type θ^a as well

[12] Please see Georgii (1989), Liggett (1985), or Kindermann and Snell (1980)

[13] Their results apply to economies with a finite number of agents with straightforward modifications. Evidently, existence results are easier to prove in that case.

[14] See the discussion at the end of this section for how to extend their ideas to more general interaction structures.

as the realizations of the types θ^b of the agents $b \in \{a+1, a+2, \ldots, a+N\}$. The vector of types whose realization is observed by the agent $a = 0$ is denoted $\theta_N := \{\theta^0, \theta^1, \ldots, \theta^N\}$; by analogy $T^a\theta_N := (\theta^a, \ldots, \theta^{a+N})$ denotes the vector of types whose realization is observed by the agent $a \in \mathbb{A}$.[15] If $N = \infty$ each agent has *complete information* about the current configuration of types when choosing his action. When instead $N \in \mathbb{N}$, an agent only has *incomplete information* about the types of the other agents. By convention, if $N = 0$, agents only observe their own types. Finally, the set of possible configurations of types of all agents $a \geq 0$ is given by $\Theta^{\mathbf{0}} := \{(\theta^a)_{a \geq 0} : \theta^a \in \Theta\}$.

The infinite number of agents assumption makes the standard existence results for finite economies unusable. Hence, in order to guarantee the existence and uniqueness of an equilibrium for static economies with local interactions, BHÖ impose a form of *strong concavity* on the agents' utility functions.

Definition 3 *Let $\alpha \geq 0$. A real-valued function $f : X \to \mathbb{R}$ is α-concave on X if the map $x \mapsto f(x) + \frac{1}{2}\alpha|x|^2$ from X to $\mathbb{R}$ is concave.*

This definition is first due to Rockafellar (1976), and is used for related purposes in Montrucchio (1987) and Santos (1991). Observe that a twice continuously differentiable map $f : X \to \mathbb{R}$ is α-concave, if and only if the second derivative is uniformly bounded from above by $-\alpha$.

In order to obtain parametric continuity of the equilibrium map, BHÖ require any agent's marginal utility with respect to his own action to depend in a Lipschitz continuous manner on the action taken by his neighbor. In this sense they impose a qualitative bound on the strength of local interactions between different agents.

Assumption 1 *The utility function u: $X \times X \times \Theta \to \mathbb{R}$ satisfies the following conditions:*

(i) *The map $x \mapsto u(x, y, \theta)$ is continuous and uniformly α-concave for some $\alpha > 0$.*

(ii) *The map u is differentiable with respect to its first argument, and there exists a map L: $\Theta \to \mathbb{R}$ such that*

$$\left| \frac{\partial}{\partial x} u(x, y, \theta^0) - \frac{\partial}{\partial x} u(x, \hat{y}, \theta^0) \right| \leq L(\theta^0)|\hat{y} - y| \quad \text{and such that} \quad \mathbb{E}L(\theta^0) < \alpha. \qquad (8)$$

The quantity $L(\theta^0)$ puts a bound on $\frac{\partial^2 u(x,y,\theta)}{\partial x \partial y}$, whereas α may be viewed as a bound on $\frac{\partial^2 u(x,y,\theta)}{\partial x^2}$. Thus, $\mathbb{E}L(\theta^0) < \alpha$ means that, *on average, the marginal effect of the neighbor's action on an agent's marginal utility is smaller than the marginal effect of the agent's own choice.* It is in this sense that (8) imposes a bound on the strength of the interactions between different agents. Notice that the *Moderate Social Influence* condition in Glaeser and

[15] Formally, $T^a : \Omega \mapsto \Omega (a \in \mathbb{A})$ is the a-fold iteration of the canonical right shift operator T on Ω; that is, $T^a((\omega_b)_{b \in \mathbb{A}}) = (\omega_{b+a})_{b \in \mathbb{A}}$; furthermore, $T^a\theta_N := (\theta^0(T^a\omega), \ldots, \theta^N(T^a\omega)) = (\theta^a, \ldots, \theta^{a+N})$.

Scheinkman (2003) corresponds to the stronger contraction condition $L(\theta^0) < \alpha$. Assumption 1 can easily be verified for the following example.

Example 2 (Local Conformity) *Let* $\alpha_1\ \alpha_2 \geq 0$ *and consider a utility function of the form*

$$u(x^a, x^{a+1}, \theta^a) := -\alpha_1(x^a - \theta^a)^2 - \alpha_2(x^a - x^{a+1})^2. \tag{9}$$

Quadratic utility functions of the form (9) describe preferences in which agents face a trade-off between the utility they receive from matching their own idiosyncratic shocks and the utility they receive from conforming to the action of their peers. The higher the ratio $\frac{\alpha_2}{\alpha_1}$*, the more intense is the agent's desire for conformity. It is easy to see that the map* $x^a \mapsto u(x^a, x^{a+1}, \theta^a)$ *is* α*-concave for all* $\alpha \leq 2(\alpha_1 + \alpha_2)$*. Moreover, Assumption 1 is satisfied with* $L(\theta^0) = L := 2\max\{\alpha_1, \alpha_2\}$ *and with* $\alpha := 2(\alpha_1 + \alpha_2)$.

BHÖ study symmetric equilibria. Establishing the existence of a symmetric equilibrium is equivalent to proving the existence of a measurable function $g^* : \Theta^{\mathbf{0}} \rightarrow X$ which satisfies

$$g^*(\theta) = \arg\max_{x^a \in X} u(x^a, g^* \circ T(\theta), \theta^0) \mathbb{P}\text{-a.s.} \tag{10}$$

Each such map is a fixed point of the operator V: $B(\Theta^{\mathbf{0}}, X) \rightarrow B(\Theta^{\mathbf{0}}, X)$ which acts on the class $B(\Theta^{\mathbf{0}}, X)$ of bounded measurable functions $f: \Theta^{\mathbf{0}} \rightarrow X$ according to

$$Vg(\theta) = \arg\max_{x^a \in X} u(x^a, g \circ T(\theta), \theta^0). \tag{11}$$

On the other hand, each fixed point of V is a symmetric equilibrium. It is therefore enough to show that V has an almost surely uniquely defined fixed point.

BHÖ are also interested in deriving conditions which guarantee that the economy admits a *Lipschitz continuous equilibrium map*. Lipschitz continuity of the equilibrium map may be viewed as a minimal robustness requirement on equilibrium analysis. In particular it justifies comparative statics analysis. They metrize the product space $\Theta^{\mathbf{0}}$ in a way that allows them to parameterize the bound on the variation of the equilibrium policy. For an arbitrary constant $\eta > 0$ define a metric d_η on the product space $\Theta^{\mathbf{0}}$ by

$$d_\eta(\theta, \hat{\theta}) := \sum_{a \geq 0} 2^{-\eta|a|} |\theta^a - \hat{\theta}^a| \quad (\theta = (\theta^a)_{a \in \mathbb{N}}, \hat{\theta} = (\hat{\theta}^a)_{a \in \mathbb{N}}) \tag{12}$$

and denote by $\text{Lip}_\eta(1)$ the class of all continuous functions $f: \Theta^{\mathbf{0}} \rightarrow X$ which are non-expanding with respect to the metric d_η, i.e.,

$$\text{Lip}_\eta(1) := \left\{ f : \Theta^0 \rightarrow X : |f(\theta) - f(\hat{\theta})| \leq d_\eta(\theta, \hat{\theta}) \right\}$$

Their main result in this section is

Theorem 4 *Let $\mathcal{S}$ be a static economy with local interactions and complete information.*

(i) *If the utility function $u : X^2 \times \Theta \to \mathbb{R}$ satisfies Assumption 1, then $\mathcal{S}$ admits a unique symmetric equilibrium g^*.*

(ii) *If, instead of (8), the utility function u satisfies the stronger condition,*

$$\left|\frac{\partial}{\partial x}u(x,y,\theta) - \frac{\partial}{\partial x}u(x,\hat{y},\hat{\theta})\right| \leq L\Big(|\hat{y}-y| + |\theta-\hat{\theta}|\Big) \text{ with } L < \alpha, \tag{13}$$

then there exists $\eta^* > 0$ such that the unique symmetric equilibrium g^* is almost surely Lipschitz continuous with respect to the metric d_{η^*}:

$$|g^*(\theta) - g^*(\hat{\theta})| \leq \frac{L}{\alpha} d_{\eta^*}(\theta, \hat{\theta}) \quad \mathbb{P}\text{-a.s.}.$$

An analogous result obtains for economies with incomplete information, where an individual agent only observes a finite number $N < \infty$ of types.

Theorem 5 *Let $\mathcal{S}$ be a static economy with local interaction and incomplete information, that is with $N \in N$.*

(i) *If the utility function $u : X^2 \times \Theta \to \mathbb{R}$ satisfies Assumption 1 and if it is* continuously *differentiable with respect to its first argument, then $\mathcal{S}$ admits a unique symmetric equilibrium g^*.*

(ii) *If u satisfies condition (13), then g^* is almost surely Lipschitz continuous:*

$$|g^*(\theta_N) - g^*(\hat{\theta}_N)| \leq \frac{L}{\alpha}|\theta_N - \hat{\theta}_N| \quad \mathbb{P}\text{-a.s.}.$$

Example 2 cont. (Local Conformity) *For the local conformity preferences described in (9), the equilibrium policy can be solved for in closed form. Let $\beta_1 := \frac{\alpha_1}{\alpha_1+\alpha_2}$* and *$\beta_2 := \frac{\alpha_2}{\alpha_1+\alpha_2}$. If the agents have complete information, i.e., if $N = \infty$, then the equilibrium takes the form*

$$g^*(T^a\theta_N) = \beta_1 \sum_{i=a}^{\infty} \beta_2^{i-a}\theta^i.$$

Observe that $\beta_1 \sum_{i=a}^{\infty} \beta_2^{i-a} = 1$. Thus, in equilibrium, the action of an agent $a \in \mathbb{A}$ is given by a convex combination of the types θ^b of the agents $b \in \{a, a+1, a+2, \ldots\}$. If the agents only have incomplete information, that is, if $N < \infty$, then

$$g^*(T^a\theta_N) = \beta_1 \left(\sum_{i=a}^{a+N} \beta_2^{i-a}\theta^i + \beta_2^{N+1}\mathbb{E}\theta^a\right).$$

BHÖ study the statistical properties of the equilibrium for an economy with the above specification. In particular, they characterize the effects of local conformity on the variance and the correlation structure of individual actions in the population as well as on the variance of the mean action across different economies. When the variance of the mean action across economies is larger than the variance of each action in the population, they say that social interactions generate a *social multiplier* effect. I postpone the discussion of this part to Section 2.3.

Economies with more general interaction structures. While the *Moderate Social Influence* assumption is generally not enough to obtain existence and uniqueness of equilibrium in economies with more general interaction structures, a stronger condition, like condition (13), in fact suffices for existence, uniqueness, and Lipschitz continuity. This is the case for both complete and incomplete information economies. Consider the case in which agents are located on the d-dimensional integer lattice $\mathbb{Z}^d$, and the preferences of the agent $a \in \mathbb{Z}^d$ are described by a utility function of the form

$$\left(x^a, \{x^b\}_{b\in N(a)}, \theta^a\right) \mapsto \hat{u}\left(x^a, \{x^b\}_{b\in N(a)}, \theta^a\right)$$

where $N(a) := \left\{b \in \mathbb{Z}^d : \| a - b \| = 1\right\}$ denotes the set of the agent's nearest neighbors. In such a more general model, each symmetric equilibrium is given by a fixed point of the operator

$$Vg(\theta) = arg \max_{x^0\in X} \hat{u}(x^0, \{g\circ T^a(\theta)\}_{a\in N(0)}, \theta^0).$$

BHÖ show that, if the utility function satisfies the contraction condition

$$\left|\frac{\partial}{\partial x^a}\hat{u}\left(x^a, \{x^b\}_{b\in N(a)}, \theta\right) - \frac{\partial}{\partial x^a}\hat{u}\left(x^a, \{\hat{x}^b\}_{b\in N(a)}, \hat{\theta}\right)\right| \leq L \max\{|\hat{x}^b - x^b|, |\theta - \hat{\theta}| : b \in N(a)\},$$

then V satisfies the contraction condition

$$|Vg - V\hat{g}| \leq \frac{L}{\alpha} \max\left\{|g\circ T^b - \hat{g}\circ T^b| : b \in N(a)\right\}.$$

Hence, V becomes a contraction that maps a set of Lipschitz continuous functions continuously into itself. Two-sided interactions are simply a special case of this general model.

Finally, BHÖ also show that the results they obtain for static economies can be reinterpreted (mathematically and economically) in two interesting ways:

(i) Equilibria in static economies can be characterized as *stationary solutions to a stochastic difference equation* derived from optimality conditions and as such a mathematical structure common to their environment and that of macroeconomic rational expectations models, e.g., Blanchard and Kahn (1980), can be unearthed;

(ii) Föllmer (1974) considers an economy where the law of the configuration of agents' exogenous types is a *Gibbs measure*. In their setup of the complete information economies with local interactions, BHÖ show that it is instead the law of the configuration of the endogenous choices of agents that is a Gibbs measure specified by a family of conditional probability distributions (agents' behavioral rules) given neighbors' equilibrium choices.

Horst and Scheinkman (2006)

Horst and Scheinkman (HS henceforth) are interested in equilibrium existence and uniqueness results in fairly general systems of static local and global interactions with an infinite number of agents. They also examine the structure of the equilibrium distribution and derive a "Markov" property for the equilibrium distribution of a class of spatially homogeneous systems.

Formally, the set of agents $\mathbb{A} \subset \mathbb{Z}^d$. Each agent $a \in \mathbb{A}$ makes a choice x^a from a common compact and convex set $X \subset \mathbb{R}^l$. The configuration space $S := \left\{x = (x^b)_{b\in\mathbb{A}} : x^b \in X\right\}$ of all action profiles is equipped with the product topology, and hence it is compact. Agent a's utility is affected by neighboring agents in varying degrees. To that end, let (J^a, θ^a) be a random variable where $J^a = (J^{a,b})_{b \neq a}$ with support $\Xi := \mathbb{R}^{\mathbb{A}\setminus\{0\}}$ capturing bilateral strength of interactions and θ^a with support Θ, agent a's taste shock. Agent a's reference group $N(a)$ is defined by the values of the realized interaction strength variable, i.e.,

$$N(a) := \left\{b \in \mathbb{A} : J^{a,b} \neq 0\right\}$$

These are the agents who interact with agent *a locally*. The agents who are not in a's reference group possibly affect his utility through a *global interaction* variable (empirical distribution) $p(x)$ associated with each action profile x. However, this way of modeling the global effect is not always appropriate for topological difficulties.[16] GS uses a two-step method to separate local (micro) and global (macro) interactions.

To that end, let $(\Omega, \mathcal{F}, \mathbb{P}) := ((\Xi \times \Theta)^{\mathbb{A}}, \mathcal{B}(\Xi \times \Theta)^{\mathbb{A}}, \mathbb{P})$ be the canonical probability space and let p be a probability measure on the action set X, and let $\mathcal{M}(X)$ be the set of such measures.[17] This way, a given aggregate belief $p \in \mathcal{M}(X)$ will simply be a parameter of the utility function without any explicit link between x and p. Thus, the preferences of agent a are represented by a utility function $U^a : S \times \mathcal{M}(X) \times \Xi \times \Theta \to \mathbb{R}$ such that

$$U^a(x^a, \{x^b\}_{b\neq a}, p, J^a, \theta^a) := u^a(x^a, \{J^{a,b}x^b\}_{b\neq a}, p, \theta^a)$$

They call the equilibrium that comes out of this structure given a common exogenous aggregate belief for all agents, a **microscopic equilibrium**, namely

Definition 4 *Given* $p \in \mathcal{M}(X)$, *an action profile* $g(p, J, \theta) = \left\{g^a(p, J, \theta)\right\}_{a\in\mathbb{A}}$ *is a* microscopic equilibrium *associated with* p *if*

$$g^a(p, J, \theta) \in \arg\max_{x^a\in X} U^a(x^a, \{g^b(p, J, \theta)_{b\neq a}, p, J^a, \theta^a\}) \quad \mathbb{P}\text{-}a.s.$$

[16] Utility functions might not be continuous w.r.t product topology if x enters in a non-trivial fashion. In addition, the configuration x does not have to have an empirical distribution. Hence, the continuity of the utility functions already imposes a decay rate on the strength of interactions.

[17] $\mathcal{M}(X)$ is compact with respect to the topology of weak convergence.

which they show to exist(not necessarily homogeneous) for any random social interactions system (purely local ones in particular). When they talk about the full-fledged general equilibrium, they require the aggregate belief p to be *consistent* with the empirical distribution of equilibrium actions, say $p(J, \theta)$.

Definition 5 *A random variable* $g(J,\theta) = \{g^a(J,\theta)\}_{a\in\mathbb{A}}$ *is an* **equilibrium** *for* $\mathcal{E}$ *if*

(i) *When* $\mathcal{E}$ *is not purely local, the empirical distribution associated with the action profile* $g(J, \theta)$ *exists almost surely, i.e., the weak limit*

$$\lim_{n\to\infty} \frac{1}{|\mathbb{A}_n|} \sum_{a\in\mathbb{A}} \delta_{g^a}(J,\theta)(\cdot) = p(J,\theta)$$

exists almost surely for some random variable $p(J,\theta) \in \mathcal{M}(X)$ *along the increasing sequence of finite sets* $\mathbb{A}_n := [-n, n]^d \cap \mathbb{A} \uparrow \mathbb{A}$ *and*

(ii) *No agent wants to deviate, i.e.,*

$$g^a(J,\theta) \in \arg\max_{x^a\in X} U^a(x^a, \{g^b(J,\theta)_{b\neq a}, p(J,\theta), J^a, \theta^a\}) \quad \mathbb{P}\text{-a.s.} \quad (a \in \mathbb{A}).$$

Unfortunately, unless some form of spatial homogeneity prevails, there is no reason to expect that the empirical distribution associated with the equilibrium actions exists (condition (i) above). For this reason, when global interactions are present, HS restrict themselves to **homogeneous** systems, i.e.,

Definition 6 *An economy* $\mathcal{E}$ *is homogeneous if* $\mathbb{A} = \mathbb{Z}^d$ *and*

(i) *There exists a measurable mapping* $U : S \times \mathcal{M}(X) \times \Xi \times \Theta \to \mathbb{R}$ *such that for all* $a \in \mathbb{A}$

$$U^a(x^a, \{x^b\}_{b\neq a}, p, J^a, \theta^a) = U(x^a, \{x^b\}_{b\neq a}, p, (T^a J)^0, (T^a\theta)^0)^{18}$$

(ii) *The distribution of the random variable* $(J,\theta) = \{(J^a,\theta^a)\}_{a\in\mathbb{A}}$ *is* stationary, *i.e.,*

$$\mathbb{P}[(J,\theta) \in B] = \mathbb{P}[T^a(J,\theta) \in B]$$

for all $a \in \mathbb{A}$ *and any measurable set* $B \in \mathcal{F}$.

The nice thing about the spatially homogenous systems, as they show, is that they can be viewed as convex combinations of ergodic systems.[19] In particular, a system where $(J^a, \theta^a)_{a\in\mathbb{A}}$ are i.i.d is ergodic. Given a homogeneous system $\mathcal{E}$, there exists a set $\mathcal{M}_0$ of ergodic probability measures on $(\Omega, \mathcal{F})$ and a mixing measure π such that

[18] T^a is simply a shift operator that individualizes a random variable to agent a as before.

[19] A homogeneous system $\mathcal{E}$ is called **ergodic** if, the robability measure $\mathbb{P}$ is ergodic, i.e., it satisfies a 0–1 law on the σ-field of all shift invariant events. See for example Fristedt and Gray (1997), section 28.5 or Billingsley (1995), section 24.

$$\mathbb{P}(\cdot) = \int_{\mathcal{M}_0} \nu(\cdot)\pi(d\nu)$$

where the measures ν are mutually singular, i.e., there exists (a.s.) mutually disjoint sets Ω_ν such that

$$\nu(\Omega_\nu) = 1 \text{ and } \nu(\Omega\hat{\nu}) = 0 \quad \text{for} \quad \nu \neq \hat{\nu}.$$

Thus one can think of a homogeneous interaction economy in two steps. Nature first picks an ergodic system using a distribution π, and then chooses an interaction pattern and a taste shock according to the distribution of the selected ergodic system. Given this description of course the equilibrium of the homogeneous system can be written as a family of equilibria of the associated ergodic decomposition, i.e.,

Proposition 4 *Let $\mathcal{E}$ be a homogeneous system of random social interactions with an associated ergodic decomposition $(\mathcal{E}_\nu)_{\nu \in \mathcal{M}_0}$.*

(i) *If g is a homogeneous equilibrium for $\mathcal{E}$, then g coincides a.s. with a homogeneous equilibrium g_ν for $\mathcal{E}_\nu$ on Ω_ν.*

(ii) *If for every ν, g_ν is a homogeneous equilibrium for $\mathcal{E}_\nu$, then the random variable g given by*

$$g(J,\theta) = g_\nu(J,\theta) \quad \textit{if} \quad (J,\theta) \in \Omega_\nu$$

defines a homogeneous equilibrium for $\mathcal{E}$.

HS argue that to show the existence and uniqueness of homogeneous microscopic equilibria in ergodic systems, they need to bound the strengths of interactions between agents and the effect of the global interactions on the marginal utility. They say that **MSI** (Moderate Social Interactions) holds if the best response function (unique optimum due to their strict concavity of the utility function assumption) of agents, say agent 0, h^0, is Lipschitz continuous and if the Lipschitz constants can be chosen to satisfy

$$\sum_{a \neq 0} L^a(\cdot) \leq \alpha < 1$$

Furthermore, **MSI** holds in **strong** form if one can choose L^a and L^p such that

$$\sup L^p + \sum_{a \neq 0} L^a(\cdot) \leq \alpha < 1.$$

If MSI holds, they prove that an economy $\mathcal{E}$ that is ergodic has a unique homogeneous microscopic equilibrium $g(p, \cdot)$ with respect to every empirical distribution p, which prepares the background for their main existence result.

Theorem 6 *If $\mathcal{E}$ is ergodic and has a homogeneous microscopic equilibrium $g(p, \cdot)$ with respect to every $p \in \mathcal{M}(X)$, then*

(i) *The empirical distribution associated to the equilibrium action profile $g(p, \cdot)$ exists and is a.s. equal to $\mu(p)$, the distribution of the random variable $g^0(p, \cdot)$. That is,*

$$\lim_{n\to\infty}\frac{1}{|\mathbb{A}_n|}\sum_{a\in\mathbb{A}_n}\delta_{g^a(p,J,\theta)}(\cdot)=\mu(p)\quad \mathbb{P}\text{-}a.s.$$

(ii) *If $\mathcal{E}$ satisfies MSI, then it has a homogeneous equilibrium whose associated empirical distribution is a.s. independent of (J, θ).*

(iii) *If MSI holds in strong form, the equilibrium is unique.*

The power of the ergodic structure is exploited fully in (ii) which says that the empirical distribution which is basically the aggregation of agents' local equilibrium behavior is independent of the realizations of local data. Given the equilibrium map, the behavior of the aggregates is not dependent of a particular interaction structure. This is a very nice result. If a system is homogeneous but not ergodic, then the empirical distribution would of course vary with (J, θ) but would still be constant in each Ω_ν.

For one-sided systems, HS obtain existence from the weaker assumption of average moderate social interactions, AMSI, which basically says that the Lipschitz bounds hold on average. Uniqueness follows when they assume strict concavity and a stronger version of AMSI (similar to strong MSI but in expectations). Finally, HS also derive a spatial Markov property for the equilibrium distribution of a class of homogeneous systems.

2.3 Multiple equilibria and social multiplier

One of the most appealing aspects of local interaction models is their ability to generate excess variation at the aggregate relative to the variation in exogenous data hence explain large differences in outcomes across populations and time with small differences in exogenous variables. Economists call this the **social multiplier** effect. The relevance of the social multiplier for policy analysis stems from the fact that when interactions are quantitatively important, policy interventions on single agents might have large aggregate effects.

The social multiplier concept is inherently related to two other issues: multiplicity of equilibria and identifiability of sources of variations. Typically, the forces that lead to multiple equilibrium also lead to large social multipliers. However, the former is not necessary for the latter as we will see below. I would like to argue in this section that local interaction models provide a natural outlet to tackle these issues; in particular, they suggest methods to obtain multiple equilibria and generate aggregate variation in a systematic way.

Cooper and John (1988) unearth the common features of Keynesian macroeconomic models. They ask what properties the economy should possess at the microeconomic level so that one obtains multiple equilibria at the aggregate. In particular, they are interested in coordination failures, that is, Pareto ranked multiple equilibria, and multiplier effects. They argue that the answer lies in **strategic complementarities**[20] at the individual level if the nature of the interaction is global.

They consider economies with $\mathbb{A} = \{1, 2, \ldots, I\}$, $X = [0, E]$ where E is finite. The interaction is through the average choice (global), i.e., $N(a) = \mathbb{A}\ \{a\}$ and agent a's utility from choosing x^a when everyone else chooses $\bar{x}$ is given by $V(x^a, \bar{x})$. They call $x^* \in X$ a symmetric Nash equilibrium choice if $V_1(x^*, x^*) = 0$. Their most important findings can be summarized as in this

Proposition 5 (Cooper and John (1988)) *In an economy with pure global interactions as described above, (i) strategic complementarity is necessary for multiple equilibria; (ii) strategic complementarity is necessary and sufficient for multipliers; (iii) given multiple equilibria and global positive spillovers ($V_2(x^a, \bar{x}) > 0$), equilibria can be Pareto ranked by the equilibrium action choice.*

This is a nice result for static games with purely global interactions. It suggests a way to generate multiplicity by focusing only on microeconomic fundamentals. However, Glaeser and Scheinkman (2003) show through the following example that the necessity of strategic complementarity is not robust in richer local interaction structures.

Example 3 (Glaeser and Scheinkman (2003)) *There are two sets of agents $\{\mathbb{A}_1\}$ and $\{\mathbb{A}_2\}$, with n agents in each set. For agents of a given set, the reference group consists of all agents of the other set. For $a \in \mathbb{A}_k$,*

$$\bar{x}^a = \frac{1}{n} \sum_{b \in \mathbb{A}_l} x^b$$

There are two goods, and the relative price is normalized to one. Each agent has an initial income of one unit, and his objective is to maximize

$$u^a(x^a, \bar{x}^a) = \log x^a + \log(1 - x^a) + \frac{\lambda}{2}(x^a - \bar{x}^a)$$

Only the first good exhibits social interactions, and agents of each set want to differentiate from the agents of the other set ($\lambda > 0$). There is NO strategic complementarity; an increase in the action of others (weakly) decreases the marginal utility of an agent's own action. An equilibrium (same choice for agents of the same set) is described by a pair (x, y) of actions for each set such that

$$1 - 2x + \lambda x(1 - x)(x - y) = 0$$
$$1 - 2y + \lambda y(1 - y)(y - x) = 0$$

[20] The term strategic complements was introduced by Bulow, Geanokoplos, and Klemperer (1985) in the context of multimarket oligopoly. Following BGK, Cooper and John say that strategic complementarities arise if an increase in one player's strategy increases the optimal strategy of the other players. More precisely, if $V_{12}(x^a, \bar{x}) > 0$ which in turn implies that $\frac{\partial x^*(\bar{x})}{\partial \bar{x}} > 0$.

Clearly $x = y = 1/2$ is always a symmetric equilibrium. If $\lambda < 4$, it is the unique equilibrium. For $\lambda > 4$, there are other equilibria too, e.g., for $\lambda = 4.040404$, $(x, y) = (.55, .45)$ is an equilibrium. Consequently, so is $(x,y) = (.45, .55)$. Hence existence of multiple equilibria does not imply strategic complementarity.

Glaeser and Scheinkman argue further that one can have a unique equilibrium (thanks to their MSI condition) in the presence of strategic complementarities $(u^a_{12}(x^a, \bar{x}^a, \theta^a, p) > 0)$ and obtain multiplier effects. Consider the effect of a change in the first component, p_1, of the parameter vector p. They show that if the partial of each agent's best response w.r.t p_1 is positive, one can write the impact of that effect on optimal choices as

$$\frac{\partial x}{\partial p_1} = (I + H)\left(\frac{\partial g^1}{\partial p_1}, \ldots, \frac{\partial g^n}{\partial p_1}\right)'$$

where H is a matrix with non-negative elements. This is equivalent to saying that there is a **social multiplier**. Holding all other choices constant

$$dx^a = \frac{\partial g^a(\bar{x}^a, \theta^a, p)}{\partial p_1} dp_1$$

whereas in equilibrium it becomes

$$\left[\frac{\partial g^a(\bar{x}^a, \theta^a, p)}{\partial p_1} + \sum_b H_{ab} \frac{\partial g^b(\bar{x}^b, \theta^a, p)}{\partial p_1}\right] dp_1$$

Then,

$$d\bar{x} = \frac{1}{n}\left[\sum_a \frac{\partial g^a(\bar{x}^a, \theta^a, p)}{\partial p_1} + \sum_{a,b} H_{ab} \frac{\partial g^b(\bar{x}^b, \theta^a, p)}{\partial p_1}\right] dp_1$$

which says that, average action changes not only because of the direct change in individual best responses (first sum inside the brackets), but also because of the interactive change (second sum inside brackets) in the behavior of all agents, of the same sign ($H_{ab} \geq 0$). The multiplier effect through shocks works in a similar fashion. The size of the social multiplier depends on the slope of the best response functions with respect to average choice. If this slope gets close to unity, one can generate arbitrarily large social multiplier effects. This is a serious concern, as argued in Glaeser, Sacerdote, and Scheinkman (2003), since it is common practice in empirical work in the social sciences to infer individual behavior from aggregate data.

Jovanovic (1987) is a critique along the same lines. He shows that any amount of aggregate variation can be generated by 'unique' equilibria of games where shocks are independent across agents. He argues that this is in stark contrast to standard macroeconomic 'aggregate shocks' methodology, either with intrinsic aggregate shocks (see Kydland and Prescott (1982)) or with extrinsic aggregate shocks (see Cass and Shell (1983)). Hence the modeling choice, just on theoretical grounds, in favor of aggregate shocks approach rather than the local interactions approach is moot.

Bisin, Horst and Özgür (2006) show through their pure conformity economies that the presence of local interactions is not sufficient for the existence of social multiplier effects. Consequently, social multiplier effects might not be robust to changes in the nature of interactions. When agents are rational and interact locally, multiplier effects may disappear and that the magnitude of social multipliers (in both static and dynamic settings) depends on the amount of local information people possess about the types of other individuals. For an interesting survey on the existence of social multipliers and their dependence on the nature of interactions see Burke (2008).

Jovanovic (1987) argues that no model is perfect and left-out variables (unobserved) might appear as aggregate shocks. A related point is in Glaeser and Scheinkman (2003), who argue that in the presence of unobserved heterogeneity, it may be impossible to distinguish between a large multiplier and multiple equilibria. It might be that either (i) within the same parameter regime, small differences in fundamentals across areas are amplified by strong social multiplier effects; or (ii) there are unaccounted influences (latent variables) that affect the aggregates in different ways in two different geographical areas.

One last important remark for this section is that, in the presence of multiple equilibria, the general framework of structural inference as presented in Koopmans (1949) (see also Koopmans and Reiersøl (1950)) is inadequate since it assumes that once the exogenous data is specified, the endogenous variables can be uniquely determined. Jovanovic (1989) warns that the set of distributions on observable outcomes that are consistent with a given structure can be quite large and consequently the model might be hard (if not impossible) to identify. For recent progress on this issue in the literature, see Bisin et al. (2009) and Galichon and Henry (2009).

A different kind of identification problem arises when one asks the question: Does one observe similar behavior by people within a group due to local interaction or due to the fact that people with similar characteristics choose to be part of the same group? (see e.g., Manski (1993)). This is an incredibly important question that permeates the social sciences. I will talk a little about how recent advances in the dynamic theory of local interactions might help in Section 3.6

2.4 Discrete choice models

There exists a number of social phenomena for which the discrete choice framework has been considered as a natural outlet, e.g., teenage pregnancy, technology adoption decisions, decision to enter or exit a market, staying in or dropping out of school, etc. Moreover, data sets rich in quantitative individual information did not exist before, and data on individual behavior have generally been categorized in a coarse yes-no, 0-1 fashion. Although this is changing now due to the advances in survey and collection technologies and availability of micro-level data, discrete choice methodology is widely used. For all these reasons, I will present two of the mostly cited studies in the literature on social interactions with discrete choice, namely Brock and Durlauf (2001) and Glaeser, Sacerdote, and Scheinkman (1996).

Brock and Durlauf (2001a)

Brock and Durlauf's (BD henceforth) framework is the basic machinery behind many models of binary choice with social interactions in the literature. I follow here their journal article closely although they present their theoretical and econometric methods in numerous other review and survey articles, e.g., Brock and Durlauf (2001b, 2002, 2007), Durlauf (1997, 2004, 2008). Their contribution is a framework to study economies with **global** (mean-field) **interactions** where agents interact through the population mean action. Their model being mathematically equivalent to logistic models of discrete choice (Blume (1993), Brock (1993)) is easily amenable to econometric analysis using the tools of the logistic models (see McFadden (1984) for the latter). This being a survey of theoretical contributions, I will not go into the details of their econometric analysis, although I will provide references for readers interested in further reading.

BD consider economies with a finite number of agents, each making a one-time choice x^a (simultaneously) from the common binary choice set $X = \{-1, 1\}$. Let $x := (x^b)_{b\in\mathbb{A}}$ and $x^{-a} := (x^b)_{b \neq a}$. Agent a's preferences are represented by

$$V(x^a) = u(x^a) + S(x^a, \mu^a(x^{-a})) + \theta(x^a)$$

where u is what they call the *private utility*, S the *social utility*, and θ a random utility term, i.i.d. across agents whose realization is known to agent a at the time of his decision. Let $m^{a,b} := E^a\,[x^b]$ be the expected value of agent b's choice with respect to agent a's subjective belief μ^a and $\bar{m}^a := (|\mathbb{A}| - 1)^{-1}\sum_{b\neq a} m^{a,b}$ be the average expected choice among agents other than a with respect to a's subjective belief of their likelihood. They impose a particular form of strategic complementarity on social utility, i.e.,

$$\frac{\partial^2 S(x^a, \bar{m}^a)}{\partial x^a \partial \bar{m}^a} = J > 0$$

which means that the marginal social utility to agent a's of choosing any action increases by an increase in the average expected action (from his point of view) in the rest of the population. They consider two classes of preferences depending on their parametric choice of the social utility. First, what they call the *proportional spillovers* case

$$S(x^a, \bar{m}^a) = Jx^a\bar{m}^a$$

and second, the *pure conformity* case (as in Akerlof (1997) and Bernheim (1994))

$$S(x^a, \bar{m}^a) = -\frac{J}{2}(x^a - \bar{m}^a)^2$$

Finally, they assume that the error terms $\theta(-1)$ and $\theta(1)$ are independent and extreme-value distributed, so that the differences are logistically distributed

$$Prob(\theta(-1) - \theta(1) \leq x) = \frac{1}{1 + exp(-\beta x)}$$

Equilibrium analysis. They first study the equilibrium of the model under the proportional spillovers assumption and claim later that the same results apply under the pure conformity case. They argue that it is well known that under the extreme values hypothesis for $\theta(x^a)$, x^a will obey

$$Prob(x^a) = \frac{\exp\left(\beta(u(x^a) + Jx^a\bar{m}^a)\right)}{\sum_{\hat{x}^a \in \{-1,1\}} \exp\left(\beta(u(\hat{x}^a) + J\hat{x}^a\bar{m}^a)\right)}$$

As $\beta \to \infty$, the effect of the error term on agent a's choice vanishes; as $\beta \to 0$, the above probability goes to .5 regardless of anything else. Under the i.i.d assumption, the joint probability of the choice profile can be written

$$Prob(x) = \frac{\exp\left(\beta \sum_{a \in \mathbb{A}} (u(x^a) + Jx^a\bar{m}^a)\right)}{\Pi_{a \in \mathbb{A}} \sum_{\hat{x}^a \in \{-1,1\}} \exp\left(\beta \sum_{a \in \mathbb{A}} (u(\hat{x}^a) + J\hat{x}^a\bar{m}^a)\right)}$$ [21]

Since choices are binary, one can write $u(x^a) = hx^a + k$ where h and k are chosen such that $k + k = u(1)$ and $-h + k = u(-1)$ and this way linearize the expression of the joint distribution above to get

$$\begin{aligned} E(x^a) = {} & 1 \cdot \frac{\exp\left(\beta h + \beta J(|\mathbb{A}| - 1)^{-1} \sum_{b \neq a} m^{a,b}\right)}{\exp\left(\beta h + \beta J(|\mathbb{A}| - 1)^{-1} \sum_{b \neq a} m^{a,b}\right) + \exp\left(-\beta h - \beta J(|\mathbb{A}| - 1)^{-1} \sum_{b \neq a} m^{d,b}\right)} \\ & -1 \cdot \frac{\exp\left(\beta h + \beta J(|\mathbb{A}| - 1)^{-1} \sum_{b \neq a} m^{a,b}\right)}{\exp\left(\beta h + \beta J(|\mathbb{A}| - 1)^{-1} \sum_{b \neq a} m^{a,b}\right) + \exp\left(-\beta h - \beta J(|\mathbb{A}| - 1)^{-1} \sum_{b \neq a} m^{a,b}\right)} \\ = {} & \tanh\left(\beta h + \beta J(|\mathbb{A}| - 1)^{-1} \sum_{b \neq a} m^{a,b}\right). \end{aligned} \tag{14}$$

[21] BD argue that their structure is equivalent to the mean field version of the Curie-Weiss model of statistical mechanics, presented in Ellis (1985).

Finally, impose rational expectations, i.e., for all $a, b \in \mathbb{A}$, $m^{a,b} = E(x^b)$. Since the tanh function is continuous and the support of choices is $\{-1, 1\}^{\mathbb{A}}$, an **equilibrium** exists, in particular it is unique if $\beta J < 1$, i.e.,

$$m^* = \tanh\left(\beta h + \beta J m^*\right) \tag{15}$$

In the rest of the paper, they study the behavior of the above fixed point equation under different regimes for the parameters. In particular, they give conditions under which there are multiple equilibria

Proposition 6 *(i) If $\beta J > 1$ and $h = 0$, there exist three roots: one positive, one equal to zero, one negative.*

(ii) If $\beta J > 1$ and $h \neq 0$, there exists a threshold H such that

(a) *for $|\beta h| < H$, there exist three roots, one of which has the same sign as h, the others possessing opposite sign;*

(b) *for $|\beta h| > H$, there exists a unique root with the same sign as h.*

Letting m^*_- be the mean choice level in which the largest percentage of agents choose -1, m^*_+ as the one where they choose $+1$, and m^* as the root between the two, they can characterize the limiting percentage of positive and negative choices as a function of the parameters β, h, and J. They then argue that if one reinterprets the equation (15) as a difference equation with m_t as a function of m_{t-1}, one can show that, if there is a unique fixed point to that equation, that fixed point is locally stable. However, if there are three roots, the fixed points m^*_- and m^*_+ are locally stable but the third one is locally unstable. For the rest, they focus on stable equilibria solely.

Since for any equilibrium, with positive probability there are agents who like the other equilibrium better and those who like the current one better, they cannot Pareto rank equilibria ex-post. However, using the ex-ante symmetry of the agents, they show that when $h > 0$ (< 0), the equilibrium associated with m^*_+ (m^*_-) gives a higher level of expected utility than the one associated with m^*_- (m^*_+). Moreover, when $h = 0$, the two equilibria give the same level of expected utility. Note that their analysis so far was based on expected average choice and expected individual choices. However, they show that as the economy gets large ($|\mathcal{A}| \to \infty$), the sample average population choice weakly converges to the expected population choice.

Local Interactions. BD argue that their global interaction model is nestled into a class of local interaction models where each agent interacts directly with only a finite number of others in the population. In other words, global interaction models are simply special cases of local interaction models.[22] They study a symmetric local interaction

[22] I discuss this issue carefully in dynamic environments in Section 3.3. When the population is finite, the claim is true. When the population is infinite, one should take care of some mathematical difficulties. Please see Section 3.3 for more details. Also see Sec 2.2 for a similar analysis in static models of continuous choice.

model where each neighborhood has the same size and each individual puts equal weights on his neighbors' choices. They find that

Theorem 7 *Any equilibrium expected individual and average choice level m for the global interactions model is also an equilibrium expected individual and average choice in a homogeneous local interactions model.*

To be clear, they add that local interactions model being more general, can exhibit a variety of other equilibria that one does not obtain in the global case.

Multinomial Choice. Concerned with the limitations of the binary choice setting in theoretical and econometric studies, BD extend their model to a multiple discrete choice environment; see Brock and Durlauf (2002). They find similar existence and multiplicity results and provide conditions under which the interactions effects can be identified.

Social Planner's Problem. One would expect a planner to make choices on behalf of the population to maximize the sum of individual utilities, as it is done in economics. Unfortunately, the sum of extreme-value distributed random variables is not extreme-value distributed. To resolve this issue, BD assume that the error term for the planner's problem, $\theta(x)$ is itself independent and extreme-value distributed across all possible configurations of x. Given this assumption however, it is the planner's error term that will determine x rather than the original individual terms. BD remark that one can interpret this as noise in planner's ability to calculate tradeoffs between individual utilities. They look at the limit behavior of the joint law for planner's allocation under proportional spillovers and conformity effects. They find that under the first, equilibria are inefficient and can be Pareto ranked. Under the second though, equilibrium m^* with the same signs as h is efficient. BD argue that this is due to the fact that utility specification under pure conformity punishes large deviations from the mean in a harsher way than the proportional spillovers case does.

Finally, BD discuss some extensions of their model where social utility might depend on past society behavior, might be asymmetric around the mean level, and private utility might be heterogeneous. Most importantly, they study **identification** of their model's parameters, provide sufficient conditions for identification and discuss why their conclusions are different than the ones in Manski's (1993) analysis of identification in linear models with social interactions. Interested reader should look at their section 6. Moreover, for good reviews of identification of social interactions in general, see Blume et al. (2010, chapter 23), Blume and Durlauf (2005), Brock and Durlauf (2007), Graham (2010, chapter 29), and Manski (1993, 2007).

Glaeser, Sacerdote, and Scheinkman (1996)

Glaeser, Sacerdote, and Scheinkman (GSS henceforth) are after an explanation for the excess variation in crime rates across time and geography relative to the observable heterogeneity in individual and area characteristics. To that end, they build a model of local interactions and empirically test it using data on crime rates across US provided by FBI (six time points between 1970 and 1994), and crime rates across New York City, by precinct, from the 1990 Census. They find that less than 30% of variation in cross-city or cross-precinct crime rates can be explained by observable differences in local area attributes. Moreover, they argue that positive covariance across agents' decisions is the only explanation for the discrepancy between the variance in crime rates observed and the variance predicted by local characteristics (*social multiplier*). They then show that their empirical findings are consistent with the existence of such local interactions. Finally, they build an interaction index (strength of local interaction) for different categories of crime and show that the value of the index is decreasing in the severity of crime.

This being a theory survey, I will present their baseline model which is inspired by the voter models in statistical mechanics. There are $2n+1$ agents, $\mathbb{A} = \{-n, \ldots, 0, \ldots, n\}$, placed on a circle. Common action set is $X = \{0, 1\}$, 1 denoting committing a crime. The interaction structure is one-sided, i.e., $N(a) = a - 1$. Type set is $\Theta = \{0, 1, 2\}$. Type 1 and 0 agents are fixed. They are *criminal* and *non-criminal* types, respectively. Their choices are their types. Type 2 agents are *marginals* who are affected by the choice of their neighbors. Their choices are equal to the choices of their neighbors. The probabilities of being of type 0 and 1 are p_0 and p_1 respectively and are i.i.d across agents. The proportion of agents who are of fixed types in a city is $\pi = p_0 + p_1$.

Conditional on the realization and perfect observation of the types in the economy, there is a unique Nash equilibrium: one observes sequences of 1s and 0s of varying sizes depending on the realization of fixed agents' locations. Then, each agent's action x^a can be thought of as a binary random variable and the process $\{x^a, -\infty < a < \infty\}$ as stationary, with expected value $p := p_1/(p_0 + p_1)$. GSS argue that the presence of fixed types create enough mixing in the system so that a central limit behavior arises.[23] Let

$$S_n := \sum_{|a| \le n} \left(\frac{x^a - p}{2n+1} \right)$$

be the empirical average of the deviations from the mean crime rate for a sample of $2n + 1$ agents. Then, as the population gets large, we have

$$\begin{aligned} \lim_{n\to\infty} \mathbb{E}[(S_n\sqrt{2n+1})^2] &= \lim_{n\to\infty} (2n+1)\mathbb{E}\left[S_n^2\right] \\ &= \mathrm{var}(x^0) + 2\lim_{n\to\infty} \sum_{a=1}^{n} \mathrm{cov}\,(x^0, x^a) \end{aligned} \tag{16}$$

[23] Choices of any two agents $a > b$ are independent conditional on the existence of a fixed type between them. The probability of that type nonexisting goes to zero exponentially as $b - a \to \infty$. Consequently, the process $\{x^a, -\infty < a < \infty\}$ satisfies a *strong mixing* condition with exponentially declining bounds and central limit theorem obtains. See for example Fristedt and Gray (1997), p. 563.

The choices of 0 and a are perfectly correlated conditional on the event that there does not exist a fixed type in the segment $[1, a]$. The probability of this event is $(1-p_0-p_1)^a$. If the complement of that event occurs, the covariance between these two agents is zero since they become independent. Since x^0 follows a binomial process, its variance is $\text{var}(x^0) = p(1-p)$. Hence, (16) can be written as

$$\begin{aligned}\text{var}(x^0) + 2\lim_{n\to\infty}\sum_{a=1}^{n}\text{cov}(x^0, x^a) &= p(1-p) + 2\lim_{n\to\infty}\sum_{a=1}^{n} p(1-p)(1-p_0-p_1)^a \\ &= p(1-p) + 2p(1-p)\frac{(1-p_0-p_1)}{(p_0+p_1)} \\ &= p(1-p)\frac{(2-\pi)}{\pi} =: \sigma^2\end{aligned}$$

Since $\pi > 0$, $0 < \sigma^2 < \infty$ and central limit behavior obtains

$$S_n\sqrt{2n+1} \to N(0, \sigma^2)$$

and they have a very clean expression of how the average crime rates will be distributed in a largely populated area. They interpret $(2-\pi)/\pi$ as the *degree of imitation*. They estimate this latter using their data to measure the proportion of the population that is immune to social influences, π, which in turn provides an index of the degree of social interaction across cities and across crimes.

GSS also provide a dynamic extension of their framework with two-sided interactions $N(a) = \{a-1, a+1\}$, in order to motivate their analysis of the variance of the distribution of crime as the stationary distribution of a myopic infinite horizon dynamic local interaction process. At time $t = 0$, each agent chooses the action 1 independently with probability $p > 0$. Then, each agent is determined either to be "frozen" or not with probability $\pi > 0$. Frozen agents are stuck in a set S with their time 0 choices. Pick an agent $a \notin S$. Associated with a is an independent Poisson process with mean time 1. At each arrival, a will choose from among the actions of his neighbors with equal probability. This defines the stochastic process $\{x_t^a\}_{a\in\mathbb{A}}$. They show that for given parameters (p, π), for any n, there exists a limit probability measure $\mu_n(p, \pi)$ defined over choices $\{x^a : |a| \leq n\}$. Moreover, for $m > n$, $\mu_m(p, \pi)$ agrees with $\mu_n(p, \pi)$ on $\{x^a : |a| \leq n\}$.

GSS then consider the normalized sum $1/\sqrt{2n+1}\sum_{|a|\leq n}(x^a - p)$ as before. They show that the presence of frozen agents, as before, provides enough mixing to obtain central limit behavior for the normalized sum, and the asymptotic qualitative behavior of the variance matrix is exactly as in the model in the text.

3. DYNAMIC MODELS

The theoretical literature studying local interactions is not yet fully integrated into the standard dynamic economic analysis of equilibrium. Economists using the tools of the mainstream equilibrium analysis have predominantly built static models of local interactions until very recently.[24] The reason for this choice is the complexities involved in dynamic models with forward looking agents forming rational expectations: interaction structures embody complicated non-convexities to render standard fixed point arguments invalid (see Durlauf (1997)).

In many social phenomena of economic significance, static modeling leads to misspecification or underestimation of social effects. For example, Binder and Pesaran (2001) study life-cycle consumption of agents who interact globally, through average consumption within local group they belong to. They consider conformism, altruism, and jealousy as forms of interaction and conclude that analyzing decisions of agents in static rather than dynamic settings is misleading. Moreover, they argue that dynamic social interactions coupled with habit formation or prudence might help solve the excess smoothness and excess sensitivity of consumption puzzles.

Recent empirical literature shifted attention to dynamic models, e.g., Kremer and Levy (2008) on the dynamically persistent detrimental effect of having drinking roommates on student GPAs; Carrell, Fullerton, and West (2009) on persistent group effects among randomly assigned students at the United States Air Force Academy; Cutler and Glaeser (2007) on the dynamic effects of smoking bans in the work place; DeCicca, Kenkel, and Mathios (2008) on the effect of cigarette taxes on smoking initiation and cessation cycles.

The theoretical counterpart of this body of work is in its infancy. There is a ton of questions to study and proper modeling to be done. In this section, I will first touch upon the early models of interactions with myopic dynamics. Then, I will present and study economies with forward looking rational agents and the implied rational expectations dynamics. As I mentioned in the Introduction and since I know more about them, I will focus my attention more on the latter, forward looking rational expectations economies.

3.1 Baseline dynamic model

The physical environment is the same as in the baseline model of Section 2.1 with the following additions: evolution of preferences, neighborhood structure, and individual and reference group characteristics. Similar to before, our theoretical object of study is a class of local interaction economies, represented by the tuple $\mathcal{E} = (\mathbb{A}, X, \Theta, N, P, u, \beta, T)$.

[24] The literature on dynamics modeled as population games and the later developed local interaction games with adaptive, myopically best-responding agents is discussed in Section 3.5.1.

Interaction horizon is represented by T and can be finite or infinite. $\beta > 0$ is the common discount factor agents use to discount future utilities. With the dynamic specification, one can allow for interactions in a 'changing environment', that is

$$N : \mathbb{A} \times \{1, 2, \ldots, T\} \to 2^{\mathbb{A}}$$

meaning that the reference group $N_t(a)$ of agent a can change from one period to another. It is important to notice that even then, this is not about group formation but about a commonly known and exogenously given law that governs the changes in the environment of agents.[25]

Given the neighborhood structure, the contemporaneous preferences of an agent $a \in \mathbb{A}$ are represented by a **utility function** u^a of the form

$$\left(x_{t-1}^a, x_t^a, \{x_t^b\}_{b \in N_t(a)}, \theta_t^a, p(x_t)\right) \to u^a\left(x_{t-1}^a, x_t^a, \{x_t^b\}_{b \in N_t(a)}, \theta_t^a, p(x_t)\right)$$

Last period choice x_{t-1}^a is introduced as an argument to study endogenous preference formation (e.g., habits, addiction, norms) due to social interactions. As it is clear from the representation, the type of an agent a is a stochastic process. The most common assumption is to assume that it is i.i.d across agents and time. In principal, one can allow for intertemporal exogenous persistence, in which case the information structure becomes very important.

3.2 Rational forward-looking interactions

This body of work argues that the study of equilibrium dynamics of economies with local interactions, by allowing for rational expectations of forward looking agents, may elucidate several important aspects of social interactions. An example of a specific socio-economic environment might be helpful to illustrate the usefulness of the proper forward looking equilibrium analysis of dynamic economies in the presence of local interactions[26]: Consider a teenager evaluating the opportunity of dropping out of high school. His decision will depend on the conditions of the labor market, and in particular on the relevant wage differentials, which requires him to form expectations about the wage and labor conditions he will face if he graduates from high school. The teenager's decision might depend also on the school attendance of a restricted circle of friends and acquaintances: dropping-out is generally made simpler if one's friends also drop-out (local interactions). But as the decision of dropping out depends on the teenager's expectations of the wage differential, it will also in part depend on his consideration of the possibility that, for instance, while his friends have not yet dropped out of

[25] I will mention a few things on group formation along the lines of the selection and sorting in Section 4

[26] The example comes from Bisin, Horst, and Özgür (2006).

school, they soon will, perhaps even motivated by his own decision of dropping out. Similarly, our teenager might decide to stay in school even if most of his friends dropped out, if he has reason to expect their decision to be soon reversed. The teenager will form expectations about his friends' future behavior as well as about the future wage rate.

In the rest of this section, I will present two recent models of local interactions with forward looking rational agents, namely Bisin, Horst and Özgür (2006) and Bisin and Özgür (2010). They are both important methodological contributions in the direction of integrating local interactions models into the standard dynamic economic analysis of equilibrium. I presented BHÖ's study of static economies with local interactions in Section 2.2. Here I will present their analysis of infinite horizon economies with local interactions.

Bisin, Horst and Özgür (2006)

BHÖ study infinite-horizon economies with local interactions and with infinitely-lived agents. While agents may interact locally, they are forward looking, and their choices are optimally based on the past actions of the agents in their neighborhood, as well as on their anticipation of the future actions of their neighbors. Their major contributions might be summarized as

(i) This is the first formal study in the literature, of rational expectations equilibria of infinite horizon economies with local interactions. They provide conditions under which such economies have rational expectations equilibria which depend in a Lipschitz continuous manner on the parameters. They show that such conditions impose an appropriate bound on the strength of the interactions across agents.

(ii) For a class of dynamic economies with *Conformity Preferences* (see e.g., Akerlof (1997), Brock and Durlauf (2001a), Bernheim (1994)), they consider local as well as global (e.g., global externalities, general equilibrium effects) equilibrium dynamics and characterize long run behavior of those joint processes. Moreover, they show formally that when agents have rational expectations, the effect of the local conformity component of their preferences on their equilibrium actions is reduced significantly with respect to the case in which agents are myopic.

Formally, BHÖ study the following class of economies: a countably infinite number of agents $\mathbb{A} = \mathbb{Z}$, common compact and convex action and type spaces X and Θ. Let $\mathbf{X}^0 := \{x = (x^a)_{a \geq 0}\}$. Each agent $a \in \mathbb{A}$ interacts with his immediate neighbor $N(a) = a + 1$ only (*local interactions*). Information is incomplete, that is, each agent observes only his own type and the history of past choices in the economy before making a choice[27] They focus attention on Markov perfect equilibrium in pure strategies as the equilibrium

[27] BHÖ argue that this is not restrictive and that all the results they obtain apply in a straightforward fashion to the complete information economies.

concept.[28] Each agent $a \in \mathbb{A}$ believes that everyone else in the economy at any period t makes choices according to a given choice function $g : \mathbf{X^0} \times \Theta \to X$ in the sense that

$$x_t^a = g\left(T^a x_{t-1}, \theta_t^a\right) \quad \text{where} \quad T^a x_{t-1} = \{x_{t-1}^b\}_{b \geq a}.$$

Denote by $\pi_g(T^a\, x_{t-1},\, \theta_t^a)$ the conditional law of the action x_t^a, given the previous configuration x_{t-1}. This latter induces a Feller kernel (a law of motion) for the system in the sense that

$$\Pi_g(x; \cdot) := \prod_{a=1}^{\infty} \pi_g(T^a x; \cdot). \tag{17}$$

The kernel Π_g describes the stochastic evolution of the process of individual states $\left\{(x_t^a)_{a>0}\right\}_{t\in\mathbb{N}}$. In this case, for any initial configuration of individual states $x \in \mathbf{X^0}$ and for each initial type θ_1^0, agent 0's optimization problem is given by

$$\max_{\{x_t^0\}_{t\in\mathbb{N}}} \left\{ \int u(x_1^0, x^0, x_1^1, \theta_1^0)\pi_g(Tx; dx^1) + \sum_{t\geq 2} \beta^{t-1} \int u(x_t^0, x_{t-1}^0, x_t^1, \theta_t^0)\Pi_g^t(Tx; dx_t)\nu(d\theta_t^0) \right\} \tag{18}$$

The value function associated with this dynamic choice problem is defined by the fixed point of the functional equation

$$\begin{aligned} V_g(x_{t-1}, \theta_t^0) = V_g(x_{t-1}^0,\, Tx_{t-1}, \theta_t^0) = \max_{x_t^0 \in X} \Bigg\{ &\int u(x_{t-1}^0, x_t^0, y_t^1, \theta_t^0)\; \pi_g(Tx_{t-1}; dy_t^1) \\ &+ \beta \int_{\mathbf{X}^0 \times \Theta} V_g(x_t^0, \hat{x}_t, \theta^1)\Pi_g(Tx_{t-1}; d\hat{x}_t)\nu(d\theta^1) \Bigg\} \end{aligned} \tag{19}$$

and the maximizer of this problem is denoted

$$\begin{aligned} \hat{g}_g\left(x_{t-1}, \theta_t^0\right) = \arg\max_{x_t^0 \in X} \Bigg\{ &\int u(x_{t-1}^0, x_t^0, y_t, \theta_t^0)\; \pi_g(Tx_{t-1}; dy_t) \\ &+ \beta \int V_g(x_t^0, \hat{x}_t, \theta^1)\Pi_g(Tx_{t-1}; d\hat{x}_t)\nu(d\theta^1) \Bigg\}. \end{aligned} \tag{20}$$

Finally, what they mean by *equilibrium* is stated in the following

Definition 7 *A symmetric Markov perfect equilibrium of a dynamic economy with forward looking and locally interacting agents is a map* $g^* : \mathbf{X^0} \times \Theta \to X$ *such that*

[28] This is for reasons of parsimony and clarity of the message delivered. Moreover, by choosing to focus on MPEs, they actually make their task more difficult since there are no generally accepted conditions that guarantee the existence of pure strategy MPEs in any game. More generally, one can of course, consider more sophisticated punishment strategies, and coordination devices to achieve particular behaviors.

$$g^*\left(x_{t-1}, \theta_t^0\right) = arg\max_{x_t^0 \in X} \left\{ \int u(x_{t-1}^0, x_t^0, y_t, \theta_t^0)\ \pi_{g^*}(Tx_{t-1}; dy_t) + \beta \int V_{g^*}(x_t^0, \hat{x}_t, \theta^1) \Pi_{g^*}(Tx_{t-1}; d\hat{x}_t) \nu(d\theta^1) \right\}. \tag{21}$$

BHÖ establish a series of results on the existence and the convergence of the equilibrium process. Such results require conditions on the policy function, and hence are not directly formulated as conditions on the fundamentals of the economy. They then introduce an economy with conformity preferences which is amenable to study. For this economy they show that their general conditions are satisfied, and hence are not vacuous.

In order to state a general existence result for equilibria in dynamic random economies with forward looking interacting agents, they introduce the notion of a **correlation pattern**.

Definition 8 *For $C > 0$, let*

$$L_+^C := \left\{ \mathbf{c} = (c_a)_{a \in \mathbb{N}} : c_a \geq 0, \sum_{a \in \mathbb{A}} c_a \leq C \right\}$$

denote the class of all non-negative sequences whose sum is bounded from above by C. A sequence $\mathbf{c} \in L_+^C$ will be called a correlation pattern with total impact C.
Each correlation pattern $\mathbf{c} \in L_+^C$ gives rise to a metric

$$d_{\mathbf{c}}(x, y) := \sum_{a \in \mathbb{N}} c_a |x^a - y^a|$$

that induces the product topology on $\mathbf{X^0}$. Thus, $(d_{\mathbf{c}}, \mathbf{X^0})$ is a compact metric space. In particular, the class

$$\text{Lip}_{\mathbf{c}}^C := \{ f : \mathbf{X}^0 \to \mathbb{R} : |f(x) - f(y)| \leq d_{\mathbf{c}}(x, y) \}$$

of all functions $f : \mathbf{X}^0 \to \mathbb{R}$ which are Lipschitz continuous with constant 1 with respect to the metric $d_{\mathbf{c}}$ is compact in the topology of uniform convergence.

The constant c_a may be viewed as a measure for the total impact the current action x^a of the agent $a \geq 0$ has on the optimal action of agent $0 \in \mathbb{A}$. Since $C < \infty$, we have $\lim_{a \to \infty} c_a = 0$. Thus, the impact of an agent $a \in \mathbb{A}$ on the agent $0 \in \mathbb{A}$ tends to zero as $a \to \infty$. In this sense they consider *economies with weak social interactions*. The quantity C provides an upper bound for the total impact of the configuration $x = (x^a)_{a \geq 0}$ on the current choice of the agent $0 \in \mathbb{A}$. Given this structure, a general existence result for symmetric Markov perfect equilibria in dynamic economies with local interaction is given in the following

Theorem 8 (Existence and Lipschitz continuity) *Assume that there exists $C < \infty$ such that the following holds:*

(i) *For any $\mathbf{c} \in L_+^C$, for all $\theta^0 \in \Theta$ and for each choice function $g(\cdot, \theta^0) \in \text{Lip}_{\mathbf{c}}^C$, there exists $F(\mathbf{c}) \in L_+^C$ such that the unique policy function $\hat{g}_g(\cdot, \theta^0)$ which solves (20), is Lipschitz continuous with respect to the metric $d_{F(\mathbf{c})}$ uniformly in $\theta^0 \in \Theta$.*

(ii) The map $F : L_+^C \to L_+^C$ *is continuous.*

(iii) *We have* $\lim_{n\to\infty} \| \hat{g}_{gn}(\cdot, \theta^0) - \hat{g}_g(\cdot, \theta^0)\|_\infty = 0$ *if* $\lim_{n\to\infty} \| g_n - g\|_\infty = 0$.

Then the dynamic economy with local interactions has a symmetric Markov perfect equilibrium g^* and the function $g^*(\cdot, \theta^0)$ is Lipschitz continuous uniformly in θ^0.

Once the existence of an MPE is obtained, a natural question to ask is how the economy behaves in the long run given that individuals make choices according to the choice function whose existence it is shown. To that effect, BHÖ study the limit properties of the t-fold iteration of the stochastic kernel $\Pi_{g^*}(\mathbf{x}; \cdot)$. To that end, they introduce the vector $r^* = (r_a^*)_{a\in\mathbb{A}}$ defined as

$$r_a^* := sup\{\| \pi_{g^*}(x; \cdot) - \pi_{g^*}(y; \cdot) \|: x = y \text{ off } a\}. \tag{22}$$

Here, $\| \pi_{g^*}(x; \cdot) - \pi_{g^*}(y; \cdot) \|$ denotes the total variation of the signed measure $\pi_{g^*}(x; \cdot) - \pi_{g^*}(y; \cdot)$, and $x = y$ off a means that $x^b = y^b$ for all $b \neq a$. The next theorem gives sufficient conditions for convergence of the equilibrium process to a steady state. Its proof follows from a fundamental convergence theorem by Vasserstein (1969).

Theorem 9 (Ergodicity) *If $\sum_{a\in\mathbb{A}} r_{g^*}^a < 1$, then there exists a unique probability measure μ^* on the infinite configuration space $\mathbf{X}$ such that, for any initial configuration $\mathbf{x} \in \mathbf{X}$, the sequence $\Pi_{g^*}^t(\mathbf{x}; \cdot)$ converges to μ^* in the topology of weak convergence for probability measures.*

Example 4 (Conformity Economies) *These are dynamic extensions of economies with local interactions that we saw in example 2. Let $X = \Theta = [-1,1]$, and assume that $\mathbb{E}\theta_t^0 = 0$, and that an agent $a \in \mathbb{A}$ only observes his own type θ^a. If the instantaneous utility function takes the quadratic form*

$$u(x_{t-1}^a, x_t^a, x_t^{a+1}, \theta_t^a) = -\alpha_1(x_{t-1}^a - x_t^a)^2 - \alpha_2(\theta_t^a - x_t^a)^2 - \alpha_3(x_t^{a+1} - x_t^a)^2 \tag{23}$$

for positive constants α_1, α_2 and α_3, then BHÖ show that the hypotheses of Theorem 8 are satisfied hence the economy has a symmetric Markov perfect equilibrium g^*. Moreover, the policy function g^* can be chosen to be of the linear form

$$g^*(x, \theta^0) = c_0^* x^0 + \gamma\theta^0 + \sum_{b\geq 1} c_b^* x^b$$

for some positive sequence $\mathbf{c}^* = (c_a^*)_{a\geq 0}$ and some constant $\gamma > 0$. For the same class of economies, one can also show convergence to a unique steady state. Consider the representation

$$g^*(x;\theta^0) = c_0^* x^0 + \gamma\theta^0 + \sum_{a\geq 1} c_a^* x^a.$$

of the policy function g^*. For any two configurations $x, y \in \mathbf{X^0}$ which differ only at site $a \in \mathbb{A}$ we have

$$|g^*(x,\theta^0) - g^*(y,\theta^0)| \leq c_a^* |x^a - y^a|,$$

Thus, assuming that the taste shocks are uniformly distributed on $[-1,1]$ we obtain

$$|\pi_{g^*}(x;A) - \pi_{g^*}(y;A)| \leq 2c_a^*$$

for all $A \in \mathcal{B}([-1,1])$, and so $\sum_{a\geq 0} r_{g^*}^a < 1$ if $\sum_{a\geq 0} c_a^* < \frac{1}{2}$. Hence the conditions of Theorem 9 are satisfied, which means that we obtain convergence to a steady state whenever α_1 is big enough and if α_3 is small enough, i.e., if the interaction between different agents is not too strong.

I mentioned in the beginning of this section that BHÖ also study local and global equilibrium dynamics together. I reserved this for Section 3.3. Finally, for their comparison of equilibria generated by myopic and forward looking behavior, see Section 3.5.2

Bisin and Özgür (2010)

Bisin and Özgür (BÖ henceforth) take up the study of dynamic economies from where they left and fill out many of the gaps they left for future research in Bisin, Horst, and Özgür (2006). Their major contribution is twofold:

(i) Existence, uniqueness, parametric continuity, ergodicity, and welfare properties of equilibria of dynamic conformity economies with general interaction structures.

(ii) Most importantly, the **identification** of local interaction effects (from hidden correlated effects) at the population, exploiting in a novel way the dynamic equilibrium behavior.

BÖ focus their attention on economies with **conformity preferences**. These are environments in which each agent's preferences incorporate the desire to conform to the choices of agents in his reference group. They argue that in many relevant social phenomena, in fact, the effects of preferences for conformity are amplified by the presence of limits to the reversibility of dynamic choices. This is of course the case for smoking, alcohol abuse and other risky teen behavior, which are hard to reverse because they might lead to chemical addictions. In other instances, while addiction per se is not at issue, nonetheless behavioral choices are hardly freely reversible because of various social and economic constraints, as is the case, for instance, of engaging in criminal activity. Finally, exogenous and predictable changes in the composition of groups, as e.g., in the case of school peers at the end of a school cycle, introduce important non-stationarities in the agents' choice. These non-stationarity also call for a formal analysis of dynamic social interactions. In order to provide a clean and simple analysis of dynamic social interactions in a conformity economy, they impose strong(er than required) but natural assumptions. Namely

1. Time is discrete and is denoted by $t = 1, \ldots, K$. They allow both for infinite economies ($K = \infty$) and economies with an end period ($K < \infty$).
2. Let $\mathbb{A} := \mathbb{Z}$ represent a general *social space*. Each agent interacts with his immediate neighbors, i.e., for all $a \in \mathbb{A}$, $N(a) := \{a - 1, a + 1\}$.[29]
3. The contemporaneous preferences of an agent $a \in \mathbb{A}$ are represented by the utility function

$$u(x_{t-1}^a, x_t^a, x_t^{a+1}, x_t^{a-1}, \theta_t^a) := -\alpha_1(x_{t-1}^a - x_t^a)^2 - \alpha_2(\theta_t^a - x_t^a)^2 \\ -\alpha_3(x_t^{a-1} - x_t^a)^2 - \alpha_3(x_t^{a+1} - x_t^a)^2$$

where α_1, α_2, and α_3, are positive constants.

4. Let $X = \Theta = [\underline{x}, \bar{x}] \subset \mathbb{R}$, where $\underline{x} < \bar{x}$, $E[\theta] = \int \theta dv =: \bar{\theta} \in (\underline{x}, \bar{x})$.

Let $\mathbf{X} := \{x = (x^a)_{a \in \mathbb{A}} : x^a \in X\}$ and $\Theta := \{(\theta^a)_{a \in \mathbb{A}} : \theta^a \in \Theta\}$. The timing of the type process and agents' choices are as in Bisin, Horst, and Özgür (2006). Each agent $a \in \mathbb{A}$ believes that everyone else in the economy makes choices according to a given choice function $g : \mathbf{X} \times \Theta \times \{1, \ldots, K\} \to X$. Similar to BHÖ, they are after

Definition 9 *A* symmetric Markov Perfect Equilibrium *of a dynamic economy with social interactions is a measurable map $g^* : \mathbf{X} \times \Theta \times \{1, \ldots, K\} \to X$ such that for all $a \in \mathbb{A}$ and for all $t = 1, \ldots, K$*

$$g_{K-(t-1)}^*(T^a x_{t-1}, T^a \theta_t) = arg \max_{x_t^a \in X} E\Big[u\big(x_{t-1}^a, x_t^a, \{g_{K-(t-1)}^*(T^b x_{t-1}, T^b \theta_t)\}_{b \in N(a)}, \theta_t^a\big) \\ + \beta V_{K-t}^{g^*}\big(\{g_{K-(t-1)}^*(T^b x_{t-1}, T^b \theta_t\}_{b \in \mathbb{A}}, \theta_{t+1}^I)\big)\Big] \tag{24}$$

Their first result shows that for finite horizon economies, there exists a unique MPE, which is characterized in a simple and intuitive way: agent *a*'s optimal choice each period is a convex combination of last period's observed choices, today's observed type realizations, and the average type in the economy. Moreover, those weights capture an important phenomenon: Although fundamentally, agent's preferences are affected only by their immediate friends, in equilibrium their optimal choices are affected by (hence correlated with) choices of everyone in the economy in a decaying fashion, that is, farther an agent *b* is from an agent *a*, lesser weight agent *a* puts on the last choice of agent *b*, as can be seen in Figure 1 for strong (high α_3) and mild (low α_3) interactions. For an infinite horizon economy, the existence of a stationary MPE that behaves similarly is guaranteed. All this is summarized formally in

Theorem 10 (Existence – Complete Information) *Consider an economy with conformity preferences and complete information.*

[29] BÖ argue that the method of proof does not rely on the dimensionality of the social space. Hence, social space can be represented, at an abstract level, by any *d*-dimensional integer lattice. Similarly for the action and type spaces. The only thing that they cannot dispense with for their analysis is the convexity of the choice problem and the interiority of the optimal trajectories.

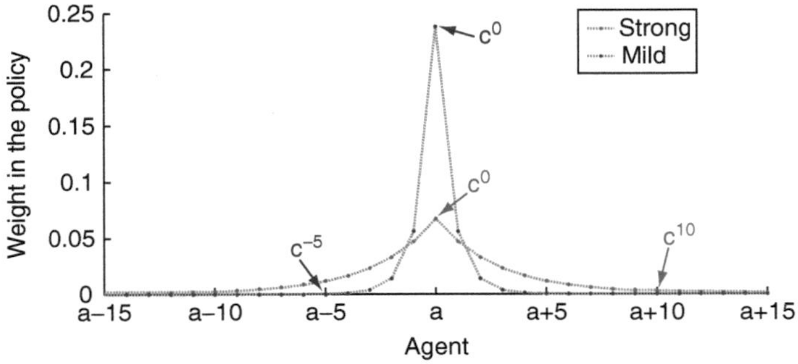

Figure 1 Weights on past history in the stationary policy function.

1. *If the time horizon is finite* ($K < \infty$), *then the economy admits an a.s. unique symmetric Markov Perfect Equilibrium* $g^* : \mathbf{X} \times \Theta \times \{1, \ldots, K\} \mapsto X$ *such that for all t, for all* $(x_{t-1}, \theta_t) \in \mathbf{X} \times \Theta$

$$g^*_{K-(t-1)}(x_{t-1}, \theta_t) = \sum_{a \in \mathbb{A}} c^a_{T-t+1} x^a_{t-1} + \sum_{a \in \mathbb{A}} d^a_{K-(t-1)} \theta^a_t + e_{T-t+1} \bar{\theta} \qquad \mathbb{P} - a.s.$$

where $c^a_\tau, d^a_\tau, e_\tau \geq 0,\ a \in \mathbb{A},$ *and* $e_\tau + \sum_{a \in \mathbb{A}} (c^a_\tau + d^a_\tau) = 1, 0 \leq \tau \leq K.$

2. *If the time horizon is infini te* ($K = \infty$), *then the economy admits a symmetric Markov Perfect Equilibrium* $g^* : \mathbf{X} \times \Theta \mapsto X$ *such that*

$$g^*(x_{t-1}, \theta_t) = \sum_{a \in \mathbb{A}} c^a x^a_{t-1} + \sum_{a \in \mathbb{A}} d^a \theta^a_t + e\bar{\theta}$$

where c^a, d^a, $e \geq 0$, *for* $a \in \mathbb{A}$, *and* $e + \sum_{a \in \mathbb{A}} (c^a + d^a) = 1.$[30]

Their method of proof is constructive and the recursive map which induces the symmetric policy function at equilibrium provides a direct and useful computation method which they repeatedly exploit to characterize equilibria and to produce comparative dynamics exercises. All these are summarized in the following

Theorem 11 (Recursive Computability) *Consider a* $K(< \infty)$*-period economy with conformity preferences* ($\alpha_i > 0$, $i = 1, 2, 3$) *and complete information. The coefficients* $(c^*_s, d^*_s, e^*_s)_{s=1}^K$ *of the sequence of Markov polices whose existence is guaranteed by Theorem 10 are* computable recursively *as the unique fixed points of the recursive maps* $T_s : L_c \to L_c$, $s = 1, \ldots, K$, *i.e., for each* $a \in \mathbb{A}$

[30] The theorems in this section can be extended with straightforward modifications to the case of incomplete information. Moreover, several assumptions can be relaxed while guaranteeing existence. In particular, the symmetry of the neighborhood structure can be substantially relaxed, adapting the analysis of Horst and Scheinkman (2006) to our dynamic environment.

$$c_s^{*a} = \Delta_s^{-1}\left(\alpha_1 1_{\{a=0\}} + \sum_{b\neq 0} \gamma_s^b c_s^{*a-b}\right)$$
$$d_s^{*a} = \Delta_s^{-1}\left(\alpha_2 1_{\{a=0\}} + \sum_{b\neq 0} \gamma_s^b d_s^{*a-b}\right).$$
$$e_s^{*a} = \Delta_s^{-1}\left(\mu_s + e_s^* \sum_{b\neq 0} \gamma_s^b\right)$$

where $\Delta_K, (\gamma_K^a)_{a\neq 0}, \mu_K$ *are the total effects on agent 0's marginal utility of an infinitesimal change in* $x_1^0, (x_1^a)_{a\neq 0}$, *and* $\bar{\theta}$ *respectively evaluated at the equilibrium path. Moreover,* $\lim_{K\to\infty}(c_K^*, d_K^*, e_K^*) = (c_\infty^*, d_\infty^*, e_\infty^*)$ *exists and is the coefficient sequence of an equilibrium policy function for the infinite horizon economy.*

Before closing this section, I would like to mention the welfare effects of local interactions. BÖ argue that the equilibrium allocations of conformity economies are generally Pareto inefficient. Individuals do not internalize the impact of their choices on other agents today and in the future. The presence of social interactions might call for **policy interventions**. Most interventions (Medicaid, Food Stamps, Social Security Act) are thought to work on the fundamentals but generated social norms, e.g., welfare stigma. Well targeted policy interventions on a few agents might spill over other agents (multiplier effect); see Moffitt (2001).

BÖ study the problem of a social planner whose objective is to maximize the ex-ante expected well-being of a generic agent, by restricting the planner to the same class of symmetric choice rules, treating individuals equally. They show that, in his optimal choice, in order to internalize the externalities generated by individual choices on other individuals, the planner puts more weight on an agent's neighbors' type realizations and past choices than the generic agent does in a laissez-faire equilibrium. Hence

Theorem 12 (Inefficiency of equilibrium) *Equilibrium of an economy with conformity preferences (finite or infinite horizon) is generically inefficient.*

One of the most important contributions of Bisin and Özgür (2010) is their study of the identification of social determinants of individual choice behavior. BÖ argue, in a novel way, that rational expectations dynamics might help the social scientist disentangle interaction effects from correlated effects. This is material for Section 3.6.

3.3 Local vs. global dynamics

This section extends the analysis of dynamic economies with local interactions to economies in which interactions have an additional **global** component. In particular, I present the methodology proposed in Bisin, Horst, and Özgür (2006) to study economies in which each agent's preferences depend on the average action of all agents. They argue that such dependence might occur, for instance, if agents have preferences for *social status*. Similarly, preferences to adhere to aggregate norms of behavior, such as specific group cultures, give rise to global interactions. More generally, global interactions could capture other externality as well as price effects. When the population is finite, global interactions are nested straightforwardly in local interaction models. When the number of agents is infinite, there are technical subtleties.

Consider a class of dynamic conformity economies, in which the preferences of each agent $a \in \mathbb{A}$ also depend on the average action of the agents in the economy,

$$p(x) := \lim_{n \to \infty} \frac{1}{2n+1} \sum_{a=-n}^{n} x^a,$$

when the limit exists. Let $\mathbf{X_e}$ denote the set of all configurations such that the associated average action exists:

$$\mathbf{X_e} := \left\{ x \in \mathbf{X} : \exists p(x) := \lim_{n \to \infty} \frac{1}{2n+1} \sum_{a=-n}^{n} x^a \right\}.$$

The preferences of the agent $a \in \mathbb{A}$ in period t are described by the instantaneous utility function $u : \mathbf{X_e} \times \Theta \to \mathbb{R}$ of the conformity class

$$\begin{aligned} & u(x_{t-1}^a, x_t^a, x_t^{a+1}, \theta_t^a, p(x_t)) \\ & = -\alpha_1 (x_{t-1}^a - x_t^a)^2 - \alpha_2 (\theta_t^a - x_t^a)^2 - \alpha_3 (x_t^{a+1} - x_t^a)^2 - \alpha_4 (p(x_t) - x_t^a)^2 \end{aligned}$$

for some positive constants α_i, $i = 1, 2, 3, 4$. As before, assume that $X = \Theta = [-1, 1]$ and that $\mathbb{E}\theta^0 = 0$. Assume also that information is incomplete so that an agent $a \in \mathbb{A}$ at time t only observes his own type θ_t^a, and all agents' past actions. Similar to before, a symmetric Markov perfect equilibrium of this economy is defined as in

Definition 10 *Let $\mathbf{x} \in \mathbf{X_e}$ be the initial configuration of actions. A symmetric Markov perfect equilibrium of a dynamic economy with local and global interactions is a map g^*: $\mathbf{X}^0 \times \Theta \times X \to X$ and a map F^*: $X \to X$ such that:*

$$\begin{aligned} g^*(x_{t-1}, \theta_t^0, p_t) = \arg\max_{x_t^0 \in X} \Big\{ & \int u(x_{t-1}^0, x_t^0, y_t^1, \theta_t^0, p_t) \pi_{g^*}(Tx_{t-1}; dy_t^1) \\ & + \beta \int V_{g^*}(x_t^0, \hat{x}_t, \theta^1, p_{t+1}) \Pi_{g^*}(Tx_{t-1}; d\hat{x}_t) \nu(d\theta^1) \Big\} \end{aligned} \quad (25)$$

and

$$p_{t+1} = F^*(p_t),$$

and

$$p_1 = p(x) \quad \text{and} \quad p_t = p(x_t) \quad \text{almost surely.}$$

At a symmetric Markov perfect equilibrium, apart from anticipating play according to the policy function g^*, all agents rationally expect the sequence of average actions $\{p(x_t)\}_{t \in \mathbb{N}}$ to be determined recursively via the map F^*. BHÖ argue that two fundamental difficulties arise in studying existence of an equilibrium of a dynamic economy with local and global interactions

(i) The endogenous sequence of average actions $\{p(x_t)\}_{t\in\mathbb{N}}$ might not be well-defined for all t (that is, $\mathbf{x}_t$ might not lie in $\mathbf{X_e}$ for some t).

(ii) Even when $x_t \in \mathbf{X_e}$, an agent's utility function depending on the action profile $\mathbf{x_t}$ in a global manner through the average action $p(\mathbf{x}_t)$ will typically not be continuous in the product topology. Thus, standard results from the theory of discounted dynamic programming cannot be applied to solve the agent's dynamic optimization problem in (25).

In order to circumvent these difficulties, BHÖ use a two-step approach in which each agent treats the global dynamic process as exogenous and independent of choices, and makes optimal choices using a stationary policy that depends on last period choices, current type realizations, and the current value of the exogenous global process. They then show that the mean choice dynamics in the economy is independent of particular choice configurations and agrees with the exogenous global dynamics.[31] To be able to do that, they show that

(i) The endogenous sequence of average actions $\{p(\mathbf{x}_t)\}_{t\in\mathbb{N}}$ exists almost surely if the exogenous initial configuration $\mathbf{x}$ belongs to $\mathbf{X_e}$, and that

(ii) It follows a deterministic recursive relation.

More specifically, they first consider an economy where the agents' utility depends on some *exogenous* quantity p, constant over time and show that agents behave optimally according to a symmetric policy function g^* that has the following linear form

$$g^*(x, \theta^0, p) = e_0^* x^0 + \varepsilon\theta^0 + \sum_{b\geq 1} e_b^* x^b + A(p) \tag{26}$$

where the correlation pattern $\mathbf{e}^* = (e_a^*)_{a\geq 0}$, and the constant $\varepsilon > 0$ are independent of p. So, a change in p has only a direct effect on the chosen action but does not affect the dependency of the action on the realized agent's type nor on the neighbors' actions. It is this independence property that allows BHÖ to separate the local and global equilibrium dynamics. To that effect, they extend the analysis to the case in which the agents' utility depends on some *exogenous* but time-varying quantity $\{p_t\}_{t\in\mathbb{N}}$ described in terms of a possibly non-linear recursive relation of the form

$$p_{t+1} = F(p_t) \quad \text{for some continuous function} \quad F: X \to X. \tag{27}$$

Since F is continuous, an agent's optimization problem can again be solved using standard results from the theory of discounted dynamic programming. They show that, in this case, the optimal symmetric policy function that each agent uses takes the form

[31] For similar separation arguments applied in the context of static economies with locally and globally interacting agents, see Horst and Scheinkman (2006) in Section 2.2. See also Föllmer and Horst (2001) for another application to interacting Markov chains.

$$g(x,\theta^0,p_1) = e_0^*x^0 + \varepsilon\theta^0 + \sum_{b\geq 1} e_b^*x^b + \sum_{t\geq 1} h_t^*p_t$$

for some correlation pattern $e^* = (e_a^*)_{a\geq 0}$ and a positive sequence $h^* = (h_t^*)_{t\geq 1}$. These sequences can be chosen independently of F and satisfy

$$\sum_{a\geq 0} e_a^* + \sum_{t\geq 1} h_t^* \leq 1.$$

Finally, BHÖ show that the recursive structure of $\{p_t\}_{t\in\mathbb{N}}$ is preserved when each element of the sequence is required to be endogenously determined as the average equilibrium action: $p_t = p(\mathbf{x}_t)$, for any t, at the equilibrium configuration $\mathbf{x}_t$. To that effect, take a continuous function $F: X \to X$ that determines recursively the sequence $\{p_t\}_{t\in\mathbb{N}}$ as in (27). Assume that the exogenous initial configuration $\mathbf{x}$ has a well defined average $p := p(\mathrm{x})$, that is, assume that $\mathbf{x} \in \mathbf{X}_e$. Let $F^{(t)}$ denote the t-fold iteration of F so that $p_t = F^{(t)}(p)$. Since the agents' types are independent and identically distributed, it follows from the law of large numbers that the average equilibrium action in the following period is almost surely given by

$$\lim_{n\to\infty}\frac{1}{2n+1}\sum_{a=-n}^{n} g(T^a x, \theta^a, p) = C^*p + \sum_{t\geq 1} h_t^* F^{(t)}(p) =: G(F)(p).$$

Thus, the average action in period $t = 2$ exists almost surely if the average action in period $t = 1$ exists, and an induction argument shows that the average action exists almost surely for all $t \in \mathbb{N}$. In order to establish the existence of an equilibrium, they first show that there exists a continuous function F^* such that, with $p_1 := p(\mathbf{x})$ we have

$$p_2 := F^*(p_1) = G(F^*)(p_1).$$

Finally, their main result can be summarized in

Theorem 13 *For the dynamic economy with local and global interactions introduced in this section, the following hold:*

1. *The economy has a symmetric Markov perfect equilibrium* (g^*, F^*) *where* $g^* : \mathbf{X}^0 \times \Theta \times X \to X$ *and* $F^* : X \to X$.
2. *In equilibrium, the sequence of average actions* $\{p(x_t)\}_{t\in\mathbb{N}}$ *exists almost surely.*
3. *The policy function* g^* *can be chosen of the linear form*

$$g^*(x,\theta^0) = e_0^*x^0 + \varepsilon\theta^0 + \sum_{b\geq 1} e_b^*x^b + B^*(p(x)) \tag{28}$$

for some positive sequence $\mathbf{e}^* = (e_a^*)_{a\geq 0}$, *a constant* $\varepsilon > 0$, *some constant* $B^*(p(x))$ *that depends only on the initial average action.*

One note of precaution: It is important for their analysis in this section that the policy functions are linear. Only in this case, in fact, can the dynamics of average actions $\{p(x_t)\}_{t\in\mathbb{N}}$ can be described in terms of a recursive relation. In models with more general local interactions, the average action typically is not a sufficient statistic for the aggregate behavior of the configuration x; hence a recursive relation typically fails to hold, as shown e.g., by Föllmer and Horst (2001). In such more general cases, the analysis must be pursued in terms of empirical fields. Interested reader should see Föllmer and Horst (2001). I also found the book by

3.4 Ergodicity

Ergodicity is the mathematical study of measure-preserving transformations in general and long-term average behavior of systems in particular. Economists are especially interested in the long-run properties of equilibrium distributions of dynamic economies and games. In this section I will present existing results on the (non)ergodicity of equilibria of economies with social interactions. Readers interested in general discussions of ergodicity should consult Halmos (1956), Petersen (1989) (ch. 1 is a gentle introduction to the kind of questions ergodic theory is concerned with), Nadkarni (1998), and Walters (2000). I also found the book by Meyn and Tweedie (1993) extremely helpful, especially when one deals with Markov processes with uncountable state spaces. For random field models, see Kindermann and Snell (1980), Liggett (1985), and Spitzer (1971).

Durlauf (1993) studies the dynamics of local interlinkages between sectors in an economy and the possibility of multiple long-run aggregate behavior emerging from the same local interactions between sectors. He uses the mathematics of random field theory to formulize his approach. Formally, at the local level, equilibrium technology, production, and capital accumulation choices give rise to

$$\mu\left(x_t^a = 1 | x_{t-1}^b = 1, \forall b \in N(a) \cup \{a\}\right)$$

a system of local conditional probabilities of choosing a particular technology (either 0 or 1) given last period technology choices of neighboring sectors (sectors that have linkages with sector a). Using a result by Dobrushin (1968), he shows that there exists at least one joint probability distribution on overall technology choices consistent with the local rules. The major economic questions Durlauf are after come from the theory of economic growth: do economies with identical technologies and preferences converge to the same long run average output? Can leading sectors tip off the economy from a low level equilibrium to a high level equilibrium due to strong interlinkages, as proposed by Hirschman (1958)? Durlauf argue that although previous models of increasing returns to scale and imperfect competition (e.g., Diamond (1982), Cooper and John (1988), Romer (1986), Lucas (1988)) have generated multiple equilibria, these latter are constant steady states entirely determined by initial conditions. Durlauf show that one can incorporate meaningful stochastic dynamics, interesting cyclic behavior, volatility of output at the cross-section of industries into the model and still characterize conditions under which the economy is ergodic with a unique invariant distribution, independent of the initial conditions. He argues that these conditions are: (i) positive and non-degenerate conditional probabilities, and (ii) not too strong local spillovers.

Durlauf's dynamics are backward looking because periodic production choices can be solved independently due to the one-lagged Markov assumption on the dependence of current production on past technology choices. Nevertheless, the analysis using random field theoretical tools to obtain aggregate probability laws consistent with sectoral stochastic linkages is novel. Bisin, Horst, and Özgür (2006) are interested in a similar issue but with fully rational forward-looking agents. At an abstract level, agents interact only with their immediate neighbors, but anticipate the future choices of these latter. Equilibrium conditions give rise to a system of conditional laws that depend on past choices on the equilibrium path. Given the conditionally independent nature of these rules, there is a unique consistent global phase. BHÖ show that under relatively mild local interactions, there exists a unique long-run joint probability distribution on the space of individual configurations to which the sequence of finite horizon global phases converge, independent of the initial conditions of the economy.

For the class of conformity economies that they study, Bisin and Özgür (2010) show that no matter how strong the strength of local interactions can be, given a stationary equilibrium policy, the Markov process jointly induced by that policy and the sequence of individual shocks converges to a unique long run probability distribution on the space of configurations. This is due to the fact that the optimal policy is a stationary trade-off between dependence on the past, adaptation to the stochastic shocks, and co-ordination on the mean shock. In the long run, iteration of the same policy makes the dependence on the initial conditions die off. Consequently, it is the path of realized shocks that determine the state of the economy. Since the system is ergodic, the empirical distribution on all such paths converge to the same probability distribution in the long run.

In this section, I focused my attention on the ergodicity of dynamic economies with local interactions and its implications on the uniqueness of long-run limit distributions. A local interaction system can be ergodic at the cross-section (space) too. We saw the implications of this on the existence of consistent aggregate laws, as presented in Horst and Scheinkman (2006), in Section 2.2. For similar ideas in the context of population games, see Blume (1993) for a study of stochastic strategy revision processes and their long run properties and see Anderlini and Ianni (1996) for an application to path dependence in local learning. A quick survey of (non)-ergodicity in economics is Horst (2008).

3.5 Myopia vs. rationality

3.5.1 Myopic Interactions

Early models of dynamic social interactions mostly subscribe to the **evolutionary** point of view. What distinguish evolutionary from the classical point of view in economics, according to Young (1998), are the concepts of **equilibrium** and **rationality**. In the mainstream economic equilibrium analysis, individual behavior is assumed to be optimal given expectations and expectations are correct, justified by the statistical evidence (**rational expectations**). Agents know their environments, use all information they have to anticipate changes in them and act accordingly. Evolutionary approach treats individuals as **low-rationality agents**. They still **adapt** to changes in their environment. However, they account for neither their actions' impact on the evolution of their environment, nor the repercussions of this latter on their own future well-being. Young argues that they too are interested in equilibrium but that equilibrium can be understood only within a dynamic framework that explains how it comes about, by observing how things look on average over long periods of time. Good surveys of this approach exist. Interested reader should consult Blume (1997), Young (1998 and 2008), Sandholm (2010), and also Burke and Young (2008, chapter 9) for applications to the study of social norms. I am going to give a quick tour of the most cited articles in the literature.

One of the earliest models of local interactions in the social sciences is Schelling (1969, 1971 and 1972). He argues that **segregation** (or separation, or sorting) might happen along many lines: income, sex, education, race, language, color, historical accidents; it might be the result of organizations, communication systems, or correlation with other modes of segregation. He is interested in segregation that results from *discriminatory individual choices*. He assumes that individuals, when making choices, are not capable of generating (often not even conscious of) changes on the aggregate dynamics of the system. **Evolutionary processes** stemming from individual actions bring about those changes in the long run. He first studies a *Spatial Proximity Model*, on a line and on a two-dimensional space. Population (finite) is divided into two permanent and recognizable groups according to color. Individuals are concerned about the proportion of their local neighbors of the opposite color. They each have a particular location at any time and can move if they are not happy with the particular color composition of their current neighborhood. Schelling uses different **behavioral rules** to represent individual choices. In one treatment, everybody wants at least half his neighbors to be of the same color and moves to another location otherwise. The rule about how agents move is deterministic and arbitrary. Nobody anticipates the movements of others (**myopic**) and agents continue moving until there is no dissatisfied agent in the system (**equilibrium**). When modeled on a two-dimensional space, agents move to the most preferred empty spaces available when dissatisfied. Once again, the dynamics come to an end when no one is dissatisfied with their neighborhood composition. In its essence, this is a **local interaction** model, with **myopically best-responding** agents. Schelling looks at the segregation (or *clustering*, or *sorting*, or *concentration*) patterns that arise once the dynamics settle: One observes clusters of same color agents living together separated from other groups along well-defined boundaries. One interesting result is that minority tends to become more segregated from majority, as its relative size diminishes. Another is that segregation is more striking as the local demand for like-colored neighbors increases.

He then studies a *Bounded-Neighborhood Model.* This is a **global interaction** model, where each agent's utility is affected by the overall color composition of the neighborhood. Given a distribution of 'tolerance' levels, each agent stays in the neighborhood if the relative proportion of people of opposite color is less than his tolerance level; otherwise, he leaves. At each moment in time, the agents with the lowest tolerance levels leave and new agents with tolerance levels higher than the current composition enter. Schelling looks at the steady state of the induced deterministic dynamic processes. There always exist two stable states involving complete segregation along with a mixed (co-habitation of blacks and whites) state whose stability depends on the tolerance distribution and the relative proportions of blacks and whites. Some interesting results are: cohabitation is more likely with similar tolerance distributions for blacks and whites; in general, for mixed equilibria to emerge, minority must be the more tolerant group. Schelling applies his analysis to *neighborhood tipping* (the inflow of a recognizable new minority into a neighborhood in sufficient numbers to cause the earlier residents to begin evacuating). He argues that main determinants of a tipping phenomenon are whether the neighborhood size is fixed, whether the new entrants are identifiable as a group, the relative sizes of the entrants with respect to the size of the neighborhood, and the availability of alternative neighborhoods for evacuating people.

A large literature using evolutionary methodology as in Schelling (1971), but more formally, studies social interaction in large populations. The common hypothesis is that individuals need not know the total structure of the game but need information on the empirical distribution of strategy choices in the population. Two pillars of this approach are a **population game**, the structure of the global interaction to occur repeatedly, and a **revision protocol**, a myopic procedure that describes who chooses when and how previous choices are revised. A population game and a revision protocol jointly induce **evolutionary game dynamics** that describe how the aggregate behavior in the population changes over time. When the resulting process is ergodic, its long run behavior will focus on a subset of states called the **stochastically stable set**.

Most of the literature focuses on the relation between **risk dominance** (Harsanyi and Selten (1988)) and **stochastic stability.** Kandori, Mailath, and Rob (1993) are the first ones to have established that link. Essentially, they argue that the periodic shocks (mutations or mistakes that are part of the revision protocol) in a 2 × 2 game reduce the set of long run equilibria by acting as a selection mechanism. Provided that the population is sufficiently large, the risk dominant equilibrium is stochastically stable. Young (1993) shows, using different techniques but the same equilibrium concept, that the connection between risk dominance and stochastic stability is not robust to an increase in the number of strategies in the population game; the resulting stochastically stable equilibrium may be neither risk dominant nor Pareto optimal.

One criticism of this approach is the speed at which an equilibrium is selected in the long run. This process might take too long. Ellison (1993) shows that if agents respond to their immediate neighbors (*local interactions*), the time to reach a stochastically stable state is reduced greatly. Moreover, in large populations with uniform matching, play is determined largely by historical factors; whereas where agents are matched with a small set of agents only, it is more likely that the evolutionary forces determine the long run outcome. Blume (1993) studies local interaction dynamics on integer lattices. He characterizes stationary distributions and the limit behavior of these dynamic systems. He relates his results to equilibrium selection as in the rest of the literature and also introduces statistical mechanics techniques to study this kind of strategic interaction. Blume (1995) extends these results to $K \times K$ games when players update using a myopic best response rule. Finally, Morris (2000) looks at the possibility of spread of a behavior initially played by a small subset of the population to the whole population through local interactions. He shows that maximal **contagion** happens in the presence of sufficiently uniform local interactions and when the number of agents one can reach in k steps is not exponential in k.

3.5.2 Does it matter?

Does it matter to model interactions myopically rather than rationally? Does the modeling choice (rational vs. myopic) affect the results that one gets significantly? The answer that Bisin, Horst, and Özgür (2006) and Bisin and Özgür (2010) give is that myopic models have the general tendency to **overestimate** the local interaction effects relative to the rational models. The main idea is that a myopic agent is unable to anticipate the effect of his current action change on others' behavior, on the evolution of the system, and the repercussions of these latter on his future well-being, whereas a rational agent anticipates and incorporates these effects into his optimal choice. Consequently, a rational agent is more immune to local behavioral and environmental changes than a myopic agent.

This idea is nicely presented in Bisin, Horst, and Özgür (2006) using their example in Section 3.2. BHÖ study a simple two-period version of their conformity economies under two distinct hypotheses: **myopia** and **full rationality** (see Section 4.3, p. 98 of their paper). They find two differences between the behavior of myopic and rational agents: (i) whereas the myopic agent is backward-looking by basing his choice on the past choices of his immediate neighbors only, the fully rational agent's choice is based on the past choices of all agents. This creates long cross-sectional correlation terms. But most importantly (ii) the fully rational choice is more weighted on the mean shock than the past actions: a rationally anticipating agent will try to smooth out local behavioral dependencies by anticipating that other agents will get a chance to change their actions next period. This further limits the component of local conformity in the choice of agents in the economy.

A similar criticism is found in Blume (1997). Blume argues that one of the most important barriers to the application of population game techniques to serious economic models is the assumption of **myopia**. The separation between choice and dynamics due to myopia makes the analysis of population games models particularly simple. But economic decision makers are typically concerned about the future as well as the present. Consequently, they try to forecast the strategy revision process, and take account of these forecasts when searching for the best response at a strategy revision opportunity. If there is any connection between the forecasts and the actual behavior of the strategy revision process, such as the hypothesis that expectations are rational, then the dynamic behavior of the strategy revision process cannot be simply computed from the choice rule. The framework used in the population games literature, to study stigma and enforcement of social norms, subscribe to the myopic formulation; hence it misses the richness of the account of individual choice that standard dynamic economic analysis offers. For instance, Blume argues, it would be hard to formulate a question about the effect of punishment duration in that framework. He points out that dispensing with the myopia hypothesis and recognizing players as intertemporal decision makers models would allow evolutionary game theory to be applicable to serious problems in the social sciences.

Blume (2003)

To exemplify such applicability, Blume (2003) models **stigma** and **social control**. Blume notes that stigma is in essence a dynamic phenomenon. Its costs are born in the future, and the magnitude of those costs are determined by the future actions of others. Hence, he **rejects myopia** and he models dynamic stigma costs as a population game (*global interactions*) with **forward looking** agents. This is a very nice and novel paper. Individuals in the model can entertain random criminal opportunities. There are two types of costs: a one-time utility cost if caught and a flow cost of stigma, when 'marked' as a criminal, that is increasing in the relative ratio of the unmarked population (*imposers of stigma*). Stigma ends at a random time when the agent gets 'unmarked'. Blume's agents perceive not only the immediate and current cost flow effects of their actions on themselves but also the externalities they generate on others and their repercussions on themselves in the future through the evolution of the marking and unmarking processes. Blume shows that apart from the *neoclassical effect* (Becker (1968)) of decreasing criminal activity, an increase in the arrest probability has a *social interaction effect*: it increases the number of tagged individuals which in turn reduces the stigma effects of being tagged as a criminal. Similar reasoning applies to the probability of getting untagged. Consequently, stigma costs of long duration will lead to increased crime rates!

3.6 Rational dynamics and identification

There are statistical problems that arise in the estimation of social interactions. Firstly, it is difficult to correctly identify individuals' reference groups. Moreover, one should distinguish between three effects in understanding group behavior (Manski (1993)): (1) correlation of individual characteristics, (2) influence of group characteristics on individuals, and (3) the influence of group behavior on individual behavior. The equilibrium allocations of economies with local interactions are in general Pareto inefficient because local interactions are a form of direct preference externalities. As a consequence, the presence of local interactions might call for policy interventions. Most policy interventions such as Medicaid, Food Stamps, Social Security Act are thought to operate on the fundamentals. However, there is documented evidence that responses of welfare recipients generated norms, and unexpected community responses due to social interactions (Moffitt (2001)). Thus, identifying the existence and nature of social interactions are of utmost importance for efficient policy implementation.

The question of identification goes back, in economics, to Pigou (1910), Schultz (1938), Frisch (1928, 1933, 1934, and 1938), Marschak (1942), Haavelmo (1944), Koopmans (1949), Koopmans, Rubin, and Leipnik (1950), Wald (1950), Hurwicz (1950). The standard definitons of identification that we still use are owed to Koopmans (1949) and Koopmans and Reiersøl (1950), both of which are very beautiful articles providing clear exhibitions of the main idea. More recent surveys on the topic exist of course; see Rothenberg (1971), Hausman and Taylor (1983), Hsiao (1983), Matzkin (2007), and Dufour and Hsiao (2008). Moreover, Blume and Durlauf (2005), Brock and Durlauf (2007), Manski (2007, 2000), Blume et al. (2010, chapter 23) and Graham (2010, chapter 29) in this volume, and Manski (1993, 2007) are good guides to the main questions pertaining to social interactions. Since the pessimistic view expressed in Manski (1993), there has been progress in the identification literature. Conley and Topa (2002, 2003) compare predictive power of different neighborhood structures to identify the reference groups. Graham (2008) uses excess variance across groups for identification. Davezies et al. (2006) use size variation across groups; Bramoullé et al. (2009) uses reference group heterogeneity for identification. Other recent contributions include Glaeser and Scheinkman (2001), Graham and Hahn (2005); De Paula (2009), Evans, Oates and Schwab (1992), Ioannides and Zabel (2008), and Zanella (2007).

The main question is easy to state. A **structure** is a specification of both the distribution of variables unobserved by the econometrician and the relationship connecting these latter to the observed variables, which implies a unique probability distribution.

A **model** is simply a collection of admissible structures. One says that an admissible structure S is **identifiable** by the model (or that the model **identifies** a given structure) if there exists no other structure S' that induces the same probability distribution on the observable variables.

Bisin and Özgür (2010) argue that dynamic equilibrium processes generated by the actions of rational agents might help identify certain interaction effects. In particular, they are interested in identifying correlated effects (unobserved to the econometrician) from local interactions. They first argue that as suspected by Manski (1993) too, dynamic specification does not necessarily solve the identification problem and the necessary support for a particular intertemporal specification should come from data. They show that in **static** as well as **stationary dynamic** models, reflection problem presented in Manski (1993) kicks back. One interesting specification, Bisin and Özgür argue, is environments where correlated effects follow a stationary law through time whereas observed behavior is non-stationary. Take the question of whether adolescents' substance use is affected by their peers and if there is variation in their propensity to consume addictive substances across grades. If, as it is argued in Hoxby (2000a,b), for instance, the school composition is stationary (with no significant trend), in the short run, and that the core friendship groups have been formed already, any significant variation in adolescent behavior through time must be due to local interactions. This simple observation is due to the **rationality** of the agents in this dynamic environment. A rational agent, if his choice is affected by the choices of his peers, will take into account how much longer he will interact with them. In particular, his propensity to consume due to his peers' consumption must be the lowest in the final year and monotonically higher as one considers earlier years. This is exactly the equilibrium behavior Bisin and Özgür obtain from a finite-horizon dynamic model with local interactions. Consequently, the probability distributions on the observed adolescent behavior generated by the correlated structure and the local interaction structure are different.

4. CONCLUDING REMARKS

This paper has presented the current state of affairs in the theoretical literature on local social determinants of individual choice behavior. I discussed a variety of models on each side of many division lines that the literature subscribes to: discrete vs. continuous choice, static vs. dynamic interactions, rational vs. myopic behavior. For all the models I surveyed, I presented findings on equilibrium existence and uniqueness, long run behavior, social multiplier effects and multiple equilibria and identification of interaction effects. There is a lot more to be done on the theoretical front combined with a better understanding of empirical social processes.

One very important issue is the **determination of individual reference groups**. Most of the literature that I surveyed takes the assumption that when interactions are modeled, the relevant reference groups and the nature of the interactions is known to the agents and to the outsiders (read econometrician). However, when doing empirical work, it is not clear whether these assumptions stand up to criticisms. This will probably be a joint effort between better survey data collection and related theorizing.

Another future area of investigation is the use of **proper dynamic models** in empirical work rather than one-shot myopic models. Needless to say, this goes once alongside the availability of rich panel data sets. These latter began to appear and although most of them initially collected by sociologists, economists started to take an interest in them.[32] The proper modeling of dynamics might help identification of interaction effects as I argued in Section 3.6.

One last, but not least, future research area is the joint modeling of **self-selection** (or sorting) and **social interactions**. There already exists a literature on network formation whose dynamic counterpart is in the development stage. The joint modeling of these two phenomena would most probably help the researcher disentangle the interactions part of individual choice behavior by correctly accounting for behavior due to *equilibrium* self-selection or sorting. This latter is due to the fact that sorting behavior of *rational* agents carry information about their attitudes towards particular interaction processes that might follow.

[32] One interesting such data set is the National Longitudinal Study of Adolescent Health (**Add Health**). See http://www.cpc.unc.edu/projects/addhealth for more info.

REFERENCES

Akerlof, G., 1997. Social Distance and Social Decisions. Econometrica 65, 1005–1027.

Anderlini, L., Ianni, A., 1996. Path Dependence and Learning from Neighbors. Games Econ. Behav. 13, 141–178.

Averintzev, M.B., 1970. A Way of Describing Random Fields with Discrete Parameter (in Russian). Problemy Peredachi Informatsii 6, 100–109.

Bala, V., Goyal, S., 2000. A Non-cooperative Model of Network Formation. Econometrica 68, 1181–1229.

Becker, G.S., 1968. Crime and Punishment: An Economic Approach. J. Polit. Econ. 76, 169–217.

Becker, G., Murphy, K.M., 1988. A Theory of Rational Addiction. J. Polit. Econ. 96, 675–701.

Bénabou, R., 1993. Workings of a City: Location, Education and Production. Q. J. Econ. 108, 619–652.

Bénabou, R., 1996. Equity and Efficiency in Human Capital Investment: The Local Connection. Rev. Econ. Stud. 62, 237–264.

Bernheim, B.D., 1994. A Theory of Conformity. J. Polit. Econ. 102, 841–877.

Bhattacharya, R.N., Majumdar, M., 1973. Random Exchange Economies. J. Econ. Theory 6, 37–67.

Bikhchandani, S., Hirshleifer, D., Welch, I., 1992. A Theory of Fads, Fashion, Custom, and Cultural Exchange as Information Cascades. J. Polit. Econ. 100, 992–1026.

Billingsley, P., 1995. Probability and Measure, third ed. John Wiley & Sons, New York.

Binder, M., Pesaran, M.H., 2001. Life-Cycle Consumption under Social Interactions. J. Econ. Dyn. Control 25, 35–83.

Bisin, A., Horst, U., Özgür, O., 2006. Rational Expectations Equilibria of Economies with Local Interactions. J. Econ. Theory 127, 74–116.

Bisin, A., Moro, A., Topa, G., 2009. The Empirical Content of Models with Multiple Equilibria in Economies with Social Interactions. mimeo, New York University.

Bisin, A., Özgür, O., 2009a. Dynamic Models of Social Interactions: Identification and Characterization. mimeo, Université de Montréal and New York University.
Bisin, A., Özgür, O., 2009b. Social Interactions and Selection. mimeo, Université de Montréal and New York University, invited session in the 2009 AEA meetings in San Francisco.
Blanchard, O., Kahn, C., 1980. The Solution of Linear Difference Models under Rational Expectations. Econometrica 48, 1305–1312.
Blume, L., 1993. The Statistical Mechanics of Strategic Interaction. Games Econ. Behav. 11, 111–145.
Blume, L., 1995. The Statistical Mechanics of Best-Response Strategy Revision. Games Econ. Behav. 11, 111–145.
Blume, L., 1997. Population Games. In: Arthur, W.B., Durlauf, S., Lane, D. (Eds.), The Economy as a Complex Evolving System II. Addison Wesley, Menlo Park, CA.
Blume, L., Brock, W.A., Durlauf, S.N., Ioannides, Y.M., 2010. Identification of Social Interactions. this volume (Chapter 23).
Blume, L., 2003. Stigma and Social Control. mimeo, Cornell University.
Blume, L., Durlauf, S., 2005. Identifying Social Interactions: A Review. In: Oakes, J.M., Kaufman, J. (Eds.), Methods in Social Epidemiology. Jossey-Bass, San Francisco.
Bramoullé, Y., Djebbari, H., Fortin, B., 2009. Identification of Peer Effects through Social Networks. J. Econom. 150, 41–55.
Brock, W., 1993. Pathways to Randomness in the Economy: Emergent Nonlinearity and Chaos in Economics and Finance. Estud. Econ. 8, 3–55; and Social Systems Research Institute Reprint # 410, University of Wisconsin at Madison.
Brock, W., Durlauf, S., 2001a. Discrete Choice with Social Interactions. Rev. Econ. Stud. 68, 235–260.
Brock, W., Durlauf, S., 2001b. Interactions-Based Models. In: Heckman, J., Leamer, E. (Eds.), Handbook of Econometrics, vol. 5. North Holland, Amsterdam.
Brock, W., Durlauf, S., 2002. A Multinomial-Choice Model with Neighborhood Effects. Am. Econ. Rev. 92, 298–303.
Brock, W., Durlauf, S., 2007. Identification of Binary Choice Models with Social Interactions. J. Econom. 140 (1), 52–75.
Bulow, J.I., Geanokoplos, J.D., Klemperer, P.D., 1985. Multimarket Oligopoly: Strategic Substitutes and Complements. J. Polit. Econ. 93, 488–511.
Burke, M., 2008. Social Multipliers. In: Blume, L., Durlauf, S. (Eds.), New Palgrave Dictionary of Economics, revised ed.
Burke, M.A., Young, H.P., 2008. Social Norms. This volume (chapter 9).
Carrell, S.E., Fullerton, R.L., West, J.E., 2009. Does Your Cohort Matter? Measuring Peer Effects in College Achievement. J. Labor Econ. 27 (3), 439–464.
Case, A., Katz, L., 1991. The Company You Keep: The Effect of Family and Neighborhood on Disadvantaged Families. NBER Working Paper 3705.
Cass, D., Shell, K., 1983. Do Sunspots Matter? J. Polit. Econ. 91, 193–227.
Choquet, G., 1969. Lectures on analysis. Benjamin, New York-Amsterdam.
Coleman, J.S., Katz, E., Menzel, H., 1996. Medical Innovation: A Diffusion Study. Bobbs Merrill, New York.
Conley, T., Topa, G., 2002. Socio-economic Distance and Spatial Patterns in Unemployment. Journal of Applied Econometrics 17 (4), 303–327.
Conley, T., Topa, G., 2003. Identification of Local Interaction Models with Imperfect Location Data. Journal of Applied Econometrics 18, 605–618.
Cooper, R., John, A., 1988. Coordinating Coordination Failures in Keynesian Models. Q. J. Econ. 103, 441–465.
Crane, J., 1991. The Epidemic Theory of Ghettoes and Neighborhood Effects of Dropping Out and Teenage Childbearing. American Journal of Sociology 96, 1226–1259.
Cutler, D.M., Glaeser, E.L., 2007. Social Interactions and Smoking. mimeo, Harvard University and NBER working paper No. 13477.
Davezies, L., d'Haultfoeuille, X., Fougère, D., 2006. Identification of Peer Effects Using Group Size Variation. IZA working paper 2324.

DeCicca, P., Kenkel, D.S., Mathios, A.D., 2008. Cigarette Taxes and the Transition from Youth to Adult Smoking: Smoking Initiation, Cessation, and participation. J. Health Econ. 27 (4), 904–917.
De Paula, A., 2009. Inference in a Synchronization Game with Social Interactions. J. Econom. 148, 56–71.
Diamond, P., 1982. Aggregate Demand Management in Search Equilibrium. J. Polit. Econ. 90, 881–894.
Dobrushin, R.L., 1968. Description of a Random Field by Means of Conditional Probabilities and Conditions of its Regularity. Th. Probability Appl. 13, 197–224.
Dufour, J.M., Hsiao, C., 2008. Identification. In: Durlauf, S.N., Blume, L.E. (Eds.), The New Palgrave Dictionary of Economics, second ed.
Durlauf, S., 1993. Nonergodic Economic Growth. Rev. Econ. Stud. 60, 349–366.
Durlauf, S., 1996a. A Theory of Persistent Income Inequality. J. Econ. Growth 1, 75–93.
Durlauf, S., 1996b. Neighborhood Feedbacks, Endogenous Stratification, and Income Inequality. In: Barnett, W., Gandolfo, G., Hillinger, C. (Eds.), Dynamic Disequilibrium Modelling: Proceedings of the Ninth International Symposium on Economic Theory and Econometrics. Cambridge University Press, New York.
Durlauf, S., 1997. Statistical Mechanics Approaches to Socioeconomic Behavior. In: Arthur, W.B., Durlauf, S., Lane, D. (Eds.), The Economy as a Complex Evolving System II. Addison Wesley, Menlo Park, CA.
Durlauf, S.N., 2004. Neighborhood Effects. In: Henderson, J.V., Thisse, J.F. (Eds.), Handbook of Urban and Regional Economics, vol 4. North Holland, Amsterdam.
Durlauf, S.N., 2008. Statistical Mechanics. In: Blume, L., Durlauf, S. (Eds.), New Palgrave Dictionary of Economics, revised ed.
Durlauf, S.N., Young, P. (Eds.), 2001. Social Dynamics. MIT Press, Cambridge, MA.
Ellis, R., 1985. Entropy, Large Deviations, and Statistical Mechanics. Springer-Verlag, New York.
Ellison, G., 1993. Learning, Local Interaction and Coordination. Econometrica 61, 1047–1071.
Ellison, G., Fudenberg, D., 1993. Rules of Thumb for Social Learning. Journal of Political Economy 101, 612–644.
Evans, W., Oates, W., Schwab, R., 1992. Measuring Peer Group Effects: A Study of Teenage Behavior. J. Polit. Econ. 100 (51), 966–991.
Föllmer, H., 1974. Random Economies with Many Interacting Agents. Journal of Mathematical Economics 1 (1), 51–62.
Frisch, R., 1928. Correlation and scatter in statistical variables. Nordic Stat. Jour. 1, 36.
Frisch, R., 1933. Pitfalls in the statistical construction of demand and supply curves. Veröffentlichungen der Frankfurter Ges. für Konjunkturforschung, Neue Folge, Heft 5, Leipzig.
Frisch, R., 1934. Statistical Confluence Analysis by Means of Complete Regression Systems. Publ. No. 5, Universitetets Økonomiske Institutt, Oslo. 1934.
Frisch, R., 1938. Statistical Versus Theoretical Relations in Economic Macrodynamics. mimeographed document for League of Nations conference.
Föllmer, H., Horst, U., 2001. Convergence of Locally and Globally Interacting Markov Chains. Stochastic Processes and Their Applications 96, 99–121.
Fristedt, B., Gray, L., 1997. A Modern Approach to Probability Theory. Birkhäuser, Boston.
Galichon, A., Henry, M., 2009. Set Identification in Models with multiple Equilibria. mimeo, Université de Montréal.
Georgii, H.O., 1972. Phasentibergang 1. Art bei Gittergasmodellen. In: Lecture Notes in Physics, vol. 16. Springer, Heidelberg-Berlin-New York.
Georgii, H., 1989. Gibbs Measures and Phase Transitions. Walter de Gruyter, Berlin.
Glaeser, E., Sacerdote, B., Scheinkman, J., 1996. Crime and Social Interactions. Q. J. Econ. CXI, 507–548.
Glaeser, E., Sacerdote, B., Scheinkman, J., 2003. The Social Multiplier. J. Eur. Econ. Assoc. 1, 345–353.
Glaeser, E., Scheinkman, J., 2001. Measuring Social Interactions. In: Durlauf, S., Young, P. (Eds.), Social Dynamics. Brookings Institution Press and MIT Press, Cambridge, MA.
Glaeser, E., Scheinkman, J., 2003. Non-Market Interactions. In: Dewatripont, M., Hansen, L.P., Turnovsky, S. (Eds.), Advances in Economics and Econometrics: Theory and Applications, Eight World Congress, vol. I. Cambridge University Press, pp. 339–369.

Graham, B.S., 2008. Identifying Social Interactions through Excess Variance Contrasts. Econometrica 76, 643–660.
Graham, B.S., Hahn, J., 2005. Identification and Estimation of the Linear-in-Means Model of Social Interactions. Econ. Lett. 88 (1), 1–6.
Graham, B., 2010. Econometric Methods for the Analysis of Assignment Problems in the Presence of Complimentarity and Social Spillovers. This volume.
Gul, F., Pesendorfer, W., 2007. Harmful Addiction. Rev. Econ. Stud. 74 (1), 147–172.
Haavelmo, T., 1944. The Probability Approach in Econometrics. Econometrica 12, July.
Halmos, P.R., 1956. Lectures on Ergodic Theory. Chelsea Publishing Company.
Harsanyi, J., Selten, R., 1988. A General Theory of Equilibrium Selection in Games. MIT Press, Cambridge MA.
Hausman, J.A., Taylor, W.E., 1983. Identification in Linear Simultaneous Equations Models with Covariance Restrictions: An Instrumental Variables Interpretation. Econometrica 51 (5), 1527–1549.
Haveman, R., Wolfe, B., 1994. Succeeding Generations. Russel Sage Foundation, New York.
Hildenbrand, W., 1971. Random Preferences and Equilibrium Analysis. J. Econ. Theory 3, 414–429.
Hirschman, A.N., 1958. The Strategy of Economic Development. Yale University Press, New Haven.
Horst, U., 2008. Ergodicity and Non-Ergodicity in Economics. In: Blume, L., Durlauf, S. (Eds.), New Palgrave Dictionary of Economics, revised ed.
Horst, U., Scheinkman, J., 2006. Equilibria in Systems of Social Interactions. J. Econ. Theory 130, 44–77.
Hoxby, C.M., 2000a. The Effects Of Class Size On Student Achievement: New Evidence From Population Variation. Q. J. Econ. 115 (4), 1239–1285.
Hoxby, C.M., 2000b. Peer Effects in the Classroom: Learning from Gender and Race Variation. NBER Working Paper 7867.
Hsiao, C., 1983. Identification. In: Griliches, Z., Intriligator, M.D. (Eds.), Handbook of Econometrics, vol. 1. North-Holland, Amsterdam.
Hurwicz, L., 1950. Generalization of the Concept of Identification. In: Statistical Inference in Dynamic Economic Models. Cowles Commission Monograph 10, John Wiley and Sons, New York.
Ioannides, Y., 1990. Trading Uncertainty and Market Form. Int. Econ. Rev. (Philadelphia) 31 (3), 619–638.
Ioannides, Y., Zabel, J., 2008. Interactions, Neighborhood Selection, and Housing Demand. J. Urban Econ. 63, 229–252.
Jackson, M.O., Wolinsky, A., 1996. A Strategic Model of Social and Economic Networks. J. Econ. Theory 71, 44–74.
Jovanovic, B., 1987. Micro Shocks and Aggregate Risk. Q. J. Econ. 102, 395–409.
Jovanovic, B., 1989. Observable Implications of Models with Multiple Equilibria. Econometrica 57, 1431–1437.
Kandori, M., Mailath, G., Rob, R., 1993. Learning, Mutation, and Long-run Equilibria in Games. Econometrica 61, 29–56.
Kindermann, R., Snell, J.L., 1980. Markov Random Fields and Their Applications. American Mathematical Society, Providence, R.I.
Kirman, A., 1983. Communication in Markets: A Suggested Approach. Econ. Lett. 12, 1–5.
Koopmans, T.C., 1949. Identification Problems in Economic Model Construction. Econometrica 17, 125–144.
Koopmans, T.C., Rubin, H., Leipnik, R.B., 1950. Measuring the Equation Systems of Dynamic Economics. In: Statistical Inference in Dynamic Economic Models, Cowles Commission Monograph 10. John Wiley and Sons, New York.
Koopmans, T.C., Reiersøl, O., 1950. The Identification of Structural Characteristics. Annals of Mathematical Statistics 21, 165–181.
Kremer, M., Levy, D., 2008. Peer Effects and Alcohol Use among College Students. J. Econ. Perspect. 22 (3), 189–206.
Kydland, F., Prescott, E.C., 1982. Time to Build and Aggregate Fluctuations. Econometrica 50, 1345–1370.
Liggett, T.M., 1985. Interacting Particle Systems. Springer Verlag, Berlin.
Lucas, R.E., 1988. On the Mechanics of Economic Development. J. Monet. Econ. 22, 3–42.
Malinvaud, E., 1972. The Allocation of Individual Risks in Large Markets. J. Econ. Theory 4, 312–328.

Manski, C., 1993. Identification of Endogenous Social Effects: The Reflection Problem. Rev. Econ. Stud. 60, 531–542.
Manski, C., 2000. Economic Analysis of Social Interactions. J. Econ. Perspect. 14, 115–136.
Manski, C., 2007. Identification for Prediction and Decision. Harvard University Press, Cambridge, MA.
Marschak, J., 1942. Economic Interdependence and Statistical Analysis. In: Studies in Mathematical Economics and Econometrics. University of Chicago Press, pp. 135–150.
Matzkin, R., 2007. Nonparametric Identification. In: Heckman, J., Leamer, E. (Eds.), Handbook of Econometrics, vol. 6. North-Holland, Amsterdam.
McFadden, D., 1984. Econometric Analysis of Qualitative Response Models. In: Griliches, Z., Intriligator, M. (Eds.), Handbook of Econometrics: Volume II. North-Holland, Amsterdam.
Meyn, S.P., Tweedie, R.L., 1993. Markov Chains and Stochastic Stability. Springer-Verlag, London.
Moffitt, R.A., 2001. Policy Interventions, Low-Level equilibria, and Social Interactions. In: Durlauf, S., Young, P. (Eds.), Social Dynamics. Brookings Institution Press and MIT Press, Cambridge, MA.
Montrucchio, L., 1987. Lipschitz Continuous Policy Functions for Strongly Concave Optimization Problems. Journal of Mathematical Economics 16, 259–273.
Morris, S., 2000. Contagion. Rev. Econ. Stud. 67, 57–78.
Nadkarni, M.G., 1998. Basic Ergodic Theory. Birkhäuser, Basel; Boston Berlin.
Nakajima, R., 2007. Measuring Peer Effects on Youth Smoking Behavior. Rev. Econ. Stud. 74, 897–935.
Pesendorfer, W., 1995. Design Innovation and Fashion Cycles. The American Economic Review 85 (4), 771–792.
Petersen, K., 1989. Ergodic Theory. Cambridge University Press.
Pigou, A.C., 1910. A Method of Determining the Numerical Values of Elasticities of Demand. Economic Journal 20, 636–640.
Rockafellar, R.T., 1976. Saddle Points of Hamiltonian Systems in Convex Lagrange Problems Having a Nonzero Discount Rate. J. Econ. Theory 12, 71113.
Romer, P., 1986. Increasing Returns and Long Run Growth. J. Polit. Econ. 94, 1002–1037.
Rothenberg, T.J., 1971. Identification in Parametric Models. Econometrica 39 (3), 577–591.
Sandholm, W.H., 2010. Population Games and Evolutionary Dynamics. MIT Press, Cambridge MA.
Santos, M.S., 1991. Smoothness of the Policy Function in Discrete Time Economic Models. Econometrica 59, 1365–1382.
Schelling, T., 1969. Models of Segregation. Am. Econ. Rev. 59 (2), 488–493.
Schelling, T., 1971. Dynamic Models of Segregation. J. Math. Sociol. 1, 143–186.
Schelling, T., 1972. A Process of Residential Segregation: Neighborhood Tipping. In: Pascal, A. (Ed.), Racial Discrimination in Economic Life. Lexington Books, Lexington, MA.
Schultz, H., 1938. Theory and Measurement of Demand. University of Chicago Press.
Shiller, R., 2000. Irrational Exuberance. Princeton University Press, Princeton, NJ.
Spitzer, F., 1971. Random Fields and Interacting Particle Systems. Mathematical Association of America, Providence.
Topa, G., 2001. Social Interactions, Local Spillover and Unemployment. The Review of Economic Studies 68, 261–295.
Vasserstein, L.N., 1969. Markov Processes over Denumerable Product of Spaces Describing large Systems of Automata. Problemy Peredaci Informacii 5, 64–72.
Wald, A., 1950. Note on the Identification of Economic Relations. In: Statistical Inference in Dynamic Economic Models. Cowles Commission Monograph 10, John Wiley and Sons, New York.
Walters, P., 2000. An Introduction to Ergodic Theory. Springer-Verlag.
Young, P., 1993. The Evolution of Conventions. Econometrica 61, 57–84.
Young, H.P., 1998. Individual Strategy and Social Structure. Princeton University Press, Princeton, NJ.
Young, H.P., 2008. Stochastic Adaptive Dynamics. In: Blume, L., Durlauf, S. (Eds.), New Palgrave Dictionary of Economics, revised ed.
Zanella, G., 2007. Discrete Choice with Social Interactions and Endogenous Membership. J. Eur. Econ. Assoc. 5, 122–153.

FURTHER READINGS

Blume, L., Durlauf, S., 2001. The Interactions-Based Approach to Socioeconomic Behavior. In: Durlauf, S., Young, P. (Eds.), Social Dynamics. Brookings Institution Press and MIT Press, Cambridge, MA.

Frisch, R., Mudgett, B.D., 1931. Statistical Correlation and the Theory of Cluster Types. J. Am. Stat. Assoc. 26, 375.

CHAPTER 14

Diffusion, Strategic Interaction, and Social Structure

Matthew O. Jackson* **and Leeat Yariv**†

Contents

1. Introduction 646
2. Empirical Background: Social Networks and Diffusion 647
   2.1 The effects of networks from static perspectives 647
   2.2 The Effects of networks over time 651
3. Models of Diffusion and Strategic Interaction Absent Network Structure 653
   3.1 Marketing models 654
   3.2 Collective action, fashion, and fads 655
4. Models of Diffusion and Strategic Interaction in Network Settings 657
   4.1 A unified setting 658
   4.2 Epidemiology models 658
      4.2.1 Random graph models 658
      4.2.2 Diffusion with recovery 661
   4.3 Graphical games 665
   4.4 Network games 668
   4.5 Adding dynamics – diffusion and equilibria of network games 672
5. Closing Notes 674
References 675

Abstract

We provide an overview and synthesis of the literature on how social networks influence behaviors, with a focus on diffusion. We discuss some highlights from the empirical literature on the impact of networks on behaviors and diffusion. We also discuss some of the more prominent models of network interactions, including recent advances regarding interdependent behaviors, modeled via games on networks.

JEL Classification Codes: D85, C72, L14, Z13

* Department of Economics, Stanford University, Stanford CA 94305, USA and the Santa Fe Institute, Santa Fe NM 87501, USA.
† Division of the Humanities and Social Sciences, Caltech, Pasadena, CA 91125.

Handbook of Social Economics, Volume 1A
ISSN 0169-7218, DOI: 10.1016/S0169-7218(11)01014-8

Keywords

Diffusion
Learning
Social Networks
Network Games
Graphical Games
Games on Networks

1. INTRODUCTION

How we act, as well as how we are acted upon, are to a large extent influenced by our relatives, friends, and acquaintances. This is true of which profession we decide to pursue, whether or not we adopt a new technology, as well as whether or not we catch the flu. In this chapter we provide an overview of research that examines how social structure impacts economic decision making and the diffusion of innovations, behaviors, and information.

We begin with a brief overview of some of the stylized facts on the role of social structure on diffusion in different realms. This is a rich area of study that includes a vast set of case studies suggesting some important regularities. With that empirical perspective, we then discuss insights from the epidemiology and random graph literatures that help shed light on the spread of infections throughout a society. Contagion of this form can be thought of as a basic, but important, form of social interaction, where the social structure largely determines patterns of diffusion. This literature presents a rich understanding of questions such as: "How densely connected does a society have to be in order to have an infection reach a nontrivial fraction of its members?," "How does this depend on the infectiousness of the disease?," "How does it depend on the particulars of the social network in place?," "Who is most likely to become infected?," and "How widespread is an infection likely to be?," among others. The results on this apply beyond infectious diseases, and touch upon issues ranging from the spread of information to the proliferation of ideas.

While such epidemiological models provide a useful look at some types of diffusion, there are many economically relevant applications in which a different modeling approach is needed, and, in particular, where the interaction between individuals requires a game theoretic analysis. In fact, though disease and the transmission of certain ideas and bits of information can be modeled through mechanical or purely probabilistic sorts of diffusion processes, there are other important situations where individuals take decisions and care about how their social neighbors or peers behave. This applies to decisions of which products to buy, which technology to adopt, whether or not to become educated, whether to learn a language, how to vote, and so forth. Such interactions involve equilibrium considerations and often have multiple potential outcomes. For example, an agent might care about the proportion of neighbors adopting a given action, or might require some threshold of stimulus before becoming convinced to take an action, or might want to take an action that is different from that of his or her neighbors (e.g., free-riding on their information gathering if they do gather information, but gathering information him or herself if neighbors do not). Here we provide an overview of how the recent literature has modeled such interactions, and how it has been able to meld social structure with predictions of behavior.

2. EMPIRICAL BACKGROUND: SOCIAL NETWORKS AND DIFFUSION

There is a large body of work that identifies the effects of social interactions on a wide range of applications spanning fields: epidemiology, marketing, labor markets, political science, and agriculture are only a few.

While some of the empirical tools for the analysis of social interaction effects have been described in Block, Blume, Durlauf, and Ioannides (Chapter 18, this volume), and many of their implementations for research on housing decisions, labor markets, addictions, and more, have been discussed in Ioannides (Chapter 25, this volume), Epple and Romano (Chapter 20, this volume), Topa (Chapter 22, this volume), Fafchamps (Chapter 24, this volume), Jackson (Chapter 12, this volume), and Munshi (Chapter 23, this volume), we now describe empirical work that ties directly to the models that are discussed in the current chapter. In particular, we discuss several examples of studies that illustrate how social structure impacts outcomes and behaviors.

The relevant studies are broadly divided into two classes. First, there are cross-sectional studies that concentrate on a snapshot of time and look for correlations between social interaction patterns and observable behaviors. This class relates to the analysis below of strategic games played by a network of agents. While it can be very useful in identifying correlations, it is important to keep in mind that identifying causation is complicated without the fortuitous exogenous variation or structural underpinnings. Second, there are longitudinal studies that take advantage of the inherent dynamics of diffusion. Such studies have generated a number of interesting observations and are more suggestive of some of the insights the theoretical literature on diffusion has generated. Nonetheless, these sorts of studies also face challenges in identifying causation because of potential unobserved factors that may contemporaneously influence linked individuals.

The empirical work on these topics is immense and we provide here only a narrow look of the work that is representative of the *type* of studies that have been pursued and relate to the focus of this chapter.

2.1 The effects of networks from static perspectives

Studies that are based on observations at one point of time most often compare the frequency of a certain behavior or outcome across individuals who are connected as opposed to ones that are not. For example, Glaeser, Sacerdote, and Scheinkman (1996) showed that the structure of social interactions can help explain the cross-city variance in crime rates in the U.S.; Bearman, Moody, and Stovel (2004) examined the network of romantic connections in high-school, and its link to phenomena such as the spread of sexually transmitted diseases (see the next subsection for a discussion of the spread of epidemics). Such studies provide important evidence for the correlation of behaviors with characteristics of individuals' connections. In the case of diseases, they provide some direct evidence for diffusion patterns.

With regards to labor markets, there is a rich set of studies showing the importance of social connections for diffusing information about job openings, dating back to Rees (1966) and Rees and Schultz (1970). Influential studies by Granovetter (1973, 1985, 1995) show that even casual or infrequent acquaintances (weak ties) can play a role in diffusing information. Those studies were based on interviews that directly ask subjects how they obtained information about their current jobs. Other studies, based on outcomes, such as Topa (2001), Conley and Topa (2002), and Bayer, Ross, and Topa (2008), identify local correlations in employment status within neighborhoods in Chicago, and consider neighborhoods that go beyond the geographic but also include proximity in other socioeconomic dimensions, examining the extent to which local interactions are important for employment outcomes. Bandiera, Barankay, and Rasul (2008) create a bridge between network formation (namely, the creation of friendships amongst fruit pickers) and the effectiveness of different labor contracts. The extensive literature on networks in labor markets[1] documents the important role of social connections in transmitting information about jobs, and also differentiates between different types of social contacts and shows that even weak ties can be important in relaying information.

There is further (and earlier) research that examines the different roles of individuals in diffusion. Important work by Katz and Lazarsfeld (1955) (building on earlier studies of Lazarsfeld, Berelson, and Gaudet (1944), Merton (1948), and others), identifies the role of "opinion leaders" in the formation of various beliefs and opinions. Individuals are heterogeneous (at least in behaviors), and some specialize in becoming well informed on certain subjects, and then information and opinions diffuse to other less informed individuals via conversations with these opinion leaders. Lazarsfeld, Berelson, and Gaudet (1944) study voting decisions in an Ohio town during the 1940 U.S. presidential campaign, and document the presence and significance of such opinion leaders. Katz and Lazarsfeld (1955) interviewed women in Decatur, Illinois, and asked about a number of things such as their views on household goods, fashion, movies, and local public affairs. When women showed a change in opinion in follow-up interviews, Katz

[1] For more references see the survey by Ioannides and Datcher-Loury (2004), Chapter 10 in Jackson(2008), and Jackson (Chapter ?, this volume).

and Lazarsfeld traced influences that led to the change in opinion, again finding evidence for the presence of opinion leaders.

Diffusion of new products is understandably a topic of much research. Rogers (1995) discusses numerous studies illustrating the impacts of social interactions on the diffusion of new products, and suggests various factors that impact which products succeed and which products fail. For example, related to the idea of opinion leaders, Feick and Price (1987) surveyed 1531 households and provided evidence that consumers recognize and make use of particular individuals in their social network termed "market mavens," those who have a high propensity to provide marketplace and shopping information. Whether or not products reach such mavens can influence the success of a product, independently of the product's quality. Tucker (2008) uses micro-data on the adoption and use of a new video-messaging technology in an investment bank consisting of 2118 employees. Tucker notes the effects of the underlying network in that employees follow the actions of those who either have formal power, or informal influence (which is, to some extent, endogenous to a social network).

In the political context, there are several studies focusing on the social sources of information electors choose, as well as on the selective mis-perception of social information they are exposed to. A prime example of such a collection of studies is Huckfeldt and Sprague (1995), who concentrated on the social structure in South Bend, Indiana, during the 1984 elections. They illustrated the likelihood of socially connected individuals to hold similar political affiliations. In fact, the phenomenon of individuals connecting to individuals who are similar to them is observed across a wide array of attributes and is termed by sociologists *homophily* (for overviews see McPherson, Smith-Lovin, and Cook, 2001, Jackson, 2007, as well as the discussion of homophily in Jackson, Chapter 12 in this volume).

While cross-sectional studies are tremendously interesting in that they suggest dimensions on which social interactions may have an impact, they face many empirical challenges. Most notably, correlations between behaviors and outcomes of individuals and their peers may be driven by common unobservables and therefore be spurious. Given the strong homophily patterns in many social interactions, individuals who associate with each other often have common unobserved traits, which could lead them to similar behaviors. This makes it difficult to draw (causal) conclusions from empirical analysis of the social impact on diffusion of behaviors based on cross-sectional data.[2]

Given some of the challenges with causal inference based on pure observation, laboratory experiments and field experiments are quite useful in eliciting the effects of real-world networks on fully controlled strategic interactions, and are being

[2] In fact, Aral and Walker (2010) use different advertising methods on random samples of Facebook users and illustrate that the similarity in attributes may be an important component in observed patterns of network effects in diffusion. This is discussed at more length in Jackson (Chapter 12, this volume).

increasingly utilized. As an example, Leider, Mobius, Rosenblat, and Do (2009) elicited the friendship network among undergraduates at a U.S. college and illustrated how altruism varies as a function of social proximity. In a similar setup, Goeree, McConnell, Mitchell, Tromp, and Yariv (2010) elicited the friendship network in an all-girls school in Pasadena, CA, together with girls' characteristics and later ran dictator games with recipients who varied in social distance. They identified a "1/d Law of Giving," in that the percentage given to a friend was inversely related to her social distance in the network.[3] Various field experiments, such as those by Duflo and Saez (2003), Karlan, Mobius, Rosenblat, and Szeidl (2009), Dupas (2010), Beaman and Magruder (2010), and Feigenberg, Field, and Pande (2010), also provide some control over the process, while working with real-world network structures to examine network influences on behavior.[4]

Another approach that can be taken to infer causal relationships is via structural modeling. As an example, one can examine the implications of a particular diffusion model for the patterns of adoption that should be observed. One can then infer characteristics of the process by fitting the process parameters to best match the observed outcomes in terms of behavior. For instance, Banerjee, Chandrasekhar, Duflo, and Jackson (2010) use such an approach in a study of the diffusion of microfinance participation in rural Indian villages. Using a model of diffusion that incorporates both information and peer effects, they then fit the model to infer the relative importance of information diffusion versus peer influences in accounting for differences in microfinance participation rates across villages. Of course, in such an approach one is only as confident in the causal inference as one is confident that the model is capturing the essential underpinnings of the diffusion process.

The types of conclusions that have been reached from these cross sectional studies can be roughly summarized as follows. First, in a wide variety of settings, associated individuals tend to have correlated actions and opinions. This does not necessarily embody diffusion or causation, but as discussed in the longitudinal section below, there is significant evidence of social influence in diffusion patterns as well. Second, individuals tend to associate with others who are similar to themselves, in terms of beliefs and opinions. This has an impact on the structure of social interactions, and can affect diffusion. It also represents an empirical quandary of the extent to which social structure influences opinions and behavior as opposed to the reverse (that can partly be sorted out with careful analysis of longitudinal data). Third, individuals fill different roles in a society, with some acting as "opinion leaders," and being key conduits of information and potential catalysts for diffusion.

[3] For a look at a few network experiments that are not based on a real-world social structure, see Kosfeld (2004).

[4] Baccara, Imrohoroglu, Wilson, and Yariv (2010) use field data to illustrate how different layers of networks (social and professional) can affect outcomes differentially.

2.2 The Effects of networks over time

Longitudinal data can be especially important in diffusion studies, as they provide information on how opinions and behaviors move through a society over time. They also help sort out issues of causation as well as supply-specific information about the extent to which behaviors and opinions are adopted dynamically, and by whom. Such data can be especially important in going beyond the documentation of correlation between social connections and behaviors, and illustrating that social links are truly the conduits for information and diffusion if one is careful to track what is observed by whom at what point in time, and can measure the resulting changes in behavior. For example, Conley and Udry (2008) show that pineapple growers in Ghana tend to follow those farmers who succeed in changing their levels of use of fertilizers. Through careful examination of local ties, and the timing of different actions, they trace the influence of the outcome of one farmer's crop on subsequent behavior of other farmers.

More generally, diffusion of new technologies is extremely important when looking at transitions in agriculture. Seminal studies by Ryan and Gross (1943) and Griliches (1957) examined the effects of social connections on the adoption of a new behavior, specifically the adoption of hybrid corn in the U.S. Looking at aggregate adoption rates in different states, these authors illustrated that the diffusion of hybrid corn followed an S-shape curve over time: starting out slowly, accelerating, and then ultimately decelerating.[5] Foster and Rosenzweig (1995) collected household-level panel data from a representative sample of rural Indian households having to do with the adoption and profitability of high-yielding seed varieties (associated with the Green Revolution). They identified significant learning-by-doing, where some of the learning was through neighbors' experience. In fact, the observation that adoption rates of new technologies, products, or behaviors exhibit S-shaped curves can be traced to very early studies, such as Tarde (1903), who discussed the importance of imitation in adoption. Such patterns are found across many applications (see Mahajan and Peterson (1985) and Rogers (1995)).

Understanding diffusion is particularly important for epidemiology and medicine for several reasons. For one, it is important to understand how different types of diseases spread in a population. In addition, it is crucial to examine how new treatments get adopted. Colizza, Barrat, Barthelemy, and Vespignani (2006, 2007) tracked the spread of severe acute respiratory syndrome (SARS) across the world combining census data with data on almost all air transit during the years 2002–2003. They illustrated the importance of structures of long-range transit networks for the spread of an epidemic. Coleman, Katz, and Menzel (1966) is one of the first studies to document the role of social networks in diffusion processes. The study looked at the adoption of a new drug (tetracycline) by doctors and highlighted two observations. First, as with hybrid corn,

[5] See Young (2010) for a complementary analysis to that of Griliches (1957).

adoption rates followed an S-shape curve over time. Second, adoption rates depended on the density of social interactions. Doctors with more contacts (measured according to the trust placed in them by other doctors) adopted at higher rates and earlier in time.[6]

Diffusion can occur in many different arenas of human behavior. For example Christakis and Fowler (2007) document influences of social contacts on obesity levels. They studied the social network of 12,067 individuals in the U.S. assessed repeatedly from 1971 to 2003 as part of the Framingham Heart Study. Concentrating on body-mass index, Christakis and Fowler found that a person's chances of becoming obese increased by 57% if he or she had a friend who became obese, by 40% if he or she had a sibling who became obese, and by 37% if they had a spouse who became obese in a previous period. The study controls for various selection effects, and takes advantage of the direction of friendship nominations to help sort out causation. For example, Christakis and Fowler find a significantly higher increase of an individual's body mass index in reaction to the obesity of someone that the individual named as a friend compared to someone who had named the individual as a friend. This is one method of sorting out causation, since if unobserved influences that were common to the agents were at work, then the direction of who mentioned the other as a friend would not matter, whereas direction would matter if it indicated which individuals react to which others. Based on this analysis, Christakis and Fowler conclude that obesity spreads very much like an epidemic with the underlying social structure appearing to play an important role.

It is worth emphasizing that even with longitudinal studies, one still has to be cautious in drawing causal inferences. The problem of homophily still looms, as linked individuals tend to have common characteristics and so may be influenced by common unobserved factors, for example, both being exposed to some external stimulus (such as advertising) at the same time. This then makes it appear as if one agent's behavior closely followed another's, even when it may simply be due to both having experienced a common external event that prompted their behaviors. Aral, Muchnik, and Sundararajan (2009) provide an idea of how large this effect can be, by carefully tracking individual characteristics and then using propensity scores (likelihoods of having neighbors with certain behaviors) to illustrate the extent to which one can over-estimate diffusion effects by not accounting for common backgrounds of connected individuals.

Homophily not only suggests that linked individuals might be exposed to common influences, it also makes it hard to disentangle which of the following two processes is at the root of observed similarities in behavior between connected agents. It could be

[6] As a caveat, Van den Bulte and Lilien (2001) add controls having to do with marketing exposure of the doctors in the study and show that the social effects may be mitigated. Nonetheless, further studies such as Nair, Manchanda, and Bhatia (2006) have again found evidence of such effects after more carefully controlling for the marketing and other characteristics in a much larger data set.

that similar behavior in fact comes from a process of selection (assortative pairing), in which similarity precedes association. Alternatively, it could be a consequence of a process of socialization, in which association leads to similarity. In that respect, tracking connections and behaviors over time is particularly useful. Kandel (1978) concentrated on adolescent friendship pairs and examined the levels of homophily on four attributes (frequency of current marijuana use, level of educational aspirations, political orientation, and participation in minor delinquency) at various stages of friendship formation and dissolution. She noted that observed homophily in friendship dyads resulted from a significant combination of both types of processes, so that individuals emulated their friends, but also tended to drop friendships with those more different from themselves and add new friendships to those more similar to themselves.[7]

In summary, let us mention a few of the important conclusions obtained from studies of diffusion. First, not only are behaviors across socially connected individuals correlated, but individuals do influence each other. While this may sound straightforward, it takes careful control to ensure that it is not unobserved correlated traits or influences that lead to similar actions by connected individuals, as well as an analysis of similarities between friends that can lead to correlations in their preferences and the things that influence them. Second, in various settings, more socially connected individuals adopt new behaviors and products earlier and at higher rates. Third, diffusion exhibits specific patterns over time, and specifically there are many settings where an "S"-shaped pattern emerges, with adoption starting slowly, then accelerating, and eventually asymptoting. Fourth, many diffusion processes are affected by the specifics of the patterns of interaction.

3. MODELS OF DIFFUSION AND STRATEGIC INTERACTION ABSENT NETWORK STRUCTURE

We now turn to discussing various models of diffusion. As should be clear from our description of the empirical work on diffusion and behavior, models can help greatly in clarifying the tensions at play. Given the issues associated with the endogeneity of social relationships, and the substantial homophily that may lead to correlated behaviors among social neighbors, it is critical to have models that help predict how behavior should evolve and how it interacts with the social structure in place.

We start with some of the early models that do not account for the underlying network architecture per-se. These models incorporate the empirical observations regarding social influence through the particular dynamics assumed, or preferences posited, and generate predictions matching the *aggregate* empirical observations regarding

[7] Of course there is also homophily based on nonmalleable attributes, in which case homophily can only be due to the connection process. For example, Goeree, McConnell, Mitchell, Tromp, and Yariv (2010) observe homophily on height, and there is a rich literature on homophily based on ethnicity, gender, and other nonmalleable attributes (see Jackson, Chapter 12 in this volume, for references).

diffusion over time of products, diseases, or behavior. For example, the so-called *S*-shaped adoption curves. After describing these models, we return to explicitly capturing the role of social networks.

3.1 Marketing models

One of the earliest and still widely used models of diffusion is the Bass (1969) Model. This is a parsimonious model, which can be thought of as a "macro" model: it makes predictions about aggregate behavior in terms of the percentage of potential adopters of a product or behavior who will have adopted by a given time. The current rate of change of adoption depends on the current level and two critical parameters. These two parameters are linked to the rate at which people innovate or adopt on their own, and the rate at which they imitate or adopt because others have, thereby putting into (theoretical) force the empirical observation regarding peers' influence.

If we let $G(t)$ be the percentage of agents who have adopted by time t, and m be the fraction of agents in the population who are potential adopters, a discrete time version of the Bass model is characterized by the difference equation

$$G(t) = G(t-1) + p(m - G(t-1)) + q(m - G(t-1))\frac{G(t-1)}{m},$$

where p is a rate of innovation and q is a rate of imitation. To glean some intuition, note that the expression $p\ (m - G(t-1))$ represents the fraction of people who have not yet adopted and might potentially do so times the rate of spontaneous adoption. In the expression $q(m - G(t-1))\frac{G(t-1)}{m}$, the rate of imitation is multiplied by two factors. The first factor, $(m - G(t-1))$, is the fraction of people who have not yet adopted and may still do so. The second expression, $\frac{G(t-1)}{m}$, is the relative fraction of potential adopters who are around to imitate. If we set m equal to 1, and look at a continuous time version of the above difference equation, we get

$$g(t) = (p + qG(t))(1 - G(t)), \tag{1}$$

where g is the rate of diffusion (times the rate of change of G). Solving this when $p > 0$ and setting the initial set of adopters at 0, $G(0) = 0$, leads to the following expression:

$$G(t) = \frac{1 - e^{-(p+q)t}}{1 + \frac{q}{p}e^{-(p+q)t}}.$$

This is a fairly flexible formula that works well at fitting time series data of innovations. By estimating p and q from existing data, one can also make forecasts of future diffusion. It has been used extensively in marketing and for the general analysis of diffusion (e.g., Rogers (1995)), and has spawned many extensions and variations.[8]

[8] For some recent models, see Leskovec, Adamic, and Huberman (2007) and Young (2010).

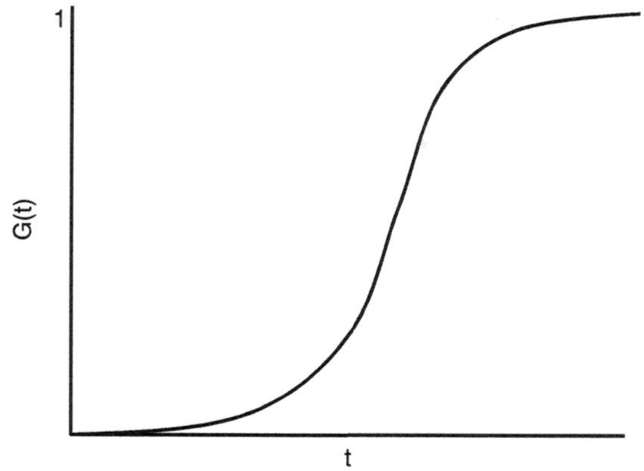

Figure 1 *S*-shape Adoption.

If q is large enough,[9] then there is a sufficient imitation/social effect, which means that the rate of adoption accelerates after it begins, and so $G(t)$ is S-shaped (see Figure 1), matching one of the main insights of the longitudinal empirical studies on diffusion discussed above. The Bass model provides a clear intuition for why adoption curves would be S-shaped. Indeed, when the adoption process begins, imitation plays a minor role (relative to innovation) since not many agents have adopted yet and so the volume of adopters grows slowly. As the number of adopters increases, the process starts to accelerate as now innovators are joined by imitators. The process eventually starts to slow down, in part simply because there are fewer agents left to adopt (the term $1-G(t)$ in (1) eventually becomes small). Thus, we see a process that starts out slowly, then accelerates, and then eventually slows and asymptotes.

3.2 Collective action, fashion, and fads

The Bass model described above is mechanical in that adopters and imitators are randomly determined; they do not choose actions strategically. The empirical observation that individuals influence each other through social contact can be derived through agents' preferences, rather than through some exogenously specified dynamics.

Diffusion in a strategic context was first studied without a specific structure for interactions. Broadly speaking, there were two approaches taken in this early literature. In the first, all agents are connected to one another (that is, they form a complete network). Effectively, this corresponds to a standard multi-agent game in which payoffs to each player depend on the entire profile of actions played in the population. The second approach has been to look at interactions in which agents are matched to partners in a random fashion.

[9] See Jackson (2008) for a more detailed discussion.

Diffusion on Complete Networks. Granovetter (1978) considered a model in which N agents are all connected to one another and each agent chooses one of two actions: 0 or 1. Associated with each agent i is a number n_i. This is a threshold such that if at least n_i other agents take action 1 then i prefers action 1 to action 0, and if fewer than n_i other agents take action 1 then agent i prefers to take action 0. The game exhibits what are known as strategic complementarities. For instance, suppose that the utility of agent i faced with a profile of actions $(x_1, \ldots, x_N) \in \{0, 1\}^N$ is described by:

$$u_i(x_1, \mathrm{K}, x_N) = \left[\frac{\sum_{j \neq i} x_j}{N-1} - c_i\right] x_i, \tag{2}$$

where c_i is randomly drawn from a distribution F over [0,1]. c_i can be thought of as a cost that agent i experiences upon choosing action 1 (e.g., a one-time switching cost from one technology to the other, or potential time costs of joining a political revolt, etc.). The utility of agent i is normalized to 0 when choosing the action 0. When choosing the action 1, agent i experiences a benefit proportional to the fraction of other agents choosing the action 1 and a cost of c_i.

Granovetter considered a dynamic model in which at each stage agents best respond to the previous period's distribution of actions. If in period t there was a fraction x^t of agents choosing the action 1, then in period $t+1$ an agent i chooses action 1 if and only if his or her cost is lower than $\frac{Nx^t - x_i^t}{N-1}$, the fraction of other agents taking action 1 in the last period. For a large population, $\frac{Nx^t - x_i^t}{N-1} \simeq x^t$ and $x^{t+1} \simeq F(x^t)$. A fixed-point $x^* = F(x^*)$ then corresponds to an (approximate) equilibrium of a large population.

The shape of the distribution F determines which equilibria are *tipping points*: equilibria such that only a slight addition to the fraction of agents choosing the action 1 shifts the population, under the best response dynamics, to the next higher equilibrium level of adoption (we return to a discussion of tipping and stable points when we consider a more general model of strategic interactions on networks below).

Note that while in the Bass model the diffusion path was determined by $G(t)$, the fraction of adopters as a function of time, here it is easier to work with $F(x)$, corresponding to the fraction of adopters as a function of the previous period's fraction x.

Although Granovetter (1978) does not examine conditions under which the time series will exhibit attributes like the S-shape that we discussed above, by using techniques from Jackson and Yariv (2007) we can derive such results, as we now discuss. Keeping track of time in discrete periods (a continuous time analog is straightforward), the level of change of adoption in the society is given by

$$\Delta(x^t) = F(x^t) - x^t.$$

Thus, to derive an S-shape, we need this quantity to initially be increasing, and then eventually to decrease. Assuming differentiability of F, this corresponds to the derivative of $\Delta(x^t)$ being positive up to some $\overline{x}$ and then negative. The derivative of $F(x) - x$ is $F'(x) - 1$ and having an *S*-shape corresponds to F' being greater than 1 up to some point and then less than 1 beyond that point. For instance, if F is concave with an initial slope greater than 1 and an eventual slope less than 1, this is satisfied. Note that the *S*-shape of adoption over time does not translate into an *S*-shape of F – but rather a sort of concavity.[10] The idea is that we initially need a rapid level of change, which corresponds to an initially high slope of F, and then a slowing down, which corresponds to a lower slope of F.

Fashions and Random Matching. A different approach than that of the Bass model is taken by Pesendorfer (1995), who considers a model in which individuals are randomly matched and new fashions serve as signaling instruments for the creation of matches. He identifies particular matching technologies that generate fashion cycles. Pesendorfer describes the spread of a new fashion as well as its decay over time. In Pesendorfer's model, the price of the design falls as it spreads across the population. Once sufficiently many consumers own the design, it is profitable to create a new design and thereby render the old design obsolete. In particular, demand for any new innovation eventually levels off as in the above two models.

Information Cascades and Learning. Another influence on collective behavior derives from social learning. This can happen without any direct complementarities in actions, but due to information flow about the potential payoffs from different behaviors. If people discuss which products are worth buying, or which technologies are worth adopting, books worth reading, and so forth, even without any complementarities in behaviors, one can end up with cascades in behavior, as people infer information from others' behaviors and can (rationally) imitate them. As effects along these lines are discussed at some length in Jackson (Chapter 12, this volume) and Goyal (Chapter 15, this volume), we will not detail them here. We only stress that pure information transmission can lead to diffusion of behaviors.

4. MODELS OF DIFFUSION AND STRATEGIC INTERACTION IN NETWORK SETTINGS

We now turn to models that explicitly incorporate social structure in examining diffusion patterns. We start with models that stem mostly from the epidemiology literature and account for the underlying social network, but are mechanical in terms of the way that disease spreads from one individual to another (much like the Bass model described above). We then proceed to models in which players make choices that depend on their neighbors' actions as embedded in a social network; for instance, only adopting

[10] Concavity, plus having a slope that is 1 at some point, is sufficient, but not necessary to have the positive and then negative property of $F'(x) - 1$.

an action if a certain proportion of neighbors adopt as well (as in Granovetter's setup), or possibly not adopting an action if enough neighbors do so.

4.1 A unified setting

Many models of diffusion and strategic interaction on networks have the following common elements.

There is a finite set of agents $N = \{1, \ldots, n\}$.

Agents are connected by a (possibly directed) network $g \in \{0, 1\}^{n \times n}$. We let $N_i(g) \equiv \{j : g_{ij} = 1\}$ be the neighbors of i. The degree of a node i is the number of her neighbors, $d_i \equiv |N_i(g)|$.

When links are determined through some random process, it is often useful to summarize the process by the resulting distribution of degrees P, where $P(d)$ denotes the probability a random individual has a degree of d.[11,12]

Each agent $i \in N$ takes an action x_i. In order to unify and simplify the description of various models, we focus on binary actions, so that $x_i \in \{0, 1\}$. Actions can be metaphors for becoming "infected" or not, buying a new product or not, choosing one of two activities, and so forth.

4.2 Epidemiology models

4.2.1 Random graph models

Some basic insights about the extent to which behavior or an infection can spread in a society can be derived from random graph theory. Random graph theory provides a tractable base for understanding characteristics important for diffusion, such as the structure and size of the components of a network, maximally connected subnetworks.[13]

Before presenting some results, let us talk through some of the ideas in the context of what is known as the *Reed-Frost model*.[14] Consider, for example, the spread of a disease. Initially, some individuals in the society are infected through mutations of a germ or other exogenous sources. Consequently, some of these individuals' neighbors are infected through contact, while others are not. This depends on how virulent the disease is, among other things. In this application, it makes sense (at least as a starting point) to assume that becoming infected or avoiding infection is not a choice;

[11] Such a description is not complete, in that it does not specify the potential correlations between degrees of different individuals on the network. See Galeotti, Goyal, Jackson, Vega-Redondo, and Yariv (2010) for more details.

[12] In principle, one would want to calibrate degree distributions with actual data. The literature on network formation, see Bloch and Dutta (Chapter 16, this volume) and Jackson (Chapter 12, this volume), suggests some insights on plausible degree distributions $P(d)$.

[13] Formally, these are the subnetworks projected induced by maximal sets $C \subseteq N$ of nodes such any two distinct nodes in C are *path connected* within C. That is, for any $i,j \in C$, there exist $i_1, \ldots, i_k \in C$ such that $g_{ii_1} = g_{i_1 i_2} = \ldots = g_{i_{k-1} i_k} = g_{i_k j} = 1$.

[14] See Jackson (2008) for a more detailed discussion of this and related models.

i.e., contagion here is nonstrategic. In the simplest model, there is a probability $\pi \geq 0$ that a given individual is immune (e.g., through vaccination or natural defenses). If an individual is not immune, it is assumed that he or she is sure to catch the disease if one of his or her neighbors ends up with the disease. In this case, in order to estimate the volume of those ultimately infected, we proceed in two steps, depicted in Figure 2. First, we delete a fraction π of the nodes that will never be infected (these correspond to the dotted nodes in the Figure). Then, we note that the components of the remaining network that contain the originally infected individuals comprise the full extent of the infection. In particular, if we can characterize what the components of the network look like after removing some portion of the nodes, we have an idea of the extent of the infection. In Figure 2, we start with one large connected component (circumvented by a dotted line) and two small-connected components. After removing the immune agents, there is still a large connected component (though smaller than before), and four small components.

Thus, the estimation of the extent of infection of the society is reduced to the estimation of the component structure of the network. A starting point for the formal analysis of this sort of model uses the canonical random network model, where links are formed independently, each with an identical probability $p > 0$ of being present. This is sometimes referred to as a "Poisson random network" as its degree distribution is approximated by a Poisson distribution if p is not excessively large; and has various other aliases such as an "Erdös-Renyi random graph," a "Bernoulli random graph," or a "$G(n,p)$" random graph (see Jackson, Chapter 12 in this volume, for more

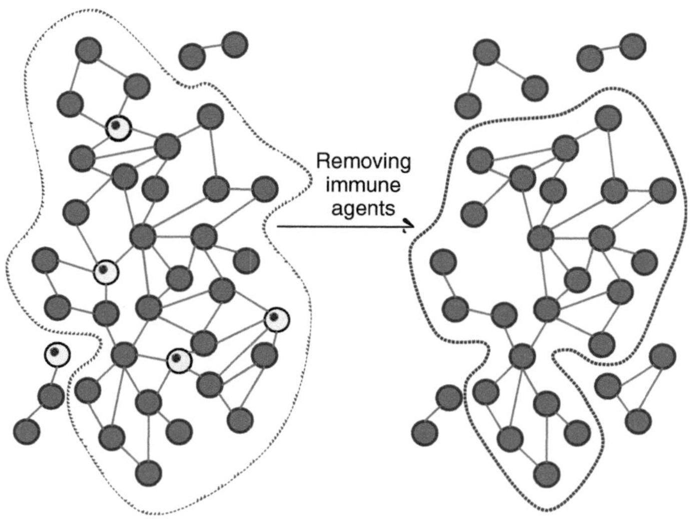

Figure 2 Network Components and Immune Agents.

background). Ultimately, the analysis boils down to considering a network on $(1-\pi)n$ nodes with an independent link probability of p, and then measuring the size of the component containing a randomly chosen initially infected node.

Clearly, with a fixed set of nodes, and a positive probability p that lies strictly between 0 and 1, every conceivable network on the given set of nodes could arise. Thus, in order to say something specific about the properties of the networks that are "most likely" to arise, one generally works with large n where reasoning based on laws of large numbers can be employed. For example, if we think of letting n grow, we can ask for which p's (that are now dependent on n) a nonvanishing fraction of nodes will become infected with a probability bounded away from 0. So, let us consider a sequence of societies indexed by n and corresponding probabilities of links $p(n)$.

Erdös and Renyi (1959, 1960) proved a series of results that characterize some basic properties of such random graphs. In particular,[15]

- The threshold for the existence of a "giant component," a component that contains a nontrivial fraction of the population, is $1/n$, corresponding to an average degree of 1. That is, if $p(n)$ over $1/n$ tends to infinity, then the probability of having a giant component tends to 1, while if $p(n)$ over $1/n$ tends to 0, then the probability of having a giant component tends to 0.
- The threshold for the network to be connected (so that every two nodes have a path between them) is $\log(n)/n$, corresponding to an average degree that is proportional to $\log(n)$.

The logic for the first threshold is easy to explain, though the proof is rather involved. To heuristically derive the threshold for the emergence of a giant component, consider following a link out of a given node. We ask whether or not one would expect to be able to find a link to another node from that one. If the expected degree is much smaller than 1, then following the few (if any) links from any given node is likely to lead to dead-ends. In contrast, when the expected degree is much higher than 1, then from any given node, one expects to be able to reach more nodes, and then even more nodes, and so forth, and so the component should expand outward.

Note that adjusting for the factor π of the number of immune nodes does not affect the above thresholds as they apply as limiting results, although the factor will be important for any fixed n.

Between these two thresholds, there is only one giant component, so that the next largest component is of a size that is a vanishing fraction of the giant component. This is intuitively clear, as to have two large components requires many links within each component but no links between the two components, which is an unlikely event. In that sense, the image that emerges from Figure 2 of one large connected component is reasonably typical for a range of parameter values.

[15] See Chapter 4 in Jackson (2008) for a fuller discussion and proofs of these results.

These results then tell us that in a random network, if average degree is quite low (smaller than 1), then any initial infection is likely to die out. In contrast, if average degree is quite high (larger than $\log(n)$), then any initial infection is likely to spread to all of the susceptible individuals, i.e., a fraction of $1 - \pi$ of the population. In the intermediate range, there is a probability that the infection will die out and also a probability that it will infect a nontrivial, but limited, portion of the susceptible population. There, it can be shown that for such random networks and large n, the fraction of nodes in the giant component of susceptible nodes is roughly approximated by the nonzero q that solves

$$q = 1 - e^{-q(1-\pi)np}. \tag{3}$$

Here, q is an approximation of the probability of the infection spreading to a nontrivial fraction of nodes, and also of the percentage of susceptible nodes that would be infected.[16]

This provides a rough idea of the type of results that can be derived from random graph theory. There is much more that is known, as one can work with other models of random graphs (other than ones where each link has an identical probability), richer models of probabilistic infection between nodes, as well as derive more information about the potential distribution of infected individuals.

It should also be emphasized that while the discussion here is in terms of "infection," the applications clearly extend to many of the other contexts we have been mentioning, such as the transmission of ideas and information. Fuller treatment of behaviors, where individual decisions depend in more complicated ways on neighbors' decisions, are treated in Section 4.3.

4.2.2 Diffusion with recovery

The above analysis of diffusion presumes that once infected, a node eventually infects all of its susceptible neighbors. This misses important aspects of many applications. In terms of diseases, infected nodes can either recover and stop transmitting a disease, or die and completely disappear from the network. Transmission will also generally be probabilistic, depending on the type of interaction and its extent.[17] Similarly, if we think of behaviors, it might be that the likelihood that a node is still actively transmitting a bit of information to its neighbors decreases over time.

Ultimately, we will discuss models that allow for rather general strategic impact of peer behavior (a generalization of the approach taken by Granovetter). But first we discuss some aspects of the epidemiology literature that takes steps forward in that direction by considering two alternative models that keep track of the state of nodes and are more explicitly dynamic. The common terminology for the possible states that

[16] Again, see Chapter 4 in Jackson (2008) for more details.

[17] Probabistic transmission is easily handled in the above model by simply adjusting the link probability to reflect the fact that some links might not transmit the disease.

a node can be in are: *susceptible*, where a node is not currently infected or transmitting a disease but can catch it; *infected*, where a node has a disease and can transmit it to its neighbors; and *removed* (or *recovered*), where a node has been infected but is no longer able to transmit the disease and cannot be re-infected.

The first of the leading models is the "SIR" model (dating to Kermack and McKendrick, 1927), where nodes are initially susceptible but can catch the disease from infected neighbors. Once infected, a node continues to infect neighbors until it is randomly removed from the system. This fits well the biology of some childhood diseases, such as the chicken pox, where one can only be infected once.

The other model is the "SIS" model (see Bailey, 1975), where once infected, nodes can randomly recover, but then they are susceptible again. This corresponds well with an assortment of bacterial infections, viruses, and flus, where one transitions back and forth between health and illness.

The analysis of the SIR model is a variant of the component-size analysis discussed above. The idea is that there is a random chance that an "infected" node infects a given "susceptible" neighbor before becoming "removed." Roughly, one examines component structures in which instead of removing *nodes* randomly, one removes *links* randomly from the network. This results in variations on the above sorts of calculations, where there are adjusted thresholds for infection depending on the relative rates of how quickly infected nodes can infect their neighbors compared to how quickly they are removed.

In contrast, the SIS model involves a different sort of analysis. The canonical version of that model is best viewed as one with a random matching process rather than a social network. In particular, suppose that a node i in each period will have interactions with d_i other individuals from the population. Recall our notation of $P(d)$ describing the proportion of the population that has degree d (so d interactions per period). The matches are determined randomly, in such a way that if i is matched with j, then the probability that j has degree $d > 0$ is given by

$$\tilde{P}(d) = \frac{P(d)d}{\langle d \rangle}, \tag{4}$$

where $\langle \cdot \rangle$ represents the expectation with respect to P.[18] This reflects the fact that an agent is proportionally more likely to be matched with other individuals who have lots of connections. To justify this formally, one needs an infinite population. Indeed, with any finite population of agents with heterogeneous degrees, the emergent networks will generally exhibit some correlation between neighbors' degrees.[19]

Individuals who have high degrees will have more interactions per period and will generally be more likely to be infected at any given time. An important calculation

[18] We consider only individuals who have degree $d > 0$, as others do not participate in the society.

[19] See the appendix of Currarini, Jackson, and Pin (2009) for some details along this line.

then pertains to the chance that a given meeting will be with an infected individual. If the infection rate of degree d individuals is $\rho(d)$, the probability that any given meeting will be with an infected individual is θ, where

$$\theta = \sum_{d} \tilde{P}(d)\rho(d) = \frac{\sum P(d)\rho(d)d}{\langle d \rangle}. \tag{5}$$

The chance of meeting an infected individual in a given encounter then differs from the average infection rate in the population, which is just $\rho = \sum P(d)\rho(d)$, because θ is weighted by the rate at which individuals meet each other.

A standard version of contagion that is commonly analyzed is one in which the probability of an agent of degree d becoming infected is

$$v\theta d, \tag{6}$$

where $v \in (0, 1)$ is a rate of transmission of infection in a given period, and is small enough so that this probability is less than one. If v is very small, this is an approximation of getting infected under d interactions with each having an (independent) probability θ of being infected and then conditionally (and independently) having a probability v of getting infected through contact with a given infected individual. The last part of the model is that in any given period, an infected individual recovers and becomes susceptible with a probability $\delta \in (0, 1)$.

If such a system operates on a finite population, then eventually all agents will become susceptible and that would end the infection. If there is a small probability of a new mutation and infection in any given period, the system will be ergodic and always have some probability of future infection.

To get a feeling for the long run outcomes in large societies, the literature has examined a steady state (i.e., a situation in which the system essentially remains constant) of a process that is idealized as operating on an infinite (continuous) population. Formally, a steady-state is defined by having $\rho(d)$ be constant over time for each d. Working with an approximation at the limit (termed a "mean-field" approximation that in this case can be justified with a continuum of agents, but with quite a bit of technical detail), a steady-state condition can be derived to be

$$0 = (1 - \rho(d))v\theta d - \rho(d)\delta \tag{7}$$

for each d. $(1-\rho(d))v\theta d$ is the rate at which agents of degree d who were susceptible become infected and $\rho(d)\delta$ is the rate at which infected individuals of degree d recover. Letting $\lambda = \frac{v}{\delta}$, it follows that

$$\rho(d) = \frac{\lambda\theta d}{\lambda\theta d + 1}. \tag{8}$$

Solving (5) and (8) simultaneously leads to a characterization of the steady-state θ:

$$\theta = \sum_d \frac{P(d)\lambda\theta d^2}{\langle d\rangle(\lambda\theta d + 1)}. \tag{9}$$

This system always has a solution, and therefore a steady-state, where $\theta = 0$ so there is no infection. It can also have other solutions under which θ is positive (but always below 1 if λ is finite). Unless P takes very specific forms, it can be difficult to find steady states $\theta > 0$ analytically.

Special cases have been analyzed, such as the case of a power distribution, where $P(d) = 2d^{-3}$ (e.g., see Pastor-Satorras and Vespignani (2000, 2001)). In that case, there is always a positive steady-state infection rate. More generally, Lopez-Pintado (2008) addresses the question of when it is that there will be a positive steady-state infection rate. To get some intuition for her results, let

$$H(\theta) = \sum \frac{P(d)d}{\langle d\rangle}\left(\frac{\lambda d\theta}{\lambda d\theta + 1}\right) = \sum \tilde{P}(d)\left(\frac{\lambda d\theta}{\lambda d\theta + 1}\right), \tag{10}$$

so that the equation $\theta = H(\theta)$ corresponds to steady states of the system. We can now extend the analysis of Granovetter's (1978) model that we described above, with this richer model in which $H(\theta)$ accounts for network attributes. While the fixed-point equation identifying Granovetter's stable points allowed for rather arbitrary diffusion patterns (depending on the cost distribution F), the function H has additional structure to it that we can explore.

In particular, suppose we examine the infection rate that would result if we start at a rate of θ and then run the system on an infinite population for one period. Noting that $H(0) = 0$, it is clear that 0 is always a fixed-point and thus a steady-state. Since $H(1) < 1$, and H is increasing and strictly concave in θ (which is seen by examining its first and second derivatives), there can be at most one fixed-point besides 0. For there to be another fixed-point (steady-state) above $\theta = 0$, it must be that $H'(0)$ is above 1, or else, given the strict concavity, we would have $H(\theta) < \theta$ for all positive θ. Moreover, in cases where $H'(0) > 1$, a small perturbation away from a 0 infection rate will lead to increased infection. In the terminology we have introduced above, 0 would be a *tipping point*. Since

$$H'(0) = \lambda \frac{\langle d^2\rangle}{\langle d\rangle}, \tag{11}$$

we have a simple way of checking whether we expect a positive steady-state infection or a 0 steady-state infection. This simply boils down to a comparison of the relative infection rate λ and $\frac{\langle d\rangle}{\langle d^2\rangle}$ so that there is a positive infection rate if and only if

$$\lambda > \frac{\langle d \rangle}{\langle d^2 \rangle}. \tag{12}$$

Higher infection rates lead to the possibility of positive infection, as do degree distributions with high variances (relative to mean). The idea behind having a high variance is that there will be some "hub nodes" with high degree, who can foster contagion.

Going back to our empirical insights, this analysis fits the observations that highly-linked individuals are more likely to get infected and experience speedier diffusion. Whether the aggregate behavior exhibits the S-shape that is common in many real-world diffusion processes will depend on the particulars of H, much in the same way that we discussed how the S-shape in Granovetter's model depends on the shape of the distribution of costs F in that model. Here, things are slightly complicated since H is a function of θ, which is the probability of infection of a neighbor, and not the overall probability of infection of the population. Thus, one needs to further translate how various θ's over time translate into population fractions that are infected.

Beyond the extant empirical studies, this analysis provides some intuitions behind what is needed for an infection to be possible. It does not, however, provide an idea of how extensive the infection spread will be and how that depends on network structure. While this does not boil down to as simple a comparison as (12), there is still much that can be deduced using (9), as shown by Jackson and Rogers (2007). While one cannot always directly solve

$$\theta = \sum_d \frac{P(d)\lambda\theta d^2}{\langle d \rangle (\lambda\theta d + 1)},$$

notice that $\frac{\lambda\theta d^2}{\langle d \rangle (\lambda\theta d + 1)}$ is an increasing and convex function of d. Therefore, the right hand side of the above equality can be ordered when comparing different degree distributions in the sense of stochastic dominance (we will return to these sorts of comparisons in some of the models we discuss below). The interesting conclusion regarding steady-state infection rates is that they depend on network structure in ways that are very different at low levels of the infection rate λ compared to high levels.

4.3 Graphical games

While the above models provide some ideas about how social structure impacts diffusion, they are limited to settings where, roughly speaking, the probability that a given individual adopts a behavior is simply proportional to the infection rate of neighbors. Especially when it comes to situations in which opinions or technologies are adopted, purchasing decisions are made, etc., an individual's decision can depend in much more complicated ways on the behavior of his or her neighbors. Such interaction naturally calls on game theory as a tool for modeling these richer interactions.

We start with static models of interactions on networks that allow for a rather general impact of peers' actions on one's own optimal choices.

The first model that explicitly examines games played on a network is the model of "graphical games" as introduced by Kearns, Littman, and Singh (2001), and analyzed by Kakade, Kearns, Langford, and Ortiz (2003), among others. The underlying premise in the graphical games model is that agents' *payoffs* depend on their own actions and the actions of their direct neighbors, as determined by the network of connections.[20]

Formally, the payoff structure underlying a graphical game is as follows. The payoff to each player i when the profile of actions is $x = (x_1, \ldots, x_n)$ is

$$u_i(x_i, x_{N_i(g)}),$$

where $x_{N_i(g)}$ is the profile of actions taken by the neighbors of i in the network g.

Most of the empirical applications discussed earlier entailed agents responding to neighbors' actions in roughly one of two ways. In some contexts, such as those pertaining to the adoption of a new product or new agricultural grain, decisions to join the workforce, or to join a criminal network, agents conceivably gain more from a particular action the greater is the volume of peers who choose a similar action. That is, payoffs exhibit strategic complementarities. In other contexts, such as experimentation on a new drug, or contribution to a public good, when an agent's neighbors choose a particular action, the relative payoff the agent gains from choosing a similar action decreases, and there is strategic substitutability. The graphical games environment allows for the analysis of both types of setups, as the following example (taken from Galeotti, Goyal, Jackson, Vega-Redondo, and Yariv (2010)) illustrates.

Example 1 (Payoffs Depend on the Sum of Actions) Player i's payoff function when he or she chooses x_i and her k neighbors choose the profile $(x_1, \ldots, x_k)$ is:

$$u_i(x_i, x_1, \ldots, x_k) = f\left(x_i + \lambda \sum_{j=1}^{k} x_j\right) - c(x_i), \qquad (13)$$

where $f(\cdot)$ is nondecreasing and $c(\cdot)$ is a "cost" function associated with own effort (more general but much in the spirit of (2)). The parameter $\lambda \in \mathbb{R}$ determines the nature of the externality across players' actions. The shape and sign of λf determine the effects of neighbors' action choices on one's own optimal choice. In particular, the example yields strict strategic substitutes (complements) if, assuming differentiability, $\lambda f''$ is negative (positive).

There are several papers that analyze graphical games for particular choices of f and λ. To mention a few examples, the case where f is concave, $\lambda = 1$, and $c(\cdot)$ is increasing

[20] There are also other models of equilibria in social interactions, where players care about the play of certain other groups of players. See Glaeser and Scheinkman (2000) for an overview.

and linear corresponds to the case of information sharing as a local public good studied by Bramoullé and Kranton (2007), where actions are strategic substitutes. In contrast, if $\lambda = 1$, but f is convex (with $c'' > f'' > 0$), we obtain a model with strategic complements, as proposed by Goyal and Moraga-Gonzalez (2001) to study collaboration among local monopolies. In fact, the formulation in (13) is general enough to accommodate numerous further examples in the literature such as human capital investment (Calvó-Armengol and Jackson (2009)), crime and other networks (Ballester, Calvó-Armengol, and Zenou (2006)), some coordination problems (Ellison (1993)), and the onset of social unrest (Chwe (2000)).

The computer science literature (e.g., the literature following Kearns, Littman, and Singh (2001), and analyzed by Kakade, Kearns, Langford, and Ortiz (2003)) has focused predominantly on the question of when an efficient (polynomial-time) algorithm can be provided to compute Nash equilibria of graphical games. It has not had much to say about the properties of equilibria, which is important when thinking about applying such models to analyze diffusion in the presence of strategic interaction. In contrast, the economics literature has concentrated on characterizing equilibrium outcomes for particular applications, and deriving general comparative statics with respect to agents' positions in a network and with respect to the network architecture itself.

Information players hold regarding the underlying network (namely, whether they are fully informed of the entire set of connections in the population, or only of connections in some local neighborhood) ends up playing a crucial role in the scope of predictions generated by network game models. Importantly, graphical games are ones in which agents have complete information regarding the networks in place. Consequently, such models suffer from inherent multiplicity problems, as clearly illustrated in the following example. It is based on a variation of (13), which is similar to a model analyzed by Bramoullé and Kranton (2007).

Example 2 (Multiplicity – Complete Information) Suppose that in (13), we set $\lambda = 1$, choose $x_i \in \{0, 1\}$, and have

$$f\left(x_i + \sum_{j=1}^{k} x_j\right) \equiv \min\left[x_i + \sum_{j=1}^{k} x_j, 1\right],$$

and $c(x_i) \equiv cx_i$, where $0 < c < 1$. This game, often labeled the *best-shot public goods game*, may be viewed as a game of local public-good provision. Each agent would choose the action 1 (say, experimenting with a new grain, or buying a product that can be shared with one's friends) if they were alone (or no one else experimented), but would prefer that one of their neighbors incur the cost c that the action 1 entails (when experimentation is observed publicly). Effectively, an agent just needs at least one agent in his

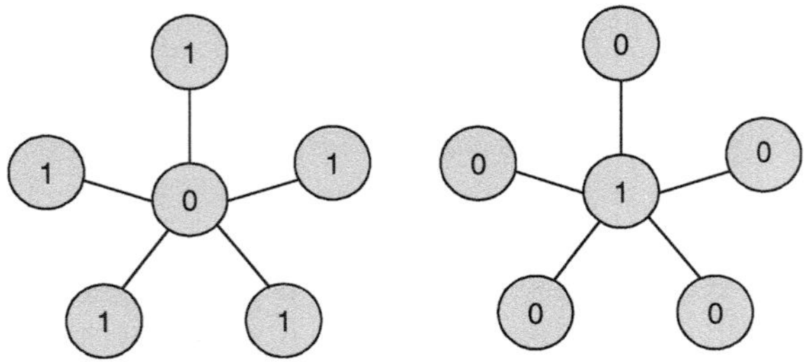

Figure 3 Multiplicity of Equilibria with Complete Information.

or her neighborhood to take action 1 to enjoy its full benefits, but prefers that it be someone else given that the action is costly and there is no additional benefit beyond one person taking the action.

Note that, since $c < 1$, in any (pure strategy) Nash equilibrium, for any player i with k neighbors, it must be the case that one of the agents in the neighborhood chooses the action 1. That is, if the chosen profile is $(x_1, \ldots, x_k)$, then $x_i + \sum_{j=1}^{k} x_j \geq 1$. In fact, there is a very rich set of equilibria in this game. To see this, consider a star network and note that there exist two equilibria, one in which the center chooses 0 and the spokes choose 1, and a second equilibrium in which the spoke players choose 0 while the center chooses 1. Figure 3 illustrates these two equilibria. In the first, depicted in the left panel of the Figure, the center earns more than the spoke players, while in the second equilibrium (in the right panel) it is the other way round.

Even in the simplest network structures equilibrium multiplicity may arise and the relation between network architecture, equilibrium actions, and systematic patterns can be difficult to discover.

4.4 Network games

While complete information regarding the structure of the social network imposed in graphical game models may be very sensible when the relevant network of agents is small, in large groups of agents (such as a country's electorate, the entire set of corn growers in the 50's, sites in the world-wide web, or academic economists), it is often the case that individuals have noisy perceptions of their network's architecture. As the discussion above stressed, complete information poses many challenges because of the widespread occurrence of equilibrium multiplicity that accompanies it. In contrast, when one looks at another benchmark, where agents know how many neighbors they will have but not who they will be, the equilibrium correspondence is much easier to deal with. Moreover, this benchmark is an idealized model of settings in which agents make choices like learning a language or adopting a technology that they will use over a long time. In such contexts, agents have some idea of how many interactions they are likely to have in the future, but not exactly with whom the interactions will be.

A *network game* is a modification of a graphical game in which agents can have private and incomplete information regarding the realized social network at place. We describe here the setup corresponding to that analyzed by Galeotti, Goyal, Jackson, Vega-Redondo, and Yariv (2010) and Jackson and Yariv (2005, 2007), restricting attention to binary action games.[21]

Uncertainty is operationalized by assuming the network is determined according to some random process yielding our distribution over agents' degrees, $P(d)$, which is common knowledge. Each player i has d_i interactions, but does not know how many interactions each neighbor has. Thus, each player knows something about his or her local neighborhood (the number of direct neighbors), but only the distribution of links in the remaining population.

Consider now the following utility specification, a generalization of (2). Agent i has a cost of choosing 1, denoted c_i. Costs are randomly and independently distributed across the society, according to a distribution F^c. Normalize the utility from the action 0 to 0 and let the benefit of agent i from action 1 be denoted by $v(d_i, x)$, where d_i is i's degree and she expects each of her neighbors to independently choose the action 1 with probability x. Agent i's added payoff from adopting behavior 1 over sticking to the action 0 is then $v(d_i, x) - c_i$.

This captures how the number of neighbors that i has, as well as their propensity to choose the action 1, affects the benefits from adopting 1. In particular, i prefers to choose the action 1 if

$$c_i \leq v(d_i, x). \tag{14}$$

This is a simple cost-benefit analysis generalizing Granovetter (1978)'s setup in that benefits can now depend on one's own degree (so that the underlying network is accounted for). Let $F(d, x) \equiv F^c(v(d, x))$. In words, $F(d, x)$ is the probability that a random agent of degree d chooses the action 1 when anticipating that each neighbor will choose 1 with an independent probability x.

Note that $v(d, x)$ can encompass all sorts of social interactions. In particular, it allows for a simple generalization of Granovetter's (1978) model to situations in which agents' payoffs depend on the expected number of neighbors adopting, dx.

Existence of symmetric Bayesian equilibria follows standard arguments. In cases where v is nondecreasing in x for each d, it is a direct consequence of Tarski's Fixed-Point Theorem. In fact, in this case, there exists an equilibrium in pure strategies.

[21] There are also other variations, such as Galeotti and Vega-Redondo (2006) and Sundararajan (2007), who study specific contexts, compatible with particular utility specifications.

In other cases, provided v is continuous in x for each d, a fixed-point can still be found by appealing to standard theorems (e.g., Kakutani) and admitting mixed strategies.[22]

Homogeneous Costs. Suppose first that all individuals experience the same cost $c > 0$ of choosing the action 1 (much like in Example 2 above). In that case, as long as $v(d, x)$ is monotonic in d (nonincreasing or nondecreasing), equilibria are characterized by a threshold. Indeed, suppose $v(d, x)$ is increasing in d, then any equilibrium is characterized by a threshold d^* such that all agents of degree $d < d^*$ choose the action 0 and all agents of degree $d > d^*$ choose the action 1 (and agents of degree d^* may mix between the actions). In particular, notice that the type of multiplicity that appeared in Example 2 no longer occurs (provided degree distributions are not trivial). It is now possible to look at comparative statics of equilibrium behavior and outcomes using stochastic dominance arguments on the network itself. For ease of exposition, we illustrate this in the case of nonatomic costs (see Galeotti, Goyal, Jackson, Vega-Redondo, and Yariv (2010) for the general analysis).

Heterogeneous Costs. Consider the case in which F^c is a continuous function, with no atoms. In this case, a simple equation is sufficient to characterize equilibria. Let x be the probability that a randomly chosen neighbor chooses the action 1. Then $F(d, x)$ is the probability that a random (best responding) neighbor of degree d chooses the action 1. We can now proceed in a way reminiscent of the analysis of the SIS model. Recall that $\tilde{P}(d)$ denoted the probability that a random neighbor is of degree d (see equation (4)). It must be that

$$x = \phi(x) \equiv \sum_d \tilde{P}(d)F(d, x). \tag{15}$$

Again, a fixed-point equation captures much of what occurs in the game. In fact, equation (15) characterizes equilibria in the sense that any symmetric[23] equilibrium results in an x that satisfies the equation, and any x that satisfies the equation corresponds to an equilibrium where type (d_i, c_i) chooses 1 if and only if inequality (14) holds. Given that equilibria can be described by their corresponding x, we often refer to some value of x as being an "equilibrium."

Consider a symmetric equilibrium and a corresponding probability of x for a random neighbor to choose action 1. If the payoff function v is increasing in degree d, then the expected payoff of an agent with degree $d + 1$ is $v(d+1, x) \geq v(d, x)$ and so $F^c(v(d+1, x)) \geq F^c(v(d, x))$ and agents with higher degrees choose 1 with weakly higher probabilities. Indeed, an agent of degree $d + 1$ can imitate the decisions of an

[22] In such a case, the best response correspondence (allowing mixed strategies) for any (d_i, c_i) as dependent on x is upper hemi-continuous and convex-valued. Taking expectations with respect to d_i and c_i, we also have a set of population best responses as dependent on x that is upper hemi-continuous and convex valued.

[23] Symmetry indicates that agents with the same degree and costs follow similar actions.

agent of degree d and gain at least as high a payoff. Thus, if v is increasing (or, in much the same way, decreasing) in d for each x, then any symmetric equilibrium entails agents with higher degrees choosing action 1 with weakly higher (lower) probability. Furthermore, agents of higher degree have higher (lower) expected payoffs.

Much as in the analysis of the epidemiological models, the multiplicity of equilibria is determined by the properties of ϕ, which, in turn, correspond to properties of $\tilde{P}$ and F. For instance,

- if $F(d, 0) > 0$ for some d in the support of P, and F is concave in x for each d, then there exists at most one fixed-point, and
- if $F(d, 0) = 0$ for all d and F is strictly concave or strictly convex in x for each d, then there are at most two equilibria—one at 0, and possibly an additional one, depending on the slope of $\phi(x)$ at $x = 0$.[24]

In general, as long as the graph of $\phi(x)$ crosses the 45-degree line only once, there is a unique equilibrium (see Figure 4 below).[25]

The set of equilibria generated in such network games is divided into stable and unstable ones (those we have already termed in Section 3.2 as *tipping points*). The simple characterization given by (15) allows for a variety of comparative statics on fundamentals pertaining to either type of equilibrium. In what follows, we show how these

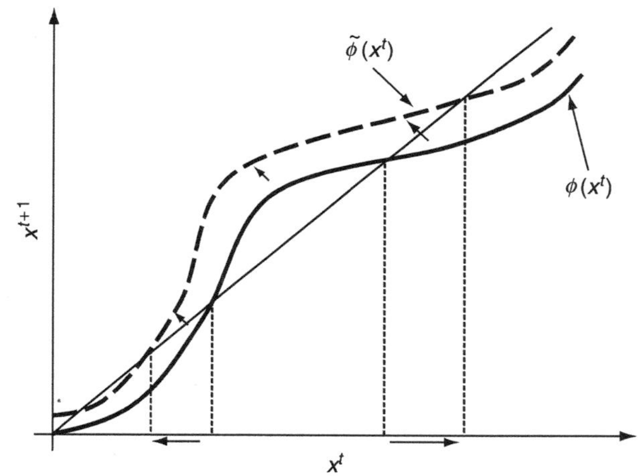

Figure 4 The Effects of Shifting $\phi(x)$ Pointwise.

[24] As before, the slope needs to be greater than 1 for there to be an additional equilibrium in the case of strict concavity, while the case of strict convexity depends on the various values of $F(d, 1)$ across d.

[25] Morris and Shin (2003, 2005) consider uncertainty on payoffs rather than on an underlying network. In coordination games, they identify a class of payoff shocks that lead to a unique equilibrium. Heterogeneity in degrees combined with uncertainty plays a similar role in restricting the set of equilibria. In a sense, the analysis described here is a generalization in that it allows studying the impact of changes in a variety of fundamentals on the set of stable and unstable equilibria, regardless of multiplicity, in a rather rich environment. Moreover, the equilibrium structure can be tied to the network of underlying social interactions.

comparative statics tie directly to a simple strategic diffusion process. Indeed, it turns out there is a very useful technical link between the static and dynamic analysis of strategic interactions on networks.

4.5 Adding dynamics – diffusion and equilibria of network games

An early contribution to the study of diffusion of strategic behavior allowing for general network architectures was by Morris (2000).[26] Morris (2000) considered coordination games played on networks. His analysis pertained to identifying social structures conducive to *contagion*, where a small fraction of the population choosing one action leads to that action spreading across the *entire* population. The main insight from Morris (2000) is that maximal contagion occurs when the society has certain sorts of cohesion properties, where there are no groups (among those not initially infected) that are too inward looking in terms of their connections.

In order to identify the full set of stable of equilibria using the above formalization, consider a diffusion process governed by best responses in discrete time (following Jackson and Yariv (2005, 2007)). At time $t = 0$, a fraction x^0 of the population is exogenously and randomly assigned the action 1, and the rest of the population is assigned the action 0. At each time $t > 0$, each agent, *including the agents assigned to action* 1 *at the outset*, best responds to the distribution of agents choosing the action 1 in period $t-1$, accounting for the number of neighbors they have and presuming that their neighbors will be a random draw from the population.

Let x_d^t denote the fraction of those agents with degree d who have adopted behavior 1 at time t, and let x^t denote the link-weighted fraction of agents who have adopted the behavior at time t. That is, using the distribution of neighbors' degrees $\tilde{P}(d)$,

$$x^t = \sum_d \tilde{P}(d) x_d^t.$$

Then, as deduced before from equation (14), at each date t,

$$x_d^t = F\left(d, x^{t-1}\right).$$

and therefore

$$x^t = \sum_d \tilde{P}(d) F(d, x^{t-1}) = \phi(x^{t-1}).$$

As we have discussed, any rest point of the system corresponds to a static (Bayesian) equilibrium of the system.

[26] One can find predecessors with regards to specific architectures, usually lattices or complete mixings, such as Conway's (1970) "game of life," and various agent-based models that followed such as the "voter model" (e.g., see Clifford and Sudbury (1973) and Holley and Liggett (1975)), as well as models of stochastic stability (e.g., Kandori, Mailath, Robb (1993), Young (1993), Ellison (1993)).

If payoffs exhibit complementarities, then convergence of behavior from any starting point is monotone, either upwards or downwards. In particular, once an agent switches behaviors, the agent will not want to switch back at a later date.[27] Thus, although these best responses are myopic, any eventual changes in behavior are equivalently forward-looking.

Figure 4 depicts a mapping ϕ governing the dynamics. Equilibria, and resting points of the diffusion process, correspond to intersections of ϕ with the 45-degree line.

The figure allows an immediate distinction between two classes of equilibria that we discussed informally up to now. Formally, an equilibrium x is *stable* if there exists $\varepsilon' > 0$ such that $\phi(x - \varepsilon) > x - \varepsilon$ and $\phi(x + \varepsilon) < x + \varepsilon$ for all $\varepsilon' > \varepsilon > 0$. An equilibrium x is *unstable* or a *tipping point* if there exists $\varepsilon' > 0$ such that $\phi(x - \varepsilon) < x - \varepsilon$ and $\phi(x + \varepsilon) > x + \varepsilon$ for all $\varepsilon' > \varepsilon > 0$. In the figure, the equilibrium to the left is a tipping point, while the equilibrium to the right is stable.

The composition of the equilibrium set hinges on the shape of the function ϕ. Furthermore, note that a point-wise shift of ϕ (as in the figure, to a new function ϕ) shifts tipping points to the left and stable points to the right, loosely speaking (as sufficient shifts may eliminate some equilibria altogether), making adoption more likely. This simple insight allows for a variety of comparative statics.

For instance, consider an increase in the cost of adoption, manifested as a First Order Stochastic Dominance (FOSD) shift of the cost distribution F^c to $\overline{F}^c$. It follows immediately that:

$$\overline{\phi}(x) = \sum_d \tilde{P}(d)\overline{F}^c(v(d,x)) \leq \sum_d \tilde{P}(d)F^c(v(d,x)) = \phi(x)$$

and the increase in costs corresponds to an increase of the tipping points and decrease of the stable equilibria (one by one). Intuitively, increasing the barrier to choosing the action 1 leads to a higher fraction of existing adopters necessary to get the action 1 to spread even more.

This formulation also allows for an analysis that goes beyond graphical games regarding the social network itself, using stochastic dominance arguments (following Jackson and Rogers (2007)) and Jackson and Yariv (2005, 2007)). For instance, consider an increase in the expected degree of each random neighbor that an agent has. That is, suppose $\tilde{P}'$ FOSD $\tilde{P}$ and, for illustration, assume that $F(d, x)$ is nondecreasing in d for all x. Then, by the definition of FOSD,

$$\phi'(x) = \sum_d \tilde{P}'(d)F(d,x) \geq \sum_d \tilde{P}(d)F(d,x) = \phi(x),$$

and, under P', tipping points are lower and stable equilibria are higher.

[27] If actions are strategic substitutes, convergence may not be guaranteed for all starting points. However, whenever convergence is achieved, the rest point is an equilibrium, and the analysis can therefore be useful for such games as well.

Similar analysis allows for comparative statics regarding the distribution of links, by simply looking at Mean Preserving Spreads (MPS) of the underlying degree distribution.[28]

Going back to the dynamic path of adoption, we can generalize the insights that we derived regarding the Granovetter (1978) model. Namely, whether adoption paths track an *S*-shaped curve now depends on the shape of ϕ, and thereby on the shape of both the cost distribution F and agents' utilities.

5. CLOSING NOTES

There is now a substantial and growing body of research studying the impacts of interactions that occur on a network of connections. This work builds on the empirical observations of peer influence and generates a rich set of individual and aggregate predictions. Insights that have been shown consistently in real-world data pertain to the higher propensities of contagion (of a disease, an action, or behavior) in more highly connected individuals, the role of "opinion leaders" in diffusion, as well as an aggregate *S*-shape of many diffusion curves. The theoretical analyses open the door to many other results, e.g., those regarding comparative statics *across* networks, payoffs, and cost distributions (when different actions vary in costs). Future experimental and field data will hopefully complement these theoretical insights.

A shortcoming of some of the theoretical analyses described in this chapter is that the foundation for modeling the underlying network is rooted in simple forms of random graphs in which there is little heterogeneity among nodes other than their connectivity. This misses a central observation from the empirical literature that illustrates again and again the presence of homophily, people's tendency to associate with other individuals who are similar to themselves. Moreover, there are empirical studies that are suggestive of how homophily might impact diffusion, providing for increased local connectivity but decreased diffusion on a more global scale (see Rogers (1995) for some discussion). Beyond the implications that homophily has for the connectivity structure of the network, it also has implications for the propensity of individuals to be affected by neighbors' behavior: for instance, people who are more likely to, say, be immune may be more likely to be connected to one another, and, similarly, people who are more likely to be susceptible to infection may be more likely to be connected

[28] In fact, Jackson and Yariv (2007) illustrate that if $F(d, x)$ is nondecreasing and convex, then power, Poisson, and regular degree distributions with identical means generate corresponding values of ϕ^{power}, $\phi^{Poisson}$, and $\phi^{regular}$ such that

$$\phi^{power}(x) \geq \phi^{Poisson}(x) \geq \phi^{regular}(x)$$

for all x, thereby implying a clear ranking of the tipping points and stable equilibria corresponding to each type of network.

to one another.[29] Furthermore, background factors linked to homophily can also affect the payoffs individuals receive when making decisions in their social network. Enriching the interaction structure in that direction is crucial for deriving more accurate diffusion predictions. This is an active area of current study (e.g., see Baccara and Yariv (2010), Bramoullé and Rogers (2010), Currarini, Jackson, and Pin (2006, 2009, 2010), and Peski (2008)).

Ultimately, the formation of a network and the strategic interactions that occur amongst individuals is a two-way street. Developing richer models of the endogenous formation of networks, together with endogenous interactions on those networks, is an interesting direction for future work, both empirical and theoretical.[30]

[29] The mechanism through which this occurs can be rooted in background characteristics such as wealth, or more fundamental personal attributes such as risk aversion. Risk averse individuals may connect to one another and be more prone to protect themselves against diseases by, e.g., getting immunized; similarly for wealth.

[30] As discussed above, there are some studies, such as that of Kandel (1978), that provide evidence for the back and forth interaction between behavior and network formation. There are also some models that study co-evolving social relationships and play in games with neighbors, such as Ely (2002), Mailath, Samuelson, and Shaked (2000), Jackson and Watts (2002, 2010), Droste, Gilles, and Johnson (2003), Corbae and Duffy (2003), and Goyal and Vega-Redondo (2005). These articles only begin to provide insight into such interplay.

REFERENCES

Aral, S., Walker, D., 2010. Creating Social Contagion through Viral Product Design: Theory and Evidence from a Randomized Field Experiment, mimeo.

Aral, S., Muchnik, L., Sundararajan, A., 2009. Distinguishing Influence Based Contagions from Homophily Driven Diffusion in Dynamic Networks. Proc. Natl. Acad. Sci..

Baccara, M., Imrohoroglu, A., Wilson, A.J., Yariv, L., 2010. A Field Study on Matching with Network Externalities, mimeo.

Baccara, M., Yariv, L., 2010. Similarity and Polarization in Groups, mimeo.

Bailey, N.T.J., 1975. The Mathematical Theory of Infectious Diseases and Its Applications, London Griffin.

Ballester, C., Calvó-Armengol, A., Zenou, Y., 2006. Who's who in networks. Wanted: The Key Player. Econometrica 74 (5), 1403–1417.

Bandiera, O., Barankay, I., Rasul, I., 2008. Social capital in the workplace: Evidence on its formation and consequences. Labour Econ. 15 (4), 724–748.

Banerjee, A., Chandrasekhar, A., Duflo, E., Jackson, M.O., 2010. The Diffusion of MicroFinance in Rural India, mimeo.

Bass, F., 1969. A new product growth model for consumer durables. Manag. Sci. 15 (5), 215–227.

Bayer, P., Ross, S., Topa, G., 2008. Place of Work and Place of Residence: Informal Hiring Networks and Labor Market Outcomes. J. Polit. Econ. 116 (6), 1150–1196.

Beaman, L., Magruder, J.R., 2010. Who gets the job referral? Evidence from a social networks experiment, mimeo.

Bearman, P.S., Moody, J., Stovel, K., 2004. Chains of Affection: The Structure of Adolescent Romantic and Sexual Networks. AJS 110 (1), 44–91.

Bramoullé, Y., Kranton, R., 2007. Strategic Experimentation in Networks. J. Econ. Theory 135 (1), 478–494.

Bramoullé, Y., Rogers, B.W., 2010. Diversity and Popularity in Social Networks, mimeo.

Calvó-Armengol, A., Jackson, M.O., 2009. Like Father, Like Son: Labor Market Networks and Social Mobility. American Economic Journal: Microeconomics 1 (1), 124–150.

Christakis, N.A., Fowler, J.H., 2007. The Spread of Obesity in a Large Social Network over 32 Years. N. Engl. J. Med. 357 (4), 370–379.
Chwe, M.S.-Y., 2000. Communication and Coordination in Social Networks. Rev. Econ. Stud. 67, 1–16.
Clifford, P., Sudbury, A., 1973. A Model of Spatial Conflict. Biometrika 60 (3), 581–588.
Coleman, J.S., Katz, E., Menzel, H., 1966. Medical Innovation: A Diffusion Study. Bobbs-Merrill, Indianapolis.
Colizza, V., Barrat, A., Barthélemy, M., Vespignani, A., 2006. The role of the airline transportation network in the prediction and predictability of global epidemics. Proc. Natl. Acad. Sci. U. S. A. 103, 2015–2020.
Colizza, V., Vespignani, A., 2007. Invasion Threshold in Heterogeneous Metapopulation Networks. Phys. Rev. Lett. 99, 148–701.
Conley, T.G., Topa, G., 2002. Socio-Economic Distance and Spatial Patterns in Unemployment. Journal of Applied Econometrics 17 (4), 303–327.
Conley, T.G., Udry, C., 2008. Learning About a New Technology: Pineapple in Ghana. Am. Econ. Rev forthcoming.
Corbae, D., Duffy, J., 2003. Experiments with Network Formation. forthcoming: Games Econ. Behav.
Currarini, S., Jackson, M.O., Pin, P. 2006. Long Run Integration in Social Networks, mimeo.
Currarini, S., Jackson, M.O., Pin, P., 2009. An Economic Model of Friendship: Homophily, Minorities and Segregation. Econometrica 77 (4), 1003–1045.
Currarini, S., Jackson, M.O., Pin, P., 2010. Identifying the roles of race-based choice and chance in high school friendship network formation. Proc. Natl. Acad. Sci. 107 (11), 4857–4861.
Droste, E., Gilles, R., Johnson, C., 2003. Evolution of Conventions in Endogenous Social Networks, mimeo.
Duflo, E., Saez, E., 2003. The Role of Information and Social Interactions in Retirement Plan Decisions: Evidence From a Randomized Experiment. Q. J. Econ..
Dupas, P., 2010. Short-Run Subsidies and Long-Run Adoption of New Health Products: Evidence from a Field Experiment. mimeo: UCLA.
Ellison, G., 1993. Learning, Local Interaction, and Coordination. Econometrica 61 (5), 1047–1071.
Ely, J.C., 2002. Local Conventions. Advances in Theoretical Economics 2 (1) Article 1.
Erdős, P., Rényi, A., 1959. On random graphs. Publicationes Mathematicae 6, 290–297.
Erdős, P., Rényi, A., 1960. On the evolution of random graphs. Publications of the Mathematical Institute of the Hungarian Academy of Sciences 5, 17–61.
Feick, L.F., Price, L.L., 1987. The Market Maven: A Diffuser of Marketplace Information. Journal of Marketing 51 (1), 83–97.
Feigenberg, B., Field, E., Pande, R., 2010. Building Social Capital through Microfinance. mimeo: Harvard University.
Foster, A.D., Rosenzweig, M.R., 1995. Learning by Doing and Learning from Others: Human Capital and Technical Change in Agriculture. J. Polit. Econ. 103 (6), 1176–1209.
Galeotti, A., Goyal, S., Jackson, M.O., Vega-Redondo, F., Yariv, L., 2010. Network Games. Rev. Econ. Stud. 77 (1), 218–244.
Galeotti, A., Vega-Redondo, F., 2006. Complex Networks and Local Externalities: A Strategic Approach, mimeo.
Glaeser, E.L., Scheinkman, J.A., 2000. Non-market Interactions. NBER Working Paper Number 8053.
Glaeser, E.L., Sacerdote, B., Scheinkman, J.A., 1996. Crime and Social Interactions. Q. J. Econ. 111 (2), 507–548.
Goeree, J.K., McConnell, M.A., Mitchell, T., Tromp, T., Yariv, L., 2010. The 1/d Law of Giving. American Economic Journal: Microeconomics 2 (1), 183–203.
Goyal, S., Moraga-Gonzalez, J.L., 2001. R&D Networks. Rand. J. Econ. 32 (4), 686–707.
Goyal, S., Vega-Redondo, F., 2005. Network Formation and Social Coordination,'. Games Econ. Behav. 50, 178–207.
Granovetter, M., 1973. The Strength of Weak Ties. AJS 78 (6), 1360–1380.
Granovetter, M., 1978. Threshold Models of Collective Behavior. AJS 83 (6), 1420–1443.
Granovetter, M., 1985. Economic action and social structure: the problems of embeddedness. AJS 91 (3), 481–510.

Granovetter, M., 1995. Getting a Job: A Study in Contacts and Careers. University of Chicago Press.
Griliches, Z., 1957. Hybrid corn: an exploration of the economics of technological change. Econometrica 25, 501–522.
Holley, R.A., Liggett, T.M., 1975. Ergodic Theorems for Weakly Interacting Infinite Systems and The Voter Model. The Annals of Probability 3 (4), 643–663.
Huckfeldt, R.R., Sprague, J., 1995. Citizens, Politics and Social Communication. Cambridge Studies in Public Opinion and Political Psychology.
Ioannides, Y.M., Datcher-Loury, L., 2004. Job information networks, neighborhood effects and inequality. J. Econ. Lit. 424, 1056–1093.
Jackson, M.O., 2007. Social Structure, Segregation, and Economic Behavior. Nancy Schwartz Memorial Lecture, given in April 2007 at Northwestern University, printed version: http://www.stanford.edu/~jacksonm/schwartzlecture.pdf.
Jackson, M.O., 2008. Social and Economic Networks. Princeton University Press, NJ.
Jackson, M.O., Rogers, B.W., 2007. Relating Network Structure to Diffusion Properties through Stochastic Dominance. The B.E. Press Journal of Theoretical Economics 7 (1) (Advances), 1–13.
Jackson, M.O., Watts, A., 2002. On the Formation of Interaction Networks in Social Coordination Games. Games Econ. Behav. 41, 265–291.
Jackson, M.O., Watts, A., 2010. Social Games: Matching and the Play of Finitely Repeated Games. Games Econ. Behav. 70 (1), 170–191.
Jackson, M.O., Yariv, L., 2005. Diffusion on Social Networks. Economie Publique 16 (1), 69–82.
Jackson, M.O., Yariv, L., 2007. Diffusion of Behavior and Equilibrium Properties in Network Games. The American Economic Review (Papers and Proceedings) 97 (2), 92–98.
Kakade, S., Kearns, M., Langford, J., Ortiz, L., 2003. Correlated Equilibria in Graphical Games. ACM Conference on Electronic Commerce New York.
Kandel, D.B., 1978. Homophily, Selection, and Socialization in Adolescent Friendships. Am. J. Sociol. 84 (2), 427–436.
Kandori, M., Mailath, G., Rob, R., 1993. Learning, Mutation, and Long Run Equilibria in Games. Econometrica 61 (1), 29–56.
Karlan, D., Mobius, M.M., Rosenblat, T.S., Szeidl, A., 2009. Measuring Trust in Peruvian Shantytowns, mimeo.
Katz, E., Lazarsfeld, P.F., 1955. Personal influence: The part played by people in the flow of mass communication. Free Press, Glencoe, IL.
Kearns, M., Littman, M., Singh, S., 2001. Graphical Models for Game Theory. In: Breese, J.S., Koller, D. (Eds.), Proceedings of the 17th Conference on Uncertainty in Artificial Intelligence. Morgan Kaufmann University of Washington, San Francisco, Seattle, Washington, USA, pp. 253–260.
Kermack, W.O., McKendrick, A.G., 1927. A Contribution to the Mathematical Theory of Epidemics. Proc. R. Soc. Lond. Series A 115, 700–721.
Kosfeld, M., 2004. Economic Networks in the Laboratory: A Survey. Review of Network Economics 30, 20–42.
Lazarsfeld, P.E., Berelson, B., Gaudet, G., 1944. The people's choice: How the voter makes up his mind in a presidential campaign. Duell, Sloan and Pearce, New York.
Leider, S., Mobius, M.M., Rosenblat, T., Do, Q.A., 2009. Directed Altruism and Enforced Reciprocity in Social Networks. Q. J. Econ, forthcoming.
Leskovec, J., Adamic, L.A., Huberman, B.A., 2007. The dynamics of viral marketing. ACM Transactions on the Web (TWEB) archive 1 (1), Article No. 5.
Lopez-Pintado, D., 2008. Contagion in Complex Social Networks. Games Econ. Behav. 62 (2), 573–590.
Mahajan, V., Peterson, R.A., 1985. Models for Innovation Diffusion (Quantitative Applications in the Social Sciences. Sage Publications, Inc.
Mailath, G., Samuelson, L., Shaked, A., 2000. Endogenous Inequality in Integrated Labor Markets with Two-Sided Search. American Economic Review 90, 46–72.
McPherson, M., Smith-Lovin, L., Cook, J.M., 2001. Birds of a Feather: Homophily in Social Networks. Annu. Rev. Sociol. 27, 415–444.

Merton, R., 1948. Patterns of Influence: a study of interpersonal influence and of communications behavior in a local community. In: Lazarsfeld, P., Stanton, F. (Eds.), Communication Research. Harper and Brothers, New York, pp. 180–215.

Morris, S., 2000. Contagion. Rev. Econ. Stud. 67 (1), 57–78.

Morris, S., Shin, H., 2003. Global Games: Theory and Applications. In: Dewatripont, M., Hansen, L., Turnovsky, S. (Eds.), Advances in Economics and Econometrics. Proceedings of the Eighth World Congress of the Econometric Society. Cambridge University Press, Cambridge, pp. 56–114.

Morris, S., Shin, H., 2005. Heterogeneity and Uniqueness in Interaction Games. In: Blume, L., Durlauf, S. (Eds.), The Economy as an Evolving Complex System III. Oxford University Press, Santa Fe Institute Studies in the Sciences of Complexity.

Nair, H., Manchanda, P., Bhatia, T., 2006. Asymmetric Effects in Physician Prescription Behavior: The Role of Opinion Leaders, mimeo.

Pastor-Satorras, R., Vespignani, A., 2000. Epidemic Spreading in Scale-Free Networks. Phys. Rev. Lett. 86 (14), 3200–3203.

Pastor-Satorras, R., Vespignani, A., 2001. Epidemic dynamics and endemic states in complex networks. Physical Review E 63, 066–117.

Pesendorfer, W., 1995. Design Innovation and Fashion Cycles. Am. Econ. Rev. 85 (4), 771–792.

Peski, M., 2008. Complementarities, Group Formation, and Preferences for Similarity, mimeo.

Rees, A., 1966. Information Networks in Labor Markets. Am. Econ. Rev. 56 (2), 559–566.

Rees, A., Schultz, G.P., 1970. Workers and Wages in an Urban Labor Market. University of Chicago Press.

Rogers, E.M., 1995. Diffusion of Innovations. Free Press.

Ryan, B., Gross, N.C., 1943. The diffusion of hybrid seed corn in two Iowa communities. Rural Sociol. 8, 15–24.

Sundararajan, A., 2007. Local network effects and network structure. The B.E. Journal of Theoretical Economics 7 (1) (Contributions), Article 46.

Tarde, G., 1903. Les Lois de L'Imitation: Etude Sociologique. Elibron Classics, translated to English in The Laws of Imitation, H. Holt and company.

Topa, G., 2001. Social Interactions, Local Spillovers and Unemployment. Rev. Econ. Stud. 68 (2), 261–295.

Tucker, C., 2008. Identifying Formal and Informal Inuence in Technology Adoption with Network Externalities. Manag. Sci. 55 (12), 2024–2039.

Van den Bulte, C., Lilien, G.L., 2001. Medical Innovation Revisited: Social Contagion versus Marketing Effort. AJS 106 (5), 1409–1435.

Young, P., 1993. The Evolution of Conventions. Econometrica 61 (1), 57–84.

Young, P., 2010. Innovation Diffusion in Heterogeneous Populations: Contagion, Social Influence, and Social Learning. Am. Econ. Rev. forthcoming.

CHAPTER 15

Learning in Networks

Sanjeev Goyal*

Contents

1. Introduction 680
2. Nonstrategic Interaction 684
  2.1 Repeated choice and social learning 684
  2.2 Naive learning 699
  2.3 Sequence of single choices 700
3. Strategic Interaction 704
  3.1 Coordination games 705
    3.1.1 Multiple equilibria *707*
    3.1.2 Dynamic stability and equilibrium selection *708*
    3.1.3 Related themes *712*
  3.2 Games of cooperation 716
    3.2.1 Imitation and altruism *717*
    3.2.2 Interaction and information neighborhoods *720*
4. Concluding Remarks 721
5. Appendix 723
References 724
Further Readings 727

Abstract

We choose between alternatives without being fully informed about the rewards from different courses of action. In making our decisions, we use our own past experience and the experience of others. So the ways in which we interact – our social network – can influence our choices. These choices in turn influence the generation of new information and shape future choices. These considerations motivate a rich research programme on how social networks shape individual and collective learning. The present paper provides a summary of this research.
JEL Codes: C72, C73, D83, D85

Keywords

Social learning
bandit arms
networks

* Faculty of Economics and Christ's College, University of Cambridge. E-mail: sg472@cam.ac.uk This paper has been prepared for publication in the *Handbook of Social Economics*, edited by Jess Benhabib, Alberto Bisin and Matthew O. Jackson. I am grateful to Larry Samuelson for very helpful comments on an earlier draft of this paper.

Handbook of Social Economics, Volume 1A
ISSN 0169-7218, DOI: 10.1016/S0169-7218(11)01015-X

influencers
incomplete learning
Bayesian learning
cooperation
coordination
evolutionary games
spatial learning
technological change

1. INTRODUCTION

In a wide range of economic situations, individuals make decisions without being fully informed about the rewards from different options. In many of these instances, the decision problems are of a recurring nature and it is natural that individuals use their past experience and the experience of others in making current decisions. The experience of others is important for two reasons: One, it may yield information on different actions per se (as in the case of choice of new consumer products, agricultural practices, or medicines prescribed); and two, in many settings the rewards from an action depend on the choices made by others and so there is a direct value to knowing about other's actions (as in the case of which language to learn). This suggests that the precise way in which individuals interact can influence the generation and dissemination of useful information and that this could shape individual choices and social outcomes. In recent years, these considerations have motivated a substantial body of work on learning which takes explicit account of the structure of interaction among individual entities. The present paper provides a survey of this research.

I will consider the following framework: There is a set of individuals who are located on nodes of a network; the arcs of the network reflect relations between these individuals. Individuals choose an action from a set of alternatives. They are uncertain about the rewards from different actions. They use their own past experience, and also gather information from their neighbors (individuals who are linked to them) and then choose an action that maximizes individual payoffs. I start by studying the influence of network structure on individual and social learning in a pure information-sharing context. I then move on to a study of strategic interaction among players located in a network, i.e., interactions where an individual's actions alter payoffs of others. The focus will be on examining the relation between the network structure on the one hand, and the evolution of individual actions, beliefs and payoffs on the other hand. A related and recurring theme of the survey will be the relation between network structure and the prospects for the adoption of efficient actions.[1]

[1] This chapter builds on Goyal (2005, 2007a). The focus here is on analytical results and there will be no discussion of the large literature on agent based modeling and computational economics, which studies similar issues. For surveys of this work, see Judd and Tesfatsion (2005), Kirman and Zimmermann (2001)).

The following examples elaborate on the variety of applications, which follow within the scope of the general approach. We start with three examples involving pure information sharing.

Consumer choice: A consumer buying a computer chooses a brand without being fully informed about the different options. Since a computer is a major purchase, potential buyers also discusses the pros and cons of different alternatives with close friends, colleagues, and acquaintances. The importance of opinion leaders and mavens in the adoption of consumer goods has been documented in a number of studies (see e.g., Feick and Price, 1987; Kotler and Armstrong, 2004).

Medical innovation: Doctors have to decide on new treatments for ailments without complete knowledge of their efficacy and side-effects; they read professional magazines as well as exchange information with other doctors in order to determine whether to prescribe a new treatment. Empirical work suggests that location in inter-personal communication networks affects the timing of prescription while the structure of the connections between physicians influences the speed of diffusion of new medicines (for a pioneering study see on this see Coleman, 1966). There is also evidence that medical practices vary widely across countries and part of this difference is explained by the relatively weak communication across countries (see e.g., Taylor, 1979).

Agricultural practices: Farmers decide on whether to switch crops, adopt new seeds and alternative farming packages without full knowledge of their suitability for the specific soil and weather conditions they face. Empirical work shows that individuals use the experience of similar farmers in making critical decisions on adoption of new crops as well as input combinations (see e.g., Ryan and Gross (1943), Griliches, 1957; Conley and Udry, 2010).

We now turn to applications in which actions of others affect individual payoffs. We will focus on games of coordination and games of cooperation. The problem of coordination arises in its simplest form when, for an individual, the optimal course of action is to conform to what others are doing. The following three examples illustrate how coordination problems arise naturally in different walks of life.

Adoption of new information technology: Individuals decide on whether to adopt, say, a fax machine without full knowledge of its usefulness. This usefulness depends on the technological qualities of the product but clearly also depends on whether others with whom they communicate adopt a similar technology. Empirical work suggests that that there are powerful interaction effects in the adoption of information technology (Economides and Himmelberg, 1995).

Language choice: Individuals choose which language to learn at school as a second language. The rewards depend on the choices of others with whom they expect to interact. Empirical work suggests that changes in the patterns of interactions among individuals – for instance, a move from a situation in which groups are relatively isolated with little across-group interaction to one in which individuals are highly mobile and groups are more integrated – has played an important role in the extinction of several languages and the dominance of a few languages (see e.g., Watkins, 1991; Brenzinger 1998).

Social Norms: Individuals choose whether to be punctual or to be casual about appointment times. The incentives for being punctual are clearly sensitive to whether others are punctual or not. Casual observation suggests that in some countries punctuality is the norm while in others it is not.[2] Similarly, the decision on whether to stand in a queue or to jump it is very much shaped by the choices of others. Likewise, the arrangement of cutlery on a table is governed by norms which have evolved spatially and across time (for a study, see Elias, 1978). These examples illustrate the role of interaction externalities in shaping social outcomes.

The problem of cooperation arises when individual incentives lead to an outcome which is socially inefficient or undesirable. Such conflicts between individual incentive driven behavior and social goals are common in many situations. The following example illustrates this.

Provision of public goods: Individuals have the choice of exerting effort which is privately costly but yields benefits to themselves as well as to others. A simple example of this is proper maintenance of a personal garden that is also enjoyed by others. Another example is the participation of parents in school monitoring associations – such as governing bodies. In such contexts, it is often the case that the personal costs exceed the personal benefits but are smaller than the social benefits. Theoretical work argues that the structure of interaction between individuals – in particular whether one's acquaintances know each other – can be crucial in determining levels of public good provision (see e.g., Coleman, 1990).

I now place the material covered in this survey paper within a broader context. Repeated choice among alternatives whose relative advantages are imperfectly known is a common feature of many real life decision problems and so it is not surprising that the study of learning has been one of the most active fields of research in economics in the last two decades. Different aspects of this research have been surveyed in articles and books; see e.g., Blume and Easley (1995), Fudenberg and Levine (1998) Kandori (1997), Marimon (1997), Samuelson (1997), Vega-Redondo (1997), and Young (1998). The focus of the present survey will be on a very specific set of issues concerning the network structure of interaction and information flow on the one hand and the process of learning on the other hand.

Actions often yield outcomes which are informative about their true profitability and so the process of learning optimal actions has been extensively studied in the economics and decision theory literatures. The initial models focused on a the prospects of single decision maker learning the optimal action in the long run; see e.g., Berry and Fristedt

[2] For a formal model of punctuality as social norm, see Basu and Weibull (2002).

(1985), Rothschild (1974) and Easley and Kiefer (1988). In many of the applications (as in the examples mentioned earlier in the introduction) experimentation with different alternatives is expensive and it is natural to suppose that individuals will use the experience of others in making their own choices. However, if the outcomes of individual trials yield information which is shared with others, individual experimentation becomes a public good and so choice takes on a strategic aspect, even though actions of others do not matter for individual payoffs. This motivates a study of the dynamics of strategic experimentation; for an elegant analysis of this issue see e.g., Bolton and Harris (1999). In this line of research the actions and outcomes of any individual are commonly observed by everyone. By contrast, the focus of this chapter is on the differences in what individuals observe and how these differences affect the process of social learning.

Similarly, the study of coordination and cooperation problems has a long and distinguished tradition in economics. The problem of coordination has been approached in two different ways, broadly speaking. One approach views this to be a static game between players, and tries to solve the problem through introspective reasoning; Schelling (1960) introduced the notion of focal points in this context.[3] The second approach takes a dynamic perspective and seeks solutions to coordination problems via the gradual accumulation of precedent. This approach has been actively pursued in recent years; see Young (1998) for a survey of this work. The present chapter takes a dynamic approach as well and the focus here is how the network of interaction shapes the process of learning to coordinate.

The conflict between personal interest driven behavior and the social good has been a central theme in economics (and game theory). One approach to the resolution of this problem focuses on the role of repeated interaction between individuals. A self-interested individual may be induced to act in the collective interest in the current game via threats of punishments in the future from other players. This line of reasoning has been explored in models of increasing generality over the years and a number of important results have been obtained. For a survey of this work, see Mailath and Samuelson (2006). Most of this work takes the interaction between individuals to be centralized (an individual plays with everyone else) or assumes that interaction is based on random matching of players. A second approach to this problem focuses on the role of nonselfish individual preferences and nonoptimizing rules of behavior. This

[3] For recent work in this tradition see Bacharach (2006), and Sugden (2004). Also see Lewis (1969) for an influential study of the philosophical issues relating to conventions as solutions to coordination problems. On the applied side, the theory of network externalities is closely related to the problem of social coordination. This theory arose out of the observation that in many markets the benefits of using a product are increasing in the number of adopters of the same product (examples include fax machines and word processing packages). In this literature, the focus was on the total number of adopters and this work examined whether these consumption externalities will inhibit the adoption of new products. For a survey of this work, see Besen and Farrell (1994) and Katz and Shapiro (1994). The models of social coordination with local interaction presented in section 3.1 can be seen as an elaboration of this line of research.

approach uses empirical and experimental evidence as a motivation for the study of alternative models of individual behavior. The role of altruism, reciprocity, fairness and inequity aversion has been investigated in this line of work. Camerer (2003), and Fehr and Schmidt (2003) provide surveys of this research. The present chapter takes a dynamic approach to the study of cooperation and the interest is in understanding how decision rules and networks of interaction jointly shape individual behavior.

Section 2 presents the model and the main results for learning for the pure information sharing problem, while Section 3 takes up learning in strategic games played on networks. Section 4 concludes the paper.

2. NONSTRATEGIC INTERACTION

This section considers learning of optimal actions in a context where payoffs to an individual depend only on the actions chosen by him. We start with a model in which a set of individuals choose actions repeatedly: they observe the outcomes of their own actions as well as the actions and outcomes of their neighbors. We then study a simpler setting in which a sequence of individuals make one shot decisions.

2.1 Repeated choice and social learning

Consider a group of individuals who at regular intervals, individuals choose an action from a set of alternatives. They are uncertain about the rewards from different actions. So they use their own past experience and gather information from their neighbors, friends and colleagues, and then choose an action that maximizes individual payoffs. Three features are worth mentioning. One, individuals choose actions repeatedly and two, actions potentially) generate information on the value of the different alternatives. Thus the amount of information available to the group is endogenous and a function of the choices that individuals make. Three, individuals may have different neighbors and this will give them access to different parts of the information available in the group.[4]

It is convenient to present the model in three parts: the first part lays out the decision problem faced by individuals, the second part introduces notation concerning networks, while the third part discusses the dynamics. The presentation here is based on the work of Bala and Goyal (1998, 2001).[5]

Decision Problem: Suppose that time proceeds in discrete steps, and is indexed by $t = 1,2,\ldots$. There are $n \geq 3$ individuals in a society who each choose an action from

[4] There is an important strand of research in which a single individual makes one choice upon observing the history of past actions (and payoffs). I discuss models of sequential choice and social learning in section 2.3 below.

[5] In an early paper, Allen (1982) studied technology adoption by a set of individuals located on nodes of a graph, who are subject to local influences. This is close in spirit to the motivation behind the framework developed here. Her work focused on invariant distributions of actions, while the interest in this chapter is on the dynamic processes of learning that arise in different networks.

a finite set of alternatives, denoted by S_i. It assumed that all individuals have the same choice set, i.e., $S_i = S_j = A$, for every pair of individuals i and j. Denote by $a_{i,t}$ the action taken by individual i in time period t. The payoffs from an action depends on the state of the world θ, which belongs to a finite set Θ. This state of the world is chosen by nature at the start of the process and remains fixed across time. If θ is the true state and an individual chooses action $a \in A$ then he observes an outcome $y \in Y$ with conditional density $\phi(y, a; \theta)$ and obtains a reward $r(a, y)$. For simplicity, take Y to be a subset of $\mathcal{R}$, and assume that the reward function $r(a,.)$ is bounded. In some examples Y will be finite and we will interpret $\phi(y, a; \theta)$ as the probability of outcome y, under action a, in state θ.

Individuals do not know the true state of the world; their private information is summarized in a prior belief over the set of states. For individual i this prior is denoted by $\mu_{i,1}$. The set of prior beliefs is denoted by $\mathcal{P}(\Theta)$. To allow for the possibility of learning of any state of the world, it will be assumed that prior beliefs are interior, i.e., $\mu_{i,1}(\theta) > 0, \forall\theta$, and $\forall i \in N$. Given belief μ, an individual's one period expected utility from action a is given by

$$u(a, \mu) = \sum_{\theta\in\Theta}\mu(\theta)\int_Y r(a, y)\phi(y, a; \theta)dy. \tag{1}$$

The expected utility expression has a natural analogue in the finite Y case. In the basic model, it will be assumed that individuals have similar preferences which are reflected in a common reward function $r(\cdot, \cdot)$. Learning among neighbors with heterogeneous preferences is discussed subsequently.

Given a belief, μ, an individual chooses an action that maximize (one-period) expected payoffs. Formally, let $B : \mathcal{P}(\Theta) \rightarrow A$ be the one period optimality correspondence:

$$B(\mu) = \{a \in A | u(a, \mu) \geq u(a', \mu), \forall a' \in A\} \tag{2}$$

For each $i \in N$, let $b_i : \mathcal{P}(\Theta) \rightarrow A$, be a selection from the one period optimality correspondence B.

Let δ_θ represent point mass belief on the state θ; then $B(\delta_\theta)$ denotes the set of optimal actions if the true state is θ. A well-known example of this decision problem is the two-arm bandit.

Example 2.1 *The two-arm bandit.*

Suppose $A = \{a_0, a_1\}$, $\Theta = \{\theta_0, \theta_1\}$ and $Y = \{0, 1\}$. In state θ_1, action a_1 yields Bernoulli distributed payoffs with parameter $\pi \in (1/2, 1)$, i.e., it yields 1 with probability π, and 0 with probability $1 - \pi$. In state θ_0, action a_0 yields a payoff of 1 with probability $1 - \pi$, and 0 with probability π. Furthermore, in both states, action a_0 yields payoffs which are Bernoulli distributed with probability 1/2. Hence action a_1 is optimal in state θ_1, while action a_0 is optimal in state θ_0. The belief of an individual is a number $\mu \in (0, 1)$, which represents the probability that the true state is θ_1. The one period optimality correspondence is given by

$$B(\mu) = \begin{cases} a_1 & \text{if } \mu \geq 1/2 \\ a_0 & \text{if } \mu \leq 1/2 \end{cases}$$

An individual chooses an action $b_i(\mu_{i,1})$ and observes the outcome of his action; he also observes the actions and outcomes obtained by a subset of the others, viz., his *neighbors*. The notion of neighborhoods and related concepts are defined next.

Directed Networks: Each individual is located (and identified with) a distinct node of a network. A link between two individuals i and j is denoted by g_{ij}, where $g_{ij} \in \{0, 1\}$. In the context of information networks, it is natural to allow for the possibility that individual i observes individual j, but the reverse does not hold. This motivates a model of links which are *directed:* if $g_{ij} = 1$ then there is flow of information from j to i, but I will allow for $g_{ji} = 0$ even when $g_{ij} = 1$. In Figure 1, there are 3 players, 1, 2 and 3, and $g_{1,3} = g_{3,1} = g_{2,1} = 1$. A directed link from i to j, $g_{ij} = 1$ is represented as an arrow that ends at j.

There is a *directed* path from j to i in g either if $g_{ij} = 1$ or there exist distinct players $j_1, \ldots, j_m$ different from i and j such that $g_{i,j_1} = g_{j_1,j_2} = \ldots = g_{j_m,j} = 1$. For example, in Figure 1 there is a directed path from player 3 to player 2, but the converse is not true. The notation "$j \xrightarrow{g} i$" indicates that there exists a (directed) path from j to i in g. Define $N_i(g) = \left\{k | i \xrightarrow{g} k\right\} \cup \{i\}$ as the set of players that i accesses either directly or indirectly in g, while $\eta_i(g) \equiv |N_i(g)|$ is the number of people accessed. The length of a path between i and j is simply the number of intervening links in the path. The distance between two players i and j in a network g refers to the length of the shortest directed path between them in the network g, and is denoted by $d_{i,j}(g)$.

Let $N_i^d(g) = \left\{k \in N | g_{i,k} = 1\right\}$ be the set of individuals with whom i has a direct link in network g. This set $N_i^d(g)$ will be referred to as the *neighbors* of i in network g. Define $\eta_i^d(g) \equiv |N_i^d(g)|$ as the *out-degree* of individual i. Analogously, let $N_{-i}^d(g) = \{k \in N | g_{ki} = 1\}$ be the set of people who observe i and define $\eta_{-i}^d(g) \equiv |N_{-i}^d(g)|$ as the *in-degree* of individual i.

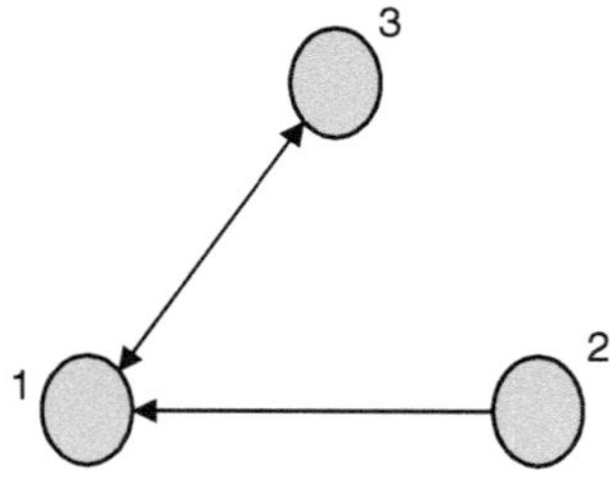

Figure 1 Directed information network.

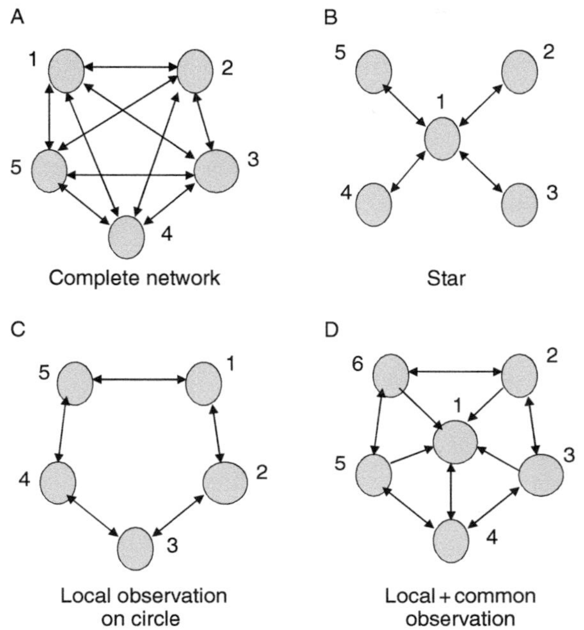

Figure 2 Simple information networks.

A network *g* is said to be connected if there exists a path between any pair of players *i* and *j*. The analysis will focus on connected networks. This is a natural class of networks to consider since networks that are not connected can sometimes be viewed as consisting of a set of connected subnetworks, and then the analysis I present can be applied to each of the connected subnetworks. For instance, consider the networks in Figure 2; each of them is connected. The last network, which combines local and common observation reflects a situation in which individuals gather information from their local neighborhoods and supplement it with information from a common source. The star represents a situation in which the in-degree and out-degree of an individual are equal, but the in-degree of the central node is higher than that of the peripheral node. By contrast, the network in Figure 2D represent a situation in which there is significant asymmetry between the in-degree and the out-degree of the central node, while the other nodes have in-degree equal to the out-degree. The central individual only observes one other node but is observed by five others.[6]

Empirical evidence on networks: The classic early work of Lazarsfeld, Berelson, and Gaudet 1948 and Katz and Lazersfeld 1955 investigated the impact of personal contacts

[6] There are, of course, networks for which the distinction between connectedness and disconnectedness is too coarse. As an example, suppose person 1 observes 2, who observes 3, and so on, until person $n-1$, who observes n. Clearly this network is not connected. However, the connected components are singletons. Learning (and payoffs) in this network is likely to exhibit very different features from learning in an empty network (which is also disconnected).

and mass media on voting and consumer choice with regard to product brands, films and fashion changes. They found that personal contacts play a dominant role in disseminating information which in turn shapes individuals' decisions. In particular, they identified 20% of their sample of 4000 individuals as the primary source of information for the rest. Similarly, Feick and Price 1987 found that 25% of their sample of 1400 individuals acquired a great deal of information about food, household goods, nonprescription drugs and beauty products and that they were widely accessed by the rest.

Research on virtual social communities reveals a similar pattern of communication. Zhang, Ackerman and Adamic 2007 study the Java Forum: an on-line community of users who ask and respond to queries concerning Java. They identify 14000 users and find that 55% of these users only ask questions, 12% both ask and answer queries, and about 13% only provide answers.[7]

The empirical research has highlighted a number of common features of social networks: *one*, the distribution of connections is very unequal. For instance, most web sites (over 90%) have fewer than 10 other web-sites linking to them (this is their in-degree), but at the same time there exist web-sites, such as google.com, bbc.com, and cnn.com, which have hundreds of thousands of in-coming links. Communication networks in rural communities have been found to exhibit a similar inequality: most people in a village talk to their relatives and neighbors and a small set of highly connected villagers leading to a skewed distribution of in-degrees (Rogers, 2003).

The *second* feature is the asymmetry between in-degree and out-degree of a node. In many contexts, there exist a small set of nodes which have a very large in-degree and relatively small out-degree, while most other nodes have an out-degree which is larger than their in-degree. This pattern of connections arises naturally if individuals have access to local as well as some common/public source of information. For instance, in agriculture, individual farmers observe their neighboring farmers and all farmers observe a few large farms and agricultural laboratories. Similarly, in academic research, individual researchers keep track of the work of other researchers in their own narrow field of specialization and also try and keep abreast of the work of pioneers/intellectual leaders in their subject more broadly defined.

Dynamics: In period 1 each individual starts by choosing an action $b_i(\mu_{i,1})$: in other words, we assume that individuals are myopic in their choice of actions. This myopia assumption is made for simplicity: it allows us to abstract from issues concerning strategic experimentation and to focus on the role of the network in shaping social learning.[8] At the end of the period, every individual i observes the outcome of his own actions. She also observes the actions and outcomes of each of his neighbors, $j \in N_i^d(g)$.

[7] Adar and Huberman 2000 report similar findings with regard to provision of files in the peer-to-peer network, Gnutella.

[8] We conjecture that the arguments developed in Theorem's 1–3 below carry over to a setting with far sighted players, so long as optimal decision rules exhibit a cut-off property in posterior beliefs (as identified for instance in example 2.1).

Individual i uses this information to update his prior $\mu_{i,1}$, and arrive at the prior for period 2, $\mu_{i,2}$. She then makes a decision in period 2, and so on.

In principle, the choices of an individual $j \in N_i^d$, reveal something about the priors (and hence private information) of that individual and over time will also reveal something about the actions and experience of his neighbors. However, in updating his priors, it will be assumed that an individual does not take into account the fact that the actions of his neighbors potentially reveal information about what these neighbors have observed about their neighbors. The main reason for this assumption is tractability. The study of social learning in the presence of inferences about the neighbors of neighbors is an important subject; see remarks below and at the end of this section on this issue.

I now describe the space of outcomes and the probability space within which the dynamics occur as the notation is needed for stating the results. The details of the construction are provided in the appendix. The probability space is denoted by $(\boldsymbol{\Omega}, \mathcal{F}, P^\theta)$, where $\boldsymbol{\Omega}$ is the space of all outcomes, $\mathcal{F}$ is the σ field and P^θ is a probability measure if the true state of the world is θ. Let P^θ, be the probability measure induced over sample paths in $\boldsymbol{\Omega}$ by the state $\theta \in \boldsymbol{\Theta}$.

Let $\boldsymbol{\Theta}$ be endowed with the discrete topology, and suppose $\mathcal{B}$ is the Borel σ–field on this space. For rectangles of the form $\mathcal{T} \times H$, where $\mathcal{T} \subset \boldsymbol{\Theta}$, and H is a measurable subset of $\boldsymbol{\Omega}$, let $P_i(\mathcal{T} \times H)$ be given by

$$P_i(\mathcal{T} \times H) = \sum_{\theta \in \mathcal{T}} \mu_{i,1}(\theta) P^\theta(H). \tag{3}$$

for each individual $i \in N$. Each P_i extends uniquely to all $\mathcal{B} \times \mathcal{F}$. Since every individual's prior belief lies in the interior of $\mathcal{P}(\boldsymbol{\Theta})$, the measures $\{P_i\}$ are pair wise mutually absolutely continuous. All stochastic processes are defined on the measurable space $(\boldsymbol{\Theta} \times \boldsymbol{\Omega}, \mathcal{B} \times \mathcal{F})$.

A typical sample path is of the form $\omega = (\theta, \omega')$, where θ is the state of nature and ω' is an infinite sequence of sample outcomes:

$$\omega' = ((y^a_{i,1})_{a \in A, i \in N}, (y^a_{i,2})_{a \in A, i \in N}, \ldots), \tag{4}$$

with $y^a_{i,t} \in Y^a_{i,t} \equiv Y$. Let $C_{i,t} = b_i(\mu_{i,t})$ denote the action of individual i in period t, $Z_{i,t}$ the outcome of this action, and let $U_{i,t} = u(C_{i,t}, \mu_{i,t})$ be the expected utility of i with respect to his own action at time t. Given this notation the posterior beliefs of individual i in period $t+1$ are:

$$\mu_{i,t+1}(\theta|g) = \frac{\prod_{j \in N_i^d(g) \cup \{i\}} \phi(Z_{j,t}; C_{j,t}; \theta) \mu_{i,t}(\theta)}{\sum_{\theta' \in \boldsymbol{\Theta}} \prod_{j \in N_i^d(g) \cup \{i\}} \phi(Z_{j,t}; C_{j,t}; \theta) \mu_{i,t}(\theta)}. \tag{5}$$

The interest is in studying the influence of the network g on the evolution of individual actions, beliefs, and utilities, $(a_{i,t}, \mu_{i,t}, U_{i,t})_{i \in N}$, over time.

Remark 1: The above formula is one way in which individual i incorporates information from own and neighbors' experience. There are simpler alternatives. For instance, in period $t+1$, an individual may apply Bayes' Rule own experience to update belief $\mu_{i,t}$ to arrive at an interim belief $\hat{\mu}_{i,t+1}$ and then take a weighted average of this interim belief and period t belief of neighbors to arrive at an overall posterior belief $\mu_{i,t+1}$. For a study of learning with such updating rules see Jadbabaie, Sandroni and Tahbaz-Salehi (2010). Observe that in this model if there is no new information coming in every period, then learning entails averaging of initial opinions across neighbors, as in the DeGroot (1972) model. I refer to this as naive learning and discuss it in Section 2.2 below.

Remark 2: An alternative and general formulation of the problem of (fully) Bayesian learning is developed in a recent paper by Mueller-Frank (2010). He considers a finite set of agents who each have a commonly known partition of the states of the world. Individuals are located in networks and observe the actions of their neighbors. At the start, each agent chooses an action that is optimal with respect to his initial partition. As individuals observe their neighbors, they refine their partitions on the state of the world. The paper develops a number of results on how network structure and levels of common knowledge (with regard to rationality and strategies) matter for the properties of long run actions.

Main results: Individual actions are an optimal response to beliefs, which in turn evolve in response to the information generated by actions; thus, the dynamics of actions and beliefs feed back on each other. Over time, as an individual observes the outcomes of own actions and the actions and outcomes of neighbors, his beliefs will evolve depending on the particularities of his experience. However, it seems intuitive that as time goes by, and his experience grows, additional information should have a smaller and smaller effect on his views of the world. This intuition is captured by the following result, due to Bala and Goyal (1998), which shows that the beliefs and utilities of individuals converge.

Theorem 2.1 *The beliefs of individuals converge, in the long run. More precisely, there exists* $Q \in \mathcal{B} \times \mathcal{F}$ *satisfying* $P_i(Q) = 1$, *for all* $i \in N$, *and random vectors* $\{\mu_{i,\infty}\}$ *such that* $\omega \in Q \Rightarrow \lim_{t\to\infty}\mu_{i,t}(\omega) = \mu_{i,\infty}(\omega)$. *The utilities of individuals converge:* $\lim_{t\to\infty} U_{i,t}(\omega) = U_{i,\infty}(\omega)$, *for every* $i \in N$, *with probability 1.*

The convergence of beliefs follows as a corollary of a well known mathematical result, the Martingale Convergence Theorem (see e.g., Billingsley, 1985). Next consider the convergence in utilities. Let $A_i(\omega)$ be the set of actions that are chosen infinitely often by individual i along sample path ω. Note that since the set of actions is finite, this set is always nonempty. It is intuitive that an action $a \in A_i(\omega)$ must be optimal with respect to the long run beliefs. Moreover, since the different states in the limiting beliefs are not distinguished by the actions, these actions must yield the same utility in each of the states that are in the support of the limit belief $\mu_{i,\infty}(\omega)$. These observations yield convergence of individual utility.

In what follows, I will take θ_1 to be the true state of nature. Note that

$$Q^{\theta_1} = \{\omega = (\theta, \omega')|\theta = \theta_1\} \tag{6}$$

has P^{θ_1} probability 1.[9] It will be assumed that the strong law of large numbers holds on Q^{θ_1}.[10] All statements of the form 'with probability 1' are with respect to the measure P^{θ_1}.

We will now turn to a key question in this literature: Do individuals choose the right action and earn the maximal possible earn the state in the long run?

It is useful to begin an analysis of this question by examining the learning problem for a single agent in the two-arm bandit. Suppose the true state is θ_1 and action a_1 is the optimal action. A well-known result from the statistical literature says that starting from any prior belief $\mu_{i,\,0}$, there is a positive probability that an agent will switch to action a_0 and remain at that action for ever. Let us now suppose that individuals choose between the two arms of the bandit and observe their own outcomes as well as outcomes of a subset of the other members of the group. Suppose individual i starts with beliefs $\mu_{i,0}$ and let $\mu_{i,0} < 1/2$ except for agent 1. Fix $\mu_{1,0} > 1/2$. Define k to be the smallest number such that if agent 1 observes k outcomes of 0 with action a_1 then his posterior $\mu_{1,k} < 1/2$. Suppose the trials of agent 1 do yield a k long sequence of 0's. It is now easy to verify that in a connected society every agent i will have beliefs $\mu_{i,k} < 1/2$ at time k. But observe that different individuals will have started with different priors and observed different experiences. So the posterior beliefs will typically differ across agents. Observe that once everyone switches to action a_0, no further information is being generated and so individual beliefs will remain different in the long run. What about the long run utilities? The following result, due to Bala and Goyal (1998), responds to this question.

Theorem 2.2 *If the society is connected then every individual gets the same long run utility:* $U_{i,\,\infty}(\omega) = U_{j,\,\infty}(\omega)$ *for every pair of individuals* $i,j \in N$*, with probability one.*

The key observation here is that, if i observes the actions and outcomes of j then he must be able to do as well as j in the long run. While this observation is intuitively plausible, the formal arguments underlying the proof are quite complicated. The principal reason for the complication is that individual i observes the actions and corresponding outcomes of a neighbor j, but does *not* observe the actions and outcomes of the neighbors of j. The claim that i does as well as j if he observes j then rests on the idea that all payoff relevant information that j has gathered is (implicitly) reflected in the choices that he makes, over time. In particular, if j chooses a certain action in the long run then this action must be the best action for him, conditional on all his information. However, individual i observes these actions and the corresponding outcomes and can therefore do as well as j by simply imitating j.

[9] There is a slight abuse of notation here; the domain of the definition of P^{θ_1} is Ω and not $\Theta \times \Omega$.

[10] For a statement of the strong law of large numbers, see e.g., Billingsley (1985).

The final step in the proof shows that this payoff improvement property must also be true if person i observes j indirectly, via a sequence of other persons, i_1, i_2,..i_m. The above argument says that i does as well as i_1 who does as well as i_2, and so on until i_m does as well as j. The final step is to note that in a connected society there is an information path from any player i to any player j.

This result shows that in any connected society, local information transmission is sufficient to ensure that every person gets the same utility in the long run. Connected societies cover a wide range of possible societies and this result is therefore quite powerful. However, it leaves open the question of whether individuals are choosing the optimal action and earning the maximal possible utility in the long run.

To study this question it is useful to fix a true state and an optimal action. Let θ_1 is the true state of the world and let $B(\delta_{\theta_1})$ be the set of optimal actions, corresponding to this state. Social learning is said to be *complete* if for all $i \in N, A^i(\omega) \subset B(\delta_{\theta_1})$, on a set of sample paths which has probability 1 (with respect to the true state θ_1). The analysis of long run learning rests on the informativeness of actions. An action is said to be fully informative if it can help an individual distinguish between all the states: if for all θ, $\theta' \in \Theta$, with $\theta \neq \theta'$,

$$\int_Y |\phi(y; a, \theta) - \phi(y; a, \theta')| dy > 0. \tag{7}$$

By contrast, an action a is uninformative if $\phi(., a; \theta)$ is independent of θ. In Example 2.1 above, action a_0 is uninformative while action a_1 is fully informative.

In any investigation of whether individuals choose the optimal action in the long run, it is necessary to restrict beliefs. To see why this is so, consider Example 2.1 above. If everyone has priors such that the uninformative action is optimal then there is no additional information emerging in the society and so an individual using Bayes' updating will retain his priors and everyone will therefore choose the suboptimal action forever. Optimism in the prospects of a new technology is by itself, not sufficient. The structure of connections is also important for learning to take place. This is illustrated with the help of the following two examples.

Example 2.2 *Incomplete Learning.*

Suppose that the decision problem is as in Example 2.1 and suppose that everyone is optimistic, i.e., $\mu_{i,1}$ $(\theta_1) > 1/2$. Moreover, for concreteness, assume that beliefs satisfy the following condition.

$$\inf_{i \in N} \mu_{i,1} > \frac{1}{2}; \quad \sup_{i \in N} \mu_{i,1} < \frac{1}{1+x^2} \tag{8}$$

where $x = (1 - \pi)/\pi \in (0, 1)$. These restrictions incorporate the idea that individuals are optimistic about the unknown action but there is an upper bound on their optimism. From the optimality correspondence formula given above, it follows that every person chooses a_1 in period 1. Suppose that individuals are arranged around a circle and observe their

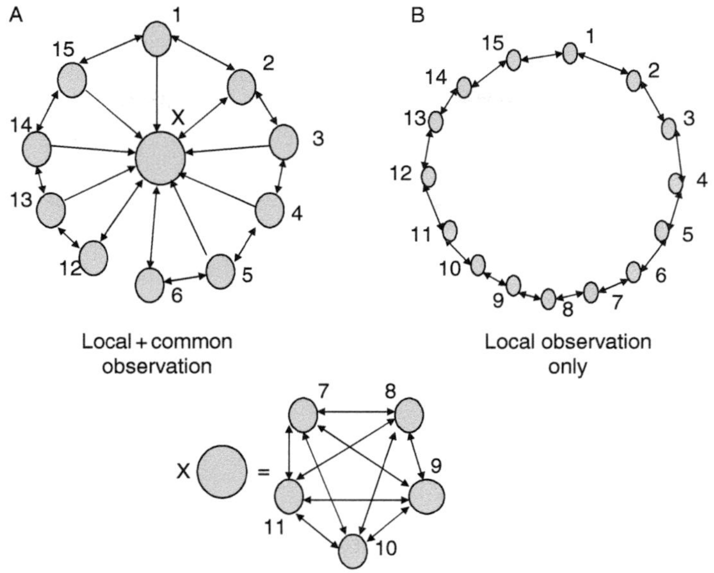

Figure 3 Local + Common Information.

neighbors and a set of common individuals: i.e., $N_i^d = \{i-1, i+1\} \cup \{7, 8, 9, 10, 11\}$. Figure 3 illustrates such a society.[11]

We now show that *there is a strictly positive probability of incomplete learning* in this society. The argument is quite simple: suppose that every person in the commonly observed set is unlucky in the first period and gets an outcome of 0. Consider any individual i and note that this person can get at most three positive signals from his immediate neighborhood. Thus any person in this society will have a minimum residual of two negative signals on the true state. Given the assumptions on the priors, this negative information is sufficient to push the posteriors below the critical cut-off level of 1/2 and this will induce a switch to action a_0 in period 2, for everyone. From then on, no further information is generated and so everyone chooses the suboptimal action a_0 forever. Notice that this argument does not use the size of the society and so there is an upper bound on the probability of learning, which is smaller than one, *irrespective of the size of the society*.

To appreciate the reasons underlying the failure of information aggregation in the above example, note that if θ_1 is the true state then, in a large society, roughly a fraction π (where $\pi > 1/2$) of individuals will receive a payoff of 1 from the action a_1 and a fraction $(1-\pi)$ (where $1-\pi < 1/2$) of people will receive a payoff of 0. Example 2.2 thus illustrates how a few common signals can block out and overwhelm a vast amount of locally available positive information on action a_1. One way of exploring the role of

[11] This Figure is only illustrative of the general structure, and must be interpreted with care: in particular, individual 6 observes 5 and 7–11, 7 observes 6 and 7–11, individuals 8–10 only observe 7–11, while individual 11 observes 7–11 and 12.

network structure is by altering the relative size of local and common information. This is the route taken in the next example.

Example 2.3 *Complete Learning.*

Consider again the decision problem as in Example 2.1 and suppose that information flows via observation of immediate neighbors who are located around a circle: for every i, $N_i^d = \{i-1, i+1\}$. Thus this society is obtained from the earlier one in Example 2.2 by deleting a large number of communication connections. Figure 2.1B illustrates this new society. What are the prospects of learning in such a society? First, fix an individual i and note that since θ_1 is the true state of the world, actions a_1 is actually the optimal action. This means that there is a positive probability that a sequence of actions a_1 will on average generate positive information forever. This means that starting with optimistic priors, individual i will persist with action a_1, forever, if he were isolated, with positive probability.

Analogous arguments show that similar sequences of actions can be constructed for each the neighbors of player i, $i-1$ and $i+1$. Exploiting independence of actions across players, it follows that the probability of the three players $i-1$, i, and $i+1$ receiving positive information on average is strictly positive. Denote this probability by $q > 0$. Hence the probability of individual i choosing the suboptimal action a_0 is bounded above by $1-q$. Finally, note that along this set of sample paths, the experience of other individuals outside the neighborhood cannot alter the choices of individual i. So we can construct a similar set of sample paths for individual $i+3$, whose information neighborhood is $\{i+2, i+3, i+4\}$. From the independent and identical nature of the trials by different individuals, it can be deduced that the probability of this sample of paths is $q > 0$ as well. Note next that since individuals i and $i+3$ do not share any neighbors, the two events, $\{i$ does not try optimal action$\}$ and $\{i+3$ does not try optimal action$\}$ are independent. This in turn means that the joint event that *neither of the two try the optimal action* is bounded above by $(1-q)^2$. In a society where $N_i^d = \{i-1, i+1\}$, and given that $q > 0$, it now follows that learning can be made arbitrarily close to 1, by suitably increasing the number of individuals.

Example 2.3 illustrates in a simple way in which the architecture of connections between individuals in a society can determine whether a society adopts the optimal action in the long run. It also helps in developing a general property of networks that facilitates learning of optimal actions. In the society of Example 2.2 (see Figure 2.1A) with a set of commonly observed individuals, the positive information generated on the optimal actions in different parts of the society is overturned by the negative information generated by this common observed group. By contrast, in a society with only local ties, negative information does arise over time but it cannot overrule the positive information generated in different parts of the society. This allows the positive local information to gain a foothold and eventually spread across the whole society.

The critical feature of the society in Example 2.3 (in Figure 2.1B) is the existence of individuals whose immediate neighborhood is distinct. This leads naturally to the idea of *local independence*. Two individuals i and j are locally independent if $N_i^d(g) \cup \{i\} \cap N_j^d(g) \cup \{j\} = \emptyset$. Moreover, a player i has optimistic prior beliefs if the set of optimal actions under the prior belief $B(\mu_{i,1}) \subset B(\delta_{\theta_1})$. The following general result on networks and social learning, due to Bala and Goyal (1998), can now be stated.

Theorem 2.3 *Consider a connected society. In such a society, the probability that everyone chooses an optimal action in the long run can be made arbitrarily close to 1, by increasing the number of locally independent optimistic players.*

The proof of this result is provided in the appendix. The arguments in the proof extend the intuition underlying Example 2.3, to allow for an arbitrary number of actions, as well as more general outcomes spaces.

Theorem 2.3 and Examples 2.2 and 2.3 have a number of interesting implications which are worth elaborating on. The *first* remark is about the relation with the strength of weak ties hypothesis due to Mark Granovetter (see Granovetter, 1974).[12] In Granovetter's theory, society is visualized as consisting of a number of groups that are internally tightly linked but have a few links across them. In one interpretation, the links across the groups are viewed as weak ties and Granovetter's idea is that weak ties are strong in the sense that they are critical for the flow of new ideas and innovations across the groups in a society. The above result can be interpreted as showing that in societies with this pattern of strong ties (within groups) and weak ties (across groups), the weak ties between the groups do carry valuable information across groups and therefore play a vital role in sustaining technological change and dynamism in a society.

The *second* remark is about what Examples 2.2 and 2.3 and Theorem 2.3 tell us about the generation and diffusion of information in real world networks. Our description of information networks in Section 2.1 suggests that they exhibit very unequal distribution of in-degrees. It is intuitively plausible that in networks with such unequal in-degree distribution a few highly connected nodes have the potential to startwaves of diffusion of ideas and technologies. The formal arguments presented above suggest, somewhat disturbingly, that these waves can lead to mass adoption of actions or ideas whose desirability is contradicted by large amounts of locally collected information. Moreover, due to the broad adoption of such actions, information generation about alternative actions is seriously inhibited and so suboptimal actions can persist.

The *third* remark is about the impact of additional links on the prospects of diffusion of a desirable action. On the one hand, Examples 2.2 and 2.3 together shows that adding links in a network can actually lower the probability of a society learning to choose the optimal action. However, if links are added to the network in Figure 2.1A

[12] For a general formulation of the role of social relation in economic activity, see Granovetter (1985).

eventually we will arrive at the complete network: clearly, the probability of adopting optimal action can be increased to 1, in a complete network by simply increasing the number of nodes. These observations suggest that the impact of additional links depends very much on the initial network and how the links are added. Can we say anything about the marginal value of different links in a network? The above discussion about strength of weak ties suggests that links which act as *bridges* between distinct groups in a society will be very valuable. However, an assessment of the marginal value of links in more general networks appears to be a open question.

The *fourth* remark is about a potential trade-off between the possibility of learning and the speed of learning. A society with common pool of observations has quick but inefficient convergence, whereas the society with pure local learning exhibits slower speed of learning but the probability of learning is higher. A similar trade-off is also present in Ellison and Fudenberg (1993), who study a spatial model of learning, in which the payoffs are sensitive to location. They suppose that there is a continuum of individuals arranged along a line. Each individual has a window of observation around himself (this is similar to the pure local learning network considered above). They consider a choice between two technologies, and suppose that technology A (B) is optimal for all locations to the right (left) of 0. For individual i, the window is an interval given by $[i - w, i + w]$, for some $w \in \mathcal{R}_+$. Each individual chooses the action which yields a higher average payoff in this window. Suppose that, at the start, there is a boundary point $x_0 > 0$, with technology A being adopted to the right of x_0, and technology B being adopted to the left of x_0. Ellison and Fudenberg show that the steady state welfare is decreasing in the size of the interval. Thus, smaller intervals are better from a long term welfare point of view. However, if w is small then the boundary moves slowly over time and if the initial state is far from the optimum then this creates a trade-off: increasing w leads to a short-term welfare gain but a long-term welfare loss.

Diversity: The discussion now turns to the third question posed in the introduction: what is the relation between the structure of connections and the prospects for diversity of actions in a society? Theorem 2.2 says that in a connected society all individuals will obtain the same utility. If there is a unique optimal action for every state this implies that all individuals will choose the same action as well. In case there are multiple optimal actions, however, the result does not say anything about conformism and diversity. To get an impression of the issues involved, start with a society that is split into distinct complete components. Now the level of integration of the society can be measured in terms of the number of cross-group links. Figure 4 presents three such societies, with varying levels of integration. Bala and Goyal (2001) study the probability of diversity as a function of the level of integration. They find that diversity can occur with positive probability in a partially integrated society but that the probability of diversity is zero in a fully integrated society (i.e., the complete network). A characterization of networks which allow for diversity appears to be an open problem.

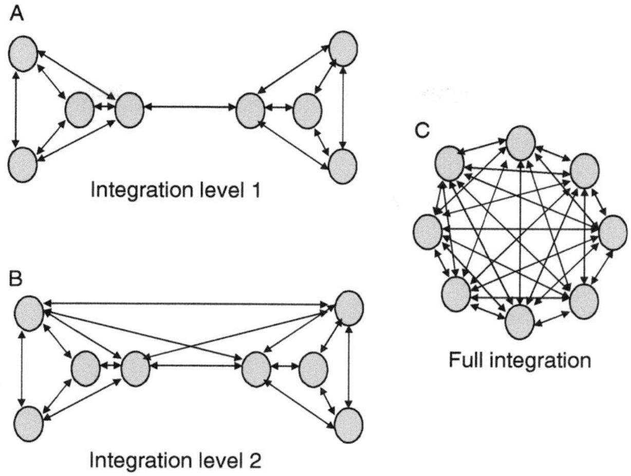

Figure 4 Network integration and social conformism.

Preference heterogeneity: This result on conformism, and indeed all the results reported so far, are obtained in a setting where individuals have identical preferences. However, individuals often have different preferences which are reflected in a different ranking of products or technologies. This raises the question: What are the implications of individual preference heterogeneity for the three results, Theorems 2.1–2.3, obtained above?

It is easy to see that the considerations involved in Theorem 2.1 do not depend in any way on the structure of interaction, so the convergence of beliefs and utilities will obtain in the more general setting with differences in preferences as well. This leads to a study of the long run distribution of utilities. In a society with individuals who have different preferences, the analogue of Theorem 2.2 would be as follows: *in a connected society, all individuals with the same preferences obtain the same utility*. Bala and Goyal (2001) show that this conjecture is false. They construct an example in which preference differences can create information blockages that impede the transmission of useful information and thereby sustain different utility levels (and also different actions) for individuals with similar preferences.

This example motivates a stronger notion of connectedness: *group-wise* connectedness. A society is said to be group-wise connected if for every pair of individuals i and j of the same preference type, either j is a neighbor of i, or there exists a path from j to i with all members of the path being individuals having the same preference as i and j. Bala and Goyal (2001) then show that the conjecture on equal utilities for members of the same preference type obtains in societies which satisfy this stronger connectedness requirement. In a setting with a unique optimal action for every preference type, this result also implies conformity in actions within preference types.

In the above discussion on heterogeneity, we have kept the proximity in preferences and proximity in social connections separate. In some contexts, it is possible that network proximity and distance on other dimensions are related. A large body of research argues that social relations such as friendships exhibit 'homophily': people tend to make friends with others from the same race and gender. For a recent attempt at understanding the ways in which homophily in networks affects social learning, see Golub and Jackson (2010b).

Sources of information and decision rules: The framework developed in Section 2.1 was motivated by the idea that social proximity is an important factor in determining the sources of information that individuals rely upon in making decisions. While this motivation appears to be sound and is supported by a range of empirical work, the framework developed to study social learning above is a little rigid in the following sense. In many situations, individuals get aggregate data on relative popularity of different actions in the population at large. Measures of popularity are potentially useful because they may yield information on average quality of the product. This type of information is not considered the analysis above. One way to model these type of ideas is to suppose that individuals get to observe a sample of other people chosen at random. They use the information obtained from the sample – which could relate to the relative popularity of different actions, or actions and outcomes of different actions – in making his choices. This approach has been explored by Ellison and Fudenberg (1993, 1995), among others. These papers examine the ways in which the size of the sample, the type of information extracted from the sample, and the decision rule that maps this information into the choice of individuals affects social learning.

In recent work, Gale and Kariv (2003) study a model with fully rational individuals who get a private signal at the start and in subsequent periods get to observe the actions of their neighbors, who in turn observe the actions of their neighbors and so on. In this setting, the choice of actions can potentially communicate the private information generated at the start of the process. Individual actions, however, do not generate fresh information unlike the model discussed in Section 2.1. However, full rationality of individuals makes the inference problem quite complicated and they are obliged to focus on small societies to get a handle on the dynamics of learning. In particular, they show that beliefs and utilities of individual individual's converge. This finding is similar to Theorem 2.1 reported above. They also show that in a connected society every individual chooses the same action and obtains the same utility. Thus social conformism obtains in the long run. The ideas behind this result mirror those discussed in Theorem 2.2 above.

Changes in decision rules will have an impact on the learning process and the outcomes may well be different with non-Bayesian rules of thumb such as imitation of the best or popularity weighted schemes. In a recent paper, Chatterjee and Xu (2004) explore learning from neighbors under alternative bounded rational decision rules.

2.2 Naive learning

The previous section focused on a model of Bayesian learning and established a number of results on the relation between the evolution of beliefs, actions, and payoffs and the structure of the network. The complexity of the learning process meant that I was able to obtain only relatively simple results concerning the effects of networks. This section simplifies the learning process and this will allow us to derive sharper results with regard to the implications of networks. The exposition in this section draws on the work of DeMarzo, Vayanos and Zweibel (2003) and Golub and Jackson (2010a).

There are n individuals, each of whom starts with a belief at date 0, a number p_i^0. In period 1 each individual i updates his belief, by taking an average of the beliefs of others and his own belief. She assigns weight $\omega_{ij} \in [0, 1]$ to each $j \in N$, with $\sum_{j \in N} w_{ij} = 1$. This yields p_i^1, for $i \in N$. Define for any $t \geq 0$, the vector of beliefs at start of that period, $\mathbf{p}^t = \{p_1^t, p_2^t, p_3^t, .. p_n^t\}$. Let $\mathbf{W}$ be the $n \times n$ stochastic matrix defined by the weights which individuals assign to each others opinions. The belief revision process repeats itself over time $t = 2, 3, 4, \ldots$ I study the evolution of $\mathbf{p}^t$ in relation to the matrix $\mathbf{W}$.

As in the previous section, our interest will be in connected societies; in the present context a society is said to be connected if for every pair of players i and j, either $\omega_{ij} > 0$ or there is a intermediate sequence of individuals $i_1, i_2, .. i_k$ such that $w_{ii_1}, \ldots .w_{i_kj} > 0$. DeMarzo et al. (2003) prove the following result.

Theorem 2.4 *Suppose that the matrix W comes from a connected society and that* $w_{ii} > 0$ *for all i. Then*

1. *The influence of j on i converges:* $\lim_{t \to \infty} w_{ij}^t = w_j$.
2. *The beliefs converge* $p_i^t \to p^*$, *for all* $i \in N$, *where* $p^* = wp^0$.
3. *The social influence vector* $\boldsymbol{w} = (w_1, w_2, w_3, \ldots, w_n)$, *is defined as the unique solution to* $\mathbf{w} \cdot \mathbf{W} = \mathbf{w}$.

The society is connected and so the Markov process is irreducible, and since $\omega_{ii} > 0$, the Markov chain is also a periodic. It is well known that such a Markov chain has a unique stationary distribution, i.e., there exists a unique probability distribution w such that $wW = w$. Moreover, starting from any state i, the probability of being in any state j at date t converges to ω_j, as $t \to \infty$.

I now turn to the prospects of complete learning in different types of networks. To study this issue, it is useful to define θ as the true state, and let individual prior belief be $p_i^0 = \theta + \rho_i$, which is distributed i.i.d with mean equal to true state θ and variance given by $0 \leq \sigma^2 < \infty$. Under what circumstances will updated individual beliefs approach the truth as n gets large?

To get some intuition for this result, let us start with a consideration of society in which every individual assigns an equal weight to every other individual. If $\omega_{ij} = 1/n$ for every i and j, then at end of period 1, with n individuals, average belief is $p_j^{1,n} = \theta + 1/n \sum_{i \in N} \rho_i$, for all $j \in N$. It follows from the law of large numbers that this belief converges to the truth as n gets large. I now present an example taken from Golub and Jackson (2010), which illustrates how network structure matters for learning.

Example: Consider a star network in which all spokes only observe the center while the center observes all the spokes. For a society with $n = 4$ the matrix is given in Table 1:

Table 1

	1	2	3	4
1	1-δ	$\delta/3$	$\delta/3$	$\delta/3$
2	1-ε	ε	0	0
3	1-ε	0	ε	0
4	1-ε	0	0	ε

It is easy to show that for general n, with 1 at the center the social influence vector is:

$$w_1 = \frac{1-\varepsilon}{1-\varepsilon+\delta}; \quad w_j = \frac{\delta}{(n-1)(1-\varepsilon+\delta)}, \quad j \neq 1 \tag{9}$$

Finally, I observe that the limit belief is given by:

$$\theta + w_1\rho_1 + \frac{\delta}{(n-1)(1-\varepsilon+\delta)}\sum_{j=2}^{n}\rho_j \tag{10}$$

does not converge to θ generally, since $w_1\ \rho_1 \neq 0$, irrespective of n. ■

Let w_i^n be the limit social influence and p_i^n be the limit belief of person i in a network with n individuals. Golub and Jackson (2010) build on the above example to prove the following result.

Theorem 2.5 *Let W_n be a sequence of connected societies, as n varies, in which $w_{ii} > 0$, for all $i \in N$. Then*

$$\text{plim}_{n\to\infty}\sum_{i\in A_n} w_i^n p_i^n = \theta, \tag{11}$$

if and only if $\lim_{n\to\infty} \max_i w_i^n \to 0$.

This result shows that vanishing social influence is both necessary as well as sufficient in a context of naive learning to guarantee that complete learning obtains in a large society. This result also nicely complements our analysis of incomplete learning in the previous section. It shows how bounds on social influence are necessary for complete social learning.

2.3 Sequence of single choices

In the framework studied in Section 2.1, it was assumed that an individual observes all the actions as well as the outcomes of the actions of his direct neighbors. There is an extensive literature that has studied a simpler formulation in which individuals move only once but they learn by observing the history of past behavior. Broadly speaking, there are two approaches here. One, where individuals observe actions and outcomes from the past; here the actions generate information and so the friction arises when individuals stop choosing actions which are informative. Two, where individuals receive individual private signals but observe only the actions from the past; here the source of friction is that individual actions may not reflect private information.

Observation of past actions and outcomes: Consider a sequence of agents entering at discrete points in time $t = 1,2,3\ldots$. Each agent enters with a prior belief, observes the entire history of actions and outcomes of actions of all past agents, updates his priors, and then chooses an action which is optimal with respond to the posterior beliefs. Do individual agents eventually learn the truth and choose the optimal action? I follow Bala and Goyal (1994, 1995) in the discussion below.

Given that there is only one agent at any point in time, I can drop the subscript i in the notation I developed in repeated action-learning model. As before let $\theta_1 \in \Theta$ be the true state. Suppose that prior beliefs at point of entry of agent are given by μ_t^0. Moreover, let these prior beliefs be drawn from some distribution $\mathcal{D}$ on the set of possible priors. I will suppose that D admits priors, which place point mass on any of the states $\theta \in \Theta$. I shall refer to this as the heterogeneous prior assumption. Agent t enters with prior belief μ_t^0, and updates this prior upon observing the history of past actions and outcomes using Bayes' Rule. Let $a_t = b(\mu_t)$ denote the action in period t, Z_t the outcome of this action, and let $U_t = u(a_t, \mu_t)$ be the expected utility with respect to his own action at time t. Given this notation the posterior beliefs of individual in period t are:

$$\mu_t(\theta|Z_t) = \frac{\prod_{t'=1}^{t-1}\phi(Z_{t'}; a_{t'}; \theta)\mu_t^0(\theta)}{\sum_{\theta'\in\Theta}\prod_{t'=1}^{t-1}\phi(Z_{t'}; a_{t'}; \theta)\mu_t^0(\theta')}. \tag{12}$$

The interest is in studying the evolution of individual actions, beliefs, and utilities, (a_t, μ_t, U_t), over time. Let δ_{θ_1} refer to a belief that the true state of the world is θ_1. Let $B(\delta_{\theta_1})$ be the set of optimal actions with this point mass belief. Let S_t be the number of times that an optimal action $x \in B(\delta_{\theta_1})$ has been chosen until time t. I shall say that actions converge in probability if for every $\varepsilon > 0$,

$$\lim_{t\to\infty} P(|1 - \frac{S_t}{t}| < \varepsilon) = 1. \tag{13}$$

The following result from Bala and Goyal (1995) characterizes long run learning.

Theorem 2.6 *Suppose that the distribution $\mathcal{D}$ respects the heterogeneity property. The sequence of actions a_t converges in probability to the set $G(\delta_{\theta_1})$. The utilities U_t converge in probability to $U(x, \delta_{\theta_1})$, where $x \in G(\delta_{\theta_1})$. Moreover, actions fail to converge to an optimal action, almost surely.*

First observe that heterogeneity is necessary for learning to obtain. To see why this is true consider the two arm bandit considered in Example 2.1 above. If every agent entered with the same prior belief (say) $\mu > 1/2$ there exists a finite sequence of 0's which will lead to posterior falling below the threshold 1/2. Once this happens, every agent will choose action 0, forever after. More generally, if priors of all agents are bounded above by a number $x < 1$ then a variant of the above argument can be used to demonstrate that there is a positive probability of incomplete learning. Second, note that if there is no upper bound on prior beliefs: but then for a period t, there exist a range of prior beliefs such that an agent with these beliefs will choose an action that is entirely independent of the history of past actions and outcomes. In other words, along almost all sample paths, the suboptimal action is chosen infinitely often. So actions fail to converge to optimal actions, almost surely.

However, as time goes by, and the informative action is chosen infinitely often, sufficient information on the true state is revealed: this implies that the set of beliefs which can be insensitive to past history shrinks. The theorem stated above tells us that the set of beliefs shrinks sufficiently quickly to ensure that there is convergence to optimal action in probability.

Observation of past actions: In many interesting economic contexts, there may be limited opportunity for direct communication and so individuals learn from others by observing their actions. Let us briefly sketch such a model. There is a single sequence of privately informed individuals who take one action each. Before making his choice an individual gets to observe the actions of all the people who have made a choice earlier. The actions of his predecessors *potentially* reveal their private information. An individual can therefore use the information revealed via the actions of others along with his own private information to make decisions. I will refer to this process as observational social learning. This model was introduced in Banerjee (1993) and Bikhchandani, Hirshleifer and Welch (1992); for a general treatment, see Smith and Sorensen (2000). An extensive literature has grown around this basic model. I will discuss some of the basic insights but a comprehensive survey is outside the scope of the present chapter.[13] The principal question is: do individuals eventually learn and choose the optimal action?

I first discuss the basic insight of the early papers by Banerjee (1993) and Bikhchandani, Hirshleifer and Welch (1992). Consider a setting in which private signals are equally accurate and individuals assign equal weight to their own and the signal of others. To fix ideas suppose that there are two actions and two states. For simplicity, suppose that in state 1 action 1 is optimal, while in state 0 action 0 is optimal. Suppose that initially agents believe that the states are equally likely. At point of entry, agent in period t, observes a private signal: probability of signal x when true state is x is q, where $q > 1/2$. The probability that signal is x when true state is $y \neq x$ is $1 - q < 1/2$. Assume that signals are drawn independently, conditional on the true state in every period. Now suppose that the first two individuals observe a signal in favor of state (and hence action) 1. They will both choose action 1. Consider agent 3 who observes this sequence of 1's. Given that the information from others is as accurate as his own,

[13] For an elegant survey of the research on observational learning see, Chamley (2004).

two signals in favor of state 1 will overrule his own signal in favor of action 0. So agent 3 will also choose action A, and this is his choice irrespective of his own signal. In that case, his action does not convey any information about his signal. In particular, agents 4 onward are in the same situation as agent 3. So they too will ignore their own private information and choose action 1. Thus the sequence of individuals may *herd* on action 1. Observe that this argument is independent of whether 1 is in fact an optimal action. So I have shown that there is a strictly positive probability that society may herd on the wrong action. Finally, observe that private signals arrive independently (and exogenously) over time: so eventually there will *always* be enough information to infer the optimal action. This illustrates how observational learning may fail to aggregate private information.

The discussion in the previous section suggests a possible way out of this inefficient herding: suppose agents draw signals that are heterogeneous and have different levels of accuracy. This will induce private beliefs which vary across agents. In particular, if some agents receive very 'strong' signals – signals which make one state much more likely as compared to the other state – then they may choose to ignore past observations and choose an action which reflects their private signal. Suppose private belief about state 0, given by μ_t^0 ranges between $\underline{\beta}$ and $\bar{\beta}$. I shall say that beliefs are bounded if there are numbers $\underline{\beta} > 0$ and $\bar{\beta} < 1$. Beliefs are unbounded if $\underline{\beta} = 1 - \bar{\beta} = 0$. Following our discussions after Theorem 2.6, it is easy to possible to verify that if agents have bounded beliefs then inefficient herding may occur, while if beliefs are unbounded then observational learning will lead to efficient choice of actions eventually; for a general analysis of this problem see Smith and Sorensen (2000).

In a recent paper, Acemoglu et al. (2010), introduce social networks in a single sequence setting with observational learning. They propose the following natural model. Suppose that agent at time t can draw a sample from the past, $N_t \subseteq \{1, 2, ..t-1\}$. Let this sample be drawn with some probability distribution $\mathcal{L}_t$. Some examples of such distributions are:

1. $L_t(\{1, 2, \ldots t-1\}) = 1$: this corresponds to the standard model in which every agent observes the entire past history of actions.
2. $L_t(\{t-1\}) = 1$: every agent observes only the immediately preceding agent.
3. L_t assigns equal probability to picking every subset of the past sequence of agents.

Acemoglu et al. (2010) obtain several interesting results with regard to asymptotic learning. I will focus on the setting with unbounded beliefs. Recall, that if observation window is the entire past history then the arguments above (from Bala and Goyal (1995) and Smith and Sorensen (2000) ensure that actions converge in probability to optimal actions. So the interest is in examining what is the minimum information needed to ensure learning.

Their result develops a sufficient condition on social networks which ensures that actions converge to optimal action in probability. A simple example illustrates the key idea: suppose that there is a positive probability that for all $t \geq 2$, $L_t(1) = p > 0$. Suppose that this agent Mr. 1 chooses action 1. Under the assumption of unbounded beliefs I know that any point there is a possibility of an agent with extremal signals and hence private beliefs which sharply favor one state over the other. But under our hypothesis there is a strictly positive probability that such an agent observes a single agent, Mr. 1, who has chosen action 1. It is then easy to see that this agent will choose an action that depends solely on his private signal. As beliefs arise independently over time and as observation neighborhoods are independent across agents, it follows that there is a strictly positive probability that agents will choose action in line with their private belief. This prevents asymptotic learning.

To rule this problem out, Acemoglu et al. (2010) develop the property of *expanding observations* in social networks. A social network is said to satisfy expanding observations if for all $k \in \mathcal{N}$,

$$\lim_{t\to\infty} L_t(\max_{b\in N_t} b < k) = 1. \tag{14}$$

If the network does not satisfy this property then it is has nonexpanding observations. Expanding observations rules out the example discussed above in which every agent samples agent 1 with strictly positive probability. The following theorem shows expanding an observation suffices to ensure asymptotic learning.

Theorem 2.7 *Assume that beliefs satisfy unbounded private beliefs property and network L_t satisfies expanding observations. Then actions converge in probability to the optimal action.*

The proof of this result rests on a set of arguments. First, the authors establish a generalized improvement principal. Suppose every agent t gets to observe one person from the past: then there is a strict increase in the probability of Mr. t making the correct choice, as compared to the person he observes. This argument builds on the 'welfare improvement' principle in Banerjee and Fudenberg (2004) and the 'imitation' principle across neighbors in Bala and Goyal (1998). The second step shows that this improvement principle can be extended to allow for multiple observations. The third step exploits expanding observations to infer that later agents will have access to new information and so the expected utilities must converge to the maximum possible value, i.e., actions must converge to the optimal one.

It is worth discussing the relationship between Example 2.2, Theorem 2.3 and Theorem 2.7. Note that the key obstacle to complete learning in the repeated action setting is the asymmetry in observation: there is a small group of agents who observe few others but are observed by everyone. In Theorem 2.7 by contrast, the expanding observations property of social networks ensures that agents eventually assign zero probability on any fixed set of early agents. This ensures that new information arrives into the system and ensures long run learning.

3. STRATEGIC INTERACTION

In this section, I will study situations in which the payoffs to an individual depend on his own action as well as the action of others players. The choice of actions of others is imperfectly known and this creates uncertainty about the payoffs that an individual can hope to earn. As in the previous sections, time proceeds at discrete points; at every point, an individual gets an opportunity to choose an action, with some probability. In choosing her action, she takes into account the past history of actions of others, forms some view of how others will move in the current period, and then chooses an action which is 'optimal' for herself. The set of actions taken together defines the profile of actions for the current period. This in turn shapes the behavior of actions over time. The focus will be on the relation between the network of interaction between individuals and the dynamics of actions and utilities. I will consider two classical types of games: games of coordination and games of cooperation. I start with the former.

3.1 Coordination games

It is useful to start with a description of a two action coordination game among two players. Denote the players by 1 and 2 and the possible actions by α and β. The rewards to a player depend on her own action and the action of the other player. These rewards are summarized in the following pay-off matrix.

Table 2

1 \ 2	α	β
α	a, a	d, e
β	e, d	b, b

At the heart of coordination games are two basic ideas: one, there are gains from individuals choosing the same action; and two, rewards may differ depending on which actions the two players coordinate on. These considerations motivate the following restrictions on the payoff parameters.

$$a > d; b > d; d > e; a + d > b + e. \tag{15}$$

These restrictions imply that there are two (pure strategy) Nash equilibria of the game: $\{\alpha, \alpha\}$ and $\{\beta, \beta\}$ and that coordinating on either of them is better than not coordinating at all.[14] The assumption that $a + d > b + e$ implies that if a player places equal probability on her opponent playing the two actions then it is strictly better for her to choose α. In other words, α is the *risk-dominant* action in the sense of Harsanyi and Selten (1988). It is important to note that α can be risk-dominant even if it is not efficient (that is even if $b > a$). Indeed, one of the important considerations in the research to date has been relative salience of riskiness versus efficiency. Given the restrictions on the payoffs, the two equilibria are *strict* in the sense that the best response

[14] In principle, players can want to coordinate on action combinations $\{\alpha, \beta\}$ or $\{\beta, \alpha\}$; games with such equilibria may be referred to as anti-coordination games. See Bramoulle (2007) for a study of network effects in this class of games.

in the equilibrium yields a strictly higher payoff than the other option. It is well known that strict equilibria are robust to standard refinements of Nash equilibrium (see e.g., Van Damme, 1991).

The focus of the analysis is on the effects of local interactions. I study local interaction in terms of neighborhoods within a model of networks. Suppose, as before, that the $N = \{1, 2, \ldots, n\}$ players are located on the nodes of an undirected network $g \in \mathcal{G}$, where $\mathcal{G}$ is the set of all possible undirected networks on n nodes. I will assume that a player i plays the coordination game with each of her neighbors. Recall that $N_i(g) = \{j \in N | g_{i,j} = 1\}$ refers to the set of players with whom i is linked in network g. Three networks of interaction – the complete network, the star and local interaction among players located around a circle – will be extensively used in this chapter. For easy reference they are presented in Figure 5.

As before, s_i denotes the strategy of player i and $S_i = \{\alpha, \beta\}$ the strategy set.[15] Let $S = \prod_{i \in N} S_i$ denote the set of all strategy profiles in the game and let s refer to a typical member of this set. In the two player game, let $\pi(x, y)$ denote the payoffs to player i when this player chooses action x, while her opponent chooses action y. The payoffs to a player i in network g, from a strategy s_i, given that the other players are choosing s_{-i} are:

$$\prod_i (s_i, s_{-i} \,|\, g) = \sum_{j \in N_i(g)} \pi(s_i, s_j) \tag{16}$$

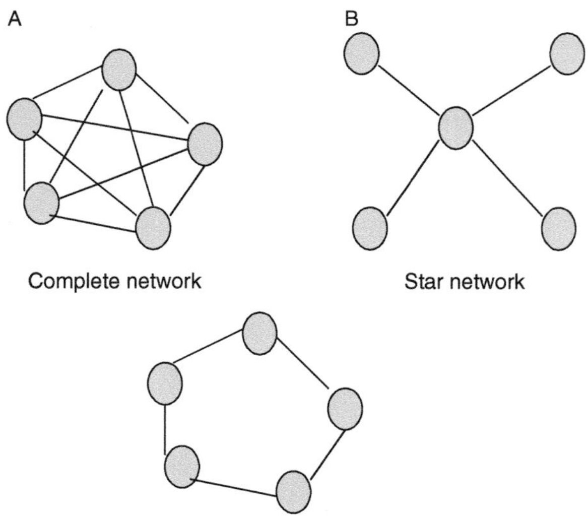

Figure 5 Simple networks.

[15] In the present model, individual choices refer to languages, word processing packages, norms for driving etc. For an influential formulation in which individuals choose where to locate on a network and their payoffs depend on who locates next to them, see Schelling (1975).

This formulation reflects the idea that a player i interacts with each of the players in the set $N_i(g)$. The players N, their interactions summarized by a network g, the set of actions for each player $S_i = \{\alpha, \beta\}$, and the payoffs 16 (where $\pi(x, y)$ satisfies 15) together define a social coordination game.

3.1.1 Multiple equilibria

This section starts by describing some Nash equilibria that can arise under different network structures. First, note that the strategy profile $s_i = x$, for all $i \in N$, where $x \in \{\alpha, \beta\}$ is a Nash equilibrium for every possible network structure. This is easily checked given the restrictions on the payoffs. Are there other types of equilibria which display diversity of actions and how is their existence affected by the structure of interaction? To get a sense of some of the forces driving conformism and diversity, it is useful to consider a class of societies in which there are several groups and intra-group interaction is more intense as compared to inter-group interaction. Figure 6 presents network structures with two groups that capture this idea. The number of cross-group links reflect the level of integration of the society.

Simple calculations reveal that equilibria with a diversity of actions are easy to sustain, in societies with low levels of integration, but that such equilibria cannot be sustained in the fully integrated society, i.e., in the complete network.

The above observations are summarized in the following result.

Theorem 3.1 *Consider a social coordination game. A strategy profile in which everyone plays the same action is a Nash equilibrium for every network $g \in \mathcal{G}$. If the network is complete, then these are the only possible Nash equilibria. If the network is incomplete then there may exist equilibria with a diversity of actions as well.*

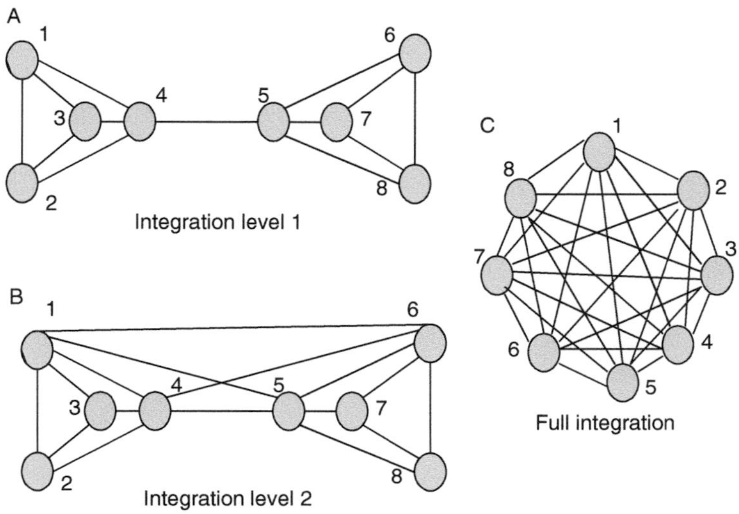

Figure 6 Levels of network integration.

This result yields two insights: one, multiple equilibria with social conformism exist for every possible network of interaction, and two, social diversity can arise in equilibrium, but the possibility of such outcomes depends on the network architecture. The result does raise a natural question: does diversity become less likely as I add links to a network? The following example illustrates why this may not be true in general.

Example 3.1 *Density of networks and diversity of actions*

Consider a star network with 8 nodes. Let node 1 be the central node. Observe that in the star network, any equilibrium must involve conformism: this is because in equilibrium every periphery node must choose the same action as the central node. Now supplement this network by adding three links between three peripheral nodes 1, 2 and 3, such that they now constitute a complete (sub) network. Now it is easy to see that if the payoffs from the two actions are similar then there is an equilibrium in which these three nodes choose action β, while the rest of the players all choose action α. Thus adding links to a network can sometimes facilitate the emergence of action diversity. Also note that the outcome with a single action remains an equilibrium in the new network. △

These observations lead to an examination of the robustness of different equilibria and how this is in turn related to the structure of interaction.

3.1.2 Dynamic stability and equilibrium selection

Assume that time is a discrete variable and indexed by $t = 1,2,3, \ldots$ In each period, with probability $p \in (0,1)$, a player gets an opportunity to revise her strategy. Faced with this opportunity, player i chooses an action which maximizes her payoff, under the assumption that the strategy profile of her neighbors remains the same as in the previous period. If more than one action is optimal then the player persists with the current action. Denote the strategy of a player i in period t by s_i^t. If player i is not active in period t then set $s_i^t = s_i^{t-1}$. This simple best-response strategy revision rule generates, for every network g, a transition probability function, $P_g(ss') : S \times S \to [0, 1]$, which governs the evolution of the state of the system s^t. A strategy profile (or state), s, is absorbing if the dynamic process cannot escape from the state once it reaches it, i.e., $P_g(ss) = 1$. The interest is in the relation between absorbing states and the structures of local interaction.

The first step in the analysis is the following convergence result and the characterization of the limiting states.

Theorem 3.2 *Consider a social coordination game. Starting from any initial strategy profile, s^0, the dynamic process s^t converges to an absorbing strategy profile in finite time, with probability 1. There is an equivalence between the set of absorbing strategy profiles and the set of Nash equilibria of the static social game.*[16]

[16] The relation between the Nash equilibria of the social coordination game and the equilibria of the original 2×2 game has been explored in Mailath, Samuelson and Shaked (1997). They show that the Nash equilibria of the static social game is equivalent to the set of correlated equilibria of the 2×2 game. Ianni (2001) studies convergence to correlated equilibria under myopic best response dynamics.

The equivalence between absorbing states and Nash equilibria of the social game of coordination is easy to see. The arguments underlying the convergence result are as follows: start at some state s_0. Consider the set of players who are not playing a best response. If this set is empty then the process is at a Nash equilibrium profile and this is an absorbing state of the process, as no player has an incentive to revise her strategy. Therefore, suppose there are some players who are currently choosing action α but would prefer to choose β. Allow them to choose β, and let s_1 be the new state of the system (this transition occurs with positive probability, given the decision rules used by individuals). Now examine the players doing α in state s_1 who would like to switch actions. If there are some such players then have them switch to β and define the new state as s_2. Clearly, this process of having the α players switch will end in finite time (since there are a finite number of players in the society). Let the state with this property be $\hat{s}$. Either there will be no players left choosing α or there will be some players choosing α in $\hat{s}$. In the former case the process is at a Nash equilibrium. Consider the second possibility next. Check if there are any players choosing β in state $\hat{s}$, who would like to switch actions. If there are none then the process is at an absorbing state. If there are some β players who would like to switch then follow the process as outlined above to reach a state in which there is no player who wishes to switch from β to α. Let this state be denoted by $\bar{s}$. Next observe that no player who was choosing α (and did not want to switch actions) in $\hat{s}$ would be interested in switching to β. This is true because the game is a coordination game and the set of players choosing α has (weakly) increased in the transition from $\hat{s}$ to $\bar{s}$. Hence the process has arrived (with positive probability) at a state in which no player has any incentive to switch actions. This is an absorbing state of the dynamics; since the initial state was arbitrary, and the above transition occurs with positive probability, the theory of Markov chains says that the transition to an absorbing state will occur in finite time, with probability 1.

An early result on convergence of dynamics to Nash equilibrium in regular networks (where every player has the same number of neighbors) is presented in Anderlini and Ianni (1996). In their model, a player is randomly matched to play with one other player in her neighborhood. Moreover, every player gets a chance to revise her move in every period. Finally, a player who plans to switch actions can make an error with some probability. They refer to this as noise on the margin. With this decision rule, the dynamic process of choices converges to a Nash equilibrium for a class of regular networks. The result presented here holds for all networks and does not rely on mistakes for convergence. Instead, the above result exploits inertia of individual decisions and the coordination nature of the game to obtain convergence.

Theorem 3.2 shows that the learning process converges. This result also says that every Nash equilibrium (for a given network of interaction) is an absorbing state of the process. This means that there is no hope of selecting across the variety of equilibria identified earlier in Proposition 3.1 with this dynamic process. This finding motivates a study of relative stability of different equilibria. There are a number of different approaches which have been adopted in the literature. I will examine the robustness with respect to small but repeated perturbations, i.e., stochastic stability of outcomes. For a general study of dynamic stability of equilibria, see Samuelson (1997) and Young (1998).

The ideas underlying stochastic stability can be informally described as follows. Suppose that s and s' are the two absorbing states of the best-response dynamics described above. Given that s is an absorbing state, a movement from s to s' requires an error or an experiment on the part of one or more of the players. Similarly, a movement from s' to s requires errors on the part of some subset of players. I will follow standard practice in this field and refer to such errors/experiments as *mutations*. The state s is said to be stochastically stable if it requires relatively more mutations to move from s to s' as compared to the other way around. If it takes the same number of mutations to move between the two states, then they are both stochastically stable.

Formally, suppose that, occasionally, players make mistakes, experiment, or simply disregard payoff considerations in choosing their strategies. Assume that, conditional on receiving a revision opportunity at any point in time t, a player chooses her strategy at random with some small *mutation* probability $\varepsilon > 0$. Given a network g, and for any $\varepsilon > 0$, the mutation process defines a Markov chain that is a periodic and irreducible and, therefore, has a unique invariant probability distribution; denote this distribution by μ_g^ε.[17] The analysis will study the support of μ_g^ε as the probability of mistakes becomes very small, i.e., as ε converges to 0. Define $\lim_{\varepsilon \to 0} \mu_g^\varepsilon = \hat{\mu}_g$. A state s is said to be *stochastically stable* if $\hat{\mu}_g(s) > 0$. This notion of stability identifies states that are relatively more stable with respect to such mutations.[18] I will now examine the effects of the network of interaction, g, on the set of stochastically stable states. I will consider the complete network, local interaction around the circle, and the star network.

Example 3.2 *The complete network.*

This example considers the complete network in which every player is a neighbor of every other player. Suppose that player 1 is deciding on whether to choose α or β. It is easy to verify that at least $k = (n-1)(b-d)/[(a-e)+(b-d)]$ players need to choose α, for α to be optimal for player 1 as well. Similarly, the minimum number of players needed to induce player 1 to choose β is given by $l = (n-1)(a-e)/[(a-e) + (b-d)]$. Given the assumption that $a + d > b + e$ it follows that $k < n/2 < l$. If everyone is choosing α then it takes l mutations to transit to a state where everyone is choosing β; likewise, if everyone is choosing β then it takes k mutations to transit to a state where everyone is choosing α. From the general observations on stochastic

[17] This follows from standard results in the theory of Markov chains, see e.g., Billingsley (1985).

[18] These ideas have been applied extensively to develop a theory of equilibrium selection in game theory. The notion of stochastic stability was introduced into economics by Kandori, Mailath and Rob (1993) and Young (1993).

stability above, it then follows that in the complete network, everyone choosing the risk-dominant action α is the unique stochastically stable outcome. ■

Example 3.3 *Local interaction around a circle.*

This example considers local interaction with immediate neighbors around a circle and is taken from Ellison (1993). Suppose that at time $t-1$ every player is choosing β. Now suppose that two adjacent players i and $i+1$ choose action α at time t, due to a mutation in the process. It is now easy to verify that in the next period, $t+1$ the immediate neighbors of i and $i+1$, players $i-1$ and $i+2$ will find it optimal to switch to action α (this is due to the assumption that α is risk-dominant and $a+d > b+e$). Moreover, in period $t+2$ the immediate neighbors of $i-1$ and $i+2$ will have a similar incentive, and so there is a process under way which leads to everyone choosing action α, within finite time. On the other hand, if everyone is choosing α then $n-1$ players must switch to β to induce a player to switch to action β. To see why this is the case, note that a player bases her decision on the actions of immediate neighbors, and so long as at least one of the neighbors is choosing α the optimal action is to choose α. It then follows that everyone choosing the risk-dominant action α is the unique stochastically stable state. ■

The simplicity of the above arguments suggests the following conjecture: the risk-dominant outcome obtains in all networks. This conjecture is false as the following example illustrates.

Example 3.4 *The star network.*

This example considers interaction on a star; recall that a star is a network in which one player has links – and hence interacts – with all the other $n-1$ players, while the other players have no links between them. This example is taken from Jackson and Watts (2002). Suppose that player 1 is the central player of the star network. The first point to note about a star network is that there are only two possible equilibrium configurations, both involving social conformism. A study of stochastically stable actions therefore involves a study of the relative stability of these two configurations. However, it is easily verified that in a star network a perturbation that switches the action of player 1 is sufficient to get a switch of all the other players. Since this is also the minimum number of mutations possible, it follows that both states are stochastically stable! ■

Examples 3.2–3.4 show that network structure has an important bearing on the nature of stochastically stable states. They also raise two types of questions. The first question pertains to network structure. Is it possible to identify general features of networks that sustain conformism and diversity, respectively, and also if some networks favor one type of conformism while other networks facilitate a different type of conformism? The second question relates to the decision rules. Is the role of interaction structures sensitive to the formulation of decision rules and the probability of mutations? The first question appears to be an open one;[19] Section 3.1.3 takes up the second question.

[19] There is a small experimental literature on coordination games which studies specific structures of local interaction; see e.g., Cassar (2007), Berninghaus et al. (2002).

I conclude this section by discussing the effects of the network of interaction on the rates of convergence of the dynamic process. From a practical point of view, the invariant distribution $\hat{\mu}_g$ is only meaningful if the rate of convergence of the dynamics is relatively quick. In the above model, the dynamics are Markovian and if there is a unique invariant distribution then standard mathematical results suggest that the rate of convergence is exponential. In other words, there is some number $\rho < 1$ such that the probability distribution of actions at time t, σ^t, approaches the invariant distribution σ^* at a rate approximately given by ρ^t. While this result is helpful, it is easy to see that this property allows a fairly wide range of rates of convergence, depending on the value of ρ. If ρ is close to 1 then the process is essentially determined by the initial configuration σ_0 for a long period, while if ρ is close to 0 then initial conditions play a less important role and dynamics shape individual choices quickly. The work of Ellison (1993) directed attention to the role of interaction structure in shaping the rate of convergence. He argued that in a complete network transition between strict Nash equilibria based on mutations would take a very long time in large populations since the number of mutations needed is of the order of the population. By contrast, as Example 3.3 showed under local interaction around a circle, a couple of mutations (followed by best responses) are sufficient to initiate a transition to the risk-dominant action. Thus local interaction leads to dramatically faster rates of convergence to the risk-dominant action.[20]

3.1.3 Related themes

The study of social coordination with local interaction has been a very active field of research and a number of themes have been explored. This section discusses two strands of this work. One, I consider other decision rules and two, I discuss the implications of different initial configurations.

Alternative Decision Rules: In the discussion above, I started with a myopic best response decision rule. I then complemented it with small but persistent mutations and looked at what happens as the probability of mutations becomes small. I now discuss alternatives to the best response rule with equiprobable mutations. A first step in this exercise is to consider an alternative formulation of decision rules in which individual experimentation is more sensitive to payoff losses. In any period t, an individual i located in network g is drawn at random and chooses (say) α according to a probability distribution, $p_i^\gamma(\alpha|s^t, g)$, where $\gamma > 0$ and s^t is the strategy profile at time t.

$$p_i^\gamma(\alpha|s^t, g) = \frac{e^{\gamma \Pi_i(\alpha, s^t_{-i}|g)}}{e^{\gamma \Pi_i(\alpha, s^t_{-i}|g)} + e^{\gamma \Pi_i(\beta, s^t_{-i}|g)}} \tag{17}$$

[20] While local interaction has dramatic effects on rates of convergence it is worth observing that it entails repeated interaction among neighbors. Repeated interaction however makes the bounded and myopic rational rules of behavior in the dynamic models less plausible.

This is referred to as the log-linear response rule; in the context of coordination games, this rule was first studied by Blume (1993). Note that for large values of γ the probability distribution will place most of the probability mass on the best response action. Define $\Delta_i(s|g) = \Pi_i(\beta, s_{-i}|g) - \Pi_i(\alpha, s_{-i}|g)$. Then for large γ the probability of action α is:

$$p_i^{\gamma}(\alpha|s^t, g) = \frac{e^{-\gamma\Delta_i(s^t|g)}}{1 + e^{-\gamma\Delta_i(s^t|g)}} \cong e^{-\gamma\Delta_i(s^t|g)}. \tag{18}$$

This expression says that the probability of not choosing the best response is exponentially declining in the payoff loss from the deviation. The analysis of local learning in coordination games when individuals use the log-linear decision rule is summarized in the following result, due to Young (1998).

Theorem 3.3 *Consider a social coordination game on a connected network g. Suppose that in each period one individual is picked at random to revise choices. In revising choices this individual uses the log-linear response rule. Then the stochastically stable outcome is a state in which every player chooses the risk-dominant action.*

This result tells us that if the mutation probabilities are payoff sensitive in a strong form – the probability of choosing an action is exponentially declining in payoff losses associated with it – then the network structure has no effects on the long run distribution of actions. To get some intuition for the result it is useful to discuss the dynamic process in the star network. In that example, the simplest way to get a transition is via a switch in the action of the central player. In the standard model, with payoff insensitive mutations, the probability of the central player making a switch from α to β is the same as the other way around. By contrast, under the log-linear response rule, matters are very different. If there are many peripheral players, then there is a significant difference in the payoff losses involved and the probability of switching from α to β is significantly smaller than the probability of switching from β to α. This difference is crucial for obtaining the above result.

The mutation structure has been the subject of considerable research over the years. In an influential paper, Bergin and Lipman (1996) showed that any outcome could be supported as stochastically stable if the order of magnitudes for mutations was different across different actions. This 'anything is possible' result has provoked several responses and two of them are worth discussing here. The first response interprets mutations as errors, and says that these errors can be controlled at some cost. This argument has been developed in van Damme and Weibull (2002). This paper shows that incorporating this cost structure leads back to the risk-dominant equilibrium. This line of research has been further extended to cover local interaction on general weighted graphs by Baron, Durieu, Haller, and Solal (2002). A second response is to argue that risk-dominance obtains for any possible mutation rule, if some additional conditions are satisfied. In this vein, a recent paper by Lee, Szeidl and Valentinyi (2003) argues that given any state dependent mutation process, under local interaction on a 2 dimensional torus the dynamics select for the risk-dominant action, provided the number of players is sufficiently large.

I turn next to a consideration of decision rules that are different in a more fundamental way from the best response principle. A simple and widely studied rule of thumb is *imitation: choose an action that yields the highest payoffs, among all the actions that are currently chosen by all others.*[21] Robson and Vega-Redondo (1996) study this rule in the context of social coordination games, and show that, taken together with random matching, it leads to the efficient action being the unique stochastically stable action.

Role of initial configuration: In the discussion of the dynamics above, no restrictions were placed on the initial configuration of actions. A number of papers have examined the nature of dynamics under restrictions on initial configuration. Two approaches are discussed here as they illustrate quite different types of restrictions on initial conditions. The first one uses a random process to determine the initial configuration: every individual independently chooses an action with some probability. This random choice determines the starting point of the dynamic process. Lee and Valentinyi (2000) study the spread of actions on a 2-dimensional lattice starting with this random assignment of initial actions. They show that if individuals use the best-response rule then all players choose the risk-dominant action eventually.

The second approach considers the following problem: If I start with a small group of players choosing an action, what are the features of the network that allow for this behavior to be taken up by the entire population? Goyal (1996) consider diffusion in the context of specific networks; Morris (2000) shows that maximal contagion occurs when local interaction is sufficiently uniform and there is slow neighbor growth, i.e., the number of players who can be reached in d steps does not grow exponentially in d.

Endogenous networks: So far I have assumed that the network of interaction is fixed and given. In this section, I briefly discuss some work which endogenizes the network. I present a simple model in which players choose their partners and choose an action in the coordination games they play with their different partners. This framework allows us to endogenize the nature of interaction and study the effect of partner choice on the way players coordinate their actions in the coordination game. The issue of endogenous structures of interaction on coordination was explored in early papers by Ely (2002), Mailath, Samuelson and Shaked (1997), and Oechssler (1997). They use a framework in which players are located on islands. Moving from an island to another implies severing all ties with the former island and instead playing the game with all the players in the new island. Thus, neighborhoods are made endogenous via the choice of islands. In my exposition here, I will follow the approach of Droste, Gilles and Johnson (1999), Goyal and Vega-Redondo (2005), and Jackson and Watts (2002), in which individuals create links and thereby shape the details of the network of interaction.

[21] This rule is also used in the study of altruism in Section 3.2.

As before I shall suppose that $N = \{1, 2, \ldots, n\}$ is the set of players, where $n \geq 3$. Each player has a strategy $s_i = \{g_i, a_i\} \in \mathcal{G}_i$, where g_i refers to the links that she forms while $a_i \in A_i$ refers to the choice of action in the accompanying coordination game. Any profile of link decisions $g = (g_1, g_2 \ldots g_n)$ defines a directed network. Given a network g, I say that a pair of players i and j are directly linked if at least one of them has established a linked with the other one, i.e. if $\max\{g_{ij}, g_{ji}\} = 1$.[22] To describe the pattern of players' links, I shall take recourse to our earlier notation and define $\hat{g}_{ij} = max\{g_{ij}, g_{ji}\}$ for every pair i and j in N. I refer to g_{ij} as an active link for player i and a passive link for player j. I will say that a network g is essential if $g_{ij}g_{ji} = 0$, for every pair of players i and j. Also, let $G^c(M) \equiv \{g : \forall i, j \in M, \hat{g}_{ij} = 1, g_{ij}g_{ji} = 0\}$ stand for the set of complete and essential networks on the set of players M. Given any profile $s \in S$, I shall say that $s = (g, a) \in S^h$ for some $h \in \{\alpha, \beta\}$ if $g \in G^c$ and $a_i = h$ for all $i \in N$.

Every player who establishes a link with some other player incurs a cost $c > 0$. Given the strategies of other players, $s_{-1} = (s_1, \ldots s_{i-1}, s_{i+1}, \ldots s_n)$, the payoffs to a player i from playing some strategy $s_i = (g_i, a_i)$ are given by:

$$\Pi_i(s_i, s_{-i}) = \sum_{j \in N^d(i;\hat{g})} \pi(a_i, a_j) - \mu^d(i; g) \cdot c \tag{19}$$

The following result, due to Goyal and Vega-Redondo (2005), provides a complete characterization of stochastically stable social networks and actions in the coordination game.

Theorem 3.4 *Suppose (15) holds and $b > a$. There exists some $\bar{c} \in (e, a)$ such that if $c < \bar{c}$ then the long run network is complete while all players choose action α, while if $\bar{c} < c < b$ then the long run network is complete and all players choose action β. Finally, if $c > b$ then the long run network is empty and actions are undetermined.*

This result illustrates that the *dynamics* of link formation play a crucial role in the model. I observe that the only architecture that is stochastically stable (within the interesting parameter range) is the complete one, although players' behavior in the coordination game is *different* depending on the costs of forming links. However, if the network were to remain fixed throughout, standard arguments indicate that the risk-dominant action must prevail in the long run (cf. Kandori, Mailath and Rob, 1993). Thus, it is the link formation *process* that, by allowing for the *co*-evolution of the links and actions, shapes individual behavior in the coordination game.

I now briefly provide some intuition on the sharp relationship found between the *costs* of forming links and the corresponding behavior displayed by players in the coordination game. On the one hand, when the cost of forming links is small, players wish to be linked with everyone irrespective of the actions they choose. Hence, from an individual perspective, the relative attractiveness of different actions is quite *insensitive* to what is the

[22] This approach to link formation builds on the work of Goyal (1993) and Bala ad Goyal (2000).

network structure faced by any given player at the time of revising her choices. In essence, a player must make her fresh choices as if she were in a complete network. In this case, therefore, the risk-dominant (and possibly) inefficient convention prevails since, under complete connectivity, this convention is harder to destabilize (through mutations) than the efficient but risk-dominated one. By contrast, if costs of forming links are high, individual players choose to form links only with those who are known (or perceived) to be playing the same action. This lowers the strategic uncertainty in the interaction and thus facilitates the emergence of the efficient action.

I conclude by discussing the relation between the above results and the earlier work of Ely (2002), Mailath, Samuelson and Shaked (1997), Oechssler (1997), and Bhaskar and Vega-Redondo (2004). The basic insight flowing from the earlier work is that, if individuals can easily separate/insulate themselves from those who are playing an inefficient action (e.g., the risk-dominant action), then efficient "enclaves" will be readily formed and eventually attract the "migration" of others who will adopt the efficient action eventually. One may be tempted to identify *easy* mobility with *low* costs of forming links. However, the considerations involved in the two approaches turn out to be very different. This is evident from the differences in the results: recall that in the network formation approach, the risk-dominant outcome prevails if the costs of forming links are small. There are two main reasons for this contrast. First, in the network formation approach, players do not *indirectly* choose their pattern of interaction with others by moving across a *pre-specified* network of locations (as in the case of player mobility). Rather, they construct *directly* their interaction network (with no exogenous restrictions) by choosing those agents with whom they want to play the game. Second, the cost of link formation is paid per link formed and thus becomes truly effective only if it is high enough. Thus it is precisely the restricted "mobility" that high costs induce which helps insulate (and thus protect) the individuals who are choosing the efficient action. If the costs of link formation are low, then the extensive interaction this facilitates may have the unfortunate consequence of rendering risk-dominance considerations decisive.

3.2 Games of cooperation

This section studies effects of interaction structure in situations where incentives of individuals are in conflict with socially desirable outcomes. Potential conflict between incentives of individuals and social desirable outcomes is clearly an important dimension of social and economic life and the importance of this problem has motivated an extensive literature on the evolution of social norms. This literature spans the fields of biology, computer science, philosophy, and political science, in addition to economics.[23] However, it seems that few analytical results with regard to the effects of network

[23] For a survey of work see e.g., Ullman-Margalit (1977), Axelrod (1997), Nowak and May (1992).

structure on social cooperation have been obtained. This presentation here will be based on Eshel, Samuelson, and Shaked (1998).

The provision of local public goods illustrates the economic issues very well: every individual contributes to an activity and all the individuals in her neighborhood benefit from it.[24] Suppose there are $N = \{1, 2 \ldots, n\}$ players (where n is assumed to be large) and each player has a choice between two actions C (contribute) and D (defect or not contribute). Let $s_i = \{C, D\}$ denote the strategy of player i and as usual let $s = \{s_1, s_2, s_3, \ldots, s_n\}$ refer to the strategy profile of the players. Define $n_i\ (C, s_{-i}|g)$ as the number of neighbors of player i in network g who choose C given the strategy profile s_{-i}. The payoffs to player i, in network g, from choosing C, given the strategy profile s_{-i} are:

$$\Pi_i(C, s_{-i}|g) = n_i(C, s_{-i}|g) - e. \tag{20}$$

where $e > 0$ is the cost associated with the (contribution) action C. On the other hand, the payoffs to player i from action D are given by:

$$\Pi_i(D, s_{-i}|g) = n_i(C, s_{-i}|g). \tag{21}$$

Since $e > 0$, it follows that action D strongly dominates action C. So, if players are payoff optimizers then they will never choose C. Thus it is necessary to have at least some players using alternative decision rules if there is to be any chance of action C being adopted.

3.2.1 Imitation and altruism

Suppose that all players use an *imitate the best action* rule: compare the average payoffs from the two actions across the different members of the population and choose the action that attains the higher average payoff. Moreover, if everyone chooses the same action then payoffs across different actions cannot be compared and an individual persists with the current action.

As in the previous sections consider a dynamic model in which time is discrete and indexed by $t = 1, 2, \ldots$ Suppose that in each period a player gets a chance to revise her strategy with some probability $p \in (0,1)$. This probability is independent across individuals and across time. Let the strategy profile at time t be denoted by s^t. The above decision rule along with an initial action profile, s^1, define a Markov process where the states of the process are the strategy profiles s. The probability of transition from s to s' is either 0 or 1. Recall that a state (or a set of states) is said to be absorbing if the process cannot escape from the state once it is reached. The interest is in the relation between the interaction structure and the nature of the absorbing state (or set of states) of the dynamic process.

[24] Clearing the snow in front of one's house, having a night light on, and controlling the level of noise pollution are some everyday activities that fit the description of local public goods.

Consider first the complete network. If both actions are being chosen in a society then it follows from simple computations that the average payoffs from choosing D are larger than the payoffs from choosing C.[25] This means that the outcome in which everyone chooses action D will obtain. Thus *starting from any initial configuration (except the extreme case where everyone is doing C), the dynamic process will converge to a state in which everyone chooses D*. This negative result on the prospects of contribution under the complete network leads to an exploration of local interaction.

So consider next the contribution game with local interaction around a circle.[26] Let $N_i(g) = \{i-1, i+1\}$ be the neighborhood of player i and let this interaction network be denoted by g^{circle}. The payoffs to player i in g^{circle} are given by $n_i(C, s_{-i}|g^{\text{circle}}) - e$ if player i chooses C and by $n_i(C, s_{-i}|g^{\text{circle}})$ if she chooses action D.

In the following discussion, to focus attention on interesting range of costs, it will be assumed that $e < 1/2$. Suppose that there is a string of 3 players choosing action C, and they are surrounded on both sides by a population of players choosing D. Given the decision rule, any change in actions can only occur at the boundaries. What are the payoffs observed by the player choosing action C on the boundary? Well, she observes one player choosing D with a payoff of 1, while she observes one player choosing action C with payoff $2-e$. Moreover, she observes her own payoff of $1-e$, as well. Given that $e < 1/2$, it follows that she prefers action C. On the other hand, the player on the boundary choosing action D, observes one player choosing action D, with payoff 0, one player choosing action C with payoff $1-e$ and herself with a payoff 1. Given that $e < 1/2$, she prefers to switch to action C. This suggests that the region of altruists will expand. Note however that if everyone except one player is choosing action C, then the player choosing D will get a payoff of 2, and since this is the maximum possible payoff, this will induce her neighbors to switch to action D. However, as they expand, this group of egoists will find their payoffs fall (as the interior of the interval can no longer free ride on the altruists). These considerations suggest that a long string of players choosing action C can be sustained, while a long string of players choosing D will be difficult to sustain. These arguments are summarized in the following result, due to Eshel, Samuelson, and Shaked (1998).

Theorem 3.5 *Consider the contribution game with local interaction and suppose that $e < 1/2$. Absorbing sets are of two types: one, they contain a singleton state in which all players choose either action C or action D, and two, they contain states in which there are strings of C players*

[25] Note that in a complete network, with a strategy profile where K players choose C, the average payoffs to a C player are $K-1-e$, while the average payoffs to a D player are K.

[26] Tieman, Houba and Van der Laan (2000) consider a related model of cooperative behavior with local interaction in games with conflict. In their model, players are located on a network and play a generalized (many action) version of the prisoner's dilemma. They find that with local interaction and a tit-for-tat type decision rule, superior payoff actions that are dominated can survive in the population, in the long run.

of length 3 or more which are separated by strings of D players of length 2. In the latter case, at least 60% of the players choose action C (on average).

It is worth commenting on the relative proportions of C players in mixed configurations. First note that a string of D players cannot be of size 3 or longer (in an absorbing state). If it is then the boundary D players will each have two players choosing C on one side and a player choosing D who is surrounded by D players. It is easy to show that these boundary players will switch to C. Likewise, there have to be at least 3 players in each string of C players; otherwise, the boundary players will switch to D. These considerations put together yield the proportions mentioned in the result above.

Given the above arguments, it is easily seen that in any string of five players at least three players will remain with action C, forever. If players strategies are randomly chosen initially then it follows that the probability of such a string of C players can be made arbitrarily close to 1, by suitably increasing the number of players. This idea is summarized in the following result, due to Eshel, Samuelson, and Shaked (1998).

Theorem 3.6 *Consider the contribution game with local interaction and suppose that $e < 1/2$. Suppose that players' initial strategy choices are determined by independent, identically distributed variables where the probability of C and D is positive. Then the probability of convergence to an absorbing set containing states with at least 60% of C players goes to 1, as n gets large.*

This result shows that with local interaction around a circle, in large societies a majority of individuals will contribute, in the long run.[27]

So far the discussion on network effects has been restricted to the case of pure local interaction among agents located on a circle. This raises the question: how likely is contribution in more general structures of interaction? In the case of pure local interaction around a circle, the persistence and spread of cooperative behavior appears to be related to the presence of C players who are protected from D players and therefore earn sufficiently high payoffs so that other C players on the boundary persist with action C as well. In higher dimensional interaction (e.g., k-dimensional lattices) or asymmetric interaction (as in a star), this protective wall can be harder to create and this may make altruism more vulnerable. The following example illustrates this.

Example 3.5 *Altruism in a star network.*

First note that mixed configurations in which some individuals choose C while others choose D are not possible in a star. Therefore, only the two pure strategy configurations – everyone choosing C or everyone choosing D – are possible in an absorbing state. What is the relative robustness of these two absorbing states? As in the previous section, let us examine the stochastic stability of the two states. It is possible to move from a purely altruistic society to a purely egoist society, via a switch by the central player, followed by imitation by the rest. The reverse transition requires

[27] Eshel, Samuelson and Shaked (1998) also study stochastic stability of different absorbing sets. They show that the states identified in the above proposition are also the stochastically stable ones.

switching of action by at least three players, the central player and two peripheral players. Thus if interaction is on a star network then all individuals will choose D and contribution will be zero, in the long run.

These arguments taken along with the earlier discussion on the pure local interaction model suggest that the structure of interaction has profound effects on the levels of contribution that can be sustained in a society. These observations also lead back to a general question posed in the introduction: Are some interaction structures better at sustaining contributions (and hence efficient outcomes) as compared to other interaction structure and what is the relation between interaction structures and diversity of actions?

Existing work on this subject seems to be mostly based on simulations with special classes of networks such as lattices and regular graphs (Nowak and May, 1992; Nowak and Sigmund, 2005).[28] This work suggests that in the absence of mutations, altruism can survive in a variety of interaction settings. There is also an extensive literature in evolutionary biology on the emergence and persistence of altruistic traits in different species. In this work the spread of altruistic traits is attributed to greater reproductive success. This success leads to the larger set of altruists spilling into neighboring areas and this in turn leads to a growth of the trait over time (see e.g., Wynne-Edwards, 1986; Eshel and Cavalli-Sforza, 1982).

So far we have taken as given the network of interaction. Ostracism is a natural way punishment strategy; thus, forming and dissolving links may be one way to sustain cooperation. For an early attempt at studying cooperation in networks, see Raub and Weesie (1990); for recent attempts at modeling endogenous networks and cooperation, see Vega-Redondo (2006), Fosco and Mengel (2008) and Ule (2008).

3.2.2 Interaction and information neighborhoods

In the discussion in the previous section, it was assumed that players observe those with whom they play, in other words the neighborhood of interaction coincides with the neighborhood of information. In this section, I will briefly explore the role of this assumption.[29] I will proceed by considering an example: As before, individuals are located around a circle and interact with their immediate neighbors. However, each individual observes her own action and payoffs and the actions and payoffs of a subset of the population drawn randomly from the population. Specifically, when faced with a chance to revise actions, an individual gets to observe actions of the set $I_{i,t}$; this set always includes $\{i\}$, and in addition includes a subset of $N\backslash\{i\}$. Suppose that the probability of drawing $I_{i,t}$ is $P(I_{i,t}) > 0$, for any $I_{i,t} \subset N\backslash\{i\}$. Assume that the draw of samples is independent across players and across time periods. I will refer to this is *local*

[28] There is also a small experimental literature that examines cooperative behavior in games with local interaction; see Cassar (2007) for an overview of this work.

[29] For recent work on information and interaction neighborhoods in the context of coordination games, see Alos-Ferrer and Weidenholzer (2008).

plus random information. If $j \in I_{i,t}$, then i gets to see $\{s_{j,t-1}, \Pi_{j,t-1}\}$. In period t, if she has a choice then player i will choose $s_{i,t} = C$ if C yields a higher average payoff in her sample of informants; else she will choose D. The above rules define a stationary Markov process, with state space $S = \{C, D\}^n$. Let $P_s s'(g)$ be the transition matrix, given a network of interaction, g. The following result, due to Goyal (2007b), summarizes the analysis of stochastically stable states.

Theorem 3.7 *Consider the contribution game. Suppose interaction is with immediate neighbors around a circle, there is local plus random information and players follow the best rule. Then universal defection is the unique stochastically stable outcome.*

Let us start with the ALL C state and suppose 1 player switches to D. She earns 2, and this is the maximum possible payoff attainable in this setting. Now get individuals outside $N_1(g) = \{-1, 2\}$, to choose an action, one by one. Suppose that for any player $j \notin N_1(g)$, $I_{j,t} = \{j, 1\}$. This player compares maximum possible payoff of $2 - e$ from action C with a payoff of 2 from D which player 1 earns. So she will switch to D. Iterate on players one at a time. Finally, suppose players -1 and 2 in $N_1(g)$ move. They compare payoff of $-e$ from action C with payoff 2 from action D earned by player 1. Clearly, they will switch to D as well. I have thus shown that a single mutation followed by standard imitation dynamics suffices for the transition to all D state.

Next start with an ALL D state. Clearly a single mutation to action C will have no effect. The individual compares $-e$ from action C with a payoff 0 or a positive payoff from D and so she will switch back to action D. Moreover, no player choosing D has any incentive to move to C. Hence, it takes two or more mutations to transit from an all D state. Similar arguments can be developed for any mixed state of actions. So I have shown that it takes relatively fewer mutations to arrive at the all D state as compared to other states with action C. Thus the state of universal defection is uniquely stochastically stable.

A comparison of Theorem 3.7 with Theorem 3.6 highlights the important role of information radius in sustaining cooperation. Recall, that if information and interaction radius are the same, then Eschel, Samuelson and Shaked (1998) show that are absorbing states with mixed action configurations and in such a mixed configuration at least 60% of players choose C. By contrast, if interaction is local around with a circle but players have access to information drawn at random from the population, then universal defection is the only possible outcome. This discussion points to the need for a more general systematic study of models in which the neighborhood of information is allowed to vary generally and its effects on long run outcomes studied.

4. CONCLUDING REMARKS

I have examined the following general framework: there is a set of individuals who are located on nodes of a network; the arcs of the network reflect relations between these individuals. At regular intervals, individuals choose an action from a set of alternatives.

They are uncertain about the rewards from different actions. They use their own past experience, as well as gather information from their neighbors (individuals who are linked to them) and then choose an action that maximizes individual payoffs.

I first studied the influence of network structure on individual and social learning in a pure information-sharing context. I then moved on to a study of strategic interaction among players located in a network, i.e., interactions where actions alter payoffs of others. The focus was on the relation between the network structure on the one hand, and the evolution of individual actions, beliefs, and payoffs on the other hand. A related and recurring theme of the survey was the relation between network structure and the prospects for the adoption of efficient actions.

The work to date provides a number of insights about how networks – connectedness, centrality, dispersion in connections – and decision rules together shape individual behavior and welfare. While much progress has been made, there remain a number of important open problems.

A first remark concerns the formation of networks. Most of the work on communication and learning uses a framework where the network is exogenously given. The systematic study of information sharing and learning in endogenously evolving networks is an important subject for further research.[30]

A second remark concerns the role of interaction neighborhood and information neighborhood. Social networks reflect patterns of interaction among individuals and they also serve as a conduit for the transmission of useful information in a society. Traditionally, interaction and information have been conflated and this has allowed for a parsimony in the details of modeling. However, interaction and information are distinct and have rather different implications. Moreover, in applications this distinction is natural and deserves more attention.

The third remark is about the formulation of individual decision-making rules in models of networks. Strategic considerations and indirect inferences quickly become very complicated in a network setting: so both descriptive plausibility and tractability motivate simple individual decision rules. However, existing results already suggest that the role of networks may be sensitive to the precise assumptions on individual decision rules. The network irrelevance property under log-linear response rule noted in Theorem 3.3. and the network effects under best-response rule identified in Example 3.4 illustrate this point. More work is clearly needed before we have a systematic understanding of the ways in which networks and different decision rules combine to shape behavior and welfare.

A fourth and final remark is about the context of social leaning. In many interesting applications, learning takes place within a context where firms and governments have

[30] For recent attempts at modeling endogenous formation of networks and groups in the context of communication and information sharing, see Acemoglu et al. (2010) and Baccara and Yariv (2010).

an active interest in facilitating/impeding the flow of information and certain behaviors. As we develop a more complete understanding of the 'pure' problem of learning and evolution in networks it is important to integrate these insights with economic models of pricing, advertising and market competition.[31]

5. APPENDIX

It is important to construct the probability space within which the processes relating to Bayesian social learning take place. Recall that the probability space is denoted by $(\Omega, \mathcal{F}, P^{\theta})$, where Ω is the space of all outcomes, $\mathcal{F}$ is the σ-field and P^{θ} is a probability measure if the true state of the world is θ. Let Θ be the set of possible states of the world and fix $\theta \in \Theta$ in what follows. For each individual $i \in N$, action $a \in A$, and time periods $t = 1,2,\ldots$ let $Y^a_{i,t}$ be the set of possible outcomes. For each $t = 1,2..$ let $\Omega_t = \prod_{i \in N}\prod_{a \in A} Y^a_{i,t}$ be the space of tth outcomes across all individuals and all actions. For simplicity, we will assume that $Y^a_{i,t} = Y$. Ω_t is endowed with the product topology. Let $H_t \subset \Omega_t$, be of the form

$$H_t = \prod_{i \in N}\prod_{a \in A} H^a_{i,t} \tag{22}$$

where $H^a_{i,t}$ is a Borel subset of Y, for each $i \in N$ and $a \in A$. Define the probability P^{θ}_t of the set H_t as:

$$P^{\theta}_t(H_t) = \prod_{i \in N}\prod_{a \in A}\int_{H^a_{i,t}} \phi(y; a, \theta)dy \tag{23}$$

where ϕ is the density of y, given action a and state θ. P^{θ} extends uniquely to the σ-field on Ω_t generated by the sets of the form H_t. Let $\Omega = \prod_{t=1}^{\infty}\Omega_t$. For cylinder sets $H \subset \Omega$, of the form

$$H = \prod_{t=1}^{T} H_T \times \prod_{t=T+1}^{\infty} \Omega_t \tag{24}$$

let P^{θ} (H) be defined as $P^{\theta}(H) = \prod_{t=1}^{T} P^{\theta}_t(H_t)$. Let $\mathcal{F}$ be the σ-field generated by sets of the type given by (24). P^{θ} extends uniquely to the sets in $\mathcal{F}$. This completes the construction of the probability space $(\Omega, \mathcal{F}, P^{\theta})$.

Let Θ be endowed with the discrete topology, and suppose $\mathcal{B}$ is the Borel σ–field on this space. For rectangles of the form $\mathcal{T} \times H$, where $\mathcal{T} \subset \Theta$, and H is a measurable subset of Ω, let $P_i(\mathcal{T} \times H)$ be given by

[31] For recent efforts in this direction, see Chatterjee and Dutta (2010), Colla and Mele (2010), Galeotti and Goyal (2009).

$$P_i(\mathcal{T} \times H) = \sum_{\theta \in \Theta} \mu_{i,1}(\theta) P^{\theta}(H). \tag{25}$$

for each individual $i \in N$. Each P_i extends uniquely to all $\mathcal{B} \times \mathcal{F}$. Since every individual's prior belief lies in the interior of $\mathcal{P}(\Theta)$, the measures $\{P_i\}$ are pairwise mutually absolutely continuous.

The σ-field of individual i's information at the beginning of time 1 is $\mathcal{F}_{i,1} = \{\emptyset, \Theta \times \Omega\}$. For every time period $t \geq 2$, define $\mathcal{F}_{i,t}$ as the σ-field generated by the past history of individual i's observations of his neighbors actions and outcomes, $(C_{j,1}, Z_{j,1})_{j \in N_i^d(g)}, \ldots\ldots, (C_{j,t-1}, Z_{j,t-1})_{j \in N_i^d(g)}$. Individuals only use the information on actions and outcomes of their neighbors, so the set classes $\mathcal{F}_{i,t}$ are the relevant σ-fields for our study. We shall denote by $\mathcal{F}_{i,\infty}$ the smallest σ-field containing all $\mathcal{F}_{i,t}$, for $t \geq 2$.

Recall that the objects of study are the optimal actions, $C_{i,t}$, the individual beliefs, $\mu_{i,t}$ and individual expected utilities $U_{i,t}$.

REFERENCES

Acemoglu, D., Bimpikis, K., Ozdaglar, A., 2010. Communication dynamics in endogenous social networks. mimeo, MIT.

Acemoglu, D., Dahleh, I., Lobel, M., Ozdaglar, A., 2010. Bayesian learning in social networks. mimeo, MIT Economic Department.

Adar, E., Huberman, B.A., 2000. Free Riding on Gnutella. First Monday 5 (10).

Allen, B., 1982. Some stochastic processes of interdependent demand and technological diffusion of an innovation exhibiting externalities among adopters. Int. Econ. Rev. (Philadelphia) 23, 595–607.

Alos-Ferrer, C., Weidenholzer, S., 2008. Contagion and Efficiency. J. Econ. Theory. 143 (1), 251–274.

Anderlini, L., Ianni, A., 1996. Path dependence and learning from neighbors. Games Econ. Behav. 13, 141–177.

Axelrod, R., 1997. The complexity of cooperation: agent-based models of competition and collaboration. Princeton University Press, Princeton, New Jersey.

Baccara, M., Yariv, L., 2010. Similarity and polarization in groups. mimeo, NYU and Caltech.

Bacharach, M., 2006. Gold, N., Sugden, R. (Eds.), Beyond Individual Choice: Teams and Frames in Game Theory. Princeton University Press, Princeton, New Jersey.

Bala, V., Goyal, S., 1994. The Birth of a New Market. Economic Journal 282–290.

Bala, V., Goyal, S., 1995. A theory of learning with heterogeneous agents. Int. Econ. Rev. (Philadelphia) 36 (2), 303–323.

Bala, V., Goyal, S., 1998. Learning from Neighbours. Rev. Econ. Stud. 65, 595–621.

Bala, V., Goyal, S., 2000. A Non-Cooperative Model of Network Formation. Econometrica 68 (5), 1181–1231.

Bala, V., Goyal, S., 2001. Conformism and diversity under social learning. Economic Theory 17, 101–120.

Banerjee, A., 1993. A Simple Model of Herd Behavior. Q. J. Econ. 107, 797–817.

Banerjee, A., Fudenberg, D., 2004. Word-of-mouth learning. Games Econ. Behav. 46 (1), 1–22.

Baron, R., Durieu, J., Haller, H., Solal, P., 2002. A note on control costs and potential functions for strategic games. Journal of Evolutionary Economics 12, 563–575.

Basu, K., Weibull, J., 2002. Punctuality: A cultural trait as equilibrium. MIT Dept of Economics Working Paper 02–26.

Bergin, J., Lipman, B., 1996. Evolution of state dependent mutations. Econometrica 64, 943–956.

Berninghaus, S., Ehrhart, K.M., Kesar, C., 2002. Conventions and local interaction structures. Games and Economic Behavior 39, 177–205.
Berry, D., Fristedt, B., 1985. Bandit Problems: Sequential Allocation of Experiments. Chapman and Hall, New York.
Besen, S., Farrell, J., 1994. Choosing how to compete: strategies and tactics in standardlization. Journal of Economic Perspectives 8 (2), 117–131.
Bhaskar, V., Vega-Redondo, F., 2004. Migration and the evolution of conventions. Journal of Economic Behavior and Organization 55, 397–418.
Bikhchandani, S., Hirshliefer, D., Welch, I., 1992. A theory of fads, fashion, custom, and cultural change as informational cascades. J. Polit. Econ. 100, 992–1023.
Billingsley, P., 1985. Probability and Measure. Wiley, New York.
Blume, L., 1993. The statistical mechanics of strategic interaction. Games Econ. Behav. 4, 387–424.
Blume, L., Easley, D., 1995. What has the rational learning literature taught us? In: Kirman, A., Salmon, M. (Eds.), Learning and Rationality in Economics. Oxford University Press.
Bolton, P., Harris, C., 1999. Strategic Experimentation. Econometrica 67 (2), 349–374.
Bramoulle, Y., 2007. Anti-Coordination and Social Interactions. Games and Economic Behavior 58, 30–49.
Brenzinger, M., 1998. Endangered languages in Africa. Rudiger Koppe Verlag, Berlin.
Camerer, C., 2003. Behavioral Game Theory: Experiments in Strategic Interaction. The Roundtable Series in Behavioral Economics. Princeton University Press, Princeton, New Jersey.
Cassar, A., 2007. Coordination and Cooperation in Local, Random and Small World Networks: Experimental Evidence. Games and Economic Behavior 58 (2), 209–230.
Chamley, C., 2004. Rational Herds: Economic Models of Social Learning. Cambridge University Press, New York.
Chatterjee, K., Dutta, B., 2010. Word of mouth learning and strategic learning in networks. Mimeo, Penn State University and Warwick University.
Chatterjee, K., Xu, S., 2004. Technology Diffusion by learning from neighbors. Adv. in Appl. Probab. 36, 355–376.
Coleman, J., 1966. Medical Innovation: A Diffusion Study, second ed. Bobbs-Merrill.
Coleman, J., 1990. The Foundations of Social Theory. Harvard University Press, Cambridge MA.
Colla, P., Mele, A., 2010. Information Linkages and Correlated Trading. Rev. Financ. Stud. 23, 203–246.
Conley, T., Udry, C., 2010. Learning about a new technology: Pineapple in Ghana. American Economic Review 100, 35–69.
DeGroot, M., 1972. Reaching a Consensus. J. Am. Stat. Assoc. 69 (345), 118–121.
DeMarzo, P., Vayanos, D., Zweibel, J., 2003. Persuasion bias, social influence, and unidimensional opinions. Q. J. Econ. 118, 909–968.
Droste, E., Gilles, R., Johnson, K., 1999. Endogenous interaction and the evolution of conventions. In: Adaptive Behavior in Economic and Social Environments. PhD Thesis. Center, University of Tilburg.
Easley, D., Kiefer, N., 1988. Controlling a stochastic process with unknown parameters. Econometrica 56, 1045–1064.
Economides, N., Himmelberg, C., 1995. Critical Mass and Network Size with application to the US FAX Market. mimeo, NYU.
Elias, N., 1978. The history of manners, Part 1 of The Civilizing Process. Pantheon Books.
Ellison, G., 1993. Learning, Local Interaction, and Coordination. Econometrica 61, 1047–1071.
Ellison, G., Fudenberg, D., 1993. Rules of Thumb for Social Learning. J. Polit. Econ. 101, 612–644.
Ellison, G., Fudenberg, D., 1995. Word-of-mouth communication and social learning. Q. J. Econ. 109, 93–125.
Ely, J., 2002. Local Conventions. Berkeley Electronic Press Journals, Advances in Theoretical Economics 2 (1), 1.
Eshel, I., Cavalli-Sforza, L.L., 1982. Assortment of encounters and evolution of cooperativeness. Proc. Natl. Acad. Sci. 79 (4), 1331–1335.
Eshel, I., Samuelson, L., Shaked, A., 1998. Altruists, egoists, and hooligans in a local interaction model. Am. Econ. Rev. 157–179.

Fehr, E., Schmidt, K., 2003. Theories of Fairness and Reciprocity – Evidence and Economic Applications. In: Dewatripont, M. (Ed.), Advances in Economics and Econometrics, Eighth World Congress of the Econometric Society. 1, Cambridge University Press, Cambridge.
Feick, L.F., Price, L., 1987. The Market Maven: A Diffuser of Market-place Information. Journal of Marketing 51, 83–97.
Fosco, C., Mengel, F., 2008. Cooperation through Imitation and Exclusion in Networks. mimeo, Maastricht University.
Fudenberg, D., Levine, D., 1998. The theory of learning in games. MIT Press, Cambridge.
Gale, D., Kariv, S., 2003. Bayesian Learning in Social Networks. Games Econ. Behav. 45, 329–346.
Galeotti, A., Goyal, S., 2009. Influencing the influencers: a theory of strategic diffusion. Rand. J. Econ. 40 (3), 509–532.
Golub, B., Jackson, M.O., 2010. Naive learning in social networks: convergence, influence and wisdom of crowds. American Economic Journal: Microeconomics 2 (1), 112–149.
Goyal, S., 1993. Sustainable communication networks. Tinbergen Institute Discussion Paper, TI 93–250.
Goyal, S., 1996. Interaction Structure and Social Change. J. Inst. Theor. Econ. 152 (3), 472–495.
Goyal, S., 2005. Learning in networks. In: Demange, G., Wooders, M. (Eds.), Group Formation in Economics. Cambridge University Press, Cambridge.
Goyal, S., 2007a. Connections: an introduction to the economics of networks. Princeton University Press, Oxford.
Goyal, S., 2007b. Interaction, information and learning. mimeo, University of Cambridge.
Goyal, S., Vega-Redondo, F., 2005. Network formation and social coordination. Games Econ. Behav. 50, 178–207.
Granovetter, M., 1974. Getting a Job: A Study of Contacts and Careers. Harvard University Press.
Granovetter, M., 1985. Economic Action and Social Structure: The Problem of Embeddedness. AJS 3, 481–510.
Griliches, Z., 1957. Hybrid Corn: An exploration in the economics of technological change. Econometrica 25, 501–522.
Harsanyi, J., Selten, R., 1988. A General Theory of Equilibrium Seletion in Games. MIT Press, Cambridge MA.
Ianni, A., 2001. Correlated equilibria in population games. Math. Soc. Sci. 42 (3), 271–294.
Jackson, M., Watts, A., 2002. On the formation of interaction networks in social coordination games. Games Econ. Behav. 41 (2), 265–291.
Jadbabaie, A., Sandroni, A., Tahbaz-Salehi, A., 2010. Non-bayesian social learning. PIER Working Paper 10–005.
Judd, K., Tesfatsion, L., 2005. Handbook of Computation Economics II: Agent based computational economics. North Holland, Amsterdam.
Kandori, M., 1997. Evolutionary game theory in economics. In: Kreps, , Wallis, (Eds.), Advances in Economics and Econometrics: Theory and applications. Cambridge University Press.
Kandori, M., Mailath, G., Rob, R., 1993. Learning, mutation and long run equilibria in games. Econometrica 61, 29–56.
Katz, E., Lazersfeld, P., 1955. Personal Influence. The Free Press, New York.
Katz, M., Shapiro, C., 1994. Systems competition and network effects. Journal of Economc Perspectives 8 (2), 93–115.
Kirman, A., Zimmermann, J.-B., 2001. Economics with Heterogeneous Interacting Agents. Series: Lecture Notes in Economics and Mathematical Systems. Springer Verlag.
Kotler, P., Armstrong, G., 2004. Principles of Marketing, tenth ed. Prentice Hall, New York.
Lazarsfeld, P., Berelson, B., Gaudet, H., 1948. The People's Choice. Columbia University Press., New York.
Lee, I., Valentinyi, A., 2000. Noisy Contagion without Mutation. Rev. Econ. Stud. 67 (1), 17–47.
Lee, I., Szeidl, A., Valentayini, A., 2003. Contagion and State dependent Mutations. Berkeley Electronic Press Journals, Advances in Economics 3 (1), 2.
Lewis, D., 1969. Convention: A Philosophical Study. Harvard University Press, Cambridge, MA.
Mailath, G., Samuelson, L., Shaked, A., 1997. Correlated equilibria and local interaction. J. Econ. Theory 9, 551–568.

Mailath, L., Samuelson, L., 2006. Repeated Games and Reputations: Long-Run Relationships. Oxford University Press, Oxford.
Marimon, R., 1997. Learning from learning in economics. In: Kreps, K., Wallis, (Eds.), Advances in Economics and Econometrics: Theory and applications. Cambridge University Press.
Morris, S., 2000. Contagion. Rev. Econ. Stud. 67 (1), 57–79.
Mueller-Frank, M., 2010. A general framework for rational learning in social networks. mimeo, Northwestern University.
Nowak, M., May, R., 1992. Evolutionary games and spatial chaos. Nature 359, 826–829.
Nowak, M., Sigmund, K., 2005. Evolution of indirect reciprocity. Nature 1291–1298.
Oechssler, J., 1997. Decentralization and the coordination problem. J. Econ. Behav. Organ. 32, 119–135.
Raub, W., Weesie, J., 1990. Reputation and efficiency in social interactions. AJS 96, 626–655.
Robson, A., Vega-Redondo, F., 1996. Efficient equilibrium selection in evolutionary games with random matching. J. Econ. Theory. 70, 65–92.
Rogers, E., 2003. The Diffusion of Innovations. Free Press, New York.
Rothschild, M., 1974. A two-arm bandit theory of market pricing. J. Econ. Theory. 9, 185–202.
Ryan, B., Gross, N., 1943. The diffusion of hybrid seed corn in two Iowa communities. Rural Sociol. 8, 15–24.
Samuelson, L., 1997. Evolutionary Games and Equilibrium Selection. MIT Press, Cambridge, MA.
Schelling, T., 1960. The strategy of conflict. Norton, New York.
Schelling, T., 1975. Micromotives and macrobehavior. Norton, New York.
Smith, L., Sorensen, P., 2000. Pathological Outcomes of Observational Learning. Econometrica 68 (2), 371–398.
Sugden, R., 2004. The Economics of Rights, Co-operation and Welfare, second ed. Palgrave, Macmillan.
Taylor, R., 1979. Medicine out of control: the anatomy of a malignant technology. Sun Books, Melboune.
Tieman, A., Houba, H., Laan, G., 2000. On the level of cooperative behavior in a local interaction model. J. Econ. 71, 1–30.
Ule, A., 2008. Partner Choice and Cooperation in Networks: Theory and Experimental Evidence. Springer.
Ullman-Margalit, E., 1977. The emergence of norms. Clarendon Press, Oxford.
van Damme, E., 1991. Stability and Perfection of Nash Equilibrium. Springer Verlag, Berlin.
van Damme, E., Weibull, J., 2002. Evolution and refinement with endogenous mistake probabilities. J. Econ. Theory. 106, 298–315.
Vega-Redondo, F., 1997. Evolution, Games, and Economic Behaviour. Oxford University Press.
Vega-Redondo, F., 2006. Building social capital in a changing world. J. Econ. Dyn. Control. 30, .
Watkins, S., 1991. Provinces into Nations: Demographic Integration in Western Europe, 1870–1960. Princeton University Press.
Wynne-Edwards, V., 1986. Evolution through group selection. Blackwell Publishers, Oxford.
Young, P., 1993. The evolution of conventions. Econometrica 61, 57–84.
Young, P., 1998. Individual Strategy and Social Structure. Princeton University Press.
Zhang, J.M., Ackerman, S., Adamic, L., 2007. Expertise Networks in Online Communities: Structures and Algorithms WWW2007. Banff, Canada.

FURTHER READINGS

Bramoulle, Y., Lopez, D., Goyal, S., Vega-Redondo, F., 2004. Network formation in anti-coordination games. International Journal of Game Theory 33, 1–20.
Golub, B., Jackson, M.O., 2010a. Naive Learning in social networks and the Wisdom of Crowds. American Economic Journal: Microeconomics 2 (1), 112–149.
Golub, B., Jackson, M.O., 2010b. How Homophily Affects Diffusion and Learning in Networks. Stanford University mimeo.
Skyrms, B., Pemantle, R., 2000. A dynamic model of social network formation. Proc. Natl. Acad. Sci. 97 (16), 9340–9346.

CHAPTER 16

Formation of Networks and Coalitions

Francis Bloch* **and Bhaskar Dutta**†

Contents

1. Introduction 730
2. One-Stage Models of Coalition and Network Formation 731
   2.1 A general framework 731
   2.2 Models of coalition and network formation 734
   2.3 Stability 737
   2.4 The degree of consent in group and network formation 741
   2.5 Some examples 742
3. Sequential Models of Coalition and Network Formation 746
   3.1 Coalitional bargaining 746
   3.2 Sequential models of network formation 751
4. Farsightedness 754
5. Group Formation in Real Time 762
   5.1 Dynamic network formation 762
   5.2 Coalition formation over time 765
6. The Tension between Efficiency and Stability 771
7. Conclusions and Open Problems 774
References 776
Further Reading 779

Abstract

This chapter surveys recent models of coalition and network formation in a unified framework. Comparisons are drawn among various procedures of network and coalition formation, involving simultaneous and sequential moves. The survey also covers models of group and network formation by farsighted players and in dynamic contexts. The chapter concludes with a discussion of efficient network and coalition formation procedures and directions for future research.
JEL Codes: C70, C71, C78, D85

* Ecole Polytechnique
† University of Warwick

Handbook of Social Economics, Volume 1A
ISSN 0169-7218, DOI: 10.1016/S0169-7218(11)01016-1

Keywords

Coalition Formation
Networks
Farsighted Players
Bargaining
Efficiency
Stability
Externalities

1. INTRODUCTION

Although much of formal game theory focuses on noncooperative behavior, sets of individuals often cooperate with one another to promote their own self-interest. For instance, groups of countries form customs unions, political parties form coalitions, firms form cartels, and so on. There is also growing awareness that there are a variety of contexts where the particular structure or *network* of interactions has a strong influence on economic and social outcomes. Typically, groups and networks form through the *deliberate* choice of the concerned individuals. Given the influence of groups and networks on the eventual outcome, it is important to have some idea of what kind of coalitions and networks may form. In this survey, we focus on this issue by discussing some recent literature on the endogenous formation of coalitions and networks.

Given the huge literature around this area, we have had to be very selective in what we cover in this survey.[1] For instance, given our focus on the *formation* of networks, we will not discuss the growing and fascinating literature on how the structure of interactions affect outcomes given a *fixed* network. In the area of cooperative game theory, we will eschew completely any discussion of solution concepts like the Shapley value. Neither will we have anything to say on solutions like the various versions of the bargaining set which essentially assume that the coalition of all players will necessarily form. Rather, we focus on coalition formation processes where there is no a priori reason to expect the grand coalition to form.[2]

In much the same spirit, while we do discuss bargaining processes that determine network structures or coalition structures along with individual payoffs, we do not cover the huge literature on bargaining and markets. Perhaps more contentious is our decision to omit the very interesting literature on the so-called Nash program.

[1] For a more exhaustive survey of group and network formations, we refer the reader to the collection of surveys in Demange and Wooders (2005), and to the recent books on coalitions by Ray (2007) and on networks by Goyal (2007) and Jackson (2008).

[2] In that respect, we share Maskin (2003)'s view that "Perhaps one reason that cooperative theory has not been more influential on the mainstream is that its two most important solution concepts for games of three or more players, the core and Shapley value, presume that the grand coalition – the coalition of all players – always forms. And thus the possibility of interaction between coalitions – often important in reality – is ruled out from the beginning."

We decided to leave out this literature, because the focus of this literature is *normative* in nature. That is, the objective has often been to describe (for instance) bargaining procedures that sustain some given solution concept rather than to focus on procedures which are *actually used*.[3]

The plan of the paper is the following. In the next section, we first describe a general framework that encompasses both coalition structures and network structures. In this section, we also discuss various issues that arise in the formation of groups through one-stage processes or normal form games when players are *myopic*. Section 3 focuses on bargaining or multistage group formation procedures. In Section 4, we go back to one-stage models but assume that players are *farsighted*. Section 5 describes some recent literature on group formation in a dynamic setting. In Section 6, we discuss the tension between efficiency and stability, essentially in the context of network formation. Section 7 concludes and discusses open questions for future research.

2. ONE-STAGE MODELS OF COALITION AND NETWORK FORMATION

In this section, we are concerned with issues that arise when agents form networks or coalitions by means of normal form games. That is, agents simultaneously choose which coalitions (or what links to form). Given these simultaneous choices, different "rules of the game" determine exactly what coalitions or networks will actually form.

2.1 A general framework

We describe a general framework within which we can discuss several issues connected with the one-shot (or simultaneous) formation of both networks and coalitions.

Consider a social environment where $N = \{1, \ldots, n\}$ is a finite set of agents or players, while X is the set of *social states*. Each individual i has a preference relation $\succeq_i$ over X. Let $\succ_i$ denote the strict preference relation corresponding to $\succeq_i$. The power of different groups to change the social state is represented by an *effectivity relation* $\{\rightarrow_S\}$ on $X \times X$, where for any $x, y \in X$, $x \rightarrow_S y$ means that the coalition or group S has the means to change the state to y if the "status quo" is x. So, a social environment is represented by the collection, $\mathbb{E} = (N, X, \{\succeq_i\}_{i \in N}, \{\rightarrow_S\}_{S \subseteq N})$.

Several different examples fit this general description of a social environment.

Normal Form Games: For each $i \in N$, let S_i denote the strategy set of player i, $S^N \equiv \prod_{i \in N} S_i$, while $u_i : S^N \rightarrow \mathbb{R}$ is player i's payoff function. Now, letting $X = S^N$, u_i is simply the numerical representation of the preference relation $\succeq_i$. Finally, the effectivity relation also has a natural interpretation. Consider $x = (s_1, \ldots, s_n)$ and $y = (s'_1, \ldots, s'_n)$. Then, for any group $S \subseteq N$, $x \rightarrow_S y$ iff $s_i = s'_i$ for all $i \notin S$.

[3] Serrano (2005) is an excellent survey on the Nash program.

Undirected Networks: A rich literature models social and economic interactions by means of networks or graphs. Identify N with the set of nodes. An arc exists between nodes i and j if i and j "interact bilaterally." The network is undirected if bilateral interaction is a symmetric relation. The specific economic or social context being modeled gives meaning to the term bilateral interaction. For instance, the nodes may be a set of firms, and bilateral interaction may refer to firms i and j collaborating in a research joint venture.[4] Alternatively, the graph may represent a friendship (or connections) network where i and j are linked if they are "friends."[5]

Let G be the set of all possible undirected networks with N as the set of all nodes. A *value function* v specifies the aggregate value of each graph, while Y is an *allocation rule* that specifies the payoff corresponding to each value function and each network.

Fix some value function. For simplicity, ignore the dependence of payoffs on the value function. So, $Y_i(g)$ denotes the payoff to i corresponding to a network $g \in G$. Letting $X = G$, we can now identify Y_i as the numerical representation of $\succeq_i$.

The implicit assumption underlying models of the strategic formation of undirected networks is that a link between any pair i and j can form only if both agents decide to form the link. However, an existing link (ij) can be broken unilaterally by either i or j. We will formally define these "rules" of network formation subsequently. However, this informal description is sufficient to describe the relevant effectivity relation. Consider any $S \subseteq N$, and any pair g, $g' \in G$. Then,

$$g \to_S g' \Leftrightarrow (ij \in g' - g \Rightarrow \{i, j\} \subseteq S \quad \text{and} \quad ij \in g - g' \Rightarrow \{i, j\} \cap S \neq \emptyset)$$

Directed Networks: The main difference between directed and undirected networks is that in the former, arcs are directed. So, i can be "connected" to j without j being connected to i. For instance, i can access j's homepage, but j need not access i's webpage. Let G^d be the set of all directed networks on node set N. It is standard to assume that i does not need j's consent to form the directed link to j. So, for any pair g, $g' \in G^d$ and subset S of N,

$$g \to_S g' \Leftrightarrow (ij \in (g - g') \cup (g' - g) \Rightarrow \{i, j\} \cap S \neq \emptyset)$$

Characteristic Function Games: The cornerstone of cooperative game theory is the *characteristic function*. A (TU) characteristic function game is a pair (N, v) where v is the characteristic function describing the "worth" of every coalition. The worth of a coalition is the maximum aggregate utility that a coalition can *guarantee* itself.

[4] See Goyal and Joshi (2003).

[5] The connections model is due to Jackson and Wolinsky (1996) (henceforth JW). See also Bloch and Dutta (2009) for an analysis that incorporates strength of links in a friendship network.

For every coalition S, let $A(S) = \{x \in \mathbb{R}^N | \sum_{i \in S} x_i \leq v(S)\}$. So, $A(N)$ is the set of feasible allocations for the grand coalition, while $A(S)$ is the set of allocations that gives members of S what they can get on their own. Identify X with $A(N)$.

Clearly, $x \succeq_i y$ if and only if $x_i \geq y_i$. Also, the effectivity relation is easy to describe. For any x and y,

$$x \rightarrow_S y \text{ iff } y \in A(S)$$

That is, the coalition S can enforce any social state y in $A(S)$ if the sum of the payoffs to individuals in S does not exceed the worth of S.

A straightforward extension to NTU characteristic function games is readily available. In the NTU version, members of a coalition cannot transfer payoffs among themselves on a one-to-one basis. For instance, the situation being modeled may not have any "money" (more generally a private good). Alternatively, even if the model has money, players' utilities may not be linear in money. For instance, consider the familiar exchange economy in which individuals have (ordinal) preferences defined over the commodity space. Individuals also have endowments of goods, and can trade with each other. So, the worth of any coalition is the set of feasible utility vectors that the coalition can get by restricting trade to within the coalition.

Thus, the NTU characteristic function specifies a *set* $V(S)$ of feasible utility vectors for each coalition S. So, $x \rightarrow_S y$ if the restriction of y to S is in $V(S)$.

Hedonic games without externalities are "ordinal" versions of characteristic function games in which players are partitioned into groups or communities, and each player's payoff is solely determined by the identity of other members in her coalition.[6] So, each player i has a preference ordering over the set of coalitions to which i belongs. Examples of group interaction that fit this description include the formation of social clubs, local communities, which provide local public goods such as roads, etc. Clearly, such games also fit into the general framework outlined here.

Games in partition function form: Characteristic functions (in either the TU or NTU version) cannot adequately describe environments in which there are significant *externalities* across coalitions - the notion of what a coalition can guarantee itself is not always meaningful. For consider situations where the payoff to a coalition S depends on the actions taken by the complementary coalition. Clearly, it may not be in the interest of the complementary coalition to take actions that minimize payoffs to S. For instance, in a Cournot oligopoly where each firm has a "large" capacity, payoffs to S are minimized at zero if the firms outside S produce so much output that prices are driven to marginal cost. But, it makes no sense for these firms to do so. So, S has to make some predictions about the behavior of its opponents.

[6] This terminology is due to Dréze and Greenberg (1980).

A more general representation-one that incorporates the possibility of externalities- is the *partition function form*. Let Π_S denote the set of all partitions of any coalition $S \subset N$. For any coalition S, S^c denotes the set $N \backslash S$. Call objects of the form $(S; \pi(S^c))$ *embedded coalitions*. Then, (N, w) denotes a game in partition function form, where w specifies a real number for every embedded coalition. We represent this as $w(S; \pi\ (S^c))$.[7] Notice that this definition incorporates the possibility of externalities since the worth of a coalition depends on how the complementary coalition is organised.[8]

In analogy with the earlier example, one can identify the set of social states with the set of embedded coalitions. Now, suppose $x = (S; (S_1, \ldots S_K))$ where $(S_1, \ldots, S_K)$ is some partition of S^c, and consider any subset T of N. What social state can T induce from x? Suppose members of coalition T believe that once they leave their current coalitions, all others will stay in their original coalitions. That is, there will not be any further reorganization of members. Let $T_0 = S \backslash T$, and $T_k = S_k \backslash T$ for each $j = 1, \ldots, K$, and $y \equiv (T; (T_0, T_1, \ldots, T_K))$. Then, under the *myopic* assumption that players in T^c will "stay put", we can write $x \rightarrow_S y$. However, the assumption of myopic agents is typically an assumption of convenience, and we will consider alternatives notions of "farsightedness."

2.2 Models of coalition and network formation

In this subsection, we describe different one-shot noncooperative procedures by which agents form coalitions and networks. These are all procedures that give rise to normal form games. Two classes of models have been discussed in the literature. In the first class, individuals are precluded from transferring money or utility. In these models, strategies are simply an announcement of the other players with whom a player wants to form a coalition or link. In the second class of models, individual strategies are *bids* to "buy" resources of other agents or "transfers" or "demands" to set up links with other agents. These bids, transfers, and demands are in money or utility. Once again, the rules of the game specify what coalitions or networks form, and *net* payoffs now depend on both the solution concept as well as the bids and transfers. We describe these different models in some detail below.

Models without transfers

The earliest model of coalition formation was proposed by von Neumann and Morgenstern (1944, pp. 243–244). Each player i announces a coalition $S(i)$ to which she wants to belong. The outcome function assigns to any vector of announcements

[7] Hedonic games with externalities are ordinal counterparts of games in partition function form. In such games, a player has a preference ordering over the set of all possible partitions of N.

[8] The derivation of a game in partition function form from a game in normal form is not without problems. One possibility is to treat each coalition as a single entity, and then assume that each such entity plays a noncooperative game among each other. If for every partition of N, this noncooperative game has a *unique* Nash equilibrium, then the unique equilibrium payoff for S corresponding to each $\pi(S^c)$ can be identified with $w(S; \pi\ (S^c))$.

$S(1), \ldots, S(n)$, a coalition structure π as follows: $S \neq \{i\} \in \pi$ if and only if, for all agents $i \in S$, $S(i) = S$. A singleton i belongs to the coalition structure π if and only if (i) either $S(i) = \{i\}$ or $S(i) = S$ and there exist $j \in S$ such that $S(j) \neq S$. In this procedure, a coalition is formed if and only if *all its members unanimously agree to enter the coalition.*

This procedure was rediscovered by Hart and Kurz (1984), who labeled it 'model γ'. They contrast it with another procedure, labeled 'model δ', where unanimity is not required for a coalition to form. In the δ procedure, the outcome function assigns to any vector of announcements $S(1), \ldots, S(n)$, a coalition structure π where: $S \in \pi$ if and only if $S(i) = S(j) \supseteq S$ for all $i, j \in S$. In other words, coalitions are formed by any subset S of players who coordinate and announce the same coalition $S(i)$. In this procedure, the announcement serves to coordinate the actions of the players, and indicates what is the largest coalition that players are willing to form.

Myerson (1991) proposes a game of undirected network formation that is very similar to models γ and δ. In particular, agents simultaneously announce the set of agents with whom they want to form links. Hence, a pure strategy in the game is a subset $S(i) \subseteq N \backslash \{i\}$ for every agent i. The formation of a link requires *consent* by both parties. Link ij is formed if and only if $i \in S(j)$ and $j \in S(i)$. Myerson's model is well suited to handle situations where both agents need to agree to form a link (e.g., friendship relations, formal agreements).

In contrast to Myerson (1991), Bala and Goyal (2000) study the formation of directed networks where agents do not need the consent of the other party to form a link. They consider situations (like the formation of communication links) where agents can freely build connections to the existing network. In these situations, one of the two agents initiates the link and incurs its cost. So, every agent announces a subset $S(i)$ of $N \backslash i$, and the directed link $i \rightarrow j$ is formed if and only if $j \in S(i)$. Bala and Goyal distinguish between two specifications of payoffs. In the *one-way flow model*, the agent initiating the link is the only one to derive any benefit from the link. In the *two-way flow model*, one agent incurs the cost of forming the link, but both agents benefit from the link formed.

Both models γ and δ are models of *exclusive membership*: players can exclude other players from a coalition by their announcements. Myerson's link formation also has this feature. Other procedures do not give players the ability to exclude other agents from the coalition: these are games of *open membership*. For example, the procedure proposed by d'Aspremont et al. (1983) to study the formation of a cartel is defined as follows: players announce their willingness to participate in the cartel (either 'yes' or 'no'). A cartel is formed by all the players who have announced 'Yes'. Alternatively, the equilibria of the cartel formation game can be characterized by the following two conditions of *internal* and *external stability*. Let $v_i^I(S)$ define the profit of an insider in cartel S and $v_i^O(S)$ the profit of an insider when cartel S forms. A cartel is internally stable if no member of the cartel wants to leave, $v_i^I(S) \geq v_i^O(S \backslash \{i\})$ for all $i \in S$. A cartel is externally stable if no outsider wants to join the cartel, $v_i^O(S) \geq v_i^I(S \cup \{i\})$ for all $i \notin S$. One drawback of the procedure of d'Aspremont et al. (1983) is that it only allows one coalition to form. The procedure can easily be generalized to the following open membership game. Every player announces an address $a(i)$ (taken from a set A of cardinality greater than $n + 1$, and with a distinctive element a_0). A coalition S is formed if and only if $a(i) = a(j) \neq a_0$ for all $i, j \in S$. Coalitions are formed by players who announce the same address. Players also have the opportunity to remain singletons by announcing the particular address a_0.

In all procedures defined above, the decision to participate in a group or to form a link was modeled as a discrete $\{0, 1\}$ choice. In reality, agents may choose the amount of resources they spend in different groups and on different links, resulting in a continuous model of participation and link formation. Bloch and Dutta (2009) and Rogers (2005) study this issue in models of link formation. They assume that agents select how to allocate fixed resources X_i on different links. In their models, agents thus choose a vector of investments on every link, $x^i = (x_1^i, x_2^i, \ldots, x_n^i)$ such that $\sum_j x_j^i = X_i$ for all i. Individual investments are transformed into link quality by a production function, $s_{ij} = f(x_j^i, x_i^j)$, assigning a number between 0 and 1, the quality of the link, as a function of individual investments. The outcome of the link formation game is thus a *weighted network* where links have different values. Similarly, one can consider a model of group participation where agents select the amount of resources they devote to different activities. If there are K different activities or tasks to perform, every agent chooses a vector $x^i = (x_1^i, x_2^i, \ldots, x_K^i)$ satisfying $\sum_k x_k^i$. These resources are combined in groups to produce surplus, according to a family of production functions, $v(S, k, (x_k^i)_{i \in S})$. In this formulation coalitions are overlapping in the sense that the same player may belong to different coalitions.

Models with transfers

In the games presented in the previous sections, agents were precluded from transferring money or utility. States were defined as coalition structures or networks, and did not include a description of individual payoffs achieved by the players. We now introduce one-stage procedures of coalition or network formation where agents are allowed to transfer utility.

Kamien and Zang (1990)'s model of monopolization in a Cournot industry was originally designed to study mergers in Industrial Organization. However, the first period game of coalition formation that they introduce is quite general and can be applied to any problem of coalition formation. They suppose that every agent i submits a vector of *bids*, b_j^i over all agents j in N. A bid b_j^i for $i \neq j$ is interpreted as the amount of money that agent i is willing to put to acquire the resources of agent j. A bid b_i^i is interpreted as the asking price at which agent i is willing to sell her resources. Given a matrix $B = [b_i^j]$ of nonnegative bids, one can assign the resources of every agent i either to another agent j (or to agent i herself, if she remains a singleton). Formally, let

$$S(i) = \{j \in N, j \neq i, b_i^j \geq b_i^k \; \forall \, k \neq j\}$$

denote the set of players other than i such that (i) the bid they offer is no smaller than the bid of any other player and (ii) the bid they offer is higher than the asking price. If $S(i)$ is a singleton, the assignment of the resources of player i to the unique player in $S(j)$ (and hence the formation of a coalition S containing $\{i, j\}$) is immediate. If $S(i)$ is not a singleton, one needs to define an exogenous tie-breaking rule to assign the resources of player i to some member of $S(i)$. As a result of this bidding procedure, resources of some players are bought by other players, resulting both in the formation of a coalition structure π and in transfers across players given by $t_i^j = b_i^j$ and $t_j^i = -b_i^j$ if player j acquires the resources of player i.[9] Multibidding games have later been extended by Perez Castrillo and Wettstein (2002) who have also uncovered a connection between bidding mechanisms and the Shapley value.[10]

Bloch and Jackson (2007) extend Myerson's model of link formation to allow transfers among agents.[11] In their basic setting, every agent announces a vector of bids, $t^i = (t_j^i), j \neq i$. The bid t_j^i may be positive (and then interpreted as an offer to pay t_j^i to player j), or may be negative (and then interpreted as a demand to receive t_j^i from player j). Given the simultaneous announcement of bids and the matrix $T = [t_{ij}]$, links are formed and transfers made as follows: If $t_j^i + t_i^j \geq 0$, the link between i and j is formed, and players pay (or receive) the transfer that they offered (or demanded). Given this specification, it may be that transfers are wasted out of equilibrium if $t_j^i + t_i^j > 0$. Alternative transfer procedures could be specified, without altering the network formed in any equilibrium of the procedure. Bloch and Jackson then proceed to define richer structures of transfers, where players are not constrained to put money only on the links they form. In one model, players can choose to subsidize links formed by other players, by announcing positive transfers t_{jk}^i on links formed by other players; in another model, players can announce negative transfers in order to prevent the formation of a link by other players. Finally, in the most general setting, Bloch and Jackson allow players to announce positive or negative transfers contingent on the entire network formed.

2.3 Stability

The processes of group formation described above tell us *how* networks or coalitions form, but not *which* group(s) will actually materialize in any specific context. Since these processes yield well-defined normal form games, it is natural to use game-theoretic notions of equilibrium to predict the network or coalition structure that is

9 Perez Castrillo (1994) independently proposed a procedure of coalition formation that bears close a resemblance to Kamien and Zang (1990)'s bidding game. The main difference is that Perez Castrillo introduces competitive outside players (the "coalition developers") who simultaneously bid for the resources of the players.

10 See also Macho Stadler, Perez Castrillo and Wettstein (2007) for partition function games, and, in the context of networks, Slikker (2007).

11 Slikker and van den Nouweland (2001) introduced an early model of link formation with transfers where agents, in addition to forming links, submit claims on the value of the network.

formed. In this section, we describe some of the equilibrium concepts that are relevant when agents are "myopic." We clarify the meaning of this term shortly.

Consider a social environment that is represented by the collection $\mathbb{E} = (N, X, \{\succeq_i\}_{i\in N}, \{\to_S\}_{S\subseteq N})$. Which social states are likely to emerge as social outcomes following strategic interaction among the agents?

Definition 1 *A social state $x \in X$ is a k-equilibrium if there is no set $S \subseteq N$ with $|S| \leq k$ such that there is $y \in X$ with $x \to_S y$ and $y \succ_i x$ for all $i \in S$.*

Implicit in this definition of stability is the idea that when a coalition contemplates a deviation from a social state x, which is "on the table" to a state y, it compares the utilities associated with x and y. The deviating coalition does not consider the possibility that y itself may not be stable. That is, it does not take into account the possibility that there may be further round(s) of deviation from y. This is the sense in which the current notion of stability is relevant only when players are "myopic." In a later section, we will consider different definitions of stability for players who "look ahead."

This general definition encompasses several notions of stability that have been used in the literature. For instance, if $k = 1$, then it is analogous to Nash equilibrium. However, in most settings of group formation, Nash equilibrium hardly has any predictive power.[12] Consider for example, a setting of hedonic games (with or without externalities) where players prefer to belong to *some* coalition rather than remain single. Then, *any coalition structure* can be sustained as an equilibrium of the γ game of coalition formation. To see this, fix any coalition structure π. Let $S \in \pi$, and suppose individual $i \in S$. If all players in $S\backslash\{i\}$ announce the coalition S, it is a best response of player i to also announce S, even though she may prefer another coalition.[13]

Given the typical indeterminacy of Nash equilibrium particularly in models of undirected networks, it is not surprising that other equilibrium notions have been considered in the literature. Because it takes agreement of both players i and j to form the link ij, it is natural to consider coalitions of size two since this is the minimal departure from a purely noncooperative equilibrium concept. JW specified a very weak notion of stability for undirected networks.

Definition 2 *A network g is pairwise stable if for all $i, j \in N$,*

(i) $Y_i(g) \geq Y_i(g - ij)$

(ii) $Y_i(g + ij) > Y_i(g)$ *implies that* $Y_j(g + ij) < Y_j(g)$.

This concept of stability is very weak because it restricts deviations to change only *one* link at a time, either some agent can delete a link or a pair of agents can add the link

[12] Somewhat surprisingly, it turns out that pure strategy Nash equilibria do not necessarily exist in Bala and Goyal's model with *heterogeneous* agents. See Galeotti, Goyal and Kamphorst (2006), Billand and Bravard (2005) and Haller and Sarangi (2005).

[13] Similar results are available in the context of both directed and undirected networks. See Bala and Goyal (2000) and Dutta, Tijs and van den Nouweland (1998).

between them. This notion of stability is not based on any specific procedure of network formation. A stronger concept of stability based on bilateral deviations uses Myerson's network formation game.

Definition 3 *A 2-equilibrium s^* of Myerson's game is a Pairwise Nash equilibrium.*

Bloch and Jackson (2006), Calvo-Armengol and Ilkilic (2009) and Gilles, Chakrabarti and Sarangi (2006) analyze the relation between pairwise Nash equilibria and alternative solution concepts. In particular, Bloch and Jackson (2006) observe that the set of pairwise Nash equilibria is the intersection of Nash equilibria of Myerson's game and pairwise stable networks. This intersection may very well be empty even when pairwise stable networks exist. Calvo-Armengol and Ilkilic (2009) characterize the class of network values for which pairwise Nash equilibrium networks and pairwise stable networks coincide.

As an alternative way to select among equilibria involving coordination failures, one may choose to consider only equilibria in *undominated* strategies, as in Dutta, Tijs, and van den Nouweland (1998). Selten's trembling-hand perfection may also prove useful, as well as Myerson (1978) concept of proper equilibrium. Calvo-Armengol and Ilkilic (2009) focus on proper equilibria, and provide a (complex) condition on network value functions for which pairwise Nash equilibria and proper equilibrium networks coincide. In a different vein, Gilles and Sarangi (2006) propose a refinement based on evolutionary stability (termed *monadic stability*) to select among the equilibria of the linking game. Feri (2007) also applies evolutionary stability arguments to Bala and Goyal's models, and characterizes the set of stochastically stable networks.

Bala and Goyal (2000) follow a different approach. Faced with the multiplicity of equilibria in their one-way and two-way flow models, they propose to concentrate on *strict* Nash equilibria, where every player plays a strict best response to the actions of the other players. Eliminating strategy profiles where players are indifferent results in a drastic reduction of the number of equilibrium networks. Hojman and Szeidl (2008) show that the set of equilibrium networks can also be drastically reduced (to periphery-sponsored stars) when the value function of the network satisfies two conditions (i) strong decreasing returns to scale in the number of links and (ii) decay with network distance.

Of course, the strongest equilibrium notion allows for deviations by any group of players, and so corresponds to n-equilibrium. For normal form games, this is the notion of strong Nash equilibrium. Dutta and Mutuswami (1997) and Jackson and van den Nouweland (2005) study the strong equilibria of Myerson's network formation game.[14] Jackson and van den Nouweland (2005) characterize the set of network value functions for which strong equilibria of the Myerson game exist as follows.

[14] Jackson and van den Nouweland allow for deviations where some players are indifferent, and so their concept of equilibrium is stronger than the version defined here.

Definition 4 *A network value function v, from the set of all graphs G to* $\Re$ *is* top-convex *if and only if* $\max_{g \in G^S} \frac{v(g)}{|S|} \leq \max_{g \in G} v(g)/n$.

Theorem 1 *The set of strong equilibria in Myerson's game is nonempty if and only if the network value function v is top-convex.*

Jackson and van den Nouweland's characterization theorem shows that strong equilibria only exist when the per capita value of the grand coalition exceeds the per-capita value of any smaller coalition. This very strong convexity property is also the property guaranteeing nonemptiness of the core for symmetric TU games, and as we will see below, also plays a role in Chatterjee et al. (1993)'s study of coalitional bargaining games.

In the context of coalition formation, Hart and Kurz (1983) focus attention on the strong equilibria of the γ and δ games of coalition formation.[15] This concept of strong equilibrium is of course closely related to the familiar concept of the *core* of a characteristic function game.

Definition 5 *An allocation x belongs to the core of the game (N, v) iff x is feasible and*

$$\sum_{i \in S} x_i \geq v(S) \text{ for all } S \subseteq N$$

Of course, not all games have a nonempty core. Bondareva (1963) and Shapley (1967) characterized the class of games that have nonempty cores. Denote by $1_S \in R^n$ the vector such that

$$(1_S)_i = 1 \text{ if } i \in S, (1_S)_i = 0 \text{ if } i \notin S$$

A collection (λ_S) is a *balanced collection of weights* if $\sum \lambda_S 1_S = 1_N$. A game (N, v) is balanced if for all balanced collection of weights (λ_S), $\sum_S \lambda_S v(S) \leq v(N)$.

The classic result of Bonderava-Shapley is the following:

Theorem 2 *A game (N, v) has a nonempty core if and only if it is balanced.*

Notice that since Definition 1 is given in terms of the effectivity relation, the stability of any given social state will depend upon the group formation procedure. Consider, for instance, the γ and δ models of coalition formation applied to the next example.

Example 1 $N = \{1,2,3\}$. *Players are symmetric and receive values given by the following partition function* $v(123) = (1, 1, 1)$, $v(1|2|3) = (0, 0, 0)$, $v(12|3) = (-1, -1, 2)$.[16]

In game γ, the grand coalition N (giving a payoff of 1 to every player) is formed at a Nash equilibrium. If any player deviates from the announcement N, the coalition structure would collapse into a collection of singletons, resulting in a payoff of 0. By contrast, the grand coalition is not formed at any Nash equilibrium of the game δ. If

[15] In a companion paper, Hart and Kurz (1984) provide an example to show that the set of strong equilibria of the procedure of coalition formation may be empty.

[16] We assume that each player in a coalition gets an equal payoff, so that individual values can easily be derived from the partition function.

a player i deviates from the announcement N, the other two players would still form the smaller two-player coalition, and the deviator would receive a payoff of 2 greater than the payoff she received in the grand coalition.

In general, the easier it is for coalitional deviations, the smaller is the set of equilibria. That is, suppose $\{\rightarrow_S^1\}_{S\subseteq N}$ and $\{\rightarrow_S^2\}_{S\subseteq N}$ are two families of effectivity relations with $x \rightarrow_S^1 y$ implying $x \rightarrow_S^2 y$ for all S and all x, y in X. Then, any k-equilibrium corresponding to $\rightarrow_S^2$ must be a k-equilibrium of $x \rightarrow_S^1 y$.

2.4 The degree of consent in group and network formation

The formation of groups and networks is an act that typically involves more than one agent, and may produce externalities on other agents. An important aspect of the procedure of group and network formation is thus the *degree of consent* it requires both from players directly and indirectly affected by the moves. In a model without transfers, this is of paramount importance, as players cannot easily be compensated for the decision taken by other players; in models with transfers, the issue is somewhat mitigated by the fact that players can propose transfers (e.g., exit and entry prices) in order to internalize the externalities due to the moves of other players. In actuality, the formation of a group may require very little or very strong consent. In international law, agreements are typically open to the signature of all countries without restriction, so that no consent is needed either to enter or to exit the coalition. By contrast, transfers of professional soccer players across European teams require the consent (and the payment of a compensating transfer) both from the team that the player leaves and from the team that the player enters. In the formation of jurisdictions, as discussed in Jehiel and Scotchmer (2001), different constitutional rules on mobility result in very different coalition structures. The following table summarizes the assumptions on the degree of consent in models of group and network formation.

	No Consent	**Consent to Enter**	**Consent to Enter, Exit**
Coalitions	*Open membership*	*Games γ and δ*	*Individually stable contractual equilibrium*
	d'Aspremont et al. (1983)	Hart and Kurz (1984)	
		Bidding games	Dréze and Greenberg (1980)
		Kamien and Zang (1990)	
		Perez-Castrillo (1994)	
		Individually stable equilibrium	
		Dréze and Greenberg (1980)	
Networks	*Directed networks*	*Linking game*	
	Bala and Goyal (2000)	Myerson (1991)	
		Pairwise stable networks	
		JW	

For cooperative games without externalities, the introduction of additional constraints on the moves of players (requiring consent to enter and consent to enter and exit) makes deviations harder, and enlarges the set of equilibria. For example, Dréze and Greenberg (1980) note that individually stable contractual equilibria may exist in circumstances where individually stable equilibria fail to exist. When externalities are introduced, the picture becomes less clear, and different rules of consent may yield different predictions on the equilibrium outcomes. Yi (1997) studies this issue by comparing equilibrium outcomes of games with open membership and consent, focussing on the difference between games with *positive externalities* where the formation of a coalition benefits outside players, and games with *negative externalities* where the formation of a coalition harms outside players. The differences between these two types of games can easily be understood considering the following two examples:

Example 2 *A game with positive externalities.* $N = \{1, 2, 3\}$. *Players are symmetric and receive values given by the following partition function* $v\ (123) = (1, 1, 1)$, $v\ (1|2|3) = (0, 0, 0)$, $v\ (12|3) = (-1, -1, 2)$.

As we saw above, the grand coalition is formed at an equilibrium of the γ game. However, if one considers an open membership game, players always want to leave any coalition, and the only equilibrium is one where all players remain as singletons.

Example 3 *A game with negative externalities.* $N = \{1, 2, 3\}$. *Players are symmetric and receive values given by the following partition function* $v(123) = (1, 1, 1)$, $v\ (1|2|3) = (0, 0, 0)$, $v\ (12|3) = (2, 2, -1)$.

In this example, the only equilibrium of the γ and δ games results in players forming a coalition of size 2. However, in an open membership game, the third player will always want to join the coalition, and in equilibrium the grand coalition will form. Yi (1997) results generalize these two simple examples. He shows that in games with positive externalities, open membership will result in less concentrated coalition structures than games that require consent to enter; in games with negative externalities, the result is reversed and open membership games yield larger coalitions than games with consent.

In networks, the absence of consent typically results in over-connections. If an agent does not require the consent of her partner to form a link, she might choose to form links that are beneficial to her, at the expense of her partner and all other agents in the network. This is illustrated by the following simple example:

Example 4 $N = 2$. *The payoffs in the graph are as follows:* $Y(\varnothing, v) = (0,0)$, $Y_1(\{12\}) = 1$, $Y_2(\{12\}) = -2$.

If consent is needed, the only equilibrium is the (efficient) empty network. If consent is not needed, player 1 can impose the formation of a link to player 2, resulting in the inefficient network $\{12\}$.

2.5 Some examples

We describe some examples to illustrate how the concepts described earlier have been applied in specific contexts.

The Connections Model

This is due to Jackson and Wolinsky (1996). In this model, a link represents social relationships (e.g., friendship). These offer benefits (favors, information). In addition, individuals also benefit from indirect relationships. However, a "friend of a friend" generates a lower benefit than a friend. In other words, benefits decrease with the (geodesic) distance between any pair of nodes. Note that the benefit available at each node i has the "nonrivalry" characteristic of a pure public good – the benefit does not depend upon how many other nodes are connected to i.

Both i and j pay cost $c > 0$ for setting up link ij.

Hence, the net utility $u_i(g)$ to player i is

$$u_i(g) = \sum_{j \neq i, j \in P_i(g)} \delta^{d(i,j,g)} - c\#\{j | g_{ij} = 1\} \tag{1}$$

where $\delta < 1$, $d(i, j, g)$ is the geodesic distance between i and j, and $P_i(g)$ is the set of j who are path connected to i in g.

In the context of networks, it has become standard to define a network to be efficient if it maximizes the overall value of the network. Notice that this is a stronger notion of efficiency than the more familiar concept of Pareto efficiency.[17]

Definition 6 *Given v, a network g is efficient if $v(g) \geq v(g')$ for all g'.*

The simplicity of the model makes it easy to characterize both the sets of efficient and pairwise stable networks in terms of the two parameters c and δ. For instance, suppose c is smaller than $\delta - \delta^2$. Then, the cost of setting up an additional link ij is $2c$. Individuals i and j each get an additional benefit of at least $\delta - \delta^2$. So, the complete network must be both the unique efficient and pairwise stable network. The complete characterization is described below.

Efficiency: The efficient network is:

(i) the complete network if $c < \delta - \delta^2$;

(ii) a star encompassing everyone if $\delta - \delta^2 < c < \delta + \frac{n-2}{2}\delta^2$; and,

(iii) the empty network for $\delta + \frac{n-2}{2}\delta^2 < c$.

Pairwise Stability:

(i) If $c < \delta - \delta^2$, then the complete network is the unique pairwise stable network.

(ii) If $\delta - \delta^2 < c < \delta$, then a star encompassing everyone is one of several pairwise stable networks.

(iii) If $\delta < c < \delta + \frac{n-2}{2}\delta^2$, then all pairwise stable networks are inefficient.

Notice that the last case illustrates the fact that there may be situations in which the efficient network is not pairwise stable.

Bala and Goyal (2000) consider a version of the connections model where each agent i can set up a directed link with j without the consent of j and agents derive

[17] See Jackson (2003) for alternative definitions of efficiency for networks.

utility from directed links (one-way flow) or from undirected links (two-way flow). They make the simplifying assumption that the value of information that i gets from j does not depend upon the distance between i and j; that is, there is no decay. In both versions of the model, there are a multiplicity of Nash equilibria. However, Bala and Goyal show that strict Nash equilibrium has a lot of predictive power. In particular, in the one-way flow model, a strict Nash equilibrium is either a wheel or the empty network. In the case of the two-way flow model, a strict Nash equilibrium is either the center-sponsored star or the empty network.

Collaboration Among Oligopolistic Firms

There is considerable evidence that competing firms in the same industry collaborate with each other in a variety of ways-forming research joint ventures, sharing technology, conducting joint R & D, etc. Goyal and Joshi (2003) analyze research collaboration among firms using a two-stage model. In the first stage, each firm simultaneously announces the set of firms with which it wants to set up links. As in the typical two-sided model of link formation, a link forms between firms i and j if each firm has declared that it wants to form a link with the other. A link between firms i and j reduces the cost of production of both firms. Firms i and j also incur a cost $\gamma > 0$ in setting up a link. In the second stage, firms compete in the product market. Assume that firms compete in *quantities*, i.e. they are Cournot oligopolists, although price competition is also easy to analyze.

In its simplest version, the model specifies that n ex-ante identical firms face a linear market demand curve

$$p = a - Q$$

where p denotes the market price and $Q = \sum_{i=1}^{n} q_i$ is the industry output when firms choose the output vector $(q_1, \ldots, q_n)$. Firms have zero fixed cost of production and and initial identical marginal cost c_0. Let $g_{ij} = 1$ if firms i and j set up a collaboration link, and $g_{ij} = 0$ otherwise. Each collaboration link reduces the marginal cost by λ.

Firm i's marginal cost is then

$$c_i(g) = c_0 - \lambda \sum_{j \neq i} g_{ij} \tag{2}$$

The gross profit of a firm is its Cournot profit in the second stage, given a particular network structure, while its net profit is gross profit minus the cost of forming links.

Given any network g, if firms i and j are not linked in g, then by forming the link ij, both firms reduce their marginal cost. This must increase their level of gross profits. Now, suppose link cost, γ, is so low that the change in net profit is always positive for firms i and j whenever the firms set up the additional link ij. Then, the network structure satisfies the general property of *Link Monotonicity*.

Definition 7 *The pair* (Y, v) *satisfies Link Monotonicity if for all* g, *for all* $ij \in /g$, $Y_i(g + ij, v) > Y_i(g, v)$ *and* $Y_j(g + ij, v) > Y_j(g + ij, v)$.

It is obvious that if the network structure satisfies Link Monotonicity, then the complete graph g^N must be the only pairwise stable network. Suppose that we define a collaboration network to be efficient if it maximizes industry profits - that is, we ignore consumer surplus. Then, it is possible to find parameter values such that the complete graph is not the efficient structure.

Risk-Sharing Networks

This is due to Bramoulle and Kranton (2007) and Bloch, Genicot and Ray (2008). It models informal risk sharing across communities. Suppose there are two villages, and the sets of individuals living in villages 1 and 2 are V_1, V_2 respectively. Individual income is a random variable. For agent i living in village v, income is

$$\tilde{y}_i = \bar{y} + \tilde{\varepsilon}_i + \tilde{\mu}_v$$

where $\tilde{\varepsilon}_i$ is an idiosyncratic shock and $\tilde{\mu}_v$ is a village-level shock. Assume that village shocks are i.i.d. with mean zero and variance σ^2_μ, while idiosyncratic shocks are i.i.d. with mean zero and variance σ^2_ε. The village and idiosyncratic shocks are also independently distributed. Individuals have the same preferences with an increasing and strictly concave utility function $u(y)$, so that individuals are risk-averse.

Formal insurance is not available, but pairs of "linked" agents can smooth incomes by transferring money after the realization of shocks. A link between individuals in the same village costs c, while a link between individuals across villages costs $C > c > 0$. Of course, links have to be established ex ante, that is before the realization of the shock. Several interesting questions arise. When will one observe only within-village networks? When will agents also insure against village shocks? Will the latter type of network improve welfare?

A Model of Political Parties

This is due to Levy (2004). She assumes that political parties are composed of factions- groups who differ in their ideological positions. Parties form in order to facilitate commitment policies that represent a compromise between the preferred policies of individual politicians comprising the party.

Assume that a continuum of voters is composed of N finite groups of equal measure. Each group has different preferences over the policy space $Q \subset \mathbb{R}^k$. Voters who belong to group i share single-peaked preferences, represented by a strictly concave utility function $u(q, i)$. The "game" has N politicians, politician i having the preference of group i. Suppose the N politicians are arranged according to some coalition structure π. Interpret each S as a party. For each $S \in \pi$, let Q_S denote the set of Pareto-optimal points for coalition S. Then, each party simultaneously announces a policy platform $q_S \in Q_S \cup \{\varnothing\}$. Let q represent the vector of policy plaforms announced by the different parties. Voters now vote sincerely and the platform with the highest vote wins, ties being broken randomly. Each politician's utility from the game is his expected utility of the electoral outcome. The Nash equilibrium of this game then generates a partition function game.

The Exchange Economy

Each of n individuals have an endowment of L goods. Let $w_i \in \mathbb{R}_+^L$ denote the endowment of individual i. Each individual i has a utility function u_i defined over $\mathbb{R}_+^L$. Each coalition of individuals can trade with each other. This defines a nontransferable utility characteristic function game - notice that there are no externalities across coalitions.

3. SEQUENTIAL MODELS OF COALITION AND NETWORK FORMATION

3.1 Coalitional bargaining

In this section, we survey sequential models of coalition formation, which are based on Rubinstein (1982)'s model of alternative offers bargaining. As in Rubinstein (1982)'s model, the representative model has an infinite horizon, players discount future payoffs, and at each period in time, one of the players (the proposer) makes an offer to other players (the respondents) who must approve or reject the proposal. Different variants of this scenario have been proposed, each reflecting different assumptions on (i) the type of admissible offers, (ii) the selection of the proposer and (iii) the order of responses.

Coalitional bargaining games extend the two-person bargaining games, by considering general gains for cooperation, which can either be described by a coalitional game with transferable utility, or a partition function game.[18] Chatterjee, Dutta, Ray and Sengupta (1993) propose a model of coalitional bargaining based on an arbitrary game in coalitional form. Players are ordered according to an exogenous protocol. At the initial stage, player 1 chooses a coalition S to which she belongs and a vector of payoffs for all members of S, $\mathbf{x}_S$ satisfying $\sum_{i \in S} x_i = v(S)$. Players in S then respond sequentially to the offer. If all accept the offer, the coalition S is formed, and the payoff vector $\mathbf{x}_S$ is implemented. The first player in $N \backslash S$ is chosen as proposer with no lapse of time. If one of the players in S rejects the offer, one period elapses and the rejector becomes the proposer at the following period.

Chatterjee et al. (1993) look for conditions on the underlying characteristic function v for which efficient equilibria exist. Efficient equilibria must possess two features: (i) agreement must be reached immediately, so that there is no efficiency loss due to delay, and (ii) the grand coalition should be formed in equilibrium. Let $m_i(S)$ denote the continuation value of player i when she makes an offer and the set of active players is S. The following example shows that for some protocols, all equilibria result in delay.

Example 5 *$N = 4$, $v(\{1,j\}) = 50$ for $j = 2,3,4$, $v(\{i,j\}) = 100$, $i,j = 2,3,4$ and $v(S) = 0$ for all other coalitions.*

[18] Early extensions of Rubinstein (1982)'s bargaining game to three players were studied by Herrero, Shaked and Sutton – as reported in Sutton (1986) and Binmore (1985).

Suppose by contradiction that all equilibria exhibit immediate agreement. Then, all players make acceptable offers, and in particular,

$$m_i(N) = \delta 100/(1+\delta) \text{ for } i = 2, 3, 4$$
$$m_1(N) = \delta[50 - 100\delta/(1+\delta)]$$

Clearly, when δ converges to 1, $m_1(N)$ converges to 0. Consider then the following deviation for player 1. Player 1 makes an unacceptable offer when the set of players is N, and waits for two players to form a coalition before making an acceptable offer. In that situation, the first coalition will be formed by two of the players 2, 3 and 4 (who will roughly obtain 50 each). Once these two players have left, player 1 and the remaining player will equally share the surplus of 50 and obtain 25 each. Hence, this deviation is profitable for player 1, who has an incentive to make an unacceptable offer (thereby inducing delay) at the beginning of the game.

A careful look at the preceding example shows that delay occurs in equilibrium because one of the players (player 1) is better off waiting for some players to leave before entering negotiations. This suggests that the following condition will be sufficient to rule out delay in equilibrium.

Condition 1 *For all coalitions S and T with $T \subset S$ and all discount factors, $m_i(S) \geq m_i(T)$ for all players i in T.*

Turning now to the second source of inefficiency, the following example shows that even if agreement is reached immediately, the grand coalition may fail to form in equilibrium.

Example 6 $N = 3$, $v(S) = 0$ *if* $|S| = 1$, $v(S) = 3$ *if* $|S| = 2$, $v(N) = 4$.

Suppose by contradiction that the grand coalition forms. Then, $m_i(N) = 4\delta/(2+\delta)$, which converges to 4/3 as δ converges to 1. But then, any player has an incentive to propose to form a two player coalition, resulting in an expected payoff of $3\delta/(1+\delta)$, which converges to 3/2 as δ converges to 1.

The preceding example shows that, as long as intermediate coalitions produce a large surplus, players have an incentive to form smaller, inefficient coalitions. A careful look at the example shows that the two-player coalition forms because this is the coalition that maximizes *per capita* payoff. In particular, if the grand coalition were to maximize the per capita payoff of all the players,(condition of top convexity) then it would clearly form in equilibrium. The next Proposition shows that top convexity is a necessary and sufficient condition for the grand coalition to form in all stationary subgame perfect equilibria and for all protocols.

Theorem 3 *The following two statements are equivalent:*

(a) *The game v satisfies top convexity;*

(b) *For every protocol, there exists a sequence of discount factors converging to 1 and a corresponding sequence of efficient stationary subgame perfect equilibria.*

Okada (1996) analyzes a coalitional bargaining game where the proposer is selected at random after every rejection. In that case, no player will strategically make an unacceptable offer, in order to pass the initiative to another player. Hence, the agreement will be reached at the beginning of the bargaining game. This agreement however may not lead to the formation of the grand coalition – the first proposer may find it optimal to form a smaller coalition. In order to guarantee that the grand coalition forms immediately, the same condition of top convexity identified by Chatterjee et al. (1993), is in fact necessary and sufficient.

If underlying gains from cooperation are represented by a game in partition function form (allowing for externalities across coalitions), players forming a coalition must anticipate which coalitions will be formed by subsequent players. Bloch (1996) proposes a coalitional bargaining game capturing this forward-looking behavior when the division of the surplus across coalition members is fixed.[19] Bloch (1996)'s main result deals with symmetric games where payoffs only depend on the size distribution of coalitions. In that case, the equilibrium coalition structures of the infinite horizon bargaining game can be computed by using the following finite procedure. Let players be ordered exogenously. The first player announces an integer k_1, corresponding to the size of the coalition she wants to form. Player $k_1 + 1$ then announces the size k_2 of the second coalition formed. The game ends when all players have formed coalitions, i.e. $\sum k_t = n$.

While Bloch (1996) assumes that the division rule of the surplus is fixed, Ray and Vohra (1999) consider a model of coalitional bargaining with externalities, where the division of coalitional surplus is endogenous, and payoffs are represented by an underlying game in partition function form. Ray and Vohra (1999) first establish the existence of stationary equilibria in mixed strategies, where the only source of mixing is the probabilistic choice of a coalition by each proposer. Their main theorem establishes an equivalence between equilibrium outcomes of the game and the result of a recursive algorithm. This algorithm, in four steps, characterizes equilibrium coalition structures for symmetric games. It can easily be implemented on computers and has been successfully applied in Ray and Vohra (2001) to study the provision of pure public goods. For any vector $\mathbf{n}$ of positive integers, $\mathbf{n} = (n_i)$, let $K(\mathbf{n}) = \sum n_i$. We construct a mapping $t(\mathbf{n})$ for all vectors $\mathbf{n}$ such that $K(\mathbf{n}) \leq n$. This mapping associates a positive integer to any vector $\mathbf{n}$. Applying this mapping repeatedly, starting at the empty set, when no coalition has formed, we obtain a coalition structure, $c(\emptyset) = \mathbf{n}^*$ that will be the outcome of the algorithm.

Step 1: For all $\mathbf{n}$ such that $K(\mathbf{n}) = n - 1$, define $t(\mathbf{n}) = 1$.

Step 2. Recursively, suppose that $t(\mathbf{n})$ has been defined for all $\mathbf{n}$ such that $K(\mathbf{n}) \geq m$ for some m. Suppose moreover that $K(\mathbf{n}) + t(\mathbf{n}) \leq n$. Then define

$$c(\mathbf{n}) = (\mathbf{n}, t(\mathbf{n}), t(\mathbf{n}, t(\mathbf{n})), \ldots)$$

[19] In this game, as in the seminal studies of Selten (1981) and Moldovanu and Winter (1995), there is no discounting but all players receive a zero payoff in the case of infinite play.

which is a list of integers, corresponding to the repeated application of the mapping t starting from the initial state $\mathbf{n}$.

Step 3 For any $\mathbf{n}$ such that $K(\mathbf{n}) = m$, define $t(\mathbf{n})$ to be the largest integer in $\{1, \ldots, n - m\}$ that maximizes the expression

$$\frac{v(t, c(\mathbf{n}, t))}{t}.$$

Step 4 Since the mapping t is now defined recursively for all vectors $\mathbf{n}$, start with the initial state where no coalition has formed, and compute $\mathbf{n}^* = c(\emptyset)$.

Ray and Vohra (1999) then show that, in symmetric games where payoffs are increasing in the order in which coalitions are formed, the preceding algorithm fully characterizes equilibrium coalition structures when the discount factor converges to 1.[20]

Political science is an important area of application of models of coalitional bargaining. Political agents have to build majority coalitions in order to secure the passing of legislation or the implementation of policies. Majority building occurs in many different political processes: in the formation of coalitional governments in parliamentary democracies, in the passing of legislation in parliament, or in the choice of policies in supranational bodies, like the United Nations Security Council or the European Council. Political scientists have developed a specific analysis of coalition formation, encompassing both theoretical models and empirical estimations. The analysis of coalition formation in political science exhibits two distinctive features: (i) the exact process by which coalitions are formed (the "rules of the game") are often well specified, either through custom or through constitutional provisions, and (ii) the coalitional game is a simple game, where coalitions are either winning or losing.

Baron and Ferejohn (1989) consider an extension of Rubinstein (1982)'s alternating offers model, where members of a legislature bargain over the division of a pie of fixed value (interpreted as the distribution of benefits to different constituencies). In order to be accepted, a proposal must receive the approval of a simple majority of members of the legislature. In the *closed rule* model they consider, a proposer is chosen at random, and his offer is immediately voted upon by the legislature.[21] Baron and Ferejohn (1989)'s first result is an indeterminacy result, showing that any distribution of payoffs can be reached in a subgame perfect equilibrium of the closed-rule game.

Theorem 4 *For an n-member majority rule legislature with a closed rule, if the discount factor satisfies* $1 > \delta > \frac{n+2}{2(n-1)}$ *and* $n \geq 5$, *any distribution x of the benefits may be supported as a subgame-perfect equilibrium.*

[20] Montero (1999) considers a version of the Ray and Vohra (1999) model where the proposer is chosen at random, as in Okada (1996).

[21] The second model they consider – the *open rule model* – is more complex and allows for amendments to the status quo.

The intuition underlying this indeterminacy result is easy to grasp. In Baron and Ferejohn (1989)'s game, a deviating player can always be punished (independently of the discount factor) by other players systematically excluding him from any coalition. These equilibrium punishment strategies can be used to deter any deviation from an arbitrary distribution of benefits x. In order to select among equilibria, Baron and Ferejohn (1989) impose a further restriction on equilibrium strategies, by assuming that strategies are stationary – namely cannot depend on the entire history of play but only on the current offer. With stationary strategies, members of the legislature cannot exclude other members in response to a deviation, and the equilibrium distribution of benefits becomes unique, as shown in the following Proposition.

Theorem 5 *For all $\delta \in [0, 1]$, a configuration of pure strategies is a stationary subgame perfect equilibrium in a closed rule game (with an odd number of legislators) if and only if a member recognized proposes to receive $1 - \delta \frac{n-1}{2n}$ and offers $\frac{\delta}{n}$ to $\frac{n-1}{2}$ members selected at random, and each member votes for any proposal in which at least $\frac{\delta}{n}$ is received.*

By contrast to Rubinstein (1982)'s game, where the shares of the proposer and respondent converge to $\frac{1}{2}$ when δ converges to 1, the proposer in Baron and Ferejohn (1989)'s game retains a large advantage over the respondents, even when all players become perfectly patient. This is due to the fact that a respondent is not sure to be included in the next majority coalition if she rejects the offer, so that the minimal offer she is willing to accept may be quite low. In an application to the formation of coalitional governments in parliamentary systems, Baron and Ferejohn (1989) note that, even if the probability of recognition is proportional to the number of seats in parliament, the proposer's advantage remains very large, and results in the first proposer (even if it is a small party) obtaining a disproportionate number of cabinet posts. In the open rule procedure, the proposer's advantage is mitigated by the fact that a second member of parliament can propose an amendment. This reduces the power of the first proposer, and results in a larger share of the benefits for the respondents. Furthermore, for low values of the discount factor, the first proposer will choose in equilibrium to make offers to a supermajority of members, in order to reduce the probability that a second member of parliament propose an amendment to his offer.[22]

An important extension of Baron and Ferejohn (1989)'s model was proposed by Merlo and Wilson (1995) to take into account uncertainty and random shocks on the surplus from cooperation. In their model of bargaining in a stochastic environment, players share a cake whose size varies from period to period according to a general Markov process. They consider a bargaining problem, where the agreement has to be unanimously

[22] The coalitional bargaining model of Baron and Ferejohn (1989) has generated a considerable theoretical and empirical literature in political science. See Harrington (1989), Baron and Kalai (1993), Winter (1996), Merlo (1997), Banks and Duggan (2000), Jackson and Moselle (2002), Norman (2002), Eraslan (2002) and Seidmann, Winter and Pavlov (2007) for theoretical contributions and Merlo (1997), Diermeier and Merlo (2004) and Diermeier, Eraslan and Merlo (2003) for empirical tests.

accepted by all players to be effective. This model is well suited to analyze the formation and collapse of coalitional governments that face an uncertain, stochastic environment.

While the coalitional bargaining models of Chatterjee et al. (1993) and Baron and Ferejohn (1989) are straightforward extensions of Rubinstein (1982) bargaining model, other more complex extensive form procedures have also been studied, often with the objective of providing a noncooperative foundation to a cooperative solution concept. Most papers in this "Nash program" vein aim at supporting solution concepts like the core or the Shapley value, where the grand coalition is *assumed to form*. Hence, these procedures are usually not well suited to analyze the formation of partial coalitions.[23] However, recent work on the Shapley value with externalities discusses procedures that can lead to the formation of partial coalitions. For example, Maskin (2003) proposes a sequential procedure where players enter the game according to an exogenous rule of order, and existing coalitions simultaneously bid for the entering player. Macho-Stadler, Perez-Castrillo and Wettstein (2007) propose a different bidding procedure that implements another type of Shapley value with externalities. Declippel and Serrano (2008) and Dutta, Ehlers and Kar (2010) propose other extensions of the Shapley value to games with externalities but do not discuss noncooperative implementation.

3.2 Sequential models of network formation

Sequential models of network formation have been proposed in order to circumvent two difficulties in models of network formation. First, in a sequential procedure, agents do not behave myopically and choose their actions anticipating the reaction of subsequent players. In the words of Aumann and Myerson (1988):

> *'When a player considers forming a link with another one, he does not simply ask himself whether he may expect to be better off with this link than without it, given the previously existing structure. Rather, he looks ahead and asks himself, "Suppose we form this new link, will other players be motivated to form further links that were not worthwhile for them before? Where will it all lead? Is the* end result *good or bad for me?"*
>
> ***(Aumann and Myerson (1988, p. 178)).***

Second, as a finite sequential game of complete information generically possesses a unique subgame perfect equilibrium, the use of sequential procedures helps to refine the set of Nash equilibria and to resolve the coordination issues involved in link formation. Both the modeling of players as forward-looking agents, and the resolution of coordination problems due to the sequentiality of decisions indicate that sequential models are more likely to produce *efficient networks* than simultaneous procedures.

[23] Some representative papers include Gul (1989), Hart and Mas Colell (1996), and Perez-Castrillo and Wettstein (2000) for noncooperative implementation of the Shapley value, Perry and Reny (1994), Lagunoff (1994) and Serrano and Vohra (1997) for the core, or Binmore, Rubinstein and Wolinsky (1986) and Krishna and Serrano (1996) for the bargaining solution.

Unfortunately, as shown by Currarini and Morelli (2000) and Mutuswami and Winter (2002) even sequential procedures may not produce efficient networks except under restrictive conditions on the underlying structure of gains from cooperation.

In the first attempt to study sequential procedures of network formation, Aumann and Myerson (1988) consider a finite game where, at any point in time, a pair of players who are not yet linked is called to form a new link by mutual agreement. Links are never destroyed. The game is finite, but the rule of order must be such that, after the last link is formed, all pairs of players who are not linked have a last opportunity to form a new link. Aumann and Myerson (1988)'s primary objective is to emphasize the role of anticipation and forward-looking behavior on the formation of networks. Consider the following example:

Example 7 $N=3$. *If* $g=\emptyset$, $Y_i(g)=0$. *If* $g=\{ij\}$, $Y_i(g)=Y_j(g)=30$, $Y_k(g)=0$. *If* $g=\{ij, ik\}$, $Y_i(g)=44$, $Y_j(g)=Y_k(g)=14$. *If* $g=\{ij, ik, jk\}$, $Y_i(g)=Y_j(g)=Y_k(g)=24$.

In this Example, the complete network is efficient, but, for any rule of order, the subgame perfect equilibrium of Aumann and Myerson (1988)'s game is for two players to form a single link. After this link is formed, if one of the players tries to form another link in order to obtain the payoff of 44, this will be followed by the formation of the last link, resulting in a payoff of 24. Hence, forward-looking players will never choose to form an additional link after the first link is formed. The same line of reasoning can be applied to characterize the subgame perfect equilibrium in an "apex game" where one large player faces four small players.

Example 8 $N=5$. *Players get payoffs that only depend on the components of the network, and not the way players are linked. There are two types of player: one large player (player 1) and four small players, (2,3,4,5). Winning coalitions either include the large player, or consist of all four small players. Payoffs are based on the Shapley value of this apex game. If coalition* $\{1, i\}$ *forms, player 1 and i get* $\frac{1}{2}$. *If coalition* $\{1, i, j\}$ *forms, player 1 gets* $\frac{2}{3}$ *and players i and j get* $\frac{1}{6}$ *each. If coalition* $\{1, i, j, k\}$ *forms, player 1 gets* $\frac{3}{4}$ *and players i, j, k get* $\frac{1}{12}$ *each. If the four small players form a coalition, they receive* $\frac{1}{4}$ *each. If the grand coalition forms, the large player receives* $\frac{3}{5}$ *and the four small players get* $\frac{1}{10}$ *each.*

In this Example, the unique equilibrium structure is for the four small players to form a coalition. By backward induction, we observe that, if coalition $\{1, i, j, k\}$ forms, small players have an incentive to form a link to the excluded small player, and the grand coalition results. Hence, coalition $\{1, i, j\}$ is stable, because the large player knows that, if she invites another small player to join, the end result will be the grand coalition, with a payoff of $\frac{3}{5}$. On the other hand, if coalition $\{1, i\}$ forms, the large player has an incentive to bring in another small player, resulting in the stable coalition $\{1, i, j\}$. At the beginning of the game, small players realize that they can either obtain a payoff of $\frac{1}{4}$ (if they form a coalition of small players) or $\frac{1}{6}$ (if they join the large player in a three-player coalition), and prefer to form the coalition of small players.

Aumann and Myerson (1988)'s model makes strong assumptions on the rule of order to ensure that the game is finite. Attempts to construct general, infinite horizon models of network formation based on the same structure as models of coalitional bargaining have so far remained elusive. One exception is Watts (2001)'s construction of a subgame perfect equilibrium in the connections model where agents' utilities can be decomposed as the sum of benefits from communication (discounted by the distance in the network) and costs of direct links. In her model, at each point in time, when a pair of players is selected, it can either choose to form a new link or to destroy the existing link, resulting in a game with infinite horizon – and a large number of equilibria. When the discount factor goes to 1, Watts (2001) exhibits one subgame perfect equilibrium where players form the circle network. To sustain this equilibrium, players employ a grim strategy, where players who fail to cooperate are punished by being ostracized. However, this is only one equilibrium among many, and Watts (2001) does not propose a full characterization of the set of subgame perfect equilibrium outcomes.

In two related contributions, Currarini and Morelli (2000) and Mutuswami and Winter (2002) propose finite procedures to study the relation between efficiency and equilibrium. In both procedures, agents are ordered according to an exogenous rule, and make announcements in sequence. In both models, one needs to impose a monotonicity condition on the value of the network to guarantee that any subgame perfect equilibrium is efficient.

Currarini and Morelli (2000) suppose that the total value of the network is given by a mapping $v : G \rightarrow \Re$, associating a real number $v(g)$ to any graph g. They suppose that the value is monotonic in the following sense:

Definition 8 *A link ij in graph g is* critical *if and only if the number of components of $g - ij$ is strictly greater than the number of components of g. The value function v satisfies* size monotonicity *if and only if for all graphs g and critical links ij, $v(g) > v(g - ij)$.*

They consider a finite procedure where each player makes a single move. At stage i, player i announces a pair (g_i, d_i) where g_i is a set of *links* to agents in $N \backslash i$ and d_i is a real number, expressing the *demand* of agent i. Given these announcements, one constructs a network g by letting link ij be formed if and only if both parties agree to the formation of that link. For any component h of g, one verifies whether the value of the component $v(g(h))$ can cover the demands of the agents in h. If the answer is positive, network $g(h)$ is formed, and every member of h receives her demand d_i. If the answer is negative, then all members of h are isolated and receive a payoff of zero. In this model, they prove that all subgame perfect equilibria are efficient:

Theorem 6 *Let v satisfy size monotonicity. Then any subgame perfect equilibrium network of Currarini and Morelli (2000)'s sequential game is efficient.*

Mutuswami and Winter (2002) consider instead a model where players have private values over the network, $v_i(g)$, face a known cost function $c(g)$, and can transfer utility only insofar as they share the cost of the network. In their mechanism, at stage i, player

i announces a pair (g_i, x_i) where g_i is a set of links that player i wants to see formed and x_i is a positive number, representing the *conditional cost contribution* of player i, that she commits to pay if the network formed is a superset of g_i. Given these announcements, the coalition S is said to be *compatible* if and only if: (i) $g_i \in G^S$ for all $i \in S$ and (ii) $\sum_{i \in S} x_i \geq c(\cup_{i \in S} g_i)$. The mechanism then selects the *largest* compatible coalition S^* among the connected coalitions 1, 12, 123,...,123...n. The network formed is $g = \cup_{i \in S^*} g_i$ and every player in S^* receives a payoff $v_i(g) - x_i$ whereas players in $N \backslash S^*$ receive a payoff of zero. Mutuswami and Winter (2002) consider the following notion of monotonicity:

Definition 9 *The value function v_i is monotonic if and only if, whenever $g \subset g'$, $v_i(g) \leq v_i(g')$.*

They prove that any subgame perfect equilibrium network is efficient.

Theorem 7 *Suppose that $c(\emptyset) = 0$ and that $v_i(\cdot)$ is monotonic for every agent i. Then every subgame perfect equilibrium network in the Mutuswami and Winter (2002) sequential mechanism is efficient. Furthermore, in equilibrium, every agent receives his marginal contribution:*

$$u_i = (\max_{g \in G^{\{1,\ldots,i\}}} \sum_{j=1}^{i} v_j(g) - c(g)) - (\max_{g \in G^{\{1,\ldots,i-1\}}} \sum_{j=1}^{i-1} v_j(g) - c(g)).$$

4. FARSIGHTEDNESS

In Section 2.3, we described the notion of a k-equilibrium. Recall that implicit in the definition of a k-equilibrium is the idea that when a group or individual contemplates deviation from the proposal x "on the table" to another social state y, it simply compares the utilities it gets under y and x. But, consider the familiar *voting paradox*.

Example 9 *$N = \{1, 2, 3\}$, $X = \{x, y, z\}$, and $a \rightarrow_S b$ for all $a, b \in X$ iff $|S| \geq 2$. The preferences of the three individuals are described below.*

$$x \succ_1 y \succ_1 z, y \succ_2 z \succ_2 x, z \succ_3 x \succ_3 y$$

No social state is a 2-equilibrium. Individuals 1 and 3 prefer to move from y to x and have the power to do so, 2 and 3 want to move away from x to z, and the cycle is completed because 1 and 2 prefer to move from z to y. Given this cycle, why does 1 agree to join 3 in moving from y to z when z itself is not a "stable outcome"? That is, what is the relevance of the utility that she derives from z when there is no guarantee that the group will agree to adopt z as the final outcome.

The answer must be that the concept of k-equilibrium models players who are *myopic* – they do not look ahead to the possibility of further deviations once they themselves have moved away from the status quo. In this section, we discuss concepts of stability in one-stage models of group formation when players are *farsighted* in the sense that they take into account the "final" outcome(s), which can result from their initial deviation.[24] Of course, since players move only once, these notions of farsightedness must involve introspection.

Notice that equilibrium predictions in the bargaining models described in the last section already incorporate this kind of farsighted behavior. For instance, an initial proposer evaluates what will happen if he makes a proposal that is rejected by some other player. Will the new proposal give him less than he is asking for now? Similarly, a player who contemplates rejecting the current proposal must also look far ahead and anticipate the proposal that is ultimately approved by the players.

There are different options in modeling players' farsighted behavior when players choose actions simultaneously, depending at least partly on the social environment. First, suppose the social environment is such that there are no externalities across groups. Consider, for instance, games in characteristic function form or hedonic games without externalities, so that "subgames" are well-defined. The standard myopic stability notion then is the core. Clearly, one implication of farsighted behavior is that the act of blocking must be credible. In particular, if a coalition S contemplates breaking away from the grand coalition, then it must also take into account the possibility that a subcoalition of itself may effect a further deviation.

It is possible to generalize this notion. For each S, let F_S be the set of feasible outcomes for S, and Θ_S be a solution concept. Then, the solution concept should satisfy the requirement that an allocation x is in Θ_S only if no sub-coalition T of S can block x with an allocation which is itself a solution for T. More formally,

Definition 10 *The solution Θ_S satisfies Internal Consistency if for all games (N, v) and for all $S \subseteq N$,*

$$\Theta_S(v) = \{x \in F_S(v) | \text{ there is no } T \subset S, y \in \Theta_T(v) s.t. y \succ_i x \forall i \in T\}$$

Greenberg (1990) and Ray (1989) prove the following.

Theorem 8 *The core satisfies Internal Consistency.*

The underlying intuition is quite simple. For suppose $x \notin C_S(v)$. Then, some $T \subset S$ blocks x with y. If y is not in core of T, then some subset of T, say R blocks y. But, notice that this implies

$$v(R) > \sum_{i \in R} y_i > \sum_{i \in R} x_i$$

So, R blocks x. And so on until some singleton coalition does the blocking.[25]

[24] In the next section, we will discuss farsightedness in the context of dynamic situations where groups interact over time.

[25] Consistency requires that a coalition can only block with allocations from its own set of unblocked allocations. Suppose "norms" dictate that all unblocked allocations are not available, but only those which pass the norms test. Dutta and Ray (1989) define a recursive notion of *Norm consistency*, which imposes the requirement that each coalition can only block with those feasible allocations that pass the norms test from its one set of unblocked allocations. Their *egalitarian solution* uses the norm of selecting the Lorenz-maximal elements in each set.

It is not straightforward to apply this definition of internal consistency to games with externalities since subgames on coalitions are not well-defined. Below, we describe other approaches to farsighted behaviour in general social environments.

Fix some social environment $\Gamma = (N, \{\rightarrow_S\}_{S \subseteq N}, \{\succeq\}_{i \in N})$. For all $x, y \in X$, define the binary relation $>$ as follows

$$x > y \text{ if } \exists S \subseteq N \text{ such that } y \rightarrow_S x \text{ and } x \succ_i y \forall i \in S$$

Now, farsighted behavior "could" mean the following:

(i) If x is not "stable," then some coalition should be able to deviate profitably to some y *and* y should itself be stable.

(ii) If x is stable, then no coalition can have a profitable deviation from x to another stable outcome y.

It is worth pointing out why (i) and (ii) incorporate farsightedness. Implicit in (i) is the idea that if a coalition S has the power to deviate from x to some stable outcome y, then the stability of y ensures that there will not be any further deviation from y. So, if members of S all prefer y to x, then they will go ahead with the deviation and so x cannot be stable. The same logic also suggests the criterion that any stable social state must satisfy. If x is stable, then no coalition should want to move to another stable state.

These considerations lead to the vNM *stable set* with respect to the binary relation $>$.

Definition 11 *The vNM stable set for any asymmetric relation* $\succ$ *over* X *is a set* $V(\succ)$ *satisfying:*

External Stability: If $y \notin V(\succ)$, *then there is some* $x \in V(\succ)$ *such that* $x \succ y$.

Internal Stability: If $y \in V(\succ)$, *then there is no* $x \in V(\succ)$ *such that* $x \succ y$.

Lucas (1969) showed that a stable set need not exist. For instance, it is empty in Example 9 for the relation $>$. Even if stable sets do exist, they need not be unique. In fact, as the following example illustrates, there may be a continuum of vNM solutions even in very simple games.

Example 10 *Let* $N = \{1, 2, 3\}$, $v(S) = 1$ *if* $|S| \geq 2$ *and* $v(S) = 0$ *otherwise. Choose any* $a \in [0, 1/2)$, *and any* $i \in N$. *Then, the set* $V_i(a) = \{x \in R^3_+ | x_i = a, x_j + x_k = 1 - a\}$ *constitutes a vNM set for the relation* $>$.

It is easy to check that $V_i(a)$ satisfies internal consistency. To check external stability, take any $y = (y_1, y_2, y_3)$ such that $\sum_{i=1}^{3} y_i = 1$ and $y \notin V_i(a)$. If $y_i > a$, then $y_j + y_k < 1 - a$, and there must exist $x \in V_i(a)$ such that $x_j > y_j$ and $x_k > y_k$. If $y_i < a$, then without loss of generality assume that $y_j \geq y_k$. Then, there exists $x \in V_i(a)$ such that $x_i > y_i$ and $x_k > y_k$.

The nonuniqueness of vNM sets is possibly one reason why this solution concept has not been very popular in applications. Harsanyi (1974) also felt that the vnM set $V(>)$ does not really incorporate farsighted behavior. The example below illustrates the nature of his criticism.

Example 11 *Let* $X = \{x, y, z, w\}$, $N = \{1, 2\}$, *and individual preferences be*

(i) $x \succ_1 y \succ_1 z \succ_1 w$.

(ii) $w \succ_2 y \succ_2 x \succ_2 z$.

Finally, the effectivity relation is:

$$x \rightarrow_2 y,\ z \rightarrow_1 w,\ w \rightarrow_1 x,\ y \rightarrow_2 z,\ z \rightarrow_{\{1,2\}} y.$$

The vnM set is $\{y, w\}$. The underlying logic is the following. Player 1 does not deviate from w to x because x itself is not stable since 2 will deviate from x to y. But, why should this deter 1 from deviating since she prefers y to w? Thus, 1 does not look sufficiently far ahead.

Harsanyi's objection can be interpreted as a criticism not of the stable set, but of the direct domination relation $>$. Notice that the problem unearthed in Example 11 arises partly because 1 does not anticipate the *chain* of deviations which might follow from her initial deviation from w. This suggests that the domination relation itself should be modified so as to consider a *chain* of deviations. The *indirect domination* relation, defined below, captures this aspect.

Definition 12 *A state* y *is indirectly dominated by* x *if there exist sequences of states* $\{y_0, \ldots, y_K\}$ *and coalitions* $\{S_0, \ldots S_{K-1}\}$ *such that* $y_0 = y$, $y_K = x$, *and for all* $k = 0, \ldots K{-}1$,

(i) $y_k \rightarrow_{S_k} y_{k+1}$.

(ii) $y_K \succ_i y_k$ *for all* $i \in S_k$.

Let $x >> y$ denote the relation that x indirectly dominates y.

The indirect domination relation incorporates the idea that coalitions look beyond their own immediate actions to the "ultimate" consequence-each coalition S_k compares y_k with the "end point" y_K. But how is the end point determined? Our previous discussion suggests that a natural candidate for the end point is that it should be stable so that there is no further deviation from it. This in turn suggests $(V>>)$ as a candidate for a farsighted consistent solution.[26]

In Example 11, $(V>>) = \{y\}$, and so $V(>>) \subset V(>)$. However, this is not true in general,[27] as the following example illustrates.

Example 12 *Let* $X = \{x, y, z, w\}$, $N = \{1, 2, 3\}$. *Preferences and the effectivity relation are as follows.*

(i) $y \succ_1 x \succ_1 z$.

(ii) $z \succ_2 w$.

(iii) $z \succ_3 y$.

(iii) $y \rightarrow_3 w,\ w \rightarrow_2 z,\ x \rightarrow_1 y$.

[26] Diamantoudi and Xue (2007) advance this as a solution concept in their analysis of hedonic games with externalities. See also Diamantoudi and Xue (2003) and Xue (1998).

[27] What is true however is that $V(>)$ can never be a subset of $V(>>)$. For suppose $V(>) \equiv V \subset V' \equiv V(>>)$. Let $y \in V' \backslash V$. Then, by External Stability of V with respect to $>$, there is $x \in V$ with $x > y$. But, $x > y$ implies $x >> y$, and so V' violates Internal Stability with respect to $>$.

Then, $y > x$, $z >> y$, $z > w$ and hence $z >> w$. So, $V(>) = \{y, z\}$ and $V(>>) = \{x, z\}$.

Chwe (1994) points out that (V >>) may sometimes be too restrictive.[28] Consider the following example.

Example 13 *Let $X = \{x, y, z, w\}$, $N = \{1, 2\}$ and preferences and effectivity functions be as follows.*

(i) $w \succ_1 y \succ_1 x \succ_1 z$.

(ii) $z \succ_2 w \succ_2 y \succ_2 x$.

(iii) $x \rightarrow_1 y$, $y \rightarrow_2 z$, $y \rightarrow_{\{12\}} w$.

Then, $y >> x$, $w >> x$, $z >> y$, and $(V >>) = \{w, z\}$. The logic ruling out x as a "stable" outcome is that 1 will move to y anticipating that $\{1, 2\}$ will deviate further to w which 1 prefers to x. But, is this anticipation reasonable? After all, once 1 deviates to y, individual 2 has the option of moving to either z or w. Surely, 2 will prefer the move to z which is worse than x as far as 1 is concerned. Thus, if 1 makes the right inference, then 1 should not plan to deviate from x.

Chwe (1994) advances a different solution concept based on the indirect domination relation.

Definition 13 *A set $Y \subset X$ is consistent if $x \in Y$ iff $\forall y, S$ s.t. $x \rightarrow_S y$, there is $z \in Y$ s. t. either $z = y$ or $z >> y$ and $x \succ_i z$ for some $i \in S$.*

Chwe (1994) shows that there is a largest consistent set, denoted LCS, and offers this as a solution concept. He proves the following.

Theorem 9 *Suppose X is finite. Then,*

(i) *The LCS is nonempty and has the external stability property with respect to >>.*

(ii) *$V(>>) \subset LCS(>>)$.*[29]

Suppose a coalition S has the power to move from x to y. When will it decide not to deviate to y? Being a farsighted solution concept, y is relevant if y itself is in the consistent set. If y is indeed in a consistent set, and some individual in S prefers x to y, then S will not move to y. Otherwise, S looks ahead to some chain of deviations from y to an element z in Y, which indirectly dominates y, and compares z to x.

In Example 13, the LCS=$\{x, z, w\}$, because 1 will be deterred from moving to y apprehending the further move to z by 2. But, while (V >>) can be faulted for being too restrictive, the LCS errs in the opposite direction by being too permissive. That is, it labels states as being "stable" when there are good reasons for declaring them to be unstable. Consider a slight modification of Example 13.

[28] Of course, it can sometimes be empty as in the voting paradox.

[29] Since the set of all networks on a finite player set is finite, this existence theorem proves very useful to Page, Wooders and Kamat (2005) and Page and Wooders (2009) in their analysis of network formation. For a different concept of farsighted network formation based on pairwise stability, see Herings et al. (2009).

Example 14 *Let* $X = \{x, y, z, w\}$, $N = \{1, 2\}$ *and preferences and effectivity functions be as follows.*

(i) $z \succ_1 x \succ_1 w$.

(ii) $z \succ_2 w \succ_2 y$.

(iii) $x \rightarrow_1 y$, $y \rightarrow_2 z$, $y \rightarrow_2 w$

Then, the LCS contains x. The argument justifying this is the following. Suppose 1 moves to y. Then, 2 could move further to w, which is in the LCS. Since $x \succ_1 w$, this should deter the move from x. But, why should 2 move to w from y when she can also move to z, which she prefers to both y and w? Notice that if 2 actually moves to z, then this justifies $1'$s deviation from x to y. Hence, in this example, x should not be deemed to be stable. Note that Chwe himself is aware of this problem. He suggests the following interpretation of the LCS - if a state does not belong to the LCS, then it cannot possibly be stable.

These examples suggest that none of these attempts to define a farsighted solution concept is completely satisfactory.

The problem with solution concepts such as $V(>>)$ and LCS is that their arguments for inclusion or exclusion vis-a-vis stability are based on some sequence of deviations. For instance, Greenberg (1990) had pointed out that the vnM stable set (with respect to any binary relation) was based on optimistic predictions. These problems are avoided by Ray and Vohra (1997) in their solution concept of equilibrium binding agreements (EBA). They study the very general framework of normal form games. Their basic idea is that once a particular structure forms, the players within each coalition will have signed a binding agreement to cooperate with one another. But, prior to joining a coalition and agreeing on any specific course of actions, each player must predict what coalition structure will form in equilibrium. And players will evaluate their payoffs in the "equilibrium" before signing any binding agreement.

In what follows, we restrict attention to normal games where for each coalition structure or partition of the player set N, the game in which each coalition plays as a single "player" has a unique Nash equilibrium. Assuming that players within each coalition also agree on how to divide the coalitional payoffs corresponding to the Nash equilibrium, we then have a hedonic game with externalities. Start from the grand coalition N. Suppose S contemplates a deviation from N. Then, the "temporary" partition will be $\{S, N - S\}$. Of course, since players are farsighted, S will not necessarily believe that this is the end of the process. There are several possible types of deviations.

(i) S itself may break up further.

(ii) $N - S$ may break up

(iii) Some group from S may join with some group from $N - S$.

Ray and Vohra (1997) allow for deviations of types (i) and (ii).[30] So, partitions can only become finer. The coalition structure of singletons, say π^*, is stable by definition since there is no finer partition. Now, consider any partition π whose only finer partition is π^*. Then, π is an EBA if no one one wants to deviate to π^*. Recursively, suppose all the set of all EBAs which are finer than a given partition π have been determined. Then, any coalition contemplating a deviation from π will compare the payoffs in π to what they can get in the next finer EBA. In other words, at each stage potential deviators predict the partition from which there will be no further deviation. The "solution" of the game is the set of coarsest EBAs.

Diamantoudi and Xue (2007) reformulate the concept of EBAs for hedonic games with externalities. For this restricted class of games, the set of EBAs is a vNM stable set of a particular binary relation. Their analysis is somewhat simpler than the original definition, and we describe their reformulation.

Definition 14 *A coalition structure π' is reachable from π via a sequence of coalitions $T_0, \ldots, T_{K-1}$ if $T_k \in \pi'$ and $\pi_k \rightarrow_{T_k} \pi_{k+1}$ for all $k = 0, K-1$, with $\pi_0 \equiv \pi$ and $\pi_K = \pi'$. Moreover, if $\pi' \succ_j \pi_k$ for all $j \in T_k$, then π' sequentially dominates π.*[31]

Suppose π' sequentially dominates π and is an EBA. Can we rule then out π as an EBA? This would mean that members of T_0 have an optimistic prediction about the order of deviations - precisely the criticism we have made about $V(>>)$. Ray and Vohra are careful to avoid this pitfall.

Definition 15 *π' RV -dominates π, π' RV π, if there exist $T_0, \ldots, T_{K-1}$ s.t. each $T_k \in \pi'$, and*

(i) *π' is reachable from π via $T_0, \ldots, T_{K-1}$*

(ii) *$\pi' \succ_i \pi$ for all $i \in T_0$.*

(iii) *If $Q = \hat{\pi}$ or Q is reachable from $\hat{\pi}$ via a subcollection of $\{T_1, \ldots, T_{K-1}\} - \{T\}$, where $\pi \rightarrow_{T_0} \hat{\pi}$, then π' RVQ.*

It is condition (iii), which avoids the problems that can arise by focusing on specific sequences of deviations. For, let T_0 be the coalition that has initiated the deviation from π. For suppose some coalition(s) in $\{T_1, \ldots, T_{k-1}\}$ deviate from the path prescribed in the move from π to π'. Then, the resulting partition is also RV-dominated by π'. Hence, condition (iii) gives the specific sequence of deviations from π to π' a certain robustness.

Diamantoudi and Xue (2007) prove the following.

Theorem 10 *The set V(RV) is the set of EBAs.*

[30] Bernheim, Peleg and Whinston (1987)'s notion of *Coalition-proof Nash equilibrium* assumes that only deviations of type (i) are possible. Yi (1997) studies coalition-proof Nash equilibria of the open membership game of coalition formation. In the context of networks, Dutta and Mutuswami (1997) and Dutta, Tijs and van den Nouweland (1998) apply coalition-proofness to select among equilibria in the Myerson network formation game. When link monotonicity holds, they show that coalition-proof equilibrium networks are equivalent to the complete network.

[31] Notice the similarity with indirect domination.

The concept of Efficient Binding Agreements captures "almost" perfectly the intuitive basis of stability in group formations. The only caveat is the restriction that coalitional deviations can only result in finer partitions. This makes the definition "workable" since π^*, the partition of singletons, is by definition an EBA. And this then allows the recursion to be well-defined. But, of course, π^* may not satisfy one's intuitive sense of stability if individuals across elements in a partition can execute joint deviations. In other words, a fully satisfactory definition of stability needs to allow for coalitional deviations that do not necessarily result in finer deviations. Unfortunately, as pointed out by Ray and Vohra (1997) and Ray (2007), this would then result in possibly infinite chains of deviations because of cycles - the same partition can figure infinitely often in any sequence.[32]

The issue of existence of EBAs is not of any interest since π^* is always an EBA. What is of interest is whether efficient outcomes can be sustained as EBAs. This issue goes back to the Coase (1937) who asserted that in a world of complete information, and if there are no restrictions on negotiations, individuals should be able to reach efficient outcomes. However, Ray and Vohra (1997, 2001) and Diamantoudi and Xue (2007) produce examples to show that this optimism is misplaced. The following example from Ray (2007) illustrates.

Example 15 *Consider a public good economy with 3 symmetric agents, where m units of a private good (money) generate m units of public good, but generates utility cost of* $(1/3)m^3$. *Individuals have endowment of money. Any coalition of s will contribute per capita amount of* $m(s)$ *to maximize*

$$sm(s) - (1/3)m(s)^3$$

If production elsewhere is z, then payoff to coalition of size s is

$$s[z + (2/3)s^{3/2}]$$

Hence, the partition function is

$$v(123) = 6\sqrt{3}, v(1|2|3) = (8/3, 8/3, 8/3), v(1|23) = (2\sqrt{2} + 2/3, 2[1 + 2/3\sqrt{8}])$$

Of course, the grand coalition is the efficient partition. But, this cannot be sustained as an EBA. The per capita payoff in the grand coalition is $2\sqrt{3} < 2\sqrt{2} + 2/3$. If i leaves N, jk will stay together. That is, $\{\{i\}, \{jk\}\}$ is an EBA. But this ensures that the grand coalition cannot be an EBA.

Levy (2004) and Ray and Vohra (2001) illustrate the possibility of applying the concept of EBAs in specific contexts.

[32] Diamantoudi and Xue (2007) extend the notion of EBAs by allowing for such deviations. Their solution concept is $V(>>)$. But, as Chwe (1994) pointed out, this can be too restrictive as a solution concept.

5. GROUP FORMATION IN REAL TIME

In the preceding sections, we have discussed the formation of networks and coalitions in a static setting; that is, one where the set of individuals form either a network or a coalition structure once and for all with payoffs being generated only once. In this section, we describe some recent literature that models group formation in a dynamic context where for instance, networks evolve over time or coalitions form and break up as individuals renegotiate for better payoffs. Although there has been relatively little work in this dynamic framework, the approach has some advantages over the more conventional approach. First, there are many contexts where it is perhaps a better description of how groups *actually* interact. For example, relationships typically evolve over time, suggesting that the structure of links in a communication network does change over time. Second, as Konishi and Ray (2003) point out, cycles in sequences of deviations that pose problems for a satisfactory definition of farsightedness can be handled easily in a dynamic setting. Payoffs from cycles can be evaluated just as any other sequence of deviations.

We first describe the dynamic formation of models of networks and coalitions where players do not bargain over payoffs. That is, these are models where in every period, each player's payoff is specified completely by the network or coalition structure which forms. We then go on to describe models where per period payoffs are determined by a dynamic bargaining procedure.

5.1 Dynamic network formation

Watts (2001) was the first to study the dynamic evolution of networks for the specific case of Jackson-Wolinsky communication networks. We describe a more general framework by not restricting attention to communication networks. Time is divided into discrete time periods $T = \{1, 2, \ldots,\}$. In any period t, g_t is the historically given graph. A pair i, j meet randomly with probability p_{ij} in period t. The selected pair can decide to:

- **(i)** Form the link ij if $ij \notin g_t$. In keeping with the usual assumption in network formation, the link forms if both i and j agree to form the link.
- **(ii)** Either i or j can unilaterally break the link ij if $ij \in g_t$.

Assume that agents are *myopic*, so that each pair of active agents in any period t choose their actions only by looking at their t-period payoff. Not surprisingly, Watts is able to show that in the case of communication networks, the dynamic process does not always converge to the efficient network. For instance, if $\delta < c$, then no link can ever form since the pair forming the first link is better off (in a myopic sense) by not forming the link.[33]

[33] On the other hand, the star network is efficient if $(\delta - \delta^2) < c < \delta + \frac{n-2}{2}\delta^2$.

Of course, the specification of myopic behavior is often an extreme assumption. Suppose, for instance, that the formation of the first link results in a payoff of $-\varepsilon$ to each agent involved in the link, while two or more links give each linked agent a payoff of 1 million. Myopic agents simply cannot get the process off the ground, and so cannot exploit even very high increasing returns to network formation. There are two ways of avoiding this phenomenon. First, one can stick to the assumption of myopic behavior, but allow for the possibility that there may be exogenous shocks or "mutations," which cause a link to form (that would otherwise not form due to myopia), and thus help the process of network process. Second, one can assume that players are farsighted and so be willing to suffer a small initial loss in order to reap large gains in the future. Both avenues have been explored in the literature, with Jackson and Watts (2002), Feri (2007) and Tercieux and Vannetelbosch (2006) adopting the first approach, while Dutta, Ghosal and Ray (2005) model farsighted behavior in the dynamic network formation. We describe each in turn.

Jackson and Watts (2002) add random perturbations to the basic stochastic process described above, and examine the distribution over networks as the level of random perturbation goes to 0. The basic stochastic process and myopic behavior gives rise to the notion of *improving paths*. An improving path from any network g is a sequence of networks $\{g_0, g_1, \ldots g_K\}$ with $g = g_0$ such that for each $k = 0, \ldots, K-1$

(i) $g_{k+1} = g_k - ij$ for some ij such that $Y_i(g_k - ij) > Y_i(g_k)$, or

(ii) $g_{k+1} = g_k + ij$ for some ij such that $Y_l(g_k + ij) > Y_l(g_k)$ for $l = i, j$.

So, an improving path is one where each pair of adjacent networks differ only by the addition or deletion of just one link, and the link addition or deletion is the result of myopic payoff-maximizing behavior by the concerned pair of agents. Improving paths must lead either to pairwise stable networks or cycles where the same set of networks is visited repeatedly over time.

Now consider a process of mutation so that in any period t, after actions are taken by the active pair, there is a probability $\epsilon > 0$ that a tremble takes place, and the link is deleted if present and added if absent. This process defines a Markov chain where the states are the networks existing at the end of every period. The Markov chain has a unique stationary distribution that converges to a unique limiting distribution as ϵ converges to 0. Call a network *stochastically stable* if it is in the support of this limiting distribution. Jackson and Watts (2002) show that the set of stochastically stable networks are those networks that minimize *resistance*.[34] Jackson and Watts provide an interesting application of their analysis to matching models like the marriage market and the college-admissions model. They show that the set of stochastically stable networks coincides with the set of core matchings in these models.

[34] The concept of *resistance* is originally due to Freidlin and Wentzell (1984). The resistance of a network measures how many mutations are needed in order to get away from the network to an improving path leading to another network.

Dutta, Ghosal and Ray (2005) modify the analysis of Konishi and Ray (2003) (to which we turn in the next subsection) to model farsighted behavior when networks evolve over time. Unlike Watts (2001) and Jackson and Watts (2002), they assume that players take into account the discounted value of all future payoffs from any sequence of networks. They also allow the active pair in period t to unilaterally break some existing links in g_t.

Define a state to be a pair (g, ij) where g represents the current network while ij is the pair of active agents in any period. A (mixed) **Markov** strategy for any player is a probability distribution over possible actions at each state s in which player i is an active agent. It is Markovian because the actions of each pair of active agents depends only on the state s, and not on the history of how the network evolved in the past.

A strategy profile precipitates for each state s some probability measure λ_s over the feasible set $F(s)$ of future networks starting from s.

So, a Markov process is induced on the set S of states; while λ_s describes the movement to a new network, the given random choice of active players moves the system to a new active pair.

The process creates values for each player. For any strategy profile μ,

$$V_i(s,\mu) = \sum_{g' \in F(s)} \lambda_s(g')[Y_i(g') + \delta \sum_{i'j'} \pi(i'j') V_i(s', \mu)]$$

where $\delta \in (0,1)$ is the discount factor, λ_s is the probability over $F(s)$ associated with μ, $\pi(i'\,j')$ is the probability that a pair $i'\,j'$ will be active "tomorrow", and s' stands for the state $(g', i'\,j')$.

An *equilibrium process of network formation* is a strategy profile μ with the property that there is no active pair at any state s that can benefit — either unilaterally or bilaterally — by departing from $\mu(s)$. Notice that this is the dynamic counterpart of the static concept of pairwise Nash equilibrium.

Define a state to be *absorbing* if there is no deviation from that state. A state is *strongly absorbing* if it is absorbing, and the process converges to that state from every other state. Strongly absorbing states are the dynamic counterpart of stable networks in the static setting.

DGR show that if the network structure satisfies Link Monotonicity, then for all δ, there will be *some* equilibrium μ^* such that the complete graph g^N will be strongly absorbing. Of course, Link Monotonicity does not ensure that the complete network is efficient. However, they also show that a strong form of increasing returns (which implies that g^N is the unique efficient network), and ensures that g^N is a strongly absorbing graph for *some* equilibrium. This positive result cannot be improved to show that the complete network is absorbing for *all* equilibria — static coordination failures can occur even with strong increasing returns to scale. This is illustrated in the next example.

Example 16 *Let* $N = \{1, 2, 3, 4\}$, $v(g^N) = 4$, $v(\{ij\}) = -100$ *and* $v(g) < 0$ *for all other* g. *Let the allocation rule be equal division within each component, and* $\delta > \frac{6}{151}$.

Let μ be such that each pair of active agents breaks all links at all networks, and also refuses to form any link. Then, the empty graph is the strongly absorbing graph.

This also turns out to be an equilibrium. For by following this strategy, $V_i(g, ij, \mu) = 0$. It is enough to check for deviation at g^N. If ij do not break any links at g^N, then

$$V(g^N, ij, \mu') = \frac{6(6 - 151\delta)}{(6 - \delta)^2} < 0$$

5.2 Coalition formation over time

Konishi and Ray (2003) (henceforth KR) study coalition formation in a dynamic setting. Let us restrict attention to characteristic function games, where for technical convenience assume that each coalition S has a nonempty and *finite* set of payoff vectors in $\mathbb{R}^S$. Let X be the finite set of possible states, where a state is a pair $x = (\pi, u)$, where π is a coalition structure and u is such that u_S is a feasible payoff vector for each $S \in \pi$.

For each coalition S, let $F_S(x) = \{y \in X | x \to_S y\}$ be the set of states that S can reach by a coalitional deviation. KR consider a scenario in which at current state x, some coalition S is selected at random, and the selected coalition then chooses (perhaps randomly) some feasible state out of $F_S(x)$. So, there is a random transition from one state to another. This process is captured in the following definition.

Definition 16 *A process of coalition formation (PCF) is a transition probability* $p: X \times X \to [0,1]$ *so that* $\sum_{y \in X} p(x, y) = 1$.

Player i's payoff from a sequence of probabilities $\{\lambda_t\}$ is

$$\sum_{t=0}^{\infty} \delta_i^t \Big(\sum_{x \in X} \lambda_t(x) u_i(x) \Big)$$

Hence, each PCF induces a value function for each i.

$$V_i(x, p) = (1 - \delta) u_i(x) + \delta_i \sum_{y \in X} p(x, y) V_i(y, p)$$

Fix x, S, p. Say that S has a *weakly profitable move* from x if there is $y \in F_S(x)$ such that $V_i(y, p) \geq V_i(x, p)$ for all $i \in S$. S has a *strictly profitable move* if the inequality is strict for all $i \in S$.

A move y is *efficient* for S if there is no z such that $V_i(z, p) > V_i(y, p)$ for all i.

Definition 17 *A PCF* p *is an equilibrium process of coalition process (EPCF) if*

(i) *whenever* $p(x, y) > 0$ *for some* $y \neq x$, *then there is* S *such that* y *is a weakly profitable and efficient move for* S;

(ii) *if there is some strictly profitable move from* x, *then* $p(x, x) = 0$ *and there is a strictly profitable and efficient* y *such that* $p(x, y) > 0$.

A PCF is an "equilibrium" if at all dates and all states, a coalitional move to another state is "justified" only if the move gives the coalition a higher present value. Notice that this incorporates farsighted behavior because individuals evaluate PCFs in terms of the discounted value of future payoffs. KR show that an equilibrium process of coalition formation exists. An equilibrium PCF may not necessarily be *deterministic*, where a deterministic PCF has $p(x,y) \in \{0,1\}$.

KR establish a striking result, which provides a strong justification for the *core* as a solution concept in this dynamic setting. Call a state x to be *absorbing* if $p(x, x) = 1$, and a PCF to be absorbing if for every y, there is an absorbing x s.t. $p^k(y, x) > 0$. A PCF has unique limit if it is absorbing and possesses a single absorbing state. They show that every core allocation can be described as the limit of some deterministic EPCF. Conversely, if a deterministic EPCF has a unique limit, then that limit must be a core allocation.

What happens if deterministic EPCFs do not have a unique absorbing limit? KR show that all absorbing deterministic EPCFs have absorbing states that lie in the LCS. They also construct an interesting example, which shows that not all states in the LCS can be supported as absorbing states of EPCFs. This illustrates the point we made in the previous section that the LCS is too "large."

This line of thought also suggests that the set of such absorbing states can itself be interpreted as a farsighted solution set. Clearly, the analysis of group formation in a dynamic setting is a very promising area, where much work needs to be done. Perhaps, it would be more fruitful to focus on specific applications rather than adopt the more abstract framework.

5.2.1 Coalitional bargaining over time

The coalitional bargaining models described in Section 3 assume that coalitions leave the game after they are formed. The extensive forms do not allow for renegotiations, and the Coasian intuition that bargaining should allow players to reach efficient outcomes is not supported by the models. Clearly, the assumption that coalitions exit the game after they are formed is a convenient device to solve the coalitional bargaining model recursively, but is hard to justify in real world negotiations. The models we discuss here allow players to renegotiate agreements continuously.

Seidmann and Winter (1998) propose a model with continuous renegotiation, which is a direct extension of Chatterjee et al. (1993).[35] At the initial phase, one player is chosen according to a fixed protocol to be the proposer. This player can either pass

[35] This is the model with "reversible" actions in Seidmann and Winter (1998).

the initiative to another player or propose an agreement (S, x) where x is a vector of payoffs for all members of coalition S satisfying $\sum x_i = v(S)$. If one member of S rejects the offer, she becomes the proposer at the next period. If all members agree, the coalition is formed, and (S, x) becomes the current state. Any state of the game can thus be described as a list of "interim agreements" (S_t, x_t) between the players. After the initial period, the game enters a phase of renegotiation. The protocol selects one player who can either pass the initiative to another player or make a proposal (R, y), which must satisfy $\sum y_i = v(R)$ and if $R \cap S_t \neq \emptyset$ then $S_t \subseteq R$. This last condition states that a proposal must include *all the members of interim coalitions* and defines the role of interim coalitions in the model.

Seidmann and Winter (1998)'s main emphasis is on the dynamics of coalition formation. They first show that stationary perfect equilibria of the game will always lead to the formation of the efficient grand coalition. However, this process can either be immediate or gradual, according to the properties of the underlying coalitional game.

Theorem 11 *If the core of the underlying coalitional game is empty, then there exists $\underline{\delta} < 1$ such that for all $\delta \geq \underline{\delta}$, the game does not possess a stationary perfect equilibrium where the grand coalition is formed immediately.*

The previous theorem clarifies conditions under which the grand coalition forms immediately. It shows that agreement *must be gradual* if the game has an empty core. While this result provides a necessary condition for immediate agreement, it does not give a sufficient condition. Seidmann and Winter (1998) note that in a class of games where the marginal worth of the grand coalition is very large (and hence the core is nonempty), there will always be an equilibrium with immediate agreement.

Okada (2000) proposes a model of bargaining with renegotiation based on Seidmann and Winter (1998) where proposers are chosen at random every period. Based on Okada (1996)'s analysis, he shows that agreements will be reached at every period, so that the grand coalition forms in at most $(n-1)$ steps.

Gomes (2005) extends the analysis to games in partition function form. In his model, proposers are chosen at random (as in Okada (2000)) and probability p_i denotes the recognition probability of player i. A contract consists in a coalition S and a vector of contingent payoffs $x_i(\pi)$, which depend on the entire coalition structure π and verify $\sum_{i \in S} x_i(\pi) = v(S, \pi)$ for all coalition structures such that $S \in \pi$. Gomes (2005)'s first result extends Okada (2000)'s analysis in showing that, when the grand coalition is efficient, it will ultimately form in a finite number of steps. He also proposes a condition on the partition function that guarantees that the grand coalition forms immediately. In order to describe this condition, define, for any collection $\mathcal{S}$ of coalitions in a coalition structure π, the coalition structure obtained by merging all coalitions in $\mathcal{S}$ by $\pi\mathcal{S}$, i.e. $\pi\mathcal{S} = \pi \backslash (\cup_{S \in \mathcal{S}} S) \cup (\cup_{S \in \mathcal{S}} S)$. (By an abuse of notation, we shall also denote $\mathcal{S} = \cup_{S \in \mathcal{S}} S$.)

Theorem 12 *Suppose that for all coalition structures π and all collections of coalitions $\mathcal{S}$ in π,*

$$v(\mathcal{S},\pi\mathcal{S})+\sum_{i\in\mathcal{S}}p_i(v(N)-\sum_{T\in\pi\mathcal{S}}v(T,\pi\mathcal{S}))\leq\sum_{S\in\mathcal{S}}(v(S,\pi)+\sum_{i\in S}p_i(v(N)-\sum_{T\in\pi}v(T,\pi))),$$

then there exists a stationary perfect equilibrium where the grand coalition forms immediately at any state. Conversely, if this condition fails, there exists a state at which the grand coalition does not form in any stationary perfect equilibrium for δ large enough.

Gomes and Jehiel (2005) extend the preceding analysis by considering a general setup, described by a set of states in the economy, and an effectivity function over the states. At every period in time, a player is chosen at random to make an offer, consisting of a transition from the current state to a new state, and a vector of transfers to members of the coalition effective in that transition. Any Markov perfect equilibrium of this game generates a Markov process, and Gomes and Jehiel (2005) first study the convergence properties of this process. Their main result shows that, if players are sufficiently patient, the aggregate value is the same in any recurrent set.[36]

Theorem 13 *The aggregate equilibrium values are approximately the same at all states in the recurrent sets for all economies when δ converges to one.*

As a consequence of this theorem, generically, the Markov process can only admit one recurrent set set. The preceding theorem does not imply that the process always converge to an *efficient* state. In fact, this may not be the case, and one needs the following sufficient condition to guarantee that the process converges to an efficient recurrent set.

Definition 18 *A state a is* negative externality free *if for all $i \in N$, all sequences of moves, $a \rightarrow_{S_1} \rightarrow \ldots \rightarrow_{S_K} b$ involving coalitions $S_k \subseteq N\backslash\{i\}$, $v_i(b) \geq v_i(a)$. A state a is an ENF state if it is efficient and negative externality free.*

Theorem 14 *Any ENF state is in a recurrent set. Hence, if there exists an ENF state, the Markov process always converges to an efficient allocation.*

Hyndman and Ray (2007) build on Gomes and Jehiel (2005) and Konishi and Ray (2003) to propose a general dynamic model of coalition formation, without imposing any stationarity restriction. Like Gomes and Jehiel (2005), they consider an abstract set of states, and an effectivity function, specifying which coalitions are effective in the transition between states. Their first result shows that, in the absence of externalities across coalitions, all equilibria are asymptotically efficient.

Theorem 15 *In characteristic function games with permanently binding agreements, any benign subgame perfect equilibrium (where players always opt for a strategy that makes other players better off when they are indifferent) results in an asymptotically efficient payoff.*

In the presence of externalities, the efficiency result fails, as the following example shows:

[36] A recurrent set of a Markov process is the set of states which are reached in the long run, i.e., a set of states that the Markov process never leaves once it has reached it, and such that the Markov process visits all states in the recurrent set.

Example 17 $N = 3$ *and payoff vectors are as follows* $v(1|2|3) = (6, 6, 6)$, $v(1|23) = (0, 10, 10)$, $v(12|3) = (5, 5, 0)$, $v\ (13|2) = (5, 0, 5)$, $v(123) = (0, 0, 0)$

In this example, the two states $\{12|3\}$ and $\{13|2\}$ are Pareto dominated by state $\{1|2|3\}$, but they are absorbing states. Player 1 will never accept to move to state $\{1|2|3\}$, because she knows that players 2 and 3 will subsequently form coalition 23. Hence, any transition out of the two states $\{12|3\}$ and $\{13|2\}$ will be blocked by player 1.

Hyndman and Ray (2007) provide sufficient conditions under which games with externalities result in efficient outcomes (e.g., "grand coalition superadditivity," which states that the grand coalition is efficient). They also provide a four-player example where, starting from any state, the outcome is asymptotically inefficient. Hence, the final conclusion of their analysis is mixed: the presence of externalities does indeed lead to inefficiencies, which can only be alleviated by placing stringent restrictions on the value functions.

The previous models assume that players have the ability to continuously renegotiate agreements until the grand coalition forms. Two studies have considered what happens when players choose *endogenously* whether to exit the game. In these contributions, the players' decisions is whether to take an outside option (defined by the current contract or agreement) or to continue negotiating. As the grand coalition is always assumed to be efficient, the issue is whether players ever choose to exit the game inefficiently early.

Seidmann and Winter (1998) argue, through an example, that this may indeed occur in a model of coalitional bargaining. The model they construct follows the same rules as the model of coalitional bargaining with renegotiation described above, with the following differences.[37] At any period, after a contract has been offered and respondents have made their decisions, players are given the opportunity to implement the current agreement. Implementation means that the players commit, in an irreversible fashion, to leave the negotiations with their current agreement. In Seidmann and Winter (1998)'s model, all players simultaneously decide whether to implement, and every player has a veto power over the decision for his coalition. In other words, a contract involving a coalition S of players is implemented as soon as one of the players in S chooses to implement it.[38]

Example 18 $N = 3$, $v(S) = v > 2/3$ *if* $|S| = 2$, $v(N) = 1$. *The protocol specifies that, after a two-player coalition forms, the next proposer is the outsider.*

In this example, all stationary perfect equilibria are inefficient, and result in players forming a coalition of size 2 and then exiting with positive probability. Note first that because the core of the game is empty, the grand coalition cannot form immediately.

[37] Seidmann and Winter (1998) call this version of their model the model with "irreversible decisions."

[38] This last hypothesis allows for "trivial" equilibria, where all players choose to implement the contract. These equilibria of course give rise to inefficient exit, but arise purely because of coordination failures among members of a coalition.

Suppose that the grand coalition indeed forms after a two-player coalition is formed. Without loss of generality, suppose that the coalition {1,2} forms. The interim contract is given by (x_1, x_2) with $x_1 + x_2 = v$. This defines the outside options of players 1 and 2. Now suppose that player 3 makes an offer, which is indeed accepted. If the outside options of the other two players are not binding, then the offer will converge to $(\delta/(1+2\delta), \delta/(1+2\delta), 1/(1+2\delta))$. But, because $v > 2/3$ either x_1 or x_2 must be larger than 1/3 and one of the two outside options has to be binding – a contradiction. If now one of the outside options is binding (say x_1) then, as long as $\delta < 1$, player 1 has an incentive to implement the contract early rather than wait to obtain his outside option.

Bloch and Gomes (2006) revisit the issue of endogenous exit in a model with random proposers and externalities across coalitions. They assume that players are engaged in two parallel interactions: they form coalitions, and take part in a game in strategic form, which determines the flow payoffs at every period. Every period is separated into two subphases. Players first take part in a contracting phase, where one of the players, chosen at random, proposes to buy out the resources of other players. Every member of the coalition then responds in turn to the offer, and resources are bought only if all coalition members agree. In the second phase, the action phase, all active players choose an action in a set that contains both reversible and irreversible decisions. Reversible decisions (or inside options) determine the flow payoff of the current period, irreversible decisions (or outside options) affect the payoff of all future periods.

Bloch and Gomes (2006) distinguish between two cases: outside options are *pure* if every player is guaranteed to obtain the same payoff by exiting, irrespective of the choices of other players. Otherwise, the model displays externalities in outside options. Bloch and Gomes (2006) first show that when the choice of proposers is random, in contrast to Seidmann and Winter (1998), there always exists a stationary perfect equilibrium where players make acceptable offers at each period. More precisely, one has to refine the set of equilibria, to take care of coordination failures arising from the fact that all players simultaneously choose whether to exit (and hence, all players exiting may be an equilibrium, even though it is a dominated equilibrium for all the players). Bloch and Gomes (2006) define $\varepsilon - R$ equilibria as equilibria where all players remain in the game with probability ε at every state.

Theorem 16 *For any underlying game with pure outside options and any ϵ, there exists $\underline{\delta}$ such that for all $\delta \geq \underline{\delta}$ an $\varepsilon - R$ stationary perfect equilibrium exists. Furthermore, as δ converges to 1, the probability of exit in all $\varepsilon - R$ equilibria converges to zero, and hence the outcome of the coalitional bargaining game is approximately efficient.*

However, Bloch and Gome (2006) note that this result depends crucially on the fact that outside options are pure, and hence the same outside option is available from one period to the next. In games with externalities in outside options, the argument breaks down, and all equilibria may be inefficient.

6. THE TENSION BETWEEN EFFICIENCY AND STABILITY

A recurrent theme in the previous sections has been that when coalitions or networks form endogenously, the efficient group structure is often not supportable as a stable outcome. Notice that the failure of the efficient group structure to be supported as a stable outcome occurs in a framework of complete information and in a frictionless world – there are no transaction costs constraining the attainment of the "optimal" structure. This seems to go squarely against the Coasian intuition that rational agents should be able to attain efficiency.

Following the work of JW, several authors have discussed the different ways in which stability can be reconciled with efficiency in the context of the endogenous formation of networks. We review some of this literature in this section.

JW show that if an allocation rule satisfies *component balance* and *anonymity*,[39] then there may be value functions for which no efficient network is pair-wise stable.

Theorem 17 *Let the allocation rule satisfy anonymity and pairwise stability. Then, there is a value function such that no efficient network is pairwise stable.*

The proof consists of a counter example. Let $N = \{1, 2, 3\}$ and consider the value function v such that $v(g) = 12$ if g is the complete graph, or if g has exactly one link, and $v(g) = 13$ if g has exactly two links.

Then, g is efficient if and only if it has exactly two links. The proof is completed by showing that no graph with two links can be pairwise stable if the allocation rule Y satisfies anonymity and component balance.

Since v is symmetric, it is sufficient to show that if $g^1 = \{ij, ik\}$, then g^1 is not pairwise stable. Let $g^2 = \{ij\}$. Now, $Y_i(g^2, v) = 6$ since Y satisfies anonymity and component balance. So, $Y_i(g^1, v) \geq 6$ if g^1 is to be pairwise stable. Otherwise, i can sever his link with k.

Hence, from Anonymity we have that $Y_k(g^1, v) = Y_j(g^1, v) \leq 3.5$. But, now both j and k have the incentive to form the link jk since both get 4 at the complete graph.

This shows that g^2 is not pairwise stable.[40]

The tension between efficiency and stability surfaces again even in a dynamic setting when networks evolve over time. DGR (2005) prove a dynamic version of the JW result by constructing an example in which no efficient network is strongly efficient if the allocation rule satisfies efficiency and *limited liability*.

Definition 19: *Y satisfies limited liability if for all $i \in N$, $i \in N(h)$ and $v(h) \geq 0$ implies $Y_i(g, v) \geq 0$ for every $g \in G$.*

[39] Component Balance means that there can be no cross-subsidization across components of a network. Anonymity means that individuals who are "alike" in the sense of occupying symmetric positions in the network as well as in terms of contribution to the value must be given equal rewards.

[40] For a similar result for directed networks, see Dutta and Jackson (2000).

Example 19 *Let $N = \{1, 2, 3\}$. Consider a symmetric value function where $v(g) = 2\alpha$ if g has just one link, $v(g^N) = 3\alpha$ and $v(g) = 0$ otherwise, where α is some positive number.*

The unique efficient graph is the complete graph g^N. However, there is no pure strategy equilibrium μ^* such that g^N is strongly absorbing.

For consider any pure strategy equilibrium μ^*. Notice that since Y is anonymous, $Y_i(\{i, j\}) = Y_i(g^N) = \alpha$. Also, for all other g, $Y_k(g) = 0$ for all $k \in N$ from limited liability.

If g^N is to be strongly absorbing, then there must be a path from a one-link network to the complete network. In particular, this means that there must be some pair (i, j) and k such i, j form the link ij and then (say) i forms the link with k.

Suppose i and j have formed the link ij. Then, i and j both have a payoff of α. Notice that no graph gives them a higher payoff while the two-link graph gives both i, j a strictly lower payoff. Clearly, neither i nor j have an incentive to form the link with k.

This is essentially a heuristic proof of the following theorem.

Theorem 18 *Suppose the allocation rule satisfies anonymity and limited liability. Then, there is a value function such that no efficient network is strongly absorbing.*

The literature on ways of resolving the tension between efficiency and stability can be divided into two broad areas. The first approach assumes that the individual agents who form the nodes can influence their payoffs or rewards only through their decisions on which network to form. In other words, the *allocation rule* itself is specified exogenously to the agents. In the second approach, the agents determine both the network as well as the allocation rule, perhaps through bargaining.

Consider the first approach, and suppose the allocation rule is such that *all* agents receive the *average* payoff $v(g)/n$. The "average rule" fully aligns individual incentives with social goals, so that there can be no conflict between efficiency and stability with this rule. However, the average rule does not satisfy Component Balance, one of the specified restrictions on the allocation rule in the J-W Theorem. Of course, one could ask why it is important to restrict attention to allocation rules satisfying Component Balance. The example used to prove the JW Theorem provides an answer. Consider any of the one link graphs g, say $g = \{ij\}$. The average rule requires that k be given 4. But why should i and j agree to this rule? If they have the option of breaking away from the "society," they will certainly exercise this option.

A rule that satisfies Component Balance but is similar in spirit to the average rule is the "Component Average Rule," which divides payoffs equally within each component. Denoting this rule as Y^a, we have

$$Y_i^a(v, g) = \frac{v(h)}{n_h} \text{ for all } i \in N(h), h \in C(g)$$

It is of some interest to ask the condition under which Y^a will ensure stability of efficient networks. For any network g, call ij a *critical link* in g if $g-ij$ has more components than g. In other words, the severance of a critical link breaks up an existing link into two components.

Definition 20 *A pair* (v, g) *satisfies Critical Link Monotonicity if for any critical link in* g *and its associated components* h, h_1, h_2, $v(h) \geq v(h_1) + v(h_2)$ *implies that* $v(h)/n_h \geq \max[v(h_1)/n_{h_1}, v(h_2)/n_{h_2}]$.

The following theorem is due to JW.

Theorem 19 *Let* g *be any efficient network. Then,* g *is pairwise stable given the allocation rule* Y^a *iff* (g, v) *satisfies Critical Link Monotonicity.*

This theorem uses Y^a. An interesting question is to characterize sets of value functions under which efficient networks can be supported as pairwise stable networks for other allocation rules.

The Mechanism Design Approach

Suppose the implicit assumption or prediction is that only those networks that correspond to Pairwise Nash equilibria or Strong Nash equilibrium of the link formation game will form. Then our interest in the *ethical* properties of the allocation rule should be restricted only to how the rule behaves *on the class of these networks*. That is, since networks outside this class will not form, why should we bother about how the allocation rule behaves on these networks?

So, suppose the prediction is that only strongly stable networks will form. Then, if we want symmetry of the allocation rule, we should be satisfied if the allocation rule is symmetric on the *subdomain* of strongly stable graphs. This gives some freedom about how to specify the allocation rule. Choose some efficient $g^* \in G$. Suppose s^* induces g^*, and we want to ensure that g^* is strongly stable. Now, consider any g that is different from g^*, and let s induce g. Then, the allocation rule must *punish* at least one agent who has deviated from s^* to s. This is possible only if a deviant can be *identified*. This is trivial if there is some $(ij) \in g \backslash g^*$, because then both i and j must concur in forming the extra link (ij). However, if $g \subset g^*$, say $(ij) \in g^* \backslash g$, then *either* i *or* j can unilaterally break the link. The only way to ensure that the deviant is punished is to punish *both* i and j.

Several simple punishment schemes can be devised to ensure that at least two agents who have deviated from s^* are punished sufficiently to make the deviation unprofitable. However, since the allocation rule has to be component balanced, these punishment schemes may result in some other agent being given more than the agent gets in g^*. This possibility creates a complication because the punishment scheme has to *satisfy an additional property*. Since we also want to ensure that inefficient graphs are *not* strongly stable, agents have to be provided with an incentive to deviate from any graph that is not strongly efficient. Hence, the punishment scheme has to be relatively more sophisticated. Dutta and Mutuswami (1997) describe conditions under which this approach will reconcile the conflict between efficiency and stability.

An example of the second approach is the paper by Bloch and Jackson (2007) on network formation with transfers. Bloch and Jackson (2007) allow payoffs to be determined endogenously since players are allowed to make transfers. They highlight two difficulties in reaching efficient networks in a model of network formation with transfers. The first difficulty is due to the presence of externalities. If the formation of a link produces positive externalities on other players, direct transfers may not be sufficient to attain efficiency, as illustrated in the following example:

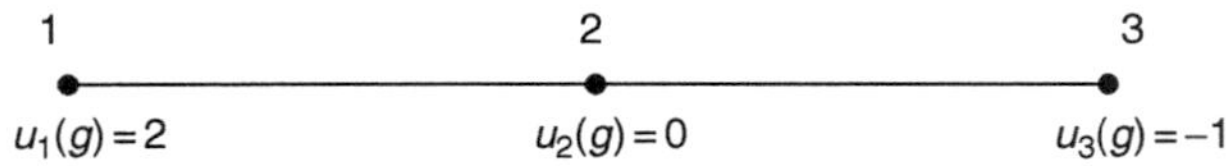

All other networks result in a utilities of 0 for all players.

The efficient network is the line $\{12, 23\}$. For this network to be supported, we must have $t^3_{23} = -1$. But if $t^2_{23} = 1$, player 2 has an incentive to deviate, so network $\{12, 23\}$ cannot be supported in equilibrium. Notice that if player 1 could subsidize the formation of link 23, this difficulty will disappear.

However, there remains another, more subtle difficulty, due to the fact that players' marginal benefits from a set of links may not be equal to the sum of the marginal benefits of every link in the set.

Example 20 *Consider a three-player society and a profile of utility functions described as follows. Any player gets a payoff of 0 if he or she does not have any links. Player 1 gets a payoff of 2 if she has exactly one link, and a payoff of 1 if she has two links. Player 2 gets a payoff of −2 if he has exactly one link, and a payoff of 0 if she has two links. Player 3′s payoff function is similar to that of player 2*

It is clear from this specification that all players' payoffs depend only on the configuration of their own links and so there are no externalities in payoffs. However, we claim that the efficient network structure (the complete network) cannot be reached in equilibrium. By setting $t^2_{2i} = 0$ for each i, player 2 gets a payoff of at least 0. The same is true for player 3. Thus, players 2 and 3 must have a payoff of at least 0 in any equilibrium. Now, suppose by contradiction that the complete network were supported in an equilibrium. It would follow that $t^1_{1i} = 0$ for at least one i, or otherwise one of players 2 and 3 would have a negative payoff. Without loss of generality, suppose that $t^1_{12} = 0$. Player 1′s payoff would then be $1 - t^1_{12} - t^1_{13}$. Suppose that player 1 deviated so that network 13, 23 forms. Then, player 1′s payoff would become $2 - t^1_{13}$, which is greater than $1 - t^1_{12} - t^1_{13}$. For this inefficiency to disappear, one needs to allow transfers that are contingent on the entire network.

7. CONCLUSIONS AND OPEN PROBLEMS

This paper has surveyed a large number of models by which agents driven by their self-interest choose to cooperate in coalitions and networks. The models belong to three broad categories. The earlier literature considered static models of group formation, where players simultaneously announce the links or group they want to form.

Following Rubinstein (1981)'s analysis of two-player bargaining, the next step has been to represent group and network formation as a sequential bargaining process. Finally, more recent work has focussed on general, abstract dynamic processes of coalition and network formation among farsighted players.

The three categories of models have advantages and disadvantages. Static games are easy to analyze, but typically exhibit multiple equilibria due to coordination failures, and refinements must be used to obtain clear predictions. Sequential bargaining models generically result in a single outcome, but the characterization of equilibrium networks or coalition structures requires complex recursive computations, and the outcome of the game may depend on details of the bargaining protocol. Dynamic processes are immune to that last criticism, as they model the process of network or group formation as an abstract game, but cannot be used to predict the exact outcome of particular models of cooperation.

What are the next steps in the study of coalition and network formation? In our opinion, three basic issues remain unexplored and should stimulate new research in the next few years.

Robustness Analysis: The large variety of models of coalition and network formation results in a large variety of predictions on the coalitions and networks that are likely to form in specific situations. For sequential games, the outcome of the process of coalition and network formation depends on fine details of the bargaining protocol. One needs to get a better understanding of the mapping between the procedure of coalition or network formation and the equilibrium outcomes. What are the features of the procedure of coalition or network formation that guarantees that efficient outcomes arise? Which processes result in single or multiple outcomes? How does the absence or presence of transfers affect the outcome of the procedure and the ability to reach efficient results? Can players manipulate procedures of coalition formation to their advantage? The answer to these important questions requires a meta-analysis of the procedures of coalition and network formation.

Coalitions versus Networks: This survey shows that networks and coalitions are related yet different modes of cooperation among agents. In one sense, networks are more general descriptions of cooperation possibilities, as they include information not only about the identity of groups of agents who cooperate (the components of the network), but also about the details of the structure of bilateral links that favors cooperation. For each network, one can derive a single coalition structure by distinguishing network components, but each coalition structure may be obtained from a large number of different networks. At another level though, networks and coalitions are different but unrelated ways of describing cooperation: some situations are inherently bilateral (e.g., face to face communication) whereas others are multilateral (e.g., large meetings). The choice between describing cooperation through coalitions or networks is then driven by the application. Even when the description of gains from cooperation is the same for bilateral and multilateral interactions (for example, when gains from cooperation are described by a game in partition function form), the process of cooperation (bilateral or multilateral) may affect the outcome. Forming bilateral links is easier than agreeing with a group of agents, inducing more cooperation in networks than coalitions. But, if agents can unilaterally sever some of their links while keeping others, they may be less likely to cooperate in the first place. Examples can be given to show that network formation models result in more cooperation as in the formation of cost-reducing alliances among firms studied by Bloch (1995) for coalitions and Goyal and Joshi (2003) for networks. But there are also examples pointing in the other direction where cooperation is easier in coalitions than networks as in the models of informal insurance in groups and networks of Genicot and Ray (2003) and Bloch, Genicot and Ray (2008).

Incomplete information: All the models considered in this survey assume that agents possess complete information on gains from cooperation. Relaxing this assumption is a difficult task, as it would introduce a number of new problems essentially revolving around the amount of information, which can be credibly shared among members of a coalition. compatibility. Wilson (1978) initiated some recent literature on the core of the exchange economy with incomplete information.[41] However, the literature group formation with incomplete information is still in its infancy, and much remains to be done.

[41] Forge et al. (2007) is an elegant survey of some of this literature.

REFERENCES

d'Aspremont, C., Jacquemin, A., Jaskold Gasbszewicz, J., Weymark, J., 1983. On the Stability of Price Leadership. Can. J. Econ. 16, 17–25.

Aumann, R., Myerson, R., 1988. Endogenous Formation of Links Between Players and of Coalitions: An Application of the Shapley Value. In: Roth, A. (Ed.), The Shapley Value: Essays in Honor of Lloyd Shapley. Cambridge University Press, pp. 175–191.

Bala, V., Goyal, S., 2000. A Noncooperative Model of Network Formation. Econometrica 68, 1181–1229.

Banks, J., Duggan, J., 2000. A Bargaining Model of Collective Choice. Am. Polit. Sci. Rev. 94, 73–88.

Baron, D., Ferejohn, J., 1989. Bargaining in Legislatures. Am. Polit. Sci. Rev. 83, 1181–1206.

Baron, D., Kalai, E., 1993. The Simplest Equilibrium of a Majority-Rule Division Game. J. Econ. Theory 61, 290–301.

Bernheim, D., Peleg, B., Whinston, M., 1987. Coalition-Proof Nash Equilibria I. Concepts. J. Econ. Theory 42, 1–12.

Billand, P., Bravard, C., 2005. A Note on the Characterization of Nash Networks. Math. Soc. Sci. 49, 355–365.

Binmore, K., 1985. Bargaining and Coalitions. In: Roth, A. (Ed.), Game-Theoretic Models of Bargaining. Cambridge University Press, Cambridge.

Binmore, K., Rubinstein, A., Wolinsky, A., 1986. The Nash Bargaining Solution in Economic Modelling. Rand J. Econ. 17, 176–188.

Bloch, F., 1995. Endogenous Structures of Association in Oligopolies. Rand J. Econ. 26, 537–556.

Bloch, F., 1996. Sequential Formation of Coalitions in Games with Externalities and Fixed Payoff Division. Games Econ. Behav. 14, 90–123.

Bloch, F., Dutta, B., 2009. Communication Networks with Endogenous Link Strength. Games Econ. Behav. 66, 39–56.

Bloch, F., Gomes, A., 2006. Contracting with Externalities and Outside Options. J. Econ. Theory 127, 172–201.
Bloch, F., Jackson, M.O., 2006. Definitions of Equilibrium in Network Formation Games. International Journal of Game Theory 34, 305–318.
Bloch, F., Genicot, G., Ray, D., 2008. Informal Insurance in Social Insurance. J. Econ. Theory 143, 36–58.
Bloch, F., Jackson, M.O., 2007. The Formation of Networks with Transfers between Players. J. Econ. Theory 133, 83–110.
Bondareva, O., 1963. Some Applications of Linear Programming Methods to the Theory of Cooperative Games (In Russian). Problemy Kybernetiki 10, 119–139.
Bramoulle, Y., Kranton, R., 2007. Risk Sharing Networks. J. Econ. Behav. Organ. 64, 275–294.
Calvo-Armengol, A., Ilkilic, R., 2009. Pairwise Stability and Nash Equilibria in Network Formation. International Journal of Game Theory 38, 51–79.
Chatterjee, K., Dutta, B., Ray, D., Sengupta, K., 1993. A Non-cooperative Theory of Coalitional Bargaining. Rev. Econ. Stud. 60, 463–477.
Chwe, M., 1994. Farsighted Coalitional Stability. J. Econ. Theory 63, 299–325.
Coase, R., 1937. The Nature of the Firm. Economica 386–405.
Currarini, S., Morelli, M., 2000. Network formation with Sequential Demands. Rev. Econ. Design 5, 229–250.
Declippel, G., Serrano, R., 2008. Marginal Contributions and Externalities in the Value. Econometrica 76, 1413–1436.
Demange, G., Wooders, M. (Eds.), 2005. Group Formation in Economics: Networks, Clubs and Coalitions. Cambridge University Press, Cambridge.
Diamantoudi, E., Xue, L., 2003. Farsighted Stability in Hedonic Games. Soc. Choice Welfare 21, 39–61.
Diamantoudi, E., Xue, L., 2007. Coalitions, Agreements and Efficiency. J. Econ. Theory 136, 105–125.
Diermeier, D., Eraslan, H., Merlo, A., 2003. A Structural Model of Government Formation. Econometrica 71, 27–70.
Diermeier, D., Merlo, A., 2004. An Empirical Investigation of Coalitional Bargaining Procedures. J. Public Econ. 88, 783–797.
Drèze, J., Greenberg, J., 1980. Hedonic Coalitions: Optimality and Stability. Econometrica 48, 987–1003.
Dutta, B., Ghosal, S., Ray, D., 2005. Farsighted Network Formation. J. Econ. Theory 122, 143–164.
Dutta, B., Jackson, M.O., 2000. The Stability and Efficiency of Directed Networks. Rev. Econ. Design 5, 251–272.
Dutta, B., Mutuswami, S., 1997. Stable Networks. J. Econ. Theory 76, 322–344.
Dutta, B., Ray, D., 1989. A Concept of Egalitarianism under Participation Constraints. Econometrica 57, 615–635.
Dutta, B., Tijs, S., van den Nouweland, A., 1998. Link Formation in Cooperative Situations. International Journal of Game Theory 27, 245–256.
Eraslan, H., 2002. Uniqueness of Stationary Equilibrium Payoffs in the Baron-Ferejohn Model. J. Econ. Theory 103, 11–30.
Feri, F., 2007. Stochastic Stability in Networks with Decay. J. Econ. Theory 135, 442–457.
Forges, F., Minelli, E., Vohra, R., 2007. Incentives and the Core of an Exchange Economy: a survey. J. Math. Econ. 38, 1–41.
Freidlin, M., Wentzell, A., 1984. Random Perturbations of Dynamical Systems. Springer Verlag, New York.
Galeotti, A., Goyal, S., Kamphorst, J., 2006. Network Formation with Heterogeneous Players. Games Econ. Behav. 54, 353–372.
Genicot, G., Ray, D., 2003. Group Formation in Risk-Sharing Arrangements. Rev. Econ. Stud. 70, 87–113.
Gilles, R., Sarangi, S., 2006. Building Social Networks. mimeo, Virginia Tech and Louisiana State Universities.
Gilles, R., Chakrabarti, S., Sarangi, S., 2006. Social network Formation with Consent: Nash Equilibria and Pairwise Refinements. mimeo, Queen's University Belfast and Louisiana State University, Virginia Tech.
Gomes, A., 2005. Multilateral Contracting with Externalities. Econometrica 73, 1329–1350.

Gomes, A., Jehiel, P., 2005. Dynamic Processes of Social and Economic Interactions: On the Persistence of Inefficiencies. J. Polit. Econ. 113, 626–667.
Goyal, S., 2007. Connections: An Introduction to the Economics of Networks. Princeton University Press, Princeton.
Goyal, S., Joshi, S., 2003. Networks of Collaboration in Oligopoly. Games Econ. Behav. 43, 57–85.
Greenberg, J., 1990. The Theory of Social Situations: An Alternative Game-Theoretic Approach. Cambridge University Press, Cambridge.
Gul, F., 1989. Bargaining Foundations of the Shapley Value. Econometrica 57, 81–95.
Haller, H., Sarangi, S., 2005. Nash Networks with Heterogeneous Links. Math. Soc. Sci. 50, 181–201.
Harrington, J., 1989. The Advantageous Nature of Risk Aversion in a Three Player Bargaining Game where Acceptance of a Proposal Requires a Simple Majority. Econ. Lett. 30, 195–200.
Harsanyi, J., 1974. An Equilibrium Point Interpretation of Stable Sets and a Proposed Alternative Definition. Manag. Sci. 20, 1472–1495.
Hart, S., Kurz, M., 1983. Endogenous Formation of Coalitions. Econometrica 51, 1047–1064.
Hart, S., Kurz, M., 1984. Stable Coalition Structures. In: Holler, M. (Ed.), Coalitions and Collective Action. Physica-Verlag.
Hart, S., Mas-Colell, A., 1996. Bargaining and Value. Econometrica 64, 357–380.
Herings, J.J., Mauleon, A., Vannetelbosch, V., 2009. Farsightedly Stable Networks. Games Econ. Behav. 67, 526–541.
Hojman, D., Szeidl, A., 2008. Core and Periphery in Networks. J. Econ. Theory 139, 295–309.
Hyndman, K., Ray, D., 2007. Coalition Formation with Binding Agreements. Rev. Econ. Stud. 74, 1125–1147.
Jackson, M.O., 2003. The Stability and Efficiency of Economic and Social Networks. In: Dutta, B., Jackson, M. (Eds.), Networks and groups: Models of Strategic Formation. Springer Verlag, Heidelberg.
Jackson, M.O., 2008. Social and Economic Networks. Princeton University Press, Princeton.
Jackson, M.O., Moselle, B., 2002. Coalition and Party Formation in a Legislative Voting Game. J. Econ. Theory 103, 49–87.
Jackson, M.O., van den Nouweland, A., 2005. Strongly Stable Networks. Games Econ. Behav. 51, 420–444.
Jackson, M.O., Watts, A., 2002. The Evolution of Social and Economic Networks. J. Econ. Theory 106, 265–295.
Jackson, M.O., Wolinsky, A., 1996. A Strategic Model of Economic and Social Networks. J. Econ. Theory 71, 44–74.
Jehiel, P., Scotchmer, S., 2001. Constitutional Rules of Exclusion in Jurisdiction Formation. Rev. Econ. Stud. 68, 393–413.
Kamien, M., Zang, I., 1990. The Limits of Monopolization through Acquisition. Q. J. Econ. 90, 465–499.
Konishi, H., Ray, D., 2003. Coalition Formation as a Dynamics Process. J. Econ. Theory 110, 1–41.
Krishna, V., Serrano, R., 1996. Multilateral Bargaining. Rev. Econ. Stud. 63, 61–80.
Lagunoff, R., 1994. A Simple Noncooperative Core Story. Games Econ. Behav. 7, 54–61.
Levy, G., 2004. A Model of Political Parties. J. Econ. Theory 115, 250–277.
Lucas, W., 1969. The Proof that a Game may not have a Solution. Transactions of the American Mathematical Society 137, 219–229.
Macho-Stadler, I., Perez Castrillo, D., Wettstein, D., 2007. Efficient Bidding with Externalities. Games Econ. Behav. 57, 304–320.
Maskin, E., 2003. Bargaining, Coalitions and Externalities. Presidential Address, Econometric Society.
Merlo, A., Wilson, C., 1995. A Stochastic Model of Sequential Bargaining with Complete Information. Econometrica 63, 371–399.
Merlo, A., 1997. Bargaining over Governments in a Stochastic Environment. J. Polit. Econ. 105, 101–131.
Moldovanu, B., Winter, E., 1995. Order Independent Equilibria. Games Econ. Behav. 9, 21–34.
Montero, M., 1999. Coalition Formation in Games with Externalities. mimeo, Tilburg University.
Mutuswami, S., Winter, E., 2002. Subscription Mechanisms for Network Formation. J. Econ. Theory 106, 242–264.
Myerson, R., 1978. Refinements of the Nash Equilibrium Concept. International Journal of Game Theory 15, 133–154.

Myerson, R., 1991. Game Theory. Harvard University Press, Cambridge.
Norman, P., 2002. Legislative Bargaining and Coalition Formation. J. Econ. Theory 102, 322–353.
Okada, A., 1996. A Noncooperative Coalitional Bargaining Game with Random Proposers. Games Econ. Behav. 16, 97–108.
Okada, A., 2000. The Efficiency Principle in Noncooperative Coalitional Bargaining. Japanese Economic Review 51, 34–50.
Page, F., Wooders, M., Kamat, S., 2005. Networks and Farsighted Stability. J. Econ. Theory 120, 257–269.
Page, F., Wooders, M., 2009. Strategic Basins of attraction, the Path Dominance Core and Network Formation Games. Games Econ. Behav. 66, 462–487.
Perez Castrillo, D., 1994. Cooperative Outcomes through Noncooperative Games. Games Econ. Behav. 7, 428–440.
Perez Castrillo, D., Wettstein, D., 2002. Bidding for the Surplus: A Noncooperative Approach to the Shapley Value. J. Econ. Theory 100, 274–294.
Perry, M., Reny, P., 1994. A Noncooperative View of Coalition Formation and the Core. Econometrica 62, 795–817.
Ray, D., 1989. Credible Coalitions and the Core. International Journal of Game Theory 18, 185–187.
Ray, D., 2007. A Game-Theoretic Perspective on Coalition Formation. Oxford University Press, Oxford.
Ray, D., Vohra, R., 1997. Equilibrium Binding Agreements. J. Econ. Theory 73, 30–78.
Ray, D., Vohra, R., 1999. A Theory of Endogenous Coalition Structures. Games Econ. Behav. 26, 286–336.
Ray, D., Vohra, R., 2001. Coalitional Power and Public Goods. J. Polit. Econ. 109, 1355–1384.
Rogers, B., 2005. A Strategic Theory of Network Status. mimeo, Northwestern University.
Rubinstein, A., 1982. Perfect Equilibrium in a Bargaining Game. Econometrica 50, 97–109.
Selten, R., 1981. A Noncooperative Model of Characteristic Function Bargaining. In: Bohm, V., Nachtkamp, H. (Eds.), Essays in Game Theory and Mathematical Economics in Honor of O. Morgenstern. Bibliographisches Institut Mannheim, Mannheim.
Seidmann, D., Winter, E., 1998. Gradual Coalition Formation. Rev. Econ. Stud. 65, 793–815.
Seidmann, D., Winter, E., Pavlov, E., 2007. The Formateur's Role in Government Formation. Econ. Theory 31, 427–445.
Serrano, R., 2005. Fifty Years of the Nash Program 1953–2003. Investigaciones Economicas 29, 219–258.
Serrano, R., Vohra, R., 1997. Noncooperative Implementation of the Core. Soc. Choice Welfare 14, 513–525.
Shapley, L., 1967. On Balanced Sets and Cores. Naval Research Logistics Quarterly 14, 453–460.
Slikker, M., 2007. Bidding for the Surplus in Network Allocation Problems. J. Econ. Theory 137, 493–511.
Slikker, M., van den Nouweland, A., 2001. A One-Stage Model of Link Formation and Payoff Division. Games Econ. Behav. 34, 153–175.
Sutton, J., 1986. Noncooperative Bargaining Theory: An Introduction. Rev. Econ. Stud. 53, 709–724.
Tercieux, O., Vannetelbosch, V., 2006. A Characterization of Stochastically Stable Networks. International Journal of Game Theory 34, 351–369.
von Neumann, J., Morgenstern, O., 1944. Theory of Games and Economic Behavior. Princeton University Press, Princeton.
Watts, A., 2001. A Dynamic Model of Network Formation. Games Econ. Behav. 34, 331–341.
Wilson, R., 1978. Information, Efficiency and the Core of an Economy. Econometrica 46, 807–816.
Winter, E., 1996. Voting and Vetoeing. Am. Polit. Sci. Rev. 90, 813–823.
Xue, L., 1998. Coalitional Stability under Perfect Foresight. Econ. Theory 11, 603–627.
Yi, S.S., 1997. Stable Coalition Structures with Externalities. Games Econ. Behav. 20, 201–237.

FURTHER READING

Dutta, B., Ehlers, L., Kar, A., 2009. Externalities, Potential, Value and Consistency. mimeo, Department of Economics, University of Montreal.

CHAPTER 17

Matching, Allocation, and Exchange of Discrete Resources[1]

Tayfun Sönmez[2] and M. Utku Ünver[3]
Boston College Department of Economics, 140 Commonwealth Ave., Chestnut Hill, MA, 02467, USA.

Contents

Introduction 783
2. House Allocation and Exchange Models 786
  2.1 House allocation 786
  2.2 The housing market 788
  2.3 House allocation with existing tenants 794
3. Kidney Exchange 801
  3.1 Directed live donations and donor exchanges 801
  3.2 The designs 803
  3.3 The model 804
  3.4 Multi-way kidney exchanges with strict preferences 804
  3.5 Two-way kidney exchanges with 0–1 preferences 808
    3.5.1 Priority mechanism 811
    3.5.2 The structure of Pareto-efficient matchings 812
    3.5.3 Egalitarian mechanism 813
  3.6 Multi-way kidney exchanges with 0–1 preferences 816
  3.7 Recent developments and related literature 820
4. School Admissions 821
  4.1 College admissions 821
    4.1.1 Differences between college admissions, student placement, and school choice problems 824
  4.2 Student placement 824
    4.2.1 Simple case: one skill category 825
    4.2.2 Current mechanism in Turkish college student placement: multi-category serial dictatorship 826
    4.2.3 Mechanisms via the associated college admissions problem 828
    4.2.4 Pareto efficiency and elimination of justified envy 828

[1] We dedicate this survey to the memory of David Gale (1921–2008), one of the two founders of matching theory along with Lloyd Shapley. This survey is based on the lecture notes of Sönmez and Ünver for the graduate level "Matching Market Design" courses that they taught respectively at Boston College and the University of Pittsburgh from 2005 to 2008. We would like to thank Aytek Erdil, Fuhito Kojima, Morimitsu Kurino, Alexey Kushnir, Muriel Niederle, and Parag Pathak for their comments.
[2] E-mail: sonmezt@bc.edu, url: http://www2.bc.edu/~sonmezt
[3] E-mail: unver@bc.edu, url: http://www2.bc.edu/~unver

Handbook of Social Economics, Volume 1A
ISSN 0169-7218, DOI: 10.1016/S0169-7218(11)01017-3

4.2.5 Strategy-proofness and elimination of justified envy 829
4.2.6 Respecting improvements 830
4.3 School choice 830
4.3.1 The Boston school choice mechanism 831
4.3.2 Incentives, Pareto efficiency, and justified-envy-freeness with strict and weak priorities 832
4.3.3 The school choice TTC mechanism 834
4.4 Recent developments and related literature 835
5. Axiomatic Mechanisms and Market Design 837
5.1 House allocation and hierarchical exchange 837
5.2 Trading cycles with brokers and owners 840
5.3 Related literature 844
6. Concluding Remarks 844
6.1 Lottery mechanisms in matching 844
6.2 Other literature 846
References 848

Abstract

We present a survey of the emerging literature on the design of matching markets. We survey the articles on discrete resource allocation problems, their solutions, and their applications in three related domains. The first domain gives the theoretical background regarding the basic models, namely "house allocation and exchange" problems. First, we investigate the allocation and exchange problems separately, and then we combine them to present a real-life application: on-campus housing at universities. As the second application domain, we extend the basic allocation and exchange models to the "kidney exchange" problem and present new theory and applications regarding this problem. We present proposed and adopted mechanisms that take very specific institutional details into account. Then, we present the school admissions problem in three subcategories: the "college admissions" model where both schools and students are strategic agents, the "school placement" model where only students are strategic agents and they induce an endogenous priority structure of schools over students, and finally the "school choice" model for the US public school districts where the students are the only strategic agents and the school priorities over the students are exogenous. In the final chapter, we investigate the basic models of the axiomatic mechanism design literature that present mechanisms that are generalizations of the mechanisms designed for the specific market design problems discussed before.
JEL Codes: C78, D78

Keywords

Matching
Market Design
House Allocation
Housing Market
On-campus Housing
Kidney Exchange
School Choice

College Admissions
Student Placement
Top-Trading Cycles
Deferred Acceptance

INTRODUCTION

Matching theory, a name referring to several loosely related research areas concerning matching, allocation, and exchange of indivisible resources, such as jobs, school seats, houses, etc., lies at the intersection of game theory, social choice theory, and mechanism design. Matching can involve the *allocation* or *exchange* of indivisible objects, such as dormitory rooms, transplant organs, courses, summer houses, etc. Or matching can involve *two-sided matching*, in markets with two sides, such as firms and workers, students and schools, or men and women, that need to be matched with each other. Auctions can be seen as special cases of matching models, in which there is a single seller. Recently, matching theory and its application to market design have emerged as one of the success stories of economic theory and applied mechanism design.

The seminal research paper on the subject was written by Gale and Shapley (1962), who introduced the two-sided matching model and a suitable solution concept called *stability*. They also showed that a stable matching always exists and proved this result through a simple iterative algorithm known as the *deferred acceptance algorithm*. Gale and Shapley were most likely unaware that this short note published in the *American Mathematical Monthly* would spark a new literature in game theory, which is now commonly referred to as *matching theory*.

Shapley and Shubik (1972) and Kelso and Crawford (1982) introduced variants of the two-sided matching model where monetary transfers are also possible between matching sides. However, Gale and Shapley's short note was almost forgotten until 1984, when Roth (1984) showed that the same algorithm was independently discovered by the National Residency Matching Program (NRMP)[1] in the United States (US), and since the 1950s, it had been used in matching medical interns with hospital residency positions (Roth 2008a also attributes the same discovery to David Gale). This discovery marked the start of the convergence of matching theory and game-theoretical field applications. In 1980s, several papers were written on the two-sided matching model and its variants exploring strategic and structural issues regarding stability.[2] Recently, new links between auctions, two-sided matching, and lattice theory were discovered (for example,

[1] See http://www.nrmp.org, retrieved on 10/16/2008.

[2] An excellent survey of these theoretical and practical developments from the 1950s to the 1990s is explored in Roth and Sotomayor (1990). Also see Gusfield and Irving (1989) on the complementary work in operations research and computer science on algorithms regarding two-sided matching theory.

see Hatfield and Milgrom 2005 for a summary of these discoveries and new results in a general two-sided matching domain).[3]

In this survey, we will focus on the other branch of matching theory, *allocation and exchange of indivisible goods*, which was also initiated by Shapley and (indirectly) Gale together with Scarf (Shapley and Scarf 1974).[4] The basic model, referred to as the *housing market*, consists of agents each of whom owns an object, e.g., a house. They have preferences over all houses including their own. The agents are allowed to exchange the houses in an exchange economy. Shapley and Scarf showed that such a market always has a (*strict*) *core* matching, which is also a competitive equilibrium allocation. They also noted that a simple algorithm suggested by David Gale, now commonly referred to as *Gale's top trading cycles algorithm*, also finds this particular core outcome.

In the two-sided matching model, both sides of the market consist of agents, whereas in a housing market only one side of the market consists of agents. Subsequent research on the housing market showed that both competitive and core allocations are unique when preferences are strict (Roth and Postlewaite 1977). Moreover, when the core concept is used as a direct mechanism, it is strategy-proof (Roth 1982a). Subsequently, Ma (1994) showed that this is the only direct mechanism that is strategy-proof, Pareto-efficient, and individually rational. Although the core as a mechanism is the unique *nice* direct mechanism (unlike in most game-theoretical models including the two-sided matching model), the research on housing market model remained limited until recently with respect to the two sided-matching model. The links between the two models were later discovered and explored by Balinski and Sönmez (1999), Ergin (2002), Abdulkadiroğlu and Sönmez (2003a), Ehlers and Klaus (2006), and Kojima and Manea (2007), among others.

The allocation model consists of objects and agents, each of whom has preferences over the objects. These objects will be allocated to the agents. Monetary transfers are not available. An exogenous control rights structure regarding the objects can be given in the definition of the problem. For example, each agent can have objects to begin with (as in the kidney exchange problem of Roth, Sönmez, and Ünver 2004, or the housing market), or some agents can have objects while others have none (as in the house allocation problem with existing tenants of Abdulkadiroğlu and Sönmez 1999). There can also be more complicated exogenous control rights

[3] For surveys on market design of the US Federal Communications Commission (FCC) auctions (see http://wireless.fcc.gov/auctions/default.htm?job=auctions_home, retrieved on 10/16/2008), electricity markets (e.g., for California market see http://www.caiso.com, retrieved on 10/16/2008), and other aspects of matching markets and their links to game theory and more specifically to auction and matching theory see Milgrom (2000, 2004, 2007), Klemperer (2004), Wilson (2002), and Roth (2002, 2008b), respectively.

[4] Nevertheless, we will also give basic results regarding Gale and Shapley's (1962) model and summarize important market design contributions on the subject in Chapter 4 under the "College Admissions" heading.

structures, as in the school choice problem, where each school prioritizes the students (as defined by Abdulkadiroğlu and Sönmez 2003a). In the simplest of these models, there are no initial property rights, and objects are socially endowed (as in the house allocation problem of Hylland and Zeckhauser 1979). Almost all of these models have real-life applications. In all of these applications, there exists a central planner (such as the housing office of a college allocating dorm rooms to students, a central health authority deciding which patients will receive kidneys, or a school board for assigning students to schools) that implements a direct mechanism by collecting preference information from the agents. The central authority uses a well-defined procedure that we will simply refer to as a *mechanism*. In this survey, we inspect properties of different mechanisms proposed in the literature for these allocation problems. Most of the mechanisms we will introduce will be implemented by intuitive iterative algorithms.

In the models with initial property rights, various fairness and individual rights protection properties should be respected by any plausible mechanism for normative, institutional, or economic reasons. Some examples are as follows:

Normatively, one would expect there to be equal chances of assigning an object to agents who have identical rights over objects. In a school choice problem, students are the agents. Students who have the same priority at a school may be given the same chances of admission. Thus, from a fairness point of view, an even lottery can be used to order such students for tie-breaking purposes. On the other hand, if there exists a student who prefers a school to her assigned school and this more preferred school has admitted a student who has lower priority than her, then she has justified envy toward this student. Besides following certain normative criteria for institutional and legal reasons, adopted school choice mechanisms are expected to eliminate justified envy. For example, if there is justified envy regarding a student, her family can potentially take legal action against the school district.

In a kidney exchange problem, if a kidney transplant patient is not assigned a kidney as good as her live paired-donor's, she will not participate in the exchange in the first place. Under incomplete information, such possibilities may cause unnecessary efficiency loss. Thus, individual rationality is important for the kidney exchange problem.

Moreover, if possible, we would like the mechanisms to be incentive compatible: decision makers such as students, patients, and doctors should not be able to manipulate these systems by misreporting their preferences. This will be important not only in achieving allocations that satisfy the properties of the mechanisms under true preferences, but also for fairness reasons. For example, not all students are sophisticated enough to manipulate a mechanism successfully (see Pathak and Sönmez 2008 and also Vickrey 1961 for similar arguments in auction design). Moreover, one can expect that implementing a strategy-proof mechanism will minimize the informational burden of the agents. They will only need to form their (expected) preference ordering correctly and will not need to guess the preferences of other agents before submitting their preferences. Hence, in this survey, besides introducing several plausible mechanisms, we will explore what properties make these mechanisms plausible.

The survey will consist of four main chapters: In Chapter 2, we will introduce the *house allocation problem* and the *housing market* and explore mechanisms in this domain. As the market design application of these models, we will introduce one additional model and mechanism, inspired by dormitory room allocation at colleges. In Chapter 3, we will introduce the *kidney exchange* models under various institutional and modeling restrictions. We will draw parallels between some of these models and the house allocation and exchange models. We will also inspect real-life mechanisms designed by economists for these problems. In Chapter 4, we will explore the *school admissions problem*, and plausible mechanisms under different institutional restrictions. We will explore school admissions under three different models, the *college admissions problem*, the *student placement problem*, and the *school choice problem*. In Chapter 5, we will introduce general classes of mechanisms that can be used to characterize desirable house allocation mechanisms.

2. HOUSE ALLOCATION AND EXCHANGE MODELS

2.1 House allocation

The simplest of the indivisible goods allocation models is known as the *house allocation problem* and is due to Hylland and Zeckhauser (1979). In this problem, there is a group of agents and houses (representing indivisible objects). Each agent shall be allocated a house by a central planner using her preferences over the houses. All houses are social endowments. Formally, a triple $(A, H, \succ)$ is a **house allocation problem** if

- $A = \{a_1, a_2, \ldots, a_n\}$ is a set of **agents**,
- $H = \{h_1, h_2, \ldots, h_n\}$ is a set of **houses**,
- $\succ = (\succ_a)_{a \in A}$ is a strict preference profile such that for each agent $a \in A, \succ_a$ is a **strict preference relation** over houses.[1] The induced weak preference relation of agent a is denoted by $\succsim_a$ and for any $h, g \in H, h \succsim_a g \Leftrightarrow h \succ_a g$ or $h = g$ (i.e., a binary relation, which is a linear order).[2]

[1] For any subset of agents B, we will use $\succ_{-B}$ to denote $(\succ_a)_{a \in A \setminus B}$ and $\succ_B$ to denote $(\succ_a)_{a \in B}$.

[2] A binary relation β defined on a set X is a linear order if

- it is complete, i.e., for all $x, y \in X$, either $x \beta y$ or $y \beta x$,
- it is reflexive, i.e., for all $x \in X$, $x \beta x$,
- it is transitive, i.e., for all $x, y, z \in X$, $x \beta y$ and $y \beta z$ imply $x \beta z$, and
- it is anti-symmetric, i.e., for all $x, y \in X$, $x \beta y$ and $y \beta x$ imply $x = y$.

There are various applications of the house allocation problem, such as organ allocation for transplant patients waiting for deceased donor organs, dormitory room allocation at universities, and parking space and office allocation at workplaces.

Throughout this subsection, we will fix A and H. A problem is denoted only through the preference profile $\succ$.

The outcome of a house allocation problem is a **matching**, which is a one-to-one and onto function $\mu : A \to H$ such that house $\mu(a)$ is the assigned house of agent a under matching μ. Let $\mathcal{M}$ be the set of matchings.

We will inspect several desirable properties of matchings. A matching μ is **Pareto-efficient** if there is no other matching ν such that $\nu(a) \succsim_a \mu(a)$ for all $a \in A$ and $\nu(a) \succ_a \mu(a)$ for some agent $a \in A$.

A (**deterministic direct**) **mechanism** is a procedure that assigns a matching for each house allocation problem. For any problem $\succ$, let $\phi[\succ] \in \mathcal{M}$ refer to the matching outcome of ϕ for problem $\succ$.

Next, we discuss several desirable properties of mechanisms. A mechanism ϕ is **strategy-proof** if for any problem $\succ$, any agent $a \in A$ and any preference relation $\succ_a^*$

$$\phi[\succ_a, \succ_{-a}](a) \quad \succsim_a \quad \phi[\succ_a^*, \succ_{-a}](a).$$

That is, in a game induced by the direct mechanism ϕ, when agents reveal their preferences and the central planner implements a matching using ϕ according to the revealed preference profile, it is a weakly dominant strategy for each agent to truthfully report her preferences.

A mechanism is **Pareto-efficient** if it assigns a Pareto-efficient matching for each problem.

Next, we introduce a fundamental class of mechanisms, commonly referred to as *serial dictatorships* (or *priority mechanisms*) (for example, see Satterthwaite and Sonnenschein 1981 and Svensson 1994). A serial dictatorship is defined through a priority ordering of agents. A **priority ordering** is a one-to-one and onto function $f : \{1, 2, \ldots, n\} \to A$. That is, for any $k \in \{1, \ldots, n\}$, $f(k) \in A$ is the agent with the kth highest priority agent under f. Let $\mathcal{F}$ be the set of orderings. Each priority ordering induces a direct mechanism. We refer to the direct mechanism π^f as the **serial dictatorship induced by priority ordering** $f \in \mathcal{F}$, and its matching outcome $\pi^f[\succ]$ is found iteratively as follows:

Algorithm 1 *The* serial dictatorship induced by f:

Step 1: *The highest priority agent $f(1)$ is assigned her top choice house under $\succ_{f(1)}$*

⋮

Step k: *The kth highest priority agent $f(k)$ is assigned her top choice house under $\succ_{f(k)}$ among the remaining houses.*

We can summarize the desirable properties of serial dictatorships with the following theorem:

Theorem 1 *A* serial dictatorship *is* strategy-proof *and* Pareto-efficient.

Moreover, Abdulkadiroğlu and Sönmez (1998) show that for any Pareto-efficient matching of a given problem, there exists a serial dictatorship that achieves this matching.

Serial dictatorships can be easily implemented in real-life applications; therefore, they are very appealing. If it is not possible to distinguish between agents to determine the control rights of houses and order them as *serial dictators*, then a random ordering can be chosen and the induced serial dictatorship can be implemented to sustain fairness.

2.2 The housing market

The second model we consider is a variant of the house allocation problem and is known as a *housing market* (Shapley and Scarf, 1974). The only difference between this problem and the house allocation problem is that now each agent *owns* a house, i.e., has the initial property right of a house. Hence, a housing market is an exchange market (with indivisible objects) where agents have the option to trade their house in order to get a better one. On the other hand, a house allocation problem has no predefined control rights structure. The houses are social endowments, and the central planner allocates them.

Formally, a **housing market** is a list $(A, (a, h_a)_{a \in A}, \succ)$ such that

- $A = \{1, \ldots, n\}$ is a **set of agents** and $\{h_1, \ldots, h_n\}$ is a **set of houses** such that each agent a **occupies** house h_a satisfying $h_b \neq h_a$ for any $b \neq a$, and
- $\succ = (\succ_a)_{a \in A}$ is a strict preference profile such that for each agent $a \in A, \succ_a$ is a **strict preference relation over houses**.

Throughout this subsection, we fix the set of agents A. We also fix the endowments of agents as above and denote the set as H. Thus, each market is denoted by a preference profile $\succ$.

There are several real-life applications of housing markets. We will focus on an important one in the next section. In this application, agents are end-stage kidney disease patients, are endowed with a live donor who would like to donate a kidney to them, and have the option to trade their donors to receive a better quality kidney.

Next, we define solution concepts for housing markets. The definitions of a matching, a mechanism, and their properties introduced for the housing allocation problem also apply to the housing market.

We also introduce a new concept about the additional structure of the housing market regarding initial property rights. A matching μ is **individually rational** if for each agent $a \in A, \mu(a) \succsim_a h_a$, that is, each agent is assigned a house at least as good as her own occupied house. A mechanism is **individually rational** if it always selects an individually rational matching for each market.

Although we focused on allocation through direct mechanisms, a decentralized solution may naturally exist for a housing market, which is an exchange economy with indivisible objects. A *competitive equilibrium* may be achieved through decentralized trading. We define a price vector as a positive real vector assigning a price for each house, i.e., $p = (p_h)_{h \in H} \in \mathbb{R}^n_{++}$ such that p_h is the price of house h. A matching - price vector pair $(\mu, p) \in \mathcal{M} \times \mathbb{R}^n_+$ finds a **competitive equilibrium** if for each agent $a \in A$,

- $p_{\mu(a)} \leq p_{h_a}$ (budget constraint), and
- $\mu(a) \succsim_a h$ for all $h \in H$ such that $p_h \leq p_{h_a}$ (utility maximization).

Under a competitive equilibrium, each agent is assigned the best house that she can afford.

Another important concept for exchange economies is the *core*. With divisibilities, it is well known that any competitive equilibrium allocation is also in the core.

We formulate the core for a housing market as follows: A matching μ is in the **core** if there exists no coalition of agents $B \subseteq A$ such that for some matching $\nu \in \mathcal{M}$ such that for all $a \in B$, $\nu(a) = h_b$ for some $b \in B$, we have $\nu(a) \succsim_a \mu(a)$ for all $a \in B$ and $\nu(a) \succ_a \mu(a)$ for some $a \in B$. That is, the core is the collection of matchings such that no coalition could improve their assigned houses even if they traded their initially occupied houses only among each other.

Although competitive equilibrium and the core are very intuitive solution concepts with nice economic properties, it is not immediately clear that they exist and are related to each other for the housing market. Shapley and Scarf also proved that the core is nonempty and there exists a core matching that can be sustained under a competitive equilibrium.

Theorem 2 *The* core *of a housing market is non-empty and there exists a* core *matching that can be sustained as part of a* competitive equilibrium.

As an alternative proof to their initial proof, they introduced an iterative algorithm that is a core and competitive equilibrium matching. They attribute this algorithm to David Gale. This algorithm is a clearing algorithm that forms a directed graph in each iteration and assigns houses to a subset of agents. In order to define the algorithm, we define the following concept:

Consider a directed graph in which agents and houses are the vertices and edges are formed by each agent pointing to one house and each house pointing to one agent. We define a special subgraph of this graph. A **cycle** is a list of houses and agents (h_1, a_1, h_2, a_2, ..., h_m, a_m) such that each agent a_k points to house h_{k+1} for $k \in \{1, \ldots, m-1\}$, a_m points to h_1, and each house h_k points to agent a_k for $k \in \{1, \ldots, m\}$. Figure 2.1 depicts such a cycle.

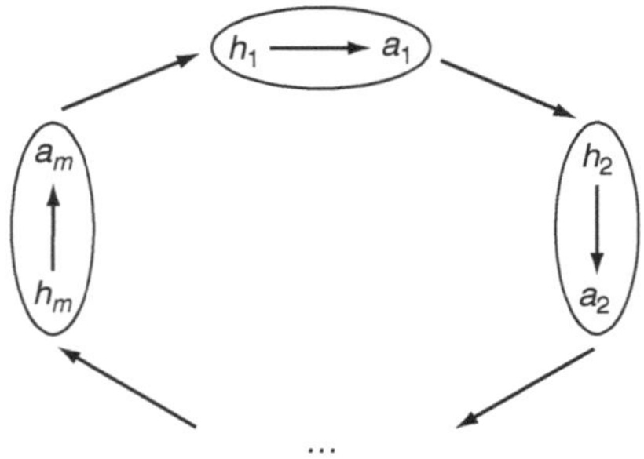

Figure 2.1 A cycle.

An interesting fact about any directed graph that is formed as explained above is the following:

Lemma 1 *Each directed graph formed by each agent pointing to a house and each house pointing to an agent has a cycle, and no two cycles intersect.*

This lemma will enable us to define the following algorithm properly:

Algorithm 2 Gale's top trading cycles (TTC) algorithm:

Step 1: *Let each agent point to her top choice house and each house point to its owner. In this graph there is necessarily a cycle and no two cycles intersect (by Lemma 1). Remove all cycles from the problem by assigning each agent the house that she is pointing to.*

⋮

Step k: *Let each remaining agent point to her top choice among the remaining houses and each remaining house point to its owner (note that houses leave with their owners and owners leave with their houses, so a house remaining in the problem implies that the owner is still in the problem and vice versa). There is necessarily a cycle and no two cycles intersect. Remove all cycles from the problem by assigning each agent the house that she is pointing to.*

The algorithm terminates when no agents and houses remain. The assignments formed during the execution of the algorithm is the matching outcome.

Shapley and Scarf also proved the following theorem:

Theorem 3 Gale's TTC algorithm *achieves a* core *matching that is also sustainable by a* competitive equilibrium.

A competitive equilibrium price vector supporting this core matching at the equilibrium can be formed as follows: Partition the set of agents as $C_1, C_2, \ldots, C_r$ where C_k is the set of agents removed in Step k of Gale's TTC algorithm. Price vector p is such that for any pair of houses h_a, h_b if the owners a and b were removed in the same step, i.e., $a, b \in C_k$ for some Step k, then we set $p_{h_a} = p_{h_b}$, if (without loss of generality) owner a is removed before agent b, i.e., $a \in C_k$ and $b \in C_\ell$ such that $k < \ell$, then we set $p_{h_a} > p_{h_b}$. That is, (1) the prices of the occupied houses whose owners are removed in the same step are set equal to each other and (2) the prices of those whose owners are removed in different steps are set such that the price of a house that leaves earlier is higher than the price of a house that leaves later.

Below, we demonstrate how Gale's TTC algorithm works with an involved example:

Example 1 ***The execution of Gale's TTC algorithm***

Let

$$A = \{a_1, a_2, a_3, a_4, a_5, a_6, a_7, a_8, a_9, a_{10}, a_{11}, a_{12}, a_{13}, a_{14}, a_{15}, a_{16}\}.$$

Here h_i is the occupied house of agent a_i. Let the preference profile $\succ$ be given as:

a_1	a_2	a_3	a_4	a_5	a_6	a_7	a_8	a_9	a_{10}	a_{11}	a_{12}	a_{13}	a_{14}	a_{15}	a_{16}
h_{15}	h_3	h_1	h_2	h_9	h_6	h_7	h_6	h_{11}	h_7	h_2	h_4	h_6	h_8	h_1	h_5
$\vdots$	h_4	h_3	$\vdots$	$\vdots$	$\vdots$	$\vdots$	h_{12}	$\vdots$	h_3	h_4	h_{14}	h_{13}	$\vdots$	$\vdots$	$\vdots$
	$\vdots$	$\vdots$					$\vdots$		h_{12}	h_{16}	$\vdots$	$\vdots$			
									h_{10}	$\vdots$					
									$\vdots$						

We depict the directed graphs that are formed in each step of the algorithm in Figures 2.2–2.6. The cycles are shown through bold arrows. Observe that we abbreviated in the graphs below the arrows through which each house points to its owner. When a cycle is removed, each agent in the cycle is assigned the house she is pointing to.

The outcome is:

$$\mu = \begin{pmatrix} a_1 & a_2 & a_3 & a_4 & a_5 & a_6 & a_7 & a_8 & a_9 & a_{10} & a_{11} & a_{12} & a_{13} & a_{14} & a_{15} & a_{16} \\ h_{15} & h_4 & h_3 & h_2 & h_9 & h_6 & h_7 & h_{12} & h_{11} & h_{10} & h_{16} & h_{14} & h_{13} & h_8 & h_1 & h_5 \end{pmatrix}$$

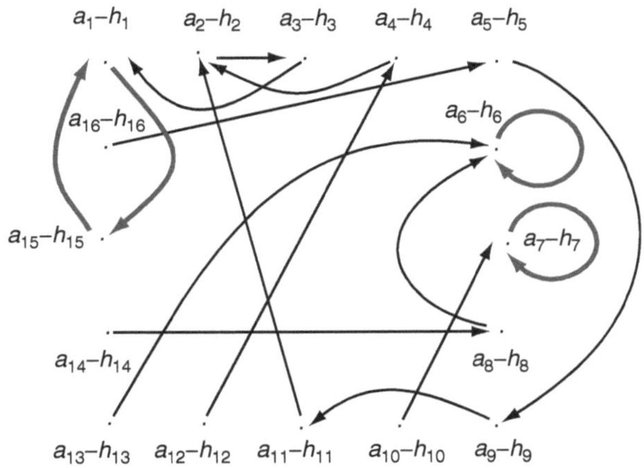

Figure 2.2 Step 1 of Gale's TTC algorithm.

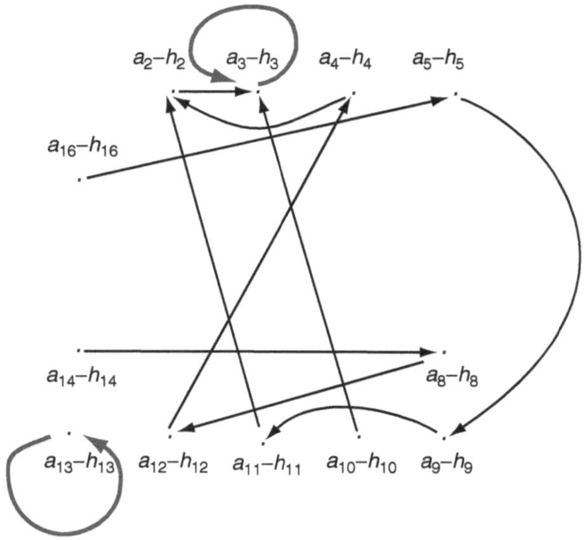

Figure 2.3 Step 2 of Gale's TTC algorithm.

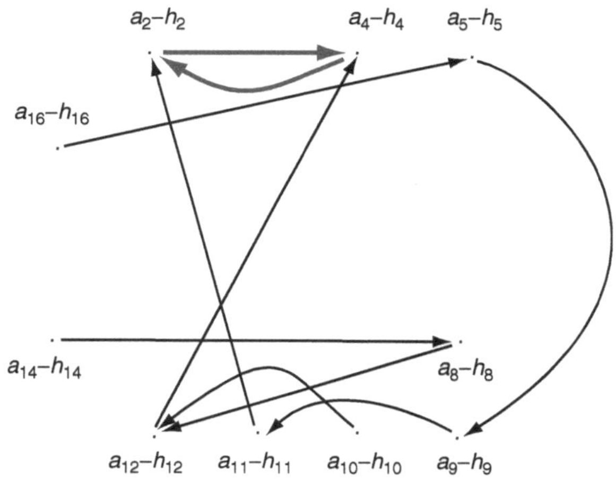

Figure 2.4 Step 3 of Gale's TTC algorithm.

After Shapley and Scarf's paper, a series of papers proved that the core of a housing market has really nice properties when it is used as a direct mechanism:

Theorem 4 ***(Roth and Postlewaite 1977)*** *The core of a housing market has exactly one matching which is also the unique matching that can be sustained at a competitive equilibrium.*

The above result together with Shapley and Scarf's result implies that the core can be used as a mechanism, and Gale's TTC can be used to find it. By definition, the core

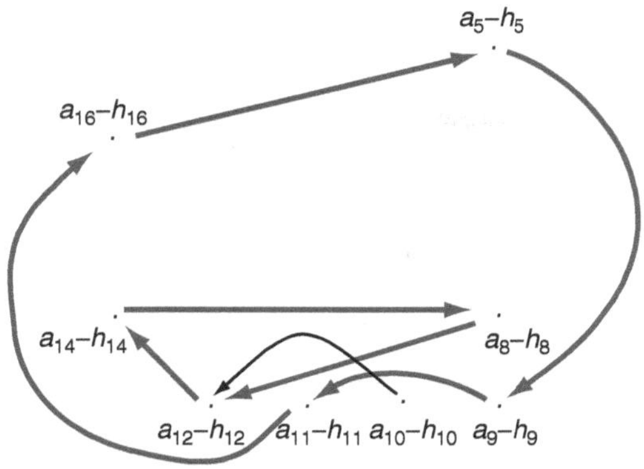

Figure 2.5 Step 4 of Gale's TTC algorithm.

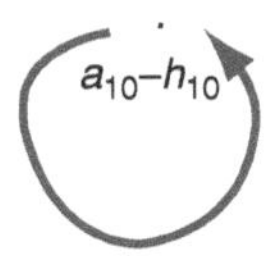

Figure 2.6 Step 5 of Gale's TTC algorithm.

is Pareto-efficient and individually rational. The following theorem shows that this mechanism also has good incentive properties:

Theorem 5 ***(Roth 1982a)*** *The* core mechanism *is* strategy-proof.

Moreover, there is no other mechanism with these properties:

Theorem 6 ***(Ma 1994)*** *The* core mechanism *is the only mechanism that is* individually rational, Pareto-efficient, *and* strategy-proof *for a housing market.*

Thus, from theoretical, practical, and economic points of view, the core is the best solution concept for housing markets. It is the decentralized solution concept and can be implemented in a centralized manner. In economics, there are very few problem domains with such a property. For example, in exchange economies with divisible goods, the competitive equilibrium allocation is a subset of the core, but both the competitive equilibrium and any other core selection are manipulable as a direct mechanism.[3,4]

[3] Positive results of this section no longer hold in an economy in which one agent can consume multiple houses or multiple types of houses. Even the core may be empty (Konishi, Quint, and Wako 2001). Also see Pápai (2003), Wako (2005), and Klaus (2008) on the subject under different preference assumptions.

On the other hand, if there are no initial property rights, serial dictatorships can still be used for strategy-proof and Pareto-efficient allocation (see Klaus and Miyagawa 2002). Also see Pápai (2001) and Ehlers and Klaus (2003) for other characterizations under different preference assumptions.

[4] See Quinzzii (1984) for the existence results of core allocations and competitive equilibria in a generalized model with both discrete and divisible goods. See Bevia, Quinzii, and Silva (1999) for a generalization of this model when an agent can consume multiple indivisible goods.

In the next subsection, we focus on a market design problem that has the features of both housing markets and house allocation problems.

2.3 House allocation with existing tenants

In some US universities, a probabilistic version of the serial dictatorship is used for allocating dormitory rooms to students. By a (usually equally weighted) lottery, a priority ordering is determined and students reveal a preference ordering over possible dormitory rooms. Then the induced serial dictatorship is used to allocate these rooms to students. This is known as the *housing lottery* at campuses.

Motivated by real-life **on-campus housing** practices, Abdulkadiroğlu and Sönmez (1999) introduced a **house allocation problem with existing tenants:** A set of houses shall be allocated to a set of agents by a centralized clearing house. Some of the agents are **existing tenants**, each of whom already occupies a house, referred to as an **occupied house**, and the rest of the agents are **newcomers**. Each agent has strict preferences over houses. In addition to occupied houses, there are **vacant houses**. Existing tenants are entitled not only to keep their current houses but also to apply for other houses.

Here, existing tenants can be likened to the current college students who occupy on-campus houses (or dormitory rooms, condos, etc.) from the previous year. The newcomers can be likened to the freshman class and any other current student who does not already occupy a house. Vacant houses are the houses vacated by the graduating class and the students who no longer need on-campus housing.

The mechanism known as the **random serial-dictatorship (RSD) with squatting rights** is used in most real-life applications of these problems. Some examples include undergraduate housing at Carnegie Mellon, Duke, Michigan, Northwestern, and Pennsylvania. This mechanism works as follows:

Algorithm 3 *The* RSD with squatting rights:

1. *Each existing tenant decides whether she will enter the housing lottery or keep her current house (or dormitory room). Those who prefer keeping their houses are assigned their houses. All other houses (vacant houses and houses of existing agents who enter the lottery) become available for allocation.*
2. *An ordering of agents in the lottery is randomly chosen from a given distribution of orderings. This distribution may be uniform or it may favor some groups.*
3. *Once the agents are ordered, available houses are allocated using the induced* serial dictatorship: *The first agent receives her top choice, the next agent receives her top choice among the remaining houses, and so on.*

Since it does not guarantee each existing tenant a house that is as good as what she already occupies, some existing tenants may choose to keep their houses even though they wish to move, and this may result in a loss of potentially large gains from trade.

In contrast, Abdulkadiroğlu and Sönmez propose a mechanism that has the features of both the core in housing markets and serial dictatorships in house allocation problems.

We refer to this mechanism as the **"You request my house - I get your turn" (YRMH-IGYT) mechanism**. Let $f \in \mathcal{F}$ be a priority ordering of agents in A. Each f defines a YRMH-IGYT mechanism. The corresponding YRMH-IGYT algorithm clears as follows:

Algorithm 4 *The* YRMH-IGYT algorithm induced by f:

- *Assign the first agent her top choice, the second agent her top choice among the remaining houses, and so on, until someone requests the house of an existing tenant.*
- *If at that point the existing tenant whose house is requested is already assigned another house, then do not disturb the procedure. Otherwise, modify the remainder of the ordering by inserting the existing tenant before the requestor at the priority order and proceed with the first step of procedure through this existing tenant.*
- *Similarly, insert any existing tenant who is not already served just before the requestor in the priority order once her house is requested by an agent.*
- *If at any point a cycle forms, it is formed by exclusively existing tenants and each of them requests the house of the tenant who is next in the cycle. (A cycle is an ordered list* $(h_{a_1}, a_1, \ldots, h_{a_k}, a_k)$ *of occupied houses and existing tenants where agent* a_1 *demands the house of agent* a_2, h_{a_2}, *agent* a_2 *demands the house of agent* a_3, $h_{a_3}, \ldots$, *agent* a_k *demands the house of agent* a_1, h_{a_1}.*) In such cases, remove all agents in the cycle by assigning them the houses they demand and proceed similarly.*

Below, we present an example showing how the algorithm clears:

Example 2 ***The execution of the YRMH-IGYT algorithm***

$$\begin{aligned} A_E &= \{a_1, a_2, a_3, a_4, a_5, a_6, a_7, a_8, a_9\} \text{ is the set of existing tenants,} \\ A_N &= \{a_{10}, a_{11}, a_{12}, a_{13}, a_{14}, a_{15}, a_{16}\} \text{ is the set of newcomers, and} \\ H_V &= \{h_{10}, h_{11}, h_{12}, h_{13}, h_{14}, h_{15}, h_{16}\} \text{ is the set of vacant houses.} \end{aligned}$$

Suppose that each existing tenant a_k *occupies* h_k *for each* $k \in \{1, \ldots, 9\}$. *Let the preference profile* $\succ$ *be given as:*

A_E								
a_1	a_2	a_3	a_4	a_5	a_6	a_7	a_8	a_9
h_{15}	h_3	h_1	h_2	h_9	h_6	h_7	h_6	h_{11}
⋮	h_4	h_3	⋮	⋮	⋮	⋮	h_{12}	⋮
	⋮	⋮					⋮	

A_N						
a_{10}	a_{11}	a_{12}	a_{13}	a_{14}	a_{15}	a_{16}
h_7	h_2	h_4	h_6	h_8	h_1	h_5
h_3	h_4	h_{14}	h_{13}	⋮	⋮	⋮
h_{12}	h_{16}	⋮	⋮			
h_{10}	⋮					
⋮						

Let

$$f = (a_{13}, a_{15}, a_{11}, a_{14}, a_{12}, a_{16}, a_{10}, a_1, a_2, a_3, a_4, a_5, a_6, a_7, a_8, a_9)$$

be the ordering of the agents. We will denote the outcome of the mechanism by $\psi^f[\succ]$. *Figures 2.7–2.26 illustrate the dynamics of the YRMH-IGYT algorithm.*

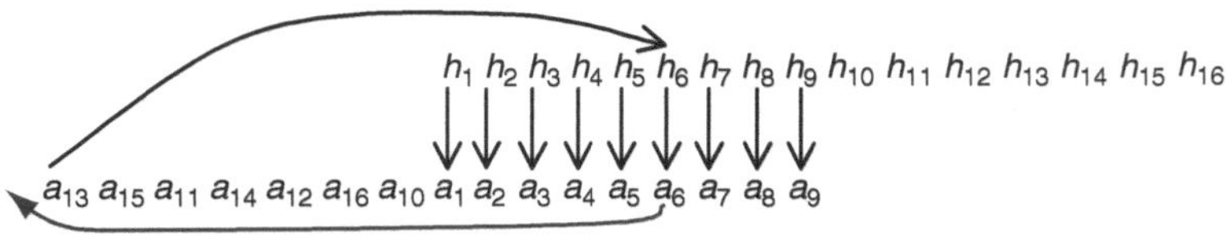

Figure 2.7 YRMH-IGYT Example - Step 1.

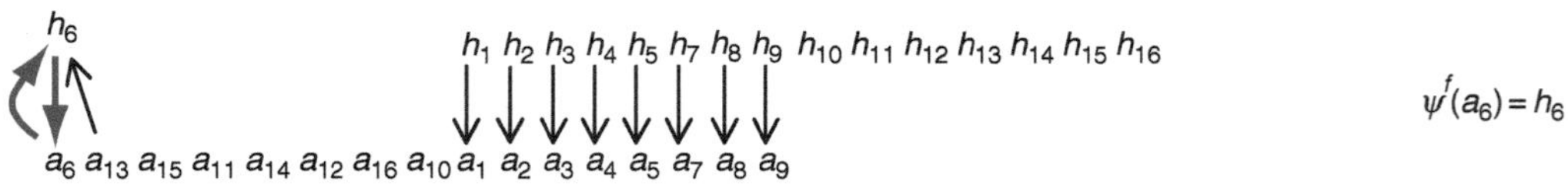

Figure 2.8 YRMH-IGYT Example - Step 2.

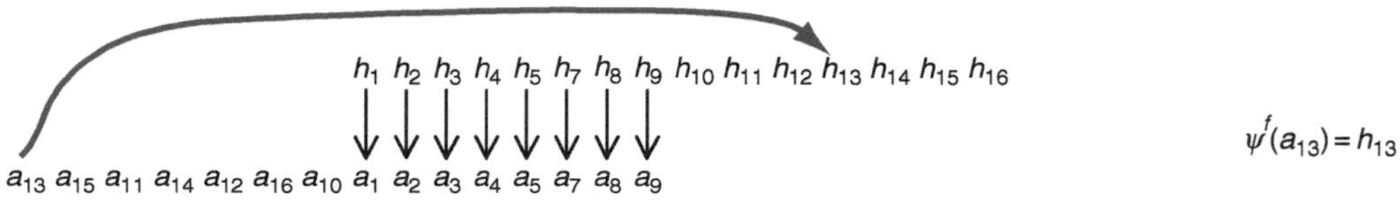

Figure 2.9 YRMH-IGYT Example - Step 3.

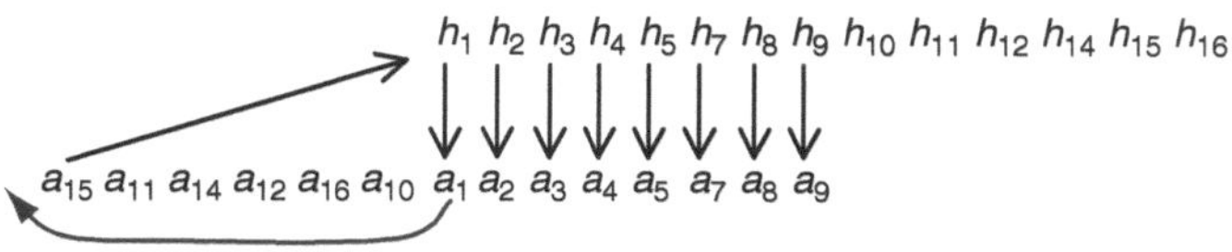

Figure 2.10 YRMH-IGYT Example - Step 4.

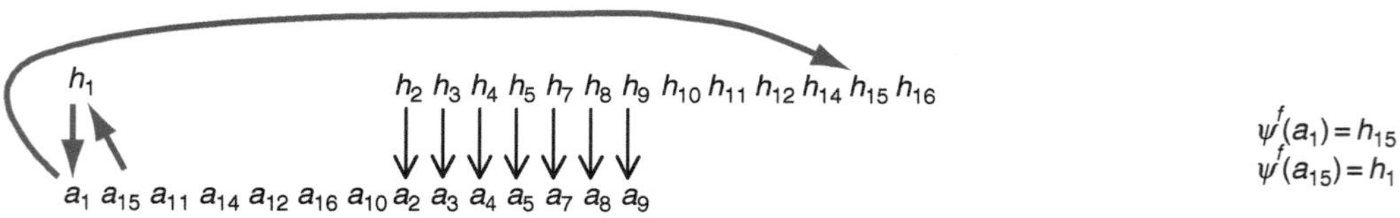

Figure 2.11 YRMH-IGYT Example - Step 5.

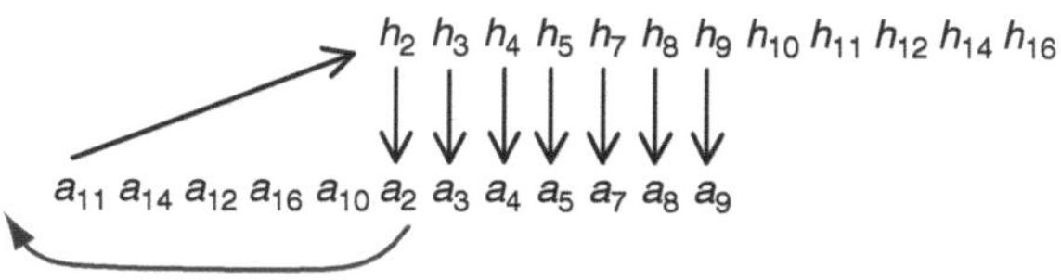

Figure 2.12 YRMH-IGYT Example - Step 6.

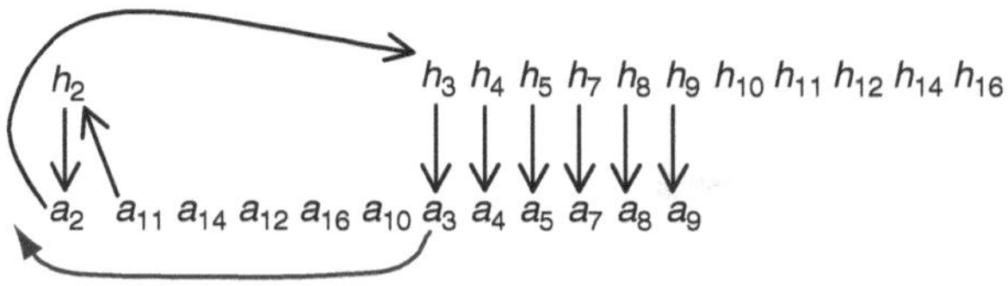

Figure 2.13 YRMH-IGYT Example - Step 7.

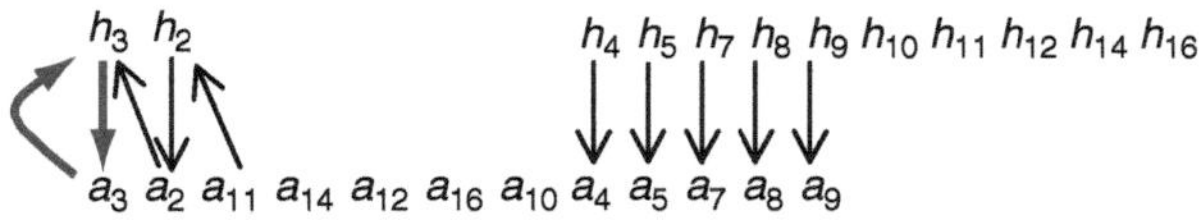

$\psi^f(a_3) = h_3$

Figure 2.14 YRMH-IGYT Example - Step 8.

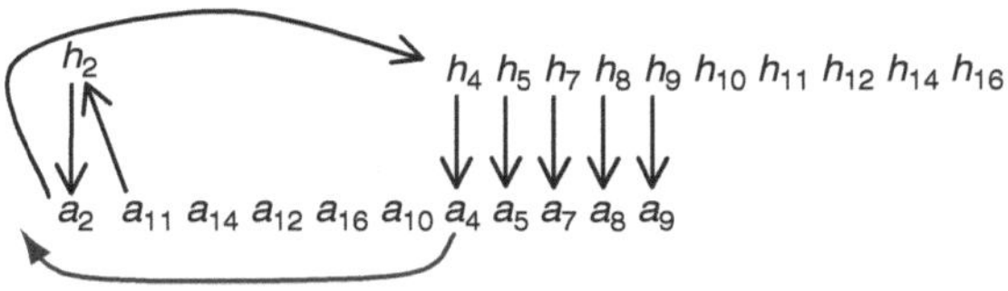

Figure 2.15 YRMH-IGYT Example - Step 9.

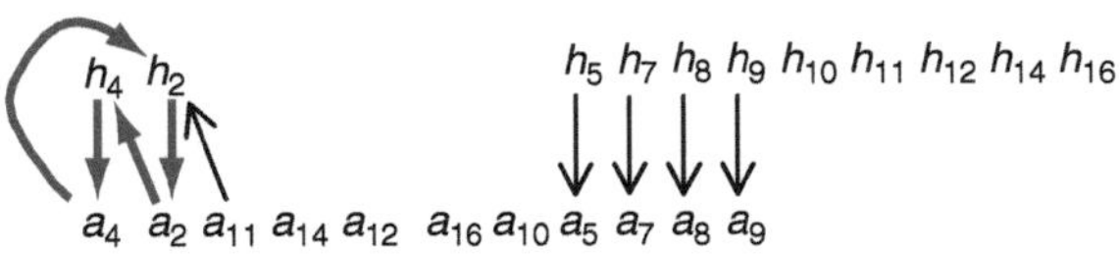

$\psi^f(a_4) = h_2$
$\psi^f(a_2) = h_4$

Figure 2.16 YRMH-IGYT Example - Step 10.

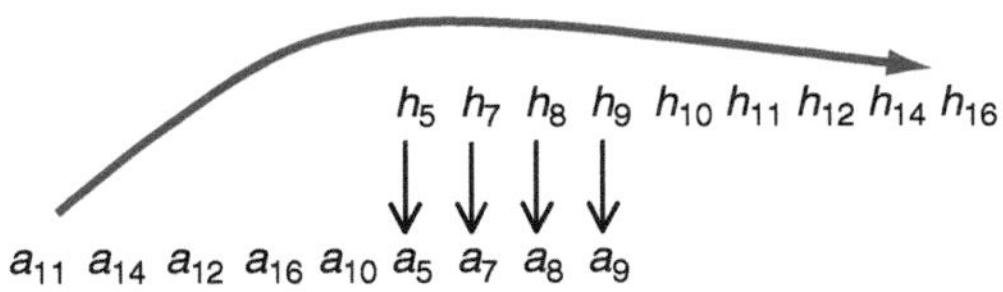

$\psi^f(a_{11}) = h_{16}$

Figure 2.17 YRMH-IGYT Example - Step 11.

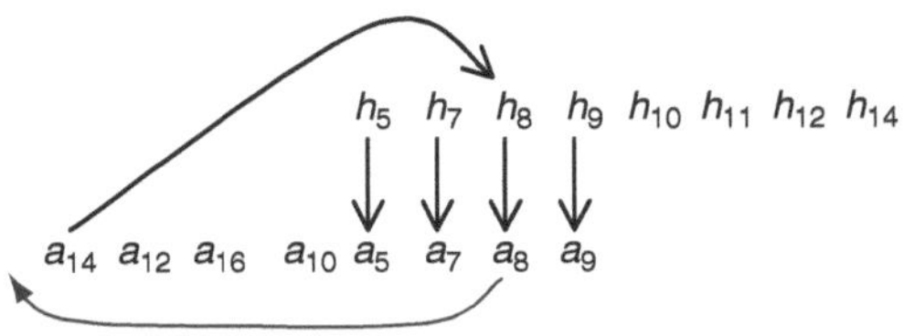

Figure 2.18 YRMH-IGYT Example - Step 12.

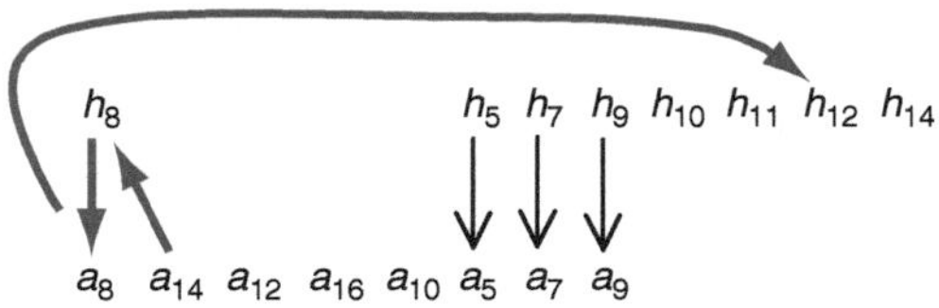

$\psi^f(a_3) = h_{12}$
$\psi^f(a_{14}) = h_8$

Figure 2.19 YRMH-IGYT Example - Step 13.

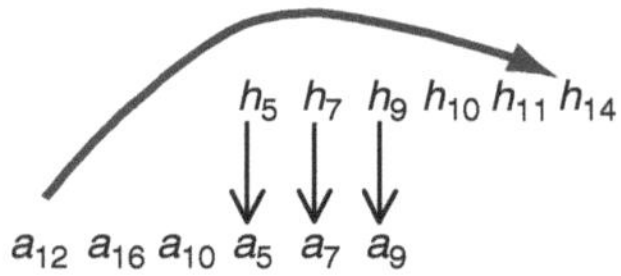

$\psi^f(a_{12}) = h_{14}$

Figure 2.20 YRMH-IGYT Example - Step 14.

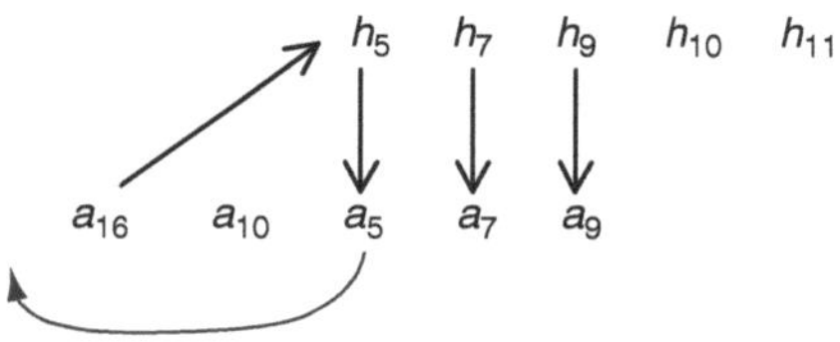

Figure 2.21 YRMH-IGYT Example - Step 15.

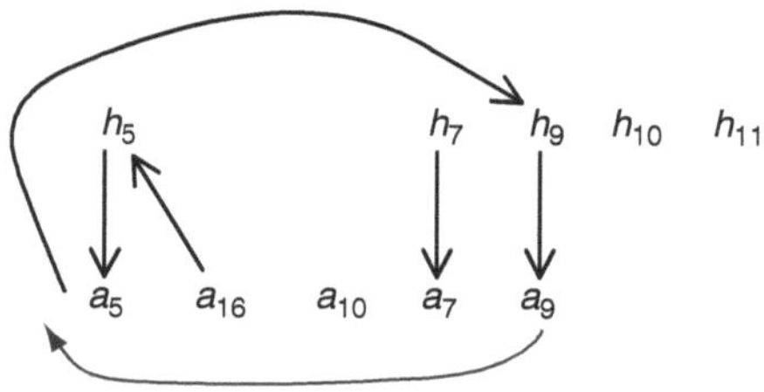

Figure 2.22 YRMH-IGYT Example - Step 16.

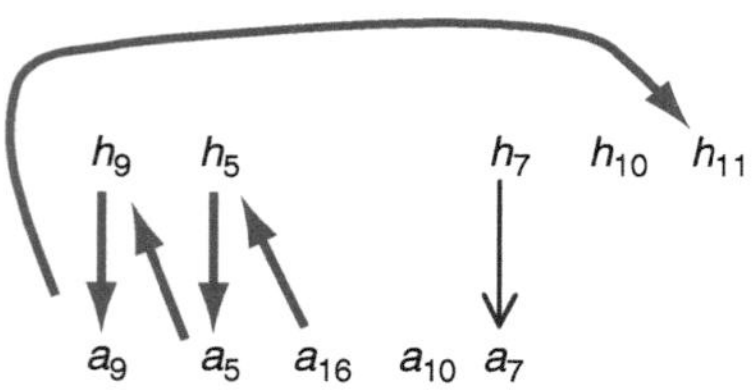

$\psi^f(a_9) = h_{11}$
$\psi^f(a_5) = h_9$
$\psi^f(a_{16}) = h_5$

Figure 2.23 YRMH-IGYT Example - Step 17.

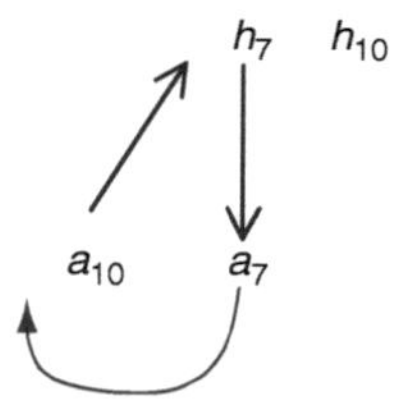

Figure 2.24 YRMH-IGYT Example - Step 18.

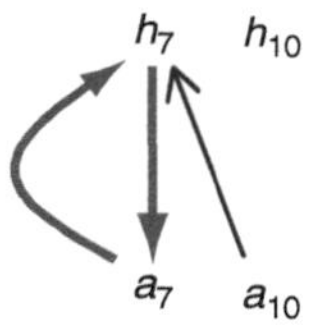

$\psi^f(a_7) = h_7$

Figure 2.25 YRMH-IGYT Example - Step 19.

$\psi^f(a_{10}) = h_{10}$

Figure 2.26 YRMH-IGYT Example - Step 20.

The outcome of the algorithm is

$$\mu = \begin{pmatrix} a_1 & a_2 & a_3 & a_4 & a_5 & a_6 & a_7 & a_8 & a_9 & a_{10} & a_{11} & a_{12} & a_{13} & a_{14} & a_{15} & a_{16} \\ h_{15} & h_4 & h_3 & h_2 & h_9 & h_6 & h_7 & h_{12} & h_{11} & h_{10} & h_{16} & h_{14} & h_{13} & h_8 & h_1 & h_5 \end{pmatrix}$$

The following theorem shows that this mechanism has desirable properties:

Theorem 7 ***(Abdulkadiroğlu and Sönmez 1999)*** *Any* YRMH-IGYT mechanism *is* individually rational, Pareto-efficient, *and* strategy-proof.

Thus, the YRMH-IGYT mechanisms have nice features. The priority ordering can be determined through a lottery. Chen and Sönmez (2002) showed through a laboratory experiment that this mechanism is practically better than the RSD mechanism with squatting rights. The treatments of the YRMH-IGYT mechanism were more efficient than the RSD with squatting rights mechanism, and manipulation did not occur to a significant degree.

Moreover, it is the unique mechanism that satisfies certain desirable properties:

A mechanism is **coalitionally strategy-proof** if for any problem there is no coalition of agents who can jointly misreport their preferences and all weakly benefit while at least one in the coalition strictly benefits.

A mechanism is **consistent** if, we remove the agents and their assigned houses by the mechanism from the problem together with some unassigned houses, provided that in the remaining problem if an existing tenant remains her occupied house also remains, then rerunning the mechanism for this subproblem does not change the assignments of agents in the subproblem.

A mechanism is **weakly neutral** if, when the vacant houses are relabeled and the mechanism is rerun, then every agent who was assigned a vacant house in the original problem is assigned the relabeled version of the vacant house, and every agent who was assigned an occupied house in the original problem is assigned the same occupied house.

The characterization theorem is as follows:

Theorem 8 ***(Sönmez and Ünver 2010b)*** *A mechanism is* coalitionally strategy-proof, individually rational, Pareto-efficient, weakly neutral, *and* consistent *if and only if it is equivalent to a* YRMH-IGYT mechanism.

We conclude by stating some other characterizations regarding restricted domains. In the restricted domains, the mechanisms characterized are equivalent to YRMH-IGYT mechanisms.

Theorem 9 ***(Svensson 1999)*** *In the house allocation problem, a mechanism is* coalitionally strategy-proof, *and* (weakly) neutral *if and only if it is equivalent to a* serial dictatorship.

Theorem 10 ***(Ergin 2000)*** *In the house allocation problem, a mechanism is* Pareto-efficient, (weakly) neutral, *and* consistent *if and only if it is equivalent to a* serial dictatorship.

On the other hand, when there are no newcomers, as in the housing market domain, Theorems 5 by Roth (1982a) and 6 by Ma (1994) imply that the core mechanism is the only desirable mechanism: A mechanism is individually rational, strategy-proof, and Pareto-efficient if and only if it is equivalent to the core mechanism. Observe that these three theorems do not follow from Theorem 8, since smaller sets of axioms are needed in characterization in the more restricted domains.

Some other recent papers on house allocation and exchange mechanisms are as follows: Jaramillo and Manjunath (2009) extends the YRMH-IGYT mechanism (more precisely, Gale's TTC algorithm) to the case where agents can have preferences with indifferences. The new mechanism is strategy-proof, Pareto-efficient, and individually rational like the YRMH-IGYT mechanism. Ekici (2009) introduces a new property call reclaim-proofness for house allocation problems with existing tenants. He shows that all reclaim-proof matchings of a problem can be found through YRMH-IGYT mechanisms induced by different priority orders. He continues defining competitive matchings in this domain and shows that competitive matchings coincide with reclaim-proof matchings.

3. KIDNEY EXCHANGE

In the recent years, the design of kidney exchange (in the medical literature also known as kidney paired donation) mechanisms has been one of the important market design applications of the house allocation and exchange models. A new theory has been developed to accommodate the institutional restrictions imposed by the nature of the problem. This chapter surveys three articles on this design problem (Roth, Sönmez, and Ünver, 2004, 2005a, 2007).

Transplantation is the preferred treatment for the end-stage kidney disease. There are more than 70000 patients waiting for a kidney transplant in the US. In 2005, only 16500 transplants were conducted, 9800 from **deceased donors** and 6570 from **living donors**, while 29160 new patients joined the deceased donor waiting list and 4200 patients died while waiting for a kidney.[1] Buying and selling a body part is illegal in many countries in the world including the US. **Donation** is the only source of kidneys in many countries. There are two sources of donation:

1. **Deceased donors:** In the US and Europe a centralized priority mechanism is used for the allocation of deceased donor kidneys. The patients are ordered in a waiting list, and the first available donor kidney is given to the patient who best satisfies a metric based on the quality of the match, waiting time in the queue, age of the patient, and other medical and fairness criteria.
2. **Living donors:** Generally friends or relatives of a patient (due to the "no buying and selling" constraint) would like to donate one of their kidneys to a designated patient.[2] Live donations have been an increasing source of donations in the last decade. The design problem determines in the most efficient manner of allocating the kidneys of these donors.

3.1 Directed live donations and donor exchanges

After a patient identifies a willing donor, the transplant is carried out if the donor kidney is compatible with the patient. There are two tests that a donor should pass before she is deemed compatible with the patient:

1. **Blood compatibility test:** There are four blood types, "O," "A," "B," and "AB." "O" type kidneys are blood-type compatible with all patients; "A" type kidneys are blood-type compatible with "A" and "AB" type patients; "B" type kidneys are blood-type compatible with "B" and "AB" type patients; and "AB" type kidneys are only blood-type compatible with "AB" type patients.
2. **Tissue compatibility test** (or **crossmatch test**)**:** 6 HLA (short for human leukocyte antigen) proteins (3 inherited from the mother and 3 inherited from the father)

[1] According to SRTR/OPTN national data retrieved at http://www.optn.org on 2/27/2007.

[2] Although the number of "nondirected," good Samaritan altruistic donors has steadily been increasing, it is still small relative to the number of "directed" live donors.

located on patient and donor DNA helices respectively play two roles in determining tissue compatibility. If antibodies exist in the patient blood against the donor HLA, then the donor kidney cannot be transplanted to the patient and it is deemed tissue-type incompatible. It is reported that, on average, there is only 11% chance of tissue-type incompatibility for a random donor and patient (Zenios, Woodle, and Ross, 2001).

Exact HLA match is not required for tissue compatibility; however, there is a debate in the medical literature about how important the closeness of HLA proteins of the patient and donor are for the long-run survival rate of a transplanted kidney.

Traditionally, if either test fails, the patient remains on the deceased donor waiting list and the donor goes home unutilized. However, the medical community came up with two ways of utilizing these "unused" donors.

An (**paired**) **exchange** involves two incompatible patient-donor pairs such that the patient in each pair feasibly receives a transplant from the donor in the other pair. This pair of patients exchange donated kidneys. For example, see Figure 3.1. Of course the number of pairs in a paired exchange can be larger than two.

A **list exchange** involves an exchange between one incompatible patient-donor pair and the deceased donor waiting list. The patient in the pair becomes the first priority person on the deceased donor waiting list in return for the donation of her donor's kidney to someone on the waiting list (see Figure 3.2).

List exchanges can potentially harm O blood-type patients waiting on the deceased donor waiting list. Since the O blood type is the most common blood type, a patient with an incompatible donor is most likely to have O blood herself and a non-O blood-type incompatible donor. Thus, after the list exchange, the blood type of the donor sent to the deceased donor waiting list has generally non-O blood, while the patient placed at the top of the list has O blood. Thus, list exchanges are deemed ethically controversial. Only the New England region in the US adopted list exchange.

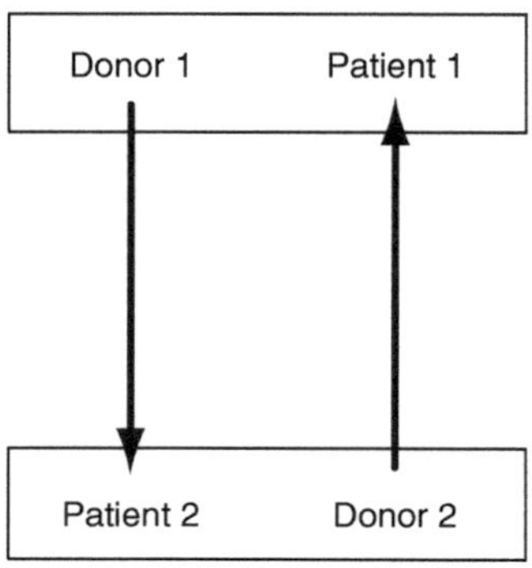

Figure 3.1 A paired exchange.

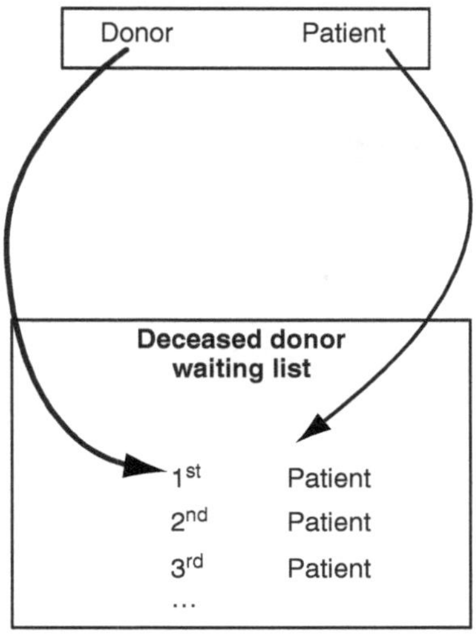

Figure 3.2 A list exchange.

A list exchange can also involve more pairs than one. Doctors also use nondirected live altruistic donors instead of deceased donors. There is no uniform national policy regarding the handling of nondirected live donors. Many regions conduct exchanges induced by nondirected live donors. Since live donor kidneys are better quality than deceased donor kidneys, such exchanges create better participation incentives for patients and their live paired donors.

3.2 The designs

Two live donor exchange programs have already been established in the US through collaboration between economists and medical doctors, one in New England and one in Ohio. A national exchange program is being developed.

The surveyed designs illustrate how the exchange system may be organized from the point of view of **efficiency**, providing consistent **incentives** to patients-donors-doctors. Although medical compatibilities are important for matching, the incentives to patients and doctors are also quite important. Patients (doctors) hold *private* information about their (their patients') preferences over several dimensions such as the geographic distance of the match or the number of willing donors they have. Under some designs, they may not want to reveal this information truthfully, since they (their patients) may benefit from manipulation of information revelation. The initial two designs we will discuss in this survey extract the private information truthfully from patients (doctors) under any circumstance (*strategy-proofness*). We impose several other important *economic* or *normative* criteria on our designs besides incentive compatibility, such as Pareto efficiency and fairness. For fairness, we consider two different approaches: (1) giving *priorities* to patients based on their exogenous characteristics or (2) making every patient as equally well off as the medical constraints permit (also known as *egalitarianism*). Finally, the last design we will discuss refines Pareto efficiency and focuses on aggregate efficiency concerns.

3.3 The model

A **kidney exchange problem** consists of:

- a set of **donor (kidney)-(transplant) patient pairs** $\{(k_1, t_1), \ldots (k_n, t_n)\}$,
- a set of **compatible kidneys** $K_i \subset K = \{k_1, \ldots, k_n\}$ for each patient t_i, and
- a **strict preference relation** $\succ_i$ over $K_i \cup \{k_i, w\}$ where w refers to the priority in the waiting list in exchange for kidney k_i.

An outcome of a problem is a **matching** of kidneys/waiting list option to patients such that multiple patients can be matched with the w option (and lotteries over matchings are possible). A kidney exchange **mechanism** is a systematic procedure to select a matching for each kidney exchange problem (and lottery mechanisms are possible).[3]

A matching is **Pareto-efficient** if there is no other matching that makes everybody weakly better off and at least one patient strictly better off. A mechanism is **Pareto-efficient** if it always chooses Pareto-efficient matchings.

A matching is individually rational if each patient is matched with an option that is weakly better than her own paired-donor. A mechanism is **individually rational** if it always selects an **individually rational** matching.[4]

A mechanism is **strategy-proof** if it is always the best strategy for each patient to:

1. reveal her preferences over other available kidneys truthfully, and
2. declare the whole set of her donors (in case she has multiple donors) to the system without hiding any (the model treats each patient as having a single donor, but the extension to multiple donors is straightforward).

3.4 Multi-way kidney exchanges with strict preferences

The first design and the set of results are due to Roth, Sönmez, and Ünver (2004). Unless otherwise noted, all stated results are from this paper. In this design the underlying assumptions are as follows:

- Any number of patient-donor pairs can participate in an exchange, i.e., exchanges are possibly multi-way.

[3] For the time being, we exclude the possibility of non-directed altruistic donors. However, such donors can be incorporated into the problem easily as w option. But, there is one difference: an altruistic donor cannot be matched to more than one patient.

[4] We will assume that an incompatible own paired-donor is the opt-out option of a patient.

- Patients have heterogeneous preferences over compatible kidneys; in particular, no two kidneys have the same quality, i.e., the preferences of a patient are strict and they linearly order compatible kidneys, the waiting list option, and her own paired-donor. Opelz (1997) shows in his data set that among compatible donors, the increase in the number of HLA protein mismatches decreases the likelihood of kidney survival. Body size, age of donor etc. also affect kidney survival.
- List exchanges are allowed.

Under these assumptions, this model is very similar to the house allocation model with existing tenants. We will consider a class of mechanisms that clear through an iterative algorithm.

Since the mechanism relies on an algorithm consisting of several rounds, let's first focus on some of the graph-theoretical objects encountered by the algorithm. In each stept

- each patient t_i points either toward a kidney in $K_i \cup \{k_i\}$ or toward w, and
- each kidney k_i points to its paired patient t_i.

In such a directed graph, we are interested in two types of subgraphs: One is a **cycle** (as defined in housing markets, where agents refer to patients and houses refer to kidneys). Each cycle is of even size and no two cycles can intersect. The other is a new concept. A *w*-**chain** is an ordered list of kidneys and patients $(k_1, t_1, k_2, t_2, \ldots, k_m, t_m)$ such that k_i points to t_i for each patient, t_i points to k_{i+1} for each $i \neq m$, and t_m points to w (see Figure 3.2).

We refer to the last pair (k_m, t_m) as the **head** and the first pair (k_1, t_1) as the **tail** in such a *w*-chain (see Figure 3.3). A *w*-**chain** is also of even size but, unlike in a cycle, a kidney or a patient can be part of several *w*-chains (see Figure 3.4).

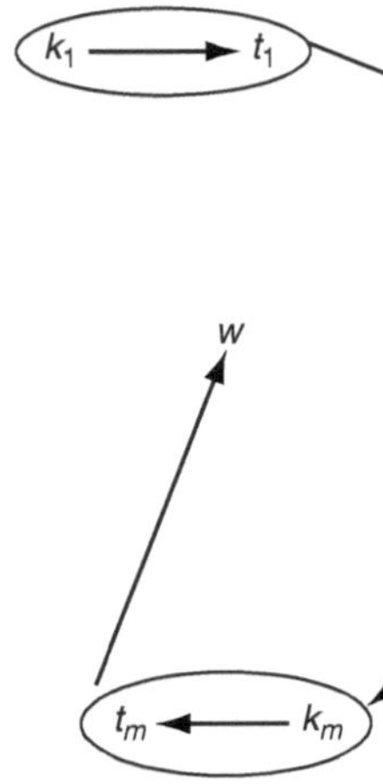

Figure 3.3 A w-chain.

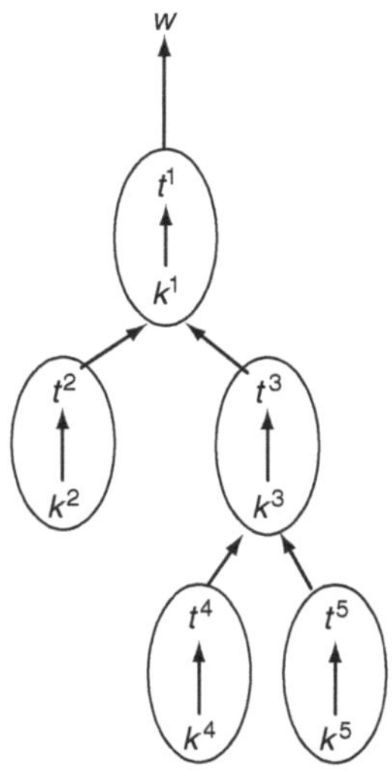

Figure 3.4 In this figure, there are 5 w-chains initiated by each of the 5 pairs: (k_1, t_1), (k_2, t_2, k_1, t_1), (k_3, t_3, k_1, t_1), $(k_4, t_4, k_3, t_3, k_1, t_1)$, and $(k_5, t_5, k_3, t_3, k_1, t_1)$

One practical possibility is choosing among w-chains with a well-defined chain selection rule. The choice of chain selection rule has implications for efficiency and incentive-compatibility.

We can now state our first result of this section:

Lemma 2 *Consider a graph in which both the patient and the kidney of each pair are distinct nodes as is the waiting list option w. Suppose each patient points either toward a kidney or w, and each kidney points to its paired patient. Then either there exists a cycle or each pair initiates a w-chain. Moreover, when cycles exist, no two cycles intersect.*

Based on this lemma, we can formulate the following exchange procedure that is referred to as the **top trading cycles and chains algorithm (TTCC) algorithm**. Fix a chain selection rule. At a given time and for a given kidney exchange problem, the TTCC mechanism determines the exchanges as follows:

Algorithm 5 *The* TTCC algorithm with a chain selection rule:

1. *Initially all kidneys are available and all agents are active. At each stage of the procedure*
   - *each remaining active patient t_i points to the best remaining unassigned kidney or to the waiting list option w, whichever is more preferred,*
   - *each remaining passive patient continues to point to her assignment, and*
   - *each remaining kidney k_i points to its paired patient t_i.*
2. *By Lemma 2, there is either a cycle, or a w-chain, or both.*
   (a) *Proceed to Step 3 if there are no cycles. Otherwise, locate each cycle and carry out the corresponding exchange. Remove all patients in a cycle together with their assignments.*

(b) *Each remaining patient points to her top choice among remaining choices and each kidney points to its paired patient. Proceed to Step 3 if there are no cycles. Otherwise locate all cycles, carry out the corresponding exchanges, and remove them.*

(c) *Repeat Step 2b until no cycle exists.*

3. *If there are no pairs left, we are done. Otherwise, by Lemma 2, each remaining pair initiates a w-chain. Select only one of the chains with the chain selection rule. The assignment is final for the patients in the selected w-chain. In addition to selecting a w-chain, the chain selection rule also determines:*

(a) *whether the selected w-chain is removed, or*

(b) *the selected w-chain in the procedure although each patient in it is henceforth passive.*

If the w-chain is removed, then the tail kidney is assigned to a patient in the deceased donor waiting list. Otherwise, the tail kidney remains available in the problem for the remaining steps.

4. *Each time a w-chain is selected, a new series of cycles may form. Repeat Steps 2 and 3 with the remaining active patients and unassigned kidneys until no patient is left. If there exist some tail kidneys of w-chains remaining at this point, remove all such kidneys and assign them to the patients in the deceased-donor waiting list.*

Below we list a number of plausible chain selection rules:

a. Choose minimal w-chains and remove them.

b. Choose the longest w-chain and remove it.

c. Choose the longest w-chain and keep it.

d. Prioritize patient-donor pairs in a single list. Choose the w-chain starting with the highest priority pair and remove it.

e. Prioritize patient-donor pairs in a single list. Choose the w-chain starting with the highest priority pair and keep it.

Each w-chain selection rule induces a TTCC mechanism. The removal and non-removal of w-chain has implications for efficiency.

Theorem 11 ***(Roth, Sönmez, and Ünver 2004)*** *Consider a chain selection rule where any w-chain selected at a nonterminal step remains in the procedure and thus the kidney at its tail remains available for the next step. The* TTCC mechanism *induced by* any such chain selection rule *is* Pareto-efficient.

In the absence of list exchanges, the kidney exchange problem is a direct application of housing markets, and therefore, Theorem 5 implies that TTCC is strategy-proof. What happens when list exchanges are allowed?

Theorem 12 ***(Roth, Sönmez, and Ünver 2004)*** *The* TTCC mechanism *induced by* chain selection rules (a), (d), or (e) *is* strategy-proof. *On the other hand, the* TTCC mechanism *induced by* chain selection rules (b) or (c) *is* not strategy-proof.

We mentioned that the current model is very similar to the house allocation model with existing tenants. There is also a close relationship between the TTCC algorithm and YRMH-IGYT algorithm, when we introduce to the house allocation problem with existing tenants a house similar to the w option of the kidney exchange problem.

Proposition 1 ***(Krishna and Wang 2007)*** *The* TTCC algorithm *induced by* chain selection rule (e) *is equivalent to the* YRMH-IGYT algorithm.

3.5 Two-way kidney exchanges with 0–1 preferences

Although the previous model is a variation of the house allocation and exchange model, there are intricate restrictions of the kidney exchange problem that this model cannot handle.

Since kidney donation is considered a gift, a donor cannot be forced to sign a contract regarding the donation. Thus, all transplants in an exchange should be conducted simultaneously, since otherwise a donor in the exchange could potentially back out after her paired-patient receives a kidney. This is an important restriction and almost always respected in real life. Since there should be a separate transplant team of doctors present for each donation and consequent transplant, this constraint puts a physical limit on the number of pairs that can participate simultaneously in one exchange. Because of this restriction, most of the real-life exchanges have been two-way exchanges including two pairs in one exchange. Roth, Sönmez, and Ünver (2005a) considered a model of kidney exchange using this restriction.

Another controversial issue in the market design for kidneys concerns the preferences of patients over kidneys. In the previous model, the assumption was that these preferences are heterogeneous. Although this is certainly the correct modeling approach from a theoretical point of view, small differences in quality may be only of secondary importance. Indeed, in the medical empirical literature several authors make this claim. In this second model, we will assume that all compatible kidneys have the same likelihood of survival, following Delmonico (2004) and Gjertson and Cecka (2000) who statistically show this in their data set. The medical doctors also point out that if the paired-donor of a patient is compatible with her, she will directly receive a kidney from her paired-donor and will not participate in the exchange.

The following model and the results are due to Roth, Sönmez, and Ünver (2005a), unless otherwise noted.

Let N be the set of pairs of all and only incompatible donors and their patients. Preferences are restricted further such that, for each pair $i \in N$, and $k, k' \in K_i$, $k \sim_i k'$, i.e., a patient is indifferent among all compatible kidneys. Moreover, we restrict our attention to individually rational and two-way exchanges in this subsection. That is, for any $\mu \in \mathcal{M}$ and pair i, if $\mu(t_i) = k_j$ for some pair j then $\mu(t_j) = k_i$, and $k_j \in K_i$, $k_i \in K_j$. By a slight abuse of notation, we treat both the patient and the donor as one entity, and rewrite $\mu(i) = j$, meaning that patient t_i is matched with donor k_j, instead of $\mu(t_i) = k_j$.[5] Since we focus on two-way exchanges, we need to define the following concept: Pairs i, j are **mutually compatible** if j has a compatible donor for the patient

[5] Moreover, throughout this section, whenever it is appropriate, we will use the term "patient" instead of "pair."

of i and i has a compatible donor for the patient of j, that is, $k_j \in K_i$ and $k_i \in K_j$. We can focus on a *mutual compatibility matrix* that summarizes the feasible exchanges and preferences. A **mutual compatibility matrix** $R = [r_{i,j}]_{i\in N, j\in N}$ is defined as for any $i, j \in N$,

$$r_{i,j} = \begin{cases} 1 & \text{if } i \text{ and } j \text{ are mutually compatible} \\ 0 & \text{otherwise} \end{cases}$$

A **two-way kidney exchange problem** is denoted by (N, R). Figure 3.5 depicts an undirected graph representation of a kidney exchange problem with $N = \{1, 2, \ldots, 14\}$, Problem (N, R) is given where the edges are the set of feasible two-way exchanges and the vertices are the incompatible pairs. A **subproblem** of (N, R) is denoted as (I, R_I) where $I \subseteq N$ and R_I is the restriction of R to the pairs in I. For example, Figure 3.6 depicts subproblem (I, R_I) of the above problem with $I = \{8, 9, 10, 11, 12, 13, 14\}$:

In Figure 3.7, we depict with boldface edges a matching for the above problem (R, N).

A problem is **connected** if the corresponding graph of the problem is connected, i.e., one can traverse between any two nodes of the graph using the edges of the graph. A **component** is a largest connected subproblem. In the above problem (R, N), there is only one component, the problem itself. On the other hand, in the above subproblem (I, R_I), there are two components, the first consisting of pairs 8, 9, and 10 and the

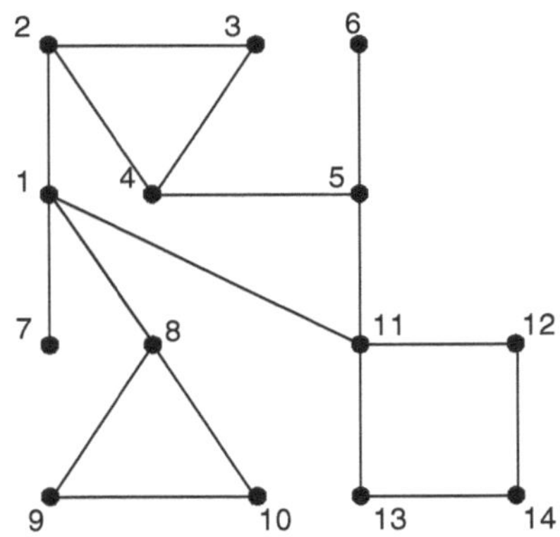

Figure 3.5 A two-way kidney exchange problem.

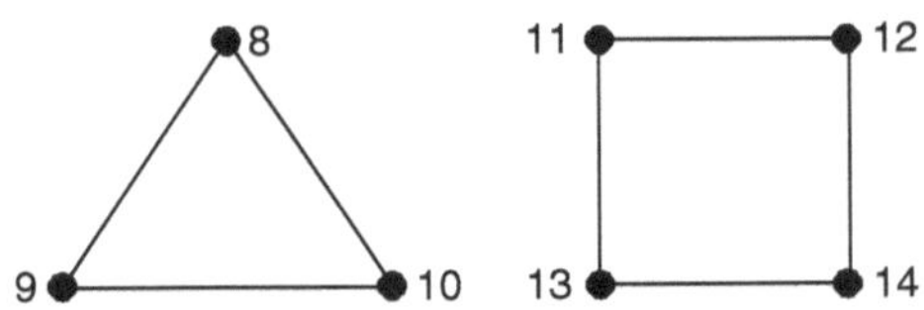

Figure 3.6 A subproblem of the problem in Figure 3.5.

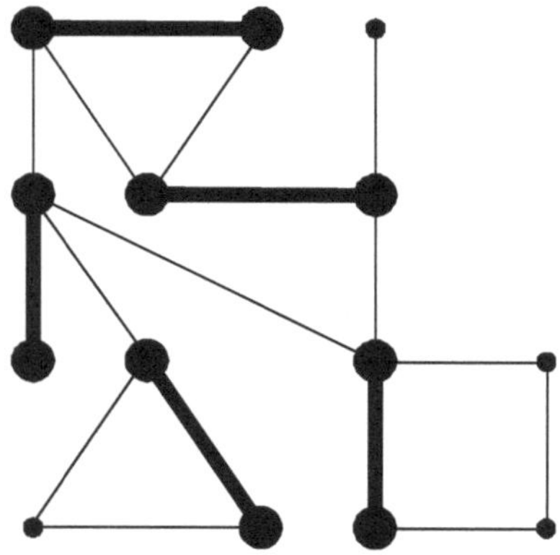

Figure 3.7 A matching.

second consisting of pairs 11, 12, 13, and 14. We refer to a component as **odd** if it has an odd number of pairs, and as **even** if it has an even number of pairs. In the above example, the first component is odd and the second component is even.

Besides deterministic outcomes, we will also define stochastic outcomes. A stochastic outcome is a **lottery** $\lambda = (\lambda_\mu)_{\mu \in \mathcal{M}}$ that is a probability distribution on all matchings. Although in many matching problems, there is no natural definition of von Neumann - Morgenstern utility functions, there is one for this problem: It takes value 1 if the patient is matched and 0 otherwise. We can define the (**expected**) **utility** of a patient t_i under a lottery λ as the probability of the patient getting a transplant and we denote it by $u_i(\lambda)$. The **utility profile** of lottery λ is denoted by $u(\lambda) = (u_i(\lambda))_{i \in N}$.

A matching is **Pareto-efficient** if there is no other matching that makes every patient weakly better off and some patient strictly better off. A lottery is **ex-post efficient** if it gives positive weight to only Pareto-efficient matchings. A lottery is **ex-ante efficient** if there is no other lottery that makes every patient weakly better off and some patient strictly better off. Although in many matching domains ex-ante and ex-post efficiency are not equivalent (for example, see Bogomolnaia and Moulin, 2001), because of the following lemma, they are equivalent for two-way kidney exchanges with 0–1 preferences.

Lemma 3 ***(Roth, Sönmez, and Ünver 2005a)*** *The same number of patients are matched at each* Pareto-efficient *matching, which is the maximum number of pairs that can be matched.*

Thus, finding a Pareto-efficient matching is equivalent to finding a matching that matches the maximum number of pairs. In graph theory, such a problem is known as a *cardinality matching problem* (see e.g., Korte and Vygen 2002, for an excellent survey of this and other optimization problems regarding graphs), and various intuitive polynomial time algorithms are known to find one Pareto-efficient matching starting with Edmonds' (1965) algorithm.

This lemma would not hold if exchange were possible among three or more patients. Moreover, we can state the following lemma regarding efficient lotteries:

Lemma 4 (*Roth, Sönmez, and Ünver 2005a*) *A lottery is* ex-ante efficient *if and only it is* ex-post efficient.

There are many Pareto-efficient matchings, and finding all of them is not computationally feasible (i.e., NP-complete). Therefore, we will focus on two selections of Pareto-efficient matchings and lotteries that have nice fairness features.

3.5.1 Priority mechanism

In many situations a natural priority ordering may arise that naturally orders patients. For example, the sensitivity of a patient to the tissue types of others, known as PRA, is a good criterion accepted also by medical doctors. Some patients may be sensitive to almost all tissue types other than their own and have a PRA=99%, meaning that they will reject 99% of donors from a random sample based solely on tissue incompatibility. So, one can order the patients from high to low with respect to their PRAs and use the following *priority mechanism*:

Algorithm 6 *The* two-way priority (kidney exchange) mechanism:

Given a priority ordering of patients, a ***priority mechanism***

matches ***Priority 1*** *patient if she is mutually compatible with a patient, and skips her otherwise.*

⋮

matches ***Priority k*** *patient in addition to all the previously matched patients if possible, and skips her otherwise.*

Thus, the mechanism determines which patients are to be matched first, and then one can select a Pareto-efficient matching that matches those patients. Thus, the mechanism is only unique-valued for the utility profile induced. Any matching inducing this utility profile can be the final outcome. The following result makes a priority mechanism very appealing:

Theorem 13 *A* two-way priority mechanism *is* Pareto-efficient *and* strategy-proof.

Although the above model did not consider multiple paired-donors, the extension of the model to multiple paired-donors is straightforward.

One can find additional structure about Pareto-efficient matchings (even though finding all such matchings is exhaustive) thanks to the results of Gallai (1963, 1964) and Edmonds (1965) in graph theory and combinatorial optimization. We can partition the patients (as a matter of fact, the incompatible pairs) into three sets as N^U, N^O, N^P. The members of these sets are defined as follows:

An **underdemanded patient** is one for who there exists a Pareto-efficient matching that leaves her unmatched. Set N^U is formed by underdemanded patients, and we will refer to this set as the set of underdemanded patients. An **overdemanded patient** is one who is not underdemanded, yet is mutually compatible with an underdemanded patient. Set N^O is formed by overdemanded patients. A **perfectly matched patient** is one that is neither underdemanded nor mutually compatible with any underdemanded patient. Set N^P is formed by perfectly matched patients.

3.5.2 The structure of Pareto-efficient matchings

The following result, due to Gallai and Edmonds, is the key to understand the structure of Pareto-efficient matchings:

Lemma 5 ***Gallai (1963,1964)-Edmonds (1965) Decomposition (GED)***: *Let μ be any Pareto-efficient matching for the original problem (N, R) and (I, R_I) be the* ***subproblem*** *for $I = N \setminus N^O$. Then we have:*

1. *Any overdemanded patient is matched with an underdemanded patient under μ.*
2. *$J \subseteq N^P$ for any* ***even component*** *J of the subproblem (I, R_I) and all patients in J are matched with each other under μ.*
3. *$J \subseteq N^U$ for any* ***odd component*** *J of the subproblem (I, R_I) and for any patient $i \in J$, it is possible to match all remaining patients with each other under μ. Moreover, under μ*
    - *either one patient in J is matched with an overdemanded patient and all others are matched with each other,*

      or
    - *one patient in J remains unmatched while the others are matched with each other.*

One can interpret this lemma as follows: There exists a competition among odd components of the subproblem (I, R_I) for overdemanded patients. Let $\mathcal{D} = \{D_1, \ldots, D_p\}$ be the set of odd components remaining in the problem when overdemanded patients are removed. By the GED Lemma, all patients in each odd-component are matched but at most one, and all of the other patients are matched under each Pareto-efficient matching. Thus, such a matching leaves unmatched $|\mathcal{D}| - |N^O|$ patients each of whom is in a distinct odd component.

A depiction of the GED Lemma for a problem is given in Figure 3.8.

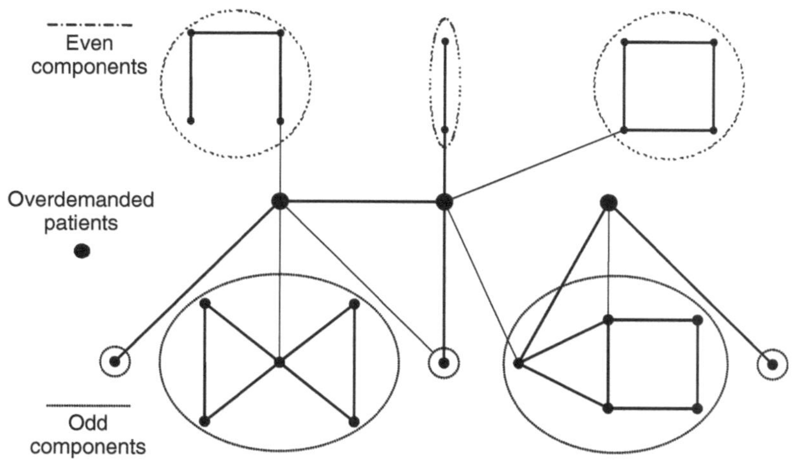

Figure 3.8 The Gallai-Edmonds Decomposition.

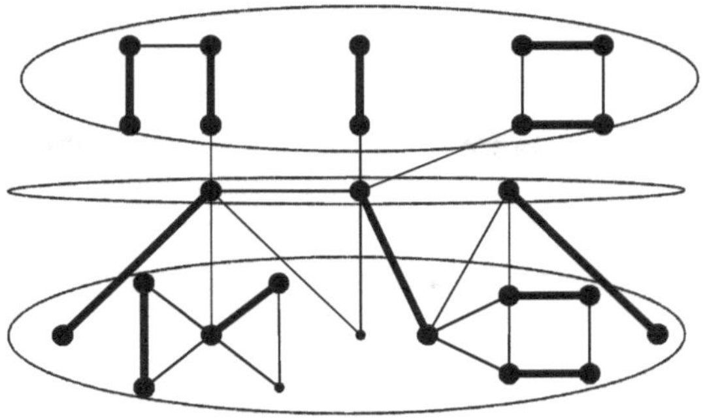

Figure 3.9 A Pareto-efficient matching of the GED given in Figure 3.8.

First suppose that we determine the set of overdemanded patients, N^O. After removing those from the problem, we mark the patients in odd components as *underdemanded*, and patients in even components as *perfectly matched*. Moreover, we can think of each odd component as a single entity, which is competing to get one overdemanded patient for its patients under a Pareto-efficient matching. An example of a Pareto-efficient matching is given in Figure 3.9 for problem in Figure 3.8.

It turns out that the sets N^U, N^O, N^P and the GED decomposition can also be found in polynomial time thanks to Edmonds' algorithm.

Below, we introduce another mechanism that takes into consideration another notion of fairness. This mechanism is also due to Roth, Sönmez, and Ünver (2005a).

3.5.3 Egalitarian mechanism

Recall that the utility of a patient under a lottery is the probability of receiving a transplant. Equalizing utilities as much as possible may be considered very plausible from an equity perspective, which is also in line with the Rawlsian notion of fairness (Rawls 1971). We define a central notion in Rawlsian egalitarianism:

A feasible utility profile is **Lorenz-dominant** if

- the least fortunate patient receives the highest utility among all feasible utility profiles, and

  ⋮

- the sum of utilities of the k least fortunate patients is the highest among all feasible utility profiles.[6]

Is there a feasible Lorenz-dominant utility profile? Roth, Sönmez, and Ünver answer this question affirmatively. It is constructed with the help of the GED of the problem. Let

- $\mathcal{J} \subseteq \mathcal{D}$ be an arbitrary set of odd components of the subproblem obtained by removing the overdemanded patients,

[6] By *k least fortunate patients* under a utility profile, we refer to the k patients whose utilities are lowest in this utility profile.

- $I \subseteq N^O$ be an arbitrary set of overdemanded patients, and
- $C(\mathcal{J}, I)$ denote the **neighbors** of $\mathcal{J}$ among I, that is, each overdemanded patient in $C(\mathcal{J}, I)$ is in I and is mutually compatible with a patient in an odd component of the collection $\mathcal{J}$.

Suppose only overdemanded patients in I are available to be matched with underdemanded patients in $\bigcup_{J\in\mathcal{J}} J$. Then, what is the upper bound of the utility that can be received by the *least fortunate* patient in $\bigcup_{J\in\mathcal{J}} J$? The answer is

$$f(\mathcal{J}, I) = \frac{|\bigcup_{j\in\mathcal{J}} J| - (|\mathcal{J}| - |C(\mathcal{J}, I)|)}{|\bigcup_{J\in\mathcal{J}} J|}$$

and it can be received only if

1. all underdemanded patients in $\cup_{J\in\mathcal{J}} J$ receive the same utility, and
2. all overdemanded patients in $C(\mathcal{J}, I)$ are committed for patients in $\cup_{J\in\mathcal{J}} J$.

The function *f* is the key in constructing an egalitarian utility profile. The following procedure can be used to construct it:

Algorithm 7 The construction of the egalitarian utility profile u^E :

Partition $\mathcal{D}$ as $\mathcal{D}_1, \mathcal{D}_2, \ldots$ and N^O as $N_1^O, N_2^O, \ldots$ as follows:

Step 1.

$$\mathcal{D}_1 = \arg\min_{\mathcal{J}\subseteq\mathcal{D}} f(\mathcal{J}, N^O) \quad \text{and}$$

$$N_1^O = C(\mathcal{D}_1, N^O)$$

⋮

Step k.

$$\mathcal{D}_k = \arg \min_{\mathcal{J}\subseteq\mathcal{D}\setminus\bigcup_{\ell=1}^{k-1}\mathcal{D}_\ell} f\left(\mathcal{J}, N^O \setminus \bigcup_{\ell=1}^{k-1} N_\ell^O\right) \quad \text{and}$$

$$N_k^O = C\left(\mathcal{D}_k, N^O \setminus \bigcup_{\ell=1}^{k-1} N_\ell^O\right)$$

Construct the vector $u^E = (u_i^E)_{i\in N}$ as follows:

1. *For any overdemanded patient and perfectly matched patient $i \in N \setminus N^U$,*

$$u_i^E = 1.$$

2. *For any underdemanded patient i whose odd component left the above procedure at Step k(i),*

$$u_i^E = f(\mathcal{D}_{k(i)}, N_{k(i)}^O).$$

We provide an example explaining this construction:

Example 3 *Let $N = \{1,\ldots,16\}$ be the set of patients and let the reduced problem be given by the graph in Figure 3.10. Each patient except 1 and 2 can be left unmatched at some Pareto-efficient matching and hence $N^U = \{3,\ldots,16\}$ is the set of underdemanded patients. Since both*

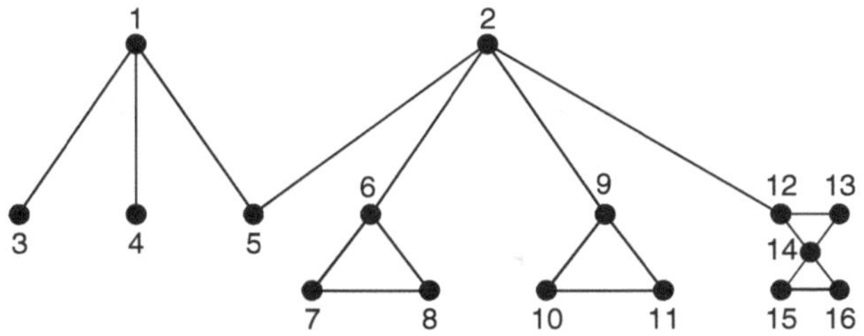

Figure 3.10 Graphical Representation for Example 3.

patients 1 and 2 have links with patients in N^U, $N^O = \{1,2\}$ *is the set of overdemanded patients.*

$$\mathcal{D} = \{D_1, \ldots, D_6\}$$

where

$$D_1 = \{3\},\ D_2 = \{4\}, D_3 = \{5\}, D_4 = \{6,7,8\}$$
$$D_5 = \{9,10,11\}, D_6 = \{12,13,14,15,16\}$$

Consider $\mathcal{J}_1 = \{D_1, D_2\} = \{\{3\},\{4\}\}$. *Note that by the GED Lemma, an odd component that has k patients guarantees* $\frac{k-1}{k}$ *utility for each of its patients. Since* $f(\mathcal{J}_1, N^O) = \frac{1}{2} < \frac{2}{3} < \frac{4}{5}$, *none of the multi-patient odd components is an element of* $\mathcal{D}_1$. *Moreover, patient 5 has two overdemanded neighbors and* $f(\mathcal{J}, N^O) > f(\mathcal{J}_1, N^O)$ *for any* $\mathcal{J} \subseteq \{\{3\},\{4\},\{5\}\}$ *with* $\{5\} \in \mathcal{J}$. *Therefore*

$$\mathcal{D}_1 = \mathcal{J}_1 = \{\{3\},\{4\}\}, \quad N_1^O = \{1\},$$
$$u_3^E = u_4^E = \frac{1}{2}.$$

Next consider $\mathcal{J}_2 = \{D_3, D_4, D_5\} = \{\{5\},\{6,7,8\},\{9,10,11\}\}$. *Note that* $f(\mathcal{J}_2, N^O \backslash N_1^O) = \frac{7-(3-1)}{7} = \frac{5}{7}$. *Since* $f(\mathcal{J}_2, N^O \backslash N_1^O) = \frac{5}{7} < \frac{4}{5}$, *the 5-patient odd component* D_6 *is not an element of* $\mathcal{D}_2$. *Moreover,*

$$f(\{D_3\}, N^O\backslash N_1^O) = f(\{D_4\}, N^O\backslash N_1^O) = f(\{D_5\}, N^O\backslash N_1^O) = 1,$$

$$f(\{D_3, D_4\}, N^O\backslash N_1^O) = f(\{D_3, D_5\}, N^O\backslash N_1^O) = \frac{3}{4},$$

$$f(\{D_4, D_5\}, N^O\backslash N_1^O) = \frac{5}{6}.$$

Therefore,

$$\begin{aligned} \mathcal{D}_2 &= \mathcal{J}_2 = \{\{5\},\{6,7,8\},\{9,10,11\}\}, \\ N_2^O &= \{2\}, \\ \text{and} \quad u_5^E &= \cdots = u_{11}^E = \frac{5}{7}. \end{aligned}$$

Finally since $N^O \backslash (N_1^O \cup N_2^O) = \emptyset$,

$$\begin{aligned} \mathcal{D}_3 &= \{\{12,13,14,15,16\}\}, \\ N_3^O &= \emptyset, \\ \text{and} \quad u_{12}^E &= \cdots = u_{16}^E = \frac{4}{5}. \end{aligned}$$

Hence the egalitarian utility profile is

$$u^E = (1,1,\frac{1}{2},\frac{1}{2},\frac{5}{7},\frac{5}{7},\frac{5}{7},\frac{5}{7},\frac{5}{7},\frac{5}{7},\frac{5}{7},\frac{4}{5},\frac{4}{5},\frac{4}{5},\frac{4}{5},\frac{4}{5}).$$

Roth, Sönmez, and Ünver (2005a) proved the following results:

Theorem 14 (*Roth, Sönmez, and Ünver 2005a*) *The vector* u^E is a feasible utility profile.

In particular, the proof of Theorem 14 shows how a lottery that implements u^E can be constructed.

Theorem 15 (*Roth, Sönmez, and Ünver 2005a*) *The utility profile* u^E Lorenz-dominates *any other feasible utility profile (efficient or not).*

The egalitarian mechanism is a lottery mechanism that selects a lottery whose utility profile is u^E. It is only unique-valued for the utility profile induced. As a mechanism, the egalitarian approach has also appealing properties:

Theorem 16 (*Roth, Sönmez, and Ünver 2005a*) *The* egalitarian mechanism *is* Pareto-efficient *and* strategy-proof.

The egalitarian mechanism can be used for cases in which there is no exogenous way to distinguish among patients. The related literature for this subsection include two other papers, one by Bogomolnaia and Moulin (2004), who inspected a two-sided matching problem with the same setup as the model above, and one by Dutta and Ray (1989), who introduced the egalitarian approach for convex TU-cooperative games.

3.6 Multi-way kidney exchanges with 0–1 preferences

Roth, Sönmez, and Ünver (2007) inspected what is lost when the central authority conducts only two-way kidney exchanges rather than multi-way exchanges. More specifically, they inspected the upper bound of marginal gains from conducting 2&3-way exchanges instead of only two-way exchanges, 2&3&4-way exchanges instead of only 2&3-way exchanges, and unrestricted multi-way exchanges instead of only 2&3&4-way exchanges. The setup is very similar to the previous subsection with only one difference: a matching does not necessarily consist of two-way exchanges. All results in this subsection are due to Roth, Sönmez, and Ünver (2007) unless otherwise noted.

An example helps illustrate why the possibility of a 3-way exchange is important:

Example 4 *Consider a sample of 14 incompatible patient-donor pairs. A pair is denoted as type x-y if the patient and donor are ABO blood-types x and y respectively. There are nine pairs, who are blood-type incompatible, of types A-AB, B-AB, O-A, O-A, O-B, A-B, A-B, A-B, and B-A; and five pairs, who are incompatible because of tissue rejection, of types A-A, A-A, A-A, B-O, and AB-O. For simplicity in this example there is no tissue rejection between patients and other patients' donors.*

- *If only two-way exchanges are possible:*
  (A-B,B-A); (A-A,A-A); (B-O,O-B); (AB-O,A-AB) is a possible Pareto-efficient matching.
- *If three-way exchanges are also feasible:*
  (A-B,B-A); (A-A, A-A, A-A); (B-O, O-A, A-B); (AB-O, O-A, A-AB) is a possible maximal Pareto-efficient matching.

The three-way exchanges allow

1. *an odd number of A-A pairs to be transplanted (instead of only an even number with two-way exchanges), and*
2. *a pair with a donor who has a blood type more desirable than her patient's to facilitate three transplants rather than only two. Here, the AB-O type pair helps two pairs with patients having less desirable blood type than their donors (O-A and A-AB), while the B-O type pair helps one pair with a patient having a less desirable blood type than her donor (O-A) and a pair of type A-B. Here, note that another A-B type pair is already matched with a B-A type, and this second A-B type pair is in excess.*

First we introduce two upper-bound assumptions and find the size of Pareto-efficient exchanges with only two-way exchanges:

Assumption 1 ***(Upper Bound Assumption)*** *No patient is tissue-type incompatible with another patient's donor.*

Assumption 2 ***(Large Population of Incompatible Patient-Donor Pairs)*** *Regardless of the maximum number of pairs allowed in each exchange, pairs of types O-A, O-B, O-AB, A-AB, and B-AB are on the "long side" of the exchange in the sense that at least one pair of each type remains unmatched in each feasible set of exchanges.*

The first result is about the greatest lower bound of the size of two-way Pareto-efficient matchings:

Proposition 2 ***(Roth, Sönmez, and Ünver 2007) The Maximal Size of Two-Way Matchings:*** *For any patient population obeying Assumptions 1 and 2, the maximum number of patients who can be matched with only two-way exchanges is:*

$$2(\#(A\text{-}O) + \#(B\text{-}O) + \#(AB\text{-}O) + \#(AB\text{-}A) + \#(AB\text{-}B)) + (\#(A\text{-}B) + \#(B\text{-}A) - |\#(A\text{-}B) - \#(B\text{-}A)|) + 2\left(\left\lfloor\frac{\#(A\text{-}A)}{2}\right\rfloor + \left\lfloor\frac{\#(B\text{-}B)}{2}\right\rfloor + \left\lfloor\frac{\#(O\text{-}O)}{2}\right\rfloor + \left\lfloor\frac{\#(AB\text{-}AB)}{2}\right\rfloor\right)$$

where $\lfloor a \rfloor$ *refers to the largest integer smaller than or equal to a and #(x-y) refers to the number of x-y type pairs.*

We can generalize the above example in a proposition for three-way exchanges. We introduce an additional assumption for ease of notation. The symmetric case implies replacing types "A" with "B" and "B" with "A" in all of the following results.

Assumption 3 *#(A-B) > #(B-A).*

The following is a simplifying assumption.

Assumption 4 *There is either no type A-A pair or there are at least two of them. The same is also true for each of the types B-B, AB-AB, and O-O.*

When three-way exchanges are also feasible, as we noted earlier, Lemma 3 no longer holds. Thus, we consider the largest of the Pareto-efficient matchings under 2&3-way matching technology.

Proposition 3 ***(Roth, Sönmez, and Ünver 2007) The Maximal Size of 2&3-Way Matchings:*** *For any patient population for which Assumptions 1–4 hold, the maximum number of patients who can be matched with two-way and three-way exchanges is:*

$$2(\#(A\text{-}O) + \#(B\text{-}O) + \#(AB\text{-}O) + \#(AB\text{-}A) + \#(AB\text{-}B)) + (\#(A\text{-}B) + \#(B\text{-}A) - |\#(A\text{-}B) - \#(B\text{-}A)|) + (\#(A\text{-}A) + \#(B\text{-}B) + \#(O\text{-}O) + \#(AB\text{-}AB)) + \#(AB\text{-}O) + min\{(\#(A\text{-}B) - \#(B\text{-}A)), (\#(B\text{-}O) + \#(AB\text{-}A))\}$$

And to summarize, the marginal effect of availability of 2&3-way kidney exchanges over two-way exchanges is:

$$\#(A\text{-}A) + \#(B\text{-}B) + \#(O\text{-}O) + \#(AB\text{-}AB) - 2\left(\left\lfloor\frac{\#(A\text{-}A)}{2}\right\rfloor + \left\lfloor\frac{\#(B\text{-}B)}{2}\right\rfloor + \left\lfloor\frac{\#(O\text{-}O)}{2}\right\rfloor + \left\lfloor\frac{\#(AB\text{-}AB)}{2}\right\rfloor\right) + \#(AB\text{-}O) + \min\{(\#(A\text{-}B) - \#(B\text{-}A)), (\#(B\text{-}O) + \#(AB\text{-}A))\}$$

What about the marginal effect of 2&3&4-way exchanges over 2&3-way exchanges? It turns out that there is only a slight improvement in the maximal matching size with the possibility of four-way exchanges. We illustrate this using the above example:

Example 5 ***(Example 4 Continued)*** *If four-way exchanges are also feasible, instead of the exchange (AB-O; O-A, A-AB) we can now conduct a four-way exchange (AB-O, O-A, A-B, B-AB). Here, the valuable AB-O type pair helps an additional A-B type pair in excess in addition to two pairs with less desirable blood-type donors than their patients.*

Proposition 4 ***(Roth, Sönmez, and Ünver 2007) The Maximal Size of 2&3&4-Way Matchings:*** *For any patient population in which Assumptions 1-4 hold, the maximum number of patients who can be matched with two-way, three-way, and four-way exchanges is:*

$$
\begin{aligned}
&2\left(\#(A\text{-}O)+\#(B\text{-}O)+\#(AB\text{-}O)+\#(AB\text{-}A)+\#(AB\text{-}B)\right)\\
&+\left(\#(A\text{-}B)+\#(B\text{-}A)-|\#(A\text{-}B)-\#(B\text{-}A)|\right)\\
&+\left(\#(A\text{-}A)+\#(B\text{-}B)+\#(O\text{-}O)+\#(AB\text{-}AB)\right)\\
&+\#(AB\text{-}O)\\
&+\min\{(\#(A\text{-}B)-\#(B\text{-}A)),(\#(B\text{-}O)+\#(AB\text{-}A)+\#(AB\text{-}O))\}
\end{aligned}
$$

Therefore, in the absence of tissue-type incompatibilities between patients and other patients' donors, the marginal effect of four-way kidney exchanges is bounded from above by the rate of the very rare AB-O type.

It turns out that under the assumptions above, larger exchanges do not help to match more patients. This is stated as follows:

Theorem 17 ***(Roth, Sönmez, and Ünver 2007) Availability of Four-Way Exchange Suffices:*** *Consider a patient population for which Assumptions 1, 2, 4 hold and let μ be any maximal matching (when there is no restriction on the size of the exchanges). Then there exists a maximal matching ν that consists only of two-way, three-way, and four-way exchanges, under which the same set of patients benefits from exchange as in matching μ.*

In fact, Roth, Sönmez, and Ünver proved a more general theorem, which states that as long as there are n object types (e.g., for kidneys, 4 blood-types) and compatibility is determined by a partial order (i.e., a transitive, reflexive, anti-symmetric binary relation, e.g., blood-type compatibility is a partial order with "O" at the highest level, "A" and "B" incomparable with each other at the next level, and "AB" at the bottom level of compatibility), if Assumptions 2 and 4 hold, and μ is any maximal matching, then there exists a maximal matching ν which consists only of 2&3&...&n-way exchanges, in which the same agents are matched as in μ.

The strategic properties of multi-way kidney exchange mechanisms are inspected by Hatfield (2005) in the 0-1 preference domain. This result is a generalization of Theorem 13.

A deterministic kidney exchange mechanism is **consistent*** if whenever it only selects a multi-way matching in set $\mathcal{X} \subseteq \mathcal{M}$ as its outcome, where all matchings in $\mathcal{X}$ generate the same utility profile when the set of feasible individually rational matchings is $\mathcal{M}$, then for any other problem for the same set of pairs such that the set of feasible individually rational matchings is $\mathcal{N} \subset \mathcal{M}$ with $\mathcal{X} \cap \mathcal{N} \neq \emptyset$, it selects a multi-way matching in set $\mathcal{X} \cap \mathcal{N}$.[7,8] The last result of this section is as follows:

Theorem 18 (*Hatfield 2005*): *If a deterministic mechanism is* nonbossy *and* strategy-proof *then it is* consistent*. *Moreover, a* consistent* *mechanism is* strategy-proof.[9]

Thus, it is trivial to create strategy-proof mechanisms using *maximal-priority* or *priority* multi-way exchange rules. By maximal-priority mechanisms, we mean mechanisms that maximize the number of patients matched (under an exchange restriction such as 2, 3, 4, etc., or no exchange size restriction) and then use a priority criterion to select among such matchings.

3.7 Recent developments and related literature

In closing of this section, we would like to note that New England Program for Kidney Exchange (NEPKE)[10] is using a priority-based mechanism that incorporates 2&3&4-way paired exchanges, list exchanges, and nondirected altruistic donor exchanges (similar to the list exchanges, instead of the pair initiating a list exchange, an altruistic donor is used, e.g., see Sönmez and Ünver, 2006 and Roth, Sönmez, Ünver, Delmonico, and Saidman, 2006; also see Roth, Sönmez, and Ünver, 2005b). The Alliance for Paired Donation (APD)[11] is another kidney exchange program that has been established with the help of economists. This program is larger than its New England counterpart in number of transplant centers participating. In 2007, remarkably most of the kidney exchanges conducted in NEPKE and APD were chain exchanges initiated by a nondirected altruistic donor.

At the time of the preparation of this survey, the United Network for Organ Sharing (UNOS), the contractor for the federal Organ Procurement and Transplant Network (OPTN) that is in charge of the allocation of deceased donor kidneys in the US, has been designing the national kidney exchange program in collaboration with medical doctors, economists, and computer scientists.

Finding maximal multi-way matchings with a size limit is an NP-complete problem unlike its counterpart for two-way exchanges. Especially in large patient pools this may create a computational handicap. In the computer science literature, Abraham, Blum, and Sandholm (2007) introduced an integer-programming algorithm that can compute the maximal multi-way exchanges with size-limit in a fast fashion exploiting the special structure of the multi-way kidney exchange problem. They use the Roth, Sönmez, and Ünver (2007) formulation of the multi-way exchange problem in their algorithm.

[7] Recall that a kidney exchange mechanism may select many matchings that are utilitywise equivalent in the 0-1 preference domain. A two-way priority mechanism is an example.

[8] We use the * superscript to distinguish this new property from the consistency property we introduced in the house allocation problem.

[9] When there are possible indifferences in preferences, nonbossiness and strategy-proofness together are not necessarily equivalent to coalitional strategy-proofness.

[10] See http://www.nepke.org retrieved on 10/16/2008.

[11] See http://www.paireddonation.org retrieved on 10/16/2008.

Ünver (2010) considered a dynamic exchange problem where pairs arrive at the pool under a stochastic Poisson process. He finds optimal dynamic matching in this framework and shows that it may always not be optimal to conduct the largest exchange currently possible. Yilmaz (2008) found an egalitarian mechanism that allows multi-way list and paired exchanges under compatibility-based preferences.

Zenios (2002) studied the optimal control of a paired and list exchange program. In addition to the simulations reported in Roth, Sönmez, and Ünver (2004, 2005b, and 2007), in the medical literature starting with Segev et al. (2005), who simulated possible gains in the US population using Edmonds' (1965) algorithm from weight-maximal two-way exchanges, several papers reported Monte-Carlo simulations estimating possible gains from various ideas in kidney exchange.

In the algorithmic design literature, there are theoretically related studies to the kidney exchange problem such as Abraham et al. (2005), Cechlárová, Fleiner, and Manlove (2005), Biró and Cechlárová (2007), Irving (2007), and Biró and McDermid (2008). These studies study computational complexity of different proposed solutions to the house allocution and kidney exchange problems.

4. SCHOOL ADMISSIONS

4.1 College admissions

In Gale and Shapley's (1962) seminal model, there exist two sides of agents referred to as colleges and students. Each student would like to attend a college and has preferences over colleges and the option of remaining unmatched. Each college would like to recruit a maximum number of students determined by their exogenously given capacity. They have preferences over individual students, which translate into preferences over groups of students under a responsiveness (Roth 1985) assumption. More specifically, a **college admissions problem** consists of:

- a finite set of **students** I,
- a finite set of **schools** S,
- a **quota** vector $q = (q_s)_{s \in S}$ such that $q_s \in \mathbb{Z}_{++}$ is the quota of school s,
- a **preference profile for students** $\succ_I = (\succ_i)_{i \in I}$ such that $\succ_i$ is a strict preference relation over schools and remaining unmatched, denoting the strict preference relation of student i, and
- a **preference profile for schools over individual students** $\succ_S = (\succ_s)_{s \in S}$ such that $\succ_s$ is a strict preference relation over students and remaining unmatched, such that when such a relation is extended over groups of students it satisfies the following two restrictions known as **responsiveness** (Roth 1985):[1]
  - whenever $i, j \in I$ and $J \subseteq I \backslash \{i, j\}$, $i \cup J \succ_s j \cup J$ if and only if $i \succ_s j$,
  - whenever $i \in I$ and $J \subseteq I \backslash i$, $i \cup J \succ_s J$ if and only if $i \succ_s \emptyset$, which denotes the remaining unmatched option for a school (and for a student).

[1] By an abuse of notation, we will denote a singleton without $\{\}$.

A **matching** is the outcome of a problem, and is defined by a function $\mu : I \cup S \rightarrow 2^S \cup 2^I$ such that for each student $i \in I$, $\mu(i) \in 2^S$ with $|\mu(i)| \leq 1$, for each school s, $\mu(s) \in 2^I$ with $|\mu(s)| \leq q_s$, and $\mu(i) = s$ if and only if $i \in \mu(s)$. A (**deterministic direct**) **mechanism** selects a matching for each problem.

The central solution concept in the literature is *stability* (Gale and Shapley 1962). A matching μ is **stable** if

- each match is **individually rational**, i.e., there is no **blocking agent** x and a partner $y \in \mu(x)$ such that $\mu(x)\backslash y \succ_x \mu(x)$, that is, no agent would rather not be matched with one of her mates under μ (if x is a student, then she prefers remaining unmatched to her mate), and
- there is no **blocking pair** $(i, s) \in I \times S$ such that
  - $s \succ_i \mu(i)$, and
  - $i \cup (\mu(s)\backslash x) \succ_i \mu(s)$ for some $x \in \mu(s)$ or $|\mu(s)| < q_s$ and $\mu(s) \cup i \succ_s \mu(s)$,

  that is, there exists no student-school pair who would prefer to be matched with each other rather than at most one of their current mates under μ.

Gale and Shapley prove that for each market there exists a stable matching that can be found through the **school-proposing** or **student-proposing** versions of the **deferred acceptance (DA) algorithm**. We state these algorithms below:

Algorithm 8 *The* school-proposing DA algorithm:

Step 1: *Each school s proposes to its top choice q_s students (if it has fewer individually rational choices than q_s, then it proposes to all its individually rational students). Each student rejects any individually irrational proposals and, if more than one individually rational proposal is received, "holds" the most preferred.*

⋮

Step k: *Any school s that was rejected in the previous step by ℓ students makes a new proposal to its most preferred ℓ students who haven't yet rejected it (if there are fewer than ℓ individually rational students, it proposes to all of them). Each student "holds" her most preferred individually rational offer to date and rejects the rest.*

The algorithm terminates after a step where no rejections are made by matching each student to the school (if any) whose proposal she is "holding."

Algorithm 9 *The* student-proposing DA algorithm:

Step 1: *Each student proposes to her top-choice individually rational school (if she has one). Each school s rejects any individually irrational proposals and, if more than q_s individually rational proposals are received, "holds" the most preferred q_s of them and rejects the rest.*

⋮

Step k: *Any student who was rejected in the previous step makes a new proposal to her most preferred individually rational school that hasn't yet rejected her (if there is one). Each school s "holds" at most q_s best student proposals to date, and rejects the rest.*

The algorithm terminates after a step where no rejections are made by matching each school to the students (if any) whose proposals it is "holding."

These algorithms have desirable properties:

Theorem 19 ***(Gale and Shapley 1962)*** The student- *and* school-proposing DA algorithm *each converge to a stable matching in a finite number of steps.*

Moreover, these algorithms can be used to determine the outcomes of important stable mechanisms:

Theorem 20 ***(Gale and Shapley 1962)*** *The outcome of the* student-proposing DA algorithm *is at least as good as any other stable matching for all students. The outcome of the* school-proposing DA algorithm *is at least as good as any other stable matching for all schools.*

We will refer to the mechanism whose outcome is reached by the student-proposing DA algorithm as the **student-optimal stable mechanism** and the mechanism whose outcome is reached by the school-proposing DA algorithm as the **school-optimal stable mechanism**.[2]

Stability implies Pareto efficiency. However, it imposes many restrictions on mechanisms:

Theorem 21 ***(Roth 1982b)*** *There is* no stable *and* strategy-proof *college admissions mechanism.*

Yet, a partially positive result exists:

Theorem 22 ***(Dubins and Freedman 1981, Roth 1982b)*** *It is a weakly dominant strategy for students to tell the truth under the* student-optimal stable mechanism.

However, we have a negative result for schools' incentives under stable mechanisms:

Theorem 23 ***(Roth 1985)*** *There exists* no stable *mechanism that makes it a dominant strategy for each school to state its preferences over the students truthfully.*

While these results are true in the college admissions setting, the hospital-intern entry-level labor markets in the US can be modeled using the same framework. In the US, the National Residency Matching Program (NRMP) oversees this matching procedure. Roth (1984) showed that the previous NRMP mechanism that was in use from 1950s to 1997 was equivalent to the school-optimal stable mechanism. Roth (1991) observed that several matching mechanisms that have been used in Britain for hospital-intern matching were unstable and as a result were abandoned, while stable mechanisms survived. This key observation helped to pin down stability as a key property of matching mechanisms in the college admissions framework. Roth and Peranson (1999) introduced a new design for the NRMP matching mechanism based on the student-optimal stable mechanism. Interestingly, the replacement of the older stable

[2] See Roth and Sotomayor (1990) for other properties of stable matchings, such as the lattice property, conflict of interest, and parallels between the model in which a school can also be matched with a single student (also known as the *one-to-one matching market* or *marriage market*) and the college admissions model.

mechanism with the newer mechanism was partially attributed to the positive and negative results in Theorems 22 and 23, respectively.

4.1.1 Differences between college admissions, student placement, and school choice problems

Although Gale and Shapley named their model as the college admissions problem, not all college admission procedures can be studied within this framework. For example, US college admissions are usually decentralized. However, there are countries, such as Turkey, Greece, and China, where the process of college admissions is centralized. In such countries, colleges are not strategic agents unlike in the college admissions model, while students potentially are. School seats are objects to be consumed, and there are priority orderings for each school over students based on their exam scores. We will refer to such a problem as a *student placement problem* (Balinski and Sönmez 1999). In the US, K-12 public school admissions are centralized in many states. Moreover, there is relative freedom of school choice freedom, i.e., students do not have to attend the neighborhood school, but have the chance to attend a different school. In such a problem, schools seats are objects to be consumed, and students are potential strategic agents. Priorities that order students for each school are exogenously determined by geography and demographics. We will refer to such a problem as a *school choice problem* (Abdulkadiroglu and Sönmez 2003a). We explore these models and real-life mechanisms below.

4.2 Student placement

A **student placement problem** consists of:

- a finite set of **students** I,
- a finite set of **schools** S,
- a **qauota** vector $q = (q_s)_{s\in S}$ such that $q_s \in \mathbb{Z}_{++}$ is the quota of school s,
- a **preference profile for students** $\succ_I = (\succ_i)_{i\in I}$ such that $\succ_i$ is a strict preference relation over schools and remaining unmatched option, denoting the strict preference relation of student i,
- a finite set of **categories for schools** C,
- an **exam score profile** for students $e = (e^i)_{i\in I}$ such that for any $i \in I$ and $e^i = (e^i_c)_{c\in C}$ where for each category $c \in C$, $e^i_c \in \mathbb{R}_+$ is the exam score of student i in this category and there are no other students $j \in I\backslash\{i\}$ such that $e^i_c = e^j_c$, and
- a **type function** mapping each school to a category type, $t : S \rightarrow C$.

Throughout this subsection we fix I, S, C, and t. Thus a placement problem is denoted through a triple $(\succ_I, q, e)$.

Each school s admits students according to the exam scores of students in category $t(s)$.

For each student placement problem, we can construct an **associated college admissions problem** by assigning each school s a preference relation $\succ_s$ based on the ranking in its category $t(s)$.

We will define a matching and mechanism in this domain together with a new concept.

A **matching** is a function $\mu : I \rightarrow S \cup \{\emptyset\}$ such that no school is assigned to more students than its capacity. When $\mu(i) = \emptyset$, we say that student i is *unmatched* or *matched to no school option.*

A **tentative student placement** is a correspondence $\mu : I \Rightarrow S \cup \{\emptyset\}$ such that no school is assigned to more students than its capacity. Observe that a *tentative student placement* allows a student to be assigned to more than one school.

A **mechanism** is a function that assigns a *matching* for each student placement problem.

Next, we will define desirable properties of student placement mechanisms.

A matching μ **eliminates justified envy** if, whenever a student i prefers another student j's assignment $\mu(j)$ to her own, she ranks worse than j in the category of school $\mu(j)$.

A matching μ is **non-wasteful** if, whenever a student i prefers a school s to her own, there is no empty slot at school s under μ.

We introduced these new concepts to relate *elimination of justified envy, nonwastefulness,* and *individual rationality* to *stability* in the college admissions model as follows:

Proposition 5 ***(Balinski and Sönmez 1999)*** *A school placement matching* eliminates justified envy *and is* non-wasteful *and* individually rational *if and only if the matching is* stable *in the associated college admissions problem. That is, there is an isomorphism with stable college admissions.*

Elimination of justified envy is a critical property in the context of Turkish college admissions. In Turkey, colleges have schools in different areas such as medicine, engineering, humanities, social sciences, and management. The score categories for these schools are typically different from each other. Medical schools usually admit based on a science-weighted score, engineering schools use a math-weighted score, management schools use an equal-language-math-weighted score, and many social sciences and humanities use a social-science-weighted score. Elimination of justified envy is used as the basic notion of fairness in Turkish placement system.

A mechanism **eliminates justified envy** (or is **nonwasteful**) if it always selects a matching that eliminates justified envy (is nonwasteful).

4.2.1 Simple case: one skill category

If there is a single category, then the following proposition follows:

Proposition 6 ***(Balinski and Sönmez 1999)*** *If there is only one category (and hence only one ranking) then there is only one mechanism that is* Pareto-efficient *and* eliminates justified envy: *The* simple serial dictatorship *induced by this ranking.*

It is also useful to observe that there is a unique stable matching in the associated college admissions model that coincides with the outcome of the above serial dictatorship.

An example from Turkey is again useful in this context. There exist merit-based Turkish high schools that admit their students using the results of a centralized exam. This exam has a single score and category. It turns out that the mechanism used in Turkey, developed independently by computer programmers, is the induced serial-dictatorship.

4.2.2 Current mechanism in Turkish college student placement: multi-category serial dictatorship

Currently, the Turkish centralized mechanism uses the following iterative algorithm:

Algorithm 10 *The* multicategory serial dictatorship:

Step 1:

- *For each category c: Consider the ranking induced by the exam scores in this category and assign the school seats in this category to students with the induced simple serial dictatorship.*
- *Assign the "no school" option to all students who are not assigned a school.*
- *This in general leads to a tentative student placement.*
- *For each student i construct $\succ_i^1$ from $\succ_i$ as follows:*
  - *If the student is not assigned more than one school then $\succ_i^1 = \succ_i^1$.*
  - *If the student is assigned more than one school then obtain $\succ_i^1$ by moving the "no school" option $\emptyset$ right after the best of these assignments, otherwise keeping the ranking of the schools the same.*

Let $\succ^1 = (\succ_i^1)_{i \in I}$ be the list of adjusted preferences.

⋮

Step k: *Construct $\succ^k$ from $\succ^{k-1}$ as it is described in Step 1.*

The procedure terminates at the step in which no student is assigned more than one school. The ***multicategory serial dictatorship*** *selects this matching.*

We give an example to show how this algorithm works.

Example 6 $I = \{i_1, i_2, i_3, i_4, i_5\}$, $S = \{s_1, s_2, s_3\}$, $q = (q_{s_1}, q_{s_2}, q_{s_3}) = (2, 1, 1)$, $C = \{c_1, c_2\}$, $t(s_1) = c_1$, $t(s_2) = t(s_3) = c_2$, *with preference profile $\succ$ and exam score profile e given as:*

$$\begin{array}{rl} i_1 : s_2 - s_1 - \emptyset & e^{i_1} = (9,9) \\ i_2 : s_1 - s_2 - s_3 - \emptyset & e^{i_2} = (8,6) \\ i_3 : s_1 - s_3 - s_2 - \emptyset & e^{i_3} = (7,7) \\ i_4 : s_1 - s_2 - \emptyset & e^{i_4} = (6,8) \\ i_5 : s_2 - s_3 - s_1 - \emptyset & e^{i_5} = (5,5) \end{array}$$

Note that these scores induce the following rankings in categories c_1 and c_2:

$$\begin{array}{l} c_1 : i_1\, i_2\, i_3\, i_4\, i_5 \\ c_2 : i_1\, i_4\, i_3\, i_2\, i_5 \end{array}$$

Step 1: *In Step 1 we first find the serial dictatorship outcomes for* $\succ$*:*

$$c_1 : \begin{matrix} i_1 & i_2 \\ s_1 & s_1 \end{matrix} \qquad c_2 : \begin{matrix} i_1 & i_4 & i_3 \\ s_2 & \emptyset & s_3 \end{matrix}$$

Step 1 yields the following tentative student placement:

$$\nu^1 = \begin{pmatrix} i_1 & i_2 & i_3 & i_4 & i_5 \\ s_1, s_2 & s_1 & s_3 & \emptyset & \emptyset \end{pmatrix}$$

Since student i_1 *is assigned two schools her preferences are truncated:*

$$i_1 : s_2 - \emptyset$$

For other students: $\succ^1_{i_2} = \succ_{i_2}$, $\succ^1_{i_3} = \succ_{i_3}$, $\succ^1_{i_4} = \succ_{i_4}$, *and* $\succ^1_{i_5} = \succ_{i_5}$.

Step 2: *In Step 2 we first find the serial dictatorship outcomes for* $\succ^1$*:*

$$c_1 : \begin{matrix} i_1 & i_2 & i_3 \\ \emptyset & s_1 & s_1 \end{matrix} \qquad c_2 : \begin{matrix} i_1 & i_4 & i_3 \\ s_2 & \emptyset & s_3 \end{matrix}$$

Step 2 yields the following tentative student placement:

$$\nu^2 = \begin{pmatrix} i_1 & i_2 & i_3 & i_4 & i_5 \\ s_2 & s_1 & s_1, s_3 & \emptyset & \emptyset \end{pmatrix}.$$

Since student i_3 *is assigned two schools her preferences are truncated:*

$$i_3 : s_1 - \emptyset$$

For other students: $\succ^2_{i_1} = \succ^1_{i_1}$, $\succ^2_{i_2} = \succ^1_{i_2}$, $\succ^2_{i_4} = \succ^1_{i_4}$, *and* $\succ^2_{i_5} = \succ^1_{i_5}$.

Step 3: *In Step 3 we first find the serial dictatorship outcomes for* $\succ^2$*:*

$$c_1 : \begin{matrix} i_1 & i_2 & i_3 \\ \emptyset & s_1 & s_1 \end{matrix} \qquad c_2 : \begin{matrix} i_1 & i_4 & i_3 & i_2 \\ s_2 & \emptyset & \emptyset & s_3 \end{matrix}$$

Step 3 yields the following tentative student placement:

$$\nu^3 = \begin{pmatrix} i_1 & i_2 & i_3 & i_4 & i_5 \\ s_2 & s_1, s_3 & s_1 & \emptyset & \emptyset \end{pmatrix}$$

Since student i_2 *is assigned two schools her preferences are truncated:*

$$i_2 : s_1 - \emptyset$$

For other students: $\succ^3_{i_1} = \succ^2_{i_1}$, $\succ^3_{i_3} = \succ^2_{i_3}$, $\succ^3_{i_4} = \succ^2_{i_4}$, *and* $\succ^3_{i_5} = \succ^2_{i_5}$.

Step 4: *In Step 4 we first find the serial dictatorship outcomes for* $\succ^3$.

$$c_1 : \begin{matrix} i_1 & i_2 & i_3 \\ \emptyset & s_1 & s_1 \end{matrix} \qquad c_2 : \begin{matrix} i_1 & i_4 & i_3 & i_2 & i_5 \\ s_2 & \emptyset & \emptyset & \emptyset & s_3 \end{matrix}$$

Step 4 yields the following tentative student placement (which is also a matching):

$$\nu^4 = \begin{pmatrix} i_1 & i_2 & i_3 & i_4 & i_5 \\ s_2 & s_1 & s_1 & \emptyset & s_3 \end{pmatrix}$$

Since no student is assigned more than one school in ν^4 *the algorithm terminates and* $\varphi^{msd}(\succ_I, e, q) = \nu^4$.

4.2.3 Mechanisms via the associated college admissions problem

We can introduce two desirable mechanisms using the isomorphism between the student placement and school admissions models:

- The **Gale-Shapley school-optimal stable mechanism**: The mechanism that selects the school-optimal stable matching of the associated college admissions problem for each student placement problem.
- The **Gale-Shapley student-optimal stable mechanism**: The mechanism that selects the student-optimal stable matching of the associated college admissions problem for each student placement problem.

The following theorem proves the relationship between the Gale-Shapley mechanisms and the multicategory serial dictatorship.

Theorem 24 ***(Balinski and Sönmez 1999)*** *The* multicategory serial dictatorship *is equivalent to the* Gale-Shapley school-optimal stable mechanism.

Next, we comment on the properties of this mechanism:

4.2.4 Pareto efficiency and elimination of justified envy

Although all stable mechanisms (including Gale and Shapley's) are Pareto-efficient in the college admissions model, in the student placement model, this is no longer true. The reason can be summarized as follows: Since schools are no longer agents in the latter model, we are no longer interested in their welfare. Moreover, unstable matchings can raise the welfare of students over the student-optimal stable matching in the college admissions model. These two results together imply that the outcome of any stable mechanism can be Pareto-inefficient in the student placement model:

Example 7 *There are three students* i_1, i_2, i_3 *and three schools* s_1, s_2, s_3, *each of which has only one seat and admit according to the following two categories* c_1 *and* c_2 *as* $t(s_1) = c_1$, $t(s_2) = c_2$, *and* $t(s_3) = c_3$. *The preferences and exam scores are as follows:*

$$\begin{array}{ll} i_1 : s_2 - s_1 - s_3 - \emptyset & e^{i_1} = (10, 7) \\ i_2 : s_1 - s_2 - s_3 - \emptyset & e^{i_2} = (8, 8) \\ i_3 : s_1 - s_2 - s_3 - \emptyset & e^{i_3} = (9, 3) \end{array}$$

These exam scores induce the following ranking for categories:

$$\begin{array}{l} c_1 : i_1 - i_3 - i_2 \\ c_2 : i_2 - i_1 - i_3 \end{array}$$

Only μ eliminates justified envy but it is Pareto-dominated by ν:

$$\mu = \begin{pmatrix} i_1 & i_2 & i_3 \\ s_1 & s_2 & s_3 \end{pmatrix} \quad \nu = \begin{pmatrix} i_1 & i_2 & i_3 \\ s_2 & s_1 & s_3 \end{pmatrix}$$

However, the multicategory serial dictatorship mechanism is not even Pareto-efficient within the set of mechanisms that eliminate justified envy.

Example 8 *Let $I = \{i_1, i_2\}$ $S = \{s_1, s_2\}$ $q = (1,1)$ $C = \{c_1, c_2\}$, $t(s_1) = c_1$, $t(s_2) = c_2$. The preferences of students are given as follows:*

$$\begin{array}{ll} i_1 : s_1 - s_2 - \emptyset & e^{i_1} = (6,8) \\ i_2 : s_2 - s_1 - \emptyset & e^{i_2} = (8,6) \end{array}$$

The algorithm terminates in one step resulting in the following Pareto-inefficient matching:

$$\varphi^{msd}[\succ_I, e, q] = \begin{pmatrix} i_1 & i_2 \\ s_2 & s_1 \end{pmatrix}$$

It is Pareto-dominated by the following matching that eliminates justified envy:

$$\mu = \begin{pmatrix} i_1 & i_2 \\ s_1 & s_2 \end{pmatrix}.$$

On the other hand, we can adopt Theorem 20 (due to Gale and Shapley) in the school placement domain for the Gale-Shapley student-optimal stable mechanism as follows:

Theorem 25 ***(Gale and Shapley 1962)*** *The* Gale-Shapley student-optimal stable mechanism *Pareto-dominates any other mechanism that eliminates justified envy.*

4.2.5 Strategy-proofness and elimination of justified envy

On the other hand, strategy-proofness is no longer at odds with the elimination of justified envy, yet the multicategory serial dictatorship is not strategy-proof:

Example 9 ***(Example 8 continued)*** *Recall that*

$$\varphi^{msd}[\succ_I, e, q] = \begin{pmatrix} i_1 & i_2 \\ s_2 & s_1 \end{pmatrix}$$

Now suppose i_1 announces a fake preference relation $\succ'_{i_1}$ where only s_1 is individually rational. In this case

$$\varphi^{msd}[\succ'_{i_1}, \succ_{i_2}, e, q] = \begin{pmatrix} i_1 & i_2 \\ s_1 & s_2 \end{pmatrix}$$

and hence, student i_1 successfully manipulates the multicategory serial dictatorship.

A mechanism is **strategy-proof** if truth telling is a weakly dominant strategy for each student in its associated preference revelation game. We can adopt Theorem 22 for the student placement model:

Theorem 26 ***(Dubins and Freedman 1981, Roth 1982b):*** *The* Gale-Shapley student-optimal stable mechanism is strategy-proof.

The following theorem shows that there is no other desirable mechanism:

Theorem 27 ***(Alcalde and Barbera 1994):*** *The* Gale-Shapley student-optimal stable mechanism *is the only mechanism that* eliminates justified envy, *and is* individually rational, nonwasteful, *and* strategy-proof.

4.2.6 Respecting improvements

Example 10 (*Example 8 continued*) *Recall that*

$$\phi^{msd}[\succ_I, e, q] = \begin{pmatrix} i_1 & i_2 \\ s_2 & s_1 \end{pmatrix}.$$

Now suppose student i_1 *scores worse in both tests and her new exam scores are* $e'^{i_1} = (5, 5)$. *In this case*

$$\phi^{msd}[\succ_I, e'^{i_1}, e^{i_2}, q] = \begin{pmatrix} i_1 & i_2 \\ s_1 & s_2 \end{pmatrix}.$$

and student i_1 *is rewarded by getting her top choice as a result of worse performance!*

Note the example is about rewarding worse performance, not respecting better performance. We define this as a property: A mechanism **respects improvements** if a student never receives a worse assignment as a result of an increase in one or more of her exam scores. The following theorems give another characterization of the Gale-Shapley student-optimal stable mechanism:

Theorem 28 ***(Balinski and Sönmez 1999):*** *The* Gale-Shapley student-optimal stable mechanism respects improvements.

Theorem 29 ***(Balinski and Sönmez 1999):*** *The* Gale-Shapley student-optimal stable mechanism *is the only mechanism that is* individually rational *and* nonwasteful, *and that* eliminates justified envy *and* respects improvements.

Thus, the Gale-Shapley student-optimal stable mechanism is the clear winner for student placement, while the Turkish student placement system uses a mechanism that is equivalent to the Gale-Shapley school-optimal stable mechanism.[3]

4.3 School choice

Next, we discuss the third model in this section: A *school choice problem* (Abdulkadiroğlu and Sönmez 2003a) models the school choice in public schools in many school districts in the US, such as Boston, St. Petersburg (Florida), Minneapolis, etc. It consists of a number of students, each of whom should be assigned a seat at one of a number of schools. Each school has a maximum capacity but there is no shortage of the total seats.

[3] See Ehlers and Klaus (2006) and Kojima and Manea (2007b) for two other characterizations regarding the Gale-Shapley student-optimal stable mechanism in resource allocation problems.

Each student has preferences over all schools and each school has a priority ordering of all students. The priorities are exogenous.

Formally, a **school choice problem** consists of

- a finite set of **students** I,
- a finite set of **schools** S,
- a **quota** vector $q = (q_s)_{s \in S}$ such that $q_s \in \mathbb{Z}_{++}$ is the quota of school s,
- a **preference profile for students** $\succ_I = (\succ_i)_{i \in I}$ such that $\succ_i$ is a strict preference relation over schools and remaining unmatched, denoting the strict preference relation of student i,
- a **priority profile for schools** $\succsim_S = (\succsim_s)_{s \in S}$ such that for each school $s \in S$, $\succsim_s$ is a binary relation over the set of students that is complete, reflexive, and transitive. That is, $i \succsim_s j$ means that student i has at least as high priority as student j at school s. Two distinct students i and j can have the same priority at school s, which is denoted as $i \sim_s j$ (i.e., $\sim_s$ is the cyclic part of $\succsim_s$). If i has higher priority than j at s, we denote it as $i \succ_s j$ (i.e., $\succ_s$ is the antisymmetric part of $\succsim_s$).

This problem has a number of differences from the college admissions problem and the student placement problem:

- Differences from college admissions:
  - Students are (possibly strategic) agents; school seats are objects to be consumed.
  - Elimination of justified envy is *plausible* but not a *must*. If imposed, then the school choice problem is *isomorphic* to stable college admissions.
- Differences from student placement:
  - Priorities are exogenous, and
  - Elimination of justified envy is *plausible* but *not a must*.

4.3.1 The Boston school choice mechanism

The most commonly used school choice mechanism is that used by the Boston Public Schools (BPS) until 2005:

Algorithm 11 *The* Boston (school choice) mechanism:

1. *For each school a priority ordering is exogenously determined. (In case of Boston, priorities depend on home address, whether the student has a sibling already attending a school, and a lottery number to break ties.)*
2. *Each student submits a preference ranking of the schools.*
3. *The final phase is the student assignment based on preferences and priorities:*

Step 1: *In Step 1 only the top choices of the students are considered. For each school, consider the students who have listed it as their top choice and assign seats of the school to these students one at a time following their priority order until either there are no seats left or there is no student left who has listed it as her top choice.*

⋮

Step k: *Consider the remaining students. In Step k only the kth choices of these students are considered. For each school still with available seats, consider the students who have listed it as their k^{th} choice and assign the remaining seats to these students one at a time following their priority order until either there are no seats left or there is no student left who has listed it as her k^{th} choice.*

4.3.2 Incentives, Pareto efficiency, and justified-envy-freeness with strict and weak priorities

The major difficulty with the Boston mechanism is that it is not strategy-proof. Moreover, it is almost straightforward to manipulate it. Even if a student has a very high priority at school s, unless she lists it as her top choice she loses her priority to students who have top ranked school s. Hence, the Boston mechanism gives parents strong incentives to overrank schools where they have high priority.

There is also some evidence in the popular media regarding the ease of manipulation of this mechanism. Consider the following quotation from the St. Petersburg Times (09/14/2003):

"Make a realistic, informed selection on the school you list as your first choice. It's the cleanest shot you will get at a school, but if you aim too high you might miss. Here's why: If the random computer selection rejects your first choice, your chances of getting your second choice school are greatly diminished. That's because you then fall in line behind everyone who wanted your second choice school as their first choice. You can fall even farther back in line as you get bumped down to your third, fourth and fifth choices."

Further evidence comes from the 2004–2005 BPS School Guide:

"For a better choice of your "first choice" school . . . consider choosing less popular schools."

The Boston mechanism does not eliminate justified envy, either. Priorities are lost unless the school is ranked as the top choice. In the previous section, we argued that if *elimination of justified envy* is plausible, then the Gale-Shapley student-optimal stable mechanism is the big winner! However, unlike in the student placement problem, in which ties in student exam scores are rare, there are possibly many students who have the same priority in the school choice problem. For example, in Boston, all students who live in the walking zone of a school and have no siblings attending the school have the same priority. Thus, the student-proposing DA algorithm can be used after breaking the tie among equal priority students through a single even lottery. This lottery preserves the strategy-proofness and justified-envy-freeness of the Gale-Shapley mechanism.

The following theorem is about the Nash equilibria of the Boston Mechanism revelation game:

Theorem 30 ***(Ergin and Sönmez 2006):*** *When priorities are strict, the set of Nash equilibrium outcomes of the preference revelation game induced by the* Boston mechanism *is equal to the set of* stable *matchings of the associated college admissions game under true preferences.*

Thus, we can state the following corollary regarding the Boston mechanism and the Gale-Shapley student-optimal stable mechanism:

Corollary 1 *When priorities are strict, the dominant-strategy equilibrium outcome of the* Gale-Shapley student-optimal stable mechanism *either* Pareto-dominates *or is* equal to *the Nash equilibrium outcomes of the* Boston mechanism.

The preference revelation game induced by the Boston mechanism is a "coordination game" among large numbers of parents in which there is incomplete information. So it is unrealistic to expect to reach a Nash equilibrium in practice.

On the other hand, if there is a limit to the number of schools that a student can reveal to the centralized match (as in Boston and New York City), then Corollary 1 no longer holds, while Theorem 30 still holds:

Theorem 31 ***(Haeringer and Klijn 2007)*** *When priorities are strict and students can reveal only a limited number of schools in their preference lists, the* Gale-Shapley student-optimal stable mechanism *may have Nash equilibria in undominated strategies that* induce justified envy.

Haeringer and Klijn (2007) also found the sufficient conditions when equilibria of the above game eliminate justified envy.

On the other hand, the following nice property of the Gale-Shapley mechanism relates its efficiency properties to any other strategy-proof and Pareto-efficient mechanism:

Theorem 32 ***(Kesten 2010)*** *When priorities are strict, the* Gale-Shapley student-optimal stable mechanism *is* not Pareto-dominated *by any other Pareto-efficient mechanism that is* strategy-proof.

When a school has the same priority for two or more students, some results under strict priorities extend, while some don't.

Under weak priorities, there can be many **student-optimal justified-envy-free** matchings, matchings that are not Pareto-dominated by any other justified-envy-free matching and Pareto-dominate any justified-envy-free matching that is not student optimal. Recall that when priorities are strict, there is a unique such matching (see Theorem 25). The above mechanism also has desirable properties for recovering such matchings:

Theorem 33 ***(Ehlers 2006, Erdil and Ergin 2008)*** *When priorities are weak, all student-optimal justified-envy-free matchings can be found by different tie-breaking rules among equal priority students using the* student-proposing DA algorithm.

This above result is a generalization of an earlier result of Abdulkadiroğlu and Sönmez (1998) who showed that when all students have the same priority, all Pareto-efficient matchings can be achieved through different serial dictatorships.

The following is a stronger generalization of the earlier result of Kesten (2010) (Theorem 32) for weak priorities:

Theorem 34 ***(Abdulkadiroğlu, Pathak, and Roth 2009)*** *When priorities are weak, the* Gale-Shapley student-optimal stable mechanism *with any tie breaking rule is* not Pareto-dominated *by any other mechanism that is* strategy-proof.

On the other hand, the Gale-Shapley student-optimal stable mechanism is not Pareto-efficient. As we discussed in the previous section, there is an efficiency cost to the elimination of justified envy. We restate a version of Example 7 below. Observe that this result does need strict priorities among at least three students to hold:

Example 11 *There are three students* i_1, i_2, i_3 *and three schools* s_1, s_2, s_3, *each of which has only one seat. Priorities and preferences are as follows:*

$$\begin{array}{ll} s_1 : i_1 - i_3 - i_2 & i_1 : s_2 - s_1 - s_3 \\ s_2 : i_2 - i_1 - i_3 & i_2 : s_1 - s_2 - s_3 \\ s_3 : i_2 - i_1 - i_3 & i_3 : s_1 - s_2 - s_3 \end{array}$$

Only μ *eliminates justified envy but it is Pareto-dominated by* ν:

$$\mu = \begin{pmatrix} i_1 & i_2 & i_3 \\ s_1 & s_2 & s_3 \end{pmatrix} \quad \nu = \begin{pmatrix} i_1 & i_2 & i_3 \\ s_2 & s_1 & s_3 \end{pmatrix}$$

Actually, the efficiency cost of justified envy is much more severe with weak priorities. The following result can be contrasted with Theorems 25 and 26, which show that the Gale-Shapley student-optimal stable mechanism is strategy-proof and Pareto-dominant among mechanisms that eliminate justified envy when priorities are strict:

Theorem 35 ***(Erdil and Ergin 2008)*** *When priorities are weak, there is no mechanism that is* constrained Pareto-efficient *(within the justified-envy-free class) among (lottery) mechanisms that* eliminate justified envy and are (weakly) strategy-proof.[4,5]

To summarize, with weak priorities, the above results show the tension between strategy-proofness and constrained efficiency for justified-envy-free mechanisms. The Gale-Shapley student-optimal stable mechanism (with a tie-breaking rule that makes it strategy-proof, such as a single tie-breaking lottery) is strategy-proof and Pareto-undominated by other strategy-proof mechanisms. Yet, there exist justified-envy-free and nonstrategy-proof mechanisms that Pareto-dominate this mechanism. An example of a constrained efficient and justified-envy-free mechanism is given by Erdil and Ergin (2008). This mechanism is nonstrategy-proof.

4.3.3 The school choice TTC mechanism

Given these negative results, one can argue that Pareto efficiency is a more important property than elimination of justified envy. School boards can interpret priorities as trading rights to a particular school. In this case, a version of the TTC mechanism becomes very plausible. Abdulkadiroğlu and Sönmez (2003a) introduced a mechanism whose outcome can be determined by the following algorithm:

Algorithm 12 *The* school choice TTC algorithm:

[4] "Weak" strategy-proofness is defined for lottery mechanisms, and requires existence of at least one von Neumann-Morgenstern utility function compatible with preferences, under which truth telling is a dominant strategy.

[5] Yilmaz (2010) obtained a similar impossibility result for the house allocation with existing tenant's domain.

- *Break the ties among equal priority students of each school through a single even lottery.*
- *Assign a counter for each school that keeps track of how many seats are still available at the school. Initially set the counters equal to the capacities of the schools.*
- *Each student "points to" her favorite school. Each school points to the student who has the highest priority.*
- *There is at least one cycle (by Lemma 2). Every student in a cycle is assigned a seat at the school she points to and is removed. The counter of each school in a cycle is reduced by one and if it reduces to zero, the school is also removed. Counters of all other schools stay put.*
- *Repeat above steps for the remaining "economy."*

TTC simply trades priorities of students among themselves starting with the students with highest priorities. TTC inherits the plausible properties of Gale's TTC:

Theorem 36 ***(Abdulkadiroğlu and Sönmez 2003a)*** *The* school choice TTC mechanism *is* Pareto-efficient *and* strategy-proof.

Chen and Sönmez (2006) conducted an experimental study and found that the Gale-Shapley mechanism outperforms TTC and the Boston mechanism in terms of truthful revelation of preferences and overall efficiency. They related this result to the fact that TTC has a tedious algorithmic description with respect to the Gale-Shapley mechanism; thus students understood the second algorithm, better than the first one, under which they tried to manipulate their preferences. On the other hand, Pais and Pintér (2008) showed that when the same games are played in an incomplete information setting then TTC resulted with more efficiency than the Gale-Shapley mechanism and the Boston mechanism.

4.4 Recent developments and related literature

In New York City (Abdulkadiroğlu, Pathak, and Roth 2005), the Gale-Shapley student-optimal stable mechanism was adopted in Fall 2003. The New York City school choice problem is a hybrid between college admissions and school choice, since there are some strategic schools. In Boston (Abdulkadiroğlu, Pathak, Roth, and Sönmez 2005, 2006), though TTC had a head start, the Gale-Shapley student-optimal stable mechanism was selected to replace the Boston mechanism.

Ergin (2002) showed that under an acyclicity condition of priorities, the Gale-Shapley mechanism finds Pareto-efficient outcomes in the school admissions domain. Moreover, the Gale-Shapley mechanism is coalitionally strategy-proof in this case.

Since in the adopted mechanisms we discussed above, ties among equal priority students are broken randomly, we may observe some unnecessary inefficiency under the Gale-Shaley student-optimal stable mechanism.

Kesten (2010) introduced a hybrid approach for the school choice domain that compensates for the inefficiency of the Gale-Shapley student-optimal stable mechanism through a compromise mechanism that introduces minimal instability while creating more efficient outcomes. Moreover, the instability is created with the consent of participating students: a blocking student will never be worse off if she gives consent for such stability violations.

Erdil and Ergin (2008) recognized that the artificial tie breaking of priorities induces inefficiencies under the Gale-Shapley student-optimal stable mechanism. Therefore, after the algorithm converges they proposed a second stage. This is also an iterative procedure. They proposed a random trading stage so that each student can trade her seat as long as other students agree. However, not all trades are acceptable. Trades involving students with the highest priority are deemed feasible. After a "stable" trading cycle is randomly found, the trades are realized. Thus, this process does not induce further inefficiencies. One can conduct feasible trades again and repeat the above procedure until no stable trades are left. Although the Erdil-Ergin mechanism is constrained ex-post efficient, it is not strategy-proof, and yet truth telling is an ordinal Bayesian-Nash equilibrium in a low and symmetric information setting. Using data from NYC schools, Abdulkadiroğlu, Pathak, and Roth (2008) showed that over 1,500 student applicants among 8th graders could have improved their assignment in the Erdil-Ergin mechanism among 90,000 students, if the same student preferences would have been revealed.

Pathak and Sönmez (2008) inspected the Boston mechanism's revelation game when not all students are sophisticated. Sincere players are restricted to report their true preferences, while strategic players play a best response. Although there are multiple equilibrium outcomes, a sincere student receives the same assignment in all equilibria. Finally, the assignment of any strategic student under the Pareto-dominant Nash equilibrium of the Boston mechanism is weakly preferred to her assignment under the student-optimal stable mechanism.

Abdulkadiroğlu and Ehlers (2007) inspected the school choice problem, when there are minimum quotas for students from different backgrounds at schools. These minimum quotas in general lead to nonexistence of justified-envy-free matchings. Thus, they introduced a new definition of justified-envy-freeness. Under this new definition, they showed that a justified-envy-free matching always exists in a "controlled" school choice problem.

There is also an emerging literature regarding the lottery mechanisms in school choice. We cite some of the recent papers below.

Abdulkadiroğlu, Che, and Yasuda (2008) introduced a new tie-breaking rule: each student has the option to designate a target school besides revealing her preferences. Whenever tie breaking is needed among multiple students for a school, students who designate this school as target get priority in tie-breaking. Then the Gale-Shapley student-optimal stable mechanism is applied on the modified priority structure. The authors found plausible properties of this mechanism over the Gale-Shapley version.

Pathak (2006) inspected lottery design in the school choice domain. He proved an equivalence result between RSD and random school-choice TTC mechanism, when all priority orders of schools are independently and uniformly randomly drawn. This corresponds to two versions of tie breaking among equal priority students: tie breaking for all schools using a single lottery or tie breaking independently for each school. However, such an equivalence does not exist for random multiple tie-breaking version of the Gale-Shapley student-optimal stable mechanism and RSD (which is equivalent to Gale-Shapley mechanism with random single tie breaking). Sethuraman (2009) generalized this result to the domain with schools with multiple quotas using a more general mechanism. He showed that his *multilottery mechanism* a generalized version of the school TTC mechanism is equivalent to RSD.

Featherstone and Niederle (2008) observed that Boston mechanism resulted with better efficiency than the Gale-Shapley student-optimal mechanism in laboratory experiments, when ties are broken randomly, and preferences are private information. Thus, Boston mechanism is effectively manipulated by the students in these experiments. They also prove this result in a symmetric environment in theory. Abdulkadiroğlu, Che, and Yasuda (2009) showed that under similar ordinal preferences of students and coarse priority structures, any symmetric Bayesian equilibrium of the Boston mechanism is better than the dominant strategy outcome of the Gale-Shapley mechanism.

Kesten and Ünver (2009) introduced two lottery mechanisms that result in lotteries over student-optimal justified-envy-free matchings according to two new definitions of justified-envy-freeness. This is the first study that employed an "ex-ante" lottery design approach in school choice, while the previous approaches were "ex-post."

5. AXIOMATIC MECHANISMS AND MARKET DESIGN

5.1 House allocation and hierarchical exchange

In the house allocation domain, Pápai (2000) introduced a wide class of mechanisms called *hierarchical exchange mechanisms* that are inspired by Gale's TTC algorithm and serial dictatorships such that they uniquely characterize the class of Pareto-efficient, reallocation-proof, and coalitionally strategy-proof mechanisms.

A mechanism ϕ is **reallocation-proof** if for any problem $\succ$, there is no pair of agents a and b and two preference relations $\succ'_a$ and $\succ'_b$ such that $\phi[\succ'_a, \succ_{-a}](a) = \phi[\succ](a)$ and $\phi[\succ'_b, \succ_{-b}](b) = \phi[\succ](b)$ and yet $\phi[\succ'_a, \succ'_b, \succ_{-\{a,b\}}](b) \succsim_a \phi[\succ](a)$ and $\phi[\succ'_a, \succ'_b, \succ_{-\{a,b\}}](a) \succ_b \phi[\succ](b)$.

The idea behind hierarchical exchange mechanisms is as follows:

Suppose that we assign houses to the agents initially according to an inheritance rule that is described by the mechanism. As the agents who have the property rights of the houses leave the market while the houses remain unmatched, their property rights are passed to other agents according to the inheritance rule.

A **submatching** is the matching of a subset of agents $B \subseteq A$ to houses $G \subseteq H$, i.e., a one-to-one and onto function σ: $B \rightarrow G$. Let $A_\sigma = B$ and $H_\sigma = G$. Let $\mathcal{S}$ be the set of submatchings. For each house h, let $\mathcal{S}_{-h}$ be the set of submatchings that do not assign house h.

Note that a **matching** is a submatching σ with $A_\sigma = A$. Let $\mathcal{M} \subset \mathcal{S}$ be the set of matchings, as before.

Formally, a hierarchical exchange mechanism is described through an inheritance function $f = (f_h)_{h \in H}$ such that each $f_h : \mathcal{S}_{-h} \backslash \mathcal{M} \rightarrow A$ determines who has the property rights of house h, once a submatching is already fixed. That is, for any $\sigma \in \mathcal{S}_{-h} \backslash \mathcal{M}, f_h(\sigma) \in A \backslash A_\sigma$, such that $f_h(\sigma)$ is the agent who has the property right of house h when the submatching σ is already fixed.[1]

We have the following restriction on f_h : For all $\sigma \subseteq \sigma'$ with $f_h(\sigma) \notin A_{\sigma'}$, we have $f_h(\sigma') = f_h(\sigma)$. That is, if an agent has the right of a house, when more matches are determined, and this agent is not matched, she does not lose her right for this house. Let $\mathcal{F}$ be the set of such f functions. Each $f \in \mathcal{F}$ induces a **hierarchical exchange mechanism**, let ϕ^f be this mechanism.

An iterative algorithm is used to find the allocation under a hierarchical exchange mechanism:

Algorithm 13 *The* hierarchical exchange induced by f:

Step k: *Suppose σ^k is a submatching already determined at the end of the previous step (we start with $\sigma^1 = \emptyset$ initially at $k = 1$). If σ^k is a matching then we terminate the algorithm, and σ^k is the outcome of the algorithm. Otherwise, each remaining house h points to its inheritance right holder f_h (σ^k), each remaining agent points to her top choice house among the remaining houses, and we obtain a directed graph. There exists at least one cycle (by Lemma 2). We clear each cycle by assigning each agent in the cycle the house she is pointing to. Let σ^{k+1} be the submatching that is determined by clearing these cycles, and the matches already determined under σ^k. We continue with Step $k + 1$.*

Below, we give examples about the relationship of hierarchical exchange and other mechanisms we introduced in the previous chapters of this survey:

Example 12 *Suppose that μ is a matching, and for each agent $a \in A, f_{\mu(a)}$ $(\emptyset) = a$. Then this inheritance rule gives a house to each agent initially. The rest of the inheritance rule is defined arbitrarily.*

The induced hierarchical exchange algorithm is equivalent to ***Gale's top trading cycles*** *algorithm and finds the core of the housing market induced by initial endowment μ.*

Example 13 *Let $p = (a_1, \ldots, a_n)$ be an ordering of agents in A. Suppose that for all h and all σ, $f_h(\sigma) = a_k$ where k is the lowest index such that a_k not matched under σ.*

This inheritance rule gives the control rights of all houses to the same agent as long as that agent is available. That is, the induced hierarchical exchange mechanism is the ***serial dictatorship*** *induced by p.*

[1] This simplified definition is due to Pycia and Ünver (2009).

Example 14 *Suppose that there are two types of agents and houses, A_E, A_N and H_O, H_V, respectively. For each $a \in A_E$, $h_a \in H_O$, we set $f_{h_a}(\emptyset) = a$. Moreover, suppose there is an ordering of agents $p = (a_1, \ldots, a_n)$ such that for all $h \in H_V$, $f_h(\sigma) = a_k$ where a_k is the agent with lowest k such that a_k is not matched under σ. For all $h_a \in H_O$, whenever a is matched under σ but h_a is not, then $f_{h_a}(\sigma) = a_k$ where a_k is the agent with lowest k such that a_k is not matched under σ.*

The induced hierarchical exchange mechanism is the ***YRMH-IGYT mechanism*** *induced by priority order p.*

Example 15 *Suppose the property rights of the houses are given according to the following inheritance table for houses $H = \{h_1, h_2, h_3, h_4\}$ over $A = \{1, 2, 3, 4\}$.*

h_1	h_2	h_3	h_4
1	1	2	4
2	2	3	3
3	3	1	2
4	4	4	1

An inheritance table refers to a specific inheritance rule profile such that regardless of the assigned house of the owner of a remaining house, this remaining house is inherited by the same new owner. The induced inheritance profile f by the above table is as follows: $f_{h_1}(\emptyset) = 1$, $f_{h_1}(\{(1,x)\}) = 2$ for any $x \in \{h_2, h_3, h_4\}$ (that is, when 1 is matched, the right goes to 2), $f_{h_1}(\{(1,x),(2,y)\}) = 3$ for all $\{x,y\} \subseteq \{h_2, h_3, h_4\}$. $f_{h_1}(\{(1,x),(2,y),(3,z)\}) = 4$ for all $\{x, y, z\} \subseteq \{h_2, h_3, h_4\}$. The rights for houses h_2, h_3, and h_4 are similarly defined.

One interpretation of the above table is that the inheritance table gives the ***priority profile*** *of houses over the students (for example, houses are school seats and the agents in A are students, and the priority profile is induced by f). Then the induced* ***school choice top trading cycles mechanism*** *(Abdulkadiroğlu and Sönmez 2003a) is a hierarchical exchange mechanism.*

Hierarchical exchange mechanisms constitute a proper superset of the mechanisms we introduced earlier. We illustrate this with an example, in which the hierarchical exchange mechanism introduced is neither a serial dictatorship, the core mechanism, a YRMH-IGYT mechanism, nor a school choice TTC mechanism:

Example 16 *Let $A = \{1, 2, 3\}$, $H = \{h_1, h_2, h_3\}$. Suppose the inheritance rule profile f induces a tree for house h_1:*

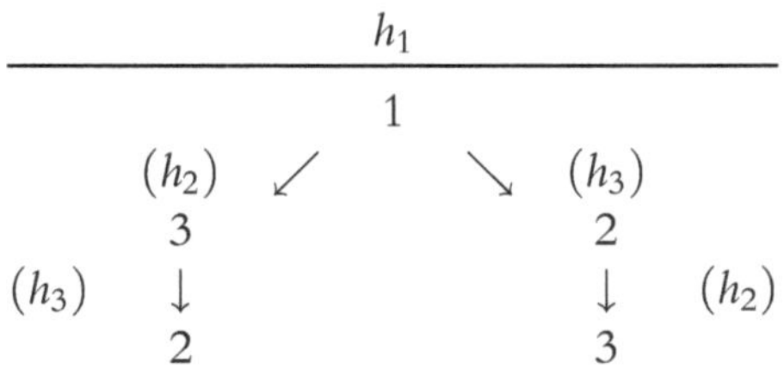

This means, $f_{h_1}(\emptyset) = 1$, $f_{h_1}(\{(1, h_2)\}) = 3$, $f_{h_1}(\{(1, h_3)\}) = 2$, $f_{h_1}(\{(1, h_2), (3, h_3)\}) = 2$, $f_{h_1}(\{(1, h_3), (2, h_2)\}) = 3$. *Suppose for houses* h_2 *and* h_3 *we have the following inheritance table for* f_{h_2} and f_{h_3}:

h_2	h_3
1	2
2	3
3	1

Let the preferences of the agents be given as:

1	2	3
h_2	h_2	h_1
h_3	h_1	h_2
h_1	h_3	h_3

The induced hierarchical exchange outcome is found as follows through the directed graphs formed:

Step 1: $1 \to h_2 \to 1$, $2 \to h_2 \to 1$, $3 \to h_1 \to 1$.

There is only one cycle: $1 \to h_2 \to 1$, *agent 1 is assigned* h_2.

Now according to h_1*'s inheritance tree the right of house* h_1 *goes to agent 3.*

Step 2: $2 \to h_1 \to 3$, $3 \to h_1 \to 3$.

There is one cycle: $3 \to h_1 \to 3$, *agent 3 is assigned house* h_1.

Step 3: $2 \to h_3 \to 2$, *there is one cycle:* $2 \to h_3 \to 2$.

No agent is left, thus the algorithm terminates. The outcome of the hierarchical exchange mechanism is given as

$$\mu = \begin{pmatrix} 1 & 2 & 3 \\ h_2 & h_3 & h_1 \end{pmatrix}$$

Our result of this chapter is as follows:

Theorem 37 *(Pápai 2000)* *A mechanism is* reallocation-proof, Pareto-efficient, *and* coalitionally strategy-proof *if and only if it is a* hierarchical exchange mechanism.

5.2 Trading cycles with brokers and owners

In this section, we introduce a new algorithm called *trading cycles with brokers and owners* (Pycia and Ünver, 2009), which is more general than hierarchical exchange. This will remove the reallocation-proofness axiom from the above characterization result.

The algorithm works as follows: In each round, it assigns the control rights of each unremoved house to some unremoved agent. This agent controls this house as an "owner" or as a "broker." The hierarchical exchange only designated control rights holders as "owners." Thus "brokers" are innovation of this new algorithm. In either case, this house cannot be matched in this round unless its control rights holder is matched. The algorithm is based on the top-trading cycles idea, yet it is substantially different.

The assignment produced by this algorithm depends on the structure of control rights. Let us define this new concept first. A **structure of control rights** (a^c, h^b) consists of a profile of **control functions** $a^c = \left(a^c_h : \mathcal{S}_{-h} \to A\right)_{h \in H}$ such that for all h and all $\sigma \in \mathcal{S}_{-h}, a^c_h(\sigma) \in A - A_\sigma$; and a **brokered house function** $h^b : \mathcal{S} - \mathcal{M} \to H \cup \{\emptyset\}$ such that for all $\sigma \in \mathcal{S} - \mathcal{M}$, if $|A_\sigma| = |A| - 1$, then $h^b(\sigma) = \emptyset$.

For all control rights structures, the assignment of houses to agents is determined by an iterative algorithm that we refer to as the **trading-cycles-with-brokers-and-owners algorithm (TCBO algorithm** for short).

Algorithm 14 *The* trading cycles with brokers and owners (TCBO) induced by (a^c, h^b):

Step k: *Let σ^{k-1} be the submatching of agents and houses removed before step k. Before the first round, the submatching of removed agents is empty, $\sigma^0 = \emptyset$.*

Determination of intra-round trade graph: *Each unremoved house h points to the agent who controls it at σ^{k-1}. If there exists a* broker at σ^{k-1}, *he points to his first choice* owned-house at σ^{k-1}. *Every other unremoved agent points to his top choice house among the unremoved houses.*

Removal of trading cycles: *There exists at least one cycle (by Lemma 2). We remove each agent in each cycle by assigning him the house he is pointing to.*

Stopping rule: *We stop the algorithm if all agents are removed (matched). The resultant matching, σ^k, is then the outcome of the algorithm.*

Since we assign at least one agent a house in every round, and since there are finitely many agents, the algorithm stops after finitely many rounds.

The terminology of owners and brokers is motivated by the trading analogy. In each round of the algorithm, an owner can either trade a house he controls for another house (in a cycle of several exchanges), or can leave in this round matched with a house he owns. A broker can trade the house he owns for another house (in a cycle of several exchanges), but cannot leave in this round matched with the house he brokers. One interpretation of this is that the owner can consume his house, but the broker cannot.

Example 17 ***(Execution of the TCBO algorithm)*** *Let $A = \{1, 2, 3\}$ and $H = \{h_1, h_2, h_3\}$. Suppose the control rights structure is such that*

- *h_1 is owned by 1 as long as 1 and h_1 are unmatched, is owned by 2 when 2 and h_1 are unmatched and 1 is matched, and is owned by 3 when 3 and h_1 are unmatched and 1 and 2 are matched,*
- *h_2 is owned by 2 as long as 2 and h_2 are unmatched, is owned by 1 when 1 and 2 are unmatched and 2 is matched, and is owned by 3 when 3 and h_2 are unmatched, and 1 and 2 are matched,*
- *h_3 is controlled by 3; he has the brokerage right as long as either 1 and 2 are unmatched and the ownership right when 1 and 2 are matched (notice that we do not need to specify who inherits h_3 when 3 is matched, because 3 may be matched only in a cycle that also contains h_3).*

The above structure of control rights may be represented as follows:

$a^c_{h_1}$	$a^c_{h_2}$	$a^c_{h_3}$
1	2	3^b
2	1	
3	3	

The^b *sign, above, next to 3 in* h_3*'s control right column, shows that* h_3 *is a brokered-house (when some agents other than 3 who controls* h_3 *are unmatched). The preferences of the agents are given as follows:*

$$\begin{aligned} &\textit{agent } 1: \ h_3 \succ_1 h_2 \succ_1 h_1 \\ &\textit{agent } 2: \ h_3 \succ_2 h_1 \succ_2 h_2 \\ &\textit{agent } 3: \ h_3 \succ_3 h_1 \succ_3 h_2 \end{aligned}$$

We run the algorithm as follows:

Step 1. *Owned-house* h_1 *points to* $a^c_{h_1}(\emptyset) = 1$*, owned-house* h_2 *points to* $a^c_{h_2}(\emptyset) = 2$*, brokered-house* $h^b(\emptyset) = h_3$ *points to* $a^c_{h^b(\emptyset)}(\emptyset) = 3$*. Agents 1 and 2 point to* h_3 *and broker 3 points to his first choice owned-house, that is* h_1*. There exists one cycle*

$$h_1 \longrightarrow 1 \longrightarrow h_3 \longrightarrow 3 \longrightarrow h_1,$$

and by removing it, we obtain

$$\sigma^1 = \{(1, h_3), (3, h_1)\}$$

Step 2. *O-house* h_2 *points to* $a^2_{h_2}(\sigma^1) = 2$ *and agent 2 points to* h_2*. There exists one cycle*

$$h_2 \longrightarrow 2 \longrightarrow h_2,$$

and by removing it, we obtain

$$\sigma^2 = \{(1, h_3), (2, h_2), (3, h_1)\}.$$

This is a matching, since no agents are left.

We terminate the algorithm, and the outcome of the mechanism is σ^2*.*

Observe that this outcome cannot be reproduced by a hierarchical exchange mechanism. Consider a modified problem obtained by changing preferences of agent 3 so that h_2 *is preferred to* h_1*:*

$$\begin{aligned} &\textit{agent } 1: \ h_3 \succ_1 h_1 \succ_1 h_2 \\ &\textit{agent } 2: \ h_3 \succ_2 h_2 \succ_2 h_1 \\ &\textit{agent } 3: \ h_3 \ \succ'_3 \ h_2 \ \succ'_3 \ h_1 \end{aligned}$$

In this case, the TCBO outcome is

$$\sigma' = \{(1, h_1), (2, h_3), (3, h_2)\}.$$

However, any hierarchical exchange mechanism that assigns h_3 *to 1 in the first problem should continue to do so in the second problem. Thus, no hierarchical exchange mechanism can reproduce this TCBOs outcome.*

We are ready to formally define TCBO mechanism class (Pycia and Ünver 2009). A control rights structure (a^c, h^b) is **compatible** if for all submatchings $\sigma \in \mathcal{S} - \mathcal{M}$,

C1. **Persistence of ownership:** If agent a owns house h at σ, and a and h are unmatched at $\sigma' \supset \sigma$, then a owns h at σ'.

C2. **No ownership for brokers:** If agent b is a broker at σ, then h^b does not own any house at σ.

C3. **Limited persistence of brokerage:** If agent h^b brokers house f at σ, agent $a' \neq b$ and house $g \neq f$ are unmatched at σ, and b does not broker f at submatching $\sigma \cup \{(a', g)\}$, then either

- **Broker-to-heir transition**: (i) there is exactly one agent a who owns a house both at σ and $\sigma \cup \{(a', g)\}$, (ii) agent a owns house f at $\sigma \cup \{(a', g)\}$, and (iii) at submatching $\sigma \cup \{(a', g), (a, f)\}$, agent b owns all houses that a owns at σ, or
- **Direct exit from brokerage**: there is no agent who owns a house at both σ and $\sigma \cup \{(a', g)\}$.

Each *compatible* pair (a^c, h^b) induces a **trading-cycles-with-brokers-and-owners mechanism** (**TCBO mechanism** for short). Its outcome is found through the TCBO algorithm that was introduced earlier. The control rights structure introduced in the previous example is compatible, thus the mechanism implemented is TCBO.

The main theorem regarding this larger class is proven by Pycia and Ünver (2009) and removes reallocation-proofness property of Pápai from the axiomatic characterization. We further assume that $|H| \geq |I|$:

Theorem 38 ***(Pycia and Ünver 2009)*** *A mechanism is* coalitionally strategy-proof *and* Pareto-efficient *if and only if it is a* TCBO mechanism.

The characterization does not need Pareto-efficiency, if the mechanisms have *full range*, i.e., mechanism ϕ has **full range** if for every matching $\mu \in \mathcal{M}$, there exists some preference profile $\succ$ such that $\phi[\succ] = \mu$.

Corollary 2 ***(Pycia and Ünver 2009)*** *A full-range mechanism is* coalitionally strategy-proof *if and only if it is a* TCBO mechanism.

As an example of a mechanism design problem in which brokerage rights are useful, consider a manager who assigns n tasks $t_1, \ldots, t_n$ to n employees $w_1, \ldots, w_n$ with strict preferences over the tasks. The manager wants the allocation to be Pareto-efficient with regard to the employees' preferences. Within this constraint, she would like to avoid assigning task t_1 to employee w_1. She wants to use a coalitionally strategy-proof direct mechanism, because she does not know employees' preferences. The only way to do it using the previously known mechanisms is to endow employees $w_2, \ldots, w_n$ with the tasks, let them find the Pareto-efficient allocation through a top-trading cycles procedure, such as Pápai's (2000) hierarchical exchange, and then allocate the remaining task to employee w_1. Ex ante each such procedure is unfair to the employee w_1. Using a trading-cycles-with-brokers-and-owners mechanism, the manager can achieve her objective without the extreme discrimination of the employee w_1. She makes w_1 the broker of t_1, allocates the remaining tasks among $w_2, \ldots, w_n$ (for instance she may make w_i the owner of t_i, $i = 2, \ldots, n$), and runs trading cycles with brokers and owners.

5.3 Related literature

Unlike the core mechanism for housing markets (see Theorem 6), there are many desirable mechanisms in the house allocation (with existing tenants) domain. We already stated some axiomatic characterization results in Theorems 8, 9, and 10. Also in the school admissions domain, we stated two characterization results (see Theorems 27 and 29, see also Ehlers and Klaus 2006, and Kojima and Manea 2007, for other characterizations in the same domain).

We will cite several other papers below:

On the other hand, if we do not insist on strict preferences, coalitional strategy-proofness and Pareto efficiency are incompatible in general. Ehlers (2002) found the largest possible preference domain under which these two properties are not at odds, and characterized the set of coalitionally strategy-proof and Pareto-efficient mechanisms. Similarly, Bogomolnaia, Deb, and Ehlers (2005) characterized two classes of strategy-proof mechanisms in the same preference domain.

There are several other axiomatic studies that focus on more specialized properties of mechanisms in different domains, such as Ehlers, Klaus, and Pápai (2002), Miyagawa (2002), Ehlers and Klaus (2007), Pápai (2007), Velez (2008), and Kesten (2009b).

6. CONCLUDING REMARKS

We would like to conclude by commenting on the literature that we left out of this survey. Our attention to axiomatic mechanism design was brief. Similarly, we did not explore lottery mechanisms in depth. Such explorations deserve their own survey papers. We give a brief summary of the literature on lottery mechanisms below, since the literature may have important implications for market design.

6.1 Lottery mechanisms in matching

In the house allocation domain, a study by Chambers (2004) showed that a probabilistic consistency property is difficult to achieve if fairness is also imposed. He showed that a uniform lottery allocation of houses is the unique stochastically consistent mechanism that is also fair in the sense of equal treatment of equals. Clearly, such an allocation is not Pareto-efficient.

On the positive side, Bogomolnaia and Moulin (2001) introduced an algorithm class, which we can refer to as *eating algorithms* that implement different lottery mechanisms. Randomization is used to sustain fairness among the agents, since as we have seen, desirable deterministic mechanisms impose an artificial hierarchical structure that can favor some agents over others. A central mechanism in the class, which gives "equal eating speeds" to all agents, is known as the *probabilistic serial (PS) mechanism*.

One shortcoming of the PS mechanism is that it is not strategy-proof. Yet, all mechanisms induced by eating algorithms including PS are ordinally efficient, in the sense that the probability distribution of houses assigned is not first-order stochastically dominated by any other (lottery) mechanism. In fact, a mechanism is ordinally efficient if and only if its outcome can be found through an eating algorithm.[1]

On the other hand, another central mechanism, obtained by randomly drawing a priority ordering of agents and implementing the resulting serial dictatorship, is not ordinally efficient. This is a surprising result, since serial dictatorships are Pareto-efficient mechanisms. On the other hand, this lottery mechanism, known as the *random serial dictatorship (RSD)* is strategy-proof.

PS and RSD mechanisms are both fair (in the sense of equal treatment of equals). Yet, it turns out that ordinal efficiency, equal treatment of equals, and strategy-proofness are incompatible properties. Thus, PS favors ordinal efficiency, while RSD favors strategy-proofness. RSD is only ex-post efficient and PS is only weakly strategy-proof.

Kojima and Manea (2010) showed that manipulability of the PS mechanism may not be a big problem. If there are sufficiently many copies of the houses (e.g., when "houses" represent "slots at schools" in the school choice domain), then PS will be a strategy-proof mechanism. In such cases, one can claim that PS is a superior mechanism to RSD.[2]

Abdulkadiroğlu and Sönmez (1998) gave a theoretical intuition in support of the use of RSD. One can imagine another fair mechanism as follows: randomly assign houses to agents and find the core of the resulting housing market (core from random endowments). It turns out that this mechanism is equivalent to RSD through their result. Pathak and Sethuraman (2010), in turn, generalized the equivalence results (as explained in the School Choice Section).

On the other hand, Sönmez and Ünver (2005) showed that in the house allocation with existing tenants domain, randomly endowing newcomers with vacant houses, and finding the core of the resulting housing market in which existing tenants initially own their occupied houses, is equivalent to randomly drawing a priority order of agents in which existing tenants are always ordered after the newcomers and implementing the induced YRMH-IGYT mechanism. Thus, the core idea favors newcomers by giving all rights to vacant houses to newcomers.

[1] Crés and Moulin (2001) and Bogomolnaia and Moulin (2002) introduced a strategy-proof and ordinally efficient lottery mechanism in a preference domain where relative preferences of the agents are identical for the houses, but opting-out can be ranked differently for each different agent.

[2] See Manea (2006) and Che and Kojima (2008) about results on asymptotic ordinal *in*efficiency and efficiency of RSD in different large economies, respectively.

Abdulkadiroğlu and Sönmez (2003b) explored why serial dictatorships, Pareto-efficient mechanisms, could result in an ordinally inefficient probability distribution over assigned houses when they are used following a uniformly random priority order drawing (i.e., RSD). They discovered that the probability distribution induced by RSD can also be generated by equivalent lotteries over *inefficient quasi-matchings*. Moreover, they also found a full characterization of ordinally efficient matchings through this intuition.

Kesten (2009a) explored the origins of ordinal inefficiencies under RSD (equivalently core from random endowments) from a different point of view. He discovered that these inefficiencies are not the results of the allocation or trading procedures used, but the deterministic problem definition. That is, if we can allocate or endow agents fractions of houses (equivalent to probabilities) through the algorithms we introduced, then RSD, PS, and Gale's TTC are essentially equivalent.

Katta and Sethuraman (2006) generalized the PS mechanism when indifferences are allowed in preferences. Yilmaz (2009, 2010) included individual rationality constraints as in the house allocation with existing agents domain and introduced a natural generalization of the PS mechanism with and without indifferences in preferences. Athanassoglou and Sethuraman (2007) allowed fractional house endowments in the house allocation domain (i.e., the existing tenants initially own a probability distribution over houses) and found a generalization of Yilmaz's mechanisms.

Budish, Che, Kojima, and Milgrom (2009) studied how to implement random matchings under certain constraints through lotteries whose support contain matchings that satisfy these constraints. They generalized Birkhoff-von Neuman Theorem by showing that when the constraints on matching probabilities can be represented as *bi-hierarchies* there exists a lottery implementation of the random matching matrix.

6.2 Other literature

We end with a series of citations pointing out new and emerging areas in discrete resources allocation and exchange problems.

First of all, there is an emerging literature on generalizations of the matching problem to different domains which simultaneously include hedonic games, housing markets, two-sided matching problems, and so on (see for example Sönmez 1996, 1999, and Pápai 2007).

Additionally, Ben-Shoham, Serrano, and Volij (2004) looked into the evolutionary dynamics that drive decentralized robust exchange in a housing market (for a generalization of this process to multiple house consumption see Bochet, Klaus, and Walzl 2007). Kandori, Serrano, and Volij (2008) inspected a similar decentralized process for housing markets with transfers when there are random and persistent shocks to the preferences of agents.

Recently, Bade (2008) studied rationalizable and nonrationalizable behavior of agents in housing problems and markets.

Market design has recently been the driving force in the advance of theory in discrete resource allocation and exchange problem. Market design applications are not limited to the ones discussed throughout this survey. Guillen and Kesten (2008) discovered that the mechanism used to assign students to rooms in an MIT dormitory is essentially equivalent to a version of the Gale-Shapley student-optimal stable mechanism that takes into consideration individual rationality constraints, and compared YRMH-IGYT and the MIT dormitory allocation mechanisms experimentally. In another market design study, Kesten and Yazici (2008) introduced an ex-post fair "discrete resource" allocation mechanism for possible applications in large corporations and organizations such as the navy or a university. However, in general such an allocation is not efficient. When multiple objects, such as courses, are being distributed to agents, such as students at a university, competitive equilibrium from equal (artificial) budgets is a natural candidate for sustaining ex-post fairness and efficiency together. Since a competitive equilibrium may not exist in general, Sönmez and Ünver (2010a) introduced a "course" allocation mechanism based on bidding under equal budgets, which can replace the most popular course bidding mechanism used in many business schools. This bidding mechanism was intended to create competitive equilibrium under equal budgets, but it fails by the impossibility result. Even under a modified definition of competitive equilibrium, this mechanism is not a competitive mechanism, while the Sönmez and Ünver proposal is. Krishna and Ünver (2008) showed that the Sönmez and Ünver (2010a) proposal is superior to the current bidding mechanisms in a designed experimental environment and in a field experiment at University of Michigan Business School. Harvard Business School course bidding mechanism tries to achieve ex-post fairness using a series of serial dictatorships with reversal of priority orders in each round of course allocation. Budish and Cantillon (2009) tested the Harvard Business School course allocation scheme in a field experiment and showed that it is manipulable and causes significant welfare losses. Budish (2009) endenized competitive prices and bidding using a direct mechanism. He proposed an approximate competitive equilibrium concept and a mechanism which finds such equilibria. The proposed direct mechanism calculates an approximate competitive equilibrium by finding approximately market clearing prices from approximately equal (artificial bid) budgets for students. This equilibrium is also approximately strategy-proof and ex-post envy-free.

There are other experimental studies on matching market design that we did not mention earlier. Calsamiglia, Haeringer, and Klijn (2007) supported the Haeringer and Klijn (2009) theoretical study on constrained school choice with laboratory experiments and complemented the Chen and Sönmez (2006) experimental study on unconstrained school choice. In the marketing literature, Wang and Krishna (2006) made an experimental study of the TTCC mechanism of Roth, Sönmez, and Ünver (2004), which was employed for time-share summer housing exchange.

Dynamic models of house allocation and exchange have been attracting attention recently: In addition to Ünver (2010), Bloch and Cantala (2008), and Kurino (2008) considered intertemporal house allocation when some agents leave and new agents join the agent population over time. Abdulkadiroğlu and Loertscher (2007) considered dynamic house allocation when the preferences of agents are uncertain.

REFERENCES

Abdulkadiroğlu, A., Che, Y.K., Yasuda, Y., 2008. Expanding 'Choice' in School Choice. Working paper.

Abdulkadiroğlu, A., Che, Y., Yasuda, Y., 2009. Resolving Conflicting Interests in School Choice: Reconsidering The Boston Mechanism. Am. Econ. Rev. forthcoming.

Abdulkadiroğlu, A., Ehlers, L., 2007. Controlled School Choice. Working paper.

Abdulkadiroğlu, A., Loertscher, S., 2007. Dynamic House Allocation. Working paper.

Abdulkadiroğlu, A., Pathak, P.A., Roth, A.E., 2005. The New York City High School Match. American Economic Review Papers and Proceedings 95 (2), 364–367.

Abdulkadiroğlu, A., Pathak, P.A., Roth, A.E., 2009. Strategy-Proofness versus Efficiency in Matching with Indifferences: Redesigning the NYC High School Match. Am. Econ. Rev. 99, 1954–1978.

Abdulkadiroğlu, A., Pathak, P.A., Roth, A.E., Sönmez, T., 2005. The Boston Public School Match. American Economic Review Papers and Proceedings 95 (2), 368–371.

Abdulkadiroğlu, A., Pathak, P.A., Roth, A.E., Sönmez, T., 2006. Changing the Boston School Choice Mechanism: Strategy-proofness as Equal Access. Working paper.

Abdulkadiroğlu, A., Sönmez, T., 1998. Random Serial Dictatorship and the Core from Random Endowments in House Allocation Problems. Econometrica 66, 689–701.

Abdulkadiroğlu, A., Sönmez, T., 1999. House Allocation with Existing Tenants. J. Econ. Theory 88, 233–260.

Abdulkadiroğlu, A., Sönmez, T., 2003a. School Choice: A Mechanism Design Approach. Am. Econ. Rev. 93, 729–747.

Abdulkadiroğlu, A., Sönmez, T., 2003b. Ordinal Efficiency and Dominated Sets of Assignments. J. Econ. Theory 112, 157–172.

Abraham, D.J., Cechlárová, K., Manlove, D.F., Mehlhorn, K., 2005. Pareto Optimality in House Allocation Problems. In: Lecture Notes in Computer Science. 3827, Springer, pp. 1163–1175.

Abraham, D.J., Blum, A., Sandholm, T., 2007. Clearing Algorithms for Barter Exchange Markets: Enabling Nationwide Kidney Exchanges. In: Proceedings of ACMEC 2007: the Eighth ACM Conference on Electronic Commerce.

Alcalde, J., Barberà, S., 1994. Top Dominance and the Possibility of Strategy-Proof Stable Solutions to Matching Problems. Econ. Theory 4, 417–435.

Athanassoglou, S., Sethuraman, J., 2007. House Allocation with Fractional Endowments. International Journal of Game Theory, forthcoming.

Bade, S., 2008. Housing Problems with Non-Rationalizable Behavior. Working paper.

Balinski, M., Sönmez, T., 1999. A Tale of Two Mechanisms: Student Placement. J. Econ. Theory 84, 73–94.

Ben-Shoham, A., Serrano, R., Volij, O., 2004. The Evolution of Exchange. J. Econ. Theory 114, 310–328.

Bevia, C., Quinzii, M., Silva, J.A., 1999. Buying Several Indivisible Goods. Math. Soc. Sci. 37 (1), 25.

Biró, P., Cechlárová, K., 2007. Inapproximability of the kidney exchange problem. Information Processing Letters 101, 199–202.

Biró, P., McDermid, E., 2008. Three-sided Stable Matchings with Cyclic Preferences and the Kidney Exchange. In: Endriss, U., Goldberg, P.W. (Eds.), COMSOC-2008: Proceedings of the 2nd International Workshop on Computational Social Choice, pp. 97–108.

Bloch, F., Cantal, D., 2008. Markovian Assignment Rules. Working paper.

Bochet, O., Klaus, B., Walzl, M., 2007. Dynamic Recontracting Processes with Multiple Indivisible Goods. Working paper.

Bogomolnaia, A., Deb, R., Ehlers, L., 2005. Strategy-Proof Assignment on the Full Preference Domain. J. Econ. Theory 123, 161–186.

Bogomolnaia, A., Moulin, H., 2001. A New Solution to the Random Assignment Problem. J. Econ. Theory 100, 295–328.

Bogomolnaia, A., Moulin, H., 2002. A Simple Random Assignment Problem with a Unique Solution. Econ. Theory 19, 623–635.

Bogomolnaia, A., Moulin, H., 2004. Random Matching under Dichotomous Preferences. Econometrica 72, 257–279.

Budish, E., 2009. The Combinatorial Assignment Problem: Approximate Competitive Equilibrium from Equal Incomes. Working Paper.

Budish, E., Cantillon, E., 2009. Strategic Behavior in Multi-Unit Assignment Problems: Lessons for Market Design. Working Paper.

Budish, E., Che, Y., Kojima, F., Milgrom, P., 2009. Implementing Random Assignments: A Generalization of the Birkhoff-von Neumann Theorem. Working Paper.

Calsamiglia, C., Haeringer, G., Klijn, F., 2007. On the Robustness of Recombinant Estimation: Efficiency in School Choice. Am. Econ. Rev. forthcoming.

Cechlárová, K., Fleiner, T., Manlove, D.F., 2005. The kidney exchange game. In: Proceedings of SOR'05: the 8th International Symposium on Operations Research in Slovenia, pp. 77–83.

Chambers, C.P., 2004. Consistency in the Probabilistic Assignment Model. J. Math. Econ. 40, 953–962.

Che, Y.K., Kojima, F., 2008. Asymptotic Equivalence of Random Priority and Probabilistic Serial Mechanisms. Econometrica forthcoming.

Chen, Y., Sönmez, T., 2002. Improving Efficiency of On-Campus Housing: An Experimental Study. Am. Econ. Rev. 92, 1669–1686.

Chen, Y., Sönmez, T., 2006. School Choice: An Experimental Study. J. Econ. Theory 127, 2002–2031.

Crès, H., Moulin, H., 2001. Scheduling with Opting Out: Improving upon Random Priority. Oper. Res. 49, 565–577.

Delmonico, F.L., 2004. Exchanging Kidneys—Advances in Living-Donor Transplantation. N. Engl. J. Med. 350, 1812–1814.

Dubins, L.E., Freedman, D.A., 1981. Machiavelli and the Gale-Shapley Algorithm. Am. Math. Mon. 88, 485–494.

Dutta, B., Ray, D., 1989. A Concept of Egalitarianism under Participation Constraints. Econometrica 57, 615–635.

Edmonds, J., 1965. Paths, Trees, and Flowers. Can. J. Math. 17, 449–467.

Ehlers, L., 2002. Coalitional Strategy-Proof House Allocation. J. Econ. Theory 105, 298–317.

Ehlers, L., 2006. Respecting Priorities when Assigning Students to Schools. Working Paper.

Ehlers, L., Klaus, B., 2003. Resource-Monotonicity for House Allocation Problems. International Journal of Game Theory 32, 545–560.

Ehlers, L., Klaus, B., 2006. Efficient Priority Rules. Games Econ. Behav. 55, 372–384.

Ehlers, L., Klaus, B., 2007. Consistent House Allocation. Econ. Theory 30, 561–574.

Ehlers, L., Klaus, B., Pápai, S., 2002. Strategy-Proofness and Population-Monotonicity for House Allocation Problems. J. Math. Econ. 38, 329–339.

Ekici, Ö., 2009. Reclaimproof Allocation of Indivisible Goods. Working paper.

Erdil, A., Ergin, H., 2008. What's the Matter with Tie-Breaking? Improving Efficiency in School Choice. Am. Econ. Rev. 98, 669–689.

Ergin, H., 2000. Consistency in House Allocation Problems. J. Math. Econ. 34, 77–97.

Ergin, H., 2002. Efficient Resource Allocation on the Basis of Priorities. Econometrica 70, 2489–2497.

Ergin, H., Sönmez, T., 2006. Games of School Choice under the Boston Mechanism. J. Public Econ. 90, 215–237.

Featherstone, C., Niederle, M., 2008. Manipulation in School Choice Mechanisms. Working paper.

Gale, D., Shapley, L., 1962. College Admissions and the Stability of Marriage. Am. Math. Mon. 69, 9–15.

Gallai, T., 1963. Kritische Graphen II. Magyar Tud. Akad. Mat. Kutató Int. Közl. 8, 373–395.

Gallai, T., 1964. Maximale Systeme unabhängiger kanten. Magyar Tud. Akad. Mat. Kutató Int. Közl 9, 401–413.

Gjertson, D.W., Michael Cecka, J., 2000. Living Unrelated Donor Kidney Transplantation. Kidney Int 58, 491–499.
Guillen, P., Kesten, O., 2008. On-Campus Housing: Theory and Experiment. Working paper.
Gusfield, D., Irving, R.W., 1989. The Stable Marriage Problem: Structure and Algorithms. MIT Press.
Haeringer, G., Klijn, F., 2009. Constrained School Choice. J. Econ. Theory 144, 1817–1831.
Hatfield, J.W., 2005. Pairwise Kidney Exchange: Comment. J. Econ. Theory 125, 189–193.
Hatfield, J.W., Milgrom, P.R., 2005. Matching with Contracts. Am. Econ. Rev. 95, 913–935.
Hylland, A., Zeckhauser, R., 1979. The Efficient Allocation of Individuals to Positions. J. Polit. Econ. 87, 293–314.
Irving, R.W., 2007. The cycle roommates problem: a hard case of kidney exchange. Inf. Process. Lett. 103, 1–4.
Jaramillo, P., Manjunath, V., 2009. Allocating objects: Dealing with indifference. University of Rochester Working Paper.
Kandori, M., Serrano, R., Volij, O., 2008. Decentralized trade, random utility and the evolution of social welfare. J. Econ. Theory 140, 328–338.
Katta, A.K., Sethuraman, J., 2006. A Solution to the Random Assignment Problem on the Full Preference Domain. J. Econ. Theory 131, 231–250.
Kelso, A.S., Crawford, V.P., 1982. Job Matchings, Coalition Formation, and Gross Substitutes. Econometrica 50, 1483–1504.
Kesten, O., 2010. School Choice with Consent. Quarterly Journal of Economics 125, 1297–1348.
Kesten, O., 2009a. Coalitional Strategy-Proofness and Resource Monotonicity for House Allocation Problems. International Journal of Game Theory 38, 17–22.
Kesten, O., 2009a. Why Do Popular Mechanisms Lack Efficiency in Random Environments? Journal of Economic Theory 144, 2209–2222.
Kesten, O., Yazici, A., 2008. A Mechanism Design Approach to a Common Distributional Problem of Centrally Administered Organizations. Economic Theory, forthcoming.
Kesten, O., Utku Ünver, M., 2009. A Theory of School Choice Lotteries. Working paper.
Klaus, B., 2008. The Coordinate-Wise Core for Multiple-Type Housing Markets is Second-Best Incentive Compatible. J. Math. Econ. 44, 919–924.
Klaus, B., Miyagawa, E., 2002. Strategy-proofness, solidarity, and consistency for multiple assignment problems. International Journal of Game Theory 30, 421–435.
Klemperer, P., 2004. Auctions: Theory and Practice. Princeton University Press.
Kojima, F., Manea, M., 2010. Strategy-Proofness of the Probabilistic Serial Mechanism in Large Random Assignment Problems. J. Econ. Theory 145, 106–123.
Kojima, F., Manea, M., 2007. Axioms for Deferred Acceptance. Econometrica forthcoming.
Konishi, H., Quint, T., Wako, J., 2001. On the Shapley-Scarf Economy: The Case of Multiple Types of Indivisible Goods. J. Math. Econ. 35, 1–15.
Korte, B., Vygen, J., 2002. Combinatorial Optimization: Theory and Algorithms, second ed. Springer.
Krishna, A., Utku Ünver, M., 2008. Improving the Efficiency of Course Bidding at Business Schools: Field and Laboratory Studies. Marketing Science 27, 262–282.
Krishna, A., Wang, Y., 2007. The Relationship between Top Trading Cycles Mechanism and Top Trading Cycles and Chains Mechanism. J. Econ. Theory 132, 539–547.
Kurino, M., 2008. House Allocation with Overlapping Agents: A Dynamic Mechanism Design Approach. Working paper.
Ma, J., 1994. Strategy-Proofness and the Strict Core in a Market with Indivisibilities. International Journal of Game Theory 23, 75–83.
Manea, M., 2006. Asymptotic Ordinal Inefficiency of Random Serial Dictatorship. Working paper.
Milgrom, P., 2000. Putting Auction Theory to Work: The Simultaneous Ascending Auction. J. Polit. Econ. 108, 245–272.
Milgrom, P.R., 2004. Putting Auction Theory to Work. Cambridge University Press.
Milgrom, P.R., 2007. Package Auctions and Package Exchanges. Econometrica 75, 935–966.
Miyagawa, E., 2002. Strategy-Proofness and the Core in House Allocation Problems. Games Econ. Behav. 38, 347–361.

Opelz, G., 1997. Impact of HLA Compatibility on Survival of Kidney Transplants from Unrelated Live Donors. Transplantation 64, 1473–1475.
Pais, J., Pintér, Á., 2008. School Choice and Information: An Experimental Study on Matching Mechanisms. Games Econ. Behav. 64, 303–332.
Pápai, S., 2000. Strategyproof Assignment by Hierarchical Exchange. Econometrica 68, 1403–1433.
Pápai, S., 2001. Strategyproof and Nonbossy Multiple Assignments. J. Public Econ. Theory 3, 257–271.
Pápai, S., 2003. Strategyproof Exchange of Indivisible Goods. J. Math. Econ. 39, 931–959.
Pápai, S., 2007. Exchange in a General Market with Indivisible Goods. J. Econ. Theory 132, 208–235.
Pathak, P.A., 2006. Lotteries in Student Assignment. Working paper.
Pathak, P., Sethuraman, J., 2010. Lotteries in Student Assignment: An Equivalence Result. Theoretical Economics, forthcoming.
Pycia, M., Ünver, M.U., 2009. Incentive Compatible Allocation and Exchange of Discrete Resources. Working paper.
Quinzzii, M., 1984. Core and Competitive Equilibria with Indivisibilities. International Journal of Game Theory 13 (41), 60.
Rawls, J., 1971. A Theory of Justice. Harvard University Press, Cambridge.
Roth, A.E., 1982a. Incentive Compatibility in a Market with Indivisibilities. Econ. Lett. 9, 127–132.
Roth, A.E., 1982b. The Economics of Matching: Stability and Incentives. Mathematics of Operations Research 7, 617–628.
Roth, A.E., 1984. The Evolution of the Labor Market for Medical Interns and Residents: A Case Study in Game Theory. J. Polit. Econ. 92, 991–1016.
Roth, A.E., 1985. The College Admissions Problem is not Equivalent to the Marriage Problem. J. Econ. Theory 36, 277–288.
Roth, A.E., 1991. A Natural Experiment in the Organization of Entry-Level Labor Markets: Regional Markets for New Physicians and Surgeons in the United Kingdom. Am. Econ. Rev. 81, 415–440.
Roth, A.E., 2002. The Economist as Engineer: Game Theory, Experimentation, and Computation as Tools for Design Economics. Econometrica 70, 1341–1378.
Roth, A.E., 2008a. Deferred Acceptance Algorithms: History, Theory, Practice, and Open Questions. International Journal of Game Theory 36, 537–569.
Roth, A.E., 2008b. What have we learned from market design? Econ. J. 118, 285–310.
Roth, A.E., Peranson, E., 1999. The Redesign of the Matching Markets for American Physicians: Some Engineering Aspects of Economic Design. Am. Econ. Rev. 89, 748–780.
Roth, A.E., Postlewaite, A., 1977. Weak versus Strong Domination in a Market with Indivisible Goods. J. Math. Econ. 4, 131–137.
Roth, A.E., Sönmez, T., Ünver, M.U., 2004. Kidney Exchange. Q. J. Econ. 119, 457–488.
Roth, A.E., Sönmez, T., Ünver, M.U., 2005a. Pairwise Kidney Exchange. J. Econ. Theory 125, 151–188.
Roth, A.E., Sönmez, T., Ünver, M.U., 2005b. A Kidney Exchange Clearing-house in New England. American Economic Review Papers and Proceedings 95 (2), 376–380.
Roth, A.E., Sönmez, T., Ünver, M.U., 2007. Efficient Kidney Exchange: Coincidence of Wants in Markets with Compatibility-Based Preferences. Am. Econ. Rev. 97 (3), 828–851.
Roth, A.E., Sönmez, T., Ünver, M.U., Delmonico, F.L., Saidman, S.L., 2006. Utilizing List Exchange and Nondirected Donation through 'Chain' Paired Kidney Donations. American Journal of Transportation 6, 2694–2705.
Roth, A.E., Sotomayor, M., 1990. Two-Sided Matching: A Study on Game-Theoretic Modelling. Cambridge University Press.
Satterthwaite, M.A., Sonnenschein, H., 1981. Strategy-Proof Allocation Mechanisms at Differentiable Points. Rev. Econ. Stud. 48, 587–597.
Segev, D., Gentry, S., Warren, D.S., Reeb, B., Montgomery, R.A., 2005. Kidney paired donation: Optimizing the use of live donor organs. J. Am. Med. Assoc. 293, 1883–1890.
Shapley, L., Scarf, H., 1974. On Cores and Indivisibility. J. Math. Econ. 1, 23–28.
Shapley, L., Shubik, M., 1972. The Assignment Game I: The Core. International Journal of Game Theory 1, 111–130.

Sönmez, T., 1996. Implementation in Generalized Matching Problems. J. Math. Econ. 26, 429–439.
Sönmez, T., 1999. Strategy-Proofness and Essentially Single-Valued Cores. Econometrica 67, 677–690.
Sönmez, T., Ünver, M.U., 2005. House Allocation with Existing Tenants: An Equivalence. Games Econ. Behav. 52, 153–185.
Sönmez, T., Ünver, M.U., 2006. Kidney Exchange with Good Samaritan Donors: A Characterization. Working paper.
Sönmez, T., Ünver, M.U., 2010a. Course Bidding at Business Schools. International Economic Review. 51, 99–123.
Sönmez, T., Ünver, M.U., 2010b. House Allocation with Existing Tenants: A Characterization. Games Econ. Behav. 69, 425–445.
Svensson, L.G., 1994. Queue allocation of indivisible goods. Soc. Choice Welfare 11, 323–330.
Svensson, L.G., 1999. Strategyproof Allocation of Indivisible Goods. Soc. Choice Welfare 16, 557–567.
Ünver, M.U., 2010. Dynamic Kidney Exchange. Rev. Econ. Stud. 77, 372–414.
Velez, R., 2008. Revisiting Consistency in House Allocation Problems. Working paper.
Vickrey, W., 1961. Counterspeculation, Auctions, and Competitive Sealed Tenders. J. Finance 16, 8–37.
Wako, J., 2005. Coalition-Proof Nash Allocation in a Barter Game with Multiple Indivisible Goods. Math. Soc. Sci. 49, 179–199.
Wang, Y., Krishna, A., 2006. Timeshare Exchange Mechanisms. Manag. Sci. 52 (8), 1223–1237.
Wilson, R., 2002. Architecture of Power Markets. Econometrica 70, 1299–1340.
Yilmaz, Ö., 2008. Kidney Exchange: An Egalitarian Mechanism. Working paper.
Yilmaz, Ö., 2010. The probabilistic serial mechanism with private endowments. Games and Econ. Behav. 69, 475–491.
Yilmaz, Ö., 2009. Random Assignment under Weak Preferences. Games Econ. Behav. 66, 546–558.
Zenios, S.A., 2002. Optimal Control of a Paired-Kidney Exchange Program. Manag. Sci. 48, 328–342.
Zenios, S.A., Steve Woodle, E., Ross, L.F., 2001. Primum non nocere: avoiding increased waiting times for individual racial and blood-type subsets of kidney wait list candidates in a living donor/cadaveric donor exchange program. Transplantation 72, 648–654.

INDEX-VOLUME 1A

Note: Page numbers followed by f, t and n indicate figures, tables and notes, respectively.

A

a posteriori block modeling, 542
Absenteeism, 503, 519
Absorbing states, 764–766, 769, 772
Abuse of notation, 208, 522, 691n9, 767, 808
Acculturation processes, 37–38
Accumulation, of civic capital, 423–428, 477
Action sets, 590
Actions
  diversity of, 708
  observations of past actions, 702–704
  observations of past actions and outcomes, 701
  outcomes of, 682–685
Activity and skill acquisition choices, 159f
A-cultural equilibrium, 159–160
Acute myocardial infarction (AMI), 327
Adaptive utility, and relative consumption, 278–287
Addictions, 624
Additive genes, 7
Additive systems, 7
Additively separable utility functions, 235
Admissibility, 275–276
Admissions. *See also* College admissions
  admission office's preferences over test scores under color-blind admission policy, 182f
  rules for, 178–183, 190
Adoptees, 1–30
  Korean-American, 21, 26
  results from economics on, 19–25
  Transmission of education in five samples of adoptees and non-adoptees, 22t
Adoption, and norms, 335
Adoptive siblings, 6–9, 12, 14
Advertising, 201–220
  empirical effects of, 211–218
  equilibrium effects of, 206–210
  forms of, 211
  GDP and, 212–215
  hours worked and, 212–218
  labor and, 207–208
  log of per capita hours against per capita advertising, 213f
  welfare, 208–209, 218
Affirmative action, 163–191
  additional issues of, 189–191
  background of, 163–164
  Coate and Loury model of, 142–147, 147f, 165–170, 167f
  college admissions and, 178–189
  color sighted *vs.* color blind, 178–189, 182f
  equilibria with, 168–170
  equilibria without, 167–168
  equilibrium wage schedules under, in Moro and Norman model, 172f
  general equilibrium in, 170–173
  in Malaysia, 173
  modeling of, 165–166
  patronizing equilibrium in, 166–170, 167f
  role model effects of, 176–178
  two-sector general equilibrium model, 173–176
Africa, mistrust in, 466
Afrobarometer surveys, 466
Agents
  Bayesian rational agents, 555
  blocking, 822
  decisions agents, 33, 263–264
  low-rationality, 633
  myopically best-responding, 635–636, 708n14
  Network Components and Immune Agents, 659f
  one-period-lived agents, 41
  rational-agent model of optimizing agents, 35–36
"Aggregate shocks" methodology, 611
Aggregate *vs.* idiosyncratic risk, 235–238, 240–242, 246, 248, 261
Aggregation, of information, 693
Aghion et al. (2008) model, 425–426
Agreeableness, 13
Agriculture
  contractual norms in, 321–327
    share contracts, 322, 325f, 327
  learning and, 681
  spread of, 237, 382n44
  spread of early farming in Europe, 380f

Alcoholism, 2, 24n15
Allocation, 781–853. *See also* House allocation problem
misallocation, of workers, 173, 194
reallocation-proof mechanisms, 837, 840, 843
rules of, 732, 765, 771–773
All-pay auctions, 190
Alternative decision rules, 712–714, 717
Altruism, 94, 107, 233
cultural transmission of, 341
evolution and, 242, 296–297
imitation and, 717–720
impure, 394
parental, 366
in star networks, 719–720
American women, and body mass index, 334
AMI. *See* Acute myocardial infarction
Amish communities, 33–34
Amoral familism, 500
Anarchy, price of, 564
Anonymity, 80–83
in network formation, 771–772, 771n39
Anti-Semitism, 384
Apartheid, 151
Aperiodic components, of networks, 558
Arcs, of networks, 680, 721
Aristocratic matching, 44–45, 48, 54n39, 507
Arms race, 235
Arrow-Debreu markets, 35, 46
Asian consumers, and status, 81n5
Assimilation, 389–392
of culture, 490
by years in the U.S., 390
Associated college admissions problem, 825, 828
Assortative matching, 507
Assortative mating, 7, 41–42, 44–46, 48
Asymmetric equilibria, 135–136, 141, 150, 154–156, 172, 194
Asymmetric information, 48n30, 59, 190, 687–688
Atheism, 374n36
Atlas Narodov Mira, 371
Austen, Jane, 48
Averages
average distances, in social networks, 525–532
generating average group wage differentials, 138–139
grade point, 189
group, 137–139
weighted, 137, 180, 357–358
Axiomatic mechanisms, 837–844

B

Balanced collection, of weights, 740
Bar passage rate, 189
Bargaining, 232, 545
bargaining games, 488
coalitional, 746–754
over time, 765–770
multilateral, 548, 775–776
through networks, 560–565
Rubinstein-Stahl bargaining game, 562
Baseline dynamic models, of local interactions, 618–619
Baseline static model, of local interactions, 589–592
Basic needs, 230
Bass model, 654–657
parsimony of, 654
Bayes' rule, 143, 167
Bayesian Nash equilibrium, 148, 157–159, 225
Bayesian rational agents, 555
Bayesian updating, 552, 554n44, 556, 560, 692
beliefs and, 425
evolution and, 229, 264, 266, 268, 276, 288
social learning and, 690, 692, 698, 701
Becker-style taste discrimination models, 191
Behavior(s). *See also* Economic behavior
coevolution of networks and, 571
economic models of, 13
evolution and, 227–234
expectations and, 314
heritability and, 236, 247, 274
other-regarding, 290
pro-social, 82
Behavioral economics, 228n10, 235, 249–250, 259, 278
Behavioral genetics, 1–3. *See also* Genetic factors
canonical results, from the literature on, 8–14
Earnings: Implied variance decomposition from the behavioral genetics model, 13t
IQ results
on education, critiques and challenges of, 14–17
Implied variance decomposition from the behavioral genetics model, 10t
model of, 5–8

and results on personality traits meta study of correlations between parents and children, 14t
years of education: Implied variance decomposition from the behavioral genetics model, 11t
Beliefs
Bayes' rule and, 425
belief flipping, 162
belief-manipulation, 368
as civic capital, 428
convergence of, 690
cultural transmission of, 369–371
direct measures of, 440–452
about poor, and redistribution, 124f
rationality of, 425
social learning and, 685–686, 688–692, 695, 697–704, 722–724
trust beliefs
civic capital as, 424–425
across countries, 441f
density functions by country, 447f
economic development and, 458f
Benchmark Economy model, 203–206
with free entry and expanding varieties, 205, 207–212
with monopoly profits, 205, 207
Benchmark model with no group choice, 157–158
Bentham, Jeremy, 278
Bequests
cumulative distribution function F of bequests, 43f
incentives to leave, 42, 44–46
Bernoulli distributed payoffs, 685
Bernoulli random graph, 659
Bertrand competition, 170, 562
Best-responding agents, myopically, 635–636, 708n14
Best-shot public goods game, 667
Beta blockers, 327
Betrayal aversion, *vs.* risk aversion, 450–451
Betting strategies, 239
Betweenness, 542
Biases, 530
Bi-hierarchies, 846
Bilateral interactions, 732, 775–776
Bilateral relationships, 514
Biological determinism, 226
Biological heterogeneity, 332
Birth control pills, 317
Bishop-seat cities, 464, 471
Bisin, Horst, and Özgür model, 600–604, 620–624
Bisin and Özgür model, 624–627
Blackmun, Harry, 164
Black-white gap, in college completion rates, 26
Black-White wage inequality, 196–197
Blinking response, 269
Block modeling, 541
a posteriori, 542
Blocking agents, 822
Blood donation, 453, 503
Blood donation across Italian provinces, 455f
Blood type compatibility, 801
Blume's dynamic model, 162
Blushing, 234
BMI. *See* Body mass index
Body language, 234
Body mass index (BMI), 14, 652
American women and, 334
Correlations in Body Mass Index For Four Types of Sibling Pairs, 15f
Body weight
correlations of, 14
norms of, 331–334
disutility function of deviation from, 331–332
ethnic variation in, 334
model of, 331–333
stable, 332
Borel σ algebra, 300, 689, 723
Boston Public Schools (BPS), 831–832
Boston school choice mechanism, 831–832
Bounded-neighborhood model, 634
Bowling Alone (Putnam), 422
"Box design" market game, 79–80
BPS. *See* Boston Public Schools
Brain activity
happiness and, 75
pleasurable, 34n7
Brock and Durlauf model, 612–615
Brokered house function, 841
Broker-to-heir transition, 843

C

Caesarian sections, 327
Caloric intake, 229
Campus Life and Learning (CLL), 189

Canada, immigrants in, 497, 499
Canonical results, from the behavioral genetics literature, 8–14
Capital, 41–42. *See also* Civic capital; Social capital
  cultural, 202
  human, 64, 73, 419–421, 423–424
    appreciation of, 427
    formation of, 135
    investment of, 137–139, 515
    unobserved *vs.* observable, 197, 496
  physical, 64, 421, 427, 452
Capitalism, spirit of, 387
Card counters, 237
Cardiac treatment, in Florida, 330
Cardinal *vs.* ordinal utility functions, 278–280
Casanova, 239
Cascades, of information, 657
Causality
  causal effects, 4–5, 15–18, 25, 77, 80, 82
    of civic capital on per capita GDP, 475f
  mutual, 317
  proximate *vs.* ultimate, 251n31
  reverse, 111, 498
CCT. *See* Conditional Cash Transfer
CDC. *See* Centers for Disease Control
Census data, 197
  of Sweden, 19
  U.S., 389, 395, 399, 589, 616
Centers for Disease Control (CDC), 333
Chains of deviations, 757–758, 761
Characteristic function games, 732–733, 740, 746, 755, 765, 768
Charity, 290
Child outcomes, 1–30
  endogeneity in, 3–4, 16, 26
  transmission coefficients in, 4–5, 18–26, 20t
Chinese writing system, 384
Choices. *See also* Continuous choice models; Discrete choice models; School choice
  activity and skill acquisition choices, 159f
  benchmark model with no group choice, 157–158
  choice-set dependence, 269–271
  by consumer, 680–681
  discriminatory individual choices, 633
  heterogeneous choices, 256
  language, 681–682
  multinomial choice model, 615
  rational choice theory, 70
  repeated choice, 684–698
  sequence of single choices, 700–704
  skill acquisition choices, 159f
  standard portfolio choice model, 61
Christianity, early, 378
Circles, local interactions around, 711
City-states, free, 341, 376, 384–385, 425, 464, 471n12
Civic capital, 417–480
  accumulation and depreciation of, 423–428, 477
  beliefs as, 428
  causal effects of, on per capita GDP, 475f
  as civic education, 425–426
  control and, 431t, 436t, 437, 462
  cooperation and, 424–425, 429, 466
  correlates of, 459–463
  across countries, 436f
  democracies and, 477
  economic development and, 456–457t
  economic effects of, 467–476
  endowments and, 437, 451, 467, 470, 473
  field experiments on, 466–467, 475–476
  GDP and, 455–456, 456–457t, 458–459, 467–470, 475f, 476
  GSS and, 419, 429, 452n10, 474, 474n14
  identification and, 468–476
  indirect measures of, 452–458
  measures of, 429–458, 432–435t
  as missing link, 417–480
  movers and, 471–474
  natural experiments on, 463–466
    in geography, 466
    in history, 463–466
  origins of, 459–467
  productivity and, 420, 454, 456t, 467–468, 468t, 473–474
  public goods and, 428, 430, 439, 464, 467
  respect and, 431t, 436t, 437, 462, 468
  social capital as, 422–423
  social infrastructure and, 467, 468t
  socialization and, 426
  transmission of, 420
  as trust beliefs, 424–425
  values as, 428–429
  WVS and, 419, 429–430, 452, 469
Civic values
  measuring, 431–432t
  parents teaching, 475–476

Civil Rights Act of 1964, 163–164
Clash of civilization, 371
Climate change, global, 237
Climatic fluctuations, 248, 466
Clinton, Hillary, 107
CLL. *See* Campus Life and Learning
Closed rule model, 749
Closure, 528
Clustering, 634
  hierarchical, 541
  high, 532–535
  in networks, 527–537, 527f
Coalitional strategy-proofness, 799–800, 835, 837, 840, 843–844
Coalitions, 729–779
  coalitional bargaining, 746–754
    over time, 765–770
  coalition-proof Nash equilibrium, 760n30
  embedded, 734
  equilibrium process of coalition process, 765
  formation of, over time, 765–770
  grand, 730, 733, 740–742, 747–748, 751–752, 755
    efficient, 767
    superadditivity of, 769
  guaranteeing of, 732–733, 740, 748, 775
  incentives in, 747, 752, 770–774
  vs. networks, 775–776
  one-stage models of, 731–746
    with transfers, 736–737
    without transfers, 734–736
  political, 749–751
  process of coalition formation, 766
  recursive algorithms in, 748–749, 760, 766, 775
  sequential models of, 745–754
Coase theorem, 548, 761
Coate and Loury model, of affirmative action, 142–147, 165–170
  multiplicity of equilibria in, 142, 147f
  Signal distributions in Coate and Loury's (1993) example of patronizing equilibrium, 167f
Co-authorship relationships, 528, 543
Cobb-Douglas aggregator, 204
Coefficient of transmission
  Comparison of Coefficient of Transmission from Parent to Child, 24f
Coevolution
  of gene culture, 382n44
  of networks and behavior, 571
Cognitive capabilities, 264
Cohesiveness, in social networks, 567–568
Cohort effects, 390n51
Collective action
  cultural transmission and, 365–369
  fashion, fads and, 655–657
Collective memory, 368
College admissions, 785, 821–824
  affirmative action and, 178–189
  associated college admissions problem, 825, 828
  differences between college admissions, student placement, and school choice problems, 824
  mechanisms of, 828
  preference profiles in, 821
College completion rates, black-white gap in, 26
College educated parents, 17
Color sighted *vs.* color blind affirmative action, 178–189
  Admission office's preferences over test scores under color-blind admission policy, 182f
Commitments, 232–235, 259, 262
Commodification, 202
  of leisure, 209–210, 218
Commodity spaces, 593
Communes, 463
Communication networks, 688, 762
Communism, 101, 484–485
Community detection, 536, 540–543
Comparative statics exercise on the steepness of the wave of advance, 383f
Comparison of Coefficient of Transmission from Parent to Child, 24f
Competition, 312, 531
Competitive equilibria, 789
Competitive matchings, 800
Competitive state, 325
Complementarities, 673
  cultural, 345, 351–352, 354, 361, 377, 400, 403
  strategic, 360–361, 363–365, 370
    in local interactions, 598–599, 609–610, 612
    norms and, 317, 424–425
    social networks and, 566, 568–570, 573
Complete
  markets, 35, 46–47

Complete information, 590–591, 600–601, 603–604, 625–626
Multiplicity of Equilibria with Complete Information, 668f
network formation and, 751, 761, 771, 776
Complete learning, 692–694, 696
Complete networks, 710–711
Component balance, 771
Components
aperiodic components, of networks, 558
component balance, 771n39
Network Components and Immune Agents, 659f
of networks, 523, 809
odd *vs.* even, 810, 812–815
Computability, recursive, 626–627
CONCOR. *See* Convergence of iterated correlations
Conditional Cash Transfer (CCT), 466–467
Conditional cost contribution, 754
Confirmatory bias model, 330
Conflict, of utility functions, 230
Conformity, 288
cultural, 353–354, 404–405
in Ising Economies, 596–597
local, 600–603
local conformity/global diversity effect, 314–315, 319, 321, 323
market imperfections, and, 49–51
network integration and social conformism, 697f
parameters of, 322
preferences, 620, 624
pure, 611
social learning and, 681, 696–698, 707–708, 711
warp of, 315, 328, 330
Connectedness
directed information networks, 522n13
group-wise, 697
of social networks, 521–522, 558, 687n6, 722
Connections model, 743–744
Conscientiousness, 13
Consensus
mistrust and, 462
networks and, 552–560, 568, 571
Consent, in group and network formation, 732, 735
degree of, 741–743, 741t
Conservative policy, 168
Consistency
internal, 755
largest consistent set, 758
of norms, 755n25
Consistent mechanisms, 800, 819
Conspicuous compassion, 82
Conspicuous consumption, 58–59, 82, 202–203
Consumer choice, 680–681
Consumerism, 202
Consumption
conspicuous, 58–59, 82, 202–203
context of, 264–272
decisions, 33
consumption-savings decisions, 42
discounting of, 41, 43, 260–262
habits of, 206, 214
investment and, 53, 61–63
joint consumption activities, 40n19, 41, 50
labor and, 206, 212
leisure and, 202–203
elasticity of substitution between, 211
maximization of, 259
preferences for, 255–256
racial differences in, 59n50
rank and, 46n27, 58
relative, 272–273, 276–278, 282, 286–290
adaptive utility and, 278–287
information and, 273–277
reproduction and, 257
status and, 84
utility functions and, 507
Contagion, 635, 665, 672, 714
Context, of consumption, 264–272
Continuous choice models, 589–590, 592–608, 619–623
Bisin, Horst, and Özgür model, 600–604
Föllmer model, 592–597
Glaeser and Scheinkman model, 597–599
Horst and Scheinkman model, 605–608
Contraception, 317, 387, 506n38
Contract Compliance Title, 163–164
Contractual norms
in agriculture, 321–327
share contracts, 322, 325f, 327
in garment industry, 517–518
Control
civic capital and, 431t, 436t, 437, 462
degree of, 331
self-control issues, 272

Conventions and customs, of norms, 313–314
Convergence
of beliefs, 690
convergence of iterated correlations, 541
Martingale Convergence Theorem, 370n34, 690
rates of, 559, 712
Convergence of iterated correlations (CONCOR), 541
"Coolness" proxies, 78
Cooperation
civic capital and, 424–425, 429, 466
in games, 437–440, 716–721, 730
norms of, 424
Cooperative firms, 429
Coordination, social, 683n3
Coordination games, 295, 314, 317–318, 571t
discriminatory outcomes with coordination failure, 140–147
learning and, 705–715
Nash equilibria of, 705–709, 712
networks and, 566n51
pure, 320
Corominas-Bosch model, 562–565
Coronary treatments, 327
Correlates of civic capital, 459–463
Correlations
of body weight, 14
correlation between change in income per capita and change in inherited trust between 2000 and 1935, 505f
correlation between trust level of country of origin and trust level of immigrants relative to Great Britain, 491f
Correlations in Body Mass Index For Four Types of Sibling Pairs, 15f
Correlations in IQ between siblings, adoptive siblings, and identical twins, 9t
of height, 14, 23–24
intergenerational, 8
personality traits meta study of correlations between parents and children, 14t
sibling correlations of IQ, 8–11
Corruption, 360–361, 452–453, 501–503
Costs
conditional cost contribution, 754
distortionary cost of taxation, 97n4, 97n5
heterogeneity in, 670
homogeneous, 670
low cost *vs.* high cost, of workers, 157
opportunity costs, 561
Counterproductive outcomes, 231
Cournot oligopolies, 733, 736, 744
Covariances, 6, 8
Crime, 100, 111, 521, 570, 588
cross-city variance in crime rates, 648
FBI crime data, 616
Cross-city variance in crime rates, 648
Cross-Country Distribution of the Ethnolinguistic Fractionalization Index, 372f
Cross-group effects
of Moro and Norman model, 149–150
of social learning, 696, 707
Cultural transmission
of altruism, 341
of beliefs, 369–371
collective action, 365–369
cultural complementarities and, 345, 351–352, 354, 361, 377, 400, 403
cultural substitution and, 345–347, 350–352, 353n19, 355, 358, 360, 377–378, 393–394, 400–404
Dynamics with cultural substitution in Bisin and Verdier, 347f
Dynamics with cultural substitution in Cavalli Sforza and Feldman, 347f
economics and, 339–416
institutions and, 363–365
intergenerational, 341, 361n27, 366n31, 392–393
modeling of, 342–371
public goods and, 366–367, 371
resilience of cultural traits, 374–377
social interactions and, 359–369
strategic complementarities and, 360–361, 363–365, 370
trade and, 362–363
Culture
A-cultural equilibrium, 159–160
assimilation of, 490
change in, 504–505
cultural capital, 202
cultural conformity, 353–354, 404–405
cultural distinction, 353–355, 393–394, 404–406
cultural heterogeneity, 344–346, 362–363, 371–374

Culture (*cont.*)
cultural intolerance, 343, 359, 370
cultural minorities, 342, 345, 353–355, 360, 368, 378n39, 394, 401
cultural norms, 114–118
cultural portability as identification strategy, 469, 471–472
dichotomous cultural traits, 342, 355
economic effects and, 504–505
economics and, 481–510
preliminaries of, 483–489
endogeneity of cultural traits, 341
fertility, 497–499
game theory and, 483–484, 488
hours worked and, 499f
infinite horizon model and, 507
labor markets and, 501
movers and, 503
multidimensional cultural traits, 355–359
redistribution, 501–503
resilience of cultural traits, 374–377
trust and cultural values, 443f, 462
Cumulative distribution function F of bequests, in preferences, 43f
Curie-Weiss model, 613n21
Current Population Survey data, 197
Customs and conventions, of norms, 313–314
Cutoff rules, 145–146, 165, 171, 180–181
Cycles. *See also* Top trading cycles algorithm; Top trading cycles and chains algorithm
in matching theory, 789, 790f, 805
in networks, 522–523, 523f
trading cycles
with brokers and owners algorithm, 840–844
preference profiles in, 843

D

DA. *See* Deferred acceptance algorithm
Darwin, Charles, 290
Darwinian dolts, 248
Darwinian model, 83
Deceased *vs.* living kidney donors, 801
Decision problems, 682, 684–685, 698
consumption decisions, 33
consumption-savings decisions, 42
decision rules, 684, 698, 709, 711, 718, 722
alternative, 712–714, 717
irreversible decisions, 769–770
reversible decisions, 770
Decisions agents, 33, 263–264
Deferred acceptance (DA) algorithm, 783, 822
Degree distributions, for social networks, 523–526, 533n31, 569
Degree of consent, in group and network formation, 741–743, 741t
Degree of control, 331
Degree of imitation, 617
Degrees of nodes, of networks, 523, 658
DeGroot model, 555–560
DeGroot updating process, 557, 557f, 558f, 559f
Delaying reproduction, 249–250
Delinquency, 653
Demand
demand theory, 592
for labor, 213n23
underdemanded *vs.* overdemanded patients, 811–815
Democracies
civic capital and, 477
education and, 366
parliamentary, 750
years of democracy since independence, 459–462
Denial, psychological, 202
Densities
of networks, 708
population densities, 349
of trust beliefs, by country, 447f
union density, 486, 487f, 501
Depreciation, of civic capital, 423–428, 477
Depression, 331
Descriptive Statistics General Social Survey, 1972–2004, 128t
Descriptive Statistics World Values Survey, 129t
Desirability, 73–74, 78–81
Determination of individual reference groups, 638
Deterministic direct mechanisms, 787, 822
Deviations, chain of, 757–758, 761
Diaspora, of Jews, 341, 374, 378
Dichotomous cultural traits, 342, 355
Dictator games, 82, 483, 489, 570, 650
Dictatorships, 95, 118, 419n2, 427
serial, 787–788, 793n3, 794, 800, 827
multi-category, 826, 828–829

random, 794, 845
simple, 825
Differences between college admissions, student placement, and school choice problems, 824
Diffusion, 645–678
on complete networks, 656–657
of disease, 519, 532, 550
epidemiological approach to, 651, 658–665
homophily and, 649, 652–653, 674
network games and, 672–674
in networks, 551
strategic interaction and, 657–674
peer effects and, 519–521
with recovery, 661–665
in social networks, 518–521, 647–653
S-shaped curves for, 651–652, 654–657, 665, 674
strategic interaction and, 653–657
in network settings, 657–674
of telephones, 519
word-of-mouth, 528, 532, 551
Direct domination relations, 757–758, 760n31
Direct vertical socialization, 341–342, 345
Directed graphs, 522
Directed information networks, 686–688, 686f, 732
connectedness of, 522n13
Directed live kidney donations, 801–803
Discounting, 340
of consumption, 41, 43, 260–262
exponential, 250–252, 256–257, 260
hyperbolic, 249–251, 254
mortality and, 248, 252n32, 262
nonexponential, 257–262
of payoffs, 746–749, 752–754, 764–765
proofs on, 298–304
Discrete choice models, 611–617
Brock and Durlauf model, 612–615
Glaeser, Sacerdote, and Scheinkman model, 615–617
Discrimination. *See also* Statistical discrimination
discriminatory individual choices, 633
dynamic models of, 161–163
economic, 138, 151, 503
as group specialization, 147–151
against minorities, 135, 138n2, 162–164, 176–183, 189–190
from search frictions, 151–156
Discriminatory outcomes
discriminatory equilibrium, 158
as result of coordination failure, 140–147
as result of inter-group interactions, 147–161
Disease diffusion, 519, 532, 550
Disparate distribution, of wealth, 60
Disparate impact tests, 136
Distinction, cultural, 353–355, 393–394, 404–406
Distortionary cost of taxation, 97n4, 97n5
Distribution, of wealth, 40–44, 58
disparate, 60
rank and, 40, 43–45
Disutility functions
of body weight norm deviation, 331–332
of hunting, 270
of socialization, 358
of work, 49, 158, 160–161, 492–493
Diversity, 371, 427, 696
of actions, 708
ethnolinguistic, 469
global diversity of norms, 314–315
local conformity/global diversity effect, 314–315, 319, 321, 323
Divisible goods, 564, 793
Dominant gene effects, 7
Domination relations, direct *vs.* indirect, 757–758, 760n31
Donor exchanges, for kidneys, 801–803
designs of, 803–804
model of, 804
"Double the difference" methodology, 6
Downward leveling, 421
Drinking
by roommates, 618
by teenagers, 588n1
transmission of, 23
Drop-out rates
from labor force participation, 529, 565, 573
from school, 588, 611, 619
Duesenberry, James, 70, 77, 243n24, 272
Dutch National Bank Household survey, 448
Dyadic exchanges, 565
Dynamic network formation, 762–765
Dynamic stability, 708–712
Dynamics with cultural substitution
in Bisin and Verdier, 347f
in Cavalli Sforza and Feldman, 347f

E

Earnings: Implied variance decomposition from the behavioral genetics model, 13t
Easterlin paradox, 76
Eating, 229, 266–267
  algorithms for, 844
EBA. *See* Equilibrium binding agreements
Economic applications, and social networks, 511–585
Economic behavior
  evolution and, 225–226, 296–297
  norms and, 311–338
  socialization and, 397–398
Economic development
  civic capital and, 456–457t
  trust beliefs and, 458f
Economic discrimination, 138, 151, 503
Economic effects
  of civic capital, 467–476
  culture and, 504–505
  of redistribution, 94–96
  of status, 84–88
Economic models
  of human behavior, 13
  Keynesian macroeconomic models, 608
  of norms, 32–35, 335
  parsimony of, 48, 53, 56, 243, 621n28
  unity of, 56–57
Economics
  adoptees, results on, from, 19–25
  behavioral, 228n10, 235, 249–250, 259, 278
  of cultural transmission and socialization, 339–416
  culture and, 481–510
    preliminaries of, 483–489
  environments and, 490–491, 506
  epidemiological approach in, 489–497
    empirical issues of, 494–496
    literature of, 497–505
    model of, 492–494
  group selection and, 295–297
  natural experiments in, 483
  of socialization, 339–416
  training in, 428
  WVS and, 482, 489, 498, 500
Edges, of networks, 522
Education
  behavioral genetics results on, critiques and challenges of, 14–17
  civic capital as civic education, 425–426
  democracies and, 366
  educational attainment, 2
  externalities in, 100
  girls to boys ratio, in tertiary education, 487f
  inequality of, 15
  "La Mala Educacion," 428
  of mother, 4, 18–22, 24
  parental, 497–498
  redistribution and, 96, 107
  years of, 5, 11, 18–19, 21–22, 24–25
  years of education: Implied variance decomposition from the behavioral genetics model, 11t
EEOC. *See* Equal Employment Opportunity Commission
Effect of social capital on income per capita across cities in Northern Italy, 471f
Effectivity relations, 731–733, 740–741, 757–759, 768
Effects of Shifting Φ(x) Pointwise, 671f
Efficiency. *See also* Pareto
  ex-ante *vs.* ex-post, 810
  maximizing view of, 101
  in models with endogenous differences, 193–195
  in models with exogenous differences, 191–193
  of networks, 565, 751
  vs. stability, 771–774
  of star networks, 762n33
  of statistical discrimination, 191–195
Efficient binding agreements, 761
Efficient grand coalitions, 767
Efficient norms, 320
Effort *vs.* luck, 95, 102–103, 121, 127
Egalitarian mechanism, for two-way kidney exchanges, 813–816
Egalitarian solutions, 755n25
Egalitarian utility profiles, 814, 816
Eigenvectors, 559
Elasticity of substitution between consumption and leisure, 211
Embedded coalitions, 734
Empathy, imperfect, 341–343, 359–361, 364, 369, 394, 403
Empirical effects, of advertising, 211–218
Empirical evidence, for redistribution, 103–127
  data, 104
  results, 105–111

Employers' risk aversion, 138
Empty networks, 742–744
'Encuentros de Cuidado,' 467
Encyclopedia Britannica, 371–372
Endogeneity
in child outcomes, 3–4, 16, 26
of cultural traits, 341
endogenizing social groups, 51–52
in exits from games, 769–770
in group formation, 156–161
in marriage model, 398f
in network formation, 730
of network structure, 572–573, 675, 714–715
in preferences, 49, 508
in skills, 183–189
of social capital, 468
of status, 74
Endogenous differences, efficiency in models with, 193–195
Endowments
civic capital and, 437, 451, 467, 470, 473
endowment effect, 233
genetic, 6, 16, 19, 226
preferences and, 41–45, 50, 61–63
Enforcement
of Civil Rights Act, 163–164
of norms, 38, 313, 331–332, 528, 636
social capital and, 421–422, 424–425, 429, 452
Environmental capacity, and evolution, 251–252
Environmental variance, 3, 6, 16
Environments
economics and, 490–491, 506
of family, 2–12, 14, 16–18, 25
heritability and, 9–13
non-shared, 3, 5–6, 9–11
separate, 5
shared, 13, 15–16
Envy
fairness and, 847
preferences and, 35, 55
school choice and, 785, 831–834, 836–837
student placement and, 825, 828–830
EPCF. *See* Equilibrium process of coalition process
Epidemiological approach, 374, 377, 391–392, 472
in diffusion, 651, 658–665
in economics, 489–497
empirical issues of, 494–496
literature of, 497–505
model of, 492–494
in medicine, 490
Epistasis, 7
Equal Employment Opportunity Commission (EEOC), 164
Equal rights, for women, 163
Equality, *vs.* individualism, 95
Equilibria. *See also* Multiplicity, of equilibria; Nash equilibria
A-cultural equilibrium, 159–160
in affirmative action
general, 170–173
patronizing, 166–170, 167f
two-sector general equilibrium model, 173–176
with affirmative action, 168–170
without affirmative action, 167–168
asymmetric, 135–136, 141, 154–156, 172, 194
competitive, 789
as consumption-savings decisions, 42
discriminatory outcomes equilibrium, 158
equilibrium binding agreement, 759–761
equilibrium effects of advertising, 206–210
equilibrium process of coalition process, 765
equilibrium wage schedules under affirmative action, in Moro and Norman model, 172f
explicit equilibrium calculation, 570
indirect general equilibrium effect, 176
inefficiency of, 627
k-equilibria, 738
laissez-faire equilibrium, 184–187
Lipschitz continuous, 600–604, 607–608, 620, 622
Markov, 600
perfect, 620–623, 625–626, 628, 630, 768
microscopic, 605
monopoly profits in, 211
neoclassical general equilibrium theory, 94
in networks, 567f
Pareto, 142, 147, 161, 189, 295, 608–609
punctuated equilibrium effect, 314, 316–317, 321
risk-dominant, 320
selection among, 294–295, 708–712
self-fulfilling, 142
Spence signaling model and, 56–57, 74
in statistical discrimination
firms and workers' best responses and, 145–147

Equilibria (*cont.*)
symmetric, 669–670
symmetric monopolistically competitive equilibrium
with free entry and expanding varieties, 205
with monopoly profits, 205
symmetric steady state, 152–154
trivial, 769n38
Equilibrium binding agreements (EBA), 759–761
Equilibrium process of coalition process (EPCF), 765
Erdös-Renyi random graph, 659
ERGMs. *See* Exponential random graph models
Ergodicity, 359, 597, 599, 606–608, 623–624, 631–633
ESS. *See* European Social Survey
Ethnicity
ethnic fractionalization, 404, 405f, 406f, 459, 462
ethnic segregation, 389–390
ethnic variation, in body weight norms, 334
ethnolinguistic diversity, 469
ethnolinguistic fractionalization, 371–372
working wives and, 497–499
Ethnologue database, 371
Cross-Country Distribution of the Ethnolinguistic Fractionalization Index, 372f
Languages spoken in Asia, 373f
Etruscan cities, 385, 464, 471
Eurobarometer surveys, 419, 429, 447–448, 466
European Council, 749
European Social Survey (ESS), 115, 419, 429, 442, 447, 500
European Union, 394, 447
Even components, 810, 812–815
Event studies, 335
Evidence, 70–72. *See also* Empirical evidence, for redistribution
overlap of, 70–71
of status, 75–84
Evolution
altruism and, 242, 296, 297
Bayes' rule and, 229, 264, 266, 268, 276, 288
behavior and, 227–234
economic behavior and, 225–226, 296–297
environmental capacity and, 251–252
evolutionary game theory, 162, 225, 231–233
replicator dynamics in, 356
evolutionary stability, 739
exogenous evolutionary rules, 344n7
of farmers, 382f
fertility and, 254–255, 261–262, 291
genetic factors of, 290–292
group selection and, 290–297
of hunters, 382f
incentives and, 286–288
indirect evolutionary approach, 231–235
local interactions and, 633
mismatches of, 230–231, 259–260
preferences and, 49, 54–56, 221–310
rules of, 226–227
status and, 83–85, 272–290
utility functions and, 227–230, 267–269
Ex-ante *vs.* ex-post efficiency, 810
Exchange economy, 733, 746, 776
Exchange theory, 565, 781–853
emerging literature on, 846–848
list *vs.* paired exchanges, 802–803, 802f, 803f
Exclusive membership, 735
Existing tenants, house allocation with, 794–800
Exogenous differences
efficiency in models with, 191–193
literature of, 137–140
Exogenous evolutionary rules, 344n7
Exogenous shock, 4, 18
Exogenous skills, 179–183
Expanding observations, 704
Expanding varieties, Benchmark Economy model with, 205, 207–212
Expectations, and behaviors, 314
Expected future income, 97–99, 108
Experimental mutations, 710–714, 716, 720–721
Experimenter effect, 439
Experiments
field experiments, on civic capital, 466–467, 475–476
Hawthorne experiments, 88
natural
on civic capital, 463–467
in economics, 483
on trust, 451–452
trust game experiments, 78, 448–452, 475
ultimatum game experiments, 79–80, 488–489
Explicit equilibrium calculation, 570
Exponential discounting, 250–252, 256–257, 260

Exponential random graph models (ERGMs), 536–540, 542
Ex-post *vs.* ex-ante efficiency, 810
External stability, 735
Externalities
in education, 100
in games, 733–734, 741
group-identity, 363
negative, 742
in networks, 543–545, 548, 561, 563–565, 683n3
positional, 84
positive *vs.* negative, 742
Extraversion, 13
Eyeglasses, 3
Eyesight, 3

F

Facebook, 649n2
Fair Employment Commission Title (FEPC Title), 163
Fairness, 13, 95, 102–103, 121, 684
envy and, 847
normative features and, 785, 804
Redistribution, Work *vs.* Luck as a Driver of Success, and Fairness General Social Survey, 1972–2004, 122–123t
social capital and, 440, 452
Familias en Acción, 466
Family
environment, 2–12, 14, 16–18, 25
income of, 4, 18, 23, 25, 282
Redistribution, Family Background, and Social Mobility General
Social Survey, 1972–2004, 109t
size of, 4, 24–25
socialization and, 345
strength of family ties, 486, 487f, 499–501
structure of, 118–120
Fang model, 156, 159f, 160, 197
Farmers
evolution of, 382f
pineapple, 519, 651
Farming
at Jericho, 379, 381
spread of early farming in Europe, 380f
wave of advance of, 380–381
comparative statics exercise on the steepness of, 383f
Farsightedness, 731, 734, 754–761
Fashion, fads and collective action, 655–657
random matching and, 656–657
FBI crime data, 616
Fears
of flying, 246
of snakes, 229n11
Feedback loops, 315, 316, 334–351
Fehr-Schmidt inequity aversion model, 77
Feller kernels, 621
FEPC Title. *See* Fair Employment Commission Title
Fertility
culture and, 497–499
evolution and, 254–255, 261–262, 291
socialization and, 346, 351–352
transmission of, 394
Field experiments, on civic capital, 466–467, 475–476
Financial participation, 503
Firms
cooperative, 429
Cournot oligopolies, 733, 736, 744
Firms' net return from qualified and unqualified workers in the complex and simple tasks, 143t
oligopolistic, 744–745
workers' best responses and, 143–145
equilibria of, 145–147
First Order Stochastic Dominance (FOSD), 673
Fisher's polygenetic model, 7
Fitnesses, 232–234, 242, 267–271, 280, 287–291
Fitting random and strategic models, 540
5 w-chains, 806f
Flying, fear of, 246
Flynn effect, 16
FNSEM. *See* Fourth National Survey of Ethnic Minorities
Focal points, 683
Folk wisdoms, 52, 290
Föllmer model, 592–597
Food stamps, 627
Foraging, 250
Formation. *See* Coalitions; Groups; Link formation; Network formation
Forms, of advertising, 211
FOSD. *See* First Order Stochastic Dominance
Foundation for International Community Assistance, 475

Fourth National Survey of Ethnic Minorities (FNSEM), 404
Fractionalization
ethnic, 404, 405f, 406f, 459, 462
ethnolinguistic, 371–372
index of, 371–372, 372f
Framingham Heart Study, 652
Fraternal *vs.* identical twins, 2–4, 6, 10
Free city-states, 341, 376, 384–385, 425, 464, 471n12
Free entry, Benchmark Economy model with, 205, 207–212
Free rider problem, 296, 419, 422–423, 428, 647
Free will, 228
Freeze response, 265n44
Friedman-Savage utility function, 243–245
Fulghum, Robert, 36
Full siblings, 7–9, 14

G

"G(n,p)" random graph, 659
Gale's top trading cycles algorithm. *See* Top trading cycles algorithm
Gale-Shapley school-optimal stable mechanisms, 828, 830
Gale-Shapley student-optimal stable mechanisms, 828–830, 832–837, 847
Gallai-Edmonds Decomposition, 812f
Game theory. *See also* Coordination games; *specific games*
bargaining games, 488
characteristic function games, 732–733, 740, 746, 755, 765, 768
cooperation in games, 437–440, 716–721, 730
culture and, 483–484, 488
diffusion and network games, 672–674
endogeneity in exits from games, 769–770
evolutionary, 162, 225, 231–233, 356
externalities in, 733–734, 741
graphical games, 566, 567f, 573, 665–668
hedonic games, 733–734, 734n7, 738, 755, 757n26, 759, 846
market games, 488
multibidding games, 737
multiplicity of equilibria in, 484
Nash equilibria in, 566
network games, 668–672
nonempty cores, 740, 767
normal form games, 731, 734, 759
population games, 618n24, 632, 634–636
public goods games, 437, 467, 483, 486, 489, 667
symmetric *vs.* nonsymmetric games, 295, 319, 748
trust game experiments, 78, 448–452, 475
ultimatum game experiments, 79–80, 488–489
Garment industry, 517–518
GDP
advertising and, 212–215
civic capital and, 455–456, 456–457t, 458–459, 467–470, 475f, 476
happiness and, 77
trust and, 473–475
Gender preferences, 497–499
General equilibrium, in affirmative action, 170–173
General morality, 364–365
General Social Survey (GSS), 95, 104, 115, 121, 486n7
civic capital and, 419, 429, 452n10, 474, 474n14
Descriptive Statistics General Social Survey, 1972–2004, 128t
Preferences for Redistribution and a History of Misfortune General Social Survey, 1972–2004, 110t
Preferences for Redistribution and Religion General Social Survey, 1972–2004, 112–113t
Redistribution, Work *vs.* Luck as a Driver of Success, and Fairness General Social Survey, 1972–2004, 122–123t
Redistribution and a History of Macroeconomic Volatility during Youth General Social Survey, 1972–2004, 119–120t
Redistribution and Cultural Origin Immigrants' Regressions General Social Survey, 1972–2004, 116–117t
Redistribution and Individual Characteristics General Social Survey, 1972–2004, 106t
Generalized moralities, 452
Generalized *vs.* personalized trust, 440–442, 444–446t
Generating average group wage differentials, 138–139
Generational factors, 63n55
Generosity, 82
Genetic factors, 2–3. *See also* Behavioral genetics
coevolution of gene culture, 382n44

of evolution, 290–292
genetic clines, 383
genetic distance and trade, 388
genetic distance between 42 populations, 388f
genetic endowments, 6, 16, 19, 226
IQ and, 8–14
nonlinear nature of, 16, 26
trade and genetic distance, 388
Genetic inputs, 5–6
Geodesic distances, 523
Geographic spread
of socialization mechanisms, 348–349
stationary constant traveling wave model of, 348f
German Socio Economic Panel, 385, 429, 450, 450n8, 452
Germany
redistribution in, 485
Turkish immigrants in, 395, 500
Giant components, of networks, 525, 533, 660–661
Gibbs measure, 600, 604
Gibbs Sampling, 539
Gini coefficient, 99, 489
Girls to boys ratio, in tertiary education, 487f
Glaciation boundaries, 322n11
Glaeser, Sacerdote, and Scheinkman model, 615–617
Glaeser and Scheinkman model, 597–599
Global dynamics
climate change, 237
diversity, of norms, 314–315
global interactions, 590–592, 600, 605–607, 609, 614–615, 634
vs. local, 627–630
local conformity/global diversity effect, 314–315, 319, 321, 323
Goods. *See also* Public goods
divisible, 564, 793
indivisible, 783–784, 786, 788–789, 793n4
intermediate, 73
positional, 46, 72
status, 63
Google, 33, 688
Google Scholar, 57
page rank system of, 559
Grade point averages, 189
Grand coalition, 730, 733, 740–742, 747–748, 751–752, 755
efficient, 767–768
superadditivity of, 769
Granger causation tests, 214
Granovetter's theory, 517, 656–658, 661, 664–665, 695
Graph terminology
Bernoulli random graph, 659
directed graphs, 522
Erdös-Renyi random graph, 659
exponential random graph models, 536–540
"G(n,p)" random graph, 659
random graphs, 532, 658–661, 674
for social networks, 522–523
undirected graphs, 522
Graphical games, 566, 567f, 573, 665–668
Nash equilibria of, 667
payoffs in, 666–667
Gratz *vs.* Bollinger, 179
Great Depression, 95
Groups
cross-group effects
of Moro and Norman model, 149–150
of social learning, 696, 707
determination of individual reference groups, 638
discriminatory outcomes, as result of inter-group interactions, 147–161
effect of group size, in Moro and Norman model, 150–151
endogeneity, in group formation, 156–161
endogenizing social groups, 51–52
formation of
consent in, 732, 735, 741–743, 741t
in real time, 762–770
generating average group wage differentials, 138–139
group averages, 137–139
group inequality, 134–136, 195–197
group interactions, from peer effects, 161
group selection
economics and, 295–297
evolution and, 290–297
group specialization, discrimination as, 147–151
group-identity externalities, 363
group-wise connectedness, 697
real time group formation, 762–770
reference groups, 588, 591
Group-wise connectedness, 697
Grutter *vs.* Bollinger, 164, 179
GSS. *See* General Social Survey

GSZ model, 424–425
Guaranteeing, of coalitions, 732–733, 740, 748, 775

H

Habits, of consumption, 206, 214
Habituation, 282
Handicapping, 191
Handshaking, 313
Haplotypes, 292
Happiness
- brain activity and, 75
- GDP and, 77
- income and, 75–77
- inequality and, 77
- *vs.* utility, 75–76

Hawthorne experiments, 88
Haystack model, 292–294
Health determinants, 2, 74
Heart attacks, 327
Hedonic utilities, 279, 282, 529
Hedonism
- hedonic games, 733–734, 734n7, 738, 755, 757n26, 759, 846
- hedonic relationships, 529
- hedonic utilities, 279, 282, 529

Height correlations, 14, 23–24
Herding, 62–63, 553–554, 702
Heritability, 2–3
- behaviors and, 236, 247, 274
- environment and, 9–13
- IQ and, 25

Heterogamous marriages, 350, 387
Heterogeneity
- biological, 332
- in choices, 256
- in costs, 670
- cultural, 344–346, 362–363, 371–374
- in markets, 514
- of preferences, 696–697, 805
- sources of, 493–495
- unobserved, 516, 518, 611

Heterozygotes, 291
Hierarchies
- bi-hierarchies, 846
- hierarchical clustering, 541
- hierarchical exchange
  - house allocation and, 837–840
  - mechanisms, 837–840, 842
- in organizations, 427
- in societies, 437, 462

High clustering, 532–535
High school friendships, homophily in, 531t, 540, 542, 550
High school graduation rates, 15
Historical map of Italy, 1167, 465f
HLA. *See* Human leukocyte antigen
Hobbes, Thomas, 70
Holy Roman Empire, 385, 463
Home-country bias, 62, 488
Homogamous marriages, 346, 349–351, 395–400
- non-linear effect of neighborhood ethnic composition on identity and homogamy, 406f
- predicted homogamy as a function of time in the U.K., 407f
- probabilities of, 398f
- probability of homogamous marriage as a function of the religious shares, by U.S. state, 396f

Homogeneous costs, 670
Homophily, 335, 519, 529–532
- diffusion and, 649, 652–653, 674
- in high school friendships, 531t, 540, 542, 550
- inbreeding, 530
- out-breeding, 530
- social learning and, 698

Homozygotes, 291
Hopwood *vs.* Texas, 178
Horizontal socialization, 341, 342n3, 345, 394
Horst and Scheinkman model, 605–608
Hours worked
- advertising and, 212–218
- culture and, 499f
- log of per capita hours against per capita advertising, 213f
- men *vs.* women, 216–217
- U.S. *vs.* European, 216
- during the U.S. boom in the 1990s, 215f

House allocation problem, 786–788
- with existing tenants, 794–800
  - TTC in, 794
- hierarchical exchange and, 837–840
- models for, 786–800
- preference profiles in, 786–788, 791, 795

Housing market, 788–794
model of, 784
housing market cycle, 790f
TTC algorithm in, 790–793, 837, 839
How the other half lives (Riis), 389
"Hub-and-spoke" pattern, of networks, 534, 665
Human capital, 64, 73, 419–421, 423–424
appreciation of, 427
formation of, 135
investment of, 137–139, 515
observable *vs.* unobserved, 197, 496
Human information processing, 264, 269, 273, 277, 287
Human leukocyte antigen (HLA), 801–802
Humphrey, Hubert, 164
Hunters, evolution of, 382f
Hunting, disutility function of, 270
Hybrid corn adoption, 519, 651
Hyperbolic discounting, 249–251, 254
Hysteresis, 341, 376

I

Identical *vs.* fraternal twins, 2–4, 6, 10
Identification, 615, 637
civic capital and, 468–476
cultural portability as strategy for, 469, 471–472
rationality and, 637–638
Identity formation, 352–355
group-identity externalities, 363
Non-linear effect of neighborhood ethnic composition on identity and homogamy, 406f
oppositional, 353, 355
predicted identity as a function of time in the U.K., 406f
racial identity *vs.* wealth formation, 353–354
Ideological preferences, 95–96, 101–102, 107, 112, 118, 121
Idiosyncratic *vs.* aggregate risk, 235–238, 240–242, 246, 248, 261
i.i.d. *See* Independent and identically distributed
Illinois Cooperative Extension Service, 322
Illiteracy, 462–463
Image motivation, 82
Imitation
altruism and, 717–720
degree of, 617
principle of, 704
Immigrants, 114, 374
in Canada, 497, 499
correlation between trust level of country of origin and trust level of immigrants relative to Great Britain, 491f
Redistribution and Cultural Origin Immigrants' Regressions General Social Survey, 1972–2004, 116–117t
redistribution preferences by group and country of birth, 492f
socialization of, 389, 426
trust and, 472n13, 504
Turkish, in Germany, 395, 500
Immigration, 389–392
within-country migration, 503
Immoral familism, 363
Immunity, 659–660
Imperfect empathy, 341–343, 359–361, 364, 369, 394, 403
Imperfect learning, 369–370
Improvements, respecting, 830
Improving paths, 545
Impure altruism, 394
Inbreeding homophily, 530
Incentives
in coalitions, 747, 752, 770–774
to conspicuously consume, 59
evolution and, 286–288
incentive effects, 100–101, 111
to invest in skills, 141–142, 145, 146f, 148–151, 164–166, 172–177
in kidney exchange, 803, 806
to leave bequests, 42, 44–46
nonmonetary, 87
in school choice, 832
tax incentives, 429
trade and, 560–561, 563, 565
Income
correlation between change in income per capita and change in inherited trust between 2000 and 1935, 505f
determinants of, 2–3, 15, 20–21, 23, 23n14
Earnings: Implied variance decomposition from the behavioral genetics model, 13t
effect of social capital on income per capita across cities in Northern Italy, 471f
expected future income, 97–99, 108
of family, 4, 18, 23, 25, 282

Income (*cont.*)
  generating average group wage differentials, 138–139
  happiness and, 75–77
  inequality of, 15, 85, 97, 101, 369n33
  parental, 4, 4n, 17, 25
Income tax, 60
  progressive, 96
Incomplete information, 590–591, 600–601, 603–604, 675
  network formation and, 776
Incomplete learning, 692–694
Incomplete markets, 35, 47, 64
In-degrees, of network nodes, 686–688, 695
Independent and identically distributed (i.i.d.), 357, 599–600, 606, 612–613, 616, 619, 630, 719, 745
Indifference curves, 254–255, 278
Indirect domination relations, 757–758, 760n31
Indirect evolutionary approach, 231–235
Indirect general equilibrium effect, 176
Indirect measures, of civic capital, 452–458
Indirect preferences, 53–58
Individual reference groups, determination of, 638
Individual selection, 292–295
Individualism, *vs.* equality, 95
Individualists, 354
Individually rational mechanisms, 788–789, 822
Indivisible goods, 783–784, 786, 788–789, 793n4
Indoctrination, 36–38, 95, 99
Industrial Revolution, in U.K., 386–387
Inefficiency, of equilibrium, 627
Inequality
  Black-White wage inequality, 196–197
  of education, 15
  of groups, 134–136, 195–197
  happiness and, 77
  of income, 15, 85, 97, 101, 369n33
  social, 94
  in utility function
    directly, 100–101
    indirectly, 99–100
Inequity aversion, 684
Infinite horizon model
  culture and, 507
  local interactions and, 617, 619–620, 625–627
  network formation and, 746, 748, 753
  norms and, 44–46, 48
  redistribution and, 98
Informal insurance, 512
Information
  aggregation of, 693
  asymmetric, 48n30, 59, 190, 687–688
  cascades of, 657
  complete, 590–591, 600–601, 603–604, 625–626, 668f, 751, 761, 771, 776
  directed information networks, 686–688, 686f, 732
    connectedness of, 522n13
  human information processing, 264, 270, 273, 277, 287
  incomplete, 590–591, 600–601, 603–604, 675
  job contact information, 514–515
  Local + Common Information, 693f
  neighborhoods of, 720–721
  private, 685, 689, 698, 701–703
  relative consumption and, 273–277
  simple information networks, 687f
  sources of, 698
  technology of, 681
Informational free riding, 157–158, 176
Inheritance tables, 839f, 840f
Initial configuration, of social networks, 714
Institutions
  cultural transmission and, 363–365
  development of, 458
  long term persistence of, 384–389
  long-lasting effects of, 425, 471
Instrumental concern for rank, 53, 58–63
Insults, 313
Insurance, 243–245
  informal, 512
  social, 96, 386
  unemployment, 189–190
Integration, of networks, 696, 707
  levels of, 707f
  social conformism and, 697f
Intensity, of interaction, 595
Interaction(s). *See also* Local interactions; Social interactions
  bilateral, 732, 775–776
  discriminatory outcomes as result of inter-group interactions, 147–161
  global, 590–592, 600, 605–607, 609, 614–615, 634

group interactions, from peer effects, 161
intensity of, 595
Markovian, 594
myopic, 633–635
neighborhoods of, 720–721
nonstrategic, 684–704
peer interactions, on networks, 565–573
strategic, 704–721
Intergenerational correlations, 8
Intergenerational cultural transmission, 341, 361n27, 366n31, 392–393
Intergenerational transmission, 423–424, 428, 470, 506
Intermediate goods, 73
Internal consistency, 755
Internal stability, 735
Internalized preferences, 36–38
International Ladies Garment Workers' Union, 518
International Social Survey Programme, 306
Intolerance
cultural, 343, 359, 370
religious, 427
Introspection, 228, 233, 247, 683, 755
Invasive treatments, 327, 330
Investment
consumption and, 53, 61–63
in human capital, 137–139, 515
incentives to invest in skills, 141–142, 145, 146f, 148–151, 164–166, 172–177
over-investment *vs.* under-investment, 564
in social capital, 420–422
trust and, 458, 473
IQ, 2–3
behavioral genetics results and, critiques and challenges of, in education, 14–17
correlations in IQ between siblings, adoptive siblings, and identical twins, 9t
genetics and, 8–14
heritability and, 25
Implied variance decomposition from the behavioral genetics model, 10t
sibling correlations of, 8–11
Irrational numbers, 566n53
Irreversible decisions, 769–770
Ising Economies, 596–597
Isomorphisms, 825, 828, 831
ISSP. *See* International Social Survey Programme
Italy
Blood donation in, 453, 455f
effect of social capital on income per capita across cities in Northern Italy, 471f
historical map of, 1167, 465f
history of, second millennium, 463–466
Referenda turnout across Italian provinces, 454f
Iteroparous life histories, 252–254

J

Java Forum, 688
Jericho, farming at, 379, 381
Jews
anti-Semitism and, 384
in Diaspora, 341, 374, 378
Orthodox, 341, 374
vanishing of American Jews hypothesis, 401
Job contact information, 514–515
Johnson, Lyndon, 164
Joint consumption activities, 40n19, 41, 50
Joint problem solving, 518
Justified envy. *See* Envy
"Just-so" stories, 227

K

Kalai-Smorodinsky solution, 320n7
K-equilibria, 738
Keynesian macroeconomic models, 608
Kidney exchange, 786, 801–821
deceased *vs.* living donors, 801
directed live kidney donations, 801–803
donor exchanges, 801–803
designs of, 803–804
model of, 804
incentives in, 803, 806
multi-way
with 0–1 preferences, 816–820
with strict preferences, 804–808
mutually compatible pairs in, 808
recent developments and related literature in, 820–821
two-way, with 0–1 preferences, 808–816
egalitarian mechanism for, 813–816
priority mechanism for, 811
Kin selection, 296–297
Knight, Frank, 312
Korean-American adoptees, 21, 26

L

Labor
advertising and, 207–208
consumption and, 206, 212
demand for, 213n23
labor markets, 86–88, 135–137, 151
culture and, 501
on networks, 573–574, 648
regulation of, 499–501
on social networks, 514–517
relations, 487f
skilled *vs.* unskilled, 140–141
supply of, 59–61, 85, 102, 212–213, 216–217
women in labor force, 395
Labor force participation (LFP), 482, 490, 494–499, 506
drop-out rates, 529, 565, 573
mothers' attitudes on women in labor force, 486–488
S-shaped curves for, 506
Lactose absorption, 382n44
Laissez-faire equilibrium, 184–187
Land titles, for squatters, 485
Language choice, 681–682
Languages spoken in Asia, 373f
Largest consistent set (LCS), 758, 766
Latent space estimation, 542n33
Lattice theory, 783
Lattices, in networks, 533, 566n51, 568, 592, 672n26
LCS. *See* Largest consistent set
Leakage, 187
Learning, 657. *See also* Social learning
agriculture and, 681
complete, 692–694, 696
coordination games and, 705–715
imperfect, 369–370
incomplete, 692–694
link formation and, 715–716
multiple equilibria and, 707–708
naive, 699–700
in networks, 551–560, 679–728
norms and, 682
social, 684–698
in social networks, 518–521
star networks and, 700, 708, 711–712
Least squares, weighted, 12
Leisure
commodification of, 209–210, 218
and consumption, 202–203
elasticity of substitution between, 211
sleep and, 218
Lemons phenomenon, 224
Leslie matrices, 252–253, 256, 260–261
Levels of network integration, 707f
LFP. *See* Labor force participation
Liberal policy, 168
Libertarian views, 101
Life histories
iteroparous, 252–254
semelparous, 248–250, 252
Limited morality, norms of, 363–364
Link formation
learning and, 715–716
in network formation, 735–737, 742–744, 751, 762–763, 772
richer sequential link formation models, 535
Link monotonicity, 744–745, 760n30, 764, 773
Lipschitz continuous equilibrium, 600–604, 607–608, 620, 622
List exchanges, 802–803, 803f
Literacy rates, 463, 470
Littering, 313, 430
Living *vs.* deceased kidney donors, 801
Local + Common Information, 693f
Local conformity, 600–603
local conformity/global diversity effect, 314–315, 319, 323, 331
Local interactions, 587–644
around circles, 711
continuous choice models of, 589–590, 592–608, 619–623
Bisin, Horst, and Özgür, 600–604
Föllmer model, 592–597
Glaeser and Scheinkman model, 597–599
Horst and Scheinkman model, 605–608
discrete choice models, 611–617
Brock and Durlauf model, 612–615
Glaeser, Sacerdote, and Scheinkman model, 615–617
dynamic models of, 618–638
baseline, 618–619
evolution and, 633
infinite horizon model and, 617, 619–620, 625–627
local *vs.* global dynamics and, 627–630
multiplicity of equilibria in, 608–611
Nash equilibria in, 609, 616

rational forward-looking, 619–627
recursive algorithms in, 626, 628–631
segregation and, 633–634
S-shaped curves for, 588
static models of, 589–617
baseline, 589–592
strategic complementarities in, 598–599, 609–610, 612
utility functions of, 591–592, 597–605, 607, 619, 623
Local monopolies, 667
Local public goods, 717, 717n21
Local *vs.* global dynamics, 627–630
Log of per capita hours against per capita advertising, 213f
Logistic differential equations, 344
Log-linear response functions, 319, 713, 722
Long term persistence, of institutions, 384–389
Longevity, of Nobel Prize winners, 74n1
Long-lasting effects, of institutions, 425, 471
Lorenz-dominant utility profiles, 813
Lorenz-maximal elements, 755n25
Lotka-Volterra equations, 381
Lottery mechanisms, 844–846
multilottery mechanism, 837
utility profiles of, 810–811
Low birth weight, 288
Low-rationality agents, 633
Luck
vs. effort, 95, 102–103, 121, 127
vs. merit, 482, 486
vs. work
Redistribution, Work *vs.* Luck as a Driver of Success, and Fairness General Social Survey, 1972–2004, 122–123t

M

"Macro" models, 654
Macroeconomic experiences, 114–118
Keynesian macroeconomic models, 608
Redistribution and a History of Macroeconomic Volatility during Youth General Social Survey, 1972–2004, 119–120t
Madoff scandal, 427
Major religions, 375f
"La Mala Educacion," 428
Malaysia, affirmative action in, 173
Managerial implications, of status, 87
Marginal signals, 268
Marginals, 616
Marijuana use, 653
Markets. *See also* Housing market; Labor
Arrow-Debreu markets, 35, 46
"box design" market game, 79–80
complete, 35, 46–47
heterogeneity in, 514
incomplete, 35, 47, 64
market design, 837–844
related literature in, 844
trading cycles with brokers and owners algorithm in, 840–844
market games, 488
market imperfections, and conformity, 49–51
marketing models, 654–655
marriage markets, 163, 245, 349–350, 387, 395, 763, 823n2
missing, 46–48
networked markets and social networks, 514–521
relationships, 518
Markov equilibria, 600
Markov perfect equilibria (MPE), 620–623, 625–626, 628, 630, 768
Markov processes, 261, 274–275, 319, 328, 699
equilibria, 600
perfect, 620–623, 625–626, 628, 630, 768
Markov chains, 539, 763
Markov chain Monte Carlo, 539
perturbed, 319n6
Markovian interactions, 594
in network formation, 750, 764, 768, 768n36
Marriage(s)
endogenous marriage model, 398f
heterogamous, 350, 387
homogamous, 346, 349–351, 395–399
non-linear effect of neighborhood ethnic composition on identity and homogamy, 406f
predicted homogamy as a function of time in the U.K., 407f
probabilities of, 398f
probability of homogamous marriage as a function of the religious shares, by U.S. state, 396f
marriage markets, 163, 245, 349–350, 387, 395, 763, 823n2
Marshall, Alfred, 312–313, 316, 334
Martingale, 239

Martingale Convergence Theorem, 370n34, 690
Marx, Karl, 70
Matching theory, 190, 514, 571n59, 781–853
  aristocratic matching, 44–45, 48, 54n39, 507
  assortative matching, 507
  competitive matchings, 800
  cycles in, 789, 790f, 805
  a matching, 810f
    wasteful *vs.* nonwasteful, 825
  Pareto-efficient matchings, 810, 812–813, 813f
  probability matching, 242
  property rights in, 785, 788, 793n3, 837–839
  quasi-matchings, 846
  random matching, 657
  stability in, 783
  submatching, 838, 841, 843
  TTC in, 846
  two-sided matching model, 783–784
Maternal nutrition, 288
Mating, assortative, 7, 41–42, 44–46, 48
Maximization
  of consumption, 259
  of efficiency, 101
  of offspring, 283
  of payoffs, 680–681, 684–685, 708, 722
  of profit, 138n5, 745
  of utility function, 94, 204, 226–232, 236, 287, 332, 493
Measures, of civic capital, 429–458, 432–435t
Measuring Civic Values, 431–432t
Mechanisms, 784
  axiomatic, 837–844
  Boston school choice mechanism, 831–832
  of college admissions, 828
  consistent, 800, 819
  deterministic direct, 787, 822
  egalitarian, for two-way kidney exchanges, 813–816
  Gale-Shapley school-optimal stable, 828, 830
  Gale-Shapley student-optimal stable, 828–830, 832–837, 847
  hierarchical exchange, 837–840, 842
  individually rational, 788–789, 822
  lottery mechanisms, 844–846
    multilottery, 837
    utility profiles of, 810–811
  priority, 787
    for two-way kidney exchanges, 811
  probabilistic serial, 845
  reallocation-proof, 837, 840, 843
  school-optimal stable, 823, 828, 830
  of socialization, 346–351, 392–407
    geographic spread of, 348–349
  strategy-proof, 784
  student-optimal stable, 823, 828, 836
  TCBO mechanism, 843
  VECM, 213
  weakly neutral, 800
  YRMH-IGYT, 795–800, 807–808, 839, 845, 847
    examples of, 795f, 796f, 797f, 798f, 799f
Medicaid, 627
Medical innovation, 681
Medical treatment norms, 327–330
  minorities and, 327
Medicine, epidemiological approach in, 490
Meiotic drive, 291
Melting pot society, 341, 359n26, 374, 389
  triple melting pot hypothesis, 401
Meltzer-Richards model, 96–98, 100, 105
Membership, exclusive *vs.* open, 735
Men *vs.* women, hours worked by, 216–217
Mencken, H. L., 87
Merit *vs.* luck, 482, 486
Mesolithic sites, 379n42
Meta-analyses, 489, 775
Metabolic function, 332
Meta-preferences, 341
  meta-preference orderings, 208n13
Metropolis-Hastings algorithm, 539
Microeconomic conditions, 593–594
Microfinance, 520
Microscopic equilibrium, 605
Military training, 36n9
Mill, John Stuart, 312
Mimics, 234–235
Mincer regressions, 496
Minimum wage legislation, 501n27
Minorities, 114
  cultural, 342, 345, 353–355, 360, 368, 378n39, 394, 401
  discrimination against, 135, 138n2, 162–164, 176–183, 189–190
  medical treatment of, 327
Misallocation, of workers, 173, 194
Misfortune, 95, 108

Preferences for Redistribution and a History of Misfortune General Social Survey, 1972–2004, 110t
Mismatches
of evolution, 230–231, 259–260
statistical discrimination and, 189, 191–192, 195
Missing link, civic capital as, 417–480
Missing markets, 46–48
Mistrust, 462
in Africa, 466
consensus and, 462
regulation and, 425–426
Mixing random and strategic models, 549–550
MLRP. *See* Monotone Likelihood Ratio Property
Modeling
affirmative action, 165–166
block modeling, 541
a posteriori, 542
cultural transmission, 342–371
impact of networks, 550–574
Models, 638. *See also* Economic models; Statistical mechanics; *specific models*
continuous choice models, 589–590, 592–608, 619–623
discrete choice models, 611–617
dynamic models of discrimination, 161–163
predictive power of, 33–34, 224–225, 335
statistical, 532, 536, 540, 548, 550
Moderate Social Influence (MSI), 598, 601, 604, 607–608
Monadic stability, 739
Money pump, 223
Monopolies, local, 667
Monopolization, 363, 736
Monopoly power, 202–203, 205, 208–210, 218
Monopoly profits
Benchmark Economy with, 205, 207
in equilibrium, 211
symmetric monopolistically competitive equilibrium with, 205
Monotone Likelihood Ratio Property (MLRP), 143–144
Monotonicity, 753–754
link monotonicity, 744–745, 760n30, 764, 773
in social networks, 569
Monte Carlo simulations, 539, 821
Markov chain Monte Carlo, 539
Moral norms, 430
general morality, 364–365
generalized moralities, 452
of limited morality, 363–364
religion and, 426–427
sources of, 461–462t
Mormon Church, 378
Moro and Norman model, 147–148
cross-group effects of, 149–150
effect of group size in, 150–151
equilibrium wage schedules under affirmative action in, 172f
Mortality, and discounting, 248, 252n32, 262
Mothers
attitudes on women in labor force, 486–488
education of, 4, 18–22, 24
Movers
civic capital and, 471–474
culture and, 503
MPE. *See* Markov perfect equilibria
MSI. *See* Moderate Social Influence
Multibidding games, 737
Multi-category serial dictatorships, 826, 828–829
Multiculturalism, 353n18
Multidimensional cultural traits, 355–359
Multilateral bargaining, 548, 775–776
Multilottery mechanisms, 837
Multinomial choice model, 615
Multiplicity, of equilibria, 35, 47–48, 63
in Coate and Loury, 142, 147f
with complete information, 668f
in game theory, 484
learning and, 707–708
in local interactions, 608–611
in networks, 568–569
redistribution and, 103
of social arrangements, 52–53
in Spence signaling model, 142n8
statistical discrimination and, 135, 141–142, 144, 146, 161
Multipliers, social, 317
Multi-way kidney exchanges
with 0–1 preferences, 816–820
with strict preferences, 804–808
Mutations, 226, 228–229, 247–248, 265
experimental, 710–714, 716, 720–721
Mutual causality, 317
Mutual compatibility matrix, 809

Mutual trust, 455, 466–467
Mutually compatible pairs, 808
Myerson's game, 739
Myopia
effect of, 635–637
myopic interactions, 633–635
myopically best-responding agents, 635–636, 708n14
network formation and, 731, 734, 738, 751, 754–755, 762–763
norms and, 332–333
vs. rationality, 589, 633–637
social learning and, 688
social networks and, 557, 572

N

Naive learning, 699–700
Nash equilibria, 45, 206, 232, 234
Bayesian Nash equilibria, 148, 157–159, 225
Coalition-proof, 760n30
of coordination games, 705–709, 712
in game theory, 566
of graphical games, 667
in local interactions, 609, 616
in network formation, 734n8, 738–740, 744, 746, 751, 759, 764
norms and, 318, 320
pairwise, 739, 773
strong, 773
Nash program, 730, 751
National Academy of Science, 12
National Health and Nutrition Examination Survey (NHANES), 333
National Longitudinal Study of Adolescent Health, 404, 530
National Longitudinal Survey of Youth (NLSY), 389, 393, 404
National Research Council, 12
National Residency Matching Program (NRMP), 783, 823
Natural experiments
on civic capital, 463–466
in geography, 466
in history, 463–466
in economics, 483
Natural selection, 226, 241, 273
Nature and nurture effects, 1–30
Negative externalities, 742
Neighborhoods
Bounded-neighborhood model, 634
of interaction and information, 720–721
neighborhood tipping, 633
non-linear effect of neighborhood ethnic composition on identity and homogamy, 406f
school choice and, 399
structure of, 591, 615, 618–619, 626n30, 637
trust and, 491n16
Neighbors, in networks, 523
Neoclassical general equilibrium theory, 94
Neolithic transition, 379
NEPKE. *See* New England Program for Kidney Exchange
Network Components and Immune Agents, 659f
Network formation, 532–550, 675n30, 729–779
anonymity in, 771–772, 771n39
complete information and, 751, 761, 771, 776
consent in, 732, 735, 741–743, 741t
dynamic, 762–765
endogeneity in, 730
incomplete information and, 776
infinite horizon model and, 746, 748, 753
link formation in, 735–737, 742–744, 751, 762–763, 772
Markov processes in, 750, 764, 768, 768n36
myopia and, 731, 734, 738, 751, 754–755, 762–763
Nash equilibria in, 734n8, 738–740, 744, 746, 751, 759, 764
one-stage models of, 731–746
with transfers, 736–737
without transfers, 734–736
resistance in, 763, 763n34
sequential models of, 746–754
stability in, 737–741
stochastic stability in, 739, 763
Network with 3 Components, 524f
Networks, 547f. *See also* Random networks; Social networks
aperiodic components of, 558
arcs of, 680, 721
bargaining and trade through, 560–565
clustering in, 527–537, 527f
vs. coalitions, 775–776
coevolution of behavior and, 571
for communication, 688, 762
community detection, 536, 540–543
complete, 710–711

components of, 523, 809
consensus and, 552–560, 568, 571
coordination games on, 566n51
cycles in, 522–523, 523f
DeGroot updating process in, 557f, 558f, 559f
density of, 708
diffusion in, 551
strategic interaction and, 657–674
diffusion on complete, 656–657
directed information networks, 686–688, 686f, 732
connectedness of, 522n13
edges, 522
efficiency implications of, 565, 751
empty, 742–744
endogeneity of structure, 572–573, 675, 714–715
equilibria in, 567f
externalities in, 543–545, 548, 561, 563–565, 683n3
games on, 565–573
giant components of, 525, 533, 660–661
"hub-and-spoke" pattern of, 534, 665
integration of, 696, 707
levels of, 707f
social conformism and, 697f
labor markets on, 573–574, 648
lattices in, 533, 566n51, 568, 592, 672n26
learning in, 551–560, 679–728
modeling the impact of, 550–574
multiplicity of equilibria in, 568–569
neighbors in, 523
Network Components and Immune Agents, 659f
network games, 668–672
Network with 3 Components, 524f
networked markets, and social networks, 514–521
nodes, 522–523
degrees of, 523, 658
in-degrees *vs.* out-degrees of, 686–688, 695
over time, 651–653
paths in, 522–523, 523f
payoffs to buyers and sellers as a function of, 562f
payoffs to each node as a function of, 544f, 546f
peer interactions on, 565–573
regular, 524
simple, 706f
simple information, 687f
star networks, 537, 572
altruism in, 719–720
efficiency of, 762n33
learning and, 700, 708, 711–712
from static perspectives, 647–650
strategic, 543–548, 570
subnetworks, 523
undirected, 732
walks, 522, 523f
weighted, 736
balanced collection, of weights in, 740
Neuroticism, 13
New England Program for Kidney Exchange (NEPKE), 820
NHANES. *See* National Health and Nutrition Examination Survey
NLSY. *See* National Longitudinal Survey of Youth
Nodes, of networks, 522–523
degrees of, 523, 658
Nonempty cores, of games, 740, 767
Nonexponential discounting, 257–262
Non-linear effect of neighborhood ethnic composition on identity and homogamy, 406f
Nonmonetary incentives, 87
Non-shared environments, 3, 5–6, 9–11
Nonstrategic interaction, 684–704
Nonsymmetric *vs.* symmetric games, 295, 319, 748
Nontradability, of status, 74–75, 81–84
Nontransferable utility (NTU), 733, 746
Nonwasteful matchings, 825
Normal form games, 731, 734, 759
Norman Kingdom, 463–466
Normative features, 731
fairness and, 785, 803
vs. positive features, 555
rationality and, 223, 428
Norms, 31–67, 311–338. *See also* Moral norms
adoption and, 335
background of, 312–313
of body weight, 331–334
model of, 331–333
consistency of, 755n25
contractual, in agriculture, 321–327
share contracts, 322, 325f, 327
of cooperation, 424
cultural, 114–118
customs and conventions of, 313–314
economic behavior and, 311–338

Norms (*cont.*)
economic models of, 32–35, 335
efficient, 320
enforcement of, 38, 313, 331–332, 528, 636
global diversity of, 314–315
infinite horizon model and, 44–46, 48
learning and, 682
long-run stability of, 316–317
of medical treatment, 327–330
myopia, 332–333
Nash equilibria and, 318, 320
norm dynamics
features of, 314–316
model of, 317–321
social interactions and, 317
of stochastic stability, 316, 319, 320n7, 572
stochastically stable, 316, 319, 320n7, 572
strategic complementarities and, 317, 424–425
NRMP. *See* National Residency Matching Program
NTU. *See* Nontransferable utility
Nursing care, 61, 63n55

O

Obama, Barack, 107
Obedience, 422, 431t, 436t, 437, 462
Obesity
rates of, 317, 652
risks of, 331, 334
transmission of, 24
Obligation, social, 482
Oblique socialization, 341–342, 345, 394
Observable *vs.* unobserved human capital, 197, 496
Observations
expanding, 704
of past actions, 702–704
of past actions and outcomes, 701
Occam's Razor, 278
O'Connor, Sandra Day, 164, 179
Odd components, 810, 812–815
OECD countries, 212, 216, 218, 482n2
OFCC. *See* Office of Contract Compliance
Office of Contract Compliance (OFCC), 164
Offspring, maximization of, 283
Oligopolistic firms, 744–745
Oligopoly, 565
One skill category, in student placement, 825–826
"1/d Law of Giving," 650
One-period-lived agents, 41
One-stage models, of coalitions and network formation, 731–746
One-way flow model, 735
Open membership, 735
Openness, 13
Opportunity costs, 561
Oppositional identity formation, 353, 355
Optimism, 99, 692, 694–695
OPTN. *See* Organ Procurement and Transplant Network
Ordinal *vs.* cardinal utility, 278–280
Organ donation, 453
Organ Procurement and Transplant Network (OPTN), 820
Organizational hierarchies, 427
Orthodox Jews, 341, 374
Other-regarding behavior, 290
Ottoman Empire, 341, 377, 384
Out-breeding homophily, 530
Outcomes. *See also* Discriminatory outcomes
of actions, 682–685
for children, 1–30
observation of past actions and, 701
social, 680, 682
stationary, 235
stochastic stability of, 710–711, 714–715, 719n24, 721
Out-degrees, of network nodes, 686–688, 695
Out-of-wedlock pregnancy, 588
Outside options, 769–770
Out-sourcing, 514
Overdemanded patients, 811–815
Over-investment *vs.* under-investment, 564
Overlap, of evidence, 70–71
Over-optimism, 99
The Overspent American: Why We Want What We Don't Need (Schor), 202–203
The Overworked American: The Unexpected Decline of Leisure (Schor), 202–203

P

Page rank system, of Google, 559
Paired exchanges, 802–803, 802f
Pairwise Nash equilibria, 739, 773
Pairwise stability, 738, 743, 745, 758n29, 771

Panel Study of Income Dynamics (PSID), 23, 23t, 399
Paradoxes, in voting, 754
Parental characteristics, 4–5
altruism, 366
college educated, 17
education, 497–498
income, 4, 4n, 17, 25
teaching civic values, 475–476
Pareto
dominated, 769, 829, 833–834, 836
efficiency, 46–47, 53, 278, 561, 743, 784, 804
Pareto-efficient matchings, 810, 812–813, 813f
school choice and, 832–834
student placement and, 828–829
equilibria, 142, 147, 161, 189, 295, 608–609
gains, 194–195
improvement, 73, 245
Pareto, Vilfredo, 525
Parking violations, of United Nations officials, 453–454, 459, 502
Parliamentary democracies, 750
Parsimony
of Bass model, 654
of economic models, 48, 53, 56, 243, 621n28
Parthenogenetic reproduction, 236, 241, 342
Partition function form, 734, 734n8, 767
Paths
improving, 545
in networks, 522–523, 523f
Patients
perfectly matched, 811, 813–814
underdemanded *vs.* overdemanded, 811–815
Patronizing equilibrium, in affirmative action, 166–170, 167f
Payoffs
Bernoulli distributed, 685
to buyers and sellers as a function of the network, 562f
discounting of, 746–749, 752–754, 764–765
to each node as a function of the network, 544f, 546f
in graphical games, 666–667
maximization of, 680–681, 684–685, 708, 722
per capita, 740, 747, 761
quadratic payoff structures, 570
PCF. *See* Process of coalition formation
Peer comparisons, 282
Peer effects, 557
and diffusion, 519–521
group interactions from, 161
peer interactions, on networks, 565–573
reversal in, 569
strategic peer interactions, 566
studies on, 516
Per capita payoffs, 740, 747, 761
Perfectly matched patients, 811, 813–814
Perron-Frobenius theorem, 253
Personality traits
Behavioral genetics results on personality traits
meta study of correlations between parents and children, 14t
determinants of, 13
Personalized *vs.* generalized trust, 440–442, 444–446t
Perturbed Markov chains, 319n6
Phelps model, of statistical discrimination, 136–139, 191–192
Phenotypic gambits, 292n62
Physical capital, 64, 421, 427, 452
Pigouvian taxation, 71
Pineapple farmers, 519, 651
Planners' problem, 193–195
Pleasurable brain activity, 34n7
Poisson random networks, 524–526, 528, 533–535, 542, 659
Poisson rate, 152
Policy interventions, 627
Policy platforms, 745
Political coalitions, 749–751
Political economy, 477
Political participation, 423, 459, 499–501, 503, 649
Political parties, model of, 745–746
Political scientists' definition, of social capital, 422
Polygyny, 245
Poor, beliefs about, and redistribution, 124f
Population dynamics, 342–346, 377–383
densities, 349
genetic distance between 42 populations, 388f
population games, 618n24, 632, 634–636
simulated, 402f
Portability, cultural, 469, 471–472
Positionality, 72–73, 75–78, 84, 230. *See also* Rank
positional externality, 84

Positionality (*cont.*)
positional goods, 46, 71
relative position, 46, 49
direct concern for, 55
in social networks, 520
Positive features
vs. normative features, 555
positive externalities, 742
Postmodernist Critique, 202–203, 206n9, 208n13, 210–212, 215, 218
Postnatal development, 264
POUM. *See* Prospects of upward mobility
Power distributions, 534n32
Power laws, 525, 534, 534n32
Predators, 230, 241, 248, 257, 290
Predicted homogamy as a function of time in the U.K., 407f
Predicted identity as a function of time in the U.K., 406f
Predictive power, of models, 33–34, 224–225, 335
Preference profiles
in college admissions, 821
in house allocation, 786–788, 791, 795
in school choice, 831
in student placement, 824, 826
in trading cycles, 843
Preferences, 31–67, 235. *See also* Evolution; Redistribution; Status
admission office's preferences over test scores under color-blind admission policy, 182f
of conformity, 620, 624
for consumption, 255–256
cumulative distribution function F of bequests, 43f
endogeneity in, 49, 508
endowments and, 41–45, 50, 61–63
envy and, 35, 55
evolutionary foundations of, 49, 54–56, 221–310
of genders, 497–499
heterogeneity of, 696–697, 805
ideological, 95–96, 101–102, 107, 112, 118, 121
indirect, 53–58
internalized, 36–38
metapreference orderings, 208n13
meta-preferences, 341
A more concentrated wealth distribution, 44f
multi-way kidney exchanges
with 0–1 preferences, 816–820
with strict preferences, 804–808
present-biased, 258, 272
reduced form, 35, 39–41, 44–46
basic model of, 41–46
revealed, 74, 160–161, 224, 228, 231, 276
reversals of, 250–251, 258–259, 262–263
social, 40–53, 77–78
social construction of, 201–220
social determinants for, 35–40
for sons, 498–499
for status, 69–91
strict, 731, 784, 804–808
transmission of, 37–38
unobserved, 234
utility functions and, 36, 53–55, 57, 63
Preferential attachment, 534–535
Pregnancy
out-of-wedlock, 588
teen-age, 611
Pre-marital sex, 387
Preschool Education and Educational Careers among Migrant Children project, 395
Present-biased preferences, 258, 272
Price auctions, 488n13
"Price of anarchy," 564
Primitive arguments, 53, 57, 166, 228n10
Priorities, weak, 832–834
Priority mechanisms, 787
for two-way kidney exchanges, 811
Priority profiles, 831, 839
Prisoners' dilemma, 34, 45n26, 73, 163, 292–296, 363–364
Privacy, 82
Private information, 685, 689, 698, 701–703
Private sector, 173–176
Private utilities, 612
Probabilistic content, of trust, 440
Probabilistic serial (PS) mechanism, 845
Probabilistic sophistication, 241
Probability matching, 242
Probability of homogamous marriage as a function of the religious shares, by U.S. state, 396f
Problem solving, joint, 518
Process of coalition formation (PCF), 765
Product topology, 605n16

Productivity
civic capital and, 420, 454, 456t, 467–468, 468t, 473–474
redistribution and, 96–100
of soil, 315, 324f
index of, 322
spillovers of, 330
statistical discrimination and, 135–140, 149, 183–185, 187, 191–194
Profiling, racial, 196n31
Profit maximization, 138n5, 745
Profitable moves, 765
Progressive income tax, 96
Proofs, on discounting, 298–304
Propaganda, 369
Proper dynamic models, 639
Property rights, 100, 111, 384–385, 485–486
in matching theory, 785, 788, 793n3, 837–839
Prophecies, self-fulfilling, 140, 142
Proportional spillovers, 612
Proposition 209, 178–179
Pro-social behavior, 82
Pro-sociality, 363, 366
Prospects of upward mobility (POUM), 98–100, 108
Proximate *vs.* ultimate causality, 251n31
"Pseudolikelihood" techniques, 539
PSID. *See* Panel Study of Income Dynamics
Psychological denial, 202
Public goods
best-shot public goods game, 667
civic capital and, 428, 430, 439, 464, 467
cultural transmission and, 366–367, 371
local, 717, 717n21
provision of, 683
public goods games, 437, 467, 483, 486, 489, 667
Public sector, 173–176
Punctuality, 682
Punctuated
equilibrium effect, 314, 316–317, 321
Punishment, 52, 233
Pure conformity, 611
Pure coordination games, 320
Pure outside options, 770
Putnam, Robert D.
Bowling Alone, 422

Q

Quadratic payoff structures, 570
Quadratic utility functions, 602, 623
Qualified *vs.* unqualified workers, 141–143, 148, 157, 166–168, 174–176
Firms' net return from qualified and unqualified workers in the complex and simple tasks, 143t
Qualitative implications, 321
Quantity/quality trade off, 352
Quantum premium, 324
Quasi-matchings, 846
Quit rates, 138n5
Quota vectors, 831

R

Racial factors
in consumption, 59n50
profiling, 196n31
racial identity *vs.* wealth formation, 353–354
racialists, 354
in redistribution, 105, 113–114
segregation, 540
Radio carbon dating, 379
Random assignment, 18–19, 21
Random graphs, 532, 658–661, 674
Bernoulli random graph, 659
Erdös-Renyi random graph, 659
exponential random graph models (ERGMs), 536–540, 542
"G(n,p)" random graph, 659
Random matching, 657
Random networks, 533–535, 659–661
fitting, 540
Poisson, 524–526, 528, 533–535, 542, 659
preferential attachment, 534–535
richer sequential link formation models, 535
small world model, 526–532, 533
strategic models and, mixing, 549–550
Random serial dictatorships (RSD), 794, 845
with squatting rights, 794
Rank, 40
consumption and, 46n27, 58
instrumental concern for, 53, 58–63
wealth and, 40, 43–45
Rational choice theory, 70
Rational forward-looking local interactions, 619–627

Rational-agent model of optimizing agents, 35–36
Rationality, 223
of beliefs, 425
identification and, 637–638
low-rationality agents, 633
vs. myopia, 589, 633–637
normative features and, 223, 428
social learning and, 690, 698
Rawlsian view, 101
Real Business Cycle literature, 214–215
Real time group formation, 762–770
Reallocation-proof mechanisms, 837, 840, 843
Reciprocity, 439, 684
Recovery, diffusion with, 661–665
Recursive algorithms
in coalitions, 748–749, 760, 766, 775
in local interactions, 626, 628–631
Recursive computability, 626–627
Redistribution, 93–131
basic model for, 96–97, 105, 108
and beliefs about the poor, 124f
culture and, 501–503
economic effects of, 94–96
education and, 96, 107
empirical evidence for, 103–127
data, 104
results, 105–111
in Germany, 485
by immigrant group and country of birth, 492f
individual characteristics for, 105–108
infinite horizon model and, 98
multiplicity of equilibria and, 103
Preferences for Redistribution and a History of Misfortune General Social Survey, 1972–2004, 110t
Preferences for Redistribution and Religion General Social Survey, 1972–2004, 112–113t
productivity and, 96–100
racial factors in, 105, 113–114
Redistribution, Family Background, and Social Mobility General
Social Survey, 1972–2004, 109t
Redistribution, Work *vs.* Luck as a Driver of Success, and Fairness General Social Survey, 1972–2004, 122–123t
Redistribution and a History of Macroeconomic Volatility during Youth General Social Survey, 1972–2004, 119–120t
Redistribution and Cultural Origin Immigrants' Regressions General Social Survey, 1972–2004, 116–117t
Redistribution and Individual Characteristics General Social Survey, 1972–2004, 106t
women and, 95, 107, 127
work ethic and, 367–368
WVS and, 121–127, 125–126t
Reduced form preferences, 35, 39–41, 44–46
basic model of, 41–46
Reed-Frost model, 658
Reference groups, 588, 591
Referenda turnout across Italian provinces, 454f
Reflection problem, 520
Regents of the University of California *vs.* Bakke, 164, 178
Regional customs, 327
Regressions coefficients, 4, 24
Regular networks, 524
Regulation
of labor markets, 499–501
and mistrust, 425–426
Relationships
bilateral, 514
between ethnic fractionalization in 1860 and the probability that individuals have professional jobs, 405f
hedonic, 529
market, 518
strong *vs.* weak, 517
Relative consumption, 272–273, 276–278, 282, 286–290
adaptive utility and, 278–287
information and, 273–277
Relative position, 42, 46–49. *See also* Positionality; Rank
direct concern for, 55
Relative weight comparisons, 331
Religion, 112–113
intolerance of, 427
moral norms and, 426–427
Preferences for Redistribution and Religion General Social Survey, 1972–2004, 112–113t
Probability of homogamous marriage as a function of the religious shares, by U.S. state, 396f
social capital and, 426–427

socialization as function of religious share, 401f
Worldwide adherents of selected major religions, mid-1998, 375f
Rent to land, 323–324, 326
Rents, 209–210
Repeated choice, 684–698
Replicator dynamics, in evolutionary game theory, 356
Reproduction
age at time of, 248–249
consumption and, 257
delaying, 249–250
parthenogenetic, 236, 241, 342
Res publica, 463
Reservation wages, 323–326
Resilience of cultural traits, 374–377
Resistance, in network formation, 763, 763n34
Respect, 83n6, 88
civic capital, 431t, 436t, 437, 462, 468
for rules, sources of, 460–461t
Trust and Respect index by country, 376f
Respecting improvements, 830
Responsiveness assumptions, 821
"Restriction of range" problem, 16
Retribution, 509
Revealed preferences, 74, 160–161, 276
axioms of, 228, 231
literature of, 224
Reversals
in peer effects, 569
of preference, 250–251, 258–259, 262–263
Reverse causality, 111, 498
Reversible decisions, 770
Revision protocols, 231, 634
Richer sequential link formation models, 535
"Rich-get-richer" pattern, 534
Riis, Jacob
How the other half lives, 389
Risk, 13, 61–64, 98, 223
aggregate *vs.* idiosyncratic, 235–238, 240–242, 246, 248, 261
attitudes toward, 236–242, 488
implications of, 246
of obesity, 331, 334
risk aversion, 675n29
vs. betrayal aversion, 450–451
employers', 138
risk dominance, 634, 705, 713–716
risk-dominant equilibria, 320
sharing, 521
status and, 243–246
Robustness analysis, 775
Role model effects, of affirmative action, 176–178
Roman Empire, 378
Roommates, drinking by, 618
RSD. *See* Random serial dictatorships
Rubinstein-Stahl bargaining game, 562

S

Salient options, 269–272
Samuelson, Paul, 278
SARS. *See* Severe acute respiratory syndrome
Savings, 42–46, 48, 61, 86, 482
Scale-free distributions, 525
School
admissions, 821–837
drop-out rates, 588, 611, 619
School choice, 830–835
Boston mechanism for, 831–832
differences between college admissions, student placement, and school choice problems, 824
envy and, 785, 831–834, 836–837
incentives in, 832
neighborhood and, 399
Pareto efficiency and, 832–834
preference profiles in, 831
recent developments and related literature in, 835–837
TTC algorithm for, 834–835, 839
Schooling. *See* Education
School-optimal stable mechanisms, 823, 828, 830
Schor, Juliet B.
The Overspent American: Why We Want What We Don't Need, 202–203
The Overworked American: The Unexpected Decline of Leisure, 202–203
Search frictions
discrimination from, 151–156
wage determination and, 152
Second best, theory of, 263n39, 264
Sectors, private *vs.* public, 173–176
Segregation
ethnic, 389–390
local interactions and, 633–634
racial, 540

Segregation (*cont.*)
self-segregation, 352
Selection
among equilibria, 294–295, 708–712
group selection
economics and, 295–297
evolution and, 290–297
individual, 292–295
kin, 296–297
natural, 226, 241, 273
self-selection, 639
Self-control issues, 272
Self-determination, 462
Self-fulfilling equilibria, 142
Self-fulfilling prophecies, 140, 142
Self-fulfilling stereotypes, 135–136
Self-segregation, 352
Self-selection, 639
Semelparous life histories, 248–250, 252
Separate environments, 5
Sequence of single choices, 700–704
Sequential models
of coalitions and network formation, 746–754
richer sequential link formation models, 535
Serial dictatorships, 787–788, 793n3, 794, 800, 827
multi-category, 826, 828–829
random serial dictatorship, 794, 845
with squatting rights, 794
simple, 825
Severe acute respiratory syndrome (SARS), 651
Sexuality
pre-marital sex, 387
sexual revolution, 387
Shapley value, 730, 737, 751–752
Share contracts, 322, 325f, 327
Shared environments, 13, 15–16
Shirking, 503
Shrewdness, 2
Siblings
adoptive, 6–9, 12, 14
Correlations in Body Mass Index For Four Types of Sibling Pairs, 15f
Correlations in IQ between siblings, adoptive siblings, and identical twins, 9t
correlations of IQ between, 8–11
full, 7–9, 14
Sick leave participation rate by cohort in Sweden, 386, 386f
Signal distributions in Coate and Loury's (1993) example of patronizing equilibrium, 167f
Signal extraction, basic model of, 137–138
Signaling, 48n30, 56, 59
Spence signaling model, 56–57, 74
multiple equilibria in, 142n8
Simple information networks, 687f
Simple networks, 706f
Simple serial dictatorships, 825
Simulated population dynamics, 402f
"SIR" model, 662
"SIS" model, 662
Skills
activity and skill acquisition choices, 159f
endogenous, 183–189
exogenous, 179–183
incentives to invest in, 141–142, 145, 146f, 148–151, 164–166, 172–177
skilled *vs.* unskilled labor, 140–141
Slave trade, 341, 376, 377, 384, 427, 466
Sleep, and leisure, 218
Small world model, 526–532, 533, 570
Smith, Adam, 58, 70
Smoking, 488
transmission of, 23
workplace bans on, 618
Snakes, fear of, 229n11
Soccer, 384, 503
Social arrangements, 44–47, 50, 52–53, 60, 63–64
Social capital, 73, 418–423
as civic capital, 422–423
effect of, on income per capita across cities in Northern Italy, 471f
endogeneity of, 468
enforcement and, 421–422, 424–425, 429, 452
fairness and, 440, 452
investment in, 420–422
political scientists' definition of, 422
religion and, 426–427
sociologists' definitions of, 421–422
of Sweden, 423, 452, 475
web sites on, 418n1
Social construction, of preferences, 201–220
Social coordination, 683n3
Social determinants, for preferences, 35–40
Social inequality, 94
Social infrastructure, 420
civic capital and, 467, 468t

Social insurance, 96, 386
Social interactions, 588, 639. *See also* Local interactions
  cultural transmission and, 359–369
  norms and, 317
Social learning, 684–698
  Bayes' rule and, 690, 692, 698, 701
  beliefs and, 685–686, 688–692, 695, 697–704, 722–724
  conformity and, 681, 696–698, 707–708, 711
  cross-group effects of, 696, 707
  homophily and, 698
  myopia and, 688
  rationality and, 690, 698
  utility functions in, 685, 689–692, 696–698, 701
Social mobility, 95, 97–99, 108–111
  prospects of upward mobility (POUM), 98–100, 108
  Redistribution, Family Background, and Social Mobility General
    Social Survey, 1972–2004, 109t
Social multipliers, 317, 597–600, 615
  social multiplier effect, 604, 608–611, 638
Social networks, 511–585
  average distances in, 525–532
  cohesiveness in, 567–568
  connectedness of, 521–522, 558, 687n6, 722
  degree distributions for, 523–526, 533n31, 569
  diffusion and, 647–653
  graph terminology for, 522–523
  initial configuration of, 714
  in labor markets, 514–517
  in learning and diffusion, 518–521
  monotonicity in, 569
  myopia and, 557, 572
  networked markets and, 514–521
  position in, 520
  strategic complementarities and, 566, 568–570, 573
  structure of, 521–532
  web sites and, 688
Social norms. *See* Norms
Social obligation, 482
Social outcomes, 680, 682
Social planner's problem, 615
Social policy, 2, 15, 49, 58
Social preferences, 40–53, 77–78
Social Security Act, 627
Social states, 731
Social structure, 645–678
Social utilities, 612
Socialization
  civic capital and, 426
  disutility function of, 358
  economic behavior and, 397–398
  economics of, 339–416
  family and, 345
  fertility and, 346, 351–352
  as function of religious share, 401f
  horizontal, 341, 342n3, 345, 394
  of immigrants, 389, 426
  mechanisms of, 346–351, 392–407
    geographic spread of, 348–349
  oblique, 341–342, 345, 394
  vertical, 394
    direct, 341–342, 345
Societies, with hierarchies, 437
Sociologists' definitions, of social capital, 421–422
Soil productivity, 315, 324f
  index of, 322
Sons, preferences for, 498–499
Sources
  of heterogeneity, 493–495
  of information, 698
  of moral norms, 461–462t
  of respect for rules, 460–461t
  of trust, 460t
Spence signaling model, 56–57, 74
  multiple equilibria in, 142n8
Spillovers
  of productivity, 330
  proportional, 612
Spirit of capitalism, 387
The spread of early farming in Europe, 380f
Squatters, 485
Squatting rights, 794
S-shaped curves
  for diffusion, 651–652, 654–657, 665, 674
  for LFP, 506
  for local interactions, 588
  S-shape adoption, 655f
  for utility functions, 283n57, 285
Stability. *See also* Stochastic stability
  dynamic, 708–712
  vs. efficiency, 771–774
  evolutionary, 739

Stability (*cont.*)
internal *vs.* external, 735
long-run, of norms, 316–317
in matching theory, 783
monadic, 739
in network formation, 737–741
pairwise, 738, 743, 745, 758n29, 771
Stable body weight, 332
Standard portfolio choice model, 61
Star networks, 537, 572
altruism in, 719–720
efficiency of, 762n33
learning and, 700, 708, 711–712
Static models, 633
baseline, 589–592
of local interactions, 589–617
Static perspectives, effects of networks from, 647–650
Stationary constant traveling wave, 348f
Stationary dynamic models, 638
Stationary outcomes, 235
Stationary policy function, weights on past history in, 626f
Statistical analysis, models for, 535–543
Statistical discrimination, 133–200
affirmative action and, 163–191
additional issues of, 189–191
background of, 163–164
Coate and Loury model of, 142–147, 147f, 165–170, 167f
college admission and, 178–189
color sighted *vs.* color blind, 178–189, 182f
equilibria with, 168–170
equilibria without, 167–168
equilibrium wage schedules under affirmative action, in Moro and Norman model, 172f
general equilibrium in, 170–173
in Malaysia, 173
modeling of, 165–166
patronizing equilibrium in, 166–170, 167f
role model effects of, 176–178
two-sector general equilibrium model, 173–176
efficiency implications of, 191–195
firms and workers' best responses and, 143–145
equilibrium of, 145–147
mismatches and, 189, 191–192, 195
multiplicity of equilibria and, 135, 141–142, 144, 146, 161
Phelps model of, 136–139, 191–192
productivity and, 135–140, 149, 183–185, 187, 191–194
Statistical mechanics, 596–597, 613n21
Statistical models, 532, 536, 540, 548, 550
Statistics Sweden, 12
Status, 69–91
Asian consumers and, 81n5
consumption and, 84
correlates of, 78
economic effects of, 84–88
effects of, 78–80
endogeneity of, 74
evidence of, 75–84
evolution and, 83–85, 272–290
features of, 72–75
goods of, 63
for its own sake, 80–81, 83
managerial implications of, 87
nontradability of, 74–75, 81–84
risk and, 243–246
visibility of, 74, 81–83, 85–86
in workplace, 74–75, 85–88
zero-sum nature of, 71, 86n10
Status goods, 63
Stereotypes, 196
self-fulfilling, 135–136
Stigma, of welfare, 627
Stochastic shocks, 316, 318, 321, 632
Stochastic stability
in network formation, 739, 763
norms of, 316, 319, 320n7, 572
of outcomes, 710–711, 714–715, 719n24, 721
sets with, 634
Stochastic transmission, 551
Strangers, trust in, 442, 452, 454, 459
Strategic complementarities
cultural transmission and, 360–361, 363–365, 370
in local interactions, 598–599, 609–610, 612
norms and, 317, 424–425
social networks and, 566, 568–570, 573
Strategic interaction, 704–721
diffusion and, 653–657
in network settings, 657–674

Strategic models
fitting, 540
random networks and, mixing, 549–550
Strategic networks, 543–548, 570
Strategic peer interactions, 566
Strategic substitution, 360, 362–363, 393–394, 666
Strategy-proofness, 784, 786–787, 829–832
coalitional, 799–800, 835, 837, 840, 843–844
mechanisms of, 784
Strength of family ties, 486, 487f, 499–501
Strict preferences, 731, 784, 804–808
Strictly profitable moves, 765
Strong mixing conditions, 616n23
Strong Nash equilibrium, 773
Strongly absorbing states, 764–765, 772
Student placement, 824–830
associated college admissions problem, 825, 828
differences between college admissions, student placement, and school choice problems, 824
envy and, 825, 828–830
one skill category in, 825–826
Pareto efficiency and, 828–829
preference profiles in, 824, 826
tentative, 825
Turkish student example of, 826–828
Student-optimal stable mechanisms, 823, 828, 836
Subcontracting, 514
Submatching, 838, 841, 843
Subnetworks, 523
Substance use, 588, 653
Substitutability, 209, 212
Substitution
cultural, 345–347, 350–352, 353n19, 355, 358, 360, 377–378, 393–394, 400–404
Dynamics with cultural substitution in Bisin and Verdier, 347f
Dynamics with cultural substitution in Cavalli Sforza and Feldman, 347f
elasticity of substitution between consumption and leisure, 211
strategic, 360, 362–363, 393–394
Suicide, 75
Superadditivity, of grand coalition, 769
Supply side response, 156
Support, 528
Survival, 225–226
Sweden
census data of, 12
sick leave participation rate by cohort in Sweden, 386, 386f
social capital of, 423, 452, 475
Swedish Twin Registry, 12
Symmetric equilibria, 669–670
Symmetric monopolistically competitive equilibrium
with free entry and expanding varieties, 205
with monopoly profits, 205
Symmetric steady state equilibrium, 152–154
Symmetric *vs.* nonsymmetric games, 295, 319, 748

T

Tabellini model, 423–425
Talented 20 Plan, 179
Talmud, 378
Tarski's fixed-point theorem, 669
Task assignment, 141–145, 148–151, 165–173, 193–194
Tax policy, 60, 86, 94, 108
distortionary cost of taxation, 97n4, 97n5
income tax, 60
progressive, 96
Pigouvian taxation, 71
tax incentives, 429
tax pardons, 476
TCBO algorithm. *See* Trading-cycles-with-brokers-and-owners algorithm
TCBO mechanism. *See* Trading-cycles-with-brokers-and-owners mechanism (TCBO mechanism)
Technological change, 317, 335, 506
Technology, of information, 681
Teenage drinking, 588n1
Teen-age pregnancy, 611
Telephones, diffusion of, 519
Tentative student placement, 825
Test scores, 14n10, 15–16
admission office's preferences over test scores under color-blind admission policy, 182f
verbal, 8
Theory of the second best, 263, 263n39
Thrift, 482
Tie-breaking, 737, 785, 833–834, 836–837
Time
coalition formation over, 765–770

Time (*cont.*)
networks over, 651–653
predicted homogamy as a function of time in the U.K., 407f
predicted identity as a function of time in the U.K., 406f
real time group formation, 762–770
time diaries, 218
trade offs over, 247–263
Time spent in total work by sex, conditional on demographics, 216f
Tipping points, 316, 656, 664, 671–673
Tissue compatibility test, 801–802
Tonsillectomies, 327
Top trading cycles (TTC) algorithm, 784, 791f, 792f, 793f
in house allocation with existing tenants, 794
in housing market, 790–793, 837, 839
in matching theory, 846
in school choice, 834–837, 839
Top trading cycles and chains (TTCC) algorithm, 806–808
Top-convex functions, 740
Topology, product, 605n16
Torusota example, 323–324, 324f
Tourist industry, 471n12
Tournaments, 139–140, 191
Trade
cultural transmission and, 362–363
genetic distance and, 388
incentives and, 560–561, 563, 565
through networks, 560–565
Trade offs, 100–102
over time, 247–263
quantity/quality, 352
Trading cycles
with brokers and owners algorithm, 840–844
preference profiles in, 843
Trading-cycles-with-brokers-and-owners algorithm (TCBO algorithm), 841
Trading-cycles-with-brokers-and-owners mechanism (TCBO mechanism), 843
Training, in economics, 428
Transferable utility (TU), 732–733, 740, 746, 816
Transition matrix of the probability of being hired to the complex job, 177t
Transmission. *See also* Cultural transmission
of civic capital, 420
Comparison of Coefficient of Transmission from Parent to Child, 24f
of drinking, 23
of fertility rates, 394
intergenerational, 423–424, 428, 470, 506
of obesity, 24
of preferences, 37–38
of smoking, 23
stochastic, 551
transmission coefficients (child outcomes), 4–5, 18–26, 20t
vertical *vs.* oblique/horizontal, 394–395
Transmission of education in five samples of adoptees and non-adoptees, 22t
Transmission of income in the Holt and Swedish samples and the PSID, 23t
Treatment effects, 15, 17–18, 25–26, 189
Triads, 528, 535–537
Trial and error, 225, 229–230, 265, 283
Triple melting pot hypothesis, 401
Trivial equilibria, 769n38
Trust. *See also* Mistrust
correlation between change in income per capita and change in inherited trust between 2000 and 1935, 505f
correlation between trust level of country of origin and trust level of immigrants relative to Great Britain, 491f
cultural values and, 443f, 462
GDP and, 473–475
immigrants and, 472n13, 504
investment and, 458, 473
mutual, 455, 466–467
neighborhoods and, 491n16
personalized *vs.* generalized, 440–441, 444–446t
probabilistic content of, 440
sources of, 460t
in strangers, 442, 452, 454, 459
surveys on, 441–451
Trust and Respect index by country, 376f
trust beliefs
civic capital as, 424–425
across countries, 441f
density functions by country, 447f
economic development and, 458f
trust game experiments, 78, 448–452, 475
trust matrix, 449t, 555
TTC. *See* Top trading cycles
TTCC. *See* Top trading cycles and chains

TU. *See* Transferable utility
Turkish immigrants, in Germany, 395, 500
Turkish student example, of student placement, 826–828
Twins, 1–30
Correlations in IQ between siblings, adoptive siblings, and identical twins, 9t
identical *vs.* fraternal, 2–4, 6, 10
Swedish Twin Registry, 12
Two-arm bandit problem, 554, 685, 691, 701
Two-period example, 42–44
Two-sector general equilibrium model, of affirmative action, 173–176
Two-sided matching model, 783–784
Two-way flow model, 735
Two-way kidney exchange problem, 809, 809f
Two-way kidney exchanges with 0–1 preferences, 808–816
egalitarian mechanism for, 813–816
priority mechanism for, 811
Type space Θ, 590

U

U.K. *See* United Kingdom
Ultimate *vs.* proximate causality, 251n31
Ultimatum game experiments, 79–80, 488–489
Underdemanded patients, 811–815
Under-investment *vs.* over-investment, 564
Undirected graphs, 522
Undirected networks, 732
Unemployment, 515–516, 573
insurance, 189–190
Unexplained factors, 5
Union density, 486, 487f, 501
United Kingdom (U.K.)
Industrial Revolution, 386–387
predicted homogamy as a function of time in the U.K., 407f
predicted identity as a function of time in the U.K., 406f
United Nations officials, parking violations of, 453–454, 459, 502
United Nations Security Council, 749
United Network for Organ Sharing (UNOS), 820
United States (U.S.)
assimilation by years in the U.S, 390
census data, 389, 395, 399, 589, 616
hours worked during the U.S. boom in the 1990s, 215f
probability of homogamous marriage as a function of the religious shares, by U.S. state, 396f
U.S. *vs.* Europeans, hours worked by, 216
vanishing of American Jews hypothesis, 401
Unity, of economic models, 56–57
Unobserved heterogeneity, 516, 518, 611
Unobserved preferences, 234
Unobserved variables, 4, 18, 25
UNOS. *See* United Network for Organ Sharing
Utility functions
adaptive utility, and relative consumption, 278–287
additively separable, 235
cardinal *vs.* ordinal, 278–280
conflict of, 230
consumption and, 507
evolution and, 227–230, 267–269
Friedman-Savage, 243–245
vs. happiness, 75–76
hedonic, 52, 279, 282
inequality directly in, 100–101
inequality indirectly in, 99–100
of local interactions, 591–592, 597–605, 607, 619, 623
maximization of, 94, 204, 226–232, 236, 287, 332, 493
preferences and, 36, 53–55, 57, 63
private, 612
quadratic, 602, 623
social, 612
in social learning, 685, 689–692, 696–698, 701
S-shaped curves for, 283n57, 285
von Neumann-Morgenstern, 236, 241, 243–245, 810
Utility profiles
egalitarian, 814, 816
Lorenz-dominant, 813
of lottery mechanisms, 810–811

V

Value functions, 732
Values. *See also* World Values Survey
civic
measuring, 431–432t
teaching, 476

Values (*cont.*)
as civic capital, 428–429
Descriptive Statistics World Values Survey, 129t
experimental measures of, 437–440
survey measures of, 429–437
trust and cultural values, 443f, 462
Vanishing of American Jews hypothesis, 401
Veblen, Thorstein, 58, 70, 82, 272
VECM. *See* Vector Error Correction Mechanism
Vector Cointegration analysis, 214
Vector Error Correction Mechanism (VECM), 213
Vengeance, 233
Verbal test scores, 8
Vertical socialization, 394
direct, 341–342, 345
Vertical *vs.* oblique/horizontal transmission, 394–395
Vidal, Gore, 53
Violence, 501–503
Visibility, of status, 74, 81–83, 85–86
Voluntary associations, 464
von Neumann-Morgenstern utility function, 236, 241, 243–245, 810, 834n4
Voter model, 568, 672n26
Voter turnout, 367, 453–454, 503
Voting paradoxes, 754
Voting Rights Act of 1965, 163

W

Wages. *See also* Income
Black-White wage inequality, 196–197
equilibrium wage schedules under affirmative action, in Moro and Norman model, 172f
generating average group wage differentials, 138–139
minimum wage legislation, 501n27
reservation wages, 323–326
Wage as a function of the signal for group j, 149f
wage determination, and search frictions, 152
Walks, in networks, 522, 523f
Walrasian price effects, 362–363
Walrasian state, 325
Warp, of conformity, 315, 328, 330
Wasteful matchings, 825
W-chain, 805f
5 w-chains, 806f
Weak priorities, 832–834
Weak ties, 517, 543, 648, 695
Weakly neutral mechanisms, 800
Weakly profitable moves, 765
Wealth
distribution, 40–44, 58
disparate, 60
rank and, 40, 43–45
formation
racial identity *vs.*, 353–354
Web sites
on social capital, 418n1
social networks and, 688
Weight. *See* Body weight
Weighted averages, 137, 180, 357–358
Weighted least squares, 12
Weighted networks, 736
balanced collection, of weights in, 740
Weights on past history in the stationary policy function, 626f
Welfare
advertising and, 208–209, 218
analysis, 508
improvement of, 704
state, 96, 118, 369n33
stigma of, 627
Within-country migration, 503
Women
American, and body mass index, 334
equal rights for, 163
in labor force, 395
mothers' attitudes on, 486–488
men *vs.* women, hours worked by, 216–217
redistribution and, 95, 107, 127
women's work, 497–499
working wives, 37, 39–40, 51n35, 484, 485f, 492–496
ethnicity and, 497–499
Word-of-mouth diffusion, 528, 532, 551
Work
disutility function of, 49, 158, 160–161, 492–493
vs. luck
Redistribution, Work *vs.* Luck as a Driver of Success, and Fairness General Social Survey, 1972–2004, 122–123t
time spent in total work by sex, conditional on demographics, 216f
women's work, 497–499
work and spend cycle, 202–203, 210, 215, 218

work ethic, 216, 385–387, 426
redistribution and, 367–368
Workers
firms and workers' best responses and, 143–145
equilibrium of, 145–147
low cost *vs.* high cost, 157
misallocation of, 173, 194
qualified *vs.* unqualified workers, 141–143, 143, 157, 166–168, 174–176
Firms' net return from qualified and unqualified workers in the complex and simple tasks, 143t
working wives, 37, 39–40, 51n35, 484, 485f, 492–496
ethnicity and, 497–499
Workplace
bans on smoking at, 618
status in, 74–75, 85–88
World Bank, 429
World Trade Center attacks, 246n27
World Values Survey (WVS), 95, 104, 115, 385
civic capital and, 419, 429–430, 452, 469
economics and, 482, 489, 498, 500
redistribution and, 121–127, 125–126t
Worldwide adherents of selected major religions, mid-1998, 375f
WVS. *See* World Values Survey

X

Xavier, Francis, 36

Y

Years of democracy since independence, 459–462
Years of education, 5, 11, 18–19, 21–22, 24–25
Implied variance decomposition from the behavioral genetics model, 11t
"You request my house - I get your turn" (YRMH-IGYT) mechanism, 795–800, 807–808, 839, 845, 847
examples of, 795f, 796f, 797f, 798f, 799f
YRMH-IGYT. *See* "You request my house - I get your turn" mechanism

Z

Zero-sum nature, of status, 71, 86n10
Zipf's law, 525

INDEX-VOLUME 1B

Note: Page numbers followed by f, t and n indicate figures, tables and notes, respectively.

A

Ability
  based peer effect, 1056, 1067, 1107
  based peer model variations, 1061–1064
  defining, 1248
  entrepreneurial, 1232
  fixed, 1179
  higher productivity related with higher, 1065
  high/low, 1076
  indicators for student, 1143
  intellectual, 1182n11
  peer, 1145
  reading and peer, 1142
  tax, 1235
  tracking, 1084–1089, 1087f, 1088t
Acceptance, peer, 1180
Accountability, standards, 1150–1151
Achievement, 1099. *See also* Racial achievement gap
  acting white's potential impact on, 1182–1186
  based peer effects, 1135–1143
  gender and peer, 1123–1124, 1135
  as measured, 1099
  measurement error in, 1143
  segregation's impact on, 1172–1173, 1173f
  of students, 968
  testing, 1127, 1147
Admission, college, 1067, 1135–1136
Affirmative action, 967, 1117
Agreements, collective bargaining, 971n8
ALC. *See* Average local complementarity
Alcohol, 1115–1116
  binge drinking of, 1116
Alienation, race and experience of, 1183
Allocations. *See also* Reallocations
  of education resources, 1076
  of effort, 1179
  equilibrium, 1077, 1080–1081
  estimation of extreme, 1000
  inefficiency in equilibrium, 1077
  inference for fixed interior, 998
  Pareto Efficient, 1081, 1081n50
  socially efficient, 1078
Altruism, 923
  for enforcement of informal arrangements, 1266
  among genetically related individuals, 1266–1267
  motives, 1269
Ambivalence, 1182
Amenities
  CBD as, 1320–1321
  dependence of indirect utility on, 1321
  endogenous, 1320–1323
  exogenous, 1320–1321
  impact of, 1317–1318
  of location, 1282, 1285
AMF. *See* Average match output function
Analysis
  cross-section, 918
  statistical, 925
  treatment effect, 857, 865
AREs. *See* Average reallocation effects
Armed Forces, 971
Assignment(s)
  classroom experiments with random, 1117–1125
  classroom peer effects studies in settings without random, 1126–1153
  feasible, 974
  groups created by random, 1112
  policies of administrative, 1144
  policies of school, 968
  problems, 968
  process, 976
  race based, 1144
  roommates by random, 1112–1113
  structure in one-to-one matching problems of feasible, 975–984, 978t
Assistance
  from family, 1256
  forms of, 1256
  from friendships, 1256
  between households, 1256
  mutual, 1256
Associational redistribution, 968
  controversial social policies involving, 968

Associations
individuals' control over choice of, 967
trade, 1232
Assumption(s), 878, 930
identifying, 1150
large market, 1007
parametric, 1330
proportionality, 1142
rationality, 924
of transferable utility, 1008
Attendance, school, 1068
Attitudes, roommate interactions influencing, 1117
Attractiveness, of communities, 1331, 1334
Average local complementarity (ALC), 986, 991
difference in differences structure of, 991–992
parameters as parametrically just identified, 1014
Average match output function (AMF), 1007
estimation of, 997–998
identifying, 1007
as recovered, 997
Average reallocation effects (AREs), 975, 984
associated with optimal assignment, 1003
with continuously-valued covariates, 1005–1006
continuously-valued match characteristics and, 993–994
with discretely-valued covariates, 998–1005
identification of, 992–995, 1007
inference for fixed interior allocations on, 998
observation of match output and estimation of, 997–1006
parametric identification when unobserved match output of, 1012–1015
possible limit distributions for maximum, 1004t

B

BDD. *See* Boundary discontinuity design
Behavior
coevolution of networks and, 894
disruptive, 1152
hypotheses, 930–931
joint, 857
joint modeling of group memberships and, 938–940
peer effects and disruptive, 1133–1135
social determinants of individual, 943
transition dynamics v. steady-state, 940–941
trust in models of economic, 924
trustworthy, 925–926
Beliefs, roommate interactions influence on, 1117
Bias
network effects and, 1227–1228
selection correction, 1291
selectivity, 1227–1228
self-selection, 898
simultaneity, 1228
sorting, 1301–1302
sources of, 1148
Bidding, 1063
Blocking pairs, 1025
Boundary discontinuity design (BDD), 1292
Business, networks, 1229, 1231–1232

C

Calibration, 1086n60
Capital
acquisition of human, 967
decline of incentives for investing in human, 1241–1252
family's working, 1224
investment in human, 1173, 1245–1247
working, 1232
Caste, 1248–1249, 1252, 1252n11
Categorization, optimal function on, 1176–1177
CBD. *See* Central business district
Census, 1310–1311
Central business district (CBD), 1288
as amenity, 1320–1321
Central Limit Theorem, 919
Centralization, 1167
Characteristics
continuously-valued match, 993–997
distribution of individuals' demographic, 1327
estimation on basis of match, 1026–1029
exogenous, 1098
explicit functions of individual, 1292
match, 975
neighborhood, 861, 1032
neighbors', 1304–1305
of others in social milieus, 1284
peer, 1136
peer exogenous, 1105
relationship of education and household, 1301
school's, 1138
simulated peer, 1146
social interactions and group, 937–938
student, 875, 1139–1140

tract, 1307–1308
variation in peer, 1137
varying, 1237n6
Children, fostering, 1260
Choice(s)
of associations by individual, 968
cluster, 1307
estimation of neighborhood, 1314
housing, 1286
joint decision of housing demand and neighborhood, 1306–1311
model of individual, 1295
model of partner, 1007, 1007n26
models of, 1286–1289
models of binary, 904–907, 953, 956–957
models of community, 1076–1084
models of discrete, 857, 920, 1007
neighborhood, 881, 1287, 1296, 1299, 1306–1311, 1314, 1335
observable v. unobservable determinants of individual, 858
partner, 1007
peer, 860
probabilities, 1288–1288
social interactions in environments with discrete, 1103
spousal, 968
teachers', 1120
two-sided model of multinomial, 1008–1012
Class(es)
peer effects across, 1102
segregation of, 1060–1061
size, 878, 971, 1060, 1102, 1148, 1159
size influencing learning, 878, 1060
Classroom(s), 969
composition, 1126–1135, 1158
composition and achievement-based peer effects, 1135–1143
disruption, 1130, 1133
experiments with random assignment, 1117–1125
peer effects, 1117–1153, 1122t, 1157
peer effects studies in settings without random assignment, 1126–1153
perception of environment of, 1129–1130
size of, 878, 972
student characteristics, 875
violence, 1130
Clubs
joining, 1284–1285
value of, 1284
Clustering, urban space and absolute, 1169
Colleges
admission, 1067, 1135–1136
peer effects among roommates in, 1112–1117, 1112n82
Collusion
identifying, 1244
social networks and, 1243–1244
Community(ies)
attractiveness of, 1331, 1334
choice models, 1076–1084, 1333
disadvantaged, 1240
formation, 1285
homogenous, 1077, 1077n45
multi-, 1076n43
networks, 1228–1231
networks supporting entrepreneurship, 1239
peer effects and, 1331–1335
settlement density of, 1317
with weak outside job options, 1240
Complementarity. *See* Average local complementarity
Composition
causal mapping of group, 968
classroom, 1126–1143
neighborhoods' racial, 937–938
peer, 1106, 1111–1112, 1144
policy altering social group, 968
Connections. *See also* Network(s)
effect of, 1229
social, 1242
Constant treatment response (CTR), 1044
Consumption smoothing, 1258
aggregate, 1259
Contacts. *See also* Network(s)
employers usage of personal, 1200–1201
gender and use of, 1201
heterogeneity in attributes of, 1206
job search use of personal, 1195, 1198–1200
personal, 1216
poverty and use of, 1201
productivity of personal, 1198
racial/ethnic difference in usage of informal, 1202
segregation in social, 1172

Contacts (*cont.*)
social, 1194, 1272
teacher, 1120
variation in usage across demographic groups of, 1202
Contagion, 1259n2
Contracts
emotions for enforcing, 1265
insurance, 1270n6
risk sharing through, 1262
teachers, 1120
Control(s)
functions as constructed, 882
over individual's associations, 967
selection corrections as functions of, 881
self-selection and, 881
used for identifying network effects, 1228–1231
Coping, devices, 1182
Costs
diversity, 1068–1069
of housing, 1285
schools' fixed, 1074n38
segregation's social, 1029
social, 1183
transactional, 1273
Counterfactuals, 862
Credit
bank, 1224
market and emergence of networks, 1225
networks, 1238, 1241
quasi-, 1268
social networks providing members with, 1224–1225
trade, 1229
Crime, rates, 918
CTR. *See* Constant treatment response
Culture, oppositional, 1182–1183

D

Data
collection, 1044
cross-section analysis of, 918
experimental, 857
individual level, 918
interpreted through identity model lens, 1187–1188
market share, 1015
from MTO program, 932
nonexperimental, 923
panel, 877–878, 895, 909–910, 1230, 1234n3, 1252
quasi-experimental, 876
relationship between individual and aggregated, 884
social multipliers/information from aggregated, 884–886
sources, 1216–1217
unobserved group effects and panel, 909–910
Decision making
baseline model of, 857
categorical, 1175–1176
in group contexts, 857–863
identity in economic, 1186–1188
model of student, 1149
Decisions, 1149
high school graduation, 861
household's local, 1282
location, 1282, 1286, 1288
Dependence
of indirect utility on amenities, 1321
interpretation of, 1008n28
measure of, 1008n27
Desegregation
court-ordered, 1031
of schools, 967
Design. *See also* Boundary discontinuity design
of dormitories, 1114
experimental, 1120, 1213–1215
monopolistic group, 1089–1092
Desirability, in matching, 970
Developing economies, community-based networks role in, 1224
Discipline, 1103
Discrimination
information-based, 1167, 1173
information-based models of, 1173–1177, 1175f
in job assignments, 1173
by private schools, 1070
racial, 937
skill acquisition impacted by information-based, 1177
statistical, 1174
Disease, 940
Disruption, 1133, 1152
classroom, 1130
Distribution. *See also* Associational redistribution

of family incomes, 1083
of income, 1300, 1330, 1332
of individuals' demographic characteristics, 1327
of teacher quality, 967–968
Diversity
cost, 1068–1069
peer effect, 1067
among peers of race, 1067–1069
roommate influence and, 1117
Dormitory, designs, 1114
Dwelling
attributes, 1304
models of choice among individual units of, 1288–1289
units, 1206–1208
Dynamics
of linear models, 869–870
peer, 1167, 1177–1178, 1177–1186, 1178t, 1181f
of social interactions, 921
steady-state behavior v. transition, 940–941

E

Economics, 943. *See also* Developing economies; Social economics
concepts central to experimental, 923
empirical literature in, 1269
empirical social, 873
of identity, 856
informal job search methods and urban models of, 1217
linear model used in, 871
matching models' role in, 970
matching problems in, 969–970
Economy(ies). *See also* Developing economies
agrarian, 1224
closed exchange, 1257
favoritism giving rise to inefficiencies in network-based, 1241
urban, 1284
Education. *See also* Racial achievement gap; School
higher, 1067
levels, 860
migrant status on attainment of, 1247
migration's effect on investment in, 1246
peer, 875
peer effects as important for outcomes of, 1054
peer group effects in, 1093
private provision of, 1075
relationship of household characteristics and, 1301
segregation in, 1167
Effect(s). *See also* Average reallocation effects; Local segregation inequality effect; Maximum average reallocation effect; Peer effects; Social effects
of alternative policies as forecasted, 972
analysis of treatment, 857, 865
of business networks, 1229–1230
of connections, 1228
contextual, 859, 1293–1296
controls used for identifying network, 1228–1231
correlated, 1094, 1101
discrete location problems with endogenous/contextual, 1293–1296
of distribution of outcomes by reallocations, 967
educational attainment by students' post-educational social, 1063
endogenous, 859, 1093, 1293–1296
endogenous contextual, 1296–1297
endogenous neighborhood and housing markets' contextual, 1303–1316
equal observable contextual, 913
estimation of housing structure demand with neighborhood, 1315
estimation of network, 1226–1241
exogenous, 1094
fixed, 909, 1156–1157
group-specific, 1105
housing demand with neighborhood, 1306–1309
housing structure demand with neighborhood, 1312–1315
identification of network, 1225–1241
on laws of large numbers/central limit theorems, 917–920
neighborhood, 1206–1211, 1284, 1317–1326, 1335, 1336
of neighborhoods on schooling, 1301–1302
non-identification with unobserved group, 909
of private school vouchers, 1069
proximity, 1146
of reallocations, 967
on resident's of poor, 931–932

Effect(s) (*cont.*)
of segregation, 1092, 1172
segregation's socioeconomic, 1042
of self-selection, 856
of social interactions on treatment effects analysis, 857
special case of no income, 1300–1302
statistical instruments used for identifying network, 1231–1237
supermodularity as type of, 924
time-invariant household, 1258
of tracking in public sector, 1086
unobserved group, 909–912, 1295
Efficiency. *See also* Inefficiency
of allocations, 1078, 1081
risk sharing and, 1257–1259
segregation and, 1031
Effort
allocations of, 1179
choices by students, 860
choices of equilibrium, 1066–1067
modeling student choice of, 1149–1153
Emotions
enforcement role of, 1266
for enforcing contracts, 1265
as grounded in brain development processes, 1266
Employees, referrals, 1195–1196
Employment
opportunities, 967
social networks effect on, 1237
Enforcement
of contracts with emotions, 1265
through guilt, 1265
of informal arrangements through altruism, 1266
of risk sharing legally, 1262
shame used for, 1266
Entrepreneurship, 1232
community networks supporting, 1239
Environments
of discrete choice, 1103
home, 1158
perception of classroom, 1129–1130
shocks to, 1136
of social interactions, 968
Equations. *See* Simultaneous equations
Equilibria(um), 920, 1175
allocations, 1077, 1080–1081
approaches to one-to-one models, 1007–1029
belief restrictions, 920–921
with different degrees of mixing across tracks, 1088t
effort choices, 1066–1067
existence of, 944–946
free entry monopolistically competitive, 1084–1085
inefficiency in allocation of, 1077, 1079
in linear in means model, 944
locational, 1319–1320
in matching problems, 973n16
multiple, 1175–1176, 1175f
non-existence of fully separating, 1181f
no-voucher, 1074
pairwise stability and, 1007
play, 930
price function, 1299
properties of discrete choice models with social interactions, 953–957
public-private schooling, 1075
schooling, 1249
uniqueness of Bayes-Nash, 946–947
Errors, covariance structure model, 872–873
Estimands
definition of target, 984–988
translating analysis into, 1040
Estimation, 856
of AMF, 997–998
of AREs when observation of match output, 997–1006
on basis of match characteristics alone, 1026–1029
BDD and, 1292
for extremal assortative matchings, 1005
of extreme allocations, 1000
of housing structure demand with neighborhood effects, 1315
maximum likelihood, 921
methods, 1046
of neighborhood choice, 1312–1315
of network effects, 1226–1241
of one-to-one matching models with match output is unobserved, 1007–1029
of one-to-one matching models with observation of match output, 974–1004
pairwise logit, 1028–1029

pairwise maximum score, 1029
strategy, 1214–1215, 1231, 1233
Ethnicity, 856, 936
segregation by, 1167
Evenness, 1167, 1168n2
Evidence
on motives, 1267–1270
for peer effects presence, 1098
of social interactions, 856, 937–938
on usage of informal search methods for jobs, 1198–1206
Exchangeability, 1024
Experiments
for administrative reasons, 1114
classroom random assignment, 1117–1125
design, 1120, 1213–1215
laboratory, 922–931, 927f
natural, 1212–1216
policy, 1153
quasi-, 931
randomized, 1212–1216

F

Fairness, 923
Family, 967. *See also* Parents
altruism and, 1266–1267
assistance from, 1256
distribution of incomes of, 1083
income, 1138
networks, 1229, 1261
risk sharing roles of, 1256
working capital from, 1224
Favoritism, 1241
Fitness, peer, 1121
Friendship(s)
assistance from, 1256
homophily property of, 888
networks, 856
racial difference in, 1184–1185
Funeral societies, 1260, 1270

G

Games
matching, 1015
trust, 923–928, 927f
Gap. *See* Racial achievement gap
Gender, 856, 1158
labor market and, 1210–1211
peer achievement and, 1123–1124, 1135
roommates and, 1112
schooling and, 967
specific peer effects, 1148
study time and, 1130
testing and, 1124
use of contacts and, 1201
variation and peer effects, 1126, 1128–1129
Geometry, of canonical urban model, 1317–1326
Gifts, 1269
between households, 1260
informal, 1268
Good(s)
household, 1256
public, 1332
Grades
as outcome measure, 882
popularity and, 1183–1184, 1185f
social status' relationship with, 1183–1184, 1183f
Graph, bipartite, 888
Group memberships, 856n3, 857
identification with, 1267
joint behavior and, 857
joint modeling of behaviors and, 938–940
prices for, 936–937
scalar categories and, 935
Groups
characteristics, 937–938
composition, 967
contacts in demographic, 1202
decision making in context of, 857–863
design as monopolistic, 1089–1092
heterogeneity of, 874, 942, 1101
identification, 856, 1100–1001
interactions, 877–879
interventions in formation of, 931–932
peer, 1093
peer effects in, 1122, 1153–1154
policies altering composition of social, 968
quality, 1089–1090
random assignment for creation of, 1112
risk sharing, 1270–1275
self-segregated, 1271
self-selection into, 878–879
size, 891–892, 891n30, 1271
unobserved effects of, 909–912
Guilt
for enforcing contracts, 1265

Guilt (*cont.*)
as inherited, 1265
as negative feedback, 1265–1266

H

Health. *See also* Mental health
care, 1167
Heterogeneity
in educational outcomes, 860
essential, 876
generating, 1009
of households, 1319–1320
income and preference, 1324–1326
individual, 1247
peer, 1159
preference, 1323–1324
unobserved fixed, 1230
unobserved group-level, 874, 942
variance of group level, 1101
Homophily, of social relations, 888
Households
education's relationship with characteristics of, 1301
formation of, 1256
goods/services, 1256
heterogeneous, 1319–1320
heterogeneous preferences of, 1323
income, 1320
location decisions of, 1282
migrants in, 1245–1246
motivation for, 1256
mutual assistance between, 1256
risk sharing between, 1256–1273
risk sharing mechanisms of, 1260
survival of, 1256
transfers between, 1270
utility maximized by, 1296–1297
utility of, 1079–1080
Housing. *See also* Dwelling; Households
choice, 1286
consumption, 1308, 1317
cost of, 1285
demand, 1287, 1306–1315
demand with neighborhood effects, 1311–1312
hedonics, 1315–1316
markets, 1075, 1288
markets' contextual effects and endogenous neighborhoods, 1303–1316
migrant, 1230, 1245–1246
models of choice among individual dwelling unit, 1288–1289
moving, 1138
price as empirical control for neighborhood quality, 1302–1303
prices, 936, 1081, 1293, 1308
proximity in, 1303–1304
public, 1212
quality, 934, 1082
quantity, 1312
randomized, 1213
segregation in, 1167
services, 1305–1306
structure demand estimation with neighborhood effects, 1315
structure demand with neighborhood effect, 1312–1315
types of, 1079
vouchers, 1212

I

Identification
alternative strategies for, 1153
of AMF, 1007
of AREs, 992–995, 1007
arising from endogeneity of group, 856
of assumption, 1150
for binary choice models, 904–907
cards, 1246
challenges facing empiricists, 856
of collusion, 1244
controls used for network effects', 1228–1231
under double randomization, 988–990
endogenous group formation and, 1100–1101
endogenous social interactions' partial, 911–912, 913
experimental approaches toward social interactions', 922–931
in experimental data context, 857
as failing for linear, 866
with group membership, 1267
group size on, 891–892, 891n30
issues, 923
of linear means model, 868, 872–873, 881
of linear social networks model, 903
multiple equilibria facilitating, 919
of network effects, 1225–1241

of networks using indirect inference, 1238–1241
under no matching on unobservables, 990–991
nonparametric, 862, 1015–1024, 1017t
in 2 x 2 matching market, 1018–1021
in K x L matching markets, 1021–1024
in one-to-one matching markets without transfers, 1025–1026
of one-to-one matching models when match output is observed, 974–1004
of one-to-one matching models when match output is unobserved, 1007–1029
of one-to-one matching models when observed match output, 974–1004
pairwise logit, 1016–1018, 1017t
parametric, 915–916
of AREs when unobserved match output, 1012–1015
partial, 910–911
of peer effects, 1093–1100
peer effects as posing challenges for, 1056
problem, 1226–1228
problem for social interactions, 883
problems arising in study of social economics, 856
results as developed, 1046
selection corrections used for, 881
of social interactions, 881, 891–892, 899
of social interactions in linear network models, 890–891
of social interactions' limits, 874
in social networks, 888–890
strategies for, 1094, 1157, 1208
structural model v. potential outcomes, 865
threats to, 1251
variance restrictions used for, 1101–1103
Identity
in economic decision making, 1186–1188
economics of, 856
models of, 1186–1189
Incentives, 990–991
private v. social, 1077
Income
distribution of, 1300, 1332
distribution of family, 1083
family, 1138
households, 1320
marginal distribution of, 1271
parametric assumptions on joint distribution of, 1330
preference heterogeneity and, 1324–1326
variance of, 1330
Inefficiency, in equilibrium allocations, 1077, 1079
Inequality, 857
aversion to, 1270
inter-type, 1042
in social context, 968
social interactions explanation of, 860
Inference
approach to casual, 1044
for fixed interior allocations on AREs, 998
Influence
endogenous, 1099
exogenous, 1099
of neighborhoods on labor market outcomes, 1303
peer, 1113–1114, 1116, 1156, 1158
of roommates on attitudes/beliefs, 1117
roommates' peer, 1116–1117
social, 887
Instruments
exogenous attributes of location as, 1295
identifying network effects with statistical, 1231–1237
Insurance
contracts, 1270n6
health, 1270
mutual, 1224
Integration, 1040
school, 1147
Interactions. *See also* Social interactions
identifying parameter for endogenous, 877–878
local, 1209
panel data for unobserved group, 877–878
peer, 857, 1055–1069, 1104n70
roommate, 1117
self-interest and repeated, 1262–1264
unobserved group, 877–879
Interest. *See* Self-interest
Interventions
in group formation, 931–932
policy, 872
Intuition, 1092
Investment
in education, 1246
family-specific, 859

Investment (*cont.*)
in human capital, 1173, 1245–1247
Isolation, racial, 1031
Issues
econometric, 1093–1110
identification, 923

J

Job(s)
ceiling, 1182
direct evidence on usage of informal search methods for, 1198–1206
formal search framework for, 1216
higher ability related with higher productivity, 1065
matching, 969
model of informal search for, 1197
personal contacts used in search of, 1195, 1198–1200
productivity of informal v. formal search methods for, 1202–1203
search and labor market outcomes, 1203–1204
search intensity, 1209
search methods, 1198–1206
social networks in search for, 1196
social networks providing members with, 1224
wages, 1196

L

Labor markets
demand side of, 1248–1249
differential access to, 1239
gender and, 1210–1211
informal hiring channels in, 1195
informal search methods in, 1195
job search methods impact on outcomes of, 1203–1204
networks, 1233
networks as emerge in, 1224
personal networks used in, 1194
policies of active, 968
referrals, 1206–1211
search/matching aspect in, 1194
segregation in, 1167
social interaction effects in neighborhood level on, 1207
of teachers, 971
Laboratory(ies)
experiments, 922–931, 927f
identification issues and, 923
Language, foreign, 1140
Law, of total probability, 1045
Law of Large Numbers, 917–920
Leadership, peer, 1121
Learning
class size affecting, 878, 1060
social, 1224
Linear models
basic structure of, 863
dynamic, 869–870
in economics, 871
linear-in-means model of, 864, 865
partial, 869
reduced form of, 865–866
of social interaction, 863–884
Literacy, 1139–1140
Loans, 1264
Local reallocation effects (LREs), as derived, 995
Local segregation inequality effect (LSIE), 1042
Location(s). *See also* Neighborhood(s); Relocation
amenities of, 1282, 1285
aspatial models with social interactions of, 1287–1304
decisions, 1282, 1288
disadvantaged, 1284
discrete problems of, 1293–1296
elements of specialization for, 1282
equilibrium for individuals of, 1319–1320
estimating models of, 1293
exogenous attributes of, 1295
factors in choosing, 1285
hierarchical models of neighborhood, 1287
models, 1293
residential, 1296
social interactions and hierarchical models of, 1326–1335
social interactions role in decisions about, 1286
urban, 1282
Logit
estimation of pairwise, 1028–1029
models, 954–955
models of nested, 938–939
pairwise, 1008
identification, 1016–1018, 1017t

LREs. *See* Local reallocation effects
LSIE. *See* Local segregation inequality effect
Lunch, 1139

M

Marijuana, 1116
Market(s). *See also* Labor markets
  assumptions of large, 1007
  housing, 1075
  identification in one-to-one matching, without transfers, 1025–1026
  nonparametric identification in 2 x 2 matching, 1018–1021
  nonparametric identification in K x L matching, 1021–1024
  outcomes of labor, 1203–1204, 1303
  share data, 1015
  thickness, 1024
  transactions and risk sharing, 1261
  valuations, 1289
Marriage, 1233–1234
  rules, 1234–1235
Match. *See also* Average match output function; Match output
  characteristics, 993–994
  characteristics as basis of estimation, 1026–1029
  estimation on basis of characteristics of, 1026–1029
  surplus as measured, 973
  surplus' parametric modeling, 1027–1028
Match output. *See also* Average match output function
  estimation of AREs when observing, 997–1006
  function, 1007
  identification/estimation of one-to-one matching models with observation of, 974–1004
  identification/estimation of one-to-one matching models with unobserved, 1007–1029
  parametric identification of AREs when unobserved, 1012–1015
Matching. *See also* Match output
  assortative, 1005
  correlated, 994–995
  desirability in, 970
  econometric research on problems with, 972–974
  games, 1015
  identification under unobservables no, 990–991
  job, 970
  markets, 1018–1026
  models, 969–974, 1029
  models examples, 970–971
  negative assortative, 1002
  as one-to-one, 1007
  problems, 975, 1007, 1026
  problems and equilibrium, 973n16
  problems in economics, 970
  structure of feasible assignments in one-to-one problems in, 975–984, 978t
  surplus and, 973, 975
  unobservables and no, 981–984
Maximum average reallocation effect (MRE), 987–989
Measurement
  of achievement, 1099
  of complementarity, 986
  Delta index and, 1168
  error, 1140, 1234n4
  error in achievement, 1143
  grades and, 882
  isolation as, 1168
  of match surplus, 973
  of networks, 1232
  of segregation, 1167–1170
  social interactions and, 934–935
  of social space, 936
  of teacher quality, 968
Memberships. *See also* Group memberships
  endogenous group, 1094
Mental health, poverty and, 933
METCO. *See* Metropolitan Council for Educational Opportunities
Metropolitan Council for Educational Opportunities (METCO), 931
Microeconomics, 873
Microfoundations, of social interactions, 941–942
Migrants
  in household, 1245–1246
  labor networks and benefit of, 1245
  networks, 1230, 1247
  referrals and, 1211
  shelter provided to migrants by, 1260
  status of educational attainment of, 1247

Migration, 1225. *See also* Migrants
accumulated schooling increased with, 1245
effect on investments in education by, 1246
empirical studies on networks and, 1232
housing and, 1230
international, 1232
labor networks and, 1245
model, 1226
model of occupational, 1240, 1246–1247
networks and, 1230
payoff and, 1226
rates, 1230
Military service
compulsory, 876
random assignment for, 1215
Mill, John Stuart, 855
Mobility
networks and, 1247–1252
restrictions on, 1250
social restrictions on occupational, 1250–1251
of students, 1137
Model(s). *See also* Linear models; Modeling
ability-based peer, 1061–1064
aspatial, 1286–1303
binary choice, 904–907, 953, 956–957
canonical urban, 1317–1326
of choice, 1286–1289
community choice, 1076–1084, 1333
covariance structure, 872–873
decision making's baseline, 857
discrete choice, 857, 920, 1007
equilibrium properties of, 953–957
self-selection for, 912–913
single agent, 1015
of social interactions, 857, 904–922
of discrimination
information-based, 1173–1177, 1175f
statistical, 1174
duration, 916–917
econometric, 868
econometric implications of matching, 972–974
economic, of racial segregation, 1167
of economic behavior, 924
of educational provision, 1064
empirical matching, 969–974
estimation of matching, 997–1006
exchange, 1259
exogenous effects as assumed by theoretical, 1094
focus, 1110
graphical, 886–888
hedonic, 1287
heterogeneous gamma, 1141–1142
hierarchical, 871–872
hierarchical choice, 1335–1336
homogeneous, 1141
identity, 1186–1189
individual choice, 1295
of informal job search, 1197
informational externality, 1065–1067
of labor market outcomes, 1303
linear in means, 864, 865, 867–868, 872–873, 1043, 1108n77, 1142
equilibrium in, 944
networks' component-level unobservables in, 893–894
partial, 869
under self-selection, 880
as study of social interactions starting point, 888
linear network, 890–891
linear social networks, 893, 903
location, 1293
hierarchical, 1326–1335
logit, 954–955
migration, 1226, 1240
misbehavior, 1060–1061
multi-community, 1076n43
multinomial choice, 913–914, 1286
of multinomial choice, two-sided, 1008–1012
nested logit, 938–939
network, 889
of network referrals, 1214
nonlinear, 1103–1105
of occupational migration, 1240, 1246–1247
one-to-one matching, 974–1004, 1007–1029
parametric, 1027–1028
parametric identification for multinomial choice, 915–916
of partner choice, 1007, 1007n26
peer, 1109–1110
of peer dynamics v. models of identity, 1189
of peer interaction, 1055–1069
Arnott and Rowse, 1055–1058
misbehavior, 1060–1061

of peer pressure, 1177–1178
properties of hierarchical v. linear in means, 872
rainbow, 1110
reflection problem and hierarchical, 871–872
rhetorical, 856
simultaneous equations, 869
social interaction, 856, 874–875, 916, 941
social network, 894–895, 902–903
sorting, 1296–1298, 1332
spatial, 886–894
spatial autoregressive, 896
spatial econometrics, 895–898
student choice of effort and, 1149–1153
of student decision making, 1149
theoretical, 1159–1160
two-audience signaling, 1181f
variance components, 884
Modeling
group membership/behavior joint, 938–940
match surplus' parametric, 1027–1037
peer effects, 1055–1058, 1140
self-selection, 880
student choice of effort, 1149–1153
Monotonicity, 1297
of peer effects, 1107
Motivation, 1160
for households, 1256
intrinsic, 1265–1267
Motives
altruism, 1269
evidence on, 1267–1270
for risk sharing, 1261–1268
Moving to Opportunity (MTO), 931–934, 932n60, 1213
MRE. *See* Maximum average reallocation effect
MTO. *See* Moving to Opportunity
Music, 1113

N

Names, race and, 1187–1188, 1188f
Necessity, sufficiency as linked with, 867
Neighborhood(s), 969
aspatial models for choice of, 1287
attributes, 1304
characteristics, 861, 1032
choice, 881, 1287, 1296, 1299, 1306–1311, 1314, 1335
choice and housing demand as joint decision, 1306–1311
demand, 1312–1313
effects, 1284, 1335, 1336
effects and geometry of canonical urban model, 1317–1326
effects and housing structure demand, 1312–1315
effects and labor market referrals, 1206–1211
effects on residents of poor, 931–932
effects on schooling, 1301–1302
endogenous choice of, 1296
estimation of choice of, 1312–1315
hierarchical models of location of, 1287
housing markets' contextual effects and endogenous, 1303–1316
information in hedonic regression, 1315–1316
information in hedonic regressions, 1315–1316
labor market outcomes as influenced by, 1303
moving from high to low poverty, 933
parents' choice of, 881
quality, 1302–1303
racial composition of, 937–938
relocation to new, 1213–1214
safety, 1285–1286
segregation of, 862
self-selection and, 878
sorting, 1328
unobservables, 1316
Network(s). *See also* Social networks
agents bridging structural holes in, 1274–1275
architecture, 1273
bias and, 1227–1228
business, 1229–1230, 1231–1232
change in use of personal, 1216
coevolution of behavior and, 894
community-based, 1224
complete, 888
component-level unobservables in linear in means model in, 893–894
controls used for identifying effects of, 1228–1231
credit, 1238, 1241
in credit market, 1224
density, 1206n17
economic activity facilitated by, 1241
economic analysis of, 1224
effects as identified in practice, 1225

Network(s) (*cont.*)
effects as identified with statistical instruments, 1231–1237
empirical studies on, 1232, 1253
family, 1229, 1261
family v. community, 1229
formation literature, 1274
friendship, 856
homogenous, 1171
identification literature for, 889
indirect inference used for identifying, 1238–1241
industry specific, 1240
information relayed through, 1260, 1265
investment in human capital and, 1245–1247
labor market, 1194, 1224, 1233, 1245
literature, 936
measuring, 1232
migrant, 1230, 1247
mobility and, 1247–1252
model, 889
negative consequences of, 1241–1252
nonidentification of social interaction in models of, 892–893
personal, 1194
presence of underlying, 1239
referrals' dynamic model, 1214
resources' misallocation and, 1241–1245
risk sharing, 1270–1275
role as provision of information about new technologies, 1224
role as provision of mutual insurance, 1224
small, 1273
of social interactions, 1170
social ties defining, 1224
star, 887–888
strength, 1226
structure of, 886, 1204
topologies, 887–888, 892, 894
transitivity, 893
use of weak v. strong, 1204–1206

O

Observability. *See also* Unobservability
of actions, 907–909
One-to-one matching models
identification/estimation when match output is unobserved of, 1007–1029
as identified when match output is observed, 974–1004
Openendedness
social interactions and, 875
theory of, 879
Opportunity(ies). *See also* Moving to Opportunity
employment, 967
moving to, 931–934
Outcomes. *See also* Match output
econometric methods for evaluating effects of reallocations on distribution of, 967
educational, 1054
heterogeneity in educational, 860
labor market, 1203–1204, 1303
measuring, 882
model of labor market, 1303
peer individual, 1106
potential, 865
by reallocations, 967
social, 968, 1284
Output. *See* Match output
Outsourcing, 1239

P

Parents
family-specific investment by, 860
neighborhoods a chosen by, 881
skills transmitted to children from, 861
Payoffs
expected, 1174
fixed, 1174
migration and, 1226
Peer(s). *See also* Peer effects
ability, 1145
ability and proximity effects, 1146
ability and reading, 1142
acceptance, 1180
achievement and gender, 1123–1124
characteristics as simulated, 1146
choices, 860
composition, 1106, 1111–1112, 1144
dynamics, 1167, 1177–1178, 1177–1186, 1178t, 1181f
economic consequences of, 1056
education, 875
fitness, 1121
group variation, 1111
heterogeneity, 1159
individual outcomes, 1106
influence, 1113–1114, 1116, 1156, 1158

interactions, 857, 1104n70
models of, 1055–1069
leadership, 1121
local complementarity between, 1039
models, 1109–1110
natural variation in composition of, 1111–1112
pressure, 1177–1178
quality, 1101
racial diversity among, 1067–1069
reading and ability of, 1142
spillovers, 1152
technology, 1089
variation in characteristics of, 1137
Peer effects
ability based, 1056, 1067, 1107
categorizing, 1055
challenges for identification posed by, 1055
across classes, 1102
classroom and school, 1117–1153, 1122t, 1157
classroom composition and, 1126–1135
classroom composition and achievement-based, 1135–1143
in classroom studies in settings without random assignment, 1126–1153
among college roommates, 1112–1117, 1112n82
communities and, 1331–1335
defining, 1054–1055
development of conceptualization of, 1055
direct, 1055
disruptive behavior and, 1133–1135
diversity, 1067
educational, 1055, 1062, 1065, 1076
empirical investigation of, 1106, 1110–1156
endogenous, 1058–1059, 1095, 1098, 1112, 1151
evidence for presence of, 1098
exogenous, 1095, 1101, 1105–1110, 1112
functional form of, 1105–1110
gender specific, 1148
gender variation and, 1126, 1128–1129
in groups, 1153–1154
identification of, 1093–1100
as important for education outcomes, 1054
indirect, 1064
low-achieving students and, 1131–1133
magnitude of, 1158
modeling, 1055–1058, 1140
monotonicity of, 1107
nonlinear operation of, 1113
operation of, 1332–1333
operation through unobservables, 1097
on primary peer group level, 1122
problems in attempting identification of, 1094
race and, 1148
relevance of, 1055
research on, 1055
role of educational, 1069–1076, 1072f
semi-parametric framework for capturing, 1145
of skill choices, 1059
theoretical research relying on, 1159
with/without vouchers, 1075
Perception
of classroom environment, 1129–1130
of teachers by students, 1132
Policy(ies). *See also* Reallocations
active labor market, 968
administrative assignment, 1144
causal mapping of group composition into outcomes for making, 968
controversial social, 967–968
debates touching on segregation, 1042
educational, 971
experiments, 1153
forecasting effects of alternative, 972
infeasible, 968
interventions, 872
persistent, 1083
reallocations v. other, 967
segregation and social, 1029, 1031
social groups' composition altered by, 967
social outcomes affected by, 1284
Popularity, grades and, 1183–1184, 1185f
Population, setup, 1031–1034
Poverty
levels, 934
mental health and, 933
traps, 1082
use of contacts and, 1201
Prediction, 921n53
Preference(s)
distribution of, 926
heterogeneity, 1323–1326
households with heterogenous, 1323
matching and, 970
social, 923
structure, 1306–1309
Price(s)
character of, 1071
equilibrium function of, 1299

Price(s) (*cont.*)
hedonic, 1296–1297
housing, 936, 1081, 1293, 1308
of housing as empirical control for neighborhood quality, 1302–1303
indices of hedonic, 1289–1291
properties of function of, 1299–1300
of segregation, 1172, 1189
of skills, 1189
social interaction and, 936–937
Probability, law of total, 1045
Problem(s). *See also* Reflection problem
assignment, 968
disciplinary, 1103
discrete location, 1293–1296
econometric research on matching, 972–974
economics' matching, 969–970
equilibrium in matching, 973n16
global reallocations as social planner's, 1034–1038, 1036f, 1038f
identification, 856, 883, 1226–1228
in identifying peer effects, 1094
matching, 975
two-sided, 1026
reallocations, 973
simultaneous equations, 855–856
for social interactions, 883
structure of feasible assignments in one-to-one matching, 975–984, 978t
Productivity
as basis for wage, 1242–1243
higher, 1065
of informal job search methods, 1198
of informal v. formal job search methods, 1202–1203
of personal contacts, 1198
worker, 1242, 1245
Profit, maximizers, 1090
PROGRESA program, 879
Prosperity, permanent, 1083–1084

Q

Qualifications, observed v. unobserved, 982
Quality
average, 1091
generalized average, 1091
housing, 934, 1082
maintaining, 1068
maxmin, 1091
multiplicative, 1091
neighborhood, 1302–1303
paying for school, 1069–1070
peer, 1101
of schools, 861, 1064, 1080, 1089
teacher, 875, 968, 971, 982, 1138
technology of group, 1089–1090
Quantity, housing, 1312

R

Race. *See also* Racial achievement gap
acting white and, 1182–1186
alienation experience and, 1183
based assignments, 1144
coping devices and, 1182
discrimination and, 937
diversity among peers of, 1067–1069
friendships and difference of, 1184–1185
isolation and, 1031
naming patterns and, 1187–1188, 1188f
neighborhoods' composition of, 937–938
peer effects and, 1148
segregation by, 1167
segregation index for, 1171
wages and, 1203–1204
Racial achievement gap
acting white and, 1186
in kindergarten, 1166
segregation explaining, 1173
slow down in convergence of, 1167
as statistically significant, 1166
trends in, 1166–1167, 1166f
as widened, 1166f, 1167
Rainfall, 1237
Randomization, 1154
conditional double, 980–981
double, 978–979
of housing, 1213
identification under double, 988–990
reshuffling and, 1155
usefulness of, 980–981
Rationality, assumptions, 924
Reading
peer ability and, 1142
scores, 1126–1127
Reallocations. *See also* Average reallocation effects; Maximum average reallocation effect

associational redistributions coinciding with, 967
changes with, 970
as distinguished from other policies, 967
effects on distribution of outcomes by, 967
feasible, 1040
global, 1034–1038, 1036f, 1038f
local, 1006, 1039–1042
problems, 972
Reasoning
microeconomic, 858
spatial, 899
Reciprocity, 923
Redistributions. *See* Associational redistribution
Referrals, 1194
dynamic model of network, 1214
employee, 1195–1196
for immigrants, 1211
informal, 1196
labor market, 1206–1211
through social networks, 1224
Reflection problem, 1094–1095
for econometric models, 868
as exhibited, 871–872
hierarchical models and, 871–872
overcoming, 872
process and instrumental variables, 866–872
as special, 872
Regression, 865, 1146
discontinuity, 1118
estimating, 1114
hedonic price, 1289–1290
instrumental variable, 1232
neighborhood information in hedonic, 1315–1316
quantile, 1151
Relatedness, patterns, 1235
Relationships
bidirectional, 887
of individual and aggregated data, 884
long-term, 1261
between peer individual outcomes and peer composition, 1106
romantic, 876
student achievement/teacher quality, 968
Religion, 856
Relocation, 1149n89
Rents, 1076n42
Repeated game theory
multiple uses of, 1265
risk sharing and, 1252–1264
Research
matching problems' econometric, 972–975
on peer effects, 1055
peer-group, 1157
theoretical, 1159–1160
Reshuffling, 1155
Resources
allocations of education, 1076
networks and misallocation of, 1241–1245
pooling, 1261
in private schools, 1071
Restrictions
equilibrium belief, 920–921
of linear in means, 1109
on mobility, 1250
of no matching on unobservables, 981–984
occupational mobility's social, 1250–1251
on trade, 1241
variance, 1101–1103
Retaliation, 1266
Risk
idiosyncratic, 1261
independent sources of, 1261
neutral agent, 1261–1262
pooling arrangement, 1271, 1274
Risk sharing
arrangements, 1257
constraints to, 1275
consumption smoothing and, 1258
through contracts, 1262
early empirical economic literature on, 1267
economic literature on, 1275
efficient, 1257–1259, 1270, 1273
egalitarian, 1263
family's role in, 1256
forms of, 1259–1261
gifts/transfers between households as mechanisms of, 1260
between households, 1256–1273
through informal gifts, 1268
in interpersonal networks, 1272–1273
legal enforcement of, 1262
links formation, 1273–1274
in market transactions, 1261
motives for, 1261–1268
networks/groups, 1270–1275

Risk sharing (*cont.*)
observability of shocks and, 1269
perfect, 1257
reduced form tests of, 1259
repeated game theory applied to, 1252–1264
self-enforcing contacts for, 1264
understanding, 1256
vulnerability and, 1275
Roommates
academic performance and, 1115
alcohol and, 1115–1116
gender and, 1112
influence on beliefs/attitudes, 1117
negative effect of drinking by, 1116
peer effects among college, 1112–1117, 1112n82
peer influence between, 1116–1117
random assignment of, 1112–1113, 1215–1216
SAT and, 1114–1115
switching, 1115
Rules, marriage, 1234–1235

S

Safety, 1285–1286
Scholastic Aptitude Test, 1172
School(s). *See also* Teachers
ability tracking within, 1084–1089, 1087f, 1088t
accumulated schooling and, 1245
assignment policies, 968
attendance, 1069
caste and, 1252
characteristics, 1138
demand for quality, 1080
differentiation, 1080–1081
discrimination by private, 1070
disparity in teacher quality across, 971
English, 1247–1250
expenditures on educational resources in private, 1071
fixed costs, 1074n38
gender and, 967
graduation decisions for High, 861
integration, 1147
lunch, 1139
paying for quality of, 1069–1070
peer effects, 1117–1153, 1122t
private, 1064, 1069–1076, 1085–1086
quality of, 861, 1064, 1089
random assignment within, 1124–1125
segregation's effects across, 1172
socioeconomic disadvantage levels of, 879
tuition, 1086
voucher program, 967, 1064, 1073
vouchers and quality of, 1064–1065
vouchers for private, 1064, 1069–1076
Segregation. *See also* Desegregation; Spectral segregation index
achievement as impacted by, 1172–1173, 1173f
of classes, 1060–1061
degree of, 1040
Delta index as measure of, 1168–1169
dimensions of, 1169
dissimilarity index and, 1168
effects of, 1172
equity/efficiency implications of, 1031
ethnic, 1167
flaws in measure of, 1169n4
high v. low, 1184
index, 1171
individual v. city-wide, 1169–1170
isolation as measure of, 1168
measurement of, 1167–1170
of neighborhoods, 862
policy debates touching on, 1042
in presence of social spillovers, 1029–1044, 1030–1031t, 1036f, 1038f
price of, 1172, 1189
quantity of residential, 1172
racial, 1167
racial achievement gap as explained by, 1173
residential, 971
role in skill development, 1167
second generation, 1173
self-, 1271
in social contacts, 1172
social costs/benefits of, 1029, 1031
social interactions and measure of, 1170
socioeconomic effects of, 1042
trends in, 1172–1173, 1173f
Selection. *See also* Self-selection
correction bias, 1291
corrections for identification, 881
Self-interest
motives, 1269
rational, 1262
repeated interaction and, 1262–1264

Self-selection, 1151
behavior represented by, 880
bias in social network formation, 898
controlling for, 881
for discrete choice models, 912–913
effects of, 856
into groups, 878–879
linear in means model under, 880
modeling, 880
preferred approach for dealing with, 879
residential neighborhoods and, 878
in social network models, 894–895
spatial, 895
unobservable group interactions v., 879
Service(s). *See also* Military service
household, 1256
housing, 1305–1306
Sex, 1116
Shame
informal arrangements enforced through, 1266
as triggered, 1266
Sharing, risk, 1256–1273
Shocks
child fostering in response of, 1260
common, 1155–1156, 1262
for environment, 1136
observability of, 1269
Simultaneity, 1094
Simultaneous equations
models, 869
problems, 856
theory, 882
Size
class, 878, 971, 1060, 1102, 1148, 1159
classroom, 878, 972
group, 1271
identification and group, 891–892, 891n30
Skills
choices and peer effects, 1059
information-based discrimination's impact on acquisition of, 1177
multi-dimensional, 1092–1093
from parents to children, 861
price of, 1189
segregation's role in development of, 1167
Smoking, 1112
Social economics, identification problems arising in study of, 855
Social effects
endogenous, 1283, 1293
of students' education attainment, 1063
types of, 1282
Social interactions
aspatial models of location with, 1287–1304
basic structure of binary choice model with, 953–954
binary choice models of, 904–907
defining, 886
as derived from direct interdependences between choices, 855–856
as derived from predetermined social factors, 856
discontinuity in adoption curves induced by, 941–942, 941n65
discrete choice models of, 857, 904–922
dynamic, 921
econometrics of, 936
effects in neighborhood level on labor market, 1207
empirical implications of, 921–922
endogenous, 866, 877, 882, 886, 911–912, 917, 924
environments of, 968
in environments with discrete choices, 1103
equilibrium properties of discrete choice models with, 953–957
evidence of, 855
experimental approaches to identification of, 922–931
as explored in sociology, 870
future directions for econometrics of, 934–942
group characteristics as evidence of, 937–938
in group structures as identified, 891–892
hierarchical models of, 872
hierarchical models of location with, 1326–1335
identification of, 881, 890–891, 899
identification of binary choice model with, 906–907
identification problem for, 883
inequality explained in terms of, 860
limits to identification of, 874
linear in means model as starting point for study of, 888
linear models of, 857, 863–884
in linear network models as identified, 890–891
local, 1207
logit models of, 954–955

Social interactions (*cont.*)
measure of segregation based on, 1170
measurement and, 934–935
microfoundations of, 941–942
models, 856, 874–875, 916, 941
multinomial choice, 924
in network models' nonidentification, 892–893
network of, 1170
openendedness and, 875
pattern reversals and, 911–912
prices and, 936–937
proximity and, 899
rhetorical models of, 856
role in location decisions, 1286
social networks of, 886–894
spatial econometrics specifications of, 895–898
spatial models and, 886–894
treatment effects' analysis as effected by, 857
types of, 865, 941, 1093–1094
as uncovered via effects on laws of large numbers/central limit theorems, 917–920
unobserved variables v., 882–884
variables operated through by, 882
Social networks, 857, 947–953
adjacency matrix of, 887
change in use of, 1216
collusion and, 1244–1245
employment as effected by, 1237
endogenous, 1197
generic identifiability of linear model of, 893
graphical models of, 886–888
identification in, 888–890
in job search, 1196
jobs/credit provided for members of, 1224
literature on, 1273
local dimension of, 1206–1207
model, 894–897, 902–903
referrals through, 1224
self-selection bias in formation of, 898
self-selection in models of, 894–895
of social interactions, 886–896
term as used, 1194
with unknown network structure, 900–903
wages as effected by, 1237
Social ties, 1224
networks defined by, 1224
Sorting
bias, 1301–1302
models, 1296–1298, 1332
neighborhood, 1328
Space, social, 936
Spectral segregation index (SSI), 1170
as defined, 1172
obtaining, 1172
Spillovers, 969
equity/efficiency implications of segregation in presence of social, 1031
peer, 1152
segregation in presence of social, 1029–1044, 1030–1031t, 1036f, 1038f
treatment response with, 1044–1046
SSI. *See* Spectral segregation index
Stability, 1025, 1025n38
pairwise, 1007
Standards, accountability, 1150–1151
Status, grades relationship with social, 1183–1184, 1183f
Stigma, toward African Americans' historical specificity, 857
Strategies, 1115
estimation, 1214–1215, 1231, 1233
identification, 1094, 1153, 1157, 1209
Strength, network, 1225
Students. *See also* Roommates
academic performance of, 1115
characteristics, 1139–1140
characteristics of classroom, 875
choice of effort as modeled, 1149–1153
decision making model, 1149
effort choices by, 860
exogenous characteristics of, 1098
graduation, 876
mobility, 1137
multi-dimensional skill of, 1092–1093
peer effects and low-achieving, 1131–1133
post-educational social effects of educational attainment by, 1063
self-selection by, 1106
teacher quality and achievement of, 967–968
teachers as perceived by, 1132
Study(ies)
of social economics and identification problems, 856
of social interactions, 888
time and gender, 1130
Sufficiency, necessity as linked with, 867

Supermodularity, 859
testing for, 1026–1027
as type of endogenous social interaction effect, 924
Surplus
form of function, 990
match, 973, 975
parametric modeling of average match, 1027–1028

T

Tax
ability, 1235
community-based, 1285
Teachers
choices, 1120
contract, 1120
labor market, 971
motivation of, 1160
quality, 875, 967–968, 971, 982, 1138
as reassigned across schools, 968
responses by, 1130
student perceptions of, 1132
Technology
of group quality, 1089–1090
network's role as provision of information about, 1224
peer, 1089
Testing
achievement, 1127, 1147
gender and, 1124
for supermodularity, 1026–1027
Ties. *See* Social ties
Tracking, 1119–1120
ability, 1084–1089, 1087f, 1088t
intensification of, 1086–1087, 1089
in public sector of, 1086, 1089
Trade
associations, 1232
credit, 1229
restrictions on, 1241
Transportation, 1080–1081
Treatment
effect analysis, 857, 865
response with spillovers, 1044–1046
as valued, 1045
Trends, in racial achievement gap, 1166–1167, 1166f
Trust
concept of, 923, 925
game, 923–928, 927f
limits to, 924
in models of economic behavior, 924
Tuition
discount, 1089n61
school, 1086

U

Unemployment, 1208, 1210, 1215
Unobservability
approached to, 883–884
peer effects and, 1097
variables and, 1094
Unobservables
density of, 911–912
identification under no matching on, 990–991
neighborhood, 1316
restriction of no matching on, 981–984
Utility
assumption of transferable, 1008
in canonical urban model, 1318–1319
conditional, 1066
dependence on amenities of indirect, 1321
expected, 1258
firm, 1025
function, 1145–1146
household, 1079–1080
maximizing, 1085, 1296–1298

V

Value. *See also* World Values Survey
of assets, 1259
of clubs, 1284
continuous, 993–994, 1005–1006
discrete, 998–1005
local, 1259
of treatment, 1045
Variables
instrumental, 866–872
social interactions v. unobserved, 882–884
unobserved group level heterogeneity dealt with by instrumental, 874–875
through which social interactions operate, 882
Violence
classroom, 1130
domestic, 1133
Votes, 921–922
Voucher(s)
effects of private school, 1069

Voucher(s) (*cont.*)
  housing, 1212
  normative effects of universal, 1073
  no-voucher equilibrium and, 1074
  private school, 1064, 1069–1076
  program for school, 967, 1110n80
  quality and school, 1064–1065
  targeted, 1075
  universal private school, 1073

W

Wages
  fixed, 1242–1243
  job, 1195
  job search and, 1203
  of manager/workers as connected, 1242–1243
  productivity as basis for, 1242–1243
  race and, 1203–1204
  realized, 1196
  reservation, 1196
  social networks effect on, 1237
Wealth, 1272
Welfare, 935
  maximizing social, 1090
World Values Survey, 925

Z

Zoning, 1082

FSC
www.fsc.org
MIX
Papier | Fördert gute Waldnutzung
FSC® C083411

Kolibri 360 GmbH
Ferdinand-Jühlke-Straße 7
99095 Erfurt, Deutschland
produktsicherheit@kolibri360.de